Film Analysis

A NORTON READER

W. W. Norton & Company, Inc. also publishes

Looking at Movies: An Introduction to Film
Richard Barsam

A History of Narrative Film, Fourth Edition
David A. Cook

Reel Music
Roger Hickman

Film Analysis
A NORTON READER

Edited by

Jeffrey Geiger
University of Essex

and

R. L. Rutsky
San Francisco State University

W. W. Norton & Company
New York London

W. W. Norton & Company has been independent since its founding in 1923, when William Warder Norton and Mary D. Herter Norton first published lectures delivered at the People's Institute, the adult education division of New York City's Cooper Union. The Nortons soon expanded their program beyond the Institute, publishing books by celebrated academics from America and abroad. By mid-century, the two major pillars of Norton's publishing program—trade books and college texts—were firmly established. In the 1950s, the Norton family transferred control of the company to its employees, and today—with a staff of four hundred and a comparable number of trade, college, and professional titles published each year—W. W. Norton & Company stands as the largest and oldest publishing house owned wholly by its employees.

First Edition

The text of this book is composed in Palatino
with the display set Univers.

Composition by TSI Graphics, Inc.

Book design by Anna Oler.

Project Editor: Christopher Miragliotta

Production Manager: Ben Reynolds

Manufacturing by the Courier Companies—Westford Division.

Library of Congress Cataloging-in-Publication Data

Film analysis: a Norton reader / edited by Jeffrey Geiger and R. L. Rutsky.
    p. cm.
Includes bibliographical references and index.
ISBN 0-393-97983-0
1. Motion pictures. I. Geiger, Jeffrey. II. Rutsky, R. L.

PN1994.F43814 2005
791.43'75—dc22   2005040530

W. W. Norton & Company, Inc., 500 Fifth Avenue, New York, N.Y. 10110-0017

www.wwnorton.com

W. W. Norton & Company Ltd., Castle House, 75/76 Wells Street, London W1T 3QT

3 4 5 6 7 8 9 0

Table of Contents

Contents

Contents

Alphabetical Table of Contents
(by film title)

Contents

Contents

Preface

Images are omnipresent in our increasingly global and digital age. They attempt to persuade us; to sell us commodities; to comfort, cajole, and stimulate us; to tell us stories and entertain us; to convey information. In this context, the importance of visual literacy, of developing strategies for critical, analytical thinking about images, can scarcely be overestimated. *Film Analysis: A Norton Reader* is an effort to help students develop the skills necessary to analyze how images are constructed, how they create meanings, how they affect us, and how they are intricately embedded in cultural and ideological frameworks. And while it may seem that film has become a rather antiquated medium in this era of digitization, the basic characteristics of technologically reproduced images remain—as Walter Benjamin foresaw—the same. In the same way, whether images are digital or analog, recorded on memory cards or celluloid film, the basic ideas and approaches for analyzing them remain remarkably similar. In short, the study and analysis of films has much to teach us about analyzing images and visual culture more generally.

Although *Film Analysis: A Norton Reader* is designed to introduce students and general readers to the analysis of films, it is not a textbook in the conventional sense. Rather than competing with the variety of film studies and film history textbooks currently available for classroom and general use, *Film Analysis* is designed to complement them, offering analyses that give practical expression to the broader descriptions of formal, historical, and theoretical issues raised in such textbooks. Consequently, this book does not attempt to give a systematic account of cinematic techniques, styles, and analytical procedures, nor does it include chapters that detail the precise workings of cinematography, editing, art design, film sound, and so on. Rather, as a classroom *reader*, it approaches film study and analysis by offering critical essays on individual films, written specifically for this volume by leading film scholars.

Film Analysis offers concise, readable analyses of a diverse selection of important films, while at the same time exposing students to a range of approaches to analytical writing about film. These essays, moreover, raise key historical and theoretical issues related to these films, which should encourage further discussion and debate. The volume's introductory essay is designed to give an overview of film analysis—summarizing what it means and its value, while providing some starting points for critically engaging with film. We have also included a glossary of film-related terms at the end of the book, which can be used in conjunction with reading the essays. Of course, the essays in *Film Analysis* need not be seen purely as pedagogical tools; they may also be enjoyed for their own merits, for the insights they provide into individual films and into the possibilities of cinema in general.

In any reader such as this one, the number of essays that can reasonably be included is necessarily restricted. In this context, the choice to include an essay on one film inevitably means the exclusion of analyses of other films. Just as inevitably, there will be—and, indeed, should be—disagreements and debate over the choice of films (those chosen, those not included) and the criteria (or lack thereof) by which such decisions were made.

The films discussed in this volume were ultimately chosen through a variety of means: polls of film instructors at different academic levels, examination of a variety of course syllabi, and the personal preferences of the contributors. It has not been our aim in this volume to produce a "best of" cinema collection. We have not attempted to compile a list of the "greatest" films of all time, nor even of the greatest of a genre, region, or historical period. Making such judgments among the very different styles of filmmaking that make up world cinema is obviously an impossible task. We happily leave the compilation of "Top Films" lists, and similar exercises, to others.

It should be clear, too, that this book makes no claim to provide a comprehensive or "representative" survey of world cinema, which would be difficult even in a much larger volume. Although we have aimed for diversity, we are conscious that this volume has omitted many films—and even whole areas of filmmaking—that are part of the vast range of world cinema. Some of these decisions, it should be noted, were based on rather practical considerations. We have, for example, attempted to restrict our selections to films that are readily available in home viewing formats. And in keeping with the time constraints of most courses, we have deliberately omitted a number of films with particularly long running times. Under different circumstances (practical and otherwise), the basis for these decisions and the resulting choices would undoubtedly have been different.

Our goal has been to produce a book that would be useful in introductory film studies and film history classes. To that end, we have attempted to balance our selections between well-known films commonly taught in these courses and films that, by virtue of their differences in style, national or cultural origin, or historical period, demonstrate the diverse array of cinematic options and alternatives. In fact, despite this volume's seeming emphasis on readings of individual films, many of the films discussed here have been chosen with an eye to comparative analysis, so that the films of a particular director, artistic movement, culture, or era might be considered in relation to different films and filmmaking traditions. Indeed, the chronological structure of the book should allow for interesting comparisons between contemporary or nearly contemporary cinema movements, such as *film noir* and the rise of Italian neorealism, "classical" Hollywood cinema and the "golden age" of Japanese and French cinemas in the 1930s, or the creative power of African American filmmaking in the late 1980s and early 1990s as reflected in the cluster of important films examined here.

We should point out, however, that it has not been our concern in this volume to propose canonical or evaluative standards for films. Rather, this volume aims to address *film analysis* as a practice. That is, unlike most film studies textbooks, which rarely have the space to provide more than a handful of examples of film analysis, *Film Analysis* focuses on *how* to analyze films, rather than describing or categorizing different aspects of and approaches to analysis. Its essays offer different models for how film analysis can be practiced, while still emphasizing the contextual, analytical, and research aspects that these essays share. In keeping with this practical approach, our goal has been simply to provide, within the scope allowed by this volume, a broad enough sample of films and filmmaking styles to give introductory students a sense of cinema's many possibilities. We hope, then, that this reader will offer useful means for analyzing and thinking critically about not only the films discussed here, but about cinema and other visual texts more generally.

Film Analysis: A Norton Reader has gone from a rather vague idea about what kind of a new volume might be valuable in the classroom to something much more substantial and expansive than we could have imagined. For this, we would like to thank our contributors, who have lent us their time, their encouragement, and their remarkable intellectual and creative insights. Individually, many of them have been far more generous with their help than we had any right to expect. And collectively, they have helped to reveal the range and depth of the work that currently constitutes film studies. We would also like to express our gratitude to those who lent their support and offered valuable ideas at various stages along the way, particularly Lisa Cartwright, Teshome Gabriel, Marilyn Manners, Robert B. Ray, and Belinda Waterman. We would also like to thank the Research Promotion Fund at the University of Essex for assistance in the final preparation of the manuscript. Finally, we are keenly aware that this book would not have been possible without the excellent editorial staff at W. W. Norton: Peter Simon, for his support, optimism, and helpful knowledge of the field; Rob Bellinger; Evan Leatherwood; copy editor Ann R. Tappert; and proofreader Susan Forsyth.

Introduction

In 1896, the Russian writer Maxim Gorky attended a screening of the Lumière brothers' new invention, the *Cinématographe*. In his well-known review of the experience, he wrote that film viewing brought with it a sense of uncertainty and unease rather than the pleasure and wonder that most people would expect. Although he realized this new medium provided the kinds of thrills and easy laughs that could make it highly popular, Gorky found little of lasting value in the cinema, noting that its images of "mute, grey life" actually disturbed and depressed him. For Gorky, film was a mere entertainment, an idle distraction for the masses, with little redeeming social value. Films catered only to the viewers' sense of enjoyment, rather than to their critical faculties.

Even today, many moviegoers see the cinema as no more than an entertaining visual experience, requiring little explanation or thought. Thus, the idea that films might be worthy of serious critical attention and detailed analysis may strike some viewers as strange. "Why bother? It's only a movie" is a common attitude. This attitude, much like Gorky's initial experience of cinema, presumes that, as entertainment, films offer little of real meaning or social value. Yet, films are not *simply* entertainment. They are also meaningful documents with the potential to yield rich insights into the cultures and times in which they are made. Even films that present themselves purely as entertainment convey a host of cultural ideas and values at a "hidden" or subconscious level. Film analysis aims to bring these ideas and values, and the means through which they are conveyed, to our awareness.

Because it examines ideas and meanings that are often latent in films, film analysis is sometimes accused of overanalyzing films. Film criticism, some have argued, "reads too much into films," inventing meanings that are "not really there." This misperception stems from the fact that film analysis approaches films differently than most casual discussions do. Casual discussions of films tend to focus on opinions about the surface level of a film: "the pace was too slow"; "the cinematography was stunning"; "the acting was superb." They accept, in other words, what happens in a film, and even what is said in a film, at face value, without questioning the film itself. Film criticism or analysis, on the other hand, is never simply a matter of opinion. Instead, film analysis strives to examine the myriad narrative, thematic, and stylistic choices that are part of every film. In analyzing these choices, film analysis promotes a more skeptical approach to films, questioning those aspects that may seem obvious or natural in order to make us aware of what might otherwise have remained invisible and unquestioned.

A related objection to film analysis is the idea that too much analysis will somehow destroy the simple pleasures of the viewing experience. Much like the common opposition that sees films as *either* entertaining *or* meaningful, this concern assumes that analysis is directly opposed to pleasure, that to approach a film critically necessarily means killing off one's enjoyment. Some students even express concerns that learning about film analysis may have a cumulative effect: that they'll never be able to watch a film "just for fun" again. Yet, a critical, analytical approach to films need not detract from the entertainment or pleasure that we find in films. Just the fact that many people enjoy talking and arguing about their favorite films suggests that people do find pleasure in articulating their ideas as they relate to film. Critical analysis of films can deepen this pleasure by showing us not only the latent meanings of films but also how and why they work. Indeed, the more we understand about a film, its style, and its cultural and historical context, the more we can appreciate it.

Film analysis, then, does not simply take for granted what a film "should be." It is a process of thinking through the surface of the film text to discover its embedded and complex meanings, meanings that enrich and heighten the cinema-going experience. It strives to make sense of our fears, our hesitations, our desires—the whole strange array of pleasures and displeasures we experience as we sit for two hours in a darkened theater. Essentially, analysis brings films and their narratives into the realm of the social, allowing us to put their effects into perspective, to compare them to other films and other kinds of cultural artifacts, and finally to begin relating the films we watch to the wider world around us.

Analysis can also enhance our enjoyment of different types of films by pointing out that not all films share the same assumptions about how films should be made. While some "Hollywood-style" films may present themselves as mere entertainment, without ideas or meanings that require analysis, other films may present an entirely different way of seeing the world (*Ceddo*); or challenge the ways in which we conceive of space, time, and characters (*Un chien andalou*); or question our expectations of cinematic storytelling (*Breathless*). From early cinema to non-Western films, from experimental films to the most seemingly one-dimensional entertainments, film analysis allows us to discover the many layers of historical, cultural, and aesthetic meaning that lie within every film. Film analysis helps us to realize that entertainment, as the Russian filmmaker Sergei Eisenstein once suggested, does not always need to be innocuous. In fact, whether we notice it or not, it rarely is.

Reading the Film

The first step toward an analytical approach to film is to recognize that every film contains a range of different meanings, which are not always readily apparent. It is only by analyzing or interpreting the film in question—"reading the film"—that these meanings can be discovered. Reading a film is not the same as simply viewing a film; it implies a more active, critical approach. To read a film is to look beyond its obvious meaning—what it says or what happens in its narrative—in order to find the often unnoticed meanings, assumptions, and beliefs around which it is organized.

In many ways, this notion of reading a film relies on the traditional linguistic distinction between denotation and connotation. Denotation is generally understood as the literal or obvious meaning of a word. Connotation, on the other hand, refers to all of the implied or associated meanings that have come to be linked to that same word. Thus, the denotation of the word "fog" refers to a level of humidity thick enough to be visible, but the connotations of "fog" include much broader, more complex notions such as mystery, fear, or the loss of understanding.

Images might be seen as even more inclined toward connotation. The denotation of an image is literally what is shown in it, but very few images are purely denotative. Although all images may convey facts or information, they are rarely reducible to a single, straightforward meaning or message. Images always carry connotations, and their connotations inevitably evoke emotional and cultural associations.

In the above photograph, for example, we can clearly identify, at a denotative level, bare trees in an unidentified countryside. The lack of leaves and perhaps the quality of light allow us to deduce that it is winter; we might also reasonably surmise, based on the evidence of trees and landscape before us, that the location is somewhere in a temperate zone. Here, we are dealing only with the factual evidence of the photograph. But the scene also carries strong connotative associations, which we may find difficult to put into words. It evokes a sense of isolation, of silence. Although the photograph is artfully rendered, many viewers will probably not find the scene beautiful. It seems almost too barren, too desolate, to convey a positive emotion. One may even read a certain stoic sadness in this scene, perhaps subconsciously personifying the solitary tree in the foreground.

In films, the emotional charge conveyed at a connotative level is even more pronounced. Because of their complexity, their combination of images, music, and spoken dialogue, their frequent reliance on stories and characters that stir our feelings at a visceral level, films always communicate much more than their obvious message. The literal or denotative meaning of a film—what it says overtly—is only one of the film's many potential meanings. Reading or analyzing a film involves a concern less with a film's explicit statements than with its connotations: the complex set of ideas, beliefs, and associations that are represented in it but that are never openly stated. Reading a film is therefore a process through which we become increasingly aware of a film's multiple connotations or meanings, as well as the means through which they are conveyed.

The fact that a film's connotations may not immediately be evident from a casual viewing does not mean that they are not there. Nor does it mean that these connotative meanings are simply a product of the critic's views or opinions. Any reasonable reading or analysis of a film or films must be based, first of all, on what is *in* those films, on evidence or examples from them. Reading a film, in other words, means treating the film as a *text* to be examined. A text in this sense refers to any cultural object or form that has potential meaning. Reading a film as a text assumes that through careful attention to the film itself, through analysis of it, we can discover not just its obvious meaning, but its more complex, sometimes even contradictory, connotations.

If texts are, by definition, meaningful, they do not, however, have only *one* meaning. We can see a demonstration of this idea of textual richness in the fact that repeated viewings of a film can often lead to new discoveries and new insights. This sense of discovery could not occur if the film had a single meaning. Yet, some films can be seen as richer and more complex in meaning than others. This connotative complexity helps explain why certain films generate a wide variety of interpretations. A film that contains a broad, varied range of connotations is inevitably more open to interpretation—that is, to different interpretations—than one whose connotations are more restricted.

Some films that offer a complex mixture of connotations are experimental or antirealist in nature, and often draw explicit attention to their range of possible meanings. But even films that seem relatively straightforward or simple in meaning contain a rich array of associations if one looks more closely. Films as diverse as *Singin' in the Rain,* *Sherlock Jr., Bringing Up Baby,* and *Peking Opera Blues* might at first strike audiences as primarily entertainment vehicles, yet even films that present themselves as having little meaningful to say can affect us through these seemingly invisible connotations. Indeed, connotations, with their emotional links, tend to work most effectively on us when we are not fully aware of them. If the denotative meaning of a film is, by definition, apparent to us, its connotations enter our minds at a *subconscious* level. We seem to absorb them rather than consciously understand them. Film analysis and interpretation aim to help us become critically aware of this subconscious, largely invisible level of meaning.

The Idea of Interpretation

Interpreting films may sometimes seem an almost mystical practice, whose rules are obscure and complicated. Precisely *how* people have read and understood texts has certainly never been a simple matter. But the way that we think critically about films today did not spring up randomly or spontaneously: it is linked to a history of reading and understanding texts that goes back to the classical era. Indeed, in Western culture, the practice of interpreting texts, discovering their meanings, has its roots in early attempts to comprehend the often cryptic words and stories of the Bible.

The method through which Scripture is interpreted is called *exegesis*. The idea behind exegesis was to uncover the mysteries of texts that might on their surface appear to be either obscure or meaningless, to understand how both simple stories and difficult verses could contain alternative or additional meanings beyond what was apparent to the uninitiated eye. These meanings could be profound philosophical meanings about the nature of life, or practical meanings for use in everyday life. The practice of exegesis was therefore based in developing symbolic or *allegorical* readings of texts that stretched beyond the literal, denotative meaning of the words and stories.

Exegesis sees scriptural texts as containing layers, or levels, that exist beyond the literal. In an exegetical interpretation, any word or passage in the Bible might have several levels of meaning. It was the reader's job to find and make sense of these meanings. Some versions of biblical exegesis called for three levels of meaning in the text, others four; for our purposes here, though, it suffices to outline three key levels: the literal, the allegorical, and the moral. If the literal level corresponds to the denotative meaning of the text—the obvious stories and accounts, the entertainments and distractions it conveys—allegorical interpretation describes the discovery of the more profound, alternate meanings in the text. The moral level corresponds to the ways that the words and stories in Scripture also serve an instructive function—teaching readers how to edify or improve their everyday lives.

It may seem far-fetched to link biblical exegesis to film analysis and interpretation, but the central concepts of these early models of interpretation—even though the rules have been adapted and modified over the centuries—remain important to contemporary interpretative work. The very question of why it is *necessary* to interpret texts—whether written or visual—goes back to this need to discover latent or disguised meanings within texts, meanings that might escape the notice of less serious, less skilled examiners. Close, rigorous study of a text, with an eye to discovering its less obvious meanings—and how these meanings are constructed—remains the foundation of contemporary criticism and interpretation.

There are, however, key differences between traditional exegesis and contemporary approaches to interpretation. Exegesis was intended to unearth the "true," hidden levels of meaning in texts, and discovering this truth was based on the desire to understand the word of God. Films are not, in most cases, designed to serve as religious texts, and few would claim that they contain a single "true" or sacred meaning. Rather than looking for a singular truth in films or other cultural and artistic texts, contemporary criticism seeks to examine the variety of possible meanings within a given text and the different ways in which the text can be read or interpreted.

Contemporary criticism has, in fact, placed increasing emphasis on how people from different backgrounds and cultures read texts and their meanings differently. In acknowledging the multiple meanings or connotations that texts can evoke, contemporary criticism also acknowledges that different interpretations, from different perspectives, can coexist, with each adding something to our understanding of a given text. This is not to say, as has sometimes been claimed, that all interpretations are purely subjective, or that each is equally valid. Some interpretations are simply more trenchant, relevant, and enlightening than others. Interpretations must, moreover, be persuasive, supporting their views with evidence from the text in question. Interpretation strives, then, to provide insight into a text, to open a new perspective on it, while still remaining faithful to the integrity of the text.

Like traditional exegesis, contemporary film interpretation seeks to make us aware of the connotations, ideas, and beliefs that lie unnoticed within the text of a film. These covert meanings—which, as we have already noted, often affect us at a subconscious, emotional level—might be described as the "unconscious" of a film. In this sense, film analysis and interpretation bear a close resemblance, as many film theorists have acknowledged, to psychoanalysis. In both cases, analysis attempts to discover and interpret elements that lie at an unconscious level. Indeed, one of Sigmund Freud's most important works on psychoanalysis was *The Interpretation of Dreams*, in which he attempted to explain the unconscious processes by which dreams are produced. As in Freud's explanation of dreams, films can be said to contain covert or *latent content,* which can be discovered through a careful analysis of the elements of its explicit or *manifest content.* Just as the latent meaning of a dream could be interpreted by examining its altered or disguised forms in the manifest content, the latent meanings of a film can be discerned by tracing the vestigal elements of these meanings in the film's form and narrative. From this perspective, virtually every element in a film, from its narrative structure to the details of its *mise-en-scène,* can be seen as evidence of the latent meanings that, while they are never spelled out, inform the film—and its effect on us.

Meaning, Culture, and Ideology

The latent or unconscious meanings within a particular text cannot, however, be viewed in isolation from the cultural and historical world of which they are a part. Connotations and meanings do not exist in a vacuum; they are always culturally and historically determined. Thus, in reading or interpreting a film, we seek to discover and understand not only the latent meanings of that film, but also the complex mixture of societal ideas and beliefs that lie within it. To take a relatively simple example, it would be difficult, if not impossible, to analyze *It Happened One Night* without taking into account the fact that the film's romantic conflict is closely linked to its populist ideas about differences and conflicts between social classes (an important issue in a film made during the Great Depression). These ideas are not, however, limited simply to the text or its author; they are, in many ways, a reflection of broadly held, although often unarticulated, societal ideas and beliefs. After all, if the ideas presented in it were not already broadly accepted, at least subconsciously, *It Happened One Night* would likely not have enjoyed the popular success that it did.

The term that contemporary film studies has generally used to refer to this level of broadly held cultural or societal beliefs and ideas is *ideology*. This usage is slightly different from the way the term is commonly used, where *ideology* suggests strongly held—or even rigid—beliefs that allow for no compromise. In popular usage, *ideology* is seen as a conscious set of ideas, but as film studies uses the term, *ideology* implies a set or system of ideas that are so widely accepted that they are only rarely examined in a conscious way. Ideology, in other words, can be seen as a culture's unconscious. *Ideology,* in this sense, is very similar to *connotation.* When we examine the latent meanings or connotations of a film text, we inevitably cross into the realm of ideology, of cultural meanings and ideas.

Because ideological beliefs usually remain at an unconscious level, analyzing the cultural ideology that inflects a film or other text can be difficult. Perhaps for this reason, ideology is often figured as something that is buried deep beneath the surface of a text (or of a culture). Yet, in many ways, ideological notions are difficult to grasp precisely because they seem so obvious to us. If we accept a belief as true, it doesn't occur to us that it is ideological. It appears simply as "the way things are supposed to be," or as "common sense." Thus, not so long ago, it seemed perfectly natural in many so-called developed countries that "a woman's place is in the home." Today, this seeming truth is generally seen as an old-fashioned, and sexist, ideological belief. Yet, when it comes to beliefs that we accept as true, whether they appear in a film or elsewhere, we find it hard to see them as ideological.

Successful films, it might be argued, are those that are able to articulate prevailing cultural beliefs effectively, making them seem natural and universal, rather than culturally and historically determined. Thus, for example, we might not question why many films focus on an individual hero who, through decisive, often violent action, triumphantly overcomes villainous people or forces that seek to control or destroy him (or, occasionally, her). It may, then, require a step back to recognize that this formula is based on an ideological belief in the power of the individual, in the ability of individual action to solve problems in short order, usually by overcoming an individual villain. The fact that we know many real-life problems cannot be attributed simply to an individual villain or solved by individual heroic action does not change our belief in individualism, nor our satisfaction in seeing this belief affirmed. Thus, this belief in individual action (as opposed to collective or societal action) appears simply to be a fact, rather than an ideological notion that can be questioned and analyzed.

In some cases, however, due to the passage of time or shifts in dominant cultural beliefs, the ideological bent of a particular film, which might have been more invisible or acceptable at the time of the film's initial release, becomes more apparent to us, as in the pervasive and problematic racism of *The Birth of a Nation* or, less sensationally, in the traditional masculine and feminine stereotypes put forward in most Westerns, including *Stagecoach*. In these cases, careful film analysis not only exposes the limits of past social beliefs and practices, but can also reveal the extent to which our own ideological perspectives cannot simply be seen as a break from the past. If our dominant societal beliefs have in ways progressed beyond the past, they are also outgrowths of it. Moreover, these beliefs will undoubtedly be taken to task by future generations.

Some films—such as *Ali: Fear Eats the Soul, Do the Right Thing, Raise the Red Lantern,* or *Ceddo*—are themselves analyses of prevailing societal structures or beliefs. Their narratives obviously contain political implications (dealing with class and racial prejudice in *Ali* and *Do the Right Thing;* gender roles and the oppression of women in *Red Lantern;* religious and sociopolitical orthodoxy, as well as class and gender roles, in *Ceddo*), but these films cannot be reduced to a single political or ideological meaning. They work, rather, to engage our intellects and encourage further thinking about the political and ideological questions they raise. Eisenstein's *Battleship Potemkin* could be seen as taking this approach further, impelling viewers to think more carefully about the film medium itself as both a reflection and producer of ideology. Eisenstein's techniques aim to disrupt complacent viewing habits, to awaken the audience to an awareness of ideological conflicts that would normally remain on an unconscious level. Of course, all such films, *Potemkin* included, are themselves culturally and histori-cally determined texts that can, through careful analysis, reveal hid-den or contradictory meanings and contexts beyond those that their filmmakers intended.

Text and Context

A number of theorists have argued that *the entire realm of culture can it-self be seen as a text*—or set of texts—to be read and interpreted. From this perspective, a film or similar text may be seen as a particular in-stance within a much larger cultural and historical text, which for sim-plicity's sake we can call *context.*

The relationship between text and context can therefore be under-stood as a continuum that stretches from the specific—the text itself—to the extremely general—as exemplified in broad cultural or ideological beliefs. Between these extremes lies a host of important contextual information, ranging from the personal backgrounds of the film's makers to the institutional and industrial circumstances in which it was made, to the social and economic conditions at the time of its making. Context must also include the relation of the film to other films and film genres, and to film history and film criticism, as well as its relation to other cultural forms and technologies, such as television, computers, music, art, and literature. Indeed, context may be taken to include anything that has an influence or bearing on a par-ticular film.

Context is, therefore, crucial to the analysis or interpretation of any text. Understanding the context that surrounds and permeates a film helps provide a framework for analyzing that film. It also reminds us that films are never culturally or ideologically neutral, but are in-formed by the complex historical, social, and economic forces of the times in which they are created. Context also helps us to more imme-diately comprehend the difficulties and obstacles encountered in mak-ing films, to recognize the struggles behind the scenes of any given film and the collective effort that goes into the finished product. Fur-thermore, context can allow us to focus our analyses: knowing the so-cial and historical conditions under which a film was made can, as in the case of *It Happened One Night,* point us toward a particular inter-pretation and to relevant information and examples.

Introduction

As crucial as an understanding of context is to our analysis of any one text, we can never assume that we understand that context fully. Our ability to analyze texts and their contexts, whether in writing or in discussion, is always open to improvement. As film scholar Stephen Prince observes,

> the film critic needs to do much more than simply watch movies. The critic must be sufficiently well read, educated, and cultured to possess numerous frameworks of reference or interpretation that can be applied to films and that can nurture works of criticism. The broader a critic's social and cultural frames of reference, the richer the criticism that is produced. (335)

As Prince suggests, film analysis depends on the critic's own knowledge of and position within a broader cultural context. Our cultural background and experience help provide a framework for analyzing and interpreting cultural texts. And as we read, watch, and analyze an increasing range of texts, the greater our skill in analysis becomes. At its best, critical film analysis and interpretation enable us to understand our cultural beliefs and our own ideas, our own ways of seeing and thinking about the world.

Approaches to Writing about Film

Many students, when faced with writing analysis for the first time, feel rather lost. Unfortunately, there is no simple answer to the question of how to write analysis, since analysis is not like some mathematical formula that can be memorized and repeated. Indeed, what analysis tests is one's ability to examine the obvious, to question what is taken for granted, to go beyond conventional ideas. If there were a formula for doing analysis, it would become a conventional, predictable, and essentially pointless task. Despite common prejudices to the contrary, good critical analysis is creative work; it strives to find new ways of seeing and thinking about films—an enjoyable and creative activity in its own right.

But just as no one can easily explain how to go about making a great film, no one can explain precisely how to write good analysis. Keeping this in mind, we offer the following as some useful starting points for writing about film.

First things first: opinion is not analysis

No analysis can take into account every aspect of a film and its context. One must, therefore, make certain choices about what aspects of a film are most relevant to an insightful analysis. These choices will, to some extent, be governed by the analyst's own interests and knowledge, but they must not ignore the evidence provided by the film and the broader cultural and historical context of which the film is a part. It often happens that a student writing about a favorite film has difficulty separating opinion from analysis. Analysis requires that we question our own opinions: our likes and dislikes, the reasons that a film seems good or bad to us. If we do not examine our preset ideas about films, then we will likely find it impossible to understand and appreciate films from other cultures or films that rely on a different idea of filmmaking. Analysis must begin, then, from a willingness to question not only the film's motivations, but our own.

Starting out

At a practical level, of course, the first and often the most difficult part of writing analysis is finding a place or point from which to begin. It is often claimed that analysis should begin with a *thesis* about the film or films in question. A thesis is not simply an opinion, but neither is it simply a statement of fact: it is an argument that can be convincingly supported with examples and evidence. Yet, it can be difficult to formulate a thesis until one has examined and researched the topic. It is therefore useful to begin one's analysis from a more provisional point of interest that can, through the process of research, be turned into a supportable argument about the topic. Thus, the starting points that may lead to a strong thesis and analysis are varied. One might begin by focusing on a very specific element in a film: for example, a repeated visual element or stylistic technique. Answering why this element is repeated and what purpose it serves in the film will often lead to a productive analysis. One might also start an analysis by pinpointing an aspect of the film that stands out from the rest of the film or that contradicts other parts of the film. Such contradictions frequently provide an insight into the issues or conflicts that a film tries to, but perhaps cannot, resolve. As well, one may begin an analysis from more general considerations, such as the ideas or beliefs that are represented in the film's characters or in its narrative conflict, or how the film compares to other films of its type. At perhaps an even more general level, one might consider the film's relations to its cultural, societal, or historical context. In each case, however, the goal of analysis is to look beyond the film's literal or denotative level in order to understand the contextual, thematic, narrative, or stylistic structures that serve to motivate and organize the film. Although context, themes, narrative, and style are always closely interrelated in any film, we can, for simplicity's sake, consider them separately here. Each can serve as a beginning point for analysis.

Don't neglect context

The context in which a film is made determines how it is made, who makes it, and even whether or not it is made. It is therefore a mistake to neglect examining a film's context or to treat contextual analysis, as some students do, merely as "extra work." It is true, however, that understanding the context of a film generally requires *research,* whether that means viewing related films, studying the culture or historical period in which the film was made, reading relevant books or articles from a library, researching studio records and documents, or tracking the film's reception by audiences. One cannot expect, of course, to understand every aspect of a film's context. Analyzing context involves a continual process of sorting or filtering information with an eye to what is most relevant to your central argument about the film or films in question. As one learns about a film's cultural and historical context, it becomes easier to distinguish which contextual elements are most appropriate to your analysis. Here we will isolate a few of the key areas: the production context, the filmic context, and the cultural and historical context.

One important but often ignored aspect of contextual analysis is the *production context* of a film, the situation in which it is financed and produced. Films financed and produced by major Hollywood studios are, for example, subject to a range of influences and pressures that affect the film's ultimate form. Financial pressures and creative vision are, in many ways, structurally at odds in this process, and the negotiation of these conflicts cannot help but define the resulting film. Often, this process has been seen in terms of a conflict between the vision of the *auteur* and the restrictive structures of Hollywood, a conflict that is well illustrated in the making of *The Godfather.* Yet, it is also important to keep in mind what the film critic André Bazin called the "genius of the system," the ability of Hollywood's factory-oriented studios to produce quality films that cannot simply be attributed to a single creator, as exemplified in *Casablanca* and *Singin' in the Rain*. Of course, Hollywood is not the only context in which films are financed and made. The very different contexts in which films are produced—from the studios of Japan or India to independent financing to the institutions that support different national cinemas—are just as important to an analysis of those films as is the production context of Hollywood films.

At a somewhat broader level, films must also be seen in the context of other films; this might be called the *filmic context*. Thus, it is often productive to consider a film in comparison to others of its type or genre, or to those that have been made by the same director, producer, or studio. One cannot, after all, entirely understand a film without knowing the other films to which it, consciously or unconsciously, refers. Moreover, films such as *Sherlock Jr., Close-up,* and *8½,* which are explicitly concerned with filmmaking and film form, can scarcely be understood without considering them in the context of other films and filmmaking styles. Thus, knowing something of the history of films and of the various approaches to filmmaking at various times and in different cultures allows one to better understand the place and importance of a particular film. Equally important is the critical context that surrounds a film. Considering, for example, the various books and articles that have been written about it, its director, or about similar films not only can provide valuable information about the film and its context, but can also offer insights that help us to situate our own understanding of the film.

Beyond the context of other films and film criticism, contextual analysis can usefully turn to the broader *historical and cultural context* in which films are made. As we see in the example of the Lumières' *Arrival of a Train at La Ciotat,* the historical events that were taking place during, or prior to, the making of a film often leave their mark on it, even if they are not explicitly depicted in it. Often, too, important cultural and political issues of the time make their way into films, as is the case with a number of the films included in this volume, in which social problems such as racial prejudice and gender inequality are portrayed, often from the perspective of those affected. Yet, the role of cultural context is scarcely limited to explicit depictions of social issues or problems. Every film draws from the culture of which it is a part, from the clothing to the language to the lifestyles depicted in each. Films, in short, reflect their cultural context, including its attitudes and way of looking at the world. Not surprisingly, films that reflect different cultural perspectives often depict the world differently, using different approaches to filmmaking. Understanding these cultural differences is therefore crucial to understanding these films. Finally, as differences in cultural attitudes and perspectives suggest, films reflect the ideological beliefs of the culture in which they are made. Analyzing ideological beliefs, as we have argued, requires a recognition that these beliefs (our beliefs) are not natural or universal but cultural. Examining different cultural contexts reminds us, then, that films reflect their culture's way of looking at the world, which is not necessarily the only or the best way.

Examine the major themes

One of the most common ways to begin a film analysis is by asking, what is the film about? This approach can, however, be easily misunderstood, leading to a mere description of the film's narrative: a plot summary. For the purposes of film analysis, summarizing the plot of a film is usually unnecessary; one can generally assume that the reader already knows the film's narrative. Analyzing what a film is about should instead focus on the film's latent meanings: the main ideas, issues, or themes with which it is concerned at an implicit level.

Perhaps the most accessible way to explore a film's basic thematic structure is to look at the film in terms of its major *conflicts* or *oppositions*. In most narrative films, these oppositions are represented through the portrayal of characters and their relationship to other characters and forces. Here again, however, one must be careful to look beyond the film's obvious meanings. The fact that a hero triumphs over a villain cannot be read simply as a triumph of good over evil. One must examine exactly what ideas or values the film presents as good or bad, positive or negative. Thus, for example, Charlie Chaplin's *Modern Times* continually contrasts the predicament of those who are economically struggling through the Depression to the rules and conformity that "respectable" society attempts to impose on them. The film therefore implicitly poses the poor in contrast to the wealthy, individual freedom in contrast to societal authority and laws, and personal integrity in contrast to social convention. The film, of course, makes readily apparent which pole of these oppositions it sees favorably, and in so doing implicitly criticizes the inequities of modern industrial society. Taking a very different example, we can observe the way that *Yeelen* pits a young sorcerer in a mythic struggle against his powerful, authoritarian father. Through this struggle, the film represents, and attempts to mediate, important cultural oppositions between youth and elders, change and tradition, social openness and closed, hierarchical rule. Moreover, films often group their characters along oppositional lines, as in *Stagecoach,* where the Ringo Kid, Dallas, and Doc Boone—the outcasts of society—turn out to be more kind, innocent, and honorable than the supposed moral stalwarts of "civilized society." Through these characters, *Stagecoach* poses notions of individual freedom and integrity against societal morality and laws, which are shown to be hypocritical and even corrupt.

But it is also important to remember: *don't oversimplify* the film. While it is possible to find oppositional thematic structures in almost any film, it is worth stressing that viewing a film merely in terms of abstract oppositional meanings can lead to a reductive analysis that oversimplifies the film and its meanings. Some films are more readily understood in terms of oppositional thematic structures than others, in which the imposition of a set of oppositions may diminish their richness and complexity. For example, viewing *The Rules of the Game* solely in terms of, say, class conflicts would neglect much of what makes the film remarkable. Moreover, even films that seem to set up a clearly oppositional structure often tend, albeit unconsciously, to undermine or complicate these oppositions. Some philosophers have, in fact, argued that the tendency to see the world in terms of binary oppositions is emphasized in Western cultures (and films), as the very idea of "the West" (as opposed to "other" cultures) makes clear. A nonbinary approach is readily apparent in films such as *The Seventh Seal* or *Ceddo,* where the array of characters and social forces in conflict with one another cannot simply be reduced to oppositional terms. Thus, while thematic oppositions may often provide a useful starting point for analysis, it is important to question such oppositions as well, looking at the ways in which they reflect a particular cultural or ideological perspective.

Introduction

Think about the role of narrative

To the extent that thematic analysis examines the conceptual structures of a film or films, it often overlaps with the analysis of narrative organization or structure. Yet, while thematic analysis tends to look at these structures without considering their temporal dimensions, narrative analysis focuses on how the narrative proceeds or develops chronologically, over time. Here we suggest thinking about how the film tells its story, looking at the narrative's ongoing patterns of repetition and exclusion, and questioning, rather than simply accepting, the resolution at the story's end.

The study of narratives, or narratology, is a complex topic, which we can only touch on here, but narrative analysis generally begins by dividing a film's action into parts or segments. These segments can then be examined for *patterns of repetition and difference,* allowing the film to be usefully compared to the narrative structure of similar films. Because, however, narrative is inevitably a way of regulating what the film shows or does not show, it is important to consider not only the actions and events that appear on the screen, but also events or information that are *excluded* or *withheld.* The narrative structure of suspense and mystery films, such as *Double Indemnity* and *Chinatown,* is defined by the deliberate withholding of plot-related information, but in many films, the narrative structure is marked by an unconscious repression or displacement of ideologically troublesome elements. In this context, it is worth noting that the classical Hollywood narrative is itself based on a restricted narrative structure, in which individual actions move the story in a linear trajectory toward a conclusion that explains and brings to completion any mysteries or conflicts previously raised.

As the Hollywood narrative model suggests, an important consideration in any narrative analysis is the question of how the film resolves, or attempts to resolve, the conflicts it establishes. It is generally through its narrative—and the narrative's *resolution* or *conclusion*—that a film privileges particular themes, ideas, or meanings over others. Although the resolution can be as simple as having a character—and the ideas or values that he or she represents—triumph over another, the situation is frequently not so straightforward. Indeed, the narrative's conclusion might be purposefully ambiguous or open ended or (as is more frequently the case) neatly tied up and clearly resolved. The open-ended approach demonstrates the complexity of the issues involved and the difficulty of resolving them in a simplistic way. This approach to narrative is common in many non-Hollywood films, and perhaps explains the sense of discomfort that some viewers, accustomed to Hollywood's generally clear-cut endings, feel when confronted with the narrative ambiguity or complexity of films such as *The Rules of the Game, Daughters of the Dust,* or *Ali: Fear Eats the Soul.*

Yet, even among Hollywood films, it frequently happens that the issues raised during the course of the narrative are so complex that they cannot be resolved in a straightforward way. They become, in a sense, almost as complex as "real-life" problems, which are not so easily or simply concluded. In order to achieve an artificial sense of resolution or closure, therefore, films often resort to standard storytelling strategies, shifting or transforming their thematic or ideological tensions into conflicts that are more easily tied up and resolved. Yet, we might notice that even these strategies for tying up loose ends are not as clear cut as they appear. Indeed, often they resolve very little beyond the more superficial aspects of the plot. Many romantic comedies (such as *Bringing Up Baby*), for example, construct the conflict between their main characters in terms of differences in economic class or social background, which are supposedly resolved or mediated when, in the course of the film's narrative, they eventually fall in love and are married. Yet, the marriage of these characters does nothing to resolve or overcome the social inequities between rich and poor; it is only by transforming this conflict from a social and economic issue into an individual issue, a matter of personal incompatibilities, that a "satisfying" narrative resolution can be achieved. A similar social and economic conflict organizes, as we have noted, the narrative of *Modern Times,* in which the difficulty of overcoming the problems of inequity in a modern industrial society is implied by the film's ending, where Chaplin's Tramp figure and his girlfriend can only depart the city in search of a better life.

Finally: keep an eye on style
The style of a film includes all the elements of how the film is constructed: its cinematography, editing, *mise-en-scène,* and sound. Even the most stylistically straightforward films make important choices about how to depict the characters, objects, and scenes within them.

These choices can tell us a great deal about the attitudes and beliefs presented in the film, as well as its relation to other films. By choosing a particular framing and camera angle; varying a scene's lighting, setting, or music; or editing shots differently, filmmakers can dramatically affect how a scene or character is represented, or even how we interpret the film as a whole. Examining the stylistic choices in a film can, then, help us to understand not only its meanings, but the means through which it affects its audience.

Many introductory film textbooks provide explanations of the various elements and uses of cinematic style in much more detail than is possible in this introduction. Yet, film style also can be analyzed at a broader, structural level. Indeed, the *classical Hollywood style* is itself a stylistic structure, a set of stylistic rules that governs the particular kinds of films that can be made within it. These rules are designed to make the stylistic structure of Hollywood films invisible, allowing all attention to be focused on the flow of the narrative. The goal of Hollywood's rules of continuity is precisely the effacement of style. Because Hollywood style is designed to make itself unobtrusive and transparent, it can be particularly difficult to analyze, requiring repeated viewings of a film (or of sequences from a film or films) to discover how its stylistic techniques work. By analyzing these techniques, however, one quickly begins to see how the stylistic structure of Hollywood films can work at a subconscious level to direct the viewer's attention and reactions. Stylistic analysis makes apparent the structural rules that govern these films' representations and, often, our responses to them.

On the other hand, the notion of the film director as an *auteur*, similar to the author of a literary work, has generally relied on the idea of an *auteur*'s ability to impose a stylistic signature or structure across the body of his or her work, even when working within the confines of a system that strives for stylistic invisibility. John Ford, for example, is well known for frequently framing characters and situations through windows and doors, creating a painterly "frame within a frame" effect. Analysis of this recurring technique might suggest the need to consider the associations evoked by thresholds, which tend to connote potential movement, transition, and change. In Ford's films, these frames also suggest important structural differences between interiors and exteriors: between the realm of safety and domestic order and the realm of danger and the unknown. A different example can be found in the prominent use of the point-of-view shot in many of Alfred Hitchcock's films, which coincides with his linkage of cinema and voyeurism, which is especially highlighted in *Rear Window.*

Of course, particular stylistic techniques have often been associated with directors working outside of Hollywood as well, from Eisenstein's montage of conflicts to Ozu Yasujiro's use of low camera placements and graphic matching to Jean Renoir's use of long takes and elaborately planned camera movements. In a similar way, certain cinematic movements have employed distinctive stylistic techniques—such as German Expressionism's emphasis on distorted elements of *mise-en-scène,* notable in *The Cabinet of Dr. Caligari*—in their followers' efforts to explore different ways of representing the world. A number of these cinematic styles have emerged in conscious opposition to Hollywood practice—from the disorienting surrealism of *Un chien andalou* to the use of jump cuts and self-reflexive techniques in *Breathless.* These *alternative stylistic strategies* point to the fact that style is never neutral or natural; style is itself ideological, allowing different ways of perceiving and understanding the world to be brought to representation.

Thus, whether a stylistic technique recurs in the work of a particular director or in the films of a particular cinematic movement, the point of stylistic analysis is not simply to observe this recurrence, but to consider how these stylistic structures match or convey certain ideas within these films, from Renoir's sense of the complex rules and mechanisms of social life to Surrealism's emphasis on the role of chance, coincidence, and the unconscious within the cultural world. In a similar way, the stylistic structures of many films from non-Western cultures differ from Hollywood and European film styles precisely because they reflect different views of the world and of representation generally. Stylistic analysis enables us to discern these cultural and ideological differences.

Reading *Film Analysis*

In much the same way that one can learn about filmmaking by studying films, one can also learn about criticism by studying examples of it. This book provides examples of critical essays on films that you are likely to encounter in film and media studies courses, though the range of films available for study could not possibly be contained in a single volume. These essays offer a variety of analytical modes and insights, while raising key issues for further discussion and critical thinking about these culturally and historically important films. The critical approaches here range from historical and industrial analyses, to readings that emphasize ideological implications or important cultural differences, to approaches that emphasize film form and close readings of the image. Yet, while it is possible to view these essays in terms of their varying critical approaches, it is also important to note that they often combine different modes of analysis, demonstrating that no single critical approach is sufficient to understanding the diverse array of cinematic possibilities—even within a single film. In their diversity, these essays also serve to illustrate a range of approaches to writing clearly and responsibly about different kinds of cinematic texts.

As we discussed earlier, these essays work to excavate the multiple meanings of these texts, while also showing how the process of interpretation requires engaging with contextual material that broadens our frames of reference, heightening our understanding of the films' social and cultural significance. Each essay therefore includes sections that highlight notions of "context" and "analysis"—though it would obviously be wrong to see these categories as somehow mutually exclusive. While it is useful here for the purposes of clarity and organization to separate these categories—differentiating external pressures and events that have worked *on* the text from meanings and associations generated *by* the text—it should remain clear that researching the contexts of a given film is always part of the process of analysis. At the same time, performing a close textual analysis of a film can provide clues that deepen our understanding of the historical, social, and economic conditions under which films are made.

The forty-four essays included here offer select analyses of particular films, of important directors, and of different genres, drawn from a variety of different cultures and filmmaking perspectives and from across the history of cinema. These essays were written for this volume by leading film scholars with an eye to providing readers not only with insightful views on these individual films, but also some useful models for the critical analysis of film. The range and depth of the critical thinking in these essays should help to challenge the assumption that most films are mere entertainment, and will hopefully enhance your understanding of films as meaningful texts. As we move into the digital age and films are available to us in a wide variety of media and venues, it might seem that the film image is now a more superficial and disposable commodity than ever before. The analyses in this book suggest that not all entertainment is so easily disposable. Indeed, they offer practical examples of how one may intervene in the seemingly ephemeral processes of culture, examining the images that increasingly surround us, providing context and offering understanding of these rich cultural texts. That is why work such as film analysis is sometimes called "culture work." It helps us to come to terms with the increasingly wide range of cultural forms, messages, and meanings in which we find ourselves immersed. In so doing, it also helps us to situate ourselves as subjects within the cultures and societies we inhabit.

Recommended Reading

Allen, Robert Clyde, and Douglas Gomery. *Film History: Theory and Practice.* New York: McGraw, 1985.

Arnheim, Rudolph. *Film as Art.* Berkeley: U of California P, 1989.

Balio, Tino. *The American Film Industry.* Madison: U of Wisconsin P, 1976.

Barsam, Richard. *Looking at Movies: An Introduction to Film.* New York: Norton, 2003.

Bazin, André. *What Is Cinema?* Ed. and trans. Hugh Gray. 2 vols. Berkeley: U of California P, 1969–71.

Bordwell, David, Janet Staiger, and Kristin Thompson. *The Classical Hollywood Cinema.* New York: Columbia UP, 1985.

Bordwell, David, and Kristin Thompson. *Film Art: An Introduction.* 7th ed. New York: McGraw, 2003.

Braudy, Leo, and Marshall Cohen, eds. *Film Theory and Criticism: Introductory Readings.* 5th ed. London: Oxford UP, 1998.

Buscombe, Edward. *Cinema Today.* New York: Phaidon, 2003.

Cook, David A. *A History of Narrative Film.* 4th ed. New York: Norton, 2004.

Cook, Pam, ed. *The Cinema Book.* 2nd ed. London: BFI, 1999.

Corrigan, Timothy. *A Short Guide to Writing about Film.* 5th ed. Boston: Pearson Longman, 2003.

Deleuze, Gilles. *Cinema 1: Movement Image.* Trans. Hugh Tomlinson. Minneapolis: U of Minnesota P, 1986.

Deleuze, Gilles. *Cinema 2: Time Image.* Trans. Hugh Tomlinson. Minneapolis: U of Minnesota P, 1989.

Diawara, Manthia, ed. *Black American Cinema*. New York: Routledge, 1993.

Eisenstein, Sergei. *Film Form: Essays in Film Theory*. Ed. and trans. Jay Leyda. New York: Harcourt, 1949.

Gianetti, Louis. *Understanding Movies*. 9th ed. New York: Prentice, 2001.

Gledhill, Christine, and Linda Williams, eds. *Reinventing Film Studies*. London: Edward Arnold, 2000.

Hill, John, and Pamela Church Gibson, eds. *The Oxford Guide to Film Studies*. Oxford: Oxford UP, 1998.

———, eds. *World Cinema: Critical Approaches*. London: Oxford UP, 2000.

Kaplan, E. Ann, ed. *Feminism and Film*. New York: Oxford UP, 2000.

Lehman, Peter, ed. *Close Viewings: An Anthology of New Film Criticism*. Tallahassee: Florida State UP, 1990.

Mast, Gerald, and Bruce Kawin. *A Short History of the Movies*. 8th ed. Boston: Pearson Longman, 2002.

Miller, Toby, and Robert Stam, eds. *Film and Theory: An Anthology*. London: Blackwell, 2000.

Monaco, James. *How to Read a Film: The World of Movies, Media, and Multimedia: Language, History, Theory*. 3rd ed. Oxford: Oxford UP, 2000.

Mulvey, Laura. *Visual and Other Pleasures (Theories of Representation and Difference)*. Bloomington: Indiana UP, 1989.

Neale, Steve, and Murray Smith, eds. *Contemporary Hollywood Cinema*. New York: Routledge, 1998.

Nelmes, Jill, ed. *An Introduction to Film Studies*. London: Routledge, 1999.

Nichols, Bill, ed. *Movies and Methods: An Anthology*. 2 vols. Berkeley: U of California P, 1983–85.

Nowell-Smith, Geoffrey, ed. *The Oxford History of World Cinema*. Oxford: Oxford UP, 1997.

Prince, Stephen. *Movies and Meaning: An Introduction to Film*. 3rd ed. New York: Allyn, 2004.

Ray, Robert. *A Certain Tendency of the Hollywood Cinema, 1930–1980*. Princeton: Princeton UP, 1985.

Robinson, David. *From Peepshow to Palace: Birth of American Film*. New York: Columbia UP, 1996.

Schatz, Thomas. *Hollywood Genres*. New York: Random, 1981.

Sklar, Robert. *Film: An International History of the Medium*. New York: Prentice, 2002.

———. *Movie-Made America: A Cultural History of American Film*. Rev. ed. New York: Vintage, 1994.

Thompson, Kristin, and David Bordwell. *Film History: An Introduction*. 2nd ed. New York: McGraw, 2002.

Thornham, Sue, ed. *Feminist Film Theory: A Reader*. New York: New York UP, 1999.

Turner, Graeme. *Film as Social Practice*. 3rd ed. London: Routledge, 1999.

Williams, Linda, ed. *Viewing Positions: Ways of Seeing Film*. New Brunswick: Rutgers UP, 1994.

Wollen, Peter. *Signs and Meanings in the Cinema*. Bloomington: Indiana UP, 1973.

Film Analysis

A NORTON READER

Arrival of a Train at La Ciotat

(1895–1897)

KARIN LITTAU

Silent Films and Screaming Audiences

Context

Film history does and does not start with the Lumière brothers' invention of the *Cinématographe*. Auguste and Louis Lumière did not give birth to pictures in motion, since optical effects of movement in the form of shadow plays and magic-lantern shows were already well loved entertainments before the nineteenth century. Nor did they invent the movies, because the public could already, even if only on an individual basis, watch films by peering through Thomas Alva Edison's coin-operated peep box, the Kinetoscope. Rather, the Lumières were the first to project a strip of film on a screen large enough to be seen by an entire audience, and therefore instituted film viewing as a collective experience. The screening on December 28, 1895, at the Salon Indien of the Grand Café in Paris, will remain forever recorded in our history books, because from then onward audiences were willing to pay regularly for this new form of entertainment.[1]

On that day, the way in which the world was seen both changed and did not change. There had never been a technology that could so accurately produce an illusion of reality. Although these moving pictures were in black and white, what they simulated was not only life as it could be seen beyond the walls of the Grand Café, but also the sensation of movement as it could be felt in the hubbub of the nineteenth-century metropolis. On the other hand, those who lined up that day on the Boulevard des Capucines were already seeing the world protocinematically. This is because they were accustomed to big-city living, which had become as fast and intoxicating as the speed

---

[1]The first-ever film screening to an audience—namely, invited scientists at the Société d'Encouragement pour l'Industrie Nationale—took place on March 22, 1895.

of the onrushing impressions about to burst onto the screen. The cinema, with its restless succession of living pictures, was the very embodiment of a modern existence in flux. The Lumières' invention of a technological apparatus that combined camera, printer, and projector, and their most famous film, *Arrival of a Train at La Ciotat*, must therefore be understood in the larger context of modernity, which had brought unprecedented changes to everyday life.

The Cinema Was on Its Way Long before 1895

Everything associated with the modern age—industrialization, mobility, and consumerism—and everything this entailed, from overpopulated urban centers, machinery working around the clock, the deafening noise of trains, to shopping as a new form of addiction, were all factors in shaping a sensibility that had become, according to Friedrich Nietzsche in 1888, "immensely more irritable" (47). During the early years of the railways, nervous energies overcame the traveler as the train swallowed up the miles at an inhuman pace, just as the anxious air traveler in our own age seems to expect with every unusual vibration that disaster is waiting (Schivelbusch 160–61). The fear of technology out of control, of accidents and collisions, were just as tangibly felt at street level. Writing about the burgeoning nineteenth-century metropolis, the cultural theorist Walter Benjamin found that "moving through traffic involves the individual in a series of shocks and collisions" to the extent that "at dangerous crossings, nervous impulses flow through him in rapid succession" (132). Even pushing through the jostling crowds, the urban stroller felt at some risk, be this a potential pickpocket's hand too close for comfort, ramming the elbow of a stranger, or, as Émile Zola's novel *The Ladies' Paradise* (1883) describes it, being swept away by a current of shoppers, which the new department stores pulled in as if "sucking in the population from the four corners of Paris" (241; ch. 9). When Nietzsche gives his diagnosis of modernity, it is befitting therefore that he also gives a flavor of the new pace of life by emulating its tempo and rhythm in the fragmentary nature of his style:

> the abundance of disparate impressions greater than ever: cosmopolitanism in foods, literatures, newspapers, forms, tastes, even landscapes. The tempo of this influx *prestissimo*; the

> impressions erase each other; one instinctively resists taking in anything, taking anything deeply, to "digest" anything; a weakening of the power to digest results from this. A kind of adaptation of this flood of impressions takes place: men unlearn spontaneous action, they merely react to stimuli from outside. *Profound weakness of spontaneity:* the historian, critic, analyst, the interpreter, the observer, the collector, the reader—all of them *reactive* talents—all science! (47; italics in the original)

If over the course of the twentieth century we have become accustomed to the sheer barrage of stimuli with which modern life assaults us, and have learned to live with its anonymity and chaos, for the nineteenth-century populace it marked an age of transition, from a more tranquil existence to a more intense one.

Just like the moving images in the picture house, life outside presented previously unseen spectacles that were altogether too fleeting to absorb in anything but fragments. One of the first to characterize modernity in such terms was the poet, Charles Baudelaire. For him, the very hallmark of modernity was "the ephemeral, the fugitive, the contingent" (13), and it is this that set into motion a different relation to, and perception of, the world. In his essay "The Painter of Modern Life" (1863), we can sense how the modern city impacted on his sensibility as an artist. Strolling through Paris, which Baudelaire saw as *the* nineteenth-century capital, meant throwing oneself into "the heart of the multitude, amid the ebb and flow of movement, in the midst of the fugitive and infinite" (9). Whether this midst was experienced with excitement as "an immense reservoir of electric energy" (Baudelaire 9), or the throng of the crowd and the vibrations of city traffic fatigued people, the point is that the modern city dweller was continually bombarded by what O. Winter, in his article "The Cinematograph" (1896), called "an endless series of partial impressions" (296). In this respect, what has been called the "mobilized gaze" of the *flâneur* (Baudelaire's term for the urban stroller), who wandered through the Parisian arcades watching faces, gestures, and movements, or that of the window-shopper transfixed by the array of consumer goods on display, is not dissimilar from that of the early film viewer (Friedberg 61–65). These spectators are all put into a state of distraction by what they see; for none of them is the eye ever allowed to rest.

In much of nineteenth-century fiction we find protagonists trying to come to terms with the experience of modernity. Take the narrator of Edgar Allan Poe's short story "The Man of the Crowd" (1840), for instance. He has been sitting in a café all afternoon, watching the movements of passersby from its window, as if looking at a screen in a movie theater. When he remarks that the "rapidity with which the world flitted before the window, prevented me from casting more than a glance upon each visage" (183), he captures in a sentence the evanescence that defines his age. If the ebb and flow of movement glimpsed from behind a café window is too fugitive to be fully legible (179, 188), the speed with which the landscape flits by from the window of a moving train carriage only exaggerates the sensation recounted by Poe's narrator, namely that it "gave an aching sensation to the eye" (183). Thus, when Russell Reynolds, in a piece on traveling, "Travelling: Its Influence on Health" (1884), says of the experience of looking out of a moving train that "the eyes are strained, the ears are dinned, the muscles are jostled hither and tither, and the nerves are worried by the attempt to maintain order," he in effect sums up the experience of the industrialized age as a whole. Modernity not only leaves its populace irritable, but also makes great demands on the organ of looking, making itself felt, suggests Reynolds, as it "pull[s] at the eyeballs on looking out of the window" (qtd. in Schivelbusch 118). In a flash, the landscape recedes and what the traveler sees are "no longer flowers," Victor Hugo writes, "but flecks, or rather streaks of red and white" (qtd. in Christie 16). Everything we see out of the train, just as what we see of it, remains impressionistic. What these descriptions by Poe and Reynolds and Hugo evoke are not only how face superimposes on face in the urban crowd, or how one image, glimpsed from behind a window, bleeds into the next, but what a small step it was from the street into the picture house, from the window to the screen, toward what Schivelbusch calls a "filmic perception" (42).

The modern perception of the world as ephemeral, fugitive, and contingent is protocinematic insofar as it involves the same two elements that define the cinema: "the juncture of movement and vision" (Charney and Schwartz 6). And it is this insight that lies at the very heart of the works cited up until this point. Since most of these accounts, critical or fictional, were written some time before the emergence of the *Cinématographe*, their insights remain visionary, a precinematic history of what was yet to come: the motion-picture industry. In one of the most famous comments on living in the modern metropolis, made by the sociologist Georg Simmel only eight years after the introduction of the Lumières' *Cinématographe,* the correlation between city life and the cinematic experience could not be implied more strongly: he describes the "rapid crowding of changing images, the sharp discontinuity in the grasp of a single glance, and the unexpectedness of onrushing impressions" that confront inhabitants on a daily basis (175). In fact, Simmel's experience of the city sounds a lot like Siegfried Kracauer's description of the cinematic experience, of which he said in 1926 that "the stimulations of the senses succeed each other with such rapidity that there is no room left for even the slightest contemplation to squeeze in between them" ("Cult of Distraction" 94). In such an environment there is no time to reflect on or to "digest" anything at leisure, but responses are, to go back to Nietzsche, necessarily "reactive." It is hardly surprising, then, that thinkers such as Simmel saw the modern condition—given the "momentary" nature of its impressions—in terms of its heightened sense of the "intensification of nervous stimulation" (175), or that Nietzsche gave a physiological explanation of the modern "sensibility" as having become "immensely more irritable." Modern life, as any New Yorker or Londoner knows only too well, causes nervousness, because the unrelenting influx of visual stimuli perpetually threatens to overwhelm and overload us. It is in this sense that we must understand Walter Benjamin's thesis that film itself is a response to modernity: "There came a day when a new and urgent need for stimuli was met by the film. In a film, perception in the form of shocks was established as a formal principle. That which determines the rhythm of production on a conveyer belt is the basis of the rhythm of reception in the film" (132). So, what happened then when that day came and the Lumières presented their *Cinématographe* to the world?

Analysis

Arrival of the Cinema at the Railway Station

Almost all the films the Lumières made were shot by operators other than themselves. However, most of the very earliest films were shot by Louis himself, and all of these were short. Lasting less than a minute, each film ended when there was nothing left in the camera of the seventeen-meter-long reel it could house. The shows, too, at which the films were exhibited, were short. Lasting no more than twenty minutes, each program comprised ten or so films, with enough time in between to change the reels for each film. The programs themselves, screened at half-hour intervals throughout the day and part of the evening, were short-lived since the repertoire of films shown was changed every few weeks. Even the venues—sometimes set up in cafés, fairgrounds, or music halls—were temporary, for when the exhibition moved on, no cinema as we conceive of it in the modern sense remained. Yet, the new technology, widely advertised in the press, could attract as many as four thousand visitors in a given day. What they came to see was a screen about nine feet wide and six feet high, and what they saw were actuality films; that is, the Lumières (or one of their operators) set up the tripod outside their factory; in their garden; on the Place du Pont in their hometown of Lyon; on a beach in Neuville-sur-Saône; at a railway station in La Ciotat; on a moving train, boat, or balloon; on the lift of the Eiffel Tower; on the Champs-Elysées; in Piccadilly Circus; on the Brooklyn Bridge; in Stuttgart, Tokyo, Venice, Constantinople, Mexico, Russia, Egypt, or Indochina, and recorded everything that moved. With each film, comprising a single shot and taken from a fixed point of view, they captured "life at its least controllable and most unconscious moments," presenting, according to Kracauer, "a jumble of transient, forever dissolving patterns accessible only to the camera" (*Theory of Film* 31). They also transmitted a sense of how the world, after the arrival of faster networks of transportation, had both shrunk as a globe and yet expanded into a cosmopolitan playground. By 1897, only two years after the introduction of their *Cinématographe*, their company had produced over a thousand films, taken at numerous international locations, and displayed them in hundreds of cities all over the world.

Not only were these films about everyday life but, unlike the dead pictures of photography, the *Cinématographe* had brought these pictures, filmed "live," to life. During a typical program, viewers would first see a projected still photograph "all frozen into immobility" (Gorky, "Review" 407). But according to the writer and dramatist Maxim Gorky, who was present at a Lumière screening in Russia in 1896, what happened next was this: "suddenly a strange flicker passes through the screen and the picture stirs to life" (407). Early projectionists, by delaying the cranking and showing a still image first, were clearly aiming to intensify viewers' first experience of the moment of filmed movement.

In addition, many of the films that the Lumière Company made were about movement, so as to show off what the *Cinématographe,* as opposed to an ordinary photographic camera, could do. Hence, many of their films recorded people walking, running, jumping, marching, or dancing, and even a toddler taking its first steps. Others featured all kinds of vehicles on the move: prams in *Procession of Baby Carriages at the Paris Nursery;* bicycles in *Leaving a Factory;* horse-drawn carriages in *Quay de L'Archevêché;* electric trolley cars in *Place du Pont;* trains either arriving at stations in La Ciotat, Perrache, or Battery Place in New York, or leaving the station in Jerusalem; boats rowing out to sea in *Boat Leaving a Port,* or gliding down a waterslide in *Water Toboggan;* cars in *Festival of Paris, 1899: Parade of Flowered Cars;* and moving pavements in *Universal Exhibition, 1900: View of a Moving Sidewalk.* For their first-ever film, *Leaving a Factory* (available in three versions), the Lumières positioned the camera like a rock in the rapids, filming workers streaming out of their own factory onto the yard outside. Similarly, in *Place du Pont,* the camera captures the ebb and flow of traffic, with trolley cars, horse-drawn carriages, and pedestrians dangerously crisscrossing each other at a busy junction in Lyon.

The Lumières also, however, shot many of their films in such a way as to manipulate and exaggerate the viewers' sensations of movement and speed.[2] In a film such as *Arrival by Train in Perrache,* the camera does not merely record motion but is itself positioned on a moving train. Although the camera itself remained immobile, because it moved *with* the train, it appeared mobile, reproducing the kind of kinesthetic effect so instantly recognizable from traveling on a train: the spectator sees a mixture of panoramic views of the city in the distance and fragments of buildings in the foreground, the latter coming into view so quickly that the naked eye can barely make out details. While *Arrival by Train in Perrache* shows us a sideways view from a moving train, presenting us with one of the very first tracking shots, *Leaving Jerusalem by Railway* belongs to the popular "phantom ride"

---

[2]See also the Lumières' film *Demolition of a Wall,* which was screened both forward and, to audiences' delight, backward.

film, where a camera is either strapped to the front of a locomotive, or, as is the case in this film, to the last carriage of the train, so as to give the illusion of moving through space, thereby allowing spectators the thrill of "identification with the viewpoint of the camera" (Hansen 35).

In contrast to *Leaving Jerusalem by Railway*, where the viewpoint of the camera coincides with that of the spectator, in films such as *Arrival of a Train at La Ciotat* and *La Place des Cordeliers*, "the position of the viewer and the camera's field of vision do not coincide" (Tsivian 147). Although the objects in both these films appear to be coming straight at the camera (in the former it is a locomotive, in the latter it is horse-drawn carriages), they do not run into the camera (and by extension into the spectator); rather, they leave the camera's field of vision. This is how Gorky describes his experience:

> Carriages coming from somewhere in the perspective of the picture are moving straight at you, into the darkness in which you sit; somewhere from afar people appear and loom larger as they come closer to you; in the foreground children are play-ing with a dog, bicyclists tear along, and pedestrians cross the street picking their way among the carriages. All this moves, teems with life and, upon approaching the edge of the screen, vanishes somewhere beyond it. ("Review" 407)

What seemed striking to viewers at the time, as is evident from Gorky's account, was the way in which people or objects moved in and out of the frame. Something first seen in the background, as if in a long shot, moves toward the camera and appears bigger and bigger as it approaches, as if in close-up, only to disappear from sight alto-gether. What is at play here is a radical "discomposition" of space. As Richard de Cordova explains, while the frame of a painting marks the borders of a composed space, film "discomposes" this space insofar as it allows movement to exit into an off-screen space (83). Movement is not contained within the frame but seemingly spills out of it. The sense of flux and instability produced in terms of the composition is further enhanced by the use of diagonal perspective.

Many of the Lumière films rely on objects moving from one corner of the frame to another corner, in diagonal motion. The *mise-en-scène* here does not make use of the vanishing point, as has been the case in perspectival painting since the Renaissance; neither does the use of a diagonal create a static view, whereby one sees where the image begins and ends. Instead, organizing the composition on a diagonal, which the Lumières so skillfully did, means that the viewer merely sees a fragment of a direction, which both emanates from and moves beyond the edges of the frame. This is one aspect of the creation of dynamic movement. Another concerns the movement of people or objects from background to foreground, which not only makes them "loom larger as they come closer," but also makes them appear to accelerate as they approach the camera, even if the object, such as the locomotive in *Arrival of a Train at La Ciotat,* actually slows down before coming to a stop (Loiperdinger 57). When, like Gorky, Georges Méliès recalls that "the train dashed towards you as if about to leave the screen and land in the hall" (qtd. in Bottomore 194), what he is describing is this effect:

> The nearer the engine comes the larger it appears, the dark mass on the screen spreads in every direction at tremendous pace (a dynamic dilation towards the margins of the screen), and the actual objective movement of the engine is strengthened by this dilation. Thus the apparent alteration in the size of an object which in reality remains the same size enhances its actual activity. (Arnheim 58)

This explanation, by the psychologist Rudolf Arnheim, written in 1932, also clues us in to the viewers' apprehension and nervousness with respect to vehicles seemingly rushing from the screen toward the auditorium. The impression the film gave, as George Brunel put it in 1897, was that the train was actually "going to hit you and run you over" (qtd. in Bottomore 186).

Whether the camera positioned the spectator in the path of a moving object, such as the locomotive in *Arrival of a Train at La Ciotat,* or whether the mobile camera conveyed the dizzying sensation of speed, as in *Arrival by Train in Perrache,* what these effects produced were not simply "the negative experience of fear but the particularly modern entertainment form of the thrill" (Gunning, "Aesthetic" 122). It is in this respect that Tom Gunning sees the early cinema's ancestry located not in the literary or dramatic arts, but in "the recently appearing attractions of the amusement parks (such as the roller coaster), which combined sensations of acceleration and falling with a security guaranteed by modern industrial technology" (122). When Gunning therefore characterizes the early cinema as a "cinema of attractions," it is to draw our attention to the differences between these early shorts, in which each scene is more or less played out from beginning to end, and the later narrative traditions of cinema, which rely on complex editing techniques to make transitions between scenes.

While the films of the now-dominant classical realist paradigm deploy narrative strategies of absorption so as to enable its spectators to get lost in the fictional world they create, early actualities were largely nonnarrative films, part of a "cinema of instants" that "favored direct visual stimulus over narrative development" (Gunning, "Heard over the Phone" 218). What Gunning notes concerning the early "cinema of attractions" (lasting until about 1908), which, "rather than telling stories, bases itself on film's ability to show something" (*D. W. Griffith* 41), is also true of the action film today: it, too, subordinates the story to the thrill, and the narrative to the spectacle. The effect of such films on their audiences is quite different from that of classical Hollywood cinema or art-house cinema. The "cinema of attractions" does not lull its spectators into a dreamy state (classical cinema), nor drive them toward a critical stance (counter-cinema), but just like in the cinema of spectacles today, its viewers are continually startled and astonished by the thrilling displays: cheering, screaming, or flinching in terror or delight.

A film such as the Lumières' *Automobile Accident,* in which a pedestrian is run over by a car, before being reassembled by passersby, is a case in point. Like the threat of the head-on movement in *Arrival of a Train at La Ciotat,* there is an "aggressive aspect" to this film, because "the attraction confronts audiences and even tries to shock them" (Gunning, "Now You See It" 75). As one of many films made during that period featuring collisions, and as a forerunner to countless contemporary Hollywood blockbusters and reality film shows that proudly present the biggest yet in thrills and spills, spins and bashes, smashes and crashes, *Automobile Accident* surely appeals less to our higher sensibilities than to our hunger for sensations.

When William Wordsworth in 1800 deplored his own age's "thirst after outrageous stimulation" (160), he in many ways foresaw a culture that had yet to take shape. Critical of urban expansion and consumer culture, he blamed cheap novels and theatrical exhibitions for sustaining this thirst. Had he lived to see the *Cinématographe,* he might well have found his worst fears come to life on the big screen. By the end of the nineteenth century, the lust for sensations had become stronger than in Wordsworth's time, not least because having become used to the pace of modernity and largely desensitized to its effects, modern men and women were, Gorky notes, "reacting less and less forcefully to the simple 'impressions of daily life' and thirst[ing] more and more eagerly for new, strong, unusual, burning and strange impressions." As Gorky already sensed in 1896, this is precisely what "the cinematograph gives you" ("Gorky on the Films" 229). This was also echoed by the German writer Friedrich Freska in 1912:

> Rarely has a time suffered so much from eye-hunger [*Augen-hunger*] as ours. This is because the telegraph, newspapers, and lines of communication have brought the whole world closer together. Here, working people, bound to their chairs, are assaulted by a welter of images from all sides. . . . That is why we suffer from eye-hunger; and as a means, at least materially, to satisfy this hunger, there is nothing so fitting as the cinematograph. Eye-hunger is just as important for us in our time as once was the potato, which made it possible to feed the rapidly amounting mass of people. (98; my translation)

The onrushing locomotive of *Arrival of a Train at La Ciotat*[3] has gone down in cinema history as the most enduring image to encapsulate the "new, strong, unusual, burning and strange impressions" that film can give its audiences. It is also very clear from early viewers' own accounts that they reacted very "forcefully" to this celebrated film. So, what exactly were their reactions, and how in turn have contemporary film critics reacted to these reactions?

---

[3]Several films featured the arrival of trains (at stations in La Ciotat, de Villesfrances-sur-Saône, and Perrache). Given that *Arrival of a Train at La Ciotat* alone is known to have existed in three versions, the first of which was possibly shot as early as 1895 and the last made in the summer of 1897 (and now the most widely known), there is considerable uncertainty, as Martin Loiperdinger quite rightly finds (50–51), as to which "train film" eyewitnesses are commenting on when they recount their reactions to an onrushing locomotive.

Reactions to Arrival of a Train at La Ciotat

The French newspaper *Le courrier du centre* (July 14, 1896) announced that the approaching locomotive made "spectators draw back instinctively fearing they'll be run over by the steel monster" (qtd. in Bottomore 213). In the British news review *The Sketch* (March 18, 1896), reporting about the first Lumière show in Britain, the reviewer made it known that "in common with most people in the front rows of the stalls, I shift uneasily in my seat and think of railway accidents" (qtd. in Christie 15). In Russia, the film director Yevgeni Ivanov-Barkov remembered that "People leaped up. Some rushed toward the exit" (qtd. in Tsivian 136). Whether the Lumière train made them "recoil in horror," as one reviewer reported in Lorraine, or utter "cries of terror," as another witnessed in Switzerland (qtd. in Bottomore 187), or whether spectators at the Lumière premiere sat there "with gaping mouths," as Méliès said he did (qtd. in Gunning, "Aesthetic" 119), what is common to all these responses is that they were physical.

Does the nature of these reactions therefore indicate that early film viewers were unsophisticated? On the surface, it would seem to suggest just this, first, because they responded not with their minds but, animally, with their bodies and, second, because they mistook a representation of a train for the real thing. A third issue that follows from this is that the cinema itself is unsophisticated because it appeals to an audience's hunger for sensations (like the cheap amusement thrills of the fairground) rather than its higher sensibilities, and as such it is a medium ideally suited for the duped masses.

So, did audiences flee the scene of the first screening of *Arrival of a Train at La Ciotat* because they were fooled by the illusion of a screen image? Given that "it all seemed absolutely real," as a French reviewer claimed in June 1896 (qtd. in Bottomore 180), this hitherto unmatched realism could well be taken as an index of this new technology's unprecedented power over its powerless, and by implication unsophisticated, recipient. Yet, if we consider the way these films were first exhibited, there is little correlation between screening venues then and the dark and largely quiet movie theaters of today. In the modern cinema, the projector is hidden in a booth to conceal from the audience the machine that produces the illusions. By contrast, the *Cinématographe* was in full view, rattling noisily, and producing black-and-white pictures, which were not only very grainy but also flickered annoyingly.

In addition, films were not projected in utter silence. Apart from the accompaniment of piano music, there would often have been a showman commenting on the films displayed (Gaudreault 275), or allegedly even issuing "calming assurances" to audiences that "it is a real train, but it cannot come off the wall" (Alexander Voznesensky, qtd. in Tsivian 145). This, taken together with other early films in which the people being filmed often looked directly at the camera, would have undoubtedly disrupted the illusion, thereby making the audience as aware of the artifice of filming as they must have been of the artifice of projection. In such an environment, it is hardly likely that spectators confused the image with reality.

On the other hand, did film have a kind of direct impact then, as Yuri Tsivian wonders, that is now forever lost to us (144)? It is feasible that early filmgoers first had to get used to the conventions of the new medium, like their ancestors had to learn the conventions of perspectival painting so as not to walk into a solid wall but recognize a *trompe l'oeil* for the illusion it is. In other words, their reactions might well have betrayed, as Michael Chanan has suggested, "that they didn't yet see the screen *as a screen*" (32; italics in the original), and were therefore "not sure," according to Tsivian, "where the limits of the space that the train intended to transcend lay" (135). A counterargument to this would be that the reactions were not real or genuine in any case but largely staged. As Martin Loiperdinger has pointed out, the story of audiences running out of the auditorium might well have been a propaganda ploy, the new industry's way of exaggerating its product's impact in a bid to attract ever larger audiences. After all, other than eyewitness accounts (potentially unreliable due to later embellishments), there were no official reports either in the press or by the police to suggest that panic-stricken audiences had actually been hurt when hurtling out of the Salon Indien (43–44). In addition, there is considerable doubt, Loiperdinger finds, about whether *Arrival of a Train at La Ciotat* was actually shown on December 28, and should therefore be taken as the "origin myth" of the cinema (50).

Conversely, we might adopt Gunning's argument, that these reactions—whether expressed in terms of flight or fright—were very much "part of the *attraction* of the new invention, rather than a disturbing element that needed to be removed" ("Aesthetic" 116; italics in the original). In this case, to take the argument a little further, spectators might not have screamed involuntarily but screamed because they would have screamed at Coney Island; in other words, they reacted in line with the conventions of the fairground amusement. This is how Gunning assesses the impact of the Lumières' (in)famous film:

> Rather than mistaking the image for reality, the spectator is astonished by its transformation through the new illusion of projected motion. Far from credulity, it is the incredible nature of the illusion that renders the viewer speechless. What is displayed before the audience is less the impending speed of the train than the force of the cinematic apparatus. ("Aesthetic" 118)

The reason audiences came to the Lumière shows, then, was not for the films themselves, but because they were curious as to what the new technology could actually do. This idea is also borne out by the way in which publicity for screenings advertised not specific films but actually named the particular projection technologies on display (the Lumières' *Cinématographe*, Edison's Vitascope, the Skladanowsky brothers' Bioskop). If early viewers therefore remained, according to Gunning, "*aware* that the film [was] merely a projection" ("Aesthetic" 119; italics mine), then we would be mistaken to assume that they were unsophisticated bumpkins.

When contemporary critics argue that spectators then were *aware* of the illusion as an illusion (Gunning), or not as yet *aware* of the filmic conventions for producing illusions (Tsivian, Chanan), or only too *aware* of the new medium's capacity for creating make-believe (Loiperdinger), it seems to me that these critics are very much in the business of rationalizing why early viewers responded to the films in the way they said they did. Tsivian's notion of viewers with "untrained *cognitive* habits" (145; italics mine) and Gunning's point that if they "screamed" then they did so in order "to *acknowledge* the power of the apparatus" ("Aesthetic" 121; italics mine) both place considerable emphasis on the *conscious actions*—as opposed to the involuntary *unconscious reactions*—of these first spectators. What is significant about the reaction of early audiences to *Arrival of a Train at La Ciotat* is that they are "reactive," to invoke Nietzsche's point once more. Felt first at the level of sensations—as reflexes—before they entered the conscious mind as reflections, these responses were immediate and visceral before they were mediated critically by the mind. Neither irrational (a naïveté that mistook the illusion for reality) nor rational (an acknowledgment of the apparatus), these reactions were prerational: the result of a forgetting of the conscious self in favor of the physical self, and as such an index of the way in which film "affects primarily the spectator's senses, engaging him physiologically before he is in a position to respond intellectually" (Kracauer, *Theory of Film* 158); that is, before he or she has the presence of mind to recognize, appreciate, or analyze the artistry of effect.

Reflex actions, such as recoiling or screaming, are not mental phenomena, but are profoundly bodily manifestations of unpleasure or pleasure. We would be wrong to assume, however, that such reactions were confined to early films and early audiences. Just like the Lumières' actuality features, contemporary action, disaster, or special-effects films, too, prompt such reactions, which is why film venues from vaudeville to the multiplex have continued to be "get-thrills-quick theatres" (Hansen 65), whose visual shocks send tremors through the bodies of their audience members. Indeed, Margaret Cohen makes a very similar point:

> Such reactions have by no means disappeared with the maturing of the cinema and its audiences. We still use our bodies to stage our participation in its half-light, a participation facilitated by our lack of self-consciousness in the darkened space where cinematic projection occurs. I bite my nails, avert my eyes, smile, feel tears welling up at moments drawing me into the cinema's zone of ambiguity with compelling force. (247)

Rarely, however, do critics now, like Cohen does here, show an interest in the flesh-and-blood viewer. In much contemporary film criticism the viewer is made into either a "spectator-fish taking in everything with their eyes, nothing with their bodies" (Metz 97) or a textual spectator—"a concept, not a person" (Doane 143). By contrast, early viewers, just as early theorists, talked about the ways in which the *Cinématographe* was a "strain on the nerves" (Gorky, "Gorky on the Films" 229), or how movies caused "blood fever" (Serner 56). What is common to such responses is that they deemphasize a cognitive moment in looking and reemphasize that which excites the nerves and makes the flesh crawl.

What Freska called "eye-hunger" in 1912 or what Edward Rees a year later in the *Manchester Guardian* referred to as the film spectator's "lust of the eyes," such cinematic modes of looking have little to do with voyeurism, the paradigmatic description of spectatorship by modern film theorists. Eye-hunger, unlike voyeurism, is neither about gratification at a distance nor part of a private activity; instead, it seeks the immediate impact of the thrill or the physical shock. It is in this sense that early film viewing has much in common with what I have elsewhere called *Schaulust*,[4] of which the antecedent can be found in nineteenth-century figures such as Baudelaire's restless *flâneur* or Zola's distracted shopper. Neither of these figures is alone, nor hides, but emerges in full view as part of the crowd: irritable and yet thrilled, eyes roaming and yet transfixed, retinas inflamed, these spectators, as Nietzsche said, "merely react to stimuli from outside."

Conclusion

The assumption throughout this essay has been that the visual pleasures audiences experienced in the nonnarrative cinema of the Lumières were also about physical sensations. If we deem these bodily responses unworthy of study, then it is only because in our present age civilization and culture tend to be measured by the very distance from the body. Contemporary spectators' reactions to the Lumières' *Arrival of a Train at La Ciotat* must not be trivialized, for the "physiological tempests" (Kracauer, *Theory of Film* 159) that raged within them, and that expressed themselves with each jolt, gulp, scream, or hollow feeling in the stomach, are symptoms that for two thousand years defined what was worthy of study in other art forms. When understood within the context of this broader history of criticism, the responses of early film spectators were by no means unsophisticated. The dictum from antiquity that the dramatic or poetic ought to *move* its audience, affect them, reduce them to tears, incite them to passion, or fill them with horror, is what major thinkers from Aristotle to Longinus, from

---

[4]*Schaulust* is the German term for rubbernecking, which has been widely, and rather misleadingly, translated from Freud and Walter Benjamin as scopophilia (pleasure of looking) rather than what it means literally and connotes very physically: the lust of the eyes (Littau 35–37).

Sir Philip Sidney to Edmund Burke have all deemed to be the hallmark of great works of art. The overly intellectual response by which we now measure art's greatness is a debt, or curse, we owe to the eighteenth century and its Enlightenment philosophy of art.

Worried about the ways in which art (in particular the poetic) was hailed for its power to unleash passions in its beholder, the philosopher Immanuel Kant, in an attempt to curb such "pathological" stimulation, offered the remedy of "disinterestedness." What this rejects is a conception of art that valorizes artworks for their affects, and instead proposes that artworks be contemplated disinterestedly for their beauty. This is to say, the moment of contemplation requires that a distance be established between the self who looks and the object being looked at, the explicit goal being to disconnect one's sensuous responses from that which inspires awe, horror, terror, or passion in us. Whereas the Lumière spectators, by their own admission, were overwhelmed by the *Cinématographe*'s affects, for Kant, we are never powerless before such "irresistible" affects, provided we disengage our affective reaction in favor of intellectual activity such as reflection and contemplation. As we have seen, however, the early cinema, because it "assaults every one of the senses using every possible means" (Kracauer, "Cult of Distraction" 92) does not allow sufficient time for reflection or contemplation. By implication, the "cinema of attractions" resists disinterestedness and is therefore—if we take Kant's argument further—harmful to the spectator because it privileges distraction over contemplation, or seeing over understanding: its eye-hunger "does not seek the leisure of tarrying observantly, but rather seeks restlessness and the excitement of continual novelty and changing encounter" (Heidegger 216). For critics of modernity, this involves the impoverishment of our senses and is directly linked to the phenomenon of mass culture that arose in the course of the nineteenth century. The distaste for popular culture, or what is called the culture industry, led critics to formulate a concept of aesthetics that removes genuine art from the realm of sensory experience, now reserved for the "lowly" forms of commodity art, placing it exclusively in the intellectual realm.[5] Such an aesthetic is deeply indebted to the Kantian principle of disinterestedness, which by creating

---

[5]I am thinking here particularly of Theodor W. Adorno and his notion of the "aesthetics of negativity," but also of Bertolt Brecht's theatrical practice.

a distance between the observer and the observed can procure the necessary *critical moment* in our relation to art and thereby resist the "Philistine" demand for immediate gratification, which is the only form of aesthetic experience the culture industry knows.

Therefore, if this critical moment is missing in the reactions of early viewers to *Arrival of a Train at La Ciotat,* what is missing in modern critical theories of film is not just a moment but an entire history of affect. Rather than downgrading film to a culinary art or, conversely, elevating its study to an air of intellectual disinterestedness, perhaps the time has come to reawaken our "primary levels of aesthetic experience" (Jauss 153), such as screaming, flinching, gaping, astonishment, terror, tears, laughter, and not suppress them "in favour of the higher level of aesthetic reflection" (21). Because only then will we understand the art that the Lumières bequeathed to us.

Note: The best source for the Lumière films to date is in the form of a collection on DVD, *The Lumière Brothers' First Films,* presented in association with the Institut Lumière and available from Kino on Video. It features eighty-five complete works (1895–97), which have been digitally remastered from 35 mm materials, with commentaries in English by Bertrand Tavernier and in French by Thierry Fremaux (director of the Institut Lumière).

Credits

France, three versions: 1895, 1896, 1897, The Lumière Company

Directors: Auguste and Louis Lumière

CAST:
Members of the public
Members of the Lumière family

Bibliography

Adorno, Theodor W. *Aesthetic Theory. Gasammelte Schriften.* Vol. 7. Frankfurt: Suhrkamp, 1970.
Arnheim, Rudolf. *Film as Art.* 1932. London: Faber, 1958.
Baudelaire, Charles. *The Painter of Modern Life and Other Essays.* Trans. Jonathan Mayne. London: Phaidon, 1964.

Benjamin, Walter. *Charles Baudelaire: A Lyric Poet in the Era of High Capitalism.* Trans. Harry Zohn. London: Verso, 1983.

Bottomore, Stephen. "The Panicking Audience? Early Cinema and the 'Train Effect.'" *Historical Journal of Film, Radio and Television* 19.2 (1999): 177–216.

Chanan, Michael. *The Dream That Kicks: The Prehistory and Early Years of Cinema in Britain.* 1980. London: Routledge, 1996.

Charney, Leo, and Vanessa Schwartz, eds. *Cinema and the Invention of Modern Life.* Berkeley: U of California P, 1995.

Christie, Ian. *The Last Machine: Early Cinema and the Birth of the Modern World.* London: BFI, 1994.

Cohen, Margaret. "Panoramic Literature and the Invention of Everyday Genres." Charney and Schwartz 227–52.

de Cordova, Richard. "From Lumière to Pathé: The Break-up of Perspectival Space." *Early Cinema: Space, Frame, Narrative.* Ed. Thomas Elsaesser. London: BFI, 1990. 76–85.

Doane, Mary Ann. Untitled entry. Spec. issue on "The Spectatrix" of *Camera Obscura* 20–21 (1989): 142–47.

Freska, Friedrich. "Vom Werte und Umwerte des Kinos." 1912. *Kein Tag ohne Kino.* Ed. Fritz Güttinger. Frankfurt: Deutsches Film Museum, 1984. 98–103.

Friedberg, Anne. "Cinema and the Postmodern Condition." *Viewing Positions: Ways of Seeing Film.* Ed. Linda Williams. New Brunswick: Rutgers UP, 1994. 59–83.

Gaudreault, André. "Showing and Telling: Image and Word in Early Cinema." Trans. John Howe. *Early Cinema: Space, Frame, Narrative.* Ed. Thomas Elsaesser. London: BFI, 1990. 274–81.

Gorky, Maxim. "Gorky on the Films, 1896." Trans. Leonard Mins. *New Theatre and Film 1934 to 1937: An Anthology.* Ed. Herbert Kline. London: Harcourt, 1985. 227–31.

———. "A Review of the Lumière Programme at the Nizhni-Novgorod Fair." Trans. Leda Swan. *Kino: A History of the Russian and Soviet Film.* Ed. Jay Leyda. London: Allen and Unwin, 1960. 407–9.

Gunning, Tom. "An Aesthetic of Astonishment: Early Film and the (In)Credulous Spectator." *Viewing Positions: Ways of Seeing Film.* Ed. Linda Williams. New Brunswick: Rutgers UP, 1994. 114–33.

———. *D. W. Griffith and the Origins of American Narrative Film: The Early Years at the Biograph.* Urbana: U of Illinois P, 1991.

———. "Heard over the Phone: *The Lonely Villa* and the de Lorde Tradition of the Terrors of Technology." *Screen Histories: A Screen Reader.* Ed. Annette Kuhn and Jackie Stacey. Oxford: Clarendon, 1998. 216–27.

———. "'Now You See It, Now You Don't': The Temporality of the Cinema of Attractions." *Silent Film.* Ed. Richard Abel. New Brunswick: Rutgers UP, 1996. 71–84.

Hansen, Miriam. *Babel and Babylon: Spectatorship in Early American Film.* Cambridge, MA: Harvard UP, 1991.

Heidegger, Martin. *Being and Time.* Trans. John Macquarrie and Edward Robinson. Oxford: Blackwell, 1962.

Jauss, Hans Robert. *Aesthetic Experience and Literary Hermeneutics*. Trans. Michael Shaw. Minneapolis: U of Minnesota P, 1982.

Kant, Immanuel. *Critique of Judgement*. 1790. Trans. Werner S. Pluhar. Indianapolis: Hackett, 1987.

Kracauer, Siegfried. "The Cult of Distraction: On Berlin's Picture Palaces." 1926. Trans. Thomas Y. Levin. *New German Critique* 40 (1987): 91–96.

———. *Theory of Film: The Redemption of Physical Reality*. Introd. Miriam Bratu Hansen. Princeton, Princeton UP, 1997.

Littau, Karin. "Eye-Hunger: Physical Pleasure and Non-Narrative Cinema." *Crash Cultures: Modernity, Mediation and the Material*. Ed. Jane Arthurs and Iain Grant. Bristol: Intellect, 2002. 35–51.

Loiperdinger, Martin. "Lumières Ankunft des Zugs: Gründungsmythos eines neuen Mediums." *KINtop* 5 (1996): 37–70.

Metz, Christian. *The Imaginary Signifier: Psychoanalysis and the Cinema*. Trans. Celia Britton, Annwyl Williams, Ben Brewster, and Alfred Guzzetti. Bloomington: Indiana UP, 1982.

Nietzsche, Friedrich. *Philosophy and Truth*. 1888. Trans. Daniel Breazale. Atlantic Highlands: Humanities P, 1988.

Poe, Edgar Allan. "The Man of the Crowd." 1840. *The House of Usher and Other Tales*. Harmondsworth: Penguin, 1986. 178–88.

Rees, Edward. "Rosalie Street and 'The Pictures.'" *Manchester Guardian* 26 Feb. 1913. Rpt. in *The Guardian* 9 Oct. 1999: 15.

Schivelbusch, Wolfgang. *The Railway Journey: The Industrialization of Time and Space in the 19th Century*. Leamington, UK: Berg, 1986.

Serner, Walter. "Kino und Schaulust." *Kino-Debatte: Texte zum Verhältnis von Literatur und Film 1909–1929*. Ed. Anton Kaes. Tübingen, Ger.: Niemayer, 1978. 53–58.

Simmel, Georg. "The Metropolis and Mental Life." 1903. Trans. Hans Gert. *Simmel on Culture*. Ed. David Frisby and Mike Featherstone. London: Sage, 1997. 174–85.

Tsivian, Yuri. *Early Cinema in Russia and Its Cultural Reception*. Trans. Alan Bodger. London: Routledge, 1994.

Winter, O. "The Cinematograph." *New Review* 1896. Introd. Stephen Bottomore. Rpt. in *Sight and Sound* 51.4 (1982): 294–96.

Wordsworth, William. "Wordsworth's Preface of 1800." Appendix. *Wordsworth and Coleridge Lyrical Ballads 1798*. Ed. W. J. B. Owen. Oxford: Oxford UP, 1967. 153–79.

Zola, Émile. *The Ladies' Paradise*. 1883. Trans. Brian Nelson. Oxford: Oxford UP, 1995.

A Trip to the Moon (1902)

TOM GUNNING

Lunar Illuminations

Context

We could say the movies began in 1902 with Georges Méliès's *A Trip to the Moon* (*Le voyage dans la lune*). Undoubtedly, it is the earliest film still screened regularly today that resembles what we think of as a movie: a continuous fictional story performed by actors and extending over space and time (that is, a number of shots edited together to create a narrative). Certainly, there were films made before *A Trip to the Moon*, including scores of films by its producer, director, and star, Georges Méliès, who began film production in 1896, a few months after the first successful projection of motion pictures in France. But the best-known earlier films, such as the views shot by the Lumière Company in 1895 or the performances of dancers and acrobats filmed by the Edison Company in the 1890s, do not tell extended stories. A few fictional films consisting of several shots edited together were also made before *A Trip to the Moon*, such as Edison's *Love and War* (1899) or even Méliès's own *Bluebeard* (*Barbe-bleue*, 1901). But *A Trip to the Moon* is still widely watched with pleasure by audiences who sense that this relatively short film already possessed in 1902 many of the patterns that define movies today. But part of our pleasure in watching this film comes from its differences from later films. Both aspects of the film are important to explore: its establishment of many basic aspects of cinema entertainment still used today as well as the ways it belongs uniquely to the era of its production more than a century ago, both in terms of cinema practices and historical context.

From almost its beginnings, cinema invoked the moon, as if the silvery light of the projector piercing through a dark theater recalled lunar illumination. The full and glowing moon sailing through the night sky provides a spectacle for the eye in a manner the blinding glare of the sun cannot. But beyond this shimmering visual pleasure, the moon teases, as if its visible clarity promised a reachable proximity. Walter Benjamin wrote of the child who learns to catch a ball by reaching for the moon (124). In 1901, two years before his more famous *The Great Train Robbery*, pioneer American filmmaker Edwin Porter produced the short film *Love by the Light of the Moon* for Thomas Edison, in which a rubbernecking and goggle-eyed moon plunges out of the sky to ogle a couple necking behind a shrubbery. There is something about the visual power of the moon that makes one dream of reaching it.

Georges Méliès, like Porter one of the very first generation of filmmakers, displayed this modern desire to bring everything closer, to try to bring the alluring into our grasp. Even before *A Trip to the Moon*, Méliès had reflected this desire either to bring the moon down to earth or to propel people through space to conquer it. A magic act staged in 1891 in Méliès's theater of illusions, the Théâtre Robert-Houdin, entitled *Les farces de la lune et les mésaventures de Nostromdomus* (*The Moon's Pranks and the Misadventures of Nostradamus*), portrayed a wizardlike astronomer who observes the moon through a telescope only to find it invading his observatory. It looms at his window in the form of a voraciously grinning, full-moon face that swallows the astronomer's telescope and threatens to devour him as well. Then a delicate crescent moon brings in a lunar lady, Phoebe, who defends him from the devouring phase of the moon. In 1898, Méliès, having become a filmmaker as well as a manager of a magical theater, produced a film of this act, entitled *The Moon from One Meter*, aka *The Man in the Moon* (*La lune à un mètre*). The title expresses the idea that the magnification of the moon through the astronomer's telescope seems to bring it within arm's length, although the moral of both stage act and film seems to be that such overcomings of distance might prove dangerous.

As a professional magician, caricaturist, and producer of theatrical spectacles, Méliès mastered the arts of visual illusion. Himself well described as an *Up-to-Date Conjurer* (the English-language title of his 1899 film *L'impressionniste fin de siècle*), Méliès followed the lead of other nineteenth-century stage magicians (Jean Robert-Houdin, whose theater he took over, and the English master of modern magic John Nevil Maskelyne) and incorporated the latest technology into his theater of illusion, whether it be an electromagnet, strongly focused electric light, or concealed mechanical contraptions. When his friends the Lumière brothers invited him to a preview of their latest photographic contraption—the *Cinématographe,* producing motion pictures—he immediately recognized it as a mechanical device that created visual illusions, much like his magic theater, and attempted to purchase one. The Lumières, however, had decided not to put their invention on the market yet, and Méliès had to work with mechanics to create an equivalent device, which he did very quickly.

Méliès's first films were imitations of the Lumières' views of everyday life: *Card Party, Arrival of a Train at the Station, Place de Opera* (all 1896), as well as films of brief gags and popular dances, genres exploited by the Lumières as well. But, by the end of the first year of production, Méliès had realized that while cinema might ordinarily present a magical illusion by projecting moving images of daily life on a screen, it could also create impossible scenes of magic and transformation through manipulations of the camera and the film.

For years, film historians described the central trick used to create magical effects in Méliès's cinema as "stop-motion," but, in fact, this is only part of the story. Stop-motion involves stopping the camera, rearranging the scene while the camera is not filming, and then resuming filming after the changes have been made. Since the action of rearrangement did not appear on film, a magical effect of instantaneous change or disappearance could be achieved. Méliès (aware that journalists love such stories) later claimed he discovered the process accidentally, when filming traffic in the Place de Opera. His camera jammed momentarily, then resumed filming a few seconds later. When the film was projected, a bus, passing in front of the camera when the camera jammed, seemed to transform itself into a hearse, which was passing when the camera resumed filming (Méliès 44).

Such stories are rarely true, expressive of Méliès's sense of humor as this one may be. The process of stop-motion would naturally occur to a master of mechanical and visual illusions, such as Méliès, whose stage illusions depended on magic's basic device of concealing the actual process from view. Concealing the labor of creating the illusion by having it occur while the camera was not filming provided a filmic equivalent of the trapdoors, disguised mechanical supports for floating women, or invisible black-clad assistants that Méliès used onstage. In fact, this device of substitution during a break in filming had already been used in an 1895 Edison film showing the execution of Mary, Queen of Scots, in order to make it appear that the queen really was beheaded (a dummy being substituted for the actress during the break in filming, before the executioner brought down the ax).

Moreover, in describing the device he used as "stop-motion" (in French, *arrêt de le caméra*), Méliès was concealing part of his actual practice, following the great tradition of magicians and chefs (and filmmakers!) who only explain their processes to a certain degree, leaving the final ingredient a secret. Careful examination of Méliès's original prints undertaken some decades ago by Jacques Malthête (a great-grandson of the filmmaker) discovered that these moments of stop-motion were supplemented by cuts and splices made in the film ("Méliès, technicien du collage" 174). By cutting and splicing, Méliès could refine the trick, eliminating frames that would be overexposed as the camera slowed down and making the substitution smooth and magical. As André Gaudreault, who first theorized this practice (which he found was common among many early filmmakers), claims, Méliès was therefore a pioneer in editing, since with a simple trick, a film that appeared to consist of a single shot might actually include over a dozen "substitution splices" (217–18).

Méliès moved away from the scenes of everyday life and travel that were the specialties of the Lumière Company. An illusionist, he explored cinema's ability to create an alternative reality, rather than capture familiar views of the world. Méliès became increasingly obsessed with filmmaking, which became a passion for him that exceeded even his love of theater (or cast that love in a new dynamic form). Founding his own film production company, eventually called Star Film, he constructed a glass-enclosed studio for filming in the suburbs of Paris. In this studio Méliès ran everything. While calling him the cinema's first film director hardly covers his many roles in film production, Méliès most certainly was cinema's first *auteur*. He ran his studio; produced every film; wrote the scenarios and engineered the tricks (both cinematic and mechanical); designed, and often painted, the scenery; cast the roles; and, more often than not, played the leading man (as he does in *A Trip to the Moon*). Quoting the title of one of his trick films, Méliès was a "one-man band." Further, he developed an international system to export his films abroad, although it was in this area that his first problems arose.

Méliès made trick or magic films of two sorts. Some simply presented a series of dazzling and often hilarious transformations, while others placed these tricks within a context of characters and stories. For his story films, Méliès drew on the genre the French called *féerique* (fairy shows) and the related British form of pantomime: elaborate programs often based on fairy tales that included dances, songs, and spectacular effects, as well as slapstick comedy and acrobatic stunts. Méliès had actually provided films that were incorporated as special effects into such stage performances at the Parisian theater of Châtelet. These stage performances packed a series of attractions into a single program, often straining (or even abandoning) dramatic logic, since the acts, dances, and stage effects were often more important than the story line. They resembled a fantastic vaudeville show with the story line linking the various parts.

Up to 1902, most of the films Méliès produced consisted of a brief succession of magic tricks and gags (with occasional actualities still being produced as well; for instance, films of the 1900 Exposition and some reconstructions of historical or contemporary events, including a series of eleven short films on the Dreyfus scandal made in 1899). Méliès's most ambitious films before *A Trip to the Moon* were adaptations of fairy tales in the *féerique*/pantomime tradition. These films, *Cinderella* (1899), *The Christmas Dream* (1900), and *Little Red Riding Hood* and *Bluebeard* (both 1901), exceeded the few minutes' running time of the simpler trick films, extending gradually to nearly fifteen minutes. Transformations, appearances, disappearances, superimpositions, and spectacular theatrical effects (such as elaborate scene changes) now became embedded within a plot, usually a well-known one with familiar characters.

Analysis

The most elaborate film Méliès had produced to this point, *A Trip to the Moon*, continued and to some degree departed from the *féerique*/pantomime tradition. At 260 meters, it was longer than any previous Méliès film (although *Bluebeard*'s 210 meters approached its length). Its topic, travel through space to the moon, seems to offer a major departure from the "once upon a time" of the fairytale adaptations. Film historians have cited *A Trip to the Moon* as the first science-fiction film.

While it is always a difficult (and possibly dubious) process to establish the first film of a genre, certainly part of the originality of Méliès's film lies in its novel subject matter, placing it in a tradition that extends from Fritz Lang's *Woman in the Moon* (1929) and William Cameron Menzies's *Things to Come* (1936) to Fred Wilcox's *Forbidden Planet* (1956) and Stanley Kubrick's *2001: A Space Odyssey* (1968).

But one must notice the difference in tone between Méliès's film and later examples of the genre. "Science" fiction implies a certain sobriety and serious concern with scientific and technological possibility. This is certainly true of Jules Verne's novels, which Méliès claimed as his sources for the film. Verne's *From the Earth to the Moon* and *Around the Moon* offer detailed discussions of theories of propulsion, orbits, and gravity (even if the portrayal of the Gun Club engineers who debate the moon launch takes a satiric tone). But Méliès cannot take his scientists seriously at all, introducing them first as wizards with pointy hats, figures out of fairy pantomimes (which often introduced contemporary figures or events in order to mock them).

Certain aspects of *A Trip to the Moon* reveal Méliès still very much working within the *féerique*/pantomime tradition of burlesque and exaggeration, rather than the serious realm of later science fiction. Theirry Lefebvre, in his exemplary work on the sources of *A Trip to the Moon*, has demonstrated that one of its sources (never mentioned by Méliès) was a comic opera produced in Paris in 1877 with music by Jacques Offenbach, also called *A Trip to the Moon* (181–84). Although the major plot of the piece, a romance between an earthly prince and a moon princess, does not appear in the film, stereoscope cards showing the various acts of the opera reveal that the opening of Méliès's film reproduces events and scenic effects from the opera—including the industrial workshop in which the projectile is constructed and the enormous cannon that fires the lunar ship into space. Méliès also adopted the opera's comic treatment of the scientists.

A Trip to the Moon shares the fairy pantomime's dual focus, balancing complex visual effects with a simple story line. Today, spectacle (such as special effects) and story line continue to vie for audience attention, especially in contemporary blockbusters, so it could be said that *A Trip to the Moon* introduced a conflict that still marks popular movies (in a sense, it was cinema's first blockbuster: costing more, lasting longer, and drawing larger audiences than any previous single film). The film's story seems little more than a pretext for its effects, especially by modern criteria. We can hardly speak of individualized characters, and the motivation of character psychology plays little role in the plot. The camera maintains the framing of a theatrical tableau, never isolating or emphasizing a character's reaction. Except for the ambiguous example of the moon face as the spaceship lands, there are no close-ups (or even medium shots) in *A Trip to the Moon*.

The action often seems to pause to let special effects take center stage. After the space voyagers arrive on the moon, they stretch out their blankets on the lunar surface and take a nap. This narrative dead time, as the characters sleep in the lower part of the screen, allows Méliès to present a series of visual attractions with little attempt to advance the story. Superimposed on the dark background of the lunar sky, a comet passes by. Then the stars of the Big Dipper appear, and the heads of showgirls pop out, looking out at us as much as at the lunar explorers. Two women stars, moon maid Phoebe (pleonastically seated in a crescent moon), and a bearded man popping out of a mock-up of Saturn appear next, figures out of the burlesque mythology of comic opera, rather than space exploration. The characters notice none of these attractions (except for being awakened by the snow the mythological beings cause to descend on them), which are presented purely as visual delights (although the Méliès catalog refers to them as the visualization of the explorers' dreams) (Malthête, Maltete-Méliès, and Quevrain 109).

Spectacle, burlesque, and even absurdity frequently dominate over scientific logic, realism, or dramatic story line throughout *A Trip to the Moon*. Thus, in the apparently scientific scene of the launching of the lunar vessel, Méliès was not behaving naively in having the projectile loaded into the breach of the cannon by a troupe of showgirls dressed in a burlesque version of sailor suits. Burlesque and fairy pantomime both relied on displays of feminine attractions (such as the showgirl's legs, here encased in tights), and Méliès favored this mode of entertainment over Verne's detailed discussion of ballistics. As Lefebvre points out, in Verne's novel the huge cannon that propels the projectile toward the moon has everything but its opening underground, while both the Offenbach opera and Méliès chose to place the enormous cannon above ground, a spectacular set being more important than scientific accuracy.

The girls who push the projectile into the cannon resemble a chorus line, precisely because that is what they are supposed to be. After the projectile is loaded, they turn toward the camera and wave their hats. We are in the realm of spectacle, in which the audience is openly acknowledged and addressed, rather than the classical narrative film, in which the rule of the "fourth wall" prevails and the camera and viewer are ignored. Likewise, the disproportion in this scene between the actors and the rooftops, above which they tower like giants, does not indicate a naive primitivism in Méliès's set design (since he personally designed and built all the sets especially for this production) but an acknowledged and whimsical theatricality.

The performances, sets, and theatrical tricks in this film contrast sharply with a later cinema practice of realism and transparency. Méliès flaunts his tricks and attractions; they are what the audience has come to see. Thus when the explorers land on the moon, the effect of the earth rising is accompanied by flats of the lunar landscape descending below the stage, a common device of the fairy pantomime theater of the era but at antipodes to the realistic three-dimensional sets being introduced around this time by naturalists in the theater, such as André Antoine in France and David Belasco in the United States. We must keep in mind that Méliès was not offering an inadequate approximation of realism but a different style, based on acknowledged theatricality and illusion—a fairyland with a sense of humor and irony about itself.

Méliès openly acknowledged the dominance of tricks and attractions over the story line in his filmmaking. He wrote some years later, "As for the scenario, the story or tale, I considered it last. I can state that the scenario had no real importance, since I utilized it only as a pretext, a context for tricks or pleasing theatrical effects." He added, "One could say the scenario in this case was little more than a thread designed to link the various effects" (qtd. in Sadoul 115). The image of a film's plot as a sort of clothesline on which Méliès pegged his various attractions certainly does seem to describe one aspect of A Trip to the Moon. This investment in the spectacular rather than narrative or character development caused me to proclaim Méliès the primary filmmaker of what I termed "the cinema of attractions," a phase of early cinema that preceded the later focus on storytelling and character (Gunning). A Trip to the Moon does tell a story, but it is secondary to the display of attractions, performing, as Méliès said, as little more than a pretext. Later cinema gave dominance to storytelling, especially character development, but it hardly abandoned attractions and special effects. Even *Jurassic Park* (1993), as dominated by special effects as it may be, provides much more character motivation and psychology than *A Trip to the Moon.*

Méliès, master of popular entertainment that he was, cobbled together numerous sources to make what Lefebvre calls this "composite" film. From Verne's 1865 novel he took essentially only the concept of the projectile (technically not a rocket, the mode of later, actual space exploration, which Verne, tied to earlier ideas of ballistics, had not foreseen). Since Verne's adventurers never land on the moon's surface (Verne was aware of how difficult liftoff from the moon would be, a problem Méliès solves quite nonsensically), Méliès added some elements from H. G. Wells's novel, *The First Men in the Moon,* published shortly before the film (such as the subterranean lunar cave with its gigantic mushrooms and the very vulnerable lunar inhabitants, the Selenites).

However, both of these sources probably reached Méliès partly through other media. Offenbach's already mentioned comic opera gave Verne a comic twist. Most curiously, as Lefebvre was the first to note, Wells's lunar caves and their inhabitants reached Méliès partly through the fairground attraction, "A Trip to the Moon," invented by Fred Thompson, later the founder of Coney Island's Lunar Park. This attraction was the hit of the Pan-American Exposition in Buffalo, New York, in 1901 and then was brought to Coney Island as a permanent attraction. Visitors were seated in a flying machine that seemed to lift off, fly over Niagara Falls, and head through space, creating an illusion both visual and kinesthetic, and apparently so convincing that many attendees truly thought they had been airborne. They then descended from the airship onto a lunar surface, wandering through caves inhabited by midgets dressed as horny-headed Selenites until they eventually reached the palace of the Man in the Moon, where they watched moon maidens dance and were fascinated by electrically illuminated fountains, before emerging back onto the exposition's midway.

It is likely that this fairground attraction served as Méliès's most direct inspiration. It is also worth noting that the Pan-American Exposition, taking place soon after the United States' victory in the Spanish-American War and its subsequent taking possession of Spain's colonial empire, celebrated the United States' entrance into the ranks of imperialist nations. The new colonial possessions, from Puerto Rico to the Philippines, were highlighted in the exposition, including the display of natives brought in from the Philippines. As Woody Register points out in his biography of Fred Thompson, the "Trip to the Moon" attraction, with its emphasis on the moon's odd inhabitants, also reflected the turn-of-the-century fascination with exploration and imperial conquest (75). The end of Méliès's film, in which a captive Selenite is paraded through the streets, also participates in, and possibly satirizes, Western imperial ambitions, now extending beyond the earth's surface.

It would be one-sided to ignore the role that story does play in *A Trip to the Moon,* especially since for audiences in 1902, already familiar with the trick films Méliès had produced for the last four years, this window dressing of plot may have seemed like a compelling narrative. Richard Abel has chronicled the enthusiastic reaction American audiences had to the "French spectacular films" such as Méliès's fairy-tale films and *A Trip to the Moon* in the vaudeville theaters, where most films were shown in the United States before 1905 (*Red Rooster Scare* 10–19). They caused a similar stir among the French *forain* cinemas, the mobile film theaters that traveled along the route of French rural festivals and that provided perhaps the major market for Méliès's product. With their simple fairy-tale plots and exaggerated performances, these films also enthralled children at another of Méliès's faithful customers in France, the cinema specially designed for children set up in the Dufayel department store, so that mothers could park their kids while they shopped. The greater popularity accorded these longer films, compared to the shorter films based purely in tricks, indicates that the story line, while perhaps only a pretext, served to renew audience interest in the tricks and attractions and create a stronger viewing experience. Therefore, although the narrative form of *A Trip to the Moon* may differ from the character-based stories of later cinema, it is worth analysis.

Méliès's style of editing develops a strong sense of continuous action. The complete film consists of seventeen shots (some versions are missing the final shots of the triumphant reception of the moon voyagers and the celebrations that greet their return). The original Méliès catalog described the film as consisting of thirty "tableaux," but these tableaux indicate key actions in the film and do not correspond to cinematic shots, since several shots include more than one tableaux (Malthête, Maltete-Méliès, and Quevrain 107–11). Nonetheless, seventeen represents almost twice as many shots as any previous Méliès film. It has been claimed (especially by French film historians Georges Sadoul and Jean Mitry) that given Méliès's reliance on rather distant theatrical framing, his lack of close-up, and the often patently theatrical inspiration in his sets, performances, and even certain tricks, he should be considered a man stuck in the ways of the theater rather than a visionary of the cinema's possibilities. Although his theatrical inheritance is unquestionable, an analysis of Méliès's editing between scenes (not to mention the substitution splices discussed earlier) reveals him as a filmmaker who thought deeply about the possibilities of his medium, even if he did not create a style identical to the later narrative film.

Although each of the shot changes corresponds to a change in decor, seventeen scene changes in less than seventeen minutes would be unusual for theatrical practice in Méliès's era, even in a period (or genre, such as fairy pantomime) in which scene changes were frequent due to their spectacular nature. Furthermore, in many prints these shot changes are linked by overlap dissolves, or "lap dissolves," a device impossible in the theater and that Méliès borrowed from magic-lantern shows, which linked their projected views in this manner (and in which a change of one slide in less than a minute would be common).

What cues Méliès's shot changes? Not simply the change in decor, but also the passage of characters. From shot 1 to shot 2, the engineers move from the lecture hall to the workshop where the projectile is being fabricated. From the workshop, they proceed to the view of the casting of the giant cannon. Shots end with the scientists departing from the set, and the next shot usually begins with their being led in by Méliès, playing the wildly bearded Professor Barbenfouillis. Even the cut from shot 3 to shot 4, as the astronauts board their projectile, is bridged partly by the group's coming onto the platform at the opening of the shot, although months presumably take place between the casting of the cannon and the actual launching. Thus Méliès employed a basic principle of continuity editing, linking shots closely together by having them follow the progress of a continuous action.

This is even stronger in the part of the film that takes place on the moon, in which clear action bridges each shot in a simple trajectory of movement. After awakening from their nap because of the lunar frost (end of shot 7), the voyagers seek shelter in the lunar cave (setting for shot 8), in which they encounter the first Selenites and, in the long tradition of Western colonizers/explorers, immediately destroy several of them. Other Selenites appear and chase the party. In the throne room of the moon king (shot 9), the invaders are led in as prisoners. They escape from their captors and are chased over a lunar landscape (shot 10) until they reach the projectile, perched on the edge of an abyss (presumably the edge of the moon itself) (shot 11). The projectile plunges through space (shot 12), pierces the surface of the sea (shot 13), and lands on the bottom of the ocean (shot 14). Each of these shots falls into a line of continuous action, as it follows a simple trajectory of characters (the explorers) or objects (the projectile) as they move through space. Thus a synthetic cinematic space could be said to dominate over the simple theatrical tableaux filmed from the viewpoint of the man seated in the orchestra seats. Or, at the very least, cinema must be said to interact with theater in this style of editing. In particular, as Gaudreault has pointed out (in a pioneering article that questioned the relegation of Méliès simply to the category of filmed theatricality), the descent of the lunar ship in three brief shots lasting a total of less than fifteen seconds seems to anticipate the rapid rate of later film editing (213).

There are other cinematic devices used here, including, of course, the use of stop-motion/substitution splices, especially for the effect of the poor Selenites' vanishing in a puff of smoke after being manhandled by the scientists. The approach of the projectile toward the moon and its landing is accomplished by a complex trick shot that includes the appearance of camera movement, as the moon becomes larger as the spaceship approaches it, and at least two uses of stop-motion/substitution splices. First we see the moon at some distance as a two-dimensional image, which grows a bit bigger. Then, thanks to a substitution splice, the moon becomes more three dimensional and gains a strongly human face (an actor, of course, encased in full moon makeup). This moon face too grows bigger on the screen until, after another splice, we see the projectile apparently embedded in the moon's right eye.

The apparent camera movement was not achieved by actually moving the camera, since Méliès was not sure he could maintain a steady image in the frame while moving the camera. Therefore, while having the camera anchored in a steady position, Méliès brought the moon face slowly closer to the camera, realizing, as an experienced visual illusionist, that the audience would not be able to distinguish the difference. (He used this device also in *The Man with a Rubber Head* [1901], filmed a few months earlier, to create the impression that a head was inflating to gigantic proportions.)

Further, as Gaudreault points out, Méliès portrayed the lunar landing with one of the devices of editing unique to earlier cinema (and rediscovered by later avant-garde filmmakers): the repeated action cut, or temporal overlap between shots. This device is best known from Edwin S. Porter's *Life of an American Fireman* (1903), in which we see the fireman's rescue of a family repeated twice from two different points of view. Here we see the spaceship land twice: first we see it hitting the moon in the eye in the shot of the moon's face; then, viewed from the surface, we see the projectile land again. Clearly we are not supposed to think the ship actually landed twice; we simply see the action repeated, once seen from above the moon, once seen from the surface. Later, continuity editing would come to smooth over such switches in point of view by eliminating these repetitions and overlaps. Certain critics, looking back at this earlier practice from the perspective of modern principles, have denounced it as primitive or even foolish. From a historical perspective, however, it is simply another sign that *A Trip to the Moon*, while clearly establishing certain ideas of filmic continuity, was still from a different era. In the realm of spectacular attractions, seeing the spaceship land twice might simply double one's pleasure.

Conclusion

There is no question that *A Trip to the Moon* caused a sensation when it appeared in 1902. Abel has quoted the vaudeville theater managers in the United States who generally proclaimed the film the most spectacular and funniest they had ever booked, holding it over to play for weeks as part of their vaudeville programs (*Red Rooster Scare* 7–8). The film found equal success in France, especially among the fair exhibitors. The film was available both in a black-and-white print and in a more expensive colored version that was tinted by hand to increase its visual attraction. However, it was certainly the much larger American audience that Méliès had his eye on when he produced a film of such unparalleled length and budget (reportedly 10,000 francs). And it was here that Méliès encountered the unregulated business practices that characterized early American cinema.

Throughout 1902 and 1903, *A Trip to the Moon* was shown across the United States. As Abel has shown, rival American companies such as Biograph, Edison, Lubin, and Vitagraph all advertised copies of the film for purchase (*Red Rooster Scare* 9). But since it was relatively easy to make photographic copies of a film, the practice known as duping, very few of these copies were being purchased from Méliès. Instead, American companies absorbed the profits that Méliès's ambition and artistry garnered, by simply selling copies they made from a single original. As a new medium, film was not covered under existing copyright laws (and would not be until 1912). Méliès sent his older brother Gaston to investigate the business conditions in the United States, and his report of widespread film piracy through duping led not only to the establishment of a U.S. branch of the Méliès business, but to Méliès's establishing Star Film as the name and logo for his production company. Since the trademark could be legally protected, Méliès incorporated it into the sets of his films. But American dupers, such as Philadelphia film producer Sigmund Lubin, simply patiently scratched the logo out frame by frame before they made copies. Méliès also began to deposit prints of his films on rolls of bromide paper with the Library of Congress in Washington, D.C., where they could be copyrighted as photographs, a practice followed by many early American film producers. Certain film companies also tried to exploit the success of Méliès's film by remaking it shot by shot. I have seen two such versions of uncertain origin, one quite elaborate and possibly produced by Charles Pathé, Méliès's main commercial rival.

Perhaps most important, as I stated at the opening of this essay, *A Trip to the Moon* endures not as a fossil of a forgotten early history of the cinema, but as a film whose energy and imagination, visual design and sense of humor, technological innovation and sense of wonder still delight audiences today. Perhaps more than any other early film, it embodies the high spirits that marked early cinema, the excitement of discovery and innovation that marked the new medium. Méliès's tongue was lodged firmly in his cheek as he presented his fairy-tale vision of the future, in which scientists still dress as wizards and the inhabitants of the moon perform acrobatic stunts. But he also expressed the human desire to reach the moon, to walk the surface of the earth's satellite, to find wonders where no one had gone before.

Credits

France, 1902, Star Film

Director, Screenplay, and Set Design: Georges Méliès

CAST:
Professor Barbenfouillis   Georges Méliès
Phoebe   Bleuette Bernon

Bibliography

Abel, Richard. *The Cine Goes to Town: French Cinema 1896–1914*. Berkeley: U of California P, 1994.

———. *The Red Rooster Scare: Making Cinema American 1900–1910*. Berkeley: U of California P, 1999.

Barnouw, Erik. *The Magician and the Cinema*. New York: Oxford UP, 1981.

Benjamin, Walter. "The Work of Art in the Age of Its Technological Reproducibility." 2nd vers. Trans. Edmund Jephcott and Harry Zohn. *Selected Writings*. Ed. Howard Eiland and Michael W. Jennings. Vol. 3. Cambridge: Harvard UP, 2002.

Frazer, John. *Artificially Arranged Scenes: The Films of Georges Méliès*. Boston: G. K. Hall, 1979.

Gaudreault, André. "'Théâtricalité' et 'narrativité' dans la l'oeuvre de Georges Méliès." Maltete-Méliès 199–219.

Gunning, Tom. "The Cinema of Attractions: Early Film, Its Spectator and the Avant-Garde." *Early Cinema: Space, Frame, Narrative*. Ed. Thomas Elsaesser. London: BFI, 1990. 56–62.

Hammond, Paul. *Marvelous Méliès*. London: Gordon Fraser, 1974.

Lefebvre, Theirry. "Le Voyage dans la lune, film composite." Malthête and Mannoni 180–208.

Maltete-Méliès, Madeleine, ed. *Méliès et la naissance du spectacle cinématographique*. Paris: Klincksieck, 1984.

Malthête, Jacques. *Méliès, images et illusions*. Paris: Exporegie, 1996.

———. "Méliès, technicien du collage." Maltete-Méliès 169–84.

Malthête, Jacques, Madeleine Maltete-Méliès, and Anne Quevrain. *Essai de reconstitution du catalogue Français de la Star-Film*. Bois d'Arcy: Centre Nationale de la Cinématographie, 1981.

Malthête, Jacques, and Laurent Mannoni. *Méliès: Magie et cinéma*. Paris: Espace Edf Electra, 2002.

Malthête, Jacques, and Michel Marie. *Georges Méliès, l'illusionniste fin de siècle?* Paris: Sorbonne Nouvelle/Colloque de Cerisy, 1997.

Méliès, Georges. "Cinematographic Views." Trans. Stuart Liebman. *French Film Theory and Criticism 1907–1939: A History/Anthology.* Vol. 1. Ed. Richard Abel. Berkeley: U of California P, 1988. 35–46.

Mitry, Jean. *Histoire du cinéma.* Paris: Éditions Universitaires, 1967.

Register, Woody. *The Kid of Coney Island: Fred Thompson and the Rise of American Amusements.* Oxford: Oxford UP, 2001.

Sadoul, Georges. *Georges Méliès.* Paris: Seghers, 1961.

Solomon, Matthew. "'Twenty-five Heads under One Hat': Quick-Change in the 1890s." *Meta-Morphing: Visual Transformation and the Culture of Quick-Change.* Ed. Vivian Sobchack. Minneapolis: U of Minnesota P, 2000. 3–20.

The Birth of a Nation (1915)

DANIEL BERNARDI

Integrating Race into the Narrator System

Context

Set during the American Civil War and Reconstruction, *The Birth of a Nation* (1915) is a powerful story about the plight of two upper-class families: the Stonemans of the North and the Camerons of the South. A historic epic, this classic film offers its audience a tender portrait of two families' struggle for unity in the dense fog of war. Yet it is committed also to a romantic vision of the "Southern Legend" in its depiction of the Reconstruction era. Beset by revengeful black brutes, self-righteous white politicians, plundering carpetbaggers, manipulative mulatto mistresses, plotting mulatto politicians, and the graphic death of a Confederate daughter, the Stonemans and the Camerons endure this turbulent period of American history, eventually coming together in a marriage that symbolizes a reunited nation.

Produced and directed by David Wark Griffith (1875–1948), *The Birth of a Nation* is widely considered to be the most important American film in history. Since its initial screening, critics and scholars have proclaimed it the first feature-length film to offer audiences a powerful melodrama told with artistic subtlety. Indeed, this classic work led American cinema into the era of the Hollywood style, a system of narrative filmmaking that marshals cinematic technique—from cinematography to editing—in the service of character psychology, causal plot development, and moral endings. Although refined and even challenged over time, this style of filmmaking is still dominant today. And for this reason, Griffith is widely considered to be the father of American cinema—"the Shakespeare of the screen."

The Birth of a Nation is based on two of Reverend Thomas Dixon Jr.'s novels, *The Clansman: An Historical Romance of the Ku Klux Klan* (1905) and *The Leopard's Spots* (1902). Not surprisingly, it is known also for perpetuating some of the most repulsive stereotypes of African Americans in history. Borrowing from the Dixon novels, Griffith offers us a binary caricature of former slaves: either "faithful souls" loyal to the belief in white superiority or overly sexualized "brutes" out for revenge. Yet with few exceptions, European American actors play African American characters in blackface, making the film more about the way in which whiteness imagines blackness than it is about blackness itself. Griffith, it is widely reported, went so far as to segregate the cast, refusing to allow black actors to touch white actresses. For the famous director, whites must remain united in their quest for racial purity and national dominance. As one of the last intertitles of the film explains: "The former enemies of North and South are united in common defense of the Aryan birthright." Using the techniques of filmmaking to support the story of white supremacy, Griffith casts the Ku Klux Klan as heroes—romantic men in white hoods who ride with apparent honor and virtue in defense of white women, white families, and, via didactic metaphor, a white nation.

The importance of this complex film lies not simply in either its contribution to the art of cinematic storytelling or its overt racism, but in the relationship between these forces in the context of film history. Segregating Griffith's contribution to the craft of narrative filmmaking from his racist imagery undermines the impact that *The Birth of a Nation* had—and continues to have—on cinematic storytelling. In many ways, Griffith developed his style of filmmaking to tell unambiguous stories of an American color line. In *The Birth of a Nation,* this color line marks a clear hierarchy of races reinforced by a romantic representation of the Old South, social segregation, antimiscegenation laws, disenfranchisement, and the natural—divine—right of white rule into the future.

Analysis

Despite the trend among critics and scholars to either ignore or excuse the articulation of white supremacy in *The Birth of a Nation* in favor of focusing on the film's artistic achievements, and despite the criticism, on the other side, that this work is nothing more than racist propaganda, Griffith's epic reveals an important moment in film history, when cinematic storytelling developed as popular art in the service of racism. In what ways does *The Birth of a Nation* reflect history? How are the techniques of cinema employed in the film to facilitate and refract the story of white supremacy? More broadly, how can we simultaneously acknowledge the film's contribution to storytelling technique while challenging its systematic embrace of racism? Can racism in film be at once ugly and painful and at the same time artistic and romantic?

Reflecting History

It is difficult and perhaps unproductive to view *The Birth of a Nation* with dispassion. The film calls out for audiences to engage with it, and to do so with critical indignation. Nonetheless, it is important to situate this classic film in the context in which it was produced and initially exhibited. The sociopolitical environment in which Griffith made *The Birth of a Nation* is reflected in the film itself. Ironically, this is most clear when looking at the way in which Griffith represented the past. In other words, we find the ideologies of race that informed the production of *The Birth of a Nation* in 1915 directing the story of the Civil War and Reconstruction (1861 to 1877) represented in the film. The history outside the film as well as the representation of history in the film comprise a key issue informing the significance of *The Birth of a Nation.*

The early twentieth century saw the growth of cinema as a popular form of entertainment. European immigrants followed their predecessors into nickelodeon theaters to discover the fictionalization of American democracy, and, in the process, they were encouraged to assimilate into the social order of things. At the same time, during this period the United States was dominated by a racial formation that positioned people of color as threats to whiteness. Although few citizens advocated a return to slavery as a means of controlling this perceived threat, Jim Crow discrimination was widespread and widely accepted. Racism was an openly supported fact of American social life.

The social reality of racism informed the development of filmmaking, facilitating a troubling yet persistent link between cinema and the politics of racism. *The Birth of a Nation* was the first film to be screened at the White House, and on seeing the classic, President Woodrow Wilson (1856–1924) reportedly proclaimed, "It is like writing history with lightning. And my only regret is that it is all so terribly true."[1] Wilson was a key proponent of the League of Nations, the forerunner to today's United Nations, and a past president of Princeton University. Before becoming president of the United States, he authored a popular nonfiction book, *A History of the American People*, which Griffith later used to help ground the story of *The Birth of a Nation* in history. Wilson was also an open and persistent supporter of segregation. Under his administration (1913–21), the U.S. government maintained "separate but equal" federal workplaces, bathrooms, and restaurants. A southern Democrat, the first to be elected president since the Civil War, Wilson reportedly encouraged screenings of *The Birth of a Nation* for Congress and at various government agencies.

Griffith not only used Wilson's *A History of the American People* to legitimize his interpretation of the Civil War and Reconstruction, but also included in the film historical facsimile scenes of Robert E. Lee's surrender to General Grant and the assassination of President Abraham Lincoln at Ford's Theater in Washington, D.C. He also loosely based the senior patriarch of the Stoneman family, Austin Stoneman, on Representative Thaddeus Stevens (1792–1868), a Republican congressman who created the "forty acres and mule" proposal and advocated strongly for an integrated postwar society. Stoneman as Stevens comes off as a well-intentioned but terribly misguided politician who eventually understands the error of his integrationist ways. In the end, he reveals his loyalty to whiteness when he reacts in horror to the idea that Silas Lynch, his handpicked mulatto politician and model of integration, aspires to marry his daughter. Taking great liberties with the historical record, Griffith represents Northern politicians as wayward souls who ultimately end up supporting the purity of whiteness.

The historical references found in *The Birth of a Nation* have less to do with the film's plot than they do with the story of whiteness that it perpetuates, as the classic work is based less on past events than on a romantic discourse with the past—one that wraps the ideology of white supremacy in the flag of historical "accuracy." Capitalizing on both popular memory and political change, Griffith used historical references to legitimize the artistic decision to represent blackness as

---

[1]Although this quote is widely attributed to President Wilson, there is no direct evidence he actually said as much. In later years he claimed not to have said it, but only after he was publicly criticized for embracing the film.

bestial or servile and whiteness as superior yet under threat. In this way, the representation of the past forms a key aspect of the film's complicated role in race relations, helping to ensure the film's and its director's place in history. In *The Birth of a Nation*, "Legend," notes Robert Lang, "rewrites history to conform to ideological imperatives" (4).

Griffith's commitment to white supremacy was legitimized by the rise of social Darwinism and the eugenics movement in the nineteenth century, two related scientific paradigms that divided "man" into biological subspecies that principally included Mongoloid, Negroid, and Caucasoid. The so-called Caucasoid race, particularly those of Aryan stock, was considered to be innately superior. Conversely, the Mongoloid and Negroid races were considered to be innately inferior and, as such, not quite worthy of the full rights of a democratic society. Coupled with socioeconomic systems supported by separate but overtly unequal civil rights, the science of race at this time worked to support the belief in and structure of whiteness. Although these scientific schools of thought are considered by current scientists to have been motivated by ideology rather than empirical evidence, as pointed out by, among others, Stephen J. Gould in *The Mismeasure of Man* (1981), they nonetheless helped shape the meaning of race that contemporaneous politicians and filmmakers used to support creative and legal decisions.

The influence of biological paradigms on *The Birth of a Nation* is illustrated in the scene, set in South Carolina, in which newly elected African American legislators during Reconstruction sit back in their chairs, shoeless feet perched on desks, eating chicken and leering at white women, apparently unable or unwilling to pay attention to the workings of democracy. In this interpretation of history, the story seems to be suggesting that African Americans are unable to think beyond primitive impulses. In the scene, blacks are represented as inherently unequal to whites. Scenes like this legitimize the South's efforts to deny African Americans the right to vote, which Griffith depicts at the end of the story, when the Ku Klux Klansmen stand guard, guns in hand, to supervise new elections and banish African Americans to the margins of the frame. This is a story about whiteness. Indeed, instead of showing the Klan committing acts of brutality and terrorism, which by the time Griffith made *The Birth of a Nation* was a matter of public record, he depicted them as heroes working to ensure a reunited white nation. As Hernan Vera and Andrew Gordon write, "In *The Birth of a Nation*, blacks simply do not matter: they are only counters in the struggle of a split white self to reunite" (20).

Griffith's representation of race in this way is linked directly to Dixon's novels. In Dixon's stories, the most treacherous and threatening characters are the mulattoes, people who are considered "half" white and "half" black. According to the social Darwinian paradigm, specifically its use in determining and supporting racial hierarchies, interracial relations improved the mind but not the morals of African Americans. For Dixon, this made mulattoes an even greater threat to white civilization. Although the racial order of things, or the socio-economic structure of contemporaneous race relations, positioned African Americans as primitive and thus not too difficult to control, mulattoes were positioned as intelligent, crafty, manipulative, and immoral. They were more difficult to control, which is why interracial relationships had to be made illegal and socially unacceptable. Mulattoes were a visible sign that the riches of whiteness were being plundered by the treachery of blackness.

In *The Birth of a Nation*, we see Austin Stoneman's mulatto maid begin to tear apart her clothing at the thought of seducing the elder statesman. Her aspirations are lascivious, as she plots an improved social standing through sexual immorality. Moreover, Silas Lynch, Stoneman's mulatto politician, aspires not only to turn the South black but to marry his daughter, Elsie. His prurient aspirations are represented as vengeful and violent. "Lynch," an intertitle reads, "drunk with wine and power, orders his henchman to hurry preparations for a forced marriage." In the end, his attempt to force the white woman to wed is stopped—in the nick of time—by the Klan.

Cinematic Technique and the Story of Whiteness

Although Griffith relied on Dixon's historical fiction and Wilson's fictionalized history, the director had a long-lasting commitment to the ideology of whiteness. This history is evident in the films he made before *The Birth of a Nation*. The father of American cinema directed over 450 short films, each roughly ten minutes long, for the American Mutoscope and Biograph Company, also known as American Biograph, from 1908 to 1913. In these works, Griffith refined his technique for creating compelling stories on film. He developed a commitment to telling a story of white supremacy that included the depiction of people of color as inferior, savage, and unrestrained. For Griffith, Asians, Latinos, Native Americans, Gypsies, Jews, as well as African Americans, posed clear threats to the sanctity of whiteness. The director went as far as to use the titles of a number of his early works to market racism, including *The Greaser's Gauntlet* (1908), *Romance of a Jewess* (1908), *The Zulu's Heart* (1908), *The Mexican Sweethearts* (1909), *That Chink at Golden Gulch* (1910), and *The Heart of a Savage* (1911). As I have argued elsewhere, the racism in *The Birth of a Nation* can be traced to the director's Biograph work (104).

Griffith also made several Civil War films for American Biograph, including most notably *His Trust* (1911) and *His Trust Fulfilled* (1911). In these works, we see a sweeping battle scene, shots of slaves running wild as Northerners pillage Southern homes, close views that reveal the inner thoughts and emotions of characters, and compositions that feature recurring symbols of the Old South—including most prominently a Confederate officer's sword. Indeed, the sequel is based on the devotion a faithful soul has for his former Confederate master's sword long after the master has died in battle and the slaves have been freed. Griffith's camera work and plot structure seem to fetishize the Confederate sword, making it a symbol of white power and pride. And, as Michael Rogin notes in perhaps the most insightful essay written on Griffith's film, "The Sword Became a Flashing Vision," these same stylistic choices are all found, refined and coherent, in *The Birth of a Nation* (275).

Most of the stylistic innovations credited to *The Birth of a Nation* can be found in the director's earlier films. This is most clear in his development of chase-and-rescue scenes. Constructed through parallel editing, which is sometimes referred to as crosscutting or intercutting, chase-and-rescue scenes consist of shots of two or more separate but usually parallel locations interwoven to advance the film's plot. In one scene, we see the person(s) being chased. In another, we see the person(s) doing the chasing. The filmmaker cuts back and forth between the locations, sometimes increasing or decreasing the tempo of individual shots to further heighten suspense. He does this until the chaser either catches his victim or is interrupted by a hero. This is famously illustrated in one of Griffith's last yet most successful films, *Way Down East* (1920), where, at the end of the film and not a moment too soon, the hero saves the damsel in distress from crushing death as her body floats precariously toward a waterfall. We see this rescue through a series of parallel edits that serve to increase the tension caused by a woman heading perilously close to a gushing waterfall while casting a male as a savior. Griffith's stagings of chase-and-rescue scenes are always dramatic and intense, facilitating narrative suspense while emphasizing the plight of the characters. They also serve nicely to advance the story to a moral conclusion.

And yet Griffith did not develop chase scenes and parallel editing simply to advance causal events. In many of his films, including the earliest instances in which the technique is employed, the person being chased is a white woman, the chaser is a person of color, and the hero is a white male. In other words, Griffith developed the technique to support the tension surrounding interracial relations. This is perhaps best illustrated in *The Girls and Daddy* (1909). In this short work, a blackface brute is distracted from a burglary after coming upon two unsuspecting white girls. Griffith goes to great lengths to represent the girls as beautiful and innocent. Several shots show them playful in bed, hugging and kissing before they fall asleep. On seeing the young beauties, the blackface brute chases them from bedroom to living room to bedroom, only to be stopped by a white burglar who, at the risk of losing his loot and getting captured, elects to defend white purity and segregation and defend daddy's girls. The white burglar jumps on and pummels the blackface brute. Throughout the scene, Griffith employs cuts and even a panning shot, a rare technique at this point in film history, to both heighten the threat posed by blackness and to create a moral ending that reveals the innate heroics of whiteness.

This chase scene foreshadows the famous sequence in *The Birth of a Nation* in which Gus, another lustful blackface brute, chases Flora, a darling daughter of the Confederacy, to her death. As in *The Girls and Daddy*, Griffith cuts back and forth between Gus pursuing Flora with an obvious intent to rape and Flora either strolling ignorant of Gus or, realizing what Gus desires, running away from the "renegade Negro" in abject fear. "You see, I'm a Captain now—and I want to marry . . . ," an intertitle linked to Gus reads. Following the earlier scene of the legislature voting down antimiscegenation laws, the scene is constructed tautly in a forest; long shadows cast by looming trees divide natural lighting in ways that add a visual rhyme to the narrative context of the scene. Moreover, the pacing of the edits adds a degree of tension to the sequence, as Griffith initially lingers on shots of Flora. There is also a close-up of Gus with a menacing and prurient expression on his face. "Wait, missie, I won't hurt yeh," a provocative intertitle reads. In the meantime, Griffith cuts to a third location, where Ben Cameron searches in despair for the young Flora. In one of the most notorious scenes in film history, Flora elects to jump off a cliff to her death rather than be defiled by Gus. Ben is too late to save his Confederate sister, but not too late to organize and rally the Klan to track Gus down and bring him to justice. As punishment, Gus is castrated and lynched (the castration scene was later cut by Griffith in response to threats of censorship by local film-review boards). Although he doesn't save Flora from tragic death, Ben is a hero nonetheless for his creation and stewardship of the Klan.

Another brilliant parallel-editing scene is found at the end of the film, as the Klan rides to save otherwise helpless whites from threatening blacks. The end of the film actually includes two chase scenes, one following the other and both including the Klan as heroic. In one, we find a Northern father, held up with the elder Cameron in a cabin, holding his rifle butt over his child's head, poised to kill her lest she be attacked by the black brutes outside. The situation apparently calls for the same fate suffered by Flora. Griffith moves the camera into a close-up of the little girl's face, revealing simultaneously fear and innocence. In the other scene, we see Lynch and his henchman on the verge of forcing Elsie to marry the mulatto politician. She falls into his dark arms as he seemingly smiles in satisfaction. Both scenes are powerful, as Griffith has the camera follow the Klan's ride to the rescue along a winding forest road. The effect of this technique is that the shots of the Klan offer viewers a sense of impending heroism. In both scenes, the Klan indeed arrives in the nick of time, narrative tension at full pressure, restoring white supremacy once and for all. The blacks are subdued, and the Klan receives a parade and, ostensibly, applause. Constructed with artistry through parallel editing, a technique now commonly employed by filmmakers around the world, these final shots are among the most racist moments in American film history.

Refracting Whiteness

Disgusted by the negative images of African Americans and the positive images of the Klan in *The Birth of a Nation*, the National Association
for the Advancement of Colored People (NAACP), as well as numerous other social and political organizations, called for protests and boy-
cotts. W. E. B. DuBois, one of America's leading intellectuals at the
time, published poignant commentaries in *The Crisis*, the NAACP's
journal. These actions resulted in exhibitions of the film being delayed,
as well as local review boards, fearful of race riots, requiring minor
changes. Even the Communist Party got involved, picketing the film as
evidence of the Fascist failings of capitalism. As Janet Staiger, quoting
Nickieann Fleener-Marzec, notes, "Between 1915 and 1973 the right to
screen *The Birth of a Nation* was challenged at least 120 times" (199).

The famous director responded to the criticism of his film in an editorial published in the *New York Globe*. Claiming that his "associates"
maintained a "dignified silence in the face of an organized attack" by
"publicity seekers and fanatics," Griffith sought to ensure both the
box-office success of the film and its place in film history:

> Most well informed men know now that slavery was an eco-
> nomic mistake. The treatment of the Negroes during the days
> of Reconstruction is shown effectually and graphically in our
> picture. We show many phrases of the questions and we do
> pay particular attention to those faithful Negroes who stay
> with the former masters and were ready to give up their lives
> to protect their white friends. No characters in the story are ap-
> plauded with greater fervor than the good Negroes whose de-
> votion is so clearly shown. (Griffith 169)

Griffith's response was clearly designed as a marketing ploy to further
ensure the success of the film. As we have seen, it reveals also a key
feature of the story. In *The Birth of a Nation*, there are "good" blacks,
African Americans who remain faithful to whiteness and segregation,
and "bad" blacks, African Americans who are bestial, lustful, untrustworthy, ignorant, and unfaithful to whiteness. This is a narrative pattern Griffith established during his days at American Biograph, as we
have seen in *His Trust* and *His Trust Fulfilled*, and it remained throughout his career a preferred marketing strategy.

The controversy over *The Birth of a Nation* did not end with Griffith's deft use of the editorial pages of the *New York Globe,* and in fact continued through subsequent exhibitions of the film. Several scholars report race rioting in major cities after screenings of the film. Equally disturbing is the apparent fact that the Klan used the classic film as a recruiting tool. According to Michael Rogin, the Klan "screened the movie in the 1920s to build membership in the millions" (290). Other scholars have reported a rise in the number of lynchings of blacks by white vigilantes due to the film's depiction of African American men as rapists.

The impact of *The Birth of a Nation* was felt not only in the political and legal spheres of American life, but also in the specific experiences and protests of the African American community. In 1920, for example, African American independent filmmaker and novelist Oscar Micheaux addressed the film when he made *Within Our Gates.* In this classic, Micheaux's ending serves as a challenging homage to the end of *The Birth of a Nation.* We see the attempted rape of a black woman by a white man as her family is being lynched for a crime they did not commit. In this scene, which is not explicitly tied to a historical event but is nonetheless far more historically accurate than any image of blackness found in Griffith's classic, Micheaux exposes the representation of African Americans in *The Birth of a Nation* as a lie that masks the horrors of white supremacy during the era of slavery and Reconstruction. It must be remembered that, in reality, white slaveholders raped African American women in numbers that were both horrific and apparent to most people living in the South.

Despite protests and direct evidence that the Klan was violent in the extreme, Griffith remained stoic and even belligerent—refusing to acknowledge the film's racism or its culpability in advancing the agenda of the Klan. In 1930, upon the release of one of his last films, *Abraham Lincoln,* the southern director sat down with Walter Huston, the star of the Lincoln film, for an interview. In this filmed interview, which is included on the Kino International DVD (*"The Birth of a Nation" and the Civil War Films of D. W. Griffith*), Huston presents Griffith with a Confederate officer's sword, an ironic recapitulation of the sword found in *His Trust, His Trust Fulfilled,* and *The Birth of a Nation.* Griffith is visibly touched by the gift, and goes on to defend his depiction of the Klan as honorable and justified. He even reminisces romantically about how Mother helped stitch their white robes as they rode in defense of the Old South.

Conclusion

Irrespective of Griffith's indifference to the history of the Klan, the controversy over the film illustrates the ways in which cinema is informed by and informs our approach to race relations. To this day, scholars continue to argue about how to situate the film in history: Should it be approached as art or as propaganda? Should it be condemned for advocating racism or for the censorship it provoked? It is not uncommon for contemporary scholars to sidestep the issue and either avoid teaching the film altogether or, on showing it, ignore the incestuous relationship between the development of cinematic style and the story of white supremacy.

The Birth of a Nation should remind film scholars of at least two critical imperatives. First, films do not simply reflect the context in which they are produced. They also inform the direction of both creative and social forces. Griffith's classic work certainly reflected the meaning of race dominating the early twentieth century, as this essay has tried to demonstrate. Yet it also refracted racial ideologies in ways that impacted the meaning of whiteness in the future. *The Birth of a Nation* greatly influenced the direction of the Hollywood style. Moreover, it prompted protests, censorship, and rigorous debate about the American color line. Scholars have linked screenings of the film to a dramatic rise in Klan membership, to lynchings, to riots, and to a vigorous national critique of stereotypes. As late as the 1940s, the NAACP organized groups to picket screenings of the film and to protest the negative stereotypes the film promotes. In response, the film was rereleased numerous times in attempts to edit, minimize, and excuse the film's racist message while maintaining its status as a classic. As KVC Entertainment advertises on the back cover of its video case, "Because the story was told from the South's point of view, *The Birth of a Nation* was denounced by various liberal and civil rights organizations, and banned by the NAACP. Yet, no film before, or ever since, has portrayed the most painful chapter of America's history with such profound realism."

A second critical imperative concerns a presumed distinction between art and ideology. *The Birth of a Nation* illustrates the fact that film can be at once stylistic and political, simultaneously imaginative, brilliant, reactionary, and racist. If *The Birth of a Nation* teaches us anything, it is the ways in which the art of cinema can construct white supremacy as history written with artistry. The innovations Griffith made in pursuit of a style of narrative filmmaking were not simply in the service of storytelling; they were in the service of white supremacy. Thus, the art of *The Birth of a Nation* is its racism, particularly its construction of whiteness through the lens of black stereotypes and the craft of cinematic technique. In *The Birth of a Nation*, art is ideological, form is content, and cinema is simultaneously moving, artistic, ugly, and painful.

Credits

United States, 1915, Epoch Producing Company

Director and Producer: D. W. Griffith
Screenplay: Thomas F. Dixon Jr. (novel and play), D. W. Griffith, Frank E. Woods, and Thomas F. Dixon Jr.
Cinematography: G. W. Bitzer
Art Direction: Cash Shockley, Joseph Stringer, and Frank Wortman
Music: Joseph Carl Breil and D. W. Griffith
Costume Design: Robert Godstein

CAST:

Elsie Stoneman	Lillian Gish
Flora Cameron	Mae Marsh
Col. Ben Cameron	Henry B. Walthall
Margaret Cameron	Miriam Cooper
Lydia Brown	Mary Alden
Austin Stoneman	Ralph Lewis
Silas Lynch	George Siegmann
Gus	Walter Long
Tod Stoneman	Robert Harron
Jeff (blacksmith)	Wallace Reid
Abraham Lincoln	Joseph Henabery
Phil Stoneman	Elmer Clifton
Mrs. Cameron	Josephine Crowell
Dr. Cameron	Spottiswoode Aitken
Wade Cameron	George Beranger
Duke Cameron	Maxfield Stanley
Mammy	Jennie Lee
Gen. Ulysses S. Grant	Donald Crisp
Gen. Robert E. Lee	Howard Gaye

Bibliography

Bernardi, Daniel. "The Voice of Whiteness: D. W. Griffith's Biograph (1908–1913)." *The Birth of Whiteness: Race and the Emergence of U.S. Cinema.* Ed. Daniel Bernardi. New Brunswick: Rutgers UP, 1996. 103–28.

Gould, Stephen J. *The Mismeasure of Man.* New York: Norton, 1996.

Griffith, D. W. "Reply to the *New York Globe.*" *New York Globe* 10 Apr. 1915. Rpt. in Lang, *"Birth of a Nation"* 168–70.

Lang, Robert, ed. *"The Birth of a Nation": D. W. Griffith.* New Brunswick: Rutgers UP, 1994.

Lang, Robert. *"The Birth of a Nation:* History, Ideology, Narrative Form." Lang, *"Birth of a Nation"* 3–24.

Rogin, Michael. "The Sword Became a Flashing Vision: D. W. Griffith's *The Birth of a Nation.*" Lang, *"Birth of a Nation"* 250–93.

Staiger, Janet. "'The Birth of a Nation': Reconsidering Its History." Lang, *"Birth of a Nation"* 195–213.

Vera, Hernan, and Andrew Gordon. *Screen Saviors: Hollywood Fictions of Whiteness.* New York: Rowan, 2003.

The Cabinet of Dr. Caligari

(1920)

PAUL COATES

Radical Modernism or Commercialism?

Context

For much of the twentieth century a fixture in critics' lists of the most significant films ever made, *The Cabinet of Dr. Caligari* (*Das Cabinet des Dr. Caligari*, 1920)[1] is often described as the founding film of "art cinema," imbuing a form of cultural production—the popular cinema—with both the critical currency and the narrational uncertainties of modernism. In *Caligari*, a tale of horror and detection becomes in the end an object lesson in the untrustworthiness of narration. As embodied in the film, art cinema was able to ensure its success in Germany by launching an imaginative publicity campaign that lured prospective spectators with the enigmatic slogan "You must become Caligari!"—a campaign that lent an extrafilmic, mass-audience dimension to a line drawn from the film. At the same time, *Caligari*'s international success came as the result of product differentiation strategies that intended to establish German cinema's distinctiveness from other national cinemas, particularly the increasingly dominant American one (Elsaesser, "Film History" 71–73; Kracauer 65).

Caligari gave Weimar German cinema a reputation for imaginative studio-art direction combined with themes of the fantastic and the uncanny. Directors interested in developing this combination would beat a path to Germany in their turn—the most famous being Alfred Hitchcock. The film would acquire mythical as well as prototypical status when Siegfried Kracauer's 1947 analysis of the interrelationship of Weimar cinema and society posited a connection between the ambiguous authority of Caligari and that of Hitler, of whom Caligari could be deemed a prophetic anticipation. Although often seen as far-fetched,

---

[1]The world premiere of *Caligari* was at Marmorhaus in Berlin on February 26, 1920.

99

this thesis may be supported by Caligari's stubbornly awkward gait and his malevolent expression, both of which breathe *ressentiment* while suggesting the genealogy of repression in envenomed compensation for a sense of impairment. Allegorical readings such as Kracauer's, which strive to scratch beneath the surface of the text, have dominated the exegesis of Caligari. This approach begins with Hans Janowitz, one of the script's authors, who presents it as an allegory of the older generation's sacrifice of the young in World War I (Janowitz 224–25). Complex and compressed, the film has proved particularly attractive to the form of allegorical decipherment practiced by psychoanalysis, and critics have enjoyed drawing parallels between Dr. Caligari and Dr. Sigmund Freud (Clément). Impressions of the film's possible pathology have been further reinforced by critics who describe it in terms that echo its subject matter: as a freak, a work that "stands almost alone" (Kael 142) or "led nowhere" (Laqueur 234). Nonetheless, its popularization of the Expressionist placement of the spectator within a radically distorted environment, its demonic fairground, its use of shadows and the striking images of its two main actors (Werner Krauss and Conrad Veidt) have all proved profoundly influential. If *Caligari* is freakish, then so perhaps is cinema, which also originated in the fairground.

Script and Production

The script for *Caligari* was cowritten by Hans Janowitz and Carl Mayer. Siegfried Kracauer's account of its gestation offers fascinating insights into how their separate contributions came together. Janowitz's prewar intuition that he may have witnessed a sex crime, and later his anger at the conduct of World War I, interacted with Mayer's experiences as a wandering actor and his resentment of a military psychiatrist who once examined him (61–63). Accounts of the script's production are confusingly contradictory, however. The difficulties involved in ascertaining intentionality in the collective art of making films loom particularly large in the case of *Caligari*, the first film to offer the very kind of narrative enigma that would come to characterize individualist modernism. The roots of these difficulties appear to be a mixture of self-promotion, poor memory, and deliberate mythmaking on the part of the film's major players.

The most conscientious effort to unravel the *Caligari* myth from reality has been that of Kristin Thompson. She tersely notes some of the disparities between the three main accounts: "[Fritz] Lang claims to have suggested the frame story, yet none of the three accounts credits him with the idea. ([Hermann] Warm claims [Robert] Wiene was responsible.) Janowitz says the Expressionist sets were based on a misunderstanding, [Erich] Pommer says he agreed to the stylization upon his first meeting with Mayer and Janowitz, and Warm attributes the film's look to a conference among the three designers when the script was already going into production" (132–33). Primary responsibility for the mythologizing rests with Erich Pommer, the best-known producer of the German silent era, who colorfully attributes the painting of light and shadow onto the sets to a need to compensate for unreliable electricity supply in the immediate postwar period, and maintains that he envisaged the film as "a comparatively inexpensive production" (qtd. in Thompson 128). Pommer also claims to have been aware even at this stage of an issue deemed problematic by later aestheticians and film reviewers: the possible mismatch between three-dimensional actors and flat sets.

Hermann Warm, however, the artistic adviser at Decla, declared that the film was produced not by Pommer but by Rudolf Meinert, whom Pommer did not replace as Decla production chief until 1920. Thompson argues convincingly that contemporary evidence confirms most of Warm's account, with German trade papers describing the film as in production by the end of 1919, and *Film Kurier* attributing production to Meinert. Since its lighting conforms to contemporary practice, the ascription of the Expressionist sets to electricity cuts is unlikely, while Pommer's suggestion that the film was not supposed to be a major one is undermined by its description in Decla advance publicity as belonging to its *"Welt-Klasse"* (world-class) production category (Thompson 136). As a result, it was perhaps Rudolf Meinert, and not Pommer, who was primarily responsible for the film—though myths and contradictions remain.

Expressionism

For Walter Laqueur, "to try to define Expressionism is a thankless task, given the inchoate character of the movement" (113). Some of the main features of the movement—embracing painting, drama, writing, and film—can be enumerated nevertheless. It was a youth movement, extending roughly between the years 1905 and 1925, characterized by a pursuit of stylistic dissonance and intensity, and it took individual madness, social chaos, and apocalypse as its primary themes. Stylistically, Expressionism was animated by a rejection of the conventionality of late-nineteenth-century realism. This antirealist reaction could yield either a hard-edged, experimental modernist dissonance (as in the poetry of August Stramm) or naively direct, emotional appeals for human renewal, as in a host of minor dramatists and, most famously, in the Thea von Harbou novel that was the basis of Fritz Lang's *Metropolis* (1927). The experiments led away from registration of the external to an inward voyage in search of the soul, its protagonists more the fragments of a single mind than anything approaching realistically conceived characters.

Expressionism took to heart Edgar Allan Poe's death sentence on the long poem ("I hold that a long poem does not exist" [889]): the world's condition was far too urgent for the luxury of prolixity. This urgency was figured in the Babylonian corruption of the city, with its industrial dehumanization and social polarization, writ large a few years later in Lang's *Metropolis*—that decadent summa of Expressionism. A putrefying reality gave the lie to the nineteenth-century aesthetic of Beauty and mellifluousness in narrative and visual style, which was replaced by ugliness, angularity, and jagged diagonals. The truth of ugliness "depicted man in all his weakness and spiritual poverty" (Laqueur 114), and only an aesthetic of shock could remove society's blinkers and disclose its true state to itself. Aesthetics and eschatology thus became commingled, and the artist was figured as a haggard prophet, driven mad either by the world's blindness to its faults or by the power of his own visions. The "free-floating, aimless militancy" attributed to Expressionism by Laqueur (113) corresponded to its status as more a mood, a reaction, and a negation than a postulation of alternative possibilities. Expressionism's scream originated in a heart of whose reasons reason knew nothing. Its practitioners' febrile production of numerous manifestos further showed their lack of any unanimous sense of how to elevate their aesthetic protest into an effective political strategy. It is thus hardly surprising that both left-wingers and Joseph Goebbels (Hitler's minister of propaganda, who authored an Expressionist novel) could be numbered among its none-too-kindred yet shaping spirits.

Expressionism in the cinema, meanwhile, may be defined either as a set of themes or as a set of visual strategies. Conceiving it in terms of the former yields a broader definition than does the latter and may help account for the movement's hold on an entire generation. Friedrich Murnau's *Faust* (1926), for example, may not employ those visual strategies associated with Expressionism (and in *Caligari*, in particular, this extends to the use of distortion to render an image of a single mind buckling under stress), but certain themes do relate *Faust* to Expressionism. Above all, the idea of the divided self and the double, of which I will say much more later, is significant here. Originating in Romanticism, this "divided self" theme becomes even more intense and urgent in Expressionism. Doubling reflects and helps manage ambivalence, often with regard to an authority that can be at the same time rejected and feared. Doubling also effects dispersal, even evaporation, of responsibility. Automaton-like, other characters carry out the desires for which the protagonist fears punishment. This structure is clearly present in Murnau's *Faust*, where Mephisto is both Faust's pander and his parody, his movements echoing the main protagonist's to a far greater extent than in Goethe's early version. Since this figure of parody is also a kind of shadow, this thematic element of Expressionism is closely linked to one of its key visual strategies, the use of shadows—and one of its key films is called just that, *Schatten* (*Warning Shadows*, 1922).

The shadow can become larger than the self, an image of the protagonist's engulfment by desire, his (and these usually *are* male fantasies) submergence in a dreamworld of desire. For example, the multiplicity of doubling relationships in *Caligari* is hinted at by the depiction of the murderer Cesare as a shadow: a device that suggests a conventionally teasing thriller, yet also functions to suggest a hidden interchangeability. That is, as the shadow waxes larger than the person casting it, it at once might recall an image of the Nietzschean Superman (*Übermensch*), while paradoxically revealing that to step beyond ordinary consciousness is to move not toward the Superman's Godlike control, but toward the dissolution of identity, since power is effectively an illusion achieved through regression to the infant's belief in what Sigmund Freud called "the omnipotence of thoughts" (240).

Expressionist *mise-en-scène* strives to objectify the state of mind of the modern viewer, where the world becomes a mirror or projection of an isolated central figure with whom the viewer identifies. This central figure's world is under the sign of death because isolation generates a continual sense of vulnerability to an ever-present threat of authority, and because though Expressionism is postreligious—the inheritor of a world emptied of God by Nietzsche—it is also haunted by religious yearnings. Expressionism's father figure is no longer a signifier of a caring God but the death-dealing punisher of those who would desire his abolition. (Expressionism's sense of the father as punitive corresponds to the popular notion of "the Old Testament God," an element of its ideology that, in condemning a view associated with Judaism, may therefore be compatible with the anti-Semitism later propagated by a former Expressionist like Goebbels.)

In Expressionism, the spiritual becomes homeless. Thus in *Caligari* a world full of walking spirits is evoked by Francis's neighbor at the outset: "There are spirits everywhere. They are all around us. They have driven me from hearth and home, from wife and child." Even the oblique lines of the sets have been read as pointing to the metaphysical (Eisner 21). The small-town world of Holstenwall should be cozy but is in fact jagged and alienating, as if the traumas of city experience—that theme of so much contemporary literature, responding to the rapid growth of Berlin in particular—had been projected onto it. In these respects, then, *Caligari* is thematically Expressionist. But whereas other Expressionist works that are, like *Caligari*, modeled on the Strindbergian *Stationendrama* (drama of the Stations of the Cross) pursue a single omnipresent individual throughout and employ image distortion to simulate the extremities of his experience, no such figure is found in *Caligari*. Francis may be telling the story, but he is not present in every scene. The framing device, however, may permit a retrospective impression of his omnipresence through a distortion that declares the madness of his unreliable narration.

Thus although *Caligari* is visually Expressionist throughout, it only becomes Expressionist in the other sense—that of the thematization of isolation—if the main body of the narrative is considered from the vantage point of the ending. The result is a film that is itself ambivalent vis-à-vis its parent, that is, the Expressionism that extends to the other arts. The film's partial extraterritoriality in relation to Expressionism is further apparent, for example, in its distinctive mixture of naturalistic acting styles with the more extreme, pathos-laden ones associated with the Expressionist theater. Hence, many contemporary commentators saw only Werner Krauss's Caligari and Conrad Veidt's Cesare as characters that were truly in accord with the film's Expressionist sets. The text's attempt to associate horror with them alone may also be read, however, as an index of the depth of its desire (mirrored in that of Francis) to recover a sense of normality that, paradoxically, is established as irretrievable only at the film's end.

Analysis

Oedipus and the Double

To speak of "Oedipal revolt" in the context of *The Cabinet of Dr. Caligari* may appear strange. For the scriptwriters Janowitz and Mayer, the father/son conflict so central to the texts of Expressionism is here present as an allegory, in that Caligari represents the mad forces of authority that sent young men to their deaths in World War I. Cesare is the hapless, helpless victim of authority, recalling the biblical son Isaac who was actually sacrificed, rather than saved, by Abraham in Wilfred Owen's poem "The Parable of the Old Man and the Young." But because such a multileveled reading of Francis's central story in *Caligari* is not immediately apparent to spectators, emerging only when one decides (or is instructed) to allegorize it, the necessity of an additional "sense-making" element seems to justify the decision to surround this story with a framing device. (Janowitz decried the later addition of the frame story, however, and suggested that its imposition was a form of submissiveness to authority, and could be seen as the commercial concealment of his script's avant-garde and political convictions.)

Of course, Oedipal revolt is widely present in any story of a youthful challenge to an older figure, not just Expressionist works. Since the mother figure is crucial to the Oedipus story, an Oedipal reading might see her absence from *Caligari* as potentially significant. It would suggest that this particular father/son (Caligari/Cesare) struggle concerns power rather than sexuality; it might also underline the tyranny of a father whose lack of female companionship betokens his lack of compassion (the phrase "no female beside him" could be reconfigured as "no female side to his character"). Indeed, though Caligari is seen "feeding" Cesare, the act might be interpreted less as one of mothering than of appropriating and controlling the feminine. This extreme gender imbalance may generate chaos.

Indeed, if the film is as ambiguous as Kracauer has maintained (rebellious yet submitting its revolt to a neutralizing framing device), the same ambiguity might extend to its presentation of authority. Despite Kracauer's argument, the figure of Caligari is not the sole locus of authority, as is shown by his humiliating encounter with the high-handed, high-seated town clerk. The staging of this meeting may recall Franz Kafka's *The Castle,* but its upshot is no Kafkaesque impotence before authority: Caligari will later avenge this enforced obsequiousness. Kracauer's conception of a unified "authority" in the film is therefore misconceived, as the film splits a notion of authority between the categories Max Weber would have called "legal/bureaucratic" and "charismatic" authority. As Weber puts it, "in its economic substructure, as in everything else, charismatic domination is the very opposite of bureaucratic domination" (249). (Weber's isolation of these two categories indicates their importance for the early-twentieth-century German system of social organization, of which he was the preeminent sociologist.) Indeed, some further remarks by Weber concerning charismatic authority seem particularly apposite to the figure of Caligari: thus, "the holders of charisma, the master as well as his disciples and followers, must stand outside the ties of this world, outside of routine occupations, as well as outside the routine obligations of family life" (248). If, according to Weber, "by its very nature, the existence of charismatic authority is specifically unstable" (248), this may also suggest the Expressionist preoccupation with instability of all kinds.

Illustrating the distinction between bureaucratic and charismatic authority, then, the clerks may occupy high chairs in the film, but they are not in themselves imposing; their image alone is not arresting, as is Caligari's. It is the split marked in *these* figures of authority—and not any precise or even metaphoric Kracauerian equivalence between Caligari and Hitler—that makes the film uncannily prophetic. Legal authority as embodied by the clerks depends entirely on its artificial aids: the elevating stilts here render it absurd.

Caligari, meanwhile, has the authority of the outlaw, the fairground, and the photogenic (his appearance is based on a photograph of the philosopher Arthur Schopenhauer). The last of these categories—the power of the photogenic—is of particular interest to the film theory of the 1910s and 1920s (Abel 138–39): it is linked to early film theory's interest in clearly separating film from theater, and prescriptively deriving the tasks facing the arts through a cataloging of their putative "specificities" (the best-known example of this practice being that of Rudolf Arnheim). By inscribing Caligari's power, and the power of his charismatic authority, Caligari's image is film's haunting revenge on the theater to which it seems to owe so much: it transcends the fairground and its theatrical amusements to assert the uncanny authority of what Lotte Eisner called "the Haunted Screen." The photogenic runs for office.

The story of Oedipal revolt widely considered central both to *Caligari* and to Weimar film in general is one of male-male relations. Feminists, meanwhile, have sought to re-vision this story by elevating the female figures it marginalizes. The strongest such reading has been that of Patrice Petro, based on the theories of Linda Williams. If traditional (Freudian) psychoanalytic theory sees works of horror as generally motivated by a male castration anxiety, the signifier of the possible loss of male sexual definition, Williams seeks to replace the image of "woman as lack" with one of simple difference—women possess power of their own rather than merely maintaining the status of a sign of impotence within a male fantasy. She argues, "the female look—a look given preeminent position in the horror film—shares the male fear of the monster's freakishness, but also recognises the sense in which this freakishness is similar to her own" (qtd. in Petro, "Woman" 211). Thus, for Petro, "the monster" Cesare becomes a double for the woman Jane (210–14). Building on this idea, one may argue that the elements of homosexuality present in Cesare's depiction and his association with the feminine (for example, his lack of independent agency, his leotard outfit, his lily near the end of the film, and his inability to murder Jane) combine with his relationship with Caligari to suggest a repression of the image of the woman, a repression that also involves the absorption into his character of one of the textual positions that would logically belong to her. This absorption is not sovereign but recoils on the male figure who embodies it, imbuing him with a different sexuality as well.

At the same time, Jane's marginality within Francis's story paradoxically corresponds to her centrality within the asylum he inhabits: a dreamlike concealment by inversion. If "the monster" Cesare threatens Jane, perhaps it is because she herself threatens the place Cesare occupies: at the side of the doctor, who is the dark, repressed, sexual, and powerful equivalent of her own anodyne, near-anonymous doctor father. The genuineness of her threat to Cesare can be gauged by her centrality in the asylum. Male fear of castration can dictate the psychic and textual displacement of the female who inspires it. There are of course good textual grounds for linking Jane and Cesare, quite apart from the more generalized theoretical one given by Williams. The Jane of the opening frame is a somnambulist, as is Cesare, and at the film's end he clutches that feminizing lily. His leotard sexualizes his body in a manner culturally coded as "feminine," and he—like Jane—sports intense eye shadow. The regal authority inscribed in his name (that of the emperor Caesar) matches that of Jane, "the Queen of Hearts." His sparing of her life indicates one of the many subterranean linkages of characters that crisscross the film; premature death of the double would end the story, just as the student's killing of his reflection encodes his own suicide in Hans Heinz Ewers and Stellan Rye's 1913 film *Der Student von Prag (The Student of Prague)*. Furthermore, the doubling of Jane and Cesare, like all doublings, suggests a link between the pleasures of narcissism and a sense of horror, like the myth of Narcissus himself: self-absorption concludes in the loss of selfhood. The inhabitant of the waking dream—the somnambulist—is in effect drowned in the self, insane.

As my remarks about the two doctors—Caligari and Jane's father—should indicate, however, Jane and Cesare are not the text's only doubles. The extent to which *Caligari* is a dizzying whirl of doubles has been suggested by Thomas Elsaesser ("Social Mobility" 181–87), who also mentions the connection between Francis and Alan, suggesting that Cesare is the unacknowledged executor of the dreams of both Caligari and Francis (Francis's dream is of the rival's destruction). Doubling becomes the repressed of the story, for the narrative's eschewal of explicit doubling permits the superimposition on, and dissolution into, one another of a series of doubles that remain implicit. The linchpin is surely Cesare, who doubles for Caligari and Francis, as well as Jane. The doubling of Francis by Caligari is the only clearly visible doubling relationship, as both are straitjacketed in otherwise identical images; and although Caligari is told of the circle closing around him, it is Francis who appears in the middle of the circle outside the asylum. Doubleness is inscribed in the very appearance of Caligari, whose glasses pushed up onto his forehead or (most often) slipping down below his eyes uncannily double them. Caligari also doubles for the doctor; Francis doubles for Alan;

while Jane, as well as doubling for Cesare, reflects Caligari's alienated "female side" and his inability to recognize it as female and other (it is cast instead as a passive, semifemale male). Jane also doubles for the crucially absent mother of the Oedipal triangle.

All of these doublings may also be described as a multileveled set of scapegoatings that set aside blame. In the ideology of Expressionism in general, the source of doubling lies in the conviction that there is a double nature to the bourgeois, whose staid exterior is really demonic: the sign of the castrating, life-denying father. In *Caligari*, though, the two identities lie on opposite sides of a sheet whose folding conceals their interrelationship. Indeed, it may be argued that this critique of the bourgeoisie is so deeply concealed that Jane's father, Dr. Olsen, who is *Caligari*'s most bourgeois figure, is also the most marginal to the story, however much his image may echo that of Caligari when the two of them stand together by the latter's caravan. Thus *The Cabinet of Dr. Caligari* is a dream of Oedipal revolt in more senses than Kracauer may have guessed, as it scrambles that revolt exactly in the manner of what Freud called "dreamwork," filtering it through oneiric mechanisms of condensation, displacement, and secondary revision. Insanity pervades the text itself, not just the story it recounts. And it is far from certain whether insanity is dispelled by the doctor's benevolent statement that he thinks he knows how to cure Francis: his stating "I think," rather than "I know," suggests the patient as victim of possibly ineffective and even cruel experimentation. The "sane" doctor's final donning of glasses resuscitates the specter of "Caligarism" by re-creating the mad doctor's image, whose possible retention of power at the end is reinforced by the persistence of the cultural stereotype of the mad scientist. Paradoxically, though, the primary avenue through which insanity enters the narrative is the very device that, on the surface, seems to assert order and control by subordinating one plot element to another (Francis's story to the impersonal storytelling of "the film itself"): the highly controversial frame.

The Framing Device
There are various accounts of the source of the framing device (*Rahmenhandlung*). Hans Janowitz attributes it to Robert Wiene, and reports that he and his fellow scenarist, Carl Mayer, were outraged by its craven transformation of an intended protest against the manipulation of the

young by the old during wartime into a safely apolitical account of a young man's insanity, thus implying a vindication of authority (Janowitz 237–38). Other accounts attribute the frame story to producer Erich Pommer. Fritz Lang, who was slated to be the film's director before Wiene, later claimed the dubious credit for himself. Frank D. McConnell comments: "Lang is not a director many would accuse of moral cowardice or of capitulation to considerations of censorship or box office. And with his authority, we may ask if the frame in *Caligari* does not tell us something important not only about the particular film but about the medium itself" (28). Regardless of whether or not one accepts Lang's claim, McConnell's willingness to take the frame seriously is worth pursuing here. Meanwhile, even Janowitz's claim that it was an unwarranted addition is complicated by the existence in the archives of the Stiftung Deutsche Kinemathek (German Cinematheque Foundation) in Berlin of a version, owned once by Werner Krauss, that also possesses a narrative frame (albeit not the one ultimately filmed) (Prawer 168–69).

Whatever its source, the framing device does not so much defuse political dynamite (after all, the original script itself was allegorically encoded and required deciphering to function subversively, and so may be called always already defused, i.e., veiled) as replace political subversion with a far more unsettling spectatorial experience of modernist, Pirandellian vertigo. As Kracauer notes, the Expressionist stylization of the central story invades the frame, and this perpetual vertigo undermines belief in the possibility of any "return to normality" (70). This vertigo affects every level in the hierarchy of narrators, and makes us just as suspicious of the film's own invisible narrator as it has persuaded us to be of Francis, the "visible" narrator. We may even suspect that there is no unified or stable narrative position at all: after all, as *Caligari* implies, a collaborative art cannot have a single narrator. Subverting transparent narration also subverts authority, albeit in a manner different—and deeper—than the one envisaged by Janowitz and Mayer: authority and authorship suffer a simultaneous demise. This radical conclusion seems to counter critical suspicions that *Caligari* merely commodifies Expressionism (Budd, *"Cabinet"* 25–26), a movement whose general social domestication is apparent in the shift from the shocking, startling beginnings of fourteen years earlier (1905) to the first museum purchases immediately after World War I and its utilization in café (or film set!) decoration.

If a domestication of Expressionism does indeed occur here, it may of course anticipate the transformation of modernism into "art cinema," as described by David Bordwell (61–62). The commodification argument may also describe the relationship between taste-making elites and mass society, and between major and minor artists, with widespread adoption of a once-radical style marking a shift in what is truly innovative. In this case, the shift is from Expressionism to a position located way beyond the thought horizon of *Caligari,* that of the New Objectivity: the stylistic and intellectual realism—even cynicism—that followed Expressionism in the mid-1920s. Following this argument, the conventionality of the unfilmed framing device surrounding the Stiftung Deutsche Kinemathek script would indicate that the naively protest-driven Expressionism of Janowitz and Mayer could not envisage the more complex Expressionism of split selfhood and radical epistemological uncertainty. Thus, *Caligari* may bear the hallmarks of an "art-cinema" commodification of the modernistic, but in its framing device, it nevertheless retains a modernist capacity to unsettle. The film's dialogue between Expressionist tenets and a popular cultural form—the cinema—may be deemed either modernist (as a text that itself critiques the linearity on which it is parasitic) or even anticipatory of the postmodern (as the erasure of distinctions between "high" and "low" cultural forms: after all, it was also conceived to be as much a detective thriller as anything else). The possibility of classifying *Caligari* in either of these two ways may itself indicate the dubiousness of any watertight modern/postmodern distinction.

Caligari's strangeness, though, is partly lodged in us, its spectators, for whom "it is difficult to imagine a time . . . when an avant-garde feature, to get made at all, had to go through the same procedures and mechanisms as any standard commercial film" (Thompson 124). As if to corroborate Thompson's point about the fusion of the avant-garde and commerce, the visual radicalism of the moment when words overrun the film image to instruct the head of the institute, "Du musst Caligari werden!" ("You must become Caligari!"), is at the same time the moment of revelation to spectators of the meaning of the key line of the film's publicity campaign. The film's capacity to unsettle us, to invite us into the psychological frame and leave us there, unresolved, moves beyond the possible gimmick of a transposition of Expressionist painting to film sets, or a more felt Expressionist protest against a patriarchal, child-sacrificing authority. Furthermore, the way the narration slips out of control is reflected in the film's capacity to spawn legends of attribution, in its lack of a strong *auteur* in Wiene as director, and in a general uncertainty over responsibility for the framing device and what it was meant to achieve (a mere intriguing twist of the plot taken too far?). Such extensive and fruitful incoherence transcends and defies calculation, and the shape finally assumed by *Caligari* arguably owes as much to chance as to the works of that other immediate postwar protest phenomenon, the Dada movement, which deliberately embraced randomness.

In the context of criminal investigation, of course, the activity of framing has dubious connotations. If a suspect's framing diverts attention from those who were truly responsible, framing becomes an extension of doubling, which has a similar effect. Thus Francis's story shuffles off responsibility by attributing evil to Caligari and Cesare, while Caligari in his turn acquires what a later American military figure (Oliver North!) would call "credible deniability" through the invocation of Cesare. Furthermore, Cesare's doubling in one scene by a doll in a box parodies his lack of real agency and the inherent implausibility of anyone being in two places at the same time. (This last consideration may either prompt questions concerning Caligari's ability to spend so much time at the fairground while not being missed at the asylum, or repress them by permitting their formulation only in connection with Cesare.) "The circle closes"—to quote Francis's words to Caligari—not just around the mountebank himself but around storytelling, as the doctor (like a psychiatric version of Don Quixote, obsessed by what he reads) is driven mad by the reading of an outdated book. Could the text itself be modernist in the sense of commenting self-consciously and self-satirically on its own textuality, and in suggesting that the inherent outdatedness of all texts fatally unfits their readers for contemporary reality?

"While Father Was Away": A Close Reading

"Anxious about the prolonged absence of her father . . . ," an intertitle tells us, Jane goes to the fairground. The sequence that follows is perhaps the film's most enigmatic. Jane proceeds to Caligari's tent, where he leaps out at her—apparently catching her unawares—and she says that she thought she might find her father, Dr. Olsen, there. Caligari draws her in—spider courting fly—by inviting her to come inside and await Dr. Olsen, deferentially removing his hat (which simulates harmlessness) when she hesitates to move. After flicking open the doors of the coffin containing Cesare, he hops aside mincingly and then stands motionless, authoritative, baton in hand, observing the spectacle's effect on the perturbed Jane. As Cesare stares at her, she leans forward to peer at him, then recoils and flees. What is the meaning of all of this?

Unsurprisingly, the scene has attracted a good deal of psychoanalytically influenced interpretation, though this interpretation has usually ignored the most obvious thing (perhaps because it goes without saying): that Caligari's presence during Jane's father's absence implies a connection inaccessible to Jane's conscious awareness. In Clément's analysis, the display of Cesare renders Jane hysterical (one could say, like the Alan who laughed hysterically on learning of his own imminent death) and so casts her as an early Freudian patient. For Elsaesser, Caligari's procedure with Jane figures as more simply sexually exhibitionistic, as "Caligari's powers compensate a kind of impotence" ("Social Mobility" 183). For Petro, meanwhile, the scene marks the entry of a female point of view. Its visual composition places Cesare between Caligari and Jane. Cesare may be weapon or buffer, a "tool" (Elsaesser, "Social Mobility" 183), an offering, or sign of the seductive father's access to youthfulness (which may also mean sexual potency); he may be the hypnotist's amulet, a means of terrorizing Jane, or all of these things at once, to a greater or lesser extent. However, Caligari may merely be using a favored method of acquainting Cesare with his next victim. In terms of the work's Oedipal concerns, Cesare's subjection indicates a crushing of revolt—the lobotomization of Oedipus—and suggests that any threat to Caligari would meet a similar fate. Perhaps Caligari wants Jane to take heed of his power and warn her menfolk? There is also a suggestion of Jane's being overwhelmed by a malevolent male solidarity between Caligari and Cesare that is an infernal doubling of the solidarity between Francis and her father. (If the males go in pairs, though, could this indicate their unacknowledged fear of division and hence rule by a Jane who is, after all, "the Queen of Hearts"?) But if Cesare is readable as the unconscious of Caligari, could Cesare's instability be a seismograph of the conflicts within his master? After all, Caligari might seek Jane's death to demonstrate a scientific hypothesis about the relationship of somnambulism and free will, but it appears that his libido simultaneously desires her and therefore he needs to keep her alive. Unlike the scene in which Alan hears his death foretold, this one is utterly wordless, completely enigmatic, susceptible to all the readings given above, and perhaps even to some others. This is surely why it has attracted a degree of critical attention that may itself be explained as seeking to explain it away—for its riddling quality places it very near "the heart of [the] mystery" (*Hamlet* 3.2.336) that is *Caligari*: a film that poses a challenge to all critical authority.

Conclusion

Legacy

If, as noted in the opening section of this essay, *Caligari* has been declared a film that "led nowhere," and is without descendants (in this sense giving the lie to the title of S. S. Prawer's book *Caligari's Children*), it may well be because of the framing device's effect on the narrative it encloses. For although, as we have seen, this device is not the simple subversion of revolutionary intent described by Janowitz and Kracauer, Weimar reviewers' general perception that the film established a linkage between Expressionist style and insanity (Kracauer 70–71) allows one to see *Caligari* as genuinely anticipating Hitler, in that he also categorized Expressionism as insane or "degenerate" art. This is, of course, ironic, as *Caligari* itself can be seen as the degenerate, final gasp of Expressionism. Its ending may be read on one level as an allegory of the displacement of the Expressionist aesthetic by the emergent one of the New Objectivity. The Expressionism that presents itself as the image of mental derangement does indeed have a double attitude to itself. Perhaps that is why *Caligari* displays a dialectical, fruitful tension between modernity and mass culture, a tension that would later collapse as the pole of modernity was subsumed under that of mass culture.

Even if it does lack easily identifiable "children," it is clear that *Caligari* influenced both the avant-garde and the commercial cinema: including such key avant-gardists of the 1920s and 1960s as Marcel L'Herbier, Louis Delluc, and Kenneth Anger (Prawer 166). It also had progeny in horror movies and pockets of the shadowy world of *film noir*. But the ambiguous and simultaneous conservatism and radicalism of its uncanny framing would give way to conventionally told tales of split selfhood on the one hand (the horror movie) and an excessive avant-garde stylistics divorced from the thematics of the divided self on the other. Few subsequent films would replicate *Caligari*'s characteristic combination of narrational ambiguity, horror, and mainstream storytelling conventions, its uneasy balancing act of the commercial and the radical. One possible candidate is Martin Scorsese's *Taxi Driver* (1976), whose nightmarish New York is associated with the troubled mind of Travis Bickle, and whose ambiguous final scene suggests closure through a framing fantasy, though no such fantasy is evoked explicitly. Far more explicit is David Fincher's *Fight Club* (1999), which echoes both *Caligari* and *Taxi Driver* in reserving its revelation of narrational uncertainty for its ending (its primary address being initially to a mass-cultural audience it is loath to alienate through an earlier disclosure of its ambiguity): only at the end do we learn that Brad Pitt's character is a projection of the protagonist. Even this narrative, though, may be deemed to end conventionally, since as buildings crumble in the background a happy ending is ensured through the unification of the romantic couple.

In all three films, the most durable legacy of Expressionism is its tracking of an isolated male character whose delusions, in the absence of any countervailing account of events, become welded to the impression of reality. That protagonist's projections are signaled as such only by their excessiveness, which furnishes an excuse for stylistic violence and eccentricity. The striking style becomes commodified, though, as a way of attracting attention: no longer a sign of the damage an older generation has inflicted on the mind of the young, Expressionist protagonist, this style becomes the spectacular announcement of the arrival of a new gun in town.

Credits

Germany, 1920, Decla-Film Gesellschaft, Holz & Co.

Director: Robert Wiene
Producers: Rudolf Meinert and Erich Pommer
Screenplay: Hans Janowitz and Carl Mayer
Cinematography: Willy Hameister
Art Direction: Walter Reimann, Walter Röhrig, and Hermann Warm
Music (for Berlin première): Giuseppe Becce

CAST:

Dr. Caligari	Werner Krauss
Cesare	Conrad Veidt
Francis	Friedrich Feher
Jane	Lil Dagover
Alan	Hans Heinrich von Twardowski
Dr. Olsen	Rudolf Lettinger
A rogue	Ludwig Rex
Landlady	Elsa Wagner

Bibliography

Abel, Richard, ed. *French Film Theory and Criticism: A History—Anthology, 1907–1939*. Vol. 1, 1907–1929. Princeton: Princeton UP, 1988.

Arnheim, Rudolf. "Dr. Caligari Redivivus." *Kritiken und Aufsätze zum Film*. Ed. Rudolf Arnheim. Munich: Carl Hanser, 1979. 177–78.

———. *Film as Art*. Berkeley: U of California P, 1966.

Bordwell, David. "The Art Cinema as a Mode of Film Practice." *Film Criticism* 4.1 (1979): 56–64.

Budd, Mike, ed. *"The Cabinet of Dr. Caligari": Texts, Contexts, Histories*. New Brunswick: Rutgers UP, 1990.

———. "Retrospective Narration in Film: Rereading *The Cabinet of Dr. Caligari*." *Film Criticism* 4.1 (1979): 35–43.

Burch, Noël, and Jorge Dana. "Propositions." *Afterimage* 5 (1974): 40–66.

Carroll, Noël. "The Cabinet of Dr. Kracauer." *Millenium Film Journal* 1.2 (1978): 77–85.

Clément, Catherine B. "Charlatans and Hysterics." Budd, *"Cabinet"* 191–204.

Coates, Paul. *The Gorgon's Gaze: German Cinema, Expressionism, and the Image of Horror*. New York: Cambridge UP, 1991.

Eisner, Lotte. *The Haunted Screen: Expressionism in the German Film and the Influence of Max Reinhardt*. Trans. Roger Greaves. Berkeley: U of California P, 1969.

Elsaesser, Thomas. "Film History and Visual Pleasure: Weimar Cinema." *Cinema Histories, Cinema Practices*. Ed. Patricia Mellencamp and Philip Rosen. Frederick, MD: U Publications of America, 1984. 47–84.

———. "Social Mobility and the Fantastic." Budd, *"Cabinet"* 171–89.

Freud, Sigmund. "The 'Uncanny'" [*Das Unheimliche*]. 1919. *Standard Edition of the Complete Psychological Works of Sigmund Freud*. Vol. 17. Trans. James Strachey. London: Hogarth, 1955. 217–56.

Grafe, Frieda. "Doktor Caligari gegen Dr. Kracauer." *Filmkritik* 5 (May 1970): 242–44.

Janowitz, Hans. "*Caligari*—The Story of a Famous Story (Excerpts)." Budd, *"Cabinet"* 221–39.

Janowitz, Hans, and Carl Mayer. *"Das Cabinet des Dr. Caligari": Drehbuch von Carl Mayer und Hans Janowitz zu Robert Wienes Film von 1919/20*. Berlin: Stiftung Deutsche Kinemathek, 1995.

Kael, Pauline. *Kiss Kiss Bang Bang*. London: Marion Boyars, 1970.

Kaul, Walter, ed. *Caligari und Caligarismus.* Berlin: Stiftung Deutsche Kinemathek, 1970.

Kracauer, Siegfried. *From Caligari to Hitler: A Psychological History of the German Film.* Princeton: Princeton UP, 1947.

Laqueur, Walter. *Weimar: A Cultural History.* New York: Perigee, 1980.

McConnell, Frank D. *The Spoken Seen: Film and the Romantic Imagination.* Baltimore: Johns Hopkins UP, 1975.

Petro, Patrice. *Joyless Streets: Women and Melodramatic Representation in Weimar Germany.* Princeton: Princeton UP, 1989.

———. "The Woman, the Monster, and *The Cabinet of Dr. Caligari.*" Budd, *"Cabinet"* 205–17.

Poe, Edgar Allan. *The Complete Tales and Poems of Edgar Allan Poe.* New York: Modern Library, 1938.

Prawer, S. S. *Caligari's Children: The Film as a Tale of Terror.* Oxford: Oxford UP, 1980.

Robinson, David. *"Das Cabinet des Dr. Caligari."* London: BFI, 1997.

Salt, Barry. "From Caligari to Who?" *Sight and Sound* 48 (1979): 119–23.

Thompson, Kristin. "Dr. Caligari at the Folies-Bergere, or, The Successes of an Early Avant-Garde Film." Budd, *"Cabinet"* 121–69.

Weber, Max. *From Max Weber: Essays in Sociology.* Trans. and ed. H. H. Gerth and C. Wright Mills. London: Routledge, 1967.

Williams, Linda. "When the Woman Looks." *Re-Vision: Essays in Feminist Film Criticism.* Ed. Mary Ann Doane, Patricia Mellencamp, and Linda Williams. Amer. Film Inst. Monograph Ser. 3. Frederick, MD: U Publications of America, 1984. 83–99.

Nanook of the North (1922)

JEFFREY GEIGER

Fiction, Truth, and the Documentary Contract

Context

Robert J. Flaherty's *Nanook of the North* was an unparalleled, and unlikely, success for a nonfiction film when it was released, and it has since been numbered among the earliest and most faithful examples of feature-length documentary filmmaking. Yet increasingly, critics have attacked the construction of the "Flaherty Myth" and have stressed the ways that his "story of life and love in the actual Arctic"—as the opening credits describe it—is semifictionalized at best. The problems lie not so much in the ways that it blurs the line between fantasy and reality as in its subtly deceptive narrative strategies, which appear to naturalize the staging and reinvention of Inuit (then known as Eskimo) life that took place for the benefit of Flaherty's camera.

Though these opposing perspectives are not easily reconciled, this discussion will suggest that even a problematic text like *Nanook of the North* might act as a touchstone for ongoing debates concerning questions of authenticity in cinema and, more specifically, questions of the depiction of racial and cultural difference in what came to be known as the "expeditionary" genre of films. For instance, is it necessary, or even possible, to differentiate between fact and fiction, actuality and artifice, in film? In what ways is the representation of cultural difference engaged with questions of power and authority? Finally, as Campbell Dixon asked in the London *Daily Telegraph* in 1947, "Is *Nanook* a fake?"

Though *Nanook of the North* lacks the explicit racial and political dimensions of a film like D. W. Griffith's *The Birth of a Nation* (1915), in many ways it presents today's viewers with a similar dilemma. Griffith's film can still alarm audiences with its images of the Ku Klux Klan coming to power in the post-Civil War South, especially as this overtly ideological content is couched within one of the most ambitious and technically sophisticated features of its time. Similarly, *Nanook of the North* can be viewed as subtly endorsing certain forms of racial and cultural chauvinism within its relatively smooth and unified visual and narrative framework.[1] Though these films might offend viewers, both texts shed light on the ways in which historical and political hindsight can problematize—and sometimes confound—our understanding of significant achievements in cinema. Certainly, both films document the often painful ways that concepts of difference evolved over the last century. In a media-saturated age such as ours, it helps to look closely at how films like these have drawn on a battery of techniques to manipulate the intellectual and emotional responses of viewers as they reproduce—and produce—popular ideology.

Explorer

Flaherty began his career not with ambitions to become a great movie director, but by following in the footsteps of his father, a mining engineer who often took the family on prospecting journeys from one gold-mining camp to another throughout Canada. "Even in my youth I was always exploring new country," Flaherty stated; "in a manner of speaking, we were a nomad family" (qtd. in Rotha 7). These formative experiences clearly served as the nucleus for *Nanook*, which would transform him from an explorer and prospector into a figure recognized as the "father" of American documentary.

Filmmaking for Flaherty can be seen as a direct outgrowth of the colonial project of exploration, mapping, and prospecting in the Canadian North. In his twenties, he met the industrialist Sir William Mackenzie, whom Flaherty would later call "the Cecil Rhodes of Canada" (qtd. in Rotha 12). He worked for Mackenzie searching for iron ore along the sub-Arctic coast of the Hudson Bay. He still "knew nothing whatsoever about films" (Rotha 22), but at Mackenzie's suggestion, in 1913 he took a diversion to Rochester, New York, where he bought and learned how to use a Bell and Howell camera. By 1916, after some disastrous attempts at filming in the extreme cold, he had

---

[1]William Rothman's chapter on *Nanook of the North* in *Documentary Film Classics* (1–20) uses Griffith's film *True Heart Susie* (1919) to map intersections between *Nanook* and overt fictions.

compiled seventy thousand feet of negative documenting his northern journeys. With the encouragement of his wife (and frequent collaborator) Frances Hubbard Flaherty, he began piecing this film together for exhibition. Then, in what is now a well-known footnote to *Nanook of the North*, Flaherty dropped a cigarette on the nearly finished nitrate negative, which instantly went up in flames. Flaherty "narrowly escaped losing his life" (26) and was left with only a single positive print (now lost), sometimes called "the Harvard Print."

Viewing this print after the fire, Flaherty became fixated on its shortcomings: "It was utterly inept, simply a scene of this and a scene of that, no relation, no thread of a story or continuity whatever, and it must have bored the audience to distraction. Certainly it bored me" (qtd. in Rotha 26–27). These observations are particularly relevant in the light of *Nanook of the North*, which resolved Flaherty's concerns about continuity by employing an episodic narrative of Nanook's search for sustenance through the changing seasons. *Nanook* also tends to focus on action over static images, perhaps because of Flaherty's worries about boring audiences that would have had little knowledge of Inuit life. Thus, in the early stages of his film career, Flaherty was hardly "the patron saint of oppositional film practices" that some have come to consider him (Langer 39), nor was he necessarily obsessed with making personal or artistic statements through the medium of film. In search of an audience, viewing pleasure was a primary concern.

It was not until 1920 that another opportunity arose to make his Eskimo film. With the help of the extant print, Flaherty convinced the French fur-trading firm Revillon Frères to sponsor another trek to the North, this time with the sole purpose of making a film. Though it made the film possible, the relationship with Revillon Frères has disturbed critics since it raises unsettling questions about the commercial and imperial influences behind *Nanook*. Throughout his career, Flaherty would have an unhappy relationship with major studios and distribution companies, and would frequently turn to corporate financing, which carried with it a set of different but perhaps no less stringent limitations on creative expression. Jay Ruby points to this moment in Flaherty's career as symptomatic of the "ambivalence" he always felt toward commercial imperatives: if there was a tension between economic demands and artistic fulfillment, financial limitations coupled with limited screening venues meant that money interests grudgingly carried the day ("Re-examination" 439). Yet on the screen, Flaherty's relationship to his sponsors hardly appears adversarial; in *Nanook*, Revillon Frères' furs show up as "product placement" in a number of scenes. In Flaherty's defense, Rotha argues that Flaherty was unaware that the film industry was at that point "strongly opposed to such gratuitous screen advertising" (28), though this still fails to address the signifying power of these images in the context of imperial trade networks.

Even with the assistance of Revillon Frères, Flaherty was held to a miniscule budget in comparison to Hollywood standards; Rotha estimates a total production and postproduction cost of $53,000. Choosing equipment to withstand extreme climatic conditions, he took with him two Akeley cameras, 75,000 feet of Kodak film, an electric light plant and projector, and a printing machine. The latter two were carried specifically for screening rushes for his Inuit subjects to view, whom he relied on for feedback concerning changes or ideas for new scenes. The filming environment was unbelievably harsh, but Flaherty did not bear all the difficulties alone, as his own account makes clear:

> I also took the materials and chemicals to develop the film, and equipment to print and project it. My lighting equipment had to be extremely light because I had to go by canoe nearly 200 miles down river before I got to Hudson Bay. This meant portages, and portages meant packing the equipment on my back and on those of the Indians I took along for the river trip. And God knows, there were some long portages on that route—one of them took us two days to pack across. ("Robert Flaherty Talking" 13)

With film equipment on his own back, and on the backs of others, Flaherty journeyed for two months before arriving at Port Harrison. The location was determined by Revillon Frères: a trading post connected to the company on the northeastern shore of Hudson Bay. The cold was severe. On one occasion, when the thermometer read thirty-five degrees Fahrenheit below zero, the negative froze and shattered in the camera "like so much wafer-glass" (R. Flaherty, "Handling" 87).

At this point, two parallel versions of making *Nanook* emerge. The first treats Robert Flaherty as a quasi-mythic figure with little professional film experience, who returned from the wastes of the frozen

North with cinema's first documentary feature: an epic of human endurance. The second story lies at the margins of this one, and concerns the four Inuit assistants who helped to make *Nanook*. Frances Flaherty names them as Nanook (Allakariallak, who is not referred to by this name in the film nor in Flaherty's writings), Wetaltook, Tookalook, and "Little Tommy." "They did everything for him," Frances wrote, diligently working on what they referred to as "the aggie [motion picture]" (13–14). Seemingly straightforward activities like washing and drying the exposed film presented a myriad of unexpected problems. To wash the film the Inuit assistants

> had to keep a hole chiseled through six feet of ice all through the winter and prevent it from freezing and then haul the water in barrels on a sledge with a dog team up to the hut. Once there, they used all their hands to clear the ice out of the water before it could be poured for the required washes over the film. The deer hair falling off the Eskimos' clothes into the water worried Flaherty almost as much as the ice did. (Rotha 31)

When the coal stove used for drying ran out of fuel, Allakariallak and the others had to hunt quickly for driftwood along the coast. Revillon Frères' budget did include remuneration for Inuit actors and technicians; still, Flaherty writes that when he arrived in Cape Dufferin without an assistant, several Inuits were turned over to him to be his "servants." He notes that Allakariallak sometimes had to continuously crank the negative's drying reel near the fire through the night, while the director "slept in [his] sleeping bag just beyond cremation range" ("Handling" 86–87). Rotha suggests that the "participation by his film subjects in the actual making of the film" was crucial to its success (31), and Flaherty's practice of training local people, including actors, to work on his films continued successfully on later projects such as *Moana* (1926) and *Man of Aran* (1934). Still, this version of "collaborative" work sometimes suggests there might be a fine line between participation and subtle forms of indenture.

Flaherty remained on location on Hudson Bay until August 1921, having spent sixteen months of intense work on the film. With Charlie Gelb, he did editing in New York during the winter of 1921–22. Paramount and First National distributors were quick to pass on the finished film, the former calling it "a film that couldn't be shown to the public" (R. Flaherty, "Robert Flaherty Talking" 17). The French-based Pathé finally premiered the film on June 11, 1922, during a raging storm, at Roxy's Capitol Theatre in New York, where it was billed for a week with another adventure tale, Robert C. Bruce's *My Country*. Initial box-office receipts were reasonably good, but the film was slow to gather more general popular support. Rotha suggests that *Nanook* had an "inauspicious beginning, accompanied by lukewarm or cautious reviews by the critics" (44); but on the day following its premiere, the *New York Times* could hardly contain its praise for the movie that brought "life itself" from far-off Hudson Bay directly into New York's Capitol Theatre, noting, "beside this film the usual photoplay, the so-called 'dramatic' work of the screen, becomes as thin and blank as the celluloid on which it is printed" ("Screen"). A month later, the *Times* again singled out *Nanook* as "one of the screen's finest achievements" ("Pictures of 1922"), and *Nanook* ultimately earned nearly $300,000 on its first American run (Murphy 10).

Flaherty would never again achieve a popular success on this scale. His follow-up, *Moana*, garnered critical praise for its innovative panchromatic cinematography, but it barely managed to make a profit. For the rest of his career, Flaherty enjoyed critical success and even collaborated on a number of mainstream productions of exotic origin, such as F. W. Murnau's South Pacific romance *Tabu* (1931) and the Zoltan Korda production *Elephant Boy* (1937), shot in India. But his relationship with studios was rarely successful, and he is still best remembered for four documentary features: *Nanook of the North, Moana, Man of Aran,* and the Standard Oil–financed *Louisiana Story* (1948).

Analysis

The box-office success of *Nanook* confirmed a wave of public interest in an emerging genre of films known as exploration or expeditionary films. *Nanook* marks a break from the already popular travelogue film, which blended "static cinematography with the probing ethnographical insights of a Baedeker guide" (Doherty 222). *Nanook* was not the first film of its kind (Sir Ernest Shackleton and Frank Hurley's *South: Ernest Shackleton and the Endurance Expedition* of 1919, for example, was a key precursor), but it set the tone for the grander scale and longer format of the expeditionary film, which tended to emphasize exploration, discovery, and adventure into realms "uncharted" and unknown. While there are key differences, especially in the ways that *Nanook* attempts to minimize any references to the white explorer/filmmaker in the *mise-en-scène*, the popularity of Flaherty's film paved the way for epics like Osa and Martin E. Johnson's safari adventure *Simba: The King of the Beasts* (1928) and Merian C. Cooper and Ernest B. Schoedsack's films *Grass: A Nation's Battle for Life* (1925) and *Chang: A Drama of the Wilderness* (1927). Several years later, Cooper and Schoedsack would achieve enormous success with the adventure-fantasy *King Kong* (1933), which is clearly the offspring of these earlier expeditionary films.

By now, the cultural and racial assumptions that underlie *Nanook of the North* and the expeditionary genre it helped launch have been subjected to extensive critique. These discussions tend to revolve around two focal issues. The first hinges on the differentiation between nonfictional and fictional cinema, and the extent to which films have reinvented cultures-at-a-distance for the benefit of Western audiences. The second issue relates more generally to power imbalances that can operate within acts of representation and to the hierarchies produced and reproduced in colonial and ethnographic images.

Fact versus Fiction

In 1926, Flaherty's second film, *Moana,* prompted John Grierson to employ the term "documentary" to describe a notable feature in nonfiction filmmaking, in this case writing that the film had "documentary value" (25). But as a pioneer of many of the conventions of what was becoming classified as the documentary, Flaherty also became the focus of its problems. Flaherty has frequently been accused of falsifying his material, and his legacy has undergone serious scrutiny with critiques such as Richard Corliss's "Robert Flaherty: The Man and the Iron Myth" (1973), which derides the "sanctimonious reverence" and "premature deification" accorded to Flaherty up to and immediately after his death in 1951 (230).

"Sometimes you have to lie," Flaherty once stated; "one often has to distort a thing to catch its true spirit" (qtd. in Calder-Marshall 97). But these admissions have hardly prevented others from investigating the authenticity of his films. Since the 1970s, the very legitimacy of universal documentary truths has come under intense questioning, with Flaherty often at the center of the debate. George Stoney's film *Robert Flaherty's "Man of Aran": How the Myth Was Made* (1979), for example, highlights the distortions and omissions of Flaherty's romanticized Aran Island survival narrative and his selective *mise-en-scène,* which omits such important details as the landowner-tenant hierarchy on the island. Claude Massot's *Nanook Revisited* (1988) likewise reveals the silences and elisions in *Nanook of the North,* and makes visible the tensions between the film's elevated status in academic circles and the reactions of Inuits to the film, who found comedy rather than serious drama in famous scenes such as the seal-hunting episode. Jo-Anne Birnie Danzker has itemized some of *Nanook's* shortcomings: "It would appear . . . that none of the leading characters were identified by their actual names; that Allakariallak's [Nanook's] clothing was not indigenous to the region; that the contrived sequences were highly amusing to the Inuit; that the seal hunt was contrived" (62).

As far back as 1947, the question "Is *Nanook* a fake?" was being raised in the public domain; indeed, critical questions about Flaherty's staging arose soon after the film was released. But documentary film has long operated under less-stringent assumptions regarding the use and value of reality as raw material. According to Grierson, documentary is "a creative treatment of actuality" (qtd. in Hardy 13). More specifically, the documentary filmmaker works at producing "art" by passing from the realm of the purely descriptive use of "natural material" into the realm of "arrangements, rearrangements, and creative shapings of it" (qtd. in Hardy 20). The term "creative" here is important, for a dilemma arises when documentary images are claimed to have direct access to authenticity and thus to be diametrically opposed to fictional images. While both the documentary film and the fiction film are obviously artificial constructs created through the filmmaker's subjective choices in shooting, framing, editing, and so on, it would be a mistake to attempt to read documentary films in precisely the same ways that we do fictional ones. It may now seem almost axiomatic, after poststructuralist criticism's interrogation of the processes of representation, that the construction of documentary truth is intimately bound to issues of power, subject position, and ideological influence, as could be said of a fictional text. Still, as Ruby has argued, most audiences will comprehend documentary images as unmediated and accurate representations of reality, unless they are explicitly manipulated ("Ethics" 313). *Nanook* on first viewing might even appear more truthful and reverent toward its subjects than other kinds of documentaries, such as *Cops* or MTV's *The Real World*. In *Nanook*'s case, the space between Flaherty's images and their audience, once defined primarily by geographic and cultural distance, is now compounded by a temporal gap of over eighty years, enhancing the perceived authority and realism of the images.

In an attempt to more clearly delineate the differences between documentary and fiction, Bill Nichols suggests that documentary film can be identified through the commonalities of style, editing, and representational codes that it shares with other films that are also agreed to be documentaries; he also allows for the idea that photographic images can be tied indexically to actual historical events. But even here, documentary images on their own terms cannot guarantee their status as truthful (162). The authenticity of documentary images is therefore always contingent and subject to external factors such as context and verification. Yet just because it requires proof, it does not necessarily mean that the documentary image is false. Poststructuralist critics have preferred to speak of the status of documentary truths in the plural, rather than appealing to a single universal standard of truth by which each image must be judged. These truths may be contingent, transient, and contested, but are no less valid for being so.

Documentary film is always spatially and temporally removed from its subjects, as well as from the viewers who watch the moving figures captured on the screen, yet a collective desire persists that clings to the immediacy of documentary images as evidence of actual events having happened. This desire may have contributed to the vocal debates concerning falsifications in Flaherty's work. *Nanook* was made long before French *cinéma vérité* and Anglo-American direct cinema began to make claims for documentary immediacy; Dziga Vertov launched his *Kino-pravda* ("film-truth") project in Russia the same year as *Nanook*'s release. Flaherty himself, though obviously striving for a style that appeared unmediated, never claimed his films were absolutely truthful. Yet even with these qualifications in mind, certain ethical doubts might linger about the film. As Nichols suggests, the problem of documentary representation often comes down to interpersonal, power-laden relations between human beings and the persistent question of "how to *represent* another person when any representation threatens diminution, fabrication, and distortion" (231; italics in the original). Furthermore, with *Nanook,* the individual act of representing another person takes place in the context of twentieth-century imperial practices; thus any distortions rendered by Flaherty's camera carry with them the burden of an ongoing history of exploitation, ethnic stereotyping, and cultural misrepresentation.

The Imperial Spectacle

Alongside debates about authenticity in *Nanook* are ideological questions relating to Flaherty's background as an explorer, mapmaker, and prospector, and the ways his films might be associated with imperial practices. Flaherty is often quoted as asserting, "first I was an explorer, then I was an artist" (qtd. in Corliss 230), and the mark of the adventurer lingers in his films. For Brian Winston, Flaherty was "a child of the last age of imperial expansion, and beneath the veneer of sympathy and understanding for the peoples he filmed there is nothing but the strong whiff of paternalism and prejudice" (20). His best-known films conjure little-known worlds on the frontiers of civilization and recall nostalgia for a life amidst uncorrupted, natural surroundings.

For Corliss, this nostalgia manifested itself in Flaherty's desire to discover elemental truths about humanity and to "project them onto the mind screens of the rest of us, who may have forgotten them in our century-long rush toward catatonic computerism" (230). This will to authenticate and narrate elemental truths did not always translate into accurate representations, and Flaherty had a tendency to project his personal beliefs onto the subjects of his films. The mystification of the bourgeois family, for example, is evident in Flaherty's reconstruction of "native" families for the screen. He did not take into account the polygamy practiced in Inuit culture when creating the domestic unit of Nanook, Nyla, and their children, and his Samoan family in *Moana* was similarly an artifice: "father, mother, son, sister, and the rest are physically representative of the culture and also attractive—not necessarily handsome or beautiful but the best of type" (Ellis 21).

Critical attention to documentary fabrication and to implications of colonial appropriation embedded in texts has taken on particular force in the context of postcolonial criticism, which has helped us to view Western representations of "others" as neither neutral nor transparent, but as historically situated social acts that are marked by their social contexts. Films of the expeditionary genre thus can be seen to present two seemingly opposed (though mutually dependent) versions of indigenous or "non-Western" peoples. In the first, primitive types are portrayed as occupying the fringes of humanity, prone to outrageous behavior and bestial tastes, and often given over to bizarre or violent rituals. *Simba* contains elements of this image, which was taken to even greater lengths in openly fictional incarnations such as the Academy Award–nominated *Trader Horn* (1931) and *King Kong*. A second version, clearly on display in *Nanook*, is more closely aligned with the tradition of the "noble savage," in which an idealized Western self is projected onto an imagined cultural or racial other, making the subjects of difference familiar while at the same time effectively robbing them of cultural autonomy and significance. *Nanook*'s narrative suggests an ambivalence between these two positions, offering images of the "happy-go-lucky Eskimo" that ultimately turn to shades of savagery. Close-ups of the blood-smeared faces of Nanook, Nyla, and Allegoo after the seal-hunting sequence (the red appearing black due to the limited tonal range of orthochromatic film) reinforce the derogatory meaning of "Eskimo" as "eaters of raw flesh."

Along these lines, Fatimah Tobing Rony has seen *Nanook of the North* as part of the colonial-era "ethnographic spectacle": a practice of representing others that is aligned with the circuslike atmosphere of late-nineteenth- and early-twentieth-century world's fairs and traveling shows, which often included live exhibitions of non-Western peoples—presented as racial and cultural "types"—from around the world. These practices can be defined as a form of cultural taxidermy, an effort to produce a cultural artifact in response to the impression that a way of life is dying, for "taxidermy seeks to make that which is dead look as if it were still living" (101). Cinematic taxidermy can be found in Flaherty's romantic ethnographies, which eschew cultural contact and conflict in favor of creating an idealized, frozen image of the (presumed dying or dead) culture in question.

The scene in which Nanook encounters a gramophone is a prime example of this practice. Here the Inuit's ignorance of technology is underscored as he listens to the machine and laughs, the intertitles explaining that the trader, "in deference to Nanook, the great hunter . . . entertains and attempts to explain the principle of the gramophone."

Apart from this scene, *Nanook* reinforces the contrast between civilized and primitive states through a nearly complete elision of the presence of the filmmaker and the trappings of the West, so that in those rare moments when technology is revealed, it paradoxically becomes a device to further exclude Nanook from the modern era. Yet as Rony points out, "Because fur prices were at their height in the 1920s, the Inuit in Quebec were introduced to a cash economy, and the Inuit portrayed in *Nanook* thus were using guns, knew about gramophones, wore Western clothing, and, although many had died from Western diseases, certainly were not vanishing" (109).

An argument that would defend *Nanook* as an unadulterated document of a lost way of life may be beyond salvaging, but the film remains important not so much because it succeeds in providing an accurate and authoritative account, but because it exemplifies a mode of cultural representation and documentary practice that was emerging in the 1920s and that still inheres in our current practices. It is an important text precisely because it continues to puzzle and to challenge viewers interested in questions of cinema and truth, of the relationship between observer and observed, and of changing attitudes and approaches toward racial and cultural difference.

Close Reading

Nanook offers its viewers intertitles before images: "The mysterious Barren Lands—desolate, boulder-strewn, wind-swept—illimitable spaces which top the world." These words were written by Carl Stearns Clancy in collaboration with Flaherty, and appear to be interpreting the setting before it is even shown, operating like the authoritative "voice of God" voice-overs of later sound documentaries. The titles introduce the scene as strange and otherworldly, providing a sense of the unknown that initiates the drama and that continues to linger somewhere beyond the space of the frame. The words give way to a slow traveling shot from shipboard across an icy sea with the sun appearing to rise in the distance. Orthochromatic film stock is sensitive to blues and greens, helping Flaherty to create images of the sublime from the Arctic's limited chromatic range and vast expanses of bare land, water, and ice. Journey is immediately established as a central theme; journey not only through space—as suggested by the ship—but also through time. This physical journey becomes metaphoric as the film progresses, taking the viewer to an ideal "primitive" place untroubled by the knowledge of money, machines, and other trappings of civilized life.

Into this setting the characters are introduced—"the fearless, lovable, happy-go-lucky Eskimo"—but Flaherty does not immediately show them. Instead the viewer is geographically situated by the display of two maps, which recall the structure of the travelogue. A transition begins from the mysterious to the familiar: Nanook's territory is "a little kingdom . . . nearly as large as England." Such small gestures begin to invite viewer identification in the midst of scenes of manifest strangeness. We are finally introduced to Nanook, the protagonist, "a great hunter famous through all Ungava—Nanook, The Bear." The following shot reveals the face of Allakariallak. His expression contains the suggestion of a smile but is very different from the laughter that often accompanies later moments when Nanook faces the camera. The shot owes much to ethnographic portraiture of the time, such as that of Edward Sheriff Curtis—who produced a twenty-volume photographic study of "vanishing" North American Indians—and it similarly presents Nanook's as a noble face worthy of prolonged contemplation. A brief, direct look at the camera seems to flash past, and perhaps there is a fleeting challenge implied here: the film is not going to be a typical travelogue designed to offer the tourist an easy voyeuristic peep at foreign lands and peoples. If so, the challenge is quickly negated as Nanook's gaze begins to wander, prefiguring later images that have the effect of disarming him and displaying him to the viewer. Nyla is introduced next, smiling while rocking back and forth, creating a rather different effect from the previous shot and exemplifying something closer to what Winston describes as Inuits "clowning" for the camera (20).

Rony further argues that the film feeds the Western conception of the Inuit as childlike, simple people, an idea reinforced in the sequence at the "white man's big igloo"—the trading post. Here critics have found some of *Nanook*'s most egregious images, especially those that emphasize Nanook's simplicity. The party's arrival is strikingly composed against a wall of white arctic fox furs, where Revillon Frères' investment is clearly on show. The intertitles state that Nanook killed polar bears "with nothing more formidable than his harpoon" and now "barters for knives and beads and bright colored candy of the trader's precious store," but these items hardly seem worth risking one's life for, and the words imply a primitive naïveté. Soon images of Nanook's puppies lying alongside Nyla's naked baby appear, images that indulge in the textures of skin and fur. Yet they also set in motion a semiotic association that persists throughout the film, where Inuit and animal are closely aligned, either within a single shot or through an associative montage. The intertitles confirm the connection, noting that, "Nyla, not to be outdone, displays her young husky too." While Nanook's amiable presence rarely denotes savagery, these visual exchanges initiate connotations that soon become more potent. Nanook's exploratory biting of the phonograph record in the ensuing encounter with the trader is a disarming aside, but is followed by Nanook biting the head from a live fish in the next scene. Highlighting the survival theme, images of teeth, ravenous mouths, and, later, blood-smeared faces are focused on with increasing frequency, leading finally to the climactic sequence following the seal hunt. Here the family's consumption of raw seal is linked, through associative montage, with images of dogs gnashing their teeth.

A key to thinking critically about *Nanook of the North*'s distinctive style comes from an early review in Robert Sherwood's *The Best Moving Pictures of 1922–23*, which suggests that *Nanook* "has no plot whatsoever, and struggled along very well without it, but it did have continuity" (4). The relationship between *Nanook*'s episodic structure and its carefully constructed sense of visual and narrative continuity is crucial to understanding how Flaherty's film language both overlaps with and diverges from fictional silent cinema. The changing seasons and Nanook's search for food help to organize the narrative, but the success of Flaherty's technique lies in the staging and editing of individual sequences. What emerges is a series of absorbing vignettes, dramatically phrased intertitles, and dynamic transitional shots. Though each episode does not always logically stem from the previous one, the film's overall narrative coherence is derived from the relationship between episodes (de Bromhead 70–72). As the audience follows Nanook and the family's activities, it acquires knowledge about, and ideally develops sympathy for, the figures on the screen, while the film's gradual shift from a light tone toward a more menacing mood provides an undercurrent of suspense that keeps the spectator engaged with the events unfolding on-screen.

A noteworthy transitional shot initiates the walrus hunt, and is a good example of Flaherty's exploitation of the limited agility of the Akeley camera. "Excitement reigns," a title card states, which fades into the image of a husky in the foreground, while a formation of kayaks plying the water in the distance confirms that a significant event is emerging offscreen. The shot is typical of Flaherty's style, which employs something akin to an empty shot to establish the setting, then follows a complete action through a seamless shot sequence. Nanook traverses the space of the screen twice before gesturing to his family, who emerge from a tent. The group begins to exit the frame right, but the camera follows them as they carry a boat to the edge of the water. For a moment we lose sight of the flotilla in the distance, but it soon reappears, slicing into the frame from the left, now surprisingly only a short distance away: a shift in scale that increases the tension. Nanook follows the boats, and the camera isolates his struggle against the waves, highlighting his heroic individualism. The economy of this sequence is striking, revealing the suitability of Flaherty's limited resources to his ambitious staging. He had acquired the Akeley cameras in order to capture shots precisely like these: "These [Akeley] cameras fascinated me because they were the first cameras ever made to have a gyro-movement in the tripod-head whereby one could tilt and pan the camera without the slightest distracting jar or jerk or vibration" (R. Flaherty, "Robert Flaherty Talking" 13). The sequence's formal precision and its in medias res dramatics belie its constructedness, yet within the context of *Nanook* it appears essentially natural and unplanned.

The suspense that marks the start of the walrus hunt is echoed again at the beginning of the seal hunt, though here, instead of initiating the sequence with a carefully staged shot, Flaherty strings together images of Nanook taken from a variety of angles, providing an excess of visual information that paradoxically withholds any clear message about what is taking place, thereby intensifying the viewer's curiosity. "Flaherty's genius, after all," notes Jean-Luc Godard, "is not so far removed from that of Hitchcock—Nanook hunting his prey is like a killer stalking his victims" (31). The shot of the seal's harpooning breaks the tension, and employs a technique similar to what Sergei Eisenstein describes as "artificially produced images of motion" (52). Nanook, shot from a low angle and deep in concentration, launches his harpoon downward into offscreen space—a motion that immediately cuts to his struggle with the attached line. A third image or meaning—an offscreen seal that Nanook combats—is produced out of our visual assumptions and the dynamic juxtaposition of shots. The viewer hardly registers the fact that when the seal is finally pulled from the ice, after a struggle composed of eleven shots over three minutes, it is very clearly already dead.

Authoritative intertitles are suspended during the seal hunt in order to facilitate the audience's absorption into the spectacle. But in other sequences information is withheld for the sake of encouraging a more active intellectual involvement. During the construction of the igloo, Nanook begins to cut out a clear block of ice from the frozen sea, but titles that fully explain his actions are curiously absent. It is not until the action is complete and the title notes that a piece of snow is used "to reflect the light through the window" that the viewer fully understands the process just witnessed. The shift from ongoing involvement in Nanook's experiences to third-person distance from his actions threatens to throw the viewer out of the structure of identification and engagement carefully constructed to this point. Yet instead of becoming alienated, David MacDougall suggests, "we find ourselves placed within the communal resonance of a small but satisfying achievement as though we were a participant in the event" (230). The next title, "Nyla cleans her brand new ice window," however, might reinforce the problems of imagining a unified or collective audience response to the film. This final, gendered division of labor might inspire something less than "communal resonance" in certain viewers. While the sequence exemplifies the variety of visual and narrative strategies that Flaherty employs within the film's episodic form, it also makes visible an ideology of gender and domestic labor that complements the film's heroic theme.

The film's final scenes return viewers to the sense of mystery evoked in the opening shots, and offer evocative images that resonate with the minimalism of the drawings made on location by Flaherty's Inuit crew. The family's sledge moves across a barren landscape until the human figures disappear, leaving only drifting snow, and the eye follows the family offscreen into a space both unsettling and unknown: danger and perhaps death linger beyond the borders of the visible and invisible. Again, this might indirectly recall Curtis's photographs: a way of life vanishes. In the following sequence, crosscutting juxtaposes shots of the sheltering family under animal skins with dogs silently becoming encrusted in snow, summing up the "melancholy spirit of the North" while recalling the thematic association of Inuit and animal. The closing image of Nanook's sleeping face returns us to the film's opening portrait, but in this case it also might imply an undercurrent of pessimism. *Nanook* is ultimately "a film about hunting and killing, about the desire for death and the desire to defy death" (Rony 115); and it is easy to imagine a death mask in this sleeping portrait of the great hunter. Allakariallak's actual death, from starvation, occurred only two years after the film was released, and was reported around the world.

Conclusion

There is little question that Flaherty falsified many of the events depicted in *Nanook,* and through his framing, editing, and reenactments invented a place and a people suspended in time, isolated from modernity. Yet some of the responsibility might also lie with Western viewers who have, over the years, collaborated with filmmakers in the process of constructing a social framework of belief in the authenticity of documentary. For example, though it is framed and presented as an interior, the igloo sequence was shot with half the roof cut away: a deception, yet also a necessity for fitting bulky equipment inside the structure and attaining adequate lighting for the shoot. Viewers who attend closely enough to these images can mark visible anomalies, such as Nanook's chilled breath, the squinting faces in sunlight, and the shadows cutting across the figures: all clues to the filming conditions. We sometimes allow our eyes to play tricks on us, even when images exceed their narrative frame and actually invite our interrogation. In this case, viewers might be allowing entertainment and the persuasive immediacy of the image to override the very questions that the visible evidence of the film might raise.

Perhaps a kind of contract might be said to exist between producers and consumers of the nonfiction genre, and both sides must maintain this contract for the illusion of authenticity to be maintained. Flaherty never promised absolute authenticity, and early audiences coming to his film were for the most part willing to overlook *Nanook's* partial truths. Meanings produced by cinematic texts are the products of social, and not purely individual, determinants. Still, the uniqueness of Flaherty's technical and narrative achievement cannot be isolated from the film's problematic cultural and racial stereotyping: both influenced the future of documentary and signaled the rise of the expeditionary genre.

Credits

United States, 1922, Revillon Frères

Director, Screenplay, Cinematography, Editing: Robert J. Flaherty
Intertitles: Carl Stearns Clancy and Robert J. Flaherty

CAST:
Nanook	Allakariallak
Nyla	Alice(?) Nuvalinga
Cunayoo	Cunayoo
Allegoo	Phillipoosie

Bibliography

Barsam, Richard Meran. *Non-Fiction Film: A Critical History.* London: Allen and Unwin, 1974.

Calder-Marshall, Arthur. *The Innocent Eye: The Life of Robert J. Flaherty.* London: W. H. Allen, 1963.

Corliss, Richard. "Robert Flaherty: The Man in the Iron Myth." 1973. *Nonfiction Film Theory and Criticism.* Ed. Richard Meran Barsam. New York: Dutton, 1976. 230–38.

Danzker, Jo-Anne Birnie, ed. *Robert Flaherty Photographer/Filmmaker: The Inuit 1910–1922.* Vancouver: Vancouver Art Gallery, 1980.

de Bromhead, Toni. *Looking Two Ways: Documentary Film's Relationship with Reality and Cinema.* Hojbjerg, Den.: Intervention, 1996.

Dixon, Campbell. "Is *Nanook* a Fake?" *Daily Telegraph* [London] 27 July 1947.

Doherty, Thomas. *Pre-Code Hollywood: Sex, Immorality, and Insurrection in American Cinema, 1930–34.* New York: Columbia UP, 1999.

Eisenstein, Sergei. *Film Form: Essays in Film Theory.* Ed. Jay Leyda. London: Dennis Dobson, 1949.

Ellis, Jack C. *The Documentary Idea: A Critical History of English Language Documentary Film and Video.* Englewood Cliffs: Prentice, 1989.

Flaherty, Frances Hubbard. *The Odyssey of a Film-maker.* Urbana, IL: Beta Phi Mu Chapbook 4 (1960). <http://nimbus.ocis.temple.edu/~jruby/wava/Flaherty/>.

Flaherty, Robert. "The Handling of Motion Picture Film under Various Climatic Conditions." *Transactions of the Society of Motion Picture Engineers* 26 (3–6 May 1926): 85–93. <http://nimbus.ocis.temple.edu/~jruby/wava/Flaherty/>.

———. "Robert Flaherty Talking." *The Cinema 1950.* Ed. Roger Manvell. Harmondsworth: Penguin, 1950. 11–29.

Godard, Jean-Luc. *Godard on Godard.* Trans. Tom Milne. New York: Da Capo, 1972.

Grierson, John. "Flaherty's Poetic Moana." *New York Sun* 8 February 1926. Rpt. in *The Documentary Tradition.* Ed. Lewis Jacobs. New York: Norton, 1979. 25–26.

Hardy, Forsyth, ed. *Grierson on Documentary.* London: Faber, 1966.

Langer, Mark. "Flaherty's Hollywood Period: The Crosby Version." *Wide Angle* 20 (1998): 39–57.

MacDougall, David. "The Subjective Voice in Ethnographic Film." *Fields of Vision: Essays in Film Studies, Visual Anthropology, and Photography.* Ed. Leslie Devereaux and Roger Hillman. Berkeley: U of California P, 1995. 217–55.

Murphy, William T. *Robert Flaherty: A Guide to References and Resources.* Boston: G. K. Hall, 1978.

Nichols, Bill. *Representing Reality: Issues and Concepts in Documentary.* Bloomington: Indiana UP, 1991.

"Pictures of 1922." *New York Times* 2 July 1922, sec. 6: 3.

Rony, Fatimah Tobing. *The Third Eye: Race, Cinema, and Ethnographic Spectacle.* Durham: Duke UP, 1996.

Rotha, Paul. *Robert J. Flaherty: A Biography.* Ed. Jay Ruby. Philadelphia: U of Pennsylvania P, 1983.

Rothman, William. *Documentary Film Classics.* Cambridge: Cambridge UP, 1997.

Ruby, Jay. "The Ethics of Image-Making." *New Challenges for Documentary.* Ed. Alan Rosenthal. Berkeley: U of California P, 1988. 308–18.

———. "A Re-examination of the Early Career of Robert J. Flaherty." *Quarterly Review of Film Studies* 5.4 (1980): 432–57.

"The Screen." Rev. of *Nanook of the North,* dir. Robert J. Flaherty. *New York Times* 12 June 1922: 10.

Sherwood, Robert E. *The Best Moving Pictures of 1922–23.* Boston: Small, Maynard, 1923.

Winston, Brian. *Claiming the Real: The Documentary Film Revisited.* London: BFI, 1995.

Sherlock Jr. (1924)

HAL GLADFELDER

The Screen and the Mirror

Context

The fourth of the thirteen feature-length silent comedies in which Buster Keaton starred between 1920 and 1929, *Sherlock Jr.* is a slapstick phantasmagoria of materials borrowed from a half dozen forms of popular entertainment of the period: vaudeville, melodrama, magic shows, detective stories, romance novels, and, of course, silent films themselves. Using the ancient form of the dream vision, Keaton and his collaborators produced a work that plays with—and, by playing, unsettles—the narrative and cinematic conventions that had already, by 1924, become familiar, even humdrum. Viewers today, some eighty years after *Sherlock Jr.*'s release, are likely to be struck by its modernity and the brilliance of its execution, and to note its affinities with the roughly contemporaneous works of surrealist and avant-garde film-makers in Europe; but reviewers at the time were more likely to complain that its jokes were hackneyed—"old hoke," in the words of *Variety* (May 28, 1924, qtd. in Horton 180)—and that the film as a whole lacked both "ingenuity and originality" (*Picture Play*, September 1924, qtd. in Meade 147).

In a way, these original reviewers were right, but they managed to totally miss the point of Keaton's incorporation of shopworn gags and worn-out story lines. If many of the comic routines were silent-film and vaudeville-circuit staples—one of the funniest bits in *Sherlock Jr.* involves a banana peel and a pratfall—Keaton's use of them refreshes them, changes their meaning, by calling attention to just how familiar they are. *Sherlock Jr.*'s protagonist carefully places a banana peel in his rival's path because he has seen that trick work in the movies. But for him, it doesn't work: his rival avoids the banana peel to carry on with his seduction of "the girl in the case," and it is the protagonist himself who, forgetting his own device, goes spectacularly bottoms up. He does what the movies have taught him, again and again, to do, and ends up paying for his credulity. *Sherlock Jr.* is a film about the way we watch films, the satisfactions and risks of spectatorship, the filling-up of our fantasy lives by the "old hoke" of all the movies we have seen. It is also, thanks to Keaton's acrobatic and actorly skills, a work of astonishing inventiveness and physical grace. Yet the complaints of the original reviewer for *Variety* are, again, a useful point of departure. "This Buster Keaton feature length comedy," he writes, "is about as unfunny as a hospital operating room" (qtd. in Horton 180). For anyone who has laughed through the film, this claim seems almost willfully wrongheaded, but the analogy is nevertheless appropriate: *Sherlock Jr.* is a film whose comedy is predicated on the fragility as well as the beauty of the body, and whose stunts underscore, by defying, the body's susceptibility to injury and pain.

Keaton and the Sources of Sherlock Jr.

The body's proneness to injury and Keaton's apparently magical immunity from feeling the consequences of his spectacular falls and collisions were at the heart of his comedy from the beginning of his career and in fact, or at least in his own legend, gave him his name. When Joseph Frank Keaton was six months old, according to his mother Myra's version of the story, he crawled out of his crib on the upper floor of a boardinghouse: "somehow he'd inched out of the room and, bang, down the stairs. Harry Houdini and his wife Bessie, who were in our [traveling vaudeville] company, got to him ahead of us. Harry grabbed him up, and the confounded kid began to laugh! Houdini gasped and said, 'That's some buster your baby took.' Joe [Keaton's father] looked down and said, 'Well, Buster, looks like your Uncle Harry has named you'" (qtd. in Blesh 4).[1] The literal truth of the story is less important than the resonance of its constituent parts: the juxtaposition of bodily calamity and laughter, the baby's fantastic invulnerability, his renaming by the most celebrated magician and escape artist of all time, Houdini, through which the young Keaton seems to acquire magical powers of his own.

---

[1] Marion Meade carefully sorts out the origins of this self-authored legend in *Buster Keaton: Cut to the Chase* (18–19).

According to another childhood legend, the not-yet-three-year-old Buster was sucked from the second-story window of a different boardinghouse by the vacuum at the eye of a cyclone on a July afternoon in Kansas. Before his parents could reach his room, as Rudi Blesh writes, "their son was sailing high over trees and houses, too amazed to be afraid, and then coasting down a slow-relaxing ramp of air to land gently in the very center of an empty street" some four blocks away (9–10). It was that event that led to Buster's joining his parents' stage act as the youngest of the (now) Three Keatons, because his mother refused to leave him alone again when she was performing. Like the story of his naming, this anecdote locates the origins of Keaton's theatrical (and later cinematic) persona in a scene of violence that is also the fulfillment—dreamlike, impossible—of a wish: a fantasy of unbreakability. And in fact one of Keaton's taglines during the years he worked in the family vaudeville act (from 1900 to 1917, from four to twenty-one years old) was "The Little Boy Who Can't Be Damaged" (Meade 33).

The addition of Buster to the Keatons' vaudeville act took them from an endless round of tent-show performances in the rural backwaters of the midwestern United States to top-billed engagements in theaters in New York, Chicago, London, and elsewhere. As with many vaudeville teams, the Keatons' act consisted of a hodgepodge of musical numbers, dance turns, acrobatic routines, comical recitations, blackface and Irish humor, and imitations of well-known entertainers, but the heart of the act was an escalating series of knockabout stunts— chases around the stage, beatings, and spectacular falls—that grew out of Buster's "interruptions" of his father Joe's routine.

The Three Keatons' act was apparently never the same from one performance to the next; improvisation was as integral to their brand of vaudeville as it was to the contemporaneously emerging musical form of jazz. But typically Joe would come to the front of the stage and start a song or recitation, and Buster, dressed and made up as a miniature copy of his father, would wander onstage and start some bit of business—chasing an imaginary fly with a broom, for instance—that would distract and provoke Joe into "disciplining" the boy. He would grab Buster and sweep up the stage with his head or toss him into the orchestra (or even, when Buster was eight years old, into an audience of disruptive Yale undergraduates, breaking one's nose and cracking another's ribs).[2] The act could only work as comic entertainment because of Buster's acrobatic skill, which allowed him to emerge unscathed from whatever dangerous place his father had thrown him, but Robert Knopf, quoting from Myra Keaton's scrapbook, has argued that "the act appears to have resonated with audiences *because* of its suggestion of child abuse. Before tossing Buster across the stage, Joe would tell audiences, 'He's got to learn to mind,' or 'Father hates to be rough,' to which Buster, following each of his falls, replied, 'I'm so sorry I fell down'" (24). As Knopf goes on to note, women in the audience were often horrified by the abusiveness on display, but men tended to laugh their way through the routine. This suggests one further point, which is that, depending on the spectator, the Keatons' act could fulfill two different kinds of wish, satisfy two conflicting desires: one, the fantasy of unbreakability mentioned before, and the other, a fantasy of license to commit violence without consequences or reprisals. Both desires are evident in the later development of film comedy, assuming particularly egregious form in the work of the Three Stooges and in cartoon characters like the Road Runner. Buster Keaton's film work was never crudely violent in this way, but there is, in *Sherlock Jr.* as in his other silent comedies, a certain play with the viewer's propensity to take pleasure in the pain of others—a pleasure made safe by the performer's reassurance that he "really" is immune from harm.

Of course, Buster Keaton had no such immunity: during the filming of *Sherlock Jr.*, he evidently broke his neck performing a stunt involving a railroad water-tank spout when the water pouring from the spout threw him down onto the tracks so that the back of his neck smashed against a rail. In this case the fall and the attendant pain were severe enough that Keaton called off filming for the day, and in fact the accident may have led him to cut short the production earlier than planned, which could explain why the film is notably shorter than any of Keaton's other features (Pearson 141–43, 154). And during his vaudeville years Buster did suffer injuries at his father's hands, such

---

[2]This version of the story appears in Blesh 46–47. Meade reconstructs an earlier and probably more accurate version of the incident (32). On the Three Keatons and Buster's vaudeville experience more generally, see Knopf 19–30; Blesh 3–82; Dardis 1–24; and Jenkins 34–36.

as when Joe kicked Buster in the head so hard he was knocked unconscious for the better part of a day (Meade 33). Joe Keaton was a notoriously abusive alcoholic—many producers and other performers refused to work with him—and as the years wore on he only grew worse, until in early 1917 Buster and Myra broke up the act. But whatever damage working with Joe Keaton must have done him, Buster returned good for bad in later years and hired Joe for small parts in several of his films (including *Our Hospitality* [1923], *Go West* [1925], and *The General* [1927]), featuring him as the girl's father in *Sherlock Jr.*

With the Three Keatons act closed down, Buster went to New York to play a bit part in a Broadway musical revue; he had only been in town a couple of weeks when he ran into a friend who invited him to come have a look around a film studio. Keaton had no interest in films at the time—like many vaudevillians, including his father, Joe, who had turned down an offer from William Randolph Hearst in 1913 to make a series of two-reel (about twenty-minute-long) comedies, Keaton resented the movies for stealing from and cheapening the work of stage performers. The year before, in fact, one of the Keaton routines, a two-man brawl with brooms to the tune of the "Anvil Chorus," had shown up in a short film by the most popular screen comic of the period, Roscoe "Fatty" Arbuckle, and another Keaton routine had been used, oddly, in a Mary Pickford film. (Pickford, "America's Sweetheart," was the most popular of all the silent-movie stars, and a framed portrait of her appears prominently in the opening sequence of *Sherlock Jr.*) But Keaton went to visit the studio all the same. There, it seems by coincidence, the same Roscoe Arbuckle who had stolen his broom routine was filming a two-reel comedy called *The Butcher Boy* (1917). Arbuckle recognized Keaton and asked if he wanted to do a bit in the next scene, and while Keaton declined, he stayed to watch how the film was shot, and as he later recalled, "I was very interested in it—the mechanics of it. I wanted to know how that picture got put together through the cutting room, and the mechanics of the camera, which fascinated me the most" (Bishop 15–16). His fascination with the cinematic apparatus was so intense that, as he said in another interview, "One of the first things I did was tear a motion picture camera to pieces and found out the lenses and the splicing of film and how to get it on the projector" (qtd. in Dardis 38). It was, at least at first, the machinery that drew Keaton to filmmaking. The same afternoon he agreed to do a scene.

Gladfelder

Keaton went on to make fifteen two-reel comedies with Arbuckle, contributing gags and soon stepping into the (uncredited) role of co-director. He moved west with Joe Schenck's Comique Film Corporation (which produced the Arbuckle movies) later in 1917, first working out of Long Beach and later Hollywood; and in 1920, when Arbuckle moved to Paramount Studios, Keaton began making his own films—nineteen two-reelers from 1920 to 1923, followed by the silent features he is still best known for. In his own short films, Keaton built on the improvisatory approach he had mastered as a vaudeville performer, and which Arbuckle had adapted to the medium of silent-film comedy, but he invested that approach with a degree of narrative and visual complexity that are actually difficult to account for, given his working methods. Recalling the period with Arbuckle, Keaton said that "in those two-reelers, they didn't bother to give you any character or name or anything, things just started happening"; and even when he started to make feature-length films, Keaton noted, "We never had a script. We didn't work by one. We just got to talking about a story and laying out all the material that we could think of, and then got it all put together—everybody connected with our company knew what we were going to shoot, anyway, and we didn't have a schedule" (Bishop 16–17). Out of this offhand, conversational brainstorming, Keaton somehow constructed finished films that exhibit an Aristotelian unity of plot and a sophistication in the treatment of cinematic space equal to that of any filmmaker before or since.

Keaton's various accounts of his own working methods, along with the generally unsystematic state of film credits in the 1920s, provide a challenge for conventional notions of cinematic authorship—the by-now standard understanding of the director as *auteur*. Keaton shared director credit on all his short films, and of the ten silent features he made for his own production company, four were credited to Keaton and a codirector, four to Keaton alone, and two to other directors; but Keaton always maintained that he directed all the scenes in which he appeared. In the 1920s, such stars as Mary Pickford, Charles Chaplin, and Douglas Fairbanks exercised almost complete control over every aspect of their films, often doing their own editing, as Keaton said he learned to do from watching Arbuckle (Dardis 105; Bishop 21). Yet if this control suggests that a star like Keaton should be regarded as his films' genuine *auteur*, his own and others' accounts of the making of

Sherlock Jr. make clear that authorship in Keaton's case was multiple, collaborative, and off-the-cuff—indeed, he hired Arbuckle as codirector of *Sherlock Jr.*, though Arbuckle's contribution to the finished film was likely minor (Pearson).

Sherlock Jr. is often, and rightly, described as a self-reflexive work, a film about film—as, in Walter Kerr's phrase, an "invitation to audiences to join him in analyzing the peculiar representation/misrepresentation of life the silent screen had embroiled them in" (227). Yet it started with a disconnected bunch of gags and magic-show illusions Keaton had picked up during his vaudeville years. As he told an interviewer:

> I laid out some of these gags, and showed the technical man how to get the sets built for the things I had to do. When I got that batch of stuff together, [Keaton's lead cinematographer, Elgin Lessley] said, "You can't do it and tell a legitimate story, because there are illusions, and some of them are clown gags, some Houdini, some Ching Ling Foo. It's got to come in a dream. To get what we're after, you've got to be a projectionist in a little local small-town picture theater, and go to sleep, after you've got the picture started. Once you fall asleep, you visualize yourself as one of the important characters in the picture you're showing. You go down out of the projection room, walk up there on the screen and become part of it. Now you tell your whole story." (Qtd. in Knopf 102)

From this account, the core idea of the film, the point that links the experience of viewing films to dreams and the unconscious, and in fact the idea that turns a series of gags into a story, was not Keaton's at all.[3] Or perhaps it would be truer to say that Keaton's practice of film authorship had nothing to do with claiming originality or ownership of ideas. If a way out of a problem or an idea for a story came from his cinematographer or art director or one of his writers—of whom Keaton

---

[3]David Pearson presents an account of the origins of *Sherlock Jr.* as told by Keaton to Kevin Brownlow that is verbally almost identical to this version, except that Elgin Lessley's idea—to make the surreal or gag part of the film a movie projectionist's dream—is attributed to Keaton himself; see Pearson 149–50.

said, "they never wrote anything but gags, vaudeville sketches, and songs. . . . They were not word guys at all" (qtd. in Dardis 102)—that was fine with Keaton. What mattered in the end was the visual realization, and that had everything to do with the actors' performance, and with the manipulation of space within which that performance took place. The idea of having a character enter and so transform the very film he is projecting, after all, is only as "brilliant" as the images by which that idea is made visible on the screen.

One further issue is raised by Keaton's recollection of the origins of *Sherlock Jr.:* the relationship between narrative and gag—that is, between integration, continuity, goal orientation, and containment, on the one hand, and rupture, discontinuity, interruption, and excess, on the other.[4] When he moved from making two-reelers to making feature-length comedies (generally six to eight reels in length, or about sixty to eighty minutes, although *Sherlock Jr.* is only five reels long), Keaton and his collaborators "learned in a hurry that we couldn't make a feature-length picture the way we had done the two-reelers; we couldn't use impossible gags like the kind of things that happen to cartoon characters. We had to eliminate all these things because we had to tell a logical story" (qtd. in Dardis 103). If the features' longer running time made a greater degree of narrative continuity necessary as a device to sustain the spectator's interest, and therefore led Keaton toward a more logical and realistic sort of narrative, *Sherlock Jr.* turns narrative itself into a gag. While, for reasons I hope to make clear later, I do not wholly agree with Robert Knopf's claim that the inner or dream film in *Sherlock Jr.* "has no effect whatsoever on the story" (110), his claim draws attention to the way in which this inner film, which occupies more than half of *Sherlock Jr.*'s running time, breaks open and transforms the story we thought we were following, calling attention to the expectations and desires with which we enter into a pact with narrative. *Sherlock Jr.* fulfills those expectations and desires, but only by making a joke of our attachment to them.

---

[4]On the critical questions posed by this relationship, particularly with regard to the notion of a "classical" Hollywood cinema, see Gunning, "Crazy Machines" and "Response," and Crafton, "Pie and Chase." Robert Knopf analyzes the tension between narrative and gag in four Keaton features; see Knopf 83–111.

Analysis

Sherlock Jr.: *A Close Reading*

The opening shot of *Sherlock Jr.* shows the interior of a movie theater, but the camera has been placed where the screen must be, so that we see the auditorium as if from the perspective of someone on-screen looking back at the audience. The audience, however, is gone, and only one figure sits in the last row, in extreme long shot: Keaton himself, it will turn out, but at this point the face is concealed by an object he is holding up at eye level. The next shot cuts to a close-up of the same figure, and the object is revealed as a paperback book: *How to Be a Detective.* The only things moving in this shot are the reader's eyes as they follow the words; he lowers the book enough to reveal himself to be the expected Buster Keaton, but he sports a fake mustache, and so the spectator's recognition is also an unmasking, the penetration of a disguise.

In the film's first two shots, Keaton has introduced a number of its central motifs, but in a curiously inverted form: in this film about spectatorship, we are shown an almost emptied-out theater whose only inhabitant is *not* looking at the screen. The moving eyes introduce the theme of looking, but in fact the protagonist (he is only described in one of the opening title cards as "a boy"), even though he works as a film projectionist, only once glances at the screen of the theater where he works, until *Sherlock Jr.*'s very last scene. (The protagonist's dream double does look at the screen, and in fact in that act of looking he sets in motion the inner or dream film mentioned earlier.) But these opening shots introduce the theme of film spectatorship in another, self-reflexive way as well. We in the real audience who are watching Buster Keaton's film *Sherlock Jr.* know that Keaton is the film's star, and we know very well what he looks like (and this would have been even more true in 1924), partly because he exhibits certain trademarks: large dark eyes, a solemn cast of face, a porkpie hat. The film's second shot plays on the audience's familiarity with the movie star Buster Keaton's face and gets a laugh, the first in the film, from the character's unsuccessful attempt to disguise the fact that he *is* Buster Keaton. The laugh (a small one) comes out of a confusion of levels that in "classical" film are ordinarily kept distinct, the levels of character and star: here, the trademarks all refer to the star, while on the level of character the protagonist pretends to be unrecognizable.

From here, the story proper begins: the movie theater's manager sees that the boy is reading when he should be sweeping up the trash from the matinee that has apparently let out a few minutes before, tells the boy off (sarcastically calling him "Mr. Detective," according to a title card), and the boy starts his cleanup, which will lead in short order to the first comic routine in the film, involving three walk-on characters who ask the boy if he has found "their" lost dollar in the trash.[5] He has in fact found a single dollar, which he needs to buy a massive three-dollar box of candy on display in the shop window next to the movie theater. (This box of candy, as an earlier cutaway shot of a Mary Pickford look-alike, whom a title card refers to as "the girl in the case," suggests, is desirable to the boy as a love offering.) Nevertheless, he ends the scene a dollar poorer instead of a dollar richer, in effect bamboozled by his own lack of guile.

In this early sequence, the character of the boy might be seen as corresponding to *Sherlock Jr.*'s working title, *The Misfit* (Meade 142): he comes across as an innocent, unwise to the duplicity in the world, and revealing, in his naive fantasy of becoming a detective, a certain alienation from the tedious routines of his everyday life. In another sense, though, the misfit label seems totally wrong, in that the boy's detective fantasy is structurally indistinguishable from the similarly movie-fueled fantasies by which the other central characters in this first part of the film, the other two points of the love triangle, are shown to define their identities. I referred earlier to the girl's resemblance to Mary Pickford, a resemblance underlined by the framed poster of Pickford on the back wall of the theater lobby in which Keaton and his cohorts perform the lost-dollar routine. Similarly, the boy's rival for the girl's affection, a decidedly unalluring seducer, is introduced on a title card as "the local sheik," a term for a ladies' man that gained currency in the early 1920s from the massive popularity of *The Sheik* (1921), starring the definitely alluring Rudolph Valentino. All three characters, in other words, have created identities for themselves in imitation of models provided for them by the motion pictures.

---

[5]Kevin Sweeney offers a detailed analysis of this "Lost Dollar Gag," which he argues is the first in a series of "tripartite disruptive gags" that run through and in some sense structure the narrative (105).

For this reason, the customary division of *Sherlock Jr.* into two parts—an outer or "real life" story and an inner fantastic or dream narrative, in which a boy enters the very film he is projecting—oversimplifies the relationship between reality and fantasy, or life and film, which turn out to be overlapping or mutually penetrable categories. I remarked before that in the opening shots of the film, the character of the boy is introduced in a way that deliberately confuses the distinction between character and star—he is both the famous Buster Keaton and an anonymous small-town nobody pretending not even to be himself—and a similar point might be made for Kathryn McGuire, who plays "the girl in the case." As Daniel Moews has written, "the heroine is already, as an imitative Pickford fan, an embodiment of that confusion" between movies and real life, "a gawky adolescent actuality comically attempting to look like an agreeable screen illusion" (82); but actually the girl is not such an easy satiric target, inasmuch as she is, in fact, starring in a movie. She not only imitates but is herself "an agreeable screen illusion," and as such is also capable of becoming, as she does in the course of *Sherlock Jr.*, the detective who solves the crime of the stolen watch, as well as the heroine of her own romance.

Following the opening sequence, set primarily in the "shallow theatrical space" of the movie-theater lobby (Sweeney 110)—a space reminiscent, as Sweeney notes, of a vaudeville stage, and thus very well suited to the rather stagy and old-fashioned routines performed there (the lost-dollar and the paper-stuck-to-the-broom gags)—the next part of the film begins to open up spatially, as the boy skips along the sidewalk, holding his one-dollar box of candy, to the girl's house. The scene then shifts to another interior space, inside the house. Here, the movements of characters within the shots, as when the girl runs forward through the hallway toward the camera to greet the boy at the door, emphasize the three-dimensionality of film space, as does the design of the shots themselves—as when the camera is placed to show the sitting room (in which the boy shyly courts the girl) in the foreground of the frame and the dining room (in which the sheik tries to seduce her) in the background. This play with the illusionistic depth of the moving image prepares *Sherlock Jr.*'s spectators for the film's most startling, disruptive, and memorable sequence: the dream boy's entries into the film-within-the-film, *Hearts and Pearls*.

Before that can happen, however, and in order to motivate the dream in the first place, the boy has to be accused of a crime (the theft of the girl's father's watch), barred from the house, and frustrated in his attempts to pin the crime on the character he guesses has really perpetrated it: his rival, the sheik. The boy's frustration coincides with a rupture in the narrative, an abrupt closing-down of the plot we have just started to get involved in. This rupture, in turn, occurs at the end of a sequence in which the boy, having consulted *How to Be a Detective* for guidance after he has been expelled from the girl's house ("Shadow your man closely," the book advises), tails the sheik through various city streets and ends up, rather inexplicably, at a train yard. Throughout most of the sequence the boy is only a few inches behind his rival, almost a literal shadow, and he duplicates, on a physically smaller scale (the sheik is big, the boy is little), his rival's every step, stumble, and gesture. Part of the sequence's comic exhilaration arises from the extended tracking shot that keeps up with them as they walk along: for the first time in the film, the camera is moving, and this contributes a new degree of dynamism to the narrative, and with it a sense of anticipation. At the train yard, however, the sheik shuts the boy into a refrigerator car—the sort of container Houdini was often locked into and from which he would magically escape— but the boy just climbs out through a hatch on top of the car. Stuck on top of the now-moving train, the boy has to run faster and faster just to stay where he is in the frame. When he reaches the last car, he grabs the water-tank spout for the stunt I referred to before, the lowering-to-earth and drenching that led to Keaton's broken neck (although broken neck or no broken neck, he finishes the scene, being chased into the distance by two railroad men who have also gotten soaked).

This is the moment of rupture that brings the story we thought we were following to a halt. There is a fade to black, and a title card reads: "As a detective he was all wet, so he went back to see what he could do to his other job." We next see the boy, dejected, enter the projection booth at the movie theater. There is no more of the boy-detective plot, and in fact the boy ceases to have any agency for the remainder of the film: it is the girl, as we see in a cutaway scene at the pawnshop where the sheik had taken the stolen watch, who solves the crime and exonerates the boy. But the film is not yet even half over; so it simply begins again. Or rather, what comes next discloses that *Sherlock Jr.* has all along been about something other than a stolen watch and a small-town romance. Its real story concerns the images that insinuate themselves into the individual (and cultural) unconscious, infecting dreams, redirecting desires, making spectators into specters.

The boy's specter, his dream double, appears as soon as the boy falls asleep at the projector, just after *Hearts and Pearls*—presented by "Veronal Film Co.," Veronal being a sleep-inducing drug of the period—has begun. The boy has fallen asleep facing away from the screen, not watching the film, but the dream boy, who emerges from the boy's sleeping body via Elgin Lessley's technically impeccable double exposure, takes a great interest in what he sees on the screen, especially after the characters on-screen morph into the characters from the film's first part: the girl, the girl's father, the sheik. Outraged by the now-tuxedoed sheik's moves on the now-flapperish girl, the dream boy tries to wake his dreamer but, failing that, marches down to join the audience. Finally, when the sheik has the girl alone in her bedroom, the dream boy scrambles into the screen to break them up; but the movie sheik pitches him out of the screen so that he tumbles onto the pianist playing in the orchestra. Being a dream boy, he is invisible to the audience watching the film (whom we see from behind), and the pianist doesn't notice him falling on top of his piano, either. But to the characters on-screen he is not only visible but bothersomely real.

The visual effect on which the sequence is founded is still impressive eighty years later. As Keaton recounted in an interview, "We built what looked like a motion picture screen and actually built a stage into that frame but lit it in such a way that it looked like a motion picture being projected on a screen. But it was real actors and the lighting effect gave us the illusion, so I could go out of semi-darkness into that well-lit screen right from the front row of the theater right into the picture" (Bishop 17). The essence of the effect is its simplicity: there is no "shimmer," nothing signals the moment of the boy's crossing and recrossing of the divide between the two worlds. In fact, for the dream boy, there seems to be no boundary separating them. Like the "mirror" in the later scene in front of which the famous detective, Sherlock Jr., checks his outfit, only to then walk through it, the film screen is penetrable, immaterial, invisible—paradoxically so, of course, for as the surface on which images are projected the screen is in a sense nothing *but* visibility.

Having been thrown out of the screen once, the dream boy makes a second foray, this time approaching from the side; but as he takes a running jump into the screen the scene changes from the girl's bedroom to the exterior of the mansion in which she lives, with her father just emerging from its front door. The disruption of space through editing is perplexing, and the boy scratches his head (as, for a different reason, he will do in the film's final shot), but after he watches the girl's father go back inside the house, he seems to accept this new scene, and goes to knock at the door. When no one answers, he turns away and starts down the stairs, but the scene changes again, to a garden at night, while the boy, continuing the movement begun before the edit, now finds himself tumbling off a bench that has taken the place of the stairs he was descending. These cuts—bedroom to exterior of house to garden at night—are the first in a series of scenic transformations in which the dream boy is now caught up for the next two minutes of real time. With each change of scene—garden to city street to cliff edge to clearing with lions to a hole in the desert to a rock amidst waves to a snow bank and back to the garden—the boy is first thrown for a loop as an action started in one space puts him in harm's way in the next, but in a matter of seconds he adapts to whatever new spot he finds himself stuck in, though it is precisely this adaptation that lands him in trouble when the scene changes yet again.

No matter how many times one watches *Sherlock Jr.*, the discrepancy between the continuity of the character's movements and the discontinuity of filmed space astonishes and confounds the eye. The filming of this "graphic-match montage" (Knopf 72) required Keaton and Elgin Lessley to, according to Keaton, "measure the exact distance from the camera to where I was standing" at the end of each shot; then "as we did one shot, we'd throw it in the darkroom and develop it right there and then—and bring it back to [Lessley]. He cut out a few frames and put them in the camera gate. When I come to change scenes, he could put me right square where I was" (qtd. in Brownlow 487). The whole sequence—which ends with a fade to black after the boy, sprawled on the grass next to the garden bench he has tumbled over a second time, looks out toward the audience and scratches his head (the second prefiguration of the film's final shot)—disrupts both the boy's narrative and that of *Hearts and Pearls*, as the scenic transformations, in Garrett Stewart's phrase, "leav[e] behind any conceivable plotline" of that inner film (354). But if the succession of disconnected locales is not part of *Hearts and Pearls,* where does it come from? Does the audience in the movie theater within the film notice this surrealist interruption of the costume melodrama they have been watching? There is no reasonable way of accounting for what *Sherlock Jr.* has now become: the unconscious has taken control.

Even though he has been buffeted around by the disjunctive montage of location shots, the dream boy has survived his cinematic hazing, or rite of initiation, and is now well and truly part of the projected space of the screen, the fade to black of the shot that contains him representing his absorption into that space. As a combined iris-out and fade-in returns us to the girl's bedroom, the camera tracks forward so that we no longer see the auditorium in which *Hearts and Pearls* is being projected, and the frames of the inner and outer films now coincide. For the moment the boy has disappeared, but it turns out that he is undergoing his own transformation, for when he reappears it is in the persona of "the world's greatest detective: SHERLOCK JR.," as we see his white-gloved hand press the mansion's doorbell, the detective having been summoned there to solve the mystery of a stolen string of pearls. From this point we can recognize the inner film as a wish fulfillment, a projection of the boy's desires; the screen is a mirror in which we see ourselves as another, identification with the character on-screen providing the mechanism for an imaginary self-assertion and mastery over all those forces that, in the everyday world, frustrate and confine us.

Or at least this is how it seems at first. Sherlock Jr. is the master detective the boy aspired to become, regarded with awe by guilty and innocent alike, suave, rich, expertly taking the measure of each member of the household with his gaze (he puts his face so close to theirs he is practically sniffing them): he can indeed seem to be viewing things "from an epistemically privileged position" (Sweeney 114). Yet through the whole series of pursuits and escapes that make up the remainder of the dream film, his successes, as Dan Georgakas has observed, "increasingly depend more on luck and magic than on cunning or skill" (136). Or rather, the character's luck depends on the cunning, skill, and magic of others: his sidekick, Gillette, and his creator, Keaton himself. Left to his own devices, Sherlock Jr. seems even less talented a detective than the boy proved in the first part of the film—which is perhaps the dreamer's recompense for his own shortcomings. Tailing the sheik, for example, "the world's greatest detective" blunders into doors and is easily spotted; and he consistently fails to penetrate Gillette's dime-store disguises. He is closer to the inept Inspector Clouseau than the masterful Sherlock Holmes.

But through Gillette's intercession, as Peter Parshall has noted (81–85), the rather passive Sherlock Jr. is enabled to perform a series of more and more amazing feats—the very "illusions . . . some of them are clown gags, some Houdini, some Ching Ling Foo" (Elgin Lessley, qtd. in Knopf 102) around which Keaton built the whole story of *Sherlock Jr.* These feats depend on a somewhat unstable mixture of what Henry Jenkins has usefully defined as tricks *for* the camera, including Keaton's various pratfalls and acrobatic stunts, and tricks *with* the camera, such cinematographic effects as double exposures and the invisible edit that makes it seem as if Sherlock Jr. has literally dived through Gillette's body (46–47). Most often, perhaps, the illusions involve a combination of the two kinds of tricks. In the climactic sequence of Sherlock Jr. racing around town on the handlebars of a motorcycle, blithely unaware that the motorcycle's driver has long since fallen off, Keaton is really on the handlebars, performing his own stunts; but some of the most spectacular effects, such as the moment when the motorcycle appears to cross a gap in a viaduct at the very instant two trucks pass underneath, filling the gap, or the later moment when he passes in front of an oncoming train, were produced, as John Bengston has shown, with the help of such devices as double exposure and filming in reverse (145–46).

Sherlock Jr. does manage to rescue the kidnapped girl, albeit accidentally, when his driverless motorcycle crashes into the criminals' hideout and shoots him like a human cannonball into her abductor's body, but though they escape their pursuers, he saves her only to catch her up in further dangers, and the boy's dream ends as the two of them sink into the deep water in which their getaway car has ended up. Indeed, the dreamer only awakens when his bodily mirroring of Sherlock Jr.'s frantic attempts to swim (pulling the girl with him) to safety causes the boy to fall off the stool on which he has been sleeping. In order to accomplish his aims, then, even the dream detective depends on the acrobatic and illusionistic skills that Buster Keaton had acquired over more than twenty years onstage and in film studios, as well as on the technical experimentation and craft of Keaton's collaborators. But he depends even more on the narrative conventions that require the girl to be saved and the heterosexual couple to be reaffirmed at the conclusion of melodrama and romantic comedy alike.

Those narrative demands are the subject, in fact, of *Sherlock Jr.*'s final sequence, in which the girl, having sorted out the stolen watch business, comes into the projection booth to convey her father's apology to the boy, thus clearing the way for a resumption of their awkward courtship. As she shyly turns away and looks down, the boy, painfully unsure how to act, cannot quite summon the courage to touch her—at which point Keaton cuts to a shot from outside the projection booth, looking back through the projectionist's window. Contained within this new frame, and now seen from the other side, the couple lose some of their three-dimensionality, become more like figures on a screen; and almost as if he senses he is being watched, the boy turns his head to glance out the window (and, of course, at the camera). Something now catches his eye, as the next shot reveals: the movie he is projecting, *Hearts and Pearls*. In it, the hero and heroine (the same as they were before their dream transformations) are also caught at a romantic moment: the hero, more sure of himself than the boy, turns the heroine around by the shoulders to face him, and takes her hands. Adopting what he sees on the screen as his model, the boy turns the girl to face him, and takes her hands. In an alternating series of shots, framed so that the movie-theater screen and the projection-booth window are the same size—almost mirror images—we see first the hero and next the boy kiss the heroine's hands, then place a ring on her finger, then take her head gently in his hands and kiss her. When the girl again looks shyly away, the boy again turns to look out at the screen. There, the hero and heroine embrace, but before the boy can imitate this action, the screen he is watching fades to black and then fades in on a new shot: hero and heroine in a domestic scene, the hero bouncing twin babies on his knee. In *Sherlock Jr.*'s final shot, the boy, seen again through the projection-booth window, pulls back in surprise, and scratches his head.

Conclusion

Buster Keaton himself had two sons by early 1924, and an unhappy marriage. If the boy seems perplexed at the end of *Sherlock Jr.*, it may be because he doesn't quite know how to translate the fictional conventions of romantic love and unending happiness into the world he inhabits, even though he does his best to mirror what he sees when he looks out the projection-booth window. When Buster Keaton, playing the boy, looks out the window, what *he* sees, as I mentioned before, is the camera; what *we* see is Keaton looking at us looking at him. As a representational medium, film imitates or reflects, at least to some degree, the world outside film; as a narrative medium, film tells stories that appear to imitate reality but that perhaps imitate more closely other stories, other already conventional plots. In that sense, what movies, like all stories, reflect is less life than our fantasies about life, our desires for certain kinds of endings. If we in the audience then try to imitate what we see on-screen, as the characters in *Sherlock Jr.* do, it is as if we have ended up in a hall of mirrors. No wonder the boy scratches his head as the film fades to black.

Credits

United States, 1924, Buster Keaton Productions

Director: Buster Keaton (and, according to some sources, Roscoe Arbuckle)
Story: Jean Havez, Joe Mitchell, and Clyde Bruckman
Cinematography: Elgin Lessley and Byron Houck
Art Direction: Fred Gabourie
Electrician: Denver Harmon

CAST:

Boy/Sherlock Jr.	Buster Keaton
Girl	Kathryn McGuire
Local sheik	Ward Crane
Girl's father	Joe Keaton
Hired man/Butler	Erwin Connelly
Theater manager/Gillette	Ford West

Bibliography

Bengtson, John. *Silent Echoes: Discovering Early Hollywood through the Films of Buster Keaton*. Santa Monica: Santa Monica P, 2000.
Bishop, Christopher. "An Interview with Buster Keaton." *Film Quarterly* 12.1 (1958): 15–22.
Blesh, Rudi. *Keaton*. New York: Macmillan, 1966.
Brownlow, Kevin. *The Parade's Gone By*. New York: Knopf, 1968.

Crafton, Donald. "Pie and Chase: Gag, Spectacle and Narrative in Slapstick Comedy." Karnick and Jenkins 106–19.

Dardis, Tom. *Keaton: The Man Who Wouldn't Lie Down.* New York: Limelight, 1988.

Georgakas, Dan. "The Purple Rose of Keaton." Horton 130–39.

Gunning, Tom. "Crazy Machines in the Garden of Forking Paths: Mischief Gags and the Origins of American Film Comedy." Karnick and Jenkins 87–105.

———. "Response to 'Pie and Chase.'" Karnick and Jenkins 120–22.

Horton, Andrew, ed. *Buster Keaton's "Sherlock Jr."* Cambridge: Cambridge UP, 1997.

Jenkins, Henry. "'This Guy Keaton Seems to Be the Whole Show': Buster Keaton, Interrupted Performance, and the Vaudeville Aesthetic." Horton 29–66.

Karnick, Kristine Brunovska, and Henry Jenkins, eds. *Classical Hollywood Comedy.* New York: Routledge, 1995.

Kerr, Walter. *The Silent Clowns.* New York: Knopf, 1975.

Knopf, Robert. *The Theater and Cinema of Buster Keaton.* Princeton: Princeton UP, 1999.

Meade, Marion. *Buster Keaton: Cut to the Chase.* New York: Harper, 1995.

Moews, Daniel. *Keaton: The Silent Features Close Up.* Berkeley: U of California P, 1977.

Parshall, Peter F. "Houdini's Protégé: Buster Keaton in *Sherlock Jr.*" Horton 67–88.

Pearson, David B. "Playing Detective: Possible Solutions to the Production Mysteries of *Sherlock Jr.*" Horton 140–57.

Perez, Gilberto. "The Bewildered Equilibrist: An Essay on Buster Keaton's Comedy." *Hudson Review* 34.3 (1981): 337–66.

Stewart, Garrett. "Keaton Through the Looking-Glass." *Georgia Review* 33.2 (1979): 348–67.

Sweeney, Kevin W. "The Dream of Disruption: Melodrama and Gag Structure in Keaton's *Sherlock Jr.*" *Wide Angle* 13. 1 (1991): 104–20.

Battleship Potemkin (1926)

BILL NICHOLS

Film Form and Revolution

Context

At the beginning of the twentieth century, Russia remained a fundamentally feudal country. Ruled by a succession of autocratic and cruel tsars, democracy, let alone Communism, remained a distant dream for most of the people. Our English word "intelligentsia" is of Russian origin and initially referred to the disaffected sector of educated Russians in the nineteenth century who had few ties with the mass of uneducated peasants and who were of no interest to the government, which ruled through a combination of surveillance and force. This intelligentsia often favored radical measures to bring Russia out of feudalism and into modernity. Democratic socialists, utopian visionaries, and Marxist revolutionaries all built their base among the intelligentsia, as did the extraordinary array of artists who gained prominence in the early part of the twentieth century. Many felt they were but biding their time before the government made its incompetence and cruelty so obvious that the new class of industrial workers would rise up in revolt.

A war with Japan for control of Manchuria and the Korean Peninsula in 1904 was intended to bolster support for Tsar Nicholas II's regime, but it went badly. The Russian navy was destroyed by the untested Japanese fleet in the Battle of Tsushima Strait in 1905, and U.S. president Teddy Roosevelt brokered a treaty that deprived Russia of any spoils (and limited Japanese gains). Protests grew as the war continued; work stoppages occurred across the country; and over two hundred thousand St. Petersburg workers took to the streets to urge the implementation of reforms they naively believed the tsar would surely understand as fair, such as an eight-hour workday and a one ruble (50 cents) per day wage. The tsar had fled the capital, and his officers ordered troops to fire on the workers. Hundreds of workers died on that "Bloody Sunday" in January 1905. Other uprisings occurred: soldiers stationed at Kronstadt and sailors aboard the battleship *Potemkin* in the tsar's Black Sea fleet mutinied, but these revolts were also contained. The tsarist government remained in power until World War I, and another set of hardships and defeats set the stage for the successful Communist revolution of 1917.

Lenin's government inherited a country in serious economic disarray and also had to wage a civil war against internal opponents. In the early years of the Soviet Union, the arts, and film in particular, suffered from shortages of raw materials, studio facilities, and a reliable means of distribution. No shortage of polemical or radical new ideas existed, however. Building on the innovations of prerevolutionary, modernist artists such as Kazimir Malevich, Alexander Rodchenko, and Vladimir Tatlin, a new wave of Constructivist artists moved to center stage. Combining a modernist emphasis on form and a Communist emphasis on mobilizing the masses, Constructivist artists embraced new technologies (steel, concrete, engines, and movement) while rejecting the "bourgeois" celebration of the individual hero. Easel painting, with its portraits and landscapes of the privileged and powerful, and narratives, with their stress on individual heroes and a series of linear actions, were cast aside in favor of found materials, collage assemblies, and abstract painting, on the one hand, and of stories that told of class struggle and provoked audience engagement, on the other.

The famous poet Vladimir Mayakovsky and the artist El Lissitzky both toured Germany in 1922. They brought back radical new ideas about the scathingly satiric photomontage work of John Heartfield and others, in which photographs and slogans were "doctored" by altering the original design and juxtaposing new elements to subvert the originally intended meaning. For example, an image of a Nazi swastika was remade in the form of ax blades dripping blood and given the title "Blood and Iron." Carrying the radical implications of such work forward, Alexander Rodchenko wrote, "Art has no place in modern life. It will continue to exist as long as there is a mania for the romantic and as long as there are people who love beautiful lies and deception" (253). Constructivists often saw themselves less as artists than as engineers, less as part of the former intelligentsia than as comrades with the workers and peasants who were to be the heart and soul of a new society. It was against this background that the work of Sergei Eisenstein emerged.

In 1923, Eisenstein published his first essay, "Montage of Attractions," in which he cited German predecessors such as George Grosz and John Heartfield and the photomontage work of his Constructivist colleague Rodchenko as models for the type of theater and film he wished to create. "Attractions," for Eisenstein, were similar to circus acts, elements of a production that galvanized attention. Their organization into a whole followed from the goal of engaging and moving the audience rather than from the goal of producing a detached representation of a situation or event. As Eisenstein put it:

> The attraction . . . is every aggressive moment . . . that brings to light in the spectator those senses or that psychology that influence his experience—every element that can be verified and mathematically calculated to produce certain emotional shocks in a proper order within the totality—the only means by which it is possible to make the final ideological conclusion perceptible. (230–31)

Eisenstein wrote this essay while he was still working in the theater, after having trained as an engineer before the revolution, but the "montage of attractions" that he described came to greatest fruition in his film work. Montage became a highly elaborated concept for Eisenstein. Montage represents both a theory, in which the juxtaposition of distinct elements generates new meanings absent from the individual components, something like the relationship between letters and the words constructed from them, and a practice, in which filmmaking hinges not on the mimetic or realist representation of reality but on the filmmaker's ability to give to the assembly of fragments and pieces an interpretation that leads the audience to a new level of understanding. Juxtaposing shots in surprising ways allowed the viewer to grasp concepts and ideas that would have escaped attention in a form more fully devoted to realist representation. Eisenstein wrote numerous articles about montage and applied his evolving theories about it to all the films he made. Montage bore resemblance to the artistic principle of collage, and it was an important way of adapting cinematic techniques, especially editing, to serve Constructivist principles that linked a rejection of traditional art practices with an embrace of new media and technologies and dedicated itself to the revolutionary goal of social transformation.

Eisenstein's theory of montage also borrowed from the work of the Formalist literary critics, who maintained that art's impact and importance was essentially a matter of form, not content, and that the purpose of artistic form was to prompt the beholder to see things in a new way. "Formalism" was, in the early 1920s, a positively charged synonym for innovation in the arts that became, by the late 1920s, under the tightening grip of Stalin and the party apparatus, a negatively charged code word for elitism and detachment from the masses. Victor Shklovsky captured the political potency of Formalism in his groundbreaking essay of 1917, "Art as Technique":

> The purpose of art is to impart the sensation of things as they are perceived and not as they are known. The technique of art is to make objects "unfamiliar," to make forms difficult, to increase the difficulty and length of perception because the process of perception is an aesthetic end in itself and must be prolonged. (12)

Written with a typically Formalist preoccupation with form and its effects, Shklovsky's point nonetheless has vivid political implications. Realism, in this scheme, would only reinforce existing habits of perception and confirm the existing order of things. Constructivism and Formalism, however, confront the habitual, render it strange, and open the door to new ways of perceiving and acting. Shklovksy cites as an example a scene in "Kohlstomer," a story by Tolstoy in which a horse is flogged to goad it to perform more work. The story is told from the point of view of the horse. The horse observes what is being done to it with a mixture of bewilderment and insightfulness, which causes the reader to see the violence used to extract additional labor in a new way. The unquestioned cruelty of a customary action stands exposed as a result of a formal shift in point of view.

Eisenstein sought a similar, defamiliarizing effect in film. He chose a "montage of attractions" to prompt the viewer to see the familiar in an altogether unfamiliar way. "Bad editing" served a new goal. It did not expose the incompetence of the director to achieve the smooth continuity favored by popular cinema. Instead, it tested his skill at seeing things in an entirely new way. The theory and practice of montage sought to draw out the political implications from actions and events by using form to galvanize the viewer to a new level of insight.[1]

Analysis

Battleship Potemkin (Bronenosets Potemkin) is a classic story of heightened political consciousness set during the failed revolution of 1905 and organized around the actual mutiny of the crew of this one battleship. In such stories the hero undergoes a set of life experiences that lead him or her to see things anew, specifically, to see how the larger social forces of capitalism and class struggle shape the more particular events that might otherwise be explained as accident, fate, or the product of individual will and determination. A heightened consciousness sees connection instead of disconnection, unity instead of alienation, class solidarity rather than personal pursuits. Individual experience becomes located in relation to the larger social and economic structures that govern social existence. To change the possibilities for social existence means not a Horatio Alger-like tale of individual determination so much as a direct assault on the already established socioeconomic structure. For someone who achieves a heightened political consciousness, this ability to see underlying linkages and structures becomes the guiding principle for his or her actions.

Eisenstein's approach to this type of story, however, differed from the work of his contemporaries, such as Vsevolod Pudovkin, who, in films such as *Mother* (1926), *The End of St. Petersburg* (1927), and *Storm Over Asia* (1928), told tales of how an individual character achieved a heightened political consciousness. Eisenstein deemphasized the individual and stressed the group. One of Eisenstein's great achievements as a filmmaker is that he provided a model for a cinema of groups,

---

[1]Noël Burch writes, regarding Eisenstein's editing technique, "These 'bad' position/direction matches are of course meant to emphasize moments of tension in the narrative flow" (91). "Tension" is too vague a word for Eisenstein's attempt to shift perception from a literal imitation to a metaphoric interpretation of reality, but Burch is certainly correct to stress that Eisenstein's style can only be judged "bad" if it is judged in terms of the conventions he deliberately set out to overturn.

crowds, and masses rather than individuals. In *Battleship Potemkin* he does so by telling the story of three distinct examples of political awakening over the course of five acts. The first example involves the sailors aboard the *Potemkin* awakening to the systematic abuse that their indenture to the tsar entails (Act I, "The Men and the Maggots," and Act II, "Drama on the Quarterdeck," sometimes titled "Drama in the Harbor"). In the second awakening, the citizens of Odessa realize and express their solidarity with the mutinous crew of the *Potemkin* (Act III, "Appeal from the Dead," and Act IV, "The Odessa Steps"). In the final awakening, sailors aboard the rest of the tsar's Baltic fleet realize that they and the *Potemkin*'s crew have the tsar as their common foe (Act V, "Meeting the Squadron").

Each awakening broadens the political scope of the film, from the revolt of one ship's crew through the rising up of one town to the rebellion of the entire fleet. Although the film concludes on a victorious note, with the battleship *Potemkin* being welcomed by the remainder of the fleet, this was clearly a form of poetic license by Eisenstein, who knew full well that the revolution of 1905 failed. The film's "montage of attractions," however, serves to demonstrate how heightened political consciousness can lead to successful revolution. In that sense, *Battleship Potemkin* is a film of retroactive wish fulfillment: it converts a historical defeat into a utopian victory. It does so by modeling, through its montage effects, how a revolutionary political consciousness perceives the world and sets about transforming it.

Battleship Potemkin was Eisenstein's second film. His first, *Strike* (1925), also addresses the events of 1905, but through the story of a strike among factory workers that is broken by the tsar's spies, the company's ruthless owners, and the repressive brutality of the military. It, too, ends on an optimistic, defiant note, as the eyes of a worker spring open in extreme close-up and one word, "Remember," appears on the screen. An awakening to political consciousness remains to be completed outside the domain of film form by the audience. In *Battleship Potemkin*, Eisenstein sets out to provide a more elaborate model, within the confines of the story itself, of what coming to political consciousness might be like. Like a good orator, he does not do so once but, instead, repeats himself, three times, so that the "lesson," as Bertolt Brecht might have called it, is driven home forcefully.

The first awakening introduces us to the central characters of Vakulinchuk and Matyushenko, two sailors who play pivotal roles in Acts I and V, respectively, without becoming so central as to take the role of protagonist or hero. The opening shots are of a turbulent sea beating against the shore. Without geographic specification these shots invite a metaphoric interpretation, especially on reviewing the film. They serve to foreshadow greater turbulence to come and to introduce the sea, a fluid, dynamic medium, as the stage on which many of the events will take place. Vakulinchuk and Matyushenko are engaged in conversation on the battleship, but not about the weather. They already agree they must support the revolution (of 1905) and find a way to act.

This lively discussion yields to shots of the ship's crew asleep. Taking the interpretation of the opening shots as a cue, these images can also be read metaphorically: the scene reveals the crew to be politically asleep, while an activist vanguard debates what to do. These shots of sailors sleeping in hammocks strung at odd angles to one another also reveal Eisenstein's penchant for montage within the frame. Each shot's composition involves angles and juxtapositions that set up contrasts and conflicts, sometimes formal ones of light and dark, sometimes political ones of domination and submission. They also convey a sensuous quality. The repose of the sailors is not simply a matter of a physiological need for sleep. Their bodies and their collective arrangement exude a sensual energy that intensifies the viewer's response to these men. Here is latent energy with the potential to be harnessed to a common purpose.

The opening scenes also introduce another crucial concept of Eisenstein's: typage (*tipazh* in Russian). Individual actors were not chosen for their acting ability (many were, in fact, amateurs, and some were members of the filmmaking team); instead they were chosen for how well they looked the part. Typage produced, for Eisenstein, another form of "attraction." The audience sees a character and immediately recognizes him as a sailor or officer just by his appearance. The character is not recognized by name as an individual person, or as a film "star," but is recognized as a social type, a member of a profession, or an example of a class. Similar to typecasting, but without the attempt to marry actor to part that typecasting usually implies, typage, when joined to montage and the extreme fragmentation of performances, allowed Eisenstein to concentrate exclusively on qualities of physical appearance and movement. Eisenstein's chief assistant, Grigori Alexandrov, for example, played the ship's officer Giliarovsky based on his looks rather than his acting skills or class allegiance.

This approach to acting, which is also one of the qualities that linked Eisenstein to the birth of the documentary film tradition, means that he chose not to depend on trained performers to engage the audience through their acting abilities. That engagement came from montage. The juxtaposition of successive shots represented the conflicts and contradictions that traditional acting would allow to emerge from *within* an individual. Montage achieved an effect that for other directors came from the performance of trained actors portraying characters in a powerful way.

In this sense, Eisenstein's theory of montage represents a break with Aristotelian drama. Instead of achieving catharsis through the story of an individual character's struggles, catharsis occurs through the effect of film form, montage itself. And instead of a tragic drama, centering on the fatal flaw of a single character, Eisenstein presents a social comedy, centering on the unification of people according to class allegiance and a common goal. Eisenstein does not need "well-developed" characters to convey the sense of social integration, which Aristotelian comedy often symbolizes in the form of a marriage (the conventional "boy gets girl" plot), since he can rely on montage to provide a way of visibly and powerfully bringing disparate peoples and distant places together.

After a ship's officer beats one of the sailors, Vakulinchuk exclaims, "Will we be last to rise?" The images clearly peg the larger political meaning of revolt to the men rising from their slumber. Things quickly come to a head when the sailors refuse to eat a stew prepared with rotten meat, something the ship's doctor (also cast on the principle of typage) literally refuses to see. He uses his pince-nez as a magnifying glass, but the maggots teeming over the meat are, for him, mere eggs that a little water will wash away. Again, Eisenstein invites a metaphoric interpretation rather than an emotional identification with individual characters: those with a vested interest in the status quo cannot see the exploitative or oppressive nature of their relation to those in the subordinate classes. Montage allows the viewer to understand how those in the subordinated classes must see things for what they are, rather than for what they can be made to appear to be. A brief close-up shot of the meat, for example, shows conclusively that maggots are present and the doctor wrong.

The exploitative nature of this episode is brought home when Eisenstein provides shots of the men buying supplementary rations from the ship's commissary. What the navy does not provide they must provide for themselves, but as an expense drawn from their own meager wages. One anonymous sailor is not quite so resigned. Staring at the motto engraved on a dinner plate, "Give us this day our daily bread," a motto that would also remind a Soviet audience in 1926 of the function of religion under the tsars as part of the state's political machinery, this sailor has finally had enough. He smashes the plate, a microcosmic "smashing" that will soon expand to the more profound destruction of a totalitarian system.

Eisenstein films this inciting incident with the plate according to his concept of a montage of attractions. He is not interested in a smooth continuity that would capture the event in real time, as if it were simply a real event. It is, for him, a metaphoric event, and it needs to be represented in a way that underscores its metaphoric significance. Hence, the smashing of the plate occurs through a montage of shots that breaks the action down into smaller pieces that less add up to the actual event than reveal its wider importance. The sailor's action of raising his arm with the plate and bringing it down so that the plate shatters on a table is captured in multiple shots that defy any strict sense of linear continuity. The shots stretch the action out in time; they repeat elements of the motion, and they intensify its emotional impact, but in a conceptual sense, detached from any audience identification with the individual sailor himself.

This opening salvo of rebellion propels the film into the second act, "Drama on the Quarterdeck." The ship's officers will not countenance defiance, even if it involves rotten meat. The order is given to identify the men who have refused to eat the meat, i.e., the men who won't swallow the lies and intimidation that has been their lot. Eisenstein uses long shots to provide images of the sailors massing on the quarterdeck and close-ups of Vakulinchuk urging the men to gather together to combine their strength as one defiant opponent. The order is given to cast a tarpaulin over some of the sailors who are slow to join the others, an act that divides the men and poses the issue of class alliance in stark terms: Will the rest of the sailors witness the execution of their fellow crew members, or will they act to defend them?

By this point in the film, it is also clear that Eisenstein has rejected the traditional narrative pattern in which a hero embarks on a quest or responds to a challenge. In classical dramatization, the bulk of the narrative involves the successive stages of the journey or investigation undertaken by the hero, and the story's resolution brings closure to the initial dilemma or challenge. Vakulinchuk and Matyushenko are the only two sailors identified by name, but the quest or challenge is not theirs alone. We do not follow their journey, and we do not observe events through their eyes. These men and, soon, other similar characters enter the story at crucial moments to contribute to the action, but they do not drive the action. Like the others, they respond to the events as they unfold but do so in a way that contributes leadership and demonstrates a heightened form of political consciousness.

The crucial moment arrives: an order to fire on the shrouded sailors brings up the rifles of the ship's militia. An officer commands, "Fire!" Vakulinchuk responds, "Brothers!" The order to punish the rebels is met with the injunction to recognize commonality. Who is the enemy? Which side are you on? These crucial questions hover, suspended during the time it takes the militia to come to a decision. As soon as their rifles falter, however, the sailors burst into action. The cry of "Brothers!" has awakened them to their common cause, and soon it is the officers who are being chased around the deck and hurled into the sea. The ship's priest attempts to rise above the fray, invoking religion as an apolitical vehicle of reconciliation, but the sailors will have none of it. Played in some of the scenes by Eisenstein himself, the priest is cast down a flight of stairs and reduced to an impotent onlooker.

Eisenstein concludes Act II with the death of Vakulinchuk, a victim of the ship's officers before they are finally routed. Vakulinchuk's death takes on metaphoric significance as a symbol of the price that must be paid for freedom. Given that the film was made two years after Lenin's own death, the loss of this brave leader also carries a more particular historical resonance that has faded with the passage of time. Vakulinchuk's sudden death and disappearance from the plot, though, like the death of Marion Crane in *Psycho* (Alfred Hitchcock,

1960), does galvanize further events. These events expand the action outward onto a broadening social plane.

The expansion begins with Vakulinchuk's funeral tent, set up on the waterfront docks of Odessa, the harbor to which the mutinous crew takes the *Potemkin*. As in Dziga Vertov's extraordinary portrait of Moscow, *The Man with a Movie Camera* (1929), the port city awakens and comes to life, but not in order to carry out the routine affairs of everyday life so much as to demonstrate a heightened political consciousness by paying tribute to this fallen hero. Eisenstein begins the process in the dawn, with the funeral tent in the middle of a long shot devoid of people. Slowly, a man approaches out of the background, then two women approach in a sinuous trajectory from the foreground, and then two men from the opposite corner of the background. It is as if the people are beginning to encircle and embrace Vakulinchuk from all sides. Other shots show streams of people filling the passageways and avenues that lead to the funeral site.

This is Eisenstein at his finest. Masses of individuals propel the action forward. Eisenstein does not need to cut to "typical" workers or civil servants to give us points of identification. He fashions the citizens of Odessa into a single character composed of many parts but all streaming toward the same site for the same purpose in shots that are memorable for their formal elegance and political persuasiveness. The city, like the ship's sailors, has awakened, come together, and acted as one in opposition to an oppressive regime.

In this sequence, the last to feature Vakulinchuk, Eisenstein establishes an approach to the relation between the masses and a leader that contrasts significantly with the approach later adopted in the Fascist documentary *Triumph of the Will* (Leni Riefenstahl, 1935) and in the democratic documentary film series *Why We Fight* (Frank Capra, 1942–45). Riefenstahl's film celebrates the dynamic, galvanizing leader above all (Adolf Hitler) and reduces those who cluster around him to an anonymous, mindless mass. Capra's film series celebrates the task given to the ordinary American soldier to combat Fascism in World War II but uses a didactic voice-over commentary to explain the task to citizens and soldiers who are not shown as capable of making decisions on their own. Eisenstein, by contrast, locates power and decision making squarely in the hands of the people. The leader is dead;

he can only provide a symbolic center, not actual leadership. Responsibility passes from the vanguard leader to the massed citizenry. Each film served the needs of a specific government to win the hearts and minds of its subjects, but each did so in a distinct manner.

Eisenstein embodies this transfer of responsibility in the speeches delivered at the funeral site. A large crowd has gathered, and different male and female speakers address the group, declaring, in one case, "We won't forget," a clear response to the injunction to "Remember" that concluded *Strike.* As the speakers exhort the crowd, Eisenstein assembles his montage of attractions, among which are fleeting shots of fists being gradually clenched. Every character we see bobs and sways within the frame. Like the waves that beat on the shore at the film's beginning, the crowd exhibits a force and vitality of its own. And like the smashing of the dinner plate aboard the *Potemkin,* the shots of clenching fists violate a realist representation of time. The process is drawn out and incorporates more than one person's fist. Begun with one speaker, the fist motif reaches its climax with another speaker as the mass of citizens thrust their fists in the air and declare their solidarity with the *Potemkin's* crew.

More speeches occur aboard the battleship as the citizens come out to the ship in their boats to express solidarity and deliver food. This display of generosity, of course, contrasts with the display of callous indifference represented by the attempts of the ship's officers to foist rotten meat on the sailors. But just as the sailors' refusal to stomach such treatment provoked the wrath of the officers, so this refusal to treat the sailors as traitors provokes the tsar's military to carry out its own brutal retribution.

Act IV contains the most famous episode in *Battleship Potemkin,* and one of the most famous in all of cinema—the military's attack against the town's citizens on the Odessa steps. It is a prime example of how the principle of a montage of attractions can expand certain decisive moments out of all realistic proportion. This entire act adds only slightly to the overall story. But like song-and-dance routines, which do not normally advance the narrative of most musicals significantly, the "Odessa Steps" sequence gives the most vivid and memorable embodiment to Eisenstein's idea of montage as the essence of cinema. Like the sailors trapped under the tarpaulin, the citizens, cornered on the Odessa steps, are an easy target for the murderous Cossacks, but in this case the attempt to call out "Brothers!" is to no avail. A woman on the stairs attempts to appeal to the soldiers' sense of decency and commonality with the people, but she is butchered with a saber blade and her glasses shattered; a mother is shot and her baby plummets down the stairs in its carriage, and another mother carries her dead son upward toward the advancing soldiers, pleading for help to no avail. The ensuing massacre, despite the battleship's own violent response, forces the mutinous sailors to leave port and, eventually, to head for a confrontation with the rest of the Baltic Sea fleet.

The individual shots in this sequence are brief and powerful, like fragments from a nightmare. Eisenstein himself, in his essay "The Structure of the Film," sketches out the principles of contrast and contradiction that organize this montage sequence:

> In this acceleration of *downward* rushing movement there is suddenly upsetting opposite movement—*upward:* the *break-neck* movement of the *mass* downward leaps over into a *slowly* solemn movement upward of the mother's *lone* figure, carrying her dead son. . . .
>
> Stride by stride—a leap from dimension to dimension. A leap from quality to quality. So that in the final accounting, rather than in a separate episode (the baby carriage), *the whole method of exposing* the entire event likewise accomplishes its leap: a *narrative* type of exposition is replaced (in the montage rousing of the stone lion) and transferred to the concentrated structure of *imagery.* Visually rhythmic prose leaps over into visually poetic speech. (170–71; italics in the original)

This passage echoes Eisenstein's earlier remarks, in which the montage of attractions amounts to "every element that can be verified and mathematically calculated to produce certain emotional shocks in a proper order within the totality—the only means by which it is possible to make the final ideological conclusion perceptible" ("Montage" 230–31). The desire to produce a *calculated* effect distances the filmmaker from the intensity of the emotion that is thus produced. Eisenstein approaches the challenge of offering a model of how political consciousness can be heightened from the perspective of the engineer he was trained to become, or from the perspective of a Formalist whose greatest preoccupation is with the formal arrangement of elements that then produce, as an inevitable by-product, the intended emotional effect. Eisenstein's exploration of film form sought a technique adequate to the challenge of representing abstract concepts such as class conflict. He wanted to represent concepts powerfully more than emotions directly. Montage, with the aid of typage to signify groups and classes, was a technique for doing so. Eisenstein's concept of film form sought to raise audience engagement to a higher level, where a metaphoric interpretation becomes as passionately important as realist interpretations had been on an earlier, more rudimentary, bourgeois level.

The final act of *Battleship Potemkin* focuses on the third and broadest political awakening. Following the mutiny of the crew and the outpouring of support from the people, Eisenstein repeats the incident on the quarterdeck with the ship's militia but this time with the entire Baltic Sea fleet representing the preexisting "thesis" of loyalty to the tsar posed against the opposing "antithesis" of insurrection. Will this clash achieve a "synthesis" in revolutionary solidarity? This is the most classically narrative of the five acts in that Eisenstein devotes considerable attention to building suspense. After the sailors confer among themselves and agree that they must confront the rest of the fleet, the act develops as an extended example of editing for suspense. What will happen next? Will the fleet destroy the rebel battleship, can the *Potemkin* surmount enormous odds, and will the defiant sailors live to foment further revolution?

Matyushenko reappears as a galvanizing force, taking the place of Vakulinchuk and the other unidentified speakers who exhorted the crowd in Odessa. He orders the crew to prepare for battle, launching an extended montage that shows the tense, purposeful crew members loading ammunition and swinging the ship's guns into position to fire. Night descends, a time for sleeping and a loss of alertness, reminiscent of the men asleep in their hammocks in Act I. But the spotting of the fleet bearing down on the battleship changes that. Called to action, the men take their battle stations and prepare for the final conflict.

Up until this point in the film, Eisenstein has shown the crew's decision as a collective one, beginning with whether to remain in port or confront the fleet. Everything prepares us for a violent confrontation. Eisenstein succeeds in making visible, in giving tangible form to, the mounting sense of inevitable conflict in which two opposing classes will fight it out until one survives. But Eisenstein is less concerned with providing an accurate historical representation of class conflict, particularly in the case of a failed revolution, than with providing a model for how ostensible conflict between oppressed groups that have been divided from one another by intimidation, bribery, and sheer habit can be overcome so that the tsar and his terrorist tactics can be identified as the true enemy. The remainder of the fleet is no more the enemy than the shipboard militia or the Odessa-based Cossacks were. Can common interests and shared perceptions prevail? Will habitual, ingrained ways of acting be seen in a new, defamiliarizing light, or will they be blindly, unthinkingly continued?

Matyushenko brings these questions to a focus. It is he who is the first to see things in a different light. Rather than issuing the command to fire, as the ship's officers had done, he issues the command "Signal them to join us." Language, in the form of an appeal, breeches the ostensible gap between the sailors already in mutiny and the fleet's sailors still caught up in habitual obedience. The refusal to eat rotten meat, the smashing of the dinner plate, the appeal to the ship's militia, the speeches at the funeral tent of Vakulinchuk, the (fruitless) appeals to the town's Cossacks, and now this appeal to the rest of the fleet's sailors are instances of symbolic actions that attempt to make something happen. These acts are symbolic because they serve to represent a state of mind and a possible course of conduct rather than to achieve results by physical force. Physical actions (shooting, killing, attacking) rely on material force, whereas symbolic actions (speeches, gestures, expressions) rely on emotional and cognitive impact. Both forms of action give rise to consequences, but they do so by very different means. Violence is clearly associated with the tsar and his instruments of repression; language or symbolic action, with the people and the process of revolution.

The final appeal to the rest of the fleet is the single word "Brothers," a clear refrain from the earlier drama on the quarterdeck, where the same word is uttered by Vakulinchuk. Just as the militia's rifles began to waiver earlier, now the fleet's guns lower and turn away. The *Potemkin* steams forward, its sailors greeted enthusiastically by their comrades aboard the other ships, the officers of which are nowhere to be seen. This conclusion might give the impression that the *Potemkin* has catalyzed a mutiny by the entire fleet, which will now sail together as one united force. The film's shots lend themselves to this interpretation, which is quite likely the metaphoric and somewhat wishful conclusion Eisenstein desired. The historical facts are somewhat different. The *Potemkin* did come face-to-face with the Baltic fleet and did receive a peaceful reception. The mutinous ship was allowed to pass on its way to Romania, where most of the crew deserted; the ship was subsequently returned to the tsar (Taylor 54). This limited victory did not lead to a conversion of the entire fleet to the side of the revolution, but in the wake of the Communist revolution of 1917, a little historical revision to make earlier events more vivid harbingers of later ones did not seem altogether unreasonable. Revising the past to account for the present is a practice not reserved for specific moments in time or specific forms of government. As a model of how political consciousness can arise and grow to sweep up the citizenry of a country in revolutionary action, *Battleship Potemkin* remains a work of considerable power.

Conclusion

Battleship Potemkin is not just a classic film of importance to the history of film form. It, along with other films by Eisenstein and his contemporaries, has served as a model for political filmmaking around the world, from Gillo Pontecorvo's story of the Algerian independence movement in *The Battle of Algiers* (1965) to Fernando Solanas and Octavio Getino's account of political struggle in Argentina in *The Hour of the Furnaces* (1968). The theory of montage as a way to generate new insight and to shift the emphasis of a film to a metaphoric level has had a lasting impact, but it has not served to guarantee the promotion of heightened political consciousness among viewers, as advocated by Eisenstein. Quite the contrary. The highly rhetorical, persuasion-oriented strategies of Eisenstein have become extremely familiar from television advertising, where typage comes to represent one group above all, the consumer, and from music videos, where montage generates a succession of "attractions" as little more than spectacle. These applications clearly serve ends diametrically opposed to those championed by Eisenstein and many of his fellow filmmakers. Dissociated from a conceptual plane of metaphoric interpretation and firmly attached to the marketing of commodities, these strategies lose their political radicalism to become tools of the very economic system Eisenstein sought to move beyond.

In the debates of the 1920s in the Soviet Union, Eisenstein and his theories proved highly contentious. Many in the budding film industry saw them as detrimental to the creation of a sound economic base, to the cultivation of a cadre of writers, actors, and directors who could produce films using a model of standardization akin to that employed by the nascent Hollywood studio system. Many in the government saw the work of Sergei Eisenstein, Dziga Vertov, Lev Kuleshov, and the other Formalists as detrimental to the goal of promoting art that would be easily accessible to the uneducated masses. For Stalin, the failure of the film industry to generate as much income as the vodka industry was a serious concern (Youngblood 127). For others, like Eisenstein, such a view failed to understand the importance of creating new forms to convey the transformed social relations of a postrevolutionary society.

Eisenstein and his allies eventually lost the debate. By 1928, artistic experimentation was in decline, and in 1934, Andrei Zhdanov, a member of the Communist Party's Central Committee with responsibility for all the arts, declared that the style of Socialist Realism would be the only acceptable style. Socialist Realism called on artists to "depict reality in its revolutionary development," which meant, in effect, celebrating the triumphs of the party and ignoring its failings through stories that returned to the basic principles of realism (Zhdanov 293). Such an official policy spelled the end of an extraordinary period of artistic experimentation and achievement in the Soviet Union. Many of the great artists of the 1910s and 1920s, such as Kazimir Malevich, Alexander Rodchenko, Lev Kuleshov, Dziga Vertov, and Sergei Eisenstein were shunted aside and their accomplishments derided. Acclaimed elsewhere more than in their native land, until well after the death of Stalin, these artists remain central to our understanding of the history of twentieth-century art and cinema. That they are celebrated as great artists is itself an irony, further pointing to the ways in which the radical intentions of these Soviet filmmakers have been recuperated by the very system of social and economic relations they sought to overturn. *Battleship Potemkin* is one of many possible entry points into a range of similar work from Russia and the Soviet Union. The film is a particularly vivid example of the dramatic expansion of the sense of the possible in film and other visual media through its rigorous application of the theories of typage and montage.

Credits

USSR, 1925/26, Goskino
The first screening took place at the Bolshoi Theater, in Moscow, on December 21, 1925, in a rough-cut form, just in time to contribute to the official celebrations commemorating the twentieth anniversary of the 1905 revolution. The public release of the finished film occurred on January 18, 1926, in Leningrad and at two theaters in Moscow, the façades of which were decorated to look like battleships, while the theater staff was dressed as sailors.

Director: Sergei Eisenstein
Producer: Iakov Bliokh
Screenplay: Sergei Eisenstein, from an idea by Nina Agadzhanova-Shutko
Cinematography: Eduard Tisse
Camera Assistant: Vladmir Popov
Assistants: Grigori Alexandrov (Assistant Director), Alexander Antonov, Mikhail Gomorov, Alexander Levshin, and Maxim Strauch
Editing: Sergei Eisenstein
Art Direction: Vasili Rakhals
Titles: Nikolai Asseev, with Sergei Tretiakov

CAST:

Vakulinchuk	Alexander Antonov
Matyushenko	Alexander Levshin
Captain Golikov	Vladimir Barsky
Chief Officer Giliarovsky	Grigori Alexandrov

Bibliography

Burch, Noël. "Film's Institutional Mode of Representation and the Soviet Response." *October* 11 (1979): 77–96.
Eisenstein, Sergei. "Montage of Attractions: An Essay." 1923. *The Film Sense* in *Film Form* [and] *The Film Sense: Two Complete and Unabridged Works*. Trans. and ed. Jay Leyda. Cleveland: Meridian, 1957. 230–33.
———. "The Structure of the Film." *Film Form* in *Film Form* [and] *The Film Sense: Two Complete and Unabridged Works*. Trans. and ed. Jay Leyda. Cleveland: Meridian, 1957. 150–78.
Leyda, Jay. *Kino: A History of the Russian and Soviet Film*. London: Allen and Unwin, 1973.

Rodchenko, Alexander. "Against the Synthetic Portrait, For the Snapshot." *Russian Art of the Avant-Garde: Theory and Criticism, 1902–1934.* Ed. John Bowlt. New York: Viking, 1976. 250–54.

Shklovsky, Victor. "Art as Technique." 1917. *Russian Formalist Criticism.* Ed. L. Lemon and M. Reis. Lincoln: U of Nebraska P, 1965. 3–24.

Taylor, Richard. *"The Battleship Potemkin."* London: Tauris, 2000.

Youngblood, Denise J. *Soviet Cinema in the Silent Era: 1918–1935.* Austin: U of Texas P, 1991.

Zhdanov, Andrei. Speech at All Union Congress of Soviet Writers. *Russian Art of the Avant-Garde: Theory and Criticism, 1902–1934.* Ed. John Bowlt. New York: Viking, 1976. 292–94.

Metropolis (1927)

R. L. RUTSKY

Between Modernity and Magic

Context

Few films have stirred as much disagreement or debate as Fritz Lang's spectacular science-fiction film *Metropolis* (1927). Often considered the culmination of the artistic tradition of German silent filmmaking in the 1920s, made by one of cinema's greatest *auteurs*, it has also been criticized for its naive solutions to social and technological problems, its stereotypical portrayals of gender, and its at times confusing narrative. Erich Pommer, the head of the German studio UFA (Universum-Film Aktiengesellschaft) at the time, had intended *Metropolis* as a combination of commercial spectacle and artistic vision that could compete on the international market with big-budget Hollywood films, similar to the success he had earlier enjoyed with *The Cabinet of Dr. Caligari* (1920). Yet, *Metropolis* was not the box-office success that Pommer had hoped, and its costs helped to drive the studio into bankruptcy. Reviewers, while impressed by the film's technical and formal achievements, derided its story. Science-fiction writer H. G. Wells called it "the silliest film" he had ever seen (4). In retrospect, even Lang himself criticized the film, saying at one point that he "detested it after it was finished" (qtd. in Bogdanovich 124). But undoubtedly the most damning criticism of *Metropolis* was the argument made by Siegfried Kracauer, in his book *From Caligari to Hitler* (1947), that the film exhibited fascist tendencies. Of course, Kracauer's thesis linking German films to the psychology that made Nazism possible has been hotly debated. In the case of *Metropolis*, however, it gains support from the following, now famous anecdote:

> Lang relates that immediately after Hitler's rise to power [Nazi propaganda minister Joseph] Goebbels sent for him: ". . . he

told me that, many years before, he and the Führer had seen my picture *Metropolis* in a small town, and Hitler had said at that time that he wanted me to make the Nazi pictures." (Kracauer 164).

The question of *Metropolis*'s relation to fascism is, of course, a complex one, to which we will return later in this essay, but it should be noted that Lang himself was hardly sympathetic to National Socialism. His *The Testament of Dr. Mabuse* (1933) was banned by Nazi authorities, and when Goebbels asked him to make films supporting the National Socialist cause, Lang immediately fled Germany, leaving behind his screenwriter wife, Thea von Harbou, who had in fact written *Metropolis,* first as a novel, then as a screenplay. The fact that Harbou joined the Nazi Party while Lang went to Hollywood to direct films has led many critics to attribute the blame for any fascist inclinations in the film to her, while absolving Lang.

Such arguments, however, tend to miss the point, for *Metropolis*—and its social and political leanings—cannot be seen simply as the product of any single author's vision. What is perhaps most remarkable about *Metropolis* is its ability to condense so many of the cultural, political, and artistic currents of its time into a single film. As even Kracauer, in a kind of backhanded compliment to the film, observed, "*Metropolis* was rich in subterranean content that, like contraband, had crossed the borders of consciousness without being questioned" (163). *Metropolis* is, in other words, a film that is jammed almost to the point of incoherence with ideas, references, allusions, and visualizations: from Oedipal triangles to Christian symbols, from futuristic modern architecture to Gothic cathedrals, from mythical figures and biblical quotations to the latest technological marvels. It is precisely the "richness" of this cultural mixture—what Thomas Elsaesser has called "the eclectic-encyclopaedic scope of the film" (68)—that explains why viewers and critics have had such varied, even contradictory, responses to *Metropolis*. The film's eclectic mixture of cultural elements also helps to explain why *Metropolis*—despite the fact that it was made in a time and in social circumstances that might seem far removed from the high-tech world of the twenty-first century—has remained remarkably popular and relevant.

In part, the film's continued popularity owes something to music producer Giorgio Moroder's 1984 rerelease of a tinted, partially reconstructed version of the film with rock songs and a techno-pop sound track, which has enjoyed considerable success as a cult favorite. Yet, Moroder's "music video" version of *Metropolis* was part of a larger rediscovery of the film in the 1980s, when a number of science-fiction films such as Ridley Scott's *Blade Runner* (1982) and Terry Gilliam's *Brazil* (1985) drew heavily on *Metropolis*'s plot, as well as its dystopian vision of a technologized city. In the 1990s, this trend continued in films such as *Terminator 2* (1991), *Batman Returns* (1992), *The Fifth Element* (1997), *Dark City* (1998), and *The Matrix* (1999), whose depictions of a technological world remain deeply indebted to *Metropolis*. The influence of *Metropolis* has, however, extended well beyond sciencefiction films; it can also be seen in, for example, Madonna's "Express Yourself" music video (directed by David Fincher, 1989), the mechanical hand of Dr. Strangelove in Stanley Kubrick's *Dr. Strangelove or: How I Learned to Stop Worrying and Love the Bomb* (1964), and the references to Lang's film in Thomas Pynchon's novel *Gravity's Rainbow* (1973). Indeed, *Metropolis* has been so widely imitated and cited that even those seeing the film for the first time often find it strangely familiar. Thus, as Tom Gunning has argued, "The enigma to be explained is not the controversy the film inspires, but its continued popularity" (53). What accounts for the continuing appeal of a silent film that was not particularly successful in its own time? What is it about *Metropolis* that has allowed it to gain such a familiar, iconic status in our contemporary cultural consciousness?

Answering these questions is further complicated by the fact that no definitive version of *Metropolis* exists. More than one-quarter of the film was cut for its U.S. release, and many of its intertitles were rewritten in an effort to make sense of the re-edited film. The resulting version left unsettling gaps in the film's narrative and provided little motivation for some of the characters' actions. Subsequent releases of *Metropolis* followed the cuts in the U.S. version fairly closely, with the result that Lang's original version was, as Enno Patalas has noted, "thoroughly and irreparably destroyed, as few other films have been" (162). Efforts to reconstruct the missing footage and intertitles in *Metropolis* have helped to restore sense to some of the film's scenes, particularly by providing the backstory that, in the original version of the film, explained Fredersen's and Rotwang's relationship. Rotwang had loved Hel, who left him for Fredersen and subsequently died giving birth to Freder. Rotwang's obsessive love of the dead Hel gives the motivation for many of his seemingly pointless actions in the film, from his building of the robot (as a means to bring Hel back to life) to his actions at the end of the film, when, thinking he has died, he goes in search of Hel and, mistaking Maria for her, attempts to carry Maria off. These attempts at restoration have also, however, resulted in the distribution of several different versions of the film. Obviously, viewers' experience of *Metropolis* can be dramatically different depending on which version they have seen—particularly when, as in the Moroder version, scenes are accompanied by songs from Queen and Pat Benatar. In its own way, then, this proliferation of different versions of *Metropolis* also contributes to the varying responses that audiences have had to the film. In the analysis of the film that follows, I have therefore drawn from all available sources, including Harbou's novel, in order to provide a comprehensive examination of the film.

Analysis

Technology and Mediation

Modern technology obviously plays a major role in *Metropolis,* but the film's attitudes toward technology are often contradictory. Andreas Huyssen has in fact argued that the film attempts to bring together "two diametrically opposed views of technology": a dystopian view that emphasizes "technology's oppressive and destructive potential" and a more utopian attitude that highlights an "unbridled confidence in technical progress and social engineering" (67). Yet, rather than seeing the two conceptions of technology that Huyssen observes in *Metropolis* as utopian and dystopian, it may be more helpful to distinguish between a notion that sees technology as a matter of rational efficiency and functionality and a view that figures technology as an irrational and chaotic force that is no longer under human control. Contrary to Huyssen's view, however, *both* the rationalist conception of technology (associated with Joh Fredersen and his rationalized city) and the idea of technology as irrational and out of control (represented in the false, or robot, Maria) are presented negatively, as dystopian, in *Metropolis*. *Metropolis* suggests, in fact, that a more utopian society only becomes possible when modern technology is reconnected to—or mediated by—human emotions and spirituality.

Metropolis attempts to accomplish this mediation through the "head, heart, and hands" metaphor that structures the film: "Between the brain that plans and the hands that build there must be a mediator." The "head" is, of course, Fredersen, the "Brain of Metropolis," who is presented as a figure of almost superhuman (or inhuman) rationality and will. The architect of Metropolis, he has constructed his technological "utopian" city according to the standards of functional, modernist design. Yet, it is not simply the architecture of Metropolis that is based on modernist ideas of reducing design to its basic, functional elements. These ideals of rationalization and efficiency are extended to the entire social structure of the city, which functions according to a hierarchical division of labor that clearly borrows from the systems of "scientific management" that had recently been devised by Frederick W. Taylor and put into practice by Henry Ford in his factory assembly lines.[1]

In this hierarchical class system, the workers are forced to adapt themselves to these principles of technological rationality, as indicated by their mechanical movements and geometric formations, which echo the abstract, geometric forms of the city (and anticipate, as Kracauer and others have noted, the similar formations of the masses of Nazi supporters in Leni Riefenstahl's *Triumph of the Will* [1935]). The "hands" of Metropolis therefore become mechanized, replaceable, much like Rotwang's prosthetic hand. In a sense, what is represented here is a dismemberment of the social body; the hands are "cut off" from the utopian plans of the brain. This fragmented social body is presented not only as technological, but as figuratively dead, lacking the spirit and emotions that define human life. The workers appear robotic, zombie-like.

At the other end of the social scale, Fredersen is similarly rigid and mechanical; he shows no emotions, as we see when he coldly fires his secretary, Josaphat. He, too, seems partially dead. If the head and the

---

[1]Taylor's *The Principles of Scientific Management* was published in 1911. Ford's first assembly line started not long after. For an account of the importance of Taylor's and Ford's ideas for cinema, and a host of other interesting ideas, see Wollen.

hands have been "cut off" from one another, reanimating this dismembered social body will require the services of a mediator that will bring these alienated and mechanized "parts" together again, that will restore a sense of life and organic wholeness to this body. In *Metropolis*, of course, this mediator is Freder. He is supposedly the "heart" that enables the division of the head and the hands, his father and the workers, to be overcome, transformed into a whole, living body once again.

Triangles and Trinities

Metropolis, however, supplements this triad of "head, heart, and hands" with a heavy dose of Christian symbology. Freder is explicitly presented as a Christ figure. He descends to the workers' level where, taking the place of an exhausted worker (Georgy/No. 11811), he is "crucified" on the control dial of a machine (identified in Harbou's novel as the *Pater Noster* [Our Father] machine), crying out to his father for relief. Thus, Freder is cast not only as the mediating "heart" in *Metropolis,* but, in Christian terms, as the intercessor between his father and humanity. *Metropolis* suggests, in other words, that Christ, too, was a mediator.

It is important to note, however, that as the son and savior of *Metropolis,* Freder also mediates between his father, Joh (Jehovah) Fredersen, and the virginal mother figure of Maria (Mary). Here, it might be argued, Maria serves to represent the spiritual aspects of the workers/humanity, with the false Maria embodying their demonic side. Yet, unlike the father/son/humanity triad, the symbolic triangle of Jehovah/Christ/Mary introduces an element that does not easily fit into *Metropolis*'s tidy symbolic structure of head, heart, and hands. That element is, of course, Maria herself.

In *Metropolis,* Maria is repeatedly linked to the workers (and to their children). Indeed, she is said to be the daughter of a worker, and she certainly seems to serve as a spokesperson for the workers' cause. Yet, her mannerisms and dress distinguish her from the rest of the workers, as does the fact that she seems to have no family or place of residence in the workers' city. Most important, however, Maria does not herself seem to work, to perform physical labor. Thus, she can only with difficulty be associated with the "hands." In contrast to her highly sexualized robotic counterpart, Maria seems less a physical being than a spiritual one. Continually framed in soft lighting and preaching love, she is portrayed as an ethereal figure, much like the "Eternal-Feminine" ideal that Goethe, the great German poet, associated in his *Faust* with the "Holy Virgin, Mother, Queen." Given this association with love, spirituality, and the Virgin Mary, Maria would seem to be much more a representative of the "heart" than of the "hands." Even more than Freder, she personifies the emotional and spiritual aspects of life that have been excluded from Fredersen's rationalized, functional world. In contrast to the virginal mother figure of Maria, the false Maria is cast as the "whore of Babylon" from the Book of Revelation; wearing a Babylonian-style headdress and gown, she performs a sexual, "decadent" dance in the pleasure palace of Metropolis, during which she appears atop a beast with seven heads. With her sexually charged, demonic spirit, the false, robot Maria serves as the inversion of Maria: a "dark heart," representing the irrational, sexual, and destructive aspects of the emotions, of the soul.

Metropolis's use of the Jehovah/Christ/Mary triad disturbs its premise of the heart mediating between the head and the hands. For although Maria would seem the logical choice to represent the heart in *Metropolis,* it is Freder who is presented as the mediator of the film. Maria's presence, then, brings the film's premise into question, suggesting that *Metropolis* is less interested in bringing together the head and the hands, Fredersen and the workers, than in reconciling the division between Fredersen and Maria, the brain and the heart, rationality and emotion, the scientific-technological and the magical-spiritual. The mediation of these opposing elements is the actual ideological project of *Metropolis,* and it is for this reason that Freder, rather than Maria, must play the role of the mediator.

The workers have almost no role in this mediation. The film presents them as incapable of any action on their own, tools that are just as easily manipulated by the robot Maria as they are by Fredersen. Thus, contrary to its premise, *Metropolis* seems to suggest that the reintegration of the hands into the social body is entirely dependent on the mediation of the brain and the heart. Once this mediation has taken place, the film seems to say, the problems of the workers will be resolved. This perhaps explains why the ending of the film—in which the mediation of the head and the hands by the heart is finally staged—has seemed to many viewers and critics an unconvincing afterthought. It is, in fact, secondary to the actual mediation that *Metropolis* wants to accomplish: the mediation between the brain and the heart.

Oedipal Triangles

Importantly, the mediation of brain and heart also involves a bringing together of masculine and feminine, paternal and maternal elements. Here, we can see that *Metropolis*'s triadic symbolic structure also depends on the Oedipal triangle, which had, at the time the film was made, recently been popularized by Sigmund Freud. Freud, drawing on Sophocles' well-known play *Oedipus Rex,* had coined the term "Oedipus complex" to describe the efforts of a son to come to terms with his affection for his mother and his jealousy of his father's relationship with her. In *Metropolis,* however, the basic Oedipal triangle of father, mother, and son is split into two separate but interconnected triangles: the triad of Fredersen/Maria/Freder and the backstory of the Fredersen/Hel/Rotwang triangle that was excised from the film by its American editors.

In the first of these triangles, the virgin-mother figure of Maria stands in for Freder's actual mother, Hel. This connection is emphasized in Harbou's novel, where Freder longs for his dead mother and Maria is continually described as a virginal mother. In the film as well, the resemblance between Maria and Hel is so close that Rotwang, in his deranged state at the end of the film, believes that Maria is Hel. The Oedipal implications of this triangle are made obvious by Freder's reaction to seeing his father's embrace of the false Maria, whom he believes to be Maria. Stunned, Freder stares into the camera in disbelief, his vision assailed by white circles of light, quickly followed by starry bursts. He seems to lose his balance, while Lang cuts between the bursts of light and brief shots of Maria, Rotwang, and the image of Death, before the room seems to disappear and Freder is shown plunging downward. As a result of this psychological and visual trauma, he falls ill, regressing to an almost infantile state while suffering nightmarish hallucinations. Thus, as a number of commentators on *Metropolis* have noted, Freder's traumatized reaction—emphasized by Lang's editing and special effects—replicates what Freud refers to as "the primal scene": the situation of a young boy witnessing sexual relations between his parents. Yet, Fredersen's embrace of the robot Maria also echoes his "theft" of Freder's mother, Hel, from Rotwang. Here, as Roger Dadoun has suggested, Rotwang is cast as the "rebellious rival son" castrated by the father, as indicated symbolically by his missing hand (146). In the restored versions of the film, it is clear that Rotwang's creation of the female robot (its form is female even before it is given Maria's features) is designed to be a mechanical replacement for Hel (just as his mechanical hand replaces his original one). The film therefore suggests that Rotwang's madness—which leads to the destructive actions of the robot Maria—stems from this loss of Hel to the father figure Fredersen, just as Freder's perception of the loss of Maria to his father provokes his illness and hallucinations. In a sense, Fredersen's "possession" of Hel becomes not only the primal scene of *Metropolis*, but a kind of original sin, upsetting the balance between rationality and spirituality, masculine and feminine, brain and heart. In many ways, the mediation that *Metropolis* strives to achieve is an attempt to restore this balance, allowing the son to overcome the "sins of the father."

Technology and the Will to Mastery

At the root of these "sins" is Fredersen's excessive will to know and control, which we can see in his attempts to spy on the workers and control their actions. In this sense, his willful possession of Hel cannot be separated from his oppression of the workers. Both are in fact portrayed as aspects of his will to mastery; he is, after all, the "Master of Metropolis." In this sense, Fredersen's role as a domineering Oedipal father figure also echoes the figure of Faust, who sells his soul for knowledge and power. Indeed, *Metropolis* borrows heavily from Goethe's version of the Faust legend, where Faust's bargain with the devil not only involves his seduction of the maiden Gretchen, but also his efforts to channel his scientific knowledge and will to mastery into conquering nature, as he attempts to build an ideal city on land reclaimed from the sea. What *Metropolis*'s combination of Faustian and Oedipal motifs makes clear, however, is the extent to which Fredersen's Faustian efforts at control are cast as the imposition of an explicitly masculine or patriarchal will on nature, spirituality, and emotions, all of which are represented in *Metropolis* as feminine.

Of course, as noted at the beginning of this analysis, Fredersen's patriarchal will to knowledge and control is closely linked to modern science and technology. Indeed, the very idea of modernity is in many ways based on the ability of humanity to understand the world rationally and scientifically, rather than relying on magical, mythical, or superstitious conceptions of how the world works. If, in previous times, human beings saw the world as governed by magical or supernatural forces that were beyond their control, the rise of modern, scientific-technological rationality involves what Max Horkheimer and Theodor W. Adorno, following the work of Max Weber, have called a de-mythologizing or "disenchantment" of the world. Through this de-mythologizing process, the world comes to be seen in rational terms: no longer viewed as populated by magical, animistic spirits or gods, it becomes merely a collection of material objects, available for human use. In this shift from a magical to a modern, rational-scientific perspective, technology serves as the tool or instrument that allows humanity to achieve a growing dominance over this objectified world. Indeed, the world comes increasingly to be seen in terms of what is often called an instrumental or technological rationality, which views everything in terms of its potential value to humanity, as a resource that can be quantified, possessed, exploited, and ultimately controlled. Often, this vision of technological progress has been seen as leading toward a utopian society, in which humanity, through scientific reason and technology, would finally gain mastery over nature. Yet, in *Metropolis*, the highly rationalized, technologized society of Fredersen's ultramodern city is portrayed as decidedly dystopian. Thus, *Metropolis* displays a certain anxiety about modernity, about the domination of nature by a modern, scientific-technological rationality. Drawing on traditional representations of science as a masculine "conquest" and control of a feminine nature, it presents this technological rationality, exemplified in the figure of Fredersen, as both patriarchal and tyrannical in its efforts to master and possess nature. In fact, Fredersen's controlling rationality is applied not only to the natural world, but also to the workers, who are treated as objects to be used, controlled, and—as we see in the scenes of the Moloch machine—consumed. In a similar way, Fredersen treats the woman/mother as an object to be possessed, stolen; indeed, it is his dominating will that is said, in Harbou's novel, to have caused Hel to succumb to him.

Technological versus Organic Mise-en-Scène

Metropolis therefore figures this patriarchal technological rationality—and modernity more generally—as involving a *repression* of the "feminine" aspects of nature, and of human nature, in much the same way that modern scientific rationality repressed magical and animistic views of the world. Nature seems to be almost entirely excluded from the space and *mise-en-scène* of the city, appearing only in the artificial space of the "Eternal Gardens" (the space is also, significantly, filled with flirtatious, compliant women). Similarly, human emotions and spirituality seem to be repressed in the city, making their appearance only in those magical/spiritual spaces that seem to have escaped Fredersen's technological surveillance. It is worth noting the extent to which the *mise-en-scène* of these spaces—Maria's cavern church, the cathedral, Rotwang's house (with its pentagrams and magically closing doors)—stands in sharp contrast to the *mise-en-scène* and architecture of Fredersen's modern city, a fact that could hardly have been lost on Lang, who once trained as an architect. On the one hand, the city's architectural style is, like most modernist architecture, based on standardized geometric forms and glass-and-steel construction that mimic the functional design of machines and bridges. The buildings of Metropolis look modern and technological; they are supposed to be, as the modernist architect Le Corbusier once claimed, "machines for living." On the other hand, those spaces that are clearly not the result of Fredersen's architecture display a marked tendency toward organic rather than geometric forms. Highlighting unbalanced compositions, nonparallel lines, and asymmetrical geometries, they suggest an architecture that is neither rational nor technological, but derived from natural or organic processes and materials (wood and stone). This distinction between geometric, technological designs and more organic, "Expressionist" forms was, in fact, central to the artistic and architectural debates of the time, as the art-design team for the film was well aware. Many of the sets, objects, and costumes in the film were, in fact, drawn directly from the contemporary arts of the era. The Expressionist tendency toward organicism is particularly apparent in the concave, irregular set design of Maria's catacomb and Rotwang's house (which are, significantly enough, connected to one another). These spaces give the impression of the interior of a body rather than displaying the clean geometry of Fredersen's man-made, modernist spaces. They are also secretive spaces, hidden from Fredersen's patriarchal view. They seem, in fact, to hide a power that has been repressed in Fredersen's modern, technological city: an ancient power—for these structures are all more ancient than the city that surrounds them—that lies in the connection of these spaces to the spiritual, the religious, and the magical.

189

The film's division between a modernist and an Expressionist style of *mise-en-scène* echoes the split between masculine and feminine, rational and spiritual, brain and heart. It also accords nicely with Lang's claim to have imagined *Metropolis* as a "battle" between modern science and technology and an older tradition of the occult or magical (Bogdanovich 124). The film suggests, in fact, that it is precisely the repression of these magical/spiritual, more natural, feminine elements by Fredersen's patriarchal technological modernity that causes the divisions that haunt not only *Metropolis* but modern society itself. Yet, as Freud argued, that which is repressed always returns in another form. In *Metropolis*, this return of the repressed takes the shape of an irrational and occult female technology: the false Maria.

The Technological Unconscious

The robot Maria serves as the counterpart to Fredersen's repressive modern machines, which seem to drain the spirit, emotions, and life of the workers who service them. Indeed, the film suggests that the life spirit of the workers is transferred to these machines, as demonstrated in Freder's vision of the machine as a devouring Moloch. In this vision—made possible by Eugen Schüfftan's mirror process, which allowed the combination of models with live action—the machine takes on a demonic life of its own, not only controlling but actually consuming the lives of the workers. In the Moloch machine, Fredersen's excessive technological rationality becomes an end in itself, rather than a means to an end. It therefore seems to have its own uncanny life. In this sense, the Moloch machine prefigures the similarly demonic coming-to-life of the false Maria. Yet, while the Moloch machine remains under Fredersen's control, the robot Maria does not. If the Moloch machine is a technology of control, an extension of Fredersen's patriarchal will to mastery, the robot Maria is its inverse: a chaotic female technology that combines all of the elements that have been repressed by Fredersen's modern technological regime.

If Fredersen's masculine technologies seek to control the emotions and energies of the workers, these repressed emotions return in the seething emotional and sexual energy of the robot Maria. In her, the chaste femininity of Maria becomes the sexuality of the machine vamp, combining, as Andreas Huyssen notes, "the destructive potential of technology" with "an active and destructive female sexuality"

(77). Her sexuality incites the passions of the city's inhabitants. Wherever she goes, emotions seem to run wild. She provokes not only fights, but riots and floods, which overwhelm the constraints and boundaries of Fredersen's rationalized, hierarchical society. In her unleashing of the floods that destroy the workers' city, the robot Maria seems almost a force of nature, destructive and uncontrollable. Although Fredersen attempts to use her as a tool, sending her to "sow discord among the workers," the destruction she incites cannot be controlled. Her only motivation seems to be the pure joy of destruction. She even laughs as she is herself being destroyed. Yet, the robot Maria's destructiveness is also linked to a return of the magical and spiritual elements repressed by Fredersen's modern technology. Here, not only is the image of the good Maria superimposed—both literally and figuratively—onto Rotwang's robot, but so is her spirit or soul. In this transfer, however, Maria's spirituality is inverted, as in a photographic negative, becoming sexualized, demonic, destructive. The process by which Rotwang brings this inverted, demonic spirit to life is as much a product of "black magic" as of technology, symbolized by the inverted pentagram—the symbol of the sorceror—that is inscribed on the wall behind his robot. This association with black magic is also acknowledged by the workers, who refer to the false Maria as a witch before burning her at the stake, a traditional punishment for witches. The false Maria, then, represents what might be called the technological unconscious of *Metropolis,* the repressed other half of the rational technological order that Fredersen attempts to impose.

Thus, *Metropolis* presents the split between these two "halves" of technology, each of them equally dystopian, as symptomatic of what it sees as the fundamental problem of modern society: the repression of an "Eternal-Feminine" nature or spirit by a modern, "masculine" technological rationality. The mediation that Freder—and the film itself—strives to achieve is an effort to reintegrate this repressed feminine "heart" and the masculine "brain," to bring spirit and rationality back together again. Since, moreover, the loss of the feminine heart is symbolized in the death of the mother Hel, this reintegration also involves a symbolic reconstitution of the family, rejoining mother and father in the figure of the son. Indeed, Freder can serve as the mediator of *Metropolis* precisely because he combines the qualities of both his mother and his father, as Harbou's novel points out: "Freder is Hel's son. Yes . . . that means he has a soft heart. But he is yours too, Joh. That means he has a skull of steel" (157). Only through the intervention of such a mediator, *Metropolis* suggests, can a divided modernity be restored to wholeness.

Mediation and Nazism

Metropolis's message of mediation, of restoring wholeness to an over-rationalized, overtechnologized modern world by reintegrating spiritual or human aspects into it, may seem attractive to many viewers. It is worth recalling, however, that it was also attractive to the Nazi Party, as demonstrated by Hitler's and Goebbels's admiration for the film. Of course, we cannot hold films, or the authors of films, responsible for the beliefs of everyone who admires them. Yet, it is worth noting that there are a number of striking similarities between the film's views of modernity and those of Nazi ideology. The Nazis, for example, also saw modern society as beset by the alienating, repressive effects of technological rationality. They, too, sought to restore wholeness to this society through a mediation of modern technology and a repressed ancient spirit: in this case, the eternal spirit of Germany. Indeed, National Socialism often cast itself as a respiritualization of a fragmented, chaotic, and degenerate modern world. Significantly, the Nazis frequently figured this respiritualization in terms that recalled the "Eternal-Feminine" qualities of the virgin mother. Hitler, for example, almost always referred to Germany as the "Motherland." On the other hand, perceived enemies of the Nazis were often presented, as Klaus Theweleit has argued, in terms of a frightening, chaotic femininity that threatened to flood the land, dissolving the standards of morality and order (1: 229–99). For the Nazis, of course, the mediator who would banish this destructive and decadent femininity and reinstill the virtues of a feminine spirituality into modern society was Hitler—whose name is itself remarkably similar to the German word for mediator, *Mittler*. Much like Freder, Hitler was seen as embodying both paternal and maternal qualities, a "steel" will and a spiritual love (for Germany, for the German people). This combination of qualities helps to explain the appeal of Hitler's seemingly paradoxical public persona, which ranged from an implacable sternness to the quivering emotionality displayed in many of his speeches. In combining these traits, Hitler, like Freder, took up the role of the son who challenges the patriarchal power of established institutions and returns the eternal spirit of the motherland to its proper place.[2] In much the same way that *Metropolis* portrayed a restitution of societal wholeness through the mediation of the technological and the spiritual, so, too, did Nazism promise a similar mediation and wholeness.

Conclusion

Despite these ideological similarities between the film and Nazism, *Metropolis* cannot be seen simply as a pro-Nazi film. It was, first of all, made well before the Nazi Party came to have any power or influence. More important, however, *Metropolis* is, as I noted at the beginning of this essay, too complex and contradictory to be aligned with a particular political ideology. If the film's message of mediation is arguably similar to Nazi ideology, *Metropolis* also includes elements that cannot easily be reconciled with its explicit message. Freder, for example, is remarkably ineffectual as the film's mediator-savior, unable to stop his father's plans, Rotwang's seizure and transfiguration of Maria, or the false Maria's destruction of the city. In a different way, the film's obvious fascination with the huge machines and skyscrapers of the city undercuts its representation of Fredersen's technologies as repressive and dystopian. In an even more telling case, the film's presentation of the false Maria's performance at Rotwang's reception involves the audience in the same voyeuristic spectacle as the men—including Freder in his hallucinatory state—who ogle her. When Lang cuts from Maria's admirers to a composite shot of multiple staring eyes in close-up, then to a single eye, he suggests that this scene is an allegory for cinematic vision, portraying the film audience's own fascination with the sexuality and destructiveness embodied in the false Maria. In fact, the process of the robot Maria's creation is, as Raymond Bellour has noted, analogous to the cinematic process: both technologies aim to produce a simulacrum, an uncanny but seductive copy of the real (127).

Here, we might take note of how *Metropolis* is very much a film about the cinema or, at least, about vision and representation, looking and being looked at, voyeurism and spectacle. Indeed, almost all the conflicts in the film can also be read in terms of looking, vision, and spectacular

---

[2]Theweleit has argued that Hitler "embodies not paternal power but the common desire of sons" (2: 373).

display, from Fredersen's controlling gaze to the visual seductiveness of the robot Maria, from Rotwang's mechanical transfer of Maria's image to Freder's continual encounter of sights that seem to shock and/or fascinate him. *Metropolis*, then, may be seen as Lang's attempt to mediate between his own directorial attempts to control the cinematic vision (his ruthless perfectionism in making *Metropolis* is well documented) and his fascination with visuality and spectacle. If the pure visuality and spectacle of the film ultimately seem to overwhelm both its ideological premise and its story, this is perhaps the secret of the continuing appeal of *Metropolis*, for it allows the film to escape from the restrictive structure of head, hands, and heart. Thus, as Moroder's pop version of the film makes even more obvious, viewers often enjoy the film less as a serious parable about modern life than as an amusing, often campy pastiche that mixes striking scenes with naive ideas, cinematic virtuosity with comically over-the-top acting. Yet, the paradox of *Metropolis* is that, however we interpret it, it continues to fascinate us, to demonstrate the power that vision, images, and cinema still exert over us.

Credits

Germany, 1926/27 (although the film was passed by the German censorship board in late 1926, it was not publicly shown until January 1927), UFA (Universum-Film Aktiengesellschaft)

Director: Fritz Lang
Producer: Erich Pommer
Screenplay: Thea von Harbou and Fritz Lang
Cinematography: Karl Freund and Günther Rittau
Music: Gottfried Huppertz
Art Direction: Otto Hunte, Erich Kettelhut, and Karl Vollbrecht
Costume Design: Aenne Willkomm
Special Effects: Ernst Kunstmann
Visual Effects: Eugen Schüfftan

CAST:
Joh Fredersen	Alfred Abel
Freder Fredersen	Gustav Fröhlich
Maria/The robot	Brigitte Helm
C. A. Rotwang	Rudolf Klein-Rogge
Slim	Fritz Rasp
Josaphat	Theodor Loos
Grot	Heinrich George

Bibliography

Bellour, Raymond. "Ideal Hadaly." Trans. Stanley E. Gray. Penley, Lyon, Spigel, and Bergstrom 107–30.

Bogdanovich, Peter. *Fritz Lang in America*. London: Studio Vista, 1967.

Dadoun, Roger. "*Metropolis:* Mother—City—'Mittler'—Hitler." Trans. Arthur Goldhammer. Penley, Lyon, Spigel, and Bergstrom 133–59.

Elsaesser, Thomas. "*Metropolis*." London: BFI, 2000.

Goethe, Johann Wolfgang von. *Goethe's "Faust."* Trans. Walter Kaufman. New York: Doubleday, 1961.

Gunning, Tom. "*Metropolis:* The Dance of Death." *The Films of Fritz Lang: Allegories of Vision and Modernity*. London: BFI, 2000. 52–83.

Harbou, Thea von. *Metropolis*. Boston: Gregg, 1975.

Horkheimer, Max, and Theodor W. Adorno. *Dialectic of Enlightenment*. Trans. John Cumming. New York: Continuum, 1989.

Huyssen, Andreas. "The Vamp and the Machine: Fritz Lang's *Metropolis*." *After the Great Divide: Modernism, Mass Culture, Postmodernism*. Bloomington: Indiana UP, 1986. 65–81.

Kracauer, Siegfried. *From Caligari to Hitler: A Psychological History of the German Film*. 1947. Princeton: Princeton UP, 1974.

Patalas, Enno. "*Metropolis*, Scene 103." Trans. Miriam Hansen. Penley, Lyon, Spigel, and Bergstrom 161–68.

Penley, Constance, Elisabeth Lyon, Lynn Spigel, and Janet Bergstrom, eds. *Close Encounters: Film, Feminism, and Science Fiction*. Minneapolis: U of Minnesota P, 1991.

Theweleit, Klaus. *Male Fantasies*. Trans. Stephen Conway, Erica Carter, and Chris Turner. 2 vols. Minneapolis: U of Minnesota P, 1989.

Wells, H. G. "Mr. Wells Reviews a Current Film." *New York Times Magazine* 17 April 1927: 4+.

Wollen, Peter. "Cinema/Americanism/The Robot." *New Formations* 8 (Summer 1989): 7–34.

Un chien andalou (1929)

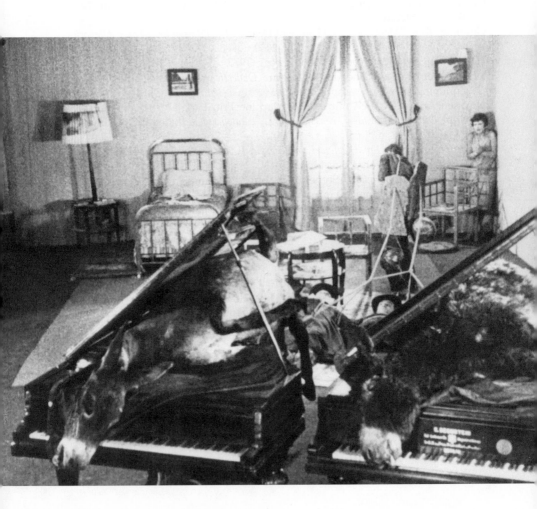

TOM CONLEY

A Rape of the Eye

Few films are so shocking, blinding, or lyrical as *Un chien andalou* (*An Andalusian Dog*, 1929). Considered frame by frame, shot by shot, Luis Buñuel and Salvador Dalí's sixteen-minute film ranks among the most dizzying and riveting films ever made. Viewers are still traumatized by the extreme close-up of a young woman's eye being sliced by a barber's razor drawn across her face by a man's hand. The violence of its beauty owes less to vanguard experimentation that historians associate with the aesthetics of surrealism or masterpieces of independent and experimental cinema than to a classical narrative and cinematic design that lays waste to contemporary bourgeois culture. *Un chien andalou* is a cavalcade of loosely connected shots but also a very tightly woven story about a concomitant rape and seduction of the viewer's vision. Viewers can return to the film not only to experience blinding shock but also to witness a comic, poignant, and compelling story of love.

How the film melds pathos and violence has been the topic of many monographs. *Un chien andalou* is the first film that Buñuel made in a career spanning six decades. His initial experiment with the medium indicates how, like most visionary directors, he was most productive in his earliest cinematic experiments. The film ultimately shows how a piece of juvenilia anticipates and distills the creative labors of a lifetime. Like the other films included in this anthology, *Un chien andalou* seems to belong to a timeless canon of films that have shaped the medium. It is a film that smashes the veneer of politeness and good conduct. It is at once a film that shows how flimsy was the veneer of post–World War I culture, a treatment of the creative possibilities of cinema in the silent era, and an essay about the limits of visibility and visuality.

The context of the birth and making of *Un chien andalou* tells a good deal about its form and the impact it bore on its first viewers. The words that follow will situate the film in Buñuel and Dalí's Paris in the

1920s before engaging a reading of its images in the mode of a *lecture de regard*, that is, a study of what it means to look at the film in accord with the way it continually stares back at us and leaves us—unlike any other film—blinded and seduced by its images.

Context

Buñuel, who is more directly responsible for the creation of the film than Salvador Dalí, was born in Calanda (in the Teruel region of Spain) on February 22, 1900. In his formative years he was trained by Marist priests and excelled in symphonic music before obtaining a degree in humanistic studies in 1917 from the University of Madrid. At that moment, living at its Residencia de Estudiantes, he met Frederico García Lorca and Dalí. He gave himself to reading and writing literature and soon completed a collection of poems under the title *Un perro andaluz* (*An Andalusian Dog*). He became a member of a group of poets that would later call themselves the Generación de 1927. In 1925 he moved to Paris, then the artistic capital of the world, to develop his talents in music, theater, and poetry. There he encountered cinema, especially that of Jean Epstein and Fritz Lang, and soon began writing theory and criticism for a French and Iberian public in *Les cahiers d'art* and in *La gaceta literaria*.[1] At the same time, he was employed by the International Institute of Intellectual Cooperation, an office in the League of Nations, which afforded him an international perspective and led him to work in the direction of cultural anthropology.

He also became involved with the Amsterdam Opera, where a commission allowed him to serve as art director for a performance of a score by Manuel de Falla. Buñuel's scenography was based on a puppet theater that anticipated the use of divided "tracks" of image and sound in film. Singers in the orchestra pit supplied the voices for the marionettes. The gap between mime and voice prepared him for his initial work on cinema under the leadership of Epstein at the Paris Film Academy. Buñuel became Epstein's assistant director (and an extra) for *Mauprat*

---

[1] Agustin Sanchez Vidal's biography *Luis Buñuel: Obra cinemátografica* is a standard point of reference. Buñuel's own memoirs were first published in French as *Mon dernier soupir* (1982), before appearing in Spanish as *Mi último suspiro* (1983) and in English as *My Last Sigh* (1984, 2003).

(1926) and figured in the making of *The Fall of the House of Usher* (1928). Buñuel also collaborated in the production of Mario Nalpas and Henri Étiévant's *Siren of the Tropics* (1927). The feature starred Josephine Baker. The production opened new doors for the director when he met, first, Pierre Batcheff and Simone Mareuil, the actor and actress who would soon be chosen to be the two leads in *Un chien andalou* and, soon afterward, Albert Duverger, the film's future director of photography.

During this time Buñuel formulated a theory of cinema in his writing. In the images of the poems he had written in Madrid, the writing on film in Paris, and the drafts of early projects, there appear flashes of the wit and invention that inspired *Un chien andalou* and informed the politics and aesthetics of his entire career. Two crucial essays on film theory make clear the importance for Buñuel of the framing of cinematic action and of *découpage,* or segmentation, in editing.[2] Work for two films (never made) on Francisco de Goya's series of drawings *Los caprichos* is indicative. He was going to make a first film, in six segments, based on Goya's drawings and another, of a biographical slant, on Goya himself. For political reasons, in early 1929 the funding for *Los caprichos* was diverted for the production of *Un chien andalou:* 1927 had been the quadricentennial of the birth of Luis de Góngora, the Baroque poet from Córdoba whose legacy Spanish writers of the vanguard had chosen to contest by way of celebrating Goya.

Goya had died in 1828, a date that Buñuel, Ramón del Valle-Inclán, and Ramón Gómez de la Serna felt far more inclined to commemorate than the birth of Góngora. For them Goya was a far greater and unremitting artist than the Baroque poet who appealed to the bourgeois establishment. The contorted expression of the latter, they contended, belonged to the horrible status quo that had given rise to the senseless butchery of World War I. To commemorate Góngora meant that Goya's devastating images of the Napoleonic invasions would be conveniently forgotten. Valle-Inclán had wished to make a film about the artist but told Buñuel that he would be the better person to do it. In 1928, Buñuel wrote to his friend Pepín Bello, "We have to fight with all the scorn and anger we possess, against all traditional poetry, from

---

[2]"Del plano fotogenico," *La gaceta literaria* 7 (1927): 1–7, and "'Découpage' o segmentación cinegráfica," *La gaceta literaria* 43 (1928): 1–10, rpt. in Sanchez Vidal 154–57 and 171–74, respectively.

Homer to Goethe, including Góngora—the foulest monster born of a mother—right up to the ruinous debris of today's poetasters. . . . You will understand the difference that separates you, Dalí and me from all our poetic friends. They are antagonistic worlds, the earth's pole and the south of Mars; and they all belong to the crater of vilest putre-faction" (qtd. in Aranda 48 and Talens 86).

Poetry and Theory

It was then that Salvador Dalí, whom Buñuel had earlier befriended in Madrid, arrived in Paris. Dalí felt that the project on Goya was overly sentimental and so urged Buñuel to develop other ideas. They toyed with a project that evolved from *El Marista en la ballesta* (The Marist in the Crossbow) to *Défense de se pencher dehor* (Do Not Lean Out of the Window), a work that soon turned into *Défense de se pencher dedans* (Do Not Lean into the Window). Dalí then suggested that they film a work based on *Un perro andaluz*, Buñuel's recent collection of poems that had been written in Madrid. The idea was timely. The title referred in part to Andalusian artists whom they felt needed to be resurrected for the anti-Góngorian politics of the moment. The work conveyed, too, images that could be reworked and realized in the film. In "No me parce ni bien ni mal" (In My View Neither Good Nor Evil), we read:

> Yo creo que a veces nos contemplan
> Por delante por detrás por los costados unos ojos rencorosos de
>   gallina . . .
> Pegajosos como un coito
> Como la gelatina que tragan los buitres
> Yo creo que he de morir
> Con las manos hundidas en el lodo de los caminos
>
> [I believe that now and again we are contemplated
> From the front from the back from the side by the spiteful eyes of a
>   hen . . .
> Slimy as a screw
> Like the jelly that the vultures carry off
> I believe I will die
> With my hands buried in muddied roads.]

The poem approximates a cinematic point of view that moves all about and around the viewer. The eye of a hen gazes on the speaker. The hen (gallina) resembles the gelatin (gelatina) that will fall from the slashed eye at the beginning of the film. And the figure of the dead speaker, his hands stuck in the mud of a road, anticipates its final shot. The image of the cadaver will be grafted onto a scene inspired by Jean-François Millet's painting *Angélus,* in which two peasants pray in a fallow field at dusk, the very painting with which Dalí would mobilize his concept of paranoid criticism. In "Pagaro de angustia" (Bird of Anguish), a landscape of love resounds with the music accompanying the death of Tristan and Isolde. The visual and musical image becomes the background for an image of love at the zenith of passion:

> *Un pleniosauro dormía entre mis ojos*
> *Mientras la música ardía en una lámpara*
> *Y el paisaje sentía una passion de Tristán e Iseo.*
>
> *Tu cuerpo se ajustaba al mío*
> *Como una mano se ajusta a lo que quiere ocultar. . . .*
>
> *[A plenisaurus was sleeping between my eyes*
> *While the music was burning in a lamp*
> *And the landscape was feeling a passion of Tristan and Isolde.*
>
> *Your body was attached to mine*
> *The way a hand attaches to what it seeks to hide. . . .]*[3]

The poem hints at how Buñuel will score his film when he uses Wagner's music to drive the pathos of love and death. The flat tenor of the verse might be said to contain the rhythm of popular music (perhaps the tango) that the director will set in contrast to the operatic material. The poem opens with a perspective that makes uncanny things large

---

[3]Translations are mine throughout. The poems are reprinted in Sanchez Vidal 135, 142. Talens notes that the two poems betray Buñuel's "virulent use of metaphors, his deliberate refusal to embellish images," and his proclivity for textures that are "rough in their bareness" (88). Talens adds cogently that the subversive quality of Buñuel's poetry and cinema is found in his realism (*su realismo*) rather than his ostensive surrealism (*surealismo*).

and small (a dinosaur between the eyes of the speaker). The play on bodies and hands that grasp and wander over each other's skin resembles what the cinema will explore with its close-up lens. The hand that "attaches to what it seeks to hide" anticipates the sequences in which the leading actor and actress contemplate a black hole, in the middle of the palm of the man's hand, swarming with ants. With these images Buñuel and Dalí went to work on *Un chien andalou*. They completed the film early in the summer of 1929. A private screening at the Studio des Ursulines was made in August before the film was first shown in public at the Studio 28 in the autumn of the same year.

Buñuel had begun to formulate a theory and practice of cinema not long before his collaboration with Dalí. In his seminal " 'Découpage' o segmentación cinegráfica" Buñuel advocates a cinema built from careful selection and forceful editing of carefully framed shots. He offered to his Spanish readers a working definition of *découpage* by noting that the French term, lacking an equivalent in Castilian, designates the "simultaneous separation and ordering of visual fragments." In order to enhance and broaden the Spanish lexicon of cinema, whose paucity he takes to be a symptom of an "intellectual and industrial insolvency," Buñuel introduces his readers to an international vocabulary that may have been lost on an Iberian public. But in a sudden and dramatic leap he turns *découpage* into an idiom of his own creation. Poetry and theory explode in a flash:

> The intuition of the film, the photogenic embryo, forever palpitates in this operation called *découpage*. Segmentation. Creation. Excision of one thing to be converted into another. What was not before now is. [Lo que antes no era ahora es.] Style. The simplest, the most complicated ways of reproducing, of creating. From the amoeba to the symphony. The authentic moment in a film, creation through segmentation. In order to be recreated through cinema this landscape will need to be segmented in 50, 100, and even more pieces. They will all move in succession in a vermicular way, ordering themselves into a colony to compose the whole of the film, a great tapeworm of silence, composed of material segments (*montage*) and of ideal segments (*découpage*). Segmentation of segmentation
>
> Film—mass of shots
> Shot—mass of images.

An isolated image represents very little. A simple monad, not yet organized, in which, at the same time, an evolution takes place and is continuous. A direct transcription of the world: a cinematic larva. The image is an active element, a cell of invisible action, but secure, in view of the shot that is the creative element, the individual likely to specify the colony. . . . The lens—"this eye lacking tradition, morality, prejudice, capable nonetheless of interpreting by itself"—sees the world. The filmmaker, in turn, orders it. Machine and man. The purest expression of our epoch, an art of our own, our authentic art of everyday life. (Qtd. in the original Spanish in Sanchez Vidal 172)

The text itself is a loose montage of intuitive sparks and a volley of surreal images containing elements of the style of *Un chien andalou.*

The ideal film scintillates where its embryonic unit, the shot, is seen as a segmentation of visual and verbal fragments—images—that amass and explode. A succession of shots is successful when it transforms what was *not* into what suddenly becomes or is. Far from a Hegelian dynamic or an Eisensteinian type of montage, Buñuel's *segmentación* embraces forms that swarm, as might a colony of bees or a mass of worms—vermin—and that give rise to a "vermiculated" whole. A film begins by being a landscape or topography, a surface seen and felt as a mosaic of an almost infinite mass of segments. The pieces, which are of different proportion, conjoin in a single shot, which in itself amasses groups of others. Segmentation makes possible creative metamorphoses.

For Buñuel, the shot is a larval mass in perpetual metamorphosis. The colony is a totality that attaches to an object and then disperses and moves elsewhere. Under the lens of a microscope, an eye that sometimes resembles the camera, the amoeba is a palpitating blob of protoplasm, a gelatinous mass dotted with mitochondria and dappled with flecks of protein in its eyelike nucleus. A sudden perception of these masses becomes the commanding *event* of a film. Buñuel conflates succession and simultaneity (evolution and continuity) by having images paradoxically commingle and follow each other in succession. Segmentation becomes both a division into parts and a composite sum of visual units. Both the film and its individual shots are a map and a landscape made of infinitesimal spatial units and lines. When they all succeed one another, they extend in the shape of a tapeworm (which resembles a strip of film), and when they are wrapped over and onto each other, they become "vermicular." The text suddenly makes manifest a poetry of its own, a personal vernacular, that appeals to entomological figures in the description of the sudden and total metamorphoses that take place when images swarm and convert from larval masses to new and unforeseen shapes.

His summary diagram effectively "segments" film and all its components where it relates wholes to parts. It is directly related to a celebrated similitude in the history of geography, in Ptolemy's *Cosmographia* (145 C.E., a manuscript edited and reprinted in many editions in the fifteenth and sixteenth centuries), in which cosmography, the description of the entire world, is related to a portrait of a man's face in profile (the icon for portraiture) just as a city view is to a depiction of an isolated eye or ear. As an entomologist, Buñuel is also a geographer: he locates isolated intensities in close-up and details in relation to greater landscapes that remain forever partial or incomplete.[4] A film is a map of a cohering group or swarm of images, if not also a picture of many agglomerated shots or local views seen in a single take. Thus, if a shot is to be a visual event, Buñuel implies, a vermicular mass of images must fill the frame. The world would be an embryonic organ, an isolated but autonomous eye or ear that moves, sees, and hears under the creative force of the shot that both distinguishes and confuses the individual creature and its colony. Buñuel suggests that no single shot can ever be subordinated to another. If it were it would lead to a predictable continuity in which, as in any keenly organized narrative, the temporal design would occlude the viewer from seeing an infinite sum of its pieces, in other words, the very crux, cause, and raison d'être of the film itself.

Buñuel goes on to note that segmentation is

> a labor that requires no labor other than the pen. The whole film, up to its last details, is to be contained in notebooks; interpretation, angles taken, the length of each segment; here a

---

[4]The opening shots of Buñuel's *Las Hurdes* (*Land without Bread*, 1932) display, first, clouds on which the credits are placed before the film cuts to four lap dissolves of maps that move from a general view of the European continent to the topography of the interior of western Iberia. In *Un chien andalou* the shot is generally seen in relation to a cityscape in which, until the end of the film, a male and a female seem to be held captive. A broad sense of mental and physical geography prevails in the film.

lap dissolve or a superimposition against a medium or American shot, a long or an Italian shot; there, fixed or moving shot, a pan, or a tracking shot. A miraculous fluency in images that spontaneously and uninterruptedly are classified and ordered everywhere in the shots (to Think, to feel with images). (Qtd. in the original Spanish in Sanchez Vidal 173)

In this passage segmentation is tantamount to writing. To film means, in a broad sense, to write with word pictures and, in the course of writing, to order images by way of decisive selection of shots, including angles, duration, depth of field, movement, cutting, and dissolves. The filmmaker perceives and apprehends the world with images that *are not subjugated to the requirements of narrative.* Crucial to the reflection is the fluency of images that move and especially translate the action and effects of writing into cinema.

Emerging from the reflection is a heightened sense of the ocular power of the medium. The eye of the camera is incarnated in the images. Yet the incarnation depends on spontaneous and immediate ruptures that turn disparate images into swarming shapes in perpetual transformation. The latter offers constantly changing perspectives in an original and originary world of time and space so pliable that spectators not only lose their sense of place and proportion but also discover physical geographies bereft of cardinal bearings.[5] *Un chien andalou* embodies a "vermicular" fluency of images that Buñuel's writing conveyed to his Spanish readers of 1927.

Analysis

A Nascent Narrative

The running time of *Un chien andalou* is sixteen minutes and fourteen seconds. Title and credits excluded (seven shots with two dissolves), it counts 290 shots. The average duration of each is slightly less than three and a half seconds. What would seem to be a frenetic rhythm is betrayed by an effect of fluid continuity. Shots tend to give way to one

---

[5]Gilles Deleuze remarks that for Buñuel the "originary world is a beginning of the world, but also an end of the world, and the irresistible slope from the one to the other" (176), a world of incommensurable cruelty, violence, and aura.

another in predictable rhythms. No shot dominates by virtue of either short or long duration with respect to others. A smooth narration leads from a shocking beginning to a conclusion that is both lyrical and morbid. The story itself is the topic of myriad interpretations. The film clearly invites spectators to make the meanings they see in the film a product of their own desire to impose a narrative on the love story that is suggested by its succession of images.

At the same time it bears traces of the classical composition of silent film. Narrative units can be discerned and distinguished by the title, the front credits, and five intertitles. The first intertitle, set between the credits and the first images, tells of what will follow in the style of a fairy tale or a fable (in a script reminiscent of art deco): "Il était une fois . . ." (Once upon a time . . .). The incipit heralds a short sequence (twelve shots, of about forty seconds' duration) in which the man (Buñuel himself) sharpens his razor before slicing the woman's eye. This cuts to a second title (in lowercase Helvetica font), "Huit ans après" (Eight years later). A long sequence ensues (totaling 152 shots lasting slightly over eight and a half minutes) before a third intertitle, in a similar font, reads, "Vers trois heures du matin" (At about three o'clock in the morning). The intertitle interprets and extends a sequence in which the male lead (Pierre Batcheff) hears a sound cue that announces the arrival of a man at the door of the apartment in which he lays bedridden. Thirty-six shots (or almost fifteen seconds) later, a fourth intertitle (of the same font, though slightly larger), states, "Seize ans avant" (Sixteen years before). It is inserted in a sequence in which the young man suddenly faces his double, a man who plays the paternal role of an elder or a teacher distraught by the childishness of a son or a pupil. Twenty-seven shots (a little over a minute) later, the last intertitle—which may not be one—"Au printemps" (In the springtime), has the look of a neon sign by which the famous French department store of that name is known. These words are the beginning of a dissolve into a static image of the man and the woman of the film, buried in sand up to their chests, who mime the pose of the two humble peasants of Millet's *Angélus* before the shot gives way to "Fin" (The End) printed in bold white letters on a black background.

Five temporal signs imply that a story is told in the order of a beginning that is truly a beginning; a middle that begins as a calculated nightmare of visual rape or castration, in which its own nocturnal time gives way to a diurnal dream of love; recession to another dream of sixteen years before; finally, an end in "springtime." The rhetoric of the writing does not really impose an order so much as mesh with the interrupted but generally cohering continuity of the images. The first section of the film depicts a calculated and almost scientific operation in which the man with the razor surgically cuts (in a literal *découpage*) the eye of the young woman who calmly stares at the camera. What "follows" is an encounter of a man and a woman. He rides a bicycle that seems to be guiding itself toward the apartment building, in the empty streets of a sunlit city, where the woman resides. Dressed in lace and frills and wearing a box with a striped cover, he approaches the apartment where the woman is reading a book that is opened to an image of Vermeer's *Lacemaker* (the one painting by Vermeer in the Louvre), in which the young woman of the painting wears the same clothing as the man. The woman in the apartment anticipates something, hurries to a window, and watches the man come to a slow halt and fall off the teetering bicycle. She rushes to help.

Back in the apartment she wishes to make him incarnate by distributing his clothing on a bed. She then sees the same man, who looks calmly at a hole in his right hand, out of which crawl a group of ants. The man and the woman look at the scene in puzzlement before the film dissolves into an armpit, and the armpit into a sea urchin, and the sea urchin into an iris shot, taken in an upward tilt, of an androgyne in a city street. The person touches a severed hand with a stick as a crowd forms a tight circle about the scene. The man and the woman in the apartment behold the event from a window above. Startled and aroused, the man watches the androgyne, who seems lost in the space of the busy street, be struck and felled by a speeding car. The man's blood pumping, he approaches the woman next to him at the window and chases her about the apartment in a pursuit that follows the rhythms of a tango. She wards him off by raising a tennis racquet (a variant of a Latin cross raised to hold a vampire at bay), before he picks up two cords and, like a beast of burden, pulls a set of tablets, two recumbent Marist priests (one played by Dalí), and a piano on which is slung the carcass of a donkey. She exits by a door. He lets go of the cords and jumps to follow her. His hand gets caught in the jamb after she slams the door shut. His hand now crawls with ants. She turns away and sees the man get embodied into the bed where she had placed his girlish effects.

The sequence that begins "At about three o'clock in the morning" moves from amorous chase and its unfinished business to the confrontation of an elder man and a young man. The young man is admonished by his double, who is dressed in a double-breasted suit, and who lashes a piece of rope and tosses pieces of the young man's clothing out of a window. The latter makes penance by facing a wall until— in the same sequence broken by the intertitle "Sixteen years before"—the elder's mood changes from anger to contrition. A shot of a desk strewn with inked papers gives way to that of the youth turning about in anger, each hand suddenly clasping a revolver. He shoots at the older man with a ferocity reminiscent of a gunfighter in a silent Western. The older man (the father who would be the son) falls, and all of a sudden his dying hands slide down the bare back of the same woman from earlier in the film, now in the pose of an odalisque. She disappears. His body lies facedown in the landscape of a park. Seen in two states at once, he returns with a group of men who carry him— that is, his cadaver—away.

A cut to a doorway, possibly of the apartment in the earlier sequence, shows the female entering and casting her eyes on a death's-head moth that is seen in increasing degrees of close-up. She stares at the lover, the same man who pursued her earlier in the film. He suddenly loses his own lips and mouth as she pouts and applies lipstick to her own. He gets bearded with the hair that seems to disappear from her right armpit. She sticks her tongue out at him in defiance, exits, and suddenly beckons a new lover (who is now Buñuel himself) dressed in knickers and sporting a knit sweater, who stands on a beach. She is reminded of the time of day by seeing the watch on his wrist, then they stroll away, her feet ambling delicately over the sticky surface. They then happen on the box (first seen in the second sequence), which now washes ashore and whose ruined contents they examine before walking away. Then, "In the springtime," they are seen immobilized in the sand of what seems to be a diorama inspired by Millet.

The mix of continuity and discontinuity reveals a miniature epic of a sentimental education. The film begins with an utterly shocking violation, indeed an inaugural castration, before it tells of the growth of two characters who are borne into sexuality, the conflicts of gender, and the symbolic order of the world. Advances and regressions mark the voyage, which leads from birth to vision and from bodily sensation, after a final projection of two lives that will be lived "happily ever after," to death and stasis. A love story of the first order, *Un chien andalou* rehearses many of the traumatic scenes that define some of the universal difficulties facing everyone who lives and grows into life. The narrative is especially remarkable insofar as the man who slits the woman's eye is also he who wins and walks away with her in an instant that promises to be both baneful and eternally blissful.

A Film about Visibility

At every juncture the film reflects on vision, eros, and cinema. Both the narrative and the order of the images are built from things signaling stakes of visibility. The first sequence (shots 1–12) begins with a close-up of two hands sharpening a barber's razor by the window of an open door.[6] Both sides of the door are evident because the two eye-like doorknobs protrude outward and inward (shot 1). It appears that a literal *découpage* is being staged. The watch on the man's left wrist suggests that the duration of the shots needs to be accounted for, while the diagonal lines defined by the crossing of the whetstone and the mullion of the window mark an angle, an angularity, hence an angst that comes with the birth of visibility itself. The man who handles the razor is seen on a dark porch, where he almost feverishly puffs on a cigarette. He raises his eyes to the sky (shots 4–9) and perhaps may be looking at the moon, shown in two reverse shots in the segment (shots 8 and 11), or simultaneously contemplating a disruptive association that will come when the film juxtaposes a cloud crossing the moon (anticipating the woman's pupil) to the razor cutting its way across the eye. The hand that holds open the eyelids resembles a giant spider or a five-legged beast (shot 10).[7] The diagonal stripes of the man's necktie correspond to those of the initial *mise-en-scène*. When the woman's eye is cut, the hatched or serial pattern on the back or dull side of the razor moves across the frame as might a strip of celluloid through a projector or camera.

---

[6]References to shots and their numbers is based on the ordering system used by Talens. His *découpage* of 358 photograms (122–66) is a valuable point of reference.
[7]It indeed may be the same hand that the young man contemplates (shot 56) when he sees ants crawling out of its black hole, a black hole that suddenly resembles both a stigma and an iris.

A casual viewer notices immediately and spontaneously that the hatching on the blade (shot 12) has as its counterpart the black and white keys of the piano in the sequence in which the lover pulls the heavy heritage of Western culture behind him (shot 148). As Buñuel had stated in a theoretical vein, "Lo que antes no era ahora est" (What was not before now is): over the keys hangs the head of the dead donkey, its eye socket bleeding and bare, enucleated, such that by suggestion the keyboard becomes an oversized razor that cuts across the now-absent eye that was indeed the one sliced at the beginning. The initial blinding was made possible by the substitution of a donkey's eye for the human eye. And an extreme and spontaneous reversal shifts the perspective *across* the film—in the manner of the slash of an imaginary diagonal—reflecting the same lines that are drawn by the ropes over the Marist priests (shots 145 and 149).

One ocular effect bleeds into another. The wheels in the second sequence (shots 24 and 52) can be likened to two eyes, which by analogy assume the form of the doorknobs (shot 11), or the illuminated pattern of whorls in the wrought-iron balustrade behind which the eye-cutter (or director or editor) looks upward, as if to the moon (shot 6). Every close-up that depicts either or both of the characters' eyes gazing at something or someone (shots 78, 106, 176–77, 183, 217, 255) configures a relation of binocularity, whereas other shots carefully put one eye in shadow, so as to underline a monocular or depthless gaze on the surface of the film (shots 90, 114, 147, 162, 179, 252, 259, 282). The framing allows the film's contents to be seen in two different ways at once. One, in depth and volume, would follow the narrative pattern by treating the characters and their actions with the illusion of spatial depth, while the other would require the eye, like that of a person with one eye, as the woman would be after the conclusion of the first sequence, to see the images as a play of tensions that moves over the entire surface of every shot.

A loose montage constructs an unconscious or oneiric cavalcade of ocular forms. One sequence begins (shot 50) when the male character disinterestedly contemplates the hole in his hand. He and the woman look closely at the "vermicular" action of the swarming ants until a montage of lap dissolves registers the hole in the hand as a dark and ostensibly pubic mass of hair in the cavity of an armpit, at which point the armpit turns into the round, pupil-like shape of the sea urchin (shots 59–60). A dissolve to an iris shot, focalized on the top of a person's head in an extreme tilt, opens its own virtual pupil (shot 62) to catch an image of a hand that hangs in the frame from the upper edge. The hand that is attached to the edge of the frame has been detached from a body, suggesting a connection with the close-ups of the hand seen on the other side of the frame, where the insects are swarming (shots 56 and 58). Two sides of the hand are seen from as many perspectives, one far and the other near.

The sequence in which the androgyne is killed (shots 85–100) underscores a similar ocular effect. The person is surrounded by a crowd that resembles the vascular membrane of a pupil. A binocular, diurnal world—a world in which depth of field and the presence of death are coequal—suddenly erupts in the film when a car, its two headlamps shining, speeds toward the hapless victim. The androgyne's gaze seems unfixed and unaware of the fact that he or she is standing in the middle of traffic on a busy boulevard. Noteworthy, too, is that in the foreplay and mating dance (shots 100–35) erotic figures bear eyelike traits. The woman's gaze prompts his lust. He touches his desired object when his two hands fondle breasts that are clothed and then, suddenly, disrobed (shots 112–13). He looks skyward, blind in orgasm, ecstasy, or death (the script states that blood drips from his lips), as his hands, reminiscent of the pose of the hand that had held open the eyelids of the woman blinded in the first sequence, fondle the breasts that suddenly get reclothed (shots 115–16). A dissolve confuses the bosoms with buttocks as the man puckers his lips (the script describes them being shaped as an anus) to form what might be imagined as a nether or anal eye in the place of the mouth. Further, in the sequence occurring "At about three o'clock in the morning," an unexpected cutaway shot (shot 173) of two arms agitating a cocktail shaker is both a sound cue and a visual reminder of the ocular allusions threaded through the film. The shaker is an "alarm clock" reminding the young man to wake up and live in the world about him, possibly imagined as two hands that extend from as many eye sockets.

A Box of Enigmas

Un chien andalou is rife with enigmas that invite and refuse decipherment. One of these is the box that bears diagonal stripes on its lid. It is first seen on the back of the young man who pedals toward the woman's apartment (shot 21). After he falls off the bike, she unlocks and finds, under a paper wrapper, a necktie with diagonal stripes (slightly wider than those on the box) and a starched collar (shot 43). Are these the effects of the man, who might be an avatar of Vermeer's *Lacemaker*? Are the stripes the connecting thread, the *fil conducteur*, of the cinematic narrative? The answer would seem to be yes until the box is seen again when the androgyne picks it up from the street and coddles it before being struck by the speeding car (shot 92). It then might be asked, since the box is placed adjacent to the corpse (shot 99), if the androgyne is a double of the lover who is now watching the spectacle with fear and lust. Perhaps: yet when the box washes up on shore, prior to the end, and the woman and her lover, who is dressed in a knit sweater with mottled crosshatching resembling the furry pattern on the death's-head moth just seen (shot 257), examine its contents, no revelation ensues. A piece of flotsam, it is adjacent to the rumpled frills and a piece of rope that have also washed up on the rocky shore. The man kicks the box (shot 287), and then the woman picks up the textile and the rope and hands them to her lover, who casts them away (shot 288).

Are the adolescent loves of time past washed up and dismissed? Has the woman found herself and her destiny? Has she broken the ties that had been connected by the piece of rope, an umbilical cord of times past, to an Oedipal scenario in an earlier life? No answer can be confirmed. One visual fact is clear: in each instance, the hands that touch or clasp the box seem to be bodily parts or animated shapes that would, in the elastic perspective of the film, at once be hands, the paws of beasts, or even the legs of crawling insects.

Conclusion

An Uncanny Title

The beginning of *Un chien andalou* is surely its most memorable sequence, but it is not its single or determining element.[8] It is already preempted by a curious play of visual writing, what, in *The Interpretation of*

---

[8]In her *Figures of Desire*, Linda Williams remarks that the editing of the opening sequence contains the "whole" of the film in its constituent parts. A gaze on an object leads to a gaze associated with a narrative event. Shots 1–12 unsettle the logic of narrative by emphasizing how the gaze generates subsequent meaning.

Dreams, Freud had called *Bilderschriften,* or picture-writing. The title bears a strong imagistic quality. Buñuel's *Un perro andaluz* (*The Andalusian Dog*) is the title of a group of poems that informed *Un chien andalou* but were not a single or decisive origin. Canines are never seen in the film unless, by the enigma of analogy, they can be imagined in the encounter of the two human beasts. In the ordering of the shots, the title stands on a black background, in a modern-style script that fills the frame (shot 1), a credit follows, "Mise en scène de Louis Buñuel" (Directed by Louis Buñuel) in a typography in a lower point size (shot 2). The third credit, "d'après un scenario de Salvador Dalí et Louis Buñuel" (based on a script by Salvador Dalí and Louis Buñuel; shot 3), dissolves into the names of the leading actor and actress (shot 5), which in turn dissolves into "Prises de vue: Duverger" (Cinematography: Duverger; shot 7); then the film begins. The cutting shows that *Un chien andalou* and the credit titled *Louis Buñuel* (hence a "French" Buñuel) are autonomous segments that bear a strange relation with what follows. Buñuel is the unnamed personage who inaugurates and who virtually concludes the narrative by directing and performing in it.

The title, however, is never accounted for by the images. The history of the context of the film indicates that it can be read in view of a politics where the cause of things Andalusian would run contrary to established norms. When glossed in French and English *un chien andalou* can refer to a creative state of obscurity, "an obscure object of desire," between nocturnal and diurnal reason. In idiomatic French, dusk is described as an atmosphere "between dog and wolf" (*entre chien et loup*). The international character of cinema and of surreal poetics already dictated that the language of film be fluid and without borders, between conscious thought and unconscious force, or even astraddle one nation and another. Can it be glossed as *un chien et un loup*? A dog *and* a wolf? The two beasts, one domesticated and the other wild, seem dissolved in the title, just as are the names that blend into each other in the sequence of credits. Buñuel and Dalí dissolve into Simone Mareuil and Pierre Batcheff, who then dissolve into Duverger, the director of photography.

The relation between the title and the credits anticipates the rhetoric of segmentation that will make autonomous takes, shots that are pictures unto themselves, often dissolve into each other so frequently that a poem seems to inhere in the alternation of straight cuts with nineteen dissolves. Many of the latter occur in moments of paroxysm and desire (the man fondling the woman, shots 113–20), or the enactment of ocular and erotic association (shots 58–61). The images accrue violence and force through juxtaposition and parataxis, on the one hand, while on the other, they often seep and meld into each other. The soundtrack that Buñuel added in 1960 underlines the effect. The alternations of tango with the musical score of Wagner's "Death of Isolde" sets whirling rhythm next to lyrical orgasm. The same sense of contrast holds for the angles and points of view chosen to produce a narrative seen through and outside of the eyes of the leading characters. The shots are taken from a variety of positions and at ranges that go from extreme close-up to great depth of field. Perspectives change so frequently that the spectator gazes on both a narrative and a cinematic adventure in Nietzschean perspective, what the philosopher called the art of extending and expanding the ways we see the world, ways that run counter to the morality that a bankrupt bourgeoisie was seen advocating at the time of World War I.

Through the enigma of the title, Buñuel and Dalí show what indeed are the virtues and limits of cinema. They do not merely convey in images an ethos and a practice entirely reflective of surrealist writers and poets. It is a cinema that goes to the technical limits of the medium in speculating on the force that images can obtain when they are cut, reassembled, and segmented. Each image owes its violence and beauty to the tension of framing elements and to the shots that are around and about it. Above all, from the very first shot, emphasis is placed on hands that seem to have an ocular tactility. The hands touch objects in the same way that the camera can rape and caress what it films. Buñuel's hands execute a *découpage,* a segmentation that "vermiculates" and goes from "the amoeba to the symphony" in the space of a little over sixteen minutes. The hands are those of a stylist, a master of a *manner* of cinema, a cinema that shows the viewer how a "desperate, passionate call to crime" is invented and constructed.[9] Few films have been handled with such creative dexterity.

---

[9]Thus Buñuel typified the film in the preface to the script he and Dalí published in *La révolution surréaliste* (no. 12) in 1929. The script itself (included in Talens' *découpage*), often at odds with the film, becomes a poem of its own form and a memory aid for the broader lines of the plot and the concatenations of images.

Credits

France, 1929, Studios des Urselines

Director: Luis Buñuel
Screenplay: Luis Buñuel and Salvador Dalí
Cinematography: Albert Duverger
Editing: Luis Buñuel

CAST:

Man	Pierre Batcheff
Woman	Simone Mareuil
Man with razor	Luis Buñuel
Seminarist	Salvador Dalí

Bibliography

Aranda, José Francisco. *Luis Buñuel: A Critical Biography.* Trans. and ed. David Robinson. New York: Da Capo, 1976.

Buñuel, Luis. *Mon dernier soupir.* Paris: Laffont, 1982.

Deleuze, Gilles. *Cinéma 1: L'Image-mouvement.* Paris: Minuit, 1983.

Sanchez Vidal, Agustin. *Louis Buñuel: Obra cinematográfica.* Madrid: Editiones J. C., 1984.

Talens, Jenaro. *The Branded Eye: Buñuel's "Un chien andalou."* Trans. Giulia Colaizzi. Minneapolis: U of Minnesota P, 1993.

Williams, Linda. *Figures of Desire: A Theory and Analysis of Surrealist Film.* Chicago: U of Chicago P, 1981.

It Happened One Night (1934)

RICHARD MALTBY

Comedy and the Restoration of Order

Context

Frank Capra and Columbia

It Happened One Night opened in New York in February 1934 to satisfactory but unremarkable business and moderate reviews. The story,
said *Variety,* was "thin and frequently illogical," but it had "that intangible quality of charm which arises from a smooth blending of the various ingredients." When the movie reached the second-run theaters in
America's smaller towns and suburbs, however, it began to draw an
almost unprecedented attendance. It was often held over for two
weeks or longer and called back for repeat bookings. By the end of the
year, it had become its studio's most successful picture to date and the
fifth-highest-grossing movie of the year, a remarkable achievement
given Columbia's distribution practices and limited access to the
country's most profitable first-run theaters. It had also garnered the
critical acclaim that led to its clean sweep of all four major Academy
Awards in March 1935. Most contemporary reviewers, however, remained puzzled by the movie's success: as William Troy wrote in the
Nation, "the wholly spontaneous response with which the picture was
received could be traced to no novelty or originality in its component
elements" (301).

   It Happened One Night's extraordinary commercial success gave rise
to a number of anecdotes about its influence on the public. Oddly, the
most enduring of these has been the story that the sales of men's un-
dershirts declined drastically after audiences discovered that Clark
Gable did not wear one in the movie's first bedroom scene. This is, of
course, a piece of nonsense invented by a Hollywood publicity agent,
but it has entered the critical folklore of the movies because it tells a
convenient fiction about the relationship between movies and their

audiences, and because it fulfills our cultural expectations that the history of entertainment must itself be entertaining.

In some respects, the two principal claims made for *It Happened One Night*'s significance in film history resemble this story by overemphasizing its originality and influence. The movie is commonly credited with inaugurating a new type of screen comedy, usually identified as "screwball" comedy, and with transforming Frank Capra into "the World's Foremost Director," a star whose "name above the title" of a movie would add to its box-office attraction. As the founding president of the Directors Guild of America, he promoted his "one man, one film" theory of movie production, a position later echoed by *auteur* theory's claim that individual creativity and "the distinguishable personality of the director" was the source of aesthetic value in Hollywood (Sarris, *American Cinema* 31). The success of *Mr. Deeds Goes to Town* (1936), *You Can't Take It with You* (1938), and *Mr. Smith Goes to Washington* (1939) allowed Capra to claim authorial control over the movies he directed and gave rise to the term "Capraesque" as a description of the sentimental expression of traditional American ideals.

In his autobiography, Capra recounts a fantastic story about being visited, after the success of *It Happened One Night*, by a "little man" who admonished him to use his talents for higher purposes (176). His biographer, Joseph McBride, believes that Capra was motivated by feelings of insecurity at his success, but whatever the explanation, after 1935 Capra's movies combined messages about the triumph of virtue over oppression with their entertainment values. His subsequent movies at Columbia confirmed his reputation for producing pictures that succeeded in pleasing critics, the industry, and the picture-going public in equal measure. His reputation did not, however, endure beyond the 1930s. Although *It's a Wonderful Life* (1946) has become an American Christmas holiday institution since the 1980s, it was not a success on first release, and Capra's career declined steadily until his retirement in 1966. Suspicious of the sentimental populism—the "Capra-corn"—of his most successful movies, auteurist critics gave Capra scant attention, and his most successful movies are now most often discussed either as examples of screwball comedy or as symptoms of their cultural moment.

Capra was, however, a prolific director of his studio's A-features before *It Happened One Night*, already regarded as "one of Hollywood's best" (Balio 80), and a central figure in the elevation of Columbia Pictures to the ranks of the major companies. The overwhelming majority of Columbia's product were B pictures and "programmers," designed to fit either half of a double bill in neighborhood and small-town theaters. As the studio's principal director of its few big-budget movies, Capra had a uniquely influential position at Columbia from the early 1930s, and after *The Bitter Tea of General Yen* (1933) was chosen to open RKO's flagship Radio City Music Hall theater in New York in December 1932, all his movies received celebrity treatment. After the success of *It Happened One Night*, Columbia concentrated its A-feature production on comedies such as *Theodora Goes Wild* (1936) and *The Awful Truth* (1937), as well as Capra's self-consciously inspirational "fantasies of goodwill."

Screwball Comedy

> Comedy usually moves toward a happy ending, and the normal response of the audience to a happy ending is "this should be," which sounds like a moral judgment. So it is, except that it is not moral in the restricted sense, but social. Its opposite is not the villainous, but the absurd. . . . Happy endings do not impress us as true, but as desirable. (Frye 167, 170)

The term "screwball" has its origins in baseball, and was coined around 1930 by New York Giants pitcher Carl Hubbell, who made baseball history in the Major League All-Star game in July 1934 by striking out six opponents with his screwball pitch. Propelled into wider public usage, "screwball" came to mean unbalanced, eccentric, unpredictable, unconventional, or lunatic. The *New Yorker* declared it "forbidden to call any character a nut; you have to call him a screwball" (qtd. in Chapman 374). The term entered the vocabulary of the movies in reviews of the 1936 comedy *My Man Godfrey*. *Variety* reported that Carole Lombard "has played screwball dames before, but none so screwy as this one. From start to finish, with no letdowns or lapses into quiet sanity, she needs only a resin bag to be a female Rube Waddell [a pitcher for the Philadelphia Athletics]" (qtd. in Balio 276). Two years later, however, *Variety* announced that there was "a very definite trend away from screwball comedies," after overproduction had exhausted audience demand (qtd. in Balio 268).

For the industry, screwball comedy represented a typical production cycle, in which the ingredients of a successful movie were cannibalized and reiterated in a series of imitations until the formula's commercial energy ran out. Such cycles were central to the major companies' organization of their annual production schedules, providing templates into which other staple ingredients, such as star personas and romance plots, could be fitted. *It Happened One Night*'s sparring lovers provided one key element for screwball comedy; others came from Carole Lombard's "dizzy" performance in Columbia's critically acclaimed but commercially unsuccessful *Twentieth Century* and the playful representation of marriage in MGM's *The Thin Man*, both released later in 1934. At the time of its release, however, none of *It Happened One Night*'s ingredients appeared particularly new. As *Variety*'s review quite accurately noted, the movie "starts out to be another long-distance bus story" (a brief and not particularly successful cycle initiated the previous year by MGM's *Fugitive Lovers* and Universal's *Cross Country Cruise*), but fortunately recognized that "the best way to do a bus story is to make them get out and walk."

As a style, screwball combined a verbally witty high comedy of manners and a low comedy of pratfalls, slapstick, and physical violence. These were the first movie comedies "in which sexually attractive, sophisticated stars indulged in their own slapstick instead of delegating it to their inferiors" (Sikov 177). The cycle's essential character was the "screwball dame," played by "exuberant, middle-class, all-American types" (Sarris, *You Ain't Heard Nothin'* 97) such as Carole Lombard, Irene Dunne, Margaret Sullavan, or Myrna Loy, who had established their reputations in drama but were willing to engage in an often quite violent physical comedy. Unusually, the screwball cycle was predominantly the product of only three studios, Paramount, MGM, and Columbia; the contract-star roster at both Warner Bros. and 20th Century–Fox seemed unsuited to the tone and upper-class settings of the cycle, while RKO's contributions relied heavily on Ginger Rogers.

Like most movie genres, however, screwball comedy has been defined retrospectively by critics seeking to classify Hollywood's output, rather than by the industry itself. As a description of a group of movies, the term had little currency outside *Variety*'s colorful prose, but it began to acquire critical status a decade later, when Richard Griffith used the term to describe their new image of courtship and marriage . . . with man and wife no longer expecting ecstatic bliss, but treating the daily experience of living as a crazy adventure sufficient to itself. And if what went on in these private worlds was mostly nonsense, what sense could be found in the great world outside, where economic crisis and the threat of approaching war barred all the conventional roads to achievement and happiness? (Griffith and Mayer 324)

Subsequent critical accounts have emphasized the movies' plot pattern, in which an initially antagonistic couple discover or rediscover romance through a sequence of combative verbal and physical exchanges, until they reconcile the sexual and ideological tensions that separate them.

In *Anatomy of Criticism*, Northrop Frye proposes that in most comedy,

what normally happens is that a young man wants a young woman, that his desire is resisted by some opposition, usually paternal, and that near the end of the play some twist in the plot enables the hero to have his will. . . . The device in the plot that brings hero and heroine together causes a new society to crystallize around the hero. (163)

What differentiated screwball comedy from other versions of romantic comedy was that the obstacle to the couple's successful romance was provided not by an external agent but by their own mutual hostility. The characteristic screwball-comedy plot was constructed around the clash of incompatible personalities and values, and much of screwball's energy comes from the escalating and apparently irresolvable conflict between its incompatible romantic couple. This conflict, however, takes place within the conventions of romance, of comedy, of classical Hollywood cinema's profound commitment to the creation of the couple, and of the social conventions of moviegoing, all of which ensure that the promise in a movie's advertising—"Together for the first time! Clark Gable and Claudette Colbert in *It Happened One Night*"—will be fulfilled by the final scene. The screwball plot, like the plots of all romantic comedies, exists to delay the moment of that fulfillment for the duration of the movie. As Eugene Vale explains in *The Technique of Screenplay Writing*:

> If a man and a woman with perfect affinity and no obvious dif-
> ficulties meet each other, there is no doubt that they will attain
> their goal. . . . All love scenes in between are without any inter-
> est. In order to show these love scenes, we must give the spec-
> tator a knowledge of some difficulties to prevent him from
> concluding to the goal. (154)

Movies consistently erect insuperable obstacles to the fulfillment of
their protagonists' desires, and then engineer an implausibly "happy
ending" that could, as they say, "only happen in the movies." One of
the most fundamental sources of the pleasure that movies offer their
audiences is the demonstration of their magical power to fulfill their
impossible promise by resolving the incompatibilities and paradoxes
around which they construct their plots. This is, of course, also the
principal occasion of their unreality, the "escapism" of which they are
so conventionally accused. If Hollywood's movies lie to us, they do so
most often by teaching us that nothing is so emotionally satisfying as
the reconciliation of irresolvable contradictions. In *It Happened One
Night,* the formation of the couple also brings about the apparent
"merging of cultural values once defined as mutually exclusive" (Altman 144–45). As Thomas Schatz has argued, this resolution can be understood in ideological terms, as suggesting "that if the working-class
stiff and the spoiled heiress can overcome their ideological disparity
and finally embrace, then we should not lose faith in the traditional
American ideal of a classless utopian society" (152). Describing *It
Happened One Night* as a "Depression romantic comedy," Elizabeth
Kendall suggests that "it pictured the Depression as an event that
taught a lesson about love. It portrayed that love as self-redefinition,
coming out of hardship, leading to reconciliation. It implied, by
metaphoric association, that the recent, nightmarish Hoover years had
been good for the national character" (54). A contemporary critic, on
the other hand, decried the unconvincing wish fulfillment of *It
Happened One Night's* suggestion that "if you stepped up to a grumpy
plutocrat . . . bawled him out, told him his daughter was a spoiled brat,
he'd at once grow enamored of you and you'd come into his millions"
(Kauffmann with Henstell 335).

The increasingly fantastic and arbitrary happy endings of Capra's
later 1930s movies incurred more intense criticism, for absolving their

audiences "from realistic thinking about the forces which governed their lives" (Griffith 452). But that was not, argued screenwriter Frances Marion in 1937, what "the average mythical audience" wanted to do at the movies. Instead,

> it wants to have its emotions aroused . . . it wants something that will pleasantly excite it, amuse it, wring it with suspense, fill it with self-approval, or even arouse its indignation; . . . above all things, it wants to be "sent home happy." . . . Something approaching the ideal life is what this audience prefers to see, rather than life as it actually knows it. . . . It seems not so interested in having situations logical, or even possible, as it is in having its pleasurable emotions aroused. (26–27)

As a way of describing the relationship between our mundane realities and the heightened realms of experience made available to us by Hollywood, "escapism" hides complexity under an apparently simple term. In examining what satisfactions entertainment offers its audience, Richard Dyer has suggested that the appeal of what is usually called "escapism" is better understood as "utopian." He argues that the movies provide a utopianism of the feelings, "what Utopia would feel like, rather than how it is organized" (5). Hollywood's version of entertainment allows its audiences' more intense, more emotional, less inhibited, less restrained selves to escape into a revised, utopian version of their everyday world, where issues are clearer, emotions more intense, and problems solved at little cost. Tina Olsin Lent has suggested that screwball comedies provided their female viewers with an escape "to a world that did not seem so remote and unattainable," since their heroines shared their objectives of finding "an emotionally satisfying, sexually exciting, physically compatible, fun-filled love-companionship" (331).

As is the case with almost all of Hollywood's genres, not all critics agree on their definitions, their chronological boundaries, or the interpretation of their cultural significance. Historian Robert Sklar places these movies in a generic tradition of "genteel romance," which had been a staple of popular magazine literature throughout the 1920s in stories that "provided reassurance that women's new freedoms—and particularly the possibility of sexual license that great wealth conferred on young women—could be safely controlled within the bounds of middle-class male imagination" (41). In Kathleen Rowe's harsh judgment, the fact that the outcome is predetermined—that the romance has to end happily with the overcoming of obstacles leading to the formation of the couple—means that *It Happened One Night* tells a "story of masculine victory which patriarchy writes as comedy. . . . Romantic comedy tolerates, and even encourages, its heroine's short-lived rebellion because that rebellion ultimately serves the interest of the hero" (47). By contrast, Stanley Cavell has produced an alternate description of an overlapping genre he identifies as the "comedy of remarriage . . . an inheritor of the preoccupations and discoveries of Shakespearean romantic comedy," in which "an essential goal of the narrative is the education of the woman, where her education turns out to mean her acknowledgment of her desire, and . . . her creation . . . as an autonomous human being" (1, 84). In contradiction to Rowe, Cavell views screwball as a utopian "comedy of equality" (82). Building on Cavell's argument that the genre requires "the creation of a new woman" (82), Maria DiBattista interprets screwball's "odd-couple" romances as an empowering comedy of female self-articulation in which the central character, the "fast-talking dame," is in revolt against the very genteel traditions that Robert Sklar sees them endorsing (x).

These contradictory critical positions suggest, at the least, that *It Happened One Night* is open to considerable flexibility in interpretation. Somewhat against these critics' own arguments, their varying formulations of screwball comedy also illustrate that Hollywood is best understood as a generic cinema rather than a cinema of discrete genres. Critics have often exaggerated the extent to which the industry conceived its product in terms of genres. Rather than establishing a number of discrete product categories, Hollywood sought to categorize its audiences, and then aimed to produce products that would appeal either to or across the demographic groupings of its audience classification (Maltby, "Sticks, Hicks and Flaps" 25). Hollywood movies are best understood as aggregations of familiar parts; their individuality is to be found in their particular combination of standardized, interchangeable elements. Romance and comedy, both staple ingredients of Hollywood's output, have been combined in a variety of ways throughout Hollywood's history. Comedies of remarriage did not, as Stanley Cavell suggests, emerge "full-blown" in the mid-1930s (27). Charles

Musser, for example, has demonstrated persuasively that the comedy of remarriage was invented in the late 1910s, with Cecil B. deMille's *Old Wives for New* (1918) and *Don't Change Your Husband* (1919), and formed part of a developing public discourse about divorce and the idea of "companionate marriage" in the 1920s (303, 313).

In locating the obstacle to the lovers' union in their mutual antagonism, the screwball plot further borrowed from the "fairy-tale" musical of the early 1930s, itself an Americanization of European operettas. Rick Altman has noted that like romantic comedies, the fairy-tale musical developed away from an overt emphasis on the sexual implications of courtship evident in Ernst Lubitsch's *The Love Parade* (1929) or *One Hour with You* (1932). Instead, the rituals of courtship were enacted "through antagonistic dialogue and especially through the characteristic plot construction whereby sexual energy is transmuted into quarreling and the progression of romantic attachment is made, paradoxically, to parallel the intensification of the conflict between the two would-be lovers" (168).

New variations on established forms created new opportunities, particularly for performers. Successful performance styles, such as the "fast-talking dame" persisted as ingredients in movies after the cycle in which they had originated had lost its audience appeal: Colbert, Katharine Hepburn, and Ginger Rogers continued to play variations on their versions of the "screwball dame" into the 1940s and beyond, for example. Screwball's generic elements can, therefore, be found in movies released long after *Variety* declared the cycle dead.

The Production Code

> Here we have all these beautiful people with nothing to do. Let us invent some substitutes for sex. (Sarris, *You Ain't Heard Nothin'* 95)

Most critics explain the emergence of screwball comedy in the mid-1930s as a consequence of the Motion Picture Production Code's restrictions on the explicit representation of sex. Andrew Sarris describes screwball as "a self-contradictory genre, the sex comedy without sex" (*You Ain't Heard Nothin'* 97). Since an overt representation of sexual desire was unacceptable under the Code, it had to be displaced onto the mutual antagonism of the central couple, and screwball's physical comedy allowed characters to touch each other without expressing desire. Indeed, screwball is one of the rare instances in which critics attach some aesthetically beneficial effect to censorship. Ed Sikov argues that screwball is defined by "the palpable clash between what can be done and what cannot be said. . . . The high wit and airy grace of screwball comedy wouldn't have been possible without enforced sublimation, an across-the-board refusal to deal with sex in a direct manner" (43, 128).

The implementation of the Production Code certainly had a determining influence on the form and structure of the screwball cycle, but in a rather more complex manner than is usually suggested. One of the great myths of American movie history is that the Production Code was not effectively enforced between 1930 and 1934. Despite a substantial body of careful historical research clearly establishing the error of this claim, it continues to be widely reproduced because, like the story of Clark Gable's missing undershirt, it tells a convenient fiction about Hollywood history. In Hollywood, history is first of all a production value, and its requirement to be entertaining is much more compelling than any obligation to be accurate. The myth of an unrestrained "pre-Code cinema" in the early 1930s maintains the commercial value of the movies it identifies as subversive or challenging to traditional values, most obviously in their circulation in seasons of "Forbidden Hollywood" on cable television.

The differences between movies made in the early 1930s and those made later in the decade are undeniable, but the change was gradual rather than cataclysmic. The Code is best understood as a system of conventions, similar to the generic conventions of romantic comedy or action movies. Such conventions evolve over time, and the early 1930s can most accurately be seen as a period in which the Code's conventions of representation, particularly its representation of sex and violence, were developed through a process of negotiation, experimentation, and expediency. The later 1930s saw the largely successful operation of these conventions in, for instance, the highly sophisticated "innocence" of the discourse on sexuality in the screwball comedies or Astaire-Rogers musicals, in which only the characters remained innocent of the suggestiveness that typically underpinned their social relations. Central to the Code's conventions was what Ruth Vasey has called "the principle of deniability," a particular kind of ambiguity that shifted the responsibility for determining the content and meaning of a movie away from the producer to the individual spectator (107).

Silent cinema was inherently flexible, since one of its major components, sound, could be varied at each performance. The Production Code was the industry's principal means of retaining the interpretative flexibility of silent cinema within the constraints of a technologically and materially much more inflexible medium. At the same time, the Code also represented the industry's reluctant acceptance of its responsibility for the moral well-being of its audiences. Its practical implementation was, however, a complex matter, involving extensive negotiation over procedure, enforcement, and interpretation at the level of textual detail. Its conventions were developed during a period of intense public debate about the moral effects of the movies, and on a number of occasions during the early 1930s—in September 1931, March 1933, and in the first half of 1934—the industry responded to public concern by increasing the stringency with which the Code was enforced. Rather than perpetuating a false distinction between movies produced before 1934 and those produced after, a more accurate history of the Production Code makes it clear that Hollywood's "Golden Age of Turbulence" (Sklar 175) was a period in which the industry negotiated a system of representation acceptable to the cultural authorities to which it deferred.

On the one hand, the Production Code strove to eliminate any moral ambiguity in a movie's narrative progression through the rigid imposition of a deterministic plotline, ascribing every character a position on a fixed moral spectrum. At the same time, however, movies constructed strategies of ambiguity around the details of action that they were not permitted to present explicitly. What could not be shown was graphic, explicit, unambiguous, unmistakable sexual behavior. Instead, what could be shown was mistakable sexual behavior, the presence of which could always be denied. The rules of both conduct and representation under these conditions were most cogently articulated by F. Scott Fitzgerald's Monroe Stahr, in *The Last Tycoon*, explaining to his scriptwriters how the audience is to understand their heroine's motivation:

> At all times, at all moments when she is on the screen in our sight, she wants to sleep with Ken Willard. . . . Whatever she

227

> does, it is in place of sleeping with Ken Willard. If she walks
> down the street she is walking to sleep with Ken Willard, if she
> eats her food it is to give her enough strength to sleep with Ken
> Willard. *But* at no time do you give the impression that she
> would even consider sleeping with Ken Willard unless they
> were properly sanctified. (51–52; episode 9)

To achieve this effect, Hollywood manufactured a product that would allow "sophisticated" viewers to read whatever they liked into a formally "innocent" movie, so long as the producers could use the machinery of the Production Code to deny that the sophisticated interpretation had been put there in the first place. So long as the story remained comprehensible at the "innocent" level, innocence was protected, because "innocent" viewers were not educated into sophistication by being forced into some half-understood suggestive interpretation. On the other hand, a "sophisticated" audience could readily find hidden, "subversive," or "repressed" meanings in almost any movie by supplying "from its own imagination the specific acts of so-called misconduct which the Production Code has made unmentionable" (Harold J. Salemson, qtd. in Inglis 183). Much of the work of self-regulation in the 1930s and 1940s lay in the maintenance of this system of conventions, which operated, however perversely, as an enabling mechanism at the same time that it was a repressive one. As Production Code Administration director Joseph Breen persistently argued, the Production Code was not so much a system of censorship as an alternative to one: a system by which censurable content could be coded and codified so as to avoid censorship.

Analysis

Clark Gable and the Restoration of Order

The demands for movie reform in the early 1930s were themselves part of a broader reaffirmation of traditional values at a moment of economic and cultural crisis, focused primarily on a fear that the family unit was in danger of disintegrating. Civic and religious groups concerned about the moral effects of the movies found cause for anxiety in Hollywood's representations of gangsters, "fallen women," and "prodigal daughters." In response, the studios sought new generic variations, in a series of attempts to fulfill the impossible promise of representing the crisis of American capitalism entertainingly, but as often as not, these variations exacerbated the problem they sought to address. Casting desirable stars as social outcasts denied audiences the satisfaction of seeing an attractive character achieve a socially acceptable and emotionally rewarding resolution, because the Code insisted that wrongdoing must be shown to result in suffering and punishment. Female-centered melodramas such as *Blonde Venus* (1932) and *Baby Face* (1933) became ever more convoluted in their attempts to achieve resolution, and initial attempts at displacing the formula into comedy, such as MGM's *Red-Headed Woman* (1932), provoked even larger torrents of criticism. As one writer complained, "our most competent stars are guilty of endowing unchastity with glamour" (Donnelly 85–86).

Men fared little better. Few successful businessmen and few successful fathers appeared in movies during the worst years of the Depression; movie gangsters, for example, invariably came from families without a father. It was almost as difficult to find a genteel romantic hero. The passionate, melodramatic male sexuality of Rudolph Valentino and John Gilbert proved vulnerable to the dictates of a sound cinema intolerant of its feminization of the male as erotic object. A 1932 fan magazine article complained that "the feminine public is wearying of rather pretty and too polished young men" in "drawing room" comedies and dramas borrowed from Broadway (Baldwin 46), but few acceptable alternatives emerged. The three top male box-office stars of the early 1930s were comedians Will Rogers, Eddie Cantor, and the plug-ugly Wallace Beery. Warner's urban ethnics—James Cagney, Paul Muni, Edward G. Robinson—were seldom more than peripheral romantic leads.

Images of aggressive male sexuality were at least as troubling to the media as images of aggressive female sexuality, and Clark Gable was criticized as "a menace to morals" for his overt expressions of a sexuality tainted with a disturbing brutality. One fan magazine article declared that "the characters which he plays today would have been repugnant a few years ago" (Quirk 278). Another observed that on the screen, while Gable might appear to "adore the current heroine to the point of madness, he might also, if sufficiently exasperated, give her a very good beating—and get away with it" (Baldwin 48). His handling of Norma Shearer in *A Free Soul* (1931), for example, was comparable with James Cagney's now more celebrated treatment of Mae Clarke in *The Public Enemy* (1931). Although this performance had been commercially successful in movies like *Red Dust* (1932), such a public image became increasingly untenable as censorship pressures mounted, and MGM experimented with Gable's persona in a series of movies in 1933. The studio's willingness to see him cast in a romantic comedy at another company's risk fitted with this experimentation.

It Happened One Night is a movie produced at the moment of the restoration of order. By late 1933 the worst of the slump had passed, and with it the fear of immediate social and political collapse. The slight signs of optimism in the economy in the summer of 1933 indicated that the Depression might have "bottomed out": theater receipts began to pick up in the fall of 1933, and the improvement was more marked in neighborhood and outlying theaters than in the downtown first-run houses. Although the public crisis over movie censorship was yet to be staged, the industry's internal mechanisms for the self-regulation of movie content were already fully operational. *It Happened One Night* was a product ideally suited to these conditions. For at least two years nonmetropolitan exhibitors had been lobbying against the "sophisticated," gangster, and "drawing-room" movies, in favor of what they termed "simple romances" (Aaronson 9). The increasing pressure of the censorship lobbies both inside and outside the industry and the box-office successes of movies such as Capra's *Lady for a Day* (released September 1933) and RKO's *Little Women* (released November 1933) endorsed such a shift in content. The *Variety* review of *It Happened One Night* noted, significantly, that it demonstrated that "a clean story can be funnier than a dirty one."

According to Capra's autobiography, the success of *It Happened One Night* resulted from Myles Connolly's critique of a script draft:

> Your leading characters are non-interest-grabbing. People can't identify with them. Take your girl: a spoiled brat, a rich heiress. How many spoiled heiresses do people know? And how many give a damn what happens to them? . . . Don't let her be a brat because she's an heiress, but because she's bored with being an heiress. More sympathetic. And the man. Forget that panty-waist painter. Make him a guy we all know and

like. Maybe a tough, crusading reporter—at outs with his pig-headed editor. More sympathetic. And when he meets the spoiled heiress—well, it's *The Taming of the Shrew*. But the shrew must be worth taming, and the guy that tames her must be one of us. (Qtd. in Capra 164)

It Happened One Night inverts the class affiliations of hero and heroine from the pattern that had dominated the "kept woman" cycle: unlike *Red-Headed Woman* or *Baby Face*, *It Happened One Night* is a romance across class lines in which the heroine is upper class and the hero is middle to working class. The entire emphasis of the story changes as a result, permitting the shift from melodrama to comedy. Where the lower-class heroine can only demonstrate her worth by sacrifice, and thus becomes the victim of the plot, the lower-class hero demonstrates his worth by overcoming class obstacles to the romance. Frye proposes that "the theme of the comic is the integration of society, which usually takes the form of integrating a central character into it" (43). In *It Happened One Night,* the character integrated into society is not, as might be conventional, the hero, Peter (Clark Gable), but the heroine, Ellie (Claudette Colbert). Peter is not in rebellion against society; he wishes to restore order; and as Kathleen Rowe suggests, the movie describes, quite overtly, the containment of the heroine under patriarchy.

The movie opens with Ellie's defiance of her father (Walter Connolly)—a defiance staged over her fitness to marry, that is, her fitness to enter the world of adult sexuality, and the fitness of her choice of a patriarchal replacement. We see a newspaper headline reading, "Ellen Andrews Escapes Father." Initially, she wants to replace her father with a bad king, King Westley (Jameson Thomas), the "high-flying" autogiro pilot who might have been the hero of a drawing-room romance. The course of the movie will ensure that she marries the good king, the people's king, Gable.[1] Before she can enter into the world of adult sexuality, however, she must be reduced to the condition of a child by Peter, and brought up again—reeducated—to assume her

---

[1]In his first scene, after his telephone argument with his editor, Peter is cheered by the crowd, who call him the "King." In 1937, Gable was declared the "King" of the movies in a fan magazine poll, and the title remained his conventional nickname.

proper, married place as property. In their first encounter on the bus, Peter claims his right of possession over her: "that which you are sitting on is mine." Having taken possession of her ticket, he again claims possession of her as an act of protection, telling Shapely (Roscoe Karns) that she is his wife. After this encounter, he reduces her to a state of financial dependence by taking her money from her. At the first autocamp he once more protects her—this time from her father's detectives—by again claiming her as his wife. Later, he quite accurately tells Shapely that he has kidnapped her.

On each occasion that Ellie seeks to assert her independence, she is punished for it. On the bus, when she leaves Peter's seat, she is first accosted by the fat man, then by Shapely. In the first autocamp, when she tries to argue with Peter, he threatens her with the sight of his sexuality by undressing; her adult resistance dissolves into a childlike response, and she runs away, an action that obliges her to accept Peter's terms over the "Walls of Jericho." In the hitchhiking scene, she proves, as she says, that "the limb is mightier than the thumb," but then they are robbed, and she again has to be protected by Peter.

On several occasions they enact her childlike dependence on him, and gradually discover that both of them enjoy and desire it. The first morning on the bus she is shown sleeping with her head on his shoulder, clutching his lapel, in the pose of a child. Shortly afterward, he tells her, "You're as helpless as a baby." In her conversation with Peter, she reveals her inexperience with men, which Peter translates as childishness. Throughout the movie, Peter constructs the rules of the childish world he has created: what to do with money, how to dunk doughnuts, what is and is not piggybacking, the Walls of Jericho. In this world Peter assumes, and learns, the role of the authoritative father, to the point of hitting Ellie when she argues with him, repeating the action of her father that led her to run away at the outset. Now that she has acquiesced in his construction of her, however, she does not try to escape again. As a vestigial remnant of Gable's earlier persona, Peter displays a noticeable enthusiasm for doing violence to children. When Shapely demands half the reward, Peter threatens him with violence to his children if he tells anyone. Later, he tells Ellie's father that "what she needs is a guy that will take a sock at her once a day whether it's coming to her or not. If you'd had half the brains you're supposed to have, you'd have done it yourself long ago." Peter not only disapproves of her father, he usurps his role, expressing patriarchal anger whenever Ellie provokes another man's desire. When she wants to charm Danker (Alan Hale) into buying her a meal, he threatens to break her neck. The movie successfully contains the explicit violence of Gable's sexuality within the acceptable bounds of a reestablished patriarchal family. At the first autocamp when, for the benefit of her father's detectives, Peter has apparently reduced Ellie to hysterical tears by his shouting and threatening to hit her, the camp owner tells the detectives, "I told you they were a perfectly nice married couple."

By the time of the haystack scene, Peter has reduced Ellie to a condition of complete childish dependence on him, but while this solves "the problem" of female sexuality by rendering Ellie too childlike to eat Peter's carrots,[2] it does not address the problem of Peter's own desire, as he realizes when he covers Ellie with his coat in imitation of the Walls of Jericho. The adult nature of Peter's own behavior remains in doubt for much of the movie. Like Ellie, he is also at odds with a father figure, Joe the editor (Charles C. Wilson). In the hitchhiking scene, the morning after the hay-field scene, Ellie refuses another carrot, and Peter responds with a braggadocio display of his prowess: "It's all in that old thumb, that old thumb never fails . . . keep your eye on that thumb, baby!" His adolescent attitude to sexual display is rewarded with failure: no cars stop, and Ellie seizes the opportunity to assert her independence and sexuality again. It is not until the more dangerous consequences of that action manifest themselves, when the driver robs them, that Peter can once again restore his patriarchal authority. On their last night together, when Ellie is seduced into his adolescent fantasy of escape to a Pacific island, Peter realizes that he must return from the transient utopia of his own invention to negotiate his rights of patriarchal possession.

---

[2] "My feeling about the carrot is that we have no more use for making its phallic symbolism explicit than Ellie and Peter would have—I mean at the time she accepts it in the car, on the way to their third night together. Surely *we* do not need to be told that their relationship has sexual overtones or undercurrents. To discover this together, and acceptably, is, rather, exactly their problem. And to suppose that this comes down to discovering the carrot's symbolism strikes me as denying the dimensions of significance I have traced in the carrot—its place as a food, uncooked, and as a gift, from a father" (Cavell 93).

From the outset of the movie, Mr. Andrews is the obstacle to Ellie's romance with Westley. The audience knows by the movie's casting that this is the wrong romance, and the plot is occupied with establishing the proper comedic pattern among the characters. First, Peter and Ellie have to recognize that they are the lovers in this comedy, a process that occupies most of the movie, reaching its discovery in their discussion of "escape" on the third night. The final discovery, however, takes place when Andrews recognizes the virtues of his younger self in Peter, and thus identifies him as a fitting man to whom he can hand over possession of his daughter.

The obstacle in the proper romance turns out to be Westley, who must be expelled from the new society not because he is the rejected lover, but because he represents the frivolous and dissipated elite, who are clearly identified with the values of the previous decade through the metaphor of the merry-go-round that goes nowhere. Peter, on the other hand, represents the solid middle-class virtues of a work ethic, even if his work is the writing of stories, and in this case the creation of a fantasy that comes true (we are, after all, in Hollywood). Peter's middle-class virtues have to do with not accepting or expecting charity, living within your means, and not taking something for nothing. These are the bourgeois virtues of dealing with money, and it is Peter's attitude to money that convinces Mr. Andrews that he is a suitable recipient for the other form of property, Ellie.

The remainder of the movie is concerned with Mr. Andrews's machinations to ensure that his daughter is given to the right man. It is the presence of this father figure—the role that was absent from the "sophisticated" plots of the early 1930s—that permits the full restoration of order at the movie's close, when the patriarch permits his daughter's entry into the realm of adult sexuality through the legal possession of a suitable substitute for himself.

Conclusion

The contradiction at the heart of *It Happened One Night* lies in the paradoxical relationship between its narrative and its performances, and this in turn explains why the movie typically requires us to maintain two contradictory ideas at the same time. The narrative enacts the restoration of social order in its establishment of proper, and proprietorial, relations between the sexes. This restoration is, however, performed through Ellie's liberation and self-discovery, and on a different level through the liberated and liberating performances of Colbert and Gable. *It Happened One Night* provided a set of mechanisms—a plot formula, a tone of comic banter—that allowed studios to reposition their stars' personae and liberate the cross-class romance from melodrama: reviews commented that *She Married Her Boss* (1935), the next movie Colbert made for Columbia, "would probably have been handled as a heavy, tragic domestic treatise with everything sour until the sweet ending" two years previously, but now it strove to maintain "the happy, easy-going mood of *It Happened One Night*" (qtd. in Dooley 40 and Balio 272).

Gable's performance was even more fundamentally made over. Capra claimed that *It Happened One Night* liberated Gable to "play himself: the fun-loving, boyish, attractive, he-man rogue that was the *real* Gable" (170), and the movie certainly established his revised persona as "the American ideal of companionable masculinity appealing to both men and women" (DiBattista 165). If *It Happened One Night*'s liberated, exuberant performances contradict its narrative, the movie is under no obligation to resolve this contradiction or to determine how individual viewers may do so. The movie's contented acceptance of its paradoxes permits the range of contradictory critical interpretations that have been discussed here; it both expresses its characters' and its audiences' desires through its performances and represses them through its containing narrative. That is the hidden reason why Hollywood movies have happy endings. The reestablishment of order renders the viewer's experimentation with expressive behavior a matter of no consequence, contained as it is within the safe, trivialized space of entertainment. No matter how vividly we have experienced Hollywood's imaginary landscapes and utopian possibilities, we leave the theater reminding ourselves that what we have seen is "only a movie."

Credits

United States, 1934, Columbia Pictures

Director: Frank Capra
Producer: Harry Cohn
Screenplay: Robert Riskin, based on the short story "Night Bus" by Samuel Hopkins Adams, published in *Hearst's International-Cosmopolitan*, Aug. 1933

Cinematography: Joseph Walker
Editing: Gene Havlick
Music Director: Louis Silvers
Song: "The Flying Trapeze," words and music by George Leybourne
Art Direction: Stephen Goosson
Costume Design: Robert Kalloch

CAST:

Peter Warne	Clark Gable
Ellie Andrews	Claudette Colbert
Alexander Andrews	Walter Connolly
Oscar Shapeley	Roscoe Karns
King Westley	Jameson Thomas
Danker	Alan Hale
Zeke	Arthur Hoyt
Zeke's wife	Blanche Friderici
Joe Gordon	Charles C. Wilson
Bus driver	Ward Bond
Bus driver	Eddie Chandler

Bibliography

Aaronson, Charles A. "Comparison of 'X' and 'Y' Proves Simple Dramatic Picture Plays." *Motion Picture Herald* 16 Apr. 1932: 9–11.

Altman, Rick. *The American Film Musical.* Bloomington: Indiana UP, 1987.

Baldwin, Faith. "Why All the Mystery about Gable's Appeal." *Modern Screen* March 1932. Rpt. in *The Best of Modern Screen.* Ed. Mark Bego. London: Columbus, 1986. 46–48.

Balio, Tino. *Grand Design: Hollywood as a Modern Business Enterprise, 1930–1939.* New York: Scribner's, 1993.

Capra, Frank. *The Name Above the Title.* New York: Macmillan, 1971.

Cavell, Stanley. *Pursuits of Happiness: The Hollywood Comedy of Remarriage.* Cambridge, MA: Harvard UP, 1981.

Chapman, Robert L., ed. *New Dictionary of American Slang.* New York: Harper, 1986.

DiBattista, Maria. *Fast-Talking Dames.* New Haven: Yale UP, 2001.

Donnelly, Gerard B. "An Open Letter to Dr. Wingate." *America* 29 Oct. 1932: 85–86.

Dooley, Roger. *From Scarface to Scarlett: American Films in the 1930s.* New York: Harcourt, 1981.

Dyer, Richard. "Entertainment and Utopia." *MOVIE* 24 (1977): 2–13.

Fitzgerald, F. Scott. *The Last Tycoon.* Harmondsworth: Penguin, 1974.

Frye, Northrop. *Anatomy of Criticism.* Princeton: Princeton UP, 1971.

Griffith, Richard. "The Film Since Then." *The Film Till Now: A Survey of World Cinema.* 1949. Ed. Paul Rotha. London: Spring, 1967.

Griffith, Richard, and Arthur Mayer. *The Movies: The Sixty-Year Story of the World of Hollywood and Its Effect on America: From Pre-Nickelodeon Days to the Present.* New York: Bonanza, 1957.

Inglis, Ruth. *Freedom of the Movies: A Report on Self-Regulation from the Commission on Freedom of the Press.* Chicago: Free, 1947.

Karnick, Kristine Brunovska, and Henry Jenkins, eds. *Classical Hollywood Comedy.* New York: Routledge, 1995.

Kauffmann, Stanley, with Bruce Henstell, eds. *American Film Criticism from the Beginnings to "Citizen Kane."* New York: Liveright, 1972.

Kendall, Elizabeth. *The Runaway Bride: Hollywood Romantic Comedy of the 1930s.* New York: Knopf, 1990.

Lent, Tina Olsin. "Romantic Love and Friendship: The Redefinition of Gender Relations in Screwball Comedy." Karnick and Jenkins 314–31.

Maltby, Richard. *Hollywood Cinema: An Introduction.* 2nd ed. Oxford: Blackwell, 2003.

———. "*It Happened One Night*: The Recreation of the Patriarch." Sklar and Zagarrio 130–63.

———. "Sticks, Hicks and Flaps: Classical Hollywood's Generic Conception of Its Audience." *Identifying Hollywood's Audiences: Cultural Identity and the Movies.* Ed. Melvyn Stokes and Richard Maltby. London: BFI, 1999. 23–41.

Marlon, Frances. *How to Write and Sell Film Stories.* London: John Miles, 1937.

McBride, Joseph. *Frank Capra: The Catastrophe of Success.* London: Faber, 1992.

Musser, Charles. "Divorce, DeMille and the Comedy of Remarriage." Karnick and Jenkins 282–313.

Quirk, James R. "Why Women Go Crazy about Clark Gable." *Photoplay* Nov. 1931. Rpt. in *The Talkies: Articles and Illustrations from a Great Fan Magazine, 1928–1940.* Ed. Richard Griffith. New York: Dover, 1971. 44+.

Rev. of *It Happened One Night,* dir. Frank Capra. *Variety* 27 Feb. 1934: 17.

Rowe, Kathleen. "Comedy, Melodrama and Gender: Theorizing the Genres of Laughter." Karnick and Jenkins 39–59.

Sarris, Andrew. *The American Cinema: Directors and Directions, 1929–1968.* New York: Dutton, 1968.

———. *You Ain't Heard Nothin' Yet: The American Talking Film, History and Memory, 1927–1949.* New York: Oxford UP, 1998.

Schatz, Thomas. *Hollywood Genres: Formulas, Filmmaking, and the Studio System.* New York: Random, 1981.

Sikov, Ed. *Screwball: Hollywood's Madcap Romantic Comedies.* New York: Crown, 1989.

Sklar, Robert. *Movie-Made America: A Cultural History of American Movies.* New York: Random, 1975.

Sklar, Robert, and Vito Zagarrio, eds. *Frank Capra: Authorship and the Studio System.* Philadelphia: Temple UP, 1998.

Stebbins, Robert. Review of *Mr. Deeds Goes to Town,* dir. Frank Capra. *New Theatre* May 1936. Rpt. in Kauffmann with Henstell 334–37.

Troy, William. Rev. of *It Happened One Night,* dir. Frank Capra. *Nation* 10 Apr. 1935. Rpt. in Kauffmann with Henstell 300–301.

Vale, Eugene. *The Technique of Screenplay Writing.* 1944. New York: Grosset, 1973.

Vasey, Ruth. *The World According to Hollywood, 1918–1939.* Exeter: U of Exeter P, 1997.

Modern Times (1936)

CHARLES J. MALAND

The Depression, Technology, and the Tramp

Context

By the 1920s, Charlie Chaplin's movie persona, the Tramp, was one of the most widely recognized human figures on the face of the globe. As we shall see, Chaplin the performer-director-writer leveraged the popularity of that persona to work himself into an enviable and highly unusual position in the American film industry: by 1923, he was making films at his own studio and distributing them through a company that he co-owned, a situation he maintained until he left the United States in a climate of turmoil in 1952. Shifting from two-reel silent comedies in the 1910s to feature-length silent comedies in the 1920s—*The Gold Rush* (1925) and *The Circus* (1928) are two notable examples—Chaplin earned the luxury of working slowly and painstakingly, creating comic pantomime narratives that satisfied huge audiences both at home and abroad.

Yet the coming of sound and the onset of the Great Depression posed significant challenges to Chaplin, and his 1936 film, *Modern Times,* stands as a fascinating work of art and document of cultural history.[1] Much anticipated, *Modern Times* was his first movie since *City Lights* (1931). In that film, released after the American film industry

---

[1]*Modern Times* has continued to enjoy a high reputation. It was among the first group of twenty-five films selected in 1989 by the National Film Preservation Board to be placed on the National Film Registry. It is eighty-first on the American Film Institute's list of the top one hundred films, bunched with two other Chaplin films, *The Gold Rush* (seventy-fourth) and *City Lights* (seventy-sixth). Four Chaplin films appear on the AFI's list of the one hundred funniest American films: *The Gold Rush* (twenty-fifth), *Modern Times* (thirty-third), *The Great Dictator* (thirty-seventh), and *City Lights* (thirty-eighth). When directors were asked in 1992 by *Sight and Sound* to list the top ten movies of all times, *Modern Times* was tied for sixth with Alfred Hitchcock's *Vertigo* (1958) and Francis Ford Coppola's *The Godfather* (1972).

had almost completely converted to talkies, Chaplin did compose a recorded musical score and included a few sound effects, but he used absolutely no dialogue. Filmgoers looked forward to the next Chaplin film for two specific reasons. They wondered whether his endearing persona, the Tramp, would talk. In addition, they were curious if Chaplin would respond in his movie to the turbulence wrought by the Great Depression and, if so, how. The first reason related more centrally to Chaplin's aesthetics, the second to his ideology. This essay examines *Modern Times* as Chaplin's sensitive response to the technology of the talkies and the ideological challenge of the Great Depression.

Talkies and the Depression: Twin Challenges

As the editors of this volume have suggested, we can achieve a richer understanding of movies by paying attention to texts—the films themselves—and their historical contexts. On the one hand, we can examine how a film's narrative, told through the medium of cinematic style, communicates meanings and evokes emotions. We will carry out this close textual analysis in the second half of this essay.[2] On the other hand, because artworks are made at a particular time and place, attention to the historical context—within both the film industry and the broader social, political, economic, and cultural milieu—can help us achieve a denser and richer understanding of them than a pure textual analysis would produce. A film like *Modern Times* encourages this dual attention to both text and context. Through linking *Modern Times* to its industrial and sociohistorical context, the film becomes a fascinating historical document, Chaplin's strategic response to his situation when he began thinking about and making the film in the early 1930s.

As we have suggested, Charlie Chaplin held an unusual—even singular—place in the industrial setting of Hollywood in the early 1930s. Born in London in 1889 to two English music-hall singers, Chaplin endured a difficult childhood after his father, struggling with alcoholism, left the family and his mother lost her singing voice. Forced to fend for himself early on, Chaplin turned to the theater, eventually rising to a successful position as a comic pantomime performer working for one

---

[2]One influential analytical framework for such textual analysis is the neo-Formalist approach presented in Bordwell and Thompson, chs. 2–10.

of Fred Karno's comedy troupes. Karno sometimes sent his acts abroad to play vaudeville houses, and in Chaplin's second North American tour, he was offered $150 a week to work as a comic for Mack Sennett's film company, Keystone. The offer doubled Chaplin's music-hall salary, and he decided to accept, arriving at Keystone in December 1913.[3]

Chaplin's rise to fame and fortune in the movie industry was meteoric. Within a few months after his arrival at Keystone, he had developed his Tramp persona—the character instantly recognizable by his moustache, cane, derby hat, tight coat, baggy pants, and outward-pointing floppy shoes. He had also, in these rough-and-tumble early days of the movie industry, begun to direct his own films, based on stories that he fashioned himself. In 1915, he left Keystone for Essanay, and his two-reel Tramp comedies became so popular that one movie commentator said that the United States was experiencing a case of "Chaplinitis" (McGuirk 85). His popularity with audiences translated into salaries that rose exponentially: Essanay paid him $1,250 per week to make fourteen two-reelers in a year, Mutual shelled out $10,000 per week (plus a $150,000 signing bonus) to make an even dozen two-reelers, and First National Exhibitors Circuit outbid several other contenders in early 1918 by offering Chaplin a cool million to make eight two-reelers with Chaplin bearing the production costs and retaining both creative control and the rights to the films (Maland 9–33).

As he was accumulating this snowballing salary and making a string of popular films, Chaplin made two business decisions that assured him a creative independence almost unheard of in Hollywood during the studio era: he built his own studio in a square block bordering Sunset Boulevard and La Brea Avenue in Hollywood, and he became—with stars Mary Pickford and Douglas Fairbanks and director D. W. Griffith—one of the cofounders of United Artists. The first choice permitted him to work on his films without having a mogul peering over his shoulder. The second guaranteed him a distribution

---

[3]Chaplin tells his own story in *My Autobiography*. For additional discussion of Chaplin's early years, see the definitive biography by David Robinson and another recent biography by Kenneth Lynn, which contains an interesting discussion of the London world in which Chaplin grew up.

company to handle his films. All of Chaplin's films from *A Woman of Paris* in 1923 (after he finally fulfilled his First National contract) through *Limelight* in 1952 were released through United Artists.

From the late 1910s through the early 1930s, Chaplin made the transition to feature-length comedies with *The Kid* (1921), *The Gold Rush* (1925), *The Circus* (1928), and *City Lights* (1931). Through his films he also probably became, via his alter ego Charlie, the most widely recognized figure in the world. In fashioning these films, Chaplin also developed what we could call a "personal genre"—a set of characteristics that audiences came to know, expect, and appreciate. We can distill them into four conventions: (1) a central comic persona, Charlie or the Tramp, with whom audiences could identify; (2) a romance with a woman character whom the Tramp admires; (3) inventive visual comedy rooted in pantomime, sometimes supplemented by scenes evoking pathos in the Tramp; and (4) serious thematic concerns stemming from contrasting moral perspectives, often rooted in the Tramp and the film's antagonist(s). Within this framework, Chaplin also promised something fresh, inventive, and unexpected to his loyal audience.

As he began to contemplate the film that would eventually become *Modern Times,* Chaplin was confronted most centrally with two challenges—the industrial/aesthetic challenge of talking films and the sociohistorical/ideological challenge of the Great Depression. The challenge of sound films predated the Great Depression. The success of two early Warner Bros. sound films—*Don Juan* (1926) and *The Jazz Singer* (1927)—helped encourage the film industry to convert almost completely to talking films by the end of 1930 (Crafton 8–18). As might be expected, many performers and directors who had flourished in the silent era were reluctant to shift to talking pictures. Although Chaplin was attuned to the ways that music could enhance silent-film narratives, he responded as an aesthetic conservative when the film industry was debating the transition to talkies. He told Gilbert Seldes in 1928, "Motion pictures need dialogue as much as Beethoven symphonies need lyrics" (qtd. in Seldes), and when asked early in 1929 what he thought about the talkies, Chaplin told the interviewer: "You can tell 'em I loath them" (qtd. in Hall). And resist the talkies he did in his next film. *City Lights,* released in January 1931, had a synchronized musical score with some sound effects, but no speech. The film, notably famous for its final scene—in which the flower girl, her sight restored, sees Charlie for the first time—proved that Chaplin still had star drawing power. Yet despite the success of *City Lights,* both with critics and at the box office, Crafton argues that the film confirmed Chaplin's "silent-comic genius while symbolically ending the era of silent production" (17).

So as he prepared *Modern Times,* Chaplin again faced the formidable challenge of the talkies, but this time with the era of silent movies long gone. As we shall see in the textual analysis of the film, Chaplin finally did include synchronized speech in his sound track, but the way he did so showed his continued conviction that the arrival of talking pictures was a mixed blessing to the movies he wanted to make.

Besides facing the challenge of the talkies in making *Modern Times,* Chaplin was confronted with a changed political climate, brought on by the stock market crash in October 1929 and the ensuing economic depression. By 1933, nonfarm unemployment had reached 25 percent in the United States, while consumption had plummeted 18 percent, construction by 78 percent, and investment by 98 percent (McElvaine 75). National income had been cut in half, five thousand banks had collapsed, and over nine million savings accounts had evaporated. These numbers had human faces, too: a Washington correspondent covering Congress wrote in his diary in January 1933, "I come home from the hill every night filled with gloom. I see on the streets filthy, ragged, desperate-looking men, such as I have never seen before" (qtd. in Leuchtenberg 18–19, 23; see also Kennedy, esp. chs. 3–4). Even after Roosevelt took office, widespread despair, deprivation, and conflict led to what McElvaine calls "rising unrest" in the country in 1934 and 1935, when Chaplin was scripting and shooting his film (ch. 10).

Shortly after the release of *City Lights,* Chaplin embarked on a world tour for sixteen months. Swarmed by crowds wherever he visited, Chaplin was also energized by discussions with world leaders and artists, often on social and economic affairs. One of the most famous encounters came in Germany with Albert Einstein, who, after Chaplin commented on the international currency crisis, told Chaplin in parting, "you are not a comedian, Charlie, but an economist" (qtd. in Robinson 429). In London he also discussed the relationship between art and propaganda with George Bernard Shaw and the double-edged sword of machinery in the industrial age with Mahat-ma Gandhi (Chaplin 433).

As he returned to California in June 1932 and contemplated his next film, however, Chaplin—like many other creative figures in literature, theater, and the movies—discovered that hard times also affect cultural life. The economic breakdown of the early 1930s had a profound impact on many American artists and intellectuals. One common shift was a weakening of what Malcolm Cowley called the "religion of art" so widespread among American expatriate artists of the 1920s and its replacement with a conviction that art should acknowledge and grapple with the social and political conflicts of the age (113–31). With the devastating effects of the Depression so vividly apparent in the cities where many artists and intellectuals lived, it is no surprise that they found themselves drawn to a more socially conscious art. The Depression resulted in political art like John Dos Passos's *U.S.A.* trilogy, Clifford Odets's play *Waiting for Lefty* and John Steinbeck's *The Grapes of Wrath*. In the movies, it helped revive the social-problem film, which had languished in the 1920s but which generated considerable attention in films like *I am a Fugitive from a Chain Gang* (1932), Fritz Lang's *Fury* (1936), and *Confessions of a Nazi Spy* (1939), among others (Balio 280–98).

This new political climate prompted some movie critics, shaped by the economic and cultural distress of the Depression, to call on filmmakers to acknowledge and engage with the social turmoil of the age in their productions. In his history of American film criticism, Myron Lounsbury writes that two varieties of criticism became more dominant during the 1930s: "social radical" criticism and "modern liberal" criticism (Lounsbury chs. 4–5, 484–86).[4] Although the social radicals were more urgent in imploring filmmakers to treat pressing social concerns in movies from a progressive and realist point of view, both groups praised films that depicted social issues and criticized those that ignored them.

---

[4]The "social radical" criticism, which appeared in such periodicals as *Experimental Cinema, New Theater,* and *New Masses,* more overtly supported radical social change and the role that a mass art like the movies could play in effecting it. The "modern liberal" criticism, appearing in such journals as the *Nation* and the *New Republic,* shared the view of the social radicals that movies played a key role in society and should engage with social issues but supported more gradual social reform.

Chaplin paid attention to some of these critics when he made *Modern Times*. In his autobiography, he describes his state of mind after returning from his world tour and contemplating his next film: "I was depressed by the remark of a young critic who said that *City Lights* was very good, but that it verged on the sentimental, and that in my future films I should try to approximate realism. I found myself agreeing with him" (483). Although it is difficult to say for certain which critic Chaplin was referring to, the two most likely candidates are two social radical critics, Harry Alan Potamkin and Lorenzo Turrent Rozas. Potamkin, writing in November 1932, and Rozas, writing in June 1934, both acknowledged Chaplin as an important film artist but criticized his sentimentality and his failure to treat social issues from a progressive perspective. Both also urged Chaplin to focus on serious social concerns instead of the wish fulfillment of romance and the emotional balm of pathos.

Chaplin's involvements in 1933 and 1934 suggest that he was wrestling with the question of how to make his films more attuned to the times. Besides commenting on social and economic issues in *A Comedian Sees the World*, a memoir of his world tour serialized in *Woman's Home Companion* between September 1933 and January 1934, Chaplin publicly supported and contributed to Upton Sinclair's EPIC (End Poverty in California) gubernatorial campaign during the 1934 elections, which took place as he was finishing his script and starting the shooting.[5] As Chaplin was working on the script between the summer of 1933 and August of 1934, it is apparent that he took to heart Gandhi's skepticism about the machine age, which he encountered on his world tour (Chaplin 344). It seems likely, too, that the events of "Bloody Thursday"—July 5, 1934, six weeks before Chaplin

---

[5]Although a number of creative film personnel supported Sinclair—among them Jimmy Cagney, Nunnally Johnson, Dorothy Parker, and Jean Harlow—studio heads generally opposed Sinclair's campaign with a passion, fearing the effect a Sinclair administration would have on the movie business. When they spread rumors that they would move their base to Florida should Sinclair be elected, Sinclair responded to the press that "They couldn't move out if they wanted to," and if they tried, he added as an aside, he might just have the state go into the business of making movies and maybe even "ask Charlie Chaplin to run that part of the show" (qtd. in Maland 145–46). MGM went so far as to produce anti-Sinclair newsreels, which were shown in theaters shortly before the election and have been credited with helping Republican Frank Merriam win a narrow 250,000-vote victory.

completed his screenplay—had some effect on the script. On that day gunshots killed two people and thirty more were wounded when dockworkers and policemen clashed during a maritime strike in San Francisco. As Kenneth Lynn has suggested, the death of the gamin's father in *Modern Times* seems modeled on this highly publicized conflict (377). Chaplin, the maker of consistently popular films since the 1910s, seemed interested in blending his popular Tramp comedies with more topical social concerns.

Chaplin finished the script in August 1934, and shot the film between October 11, 1934, and August 30, 1935, after which he supervised the editing and scoring, which was finally completed on December 22 (Robinson 465–72). This allowed time for two previews and subsequent adjustments before the February 5, 1936 New York premiere. In the fall of 1935 the film generated some prerelease publicity that Chaplin could have done without. In late July or early August, as shooting was winding down, Chaplin arranged a screening of a rough cut of *Modern Times* for Boris Shumiatsky, the head of the Soviet film industry, who had led a delegation to Hollywood to observe production methods. Shumiatsky had been appointed the Soviet film czar in December 1930, partly to make Soviet production more efficient and Soviet films more entertaining. "A film and its success," he wrote in 1933, "are directly linked to the degree of entertainment in the plot. . . . That is why we are obliged to require our masters to produce works that have strong plots and are organized around a story line" (qtd. in Taylor 194). Where better to learn about entertaining, plot-driven films and efficient production methods than Hollywood?

Precisely what went on between Chaplin and Shumiatsky during and after the screening will likely never be known.[6] On returning to Moscow, however, Shumiatsky wrote an article and gave an interview about the film, both published in *Pravda*. In September 1935, *New Masses* published a translation of the article as: "Charlie Chaplin's New Picture." It primarily describes the opening factory scenes of the

---

[6]Robinson notes (468) that Chaplin and his assistants screened a rough cut of *Modern Times* on July 25, 1935, and discussed a new ending. That may have been the screening Shumiatsky attended, or it may have been a bit later.

film, the scene in which Charlie picks up a red flag and is arrested, as well as the scene of Charlie in jail. Although Shumiatsky's article may have whetted the appetite of the left for the new Chaplin film, it didn't generate much of a stir in the United States.

More troublesome for Chaplin was the interview, some of which was translated in the *Daily Worker* and then picked up by the *New York Times,* which reported in late September that "The last reel of Charles Chaplin's forthcoming picture has been materially affected by a conversation between the producer and B. Z. Shumiatsky, head of the Russian film industry, according to a statement made by the latter in Moscow immediately following his return from his recent visit to Hollywood." It then quotes Shumiatsky, who says that the humor in *Modern Times* "is filled with fearful accusation. It shows the starvation of the unemployed, their lodgings; it unmasks capitalistic rationalization. As the result of chats with us Chaplin decided to remake the ending of his picture" ("Modern Times"). This claim was more troublesome to Chaplin. Although Chaplin probably wouldn't have minded Russian audiences knowing he had treated one of their countrymen courteously—his films generally did well in the Soviet Union, as they did in most countries—he wasn't keen on having American audiences believe that the head apparatchik of the Russian film industry was his script doctor.

Chaplin's response to Shumiatsky's claims, filtered through his trusted aide Alf Reeves, was to publicly deny any Communist influence on *Modern Times.* The front-page headline of Terry Ramsaye's December 7 *Motion Picture Herald* piece—"Chaplin Ridicules Reds' Claim Film Aids 'Cause'"—pretty much sums up Reeves's claims on Chaplin's behalf. The essay quotes some of Shumiatsky's assertions from the *Pravda* interview, as well as Reeves's disclaimer: "The Russian story reads deep, terrible social meanings to sequences that Mr. Chaplin considers funny. I can assure you that this picture is intended as entertainment, and perhaps it might be said, too, that Mr. Chaplin's purpose in making this picture is to make money" (1). Acknowledging that the film will end on a "somewhat more optimistic note than was first designed," Reeves, speaking from first-hand experience, added, "it is not true that anybody can ever tell Mr. Chaplin anything about such matters—he, as you know, has very much his own way and he has his own ideas—always" (2). Chaplin, through Reeves, reasserted his creative control of *Modern Times*.[7] Nevertheless, these claims and counterclaims about the ending of *Modern Times* simply whetted the appetites of American moviegoers who hadn't seen a Chaplin film in five years.

Analysis

Talking about the Depression

In his impressionistic study of Chaplin and his films, Parker Tyler makes an observation that helps us understand the tensions embedded in *Modern Times:*

> Gestures without speech, without sound—this was the fate of the Little Tramp; a fate accepted without protest. Silence was, finally, the supreme armor against the reality of the world. And yet, because a certain professional ego grew strong in Chaplin, the hermetic silence of the Little Tramp became hatefully irksome. (136)

Chaplin was between a rock and a hard place when he made *Modern Times.* On the one hand, he knew that a central appeal of his Tramp character rested in pantomime, not in speech. The Tramp's personality and worldview had emerged in the films through actions, not words.

---

[7]Shumiatsky had claimed that in the ending he saw, after the Tramp is released from jail and goes "through another war," he meets the gamin—now a Red Cross nurse—who refuses to return to him, leaving the Tramp to return "to his old joyless life, a shrunken, bent and solitary man." This description seems based on a misunderstanding. Robinson discusses (462–63) the original script ending, which was shot and discarded. There's no reference to any war, and in it the gamin becomes a nun and visits the Tramp as he's about to be released from the hospital, wishing him well before he goes off alone. In a reverie she separates from her body and circles around him, dancing, but the Tramp can't see the apparition. In the final shots, the nun smiles at her Mother Superior and together they walk back into the hospital. Robinson speculates that Chaplin was both hoping to please Joseph Breen at the Production Code Administration through the religious ending and to surpass the ethereal pathos that concluded *City Lights.* But Chaplin and his staff agreed that the scene didn't work, and they shot the present ending in August 1935, at the very end of shooting.

On the other hand, Chaplin's interactions as an artist with other artists, politicians, and intellectuals on his world tour, as well as the pressures placed on him by socially committed critics, made him want to speak out, to comment on the modern world in his films. To this impulse the Tramp's silence had become "hatefully irksome." It boils down to this: Chaplin knew how to make silent comedies, and he hated the tyranny of speech, but he knew that it would be professionally and financially risky, even suicidal, to turn back the clock and refuse speech entirely. The battle between his hatred of talkies and his desire to be heard lies at the core of *Modern Times*.

A formalist discussion of *Modern Times* reveals that in many ways Chaplin returned to the conventions of his "personal genre" in making this film. The central character, Charlie—called a "factory worker" in the credits—is very much the Tramp of old, in costume, makeup, and demeanor. The female lead is the gamin, played by Paulette Goddard, who would later become Chaplin's third wife. A central strand in the film traces their individual struggles to survive during these hard times and their growing mutual support for one another after they begin to interact. The film contains considerable pantomimic comedy, another convention of Chaplin's genre; one thinks particularly of the opening factory sequence, including the Billows Feeding Machine sequence and Charlie's comic ballet after he has a nervous breakdown, as well his antics in jail after the "nose powder" scene, his blindfolded skating in the department store sequence, and dozens of smaller gestures and movements so common in Chaplin's repertoire. Finally, the film sets up two contrasting moral perspectives, one represented by Charlie and the gamin, two people struggling economically like many others during hard times, the other by a wide range of authority figures, including the factory owner, various policemen, juvenile officials, and various other "respectables," such as the woman who sees the gamin steal a loaf of bread and insists on her arrest. This familiar framework of conventions meant that audiences who knew Chaplin's earlier work would find something to meet their expectations.

The plot is linear, and it starts with Charlie going to work in the factory. The logic of development thereafter follows Charlie as he goes between jail and new jobs throughout much of the film. Folded into this strand is the gamin's story: her struggle to help feed her family—

an unemployed father and two sisters—her father's death, her sisters' move to the custody of juvenile officials, and her own growing relationship with the Tramp.

The plot may be divided into fourteen segments: (1) the opening factory scene, including the Billows Feeding Machine experiment; (2) Charlie's breakdown and comic ballet, ending when he's put in an ambulance; (3) the parade, in which Charlie inadvertently finds himself leading a Communist march, ending in his arrest; (4) our introduction to the gamin and her family; (5) Charlie's first stint in jail; (6) the tragedy—the death of the gamin's father and the gamin's escape as her younger sisters are taken away by juvenile officials; (7) Charlie's release from prison, including his interaction with the minister's wife and his brief shipyard job; (8) the gamin's struggle for food and Charlie's struggles to get back to jail, ending with the couple escaping from the paddy wagon; (9) Charlie and the gamin's dream of a life of plenty; (10) the department store job, including the skating sequence, ending in Charlie's second trip to jail; (11) the couple's new ramshackle home; (12) Charlie's return to factory work, the strike, and his third trip to jail; (13) the couple's new jobs in the café; and (14) the epilogue: on the road.

Within this narrative framework, Chaplin responds to his first challenge—the challenge of the talkies—in an ingenious way. Recall Chaplin's 1928 assertion that movies need talk as much as Beethoven's symphonies need lyrics, but remember, too, that the talkies had completely dominated American movies for over half a decade. As he planned the film, Chaplin realized that he could not ignore dialogue. In fact, at one point he considered making the film a regular talkie. Robinson notes that in November 1934, the month after he had started shooting the film—Chaplin and Goddard made sound tests to prepare for the dialogue he had written for a number of the scenes (466–67).[8] Fortunately (to my mind, at least), Chaplin resisted that temptation. Instead, he created his first film with recorded speech but made it a film that stands as an outstanding meditation on the ways that speech can inhibit, manipulate, or tyrannize human life, just as, in Chaplin's

---

[8]The CBS/Fox Video laser disc of *Modern Times* includes some of that dialogue on side 4, ch. 18.

view, speech had tyrannized the art of the silent pantomimic comedy that he had done so much to perfect.[9]

Overall, the film has a complex sound track, largely made up of a richly orchestrated score conducted by Alfred Newman and composed by David Raksin, supplemented by sound effects like whistles, sirens, and bells. Spoken language occurs in just four of the film's fourteen sequences—at the very start of the film (sequences 1 and 2), the middle (sequence 7), and near the end (sequence 13). In the first two sequences, where much of the speech occurs, the language we hear is mass-mediated—it's spoken to humans by machines: principally through the factory president's closed-circuit television and the "mechanical salesman's" phonograph used to market the Billows Feeding Machine. Well over a decade before commercial television started to broadcast widely in the United States, the president of the Electro Steel Corporation uses it to speed up the assembly line and spy on his workers. The president can broadcast his image and voice to Mack, the worker who controls the speed of the assembly line. Significantly, the first words of speech in a Chaplin film are the president's order to Mack: "Section five. Speed her up. Four one." He orders greater speed two more times that day, ending by saying, "Section five. Give 'er the limit." With this torrid pace, Charlie falls into the machinery and, in a famous image, begins winding through the gears in a way "unmistakably similar to film being threaded through a projector" (Booker 50). This drives Charlie mad, leading to his comic ballet, which ends when he's driven off in an ambulance. We also hear the president's mass-mediated words when Charlie, on a brief break, leans on a sink and tries to enjoy a smoke; the TV screen on the wall shows the president's face and emits his orders: "Hey. Quit stalling. Get back to work. C'mon." Language, to the president, is the means to prevent rest and to speed up the pace of production-line work.

Mass-mediated language is also used in the first sequence to sell products. The Billows Feeding Machine staff try to peddle their wares on a phonograph with its "mechanical salesman." In the longest stretch of speech in the whole film, the salesman delivers the pitch: "Don't

---

[9]One of the best essays on the self-reflexiveness of *Modern Times*—looking at the film as Chaplin's often subtle critique of talking films—is Garret Stewart's "Modern Hard Times."

stop for lunch. Be ahead of your competitor. The Billows Feeding Machine will eliminate the lunch hour, increase your production, and decrease your overhead." The speech also gilds the machine by trumpeting such features as the "counter-shaft, double-action corn feeder with synchromesh transmission, which allows you to shift from high to low gear with the mere tip of the tongue." The mechanical salesman concludes by saying that "actions speak louder than words"—lines that Chaplin, the talented performer and director of pantomime, would agree with wholeheartedly. The comically disastrous trial run of the feeding machine, with Charlie as the unfortunate guinea pig, ends with the president's decision, not in recorded and synchronized speech but on a title card: "It's no good. It isn't practical."

In sequence 7, speech comes through another device: the radio. We first hear a brief local news item that the prisoner "who recently thwarted the city jail break" will be granted a pardon by the warden. Here speech provides narrative exposition and directs a character: the warden hears the news report and orders that Charlie be brought to his office. As he's being summoned, a minister and his wife arrive in the office. The minister goes off to visit a prisoner, leaving his wife and Charlie to sit on a bench and sip tea. When both suffer with gurgling stomachs after doing so, Charlie turns on the radio to disguise the sounds. When the first words are "If you are suffering from gastritis," Charlie lunges to turn off the radio before it can go further. Here speech again tries to sell something, which Chaplin suggests is often the case in modern times.

In the café scene we hear speech through music, and Chaplin makes a final, clever defense of pantomime and critique of talkies. Here—for the only time—speech is not mass-mediated: we first hear a group of waiters sing a fatuous song, "In the Evening by the Moonlight," most of which is accompanied by images of Charlie in the next room practicing *his* song with the gamin. As the song ends, we hear sounds of disapproval from the audience. When Charlie takes his turn, he loses the cuffs on which the gamin has written his lyrics. Unable to remember them, he sings the song in gibberish that sounds like a blend of Romance languages; however, he accompanies the story of two lovers with pantomime that is both funny and entirely satisfying. Chaplin's brilliant performance and his nonsensical language constitute the period to the film's statement on language: too often in the modern world, particularly in the movies, speech is tyrannical, manipulative, or bland. Charlie proves, as the mechanical salesman contended, that actions *do* speak louder than words.

If Chaplin used speech in *Modern Times* only to critique it, he also responded to critics calling for greater social realism. Robinson says that the original working title of the film was *Commonwealth*. Chaplin then used the title *The Masses* during some of the production stage, before releasing the film as *Modern Times*.[10] This seems significant: the first title suggests a concern about society, but using a term associated more with the United Kingdom, as in "the British commonwealth." The second, with its link to *New Masses*, then a popular radical magazine, was more politically charged. The release title promises a connection to current society but tempers any more overt leftist connotation.

In making the film Chaplin did engage with current social reality within the framework of his "personal genre"—the aesthetic contract he had established with viewers through his previous comic features. One convention of Chaplin's personal genre was the contrast between two opposing moral perspectives, and in *Modern Times* Chaplin developed that theme in the conflict between the desires of two marginalized characters—Charlie and the gamin—and the forces of society that make it difficult for them to make ends meet. By setting up this basic contrast, the film evinces sympathy for the have-nots of society, particularly their dreams of getting by, and hostility for the haves in society who desire profit and control of others at whatever cost.

The film opens with a shot of a clock nearing six o'clock, after which, following the credits, these words appear: "A story of industry, of individual enterprise—humanity crusading in the pursuit of happiness." The phrase is ambiguous: "industry" can refer to either a sector of the economy or a personal trait; "humanity" suggests a link to all

---

[10]Robinson discusses this early version of the screenplay (462). Although Chaplin would later deny that the film's working title was ever *The Masses*, both the CBS/Fox laser disc and the Image Entertainment DVD of *Modern Times* reproduce the first page of a script using that title. It's worth mentioning that the leading Communist Party magazine in the United States at this time was *New Masses*. Its forerunner, *The Masses*, was for a time edited by Chaplin's friend Max Eastman.

people; and "the pursuit of happiness" may well bring to mind for American viewers the two words that precede that phrase in the Declaration of Independence: "life" and "liberty." We're not sure whether the film is going to be a defense of collective effort or of individualism.

The film's next two shots suggest its direction. They constitute what Sergei Eisenstein, whom Chaplin met in the early 1930s (Manvell 180–82), would have called an "intellectual montage": two shots that create a third meaning through their juxtaposition. The first is a high-angle long shot of a flock of sheep moving forward. Chaplin then dissolves to a similarly framed high-angle long shot of workers emerging from a subway stop on the way to work. The shots suggest workers being treated like animals. To those who know the herd mentality of sheep, they may also suggest that workers behave as a herd, lacking individual discernment. But one more small detail may be even more telling. In the middle of the flock of white sheep is a black sheep. Although *Modern Times* shows general sympathy for the dilemmas of workers in the modern age, its focus is more centrally on one worker, Charlie, and the way his experiences and desires develop in the film, increasingly in relationship to another black sheep, the gamin.

The film's first and perhaps most pointed critique is of the factory president in the first two sequences. We have already seen how he uses language to hasten production, driving his workers mad from the strain, and to spy on workers during their breaks. Yet when we first see him he's working on a puzzle on his office desk, and then reading the funny papers. In the world of this film, his employees work; he doesn't. Yet he pushes them at a brutal pace that he sets without regard to their health and well-being. At a time when wealthy industrialists were often targets of social critique—FDR won a landslide reelection campaign the same year *Modern Times* was released by attacking "economic royalists"—Chaplin's depiction of the factory president caught the temper of the times.

Critics had called on Chaplin to work more social realism into his film, and he did so in *Modern Times.* At various points in the film we see factories closed because of the Depression; unemployed workers marching on the streets; crowds scuffling with police, leading to the death of the gamin's father; the gamin scrounging for food and firewood to keep the family going; one of Charlie's unemployed coworkers driven to burglary because of his hunger; and headlines announcing strikes, riots, and fights in breadlines, to name just a few examples. The film also draws a stark contrast between the haves— those who can purchase the luxury items in the department store— and the have-nots. Besides the more general social disorder and inequality, Chaplin sometimes highlights his empathy for the victims of the Depression, as when in sequence 4 the gamin's father is introduced as "one of the unemployed." Chaplin gives the gamin's father a medium close-up; when he runs his hand through his hair, then rests his forehead on his palm, he's the picture of dejection. It's no wonder that in sequence 7, Charlie seems completely content in jail: with his picture of Lincoln and a "Home Sweet Home" needlepoint on his wall, three square meals, and secure protection from the social disorder on the streets, Charlie seems satisfied with his place. By sequence 8, he even tries hard to get returned to jail, only giving up that desire when the gamin shows him kindness and companionship. This overt social realism amidst the satire and pantomime pleased most leftist reviewers. The *New Masses* reviewer, for example, addressed his readers: "If you had fears, prepare to shed them; Charlie Chaplin is on the side of the angels. . . . I came away stunned at the thought that such a film had been made and was being distributed. . . . To anyone who has studied the set-up, financial and ideological, of Hollywood, *Modern Times* is not so much a fine picture as an historical event" (Crichton).

However, despite its critique of the wealthy, sympathy for the have-nots, and references to the social realities of the Depression, *Modern Times* may soften the critique a bit through the Tramp-gamin subplot. As the relationship between Charlie and the gamin develops, we get the feeling that Charlie and the gamin have basic desires: companionship, food, and shelter. It's true that their dream of a prosperous middle-class home life in sequence 9 contrasts starkly with the reality of their disintegrating shack in sequence 11. But they are happy with it. They decide to keep trying together. Following the ups and downs in the factory and café sequences, the couple must leave the city entirely.

In the final scene, with "Smile" playing on the sound track, the gamin, weeping, asks in a title, "What's the use of trying?" to which Charlie—ever resilient—replies: "Buck up—never say die. We'll get along!" Lip-readers see the gamin's response: "you betcha—c'mon, let's go!" We see the couple smile; then, holding hands in long shot, they walk away from the camera toward the mountains at dawn on a sunny day, away from the turmoil of the city. On the one hand, they may seem like Huck Finn lighting out for the territory at the end of Twain's novel, fleeing civilization for a simpler, natural world. On the other, they're going off together, affirming their companionship and a conventionally optimistic conviction to keep trying. Following Charlie's isolation at the end of *The Circus* and the magnificently open ending of *City Lights*, Chaplin decides on a closed ending in *Modern Times*, one that affirms community, albeit a tiny community of two. This may be a happy ending. It may be an escape hatch. Yet this sentimental optimism is balanced by a sense that none of the problems depicted in the film—a brutal assembly-line work pace, economic inequality, poverty, hunger, unemployment—is solved by the film's resolution.

Conclusion

Modern Times did quite well at the box office: it was among the ten highest-grossing films of 1936 (Balio 405). The film was also widely and generally enthusiastically reviewed, with the left approving of its social realism (see Crichton's comments above) and more conventional reviewers praising the film's entertainment values (Maland 155–58). Yet a few critics demurred. Otis Ferguson, remarking on its old-fashioned look and its refusal to capitulate entirely to the talkies, groused in the *New Republic*, "*Modern Times* is about the last thing they should have called the Chaplin picture" (48). And economically, Chaplin's desire to blend his Tramp comedies with social realism did not fully succeed: *The Gold Rush*, for example, grossed nearly a million dollars more than *Modern Times* domestically, placing the latter in the unusual situation, for Chaplin, of having to wait for foreign rentals to turn a profit. In part because of the box-office results, Chaplin's next film, *The Great Dictator* (1940), abandoned the Tramp and his "hatefully irksome" silence for conventional dialogue.

Looked at from the perspective of the new millennium, *Modern Times* can best be remembered as Chaplin's aesthetic and ideological response to his situation in the mid-1930s. Refusing to capitulate fully to talking films, he nonetheless used speech in a self-reflexively ingenious way, condemning the way that language can be used to manipulate and oppress people. Because of his relative creative independence,

Chaplin was also free to respond to critics who urged him to temper his sentimentality with more overt social realism in his movies. Embracing the era's sympathy for industrial workers and skepticism about the motives of factory managers, *Modern Times* also captures within the framework of Chaplin's "personal genre" some of the social turbulence and anxieties of American culture in its era. As a cultural artifact of the mid-Depression years, made by one of the cinema's greatest *auteurs* and performers, it has earned a significant spot in the canon of American film comedy.

Credits

United States, 1936, Chaplin—United Artists

Director, Producer, Screenplay, and Music: Charlie Chaplin
Cinematography: Roland Totheroh and Ira Morgan
Assistant Directors: Carter De Haven and Henry Bergman
Musical Director: Alfred Newman
Music Arrangers: Edward Powell and David Raksin
Art Directors: Charles D. Hall and Russell Spencer

CAST:

A factory worker	Charles Chaplin
The gamin	Paulette Goddard
Café owner	Henry Bergman
Big Bill	Stanley J. Sanford
Mechanic	Chester Conklin
Burglar	Hank Mann
Burglar	Louis Natheaux
Company boss	Allan Garcia
Foreman	Sam Stein

Bibliography

Balio, Tino. *Grand Design: Hollywood as a Modern Business Enterprise, 1930–1939.* New York: Scribner's, 1993.
Booker, Keith. *Film and the American Left: A Research Guide.* Westport: Greenwood, 1999.
Bordwell, David, and Kristin Thompson. *Film Art.* 6th ed. New York: McGraw, 2001.
Chaplin, Charles. *My Autobiography.* New York: Simon, 1964.
Cowley, Malcolm. *Exile's Return.* New York: Viking, 1951.

Crafton, Donald. *The Talkies: American Cinema's Transition to Sound, 1926–1931.* New York: Scribner's, 1997.

Crichton, Kyle. "Chaplin in *Modern Times.*" *New Masses* 18 Feb. 1936: 29–30.

Ferguson, Otis. *"Modern Times." New Republic* 18 Feb. 1936: 48.

Flom, Eric L. *Chaplin in the Sound Era.* Jefferson, NC: McFarland, 1997.

Hall, Gladys. "Charlie Chaplin Attacks the Talkies." *Motion Picture* 37 (1929): 29.

Kennedy, David M. *Freedom from Fear: The American People in Depression and War, 1929–1945.* New York: Oxford UP, 1999.

Leuchtenberg, William E. *Franklin D. Roosevelt and the New Deal: 1932–1940.* New York: Harper, 1963.

Lounsbury, Myron. *The Origins of American Film Criticism.* New York: Arno, 1973.

Lynn, Kenneth. *Charlie Chaplin and His Times.* New York: Simon, 1997.

Maland, Charles J. *Chaplin and American Culture: The Evolution of a Star Image.* Princeton: Princeton UP, 1989.

Manvell, Roger. *Chaplin.* Boston: Little, 1974.

McElvaine, Robert S. *The Great Depression: America, 1929–1941.* Rev. ed. New York: Random, 1993.

McGuirk, Charles J. "Chaplinitis." *Motion Picture Magazine* 9.6–7 (1915): 85+.

"Modern Times." *New York Times* 29 Sept. 1935: 4.

"Mr. Shumiatsky on American Films." *New York Times* 4 Aug. 1935: 3.

Potamkin, Harry Alan. *The Compound Cinema.* New York: Teachers College P, 1977.

Ramsaye, Terry. "Chaplin Ridicules Reds' Claim Film Aids 'Cause.'" *Motion Picture Herald* 7 Dec. 1935: 1–2.

Robinson, David. *Chaplin: His Life and His Art.* New York: McGraw, 1985.

Rozas, Lorenzo Turrent. "Charlie Chaplin's Decline." *Living Age* 396 (1934): 319–23.

Seldes, Gilbert. "The Movies Commit Suicide." *Harper's* Nov. 1928: 711.

Shumiatsky, Boris. "Charlie Chaplin's New Picture." *New Masses* 24 Sept. 1935: 29–30.

Stewart, Garret. "Modern Hard Times: Chaplin and the Cinema of Self-Reflexiveness." *Critical Inquiry* 3 (1976): 295–315.

Taylor, Richard. "Ideology as Mass Entertainment: Boris Shumyatsky and Soviet Cinema in the 1930s." *Inside the Film Factory: New Approaches to the Russian and Soviet Cinema.* Ed. Richard Taylor and Ian Christie. London: Routledge, 1991. 193–216.

Tyler, Parker. *Chaplin: Last of the Clowns.* New York: Horizon, 1972.

Osaka Elegy (1936)

JOANNE BERNARDI

Revisiting 1930s Mizoguchi

Context

Mizoguchi Kenji's *Osaka Elegy* (*Naniwa erejii*, 1936) marked a critical turning point in the second decade of the director's career, but its imprint on our conception of 1930s Japanese cinema underscores its significance as much more.[1] When such terms still had critical currency, "Japan's first Golden Age" was the label given to the period this film helped define, but in hindsight this was a hastily devised response to the "discovery," through an increasing number of revivals and retrospectives, of works that predated the international film festival winners of the 1950s, beginning with Kurosawa Akira's *Rashomon* (1950). Scholarship in the last twenty years has led to fresh perspectives on how we think about Japanese cinema, making it easier to comprehend in a more nuanced cultural and historical context. The recuperation of previously neglected fragments of Japanese film history has also uncovered films and working styles beyond those attributed to Mizoguchi (1898–1956), Ozu Yasujiro (1903–1963), and Kurosawa Akira (1910–1998). These three directors were transnationally confirmed as "Japan's major directors" against the backdrop of festival awards in the 1950s and the entrenchment of *auteur* studies, with its emphasis on the authorial position of the film director. At the time of this first international recognition of Mizoguchi's work, critique of his films was concerned more with the director as an individual and an artist than with a historically specific appreciation of his films. Subsequent research has helped fill gaps in our understanding of both Japan and the film world in which these films were made. More than ever before,

---

[1] The original title uses the word *Naniwa,* an old name for Osaka, and the title is also translated into English as *Naniwa Elegy.*

Osaka Elegy can be appreciated as a representative example of prewar cinema for reasons beyond its association with a major director. To the extent that space allows, this essay revisits *Osaka Elegy* in the context of recent film scholarship and the landscape of Japanese cinema, culture, and society in the 1930s.

In "Reconstructing Japanese Film," Donald Kirihara focuses on Japanese cinema in drawing attention to the complex negotiations between culture, film practice, and film viewing. His reflections on the subject counter the revisionist scholarship of Noël Burch (*To the Distant Observer: Form and Meaning in Japanese Cinema*, 1979), which despite its inconsistencies engendered unprecedented attention toward Japanese cinema of the 1920s and 1930s. Kirihara ponders Donald Richie's assertion that Mizoguchi's films represent, for many Western viewers, what Japanese films are supposed to look like and identifies three "overlapping assumptions" used by film historians "to explain what makes a Japanese film Japanese" (501, 505). All three of these assumptions revolve around a concept of "difference": Japanese film is different because it is isolated; there is a different aesthetic temperament involved in film production (and consumption); and Japanese culture is a non-Western culture (501–3). The last assumption (the first is generally acknowledged to be ungrounded, and the usefulness of the second is questionable) is the springboard for Burch's approach in identifying what he sees as a unique dynamic between Japanese cinema and its cultural heritage. This entails a comparison between Japanese cinema in the context of the Japanese traditional arts and a lump sum of film practice that Burch calls "the Institutional Mode of Representation," or IMR (filmmaking as it developed in the United States and Europe between 1907 and 1928). This critical framework essentially pits the virtues of the traditional culture of the East against (a hegemony of film style originating in) the West. For better or for worse, defining Japanese cinema in relation to dominant film practices has been, as Kirihara puts it, one of Burch's "enduring points" (509). Debate over whether such an approach is feasible, helpful, or even appropriate has been a pivotal issue in studies of silent and early sound Japanese cinema ever since.

How is this historiographical point relevant to understanding *Osaka Elegy* in the context of the specific historical and cultural moment at which it appeared? Burch makes value judgments according to distinctions between a cinema aligned with Japan's historical cultural heritage and a cinema characterized by the "classical" Hollywood-dominant mode of representation. This framework readily promotes an antithetical, oppositional East-West critical construct in which, at its most simplistic, "East" represents "old" in a positive sense and "West" becomes conflated with a negative sense of "new." But as Frieda Freiberg points out, Burch's use of Japan's cultural heritage as central to his rationale is inconsistent, because ultimately his formal analyses overshadow the (often shaky) references to culture (7). For Burch, *Osaka Elegy* is a disappointment, "a prefiguration of Mizoguchi's post-war decline" because of the degree to which it follows "Western codes of editing." He concludes that here "Mizoguchi seemed to be hesitating not between originality and conformity—the classic Western choice—but rather between East and West, in this era the crucial choice facing the Japanese" (224).

Kirihara's own study of *Osaka Elegy* (in *Patterns of Time: Mizoguchi and the 1930s*, 1992) complements David Bordwell's interpretation of 1930s Japanese cinema as the product of a "fruitful *commingling* of international film styles with contemporary Japanese impulses" (28; italics mine). This approach comprehends 1930s Japanese cinema as a distinct style "best understood as a transformation of norms of Western decoupage" (Bordwell 5). It also enables a perception of Japanese film during this period as the product of a national culture that, however government policy might swing to the right, knows a thing or two about being cosmopolitan. As a highly self-conscious culture, it is nevertheless a fluid entity open to continuous "tactical redefinition" (16). Any "East-West" problematic involved here is not automatically a clash between two cultural extremes. This way of thinking acknowledges that, in terms of film practice, assimilation or adaptation does not necessarily preclude innovation or the cultivation of a palpable style that is varied, dynamic, highly expressive, and "Japanese."

As a depiction of a woman's self-assertiveness and agency undermined by social and cultural forces beyond her control, *Osaka Elegy* belongs to a Japan and a meaning of "Japaneseness" that is in constant, complex flux, not always the result of a clear-cut East-West dilemma. It follows that Bordwell's and Kirihara's critical framework, by allowing for a more historically specific cultural context for 1930s film, would better facilitate comprehension of the actual climate of the time. But is this context specific enough? This is the challenge that Mitsuyo Wada-Marciano takes up in her detailed examination of the 1920s and 1930s silent and early talkie films produced by the Shochiku Kamata studio.

Conventionally, the Shochiku Kamata contemporary drama film (*gendai-geki*) is described as having been strongly influenced by Hollywood, hence its routine characterization as, aesthetically, the polar opposite of films of Shochiku's rival, Nikkatsu studios. Nikkatsu was first in championing the *shinpa* film, a form of contemporary drama film that grew from the Japanese *shinpa* ("new school") theater. By 1908, when the *shinpa* film became popular, *shinpa* itself was synonymous with a distinctive formula of melodrama. Mizoguchi's career began at Nikkatsu, and *shinpa* drama is regarded as an early influence on his work. The Nikkatsu *shinpa* film's monopoly on the domestic market throughout the 1910s was a prime motivation in the 1920 establishment of the Shochiku film studio (in its first location, Kamata, on the western outskirts of Tokyo), which professed to follow Hollywood as a model. Wada-Marciano argues against this version of Japanese film history because of its resemblance to a triumphal modernization narrative in which the "modern" (new and Western-influenced) Shochiku film usurps, if not completely vanquishes, the popular, more "traditional" (old and domestically bred) Nikkatsu *shinpa* film. This conflation of "modernized" with "progressive," coupled with the lack of extant *shinpa* films that might serve as a tangible reference, reduces the *shinpa* film to a trivialized, even villainized cipher. The *shinpa* film remains well out of our reach, and by rendering this part of the equation opaque, we effectively erase what was surely a defining ingredient in the evolution of Japanese contemporary drama on-screen. Wada-Marciano reminds us that with *shinpa* out of the picture, so too are all traces of the cultural, social, and historical complexity from which it, in turn, evolved (7, 76).

Wada-Marciano advocates for less focus on the influence of a dominant IMR or classical Hollywood style in order to avoid glossing over, generalizing, or downplaying other key influences on Japanese cinema. She proposes focusing instead on how the Japanese cultural system might have informed the process of stylistic fusion and differentiation that produced a modern Japanese cinema (3–4, 96). A narrative of Japanese film history that relies on a Hollywood-dominant style as its point of departure is undeniably of limited use if it is no more than an attempt to define the "East" as that place "where one ends up when starting from the geographical West" (Harootunian 26). But has that ever been the sole intention? In identifying commingled film styles, Kirihara's and Bordwell's research maintains a relative focus on Hollywood. This might not be the only approach, but that doesn't deny its usefulness as *one* approach (as Wada-Marciano also allows), presumably more appropriate in some cases than in others. This essay's working premise is that in polishing the finer points of historiography, no single historical frame suffices (Klinger 107–15, 127–28).

The Film World in the 1930s

From the moment it opened in May 1936, *Osaka Elegy* received critical praise as a groundbreaking work of "realism" or even "social realism." Iijima Tadashi recalls writing at the time that although he found *Osaka Elegy*'s continuity, editing, and acting poor, in his opinion the film was a "masterpiece" because of its unprecedented treatment of contemporary social conditions (*Nihon eigashi* 222–23). It is well known that Mizoguchi intended the film to signal a departure from a run of Meiji period (1867–1912) films that had become progressively unsuccessful, but this was not the first time he ventured away from material generically identifiable with his own Nikkatsu *shinpa* roots. By 1936, he had already made over sixty films in a variety of forms, including the short-lived "tendency film" (*keiko eiga*), and the "proletarian film" (*puroretaria eiga*). In fact, the author of the story that inspired *Osaka Elegy*, Okada Saburo, had earlier contributed to the making of Mizoguchi's 1929 tendency film, *Metropolitan Symphony* (*Tokai kokyogaku*). "Tendency film" was the term used to refer to narrative feature films distinguished by varying degrees of leftist political expression. They had already run their course by 1936, having peaked in commercial popularity around 1929–30. In spite of (or perhaps because of) their lack of any firm ideological base, they had an impact on subsequent films that, like *Osaka Elegy*, could be seen as taking a critical view of the existing social order.

The production of *Osaka Elegy* took place in a political climate that was unstable to say the least. Tokyo was still technically under martial law as a result of an attempted coup d'état by a group of army officers that resulted in the deaths of several political figures and a temporary seizure of the city center. The film industry was already heading toward its eventual, full-fledged promotion of imperialist military campaigns to plant Japanese flags throughout Asia. By 1937, foreign journalists in Tokyo were frequently making note of the Japanese government's readiness to exploit the educational and propaganda value of film, citing as examples titles like *High Seas of the Pacific* and *Death in Action*. *Osaka Elegy* squeaked by the censors, but not without extra footwork by Mizoguchi and his assistant director, who were summoned to Tokyo for questioning. Conceivably, their arguments on the film's behalf were bolstered by its open ending, which accommodated a wide spectrum of ideological interpretation. Another possibility is that Mizoguchi and his screenwriter, Yoda Yoshikata (1909–1991), chose their agendas carefully. *Osaka Elegy* condemns the male capitalist elite and the patriarchal family order (beyond its general depiction of men as either unreliable or abusive), but for a brief moment at the beginning of the protagonist Ayako's interrogation the police are almost uncharacteristically sympathetic.

By mid-decade, the 1930s also had brought significant changes to Japanese film production and exhibition. The separation of motion-picture theaters into those screening imported films and those specializing in Japanese films (standard practice during the silent period) was no longer the norm. The popularity of live, in-theater narration by *benshi* (silent film narrators), another industry standard during the silent period, had slowed Japan's transition to sound, resulting in a surge in foreign imports in the first half of the decade. In 1935, the biggest U.S. box-office releases in Japan included Paramount's *The Lives of a Bengal Lancer,* Metro's *Public Hero #1,* and RKO Radio's *The Son of Kong* (1933). Gary Cooper, Harold Lloyd, and James Cagney topped the list of U.S. box-office stars in Japan, followed by names like William Powell, Shirley Temple, and the team of Ginger Rogers and Fred Astaire. Hollywood movie stars were being credited with inspiring a whole new generation of Japanese women. Despite the popularity of imports, domestic production peaked as well. Most major studio (Shochiku and Nikkatsu) pictures in 1935 were sound productions, and by January 1936, Shochiku had moved from Kamata to new sound facilities in Ofuna, also on the outskirts of Tokyo. By this point, over 80 percent of Japanese theaters were equipped for sound.

Japan's position in the international community was also tenuous, despite the 1936 declaration that it would host the next Olympics, a coup (later called off) in Japan's favor. Although Japan's imperialist agenda was at odds with its bid to be accepted as an international community member, there is evidence that the film industry, newly equipped for sound, was considering crossing national borders. It is unclear how seriously this was pursued. Some film veterans note that they were not at all conscious of the possibility of export at the time, but announcements of plans to set up an export system did appear in the English-language press. Between 1934 and 1937, taglines like "Tokyo's Pics and Plays to Stir Up the Patriots" are interspersed with comments on the high volume of Japanese film production, Japan's desire to counter its large import market, and steps being taken to introduce films overseas. The opening of Naruse Mikio's *Wife! Be Like a Rose!* (*Tsuma yo bara no yo ni*, 1935) at the Filmarte in New York City in 1937 under the title *Kimiko* appears to have been a test run for such prospects. Billed as the first Japanese talking picture shown in the United States and coupled with the "musical travelogue" *Melodies of Japan*, *Kimiko* had been chosen by some Chicago professors as "most representative of the life and literature" of contemporary Japan, according to Burton Crane in the *New York Times*. New York critics panned it anyway, but admittedly were charmed with the central character Kimiko, described in the *Daily News* as an "ultra modern maid of Tokyo" (Cameron), an office worker who meets her boyfriend ("a typical, modern Japanese youth," according to the Filmarte program ["Kimiko"]) on the corner after work. Naruse's film is intentionally lighthearted—Kimiko is equally at ease in a kimono or a smart business suit, pokes fun at her bourgeois uncle, and boasts of a salary almost as high as her boyfriend's—but it shares with *Osaka Elegy* a preoccupation with a distinct phenomenon of the times, the new "modern woman."

Topicality

The singular changes in the contemporary drama film that took place in the 1930s reflected not only contemporary shifts in film and politics, but fluctuating and often paradoxical social and cultural conditions as well. Mizoguchi is attributed with the original idea for *Osaka Elegy*, but he and Yoda both acknowledged Okada Saburo's contemporaneous short story "Mieko," which was published in the literary journal *Shincho* in September 1935.[2] "Mieko" was recommended to Mizoguchi by an assistant, who anticipated the story of a young woman's individual emotional and material well-being compromised by the economic needs of her parents as being compatible with the director's interests. In a roundtable discussion in January 1937, Mizoguchi explained that he pursued "Mieko" because he found the eponymous protagonist so compelling ("Mizoguchi Kenji zadankai" 14). As Yoda described it in a 1985 interview, "women had not been looked at this way before" (20 Apr.). Early in Okada's story, we know that Mieko, a young working girl of Tokyo, is keenly aware of her existence as one person in the crowd "spit out" every morning from Tokyo Station's Yaesu gate, then "swallowed up" when the workday is over (Okada 3–5). Living with and supporting her unemployed and ineffectual father and her mother, she takes action (albeit thwarted) toward living her own life by marrying a young man of her own choice. Such a "free marriage" (*jiyu kekkon*) was the modern alternative of an arranged marriage, which was more of a strategic union of the two families. Together with employment and self-sufficiency, "free marriage" was a defining characteristic of the contemporary phenomenon known as the *moga* (short for *modan gaaru*, or "modern girl").

The term *moga* first appeared in print in the early 1920s. Significantly, its meaning was much debated as it took on different shades of meaning over the years, until being outrun by the exigencies of nationalism. By the mid-1930s, *moga* implied more than a free spirit with bobbed hair and fashionable Western clothes. It also encompassed the working woman, particularly one employed in some unprecedented capacity: an office worker (commonly a receptionist or typist), a telephone operator (like Ayako), or a café or tearoom waitress or other service worker (e.g., "gasoline girls," "bus conductresses," shopgirls, and theater-ticket takers). Broader in meaning than "vamp" or "flapper," it also applied to a woman headed toward self-sufficiency. A 1935 photogravure article in English notes that women's wages at the time varied "according to the education and experience required," but adds that the growing number of women workers proved women

---

[2]Okada Saburo (1890–1954) was both a poet and a writer. A temporary sojourn in Paris had left him with a fascination with the French *conte*, or short story, and he coined the word *konto* for his own similar short stories. He had also contributed source material for Mizoguchi's *Metropolitan Symphony* (*Tokai kokyogaku*, 1929), about a wronged café waitress.

were now "stepping gradually out of [their] traditional role in order to engage in all sorts of breadwinning occupations." In the same breath is the observation that this unprecedented degree of female employment was creating a "serious problem" by supplanting men in many jobs that previously had been unavailable to women ("Women Breadwinners of Japan" 184–85).

The ability to find employment outside the home was the crux of the *moga*'s transgression: this marked her as a social threat inasmuch as she crossed gender and class boundaries. Worse still, the relative autonomy of self-sufficiency also implied an ability to cross moral, political, and ideological boundaries (Silverberg 246, 260–63). A marker for social mobility and changing values, the image of *moga* as consumer complemented new forms of leisure and urban consumption, including Western-style cinemas, cafés, theaters, and department stores. An increasingly conspicuous association between culture, commodities, and individual agency was indeed an important dimension of "modernism" in the 1930s. It is no wonder that the *moga* was already a target for nationalism, as seen in the following excerpt from a late 1935 article entitled "Japanese Woman Faces New Outlook on Life": "In contrast to the culturism which emphasizes individual liberty, the nationalist morality prescribes that individual liberty should be sacrificed for the sake of the nation as a whole. . . . With nationalism being stressed in every field of public life, it is only natural that the women's cultural or emancipation movement on the basis of internationalism has lost its former influence" (Chiba 8–9).

What better city than Osaka in which to stage a drama on the commercialization of Japanese culture? As a commercial, industrial, and manufacturing center, Osaka in 1936 was second only to Tokyo. In tourist guidebooks it became the "Venice of Japan" (because of the number of rivers, canals, and bridges), but was even more often "the city of smoke" or the "Pittsburg [sic]" or "Manchester" of Japan (see *Charm of the East* 38–39; *Present Day Osaka*, intro.; *Pocket Guide to Japan* 104). Its harbor had long ensured the city's status as a hub of industrial trade: the Osaka Iron Works (the type of location the script indicates for the early scene in which Ayako asks her boyfriend for financial aid) was one of a number of shipyards highly active in the mid-1930s. In the *Cinema Yearbook of Japan, 1936–1937*, Iijima Tadashi notes Osaka's "urban tradition of more than a thousand years," describing it as "a city that is given to action." "What is more," he writes, "action here is dominated by the purely commercial tradition of its inhabitants" (20). As early as 1919, guidebooks described the city's inhabitants as "the sharpest and most daring businessmen of Japan" (*Charm of the East* 39). Indeed, the association between Osaka merchants and a preoccupation with financial gain had been eternally memorialized in stories by Ihara Saikaku (1642–1693), one of Mizoguchi's favorite writers. Yoda writes that when he first heard Mizoguchi's idea for *Osaka Elegy,* he thought it would be interesting to write a love scene with dialogue only about money ("Mizoguchi sakuhin" 60).

Mizoguchi's fascination with this sense of commercial, even mercenary vitality was one reason why he relocated the story from Tokyo, conspicuously the location in Okada's story, to Osaka. In general, *Osaka Elegy* offers a glimpse of phenomena that were new to most large cities and their inhabitants anywhere in Japan, but the specificity of its locations makes Osaka immediately identifiable. For example, again in late 1935 we find an article on the new edifice, the concrete *apaato,* or apartment house, that was presently replacing wooden lodging houses. It explains the appeal of apartments as their ability to "accommodate families, each unit having running water, a kitchen, and the necessary plumbing" ("Apartments—Something New in Japan" 58). Mizoguchi later said the apartment Asai procures for Ayako was in fact modeled after one of Osaka's own "semi-deluxe buildings," built in 1931 ("Mizoguchi Kenji zadankai" 24). In the 1930s, department stores, which had catered to the upper classes when they first appeared, were now frequented by a more economically diverse clientele. The Sogo Department Store, where Ayako encounters Nishimura after having quit her job, was considered the most modern of Osaka's seven large department stores in 1936. It had been built just the previous year. A new trend in consumption, the "tearoom craze," is acknowledged in the scene in which Nishimura and Ayako share an intimate conversation in the department store's café. Complex public transportation systems were growing in cities throughout Japan, but in 1936 this was a special source of local pride. Osaka boasted municipal (and private) buses, streetcars, a new subway with plans for an extension, and suburban and interurban electric railways. In Yoda's script, Ayako's family home is located in a lower-class area of Sumiyoshi, halfway between Osaka and the neighboring city of Kobe. At the time, the distance between Osaka and Kobe could be covered by the Hanshin Electric Railway in thirty-five to forty minutes for a fee of 40 sen.

Mizoguchi's and Yoda's generous use of Osaka's neighborhoods, architecture, and other readily recognizable locations is evident in the published version of Yoda's film script. Script and film both open with the neon-lit night sky of the longtime entertainment center of the city, Dotonbori, a mecca of stage and movie theaters, variety halls, cafés, bars, restaurants, and novelty shops. Night dissolves into day. The script then moves, as does the film, to the Asai residence in Doshomachi. This Osaka neighborhood, historically associated with the pharmaceutical business since the early eighteenth century, is the perfect location for the Asai home and the adjacent Asai Pharmaceuticals, Ayako's and Nishimura's place of employment when the film opens. Later, the Bunraku puppet theater, arguably Osaka's prize cultural attraction, is another key ingredient that contributes to the film's topicality.[3] The play that appears in *Osaka Elegy* is "The Village of Nozaki" (*Nozakimura*), specifically, the scene known as "Kyusaku no ba." The encounter onstage between a man's lover and his betrothed mirrors what simultaneously takes place in the theater lobby, as Asai's wife discovers him in the company of Ayako. Finally, the film ends on the Ebisu Bridge, an extension of the Shinsaibashi shopping district just north of Dotonbori. As Ayako turns away from the railing, she begins to walk south, toward Dotonbori, Sennichimae, and the seamier parts of the city, resolutely leaving Asai Pharmaceuticals and her own family home behind.

Conception

After the Great Kanto Earthquake of 1923 leveled Tokyo, Mizoguchi migrated to the western region of Kansai with a Nikkatsu unit, adopting the area as his home. By 1936, he had already left Nikkatsu Kyoto in order to join his friend and associate, the producer Nagata Masaichi, in forming Daiichi Films, also located in Kyoto. Mizoguchi later remarked that conflicting male-female relations was the easiest subject at

---

[3]Bunraku is an art form native to Osaka, originating there as an offshoot of the Kabuki theater.

the time given the increasingly restrictive censorship situation ("Mizoguchi Kenji zadankai" 19). But the motivation for *Osaka Elegy* and its subsequent companion piece set in Kyoto, *Sisters of the Gion* (*Gion no kyodai*, 1936), was also a combination of Mizoguchi's fascination with Kansai culture and his determination to break a pattern of increasingly unfavorably received films. Because Daiichi built a reputation as a producer of period films, *Osaka Elegy* marked a radical change for the company as well.

According to Mizoguchi, Daiichi's financial instability by this point was another factor in choosing "Mieko" and transporting it to Osaka. He later explained that one reason he collaborated with a relatively unknown scriptwriter like Yoda was that the budget at hand was too meager to engage a well-known writer with original material. With a few exceptions (notably Yamada Isuzu and the veteran actress Umemura Yoko as Asai's wife, Sumiko), Mizoguchi also cast local, retired stage actors conversant in the regional dialect as another cost-saving measure ("Mizoguchi Kenji zadankai" 14–16). Takegawa Seiichi (Ayako's father) and Shiganoya Benkei (Asai) are two examples. *Osaka Elegy* also marks the screen debut of Shindo Eitaro (Fujino), a former *shinpa* stage actor who subsequently enjoyed a long alliance with Mizoguchi in a number of memorable roles.

The most conspicuous long-term working relationship launched by *Osaka Elegy* was that of Mizoguchi and Yoda. Illness had forced Yoda to leave Nikkatsu Kyoto, where he had worked since 1930 first as an apprentice with the director Minoru Murata and then as a writer. Yoda literally crawled out of his sickbed in order to visit Mizoguchi and ask him for a job, and he regarded Mizoguchi's answer as decisive in whether or not he would ever return to work as a scriptwriter full time. Yoda had been in the contemporary drama division of Nikkatsu while Mizoguchi worked there and was familiar with his films, although he had not thought seriously of working with him before. He had, however, been deeply impressed by a preview screening of Mizoguchi's *And Yet They Go On* (*Shikamo karera wa yuku*, 1931) as the type of film he himself would like to make (Yoda, *Mizoguchi Kenji* 41–42). There is no known extant print of this film, but a synopsis shares common elements with *Osaka Elegy:* bad experiences at the hands of men harden a young innocent who must work as a café waitress in order to support herself and her mother.

Yoda's ordeal during this first collaboration is famous. Mizoguchi demanded countless rewrites; according to Yoda, the director wasn't satisfied until at least ten versions and two thousand sheets of paper later (Shindo 25–26). Yoda had experience working on over a dozen silent scripts but this was his first time writing for sound, and he was still relatively unknown. *Osaka Elegy*'s limited success (primarily with critics) is attributed to the inadequate publicity it received from its distributor, Shochiku, because of its potentially controversial subject. Even so, publicity material for *Sisters of the Gion* a few months later already advertised Mizoguchi and Yoda as "the famous team from *Osaka Elegy*." What made this first collaboration so remarkable?

Yoda is the source of much commentary on *Osaka Elegy*, and he has made certain points repeatedly. For one, at the time of *Osaka Elegy*, Mizoguchi was apparently interested in *manzai*, a form of popular entertainment consisting of comic dialogue between two characters, usually a dimwit (*boke*) and a bully or "clever guy" (*tsukkomi*). *Manzai* was already being broadcast on radio, but in Osaka it was especially in vogue as a cheap vaudeville (*yose*) act with broad appeal. The Osaka dialect was a requisite of this frequently vulgar entertainment. Mizoguchi and Yoda's preoccupation with *manzai* surfaced in a subsequent collaboration, *The Straits of Love and Hate* (*Aienkyo*, 1937), where it becomes the protagonist's profession, but moments in *Osaka Elegy*'s dialogue carry a hint of clever repartee. Sumiko and Asai's early breakfast banter is a good example, and there are moments when Asai and Dr. Yokoi even seem to be a likely *manzai* pair. The breakfast banter, Asai's misadventure at the Bunraku theater, and the fiasco when Sumiko finds Asai at Ayako's apartment (all scenes featuring the bumbling Dr. Yokoi) are the closest we get to humor. The Osaka dialect has a long association with comic performance, but its unprecedented use in a dramatic context here was striking. Yoda later admitted that Osaka speech did not come as readily to him as his own Kyoto dialect in *Sisters of the Gion*, and he was frequently called to the set to rework dialogue in midscene, using a blackboard to rewrite lines that the actors found awkward (*Mizoguchi Kenji* 53). The result is a sense of verbal compression, concentration, and leanness that becomes even more apparent in comparison to the script.

According to Yoda, Mizoguchi asked for writing that "smelled" of life, and "he was happy when true-to-life human nature came through" (Personal interview, 13 July 1985). This brings us to the issue of *Osaka Elegy's* reputation as a landmark of cinematic realism. It is interesting to note that both in interviews and in print, Yoda remarks that Mizoguchi was more disposed toward naturalism than realism. As Wada-Marciano points out, realism, naturalism, and modernism in Japanese literature, theater, and cinema historically share a complementary and often overlapping relationship (48–57). This tangled history defies a brief summation, but Wada-Marciano's analysis of the hybridity of realism during this period helps clarify Yoda's observation. An important aspect of realism in the arts during the 1930s was that it was able to take on new meanings, each "often irrespective of its original referent" (49). Naturalism had been part of a modern impulse toward realism in Japanese fiction since its introduction as a literary movement in the early 1900s, and the overlap (as opposed to aesthetic conflict) between modernism and realism in 1930s Japan allowed for "the challenge of modernist aesthetics [to be] assimilated within the naturalist tradition" (50). At naturalism's core is the idea of scientific objective truth, and Yoda's frequent references to the raw "crudeness" that Mizoguchi requested of him often precede a description of how he relied on detailed observation in realistically projecting *Osaka Elegy's* mise-en-scène. He later commented on the cultural chaos inherent in the times: "there was so much that was unusual for us. . . . cafés, dance halls . . . in reality, there was everything new . . . lighters, elevators, apartments. . . ." (Personal interview, 18 July 1985). Many of these phenomena give *Osaka Elegy* the zeitgeist of the time.

Mizoguchi retained the same focus on the lower classes in *Osaka Elegy* as he had in his tendency films. Here the focus is specifically the underclass, the social outcasts. Yoda had his own predilection for the lower classes and the dregs of society. Before working in film he had been arrested for distributing leftist propaganda, and at Nikkatsu he continued to be a potential target for interrogation by secret police. In interviews years later, he often named Josef von Sternberg's *The Salvation Hunters* (1925), which opens with a title card dedication "to the derelicts of the earth," as a favorite film during his formative years. Yoda's script for *Osaka Elegy* includes details that communicate the ambience of Osaka's low-end nightlife and new, untidy forms of popular consumption. This was not at the expense of capturing fragments of the everyday. The whistle of the tofu cart when Nishimura visits

Ayako's house is one example of a true-to-life detail that helps create a semblance of daily routine, a technique that Yoda and Mizoguchi developed further in *Sisters of the Gion*. In both films, Yoda and Mizoguchi worked toward achieving audience identification by being as specific and personal as possible.

Mizoguchi's casting of Yamada Isuzu (b. 1917), an Osaka native, as Ayako is another example of this intimate approach. Yamada and Mizoguchi had worked together previously at Daiichi studios and Nikkatsu, and Mizoguchi knew that Yamada had recently married a fellow Daiichi actor against both her father's and her employer's wishes. In addition to this personal crisis, professionally she faced the challenge of maintaining her popularity despite now being married. Yamada remembers this period as a trying time. As if these problems weren't enough, she was also financially supporting her parents, and because they were separated she shouldered responsibility for three households. Mizoguchi questioned her in detail about these aspects of her personal life. Uncovering what Yamada herself describes as a core of loneliness and rebelliousness, scars of a complicated and difficult childhood, was the finishing touch in Mizoguchi's preproduction technique (Yamada 53–57).

Analysis

Construction

Osaka Elegy went into production in December 1935 and was shot in about twenty days. Yoda and Mizoguchi were disappointed in the final title agreed to by the Daiichi producers. "A Woman's Enemy" (*Onna no teki*) had been a working title, and in comparison *Osaka Elegy* seemed too low-key (Yoda, "Mizoguchi sakuhin" 60). Fewer cuts, a fluid camera, frequent ellipses in the narrative, and lean dialogue help to steady the acceleration of dramatic tension, but subdued is hardly a quality that applies to this film. Mizoguchi's contemporaries recognized an emergent stylistic maturity as early as the lost *A Paper Doll's Whisper of Spring* (*Kami ningyo haru no sasayaki*, 1926), and many recall Mizoguchi beginning to experiment with long takes, a major component of his style, in the 1930 *Mistress of a Foreigner* (*Tojin Okichi*). Yoda recalls Mizoguchi already using this "one scene–one cut" style (alternatively called "one scene–one take" or "one scene–one shot" style) when he entered Nikkatsu that year (Personal interview, 1 July 1985). Some of Mizoguchi's other preferences complemented this basic stylistic unit: his use of deep-focus compositions; medium- to long-range shots (close-range camera work is very rare); and a continuously tracking camera, constantly repositioning itself in relation to its object. The camera's often relentless following of a specific character's movements, at a set distance and within the circumscribed *mise-en-scène,* creates a perceptual effect of intensified, even claustrophobic objectivity.

There are as many explanations of the origins of Mizoguchi's stylistic system as there are interpretations of the way in which it functions. The mechanics of the long take are often traced back to one of Mizoguchi's friends, the son of the psychologist Naito Konan. Camera in hand, Naito had experimented with the expressive potential of uninterrupted dramatic action and studied its effects on viewer response and perception (Kishi 601–2). Mizoguchi's early training in Nikkatsu's *shinpa* film tradition, centered more on the concept of stage drama, was surely an influence. Nikkatsu's stage drama affinities, a commonality shared with increasingly popular and influential German and Russian films, also account for *Osaka Elegy's* use of chiaroscuro. Extant works reveal that hard lighting is in fact characteristic of Nikkatsu's contemporary silent and early sound urban dramas. Specific structural features of *Osaka Elegy* have been explained as conscious variations or transformations of classical Hollywood norms; for Kirihara and Bordwell, such transformations are a fundamental characteristic of 1930s Japanese cinema. The use of a 360-degree rule in editing is a key example. Instead of conforming to the Hollywood norm of 180-degree editing, Mizoguchi's camera is, as Kirihara explains, constantly "cutting around and maintain[ing] its distance from conversation." This technique allows character interaction to remain intact instead of being broken up by alternating shot/reverse shots (*Patterns of Time* 105).

In adapting Okada's story, Yoda and Mizoguchi trimmed down the number and variety of Mieko's male relationships but retained the basic premise of a young working woman's attempt to balance a sexual alliance of financial expedience with her own hopes for a desirous "free marriage." "Mieko" begins and ends with the protagonist's feelings of indignation at her parents' feigned ignorance of the harsh reality that provides for their financial well-being. How could they think she was supporting them on her meager salary alone when they knew she was just a small company's "female employee"? In fact, her job is a bonus for a sexual relationship with the company's owner. As the story develops, Mieko's chances to escape a life of disappointment and drudgery by marrying her young male friend begin to look hopeful, but in the end she is tricked into a sexual compromise in exchange for a job for her father. She is forced to relinquish all of her own individual aspirations. Like *Osaka Elegy*'s Ayako, Mieko does not anticipate her final betrayal, in Mieko's case by a (male) family friend.

The extent to which on-screen divergences from Yoda's script emphasize Ayako as the center of our focus is impressive. One way in which this is done is by cutting material that would have created more well-rounded characters. This is especially true for the male characters. The film does not, for example, include a conversation that is in the script between Asai and Dr. Yokoi after breakfast in which the good doctor suggests Asai find a mistress, specifically a "working girl" like a café waitress. Asai scoffs at the idea—not of a mistress, but that he might take up with a cheap waitress. He already has Ayako in mind. In the film this dialogue is replaced by a low-angle shot of a brief verbal exchange between Asai and Fujino after leaving in the direction of a departing Ayako. In addition to preserving the neutrality of Dr. Yokoi's semicomical character, this deletion intensifies the effect of on-screen details that inform us of Asai and Fujino's weak characters: for example, the way they both bully women, bullying either Ayako (as does Fujino) or those in service positions (as do both men). As for Nishimura, a brief scene in the script has him at Asai Pharmaceuticals, distracted by worry over Ayako's absence from work, a small suggestion of his moral fiber. On-screen, Nishimura comes across as so shallow (or dimwitted) that it stretches the limits of our credulity. Ayako's father is more visible in the script, where we see his favorite way to kill time (getting drunk at a local watering hole with fellow members of the "lumpen proletariat"), but this is elided in the film. So, too, is the father's conversation with Asai after he is summoned to Asai's office. Situations that might have sentimentalized Ayako and Asai's relationship, including a remarkable sequence that begins with Asai shopping for groceries at the local market, are also deleted on-screen.

In both the script and the film, Ayako is conspicuously without allies, except for the brief appearance of the sympathetic apartment-house employee, but the contrast between Ayako's and Sumiko's freedom of movement and range of options is more pronounced in the film. In the script, Sumiko's secure position in the hierarchy of power as the biological heir to the family business is re-inscribed by extra scenes and dialogue. Her self-assuredness is communicated on-screen by her mannerisms and comportment (with the exception of her outburst at the theater). At one point her portrayal resembles, in terms of self-possession and agency, that of a man. The elaborate tracking shot of a smiling Sumiko as she leaves breakfast for the adjacent business where she casually flirts with a male employee (Nishimura) is similar to the two prolonged tracking shots of Asai and Nishimura as they each climb Ayako's stairs for a rendezvous.

Actually, after the establishment of the characters and the initial situational setup, there are very few scenes in the film without Ayako. The most conspicuous ones of the few that occur are ones in which her actual location is unknown, immediately after she leaves home for the first time. Just as the transition shots in the narrow alleys of Kyoto form a pattern in *Sisters of the Gion,* the image that links the disparate scenes in *Osaka Elegy* is the very appearance of Ayako.

Conclusion

The final shots of *Osaka Elegy* are the most striking deviations from the script. Mizoguchi embellished Yoda's more muted endings in both *Osaka Elegy* and *Sisters of the Gion.* The end of *Osaka Elegy* follows the script in every detail up to the point where the doctor takes leave of Ayako. Yoda leaves her standing at the bridge railing, but in the film she then walks off, to a surge of background music, in the direction of Dotonbori. We last see her walking toward us, her face filling the screen. According to Yoda, Mizoguchi made the change because he "didn't want to just leave her standing there" (Personal interview, 13 July 1985). Mizoguchi was later criticized for this ending (as well as that of *Sisters of the Gion,* although in the latter case he admitted Yoda's version was probably better) ("Mizoguchi Kenji zadankai" 14). Perhaps his addition was not necessary, but it visually reinforces our desire for an answer to the question we are left asking at the end, that of where Ayako will go.

We have seen how the city of Osaka maintains a palpable presence in this film, but does understanding Ayako's geographic direction tell us everything we want to know? Throughout the film strategically placed visual details comment on Ayako's situation: cutaways to a closed office door; moments stripped of sound; unsettling oblique compositions and low angles. As Ayako works the switchboard at Asai Pharmaceuticals, the article in front of her reads, "Woman Ruined, All for Money," an explicit sign of things to come. In the early office sequence her face is framed along with a single, delicate cyclamen plant, a sharp contrast to her cigarettes, which become a more frequent prop throughout the film. In attire and demeanor, Ayako has switched roles dramatically during the course of the film, so much so that her appearance itself, and the way it is presented, is the best indication of the swiftness and decisiveness with which she falls. By the final scene, we easily see the association between Ayako and the debris floating below her, and she declares herself a delinquent and a social stray. On the other hand, there is something about the way she tugs at her hat and sets off that suggests dogged resiliency. We might be struck with the realization of how much of her future, given her limited options, is out of her control.

Donald Kirihara points out that the film's lack of closure leaves it open to interpretations that could speak to everyone, regardless of their ideological bias. Those on the right could feel justified in their criticism of the "hollow goals of Westernization," seeing the film as a confirmation of the need for cultural reform. For those on the left, the film becomes a critique not only of twentieth-century capitalism, but of the process of reducing human relations to patterns of financial exchange (*Patterns of Time* 35, 38). In either case, the ending suggests a statement with a timelessness and universality above and beyond the individual case of Ayako alone.

Credits

Japan, 1936, Daiichi Eiga Sagano

Director: Mizoguchi Kenji
Producer: Nagata Masaichi
Screenplay: Yoda Yoshikata (based on Okada Saburo's "Mieko")
Cinematography: Miki Minoru
Assistant Director: Takagi Koichi
Editing: Sakane Tatsuko
Music: Takagi Koichi

CAST:

Murai Ayako	Yamada Isuzu
Asai Sonosuke (Asai Pharmaceuticals)	Shiganoya Benkei
Asai's wife, Sumiko	Umemura Yoko
Ayako's father, Junzo	Takegawa Seiichi
Ayako's younger sister Sachiko	Okura Chiyoko
Ayako's elder brother Hiroshi	Asaka Shinpachiro
Nishimura Susumu (Ayako's boyfriend)	Hara Kensaku
Fujino, a stockbroker (Asai's friend)	Shindo Eitaro
Dr. Yokoi	Tamura Kunio
Detective Nishi Goro	Shimura Takashi
Fukuda Mine (apartment maid)	Takizawa Shizuko

Bibliography

"Apartments—Something New in Japan." *Japan Today & Tomorrow, 1935–1936.* Printer and publisher, Araki Riichiro. Osaka: Osaka Mainichi, 1935. 58.

Bernardi, Joanne. "Catching a Film Audience Abroad." *Japan Quarterly* 32.3 (1985): 294–95.

Bordwell, David. "Visual Style in Japanese Cinema, 1925–1945." *Film History* 7.1 (1995): 5–31.

Burch, Noël. *To the Distant Observer: Form and Meaning in the Japanese Cinema.* Berkeley: U of California P, 1979.

Cameron, Kate. "First Made-in-Japan Picture at Filmarte." *Daily News* [New York] 13 Apr., 1937. Billy Rose Theatre Collection File, New York Public Library.

The Charm of the East (Guide to Japan and China). Tokyo: Nippon yusen kaisha, 1919.

Chiba, Kameo. "Japanese Woman Faces New Outlook on Life." *Japan Today & Tomorrow, 1935–1936.* Printer and publisher, Araki Riichiro. Osaka: Osaka Mainichi, 1935. 8–9.

Crane, Burton. "Nippon and the World Film Mart." *New York Times* 4 Apr. 1937: 174.

Freiberg, Frieda. *Women in the Films of Mizoguchi Kenji.* Melbourne: Japanese Study Center, 1981.

"'G-Men' Best B.O. Pic in Japan During '35." *Variety* 11 Mar. 1936: 19.

Harootunian, Harry. *History's Disquiet: Modernity, Cultural Practice, and the Question of Everyday Life.* New York: Columbia UP, 2000.

Iizima [Iijima] Tadashi. "Naniwa Elegy." *Cinema Yearbook of Japan, 1936–1937.* Ed. Iizima et al. Tokyo: Sanseido, 1937. 20.

Iijima Tadashi. *Nihon eigashi.* Vol. 1. Tokyo: Hakusuisha, 1955.

"Japanese War Shows." *Variety* 18 Aug. 1937: 25.

"Kimiko." Screening premiere program. Filmarte Theater, New York City, 12 Apr. 1937.

Kirihara, Donald. *Patterns of Time: Mizoguchi and the 1930s.* Madison: U of Wisconsin P, 1992.

———. "Reconstructing Japanese Film." *Post Theory: Reconstructing Film Studies.* Ed. David Bordwell and Noël Carroll. Madison: U of Wisconsin P, 1996. 501–19.

Kishi Matsuo. *Jinbutsu Nihon eigashi*. Tokyo: Dabbidosha, 1970.

Klinger, Barbara. "Film History Terminable and Interminable: Recovering the Past in Reception Studies." *Screen* 38.2 (1997): 107–28.

Menzies, Jackie, ed. *Modern Boy Modern Girl: Modernity in Japanese Art, 1910–1935*. Sydney: Art Gallery of New South Wales, 1998.

"Mizoguchi Kenji zadankai." Roundtable discussion with Kenji Mizoguchi. *Kinema junpo* 1 Oct. 1938. Rpt. in *Mizoguchi Kenji shusei*. Ed. Nishida Nobuyoshi. Tokyo: Kinema junposha, 1991. 14–30.

"Movie-Mad Japan Outdoes America." *New York World Telegram* 10 Apr. 1937. Billy Rose Theatre Collection File, New York Public Library.

"New Jap Prod. for World Market." *Variety* 2 Aug. 1937: 12.

Okada Saburo. "Mieko." *Shincho* Sept. 1935: 2–25.

Pocket Guide to Japan. Tokyo: Board of Tourist Industry, Japanese Government Railways, 1939.

Present Day Osaka. Osaka: Osaka Municipality, 1919.

Richie, Donald. "Kenji Mizoguchi." *Cinema: A Critical Dictionary*. Vol. 2. Ed. Richard Roud. New York: Viking, 1980. 697.

Saso Tsutomu, Nishida Nobuyoshi, eds. *Eiga dokubon Mizoguchi Kenji*. Tokyo: Firumuaatosha (Film Art), 1997.

Sato Tadao. *Mizoguchi Kenji no sekai*. Tokyo: Chikuma shobo, 1982.

Shindo Kaneto. *Aru eiga kantoku no shogai Mizoguchi Kenji no kiroku*. Tokyo: Eijinsha, 1975.

Silverberg, Miriam. "The Modern Girl as Militant." *Recreating Japanese Women, 1600–1945*. Ed. Gail Lee Bernstein. Berkeley: U of California P, 1991. 239–66.

"The Tea-Room Craze in Tokyo." *Japan in Pictures*. Asahigraph Overseas Edition 3.8 (15 Aug. 1935). Tokyo: Asahi shinbunsha. 268.

Uenoda Setsuo. *Japan and Jazz: Sketches and Essays on Japanese City Life*. Tokyo: Taiheiyosha, 1930.

Wada-Marciano, Mitsuyo. "The Production of Modernity in Japanese Cinema: Shochiku Kamata Style in the 1920s and 1930s." Diss. U of Iowa, 2000.

"Women Breadwinners of Japan." *Japan in Pictures*. Asahigraph Overseas Edition 3.6 (15 June 1935). Tokyo: Asahi shinbunsha. 184–85.

Yamada Isuzu. *Eiga to tomo ni*. Kyoto: Sanichi shobo, 1953.

Yamaguchi Takeshi, ed. *Eiga kantoku Mizoguchi Kenji*. Tokyo: Heibonsha, 1998.

Yoda Yoshikata. Personal interviews. Kyoto, Japan. 20 Apr. 1985; 1, 13, 18 July 1985.

———. *Mizoguchi Kenji no hito to geijutsu*. Tokyo: Tabata shoten, 1970.

———. "Mizoguchi sakuhin ni tsuite omoide o kataru." *Jidai eiga* 2.10 (1956): 60–62.

———. "Naniwa hika." *Yoda Yoshikata shinario shu 2*. Tokyo: Eijinsha, 1984. 6–62.

Bringing Up Baby (1938)

S. I. SALAMENSKY

Screwball and the Con of Modern Culture

Context

Howard Hawks's *Bringing Up Baby* (1938) explores the trials and tribulations of a shy, bumbling paleontologist (Cary Grant) detoured from the altar by a forward, zany young socialite (Katharine Hepburn) and her pet leopard. The scientist is gradually drawn to ditch his dull intended for the ravishing heiress in a romp of hectic misadventure.

Bringing Up Baby's madcap plot—a complex series of misunderstandings, antics, pratfalls, and disasters—rapid timing, lavish settings, and sentimental appeal render it a central representative of the screwball comedy genre. The film not only offers spirited romance and quirky humor, but explores wider economic, social, and sexual anxieties at once endemic to modern Western culture and specific to the screwball period.

Screwball and Its Era

The height of the screwball comedy genre lasted roughly from 1934, with Frank Capra's *It Happened One Night,* to 1941, with Preston Sturges's *Sullivan's Travels.* Screwball may have proved too lighthearted and hard-edged for World War II and postwar audiences. It waned as studios began to concentrate on homey, sentimentalist productions aimed at family viewing.

With its chatty, slapstick story lines, lush architectures and landscapes, and fashionable, leisured characters, screwball provided Depression-era American audiences comic relief and escapist pleasure. The speculation-based economy that had led to the nation's economic collapse had destabilized long-held American faith in hard work, thrift, and responsibility as the sources of wealth and cultural power. The once agrarian, then industrial nation increasingly now traded in intangibles. Meanwhile, women's rights were on the rise, along with the divorce rate (May 2). Traditional employments, knowledge, and mores were subject to reexamination.

With changing lifestyles arose anxiety over work, gender, and the family. Screwball characters, unlike their primarily working-class contemporary audiences, are generally unencumbered by such pressures and, as such, free to examine a range of choices in their full complexity. As one critic describes it, screwball "is both a satire of actual social solidity and an indication of possible social fluidity" (Bourget 55). Those more subject to constraint could investigate different, perhaps more desirable—richer, freer, "exotic," more "erotic" (Shumway 389)—manners of living by proxy in the dark of the movie theater, see troubling issues ostensibly resolved in happy endings, and return to the daylight world refreshed.

Screwball broke ground with the advent of synchronized sound, exploiting the new "talkie" form with a vengeance. Films of the genre stage language with a speed, subtlety, and intensity previously reserved for theater, further emphasized through close-ups, reaction shots, and intercutting. The fast-talking trickster figures central to the genre deliver witty dialogue at breakneck pace, achieving discursive feats that intertitled silents did not permit. Screwball comedy represents, in a sense, "the underside of, and compensation for, the action drama" (Haskell 137), and its characters' strengths lie, accordingly, far less in action, kindness, humility, or moral rectitude than in sophistication, articulateness, and finesse.

The male screwball lead is typically an antihero: immoral, amoral, or weak. If ignoble, he appears admirable because handsome and winning. He is generally nonphysical or even quite effete, as compared to "strong, silent" men of deeds. The female lead, reflecting early feminist trends, tends to be headstrong, self-directed, and accomplished while still charming, vulnerable, and appealing. Both, unlike traditional heroes and heroines, are able to laugh at life and themselves. Little is to be taken overearnestly or overseriously. Moral character, as conventionally conceived, holds little weight in the genre. The dependable, law-abiding authority figure, societal pillar, or "straight man" appears a buffoon in this context.

In Hawks's films, particularly, as Michael Wood has observed, elements such as desirability or style create their own kind of ethic. That which is beautiful or successful is presented, in some sense, as morally right, while that which is dull or fails is presented as, in some sense, wrong. The term for the genre—a categorization assigned only retrospectively by critics—is drawn from baseball, denoting an erratic pitch. In screwball, aberrant, even illegal or deviant behavior reigns, as opposed to "playing it straight." Indeed, in a context such as the Depression, in which economics and self-interest appear to trump more traditional human values, dullness and failure have no earthly compensation, while beauty and success are well rewarded. The screwball universe may thus be taken as wistful modern fantasy—or as ironic social commentary.

Background, Making, and Reception

The script of *Bringing Up Baby* was drawn from a *Collier's* magazine story of the same title by the writer Hagar Wilde. It was adapted by Wilde and screenwriter Dudley Nichols, with the gag writer Robert McGowan later adding material. The original story involves a couple in pursuit of an escaped panther. They are engaged, and the situation threatens to divide them. In subsequent script versions, the hero becomes a scientist engaged to someone else, and more—and more elaborate—comic scenarios and characters are added. The fun of the collaboration—and, perhaps of Wilde's and Nichols's affair during it—is evident in notes in script drafts. One note, for instance, regarding a lapse in continuity, reads: "The off-stage noise you hear is two authors being slightly sick because they don't know what Susan and David have been doing until sunset" (qtd. in Mast 5).

When a suitably trained panther could not be located for filming, the animal in question was changed to a leopard (played by Nissa; cast as George, the dog, was *The Awful Truth*'s Asta). Katharine Hepburn was cast as the female lead from the beginning. Cary Grant was chosen over the studio's suggestions: Leslie Howard, Ray Milland, and Fredric March. Gerald Mast surmises that the choice was inspired by Grant's noted comic work in Leo McCarey's *The Awful Truth* (1937) then in production (Mast 7). The director and writers envisioned the film as heavy with vaudevillian shtick. An early draft, for instance, has the lovers start a pie fight. Though the film is wordy, with dialogue echoing already evident visual cues, the initial versions were more so, and included lengthy love dialogues. Hawks shot but then discarded much of this footage as excess, relying on the actors' chemistry and charisma to carry the message. Dialogue and physical business were often improvised, with Hawks's encouragement, on the set.

Gerald Mast describes the tone of the film thus:

> [The] breathlessly rapid chatter not only gives the film's dialogue a spontaneous energy; it also converts articulate patterns into the pure physicality of sound, a kind of verbal music. . . . *Bringing Up Baby* has no musical score whatever. . . . Its music is the breathless chatter of human speech. . . . Uniquely Hawksian about the film is its physicality, whether the physicality of sound and gesture or the building of scenes around concrete props and objects, easily overlooked but as important as the dialogue. . . . For Hawks, this contact with concrete objects anchors a wildly improbable farcical tale in the solid stuff of physical reality. . . . Hawks' shooting style works similarly. [Many shots] are extraordinary in their complicated choreography of movement, space, and time. . . . A single shot tells a complete little story. (9–11)

Hawks, in interviews, was notoriously reticent to discuss his directorial choices, but seems to have worked primarily, as he claimed, on instinct. The film was extensively edited, more for length than for the Production Code censors, who seem to have overlooked the numerous bawdy references and puns in the dialogue as subtle enough to place the onus of dirty-mindedness on viewers.

The film ran far over schedule and budget, but, according to Mast, RKO retained faith in its stars, as well as its director. Grant, whose career as passive male lover—called by Pauline Kael "the most publicly seduced male the world has known" (qtd. in Harvey 298)—had begun with his youthful turn opposite Mae West in *She Done Him Wrong* (1933). He would move after *Bringing Up Baby* to darker, more aggressive roles: the suave, shifty editor in Hawks's *His Girl Friday* (1940), the society rake in George Cukor's *The Philadelphia Story* (1940), the moody, caddish pilot in Hawks's *Only Angels Have Wings* (1939). Hepburn, "whose problem had been that audiences perceived her as cold, lofty, and contemptuous" (Mast 15), tempered the typical Hawks "tough woman" character with absurdist, often slapstick humor, and would draw acclaim from this point forward for patrician, peppery, but finally tender roles, for instance with James Stewart and Grant, again, as a high-strung debutante in *The Philadelphia Story,* or as a career woman with real-life partner Spencer Tracy in George Stevens's *Woman of the Year* (1942) and Cukor's *Adam's Rib* (1949). Both Grant and Hepburn "emerged" after the film as "more valuable commodities" (Mast 15–16) than they had been. Hawks, who had begun his career with silent films, would continue to direct masterful films across all genres—screwball, *noir,* Westerns, musicals, even science fiction and a biblical epic—in Jacques Rivette's words, "fusing [comedy and drama] so that each, rather than damaging the other, seems to underscore their reciprocal relation: the one sharpens the other" (70). However, Hawks would fail to garner a single Oscar nomination for this, or his other finest and most famous films: *Scarface* (1932), *His Girl Friday* (1940), *To Have and Have Not* (1944), *The Big Sleep* (1946), and *Gentlemen Prefer Blondes* (1953). Suffering less from critical "vituperation" than "silence" (McBride 5), Hawks would remain "the least known and least appreciated giant in the American cinema" (Sarris 35).

Upon its release, *Bringing Up Baby* showed poorly at the box office and in the critical eye. As one reviewer typically decried:

> To the Music Hall yesterday came a farce which you can barely hear above the precisely enunciated patter of Miss Katharine Hepburn and the ominous tread of deliberative gags. . . . After the first five minutes . . . we were content to play the game called "the cliché expert goes to the movies" and we are not at all proud to report that we scored 100 percent against . . . Howard Hawks, who . . . produced the quiz. Of course, if you've never been to the movies, *Bringing Up Baby* will all be new to you—a zany-ridden product of the goofy farce school. But who hasn't been to the movies? (Nugent 265)

Hawks himself, in retrospect, found one "fault" with the film from which he "learned an awful lot. . . . There were no normal people in it. Everyone you met was a screwball. Since that time I have learned my lesson and I don't intend ever again to make everyone crazy. . . . As it is they were all way off center" (qtd. in Henderson 311). The film would, however, be recouped by later generations of critics, as well as filmmakers, who would view Hawks as an important *auteur* and discover in his work deeper meanings and stylistic motifs. Philosopher

Stanley Cavell, for instance, reads *Bringing Up Baby* as illustrative of the thought of Shakespeare, Kant, and Emerson (*Pursuits* 111–32). Meanwhile, directorial homages have appeared in Peter Bogdanovich's *What's Up, Doc?* (1972), with Barbra Streisand as a Brooklyn Jewish incarnation of the resolutely Connecticut Anglo-Saxon Hepburn figure, as well as in Jonathan Demme's *Something Wild* (1986); James Foley's *Who's That Girl?* (1987), a Madonna vehicle; and Catherine Corsini's *The New Eve* (1999). *Bringing Up Baby* is a now well-canonized revival film, frequently shown and taught as an exemplar of the genre.

Analysis

The film opens with establishing shots of a large, solid brick edifice resembling the New York Museum of Natural History. Inside Brontosaurus Hall, filled with fossils and artifacts, paleontologist David Huxley perches high atop a scaffold, assembling a dinosaur skeleton. Swathed in a cumbersome lab coat, in the pose of Rodin's sculpture *The Thinker,* he ponders: his great life project is nearly complete, but something doesn't fit. With a colleague and his assistant, Miss Alice Swallow, he awaits the delivery of a final piece from an expedition.

David is set to wed Alice the next day. His fiancée—cheerful but prim in a male-tailored suit and slicked-down coif—reveals herself as alarmingly unromantic:

> ALICE: As soon as we're married, we're coming directly back here and you're going on with your work.
> DAVID: Oh, Alice, gee whiz. . . .
> ALICE: Now, once and for all, David, nothing must interfere with your work.
> DAVID: Oh. . . .
> ALICE: Our marriage must entail no domestic entanglements of any kind. . . .
> DAVID: You mean, you mean . . .
> ALICE: I mean, of any kind, David.
> DAVID: Oh, well, Alice, I was sort of hoping . . . well, you mean, you mean children and all that sort of thing . . .
> ALICE: Exactly. (*David mutters to himself.*) This . . . (*making a long, sweeping gesture . . .*) . . . will be our child.

DAVID: Huh? (*He looks . . . at the brontosaurus. . . .*)

ALICE: Yes, David, I see our marriage purely as a dedication to your work. . . .

DAVID: Well, gee whiz, Alice, everybody has to have a honeymoon. And . . . and . . .

ALICE: But we haven't time. (Mast 37–38)

Alice reminds him that he has a golf date with the representative of a wealthy patroness who may, if he plays his cards right, fund a big museum grant. She reminds him, prudently, to let the representative win. David has literally climbed the ladder to hard-earned career achievement and is poised to join his fate to a conscientious partner. David's life, following an ancient pattern like that of the skeleton, is falling into place. Yet, equally, David's life plan is precarious, prime for collapse, and as yet incomplete.

Enter Susan Vance, a rakishly elegant, wild-haired fellow golfer. Susan, with a masterful swing, hijacks David's ball, and then David himself, as well as his car, which she takes for her own, like his ball, and smashes. David's effort to recoup his meeting, in a restaurant, is similarly foiled when Susan causes him to slip, ripping his jacket and sparking a trail of mishaps through which they each lose large parts of their outfits. Susan exhibits blithe disregard for the conventional values embodied by Alice: honest labor, obsequiousness, stoicism, self-surveillance. Susan commits grand extravagances, not only wrecks cars but steals them, evades summonses, and—beyond all—harbors a wild animal in genteel Connecticut. Property, law, and common sense are thrown to the wind in her ruthless pursuit of pleasure—and of David. David's attempts at the dignity and seriousness that his profession and Alice require are consistently destroyed in Susan's maelstrom of frivolity and misadventure. His career, it appears, will be ruined. This seeming roadblock turns out to be a long, wacky shortcut to success. The man he is meeting turns out to be Susan's doting friend, the potential donor her aunt, and the money hers, essentially. Rules—David, along with the audience, is shown—are meant to be broken. The proof of this lies in Susan's success, and in her glamour and attractiveness while achieving it.

Like the dinosaur Alice denotes as their future child, David's marriage to Alice is doomed to end in extinction. By contrast, Susan, with her libertine ways and leopard pet—the sexualized half of the typical "Hollywood female opposition" (R. Wood 64)—seems a willing, even animalistic partner, and a more fertile mate. Robin Wood links an "explicit comparison of women to cats," from *Bringing Up Baby* to horror film, melodrama, and psychological thriller (62), to the suggestion of a seductive, dangerous, dark quality of the feminine, a vital factor Alice lacks. David, as the film is generally interpreted, is as dead as a brontosaurus carcass when he meets the correct woman for him, who leads him to a full life and fruition. David's journey from overcerebral repression to sexual and spiritual fulfillment tends to be the central focus of most readings. Stanley Cavell even ties a Kantian notion of immorality to the self-exile from community of those, like David, who retreat from coupledom, and Kantian good to a return to community via the marriage relationship (*Pursuits* 79). However, subtler—and often near-obscene—verbal and visual clues suggest deeper issues. At the heart of Hawks's comedy lies a vision if not, as in one critic's words, "bitterly tragic" (Prague 21), then, at least dark and complex.

Gender Questions

Early in the film, foreign-accented psychiatrist Dr. Lehman (Fritz Feld) cautions Susan against believing in stereotypes of insanity, while blinking, rolling his eyes, and exhibiting a tic. It is Lehman, authority of the normative and member of the aberrant, who first assumes that David and Susan are a couple, at once officiating the union and positioning it in his mad realm. Lehman, in a lampoon of Freudian therapy, translates David's initial resistance to Susan as the "conflict" that stems from the "love impulse" and David's encounters with Susan, who follows him, as evincing his "fixation" on her. Susan seizes on Lehman's words as a justification to pursue David, yet this functionalist explication is distinctly antiromantic. David's urges, applicable to any more or less appropriate object, may have less to do with Susan as an individual than with her as one of many possible answers to his need.

David is easy prey for smart, strong women: the smarter the better. He is transported from Alice's to Susan's jurisdiction with none but the faintest quibble. Neither Alice, charged to keep him, nor Susan, primed to steal him, pay regard to his wishes, which both ignore as irrelevant and/or suppress as insurrectionary. While Susan engages in strenuous antics to prevent his return to Alice, these appear less aimed at winning him over than at incurring delay, in an amorous habeas corpus. As with an imperiled woman ingenue, possession of David appears to fall to whichever rival exerts greater might to claim him. When he professes a preference for one woman over the other, it is done so perfunctorily, and markedly late in the story. As one critic notes:

> Norman Mailer in 1960 described the male movie star ideal as the sort who "could fight well, kill well (if always with honor), love well and love many, be cool, be daring, be dashing, be wild, be wily, be resourceful, be a brave gun." It's a nearly inarguable list in its way . . . but not much of it fits Grant. . . . One of the oddest and most interesting things about Grant is how he manages at once to be a paradigm of masculinity and yet at the same time to elude and even to defy most of the categories of the masculine romance. (Harvey 301)

Susan, meanwhile, is an unusually assertive, predatory figure, stalking David with obsessive desire—as well as with the entitlement, loneliness, and/or frantic ennui of the overleisured. Cavell compares Susan and David, respectively, to the heroines of Old Comedy and the heroes of New Comedy. In the first of these classical-period genres, a clever, bold heroine overcomes obstacles preventing her union with her beloved; in the second, a would-be couple, thwarted by a parental figure, is saved by the machinations of the male. Cavell describes *Bringing Up Baby* as a blend of the two: a "comedy of equality" (*Pursuits* 122). The film, however, more than redressing gender imbalances, wholly inverts them. Susan appears thoroughly dominant, ordering the undressed David while she showers to "be patient" until "I'm finished." Speaking to others, she refers to David as "Mr. Bone," as if that aspect of him were sufficient.

References abound to David's problematic "bone." The one he needs, shipped to him, goes missing, while the one in his possession malfunctions despite unorthodox attempts:

> DAVID (*shaking his head*): Alice, I think this one must belong in the tail.
> ALICE: Nonsense. You tried it in the tail yesterday and it didn't fit. (Mast 34)

The rear, as entity, position, or predicament, makes another appearance at the restaurant when Susan rips the tail of his jacket. David, stepping on her skirt, tears that. To cover her behind, he claps his hat over it, then backs her up against a pillar. David presses his pelvis to her backside and they move together, as one, to the exit. Susan has graphic and unusual proclivities as well. Jailed and approximating the pose of a stoolie, she threatens to "unbutton my puss and shoot the works!" In jail, she also promotes David as "a lady-killer" and "a wolf," attributing to him hidden savage, perhaps misogynist, and feral qualities. Where Alice proffers a fossil as a child, Susan lures David in with a leopard named Baby, on top of a babied dog called George. David even becomes a dog, crawling around in the garden. Susan, David, and what they will produce together belong to the outlaw and wild-animal realms.

On this verge of his wedding night, David has had relations neither with his fiancée nor with Susan, nor, perhaps, with any woman previously. His only other encounter with a young woman, a hatcheck girl, begins with his uncertainty over services, and ends with them bumping heads. David seems oblivious to her, while she eyes him, bemused, with unreturned desire. Soon after, David holds a purse, appearing as a cross-dresser. A deliveryman, looking David up and down in an ogling manner, congratulates him for a statement repudiating women. A nude hostage when Susan steals his clothing, David dons Susan's negligee, telling her aunt he "just went gay all of a sudden." David's hesitance, and choice of Susan over other women, may well be explained in this manner. The prudish Alice will not satisfy him. Susan appears able, but the nature of what he wants and what she offers him remain unclear.

Mores and Modernity

In the golf scene, Susan employs a Groucho Marx–like series of linguistic interruptions, substitutions, free associations, elisions, and absurd logics to detain the reluctant David:

> SUSAN: You shouldn't do that, you know....Talk while someone's shooting.
> DAVID: But that was my ball.
> SUSAN (*overlapping*): Well, anyway, I forgive you . . . because I got a good shot.

DAVID: What kind of ball are you playing?

SUSAN: PGA. . . .

DAVID: Well, I'm playing a Crowflight.

SUSAN: Uh huh, I like a PGA better. . . .

DAVID: No, I'm just trying to prove to you that you're playing my ball. You see, a PGA has two black dots and a Crowflight has a circle. . . .

SUSAN: I'm not suspicious about things like that. . . . Stop talking for a moment, will you please? . . . (*Susan putts the ball.*)

DAVID: There, you see? It's a circle.

SUSAN: Well, now, of course it is. Do you think it would roll if it was square?

DAVID: No, I have reference to a mark on a ball.

SUSAN: (*Laughs.*) I know. I was only being silly. . . .

DAVID: You . . . (*holding the ball*) . . . you don't mind if I take this with me?

SUSAN: No, not at all. Tell the caddy master to put it in my bag when you're finished. (Mast 41–44)

Susan is a type of "con" figure, a civil criminal who operates less through force than through the powers of representation. The con, lacking adequate material or physical means, compensates via performance-based forms of illusion, above all through the use of clever language. Language may be thought of as a kind of con itself, mimicking, manipulating, and distorting perception of the object world for which it purportedly stands. The poor, disenfranchised "immigrant" characters played by the Marx Brothers in their films, for example, ascend to wealth, social status, and political power through no other tool but clever language (Cavell, "Everything" 95–103). Just as conversation, in screwball, takes much of the place of action, it also tends to stand in for sexual interaction. The physically weaker Susan, unable to hold David literally in place, captivates him through ingenious language play.

Each assertion Susan makes is only loosely tied to the last, and insistently veers off the straightforward line of David's argument. The multidirectional nature and very speed of Susan's talk render the trail of her logic untraceable, untrappable, and, finally, irrefutable. In an even more complex tactic, she momentarily reverts to David's objective plane, admitting that her deception of him has been conscious. However, she then closes their conversation with a return to her initial stance. With no witness to adjudicate—even, later, when others are present, they will be confused and/or charmed into Susan's position—David is forced to concede the role of adjudicator of truth to Susan and, thus, essentially, to live according to her altered truth. As with David's ball, Susan kidnaps reality and reworks it as she wishes.

Truth, in the screwball, is a shifting, slippery concept. This may have seemed true as well in screwball-era American society, with the increasing role of the speculative economy, a force based less in material holdings than in futures, rumors, and appearances. Class mobility and the media, including film, may have provoked similar cultural anxieties. Modern power, it may have appeared, resided in whomever most persuasively, authoritatively, or powerfully claimed it (I discuss this more extensively elsewhere; see "Dangerous Talk"). Like the compelling outlaw of *noir* crime drama, the screwball con is presented as a magical, romantic figure superior to the dross and stress of everyday living. The con, drawing only on inner resources of daring and wit, makes something out of nothing, gains without paying—and gets away with it.

The name of Susan's leopard springs from the odd fact that it responds only to a vaudevillian tune:

> *I can't give you anything but love, Baby*
> *That's the only thing I've plenty of, Baby*
> *Dream a while, scheme a while*
> *We're sure to find*
> *Happiness, and I guess*
> *All those things you've always pined for*
> *Gee, I'd like to see you looking swell, Baby*
> *Diamond bracelets Woolworth doesn't sell, Baby*
> *Till that lucky day*
> *You know darned well, Baby*
> *I can't give you anything but love.* (Qtd. in Mast 164–66)

The centrality of this plot point, and its frequent repetition, thrusts the song lyrics into awkward emphasis. Passion may be one precondition for love, but the institution of marriage—which the song may well eschew along with the diamond bond—is expected to provide anything and everything else in addition. While marriage has religious and romantic signification, its sociological uses are thought to lie largely in socioeconomics. Marriage supports economic and social production, bolstering the workforce, as well as heterosexually reproducing it. In intoning the lyric—Susan leads, with David gradually chiming in—the couple pledge, in a sense, to uphold the song's dictates: to live for, and on, love. They will flaunt their hedonism, glee, and freedom, in a joke on tradition.

David's manhood, Susan's womanhood, David's sexual preference, and their humanity at large are all at issue. As their influence spreads—even stuffy Aunt Elizabeth, strolling, suddenly runs for pure joy—anarchy, barely contained by romantic convention, threatens widespread lawlessness, deviance, and disorder as a form of happy social contagion. Like their adopted wild animal progeny, their union, while exotic and appealing, may not only fail to contribute to but actually endanger the stability of civilized convention.

The song lyrics, taken literally, celebrate devotion despite poverty. David, however, appears comfortably off, and Susan, well connected and wealthy, can give David more than love, indeed. At the film's end, Susan destroys the dinosaur. However, David need not work at all once he marries the heiress, who will, in any case, due to her family's connections and funding, essentially be his employer. David's new life with Susan is figured as one of pure unfettered spirit and freewheeling fun without consequences. However, this love story obscures its own material basis. In a perhaps slightly sour modern twist on pious romantic cliché, the rich con of a lover happens to win, while Alice, who works for a living and worries for David's career, is disregarded. David has sold himself to the highest bidder, and sold diligent, faithful, well-meaning, if less attractive, Alice out as well.

Leaving David, Alice—in one final animal metaphor—pronounces him "a butterfly": pretty, flighty, distinctly unmasculine, and effete, useless to any solid, productive project, and perhaps homosexual, as suggested by one common association. David—once naive and noble-minded, attaining happiness and success through the "back" way, neither developing character, nor contributing to the community, nor paying the price expected—has become a con himself: a thoroughly modern hero.

Close Reading

The final scene is oddly somber. David—freed of Alice and, ostensibly, Susan—has returned to his work, when Susan enters. The lighting is bright, undifferentiated, and the black-and-white contrast crisp. Susan wears a black dress and black-dotted veil, looking far more like a widow than a lover. The dinosaur's rib cage creates a spiky prison-bar effect; David, back atop the ladder, glares down at Susan like a chased animal. Susan has come to bring David the bone he has been missing: completing his search for manhood, perhaps. He accepts it, though without excitement, and rejects her, coldly demanding she leave it on a table and go away.

She climbs, unsteadily swaying, to meet him. He says that he is afraid of her. She implies that his fear must be a sign of love and offers him a million dollars of her own inheritance. He begins to warm to her, as they rock on the scaffolding in tandem:

> SUSAN: Did you really have a good time?
> DAVID: Yes, I did.
> SUSAN: Oh, that's . . . but that's wonderful. Do you realize
>   what that means? It means you must like me a little bit.
> DAVID: Oh, Susan, it's more than that.
> SUSAN: Is it?
> DAVID: Yes. I love you, I think. . . .
> SUSAN: That's wonderful, because I love you too. (Mast 203)

Susan slips from the platform and, in grappling back up, causes the brontosaurus to collapse. David is shocked and disconsolate. The couple sits marooned above the wreckage together.

> SUSAN: David, can you ever forgive me?
> DAVID: I . . . I . . . I . . .
> SUSAN: You can? And you still love me?
> DAVID: Susan, that . . . that . . . that . . .
> SUSAN: You do! Oh, David.
> DAVID: Oh, dear. Oh my. Hmm.

"I Can't Give You Anything But Love," in "a bouncy orchestral version" (qtd. in Mast 206), comes up, as the couple embraces: The End.

The standard reading of the scene positions the destruction of the dinosaur as a metaphor not just for the end of David's fossilized bachelorhood, but for the end of his former life and entrance into a new, sexually vibrant, productive order. One critic further situates the collapse as effecting a complicity with the viewer who, laughing at social disorder, becomes an agent of it (Grant 127).

However, it appears less here that anarchy triumphs than that social norms are reinforced, in this case uncomfortably for both of the characters. The scenario is grim. David remains hostile until the final moments. When his love declarations come, they are cursory. Susan essentially purchases him, and nervously continues to pursue him and to ventriloquize his answers even after he acquiesces, with seemingly justifiable anxiety that she has not fully won him, or that she will lose him again. They have fun, but their partnership is less than mutual and runs on denial, irresponsibility, and money.

Conclusion

Bringing Up Baby is related by Stanley Cavell in *Pursuits of Happiness* to what he classes as Shakespeare's "comedies of remarriage." In these, Cavell argues, an audience is led to understand marriage through a separated couple's reacquaintance with it. Although they have just met, Cavell explains, David and Susan's previous alienation is so extreme, and their recognition of each other so intense, as to constitute reunion.

As David Shumway notes, however, countering Cavell, "[Screwball comedies] do just the opposite [of enlightening us about marriage]: they mystify marriage by portraying it as the goal—but not the end—of romance" (381). The film emphasizes attraction, danger, and fun over the more quotidian civic and reproductive values adherent to marriage as institution. Further, what qualities the pair detect in each other remains in question. *Bringing Up Baby* might stand, rather, as a comedy of queer marriage—if not homosexual, then queering marriage: estranging it from clichéd unseeing to highlight what might be peculiar in marriage, or in certain arrangements of it, as a project.

The standard reading of *Bringing Up Baby* has it that Susan will inspire David to grow to become his best self, and vice versa. However, David's faint acquiescence to Susan's ardor appears less than wholehearted or convinced. And Susan's lead might just as well release

David to recede further into confusion and impassivity, with her lonely again, at the top. The marriage plot, Shakespearean or otherwise—D. A. Miller cites Jane Austen—may appear to "end well" while remaining inconclusive and unsettling. Alternatively, a noncomedic reading might situate *Bringing Up Baby* as a noirish drama of induction by one con of another, or a cynical "education" tale after the mode of Balzac: a handsome young man, well intentioned but naive and lacking distinct character, discovers romantic, economic, and class shortcuts and succeeds in what turns out to be a similarly ignoble society.

Bringing Up Baby—like *His Girl Friday*, Hawks's next comedy, and his dark dramas such as *To Have and Have Not* and *The Big Sleep*—appears to be formulaic entertainment but ultimately proves troubling below the surface. It is in this complexity, as well as its fine comic sense, that *Bringing Up Baby* deserves the now-common claims to its artistry. It is a critical text for intensive study, both in the context of the period and that of today.

Credits

United States, 1938, RKO

Director and Producer: Howard Hawks
Associate Producer: Cliff Reid
Screenplay: Hagar Wilde (story), Dudley Nichols and Hagar Wilde
Cinematography: Russell Metty
Music: Dorothy Fields, Jimmy McHugh, and Roy Webb
Art Direction: Van Nest Polglase and Perry Ferguson
Costume Design: Howard Greer
Special Effects: Vernon L. Walker

CAST:

Susan Vance	Katharine Hepburn
David Huxley	Cary Grant
Major Applegate	Charles Ruggles
Slocum	Walter Catlett
Gogarty	Barry Fitzgerald
Aunt Elizabeth	May Robson
Dr. Lehman	Fritz Feld
Mrs. Gogarty	Leona Roberts
Mr. Peabody	George Irving
Mrs. Lehman	Tala Birell
Alice Swallow	Virginia Walker

Elmer	John Kelly
George, the dog	Asta
Baby, the leopard	Nissa

Bibliography

Bourget, Jean-Loup. "Social Implications in the Hollywood Genres." Grant, *Film* 50–58.

Cavell, Stanley. "Everything Goes without Saying: The Marx Brothers' Immigrant Talk." *Talk Talk Talk: The Cultural Life of Everyday Conversation.* Ed. S. I. Salamensky. New York: Routledge, 2001. 95–103.

———. *Pursuits of Happiness: The Hollywood Comedy of Remarriage.* Cambridge, MA: Harvard UP, 1981.

Grant, Barry Keith. "Experience and Meaning in Genre Films." Grant, *Film* 114–28.

———, ed. *Film Genre Reader.* Austin: U of Texas P, 1986.

Harvey, James. *Romantic Comedy in Hollywood, from Lubitsch to Sturges.* New York: Knopf, 1987.

Haskell, Molly. "Man's Favorite Sport? (Revisited)." McBride, *Focus* 135–38.

Henderson, Brian. "Romantic Comedy Today: Semi-Tough or Impossible." Grant, *Film* 309–28.

Mast, Gerald, ed. *"Bringing Up Baby."* New Brunswick: Rutgers UP, 1988.

May, Elaine Tyler. *Great Expectations: Marriage and Divorce in Post-Victorian America.* Chicago: U of Chicago P, 1980.

McBride, Joseph, ed. *Focus on Howard Hawks.* Englewood Cliffs: Prentice, 1972.

Miller, D. A. *Narrative and Its Discontents: Problems of Closure in the Traditional Novel.* Princeton: Princeton UP, 1981.

Nugent, Frank S. Rev. of *Bringing Up Baby,* dir. Howard Hawks. *New York Times* 4 Mar. 1938. Rpt. in Mast, *"Bringing"* 265.

Prague, Leland A. *Howard Hawks.* Boston: Twayne, 1982.

Rivette, Jacques. "The Genius of Howard Hawks." McBride, *Focus* 70–77.

Salamensky, S. I. "Dangerous Talk: Phenomenology, Performativity, Cultural Crisis." *Talk Talk Talk: The Cultural Life of Everyday Conversation.* Ed. S. I. Salamensky. New York: Routledge, 2001. 15–35.

Sarris, Andrew. "The World of Howard Hawks." McBride, *Focus* 35–64.

Shumway, David. "Screwball Comedies: Constructing Romance, Mystifying Marriage." *Film Genre Reader II.* Ed. Barry Keith Grant. Austin: U of Texas P, 1995. 381–401.

Wollen, Peter. "The *Auteur* Theory." Mast, *"Bringing"* 271–74.

Wood, Michael. "Looking Good." *New York Review of Books* 20 Nov. 1997: 20–21.

Wood, Robin. "Ideology, Genre, Auteur." Grant, *Film* 50–58.

The Rules of the Game (1939)

CHRISTOPHER FAULKNER

A Film Not Like the Others

Context

The Rules of the Game (*La Règle de jeu*) premiered in two Paris cinemas simultaneously on July 8, 1939, less than two months before the outbreak
of the Second World War. The Colisée was a cinema on the Champs-
Elysées that catered to the well-to-do, while the Aubert-Palace, on the
Boulevard des Italiens, attracted a clientele of middle-class and lower-
middle-class spectators. Members of the audiences in both of these cinemas were so displeased with the film that they are said to have
hooted, whistled, and set fire to newspapers during screenings. Apparently, audiences knew a war film when they saw one, even though, as
Jean Renoir observed many years later, *The Rules of the Game* is "a war
film" which makes "no reference to the war" (171).

Meaning is never immanent in a film, as some hidden truth, waiting
to be revealed once and for all. Audiences alone make films mean,
within specific contexts, and according to their own largely extracinematic necessities. Only the fertile imaginations of spectators in their
context-driven states will determine the repertoire of possible interpretations of a film at any one point in time. Films do not transcend history
and neither do spectators. Because people do not make meaning out of
movies in the abstract, removed from their everyday existences, what is
therefore always to be valued about a film can never be easily essential-
ized or universalized. This suggests that interpreting or analyzing films
is a form of social practice, not just an aesthetic exercise.

These remarks raise the issue of the relationship of the past to the
present, and of our present to the past as mediated for us by the cinema. How are we to make history mean for us? Is history to be understood as a continuous narrative, a relentless forward march of events,
whose chain of cause and effect places us at an increasing distance

from our ever-receding past so that it has no more than antiquarian interest? Or might we take our cue from Walter Benjamin, and think of the relationship of the present to the past as a discontinuous one, as a relationship of shock—a montage of attractions, as it were—one in which an "image" in the past is to be seized as it "flashes up" at a moment of present danger ("Theses" 257)? Coincidentally, I am actually writing these lines and thinking about *The Rules of the Game* on the eve of the second Gulf War and am reminded that films never fail to be contemporary with the moment at which one writes about them, just as they have never failed to be contemporaneous with all those other moments in the past at which people have written about them.

The Rules of the Game is a report on the condition of French society on the eve of the Second World War. In January 1939, while Renoir was working on the screenplay for his film, he told the journalist Marguerite Bussot that *The Rules of the Game* was to be "a precise description of the bourgeoisie of our time." The film exposes the apparent hypocrisy, ignorance, cynicism, and moral turpitude of a society in the face of what it perceives to be imminent threats to its security (which explains why audiences got so upset at seeing themselves mirrored on the screen in this way). To be fair, not all of French society was captured by the acerbic wit of *The Rules of the Game*. There are no peasant characters in the film, no urban proletariat, no representatives of a petty bourgeoisie of shopkeepers or government functionaries, all of whom counted significantly in the French population in the years before the war. More specifically, as Renoir said, the social class that is being indicted here is the French bourgeoisie. In effect, the ruling ideas, attitudes, convictions, and beliefs in French society belong to this ruling class. That means that the balance of power lies with this social class as well, and that no change is possible that does not contend with its authority and influence. To some extent, the film conveys these "truths" by having the servants impotently echo the judgments, fashions, and prejudices of their masters. This is one of the purposes of the parallel upstairs/downstairs spaces, the common gossip, and the crisscrossed love intrigues in the film. This is also why *The Rules of the Game* is an ensemble film, with at least eight characters of more or less equal importance rather than a single protagonist who drives the action. If there were other, competing ideas, attitudes, convictions, or beliefs in French society at this time (from the urban working class, say), the film does not choose to let them be heard. For this reason, *The Rules of the Game* must persuade us that the hopes for political, economic, and social change to which Renoir had committed himself earlier in the 1930s, when he worked for the French Communist Party and supported the government of the Popular Front, have now been frustrated once and for all (Faulkner 58–122). With the advantage of hindsight we can very easily point to the film's anticipation of the war, but the argument can also be made that the film is about a society that is already at war with itself. The hunt sequence recalls a scene in Renoir's *La Vie est à nous* (*Life Is Ours*) of 1936, in which members of the upper class dressed for the hunt take target practice at cardboard cutouts of French workers. The war to which "no reference" is made can be understood as class war as well as international war. In any event, one has the impression of a hopelessly closed and very conservative world.

Analysis

The Hunt

By the summer of 1939 all of Europe knew that war was imminent, especially following the violation of the Munich agreements with the German invasion of Czechoslovakia and the disputed Sudetenland in March. Two years earlier Renoir had made his own pacifist statement against war with *Grand Illusion* (1937), a film set mostly in various prison camps during the First World War but which deliberately lacks any scenes of armed conflict. *The Rules of the Game,* on the other hand, which makes no direct reference to current events playing out on the European stage, includes the most violent (and brilliant) set piece Renoir ever filmed, a ritual hunt (in which one of the characters taking part is a former First World War general) that shows the killing of many dozens of birds and rabbits in such a way that we have the impression of a wanton (and exhilarating) slaughter of war-trapped innocents. From the moment the beaters are given the signal to advance, to the last, lingering shot of the fallen game spread out across the field, this sequence comprises less than 4 minutes out of 105 minutes and 50 seconds of screen time, but 50 shots, or almost a seventh of the 336 shots that make up the total film. The shouts, trills, and whistles of the gamekeeper and his men; the whack of wood on wood of the beaters' sticks; the quick pans that catch the scurry of rabbits in the camera's sights (so that it, too, seems a weapon in the hunt, and makes us complicit in our fascination); close-ups and the sharp report of guns; the following tracks of fleeing game birds; more gunshots in the air; the fall to earth of a flutter of wings; and, as the slaughter mounts, an accelerated cutting rate and shots of shorter and shorter duration—all propel us toward the climax and the close shot of a last quivering rabbit, paws in the air, and the paroxysm of death. The number of shots in this sequence testifies to its importance to the meaning of the whole, while its visual and aural construction is designed to produce emotional "shock and awe" in the spectator. Sixty-five years on, this sequence still gets inside one's head.

The film's conclusion is explicitly linked with this hunt sequence when the poacher Marceau (who should know about these things) remarks that André Jurieux pitched forward like a fallen rabbit when he was hit. Thus, the celebrated close-up of the quivering rabbit in its death throes anticipates the film's fatal conclusion. Prophetically, Octave had warned André at the start of the hunt that they risked being mistaken for rabbits. Is André killed because, like the rabbits, he has turned out to be a nuisance, with the innocent sincerity of his feelings for Christine? Perhaps because Robert has said that he doesn't want fences and he doesn't want rabbits, such pests have to be eliminated by all means necessary. Is André's life therefore of no more value than that of a rabbit? One might be tempted to such a conclusion. On the other hand, the forceful representation of the hunt and the pity and terror it can arouse in us suggests that even the life and death of a rabbit is not negligible and might be the stuff of tragedy.

A New Definition of the Word "Accident"

We can turn to the conclusion of *The Rules of the Game* to demonstrate something of the film's interpretive complexity. If *Grand Illusion* concludes with the qualified hope that the world will return to peace, *The Rules of the Game* ends with a murder that is explained away as "a deplorable accident" to persuade us of the inevitability of war, whether that be international war or war against one's own people. Are we to take this explanation at face value, as the General does, or share the cynicism of Saint-Aubin at a bald-faced lie? I think it is important to note that the choice before us is not easily either/or; consequently, we have to be prepared to weigh the complexities of an irresolvable both/and situation. First of all, plot developments in *The Rules of the Game* tend to escape the motivations of individual characters, no matter whether they act with deliberation or express their interests unconsciously. Schumacher, in his proper domain on the grounds of the estate, thought he was firing on Octave, not André, to prevent his rendezvous with Lisette, not Christine. From his perspective, the death of André was indeed an accident, although Schumacher has certainly committed a willful murder. Here, as elsewhere, what characters think they see turns out to be contradicted by objective reality. They are often, as here, literally in the dark, and metaphorically sometimes so even in broad daylight: consider Christine's mistaken interpretation of the embrace between Robert and Geneviève seen through her field glass after the hunt.

Furthermore, Schumacher acts out a private passion (and not just his own), which turns out to be in the public interest, since he rids the world of an interloper who is a threat to the "rules" and conventions designed to maintain the status quo. Through inadvertence, Schumacher was protecting his master's "property" from being "poached," at the same time that he was fulfilling Robert's unconscious wish for André's death. We may surmise Robert's deepest desire when, after the fête, in conversation with André about Christine, he expresses his concern that André's profession as a flier may make him liable to accidents. By this moment in the film we are already aware that André is drawn to accidents, and comes out of them looking something less than heroic. Doesn't the film in effect begin with his gaffe over the radio? Shouldn't we remember the automobile accident that tests Octave's patience and his life? Hasn't Octave told Christine that up in the air André may be a modern hero but that down on the ground he can barely get himself across the Champs-Elysées without mishap? Are we not here (yet again in the film) therefore being prepared for the tragic ignominy of André's (imminent) death and the probable excuse of a "deplorable [hunting] accident"? Because the film has prepared us for its end in its beginning, and reminded us of that inevitability at opportune moments, its fatalism, beyond the power of any individual character to effect change, must seem difficult to overlook. It is because André's death can be both a murder *and* an accident that the world can be a dark, if complicated, place. In this film, the temptation to let one's analysis rest on mutually exclusive opposites is not to be trusted lest they reduce the film's meanings to a poverty of choices.

A Comedy of Manners

The publicity campaign for *The Rules of the Game* advertised it as "a film not like the others." A title card at the beginning of the film reads: "This entertainment [which takes place on the eve of the 1939 war] does not claim to be a study of morals. The characters that it presents are entirely imaginary."[1] A comedy of manners that features a massacre (of animals) and a murder (of the would-be hero), but with no pretensions to social criticism, is certainly not a film like the others. Like so many of the film's characters, the promise of the film's title card both lies and tells the truth, a contradiction not easily sustained. There is no doubt that with *The Rules of the Game* Renoir set out to make something different and that this was to be his most intellectually and financially ambitious film to date. Because he had created his own production company for the purpose, and would write, direct, and act in his own film, he felt he could risk making an experimental, commercial feature, a film that pushed the boundaries of current practice and tested the limits of audience expectation. Years later, in his autobiography, he admitted that he may have gone too far: "During the shooting of the film I was torn between my desire to make a comedy of it and the wish to tell a tragic story. . . . I was utterly dumbfounded when it became apparent that the film, which I wanted to be a pleasant one, rubbed most people up the wrong way" (170, 172).

In Renoir's own mind, the "others" against which he measured *The Rules of the Game* were no doubt all French films and most certainly those in the genre of the comedy of manners. A comedy of manners usually takes as its subject the amorous intrigues of a sophisticated

---

[1]This is a somewhat more literal translation of the French original than that which appears at the head of current subtitled prints of the film. The bracketed phrase was added to the titlecard in 1959. The film that Renoir premiered on July 8, 1939, ran approximately 94 minutes. Today's 106-minute version was put together in 1959 from rushes and discarded footage on the mistaken assumption that Renoir's original intentions were finally being satisfied. The curious history of the different versions of the film is explained on one of the special features to the Criterion Collection's handsome DVD release of *The Rules of the Game*.

social milieu (servants included) and is distinguished by dialogue notable for its witty repartee. Such comedies are designed to instruct as they delight and move toward a happy ending in which the rewards (of wealth, of station, of marriage) go to the true and steadfast of heart. The quote at the beginning of the film, from Beaumarchais' *The Marriage of Figaro,* is intended to flag the long tradition of comedy to which *The Rules of the Game* is indebted. (Did audiences remember that the Beaumarchais play was performed on the eve of another cataclysm, the French Revolution, another "image" of the past that might have "flashed up" in their moment of present danger had they been attentive to the shocks of history?) Like Beaumarchais in his time, Renoir broke the rules by creating a hybrid tragicomedy, what he called, in French, a *drame gai* (thereby predicting neither his meaning nor the audience's response), even while he borrowed from the comedy of manners some of its character types (all maids are named Lisette; Octave is a go-between), familiar stage business (mistaken identities and disguises: Christine wears the cloak with the hood that Schumacher has given Lisette; André goes to his death in Octave's overcoat), conventional plot elements (the parallel games of love between masters and servants, in which the Robert-Christine-André and Schumacher-Lisette-Marceau triangles double for one another), and a generally theatrical *mise-en-scène* (the importance assigned to performance altogether).

Furthermore, the action of comedy is usually set in motion by an interloper (like André Jurieux) who challenges the rules that hold the social world together. Such a character would ordinarily be the hero. In the years between the wars, aviators, those knights of the air, with their risk taking and their record breaking, were the heroes of the modern age (like Charles Lindbergh, with whom André Jurieux is expectantly compared). But far from being the very model of the reckless man of action, André also turns out to be a reckless man of feeling, by announcing his private affections over the public radio. We should note, too, that he expresses these feelings out of the darkness at the airport, while he is heard, by contrast, in the bright lights of Christine's boudoir and Robert's office (O'Shaughnessy 147). Another impossible antithesis, therefore. Would one not expect to associate the truth with the light and deception with darkness? However, in giving vent to his feelings out of the tumult of the dark, André speaks the repression of those who live by conformity to the rules. We know this to be the case, because both Christine and Robert first turn off the radio, as though to bury André's outburst, and yet respond immediately to his confession, the former by questioning the possibility of friendship with a man, the latter by reconsidering his feelings for Christine and his relationship with Geneviève. (Note, however, that the darkness returns for the film's conclusion, and ends there, with Robert's speech to the assembled company confessing the "deplorable accident.") In any event, from this moment at the airport, André is marked as a victim, not a hero, and the film has a priori begun its turn away from comedy toward tragedy.

A Theatrical Mise-en-scène

Under the influence of André Bazin, criticism of *The Rules of the Game* has tended to emphasize Renoir's clever use of long takes, a moving camera, and an extended depth of field in support of his guarantee of a phenomenological realism. (If we take away the hunt sequence, the *average* shot length in *The Rules of the Game* is a breathtakingly long twenty-two seconds!) In Bazin's view, the purpose of Renoir's depth of field is to confirm "the total interdependence of everything real" (90). For its part, the moving camera overcomes the impression given by most fixed camera positions of looking at a boxed rectangle like a theater set with its imaginary offstage. Instead, Bazin claims, Renoir's image is the opposite of a proscenium arch frame: "The screen is a mask whose function is no less to hide reality than it is to reveal it. The significance of what the camera discloses is relative to what it leaves hidden." Reality is always lying in wait for the camera. For Bazin, the presence of the camera during the fête is like an "invisible guest" (87), the you-are-there of a televised reality. Bazin's argument is that Renoir's style brings us into a relation with the real that is closer to what we enjoy in everyday life. The effect of characters moving in and out of the frame, or of the camera moving to include them, and of three or four actions occurring in depth on different planes simultaneously is an approximation of the "real" space and time of the continuum of reality that is much greater than that achieved by most classical filmmakers.

While this is an important argument, the numerous theatrical *mise-en-scènes* in the film cannot be ignored either. There is, of course, the stage that has been set up in the salon of the château for the costumed performances and musical numbers during the fête. But there are also the uses of interior and exterior spaces, sometimes with the action framed frontally, which give the impression of a stage on which the characters are playing out their roles. The most obvious examples are the two moments on the steps, with Octave's failure to conduct the imaginary orchestra contrasted with Robert's successful account of the "deplorable accident." These framings put us on the outside looking in, spectators to the spectacle of those other spectators, imagined or real, at the performances of Octave and Robert. The kitchen set, with its upstage and downstage playing spaces cleverly separated by the internal frame of a wall with an open doorway to the right and windows to the left, allows us to see different actions taking place simultaneously that are sometimes independent of one another (the chef going about his business while the servants eat) and sometimes in tension (as with Schumacher's pursuit of Marceau). To this example can be added the brilliant use of the château corridor, seen lengthwise on more than one occasion in great depth of field. The bedrooms of the characters lead into this public playing space like so many offstage entrances and exits into their private lives. A clever use of mirrors, first in the La Chesnaye Paris residence and later during the fête (e.g., the reflected skeleton, Christine in hiding), serve both to extend the visual field available to the camera's view and to draw attention to the representational illusion embedded within the "real" of the film. (After all, the characters are playing parts layered on top of those they already play in the film's "real life.") Something of the same illusory effect is differently achieved with the boxed rooms of the château during the fête, as the camera allows us a trick of the eye that sees a succession of rooms stretching into a distance one beyond another, and also sees each room smaller than the next, contained one inside the other. On the face of it, all of these uses of space seem to announce theater or performance as a countervailing principle to reality and authenticity in the film, both phenomenologically and morally.

However, consistent with my suggestion of the desirability of a both/and practice of interpretation, we might do better to see the film's many antitheses as only superficially opposed, whether we invoke theater and life, performance and authenticity, appearance and reality, artifice and nature, passion and reason, love and friendship, lies and truth, darkness and light, design and accident, blindness and sight, ignorance and knowledge, or any others that come to mind. We have already seen how easily the terms in these sets can be inverted, exchanged, or identified.

In this spirit, we might think of the fête sequence not so much as the embodiment of the first term in each set of oppositions enumerated above, but as the return of the repressed of the hunt—as the eruption of all those passions that were brutally put down in the cold light of a fall day. The fête is like a second hunt sequence in the film, but this time out of control, which is why it has echoes of the first hunt in the *danse macabre* of the skeletons, who are strangely reminiscent of the white-coated beaters, those earlier valets of death. And, in a parody of the first hunt, Schumacher, the hunter, pursues Marceau, the fleeing rabbit, downstairs, through doors, across rooms, and around corners in the château—except that this "parody" is in deadly earnest, even though its reality is mistaken for theater by the guests and confused with a parallel reality (or theater) by the servants. "Stop this farce!" Robert commands. "Which one?" Corneille replies. These correspondences remind us that the first hunt was itself a form of theater, with its ritualized staging, language, gestures, and role-playing, while the theater of this second hunt will also end in the reality of death. If the fête is the world of misrule, in which passions and desires usually held in check are let loose, in which the clockwork mechanism that ordinarily holds everyone in place like so many moving parts (Robert's toys) has broken down (Robert's mechanical organ, the pride of his collection), then the line between a world ordered and a world disordered is very thin indeed, especially if the one is always already embedded within the other.

The Rules of the Game

There is every reason to think that "the rules of the game" can be taken to refer just as much to the rules of narrative as to the rules of social convention. To do so would be to allow the film a dimension of self-reflexivity about narrative as a complicated form of aesthetic play with certain rules (which can sometimes be broken to effect). The dizzying confusion between theater or performance and the real that we just considered tends to ensure this self-reflexivity, but so does Renoir's presence in the film as Octave (the only character whose double is *outside* the film). In an interview in June 1939, just before the film's release, Renoir said of Octave that he is "a hero in spite of himself" because he is "the confidant of all the others" and can move with ease between masters and servants and apparently negotiate their conflicting interests ("F." 11). However, Octave is also the one character in the film who fails at role-playing, whether as hunter (he doesn't carry a gun), musician (his collapse on the steps of the château), or lover (he abandons Christine to André). His ineptitude (at performance, at self-deception) is conveyed when he becomes helpless and impotent in the very costume that might have connoted strength and independence. Octave is cursed (or blessed?) with a degree of self-awareness apparently denied any of the other characters. He is the one character in whom all antitheses, paradoxes, and contradictions collapse. Robert's comment that Octave is "a poet, but a dangerous poet" is a reminder that he is the *metteur en scène* who has set the plot in motion by getting André invited to La Colinière in the first place. It is also a reminder that this is a dangerous game, that there are risks involved in trying to stage-manage the expected narrative outcomes of the comedy of manners. And indeed, Octave is inept at narrative, too, for it is he who inadvertently brings the game to a close with the unexpected plot reversal that sends André to his death with the loan of his coat.

In other words, not even Octave-Renoir, the author, is in control of his world or can make sense of it. Furthermore, by frustrating the conventions of comedy, Renoir (Octave?) would seem to have ensured as a self-fulfilling prophecy Octave's (Renoir's?) complaint to Christine of his failure to make contact with a public and have any impact on events unfolding in the world outside the cinema. The author lacks confidence in his powers as a hero for his time, as a prophet in his own country, and banishes himself at the end.

Does the Cinema Lie?

Not only Renoir in the part of Octave encourages us to contemplate the implications of the film's self-reflexive potential. Sound and image technology, the two component apparatuses of the cinema, are also foregrounded. The first frames of *The Rules of the Game* show us a radio technician seated in his on-location recording and transmission studio, until the camera tilts down and pans right, along the cable to the announcer at her microphone (the part played by a well-known radio personality of the day). Her words and the words of her on-air interviewees become the audio bridge that justifies our visual introduction to the three linked spaces of Christine's boudoir, Robert's office, and Geneviève's apartment. At Christine's, our attention is directed to the materiality of the apparatus when the first shot includes the back of the radio receiver with its tubes and wiring. The initial responses of Christine, Robert, and Geneviève have each been determined by what they hear. The whole opening sequence of the film thus becomes a marvelous demonstration of the power and technique of sound cinema.

Similarly, Christine's field glass in the scene after the hunt easily becomes a metaphor and demonstration of cinema's place within regimes of the visual. "The camera introduces us to unconscious optics as does psychoanalysis to unconscious impulses," wrote Walter Benjamin at the conclusion of a famous passage in which he extolled the virtues of the cinema ("Work of Art" 239). The lens that brings Christine into indecent proximity with the intimate life of a squirrel also magnifies her interpretation of the embrace between Robert and Geneviève. Here, as elsewhere in the film, notably at the hunt, and especially in connection with André, disavowed human passions are projected onto animal life. Indeed, it is Christine's own "unconscious impulses" that the camera brings to the surface, since the lens lies about the objective truth of the relationship between Geneviève and Robert. "Optics" (the lens of the camera, the field glass with the lens substituting for the lens of the camera) and "impulses" (those understood, those misunderstood) determine the possible meanings of the scene. This is a compelling paradigm of the condition of spectatorship. So as not to break the spell of her illusion, Christine dare not put aside her suspension of disbelief that what she sees may not be true, just as we cannot put aside our suspension of disbelief that what we see may not be true, for fear of breaking our own illusion of involvement in the fiction of *The Rules of the Game*. When it comes to "the rules of the game," one fiction deserves another, as it were.

If the film takes some pains to make us aware of its representation of the means of representation—the acoustic and the visual, separately and together, which define the cinematic apparatus and its effects— perhaps that is because we are being encouraged to think of the entire film as a meditation on Octave's observation to Christine that we live in a period when everyone tells lies (governments, newspapers, advertising brochures), even and including the cinema. Is that the film's ultimate paradox, that *The Rules of the Game* lies—in the way that art lies—so that we may know the truth? There is a deadly honesty about such a fateful conclusion in a world bent on self-destruction.

Everyone Has His Reasons

"Everyone has his reasons," Octave says, in the film's most famous (if most misunderstood) speech. This state of affairs is "terrible," Octave points out, so much so that he would like to disappear down a hole (like a rabbit, one supposes, to escape the fatality such a situation implies). Critics have usually taken Octave's remark to heart in a positive, humanist sense to mean that it is a good thing that we live in a world comprised of so many unique individuals each with his or her own commendable motives and that such a generous view of human beings is to Renoir's credit. I want, however, to suggest that what Octave means is that while everybody may indeed have his or her reasons, it does not follow that they know what they really are, or why they have them, or whether they are actually in control of the consequences that follow from acting on them. In short, as we have discovered, motive and consequence, apparent cause and real effect, and the relations between them may be multiple, unfathomable, and even contradictory. Such a situation makes ethical judgment, makes any distinction between what's "good" and what's "bad," impossible.

At the same time, it is one of the riches of this film that the members of its ruling class turn out to be highly individuated and not easily homogenized. Among others, as we have seen, there is a French Jewish marquis (Robert), with an Austrian wife (Christine) and a Parisian mistress (Geneviève); an industrialist and his wife from the provincial city of Tourcoing (M. and Mme. La Bruyère); a young woman who is studying pre-Columbian art and culture (Jackie); a gay (Dick) and lesbian (Charlotte) pair;[2] an Italian guest (Cava), possibly gay (and a few words of Italian in the dialogue). Their servants turn out to be no less idiosyncratic: a gamekeeper from Alsace, Schumacher (the pronunciation of whose name is as disputed as the territory he

---

[2]Unlike Dick, Charlotte does not self-identify as homosexual. In the shooting script (see Curchod and Faulkner), Charlotte has a female companion whose name is Juliette. She can be spotted as an extra in some scenes of the film, but is given no lines.

comes from), with a wife, Lisette, who spends most of her time in Paris; an English chauffeur, William (and we hear a few words of English in the dialogue); a ladies' maid, Mitzi (and we hear a few words of German in the dialogue); a majordomo, Corneille, named for both a bird and a playwright. So many differences; so few similarities.

If the hunt is the centerpiece to which everything else refers, we should remark that not everyone hunts. Octave, as I have already noted, does not carry a gun; Christine carries a gun but is not seen to use it. Furthermore, Dick, Charlotte, and Cava (and Mme. La Bruyère) are not at the hunt at all and prefer card games and ping-pong. Do these latter amusements belong to a "feminine" thematics in the film and hunting to a "masculine"? Yet another of the paradoxes of the film is that it confounds the absolute separateness of these two gender thematics by, for example, André's display of (feminine) weakness in matters of the heart, which is at odds with his (masculine) aviation exploits, or by the evidence that he is at the hunt but doesn't shoot because he is too distracted by his passion for Christine. Is it everywhere in the film the crossing of these thematics that announces boundary problems requiring excessive remedies (such as the death of André)? Are, therefore, animals and the hunted associated with instinct (or passion), nature, and the feminine, while the hunters and the majority are associated with reason (or rules), culture, and the masculine? However, one function of Dick, the homosexual (in his very presence as a character), as well as of Charlotte, is to register the slippages between these two thematics. So Dick's obvious wearing of makeup is echoed by Robert's obvious wearing of makeup. He is Robert's secret sharer. In short, the line between a feminine and a masculine thematics is a constantly moving one, not fixed or static (thus, André's death can still be a murder *and* an accident). This indifference extends, for example, to competing interpretations of the meanings of love or friendship. "Did they or didn't they?" is an explicit question about the putative sexual relations between Christine and André, to which no one other than Dick and Charlotte can give voice. This is to be set alongside Christine's public testimonial about her "friendship" with André. As we have discovered, almost every attempt to be definitive about almost anything in this film imposes a limit that will not hold. Does the film prefer one thematic over the other, or is the undecidability of their relation, of their *difference,* and what their roles are to be (in history), another of the film's tragedies that has descended into farce? I don't mean to say that they must be defined oppositionally, or essentially; I simply mean that the undecidability of their relation is a sign of deeper troubles. One such problem for which this undecidability might be the metaphor is of course that between domestic peace and (inter)national war. Is the General thus the homosexual's opposite, masculinist number? After all, why have a general, as a character, at all? He's there, unequivocally, and on his own admission, for one purpose only, to hunt, not, as he points out, to write his memoirs. If he were to write his memoirs, they would be of his actions in the First World War, wouldn't they? Not so coincidentally, the General is also given the role of insisting that everything is always all right, including the "friendship" of André and Christine and the "accidental" death of André, in spite of persuasive evidence to the contrary.

Conclusion

What Does It Mean to Be French?

Renoir's films of the 1930s (of which *The Rules of the Game* is the climax) challenged the limits of what it meant to be French. No other body of work through that decade went so far in proposing the radical transformation of French society. In addition to projecting new forms of social organization and new relations of economic production, Renoir's films also envisioned a society in which human differences would be acknowledged in the form of what we now call identity politics. Interrelations with others who shared one's occupation, kinship, locality, gender, ethnicity, religious faith, sexual orientation, or identifying feature at some other affective register were as important in securing a sense of identity or belonging as were abstractions like social class or the French nation. People's allegiances are always first of all concrete and local and only secondarily general and abstract. This is a recognition both that identity is not easily secured and that the ways to identity are multiple.

We may take the famous scene of "racial" profiling in the film, in which Robert's Jewishness is held against his claims to Frenchness—until the chef defends him as a true aristocrat because he knows how to make potato salad—as a judgment on the failure of political agendas to credit the richness and variety of everyday life in the formation of people's deepest allegiances. The film's concern with otherness, with anti-Semitism and racism, and with xenophobia generally, is a function of the rise of European Fascism toward the end of the 1930s and on the eve of war. Mme. La Bruyère's historical ignorance, with her references to "Negroes" and "Buffalo Bill" is one example; the deeper meaning of Schumacher's reference to shooting poachers in Alsace, with its historically large Jewish population, is another. There is a case for arguing that the failure of the 1930s is a failure we are re-living today: an acquiescence to inflationary ideological appeals that lead to war, and an inability to respect, accept, and negotiate the human differences that foster peace.

Credits

France, 1939, La Nouvelle Edition Française, Paris

Director: Jean Renoir
Screenplay: Jean Renoir, Carl Koch, and André Zwobada
Cinematography: Jean Bachelet
Editing: Marguerite Houllé
Sound: Joseph de Bretagne
Art Direction: Eugène Lourié
Costume design: Coco Chanel

CAST:

Robert de La Chesnaye	Marcel Dalio
Christine de La Chesnaye	Nora Gregor
André Jurieux	Roland Toutain
Octave	Jean Renoir
Lisette	Paulette Dubost
Schumacher	Gaston Modot
Marceau	Julien Carette
Geneviève de Marras	Mila Parely
The General	Pierre Magnier
Saint-Aubin	Pierre Nay
Corneille	Eddy Debray
M. La Bruyère	Richard Francoeur
Mme. La Bruyère	Claire Gérard
Jackie	Anne Mayen
Dick	Georges Forster
Charlotte	Odette Talazac
The chef	Léon Larive

Bibliography

Bazin, André. *Jean Renoir.* New York: Simon, 1973.

Benjamin, Walter. "Theses on the Philosophy of History." *Illuminations.* Ed. Hannah Arendt. New York: Harcourt, 1968. 255–66.

———. "The Work of Art in the Age of Mechanical Reproduction." *Illuminations.* Ed. Hannah Arendt. New York: Harcourt, 1968. 219–53.

Bussot, Marguerite. "Propos de Jean Renoir." *Pour Vous* 25 Jan. 1939: 3.

Curchod, Olivier, and Christopher Faulkner. *"La Règle du jeu": Scénario original de Jean Renoir.* Paris: Nathan, 1999.

"F". "Jean Renoir, acteur." *Pour Vous* 28 June 1939: 11. Rpt. in *Premier Plan* 22-23-24 (1962): 278–79.

Faulkner, Christopher. *The Social Cinema of Jean Renoir.* Princeton: Princeton UP, 1986.

O'Shaughnessy, Martin. *Jean Renoir.* Manchester: Manchester UP, 2000.

Renoir, Jean. *My Life and My Films.* New York: Atheneum, 1974.

Sesonske, Alexander. *Jean Renoir: The French Films, 1924–1939.* Cambridge, MA: Harvard UP, 1980.

Stagecoach (1939)

MATTHEW BERNSTEIN

The Classical Hollywood Western Par Excellence

Context

Since its premiere in early 1939 (itself a banner year for Hollywood), John Ford's *Stagecoach* has been widely acclaimed as the first great sound-era Western and as a superior example of classical Hollywood style. Dudley Nichols's tightly structured script, under Ford's direction, compares and contrasts with intelligence and compassion the diverse passengers who undertake an uncertain, dangerous journey on the American frontier to greater self-knowledge. The film's casting draws on some of the period's finest character actors, whose detailed embodiment of Western types provides a vivid setting for the lead roles of Dallas (Claire Trevor) and especially the Ringo Kid (a young John Wayne); *Stagecoach* is in fact the film that made Wayne a major Hollywood star and inaugurated his transformation into an American icon. Ford and cinematographer Bert Glennon designed a remarkably varied visual style for the film that ranges from the epic, foreboding landscape of Monument Valley for the action and chase sequences to the intimate, Expressionistic, darkly lit interior scenes of the way stations and the stage's destination, Lordsburg.

While all these elements make *Stagecoach* a superlative cinematic entertainment, the film compels analysis for its embodiment of American ideals and realities of the late 1930s, when the United States was emerging from the dislocations of the Great Depression. *Stagecoach* appears to glorify American history, particularly its expansion westward at the expense of Native Americans, and it seems to extol the opportunities for democratic life on the frontier. Yet the film intriguingly

This essay was researched and written during my fellowship at Emory University's Center for Humanistic Inquiry. I thank the CHI (and director Martine Brownley) for providing me with the space and time to write it.

expresses ambivalence about the bringing of civilization to the frontier and the compromises to democratic ideals and individual freedom that process entails. Thus *Stagecoach* can be appreciated for its evocative, eloquent style but also its rich and varied meanings, for it is a film that demonstrates the ways in which apparently straightforward texts can be seen to embody contradictory ideas.

Horizons West

Stagecoach was the most critically acclaimed of several major studio 1939 Westerns that historians credit with raising the genre into big-budget production from the rut of B-studio, B-movie status (Schatz, "*Stagecoach*"; Stanfield). Ford himself had not directed a Western since his 1926 *Three Bad Men,* though he had previously directed the transcontinental railroad epic *The Iron Horse* (1924) and a considerable number of other Westerns from the start of his career in 1916. Beginning in 1937, Ford spent two years attempting to interest the major studios in *Stagecoach* before the semi-independent producer Walter Wanger signed on (Bernstein 146–49), although this may have been in part because the majors were producing their own big-budget Westerns at the time (Schatz, "*Stagecoach*" 24). They may also have been put off because its script was riddled with B-movie Western clichés: the familiar stagecoach passenger types; the Apache attack on the stagecoach; the cavalry's last-minute ride to the rescue; the "good-badman" hero (Ringo) who is redeemed by the heroine's (Dallas's) love; even the saloon's piano playing that stops when the villain learns the hero is in town (Slotkin 304; Grant, "Spokes" 11). What the studios could not anticipate was that *Stagecoach*'s script and direction would revitalize such conventions and demonstrate new possibilities for the genre.

The Western has virtually disappeared early in the twenty-first century, having made infrequent reappearances such as Clint Eastwood's *Unforgiven* (1992), even while its conventions subtend other genres, such as the science-fiction film (*Star Wars* [1977] is an example). In fact, classical-era Westerns may appear to today's first-time audiences like the films of a foreign, even exotic culture. Yet the Western is a uniquely American genre, with a history that extends back well before the invention of the cinema. Westerns inherited narrative formulas developed most notably in James Fenimore Cooper's *Leatherstocking Tales,* of the early 1800s, and from dime novels of the late nineteenth century

(Cawelti; Grant, "John Ford"). While becoming a staple of the early American film industry, the movie Western also inherited visual iconography crystallized in Western genre painting (such as the action-filled works of Frederic Remington (Buscombe, "Paint the Legend") and Wild West shows of the late 1800s. As the western frontier itself disappeared, the Western genre became a popular national myth, disseminated most effectively through the cinema (Schatz, "The Western" 46).

Certainly, *Stagecoach* adheres to many of the genre's basic conventions (as distinguished from the specific clichés mentioned above). Westerns are typically set west of the Mississippi River, sometime between 1860 and 1900, from about the start of the Civil War to the turn of the century, a transitional period in American history when civilization met the wilderness; *Stagecoach*'s story transpires in the 1880s during the Apache wars in the Arizona territories. The frontier setting provides the basis for any Western's fundamental conflict, be it the struggle to subdue "savage" Native Americans or to eliminate immoral white killers. In *Stagecoach,* the central characters are faced with both these antagonists: in two successive climaxes, the passengers must fight off a group of attacking Apaches and the Ringo Kid must kill the Plummer brothers to avenge the murder of his brother and his father. Typically in a Western, a frontier town is incapable of solving such problems itself; one price of frontier living is an overburdened legal and judicial system, which cannot address every instance of violent subjugation that arises from the amoral wilds of nature. Instead, the town relies on a visiting Western hero who, while "a killer of men" like the villains (Warshow 659), is allied with the community values of the besieged town. For example, in Ford's film, stagecoach driver Buck (Andy Devine) gets Sheriff Curley Wilcox (George Bancroft) to admit that "There'd be a lot more peace in this territory if that Luke Plummer was so full of lead he couldn't hold his liquor." Accordingly, as in other classic Westerns, *Stagecoach* culminates in a climactic shootout on a lonely street, where the Ringo Kid eliminates the threat of the Plummers alone.

While Westerns present an epic, mythicized history of America that celebrates pioneer fortitude and the progressive conquest of the wilderness, they also address many other compelling issues and ideologies in American life. For one thing, they depict American democracy as a superior social system to European class-riven cultures. They do so in part by incorporating the popular notion that the frontier allowed degraded, disinherited, or unjustly judged Americans to begin anew with a fresh, vital connection to the land in a community far from Europe. Inheritance, class, and other social distinctions are not firmly established on the frontier (Slotkin; Studlar, "'Be a Proud'"); in *Stagecoach*, however, the prostitute Dallas, the alleged outlaw Ringo Kid, the alcoholic Doc Boone (Thomas Mitchell) and the former Confederate Virginian Hatfield (John Carradine) are all social outcasts whom even frontier society in the town of Tonto has rejected or condemned. While they have the opportunity to redeem themselves on the journey, Dallas and Ringo must ultimately flee the American frontier.

Second, Westerns have been popular with American audiences in part because they suggest in their narrative formulas the ways in which unique individuals (who embody the values of self-interest) can be reconciled with the shared, communal values of a town that discounts extreme individuality. The Western hero temporarily allies himself with the town because he alone can defeat the evil menace that terrorizes it. Once that threat is eliminated, the Western hero typically leaves, his individuality intact (Wright 130–55). In fact, his completed mission makes his very presence in the town unnecessary; in this light, the Western hero can also be viewed as a tragic figure, one whose skills and sensibilities ensure his obsolescence (Warshow 659–60). Ironically, in killing the Plummers in a personal dispute, the Ringo Kid has paved the way for Lordsburg to become a more settled town like Tonto. Part of *Stagecoach*'s richness resides in its suggestion that this development may not be a desirable thing.

A third abiding appeal of Westerns, and one closely related to the individual versus communal tensions the films depict, arises from the genre's treatment of violence and the question of when it is justified in American democratic life. Violence and murderous villains are of course extreme expressions of individual will and power that must be subdued for the common good of society (an assumption Westerns share with gangster films). The hero who is provoked beyond reason into fighting a serial-killer villain is a mainstay of the Western genre and more broadly of American culture (and even its foreign policy). Since Sam Peckinpah's *The Wild Bunch* (1969), however, Westerns have sometimes opened with intense violence and built to even more climactic violence by their conclusion; *Stagecoach*, more traditionally, spoons out the threat of violence and then builds to the two climaxes with the attacking Apaches and then the Plummers. The story justifies these violent confrontations, for they purge the frontier of destructive elements and allow American democratic society to flourish (Slotkin 10–16).

In *Stagecoach* these climaxes come near the end of a journey that suggests how fragile frontier life is; one might even label *Stagecoach* a road film. The film combines the two story lines of combating (but not subduing) the Apaches and the Ringo Kid's mission of vengeance. The itinerary begins in the comparatively well-established town of Tonto, so civilized that it features a church on its main street and harbors its own Law and Order League of reform-minded, intolerant women. The stagecoach journeys through progressively less-established settings—the Dry Forks station, where the passengers vote on whether or not to proceed; the Apache Wells station, where "Little Coyote" is born to Mrs. Lucy Mallory (Louise Platt); and Lee's Ferry, which the Apaches have destroyed (Wood 29). The final destination, the ironically named Lordsburg, seen only at night, is a much wilder, rowdier town than Tonto, a place where prostitutes gambol with their johns freely in their own district, and where a climactic shoot-out can transpire on one of its main streets. As Peter Stowell notes, both "the existing examples of civilization, the frontier towns of Tonto and Lordsburg, are pest holes of bigotry and debauchery," from which the Ringo Kid and Dallas must escape (27).

Like any journey, that undertaken by *Stagecoach*'s passengers is also a voyage of discovery. The travelers' hardships gradually reveal their true natures beneath their apparently simple veneers. *Stagecoach* celebrates their potential growth and transformation.

Analysis

Ideology, Class, Gender, and Region within the Stagecoach

The key dramatic focus of *Stagecoach* concerns the inherent unfairness of prejudging individuals, or as Doc Boone describes it in Tonto, the "foul disease of social prejudice." The film indicts social prejudice most forcefully by demonstrating the moral superiority compared to their social betters of the most prejudged, dejected, and rejected characters:

Dallas,[1] the innocent but notorious Ringo Kid, and Doc Boone, the alcoholic, destitute, but erudite physician. In response, Lucy Mallory and even the whiskey salesman Peacock (Donald Meek) display greater compassion and kindness than we initially anticipate when we first meet them.

The temporary social microcosm of characters in the stagecoach creates a cross section of society that itself testifies to "the democratic promise of the frontier" (Grant, "Spokes" 10). Yet the coach travelers are riven with conflicting ideals and values. For example, Doc Boone and Hatfield fought on opposite sides of what Boone calls "the War of the Southern Rebellion" and what Hatfield labels "the War for the Confederacy"; twenty years after the Civil War, this would be grounds alone for a fatal fight, aside from Doc Boone's insinuations that Hatfield shoots his opponents in the back. The banker Henry Gatewood (Berton Churchill) makes constant complaints about government overregulation of banks, but he finds no agreement in the stagecoach; in fact, screenwriter Nichols created Gatewood to express anti-big-business sentiments that would resonate with audiences who had lived through the Great Depression (Maland 61–64). Moreover, Gatewood's condemnation of the cavalry for not escorting their coach through Apache territory implicitly criticizes Mrs. Mallory's husband, a cavalry captain. Eventually, at Apache Wells, Gatewood gets a curt rebuttal in Ringo's observation, "Looks to me like the army's got its hands pretty full, mister." Gatewood is irredeemably selfish, the one character who is not affected by the trip and does not change. His late apology for his rudeness

---

[1]It is notable that *Stagecoach* never identifies Dallas explicitly as a prostitute through dialogue; this reflects the very strong stipulations of the Production Code Administration, which endeavored to represent crime and what it considered illicit (i.e., unmarried) sex either implicitly or ambiguously, rather than explicitly. In this way, adult viewers could recognize why Dallas was being run out of town, while children would simply think Tonto's Law and Order League did not like her. This stricture ironically makes Ringo's ignorance of Dallas's status as a prostitute more plausible. In addition, the PCA insisted that filmmakers deemphasize the female figure. Thus *Stagecoach* uses the convention that Mrs. Mallory's near-term pregnancy be physically invisible and hence a surprise to the audience as well as the other passengers. This provides *Stagecoach* with another instance of a misjudged character: when we learn that Mrs. Mallory is pregnant, we retrospectively understand her extreme physical discomfort on the journey and her urgent determination to reach her husband.

on the trip rings hollow. Accordingly, he is arrested on arrival at Lords-burg (Maland 63).

More potent tensions among the characters in *Stagecoach* contradict the agrarian ideals and popular conceptions of democracy on the frontier, for here we find that social class still matters a great deal. Tonto's Law and Order League, a group of middle- and upper-middle-class mainstream "society" women, ceremoniously escort Dallas to the stage and pair her with Doc Boone. On the journey, Mrs. Mallory, the cavalry captain's wife, regards Dallas, Doc, and the Ringo Kid with restrained but unmistakably cool contempt. Mrs. Mallory's Tonto acquaintances warn her about "that creature" Dallas and about Doc Boone, who "couldn't doctor a horse." Accordingly, Lucy suffers Doc's cigar smoke in annoyed silence and more pointedly rebuffs each of Dallas's attempts to comfort her, at Dry Forks (where she learns her husband has left) and in the coach to Apache Wells (where she grows increasingly uncomfortable). Only her physical incapacity—labor—enables Dallas to care for her and her infant.

Lucy is joined in her contempt for her alleged social inferiors by Hatfield, the Confederate Army veteran who served under Lucy's father and is likewise a Virginian. He has little use for Ringo, uselessly berates Doc Boone as a "Drunken beast!" while Doc sobers up for the delivery of Little Coyote, and in a justly famous scene, guides Lucy to the other end of the dining table at the Dry Forks station so she need not sit next to a prostitute. Both Lucy and Hatfield, as Southerners, embody the most class-defined segment of eastern American society; they are closest to the European social system to which the democratic frontier is opposed. They would take a first-class cabin on the stagecoach were one available (Studlar, "'Be a Proud'" 140–42). Hatfield's death signifies the irrelevance of class-bound society for the idealized frontier; the birth of Little Coyote signals hope for new life free from such prejudices.

The remaining passengers assume various class positions relative to the "aristocratic" Mrs. Mallory and Hatfield. Gatewood, with his self-inflated sense of worth, joins them. Peacock, the fearful, forgettable middle-class family man and whiskey salesman, is far less contemptuous, largely because of his timidity. He must endure the attentions of Doc Boone, the loss of his whiskey samples, and everyone's assumption that he is a reverend, with ineffectual protests. Even his response to Little Coyote, making faces silently, contrasts with the loud celebrating of Buck the stagecoach driver and the others. Buck, while like Peacock a coward, has no particular ax to grind with Doc, Ringo, or Dallas; he is in fact fond of Ringo, who knows his family. And Sheriff Curley Wilcox, while arresting Ringo, is revealed to be motivated by his desire to protect the son of a good friend from the murderous Plummers, rather than his desire to collect a reward for Ringo's capture.

Even so, the overwhelming social prejudice of the firmly established members of the stagecoach community continues that of Tonto's Law and Order League. For example, at Dry Forks, Curley proposes that the group decide "democratically," i.e., by a vote, whether the stagecoach should press on to Lordsburg without an army escort. But the vote doesn't unfold according to pure democratic principles. Curley appoints himself a proxy for Ringo's vote and prevents the cowardly Buck from voting to go back to Tonto. He also solicits Lucy's sentiments, but then bypasses Dallas, leading Ringo to ask him, "Where's your manners, Curley? Aren't you going to ask the other lady first?" This question compels Curley to be more democratic than he had planned (Slotkin 307). (Ironically, once given the chance to vote, Dallas claims it makes no difference to her which way they go, even though she does not wish return to Tonto, where there are "worse things than Apaches.") Ringo's bounteous chivalry in insisting that Dallas be treated as a lady provides a telling contrast to Hatfield, whose gallantry is strictly reserved for a fellow Virginian (Slotkin 308). In this scene, and later in the stagecoach when the Ringo Kid offers water to "the other lady," he embodies the democratic ethos of the idealized West (Studlar, "'Be a Proud'" 148). The Ringo Kid's exceptional status in this regard enables *Stagecoach* to suggest that social stratification destructively infects the frontier and mitigates its promise of democratic freedom. No wonder Dallas and the Ringo Kid, aided by Doc Boone and Curley, flee to Ringo's ranch in Mexico to escape such hierarchies. As Doc Boone famously and sarcastically observes of their departure, "Well, they're saved from the blessings of civilization."

As his final observation suggests, Doc Boone is also the most articulate among the film's outcasts: with his allusions to the French Revolution ("the tumbril awaits") and classical poetry ("Is this the face that launched a thousand ships and burned the topless towers of Illium?"), he is comically conscious of his predicament; as a compassionate father figure, he dispenses tentative advice to Dallas and later aids in her escape with Ringo (Maland 66–69). While we don't know what has brought Doc Boone to his inebriated state, we do learn at Apache Wells that both Dallas and the Ringo Kid are orphans, a status that has special meaning in Ford films because of its concomitant emotional and economic deprivations (Studlar, "Sacred Duties" 52–53). In their cases, it has brought each of them to their present, marginal status, a downward trajectory that broadly reflects the dislocations of the Great Depression (Studlar, "'Be a proud'" 133–34). Dallas can only survive as a prostitute ("Don't I have a right to live?" she asks Doc Boone in Tonto), and the Ringo Kid has to avenge the murder of his father and kid brother by the Plummer brothers, who framed him for the crime. As Dallas tells Ringo resignedly, "You have to live, no matter what happens" (Studlar, "Sacred Duties" 53). Mrs. Mallory and Peacock do not know of Dallas's and Ringo's pasts, but at least they come to recognize their innate kindness and nobility by the end of their journey.

The birth of Little Coyote marks a major step toward this realization, and is in fact the first turning point of the journey. While Gatewood complains about the delay to his schedule and Hatfield fumes helplessly about Doc's unfit state, Dallas instantly asks Ringo to make hot water; cradles the baby in presenting her to the men in the hallway; sits up all night with the baby while Lucy sleeps; and protects the infant, while Lucy huddles in a corner, during the Apache attack (Studlar, "'Be a Proud'" 149). Dallas's fitness as a mother persuades the Ringo Kid to propose, and to do so in such a classically inarticulate way that it builds plausibly on John Wayne's "minimalist" performance in the role (Schatz, "Stagecoach" 39).[2] Ringo is not the only one who is impressed; all the men are awed when Dallas presents the infant to them. Peacock later acknowledges that Dallas *is* a lady when he urges the men in the coach to have some consideration for "the ladies." In Lordsburg, he invites Dallas to visit his family (though he made the same offer to Jerry the bartender in Tonto).

---

[2] "Look, Miss Dallas—you got no folks—neither have I. Maybe I'm crazy to ask you—but—well—I still got a ranch across the Border. It's a nice place—a real nice place—trees—grass—a house half built. You see I'm asking—well, what I mean is—a man could live there—and a woman."

Meanwhile, Doc Boone likewise proves his mettle by successfully delivering the baby far from any medical facility. His ruthless sobering-up routine with black coffee and his recovered pride after the successful delivery give him the first opportunity in months, perhaps years, to feel useful and capable in his profession. His newfound confidence stays with him to the end of the film, when he unthinkably challenges Luke Plummer in Lordsburg to leave his rifle at the bar before leaving to meet Ringo. Even Peacock is affected by the baby's birth; while he voted at Dry Forks to return to Tonto, at Apache Wells he wants Mrs. Mallory to rest as long as needed, in spite of the Apache threat (Stowell 28–29).

The second stage in forging the stagecoach community is the climactic Apache attack. Doc is able to save Peacock's life from an arrow wound. Dallas protects Little Coyote. In Lordsburg, Lucy is inspired to start to make the same offer of aid Dallas had previously made to her at Dry Forks ("If there's anything I can do . . ."), even though she and Dallas both know nothing can come of it. Ringo's heroics in fighting the Apaches—though he selfishly saves three bullets for the Plummers even when the coach seems on the verge of destruction (Kalinak 183)—apparently earns from Curley the opportunity to confront the Plummers. While the Ringo Kid may have the reputation of a dangerous killer—a reputation his introduction in the film, complete with rifle shot and dramatic tracking into a close-up, reinforces—he is revealed to be in fact a naive, morally innocent, and upright individual, who like Dallas has endured more than his share of misfortune on the frontier. He shows his greater mettle in his innocent courtesy to Dallas, in his kindness to everyone ("Hey Buck, how's your folks?" is his greeting to the driver when he stops the stage), and in his tolerance of human frailty (his compliment to Doc Boone's inebriated handiwork on his brother's broken arm and his acceptance of Dallas's fallen state). The Ringo Kid embodies in fact the true, native, and natural American democratic ideal. In recognition of the Kid's inherent goodness, Curley lets him not only confront the Plummers but escape to Mexico and avoid the official frontier law's shortsightedness.

Thus, if *Stagecoach*'s social snobs contradict the Western's vision of the democratic West, that promise is reaffirmed in the redemption of its wayward characters. Ringo, Dallas, and Doc Boone form an aristocracy of spirit, gallantry, and loyalty that contrasts with the ultimately superficial social distinctions to which Mrs. Mallory, Hatfield, Peacock, and Gatewood adhere. We are positioned in every possible way—visually as well as narratively—to cheer these characters on, and to welcome their acceptance by their presumptive social betters, who are representatives of mainstream society. As Joseph McBride and Michael Wilmington have put it, "What seemed to delight Ford most in *Stagecoach* was the possibility of glorifying disrepute by plunging a group of pariahs into danger and having the most apparently abject of them emerge as heroes" (54). This sympathy for the disinherited, the marginal, may have arisen from Ford's proud Irish heritage (Berg 75). Whatever its source, Ringo and Dallas's flight along with the birth of Little Coyote are events that embody the promise of the future with new lives, literally and figuratively, that begin on the frontier. Still, the fact that Ringo and Dallas must flee to Mexico to live tempers that promise in a disturbing way.

Present-day viewers may also find troubling the evident limits to the film's idealization of the West as the incubator of democratic ideals. Traditional gender roles abound in the film, appropriately for the period, as Dallas proves her worth by assuming a maternal role rather than acting out a rebellious pose as a woman of independent economic means (Studlar, "'Be a Proud'" 144). Mrs. Mallory's grim determination to be with her husband is that of the devoted spouse. Yet, both women's toughness as they confront the hardships of the frontier tentatively suggest the taking on of masculine qualities, while Doc Boone's fatherliness, Curley's solicitousness toward the Ringo Kid, and the Ringo Kid's gentleness toward all demonstrate a feminine tenderness that does not compromise their masculinity (Studlar, "Sacred Duties"). Thus, Ford's film evidences a surprisingly flexible consideration of gender roles on the frontier for a film of the late 1930s.

Another, more striking limit to democratic ideals in *Stagecoach* is the assumed exclusion of ethnic others. There are conventional (for the 1930s) comic moments created at the expense of Mexicans, although their presence enables *Stagecoach* to more accurately depict "the cultural pluralism and intermingling of the West" than other Westerns (Dagle 109–10). The Mexican Apache Wells host Chris (Chris-Pin Martin) mourns the loss of his horse rather than the loss of the wife who stole it, and Buck complains about his Mexican wife's large family and their monotonous fondness for beans. In such casually delivered dialogue and scenes, *Stagecoach* embodies its era's assumptions about nonwhite nationalities, though one can argue that Ford evokes multi-culturalism in more complex and insightful ways than he is usually credited with (Berg). Certainly, fleeting moments like the cavalry officer's questioning of a Cheyenne scout's reliability or Peacock's hysteria over Chris's "savage" wife suggest the overwhelming power of the white characters' fantasies and fears of the Native Americans. Such prejudice is more extreme, but still related, to the social prejudice Doc Boone identifies in Tonto (Dagle 105; Telotte).

The Varieties of Visual Style:
Intimate Scenes and Inspiring Landscapes
In its interior scenes—in the coach, the way stations, or the towns—*Stagecoach* dramatizes social prejudice and plays on character misperceptions through visual style as well as dialogue. Consider the early shot of Lucy Mallory inside a Tonto hotel tearoom with her friends. Hatfield has just bowed to her as she came through the door, and his gallant manner and dandyish figure piques her interest. Now sitting inside by the window, she looks out at Hatfield through the window in a medium long shot in which the midground and background are in sharp focus. (Though the great theorist André Bazin labeled Ford an unapologetic devotee of continuity editing, which fragments cinematic space rather than presenting it whole for viewer contemplation [Gallagher, *John Ford* 152–53], this shot and others in *Stagecoach* —Dallas in the hallway at Apache Wells, for example—show Ford's use of deep space and deep-focus.) Hatfield himself is framed by the curtains of the window in the left half of the screen, as he looks in and back at Mrs. Mallory; Mrs. Mallory's friend's husband stands in the right half. "Who is that gentleman?" Lucy is moved to ask her friends, who reply that Hatfield is no gentleman at all, but a notorious gambler. Lucy and Hatfield's early, mutual fascination will of course culminate in Hatfield's decision to escort Mrs. Mallory on her journey to her husband.

This medium long shot of Lucy, her friends, and Hatfield is also one of the earliest instances of many in the film in which one character is initially labeled and judged by others, only to reveal surprising and nobler dimensions before the end of the film. In this way the film extends its indictment of social prejudice to a general portrayal of misleading assumptions about people (even Cheyenne scouts and Apache wives). From the silver drinking cup Hatfield hands to Lucy—it is embossed with the Greenfield Manor crest—and Hatfield's dying words to tell Judge Greenfield about his son, we learn that Hatfield has fled the defeated South for the life of a murderous gambler on the frontier; he, too, for whatever reason (the film doesn't tell us, though we can imagine several scenarios), is an outcast from his home. Like Ringo, Dallas, and Doc Boone, Hatfield proves himself worthy in the ordeal of the journey. Having served in Lucy's father's regiment, he recognizes her as a great lady, protects her, and ably defends the coach from the Apaches.

It is part of Lucy's ingrained snobbery, that of a planter-class Virginia aristocrat, that she delivers no overt, verbal judgments of Dallas, Doc, or Ringo. Rather, Lucy's distaste for Dallas is conveyed to us through repeated eyeline match cuts and point-of-view shots, which occur first as the Tonto ladies speak of "that woman" Dallas in the coach as if she were not nearby. A shot/reverse-shot exchange of looks ensues to show Lucy looking directly at Dallas in the coach, and Dallas in the subsequent shot dropping her eyes downward in abject embarrassment.

This same dynamic occurs in the celebrated Dry Forks Station interior scene. After the group has decided to go on without cavalry escort, they sit down to eat, and Ringo unwittingly offends Mrs. Mallory by offering Dallas a place at the table to Lucy's left. Hatfield subsequently invites Mrs. Mallory to move to a seat by the window that is "cooler." (Ringo assumes their social rejection is directed at him— "I guess you can't break out of prison and into society in the same week"—and he infers that he has also offended Dallas: he starts to move away before she implores him to stay.) But nothing is cooler than Mrs. Mallory's regard for Dallas. As Nick Browne and Tag Gallagher (in *John Ford*) have shown in meticulous detail, Hatfield's suggestion is preceded by a silent exchange of looks in alternating shots of Dallas looking ashamed from Mrs. Mallory's disapproving point of view with shots of Mrs. Mallory and shots of the onlookers (Ringo and Hatfield) as they respond to this situation. Though seeing Dallas through Mrs. Mallory's eyes might visually encourage us to identify with Mrs. Mallory and share her judgments of Dallas, the editing of the scene and our observations of the characters in previous scenes in fact compel us to sympathize with Dallas, to note Mrs. Mallory's unjust ostracism, and perhaps even to recognize that Mrs. Mallory is entrapped in her own social class (Browne; Gallagher, *John Ford* 153–61). In other words, if Nichols's script encourages audience identification with the socially disdained characters, Ford's deployment of shot composition and editing reinforce its sentiments.

Stagecoach's reliance on the characters' looks and perceptions of each other obtains within the stagecoach as well. (The importance of this element in the design of the film is apparent in the seating charts appended to Dudley Nichols's final revised script, which outline the placement of each passenger within the coach on each leg of the journey, so the filmmakers could keep their continuity straight [Nichols].) The fragmenting of space, carving the passengers into groupings of two and three, visualizes these divisions. As Joan Dagle has pointed out, "A sense of separateness and conflict is thus constantly constructed inside a very intimate and communal space, capturing the ambivalent nature of this 'community'" (106). What connection exists is shown through the eyeline reactions of the passengers to one another. For example, everyone looks at Ringo when he informs Doc Boone that his kid brother with the broken arm was murdered, while Ringo himself stares off with a look of determination in his eye. Dallas often eyes Ringo with curiosity, piqued by his singular courtesies to her, such as offering her the canteen. (Gatewood, fittingly, seems oblivious to many of these eyeline observations as he sits stolidly between Dallas and Lucy, staring straight ahead.) At Apache Wells, Dallas and Ringo also share a meaningful exchange of looks as she holds Little Coyote in a madonna-and-child image that impresses Ringo greatly and in fact persuades him to propose to her.

Part of *Stagecoach*'s emotional power derives from the way in which it situates such intimate scenes within the open landscapes of the West, particularly the striking Monument Valley. The film opens with various shots of this locale, stressing its grandeur and vastness as the stagecoach and the cavalry ride through it to Tonto, all to the accompaniment of an assortment of American folk tunes and clichéd Native American music (Kalinak 176–87). In *Stagecoach* as in most Westerns, the open landscape visualizes the idea of America's limitless possibilities and individual opportunities. It's important to recognize that for 1939 audiences such majestic location scenery was akin to the most jaw-dropping visuals in today's Imax films. As Richard

Slotkin notes, "In *Stagecoach* it is the landscape's visual oddity that gives it authenticity. . . . Its peculiarity effectively represents the alien quality of the Frontier—which had been in its time as uncanny a place for pioneers as a moonscape might be" (305). No wonder Ford would shoot several more Westerns there during his career.

But such unsettled vistas, with their untarnished beauty, are in *Stagecoach* represented ambivalently, as a source of admiration and of fear, the locale from which both strong heroes and murderous villains spring. For example, it is entirely appropriate that the "notorious" Ringo Kid enters the film on the trail from out of nowhere with a rifle shot. Equally famous are the extreme long shots of the stagecoach on the floor of Monument Valley, which quickly pan left to a group of Apaches in medium-long-shot range planning their attack on the coach (Dagle 104–5). These shots, and the musical juxtaposition of grand symphonic melodies that quickly become dangerous Native American rhythms stress at once the grandeur of western expansion and the hazards it entails, showing how the wide-open spaces encourage individual freedom but also great vulnerability. In Westerns of *Stagecoach*'s vintage, Native Americans are cast as a force of nature. Their motives for violence go unexplained (Geronimo's leaving the reservation on a mission of vengeance parallels the Ringo Kid's jailbreak); their individuality and humanity are denied (Wood 29); and their elaborate and admirable culture is not depicted even minimally. They are simply a phenomenon to be evaded, tamed, or conquered. Indeed, this may be the most jarring aspect of *Stagecoach* for contemporary viewers.

The climactic Apache attack is staged, shot, and edited with turbulent motion and diverse camera angles (including one shot under the horses and coach), as if to counterbalance the relative stillness of the film's interior scenes. Backward tracking shots capture the furious pace of the chase, as the Apaches ride at full speed, shoot, reload their guns, and even, in an amazing stunt by the legendary Yakima Canutt, jump to the lead stage horse, only to be shot and dropped underneath the galloping horses and coach. In several shots the Apaches and the passengers aim right at the camera (but only the passengers have implausibly one-sided, perfect aim). The force of the sequence is so great that Ford could afford to violate the 180-degree rule of shooting and editing, crossing the axis of action while the attack continued, without disorienting the audience (Bordwell and Thompson). While the convention of the attack may seem clichéd, Ford's version gives it a ferocity that is as stimulating in its sensuality as any thrill-ride car-chase shot in Hollywood of the past twenty years. This holds true in spite of the rear-projection shots of the coach's flight juxtaposed with long shots on location.

During the Apache attack Ford takes pains to emphasize the passengers' vulnerability through his play with offscreen space. While earlier instances of on-screen/offscreen relations are comic (Doc Boone learning in midswallow from Jack the bartender that Peacock is a whiskey drummer; Doc Boone daintily adjusting Peacock's scarf while Gatewood drones on offscreen about needing a businessman for president), during the attack they are fatal and frightening. Peacock is struck with an arrow from offscreen just after Doc's farewell toast to everyone's health. In one of the film's climactic moments, as the prospects of surviving the attack grow thin, only Hatfield's gun intrudes on the close-up of the praying Mrs. Mallory. We hear a gunshot, see Hatfield's hand and gun falter, and hear, cued by Mrs. Mallory, the cavalry bugler's charge intermixed with the film's score.[3] A comparable, indirect effect informs the climactic sequence of the Ringo Kid's showdown with the Plummer brothers, as Ford cuts away from the Kid as he falls to the ground and fires off a shot, to Dallas, waiting in a ravine to learn what has happened. We learn of that outcome only after she does, in her tentative smile as the camera tracks in with the approaching, still-offscreen Kid as he comes to embrace her (this "cutaway" technique is, it should be noted, in Ernest Haycox's short story as well). In all these ways, Ford and Glennon's shot compositions, their very decisions about what remains on-screen and off, heighten the excitement of these two climactic scenes by deepening our sense of the characters' dread and their surprising and welcome exultations.

Such framings and stagings express an ethos that imbues *Stagecoach:* the darkest hour comes just before the dawn. At Apache Wells, the uncertainty of their safety and their future envelops the passengers as

---

[3]First-time viewers of *Stagecoach* may wonder about Hatfield's actions. Pioneer lore and Western narratives had it that white women captured by Native Americans faced a fate worse than death, including rape or intermarriage. Hence it was deemed an act of charity to kill them rather than let them be captured. Hatfield is acting on this assumption. See Telotte 115–21.

night falls. Hatfield's curses and epithets for Doc Boone as he sobers up ("A fine member of the medical profession!") and the pronounced, low-key side lighting on the men as Doc goes down the hall give way to the more brightly lit, joyous discovery that he has successfully delivered Mrs. Mallory's baby. A film that flourished with daytime location shooting of magnificent landscapes and cloud formations becomes at Apache Wells a study in Expressionistic shadows as the Ringo Kid watches Dallas walk out a back door in darkness, lights a cigarette from Chris's lamp in dramatically low-level lighting, and shares revelations of his devastating past with Dallas. These nighttime scenes are lit and staged with sympathetic melancholy.

A comparably dark, Expressionist aesthetic informs the rowdy town of Lordsburg. Here Dallas's greatest hopes commingle with her sense of despair that Ringo will abandon her once he learns "all about" her, as Doc puts it. As the camera tracks back with Ringo and Dallas (an echo of the dolly shots of Dallas's forced march to the stagecoach in Tonto), Lordsburg "suggests an urban-Western nightmare. . . . As Ringo walks Dallas home through these mean streets, the bars and whorehouses they pass—brief bursts of garish light and harsh sound, hysterical laughter, cries—suggest a journey into hell. Each new street brings closer to the surface the truth that Dallas cannot voice to the innocent Ringo: that she is a whore, that she is returning to a whore's life, and that from here on things will only become more vile for her" (Slotkin 310). This is the very darkest hour for Dallas—"I'll never forget you asked me" is her reply when the Kid reminds her of his marriage proposal. She can hope for little more. Yet out of these dark scenes and situations, a brighter future emerges from the most slender of hopes, thanks to the Ringo Kid's gunmanship and to the paternal goodwill of Curley and Doc Boone, who, like the audience, recognize that Dallas and Ringo deserve much, much better, and let them flee to start their new life.

Conclusion

Orson Welles claimed he watched *Stagecoach* forty times in preparation for directing *Citizen Kane* (1941) (Grant, "Spokes" 3). Film scholars and historians happily enjoy that same option, for *Stagecoach* rewards repeated viewings. André Bazin summed up *Stagecoach*'s achievement when he described it as "the ideal example of the maturity of a style brought to classic perfection." He continued: "John Ford struck the ideal balance between social myth, historical reconstruction, psychological truth, and the traditional theme of the western *mise-en-scène*" (Bazin 149). That balance resides in the film's acute social observation, its compassionate sensibility, its visual splendors, its precise narrative structure, its sense of nature's grandeur, and its faith in downtrodden people. Though it could be viewed as a simple celebration of American greatness, *Stagecoach,* in dramatizing the travails of its outcasts, leaves unresolved certain profound questions about the process, costs, and significance of white America's conquest of the wilderness during its westward expansion. Ford would continue to explore these troubling questions in his later Westerns, such as *My Darling Clementine* (1946), *Fort Apache* (1948), *The Searchers* (1956), and *The Man Who Shot Liberty Valence* (1962). Like *Stagecoach,* these are all films that shaped the course of the Western genre and, by extension, Americans' sense of their history and their identity.

Credits

United States, 1939, Walter Wanger Productions

Director: John Ford
Producer: Walter Wanger
Screenplay: Dudley Nichols
Story: Ernest Haycox
Cinematography: Bert Glennon
Editing: Otho Lovering, Dorothy Spencer, and Walter Reynolds
Music: Richard Hageman, Franke Horling, John Leipold, Leo Shuken, and Louis Gruenberg
Art Direction: Alexander Toluboff and Wiard B. Ihnen
Costume Design: Walter Plunkett
Stunt Coordinator: Yakima Canutt

CAST:
Dallas	Claire Trevor
Ringo Kid	John Wayne
Doc Boone	Thomas Mitchell
Hatfield	John Carradine
Peacock	Donald Meek
Curley	George Bancroft
Buck	Andy Devine

Lucy Mallory	Louise Platt
Calvary lieutenant	Tim Holt
Henry Gatewood	Berton Churchill
Chris	Chris-Pin Martin

Bibliography

Bazin, André. "The Evolution of the Western." *What is Cinema?* Ed. and trans. Hugh Grey. Vol. 2. Berkeley: U of California P, 1971. 149–57.

Berg, Charles Ramirez. "The Margin as Center: The Multicultural Dynamics of John Ford's Westerns." Studlar and Bernstein 75–101.

Bernstein, Matthew. *Walter Wanger, Hollywood Independent.* Minneapolis: U of Minnesota P, 2000. 146–50.

Bordwell, David, and Kristin Thompson. "Sample Analyses: *Stagecoach.*" *Film Art: An Introduction Web Site.* <http://www.mhhe.com/socscience/art-film/bordwell_6_filmart/instructor/olc/analysis_stage.mhtml>.

Browne, Nick. "The Spectator-in-the-Text: The Rhetoric of *Stagecoach.*" *Movies and Methods.* Ed. Bill Nichols. Vol. 2. Berkeley: U of California P, 1985. 458–75.

Buscombe, Ed. "Painting the Legend: Frederic Remington and the Western." Studlar and Bernstein 154–69.

———. *Stagecoach.* London: BFI, 1992

Cawelti, John. *The Six Gun Mystique.* Bowling Green, OH: Bowling Green U Popular P, 1984.

Dagle, Joan. "Linear Patterns and Ethnic Encounters in the Ford Western." Studlar and Bernstein 102–31.

Eyman, Scott. *Print the Legend: The Life and Times of John Ford.* New York: Simon, 1999.

Gallagher, Tag. *John Ford: The Man and His Films.* Berkeley: U of California P, 1986.

———. "Shoot-Out at the Genre Corral: Problems in the 'Evolution' of the Western." *Film Genre Reader.* Ed. Barry Keith Grant. Austin: U of Texas P, 1986. 202–16.

Grant, Barry Keith. "John Ford and James Fenimore Cooper: Two Rode Together." Studlar and Bernstein 193–219.

———, ed. *John Ford's "Stagecoach."* Cambridge: Cambridge UP, 2003.

———. "Spokes in the Wheels." Introduction. Grant, *John Ford's* 1–20.

Kalinak, Katherine. "'The Sound of Many Voices': Music in John Ford's Westerns." Studlar and Bernstein 169–92.

Maland, Charles. "'Powered by a Ford?': Dudley Nichols, Authorship, and Cultural Ethos in *Stagecoach.*" Grant, *John Ford's* 48–81.

McBride, Joseph, and Michael Wilmington. *John Ford.* New York: Da Capo, 1975.

Nichols, Dudley. *Stagecoach.* Rev. Final Script. Walter Wanger Collection. US Mss 136AN. Box 93, File 8. Wisconsin Center for Film and Theatre Research, Madison, WI. 11 Nov. 1938.

Schatz, Thomas. "*Stagecoach* and Hollywood's A-Western Renaissance." Grant, *John Ford's* 21–47.

———. "The Western." *Hollywood Genres.* New York: Random, 1981. 45–80.

Slotkin, Richard. *Gunfighter Nation: The Myth of the Frontier in Twentieth-Century America*. Norman: U of Oklahoma P, 1998.

Stanfield, Peter. *Hollywood, Westerns and the 1930s: The Lost Trail*. Exeter: U of Exeter P, 2001.

Stowell, Peter. *John Ford*. Boston: Twayne, 1986.

Studlar, Gaylyn. "'Be a Proud, Glorified Dreg': Class, Gender and Frontier Democracy in *Stagecoach*." Grant, *John Ford's* 132–57.

———. "Sacred Duties, Poetic Passions: John Ford and the Issue of Femininity in the Western." Studlar and Bernstein 43–74.

Studlar, Gaylyn, and Matthew Bernstein, eds. *John Ford Made Westerns: Filming the Legend in the Sound Era*. Bloomington: Indiana UP, 2001.

Telotte, J. P. "'A Little Bit Savage': *Stagecoach* and Racial Representation." Grant, *John Ford's* 113–31.

Warshow, Robert. "Movie Chronicle: The Westerner." *Film Theory and Criticism*. 5th ed. Ed. Leo Braudy and Marshall Cohen. New York: Oxford UP, 1999. 654–67.

Wood, Robin. "'*Shall* We Gather at the River?': The Late Films of John Ford." Studlar and Bernstein 23–42.

Wright, Will. *Six-Guns and Society: A Structural Study of the Western*. Berkeley: U of California P, 1975.

Citizen Kane (1941)

JAMES NAREMORE

The Magician and the Mass Media

Context

Citizen Kane is an unusually important motion picture, but critics and historians disagree about the nature of its achievement. Some view it as a collaborative product that owes a great deal to the classical studio system; others, including myself, see it as chiefly the work of the young Orson Welles, who was only twenty-six when he produced, directed, cowrote, and starred in the film. Obviously, *Kane* would not look the same nor be so fascinating had it been made anywhere other than RKO in the early 1940s. Even so, a good deal is at stake when we emphasize Hollywood over Welles. To do so is to promote the myth of a "golden age" of studio production and to transform *Kane* into an artifact of the American heritage—all the while forgetting or repressing its controversial politics and artistic difference.

Kane was the direct outgrowth of Welles's work as a prodigious director in the New York Federal Theater and in his own Mercury Theater, both of which espoused leftist, Popular Front ideas. His spectacular success on the stage and in radio during the 1930s was closely connected to major political events of the day—the New Deal, the rise of European Fascism, and the impending world war. His infamous *War of the Worlds* broadcast, which created a national panic, led to a generous contract at RKO, where he was briefly given a remarkable degree of control; as a result he brought the entire Mercury Theater to Hollywood and attempted to create an independent production company analogous to the one he and producer John Houseman had established in New York. Radio drama had made him interested in forms of first-person narration, and perhaps because of the Mars panic created by his *War of the Worlds* broadcast, he was drawn to stories about proto-Fascist demagogues who manipulate the masses. (The first words his character speaks in *Kane,* after the whispered "Rosebud," is "Don't believe everything you hear on the radio.") He tried to adapt Joseph Conrad's *Heart of Darkness,* updating the story to reflect present-day Fascism, but when that project proved too expensive he became attracted to the idea of a thinly disguised life of a famous American, told from the "prismatic" perspective of several characters. Hollywood scriptwriter Herman Mankiewicz suggested a perfect subject for such a film: William Randolph Hearst, the multimillionaire newspaper publisher who was regarded as the creator of "yellow journalism." An American imperialist, Hearst had used his newspapers to promote the Spanish-American War and to back various jingoistic causes. When his attempts at a political career failed, he retreated to his magnificent California estate, San Simeon, where he lived openly with his mistress, movie star Marion Davies, and gave fabulous parties for the Hollywood elite. He also established his own film production company at MGM, where he sponsored the quasi-Fascistic *Gabriel over the White House* (1933) and sometimes burdened Davies, a charming comedienne, with leaden, elaborately mounted costume pictures. Meanwhile, the Hearst newspapers opposed FDR and continued to favor reactionary politicians—including, for a time, Hitler and Mussolini.

Part of the impact of *Kane* for its original audience lay in the exhilarating sense it gave of a bright, iconoclastic young director using the means of production against one of America's most wealthy media moguls. But *Kane* would have been of merely topical relevance if it were not also a powerful example of film art. On a purely formal level, the picture is important for many reasons, among them its ingenious juggling of time and perspective, its carefully designed sound track, and its influential use of wide-angle, deep-focus photography. The last of these qualities is especially striking. There was nothing new about elaborate depth of field per se; studio lighting and film stocks in the early 1930s had inhibited its use, but we can find it in earlier films by Charlie Chaplin and F. W. Murnau. What makes *Kane* different from its predecessors is Welles's tendency to openly display the spatial distortions created by photographer Gregg Toland's short lenses, plus his ability to explore the possibilities these lenses offer for long takes or sequence shots. The peculiar exaggeration of perspective in *Kane* is akin to the effects one finds in German Expressionist cinema, where sets were sometimes built in tunnel-like designs. Space becomes demonic, almost oppressive: shapes bend slightly at the edge of the screen, figures tower above us, and ceilings look unnaturally low, as if they were about to squash the characters. At Xanadu, the rooms are so large that people shrink, grotesquely dominated by their possessions. Meanwhile, the elaborately showy montage sequences (such as the ones depicting Kane's first marriage and his election campaign) tend to alternate with sequences involving only one or two shots, in which camera movements and the blocking of actors within the wide-angle space are deployed in unobtrusive but complex ways.

Welles frequently staged the action along three planes of interest. Consider the boardinghouse sequence near the beginning of the picture. Mrs. Kane (Agnes Moorehead) calls out a window to her son, closes the window, and walks the length of her parlor, the camera facing her and tracking backward until she sits at a table. From this vantage we look down the full length of the room toward the window that frames and encloses young Charles as he plays in the snow. ("The Union forever!" he shouts, just as his mother gives him away to a bank.) Mrs. Kane sits at the right foreground, her face the very image of stern puritanical sacrifice. Just beyond, the officious Thatcher (George Coulouris) shows her a document, while in the middle distance the weak, irresponsible Mr. Kane (Harry Shannon) keeps pacing back and forth and saying he doesn't like turning the boy over to a "gardeen." Dialogue overlaps and several actions occur at once; meanwhile, the faces, postures, and clothing dramatically contrast with one another, just as the blurred, limitless world of snow outside the window contrasts with the sharp, gray interior. After signing the document, Mrs. Kane rises and walks back toward the window, the camera slowly following. She pauses, opens the window, and we cut to a reverse angle, the exaggeration of space caused by the wide-angle lens giving the new vantage point an unusually dynamic force. Mrs. Kane's unhappy face looms up in the foreground as she calls out the window to Charles. Behind her, the banker and the father stand awkwardly, dwarfed by her head.

French theorist André Bazin described this technique as a dialectical leap forward in the language of the cinema, enabling directors to preserve the "realism" and "ambiguity" of dramatic space (Bazin, "Evolution" 33–36). But if Welles avoided analytical editing and allowed some scenes to play in real duration, he also distorted the spatial and temporal dimensions of the images and kept the *mise-en-scène* under fairly rigid control. Some of the so-called deep-focus shots in the film (such as the scene of Kane typing an opera review) were made not by simple photography but by matte printing, which imperceptibly combined two separate shots. *Kane* is in fact one of the most stylized and "magical" movies ever made, the RKO art department's contribution so great that many scenes look like animation. The real significance of Welles's work was not in its phenomenal realism, but in its defamiliarizing, "strange-making" qualities.

More could be written (and has been) about *Kane*'s witty sound track, which plays with aural perception, and about its gifted ensemble of actors, who give somewhat heightened performances. Suffice it to say that the film declares the director's presence at every turn, and in the process runs slightly against the grain of studio practice. In this sense its style is homologous with its political concerns. And yet *Kane* never seems a narrowly tendentious film. It has a complex attitude toward its central character, criticizing his public life but showing a fair amount of sympathy for his private problems. Throughout, it brilliantly uses the talents and technical resources of RKO, neatly balancing psychological melodrama and political satire. The following analysis tries to give a sense of how it manages these contradictions.

Analysis

There are two snow sleds in the film. As everyone knows, the first is named "Rosebud" and is given to Kane by his mother. The second is a Christmas present from Kane's guardian, Thatcher, and is seen so briefly that audiences are unaware that it, too, has a name. If you press the "pause" button on the DVD edition of *Kane*, you will discover that for a few frames sled number two, which is called "Crusader," is presented fully to the camera. Where the original has a flower, this one is embossed with the helmet of a knight. The symbolism is fairly obvious: Kane repays Thatcher's gift by growing up to be a crusading, trust-busting newspaperman, out to slay the dragon Wall Street. Deprived of maternal care, he turns himself into a phony champion of the people, a phallic overreacher who dies like a medieval knight amid the empty Gothic splendor of Xanadu.

"Crusader" was a tiny joke Welles could throw away in a movie that bristles with clever asides. I mention it because I'm foolishly proud of knowing such trivia, but also because it's a convenient way to point up the duality of almost everything in *Kane*. The title character has not only two sleds but two wives and two friends. The camera makes two visits to Susan Alexander and two journeys to Xanadu; it even shows two close-ups of "Rosebud," once as it is being obliterated by the snows of Colorado at Mrs. Kane's boardinghouse and again as it is incinerated in the basement of Kane's Florida estate. Finally, in the most vivid clash of all, we have two endings: first the reporter Thompson quietly tells his colleagues that a single word can't sum up a man's life, and the camera moves away from him, lingering over the jigsaw pieces of Xanadu's art collection; after Thompson's exit, however, the camera begins tracking toward a furnace, where it reveals the meaning of "Rosebud" after all. In its last moment, the film shifts from intellectual irony to dramatic irony, from apparent skepticism to apparent revelation.

Similar tensions can be seen in the two opening "movements" of the film—a dreamy, Expressionistic portrayal of Kane's death, followed by a newsreel depiction of his life. As David Bordwell has pointed out, Welles seems to be paying homage to the fountainheads of cinematic perception—the fantasy of Georges Méliès and the realism of the Lumières (183). But even though the two modes are placed in dialectical relation, they don't achieve a synthesis; each suggests the voyeurism inherent in the medium, and each leaves Kane an enigma. In the first shot, for example, we see a "No Trespassing" sign that the camera promptly ignores. To the strains of Bernard Herrmann's funereal "power" music, we pass beyond a gigantic "K" atop a fence and progressively nearer to a lighted window in a dark castle, all the while encountering a bizarre montage: monkeys in a cage, gondolas in a stream, a golf course. The castle looks a bit like the home of a sorcerer, its strangeness enhanced by the stereoptic quality of the artwork, which was created by the Walt Disney animators. (The Disney unit worked at RKO in this period, and was ideally suited to design the spooky, compellingly kitschy Xanadu, which seems both a wonder of the world and a monument to bad taste—a fairy-tale castle of the sort that Disney himself would later use to symbolize his theme park.) Our approach to this weird domain is as voyeuristic as anything in a

Hitchcock movie; the camera is drawn like a moth to the lighted window, but as soon as it arrives the light clicks out.

Other forward movements, usually accompanied by dissolves, are used throughout—for example, when the camera twice crawls up the walls of the El Rancho nightclub and moves toward a broken skylight, enabling us to peer at Susan Alexander. Often the movement is blocked or slightly inhibited, as in the climactic moments, when we glide forward over the flotsam of Kane's life and approach the snow sled only to have it carried away by a workman; a dissolve then takes us to a furnace, where the camera continues moving forward directly into the flames, at last coming to rest on the burning "Rosebud." Here and elsewhere, the camera functions as a restless, ghostly observer, more silent and discreet than the journalists who poke about among Kane's belongings, but similar to them in certain ways. Like Kane's own newspapers, the camera is an "inquirer," and the periodic frustrations it encounters (a door closing, a light clicking out, a sled being pulled away) are like teasing affronts to our curiosity.

Our glimpses of Kane's death, shot in the style of the early European avant-garde, hide more than they reveal, tantalizing the audience and then capping the effect suddenly by introducing a blare of music and the "News on the March" title card. Once the newsreel gets under way, we settle into a more logical mode, grounded in presumably objective, documentary facts that provide a sort of cognitive map. But if the private Kane was seen too subjectively and too close-up, the public Kane is seen too objectively and usually from too far away. Welles and about a fourth of the Mercury players had previously worked on the radio version of Henry Luce's famous newsreel series, "The March of Time," and they create a wonderfully accurate parody of its hyped-up journalism, borrowing freely some of its catchphrases, such as "this week, as it must to all men, death came to . . ." (As many critics have observed, the allusion to the Luce press serves to historically expand the film's critique of mass media.) For all its self-important tone, however, "News on the March" offers mainly a compilation of Kane's public appearances, the shots usually filled with scratches and photographed from awkward vantage points. Repeatedly, Kane is shown alongside politicians, aligning himself first with the progressives and then with the Fascists. In his early career he waves and smiles in awkward gaiety, but later he becomes somber and camera shy. We are told that "few private lives were more public," but are given only a few images of the Great Man's domestic habits. Even "1941's biggest, strangest funeral" is only a brief shot from an awkward angle; the image is grainy (Toland's imitation of newsreel stock is always perfectly accurate), and we see only a few rich mourners in the distance, over the massed heads of reporters. There is an almost comic disparity between the awesomeness of Kane's possessions and the stilted old codger we sometimes see, as if the newsreel were trying to establish him both as a mythical character like Noah or Kubla Khan and as something of a joke. He marries a president's niece and gets caught in a sex scandal; he drops wet concrete over his coat at a public ceremony; he vouches for the peaceful intentions of Hitler. He is so bumbling and foolish that little remains but his wealth, and even that is treated as a believe-it-or-not curiosity. But Welles also invites us to dislike the reporters who poke microphones and cameras in Kane's face. This feeling is reinforced when we suddenly cut to a side view of the newsreel screen: the projector clicks off and the pompous musical fanfare groans to a stop, as if somebody were giving "News on the March" a raspberry.

The ensuing conversation among reporters was shot in an actual RKO screening room. The air is smoky and the reporters sinister shadows, as they will remain throughout the film. Rawlston, the newsreel editor (Philip Van Zandt), is shown from a radically low angle, gesturing against what Welles called a "Nuremberg" light beaming down from the projection booth. He and his yes-men correctly perceive the emptiness of the newsreel, but their solution is to find an "angle." "It isn't enough to tell us what a man did," Rawlston says, "you've got to tell us who he *was*." The solution is a gimmick typical of Hearst's yellow journalism: Rawlston gives Thompson (William Alland) a tap on the shoulder and a shark's smile, ordering him to go out and get "Rosebud" "dead or alive." And yet the audience isn't allowed to feel superior. We, too, have been made curious about "Rosebud," which has the same function for Welles and Mankiewicz as it does for Rawlston. Just as the newsreel lacks impact until some key has been concocted to explain Kane's life, so the movie itself lacks force without an enigma and a nicely punctuated ending. Perhaps significantly, Herman Mankiewicz, Joseph Cotten, and Erskine Sanford (the last two of whom appear later as characters in Kane's life) are barely visible in the shadows of the room, acting in the role of reporters who scoff at Kane's dying words. Everybody is involved in a dubious pursuit. The opening sections have initiated a search, but they are filled with so many ironies and opacities that they threaten to undermine the project before it starts.

The story now becomes a series of reminiscences by witnesses to Kane's life. In this regard it should be emphasized that *Citizen Kane* is fundamentally different from a film like Akira Kurosawa's *Rashomon* (1950): it doesn't present separate versions of an unknowable reality, but instead gives different facets of a single personality. Kane's biography is depicted more or less chronologically, through the memories and judgments of five characters who knew him at progressively later stages. We never have the feeling that these characters are distorting the truth (even though Leland recounts domestic events he could not possibly have seen). In other words, for all its interest in subjectivity and psychology, *Kane* has a rational structure; it's a film about complexity, not about relativity.

Thompson's quest is initiated with a thunderclap and a Gothic rainstorm, in comically scary contrast to Rawlston's last words ("It'll probably turn out to be a very simple thing"). We see a garish, dripping poster of a blonde woman, and the camera moves upward, sliding over the roof of the El Rancho and down toward the skylight. Once again the search for "Rosebud" seems tawdry, notably so in a deep-focus shot that concludes Thompson's abortive interview with Susan (Dorothy Comingore). As Thompson steps into a phone booth and closes the door, a curious waiter (Gus Schilling) moves just a fraction to the left and is visible through one of the glass panels, listening in on the conversation. In the distance, Susan is bowed drunkenly over a table. (Marion Davies was known to Hollywood insiders as an alcoholic.) When Thompson completes his conversation with his boss, he exits the booth and tries to bribe the waiter, who comments innocently, "Thank you, thanks. As a matter of fact, just the other day, when the papers were full of it, I asked her. She never heard of Rosebud." Fade out with an ironic, playful chord of Herrmann's music.

Nearly all the fragments of the narrative are structured this way, with a mild shock or a witty image at the beginning and a joke or an ironic twist at the end. The ultimate feeling, however, is inflected by Welles's Germanic staging and by the indirect influence of impressionist novelists like Joseph Conrad and F. Scott Fitzgerald, who provided a model for the film's prismatic narrative. The Thatcher portion of the film, which grows out of Thompson's reading of the diary, is at first somewhat Dickensian in mood, telling how a poor child rises suddenly to great expectations. Within a few moments Charles Foster Kane is lifted from a snowy playground in front of his mother's boardinghouse and set down at a richly Victorian Christmas celebration, although in both places the atmosphere is chilly and the boy is surrounded by menacing adult figures. George Coulouris (made up to look like John D. Rockefeller) plays Thatcher in broad caricature, delivering his lines at top speed. In a charmingly exuberant and altogether antirealistic montage, he constantly turns to face the camera, muttering in disgust as the young Kane grows up, founds a newspaper, and then attacks Wall Street. But Kane rises only to have an ignominious fall; the narrative as a whole covers the period between the winter of 1871 and the winter of 1929, when Kane, forced by the Depression to turn part of the control of his newspapers over to his former guardian, broods on his failure, telling Thatcher that he would like to have been "everything you hate." Capital, it seems, is always in charge of Kane's life, and the market crash does little more than solidify the power of America's major bankers. At the same time, a nostalgic evocation of the nineteenth century gives way to a somber present.

The portrait of Kane that emerges from these memoirs contains many ironies. For example, he is at his most charming during an early scene in the newspaper office, where his potential danger is underlined. Thatcher, who has been reading a succession of *Inquirer* headlines, lowers a paper containing a scare headline ("Galleons of Spain off Jersey Coast") to reveal Kane sitting at his editorial desk, clad in shirtsleeves, sipping coffee with a bemused, Machiavellian glint in his eye. In the same shot, Leland (Joseph Cotten) and Bernstein (Everett Sloane) enter the frame, Leland taking a cigar from the desk (he is an addict, as we see later) and Bernstein scurrying past on official business. Kane blithely dictates a telegram that echoes one of Hearst's most famous comments to a reporter ("Dear Wheeler, you provide the prose poems and I'll provide the war") and, in a large, climactic close-up, thumbs his nose at Thatcher's warnings ("You know, Mr. Thatcher, at the rate of a million dollars a year I'll have to close this place—in sixty years"). In this scene Kane is generous with money and disrespectful toward stuffy Victorian authority; perhaps most important, he says he is committed to "the people" as opposed to "the trusts." Thatcher and the elderly editor Carter—a harrumphing old banker and a genteel incompetent—are foils to his rebelliousness, making his yellow journalism and attempt to start a war in Cuba seem like creative energy. But beneath the surface Kane is a totally different sort of character. "The trouble is," he tells Thatcher, "you don't realize you're talking to two people." On the one hand is the pretty young man who claims to represent the public; on the other is the Kane who has investments in Wall Street and knows down to the penny the amount of his holdings ("eighty-two thousand, three hundred and sixty-four shares of Public Transit Preferred"). "If I don't look after the interests of the underprivileged," he remarks, in one of the places where contradictions are reconciled and class loyalty revealed, "maybe somebody else will—maybe somebody without any money or property."

When Thompson exits the Thatcher Library ("Thanks for the use of the hall"), he goes to interview Bernstein, who maintains the spell of Kane's charm. Bernstein talks mainly about the period between the founding of the newspaper and Kane's marriage to Emily Norton (Ruth Warrick), a woman who "was no Rosebud." An apologist for Kane, he is also kindly and unpretentious—the only person who has remembered Susan after Kane's death. Realistic about old age ("the only disease you don't look forward to being cured of") as well as about his position in life ("Me? I'm chairman of the board. I got nothing but time"), he looks spry and at peace with himself, and the setting for his interview is conducive of a melancholy serenity. Bernstein sits in a leather chair, his face reflected in the polished surface of his desk as if in a quiet pool. Here, in a long take that contains some of the most discreet camera movements in the film, he tells a story about seeing a girl in a white dress on the Jersey Ferry (Welles's favorite moment, beautifully acted by Everett Sloane) and reminds us that he is the only character who has been with Kane until "after the end." And yet the kindness and the cozy atmosphere don't conceal the fact that Bernstein is an overfaithful associate from a different social class than Kane. Although Kane later tells Emily in no uncertain terms that the Jewish Bernstein may pay a visit to the family nursery, there remains a significant distance between the two men. Kane and Leland arrive together at the *Inquirer* offices in a hansom cab, dressed in the height of

New York fashion, while Bernstein tags along atop a delivery wagon. Later, at the political rally and at Susan's concert, Bernstein can be seen in the company of Kane's goons. As Kane's financial agent, he is responsible for whatever dirty work needs doing, and he always places personal loyalty above principle. His prosperity has therefore come to him like a tip from his employer.

Bernstein's reminiscences are chiefly about adventure and male camaraderie. We see Kane sweeping into the *Inquirer* and turning it into a twentieth-century paper, meanwhile promising to become a knight-errant for the people, "a fighting and tireless champion of their rights as citizens." Only a few moments earlier, he concocts a lurid news item about sex and murder, telling Carter, "If the headline is big enough, it makes the news big enough." Bernstein acknowledges these warts on Kane's character, but defends him anyway, describing him as a man connected with the destiny of the country; and, indeed, the *Inquirer* newsroom becomes a focal point of social history, where we see the country moving through different stages of liberal democracy, each attempt at progress generating new conflicts and new evils. America passes from the age of the tycoon and into the era of "mass communications," with turn-of-the-century types like Kane being destroyed by the very process they have set in motion.

Leland, whom Thompson now visits in a geriatric ward, is often regarded as the spokesman for the "moral" of the film, but he is as flawed and human as the doggedly loyal Bernstein. The ultimate product of a fading and effete New England aristocracy ("One of those old families where the father is worth ten million bucks and then one day he shoots himself and it turns out there's nothing but debts"), he is an aesthete who despises the capitalists but can never join the workers. A dandy and a puritan, he is very much the "New England schoolmarm" Kane has named him, and the film may be hinting that his involvement with Kane has sexual implications. Mankiewicz and Welles were prohibited from showing a scene in a bordello where Kane unsuccessfully tries to interest Leland in a woman, but even without that scene he seems to have no active sex life. As a young man he barely conceals his admiration for Kane, and when he grows disillusioned there is inevitably a "loose" woman involved. At the big *Inquirer* party, his frowns of disapproval and complaints about the war with Spain are played off against Kane making time with one of the chorus girls. When the "love nest" with Susan Alexander brings an end to Kane's political career, it is Leland, not Emily Kane, who behaves like a jilted lover.

The two women Kane marries are as much physical and social opposites as Leland and Bernstein, yet in their own way both are connected to his desire to assert mastery. The celebrated breakfast table montage showing the disintegration of Kane's marriage to Emily (whom Leland describes as "like all the girls I knew in dancing school") is followed by the comic toothache scene in Susan Alexander's apartment, the allegro pace dissolving into a sweet, intimate rendezvous. Aided by the least ostentatious, most persuasive makeup job in the film, Welles turns rapidly from an ardent husband wooing a president's niece into a tired businessman courting a salesgirl. Kane sentimentally imagines that Susan has a mother like his own, and the scene where he presides quietly over her "recital" is followed immediately by the opening of his campaign for governor, his sexual conquest linked to his attempt to dominate the populace. In fact, the closing line of Susan's song concerns the theme of power: it comes from *The Barber of Seville,* and roughly translates "I have sworn it, I will conquer."

The ensuing political rally is a good example of how the film creates large-scale effects with a modest budget. The atmosphere is both American and Germanic, the stem-winder of a campaign speech subtly evoking newsreel shots of Hitler's harangues to his political hacks. In place of a crowd of extras, we see a painted, Expressionistic image suggesting Kane's delusions of grandeur and the crowd's lack of individuality. Everything is dominated by Kane's ego: the initial "K" he wears as a stickpin, the huge blowup of his jowly face on a poster, and the incessant "I" in his public speech. He talks about "the workingman and the slum child," and meanwhile the frock-coated men behind him are arranged to resemble the bloated rich of a Thomas Nast cartoon. Occasionally we see Kane's supporters—Leland, Bernstein, Emily, and Kane's young son—isolated in contrasting close-ups; but his political rival, "Boss" Jim Gettys (Ray Collins), stands high above the action, the stage viewed over his shoulder, dominating the frame like a sinister power.

The showdown Gettys arranges between himself, Kane, Emily, and Susan—a private conversation in contrast to the rally—is one of the most emotionally tense scenes in the film. There are over a dozen shots in the sequence, one of them a rather long take, but no close-ups; throughout, the characters are dynamically blocked, with Kane, Susan, and Gettys alternately stepping into complete shadow. Gettys is underplayed by Collins; knowing his power, he behaves courteously to Emily, even though he proudly tells Kane that he is "not a gentleman." "You see, my idea of a gentleman . . . Well, Mr. Kane, if I owned a newspaper and didn't like the way somebody was doing things . . . I wouldn't show him in a convict suit with stripes, so his children could see him in the paper, or his mother." One mama's boy has taken revenge on the other, and Kane explodes, following Gettys out of the room and down a stairwell. "I can fight this all alone," he shouts. ". . . Gettys! I'm going to send you to Sing Sing!" The last words fade weakly into traffic sounds as Gettys exits the apartment building and closes the front door.

Just at the moment when Kane's political ambitions are wrecked, the film shifts into its examination of his sexual life. In fact, the only concrete evidence we are given of his tyranny is his treatment of Susan. According to Ferdinand Lundberg's *Imperial Hearst* (1936)—one of the sources of the film's script and the subject of an absurd plagiarism case against Welles and Mankiewicz—Hearst had employed gangsters to rout his competitors during the newspaper wars of early-twentieth-century Chicago, while Hearst's editors blamed the trouble on "labor agitators." Throughout the early decades of the century, Hearst was a vigorous opponent of unions and child-labor legislation, and his mining interests in Peru were more or less forced labor camps. *Kane*'s only apparent reference to such things is to show Bernstein in the company of hired toughs and to have Leland berate Kane for his paternalistic attitude toward workers. In effect, Mankiewicz and Welles were condensing and displacing the social issues, using a love story to illustrate the character flaws that would presumably make the tycoon a danger to the public. If Susan Alexander is only roughly similar to Marion Davies, that is partly because Welles and Mankiewicz converted her into a symbol of the society at large. As Leland says, she represents for Kane a "cross-section of the American public." When Kane meets her she is a working girl, undereducated and relatively innocent, and his relationship with her is comparable to his relationship with the masses who read his papers. He showers her with wealth, but this merely confirms Leland's remark in the desolated, postelection newspaper office:

"You just want to persuade people that you love them so much that they ought to love you back." Indeed, all of Leland's accusations and prophecies are confirmed in Susan's part of the film. "You talk about the people as though you owned them," Leland says. Kane's treatment of Susan illustrates the truth of this charge and also reminds us of the violence Kane is willing to use to have his way; thus in the last reels, which show Kane retreating more and more from public life, Susan is reduced from a pleasant, attractive girl to a near suicide.

After his marriage to Susan, Kane tells reporters, "We're going to become an opera star," and he hires Matisti (Fortunio Bonanova) to begin the arduous, comically inappropriate series of music lessons. The settings grow more opulent, while Susan becomes increasingly driven and humiliated. As a result, her resemblance to Marion Davies fades. She looks more like those Peruvians toiling at gunpoint in Hearst's copper mines, though she is certainly getting better pay. Notice also that the choice of opera rather than movies for Susan's career is significant; it highlights the difference in social class between her and the patrons for whom she works. In a skillful operatic pastiche composed by Herrmann, we see her kneeling on satin pillows, pitifully frightened and garishly made-up, singing "Ah! Cruel" in a register beyond the capabilities of her voice. Meanwhile, a tuxedoed audience dozes, and, in a trick shot, the camera seems to drift up to the rafters to show a laborer holding his nose and shaking his head sadly.

"I'm not high class like you," Susan tells Kane in an even shriller voice when she kneels again on the floor and reads the Leland-Kane review, "and I never went to any swell schools." She attempts to quit the opera, but Kane orders her to continue because "I don't propose to have myself made ridiculous." In a scene remarkable for the way it shows the pain of both people, his shadow falls over her face—just as he will later tower over her in the "party" scene, when a woman's ambiguous scream is heard distantly on the sound track. Ultimately, however, Susan asserts her own power. Leland has warned that the workingman will not always tolerate Kane's patronage: "You're not going to like that one little bit when you find out it means your workingman expects something as his right and not your gift." This is more or less why Susan leaves Kane. In some ways her story may seem to replace political with personal concerns, but in other ways it shows how the public and the personal are interrelated.

Throughout, Kane is presented with a mixture of awe, satiric invective, and sympathy. To Thatcher, he is a spoiled do-gooder who is a menace to business; to Bernstein, a hero who helped build the country; to Leland, an egomaniac who wants everybody to love him but who leaves only "a tip in return." No single response is adequate, and near the end, the disparate judgments take the form of a contradictory emotion. Thompson remarks to Susan, "You know, all the same I feel sorry for Mr. Kane." Susan, the only character we've actually seen Kane victimize, gives Thompson a harsh look and a terse reply: "Don't you think I do?" Her comment crystallizes the film's mixed attitude. In the later sequences, when Kane nearly destroys her, we fear along with Susan, but we also feel Kane's age, frustration, and desire. This feeling is especially strong toward the end, where the most powerful and intense moments—Kane's enraged breaking-up of Susan's room and his discovery of the paperweight—are played off against the predatory Raymond (Paul Stewart) and the vast, mirrored labyrinth of Xanadu. As the psychological inquiry deepens, the tone of the film changes slightly. The comic blackout sketches typical of the Thatcher and Bernstein accounts are replaced by a more grotesque comedy that belongs to Susan—the scenes near the big Xanadu fireplace, for example, with Susan's voice echoing, "A person could go crazy in this dump"; or the surreal picnic, with a stream of black cars driving morosely down a beach toward a swampy encampment, where a jazz band plays "This Can't Be Love" against a matted background of sinister RKO bats borrowed from *The Son of Kong* (1933). Each phase of the story becomes more painful than the one before, until we arrive at the most cynical of the witnesses, Raymond, who is ironically responsible for the most intimate details: Susan leaves Kane, moving down a corridor into infinity and exiting Xanadu to the sound of an enraged cockatoo. (Both shots are impressive uses of optical printing.) In response, Kane blindly destroys her room and remembers his childhood loss.

Thompson never emerges from the shadows, but at the end he becomes a slightly troubled onlooker. Finally, he gives up his search, knowing too much to expect a simple answer. We are in a similar position, but are given, if not a rational explanation, a vision of "Rosebud" that appears to transcend the various witnesses. Here it might be noted that Welles was uneasy about the whole snow-sled idea. He dismissed "Rosebud" in a famous remark, calling it "dollar-book Freud" and emphasizing that Herman Mankiewicz thought it up. Even so, some of the psychoanalytic ideas that he and Mankiewicz used in the film might have come straight from a textbook. According to Freudian terminology, Kane can be described as a regressive, anal-sadistic personality. His lumpen-bourgeois family is composed of a weak, untrustworthy father and a loving, albeit puritanical mother; he is taken away from the mother during a period of sexual latency and reared by a bank, and as an adult he "returns" to what Freud describes as a pregenital form of sexuality in which "not the genital component-instincts, but the sadistic and anal are most prominent" (336). Thus Kane is partly a sadist who wants to obtain power over others and partly an anal type who obsessively collects things. A child-man, he spends all his energies rebelling against anyone who asserts authority over his will. He despises Thatcher, and when he can no longer "look after" the little people, he begins to hate them, too. When we last see him he throws a tantrum, like a baby destroying a nursery.

Imprisoned by his childhood ego, Kane treats everything as a toy: first the sled, then the newspaper, then the Spanish-American War. (Notice how the war is depicted as a child's game, with the *Inquirer* reporters sporting little wooden rifles and funny hats.) Toward the end there is Susan, with her marionette-style opera makeup and her doll-house room in a fantasy castle. The final toy, the snowy paperweight, is symptomatic of his need for a self-enclosed realm, immune from change, where he can feel autonomous. The sled burning at the heart of the furnace recalls that same realm, and like the paperweight is linked to his memory image of his mother. After our discovery of the sled, however, *Citizen Kane* concludes with another reminder of our inquisitiveness and a comment on the vanity of Kane's worldly enterprises. The camera retreats from the magic castle, staring at the smoke of corruption that drifts off into the sky, ultimately settling on the "No Trespassing" sign outside the gate. We are back where we began. Even the film's title has been a contradiction in terms.

Conclusion

Kane has become part of American folklore, and its situations keep returning in the news—Richard Nixon secluding himself in San Clemente or Howard Hughes, before his death, owning a retreat in the

Bahamas that he called the "Hotel Xanadu." Before leaving the film, therefore, we need to return to its politics. We might begin by noting that Welles was at least technically correct when he repeatedly told interviewers that Kane was a fictional character based on several turn-of-the-century tycoons. In translating Hearst into a creature of fiction, he and Mankiewicz borrowed freely from the lives of other American capitalists (among them Samuel Insull and John McCormack). They salted the story with references to Welles's own biography, and at several junctures they departed from well-known facts about Hearst, each of them important to the dramatic and ideological effect of the film. For example, they gave Kane a humble birth, which was not true of Hearst or of any other real-life figure to whom he could be compared. Equally significant, because more than anything else it aroused the ire of the Hearst press, they made Susan Alexander into a tormented, unhappy creature who walks out on her supposed benefactor—this in contrast to the Hearst-Davies relationship, which seemed generally happy. Indeed, when death finally came to Hearst, it was very different from Kane's death in the film. He did not spend his last days alone in the caverns of his estate; several years earlier he had moved to the Beverly Hills mansion of his mistress, and he died with her close at hand. His last words were unrecorded.

Most of these changes tend to create sympathy for Kane. As a poor boy suddenly given wealth he becomes less representative of his class, and as a tycoon in the grip of a psychological compulsion he seems doomed and lonely, an embodiment of the cliché that money can't buy happiness. Even so, it should be noted that throughout the 1930s, writers of the left had relished giving Hearst's career the structure of a morality play. In *The Big Money* (1936), John Dos Passos saw Hearst as a "spent Caesar grown old with spending," and in his preface to the biography of Hearst by Ferdinand Lundberg, Charles Beard predicted that the old man would die lonely and unloved. By showing Kane as a tragicomic failure, Mankiewicz and Welles were doing no more than what these writers had done, and when they changed the facts to suit the demands of melodrama they were, in principle, responding to a plea made by Lundberg, who argued that popularized criticism of Hearst's deceptions was badly needed.

In any case, *Kane* clearly does satirize Hearst's public life. It shows Kane's manipulative interest in the Spanish-American War, it reveals his exploitative "philosophy" of journalism, and it makes several references to his attacks on organized labor. In the election scenes it depicts the corruption of machine politics with the force of a great editorial cartoon. In regard to Kane's so-called progressive youth, the film is explicit in its denunciation, showing his supposed democratic aspirations as in reality a desire for power. We even see him on a balcony conferring with Hitler, an image that colors everything the character does. Equally interesting and more unorthodox, the film brings its own workings under scrutiny. From the beginning, when "Rosebud" is introduced as a cheap means of spicing up a newsreel, until the end, when Thompson confesses the futility of searching out the meaning for a single word, *Kane* suggests that the process of discovery is more important than any pat conclusion. All the while, Welles's manipulation of cinematic technique keeps reminding us that we are watching a movie rather than reality itself.

The political significance of the film was certainly not lost on Hearst, who was alive and kicking—a danger not only because of his publishing empire, which refused to advertise the film, but also because of the power he wielded in Hollywood. As a result of a vendetta by the Hearst press, *Kane* never received the block theatrical booking normally accorded to RKO's major releases. Independent theater managers everywhere were concerned about Hearst's wrath, to say nothing of what they regarded as the potential artiness of the film. Meanwhile, Hearst influenced the FBI to initiate a secret investigation of Welles that lasted for thirty years, during which time he was branded a subversive. *Kane* was recognized by many reviewers (especially in the Luce press, which was Hearst's major rival), by Hollywood professionals, and even somewhat reluctantly by the Motion Picture Academy. At the same time, it made Welles's future in American movies problematic. The paradox—and one of the biggest contradictions of them all—is that Welles had no desire to wreck the motion-picture industry. *Kane* was held to a relatively modest A-picture budget ($749,000). Nevertheless, industry bosses perceived Welles as an "artist" and a left-wing ideologue who might bring trouble. His film may not have been a thoroughgoing anticapitalist attack or a truly avant-garde experiment, but it was close enough to ensure that he would never again be allowed such freedom at a major studio.

Credits

United States, 1941, A Mercury Production at RKO

Director: Orson Welles
Producer: Orson Welles
Screenplay: Herman J. Mankiewicz, Orson Welles, and (uncredited)
  John Houseman
Cinematography: Gregg Toland
Assistant Director: Richard Wilson
Editing: Robert Wise and Mark Robson
Music: Bernard Herrmann
Sound: Bailey Fesler and James G. Stewart
Art Direction: Van Nest Polglase and Perry Ferguson
Set Decoration: Darrel Silvera
Costume Design: Edward Stevenson
Special Effects: Vernon L. Walker
Optical Printing: Linwood G. Dunn

CAST:

Charles Foster Kane	Orson Welles
Jed Leland	Joseph Cotten
Bernstein	Everett Sloane
Susan Alexander	Dorothy Comingore
Jim Gettys	Ray Collins
Thompson and newsreel narrator	William Alland
Mary Kane	Agnes Moorehead
Emily Norton	Ruth Warrick
Walter Parks Thatcher	George Coulouris
Herbert Carter	Erskine Sanford
Jim Kane	Harry Shannon
Rawlston	Philip Van Zandt
Raymond	Paul Stewart
Matisti	Fortunio Bonanova
Curator of Thatcher Library	Georgia Backus
Kane, age 8	Buddy Swan
Kane, Jr.	Sunny Bupp
Waiter	Gus Schilling
Entertainer	Charles Bennett
Nurse	Edith Evanston
Reporters	Alan Ladd, Louise Currie, Eddie Coke, Walter Sande, Arthur O'Connell, Katherine Trosper, and Richard Wilson

Bibliography

Arthur, Paul. "Out of the Depths: *Citizen Kane,* Modernism, and the Avant-Garde Impulse." Gottesman, *Perspectives* 367–82.

Bazin, André. "The Evolution of Film Language." *What Is Cinema?* Vol. 1. Ed. and trans. Hugh Gwen. Berkeley: U of California P, 1967. 23–40.

———. *Orson Welles: A Critical View.* Trans. Jonathan Rosenbaum. New York: Harper, 1978.

Bordwell, David. "The Dual Cinematic Tradition in *Citizen Kane.*" *The Classic Cinema.* New York: Harcourt, 1973. 181–97.

Bordwell, David, and Kristin Thompson. "Style in *Citizen Kane.*" *Film Art: An Introduction.* 4th ed. New York: McGraw, 1993. 60–69.

Callow, Simon. *The Road to Xanadu.* New York: Viking, 1995.

Carringer, Robert L. "*Citizen Kane, The Great Gatsby,* and Some Conventions of American Narrative." *Critical Inquiry* 2.2 (1975): 307–25.

———. *The Making of "Citizen Kane."* Berkeley: U of California P, 1985.

———. "Rosebud Dead or Alive: Narrative and Symbolic Structure in *Citizen Kane.*" *PMLA* 91.2 (1976): 185–93.

———. "The Scripts of *Citizen Kane.*" *Critical Inquiry* 5.6 (1978): 369–400.

Cook, David. *A History of Narrative Film.* 3rd ed. New York: Norton, 1996.

Dos Passos, John. *The Big Money.* New York: Harcourt, 1936.

Freud, Sigmund. *A General Introduction to Psychoanalysis.* Trans. Joan Riviere. New York: Washington Sq., 1962.

Gottesman, Ronald, ed. *Focus on "Citizen Kane."* Englewood Cliffs: Prentice, 1971.

———, ed. *Perspectives on "Citizen Kane."* New York: G. K. Hall, 1996.

Ishaghpour, Youssef. *Les films de la périodé américaine.* Paris: Editions de la Différence, 2001. Vol. 2 of *Orson Welles cinéaste: Une camera visible.* 3 vols.

Kael, Pauline. "Raising Kane." *New Yorker* 20 and 27 Feb. 1971. Rpt. in *The "Citizen Kane" Book.* Boston: Little, 1971. 3–84.

Lundberg, Ferdinand. *Imperial Hearst.* New York: Modern Library, 1937.

McBride, Joseph. *Orson Welles.* 1972. Rev. ed. New York: Da Capo, 1996.

Mulvey, Laura. "*Citizen Kane.*" London: BFI, 1992.

Naremore, James. *The Magic World of Orson Welles.* 1978. Rev. ed. Dallas: Southern Methodist UP, 1989.

———. "The Trial: The FBI vs. Orson Welles." *Film Comment* Jan.–Feb. 1991: 22–27.

Rosenbaum, Jonathan. "The Battle over Orson Welles." *Cineaste* 22.3 (1996): 6–10.

Simon, William G., ed. *Persistence of Vision* 7 (1989). Spec. issue on Orson Welles.

Thomas, François, and Jean-Pierre Berthomé. *Citizen Kane.* Paris: Flammarion, 1992.

Welles, Orson, and Peter Bogdanovich. *This Is Orson Welles.* Ed. Jonathan Rosenbaum. New York: Da Capo, 1998.

Wollen, Peter. "*Citizen Kane.*" *Readings and Writings.* London: Verso, 1982.

Casablanca (1942)

DANA POLAN

The Limitless Potentials and the Potential Limits of Classical Hollywood Cinema

Context

You can pretty much see it coming. The American Film Institute is doing its glossy television show on the "100 Most Romantic Films of All Time," and the broadcast has just come back from its last commercial break to the final countdown of the top choices. The runner-up is announced: *Gone with the Wind.* You probably know now what the top one will be. You can probably even guess which clip they'll use. There it is: at the airport in the blur of the fog, smoke, and mist (and teardrops welling up in the woman's eyes), Rick Blaine (Humphrey Bogart) tells his great love Ilsa (Ingrid Bergman) that he is staying to fight in the war and that she must go off with her husband. "You're part of his work. The thing that keeps him going," Rick tells her. "If that plane leaves the ground and you're not with him, you'll regret it, maybe not today, maybe not tomorrow . . . but soon, and for the rest of your life." These lines will be repeated at the end of the homage film *Play It Again, Sam* (1972) by Allan Felix, the Bogart wannabe that Woody Allen plays, as he also heroically sends his great love off to go back to her husband. "That's beautiful," waxes the woman (Diane Keaton). "It's from *Casablanca,*" replies Allan, "I've waited all my life to say it."

One of the great films of cult veneration, *Casablanca* is the perfect example of Hollywood perfection. By this double formulation, I mean to get at two things: (1) *Casablanca* comes closest for many fans to embodying Hollywood cinema in its classic moment insofar as (2) we imagine this classic cinema to encapsulate a certain high level of achievement in escapist entertainment and storytelling accomplishment. *Casablanca* appears to have it all: to cite just a few of its qualities, elegance and escapism blended with gripping topicality; drama and suspense but also wit and charm; lush visuality matched with melodious sound (the romantic wall-to-wall music of the great romantic composer Max Steiner); exoticism mixed with recognizable world-weariness in the figure of its cynical antihero; and a narrative style of seeming effortlessness, each great shot and each great scene gliding into the next with verve, but grace, too. The film seems perfectly acted, perfectly shot and put together, perfectly written (both at the level of those great individual lines and of the larger construction of a gripping narrative).

For Umberto Eco, *Casablanca* is not just a great case of Hollywood cinema. Rather, it is an incarnation of an idea of cinema per se as entertainment. As Eco puts it, "*Casablanca* became a cult movie because it is not *one* movie. It is 'movies'" (208). Working through the beginning of the film scene by scene, Eco shows the extent to which many myths, archetypes, and references to other narratives (filmic and otherwise) run through *Casablanca*. And it is not just that the film is so rich in offering resonances of a whole history of popular culture; it matters that the film does so well in presenting all of this with style but also with seeming ease. *Casablanca* is a film that seems to come to its spectator with confidence—that confident well-being that we take to be one of the trademarks of the Hollywood studio system.

Take, for instance, the first sequences after the credits. With an air of effortlessness, but which the spectator knows to be the result (as the credits have just informed him/her) of the crafted professionalism of the labor-intensive Hollywood film industry, the film guides us into its fictional world by gliding into it: music that plays over shots, dissolves that blend one shot into the next and thereby smooth over the transitions, and cuts that maintain screen directions and match action between shots all work to construct a faultless narrative flow that pulls the spectator in. At the same time, in a seeming divergence from mere escapism, the first moments after the credits assail the spectator with background material that is virtually documentary or even pedagogical in nature—a rush of information conveyed through newsreel footage, maps, and an authoritative masculine voice-over. Later in this essay, we will examine in greater detail some of the ways *Casablanca* may diverge from the classical Hollywood cinema that it is held to be a perfect example of, and, for the moment, it is worth noting the extent to which this opening gives some signs of the film's nonclassical aspects. In this period of war—an historical moment in which it is assumed that citizens will need factual information as much as entertainment—numerous Hollywood films began to be infiltrated by instances of didacticism and direct address to the audience. In such instances, the films presented not a fictional world that the viewer can watch from the safe distance of escapism but a world of immediate pertinence presented directly and explicitly to the spectator.

Nonetheless, *Casablanca* also has romantic escape and fantasy on its mind, and it quickly leaves its didacticism behind (although it will return later in the film's central choice between isolationism and war commitment). Soon a seamless dissolve moves us from the world of documentary into the studio-constructed exoticism of an artificial Casablanca. In this imaginary version of a real city prominent in the headlines when the film came out, a fictional narrative can emerge. And this will be a narrative conveyed with precision, economy, confidence, and perfection.

Look, for instance, at a series of four shots that enable the story to get going. In an effort to track down the killers of couriers who had been carrying valuable transit papers, the value of which was established in large part by the opening narration, which informed us about the need to flee Nazism and about Casablanca's importance as a key point in the trajectory of escape, the police in Casablanca have been told to round up all suspicious characters. A montage of shots shows a series of arrests and gives this incident an anecdotal quality: here, the montage appears to tell us, are examples of the sorts of shady figures that people the town. But suddenly, out of this series of anonymous anecdotes of ongoing police arrest, one suspect looks offscreen left and then dashes off in that direction, the camera pivoting to follow him as he moves past his potential captors. The camera ends its pivot, and he moves out of the frame, which now focuses on a young man and woman whom we've not seen before and who in alarm look left in the direction the suspect has fled. A cut leaves behind the couple to give us the predictable object of their look: the suspect who is continuing to run toward the left (with the police now joining him again in the frame, following in hot pursuit).

The couple would seem to have only an incidental function here: they would appear to be mere momentary bystanders whose primary function is less narrative than stylistic, the direction of their look allowing a seamless cut to take place. But through the narrative economy that is so central to the classical Hollywood cinema—a veritable

rule that one should introduce nothing that won't be of use somewhere else in the plot—these two people will play an important narrative function through the course of the film. They, it turns out, are
young lovers hoping themselves to flee Casablanca, and their plight
will eventually touch Rick in ways that reveal chinks in his cynical antiromantic armor.

But for the moment, the spectator's concern is with the suspect
running through a frame that also includes the police pursuing him.
They stop and take aim at him as he moves past a poster toward a passageway he obviously intends to escape through. With just these two
shots—the pivoting one in which the suspect leaves his potential captors behind and out of frame, and the static one in which those captors
have regained the foreground and are taking aim at his fleeing figure
near the passageway—the film gives evidence of that balancing and
rhyming function that a number of film scholars have seen as central
to the functioning of classical Hollywood storytelling. Each moment
of the story builds tightly from the previous one, each one flows into
the next, and sequences of such moments will serve as building blocks
for the larger narrative that the film tells. The second shot "answers"
the first and makes their conjunction into a veritable mininarrative:
the promise of escape and the immediate and seemingly inevitable
dashing of that promise.

From the image of the police taking aim, then, the cut to the next
image appears consequential, logical, and even natural: the camera
has moved close to the fleeing suspect, the blasts of guns ring out, and
he falls dead. As he drops to the bottom of the frame, the camera cuts
in even closer, showing us the details of a poster next to the passageway the man had intended to flee through: it is of Marshall Pétain, notorious in the public imagination of the time for selling out France to
the Nazis. The increasing emphasis by moving the camera closer to
Pétain's image adds a symbolic dimension to the scene: *Casablanca*, we
are being told, will be a story of betrayal, both personal and political.
The police move into frame once again and bend down to the body,
the camera following their every gesture and moving in close as they
discover Free French resistance documents on him.

These are four quick shots of seemingly incidental nature. After all,
they introduce and fully dispatch a character we have never seen and
who will never be referred to again. Yet so much has been enabled by

them. With precision and brevity, the film has indicated that one genre it will belong to is that of wartime action: out of the picturesque exoticism of the Casablanca market there abruptly emerges a narrative of violence. Likewise, it signals to us that suspense will be key to the workings of this film: there is the sudden hope of escape and, just as suddenly, with a cut, we are in a world of gunfire and death. With economy, the shots have set up some of the political conflict that will be one of the film's central themes—the threat of betrayal and the need to oppose to it the wartime fight for freedom—but they also indicate that nothing about this conflict is decided in advance. A freedom fighter might seem to be getting away from the forces of oppression, but one single cut can lead to the destruction of that hope. Will this be the fate of all such resisters?

To be sure, the overwhelming omnipresence of the Hollywood happy ending at this moment in film's history (the 1940s) might lead one to suppose that the end of the film is given in advance: this one anonymous freedom fighter may die at the beginning of the film, but the conventions of Hollywood storytelling necessitate a greater victory for the forces of good over the course of the whole film. Yet *Casablanca*'s narrative will reveal itself to be less conventional, conformist, and predictable than that. In fact, it is not clear for much of its narrative how it is defining the very notion of "good," and it is therefore not clear just how it will end: Do the film's deepest sympathies lie in the romantic and very American myth of the independent loner that Rick performs until his final political conversion? Or do they find their value in the commitment to the higher communal good that Laszlo represents? What precisely would a happy ending be in such a context? As a film of the war moment, it would seem that its explicit allegiance is to Laszlo and the need for engagement in the war, but it is also clear that there is something just a little too pure, too squeaky-clean, about Laszlo for audience identification to be wholly and wholeheartedly with him. Caught in a moment of transition from the innocent classicism of Hollywood's golden age in the 1930s to a wartime and then postwar context, which is much more downbeat and even cynical about innocence and the purity of romance—and about the ability of Hollywood entertainment to convey that innocence and purity unproblematically—*Casablanca* offers up a contradictory, even confused, ideology that suggests that its impression of confident classicism is in fact far from assured.

Production History

Indeed, if we look at some of the history of *Casablanca*—and less the history of its reception (so much of which has been about turning it into an unassailable object of cult veneration) than the history of its production within the studio as well as the wartime social history to which it is responding—suddenly the surface impression of effortless perfection seems less apparent. *Casablanca*'s "perfection" comes at a price: ironically, the film that seems to sum up Hollywood cinema is also a "perfect" symptom of the forces brewing in the 1940s that would spell an end to classical Hollywood cinema and its escapist romantic confidence. Production history and social history reveal imperfections in *Casablanca*'s glossy veneer.

Like so many Hollywood films, *Casablanca* achieved its image of perfection only as the result of a complicated production trajectory made up of compromises, last-minute improvisations, and seemingly arbitrary decisions. Despite the assembly-line-like efficiency of the Hollywood production process, there could be something haphazard in the making of any particular film; in fact, much of the specific production history for *Casablanca* shows that its makers were unsure of many things and made often random decisions along the way. The files on *Casablanca* in the Warner Bros. Archives at the University of Southern California reveal a production in which virtually every major decision was subject to modification, in which every element that ended up on the screen came as the result of complicated debate, revision, and downright improvisation. Even the title of the film was not fixed: only on the last day of 1941 was the title for this 1942 production decided on as *Casablanca* and not *Casa Blanca*. With an imminent early spring date for the start of shooting, *Casablanca* would be the object of endless negotiation during the preproduction phase. For example, on January 7, 1942, press releases went out to say that Ann Sheridan and Ronald Reagan would play the leads in the film with Dennis Morgan as Laszlo, suggesting that the studio was thinking of it at this point as something quite other than a prestige picture, since none of these actors was an A-list lead. There is some possibility, however, that Warner Bros. never really planned to cast Reagan but was mentioning his name just to build up publicity around him. (More than one film critic has speculated that if this casting had actually happened and Reagan had garnered success, he would not have remained consigned to the lesser ranks of

Warner Bros. actors and may have had a more successful acting career, thereby removing the temptation to leave acting for politics. World history might have been very different, the speculation goes!)

But even the announced casting was not fixed in stone. Even though Reagan was soon dropped from press releases about the casting and announcements made of Ann Sheridan's pairing with Humphrey Bogart, memos from studio head Jack Warner show that he was dissatisfied with the female casting and appeared to want someone with European connotations: thus, with a very short time to go before production began, Warner contemplated recently arrived French émigré actresses like Michèle Morgan or Edwige Feuillère (on March 30, 1942, Warner wrote that he would take the latter "in a minute for the leading woman" [Warner, File 18882]) or the more established émigré Hedy Lamarr. Warner's borrowing of Ingrid Bergman from independent producer David O. Selznick finally gave the studio its exotically European actress, but it also brought a series of problems with it: for example, to get Bergman, Warner had to accept certain contractual stipulations such as "all calls about tests for wardrobe or makeup or hair must go through Selznick," thus interfering with the studio's own control of the project (Warner, File 12732).

Even the casting of Dooley Wilson, who was borrowed from Paramount, as Sam, came from compromise and improvisation. Jack Warner very seriously considered the *female* African American singers Lena Horne and Ella Fitzgerald for the role, and just as it is perhaps amusing to imagine Ronald Reagan as Rick, it is intriguing to wonder what the casting of either Horne or Fitzgerald would have done to this film that is so much about gender relations and whose plot involves Rick going from one male buddy (Sam) to another (Louis), with Ilsa as only an impossible heterosexual interlude between long moments of homosocial bonding. (It is also saddening to realize from the Warner records that Hollywood racial fears meant that Dooley Wilson was contracted to $3,500 for seven to eight weeks of shooting but did not get major billing in the credits, while Conrad Veidt, in the role of Major Strasser—chosen after Warner contemplated Otto Preminger for the part—got $25,000 for five weeks and had his name in the fifth position in the credits.)

Records show that until at least thirty-two days into shooting, not all of the script issues of *Casablanca* had been resolved. This is probably more typical of the Hollywood mode of production than the seemingly efficient and elegant sheen of its products would lead us to imagine. From its opening credits—where the names of Bogart and Bergman on one line and the lesser star Paul Henreid on the next signal that this will be the story of a love triangle, and seem to indicate how this rivalry of love will work out (the star system will triumph and Bogie will get the girl)—*Casablanca* seems simultaneously to work with the inevitable logic of formula that we have come to associate with Hollywood classicism *and* to emphasize how any logic, any one outcome to its narrative, is random and accidental. Throughout the film, the spectator is unsure of plot twists and unsure of the motivations and commitments of characters.

Film historian Richard Maltby aptly describes the film's open-ended quality in an essay entitled "'A Brief Romantic Interlude': Dick and Jane Go to 3½ Seconds of the Classical Hollywood Cinema." *Casablanca,* he says, "quite deliberately constructs itself in such a way as to offer distinct and alternative sources of pleasure to two people sitting next to each other in the cinema" (443); it "presents an incomplete narrative requiring of its viewers a good deal of basic work in hypothesis-forming and -testing before the movie's story can be constructed" (449).

The 3½ seconds in the subtitle of Maltby's essay refers to the end of the sequence in the film in which Ilsa has come to Rick's apartment to do whatever she can to get the letters of transit from him so that Laszlo can escape to freedom. After several shifting power plays—Ilsa unexpectedly pulls a gun on Rick, Rick unexpectedly disarms her by the sheer force of his seductiveness, and so on—there is the swelling up of irrepressible love and reconciliation as the two lovers overcome everything that has held them back from each other. There is the deep kiss and then a curious sequence with a dissolve to an airplane tower and back to the apartment at a moment later in time, with the two lovers acting casually as if nothing has transpired. As Maltby shows, there are incompatible meanings at work here: some things tell us that Rick and Ilsa have just slept together, and other details tell us they have not. (Amusingly, when the Hays Office, the censorship arm of Hollywood, examined the scripting for this scene, its recommendation was that any fade-outs be replaced by dissolves since the former were known by savvy audience members to be coded signals that sex was happening.)

But the undecidability of this key moment—a moment whose interpretation, for instance, inflects how we read Rick's final conversation with Laszlo, in which Rick reconciles the husband to Ilsa by ensuring him that no sex happened—spreads throughout the film and makes much of the experience of *Casablanca* a guessing game. When precisely does Rick decide to help Ilsa and Laszlo? When does Louis make his decision? How much does Laszlo really know or suspect about Rick and Ilsa? Can we fully believe Ilsa when she explains to Rick her motives in Paris for not telling him about Laszlo—first, she thought Laszlo was dead; then, she felt she had to protect him when he was found to be alive? What do we make of the ending of the film with Rick and Louis walking off into a nebulous fog toward an ambiguous future, a finale that is simultaneously open ended (will they live? will they die?) and yet closed by a perfect poetic justice and political logic (life or death doesn't matter; what is important is that these two men have committed to the war effort)? This structure of undecidability helps explain why spectators can go back to *Casablanca* as a cult object and find so much to work with in it. Indeed, one of the most amusing documents in the papers in the Warner Bros. Archive has to do with the evident frustration of a fan who does not take the ending to be satisfactory at all. This fan, Verne Chute (later a somewhat successful writer of science fiction), writes to producer Hal B. Wallis in 1943 to propose the film be reshot with a happy ending. At the last minute, he suggests, it should be revealed that Laszlo and Ilsa are actually brother and sister who, for complicated plot reasons, pretended to be husband and wife, thus freeing Rick and Ilsa to go off together! Intriguingly, Wallis politely and predictably dismisses the suggestion (he pleads the expense such reshooting would involve), but he does declare, "some consideration is being given to doing a sequel to CASABLANCA; and this may materialize" (Chute). (It might be worth noting that in the 1990s there was in fact a follow-up novel to *Casablanca, As Time Goes By,* by one Michael Walsh, in which Rick, Louis, and Ilsa team up to try to assassinate a Nazi general.)

For all the zaniness of his suggestions, Verne Chute was registering the sense in which the perfect and perfected *Casablanca* can also seem unfinished. There has long been a legend that the ending of *Casablanca*—Ilsa caught between Rick and Laszlo, Rick caught between love and a newfound commitment to the war effort, and each choosing something of the greater good—was improvised at the last minute. While this might seem to overstate the case—it is clear that renunciation of love is the only possible ending to such a wartime film—there nonetheless is something unsettled about *Casablanca,* something ambiguous and open ended.

Analysis

Deconstructing the Classical Hollywood Film

Perfection for the Hollywood film came at a cost (literally so since all the production compromises added up), but in the specific case of *Casablanca,* the difficulties of production—the studio's typical indecision as to just how the product should be put together—seem to have been compounded by its historical moment. If the Hollywood dream machine had ever been a competent apparatus for generating escapist diversions, the moment of the Second World War posed a specific threat to the efficient workings of that machine. How to make audiences believe in fictive happy endings when the outcome of their real lives was in jeopardy—especially early in the war when there had been so many defeats? How to make audiences swallow perfect stories when the world around them was lacking in such perfection? (*Casablanca* at least could exploit the fact of the first Allied victories in North Africa, but still it was released at a moment when ultimate victory was far from assured.) How to continue promoting an ideology of romance when so many couples were being torn apart and where such separation was a sanctioned government policy? As his newlywed wife says to the Bogart character in another Warner Bros. film from just a year later (*Action in the North Atlantic,* 1943) when he is called back to the ship he is commander of, "We can't go around holding hands at a time like this!" Or as the title heroine of the 1943 war-recruitment comedy *Reveille with Beverly* sings to the two men in her life in that film, "I'm taking a rain check on love."

Classic Hollywood revolves around love—around plots that so frequently lead to the formation of a couple and the sealing of their relationship in the happy ending of a kiss that seems to last forever. But the war renders the promise of eternal love unstable. Heterosexual virtues—family, marriage, domesticity, and so on—are some of the values supposedly being fought for, but the fight itself leads to their being put on hold, bracketed out, and even rendered fragile. For instance, the war sends men away from home and offers them new experiences—ones that are both horrific and energizing in their exotic difference—that often make the return home seem alien. Likewise, women at home discover new opportunities (for example, in the realm of work) that lead to frustration when these are taken away from them in the postwar period. The reuniting of men and women can be joyous, but it can also be a source of suspicion—just what has my partner been doing during our separation? Just as there is an onslaught of sudden marriages during the war, there is as great a rush to divorce in the postwar period, as men and women frequently come to realize they are strangers to each other. *Films noirs* (men realizing the perfidy of seemingly seductive *femmes fatales*) and women's gothic films (women realizing the threat of strangers they've married and who they suspect are out to kill them) register these tensions, but similar anxieties also play through a wartime film like *Casablanca,* a film seemingly more confident in its ideology of romance but already giving in to suspicion about love and romantic commitment. It is standard in the literature on film to imagine that cynicism, suspicion, and doubt entered American cinema in the postwar period of *film noir,* but these were already operative in the moment of the war (where *noir* was already beginning to develop as a genre). For instance, central to the plot of *Casablanca* is the discovery by the man and the woman that each of them has gone in other directions during their separation: being apart has not meant eternal devotion. The war has upset relationships—Ilsa, for instance, first thinks Laszlo is dead and therefore out of her life, and then she has to deal with the fact that he is back—and there is every implication that the stability of romance will not be repaired in any easy fashion. *Casablanca* is immersed in a world of suspicion, and one of the very qualities to be suspected is the profundity of love itself.

With the war, lovers in Hollywood movies go out of sync. First, they are separated *spatially:* the men are "over there," and the women are on the "home front," the second word implying that they are also in a battle, but the first recognizing that they are relegated to a sphere of action other than that of men. A few films during the war will bring men and women together in a united front—for example, stories of nurses or women journalists allow for women to be shown fighting alongside the men in their lives. But for the most part, men and women move in the war film in separate spheres and come together only in mythical places—mythical because such places allow love to bloom but mythical also because love there can only be ethereal and dreamlike, utopian and unreal, all too doomed and impermanent. Thus, in the exotic space of Casablanca, Rick and Ilsa can find love again and can find their separate narratives coming together as one. Given its snappy dialogue, its high-society locale (for example, the nightclub electrified by seductive ambience), and its story of wizened and experienced lovers who have split from each other but are beginning to scope each other out toward a rekindling of romance, *Casablanca* might seem to echo back toward one of the great romantic genres of the 1930s—namely, screwball comedy—as much as it looks forward to the disruptions war brings to romance.

Like the screwball films that the philosopher Stanley Cavell calls comedies of "remarriage"—in which lovers who have known each other intimately have split up but now find occasions to begin furtive first steps to coming back together—*Casablanca* narrates how in a space apart, an exotic and erotic space, a magical space, lovers who had gone their separate ways can once again appear to share in one single story of love. But if screwball can end optimistically with a static image of the couple united forever, it would seem, in love (as in the last shot of *Bringing Up Baby,* where the man and woman are solid in their love as the world crashes down around them), the wartime film generally can represent romantic togetherness as only a temporary state. In a time of war, there are no private islands for lovers, no natural green places where one can repair to find romantic stasis. As the focus of so much of its plot on letters of transit reminds us, *Casablanca* is about a world of love in transition, a world of diasporic and displaced figures who can come together for a moment, only to find the larger forces of history pulling them apart.

But this is to suggest that the separation of the couple in wartime narratives is as much *temporal* as spatial: they are also out of sync insofar as they cannot be together in the present. On the one hand, the wartime film holds out the intangible promise of a future in which the couple will once again be united: this is intangible *of necessity* since the extracinematic reality of the moment means that one cannot really know what the future will bring, one cannot really be sure that the men will come back from "over there" and that there will be a future for love. On the other hand, then, many wartime films will look back with profound nostalgia to a past in which the couple was once perfectly united, perfectly in sync. "We'll always have Paris," Rick tells Ilsa: there will always be the memory of a moment that had seemed out of time (although in fact the disruptive time of history and world events came crashing inevitably in on it).

This suggests the importance of the flashback to so many films of the war period. The flashback actualizes on the screen the image of a lost past. In a moment when men and women have to go their separate ways, it allows for the vision of them together and directly puts this vision in the present tense. For example, in another film from the same year as *Casablanca*, *Joe Smith, American,* the eponymous hero is captured by Nazis but resists torture by remembering great moments from his courtship and marriage with his beloved wife, his memories rendered in flashbacks that unfold in the present tense. Likewise, *Casablanca*'s Paris flashback takes up a fair amount of screen time and by doing so pushes the real present tense of 1942 and its disruptive events offscreen: the Paris sequence becomes for a while an all-consuming utopian flight that holds history at bay and lets the unities of love unfurl in a seemingly atemporal idyll.

But to try to live life as an eternal present of everlasting bliss is a fiction. There is the danger that one will live in the fantasy so obsessively that one will be fully unprepared for the inevitable harsh moment when the forces of history reassert themselves—the moments when fantasy reveals its limits. Hence, the extremity of the shock Rick experiences when he feels himself betrayed by Ilsa: from a man who lived in the eternal present tense of love, he turns into one who lives in an unchanging eternity of bitterness and cynicism. Rick here is already like the postwar antihero of *film noir*—and of course Bogart would be one of the central figures of that tradition, in films like *In a Lonely Place* (1950)—who is so unprepared for life's betrayals that he retreats into coldness, hardness, or, at worst, a despairing inertia. The images of Rick drinking himself into stupor over Ilsa are not so far from those of brooding, morally wounded *noir* figures like "the Swede" in *The Killers* (1946) who have been defeated by life and passively wait for extinction. They dreamed of a space and time of unchanging romance and were unprepared for all the changes the world was holding in store for them.

Conclusion

In a sense, there are two predominant cinematic images of timelessness in the period of transition from prewar classicism to a postwar
period in which American film increasingly moves in new directions
and into new stylistic and thematic territories. On the one hand, as in
the screwball comedies of the classic 1930s, there is the affirmative
timelessness implicit in the notion of eternal romance and encapsulated in the final image of the couple united in an embrace. If the narratives of the screwball comedies of remarriage have been filled with
madcap actions as the lovers scheme and counterscheme to win back
their former partners, the endings to those narratives are about a glori-
ous leap into inaction—into the blissful stasis of a kiss. On the other
hand, as in the *films noirs* of the postwar period, there is the pessimistic
timelessness implicit in the existential brooding that comes when one
has seen all the perfidy of the world and understood that there's no
path to eternal bliss. Here the stasis is that of the psychologically
wounded male who has been betrayed by life (represented by the
erotically vital but dangerous *femme fatale*) and has given up and
awaits his end. Often the only way out of his existential funk is to suddenly discover in himself resources of stereotypically masculine
strength and reassert his machismo: thus, in *Dead Reckoning,* a 1947
film noir, Bogart plays a returned GI who, when he discovers the
woman he loves is irremediably evil and has played him for a sucker,
turns soldier once again and blows her up with a grenade. The Bogart
of *Dead Reckoning* could almost be a later version of *Casablanca*'s Rick
Blaine emerging from the passivity and funk of his own cynicism and
rediscovering the affirmative values of engagement in a masculine
cause. Certainly, the postwar *films noirs* are as much a legacy of
wartime as a cynical response to it: they narrate what the period imagines as the vulnerabilities of men not masculine enough to rise above
the seductions of dangerous femininity.

Between the joyous stasis of eternal love and the pessimistic stasis
of a brooding wounded masculinity, the wartime film holds out the
option of warrior masculinity. Even as he continues to be inspired by
the memory of romance ("We'll always have Paris"), Rick separates it
out of his present and future and becomes a man of action who bonds
in homosocial relationships with other newfound men of action (as

he says to Louis, "I think this is the beginning of a beautiful friendship"). Love can still occur in this world, but only in one's past or only to other people: it is noteworthy that several times in the film, Rick is instrumental in enabling other couples to solidify (the young lovers we saw in the three-shot sequence; Ilsa and Laszlo) but gives up on romance for himself. The wartime warrior discovers bonds with others, but these cannot be bonds of romantic love: in that, he is still an isolated individualist. Even as it upholds a mythology of love, *Casablanca* announces the more-than-partial irrelevance of romance to the new present and future needs of a world that is growing up. Seemingly the prime example of classical Hollywood cinema, *Casablanca* also appears to announce a transition from the purity and perfection of that cinema into one that is much more modern, tough-minded, questioning, and suspicious of the resonant romantic myths of an earlier time.

Credits

United States, 1942, Warner Bros.

Director: Michael Curtiz
Producer: Hal B. Wallis
Screenplay: Julius J. Epstein, Philip C. Epstein, and Howard Koch
Cinematography: Arthur Edeson
Editing: Owen Marks
Music: Max Steiner
Art Direction: Carl Jules Weyl
Costume Design: Orry-Kelly

CAST:

Rick Blaine	Humphrey Bogart
Ilsa Lund Laszlo	Ingrid Bergman
Victor Laszlo	Paul Henreid
Captain Louis Renault	Claude Rains
Guillermo Ugarte	Peter Lorre
Signor Ferrari	Sydney Greenstreet
Major Heinrich Strasser	Conrad Veidt
Carl	S. Z. Sakall

Bibliography

Anobile, Richard, ed. *Casablanca*. New York: Darien, 1974.

Black, Joel. "'You Must Remember This': The Intimate and the Obscene in Filmic Narrative." *Yearbook of Comparative and General Literature* 40 (1992): 83–89.

Card, James. "Confessions of a *Casablanca* Cultist: An Enthusiast Meets the Myth and Its Flaws." Telotte, *Cult* 66–78.

Casablanca. Spec. issue of *Journal of Popular Film and Television* 27.4 (2000).

Cavell, Stanley. *Pursuits of Happiness: The Hollywood Comedy of Remarriage*. Cambridge, MA: Harvard UP, 1981.

Chute, Verne. Letter to Hal B. Wallis (1943). File 2456, *Casablanca* Sequel File. Warner Bros. Archives. U of Southern California, Los Angeles.

Davis, John H. "'Still the Same Old Story': The Refusal of Time to Go By in *Casablanca*." *Literature/Film Quarterly* 18.2 (1990): 122–27.

Deutelbaum, Marshall. "The Visual Design Program of *Casablanca*." *Post-Script* 9.3 (1990): 36–48.

Eco, Umberto. "*Casablanca*: Cult Movies and Intertextual Collage." *Travels in Hyperreality*. Trans. William Weaver. New York: Harcourt, 1986. 197–211.

Gabbard, Krin, and Glen O. Gabbard. "Play It Again, Sigmund: Psychoanalysis and the Classical Hollywood Text." *Journal of Popular Film and Television* 18.1 (1990): 6–17.

Godden, Richard, and Mary A. McCay. "Say it Again, Sam[bo]: Race and Speech in *Huckleberry Finn* and *Casablanca*." *Mississippi Quarterly* 49.4 (1996): 657–82.

Green, Gary. "'The Happiest of Happy Accidents'? A Re-evaluation of *Casablanca*." *Smithsonian Studies in American Art* 1.2 (1987): 3–13.

Greenberg, Harvey Roy. *The Movies on Your Mind: Film Classics on the Couch, from Fellini to Frankenstein*. New York: Dutton, 1975.

Harmetz, Aljean. *Round Up the Usual Suspects: The Making of "Casablanca": Bogart, Bergman and World War II*. New York: Hyperion, 1993.

Kellman, Steven G. "Everybody Comes to Roquentin's: *La Nausée* and *Casablanca*." *Mosaic* 16.1–2 (1983): 103–12.

Key, Sarah, Jennifer Newman Brazil, and Vicki Wells. *The Casablanca Cookbook: Wining and Dining at Rick's*. New York: Abbeville, 1992.

Koch, Howard, ed. *Casablanca: Script and Legend*. Woodstock, NY: Overlook, 1973.

Lapsley, Robert, and Michael Westlake. "From *Casablanca* to *Pretty Woman*: The Politics of Romance." *Screen* 33.1 (1992): 27–49.

Maltby, Richard. "'A Brief Romantic Interlude': Dick and Jane Go to 3½ Seconds of the Classical Hollywood Cinema." *Post-Theory: Reconstructing Film Studies*. Ed. David Bordwell and Noël Carroll. Madison: U of Wisconsin P, 1996. 434–59.

Marks, Martin. "Music, Drama, Warner Brothers: The Cases of *Casablanca* and *The Maltese Falcon*." *Michigan Quarterly Review* 35.1 (1996): 112–42.

Paulus, Irena. "Du rôle de la musique dans le cinéma hollywoodien classique: Les fonctions de la musique dans le film *Casablanca* (1943) de Michael Curtiz." *Irasm* 28 (1997): 63–110.

Raskin, Richard. "*Casablanca* and United States Foreign Policy." *Film History* 4.2 (1990): 153–64.

Ray, Robert. *A Certain Tendency of the Hollywood Cinema, 1930–1980.* Princeton: Princeton UP, 1985.

Robertson, James. *The Casablanca Man: The Cinema of Michael Curtiz.* New York: Routledge, 1993.

Rosenzweig, Sidney. *"Casablanca" and Other Major Films of Michael Curtiz.* Ann Arbor: UMI Research, 1982.

Schickel, Richard. "Some Nights in Casablanca." *Favorite Movies: Critics' Choice.* Ed. Philip Nobile. New York: Macmillan, 1973. 114–25.

Telotte, J. P. "*Casablanca* and the Larcenous Cult Film." Telotte, *Cult* 43–53.

———, ed. *The Cult Film Experience: Beyond All Reason.* Austin: U of Texas P, 1991.

Vonalt, Larry. "Looking Both Ways in *Casablanca*." Telotte, *Cult* 55–65.

Warner, Jack. Memo. File 12732, *Casablanca* Legal File. Warner Bros. Archives. U of Southern California, Los Angeles.

———. Memo. File 18882, *Casablanca* Story File, pt. 2. Warner Bros. Archives. U of Southern California, Los Angeles.

Double Indemnity (1944)

GAYLYN STUDLAR

Hard-boiled *Film Noir*

Context

Double Indemnity is now regarded as a classic *film noir,* an archetypal demonstration of all those traits that came to the foreground in post–World War II Hollywood crime melodramas: highly stylized low-key lighting, circular or convoluted narrative, and an atmosphere of corruption in which violence, paranoia, and obsessive desire hold sway. However, at the time of the film's release in 1944, French critics had not yet applied this critical category to American films. Indeed, the occupation of France by German troops had made the distribution of American films an impossibility during most of the war, and so it would be the pent-up flood of films into France at the end of the conflict that would allow French critics to see immediately the connection between films that, under normal circumstances, they would have viewed over a number of years. Seeing these films in rapid succession led some of them to notice the striking stylistic and thematic resemblances between such films as John Huston's *The Maltese Falcon* (1941), Frank Tuttle's *This Gun for Hire* (1942), Billy Wilder's *Double Indemnity* (1944), Edward Dmytryk's *Murder, My Sweet* (1944), Otto Preminger's *Laura* (1944), Robert Siodmak's *Phantom Lady* (1944), and Fritz Lang's *Woman in the Window* (1944). Nino Frank, writing in *L'ecran français* in 1946, is generally credited as the first French film critic to suggest that these thrillers or crime melodramas were *films noirs,* films that figuratively and literally created a cinematic "black" world (Naremore 15–16). To critics like Frank, they marked an important new trend characterized by a more morally ambiguous, structurally complex, and sexually bold American crime film.

Yet, the war years had brought changes to Hollywood film that made these *films noirs* the exception rather than the norm of mainstream commercial production. Through the Office of War Information (OWI), the government very explicitly called on Hollywood filmmakers to perform a role in boosting wartime morale. Hollywood was asked to support the war effort by making films that would speak to the concerns of wartime America and disseminate a positive view of American society (Krutnik 36–37). In fact, the OWI demanded that its Bureau of Motion Pictures be allowed to vet every script, a request that all major studios assented to, with the exception of Paramount.

Hollywood's negotiation of the government's demand to control the content of its films was nothing new, for the industry had a long history of coping with the demands of state and local censorship boards and reformist organizations that wanted Hollywood to curb its excesses, either on or off the screen. In 1930, in response to public concerns about depictions of sex and violence in Hollywood film, the industry's chief representative, the Motion Picture Producers and Distributors of America (MPPDA), attempted to avoid government-imposed censorship by publishing a code of principles and rules ("The Motion Picture Production Code") to guide Hollywood filmmakers in controlling the moral content of their films. After a period of voluntary adherence to the Code that favored the desires of the film industry, in 1934, the MPPDA created the Production Code Administration (PCA) to quell another tide of public criticism of the low standards of screen morality. Under the auspices of Joseph Breen, the Production Code Administration applied stricter enforcement standards of the Code to Hollywood films. To make sure that this moral self-regulation was systematic and meaningful, the studios agreed that any film without a PCA certificate would be denied exhibition in theaters nationwide.

These new enforcement standards had a particular impact on the depiction of crime in film. One of the two general principles of the Code made the basic standards of representation clear: "No picture shall be produced which will lower the moral standards of those who see it. Hence the sympathy of the audience should never be thrown to the side of crime, wrongdoing, evil or sin" (qtd. in Leff and Simmons 286). As a result of the PCA's stricter enforcement of the Code, filmmakers were discouraged from centering a film around sympathetic criminal protagonists, as they had in the early 1930s gangster film hits like *Little Caesar* (1931) and *The Public Enemy* (1931), which capitalized on the extensive print and broadcast media coverage of real-world gangsters of the era, such as Al Capone and John Dillinger, who fascinated Depression-era audiences. With the advent of the PCA, film-makers were forbidden to depict details of a crime that might permit its imitation in real life. Nevertheless, in spite of protestations, censorship, and reform, box-office figures still suggested that American audiences enjoyed seeing criminal activities as screen entertainment, and Hollywood found ways to satisfy the public's desire for stories that involved murder and mayhem: private detectives, federal agents ("G-men"), and other assorted figures aligned with the law largely replaced criminal protagonists in A productions. The post-PCA ubiquity of this convention of changing protagonists from tough "bad" guys to tough "good" guys is illustrated by the reaction of actor George Raft to the role of insurance-salesman-turned-murderer Walter Neff in *Double Indemnity*. In an effort to interest Raft in playing the part, director Billy Wilder told him the film's plot. Raft responded: "Where's the lapel?" Wilder responded: "What lapel?" Raft: "You know, when the guy flips his lapel over and shows his badge" (qtd. in Schickel 58–59).

This movement away from criminal protagonists that had taken hold as the result of the PCA intensified after war came to America in December 1941. Reflecting government and industry concerns about the appropriateness of screen depictions of social problems during a time of national crisis, the Office of War Information made a focused attempt to prevent U.S. films from depicting "lawlessness or disorder" as the "main theme of a picture" (Koppes and Black 125–26). A notable change occurred in December of 1942, when the Office of Censorship released a new code of regulations that took an even tougher tack when it came to the depiction of gangsters and other lawless elements of American life, unless the depicted offenders were punished.

However much it wanted to be perceived as upholding its patriotic duty, Hollywood rankled at government control over its product. The film industry pushed Congress to defund the OWI, and in mid-1943, the Hollywood office of the OWI (known as the Bureau of Motion Pictures) was closed. Nevertheless, OWI's Ulric Bell remained in control of export licenses for films seeking foreign markets, and Bell was reputed to have a particular dislike for gangster films (Koppes and Black 126–32). Bell's attitude toward such films, combined with Hollywood's desire to gain access to newly opened foreign markets, may have played a significant role in gangsters' virtual disappearance from the screen between 1943 and the end of the war.

In spite of this, crime did manage to return to the screen during the war years, and *Double Indemnity* was the crucial film in reestablishing the dramatic value of criminality in American films. It did so in a way that set a new course for crime dramas. In this respect, *Double Indemnity*, which went into production not long after the Bureau of Motion Pictures closed, challenged the bravely hopeful, morally uplifting, and propagandistically positive filmic representations that the government wanted of Hollywood. Its story of an insurance salesman who helps his lover kill her husband obviously went against the grain of the government's desire for Hollywood to affirm community and family-centered values, but *Double Indemnity* accomplished even more. Its enormous critical success (seven Academy Award nominations) and box-office popularity (a gross of over $2.5 million) set the precedent for other films. Writing in the *New York Times* in August of 1945, Lloyd Shearer noted that *Double Indemnity* was clearly the "first of the new rough, tough murder yarns" that were establishing a new cinematic "cycle of crime" (Shearer 17). The cycle that *Double Indemnity* inspired by its success would result in one of the most influential groups of films to emerge from the studio era—those films, largely from the postwar period, that would come to be called *film noir*.

Raising Cain (and the Ire of the PCA)

Months before the release of *Double Indemnity*, as American involvement in the war dragged into its second full year, Hollywood filmmakers had begun to worry about the commercial viability of a steady diet of propaganda-infused films, or those directly based on war-related topics, including combat films (Krutnick 37). To breathe some vitality into their productions, studios tried to find fresh material and new talent, including writing talent, but the industry operated under the same kinds of economic strictures, wartime rationing systems, and loss of manpower that hindered every other U.S. business. Much of its talent, both behind and in front of the camera, was engaged in the war effort, at home or abroad. Increasingly, the studios looked at remaking properties they already owned and had made as recently as the 1930s, and revived attempts to acquire source materials with proven audience appeal, such as popular novels and plays. They even turned to sources that were previously thought to be too "low" or unsavory for mainstream productions.

In November 1943, *Variety* suggested that the "shortage of story material and writers now has film companies seriously ogling the pulp magazine scripts and scripters. It marks the first time that Holly-wood has initiated a concerted drive to replenish . . . its scripter ranks from the 20c[ents]-a-word authors of the weird-snappy-breezy-argosy-spy-crime-detective mag school" ("Pulp Mags Resent"). By turning to pulp fiction and the school of "hard-boiled" writers, Holly-wood inevitably would return to the subject of crime and, in doing so, bump up against the prevailing enforcement standards of screen morality. The surprise was that any milestone in opening new avenues for the frank portrayal of sexuality and criminality on-screen in the mid-1940s could be based on the work of James M. Cain, a former "20c[ents]-a-word author" whose work had been all but banned from the screen by the PCA in the mid-1930s.

A Hollywood-based writer, Cain was a former journalist who had unsuccessfully tried his hand as a scriptwriter in the early thirties. He entered into public consciousness with the 1934 publication of *The Post-man Always Rings Twice*, which was a controversial best seller. The book's plot was simple: a drifter, Frank Chambers, wanders into a roadside diner. There he meets Cora Papadakis, who arouses his lust. Cora is ambitious. She wants to better herself, while Frank wants only Cora. So that Frank can have her, he helps her kill her husband. After-ward, they turn against each other, but escape justice. They reconcile, but then "the postman rings twice." Cora is killed in a car accident, and Frank is put on trial for her murder. The story ends as he sits in the death house, awaiting execution for the murder he did not commit.

Postman was accused of being low in tone and of trading on the sensationalism of torrid sex scenes. The story, said Cain, was inspired by real-life events. While driving the back roads of southern Califor-nia, he saw a sexy but common woman tending a gas station, and sometime later he read a newspaper headline indicating that she had killed her husband with the help of her lover. Cain's book used this situation as the basic narrative pattern present in much of his work, including *Double Indemnity*: the male protagonist wants some woman forbidden to him by sexual and social taboo and goes outside the law to obtain her. It was a pattern that Cain recognized and worried over because he knew that Hollywood, under the grip of the PCA, didn't want racy stories about lawbreakers. In 1936, the year *Double Indem-*

nity appeared in serialized form in *Liberty* magazine, Cain told his publisher, "I wish . . . I could get hold of an idea that wouldn't be censorable, and that for this reason might be available for pictures. . . . God knows what twist there is in my mind that makes it run in these directions" (qtd. in Hoopes 276–77). That "twist" was consistent as far as *Double Indemnity* was concerned, for *Postman* was a veritable blueprint for the hastily written narrative of *Double Indemnity,* perhaps part of the reason that Cain was not particularly proud of the latter.

Like *Postman, Double Indemnity* also drew on real-life events, most particularly a highly publicized 1927 New York murder case involving Ruth Snyder and Judd Gray. Snyder, a suburban Long Island housewife, enticed her lover, a corset salesman named Gray, to help her murder her husband. After the duo killed the husband, Snyder turned on her lover, and attempted to kill him also (with poisoned wine). A popular magazine suggested at the time that "the whole gruesome story" illustrated a new twist to lawlessness. Instead of involving "criminals by impulse" or professionals, "this brutal, inhuman murder was the product of . . . that moral degeneration that is the inevitable production of long-continued self-indulgence . . . [and an] insensate desire for material satisfaction" ("Snyder Murder Mystery").

Like *Postman,* Cain wrote *Double Indemnity* from the point of view of the woman's lover, a man who is portrayed as both victim and victimizer. It tells the story of a self-destructive protagonist: in this instance, Walter Huff, an insurance salesman who starts as a likeable, if slightly sleazy, middle-class everyman. He succumbs to the charms of a woman, Phyllis Nirdlinger, and, as a result, is drawn by lust and greed into becoming a murderer. Along the way, Huff is aware that the woman is drawing him into something unthinkable, but he also admits that he was ready to use his insider's knowledge of insurance investigation to murder and reap the cash benefits—the "double indemnity" clause in the life insurance policy he has written for Phyllis's unsuspecting husband. To enhance the verisimilitude of his story, Cain extracted details of the insurance business from his father, an academic who had become an insurance executive late in life (Hoopes 294).

When things go wrong, Walter blames the chance occurrence of meeting Phyllis as the random moment of fate that began his downward spiral into crime. By the final chapter, Phyllis is revealed to be a raving psychopath, and Walter has been reduced to her accomplice, criminal fodder for sensational tabloid journalism. In an ending so melodramatic that it is worthy of grand opera, the lovers have nowhere to go except literally into the ocean, where the sharks are circling.

In *Double Indemnity* and *Postman,* the central figure of the *femme fatale* is crucial. In Cain's world, the protagonist's meeting of a woman governs his direction and his doom, a situation that would be repeated, with variations, throughout much of *film noir* in Hollywood's postwar years. In *film noir,* as in Cain's fiction, women are dangerous, not only because they kill, but because they arouse the man's desire; in unleashing his sexual desire, the woman also arouses his ability to act on other—heretofore repressed—desires, including murderous ones.

For this and other "low" elements, Cain's *The Postman Always Rings Twice* and *Double Indemnity* came to be regarded by Hollywood as "too hot" to film. Cain's novellas were not pornographic, and their "steaminess" actually was more implied than overtly stated. They didn't contain "dirty words." But to many people they seemed dirty. Raymond Chandler, who would be hired to cowrite the *Double Indemnity* screenplay when Cain proved unavailable, scathingly wrote: "Everything he [Cain] touches smells like a billygoat. He is every kind of writer I detest, a faux naïf, a Proust in greasy overalls, a dirty little boy with a piece of chalk and board fence and nobody looking" (*Selected Letters* 23). Dirty as Cain's work might have seemed to some, in October of 1935, even before the serialized version of *Double Indemnity* was in print, five studios expressed interest in buying it for screen adaptation. That interest evaporated when the PCA reported on the treatment of the story submitted by MGM. Its verdict as to whether a film made from Cain's story could pass its censorial scrutiny was unequivocal: "Under no circumstances, in no way, shape, or form . . ." began the letter from Joseph Breen (qtd. in Hoopes 268). After a fleeting indication of interest by 20th Century–Fox, the novel was, as far as Hollywood was concerned, untouchable. Then, in 1943, *Double Indemnity* was reprinted in a collection of Cain's fiction, and Paramount went back to the PCA in order to gain permission to proceed with adapting Cain's novella into a film that would be directed by the German émigré Billy Wilder, who wanted the novella to serve as the basis of his third U.S. directorial effort.

At first, the PCA seemed immovable. Breen's office did not even bother to draft a new response to Paramount but instead sent a copy of the "in no way, shape, or form" letter they had sent MGM eight years before. Yet the PCA ultimately pronounced the story acceptable under the Code after Paramount representatives reassured Breen's office that new talent would be brought on board to shape this film version. The studio also agreed to restrain the film version at several points in the story (that is, not show the murder in detail, deal with the theme of adultery in an acceptable—i.e., morally condemning—way, and bring at least one of the murderers to justice).

Now that the primary hurdle to bringing *Double Indemnity* to the screen was overcome, there arose an unanticipated problem. Wilder's usual writing partner, Charles Brackett, found Cain's novel so repugnant that he refused to work on the project (Zolotow 111). Cain was busy, so producer Joseph Sistrom suggested Paramount hire detective fiction writer Raymond Chandler to help Wilder craft a screenplay. Chandler appeared to be a logical choice because, like Cain, he was the author of tough, "hard-boiled" fiction that was "realistic" in the sense of illustrating low behaviors (violent crime and illicit sexuality). Even more than Cain, Chandler's characters were distinctly American types who used slang and spoke in contemporary common vernacular. Like Cain, he was known for tales that unfolded within that distinctly American setting, the greater Los Angeles area of Southern California.

Because of these perceived convergences, Paramount regarded Chandler and Cain as "two peas in a pod" of hard-boiled fiction, but other factors made Chandler an equally unlikely candidate for helping Wilder bring Cain's novel to the screen. Chandler had never before written a screenplay, he had no idea how Hollywood worked, and he was an alcoholic. To complicate matters, Chandler was being asked to adapt for the screen the work of a novelist he detested. In spite of despising Cain's "billygoat" fiction, Chandler agreed to Paramount's offer. The reason was simple: he needed the money.

The likelihood that a viable screenplay would emerge from the process seemed more remote when it became clear that Wilder and Chandler worked uncomfortably together. In spite of this, the results of their effort were stunning. Separating out their various contributions to the screenplay is virtually impossible since both claimed credit for the lion's share of the changes that transformed Cain's novella into an Academy Award–nominated screenplay. They streamlined the plot and gave the film its memorable flashback structure. They threw out the last third of Cain's novel, which was overly complicated and led to an ending that the PCA would not allow: the insurance company is complicit in the murderers' escape. While Cain's novel employed first-person storytelling typical of the author's other novellas, the screenplay's voice-over narration lends a different intensity and quality to the film. Unlike the novel, the film's voice-over addresses a specific person, insurance investigator Barton Keyes; spoken in a deadpan delivery by Fred MacMurray, it adds to the sense of the protagonist's inevitable, impending doom. The film is rapid in tempo, as was Cain's novella, but there is more economy in the dialogue, too, which is less symbolic than Cain's, more cleverly cynical, and caustically witty. Chandler had insisted, against Wilder's initial objection, that much of Cain's dialogue be replaced. The new dialogue successfully tones down the overheated aspects of Cain's original writing, even as Miklós Rózsa's dirgelike theme music and John Seitz's stylized, dark photography establishes an overall sense of doom that achieves the nonverbal equivalent of Cain's original dialogue and descriptions. The result is a suspenseful, emotionally intense film, but one that is also often darkly humorous and avoids the melodramatic excesses of Cain.

Analysis

Double Indemnity starts with credits that are presented over the silhouetted figure of a man on crutches, walking closer and closer to the camera until the entire frame is enveloped in darkness. This is a marvelously overdetermined image, for this man could be the antihero, Walter Neff (Fred MacMurray), or his victim, Mr. Dietrichson (Tom Powers), since the killing of Dietrichson entails Walter's masquerading as his victim, who has broken his leg. In fact, as William Luhr has suggested, it can be read as a visual motif that comments on the damaged status of all Phyllis's sexual partners: Walter, Dietrichson, and even Nino Zachetti (Byron Barr) (27).

The film's action starts with a car careening crazily down the streets of downtown Los Angeles at night. When it stops, Walter Neff emerges, and enters the Pacific All-Risk Insurance building, where he works. Although it is the middle of the night, he goes to his office and starts to dictate a report to his boss and best friend, Barton Keyes (Edward G. Robinson). He is sweating and obviously in pain. Something is wrong, and his voice-over monologue tells us what is wrong and how it got that way. He speaks into a Dictaphone machine, an addition to Cain's story based on Chandler's habit of dictating his novels. For once, says Neff, his boss's unerring instincts for spotting insurance fraud has been blinded by friendship and, indeed, love. "Hold tight to that cheap cigar of yours, Keyes," Neff says into the microphone. "I killed Dietrichson." After this startling confession, Walter Neff's voice-over continues to guide the action of the entire film, which is told primarily in flashbacks. In this respect, it became a model for many subsequent *films noirs* on how to structure a crime story. This narrative structure conveys a sense that the protagonist's future is foreclosed and so contributes to the cycle's signature quality of an oppressive atmosphere, which has sometimes led *film noir* to be linked to existentialism (Porfirio 212–17).

Setting up Walter's confession within the temporary haven of the Pacific All-Risk Insurance building is a conceit that allows the film to establish quickly the triangulated relationship between Walter, Phyllis, and Keyes. It also immediately adds poignancy to Walter's situation. In Cain's novel, the protagonist confesses to no one in particular. In the film, Walter confesses to Keyes, his only friend. Because of Walter's close relationship with Keyes, the office becomes Walter's real home, the only site where he is shown engaged in normal social interaction. In a flashback, Walter is shown sitting and smiling as Keyes, an obsessive workaholic, excitedly goes on and on about the sloppy business practices of their company. Keyes searches for a match to light his cigars. Walter teases him. In response, Keyes threatens to throw his desk at Walter. Walter looks warmly at Keyes as he lights a match for him and says, "I love you too." The voice-over returns to the image of Walter walking to his office: "I really did too, you old crab. . . . I kinda always knew . . . you had a heart as big as a house." The development of the close personal relationship between Walter and Barton Keyes, both in the confessional and in such scenes, allows the audience to understand that the film is not just about adultery or murder, but is also about the struggle for Walter's soul, a struggle between Keyes and Phyllis, between boring goodness and exciting evil, and how and why Phyllis won this struggle.

By defrauding the insurance company, Walter betrays Keyes's trust in him. In Wilder's original ending for the film, this relationship of trust and love reaches its apex in the film's final sequence when Keyes, in accordance with his friend's request, shows up at the penitentiary to witness Walter being led to the gas chamber and being executed. The scene is now lost, but script materials and stills have been studied by James Naremore. He believes that this ending would have made the film a powerful indictment of the established moral order, for after Walter is executed, Keyes's departure from the prison indicates that he has been shaken out of his moral complacency. Walter's death at the hands of the state leaves Keyes a broken man, or as the scene in the script describes him, "a forlorn and lonely man" (Naremore 91–93). Although the PCA originally told Paramount that at least one of the murderers had to be brought to justice in the film, when faced with a scene that explicitly showed the workings of the death penalty, the PCA reversed itself, demanding that Paramount delete this "gruesome" ending (92).

Walter's voice-over introduces and accompanies the first of many flashbacks, one that takes us to where Cain's original story began, to the ordinary but fateful day when insurance salesman Neff went on a routine call and encountered housewife Phyllis Dietrichson (Barbara Stanwyck). Walter recalls how one day he remembered an insurance policy that needed renewal. He decided to stop at the client's house. There, he gets by the slovenly and suspicious maid (Betty Farrington) and glimpses the client's wife, who is perched on a balcony at the top of a stairs. She is a comely blonde clothed in nothing but a towel. She stands above Walter as he grins from ear to ear at her immodesty and makes suggestive, flirtatious comments about her "coverage." Instead of offering us a filmic version of Cain's Phyllis, a curvaceous woman with freckles and a disarmingly innocent manner, the film's Phyllis is a hard-bodied, brassy blonde whose cold manner and overtly stated sexual allure marks her immediately as a temptress. She unblinkingly greets the stranger who has entered her house. As written by Wilder and Chandler and interpreted by Stanwyck, the film's Phyllis emerges as more psychologically complex than Cain's. She is a rotten temptress rather than a psychopathic one.

Phyllis retreats from the balcony to dress. When she strides into the living room, she is still in the process of dressing. After she finishes buttoning up her dress, she turns to the mirror to put on her lipstick. Walter follows her every move. These shots suggest she is a calculating tease who knows full well the effect of her overt sexuality on Walter, who is immediately interested in her "honey of an anklet." Middle-class norms are conveyed visually by the house, with its solid Spanish style and its grand piano, adorned by the framed pictures of her husband and stepdaughter, Lola (Jean Heather). By way of contrast, Phyllis's sexuality is immediately associated with class-transgressing indecency. She starts to quiz Walter about the details of the insurance business.

In voice-over, Walter claims he wasn't yet aware of her motives. We can believe that Phyllis's sexual effect on Walter leaves him blinded to her ruthless nature. He is too busy making a verbal pass at her. Coolly, she tells him he is breaking "the speed limit." "How fast was I going, officer?" he asks with a self-satisfied smile. Slick, overly confident, and unapologetically "fresh," he banters with her in Chandleresque dialogue that substitutes driving metaphors for overt sex talk. "How could I have known that murder can sometimes smell like honeysuckle?" Walter asks in voice-over as we see him leaving the Dietrichson home and walking out to his car in the sunshine.

As this scene demonstrates, Wilder and Chandler's script was sexually suggestive, but theirs was a sophisticated approach to filmmaking, one that was bold in depicting a middle-class protagonist who willingly gets involved with a married woman and turns to crime. However, in terms of presentation, the film had considerable precedent established in Hollywood under the Code. Hollywood conventions of expression allowed audiences to understand that characters engaged in all sorts of behaviors that could not be directly represented on-screen because of the guidelines of the Production Code. Audiences learned to read conventionalized filmic signs that indicated a couple had engaged in sex. In *Double Indemnity,* Walter goes to the Dietrichson house a second time. He and Phyllis quarrel after he accuses her of wanting to kill her husband and defraud the insurance company. Then Phyllis arrives at Walter's apartment. He opens the door. Darkness predominates, as it does in so much of the film. Close-ups are offered, but because of the low-key lighting, they reveal little. Walter and Phyllis kiss and embrace in the darkness. Sitting on the couch, Phyllis recounts her history with her husband; her face is half in shadow. She admits she wants to kill him and collect the insurance money. She starts to cry. Walter holds her and kisses her again. As they embrace, the camera tracks out, and the film dissolves to Walter at the Dictaphone. He confesses that he had been thinking about such a scheme for years, to "crook the house," like the "guy behind the roulette wheel" who is hired to keep the customers from cheating. "And then one night, you get to thinking how you could crook the house yourself. And do it smart." The film then returns to the scene in the apartment. Walter and Phyllis are both sitting on the couch, still fully clothed, but the mood has changed. Walter is reclining, relaxed and smoking. Phyllis reapplies her lipstick and is preparing to leave. They kiss again. Walter then seizes her roughly and tells her that he will help her commit the perfect murder.

What has led to Walter's change of mind? Why will he kill for Phyllis? Contemporary audiences unfamiliar with the conventions of Hollywood filmmaking under the Code may have difficulty discerning how the film's ellipsis and the subtle behavioral signs after it substitute for the overt depiction of the sexual act. Adult audiences of the 1940s would have been familiar with the cues that indicate that sex has taken place offscreen: the change in mood, the characters' placement on the couch, even Walter's relaxed smoking of a cigarette would have conveyed that a sexual encounter beyond the visualized kiss has occurred in the interim filled by the return to Walter's Dictaphone confession. In translating Cain's novel to the screen, Wilder and Chandler made use of these conventions and masterfully communicate potentially offensive material through verbal allusions (like the motorcycle-cop dialogue between Walter and Phyllis) and behavioral implications (like the apartment "sex" scene) that would appeal to the sophisticated viewer but would likely mean little to those who were less sophisticated.

Similarly, the PCA's demand that the filmmakers not show details of the killing of Mr. Dietrichson is handled in a way that actually adds to the psychosexual complexity of the film. When Walter, from the back seat of the Dietrichson family car, reaches over and strangles Dietrichson, the camera cuts to Phyllis, who sits behind the steering wheel. This satisfied the PCA's demand to avoid details of the murder, but revealed in close-up, Phyllis's face takes on a strange look of arousal and pleasure that has not been glimpsed before, even in her embraces with Walter. Her reaction suggests sadism, forbidden under the Code as a perversion, but how would the PCA *prove* that this is being suggested? We may regard moments like these as ambiguous, and, indeed, that is exactly the point.

In the early years of the Code, when it was enforced by the Studio Relations Committee and the leadership of Jason S. Joy, Hollywood filmmakers were encouraged to cultivate conventions of expression that would provide multiple levels of meaning. Joy was adamant that the viability of the Code actually depended on filmmakers engaging in an allusive system of representation, "from which conclusions might be drawn by the sophisticated mind, but which would mean nothing to the unsophisticated and inexperienced" (qtd. in Balio 40). This strategy of cultivating ambiguity in meaning was necessary because Hollywood had not yet developed a ratings system, and so filmmakers were obliged to aim their product at a general audience that could include persons from every possible demographic. *Double Indemnity* pushed some of the limits of established representational conventions and Code standards to suggest the fragility of middle-class norms and, consequently, of Hollywood's wartime vision of an ideal America. Middle-class boredom and sexual alienation led to the enticing thrill of criminal behavior. As a milestone in breaking through Production Code standards, *Double Indemnity* also suggested, quite daringly, the link between criminality and sexual arousal.

This is one important way in which the film anticipates a key aspect of postwar *film noir*'s major revision of the American crime film. By linking crime so securely to trangressive sexuality, *Double Indemnity*, and *films noirs* in general, placed crime within the territory of psychoanalysis and psychosexual complexity. As Borde and Chaumeton assert, *film noir* accentuated the "veiled eroticism" of the crime thriller and created "an atmosphere of latent sexuality, nebulous and polymorphous, that, as in projective tests, each individual can people with his own desires and 'structure' as he sees fit." Thus, because of self-regulation or censorship, Hollywood "made a virtue out of necessity" (144–45).

Wartime economic restrictions were another necessity made into a virtue by *Double Indemnity*. These restrictions on production included material cutbacks caused by war rationing that set limits on set construction, on the use of electricity, and on the ability to shoot on location due to gasoline rationing. On the West Coast, dimouts and blackouts were common because of the fear of a Japanese invasion (Biesen 12). As a consequence, shooting in natural (available) light and using shadow to disguise economically constructed sets were not uncommon. The development of faster (more sensitive) film emulsion allowed shooting in limited lighting. Filmmakers could adapt and shoot in a manner familiar to documentary filmmakers.

Cinematographer Seitz has suggested that *Double Indemnity* was purposefully shot in this "newsreel style" to add to its realism (Smith 177). Low-key lighting is displayed in much of the film, which largely takes place at night. Seitz's dark visual style incorporates "realistic" techniques such as night-for-night shooting, depth-of-field shooting, and on-location shooting, the latter within the confines of the Los Angeles area because of wartime restrictions on gasoline and tires. These techniques, which might be associated with "newsreel style," are most evident in the climactic outdoor scene in which Walter impersonates his victim, Dietrichson, after he has murdered him. Masquerading as Dietrichson (on crutches), Walter boards the train. He slips off the back of the last car so that he and Phyllis can plant Dietrichson's corpse on the tracks and she can claim her husband met an accidental death (by falling off a moving train). The lovers execute their plan in almost complete darkness, in night-for-night shooting that takes advantage of the wartime dimout situation under which this three-night shoot worked (Lacey). More sensitive film allowed the characters to be photographed even as they are enveloped in darkness. Full and long shots, often favored by documentary filmmakers because of the ease of focusing the subject at these distances, predominate, and serve to emphasize the lovers' isolation. These techniques might be associated with documentary style, but *Double Indemnity* also displays carefully conceived visual framing, match-on-action editing, and an often highly stylized use of shadows, the latter recalling the aesthetic preferences of German Expressionist filmmaking. As a result, visual elements associated with the "newsreel style" are offered within an overall framework of a highly controlled and stylized strategy of visual representation reflecting both European and Hollywood fiction film traditions.

But the darkness surrounding the lovers is figurative as well as literal. Keyes has a "hunch" that Dietrichson was murdered. When he goes to Walter to offer his theory of the murder, little does Keyes realize that his best friend committed the crime. The police give up on the case, but Walter knows that Keyes will not be deterred from uncovering the truth. Although he is not yet a suspect, Walter feels that it is the beginning of the "end of the line" for him and Phyllis. To avoid suspicion, they do not see each other. Walter feels guilty. He begins to cultivate a friendship with Lola Dietrichson, who tells him of her own suspicion that Phyllis not only killed her father but also caused her mother's death when Phyllis was a hired nurse to the sick woman. Walter knows Lola is in danger. He also knows that Phyllis is cheating on him with Nino Zachetti, and she may be plotting to have Zachetti eliminate him. Walter goes to the Dietrichson house at night to tell Phyllis he is "getting off the trolley car."

As Walter remarks, they are back in the living room where it all started. Phyllis sits in darkness as Walter enters, his shadow preceding him. The room is dark except for abstract lines of light and shadow created by venetian blinds. As Walter goes to close the window he plunges the room into deeper blackness. Suddenly shots ring out. Phyllis has turned her gun on him. The camera tracks in with Walter as he slowly advances toward Phyllis. He tells her to shoot again, but she can't. Something close to love has overtaken her, even though she is, as she remarks, "rotten to the heart." Photographed in close-up, Phyllis asks him to embrace her. He does, and then he shoots her. "Goodbye, baby," he says. Wounded by his lover's bullet, Walter leaves the house and makes his way to the insurance company. At the office, he finishes his confession. Keyes appears. Walter tries for the door to effect an escape to Mexico, but he is too weak from the loss of blood. He collapses at the doorway. Keyes calls for an ambulance—and the police. He then goes to Walter, who tells him that he couldn't find the killer because "the guy you were looking for was too close." Walter takes out a cigarette, and Keyes lights it for him. Whether he dies in the doorway or lives to walk into the San Quentin death house, the audience knows that Walter's life is finished.

Conclusion

Upon its release, critics recognized the film's status as a milestone in terms of its artistic quality and its daring defiance of Production Code assumptions. *Los Angeles Times* reviewer Philip K. Scheuer called the film "the most decisive step forward taken by a major studio in . . . many months. . . . As for the movie 'don'ts' it violates, they should make even a Warner brother's eyes pop." The *Hollywood Reporter* suggested that, rather than encouraging crime, *Double Indemnity* was a "crime shocker with a moral" and so discouraged imitation because of its grim take on criminality (W. H. M.). This view of the film would later be echoed by Borde and Chaumeton in reference to all of *film noir.* They note that *film noir* may entertain the audience with the "attractive side to evil," but it almost never fails to have "the long shadow of the gallows fall" over the characters (146). James M. Cain himself praised Billy Wilder's film copiously and declared that "It may be, since the word 'adult' is the one reviewers use most frequently in connection with it, that a new field for moving pictures has been opened up" (qtd. in Hoopes 348). Indeed, it had. Writing in the *New York Times*, Lloyd Shearer recognized that *Double Indemnity* was creating a trend: "Forever watchful of audience reaction, the rest of the industry almost immediately began searching its story files for properties like 'Double Indemnity'" (17).

If *Double Indemnity* was a milestone in opening new avenues for the frank portrayal of sexuality and criminality on-screen, other dramatic and formal qualities deserve consideration as much as its story line in capturing attention and spawning imitation. The acting is one of the great strengths of the film. The casting of the film was a difficult process. MacMurray, a Paramount leading man associated almost exclusively with lightweight romantic comedy, was cast against type in *Double Indemnity* in a role he was reluctant to take. Stanwyck had worked in a broad range of genres, including comedy and drama; nevertheless, she, too, was cast against type. She had become a star in the 1930s in Frank Capra–directed films by playing sympathetic, if flawed, women of great emotionality. In *Double Indemnity,* she plays against this established strength to essay Phyllis Dietrichson as a woman who is as unemotional as she is deadly. Both MacMurray and Stanwyck would use the film as a springboard to other successes, including important roles in postwar *films noirs.*

It could be argued that *Double Indemnity* did not really offer anything completely new or even unusual in terms of visual or narrative technique, but its successful combination of qualities, including its surprise casting, made it unusual, as did its daring antipropaganda articulation of middle-class sexual alienation and social disaffection. Its articulation of repressed aspects of the crime film (such as sexual perversity's link to criminality) confirmed that Hollywood filmmakers could take a sophisticated, artistically complex approach to crime, even while operating under the moral restrictions of the Code and wartime economic restrictions and morale-building imperatives. *Double Indemnity* also came at the right time. The film could make its sophisticated appeal to wartime audiences who knew the horrors of war's legalized murder and were no longer shocked by stylized fictional violence, no matter how realistic it might be in comparison to previous Hollywood fare.

Studlar

From its shadowy visuals to its centralizing interest in criminal psychology, from its construction of a classic *femme fatale* to its flashbacks and voice-over that convey an uneasy sense of a predetermined closure to events, *Double Indemnity* is archetypal of *film noir* in almost every way we now conceive of this major film cycle. Most important, it remains a film with a powerful impact on audiences. In spite of the developments in forensic science that may make its depiction of the "perfect murder" unbelievable to twenty-first-century audiences, *Double Indemnity* retains considerable force as a film experience. Its daring break with PCA norms and its stylistic and thematic influences on *film noir* not withstanding, Wilder's film would deserve its status as a dark masterpiece of American filmmaking by virtue of its remarkable demonstration of the experiential power of "against-the-grain" filmmaking, Hollywood style.

Credits

United States, 1944, Paramount Pictures

Director: Billy Wilder
Producers: Buddy G. DeSylva (exec. producer) and Joseph Sistrom
Screenplay: Billy Wilder and Raymond Chandler
Story: James M. Cain (novel)
Cinematography: John F. Seitz
Editing: Doane Harrison
Music: Miklós Rózsa
Art Direction: Hans Dreier and Hal Pereira
Costume Design: Edith Head
Makeup: Wally Westmore

CAST:
Walter Neff	Fred MacMurray
Phyllis Dietrichson	Barbara Stanwyck
Barton Keyes	Edward G. Robinson
Lola Dietrichson	Jean Heather
Mr. Dietrichson	Tom Powers
Edward S. Norton Jr.	Richard Gaines
Nino Zachetti	Byron Barr
Mr. Jackson	Porter Hall
Nettie the maid	Betty Farrington
Sam Gorlopis	Fortunio Bonanova

Bibliography

Balio, Tino. *Grand Design: Hollywood as a Modern Business Enterprise, 1930–1939.* Berkeley: U of California P, 1995.

Biesen, Sheri Chinen. *The Hard-Boiled Homefront: Film Noir and World War II.* Philadelphia: Temple UP, 1999.

Borde, Raymond, and Etienne Chaumeton. *A Panorama of American Film Noir, 1941–1953.* Trans. Paul Hammond. 1955. San Francisco: City Lights, 2002.

Cain, James M. *Double Indemnity.* 1936. New York: Vintage, 1978.

Chandler, Charlotte. *Nobody's Perfect: Billy Wilder, A Personal Biography.* New York: Simon, 2002.

Chandler, Raymond. *The Selected Letters of Raymond Chandler.* Ed. Frank MacShane. New York: Columbia UP, 1981.

Frank, Nino. "Un nouveau genre 'policier': L'aventure criminelle." *L'ecran français* 28 Aug. 1946: 14–16.

Hoopes, Roy. *Cain.* New York: Holt, 1982.

Koppes, Clayton R., and Gregory D. Black. *Hollywood Goes to War.* London: Tauris, 1988.

Krutnik, Frank. *In a Lonely Street: Film Noir, Genre, Masculinity.* London: Routledge, 1991.

Lacey, Norman. "Existing dimout regulations . . . " Interoffice memo to Frank Caffey. 6 Oct. 1943. Paramount Collection Production File. Special Collections, Academy of Motion Picture Arts and Sciences Study Center, Beverly Hills, CA.

Leff, Leonard J., and Jerold L. Simmons. *Dame in the Kimono: Hollywood, Censorship, and the Production Code.* 2nd ed. Lexington: UP of Kentucky, 2001.

Luhr, William. *Raymond Chandler and Film.* New York: Ungar, 1982.

Naremore, James. *More Than Night: Film Noir in Its Contexts.* Berkeley: U of California P, 1998.

Porfirio, Robert G. "No Way Out: Existential Motifs in Film Noir." *Sight and Sound* 45.4 (1976): 212–17.

"Pulp Mags Resent Attempt to Lure Penny-a-Liners for Film Studios." *Variety* 10 Nov. 1943: 2.

Scheuer, Philip K. "Film History Made by 'Double Indemnity.'" *Los Angeles Times* 6 Aug. 1944: C1+.

Schickel, Richard. *"Double Indemnity."* London: BFI, 1992.

Shearer, Lloyd. "Crime Certainly Pays on the Screen: The Growing Crop of Homicidal Films Poses Questions for Psychologists and Producers." *New York Times* 5 Aug. 1945: 17+.

Smith, Ella. *Starring Miss Barbara Stanwyck.* New York: Crown, 1973.

"The Snyder Murder Mystery." *Outlook* 16 May 1927: 78.

W. H. M. "Tidings." *Hollywood Reporter* 11 Aug. 1944: 2.

Wilder, Billy, and Raymond Chandler. *Double Indemnity.* With an intro. by Jeffrey Meyers. Berkeley: U of California P, 2000.

Zolotow, Maurice. *Billy Wilder in Hollywood.* New York: Putnam, 1977.

Rome Open City (1945)

MARCIA LANDY

From Movie to Method

> The term of neorealism was born with the success of *Open City*.
> . . . When the film was shown in Cannes in 1946, it went quite
> unnoticed. It was discovered much later, and I am not yet sure
> its message has been fully understood. (Rossellini 44)

Context

Roma città aperta (*Rome Open City*) is one of the most cited, and most
discussed, films in world cinema, and its director, Roberto Rossellini,
is one of the preeminent initiators of a new form of filmmaking—neorealism. *Open City* provides a map to trace Rossellini's—and neorealism's—contributions to the language of cinema. It introduces different
cinematic conceptions of landscape, character, action, situation, femininity, and masculinity. The legendary status of *Open City* resides not
in its adherence to documentary traditions but in its challenge to forms
of realism that uncritically assume that "to see is to believe." The film
uses cinema as an instrument for questioning memory and belief in
what is seen and heard. While the film provides documentary-style
images of a city in the grip of its Nazi occupiers, it questions and subverts familiar images and sounds associated with newsreels, documentaries, and commercial feature films. The city of Rome becomes a
text for the spectator to contemplate critically, while the film's reflexive
attention to spectatorship underscores distinctions between open and
closed conceptions of the world.

The Ruins of War

Open City appeared in 1945 in the last year of World War II. For twenty
years, Italy had been subjected to the power of the Fascist regime
under Benito Mussolini. The path of the regime led to Italy's entry into

World War II on the side of the Germans and resulted in the ouster of Mussolini in 1943 by the Fascist Grand Council, as dictated by Hitler. The war had already brought about devastating losses for the Italian populace. The country was divided in two. In the South, the Allies fought to liberate the country from the Germans. In the North, partisan groups of Socialists, Communists, and Catholic Action militants fought to liberate cities and the countryside from Fascist and Nazi occupiers.

While Rossellini's *Paisà* (1946) traces the efforts around Italy to liberate the country, *Open City* takes place in Rome during the last months of the German occupation; but the events are nonetheless emblematic of the broader situation confronted by the nation. The term "open city" was not Rossellini's. The concept derived from the conventions of warfare that decreed that "international cities" were "open" and thus protected from destruction; however, the notion of "openness" was not observed by the German occupiers who destroyed buildings and imposed severe martial law on the city. Dire consequences were brought down on those considered to be enemies of the law. In particular, German brutality was directed against those who supported the Allies and were identified with Resistance and leftist activities. The concept of "openness" is therefore central to the style and motifs of *Open City*.

Open City was produced under the most adverse circumstances. The Germans had only recently departed, and the effects of the social and economic devastation of the occupation were evident everywhere. Not only were filmmaking facilities destroyed, the general social infrastructure was in ruins. Money was hard to come by, as was raw film stock, but Rossellini and his associates were able to put a script together, hire professional actors, and film the sequences on the desired locations. The film was shot on the streets, in churches, in scriptwriter Sergio Amidei's apartment, and in Capitani Studios. Filming was delayed by crowds hostile to the sight of Nazis, in this case actors playing Nazis, as well as by lighting problems and conflicts among the actors.

Pierre Leprohon viewed the film as exemplifying "the hoary truth that scant resources and difficult conditions of work are often beneficial to art." These "difficulties" did not "create the inspiration, but they forced the director to find solutions, and in so doing to draw on his invention and his genius" (93). Moreover, Leprohon does not regard the film as completely "new," and he indicates where earlier filmmakers had experimented with neorealist techniques. Likewise, in his characterization of *Open City,* David Forgacs is mindful of the film's relations to the cinema that preceded it. Therefore, he regards the film as "a transitional film—for Rossellini, for the cinema, for a society coming out of two decades of Fascism—rather than a wholly new work" (11–12). These critics' comments reveal continuing struggles to characterize the quality and impact of the Rossellini film, as well as of neorealism.

Looking at Neorealism

Too often in histories of film, the Italian cinema of the Fascist years is dismissed as being comprised of fluffy comedies (*telefoni bianchi*), melodramas, and propaganda films. However, in the 1970s, many of these films became available for screening, and film critics formed a new impression of them. The feature films were highly influenced by Hollywood genres; they were not only blatant propaganda. In fact, they, like Hollywood films cast in the genre mold, addressed social differences and the changing landscape of modernity.

After 1939, Italian films began to assume a more overtly critical posture toward Fascist culture. A group of films identified as "calligraphic," or "Formalist," offered a somber portrait of a disintegrating world, drawing on a *noir*-like cinematic style (Landy, *Folklore* 169–236). However, according to Pierre Sorlin, "After the Liberation, Neorealism was much sharper and more systematic in its critique of injustice or inequality, but its techniques were those tested in the late 1930s" (83). One of neorealism's creators, Cesare Zavattini, described neorealism as a reaction to the cinema of the Fascist years and to Hollywood's commercial cinema with its "invented stories," tightly controlled scenarios, use of stars, and stylized treatment of character and situations. "Substantially, then," wrote Zavattini, "the question today is, instead of turning imaginary situations into 'reality' and trying to make them look 'true,' to make things as they are, almost by themselves, create their own special significance. Life is not what is invented in 'stories': life is another matter. To understand it involves a minute, unrelenting, and patient search" (219). Similarly, André Bazin lauded the work of the neorealists as giving back "to the cinema a sense of the ambiguity of reality" (37). Neorealist cinema "reveals to the anxious and alert spectator a world alive with possibilities, where perception results in care and where aesthetics finds its fulfillment in morality" (Andrew 82). A film such as *Open City* was "to be the repudiation of an industry as wedded to rhetoric as the Mussolini regime under which it flourished. The filmmaker's most obvious antirhetorical ploy was to dispose of all the physical trappings of prewar cinema, making a virtue of the necessity imposed on him by the straitened circumstances of a war-torn industry" (Marcus 34).

The style and subject matter of neorealism resided in a predominant use of location shooting, deep-focus and long-take photography, nonprofessional actors, a loose form of narration, and a documentary look, plus in the intermingling of fiction and nonfiction, the privileging of marginal and subaltern groups, and a focus on contemporary situations. Surprisingly, many of these characteristics can also be identified with films of the Fascist era and Hollywood films, suggesting that stylistic criteria alone cannot explain the quality, longevity, and effects of neorealism as expressed in the treatment of landscape, character, and narration in *Open City*.

Looking to philosophical rather than formal criteria to understand the impact of neorealism, Millicent Marcus has argued, "Neorealism is first and foremost a moral statement with all the ethical responsibility that such a vision entails" (23). In more specific terms, Gian Piero Brunetta has attributed the film's determining impact on postwar Italian cinema to its social and political momentum: "Most aspects of the postwar Italian cinema derive from *Open City*, direct testimony of the fight for liberation and a tribute to the will for rebirth among the Italian people. Born of an unpredictable break with the past, Rossellini's film is a prototype, a model, and even today, an unavoidable starting point" (343).

The Italian cinema "could point to a resistance and a popular life underlying oppression, although one without illusion." Films such as *Open City* began "again from zero, questioning afresh all the accepted facts from the American tradition. The Italians were therefore able to have an intuitive consciousness of the new image in the course of being born" (Deleuze, *Cinema 1* 211–12). This "new image" situates neorealism within parameters that are larger than a national tradition and more all-encompassing than the reductive notion of neorealism as "redemption" from Fascism. The philosopher Gilles Deleuze argues that Rossellini's work is exemplary of the landscape of post–World War II cinema. Rossellini's filmmaking career, which began during the Fascist regime and continued through World War II, was part of a growing tendency to challenge organic and unified conceptions of the world and the illusion of progress. The war resulted in the ruin of cities and the death of whole populations and undermined belief in the efficacy and power of leadership expressed in the demagoguery of individuals and the manipulation of masses. Yet most commercial cinema was incapable of producing the necessary shock that could give rise to thinking about the world.

Rossellini and the Road to Neorealism

In 1937, Rossellini began his career as a filmmaker, writing scripts, assisting directors on productions, and finally creating his own films. His first cinematic creations were short and poetic documentaries of natural life. His first features, a trilogy of war films, appeared in the early 1940s—*La nave bianca* (*The White Ship*, 1941), *Un pilota ritorna* (*A Pilot Returns*, 1942), and *L'uomo della croce* (*The Man with the Cross*, 1943)—and have been considered by some critics to be anticipatory of neorealism. In the spirit of the war film, the trilogy relied on a fusion of fictional elements, focusing on personal hardship, sacrifice, and romance, and on documentary-style footage conveying the brutal and machinic character of war on sea and land. The films undoubtedly reveal the character and demands of both commercial and state-sponsored cinema under the regime. They also reveal the idiosyncratic and changing treatment of cinematic narrative, perspective, and images that were to develop over the course of Rossellini's career.

In one sense, *Open City* is not a rupture from the cinema that preceded it, since the cinema under late Fascism was already engaged with a critique of the status quo through the films of Vittorio De Sica (*I bambini ci guardano* [*The Children Are Watching Us*, 1943]) and Alessandro Blasetti (*Quattro passi fra le nuvole* [*Four Steps in the Clouds*, 1942]). However, *Open City* was able more directly and more freely to tackle the nature and consequences of Fascism and war. No longer reliant on the mode of production that had distinguished commercial and state-supported cinema during Fascism, Rossellini had to generate his own sources of funding. He had also to locate producers who would invest in the film (Chiara Politi, Giuseppe Amato, and Aldo Venturini), find actors (Anna Magnani and Aldo Fabrizi) who were willing to lend their names to such a project, locate and purchase hard-to-find film stock, and enlist the talents of professional screenwriters (Sergio Amidei and Federico Fellini) and a world-class photographer (Ubaldo Arata).

The final script focused primarily on eight characters: a working-class woman, Pina (Anna Magnani); her fiancé, Francesco, a typesetter and member of the Resistance (Francesco Granjacquet); Manfredi, a Communist Resistance fighter (Marcello Pagliero); Don Pietro, a partisan priest (Aldo Fabrizi); Nazi commandant Major Bergmann (Harry Feist) and his German henchwoman, Ingrid (Giovanna Galetti); Lauretta, Pina's sister (Carla Rovere); and an Italian actress, Marina (Maria Michi). These fictionalized characters were either based on actual individuals of the time or were conflations of several figures, and the various threads of the narrative are woven together to portray the desperate conditions under the Nazi occupation, culminating in scenes of betrayal, torture, and execution (Forgacs 13–19).

In many ways this description of *Open City* would qualify it as a wartime melodrama, and critics have commented on its conventional dimensions (Brunette 41–60). However, the style and method of the film reveal that it exceeds generic categorization as war film, melodrama, or fictionalized documentary. The innovativeness of the film resides in a subtle stylistic treatment that I define as "conceptual realism." Conceptual realism depends on a self-reflexive treatment of images that situates them within an identifiable narrative but calls attention to their status as artifacts. *Open City* invokes the memory of earlier cinematic narratives, but places them in a new context, casting doubt on their clichéd and conventional meanings. To be specific, the film uses images of the Roman landscape to challenge spectators' ideas about their meaning and to solicit new associations, but without diminishing the specificity of place or the immediacy and tragedy of the events that transpire in it.

Analysis

Landscape, Allegory, and Conceptual Realism
The eponymous Rome of the title announces not merely the locale of the film but also the importance of the city in the events that take place in the five days spanned by the narrative. Movement through the city

guides the narrative from the opening high-angle shots of the German soldiers marching through the streets to the final images of the youths marching toward Saint Peter's. The images of the city are not modeled on familiar tourist photographs but on working-class areas such as Pina's tenement, the bakery looted early in the film, and the restaurant where the German soldiers bring two lambs to be slaughtered. In keeping with this working-class emphasis, the city's streets are an important locus for the film's action: trucks carrying German troops roam the streets; civilians are arrested there. The execution of Pina occurs on the street during a roundup, and the shooting of Don Pietro takes place outdoors, followed by the march of the young people. In effect, the members of the Resistance are linked to the city's open spaces.

By setting its action in the city's quotidian spaces, "the film in effect reappropriates Rome for its ordinary citizens and erases traces of the regime, freezing the city in the moment of occupation and resistance" (Forgacs 44). The film does not, however, merely attempt to document the city milieu but focuses on the camera's and the viewer's observation of the events within that milieu. *Open City*'s treatment of landscape emphasizes the movement and the constraints on the movement of the characters through the city, movement closely associated with vision—of the characters as they observe each other and of the spectator who follows their movement.

The restraints imposed on the city's populace by the occupying forces and these inhabitants' efforts to evade capture produce different angles of vision. The first half of the film emphasizes distinctions between interiors and exteriors conveyed through shots of characters as they gaze out of windows. Manfredi's landlady peers out to discover the arrival of the Nazis in search of him, and on the morning of the wedding, Pina observes the Nazis rounding up the residents of the tenement. The youths also observe the movements of the Nazis from their hideout in the upper reaches of the apartment house.

David Forgacs has observed that the film relies on several views of Rome, corresponding "to two different types of power and two different intentions: that of domination and that of resistance." The former type is associated with the system of domination instituted by the Nazis via the establishment of the Schroeder Plan, which mandated the division of the city into fourteen zones. These zones were coordinated through centralized intelligence operations and permitted the surveillance and arrest of suspects, as dramatized in the film by Major Bergmann's activities. The latter type of power, associated with the Italian populace, is decentralized, "hidden from the occupiers' gaze . . . full of hidden routes on foot," and includes escape routes via rooftops, basements, and alleyways (36).

These different views of Rome are also apparent, as Marcus has noted, in "the several maps that recur throughout the film [which] serve to remind us of [the city's] thematic importance and the different meanings attached to the city" (46). Yet these maps not only offer different perspectives on city life, they also evoke different forms of cinematic viewing. Bergmann's Rome, as conveyed through his maps, is a dominated city. The maps that hang in his office are blueprints of centralized power and control over the movement of others. By contrast, the world of the Resistance is dispersed and identified with images of constantly shifting movement. Similarly, the structure of the film relies on constantly shifting elements of tone (from tragic to comic), style (from documentary to theatrical), and perspective (the differing characters' visual perceptions of events).

Allusions to vision appear throughout *Open City*, suggesting connections between the events filmed and cinema's ability to generate different ways of seeing. Bergmann's reliance on maps and surveillance is, for example, similar to forms of cinema that strive to give a totalizing picture of the cinematic milieu, controlling what the viewer sees and how actions are construed. Thus, the maps of the city function not merely as a thematic device to underscore a contrast between oppressive mastery and the contingency of resistance, but as a strategy for commenting on forms of visual control. In a similar way, the film presents the images of Bergmann's office and torture chamber as unbearably compressed, rendering it impossible to escape the sight of torture in the closed and oppressive space. Yet this contained world is antithetical to *Open City*'s overall narrative and style, which is characterized by openness, especially in its episodic plot and in its juxtaposition of different angles of vision through which to regard characters and events. When space is no longer unified and controlled, but fragmented and dispersed, then chance and opportunity can be entertained, and the "text" of the film becomes open to different interpretations. An open text introduces the potential for allegorizing, for creating layers of meaning that extend beyond the specific events portrayed in the film. As critics have acknowledged, the images in the film resonate beyond their contemporary context. The image of Rome as the "eternal city" can thus be read as one of ruin and devastation, like the world of destruction and death that Major Hartmann invokes in his drunken speech to Bergmann. The city is comprised of the ruins of the past and present. These ruins are literal as well as historical; they are the consequence of the ravages of this war, and of all wars. They are also the consequence of Fascism's devastation of the cultural and political landscape.

Specifically, the film's treatment of Pina's death on the Roman street resonates with allegorical significance, linking her individual death to the landscape of the fallen city. She is a tragic example of the many victims of the Germans and of their cruelty in killing a pregnant woman. Her death becomes an emblematic event, evoking a religious iconography of martyrdom. After she falls, Don Pietro cradles her body in Pietà fashion. Yet Pina's martyrdom is also strikingly different from conventional religious iconography and its spiritualized landscapes. Her death is endowed with historical meaning, tying her to the fate of Italy as a nation threatened with the destruction of its present and future. Pina is associated with the fallen city of Rome and more generally with the fallen condition of Italy. Pier Paolo Pasolini would later reaffirm this connection when he cast Anna Magnani as "Mamma Roma" in his exploration of the maternal body, the city of Rome, and the Italian nation (*Mama Roma*, 1962), thus reinforcing connections between the feminine body and the Italian cultural past.

The landscape of Rome invokes still other historical associations. For example, Marcus cites the significance of the name of the leader of the young boys, Romoletto, "little Romulus," a reminder of the founding of Rome. She stresses how the film evokes three different conceptions of this founding: its mythical moment, the Fascist march on Rome with its fusion of classical and Fascist images of a new empire, and the young boys "march" on Rome at the end of the film as an anticipation of a future rejuvenation of the city. This last march, notes Marcus, is "the corrective to the initial march of the occupying troops as the boys reclaim their city for the future of justice and hope that their political activism speaks" (49). Unlike the meanings assigned to the past history of Rome, the ending of the film is highly ambiguous or open about future directions for Italy and for its cinema.

The ending of the film visually portrays space as open, both in the field where Don Pietro is shot as well as in the image of the road on which the boys travel. The dispersed sense of the narrative, the juxtaposition of different modes of cinematic representation in the film, and the somber images of the deaths of Manfredi and Don Pietro would seem to leave open the nature and possibility of a third "founding" of the city. The strength of the film is that it defies, and even subverts, closed forms of interpretation and focuses on means rather than ends in relation to the role of politics and of cinema. The film's conceptual realism relies on its transforming the cinematic landscape into an active cognitive register that generates indeterminate, open meanings. The film's allegorizing of landscape proposes strategies of reading that orchestrate a complex sense of time, bringing past, present, and future into consideration.

Deciphering Clichés of Femininity and Theatricality

The most memorable, often cited, and enigmatic image in *Open City*, if not in all of cinema, is that of Anna Magnani as Pina as she is shot down in the street while chasing Francesco. Yet she is not the only female figure in the film, and actually disappears quite early in the narrative. Pina and the other female characters—Ingrid, Marina, and Pina's sister, Lauretta—are an index to the method of the narrative and its designs on the reader. Femininity is central to the film's form. The viewer is given familiar associations of woman as maternal figure, lesbian dominatrix, actress, and prostitute. The female characters are not conceived in the language of technical realism as rounded and individuated characters, with whom the viewer is expected to identify. Instead, they are ciphers, provoking uncertainty about the quality and direction of their roles in the narrative.

Peter Bondanella and Peter Brunette have each identified elements of the film as "melodramatic," and the concept of melodrama is a starting point for understanding how the film treats character. Melodrama is associated with emotion; it is also identified with the clichés that circulate not only "in the external world, but . . . penetrate each one of us and constitute his internal world" (Deleuze, *Cinema 1* 208). Unlike traditional melodrama, however, *Open City* does not reinforce clichéd and predictable responses to suffering and injustice but rather subjects them to investigation. Rossellini's method involves an unsentimental unmasking of conventional notions of truth, heroism, good, and evil, as demonstrated in the film's portraits of the female figures. Surprisingly, in a film identified as "realistic," the female characters are drawn in a stylized fashion, leading critics to regard the film as still tied to classical cinema, as a "transitional" film. In keeping with the film's self-reflexive method, however, the female characters are central to its investigation of relations between the cinema and Fascism.

Pina seems a cliché of an idealized maternal figure, but her presence is indeterminate, raising a number of questions about her "martyrdom." Her appearances in the film are cryptic. She is portrayed as a defender of the family, an opponent of the Nazis, a penitent, and, finally, sacrificial victim. The brief images establish Pina not as a narrative agent but as a figure acted on by other forces, including the filmmaker. Specifically, Magnani's ample body, disheveled look, husky voice, and passionate acting are indicative of the film's departure from earlier cinematic conceptions of femininity. Although the cinema of the Fascist years had featured working-class women, they were largely figures in need of redemption whose appearance reflected traditional Hollywood images of beauty. Pina's character can be identified with her working-class origins, her "fallen condition" as an "unwed mother" ("I've lived badly," she confesses to Don Pietro), but not with conventional standards of beauty. Her unkempt appearance, "her status as a *popolana* [ordinary woman, woman of the people] whose identity is very much bound up with her community," and her "colloquial language," have been noted by critics (Marcus 39).

Magnani, whose role in this film catapulted her to international stardom, had been identified with comic plays and films during the Fascist era, and Rossellini's choice of her to play Pina (although he had originally wanted Clara Calamai, who had starred in Luchino Visconti's *Ossessione* [1942]) went against the grain of her past performances, though not against her own working-class origins. Consonant with the film's allegorizing, Pina's role is in many ways a reminder of the cinema of the Fascist era. Documentaries by LUCE (the state-sponsored organization for the creation of propaganda) and certain commercial feature films had focused on the project of returning women to the domestic sphere and to their "primary" role as mothers. Government campaigns were waged to enhance the birthrate as well as to promote the primacy of the family, presumed to be under siege (de Grazia 78). This valorization of motherhood corresponded with an attack on feminist aspirations. The maternal figure was often presented as either a paragon of self-abnegation or errant and destructive.

Though Magnani's character may seem to bear affinity to portraits of the mother in earlier Italian cinema, her role is nonetheless more ambiguous. In her embodiment of conformity and resistance, her character presents links to the past but also deviates from it. Her conventional role as mother and fiancée is exemplified in her domineering treatment of Marcello and her dependence on Francesco. Yet her physical appearance, her status as an unwed mother, and her resistance to Nazi authority undermine clichés of maternal femininity. While Pina is portrayed as adhering to family and church ritual (confession and marriage), her observance is, as she herself says apologetically to Manfredi, a matter of belief, not blind adherence. As she tells Manfredi, she would prefer to be married by a partisan priest than a Fascist official in the municipal hall.

Her feminine image is further complicated at the moment of death, when the film suggests a significant reversal of gendered representation. Classical representations of the Pietà are inverted by placing Pina in the position of Christ and Don Pietro in the position of the Madonna, producing further contradictions about the nature of femininity and setting Pina apart from the other feminine characters and from dominant cultural representations of femininity. Her precipitous removal from the narrative is due, in part, to the film's adherence to actual events, but it also anticipates *Open City*'s reflections on the deaths of Manfredi and Don Pietro. Like their deaths, hers cannot readily be reduced to formula, as in the case of films that elevate "great actions and great deeds" (Rossellini 210).

Pina's character is also distinguished by its contrast to the film's other female figures. Lauretta, Pina's sister, offers a rather unspectacular and unsympathetic image of prostitution. Lauretta is portrayed as pleasure-seeking and unthinking, with a cynical, self-interested view of the world that leads to her collaboration with the Nazis. Her vulgarity is revealed in her clichéd response to Francesco on his wedding night. Unaware of Pina's death, she laughs and asks him if Pina has already thrown him out. Unlike Marina, whom she seeks to emulate, she is not malign, but, as Pina describes her to Manfredi, "Stupid." Indeed, Lauretta acknowledges that her collaboration may not ultimately be in her best interest when she says to Marina, "Perhaps Manfredi is right. Maybe we are stupid."

Marina provides a familiar portrait of femininity—the *femme fatale*. She is attractive but deadly. An actress, she is constantly associated with appearances and with a melodramatic theatricality that recalls the diva—a figure of decadence, fiery passion, and death—or, even more, the domesticated, youthful, middle-class female star of popular Fascist film. In *Open City,* however, Marina's apartment, her clothes, and her attention to her own appearance are contrasted to the cramped world of the tenement and to Pina's unadorned physical appearance and her plain clothing. The repeated shots of Marina seated or standing before a mirror are suggestive of her narcissistic self-interest and her concern with image and appearance. The film presents Marina's seductive look and melodramatic temperament as deceptive, untrustworthy, and ultimately empty. She serves as an informer for the Nazis and betrays Manfredi. Her restricted vision is further evident when she collapses on seeing his mutilated body, becoming herself an inert body shorn of the fur coat that was the price of her betrayal. The very objects she sought in order to enhance her feminine image finally reveal her as a cipher. Rather than an independent woman, she emerges as a somnambulist or a marionette set in motion by external forces. Through Marina, then, the film critiques the "false" theatricality and seductive images of earlier Italian cinema, which are linked to the bombastic theatricality and emphasis on images employed by Fascism.

The character of Ingrid conveys another category of femininity. Ingrid's clothing and movements reenact the stereotype of masculinized feminine figures suggestive of lesbianism and misogyny and often identified with cinematic melodrama. These "women" are portrayed as obsessed with control and power, as unscrupulous, cold, and cruel. Ingrid's dress, hairdo, and makeup are, like her mannerisms, severe. Her movement is restricted to interiors: she is not seen in the city. She is seen primarily in the Nazi headquarters, their lounge, Bergmann's "office," and his torture chamber. Like Bergmann, Ingrid is a figure out of melodramatic cinema, with its stark opposition between the forces of good and evil. The stylized, clichéd nature of Ingrid's character is not, however, merely a device to identify her as "evil." Her character, like that of Marina, implies that theatricality is inherent in Fascist culture: it is an expression of the victory of artifice. Ingrid's character may not "explain" power, but it dramatizes its reliance on staging and on performance.

Masculinity: Theatricality and the Machine

If Ingrid plays out a stereotypical image of the lesbian, Bergmann is a formulaic incarnation of an effeminate male homosexual presented as fastidious in dress and in his manner of speaking. His hand gestures are florid, his walk mincing, and his voice high pitched (Ginsberg). Bergmann invokes familiar connections between Nazism and homosexuality explored by critics and later portrayed in Visconti's *La caduta degli dei* (*The Damned*, 1969) and Bernardo Bertolucci's *Il conformista* (*The Conformist*, 1970). If in these later films Fascism and homosexuality are explicitly linked, in the Rossellini film Bergmann is a caricature, a cartoon figure who is always onstage, preoccupied with his theater of operations that involve surveillance and torture.

Bergmann, more than Ingrid, is portrayed within the confines of Nazi headquarters. He describes his world largely in terms of surveillance from afar. His "stroll" (or "cruising") through the city of Rome "every night" occurs through the maps on the wall of his office and the photographs that he collects. He is a cinematic incarnation of the methodical, manipulative, and unscrupulous Nazi that inhabits so many melodramas. To assume that Rossellini conceived of him as a character is an injustice to the film. Bergmann's character is merely a cipher, presenting the impersonal quality of power in theatrical terms. Instead of expressing freedom of movement, Bergmann's gestures are choreographed as if he were a puppet without spontaneity. His role is another indication of the film's focus on the destructive apparatuses of power and on forms of cinema that perpetuate these representations.

Bergmann's character, like that of Ingrid, is symptomatic of what has happened to the promises of cinema as an art of the masses. The world he inhabits is one of simulacra and information networks, a world where distinctions between inside and outside have collapsed. Similarly, another character, Major Hartman (Joop van Hulzen), despite his seemingly insightful and gloomy speeches on how the Nazis "have strewn Europe with corpses" and "will perish without hope," is revealed as mechanistic, as he ultimately performs his duties automatically in executing Don Pietro. Thus, Hartman's words illuminating the horror of Nazism become ironically nothing but clichéd, hollow rhetoric.

Masculinity and Abjection

Open City offers another, contrasting world through the characters of Don Pietro and Manfredi—but this world is not easily reducible in narrative terms to conventional notions of heroic action, despite certain critics' assertions that Rossellini could not himself escape the clichés of heroism. Though the emphasis in *Open City* is on different conceptions of leadership and readiness to sacrifice, the characters are not portrayed as actively altering the dreadful plight of the city. In fact, while Francesco escapes, the Austrian deserter takes his own life, and the last part of the film is relentless in dramatizing the passive suffering of the Communist and the priest—not their escape or their overcoming the Nazis. The image of masculinity that the film offers through these characters is one of abjection. Through incarceration, verbal intimidation, and torture, the men inhabit a debased world where their survival is reduced to the power of another. Through their mortification, the spectator envisions annihilating forms of power. Yet in Manfredi's and Don Pietro's refusal to assent to the demands of the Nazis, the spectator confronts resistance to this condition of abjection.

Their refusal to give in to the Nazis, to inform on their colleagues in the Resistance, results in Manfredi's torture and death. His mutilated body invokes, for a second time in the film, the iconography of Christ. A crucial reflexive moment occurs when Don Pietro is brought in by Bergmann to look at the dying man. Don Pietro approaches Manfredi and says, "You didn't talk." Throughout, the film emphasizes not only vision but also speech: Marcello refuses to tell the priest or Francesco about his activities with Romoletto; Manfredi's landlady refuses to give information to Marina; the Austrian deserter hangs himself rather than confess; and Manfredi suffers excruciating pain (conveyed through brief images of him with his torturers and of their instruments as well as through the sounds of his groans) for his refusal to talk.

Don Pietro and the cinematic spectator are the audience for this drama. He is filmed in close-up gazing into the torture chamber, and if his vision is limited (his glasses have been broken), he can hear the screams of the tortured man perfectly. Thus, the film is concerned with different ways not only of seeing but also of hearing and speaking. In reflexive fashion, the film counterposes sight and sound, the two major components of cinema, indicating a struggle over the exchange of information and knowledge. In keeping with the film's unrelenting examination of the corruption of vision, the emphasis on silence suggests a mode of communication other than verbal language. The motif of silence also disrupts familiar cinematic techniques of fusing word and image identified with the theatricality and rhetorical flourishes of the cinema of the Fascist years. The film's insistence on silence is directed to a form of belief that cannot be reduced to verbal or visual formulas but is a matter of perception and feeling conveyed through gesture. In Manfredi's portrayal, the emphasis is not on action but on passivity, a characteristic not often associated with dominant forms of masculinity in action, adventure, and historical films.

Through the characters of Manfredi, Don Pietro, and Pina, *Open City* creates a conceptual bridge between Marxism and Catholicism. *Open City* is not, however, a polemic: it offers a more complicated conception of belief, one that flouts institutional values belonging to the church and political parties. Manfredi's portrait undermines the cinematic conventions of the Communists. The film does not provide the specifics of Marxism beyond identifying Manfredi with resistance against Nazism, injustice, and crass materialism. And in contrast to religious portraits that emphasize priestly piety, antiworldliness, and moral purity (or its violation), Don Pietro is cast in worldly terms as a political figure, a courier for the Resistance. Like many of Rossellini's later religious figures, the priest's portrayal defies the institutional constraints of both the Roman Catholic Church and the Fascist state. He is a lens through which the spectator can observe events. Observation and reflection—not action—are central to his role, traits identified with Manfredi as well.

Rossellini's conception of cinema spectatorship is particularly dramatized through Don Pietro, who becomes, in effect, an incarnation of the "new image" that demands a transformed mode of looking. He is associated with traits that characterize the method of neorealism. In contrast to Bergmann's visual strolls through Rome by means of maps and images, Don Pietro is associated with physical movement through the ravished city. He is a bridge between the various characters—Pina, Francesco, Manfredi, and Bergmann. He travels between the school, the church, the street, and Nazi headquarters. He also bridges the different stylistic modes of the film: comedy, as in the Fellini-written scene where the priest has to knock the grandfather unconscious with a frying pan in order to save him from the Nazis, or when he turns a nude statuette of a woman away from a statue of Saint Rocco; and tragedy, as in the final episodes.

Similarly, Manfredi is constrained by circumstance to assume a role in which he becomes acted upon rather than active. Although we see him briefly as one of the participants in the attack on the trucks after Pina is killed, his heroism does not consist in his confronting his oppressors in militant actions but primarily in his refusal to collaborate, in his maintaining silence in the face of excruciating torture. In the case of both Don Pietro and Manfredi, the film has transformed conceptions of masculinity inherent to the early Fascist commercial cinema.

Thus, *Open City* subverts clichéd and conventional expectations of masculine action. The lengthy scenes in which Manfredi is asked to provide information and is physically mutilated by his torturers cannot be reduced to a pious interpretation of heroism under adversity. The priest and the Communist both offer a sense of character different from classical cinema. Here, character is "reduced to helplessness, bound and gagged . . . prey to a vision, pursued by it or pursuing it" (Deleuze, *Cinema 2* 3). Similarly, the priest is "prey to a vision," forced to sit and observe the torture of Manfredi. Don Pietro and Manfredi are involved in a situation that is no longer reducible to overcoming and transforming situations through unilateral and heroic action. Instead, the film evokes the possibility of thought filtered through the spectator's vision, by which he or she can develop a different, noninstitutionalized relation to what is seen and heard.

Ambiguous Visions of the Future

In a film that focuses on a world of devastation and death, openness and hope reside in the spectator's engagement with the events. Certain critics have attached a hopeful interpretation to the youths, particularly to the final images of their marching toward Saint Peter's (Marcus 52–53). Their portraits function against the grain of many preexisting cinematic presentations of young people. During the films of the Fascist era, children were frequently portrayed as victims of callous parents or grandparents or, in some instances, as fanatic devotees to the cause of Fascism, and occasionally as domestic rebels. Here, the boys contribute to both the comedic and tragic elements in the film.

The priest's disarming of Romoletto with Marcello's assistance has its humorous side in the silencing of the grandfather with a frying pan. In the scene where the youths return to their apartments after a raid and are, one by one, unceremoniously yanked inside by their irate parents, the film suggests their vulnerability. The youths are presented as observers of their world, and as burgeoning Resistance fighters. Marcello and the other boys are not naive; they are perpetrators of death and also witnesses to it—Marcello, to the shooting of his mother, and the group of boys, to Don Pietro's execution.

The film briefly introduces a counterpoint to their youthful masculine pretensions when Marcello responds to Andreina's question of why women cannot also be heroes with the reductive assertion that "women are trouble," and it is certainly the case that Lauretta, Ingrid, and Marina are a source of "trouble." Furthermore, the one female character, Pina, who differs from them, is killed. The film thus dramatizes gender trouble, but it is not unreflexive in its treatment of masculinity and femininity. The boys' pretensions to heroism are undercut when the priest deflates their potentially foolhardy imitation of heroic masculinity by removing the gun and the bomb before innocent people die. The final images of the film belong to youth and to the spectator. If Don Pietro is the witness to Manfredi's death, the youths are the spectators to his. Their observation of his execution is not accompanied by dialogue, and their departure from the scene is fraught with ambiguity about the future: and specifically what they, and the spectator, will do with what they have seen.

Conclusion

Open City is not a text frozen in time, limited to the immediate years following the end of World War II. The film cannot be categorized by its fidelity to technical definitions of realism, since the techniques it employs—deep-focus, long-take photography and the use of nonprofessional actors, location shooting, elliptical forms of narration, and a documentary treatment—are all part of the history of cinema. Nor can *Open City* be interpreted in unidimensional terms as a document that expresses faith in a new Rome of justice and Christian charity. Rather, the film is an instance of what the novel elements in neorealism signify: it is an expression of a mode of conceptual realism that operates at "the level of the 'mental,' in terms of thought" (Deleuze, *Cinema 2* 1). This form of realism prevents perception from being put in the service of formula and cliché, so as to enable the possibility of challenging habitual modes of response to visual and auditory images.

This kind of filmmaking, exemplified powerfully by *Open City,* immerses the spectator in an awareness of time through images that are open rather than closed, a time that does not order but creatively disorders (Deleuze, *Cinema 2* 145). Its "realism" is thus not technical but conceptual. It is a portent of the attention that must be paid to the visual image in a world where image and gesture have increasingly become debased through the emphasis on modes of distraction and automatic response. *Open City*'s novel method relies on challenging automatism: subverting cinematic clichés by making self-conscious its application of image and sound in relation to their past uses. In the wake of the horrendous events that had transpired as a consequence of Fascism and World War II, images of landscape, masculinity and femininity, the body, and seeing and hearing could no longer be taken for granted.

Credits

Italy, 1945, Excelsa Film

Director: Roberto Rossellini
Screenplay/Dialogue: Sergio Amidei (based on his story) with collaboration by Federico Fellini
Cinematography: Ubaldo Arata
Assistant Directors: Sergio Amidei, with Federico Fellini, Mario Chiari, Albert Manni, and Bruno Todini
Editing: Eraldo Da Roma
Music: Renzo Rossellini

Landy

CAST:

Pina	Anna Magnani
Don Pietro Pellegrini	Aldo Fabrizi
Giorgio Manfredi (alias Luigi Ferraris)	Marcello Pagliero
Francesco	Francesco Granjacquet
Marcello	Vito Annichiarico
Major Bergmann	Harry Feist
Marina	Maria Michi
Ingrid	Giovanna Galletti
Lauretta	Carla Rovere
Major Hartman	Joop van Hulzen

Bibliography

Andrew, Dudley. "André Bazin's 'Evolution.'" *Defining Cinema*. Ed. Peter Lehman. New Brunswick: Rutgers UP, 1997. 73–96.

Bazin, André. "An Aesthetic of Reality." *What Is Cinema?* Ed. and trans. Hugh Gray. Vol. 2. Berkeley: U of California P, 1972. 16–40.

Bondanella, Peter. *The Films of Roberto Rossellini*. New York: Cambridge UP, 1993.

Brunetta, Gian Piero. "Italian Cinema and the Hard Road to Democracy, 1945." *Historical Journal of Film, Radio, and Television* 15.3 (1995): 343–48.

Brunette, Peter. *Roberto Rossellini*. New York: Oxford UP, 1987.

de Grazia, Victoria. *How Fascism Ruled Women: Italy, 1922–1945*. Berkeley: U of California P, 1992.

Deleuze, Gilles. *Cinema 1: The Movement-Image*. Trans. Hugh Tomlinson and Barbara Habberjam. Minneapolis: U of Minnesota P, 1986.

———. *Cinema 2: The Time-Image*. Trans. Hugh Tomlinson and Robert Galeta. Minneapolis: U of Minnesota P, 1989.

Forgacs, David. *Rome Open City*. London: BFI, 2000.

Forgacs, David, Sarah Lutton, and Geoffrey Nowell-Smith, eds. *Roberto Rossellini: Magician of the Real*. London: BFI, 2000.

Gallagher, Tag. *The Adventures of Roberto Rossellini: His Life and Times*. New York: Da Capo, 1998.

Ginsberg, Terri. "Nazis and Drifters: The Containment of Radical (Sexual) Knowledge in Two Italian Neorealist Films." *Journal of the History of Sexuality* 1.2 (1990): 241–61.

Guarner, José Luis. *Roberto Rossellini*. New York: Praeger, 1970.

Landy, Marcia. *The Folklore of Consensus: Theatricality in the Italian Cinema, 1930–1943*. Albany: State U of New York P, 1998.

———. *Italian Film*. London: Cambridge UP, 2000.

Leprohon, Pierre. *Italian Cinema*. Trans. Roger Greaves and Oliver Stallybrass. New York: Praeger, 1972.

Marcus, Millicent. *Italian Film in the Light of Neorealism*. Princeton: Princeton UP, 1987.

Michelone, Guido. *Invito al cinema di Rossellini.* Milan: Mursia, 1996.

Rossellini, Roberto. *My Method: Writings and Interviews.* Ed. Adriano Apra. Trans. Annapaola Cancogni. New York: Marsilio, 1992.

Seknadje-Askénazi, Enrique. *Roberto Rossellini et la second guerre mondiale.* Paris: L'Harmattan, 2000.

Sorlin, Pierre. *Italian National Cinema, 1896–1996.* New York: Routledge, 1996.

Zavattini, Cesare. "Some Ideas on the Cinema." *Film: A Montage of Theories.* Ed. Richard Dyer MacCann. New York: Dutton, 1966. 216–28.

Bicycle Thieves (1948)

GEOFFREY NOWELL-SMITH

The Resilience of Neorealism

Context

Bicycle Thieves is a film that is famous without in fact being particularly well known. As a result, many confusions have grown up around it, and it is not easy to approach unless some of these confusions are removed. The confusion begins with the title itself. The original Italian title is *Ladri di biciclette,* which translates as "Bicycle Thieves," and it is as *Bicycle Thieves* that it was released in Britain. But in France it was released as *Le voleur de bicyclette,* and in the United States as *The Bicycle Thief,* suggesting that it is first and foremost a drama about a man who steals a bicycle (or even several bicycles). In fact, it is a story about a man whose bicycle is stolen and who then attempts to steal a bicycle himself. There are therefore two thefts (one of them unsuccessful) and two thieves, and the point of the film's rather slender plot lies in the tit-for-tat nature of the theft. In this essay I shall use the British (and Italian) title *Bicycle Thieves* throughout, to respect the actual dynamic of the plot.

The second confusion concerns the author. Most sources assign the film simply to Vittorio De Sica, who was the director. But some writers describe the film as being by De Sica and Zavattini, on the grounds that Cesare Zavattini, who was principal scriptwriter on the film, played a shaping role not only in creating *Bicycle Thieves* but in creating other films on which the two men collaborated in the 1940s and 1950s. This fact was widely recognized at the time and is so again today. But the "auteurist" criticism in the mid-1950s has tended to downplay the role of collaborators of all kinds and scriptwriters in particular, and Zavattini's importance has thus been obscured. It is also the case that the credits of the film describe Zavattini only as the author of the treatment (*soggetto*) and as just one of many writers who contributed to the final script. De Sica was in fact the only actual director and was solely responsible for what many critics regard as the most remarkable feature of the film, the direction of the nonprofessional actors, so calling it a De Sica film is in a technical sense correct. But this, as I shall show, is by no means the whole story. In this essay I shall treat the film as a joint creation, attributing individual contributions where the known facts permit, but leaving this open in cases where the symbiosis of the two authors makes precise attribution impossible.

A third confusion arises from the film's connection with the Italian neorealist movement, of which it is a much-cited exemplar. This particular confusion manifests itself in two ways. First, although the film is generally (as mentioned above) ascribed to De Sica as its director, it is also widely thought to be an enactment of a distinct neorealist poetics, attributed to Zavattini. In his writings on film, Zavattini did indeed propose a poetics of neorealism, radically different from that of mainstream cinema, but it is not difficult to show—as has been done for example by Kristin Thompson—that *Bicycle Thieves* does not enact it.

Meanwhile, the film has also suffered from the equally widespread belief that neorealist films were badly made and generally shot on "grainy" black-and-white stock, which in the case of *Bicycle Thieves* is simply not true. This misconception has gained credence from the fact that it is rarely shown theatrically, so that two generations of viewers have gone by, one watching it on 16 mm and the other on VHS video, who have no firsthand knowledge of what it should look like. Shown on 35 mm it is a very beautiful film to watch, a fact that undoubtedly contributed to its original reputation. With any luck, rerelease on DVD will help bring back a sense of what the film ought to look like.

A fourth and final confusion surrounds its seesawing reputation. Over the years *Bicycle Thieves* has sunk from being regarded as a pinnacle of film art to becoming one of those films shown only as monuments to changes in critical fashion. It has also been pointed out, not without malice, that even when its reputation was at its peak, it was never popular with a mass audience, at home or abroad. This contrast between critical acclaim and popular disdain has, however, been much exaggerated. *Bicycle Thieves* was one of the better performing films at the box office in Italy when it came out, though its greatest success was in art-house distribution—in France, Britain, and the United States, in particular. The rest of this essay will be devoted to showing why the film deserves better than to be regarded as a historical curiosity.

Background

In 1948, when *Bicycle Thieves* came out, Italy was slowly recovering from the devastation caused by the Second World War. Aid under the Marshall Plan had started flowing, but its effects were still to be felt. There was widespread unemployment and a continuing shortage of food and raw materials. The film industry had been dismantled during the war and was just beginning to put itself back together. But it faced overwhelming competition from the backlog of American films that the Italian public had not been able to see during the war years and that were being released en masse from 1946 onward. It was while the commercial industry was in disarray and before the trickle of American films entering the country had become a deluge that the neorealist movement established itself.

Neorealism has never been easy to define precisely, but its most important characteristic, in literature as much as in the cinema, was the bearing of testimony. Neorealist stories and films tended to be about ordinary life, whether in extraordinary circumstances such as under the German occupation or ordinary ones such as the times of deprivation that followed. The neorealist writers and filmmakers were mostly left wing in politics, and many had taken part in the Resistance. They had a vision of reconstruction that looked forward to a future radically different from the recent Fascist past.

In the immediate postwar years, two Italian films in particular had enjoyed wide success: they were Roberto Rossellini's *Rome Open City* (*Roma città aperta*, 1945) and De Sica and Zavattini's *Shoeshine* (*Sciuscià*, 1946). *Open City* had been a box-office hit both in Italy and abroad, especially in the United States. *Shoeshine* had been less successful commercially, but it won an Oscar for best foreign film, and on that basis American producers had begun to express interest in investing in Italian films. But these were the years of the onset of the Cold War, and conservative opinion, both in Italy and in the United States, was suspicious of the pro-Communist leanings of the neorealist filmmakers. It was also widely thought, and probably rightly, that a cinema that made a virtue of making films without star actors had restricted commercial prospects with a mass audience.

By the time *Bicycle Thieves* came out, neorealism had lost much of its novelty value in its home country. Audiences were showing a clear preference for American films on the one hand and the product of the revived commercial industry on the other. The most successful "neorealist" film at the box office was *Bitter Rice* (*Riso amaro*), directed by Giuseppe De Santis and produced by Dino De Laurentiis in 1949. But *Bitter Rice,* although it shared the leftist politics characteristic of neorealist filmmakers, was a down-the-line commercial product, with a star-studded cast (including Raf Vallone, Vittorio Gassman, and the sexy "newcomer" Silvana Mangano) and a highly melodramatic subplot. Thereafter the neorealist movement began to crumble away, with a few prized directors plowing their own distinctive furrows and the remainder sinking into what became disparagingly known as "rose-tinted" neorealism (*neorealismo rosa*), in which the original radical impulse of the movement was dissipated into sentimental pictures of the lives of the deserving and not-so-deserving poor.

Internationally, however, the reputation of neorealism remained high, and the pioneers of the movement could count on a sympathetic reception at festivals and on the art-cinema circuit, and sometimes on foreign finance as well.

The Filmmakers

When De Sica and Zavattini joined forces to make the film *The Children Are Watching Us* (*I bambini ci guardano*) in 1943, De Sica was already famous as one of Italy's leading theater and film actors, while Zavattini was an up-and-coming young writer with a successful sideline as a cartoonist. De Sica had made his first film appearance as a teenager in 1917 and had then joined the theater, becoming a recognized leading actor from 1930 onward. Popular screen success came with his starring role in Mario Camerini's *Gli uomini, che mascalzoni!* (*Men—What Scoundrels*) in 1932, and for the rest of the decade he divided his time between cinema and theater (where he now had his own company), specializing as the debonair (and sometimes fraudulent) man-about-town with a delightful, self-regarding sexual charm. It was therefore somewhat of a surprise when he reemerged after the war as a director of films with proletarian subjects and a gritty, neorealist content.

Zavattini was an equally engaging character, an acerbic cartoonist and a writer whose early stories display a delightful mix of realism and whimsy. From 1935 he took to earning his money as a screenwriter, at which he soon developed a great facility. He wrote the script for Camerini's *Darò un milione* (*I'll Give a Million,* 1935), in which De Sica had one of his most famous starring roles, and was a writer (uncredited) on De Sica's second film as director, *Teresa Venerdí* (1941). But the two were not intimate (until 1940, Zavattini lived mostly in Milan, De Sica always in Rome), and the partnership proper did not begin until two years later. Unlike De Sica, whose life was totally immersed in theatrical and film work, Zavattini was involved in all sorts of different circles, journalistic and political as well as artistic. In 1944, just after the liberation of Rome, he called a meeting of filmmakers to debate what cinema should be like after the war was over. Later on, Za, as he was referred to, called many meetings, but this first was one of the most important and a founding moment of neorealism.

The Production

The title of the film was taken from a novel by Luigi Bartolini, but the core idea—the tit-for-tat theft—was basically Zavattini's. He read the novel, liked it, and dashed off a treatment, which, however, bears precious little relationship to the original. (This was to lead to trouble later, when Bartolini objected to the cavalier way his book was treated.) The action was pared down until all that was left was a man whose bicycle is stolen and who engages in a desperate search, accompanied by his small son, to find the bicycle and the thief who stole it. In desperation, he becomes a thief in his turn, but is spotted, chased down and captured, and finally released by a crowd of fellow workers.

Zavattini showed the treatment to De Sica, who decided it was worth trying to raise finance for the film. But Italian producers were wary, while an American producer who had been approached was prepared to finance it on condition that Cary Grant played the lead. So desperate were the filmmaking team to get the project off the ground that they even took this idea seriously, although, as co-scriptwriter Suso Cecchi D'Amico said later, they should have laughed it out of court immediately (Faldini and Fofi 135). Eventually money was found from private sources, and De Sica formed a production company of his own to make the film.

Besides De Sica and Zavattini, five other writers receive screen credit for the script. On the credits these names are put in alphabetical order, so that Zavattini appears at the bottom (although he was by no means least, and was in fact the only writer involved in the project at all stages of preparation).

Scripting took place in late 1947 and early 1948. Members of the script team visited a number of prospective locations, including a licensed brothel, a Catholic soup kitchen, and the home of a popular fortune-teller, in order to immerse themselves in the required atmosphere. A complete shooting script was prepared, which De Sica adhered to very closely, possibly too closely, since it proved quite constricting at times. One scene, however, was improvised. During the shooting, a group of German seminarists was encountered sheltering from the rain. As it happened, a high school student called Sergio Leone was acting as unpaid assistant on the production. According to his account, De Sica was so enchanted by the spectacle he decided to include it in the film (Faldini and Fofi 135). Leone came back the next day with a group of schoolmates and a set of costumes, and a scene was filmed inspired by what the filmmakers had seen.

Casting sessions were held to find a child actor for the film. No suitable child was found, but at one session a man walked in with his small son. The boy was rejected, but the man, an engineering worker at the Breda works called Lamberto Maggiorani, was instantly selected to play the male lead. A child was eventually found among the bystanders watching the filming (Nuzzi and Iemma 102). The actress playing the hero's wife was a journalist in real life. Other parts were mostly filled by professionals.

Filming took place over the spring of 1948. The length of the shoot was partly due to variable weather on location, which made continuity difficult and also created problems during editing. The director of photography was Carlo Montuori, and the film was shot on Gevaert stock. As was customary in Italy, no sync dialogue was recorded, and dubbing sessions were held after the rough cut was assembled. The editor was Eraldo Da Roma, who went on to be Michelangelo Antonioni's editor on a number of films, beginning with *I vinti* in 1952. Zavattini, who had taken a backseat during the shooting, returned to join in the supervision of the editing, and subsequently claimed credit for its being so tight (Nuzzi and Iemma 110). The editing is indeed tight (much tighter than in Da Roma's work for Antonioni, for example), and there are very few lingering shots and a surprisingly large number of close-ups.

Analysis

It is sometimes said that the narrative of *Bicycle Thieves* is quite sparse and that there is not much narrative or dramatic action. While it is true that the action of the film is not particularly dramatic, the narrative is in fact quite full of incident. (Rather too full, in Zavattini's later judgment.) But the structure of the narrative is episodic and resembles a road movie more than a conventional action film.

First and foremost, *Bicycle Thieves* is a film about Rome. Not, on the whole, the Rome that tourists see—though some do venture to the flea market at Porta Portese, where the hero first catches sight of the thief, and even more go to Trastevere, where the thief is finally tracked down. Rather, it is the Rome of working-class suburbs and the old popular center, districts later frequented by other Italian directors such as Federico Fellini and Pier Paolo Pasolini. It is also a film about one man, disappointed, bewildered, and angry, on a vain search for the object that symbolizes his connection with the world of work and honorable survival. In between the man and his setting stands the social world, the world of work and no work, of mutual help and mutual suspicion, and the manipulations practiced by politicians and bureaucrats.

The Story

The film is divided into forty-four scenes, with breaks in continuity marked by lap dissolves or, in the case of longer time lapses, by fades to black. The uniformity of this division may suggest a formalist impulse, cutting up the film into discrete chunks whose interrelation would be significant for its understanding. But the fact is that the dissolves, although noticeable to scholars (Thompson; Moneti) as they play through the film on a Moviola or on video, are pretty much imperceptible to the ordinary viewer, and their uniformity is more a matter of conforming rather slavishly to the editor's rule book than a major signifying feature. If anything, they serve as a reminder that the film, while original in many respects, is also quite conventional in others.

The action of the film takes place over three days. On Friday the hero is offered a job. On Saturday he starts it, but when his bicycle is stolen from him he is unable to continue it. On Sunday he searches for the bike and commits his impulse theft.

The first scene takes place outside a labor exchange. Groups of unemployed are standing around, waiting without much hope for their name to be called. Bricklayers are complaining that they never get offered anything, which might seem unfair but whose logic would be appreciated at the time: they have a skill which is going to be needed in due course, and the authorities are not keen to see this pool of labor dispersed.

Among the men with no particular skill, Antonio Ricci is one of the lucky ones. He is offered a job as a bill poster. But to get the job he needs a bike, and he doesn't have one. Or rather he does, but it is in pawn. On his return home, his wife Maria, who is shown as a competent and resourceful woman, at first upbraids him for pawning the bike but then decides that it would be better for the family to do without sheets than for Antonio to pass up this chance of a job.

Husband and wife therefore set out to the pawnshop, which is no ordinary shop but a giant and rather historic looking building with shelves reaching up to its lofty vaulted ceiling—testimony, if it were needed, to the dire circumstances of the many poor people forced to dispose of precious property in order to raise much-needed cash. They redeem the bike, and Antonio calls in at his new place of employment, where he is told to report for work at 6:45 the next morning.

Husband and wife then set off home. On the way, she asks to stop and enters a house, from which she does not come out for some time. Antonio gets impatient. With an anxious glance at his bike, which he asks a bystander to look after for him, he goes upstairs to find it is the house of "la Santona," a fortune-teller. His rationalist sensibilities offended, Antonio drags Maria away.

After a fade to black the film reopens in the Riccis' apartment. It is 6:30 the following morning and Bruno, their seven-year-old son, is cleaning Antonio's bike. As he has done earlier, De Sica takes a pretty functional view toward filming the apartment. It is clearly lit and in deep focus, with no attempt to make it seem other than it is—average sized, modestly furnished, certainly not luxurious but not desperately poor either. Besides Antonio, Maria, and Bruno, there is also a baby, shown in a brief cutaway, another of the trappings of family life.

Antonio drops Bruno off at the gas station, where the boy works as an attendant, and reports for duty. After a brief training in how to put a poster up without creasing it, Antonio is on his own. But hardly has he learned the art of how to smooth Rita Hayworth's voluptuous curves onto a flat surface, than disaster strikes. A lurking thief has spotted his unguarded bike, and makes off with it at high speed. Antonio gives chase, assisted by a bystander, but to no avail. He returns disconsolately to the scene of the crime, gives a final smoothing down to Rita, and goes to report the theft to the police. The police, however, are far more interested in despatching the riot squad to suppress a workers' demonstration, and little attention—in Antonio's opinion—is paid to his complaint.

Up to the moment of the theft the manner of the film has been mainly expository. We have been introduced to the world of economic, urban, and family life. The narrative has been tied together with cross-cutting, which also serves to relate the world of individuals to a wider social environment. Features of this manner will characterize the film throughout. But as we enter into the theme of Antonio's desperate search for the missing bike there is a shift of focus. The narrative becomes more strung out, with events following each other according to the rhythm of the search and with the psychological focus almost entirely on the searcher, Antonio, and his emotions. The family takes a backseat (we hardly see Maria anymore, though Bruno becomes more important), while Rome is viewed more and more through the prism of Antonio's frantic anxiety.

After the visit to police headquarters, Antonio sends Bruno home to break the news to Maria. He himself sets out to an unnamed building where a political meeting is being held while in the basement a group of people are rehearsing a variety routine. The building is in fact a Communist Party social club and would have been recognizable as such to audiences at the time. One of the comrades, Baiocco, a garbage collector, agrees to help Antonio and gives him a rendezvous for the following day.

Antonio and Bruno set out at dawn to join Baiocco and his team, and together they comb the market at Piazza Vittorio. After an altercation with a man refurbishing what is probably a stolen bike (but not Antonio's), Antonio and Baiocco collect Bruno, who has attracted the attentions of a dubious-looking man in a straw hat. They then set out in the rain to another market, at Porta Portese, where Baiocco leaves them—another character who will not be seen again. It is here that the unscripted scene occurs with the German priests sheltering from the rain. Antonio and Bruno then have a lucky break. They see the thief talking to an old man and give chase. The thief escapes, but they pursue the old man to a church where some charitable ladies have organized a soup kitchen for the poor.

The scene in the church is played as anxiety-comedy. Antonio tries to force information out of the old man, but the harder he tries the more disturbance he creates (this motif has already surfaced in the visit to the Communist club) and the less he is able to achieve. During the disturbance the old man manages to escape. Antonio is detained by a couple of young men in suits, who would appear to be the sons of the charitable ladies, but evades their clutches. Bruno follows, pausing to cross himself as he scampers past the altar.

The scene that follows offers respite from the chase, but not from Antonio's anxiety. Bruno ticks his father off for his incompetence and is rewarded with a slap in the face. Antonio apologizes and then asks Bruno to wait for a moment near the river. During their separation Antonio is distracted by the sight of a body being recovered from the water, which he thinks must be Bruno's, though it is not.

To pacify his son, Antonio decides to take him to a restaurant. This scene too is comic, but not without its moments of embarrassment and pathos. Antonio plies his son with wine, which is not as outlandish an idea in Italy as it may appear to present-day Americans. Even so, Bruno seems to accept more to show his precocious manliness than because he enjoys it. The comedy derives mainly from the byplay between Bruno and an overdressed middle-class child at the next table.

After leaving the restaurant, father and son pass by the house of the fortune-teller and decide to go in. Asked about their chances of recovering the bike, she offers the wise, if statistically unremarkable, prediction, "Either you'll find it immediately, or you won't find it."

The chase now resumes. Antonio and Bruno spot the thief, who recognizes Antonio and shuffles off, breaking into a run as he turns into a side street. They pursue him into a place that turns out to be a brothel where the young ladies, as they are referred to, are just taking their lunch break. Back in the street, Antonio confronts the thief, who falls down in a fit. A gang of heavies now surrounds Antonio, and a policeman, summoned by Bruno, refuses to take Antonio's side. The camera tracks in on Antonio as he retreats from the scene, defeated and utterly disconsolate.

The film now moves to its denouement. As Antonio and Bruno retreat toward the river, the sound of cheering is heard from a soccer stadium. Thousands of spectators have left their bikes unattended. As they stream away from the stadium, Antonio makes a decision. Sending Bruno away to catch a tram, he snatches a bike from a doorway and makes off on it but is instantly caught and hauled back. A crowd assembles, threatening punishment, but the bike's owner is forgiving. Bruno, who—probably deliberately—never caught his tram, takes his father's hand and leads him away. Father and son, both with tears in their eyes, merge into the crowd as it disperses.

Realism

God, as Gustave Flaubert is reputed to have said, is in the detail, and this remark is as true of *Bicycle Thieves* as of Flaubert's own novels. If the above account of the plot of the films seems unduly intricate, it is because the life of the film is not in any broad narrative sweep but in the accumulation of psychological, social, and visual detail, not all of which is instantly and unambiguously clear. For modern viewers it is probably the psychological aspect that is most interesting. We follow events through Antonio's eyes, identifying with his suffering and anxiety even if we are not always clear what emotions are coursing through his lanky frame. The acting is little help. Although Maggiorani's performance seems authentic, it is lacking in expressive intentionality such as a professional actor would have provided. The spectator is therefore engaged in a constant guessing game: What is really going on in this man's head, and how does it relate—other than in the most obvious way—to what is going on around him? Which of the many random-seeming details presented to our view is in fact the significant one that will guide us to a clear understanding of the man and his predicament?

Bicycle Thieves' use of a causally loose-knit narrative, coupled with the piecemeal introduction of sociological detail, is central to its effect. But the film's sociopolitical message, which nowadays comes across as vaguely humanist and at times almost sentimental in its stress on the sufferings of the poor, would have asserted itself much more starkly in 1948. As contemporary critics noted, the "poor" in the film are not an undifferentiated mass but clearly divided into two basic groups. Antonio finds support and solidarity among regular working-class people and suspicion and hostility among the shiftless subproletariat clustered around the street markets and the stews of

Trastevere. The institutions to which the poor have recourse are also differentiated. The fortune-teller is a fraud, the charity offered by the middle class via the Church is meaningless and ineffective; only the Communist Party seems committed to helping not just Antonio but others like him, and if in the event it cannot do much for Antonio himself it is because his problem is only a symptom of a wider social malaise that can only be tackled by collective action.

The ambiguity of the film is also much limited by the way it is edited, which is full of narrative and psychological clues. In particular, the prevalence of shots of unattended bikes from (broadly) Antonio's point of view makes it clear that the idea that bicycles might be stolen is never far from his mind and acts as a leitmotif for the action. While this helps keep the narrative focused, an alternative reading is also hinted at. For although the story would appear to be one of real events, precisely located in space and time, there is also a strong sense emanating from the film that what we are seeing is not entirely real but an enactment of Antonio's nightmare.

The main thrust of the film, however, is toward realism, and in several senses. It is, despite the occasional hints in the direction of a subjective reading, on the whole firmly objective. Events are placed in a carefully observed social reality, which is sometimes pointed up but more often simply forms part of the overall texture of the film. The plot mimics the ups and downs of everyday life, in which both chance and determinism play a part. Clever though the narration is in blending elements of alternating good and bad luck for its protagonist, it does not force the twists and turns of the action into an overly purposeful narration, in the Hollywood manner. Furthermore, the narrational stance occupies a position both within the action and at a slight distance from it. There are very few overt marks of a directorial point of view engaging the spectator's attention from a position outside the action in order to show scenes as more comic or more pathetic than they intrinsically are, while at the same time the narration holds a certain distance from the characters so that their actions are always seen in the context of what others are doing around them. It is not surprising, under the circumstances, that *Bicycle Thieves* is so often held up as a model of cinematic realism.

But caveats remain. The plot of *Bicycle Thieves* is not as "slender" (*gracile*) as Zavattini thought the ideal neorealist story should be.

Zavattini's dream was to write a film that aimed "not to invent a story which was like reality, but to tell reality as if it was a story" (Zavattini 103), and he envisaged a *mise-en-scène* that followed the characters in their everyday life without anticipating their next move and directing the spectator's attention to what was about to happen. Clearly, *Bicycle Thieves* does not fit this idealized and probably unrealizable model.

Other objections can also be made to the claims for *Bicycle Thieves* as a work of pure realism. Thompson has pointed out that its style, while generally conforming to canons of realism, also contains many elements of "classical" Hollywood narration, notably a time-driven narrative that gives shape and momentum to its otherwise sprawling construction (209). For his part, Christopher Wagstaff makes the telling point that the comic moments in the film are very deliberately staged and belong to a different mode from observational realism. It is not that realist works cannot be comic—indeed their realism would not be complete if it did not recognize the funny side of life—but rather that comedy entails a form of address to the audience that invites an active response. De Sica, who always had an eye for comedy, whether as an actor or as a director, undoubtedly intervenes in scenes such as that in the church in ways that alert the audience to how the scene is being staged for their conscious amusement.

Even so, while modern scholars (and audiences) have no difficulty in relativizing the film's realism and spotting its not infrequent moments of obvious artifice, the fact remains that in the context of its time the film was clearly locatable in a movement that made great and on the whole justifiable claims to a realistic approach to life in general and to how that life should be portrayed in cinema.

The Critics and the Public

As mentioned above, *Bicycle Thieves* was a huge critical success and a more modest one with the public. De Sica describes a rapturous reception at the Paris premiere, where he was publicly embraced by René Clair and André Gide, while a few days earlier in Rome he had heard angry working-class spectators ask for their money back (Faldini and Fofi 136). In fact, it did quite well at the box office, grossing 250 million lire (approximately $650,000). It then went on to do very well abroad, mainly on the art-house circuit but also on wider release.

While the film's aesthetic achievement was admired pretty universally, its politics proved divisive. The left applauded it, but right-wing Catholics were offended by its satire on the Church, while the Christian Democrat politicians in power in Italy were alarmed by its general portrayal of Italy as poor and backward and considered refusing it an export license.

Perhaps the most influential voice in support of the film came from outside Italy, where André Bazin wrote enthusiastically about it in the left-leaning Catholic magazine *Esprit*. Bazin praised both its realism and its political forthrightness, calling it "the only valid Communist film of the last decade" (*"Bicycle"* 51)—a barbed comment designed as much to cast suspicion on certain other neorealist films as to praise *Bicycle Thieves* itself. Politically, he praised the film for having a universal, rather than sectarian, message, while aesthetically he particularly admired what he called its transparency, meaning by this the way its components—acting, *mise-en-scène*, even the story—merged into near invisibility as if in the presence of life itself. This presumed transparency is the great enduring myth about *Bicycle Thieves*. We may not believe it so much now, but it made the film's reputation.

Conclusion

Bicycle Thieves remained on a pinnacle of critical admiration for well over a decade. It tied for third in an international critics' poll of best films, which was conducted by the magazine *Sight and Sound* in 1952. A similar poll on the occasion of the Brussels International Exhibition in 1958 named it the best film ever. But when *Sight and Sound* repeated its poll in 1962, it had fallen to seventh, and in 1972 it dropped out entirely, and has not returned.

It was not just *Bicycle Thieves* that rather dropped out of sight in the 1960s and 1970s; it was neorealism itself, under attack from both nonpolitical and "new left" standpoints. In France, François Truffaut declared roundly in *Cahiers du cinéma* that he had no interest in any Italian neorealist directors except Rossellini, while in England, *Movie* pronounced *Bicycle Thieves* and films like it merely boring.

The "new left" critique started in Italy and France, where the generation of 1968 denounced the claims of neorealism as political cinema, finding the universalism praised by Bazin merely a cover for a reformist and antirevolutionary stance. This virulent attitude spread to the English-speaking world through the magazine *Screen* (Cannella), merging with the view once expressed by Jean-Luc Godard that a political film was not one with a political content but one that was "made politically." Neither *Bicycle Thieves* nor any neorealist film matched up to Godard's criterion, nor were they intended to.

But history has a habit of making fools of people who make extreme pronouncements. *Bicycle Thieves* is a resilient film. Its richness and density underlying an apparently simple story never cease to surprise viewers—whether they come expecting a boring masterpiece or nothing in particular.

Credits

Italy, 1948, Produzioni De Sica S.A.

Director: Vittorio De Sica
Screenplay: Oreste Biancoli, Suso D'Amico, Vittorio De Sica, Adolfo Franci, Gherardo Gherardi, Gerardo Guerrieri, and Cesare Zavattini
Story: Cesare Zavattini (based on the novel by Luigi Bartolini)
Cinematography: Carlo Montuori
Camera Operator: Mario Montuori
Assistant Director: Gerardo Guerrieri and Luisa Alessandri
Editing: Eraldo Da Roma
Music: Alessandro Cicognini
Song: Giuseppe Cioffi
Music Direction: Willy Ferrero
Sound: Gino Fiorelli
Art Direction: Antonino Traverso

CAST:

Antonio Ricci	Lamberto Maggiorani
Bruno Ricci	Enzo Staiola
Maria Ricci	Lianella Carell
Patroness	Elena Altieri
Baiocco	Gino Saltamerenda
The pauper	Giulio Chiari
The thief	Vittorio Antonoucci
Beggar	Carlo Jachino

Bibliography

Bazin, André. *"Bicycle Thief." What Is Cinema?* Ed. and trans. Hugh Gray. Vol. 2. Berkeley: U of California P, 1972. 47–60.

———. "De Sica, metteur en scene." *What Is Cinema?* Ed. and trans. Hugh Gray. Vol. 2. Berkeley: U of California P, 1972. 61–78.

Caldiron, Orio, and Manuel De Sica, eds. *"Ladri di biciclette" di Vittorio De Sica.* Rome: Pantheon, 1997. Contains Italian shooting script.

Cannella, Mario. "Ideology and Aesthetic Hypotheses in the Criticism of Neo-Realism." 1966. *Screen* 14.4 (1974): 5–60.

Faldini, Franca, and Goffredo Fofi. *L'avventurosa storia del cinema italiano.* Milan: Feltrinelli, 1979.

Micciché, Lino, ed. *De Sica: Autore, regista, attore.* Venice: Marsilio, 1992.

Moneti, Guglielmo. *"Ladri di biciclette."* Micciché 247–85.

Nuzzi, Paolo, and Ottavio Iemma. *De Sica e Zavattini: Parliamo tanto di noi.* Rome: Riuniti, 1997.

Thompson, Kristin. *Breaking the Glass Armor.* Princeton: Princeton UP, 1988.

Wagstaff, Christopher. "Comic Positions." *Sight and Sound* ns 2.7 (1992): 25–27.

Zavattini, Cesare. *Neorealismo ecc.* Milan: Bompiani, 1971.

Singin' in the Rain (1952)

JANE FEUER

Winking at the Audience

Context

Singin' in the Rain has come to represent the golden age of the MGM musical, but it may not at first appear a worthy candidate for serious analysis. A light, witty entertainment, the film seems to evaporate under the kind of scrutiny film analysis is likely to provide. Although it remains a much-loved and widely admired singing and dancing extravaganza, there does not at first seem to be very much to say about this delightful piece of fluff beyond exclaiming over its perfection. Its entertainment value is self-evident, and the title number would seem to need no explanation beyond being a simple ode to the joy of life. In fact, an HMO provider once simply ran the number as an advertisement for itself. No explanation was deemed necessary to establish the connection between Gene Kelly's happiness at being in love and the presumed benefits of health-care coverage.

Yet to believe that *Singin' in the Rain* is simply *there* is to misunderstand the goals of film analysis. This essay will attempt to show that, underneath the icing, we can uncover a multilayered work that shares many thematic concerns with more seemingly "serious" films, films that—like Woody Allen's *The Purple Rose of Cairo* (1985)—film critics have labeled "self-reflexive" or "intertextual." In the case of Woody Allen's film, a character who believes in the promises made by Depression-era films actually finds herself being addressed by characters in the film she is watching. Soon she finds herself up on the screen and taking part in the narrative. The filmmaker does this to question the illusions created by classical Hollywood movies. Such "self-reflexive" films make references to earlier films in a way that causes the audience to think either about the nature of those earlier films or about the film's own status as a cinematic production. As a "Hollywood on

Hollywood" film, then, *Singin' in the Rain* cannot help but say something about the nature of the film medium and about the film industry it "winks" at. And in saying something about Hollywood, the film inevitably exposes itself as a product of the system it pretends to mock.

In addition to being a much-analyzed film, *Singin' in the Rain* is also a film whose production has been much documented. The Special Edition DVD, released in 2002 for the film's fiftieth anniversary, is a virtual archive of information. It includes not one but two documentaries about the making of this and other Freed Unit MGM musicals, plus commentary by Debbie Reynolds, Donald O'Connor, Cyd Charisse, Kathleen Freeman (who played the elocution teacher), codirector Stanley Donen, screenwriters Betty Comden and Adolph Green, filmmaker Baz Luhrmann, and author/film historian Rudy Behlmer; excerpts from the original films for which the Arthur Freed and Nacio Herb Brown songs were written; outtakes of cut musical numbers; and even clips from early sound films whose look influenced *Singin' in the Rain*. Although these sources contain sometimes conflicting information (and information that conflicts with other histories), they combine to establish that *Singin' in the Rain* is a classic, a film that has been thoroughly studied and one deserving of much study. These study aids also agree that *Singin' in the Rain* tells the true story of the coming of sound to Hollywood in 1927.

Yet the genesis of *Singin' in the Rain* had little to do with a desire on the part of its makers to do an exposé on Hollywood. In this sense it was typical of many other musicals that had already been made by the artists at what has come to be known as the Freed Unit at MGM Studios. Producer Arthur Freed assembled the best and the brightest musical-making artists, and MGM let them create relatively free from interference. Freed had been a lyricist in the 1920s and 1930s and, although credited as associate producer, he was responsible for MGM's purchasing the book and filming *The Wizard of Oz* (1939). He went on to produce some of the best-loved screen musicals: *Meet Me in St. Louis* (1944), *Easter Parade* (1948), *On the Town* (1949), and *An American in Paris* (1951). By the time *Singin' in the Rain* went into production in 1951, Freed had already hired screenwriters Betty Comden and Adolph Green to write a script that spoofed the theater (*The Barkleys of Broadway*, 1949), and with it gently mocked screen legends Fred Astaire and Ginger Rogers, who were reunited for that film. Freed was still involved in the production of *An American in Paris* (at the time considered a much more important musical than *Singin' in the Rain*), a film whose conception was similar to that of this film. That is, MGM would purchase the entire catalog of a songwriting team (in the case of *An American in Paris,* George and Ira Gershwin) and hire scriptwriters to fashion a film around a selection of these songs. This was possible because popular songs tended to express the same range of emotions as the musical film genre itself. They were about falling in love, being in love, rejection in love, the joys of singing and dancing, the joys and sorrows of being alive, and other subjects adaptable to almost any musical. The musical "number" could run the length of the song, much as a music video does today.

In this way Comden and Green were instructed to create a film based on the song catalog of Freed himself and his partner Nacio Herb Brown. The conception of the film was thus not the desire of a team of freely chosen artists to express themselves by mocking Hollywood; it was rather the much more commercial command to do something with a valuable and already presold property—the song catalog. And yet, Comden and Green had already "winked" at the legitimate theater and would go on to spoof the production of Broadway musicals (in *The Band Wagon,* 1953) and the overly commercialized nature of early TV shows (in *It's Always Fair Weather,* 1955). Somehow, the idea that Comden and Green came up with for *Singin' in the Rain* (that is, to base the script in the period of very early film musicals, for which many of the songs had originally been written, and therefore to take an affectionate but tongue-in-cheek look at the idiocies of that period) was also in line with their own themes as expressed across a series of musicals. In this sense, it both is and is not valid to say that *Singin' in the Rain* was an "original film musical" rather than one adapted from another medium, a book or a Broadway show. The fact that the script had to accommodate an already written collection of popular songs dictated that it would be created within the commercial imperatives of the film industry. The fact that it was to be an MGM musical meant that it would be a genre film like so many others, and not the original creation of its author or director. These circumstances shaped the kind of film *Singin' in the Rain* would become, but they have not prevented it from becoming a classic fifty years later, nor from being analyzed as a work of art that has distinctive form as well as content.

One of the circumstances of this method of creation was that Freed Unit musicals were never really "integrated" in the way that they are said to be. Unlike, say, *Oklahoma!* (1955), the songs were not conceived alongside the book. They are generic songs that fit a generic moment rather than the organic product of a single vision. Even *Singin' in the Rain*'s title number, with its perfect fit to the situation of falling in love, and to that of "singin'" and (added for the film) "dancin'" in the rain, is not about the specific situation, as are songs in a more fully integrated musical such as *Oklahoma!*, which goes so far as to describe a particular surrey with a particular fringe on top in the lyric. It is hard to imagine a song about such a historically specific mode of transportation (with "isinglass curtains") being transferable to another show. When songs similar to the 1943 Broadway production of *Oklahoma!*'s "Surrey with the Fringe on Top" were written for MGM musicals—say, "On the Atchison, Topeka and the Sante Fe" for *The Harvey Girls* (1946)—the numbers were not expected to fill slots in later musicals. But Freed and Brown wrote Tin Pan Alley–type songs that were expected to be "hits" when sold as sheet music. These songs were sufficiently generic to fill up virtually every song slot in *Singin' in the Rain.*

Thus the numbers in *Singin' in the Rain* might be described as "modular" rather than "organic." It was the job of the scriptwriters, musical arrangers, choreographers, scenic artists, and directors to make the prewritten songs *appear* to be organic and fully integrated into this particular musical. A successful musical like this one gives the illusion of being conceived as a whole, but this is one of many "illusions" perpetuated by the film. In fact, it can be said that *Singin' in the Rain* is a film *about* the differences between illusion and reality. It is thus a film with a theme. But in expressing this theme, *Singin' in the Rain* does not just show us the value of illusion for the characters in the film and for audiences of films; it also perpetuates a whole series of other illusions about itself. Thematic analysis can trace the development of the illusion-versus-reality theme through the film; ideological analysis can reveal the film's own confusion between illusion and reality.

Analysis

The film's opening sequence provides a good illustration of the way it sets up an opposition between illusion and reality by creating a contradiction between what we are told on the audio track and what we are shown on the visual track. As Don Lockwood narrates the story of his career for the audience of fans at the movie premier, we see a series of images that contradict the narration. While Lockwood speaks of "dignity," the images are far from dignified. Lockwood tells the fans that he performed for mom and dad's society friends, but we are shown images of two very young punks (Don and Cosmo) hoofing in sleazy pool halls and even being evicted. As Lockwood describes his early experiences of Shaw and Molière, we actually see the two young punks trying to sneak into a horror film. The high-class parents are nowhere to be seen. The Conservatory of Fine Arts is revealed to be a honky-tonk café where Don played not the violin but the fiddle. And the exclusive dramatics academy consists of vaudeville routines performed at amateur night—and so on, until we see the beginning of Don's film career as a (replacement) stunt double. The sequence not only contrasts the self-aggrandizement of the voice-over with the presumed true story shown in the visuals, it also sets us up for Don's first encounter with Kathy Selden. Both are revealed as having intellectual pretensions that they must shed in order to come together as a couple both professionally and offscreen; for "refinement," as a fan in the premier audience notes, is characteristic of Lina Lamont in *The Royal Rascal* and therefore must be a phony quality. And the fact that we in the audience "secretly" get to delight in scenes from lowbrow art, sets us up for the film's final claim that the best art in any category is the Hollywood musical itself.

In his audio commentary, *Moulin Rouge!* (2001) director Baz Luhrmann admires this sequence for its economy in providing exposition at the beginning of the film. Moreover, as Luhrmann notes, the sequence "winks" at the viewer and reminds you that you are watching a movie. This self-reflexive effect makes *Singin' in the Rain* seem both modern and modern*ist*, the latter implying that, like all great modernist works, the film is acutely aware of its own status as a created artifact.

The opening sequence sets up an obvious split between sound and image, truth and lies. Put in the context of the film as a whole, it corresponds to another opposition: that between Lina Lamont, who thinks Don loves her because he makes love to her in films, and Kathy Selden, who is destined to be his "true" love and who—at least initially—scorns the "dumb show" of silent cinema. Lina represents fakery because her image and her voice do not correspond to each other. Kathy represents sincerity and authenticity because her voice and image correspond perfectly. Lina is associated with the dishonesty of silent cinema, which fools audiences into thinking that actors are what they appear to be; Kathy is associated with the authenticity of musical performance in which singing and speaking always come "from the heart." There is even an implied contrast between the black-and-white sequences we are shown both of *The Royal Rascal* and *The Duelling Cavalier* and the vibrant Technicolor of the "Broadway Ballet" sequence that Don "describes" for the producer. Since the only other footage from *The Dancing Cavalier* we ever get to see is the tail end of the recording process for "Would You?" the presentation of the ballet implies a switch from stiff and motionless black-and-white footage with bad sound to fully mobile 1952 Technicolor footage with all the dynamism of an MGM musical. The device of having Don describe the "Broadway Ballet" and then having viewers see it completed is obviously one of "winking." This is acknowledged when the producer says (after fourteen minutes of our viewing the ballet) "I can't quite visualize it. I'll have to see it on film first," and Cosmo replies, "on film it'll be better yet." The filmmakers acknowledge that they know and we know that the elaborate number we are viewing would not actually have been possible in the 1920s: *Singin' in the Rain* sometimes appears to be taking place just as *The Jazz Singer* was released in December 1927, even though MGM didn't make its first musicals in that year since the conversion to sound stages took until 1929. In the film, the studio closes down to make the conversion "for a few weeks." And although many musicals from 1929–30 were shot entirely—or included some numbers—in two-strip Technicolor, they did not include three-strip Technicolor ballets. All of these factual "errors" seem curious in a film whose makers claim it tells the "true story" of the coming of sound.

Yet, elsewhere in the film the "winking" effect is not as obvious. For instance, there is a montage sequence showing the transition to sound in which we are escorted through a series of numbers presumably being shot at Monumental Studios. The ensuing "Revolution in Hollywood" takes us through an elaborate montage sequence presumably of footage from 1927 or early 1928 talkie musicals—with all the musical production numbers done to Freed and Brown songs (this is doubly ironic: not only were there few talkies in 1928, but also many of the

Freed and Brown songs were written in the 1930s). The numbers are fully formed and shot in 1950s Technicolor with elaborate moving camera effects and post-1933, Busby Berkeley–style high shots. Although Busby Berkeley did stage a high-angled color musical number for the 1930 film *Whoopee!* it did not look like this one. The sequence even uses animated footage of chorus girls' legs. While the songs and motifs (for example, a "college musical" in which a young man sings into a megaphone) may be true to the period, the film techniques and actual settings of the numbers most assuredly are not, as the inclusion of the originals of some of these numbers on the DVD demonstrates. For example, if you look at the original presentation of what the DVD calls Freed and Brown's first hit love song, "You Were Meant for Me," in *The Broadway Melody* (1929), it has none of the dynamic camera movement of the self-reflexive soundstage presentation in *Singin' in the Rain.* The male lead simply croons it in a static two-shot to the showgirl "Queenie," who is trying to resist him because her sister is in love with him (and yet the lyric was clearly intended for the original situation, with its dialogue reference to staying up all night thinking about her). The "coming of sound" montage sequence implies that these early talkies sprang up instantaneously in 1927 when *The Jazz Singer* premiered: but of course none of the "original" MGM numbers were shot before 1929. And the fashion-show sequence seems borrowed from the Gene Kelly Columbia Studios film *Cover Girl,* which was not made until 1944.

The elaborate moving-camera effects and full MGM audio stand in complete contrast to the inept and technologically crude sequences that are being shot contemporaneously for Don and Lina's first talkie. Here the immobilized camera is enclosed in a soundproof booth, and Lina's microphone is attached to a cable that is not even taped to the floor, so that when the producer pulls on it, Lina herself topples over. There is a discrepancy between the on-screen 1920s camera that is supposed to be shooting the number on the soundstage and the 1950s MGM camera that is really recording what we the audience are seeing (and not just recording it, but editing it, too). Unlike the "Dignity, Always Dignity" voice-over, which clearly marks the gap between "reality" and appearance, there is no clear acknowledgment that the filmmakers know that we know the technology we are witnessing is far in advance of the period shown.

A similar sleight of hand occurs in the love song Don sings to Kathy on the soundstage, "You Were Meant for Me." Don confesses that he is unable to express his feelings in the mundane world of the studio lot. He lures her into what Luhrmann calls the "heightened world" of the soundstage where he employs every cinematic trick to add to the illusion of romance that he wants to convey. The soundstage sequence is prefaced by Kelly's declaration, "I'm such a ham, I guess I'm not able to [say how I feel] without the proper setting." He leads Kathy inside to a deserted soundstage strewn with bits of moviemaking paraphernalia. "This is the proper setting," he tells her, and when she replies, "Why, it's just an empty stage," Kelly creates an entire number to show her that the world of the imagination is just a step away from the real world of the studio lot. Kelly sets the scene: he pulls a switch to reveal "a beautiful sunset." Another machine produces "mist from the distant mountains." He switches on "colored lights in a garden" and "directs" Kathy in a scene wherein "milady is standing on her balcony in a rose-trellised bower." He floods the scene with moonlight and adds "500 kilowatts of stardust" and a soft summer breeze created by turning on the wind machine. But none of this artifice seems to matter when Don says his first line, "You sure look lovely in the moonlight, Kathy," and we do not doubt his sincerity. Even though we have winked at all the technologically created illusion, we know that the simplicity of the scene and the sincerity of the song must be "real." At first, the shooting of the number reveals the lights and the wind machine, but as we are drawn into the number with the words of the song, the camera arcs around to conceal the technology of the image-making, choosing instead to reveal only a romantic view of the lovers on the ladder. The ultraromantic lyric of this old-fashioned love ballad (after all, it was written in 1929) covers the scene in stardust, especially when matched with the sincerity of Gene Kelly's delivery. The dance that follows is a curious blend of authenticity and artifice. The steps are simple and almost childlike (skipping). At the end, we come to realize that artifice is at the heart of the reality effect of cinema.

Luhrmann sees this number as an example of "winking," of making the audience aware they are watching a movie. Yet the way this number is shot first reveals and then conceals the sources of cinematic illusion. The film uses the technique of demystification and remystification, first exposing the technology of film production and then covering it up with cinematic magic. By the number's end, we are fully drawn into the romantic setting we now are supposed to believe is as real as Don's love for Kathy. Moreover, in at least two other places in *Singin' in the Rain*, the use of the wind machine is concealed entirely: first, when Kathy's scarf blows in the wind just outside the sound-stage where "You Were Meant For Me" takes place; and, later, in the "veil dance" segment of the "Broadway Ballet," where, according to the archival materials, great effort was expended to make Cyd Charisse's veil blow in time with the music.

These observations point to an aspect of *Singin' in the Rain* that only ideological analysis can reveal. On a thematic level, the film makes a clear statement about the kind of illusion only film technology can create. Bad films and bad actors are ones that let the technology interfere with the illusion of a fantasy world that musicals strive to create. These are associated with silent, black-and-white, and early sound films, but also with the bad character Lina Lamont, whose image is always in excess of her talent (a talent that is revealed through the voice). Up until the very end of the film, Lina Lamont is still attempting to conceal her lack of vocal talent, a lack that is finally revealed when Don and Cosmo pull aside the curtain at the final premiere to reveal the actual source of the audio track. We see Lina's final performance from the most demystifying camera angle in the film: the shot from the wings that shows in equal proportion Lina mouthing in front of the curtain and Kathy singing behind it. Throughout *Singin' in the Rain*, the good characters make music effortlessly and spontaneously, while the bad character (Lina) has to expend tremendous effort to do anything besides appearing to look good. For example, when Lina, Don, and Cosmo have to take elocution lessons to prepare for their first talkie, Lina struggles unsuccessfully to achieve round tones, while Don and Cosmo move effortlessly into the "Moses Supposes" number. Not only do they spontaneously master proper diction, but they also manage to flawlessly pull off a competition dance sequence using the props at hand in the teacher's office.

Spontaneity thus becomes the hallmark of a successful musical performance. The DVD archives describe the way Donald O'Connor was encouraged to improvise in the number "Make 'Em Laugh," which appears to be a spontaneous outpouring of pratfalls and sight gags on Cosmo's part but which naturally had to be choreographed to the music. Surely, the climax during which Cosmo does three consecutive running-up-the-wall backflips could not have been filmed in one spontaneous take. In "Good Mornin'," the trio spontaneously come up with a solution to the problems of The Duelling Cavalier when they realize it could be made into a musical, The Dancing Cavalier. But no number is more dependent on the idea of spontaneity than the famous title number performed by Gene Kelly seemingly alone on a simple set. The set, the steps, and the song could not be more basic, but this apparent simplicity only conceals the fact that this was a highly technical and carefully produced number. Holes had to be excavated to create puddles, "rain" had to be piped in, even the taps of Gene Kelly's feet had to be laboriously postsynchronized. Codirector Stanley Donen describes the problems that occurred when Los Angelenos came home after work and turned on their sprinklers en masse, thereby creating a drought on the set. Yet the cinematic illusion of spontaneity is perfect. That the nature of this illusion is purely cinematic became obvious to me in the 1980s when I attended the original Broadway stage version of Singin' in the Rain. The show followed the film closely, even attempting to re-create the title number on the stage with "real" stage rain. Although the choreography was virtually the same, the technology required to produce rain on the live stage completely broke my fascination with the dancing. In 2002, Pittsburgh's Civic Light Opera staged a wonderful version of the Broadway show in honor of the film's fiftieth anniversary. Unfortunately, on opening night the sprinkler system failed to shut off, and it "rained" for the rest of the show (including during the "Broadway Ballet"). Instead of enjoying the show, I spent the entire second act worrying that the dancers would slip and fall on the drenched stage. Of course, the movie addresses these potential technical problems only in self-consciously localized and isolated moments, such as the sequence of filming of The Dancing Cavalier.

Never has a film gone so far to give the appearance of effortlessness while condemning those who use the same techniques to fool the audience. At the preview screening of The Duelling Cavalier, the fact that Lina's and Don's voices go out of sync is cause for great hilarity at their expense on the part of the not-very-appreciative audience. The irony is revealed in rumors relating that Jean Hagen actually had a good singing voice and at one point dubbed one of Debbie Reynolds's numbers! Various sources cite a voice double for Debbie Reynolds in "Would You?"; whether or not this is true, we know that MGM regularly dubbed the voices of actresses (Cyd Charisse had different voice doubles in several of her Freed Unit musicals; nobody seemed to notice or care). And even more fundamentally, we know that musical numbers at MGM were never recorded live, but always lip-synced to prerecorded song tracks, whether one's own or dubbed. Since all numbers were prerecorded, the issue of vocal "authenticity" was beside the point at MGM: no one's vocals were "real." Yet they made a claim to being real.

The artifice of the dubbing process is revealed to startling effect in the 2001 TV film *Life with Judy Garland: Me and My Shadows*. Actress Judy Davis re-creates some of Judy Garland's best-remembered film performances by using the prerecordings Judy Garland herself had made at MGM. The uncanny effect of Judy Davis's body producing Judy Garland's voice is compounded during a sequence when Judy/Judy is seen on a soundstage recording "The Man That Got Away" for the 1954 version of *A Star Is Born*. Judy Davis lip-syncs her way through one of the torch songs most identified with Judy Garland, but at one point the recorded voice soars onward while the actress halts the filming of the number to tell the George Cukor character that she has missed a mark. While the 2001 film never winks at its own artifice or the fact that one Judy is impersonating the other in body but not in voice (indeed, admirers of this telefilm believe that Judy Davis was actually "channeling" Judy Garland), it is perfectly willing to demystify the playback process through which all Hollywood musicals were made in the 1950s.

Probably the most outrageous claim made in the plot of *Singin' in the Rain* is that Kathy Selden would ever under any circumstances have been given screen credit for her vocals dubbed for Lina. In short, this most beloved of films, which cherishes spontaneity and authenticity, is lying to us at every level. The question for an analysis of the film is, what are we to say about these lies? In the most fundamental sense, all art lies in being more perfect than life and in concealing the difficulty of its own creation. Because they are technological, films lie even more. Although Jean-Luc Godard once said that cinema is "truth 24 times a second," no film can be totally honest about the labor that went into its making. Whereas some (modernist) films attempt to reveal their own conditions of production, it is impossible to do so always and fully.

Each act of demystification inevitably brings with it a moment of re-mystification. So to condemn *Singin' in the Rain* for concealing its own technology would be unfair, and not very illuminating.

What we can do is to explain the paradoxes that a satiric film like this reveals. To reveal paradoxes is to believe that the film cannot help but remystify every time it cuts from an exposing camera angle to a concealing one. It is to believe that it is the nature of art to be ultimately unable to distinguish between illusion and reality, even to believe that the function of art is to make illusion real. In this sense, my reliance on archival sources about the production of the film is really cheating. Aside from providing amusing anecdotes, the knowledge that, say, Debbie Reynolds did not know how to dance before this film, might be construed not just as irrelevant to an interpretation of the film but as a positive hindrance to reading the film. Does she dance in the film? Does she dance well enough to keep up with professional hoofers Kelly and O'Connor? If so, the revelation of her amateur status can only detract from our enjoyment of her dancing in the film. Following this line of reasoning places *Singin' in the Rain* well within a long tradition of literary and filmic works that try to capture the essential paradox of art: that it is both illusory and real.

Conclusion

Ideological analysis of the film goes even further. As Carol J. Clover has written, "So wide is the gap between what *Singin' in the Rain* says and what it does that one is tempted to see a relation between the two—to see the moralizing surface story of *Singin'* as a guilty disavowal of the practices that went into its own making" (158). That is to say, the film's lies—its gaps and omissions—are symptoms of underlying anxieties that speak to its own status as a classical Hollywood film. While Clover wants to trace the way the film covers over its racial origins in African American music and dance, one could interpret *Singin' in the Rain* as a film that expresses anxiety at many other levels. In particular, as a self-reflexive Hollywood-on-Hollywood musical, it seems especially troubled by the studio system as a whole and the kind of illusionistic films produced therein. Just before the film began shooting, the long-reigning head of MGM studios, Louis B. Mayer, was replaced by Dore Schary as head of production. As Cyd Charisse explains in her audio commentary on the DVD, Dore Schary wanted MGM to make more serious, "theatrical" films. Although this had no *direct* influence on *Singin' in the Rain*, indirectly it does mark the beginning of the end of the era of musicals that this film is considered to crown. Both the kind of entertainment represented by the MGM musical and the kind of production system represented by MGM were coming under threat. Yet by making *The Duelling Cavalier* into *The Dancing Cavalier*, *Singin' in the Rain* appears to be telling us that the proper response to all artistic and economic changes is to make a musical, preferably one that very much resembles the MGM musical itself. Making musicals becomes the means to salvation for the studio system itself. The film suggests that the musical is the type of film that can respond to any and all technological changes in the industry.

Other Comden and Green films of this period address the threat posed by television to the film industry (in *It's Always Fair Weather*) and the threat that the greater high-culture pretensions (associated with Schary at MGM) posed to films that were merely entertaining (in *The Band Wagon*). But *Singin' in the Rain* deals directly with the Hollywood filmmaking process and considers the direct threat posed to the kind of entertainment Hollywood represented at the time of the transition to talkies. Although in 1952 musicals were, in hindsight, on their way out, *Singin' in the Rain* is especially clever at memorializing the time when they were charging in to rescue Hollywood itself.

Credits

United States, 1952, MGM

Directors: Stanley Donen and Gene Kelly
Producer: Arthur Freed
Screenplay: Betty Comden and Adolph Green
Cinematography: Harold Rosson
Editing: Adrienne Fazan
Original Music: Nacio Herb Brown and Lennie Hayton
Art Direction: Randall Duell and Cedric Gibbons
Set Decoration: Jacques Mapes and Edwin B. Willis
Costume Design: Walter Plunkett
Makeup: Sydney Guilaroff and William Tuttle
Other Crew: Jeff Alexander (music arranger: vocal arrangements), Arthur Freed (lyricist), Lennie Hayton (musical director), and Wally Heglin

Feuer

CAST:

Don Lockwood	Gene Kelly
Cosmo Brown	Donald O'Connor
Kathy Selden	Debbie Reynolds
Lina Lamont	Jean Hagen
R. F. Simpson	
(President, Monumental Pictures)	Millard Mitchell
Dancer	Cyd Charisse
Roscoe Dexter	
(Director, Monumental Pictures)	Douglas Fowley
Zelda Zanders aka Zip Girl	Rita Moreno

Bibliography

Altman, Rick. *The American Film Musical.* Bloomington: Indiana UP, 1987.

Barrios, Richard. *A Song in the Dark: The Birth of the Musical Film.* New York: Oxford UP, 1995.

Clover, Carol J. "Dancin' in the Rain." *Critical Inquiry* 21 (1995): 722–47. Rpt. in Cohan 157–74.

Cohan, Steven. "Case Study: Interpreting *Singin' in the Rain.*" *Reinventing Film Studies.* Ed. Christine Gledhill and Linda Williams. London: Edward Arnold, 2000. 53–75.

———. *Hollywood Musicals: The Film Reader.* London: Routledge, 2002.

Feuer, Jane. *The Hollywood Musical.* 2nd ed. Bloomington: Indiana UP, 1993.

Singin' in the Rain. Dirs. Stanley Donen and Gene Kelly. 1952. Two-disc Special Edition DVD. Warner Home Video, 2002.

Wollen, Peter. *"Singin' in the Rain."* London: BFI, 1992.

Tokyo Story (1953)

DAVID DESSER

The Space of Ambivalence

Context

A plot synopsis of Ozu Yasujiro's *Tokyo monogatari* (*Tokyo Story*) would hardly indicate why or how such a (deceptively) simple picture has consistently found its way onto numerous lists of the ten best films of all time. For instance, in the 2002 poll conducted by *Sight and Sound*, *Tokyo Story* was voted by critics as the No. 5 film of all time ("Sight and Sound Critics Top Ten Poll"). As Arthur Nolletti Jr. has convincingly shown, in many central and significant ways, Ozu's 1953 masterpiece is a remake or at least significant reworking (Nolletti borrows David Bordwell's notion that it is a "recasting") of Leo McCarey's 1937 *Make Way for Tomorrow* (Desser 25). Yet McCarey's film is all but forgotten, probably kept alive in critical discourse simply because of its connection to Ozu's film. Ozu's story of aging parents visiting their grown-up children who now live far away from them has little overt drama—there is a paucity of genuine affection expressed between parents and children, and the death of the old mother is all, essentially, that "happens" in the film. McCarey's film, in fact, is much more dramatic. If it is not a spectacular story or a complex and compelling plot that so enamors both film fans and scholars to Ozu's film, it may not either be so simple a matter as Ozu's demonstrable and now-famous style and technique. After all, stylistic consistency is a hallmark of any *auteur* director (by definition), and indeed the cohesion of style and approach in the films Ozu made around the time of *Tokyo Story* is abundantly apparent even to the casual viewer. Of course, to many admirers, Ozu's films like *Banshun* (*Late Spring*, 1949) and *Bakushu* (*Early Summer*, 1951) are quite as effective as *Tokyo Story*, and indeed in most respects they are. Perhaps it is a special combination, then, of the subtle, deceptively simple yet emotionally powerful story merging with Ozu's vaunted, playful, and challenging cinematic grammar that makes *Tokyo Story* truly a special film.

Background

Too much in film history has been allowed to enter the canon of received wisdom without much examination. Thus, there is the well-known cliché that Ozu's films were not released in the United States in the 1950s because he was, for the Japanese film industry executives who controlled distribution, "too Japanese" for Western audiences. Perhaps this contributed to the subsequent cliché in film history that he is Japan's "most Japanese director." Aside from the obvious question of how someone born and raised in Japan can be more or less "Japanese," the fact of the matter is that Ozu's films received a later distribution in the West than films by Kurosawa Akira and Mizoguchi Kenji (not to mention lesser-known directors like Kinugasa Teinosuke and Inagaki Hiroshi) because they were modern stories (*gendai-geki*) and not the period films (*jidai-geki*) that marked the first wave of Japanese film distribution to the United States and Europe. On the acclaim given to Kurosawa's *Rashomon* (1950), Daiei Studios also released Mizoguchi's *Ugetsu monogatari* (*Ugetsu*, 1953) and Kinugasa's *Jigokumon* (*Gate of Hell*, 1953), and films like *Sansho dayu* (*Sansho the Bailiff*, 1954) and *Shichinin no samurai* (*Seven Samurai*, Toho Studios, 1954, not shown in the United States until 1956) followed shortly thereafter. This cliché regarding the lack of distribution of Ozu's films before the 1960s also obscures the literally hundreds of other Japanese films similarly kept at home for the domestic audience. Never the recipient of an Academy Award or other prestigious acclaim outside of Japan, Ozu's reputation only came to the attention of the Euro-American film world over time, starting in 1959 with the gradual and occasional release of his films. It would take retrospective screenings beginning in the 1970s and the emergence of academic film studies, which came to prize Japanese cinema as a whole and Ozu in particular, to solidify Ozu's reputation as a world-class filmmaker and *Tokyo Story* as one of his finest achievements.

Of course, in Japan it was a different story. Winner of more Kinema Jumpo "Best One" awards than any other single director (six such honors, although ironically *Tokyo Story* managed to rank only No. 3 in 1953), Ozu was a consistently popular and respected filmmaker. *Tokyo*

Story emerged during a period of great productivity, as Ozu had consistently directed one film per year from 1947 to 1953. Working for the most part at Shochiku studios in their Ofuna branch outside of Tokyo, Ozu could count on a relatively free hand in his films, relying on the same scriptwriter, cinematographer, and star cast in film after film. Actors like Ryu Chishu, Hara Setsuko, Sugimura Haruko, Miyake Kuniko, and Yamamura So served as a virtual Ozu repertory company, playing variations on their roles and enacting the life and times of Japan in the 1940s and 1950s. At once a filmmaker of the moment—contemporary events show up consistently in Ozu's films—and a filmmaker interested in more timeless issues and themes, Ozu made films that in their aggregate can and do seem to be variations on one major motif: ordinary life. It would take a remarkably astute and sensitive observer to note, for instance, any change in Ozu's style and theme in *Tokyo Story* as compared to his previous films, despite the end, in 1952, of the American occupation of Japan. Ozu's films are steeped in their culture and their moment. Just as Ozu's postwar films make only occasional references to the Second World War—as virtually no audience member would need reminding of such an event—so, too, something like the end of the occupation hardly needs referencing. Instead, Ozu paints a picture of life as it is lived by ordinary people at that very moment. Perhaps this accounts, when all is said and done, for Ozu's quietly consistent hold on the Japanese imagination then and, to a large extent, now, and explains as well his ongoing cross-cultural appeal.

Analysis

General Principles

In most of the early critical assessments of Ozu's films, even the highly influential, Formalist-inflected work of Noël Burch, the unique and striking characteristics of his films were attributed to aspects of traditional Japanese culture, especially Zen Buddhism and haiku poetry. Charles Michener, writing in *Newsweek*, described Ozu's most common camera angle as being "about 3 feet above the floor, the vantage point of a haiku master kneeling on his tatami mat" (157). Traditional culture was the foundational point of film-critic-turned-director Paul Schrader in his suggestive and perceptive *Transcendental Style in Film:*

Ozu, Bresson, Dreyer. The highly influential and sharp-eyed view of Ozu's films by film and art historian Kathe Geist attributes aspects of Ozu's style to the pervasiveness of Buddhist art and thought in Japanese society (101–17). Given Ozu's widespread influence on filmmakers as diverse as, say, Taiwan's fiercely formalist and historicist Hou Hsiao-hsien and maverick American indepedent Jim Jarmusch, it seems at this point in time somewhat less than productive to rehearse the (alleged) cultural determinants of Ozu's style, his "Japaneseness." Instead, the sophisticated and challenging narrative strategies and spatial handling seem worth pursuing for their own effects and in terms of the ways in which audiences must be actively attentive to the cinematic workings of the text itself. Thus, we will examine *Tokyo Story* from the point of view of its narrative procedures and treatment of cinematic space. But it is first worth establishing some general principles and defining characteristics of Ozu's cinematic world.

What audiences might first recognize is Ozu's penchant for dedramatization. Though related to the narrative principle of ellipses, discussed below, the tendency toward dedramatization is a particularly noteworthy characteristic of Ozu's cinema. It seems at every moment of potential drama—whether the small drama of a family reunion at the train station when the aging parents first arrive in Tokyo, the minicrisis when the children tell their parents they are to go to Atami instead of staying with them, or the more obviously dramatic moment when the mother is afflicted by the stroke that will eventually kill her—Ozu eliminates the scene. An exception in *Tokyo Story* is the rather lengthy funeral scene (almost three minutes in duration), but then Ozu has famously remarked that this film is his most melodramatic and, as Tony Rayns cogently reminds us, we should take him at his word (164). Typically, however, such moments of drama—large and small—are eliminated.

In place of drama, Ozu emphasizes dailiness. Through such an emphasis on Ozu's part, famed Japanese scholar Donald Richie claimed, "Ozu illuminated the mundane to bring out the transcendental" (qtd. in Michener 157). Whatever the effects of such a strategy, it is certainly the case that Ozu's films revolve centrally around the ordinary and the daily—sweeping or dusting the house, arguing with a typically petulant child, borrowing a cup of sake from a neighbor, drinking with old friends in a neighborhood bar, and, most particularly, exchanging the ordinary pleasantries that smooth over daily conversation, especially the by-now most characteristic of all of Ozu's paeans to dailiness, "Isn't it a fine day!" Dailiness also allows Ozu to utilize one of his most suggestive intermediate spaces: clothes hanging out to dry. A sight typical in Japan—clothes waving in the breeze on suburban clotheslines or defiantly hanging on the balconies of urban high-rises—has become one of the images most characteristic of Ozu.

Ozu's focus on dailiness is also a function of his preferred characters and setting. His films belong to a Japanese genre known as the *shomin-geki,* stories of the lower middle class, but diverge from them in precisely the same way they diverge from the American, and indeed international, genre known as the "family melodrama." Though the melodrama may be something of an equivalent, it is precisely the lack of melodrama that Ozu adds or, should we say, the melodrama he refuses to add to his version of the *shomin-geki* that is notable. In relying on the *shomin-geki* as a basis for characters and setting, Ozu thereby restricts his films to the more ordinary trials in a lifespan—married life, child rearing, separation from family due to marriage or death—but typically eliminated those precise moments, such as a marriage ceremony, a tearful good-bye, that interrupt the flow, the dailiness, of such a life.

Another cliché in the Ozu scholarship rests on the surprisingly thorny issue of his favored camera position, generally, as the quote from Michener above notes, given as three feet off the ground, the (alleged) eye-level view of someone seated on a tatami mat—the traditional floor covering in a traditional Japanese home. In fact, a simple close look at any of these countless shots in this or any other Ozu film reveals that the camera is positioned slightly lower than the eye level of an adult sitting upright. It is never angled up, but it is as if the point of view were of someone lying prone, head resting on hands and vaguely looking up and across the room. To read too much into this "tatami-level" angle is to miss the fact that it is simply a favored angle of Ozu and not some transcendent statement about contemplating the universe in a Zen-like trance. In fact, the angle is a very convenient one for revealing the full bodies of characters seated on tatami—a standing eye-level view would cut off their feet, for instance, and not allow Ozu the ability to capture the full figures of characters rising from the floor or entering full-figured into a room without tilting the camera. In other words, the angle has a compositional function in that it allows for a greater perspective on the entire space of the room—in order also, for instance, to reveal clearly the ever-present teapots or rice cookers resting next to dining tables. In addition, Ozu utilizes this angle for exteriors, which, of course, have no tatami mats. Note the angle used to show the seawall at Atami, for instance, which takes the same slightly-lower-than-eye-level view across the water.

With dailiness substituted for more traditional notions of drama and action, and a favored camera position perhaps best able to capture and inculcate this dailiness, Ozu's cinema immediately strikes the viewer as the product of a unique sensibility. A close look at the narrative strategy and spatial handling within *Tokyo Story* will show the meticulousness of Ozu's style and the way it works consistently but surprisingly to hold a viewer's attention as much as any action-packed Hollywood offering.

Narrative

Any transition in a film threatens to break the narrative flow. A shift in cinematic space and time requires a viewer to make a mental adjustment, which threatens the integrity of the diegesis. Classical narrative strategy, the one typically employed in Hollywood films, ensures that such transitions are both clear and brief, one or two shots serving to (re)orient a viewer to the new place and/or time. Ozu's strategy is quite different, typically offering up a delay in plot comprehension and an ellipsis in story material. Thus, in the opening scene of *Tokyo Story* we are prepared to see Tomi and Shukichi go to the train station; to see them be met there by daughter Kyoko, who will see them off; to see something of their journey to Tokyo (much is made of a missing air pillow [*kuki makura*] they will need for their train ride); to see them meet their son Keizo in Osaka; and, most particularly, to be met at Tokyo Station by their son Koichi, whom they have not seen for some years. In fact, we see none of that action. It is all elided, every bit of it. However, it is not until some many minutes into the next scene that we realize this. For from a shot of Tomi and Shukichi seated side by side in their home, Ozu cuts to a shot of industrial chimneys, followed by four more "contentless" shots (no characters we know or will know appear), until finally offering a shot of a character whom we soon will know to be connected to our central story. Though a sign in shot 35 informs us of the Hirayama Medical Clinic, it will take some time yet to establish that the woman in the house is Fumiko, wife of Koichi, the oldest of the Hirayama children. Not only has Ozu thus delayed our comprehension of the relation of all these shots to the previous scene—we finally realize that Fumiko is their son's wife—he takes even more time to reveal that the old couple has already completed their journey to Tokyo, been met at the station, and is now at their oldest son's home. If Hollywood filmmakers prefer to use only one or two shots to make a transition clear, and perhaps no more than a few seconds of running time, Ozu takes fully two minutes and thirteen shots (shots 32–44) before a dialogue exchange ensures that the old people of the first scene are the "grandparents" referred to in shot 44, and another 1.5 minutes, requiring fifteen shots, before we learn that "they're here." All told, then, Ozu uses twenty-eight shots, taking up 3.5 minutes of running time to get back to the grandparents of the opening scene, completely eliding every bit of action that they discussed would occur.

This pattern of ellipses continues, as noted above, to eliminate moments of drama and emotion. Thus, when Koichi and Shige decide to send their old parents off to Atami, Ozu cuts from a two-shot of them to a long shot of people seated on a seawall at the famous resort. We assume, then (correctly), that the parents have been informed of the decision and been packed off to Atami, where we now find them, but only after a few more shots, thus delaying what we need confirmed. Ozu employs another ellipsis after the aged parents have been forced to spend a night separated from each other. Ozu has emphasized the drama of this separation by a rare sequence in which he relies on standard crosscutting between scenes, showing, alternatingly, the father's activities with his old drinking buddies and the mother's emotion-filled time with her sympathetic daughter-in-law. Yet, from a shot of the two women leaving the apartment, Ozu goes directly to Tokyo Station, where the entire family is gathered for the parents' return trip. This particular scene is quite dramatic and portentious, and yet the parents' reuniting has been elided.

The most daring of the ellipses, however, is surely the offscreen occurrence and retrospective revelation of Tomi's stroke on the way home from Tokyo. The parting scene at Tokyo Station has indicated a quick stop in Osaka, where they will see Keizo again (the trip to

Tokyo contained an elided scene of meeting Keizo), but which we are thoroughly convinced by now will not be shown. And indeed it is not. But Keizo in Osaka is shown, except it is the next day, and we learn that on the previous day Tomi and Shukichi had to leave the train because Tomi was taken ill. This is revealed through a conversation that starts off somewhat mysteriously, Keizo apologizing to his coworker, "Sorry about yesterday," thus referring to events we have not seen, and thus delaying revelation of the information about the elided dramatic occurrence. Certainly, in this instance, showing Tomi and Shukichi in Osaka would have been preferable. After all, nothing extraordinary occurred the first time they passed through Osaka, and thus eliding it was a perfectly "reasonable" strategy. If nothing happens, why show it? But in the return trip through Osaka, something did happen, Tomi's illness, yet we learn about this only indirectly, and when we next see Tomi she seems to be much better.

Despite our continued experiencing of ellipses, are we prepared for yet another dramatic elision, Tomi's return home and her falling into a coma from which she will not emerge? By way of preparing us, so to speak, for yet another dramatic revelation, Ozu engages in a narrative strategy quite rare for him, though one typical of Hollywood cinema: repetition of narrative information. At home in Tokyo, Koichi and his wife, Fumiko, discuss Tomi's illness and the unexpected stopover in Osaka—something we have just learned and thus giving us narrative information we already have. The narrative stress at this moment is that Tomi has not only (seemingly) recovered, but she is now back in Onomichi. Ozu has therefore elided the return to Onomichi from Osaka. More significantly, we soon learn that Tomi's fatal stroke has also been elided. This information is transmitted first by a phone call from Shige and then by a telegram that arrives at the same time. In fact, then, through ellipses and delay, Ozu has created a quite dramatic progression from the retrospective revelation that Tomi was stricken on the train ride from Tokyo to her seeming recovery to her sudden turn for the worse. All the actual events took place offscreen, but their effect is nevertheless quite surprising and intense.

Ozu's use of ellipses requires that an audience pay attention to character interaction. For instance, at Koichi's house, Shukichi remarks that they will go stay at Shige's house. But it is not until more than two minutes later that they are there, Ozu eliding their departure and arrival at Shige's home/beauty parlor (which, contrary to the subtitles, is not named "Urara" but rather should be translated as "Ooh La La"). Similarly, Ozu is loath to introduce characters in the typical Hollywood manner—by highlighting them in some fashion. Thus, the careful viewer might note the presence of Shige in the background of shot 59, but it is a difficult thing to do, and so Ozu makes sure she is visible, yet still in the background, of shot 60. It is not until six shots later that Ozu allows her character her first line of dialogue and her first narrative moment, when we learn who, and what, she is.

As if in recognition of Ozu's often difficult transitions and character introductions, the subtitles in the standard English-language print often give more information than the original text. Shot 31, of the industrial smokestacks, contains a subtitle that indicates "an industrial section of Tokyo." But there is no such information in the original version. That the transitional space(s) is clearly not Onomichi is obvious, and it may be obvious as well that it is Tokyo, but Ozu is unwilling to give that definitive information just yet. Similarly, the first mention of the character of Noriko contains the added information, attributed to Fumiko speaking to Shige, that she is "your brother's widow." No such dialogue to that effect is delivered in the Japanese conversation. Family relationships may be clear, to some extent, to the Japanese audience, but Ozu might well allow some temporary ambiguity. It certainly becomes clear soon who Noriko is, and a conversation a few scenes later gives all the background we may need, which Ozu will always do—sooner or later.

Space

The way in which Ozu delays plot progression is through his utilization of intermediate spaces. As described above, Ozu handles the transition from Onomichi to Tokyo through a series of shots that delay the revelation of new screen space and time. Such shots may be understood precisely as intermediate spaces in that the spatial location of the transitional shots relate to the new space in some way without being a necessary part of the actual locale in which the subsequent action will occur. Thus, from the shot of the old couple seated in their home in the first scene, Ozu cuts to industrial chimneys. Such chimneys are associated with Tokyo and certainly not Onomichi, and therefore we know that the locale has changed, but these chimneys are never oriented precisely as being near to or visible from Koichi's house.

Similarly, shot 33, of a train crossing; shot 34, of women speaking; and shot 36, of clothes on a line in the foreground, are not precisely located vis-à-vis Koichi's house (though the clothes may be his family's). This is to say that such shots function both as transitions and as delay. Before we see Shukichi drinking with his old buddies, Ozu relies on a long shot of a street crowded with bars and restaurants. Before showing us the old couple at Atami, Ozu uses a few shots of the sea and the resort itself. Before showing us Koichi and Fumiko discussing Tomi's illness, we see two shots of their neighborhood and a shot of clothes on a line (the same clothesline as in shot 36, but from a different angle). This works particularly well for dramatic effect when we are shown two shots in Osaka precisely when the parents are not supposed to be there. From the farewell at Tokyo Station, Ozu cuts to a low-angle shot of Osaka Castle followed by a shot in a train yard with Osaka Castle in the background. Here Keizo makes his appearance to discuss the elided action of Tomi's illness on the journey home. The intermediate space has thus functioned as a typical transition as well as a space for dramatic elision.

Along with intermediate spaces, Ozu's most characteristic stylistic choice is to employ 360-degree space. This is apparent in two different ways. The first is that characters across a cut may seem to "flip" their position. This comes from Ozu's refusal to follow one of the principal methods of ensuring the diegetic or "suture effect," the 180-degree rule. This bisecting of profilmic space ensures that characters always seem to face the same direction vis-à-vis objects and vis-à-vis each other across contiguous cuts. In order to disguise such moments of seeming discontinuity that may occur, Hollywood editors must employ a cutaway so that character positions do not appear to have flipped when the image returns to the original setup. Ozu, however, will not employ a cutaway. This may be seen in a simple moment in *Tokyo Story*. Seated behind her mother-in-law on the right side of the screen, Noriko gives the old woman a massage. When she stands up, Ozu cuts on her movement, but in so doing shifts her orientation so that now when she is standing she is screen left, with Tomi occupying the right side of the frame. A careful analysis of the opening scene will reveal both the playful and narrative elements to such a strategy.

When first seen in shot 6, Shukichi and Tomi sit side by side (a commonality in Ozu's cinema, in contrast to characters in Western films, who typically sit opposite each other). He is screen right, she on the left. In shot 8 (interestingly not simply a return to shot 6, as discussed in a moment), we see them in the same orientation, as we do in shot 14. The camera follows daughter Kyoko out of the house. When we return to the old couple in shot 18, they have switched sides of the frame: Tomi on the right, Shukichi on the left. This is not particularly a "problem," since in essence the shots following Kyoko out of the house function as cutaways. Yet, after intercutting shots 19 and 20 (matched medium close-ups as they converse), in shot 21 they have switched position: Shukichi on the right side of the frame, Tomi on the left, as in shots 8 and 14. No cutaway has been employed; Ozu has simply switched their position. It is at this point that the neighbor enters from screen left in the background. Here follows a series of shots with their neighbor, whose importance is to establish the trip's significance, but also to prepare us for her return at the end, when she will again enter the frame from the left to talk to Shukichi, helping to complete the film's overall circular pattern. Now, when the neighbor exits, Ozu returns the couple to their screen orientation as in shots 8, 14, and 21. In shot 25, he continues the orientation as in shot 21. But in shot 31, the couple has flipped once more, Tomi on the right, Shukichi on the left. In what we can take as a playful moment, Ozu has a reason for the matched positioning of shots 18 and 31: in both these shots, Tomi on the right and Shukichi on the left, they discuss the temporarily missing air pillow. Thus Ozu has linked this spatial arrangement to this particular conversation topic. It is playful precisely because there was no great reason to set things up this way in the first place. In shot 21, it is important to have Shukichi on the right and Tomi on the left in order for the camera to be able to take in the view outside to enable the neighbor to enter the frame in the background. This is an anticipatory angle, as the narrative knows that the neighbor will enter the frame and is thus positioned to capture that action without an edit. Alternately, however, there was no narrative reason to switch the couple's orientation as in shots 18 and 31. Space, then, is not reducible to narrative needs, but exists as a playful and attention-grabbing component in its own right.

This may also be shown in Ozu's lack of master shots. The introduction of the Hirayamas, in shot 6, is followed by a cut-in of Shukichi conversing with Tomi. Shot 8 returns us to the spatial arrangement of shot 6, except a careful viewing of the shot reveals it is a little longer and slightly to the right of shot 6. This enables Kyoko to enter the frame and be seen in a full shot. Had the composition been as in shot 6, her head would have been cut off.

The refusal to utilize master shots extends to the lack of establishing shots. That is, Ozu allows the geography of his spaces to remain vague. Used in interiors this technique also promotes an appreciation of the modularity of the traditional Japanese home. This is seen most amusingly in the shots of Fumiko and Minoru marching around their house in what is initially a very confusing manner, as the principle of spatial contiguity seems to be absolutely refused. Shot 37 reveals Fumiko sweeping; she exits from the left. In shot 38 she enters from the right, thus establishing spatial contiguity and smoothing over the cut with a natural progession of eyeline transfer. She then exits from the right, but in shot 39 enters from the right, a seeming mismatch. But, in fact, in shot 39 she has not returned to the room of shot 37, but has entered another room. She crosses this new room and exits left. In shot 40 she enters again from the left into yet another room. Ozu has thereby given us a taste of the geography of the house, but one that fails to orient us clearly. Rather, we are alerted to the possibilities of multiple exit and entrance points and seemingly mismatched action. The argument between Fumiko and Minoru retraces these steps through these rooms, with seemingly mismatched entrances and exits playfully calling attention both to the camera's position and to the modularity of the Japanese house, where rooms, entrances, and exits can be shifted simply by opening and closing interior screens (*shoji*).

Themes

"Isn't life disappointing?" muses Kyoko near the film's end. To which the sad and pensive Noriko can only add, "I'm afraid so." This exchange between two young women may seem surprising. Certainly, the old couple's discussions of their life, their children, their disappointments strike one as expected. After all, old age brings contemplation. Linda Ehrlich sensitively points out that the real journey in *Tokyo Story* is an inward one: "The father and mother in *Tokyo Story* are not traveling to see their city-dwelling children as much as they are hoping to confirm that their life's work has been worthwhile" (69). The best the old couple can come up with is ambivalence; things have not been so great, but then they could have been worse. Yet, the young women are forced into that same conclusion, and the best they can manage is a similar ambivalence. This is Ozu's great theme—that life is disappointing, and this disappointment is inevitable. People inevitably change—families drift apart through distance, marriage, and death. People change—a married woman is like a stranger, Tomi and Shukichi realize, a truism that one and all will come to realize. Though critics make much of the film's focus on postwar economic changes and the cost of modernity to the extended Japanese family, Ozu is interested in more timeless and transcendent issues. Tony Rayns is right to an extent that *Tokyo Story* "is an almost didactic film about the disintegration of Japanese family values [and it is] absolutely a film of its moment: Tokyo's postwar rebuilding boom, the raucous and hedonistic behaviour of young people in a hot-spring resort . . . the chasm between traditionalist, rural parents and their city-based sons and daughters . . ." (164–65). But all of Ozu's films are of their moment, and at any given moment change is inevitable. The breakdown of the Japanese family is no different in the 1950s *Tokyo Story* than it is in the 1930s *I Was Born, But . . .* (*Umarete wa mita keredo,* 1932), in which the young sons of a salaryman disrespect their father and must accommodate themselves to the immutable laws of economic power and social inequality.

Thus, it is ambivalence that characterizes Ozu's attitude here: no simple good versus evil, right versus wrong. Trains, for instance, make their regular appearance in *Tokyo Story,* even in Onomichi, perhaps therefore wrongly thought of as a repository of tradition and stasis. Trains may indeed be a source of a kind of modernity that is harmful. As Linda Ehrlich carefully notes, it is the train that took son Keizo away on business, so that he failed to return to Onomichi in time (65–66). Yet it is train travel that causes Tomi to exclaim that she didn't realize Tokyo was so close. "Imagine," she says, "yesterday I was in Onomichi, today I'm in Tokyo."

Transience, mutability, the sense of the ever-changingness of things—this is Ozu's real theme. Images of the transitory abound—smoke from chimneys or from trains; even trains themselves, whose passing is momentary, there and gone. Boats chugging through the harbor, children walking to school, clothes hanging on a line—images of the daily and the ordinary, to be sure, but whose recurrence in *Tokyo Story* and the rest of Ozu's cinema imbues them with the drama of change, of the transitory. For a film so concerned with train travel, only once do we actually see anyone on a train. And it is perhaps no surprise to find it is Noriko whom we see, looking at the watch her father-in-law gave her, another indication of her, and the film's, sensitivity to the passing of time and the inevitability of change.

Conclusion

Tokyo Story ends where it begins—in Onomichi, with Shukichi sitting in his house with the *shoji* open to take in the view and the sea breezes. The same neighbor as in the first scene passes by, offering the remark "You'll be lonely" in much the same tone in which she earlier breathed, "Isn't it a nice day." Of course, one essential difference must be noted: no longer is Tomi sitting next to the aged Shukichi. This circular pattern obviously, but no less significantly, suggests the notion of a cycle. Less linear, then, than cyclical, the narrative pattern asks to be compared to the life cycle, the ceaseless turning of the seasons. But not the seasons that are so thoroughly implicated in the (stereotypically) traditional Japanese arts. Hasumi Shigehiko cogently reminds us that "In fact, nothing could be further from Ozu's work than the rhetoric referring to the seasons found in haiku poetry" (120). Instead, these are the seasons of the human life cycle. And that is why the grandchildren, only minimally highlighted earlier and completely eliminated in the climactic moments of Tomi's death, are so memorable in the film. Though Ozu almost always sets his films in summer, the sense of time passing, seasons changing, and life going on in a perpetual cycle seem clearly implicated. Three generations of one family are shown to us, and the sense of the inevitability of change—the famous scene of Tomi wondering what little Isamu's life will be like in the future and if she will be around to see it—leaves a deep and lasting impression on us. So, too, we must understand why another relatively minor character is given such prominence in the film's final scenes. For if Kyoko expresses a major theme of the film—life's inevitable disappointments—she also, by implication, is a major part of the life cycle the film so subtly highlights. For at the film's end, we find the very family structure so central to other of Ozu's most beloved films: the marriage-age daughter at home with a widowed father.

In this respect, we may see *Tokyo Story* as part of another cycle—Ozu's film cycle, which returns again and again to the same themes, approaching them from a different perspective in each film. One of the perhaps most puzzling aspects in films like *Late Spring, Early Summer, Akibiyori* (*Late Autumn,* 1960), and *Sanma no aji* (*An Autumn Afternoon,* 1962)—the first and the last specifically focusing on a widowed father attempting to convince a marriage-age daughter to wed—is the question of the daughter's reluctance to marry. Certainly, the life of a middle-class housewife may be nothing to brag about. The long working hours of the salaryman and the lack of socializing between husband and wife do not typically create a picture of wedded bliss. A woman's identity as a wife and mother in Japanese (and other Asian) society tends to outweigh any previous sense of a more individualized self. And the tradition that a wife marries not just her husband but into his extended family as well has meant a lessening of association with one's birth family. To this extent, Noriko does have obligations to the Hirayamas, her marriage family, despite claims by critics and even by Hirayama Shukichi in the film itself that she does not. By concluding *Tokyo Story* with an intense scene between daughter-in-law Noriko and marriage-age daughter Kyoko, Ozu addresses, as it were, the very issue of this reluctance and sees it as a resistance to change, a desire not to become someone or something else. But change is inevitable. And thus to the pathos of having lost his wife must be added the pathos that Shukichi will also and inevitably lose his daughter. And yet the sheer artistry of Ozu's film, the penetrating insight into the ordinary, allows a space for contemplation and satisfaction. Indeed, life is disappointing, change is inevitable, but the ordinary pleasures of daily life, including the transcendental artistry of Ozu's cinema, certainly help overcome these feelings from time to time.

Credits

Japan, 1953, Shochiku

Director: Ozu Yasujiro
Producer: Yamamoto Takeshi
Screenplay: Ozu Yasujiro and Noda Kogo
Cinematography: Atsuta Yuharu
Editing: Hamamura Yoshiyasu

Desser

Music: Saito Takanobu
Production Design: Hamaka Tatsuo and Takashashi Itsuo
Costume Design: Saito Taizo

CAST:

Noriko	Hara Setsuko
Hirayama Shukichi	Ryu Chishu
Hirayama Tomi	Higashiyama Chieko
Koichi	Yamamura So
Shige	Sugimura Haruko
Fumiko (Koichi's wife)	Miyake Kuniko
Kyoko	Kagawa Kyoko
Numata	Tono Eijrio
Minoru	Murase Zen
Isamu	Mori Mitsuhiro

Bibliography

Bordwell, David. *Ozu and the Poetics of Cinema*. Princeton: Princeton UP, 1988.

Burch, Noël. *To the Distant Observer: Form and Meaning in the Japanese Cinema*. Berkeley: U of California P, 1979.

Desser, David, ed. *Ozu's "Tokyo Story."* New York: Cambridge UP, 1997.

Ehrlich, Linda C. "Travel Toward and Away: *Furusato* and Journey in *Tokyo Story*." Desser 53–75.

Geist, Kathe. "Buddhism in *Tokyo Story*." Desser 101–17.

Michener, Charles. "A Master from Japan." *Newsweek* 27 Mar. 1972. Rpt. in Desser 156–58.

Rayns, Tony. "*Tokyo Monogatori (Tokyo Story)*." *Sight and Sound* 4.2 (1994). Rpt. in Desser 163–67.

Schrader, Paul. *Transcendental Style in Film: Ozu, Bresson, Dreyer*. Berkeley: U of California P, 1972.

Shigehiko, Hasumi. "Sunny Skies." Desser 118–29.

"Sight and Sound Critics Top Ten Poll." *Sight and Sound* 30 Oct. 2002. <http://www.bfi.org.uk/sightandsound/topten/poll/critics.htm>.

Rear Window (1954)

ELIZABETH COWIE

Rear Window Ethics

I suggest that Hitchcock belongs—and why classify him at all?—among such artists of anxiety as Kafka, Dostoyevsky, and Poe. In the light of their own doubts these artists of anxiety can hardly be expected to show us how to live; their mission is simply to share with us the anxieties that haunt them. Consciously or not, this is their way of helping us to understand ourselves, which is, after all, a fundamental purpose of any work of art. (Truffaut 26)

Context

Rear Window has been described by Robin Wood as "perhaps the first of Hitchcock's films to which the term masterpiece can reasonably be applied" (100). A highly successful film at the box office (it was fifth highest in revenues for 1954, taking in $5.3 million in the United States), it was acclaimed by the industry, by reviewers, and by audiences. It was voted third of the ten best films for 1954 by *The Film Daily Year Book*, gaining four Oscar nominations (though not winning in any of the categories). *Rear Window* has now been recognized as a classic of American cinema, being placed on the National Film Registry in 1997, and listed among the American Film Institute's best one hundred American films of all time in 1998. The film is indeed masterful cinema, entertaining its audience on a number of levels as a light comic romance and suspenseful mystery thriller. But is it a masterpiece, and, if so, in what ways?

James Stewart plays L. B. "Jeff" Jeffries, a professional photographer confined to his New York apartment with a broken leg, injured while he was getting an action shot at an auto race. Now he spends his time observing his neighbors from his window, which looks onto the rear of the apartment buildings that form the three sides adjoining his own, and from this vantage point Jeff begins to suspect that the salesman in the apartment opposite has killed his wife. The action of the film takes place over four days and centers on Jeff's pursuit of clues and evidence, eventually aided by his girlfriend Lisa and nurse Stella, who also provide the comedy and, in Grace Kelly's Lisa, the romance in the film. But these plot elements are not mere adjuncts; rather, the murder story serves as the setting for the dramatic conflict between Jeff and Lisa arising from her wish for—and his fear of—marriage. The series of vignettes of Jeff's neighbors form a kind of filmic essay on love, desire, and marriage that is alternately humorous, sardonic, and tragic, while acting as a counterpoint to the central conflict of Jeff's own relation to love, desire, and marriage. For what the film narrates through Jeff and Lisa's conjoined fascination with the enigma of the missing wife and their hypothesis of the salesman's guilt is the resolution of the opposition between disorderly and exciting desire and the banality of married love.

Central to *Rear Window* is a look that sees without being seen, and it is the desires, and consequences, involved in such looking that are explored in the film. *Rear Window* has thus also become celebrated as a film about cinema itself. Displaying the cinematic nature of film, it mirrors both the process of filmmaking and the experience of film spectatorship. The interrelationship between *Rear Window*'s system of looks and the elements of romance, comedy, and suspense in the process of its narration will be the focus of this essay, together with the diverse modes of allusion in the film and their role in the narration. What does the film narrate? How knowing or reflexive is the film? That is, how far and in what ways does it acknowledge itself as a film? Does the film present a celebration or a critique of the cinema's voyeurism, and how does this relate to questions of gender and spectatorship?

Hitchcock is, of course, known as the "master of suspense," but suspense, as François Truffaut observes, "is simply the dramatisation of a film's narrative material, or, if you will, the most intense presentation possible of dramatic situations" (15). Hitchcock has famously contrasted surprise and suspense (Truffaut 78–80), arguing that suspense depends on the spectator having knowledge about the events and often knowing more than the characters, so that we are in a state of tense anticipation or apprehension on behalf of our characters, who may nevertheless remain oblivious of the dangers they face, and whom we would warn, if we could. All storytelling depends on suspense, on holding off the answers to the questions it poses of how, when, and who; *suspenseful* cinema intensifies this process, introducing the pressure of time, as well as the urgency of danger. In *Rear Window*, Jeff himself is prey to such suspense, for, like the film spectator, he cannot act but can only watch.

One of the pleasures of *Rear Window* is the deftness of Hitchcock's direction, both in the ease with which he moves us from comedy to pathos to suspense in the dialogue, action, and reactions of characters, and in the way he employs the set as a space not only of action, but also of desire, and of moral understanding. Such deftness makes *Rear Window* a seemingly very obvious film, with everything plainly in view. Yet *Rear Window* is also a highly playful film, and the visual and auditory puns and reversals, metaphors and associations that abound are central in the creation of its humor, its pathos, and also its suspense. Hitchcock toys with our expectations through the parallels he suggests but then reverses in relation to Jeff and his neighbors. Jeff fears the fate he sees his neighbor Lars Thorwald suffer in his marriage; subsequently, however, Jeff's investigation of the wife's murder becomes the means whereby he and Lisa reconcile their opposed demands in their relationship.

Such playfulness makes *Rear Window* appear exhibitionist, for it draws attention to itself as a device in its camera movements, framing, editing, and presentation of its themes—and knowingly so, for by soliciting us to read its reversals and parallels, it thereby also alludes to itself. In this the film displays a certain self-consciousness, demanding that we recognize that it is not merely a window onto the fictional world but a highly organized view that must be read at a figurative, or metaphoric level. The set is the *mise-en-scène* for the action, and a specular—and spectacular—audio-visual attraction, revealed by the swooping and panning of Hitchcock's highly mobile camera. Manifestly artifice, it is nevertheless highly realistic in its detail, achieving a compelling verisimilitude that is supported by Hitchcock's extremely rich and complex sound design and its frequent use of snatches of conversation, the sound of a radio, and street noises we hear or half hear. In contrast, the woman soprano heard—but never seen—practicing musical scales brings, as Michel Chion has suggested, "a free element, escaping all requirement of spatialization, to the localized, everyday fabric of music and noises that arrives from the courtyard as if from an enormous burial pit of sounds" (114). The musical score incorporates well-known melodies, producing a further layer of reference that, together with the lyrics of many of the songs in the diegetic music, comments on the actions on-screen. For example, the melody of "That's Amore" can be discerned in Franz Waxman's score as the newlyweds arrive, while a song that begins "To see is to love you, and I see you everywhere" is heard as "Miss Lonelyhearts" prepares for her make-believe dinner guest. At the composer-neighbor's party, "Mona Lisa" is being sung by his guests; his own composition "Lisa" later enchants Lisa herself, while also prompting Miss Lonelyhearts to halt her attempted suicide.

Rear Window's allusions extend beyond its fictional world, moreover, to Hitchcock's other films. For example, Lisa speculates that the pet dog may have been killed because "he knew too much," invoking Hitchcock's two versions of *The Man Who Knew Too Much* (1934 and 1956). Here, as with his own signature appearances in his films, Hitchcock makes reference to himself as an author, producing yet another layer of self-referentiality. Hitchcock's playfulness is also apparent in a different, more personal, and esoteric set of references in *Rear Window*, such as his insider joke at the expense of producer David O. Selznick, for whom Hitchcock had first worked in Hollywood. The mannerisms and gestures he coached Raymond Burr to use in playing the salesman Thorwald, Scott Curtis suggests, were those of Selznick himself, together with the producer's famous curly gray hair, glasses, and cigar (6). Even more elaborate is the reference, in Jeff and Lisa, to the love affair between Ingrid Bergman—Hitchcock's star in *Spellbound* (1945), *Notorious* (1946), and *Under Capricorn* (1949)—and the prize winning photojournalist Frank Capa (Curtis 2–7). Adding to Cornell Woolrich's original story, Hitchcock and Hayes gave Capa's profession, photojournalism, to Jeffries, as well as giving him a girlfriend whose job depends on her beauty—here a model rather than an actress. Moreover, Jeff works for a magazine clearly modeled on *Life*, which employed Capa; lives in Greenwich Village, as Capa did; and, like Capa, frequently eats at the "21" Club. The romantic plot follows closely what many have inferred was the course of the affair between

Bergman and Capa, itself closely observed by Hitchcock who—himself obsessed by Bergman (Spoto 307–8)—noted her passion for Capa and desire to marry him, together with Capa's fear of marriage, which may have motivated his noncommittal response. Certainly, in making such allusions, Hitchcock created a work that exceeds the boundaries of its fiction, marking it as not only a public but also a personal construction. Perhaps, as Steve Cohen suggests, Hitchcock was amazed that Capa rejected a glamorous woman who offered herself so freely to him (2–7). What is clear, however, is that in his re-creation of the Bergman/Capa relation, Hitchcock explores the dilemma of a man who cannot desire a desirable woman who desires him. The apartments—whose windows appear, in another punning gesture, like a bank of television screens in a store window—and their myriad stories onto which Jeff's window gives him sight are also spaces in relation to which he may obtain insight.[1] What Hitchcock achieves is a rich and subtle account of the ambivalences in desire and love, only apparently resolved when Lisa comes to mirror Jeff's desire for the adventurous.

The making of *Rear Window*, Hitchcock explained to Truffaut, gave him the "possibility of doing a purely cinematic film. You have an immobilized man looking out. That's one part of the film. The second part shows how he reacts. This is actually the purest expression of a cinematic idea" (265). The "purely cinematic" for Hitchcock here is the editing of looks within film. First and foremost, there is the camera's look at the scene, often called an "objective" look to distinguish it from, second, the subjective looks of characters. The latter may be looks to other characters or objects within the shot, or a character's look may be directed offscreen, beyond the frame, to a space that we therefore expect to be shown and thus understand as a continuous part of the fictional world of the characters. Third, there is the spectator's look at the screen, who takes as her own the camera's look, and hence also takes the position, optically, of a character's look, but who may also scan the screen or look away. Motivating the view by implying a

---

[1]Scott Curtis provides a fascinating account of the building of the set and the camera setups (27–32). Screenwriter John Michael Hayes acknowledged that he saw the neighbors' roles as "side stories" that provided "relief" from the action and "stretched out the story," and that it was Hitchcock who developed their importance in the film.

character's optical point of view introduces perspective, for while it is simply a physical place of view, it can become understood—or projected—as also a mental space. We are prompted, that is, to infer a character's mental and emotional response by seeing what she is seeing. Hitchcock, in the example he gives from *Rear Window*, places himself in the tradition of Soviet montage editing when he cites the famous experiment by Lev Kuleshov:

> In the same way, let's take a close-up of Stewart looking out of the window at a little dog that's being lowered in a basket. Back to Stewart, who has a kindly smile. But if in place of the little dog you show a half-naked girl exercising in front of her open window, and you go back to a smiling Stewart again, this time he's seen as a dirty old man! (Interview 265)[2]

Here the camera reveals the observing eye while itself being an observing eye that can be observed. A *mise-en-abyme* of observer observed is thus invoked, which we cannot be sure ends with Hitchcock as author, for he is only a stand-in or double for the omniscient gaze of the Other.

Analysis

The Story and Its Narration

The film's opening credits appear over bamboo blinds at a rectangular bay window; the camera then moves through the window and cuts to show, in a series of craning and panning movements, the apartments with their occupants, finally revealing Jeff, asleep by his window. The third shot repeats this movement, showing everyone getting ready for their day. The camera returns continually during the film to explore this enclosed space in shots at times marked as a character's—usually Jeff's—look, but also (on some six further occasions) as simply the camera's look. After a fade, the next shot shows Jeff on the phone talking with his editor. Their conversation provides us with background on how Jeff broke his leg, on his appetite for dangerous assignments,

---

[2]Hitchcock draws on the account of the experiment given by the Soviet filmmaker and theorist Vsevolod Pudovkin, who had been a student with Kuleshov.

and on the fact that he still has a week more before he gets out of his plaster cast. The camera, however, remains within Jeff's apartment (although shots of Jeff's editor were filmed, these were not used), and we are now given Jeff's look as he gazes around at the buildings outside. All at once, what he and we see is juxtaposed with what we hear, becoming a visual comment or counterpoint when, as the two consider the dangers of marriage and Jeff's editor retorts, "women don't nag, nowadays, they discuss," we observe with Jeff the altercation of the married couple opposite. Introduced here are Jeff's views—and fears—about marriage.

Later, Jeff is visited by Stella, his nurse, who berates him both for his obsessive window gazing and his failure to recognize Lisa's love for him by marrying her. To Stella's advocacy of Lisa as "perfect," he replies that yes, she is, but this is just what he finds a problem! Lisa is sheer spectacle when she visits him that evening, wearing a stunning couture dress and bringing an extravagant lobster dinner, complete with waiter, from the "21" Club.[3] The powerful sensuality of their relationship is established in the shot of Jeff asleep when Lisa, in a big close-up, enters the frame and kisses him as he awakes.[4] Their conflicts—ostensibly arising from their different styles of living and expectations of life—are explored in their witty and rebarbative dialogue, which gives us a vivid portrayal of their contrasting desires and suggests that Jeff is largely immune to the attractions of the spectacle Lisa offers of herself. As he compares her to his neighbor, whom he has dubbed "Miss Torso," and her "male drones" (in contrast to Miss Lonelyhearts, whose preparations for a dinner guest, paralleling Lisa's, prove to be make-believe), Lisa acidly challenges his limited understanding of femininity, declaring that it is clear that Miss Torso

---

[3]Sarah Street offers a fascinating analysis of Edith Head's costume design.

[4]Hitchcock refers to this as a "surprise kiss," in contrast to a suspense kiss. The film here captures Grace Kelly's perfect, shimmering beauty, but there is, perhaps, something uncanny when, as she bears down on Jeff, he suddenly opens his eyes, ending the connotations of a Princess Charming awakening her sleeping Prince and opening the way to the suggestion of a terror in the surprise. A similar shot, with further and different implications, is used by Hitchcock in *Marnie* (1964), when Mark Rutland (Sean Connery) bears down on the terrified Tippi Hedren as he abandons his "nice-guy" response to her sexual frigidity and consummates their marriage by force.

doesn't love any of the men, and suggesting that she, too, is not immune to loneliness. Then, realizing that her "good-bye" is intended as a permanent farewell, Jeff quickly changes his tone and pleads with her to keep their relationship as it is. While he does not wish to marry her, neither does he want to end their relationship. Lisa hesitates, reiterates her good-bye, then qualifies it with "until tomorrow."

Here, then, is the first narrative enigma: How, if at all, will Jeff overcome his fears and marry Lisa? For Jeff rejects the loss of freedom involved in the kinds of compromises that would be required of him by Lisa's picture of their possible married life together, wanting to keep the pleasures of bachelorhood and the excitement of sexuality outside the legal confines of marriage. Such a view, Robin Wood suggests, sees marriage as a form of disempowerment—castration—of the male (376). Classical Hollywood, however, has been characterized as a cinema that moves its male protagonist from lawless to lawful, from unmarried to married. The woman's desire must be brought to mirror the man's, to complement him and no longer confront him with her otherness as a subject, and object, of desire (Bellour). For Stanley Cavell, the goal of Hollywood's romantic comedies of remarriage is "the creation of a new woman," namely, as partner to the man (262). In *Rear Window*, however, it seems that it is not Lisa who changes (despite her very different costume at the film's close), but Jeff. Could we not say, then, that what we have here is the creation of a new man, that is, as partner to the woman? For the exploration of the problem of marriage and the curtailment of desire that Jeff fears is not resolved through narrating the subordination of Lisa's desire; rather, Jeff comes to be able to desire her as desiring.

Following Lisa's departure, Jeff resumes his observations when suddenly a woman's scream, followed by a crash, is heard. A little later Jeff sees the composer returning home, drunk, and Miss Torso firmly refusing the advances of her male friend as she shuts her door on him, implicitly confirming Lisa's earlier comment. Jeff also observes the husband of the nagging invalid wife in the apartment opposite—whom Lisa will later discover is Lars Thorwald—going out and returning several times with his salesman's bag. Jeff is puzzled by the salesman's actions, but, finally falling asleep, he does not see the salesman go out one final time, now accompanied by a woman we may assume is his wife.

The following day Stella remonstrates again over Jeff's window watching: "What are you going to do if one of them catches you?" She, too, however, is interested in his neighbors, and, moved by his account of Miss Lonelyhearts' dinner the night before, Stella voices the hope that she might find someone. Jeff wonders if the salesman might "be available soon," given his wife's disappearance, and thus opens the way to a thought not yet fully articulated—that the salesman may have disposed of his wife—which is the film's second enigma.

Two narrative spaces have been established: First, the apartments Jeff spies on with their many stories played out in front of us by their diverse occupants, to which Jeff is like a camera/filmmaker whose looks open up these narrative spaces, revealing their scenes, and second, Jeff's apartment, which is the *mise-en-scène* for his interrelation with Lisa and for his pursuit of the truth about the nagging wife who disappears. A third space is invoked, namely the exterior of Jeff's own apartment and its adjoining spaces. While Lisa and Stella each traverse this space, their look back at Jeff is, curiously, not shown in a point-of-view shot. This space is revealed only much later, in three separate but climactic shots: on the discovery of the dead dog; then when the salesman, Thorwald, looks back at Jeff; and when Jeff falls from his window. Unseen by Jeff, it is therefore a space that his look cannot control. Jeff is also subject to a fascinating curiosity, which drives him to make sense of the stories he overlooks, drawing on the bits of information his eyes chance on, trying to fit them together as a plot—that is, as motivated actions—just as we, the audience, are doing. Stella and Lisa, too, are fascinated by these dramas and the comedy and pathos of the everyday lives they narrate. They, like Jeff, as well as the spectator, are also at the same time enjoying the very act of looking itself, insofar as it enables them and us to see what might otherwise be hidden and secret, while being ourselves unseen. We are voyeurs, for what defines the voyeur's look is an over-looking; it is a look that is never returned. What is hidden and what the voyeur wants to see is conventionally the sexual, of course, which Hitchcock affords in the views of the voluptuous dancing of Miss Torso, or which can be imagined in the shots of the newlyweds on their first night and, later, when we see the husband half-dressed at the window. The visual pleasure of looking arises not simply from what is seen (the woman's body, for example), but in the uncovering of the secret of the seen, which is the secret of the woman's—or man's—enjoyment, without being seen ourselves. It is here that the sadism intrinsic to voyeurism, as Laura Mulvey notes, is located (21).

Rear Window, however, displays a self-consciousness or reflexivity in relation to its voyeurism, not only in the many comments by characters throughout the film, but also by showing the overlooking of others who are being watched by a third party, as when Jeff observes the young women on the roof, who, we may infer from their gestures, have stripped to sunbathe nude but now scurry to cover up when a helicopter appears overhead. The film also foregrounds the reversal—often comically—of implicit narratives of desire assumed in many of these scenes. For example, in the epilogue we discover that Miss Torso loves not one of her many male admirers but her less than conventionally handsome GI boyfriend.

We are not left to enjoy our voyeurism in peace, however. Suspense is introduced by Hitchcock precisely in relation to the possibility of the look returned. When Jeff suddenly notices that Thorwald is himself surveying the apartments that can be viewed from his own window and that therefore he, Jeff, might be espied, he quickly urges Stella to step back as he wheels himself away from the window. The voyeur's titillating pleasure is undermined as Hitchcock plays with our expectations—and our pleasures—introducing a narrative development that disrupts the act of overlooking the sexual scene. The film continually shifts its characters, and spectators, between a more proper curiosity and an "improper" voyeuristic looking, both of which are subject to comic irony in the dialogue, reversals of expectation, and visual puns.

Jeff cannot see clearly enough on his own, and as a result enlists the help of some mechanical devices as visual aids, which become physical extensions or prostheses. The binoculars that Jeff asks Stella for as she leaves are not sufficiently powerful, and instead he wheels himself over to a cupboard where he takes out a telephoto lens and fixes it to his camera. With this addition, Jeff is empowered to see all, a mastering that Hitchcock underlines in the framing of Jeff as he views Thorwald through his telescopic camera-eye—with all its considerable phallic connotations. He sees Thorwald wielding a large knife—itself a kind of phallic mirroring that further suggests a doubling of Jeff/Thorwald—which he wraps in newspaper. Hitchcock, well known for his interest in Sigmund Freud's theories of the unconscious and human sexuality, no doubt intended such references. The image is all the more potent given Jeff's immobility as a result of his enormous leg and waist cast, and this can be read metaphorically as a "castration": a disabling that is symbolized as well by the image of his smashed camera at the beginning of the film. (Of course there is also a parallel between Jeff and the bedridden Mrs. Thorwald, each of whom spy on Thorwald and become subject to his murderous desires.)

These tropes of empowerment and disempowerment in relation to the look culminate in the confrontation between Jeff and Thorwald at the end of the film, as Jeff tries to defend himself by shooting off flash-bulbs, but can only temporarily blind Thorwald. Jeff's impaired potency, represented by his broken leg, connects him by association to the impairment—or castration—that he believes marriage itself threatens, and which is seen vividly and with all its murderous consequences in the example of the henpecked Thorwald. The metaphor of impairment refers not to an irreversible loss or literal castration, but to the threat of loss, to being made weak, impotent. In contrast to the solution to which Thorwald resorts in murdering his wife, Jeff comes to view Lisa differently, a change signaled within the film through his point-of-view shots of her. At the same time, in the course of the film's action, Lisa is also transformed: her desire for marriage no longer threatens him with loss.

The next scene, that evening, opens once more with a camera pan across the apartments, coming to rest in close-up on Jeff and Lisa kissing. Lisa, however, complains that Jeff seems distracted, saying, "I want all of a man . . ." When Jeff explains his growing suspicion that his neighbor has murdered his wife, she declares she is worried about his mental state: "What is it you're looking for?" she asks; "I just want to know what happened," Jeff replies. "There's nothing to see," she retorts, and, pulling his wheelchair back around from the window to face her, she challenges all his suppositions (just as Lieutenant Doyle will do later). She then taunts him, saying, "Why, for all you know there's probably something a lot more sinister going on behind *those* windows," pointing off right, and Jeff turns to look, then realizes her trick, for there is nothing to be seen. Just then Lisa's gaze is caught by Thorwald's activities opposite, and her expression suddenly changes. Hitchcock, however, does not give us Lisa's point of view, but instead cuts to Jeff watching her and then to his view, through the binoculars, of Thorwald tying up a large trunk with heavy rope. "Let's start from the beginning again, Jeff," she demands. "Tell me everything you saw. And what you think it means." Nevertheless, Hitchcock has shown that Lisa's conversion arises not from what Jeff says, but from what she herself sees.

Jeff's reply is elided as the film fades to black, giving further rhetorical emphasis to Lisa's sudden conversion. We next see Jeff alone beside a phone, looking down; the film cuts to the apartment opposite, the room unlit except momentarily by the flare of a match, betraying the presence of an occupant—presumably Thorwald—smoking in the dark. Hitchcock uses fades throughout the film for scene transitions that are, in classical Hollywood films, always ellipses in time of some considerable length. Here, however, he reverses our expectations: when the phone rings, the call is from Lisa reporting the name of the occupant of the apartment opposite as Lars Thorwald, implying only a brief elision of time. Lisa remains unseen, however, and instead she invokes Jeff's look when she asks, "But what's he doing now?" Jeff answers, "He's just sitting in the living room," but the reverse shot shows not Thorwald as such but a metonymic stand-in for him as his cigar flares brightly before dying out.

The following day Stella serves Jeff a bacon-and-egg breakfast, but as he eagerly starts to eat, Stella—herself nibbling on a piece of bacon—begins to muse, "Just how do you suppose he cut her up?" Jeff returns his fork to his plate with the mouthful uneaten, apparently put off his food. Then, as Stella considers the problem of leaking blood if the trunk were used to move the wife's body, Jeff abandons drinking his tea. The deft visual comedy here is superb macabre humor, while also revealing that Stella is now a convert to Jeff's theory of wife killing.

Jeff has seduced both Stella and Lisa with his story, but fails later that day to convince his old wartime friend, now a police detective, Lieutenant Thomas J. Doyle, who nevertheless agrees to make further inquiries. The film now plays with a series of repetitions and reversals of its various stories. Jeff notices the dog of the childless couple who live above Thorwald digging at his flowerbed. Later that evening, surveying his neighbors again, he sees the dog let down in its basket as usual, while Miss Lonelyhearts dresses to go out; the pianist is giving a party; Miss Torso is practicing dance steps with a male partner. Seeing Thorwald packing his clothes, Jeff phones Doyle and asks him to come over again, then watches Thorwald make a long-distance phone call while taking jewelry out of his wife's alligator handbag, which Jeff recounts to Lisa when she arrives. She responds with firm feminine intuition, saying that no woman would go away without her jewelry, nor would she leave it tangled up in her favorite handbag. Delighted, Jeff kisses her with an enthusiasm not apparent earlier, and Lisa then reveals her plan to spend the night with him, showing him her case, diminutive but sufficient for her needs, she says, in a riposte to his earlier incredulity at her claim that she could pack for the kinds of journeys he makes. Leaving it to one side, she goes to the kitchen to make coffee and warm some brandy.

When Doyle arrives, his gaze is caught by the open case and the negligee spilling out of it, returning to this several times. Overseen by Doyle, its sexual implications are emphasized; but the policeman, observed by Jeff, is warned against jumping to conclusions. His look here echoes both his earlier fascination with the surreal painting above the fireplace and his rapt gaze at Miss Torso—a look noticed by Jeff, who asks pointedly, "How's your wife?" When Doyle quickly withdraws his gaze, we can infer both his visual pleasure and its firm repression. After receiving a phone call, and with a backward look at Lisa's case, Doyle walks forward into the room and, in a low-angle close-up, declares that Thorwald did not kill his wife. With the cold reasoning of a policeman, in contrast to the amateur imaginings of Jeff and Lisa, Doyle presents an alternative narrative account, dismissing each of their arguments—their "jumping to conclusions"—while also posing back to them an image of how their own actions might appear under the gaze of rational skepticism. But Doyle's view of things already has been subtly questioned by Hitchcock in his showing the policeman's uncomprehending gaze at the painting, with its bizarre array of objects whose sensible significance is drawn as much from our unconscious as our conscious recognition. That the complexity of desire and its dangers escapes the understanding of the law is underlined in the subsequent comedy when Doyle spills his brandy as he knocks it back, unused to drinking from a snifter glass; that is, he lacks the sophistication of Jeff and Lisa (suggesting his class difference as well). It is only as he leaves that Doyle reveals final proof that Mrs.

Thorwald is not dead when he announces that the trunk—containing her clothes and not her body—had been collected by Mrs. Anna Thorwald. Doyle delays revealing the information from his phone call—just as he did on his earlier visit—mirroring Hitchcock's own role in revealing and withholding information in the film.

Despondently, Lisa and Jeff gaze out at their neighbors. Watching as Miss Lonelyhearts brings a—younger—man home, then throws him out when he gets too fresh, Jeff calls it "pretty private stuff," and asks, "I wonder if it's ethical to watch someone with binoculars and a long focus telephoto lens?" Lisa's reply, "I'm not much on rear window ethics," echoes his implicit recognition of the dubious morality of their spying, and at the same time implicates the cinema audience as well. Visual pleasure remains the theme, however, when, closing the blinds, Lisa declares, "the show's over for tonight," but offers a "preview of coming attractions" and reappears, to Jeff's noticeable appreciation, in her negligee. A second murder then interrupts this apparent closure when a woman's scream leads Lisa to open the blinds again, discovering Miss Lonelyhearts bending over the childless couple's dog, its neck broken. The wife on their balcony above demands to know who did it, fiercely rebuking the apartments' occupants for their lack of neighborly feeling. Meanwhile, the camera—quite independent of Jeff and Lisa's look—swoops and circles to reveal the watching neighbors, including Lisa and Jeff framed at his window in the first of the three reverse-angle shots from the space of the courtyard. Jeff, noticing that Thorwald—sitting in the dark, betrayed again by the flare of his cigar as he smokes—is alone among the neighbors in not having come to his window, is again convinced of his guilt.

The next evening Stella, Lisa, and Jeff are gathered at the window again, as the film moves quickly to its denouement. Jeff discovers that the flowers where the murdered dog had been digging have grown shorter, suggesting Thorwald has replanted them. With this new evidence, Lisa—despite Jeff's reluctance—delivers a note to him, asking, "What have you done with her?" Seeing Thorwald's guilty change of expression through the telephoto lens, Jeff is gripped by fear that Lisa will be caught as she leaves, when Stella, noticing Miss Lonelyhearts, asks for the telephoto to look more closely at what she is laying out—namely, enough sleeping pills to kill herself. Here the scene is set for a second and parallel drama to unfold, which functions both to create suspense and to revalue their voyeurism as the nosiness of concerned neighbors. Lisa, returning, appears transformed as, filmed at the door, her half-lit face is flooded with excitement as she looks toward Jeff. The reverse shot reveals Jeff's rapt gaze mirroring hers, his eyes highlighted, smiling, suggesting that his view of Lisa has also been transformed. As Laura Mulvey writes, "When she crosses the barrier between his room and the block opposite, their relationship is reborn erotically" (23). Lisa has entered the field of Jeff's desire by stepping into the space of his gaze not as an image but as a subject who acts, and desires.

Now determined to find evidence, Jeff lures Thorwald from his apartment by arranging a meeting with him nearby. Stella and Lisa explore the flower bed, but, discovering nothing, Lisa—the full skirt of her dress billowing around her—climbs up and enters Thorwald's apartment. But she fails again, for the handbag she finds proves empty. Just then, Stella and Jeff see Miss Lonelyhearts about to swallow her pills, and Stella urgently demands that Jeff call the police to stop her, but as he does so the composer's song—"Lisa"—is heard, and she abandons her suicide attempt. Still connected to the police, Jeff is unable to warn Lisa when he sees Thorwald returning to his apartment and alerts the police instead. He and Stella then watch helplessly as, discovered by Thorwald, Lisa calls out to Jeff for help. Nevertheless, once rescued by the police, she manages to hide on her own finger the wedding ring she found, displaying it behind her back to Jeff. The ring, symbolizing authorized sexual union, passes from the nagging wife to the girlfriend. Worn triumphantly as a clue to—and thus trace of—a murder, it is also a symbol of Lisa's own desire. We see in close-up through Jeff's telephoto lens—thus from his point of view—her gesture, which is overlooked by Thorwald, who now looks back at Jeff to discover his mysterious pursuer. The reverse shot shows Jeff in medium close-up, but as Stella goes to extinguish the light, the camera pulls back to frame Jeff at his window from Thorwald's point of view.

This look returned presages a violence to which Jeff will become prey, as if the object of his look now returns all the aggression Jeff has projected. Alone and realizing that Thorwald knows where he is, Jeff anxiously listens for footsteps outside his apartment signaling Thorwald's arrival. Entering, Thorwald is framed in half light (just as Lisa had been) and repeats, "What do you want from me?" wrongly assuming blackmail given Jeff's earlier phone call and Lisa's failure to turn him in (which remains unexplained). But what Jeff wants is the truth of Thorwald's desire—that is, to be rid of his wife—yet the desire to be unwed is also Jeff's own. The evidence of Thorwald's guilt is his wife's ring, now worn by Lisa, making her, too, a participant in this circuit of desire. Thorwald's confession later, however, displaces the ring's evidentiary function, and, unused, it becomes a Hitchcockian "MacGuffin." Through this, and like many of the denouements in Hitchcock's films, the sequence conjoins desire and violence.[5] While blinding Thorwald momentarily by setting off his flash, Jeff's impotence is nevertheless apparent. *Rear Window* concludes with farce as Jeff is pushed out of the window. While saved from Thorwald's clutches by the police, Jeff acquires—it emerges later—a second broken leg. Cradled in Lisa's arms, we may wonder if, in this reference to the film's opening, we should understand Jeff to now be doubly castrated or on the contrary, we should see him as transformed and actually newly empowered by his changed relation to Lisa.

The film closes with an epilogue presenting a series of vignettes—alternately comic and poignant. The couple have a new dog, Miss Torso greets her returning GI fiancé, and Miss Lonelyhearts and the composer find friendship. The newlywed wife, however, is seen berating her husband since, despite all the sexual enthusiasm the film has led us to infer from her, she would never have married him if she had known he'd lost his job! As the camera tracks back through Jeff's apartment, it shows him asleep, in a reprise of the film's opening shot, but now with both legs in casts. Lisa (in slacks and shirt appropriate to her new role), noticing she is unobserved by Jeff, puts down a book on the Himalayas and picks up her copy of *Harper's Bazaar*. Hitchcock, playful to the end, gives the woman the last laugh in giving Lisa, as Tania Modleski notes, the final look. He also introduces a certain undecidability here, keeping open the question of desire and the problem of its orderly transaction within human relations such as marriage.

---

[5]For example, in *Blackmail* (1929), *Strangers on a Train* (1951), *North by Northwest* (1959), and *The Birds* (1963).

Conclusion

The Voyeurism of Rear Window

"We've become a race of Peeping Toms," Stella tells Jeff at the beginning of *Rear Window*, after chastising him for his obsessive window gazing. Her words, of course, apply equally well to the cinema as to real life, and indeed *Rear Window* is often referred to as an essay on voyeurism. Moreover, in her reference to Peeping Toms Stella invokes the specifically sexual pleasure of looking that is identified as exemplary of classical Hollywood. For, Laura Mulvey argues, the look in Hollywood's cinema is held by the male, and its films were "cut to the measure of male desire," tailored to the fears and fantasies of the male spectator (25). Many critics, like Donald Spoto, have assumed that a majority of the film is seen through Jeff's visual point of view and his mental perspective (241),[6] whereas on closer viewing it becomes apparent that such shots are a minority, while Jeff is himself the object of looks from Stella, Lisa, Doyle, and, finally, Thorwald. Yet it seems that we assimilate the "objective," or non-character-motivated shots, from Jeff's apartment with those that are motivated as being Jeff's look. Camera views motivated as point-of-view shots allow the spectator to see *as if* they were the character. In *Rear Window*, however, we also project onto Jeff our own, that is, the camera's look, *as if* it were his. This, despite numerous shots of Jeff *asleep* that Hitchcock has playfully included, and which show him subjected on two occasions to another's look, namely Lisa's—most tellingly at the film's close.

Stella's words might sum up Hitchcock's broader project as a filmmaker, namely, to implicate us as spectators in the ethics of our looking by making us, too, into Peeping Toms. The film is not only about its characters' voyeurism, their prying curiosity, and, for Doyle and Jeff, their visual pleasure, for, by failing to offer a simple critique or condemnation, *Rear Window* explores the limitations such voyeurism produces in our relations to others. Instead, it demands that we recognize our implication, and pleasure, in voyeuristic looking and what this makes us blind to.

---

[6]Wood notes, "With one brief exception . . . we are allowed to see only what he sees, know only what he knows." The exception Wood is referring to arises when, as Jeff sleeps, Thorwald leaves his apartment with a woman (103).

Stella introduces a quite different issue of looking, however, when she goes on to say, "People ought to get outside and look in at themselves," and it is this which I suggest is also central to *Rear Window* and to Hitchcock's films in general, namely, the look back at ourselves—a self-reflexivity. It is a look from elsewhere that may be—as Stella suggests—imagined by us, that is, a mental look. The set of *Rear Window* enacts Stella's metaphor, enabling us to come to know and identify with the various residents and their lives and stories, looking in on them as we might on our own lives and stories. But this is a look that may be not our own, but another's. It is a look that may be solicited, just as Lisa—seeking to impress Jeff—displays the beautiful and expensive clothes she wears. Or it may be a look fearfully anticipated, for Jeff does not wish to be seen seeing his neighbors, and certainly not spying on Miss Torso, as Stella also acidly observes. What is involved here is both our self-scrutiny and self-knowledge and our subjection to a scrutiny by an other who may praise (the ego ideal) or judge (the superego, the law). The spectator is caught in the play of the gaze (with its anxieties as well as pleasures), while, in displaying its devices and exposing its fictions, *Rear Window* disrupts our identification not only with the characters but also with the cinema's look as a distant, mastering vision. Hitchcock's film is about a gaze that finds itself seen; embodied and desiring, it is a gaze implicated in the scene.

Credits

United States, 1954, Paramount Pictures

Director: Alfred Hitchcock
Producer: Alfred Hitchcock (uncredited)
Screenplay: John Michael Hayes (based on a story by Cornell Woolrich)
Cinematography: Robert Burks
Editing: George Tomasini
Music: Franz Waxman, Jay Livingston and Ray Evans (song "Mona Lisa")
Art Direction: J. McMillan Johnson (Joseph MacMillan Johnson) and Hal Pereira
Set Decoration: Sam Comer and Ray Moyer
Costume Design: Edith Head

CAST:
L. B. "Jeff" Jeffries	James Stewart
Lisa Carol Fremont	Grace Kelly
Lt. Thomas J. Doyle	Wendell Corey

Stella	Thelma Ritter
Lars Thorwald	Raymond Burr
Miss Lonelyhearts	Judith Evelyn
Songwriter	Ross Bagdasarian
Miss Torso	Georgine Darcy
Woman on fire escape	Sara Berner
Man on fire escape	Frank Cady

Bibliography

Allen, Richard, and S. Ishij Gonzales, eds. *Alfred Hitchcock: Centenary Essays.* London: BFI, 1999.

Bellour, Raymond. "Alternation, Segmentation, Hypnosis: Interview with Raymond Bellour—An Excerpt." By Janet Bergstrom. *Feminism and Film Theory.* Ed. Constance Penley. New York: Routledge, 1988. 186–95.

Belton, John, ed. *Alfred Hitchcock's "Rear Window."* Cambridge: Cambridge UP, 2000.

Cavell, Stanley. "*North by Northwest.*" *A Hitchcock Reader.* Ed. Marshall Deutelbaum and Leland Poague. Iowa: Iowa State UP, 1986.

Chion, Michel. "Alfred Hitchcock's *Rear Window*: The Fourth Side." Belton 110–17.

Cohen, Steve. "*Rear Window*: The Untold Story." *Columbia Film View* 8.1 (1990): 2–7.

Curtis, Scott. "The Making of *Rear Window.*" Belton 21–56.

Hayes, John Michael. Interview. "*Rear Window" Ethics: Remembering and Restoring a Hitchcock Classic.* DVD of restored print. Universal Collector's Edition, 2001.

Hitchcock, Alfred. *Hitchcock on Hitchcock: Selected Writings and Interviews.* Ed. Sidney Gottlieb. Berkeley: U of California P, 1995.

Hitchcock, Alfred. Interview. *Hitchcock.* By François Truffaut. London: Paladin, 1978.

Modleski, Tania. *The Women Who Knew Too Much.* London: Routledge, 1988.

Mulvey, Laura. *Visual and Other Pleasures.* London: Macmillan, 1989.

Pudovkin, V. I. *Film Technique: Five Essays and Two Addresses.* London: George Newnes, 1933.

Raubichek, Walter, and Walter Srebnick, eds. *Hitchcock's Re-released Films: From "Rope" to "Vertigo."* Detroit: Wayne State UP, 1991.

Spoto, Donald. *The Art of Alfred Hitchcock.* London: W. H. Allen, 1977.

Stam, Robert, and Roberta Pearson. "Hitchcock's *Rear Window*: Reflexivity and the Critique of Voyeurism." *A Hitchcock Reader.* Ed. Marshall Deutelbaum and Leland Poague. Iowa: Iowa State UP, 1986. 193–206.

Street, Sarah. "The Dresses Had Told Me: Fashion and Femininity in *Rear Window.*" Belton 91–109.

Wood, Robin. *Hitchcock's Films Revisited.* New York: Columbia UP, 1989.

Žižek, Slavoj, ed. *Everything You Always Wanted to Know About Lacan (But Were Afraid to Ask Hitchcock).* London: Verso, 1992.

Seven Samurai (1954)

MITSUHIRO YOSHIMOTO

A Search for a National Community

Context

Kurosawa Akira's *Seven Samurai* (*Shichinin no samurai*) has consistently been regarded as one of the best epic action dramas in the history of the cinema. It regularly appears on various lists of the ten best films of all time, and a stream of publications on the film seems to continue endlessly. The most visible sign of the great impact of *Seven Samurai* can be arguably observed in Hollywood cinema. From *The Magnificent Seven* (1960) to *The Wild Bunch* (1969), the basic setting and plot of *Seven Samurai* and Kurosawa's signature use of slow motion and stylized representations of violence have left an indelible mark on Hollywood filmmaking. *Seven Samurai* and many other Kurosawa films have not only influenced Hollywood genres such as the Western and the war film but have also inspired film directors from different generations and from around the globe, including Sam Peckinpah, Sergio Leone, Francis Ford Coppola, George Lucas, Steven Spielberg, Andrey Tarkovsky, Kitano Takeshi, John Woo, and Miyazaki Hayao, among many others. As an increasing number of Japanese films are now remade as Hollywood films, *Seven Samurai* appears as a pioneering work whose significance and popularity truly transcend the local Japanese context of film production, distribution, and reception.

What accounts for the global influence of *Seven Samurai*? The film's attraction comes first and foremost from the intensity of images drawn with bold brushstrokes. Every single shot is well calculated as to its compositional and kinetic effects, which are further enhanced by Kurosawa's superb editing. In *Seven Samurai*, the story is not some semiautonomous construct existing separately from the images; on the contrary, it is literally impossible to discuss the film's story without first referring to the images' concrete specificity. Despite its three-

and-a-half-hour length, *Seven Samurai* successfully sustains the narrative tension throughout by presenting gripping images one after another. By often subordinating dialogue to precise shot composition and kinetic energy generated by montage, Kurosawa makes it possible for the spectators to concentrate on the images on the screen yet still comprehend the film's plot without much difficulty.

While every critic seems to agree on the sheer visual power of *Seven Samurai*, there is no clear consensus on what *Seven Samurai* is finally about from a thematic perspective. In spite of—or perhaps precisely because of—the simplicity of the story, *Seven Samurai* has generated many diverse interpretations and reactions. Stephen Prince argues that *Seven Samurai*, organized around the tension between collectivism and individualism, uses a historical past to explore the possibility of individual heroism in society where self is constructed as an effect of human interaction rather than an autonomous individual. Bert Cardullo sees in *Seven Samurai* a uniquely "Eastern" worldview, in which self is displaced by circumstance as a driving force of history. For Frederick Kaplan and many other critics, the film is about "class struggle and the role of intellectuals in that struggle" (42). Similarly, Kida Jun'ichiro argues that *Seven Samurai* shows the powerlessness of Japanese intellectuals as political agents working in an environment where civil society has yet to emerge (232–33). Sato Tadao contextualizes the film by establishing a direct link between the film's story and a contemporary event, i.e., the creation of the Self-Defense Force in 1954 despite the fact that Article 9 of the Japanese postwar constitution explicitly prohibits the use of the military to solve any international disputes. In contrast, Donald Richie finds a universal humanistic message of hope in the film's final sequence: "We are all, after all, human; we all feel the same—we are all peasants at heart" (107).

Interesting as they are, none of these interpretations and allegorical readings is completely satisfying because they fall short of explicating the sheer power of *Seven Samurai* as an epic drama. For example, Sato's criticism of *Seven Samurai* as an ideological accomplice of Japanese remilitarization slightly misses the mark because once the bandits are all vanquished, the samurai do not remain in the village to protect it from other potential threats. The binary of East and West is mostly a fiction, i.e., a product of geopolitical imagination, which cannot be a useful tool for interpreting *Seven Samurai* or any other "Eastern" film. Even critics who seem to pay attention to the specific sociohistorical context of the film's production and its textual content often mix up history and ideology, and perhaps unintentionally end up reducing the film to an illustration of Japanese national character or cultural essence.

Analysis

Samurai's Self-Discovery

The story of *Seven Samurai* is actually very simple. As its opening titles tell us, the setting of the film is the Japanese warring-states period of the sixteenth century. In the film's first sequence, farmers learn that bandits are coming to loot their small mountain village once they finish harvesting their barley. They all gather in a village square and debate how to prepare for the coming calamity. When their intense discussion fails to reach any conclusion, they visit a village patriarch, who decides to fight against the bandits by hiring a small group of samurai. Four villagers go to a town to recruit samurai who are willing to work for the village without any reward except daily meals. At first they have difficulty in identifying, let alone recruiting, any samurai for this dangerous yet thankless task, but they eventually find seven samurai who are willing to take on the mission of protecting the village from the bandits. Although there are some tense moments between the farmers and the samurai, thanks to the mediating character Kikuchiyo, they overcome those problems and methodically prepare for a coming war against the bandits. Soon a series of battles starts, and after paying a heavy price, the samurai-farmer force kill all forty bandits. Peace returns to the village, and the villagers happily plant rice seedlings accompanied by festive music and songs. The three surviving samurai look at this scene, and quietly leave the village.

The film is consciously conceived as a collective drama, so that there is no central hero in a conventional sense. Yet there are two characters whose presence is absolutely essential for the film's narrative. When they almost give up the idea of hiring samurai, the four farmers—Rikichi, Manzo, Yohei, and Mosuke—see Kanbei saving a small boy from an armed thief. They are impressed by Kanbei's martial skill and above all his personality. To disguise himself as a Buddhist monk, Kanbei does not hesitate to cut off his topknot, a symbol of samurai, and shave his head. He kills the thief and saves the child, yet apparently does not demand any reward afterward. Equally awed by this rescue scene is a young samurai Katsushiro, who idealizes Kanbei as a master swordsman with high moral standards and asks him for permission to become his apprentice. There is another young man carrying a long sword who intently observes Kanbei from the beginning of the rescue preparation. This is Kikuchiyo, played by Mifune Toshiro. Although they never exchange any words, a special relationship is established between Kikuchiyo and Kanbei through an unanswered exchange of looks. Kanbei is being looked at by the farmers and Katsushiro, yet he is not aware of their looks. Kikuchiyo's look is also fixed on Kanbei, and the film emphasizes how much Kanbei is aware of the look of Kikuchiyo. While shaving his head and changing his clothes, Kanbei looks back to Kikuchiyo three times. Yet, strangely, Kikuchiyo, who watches Kanbei's every move, does not seem to notice Kanbei's look. This is a very peculiar shot/reverse-shot scene, in which two characters look at each other yet no apparent communication occurs between them. Whereas the unanswered looks of the four farmers and Katsushiro put them in the position of students, from which they admire Kanbei as their teacher, Kikuchiyo's strange look marks him as a special character who plays the double role of student and teacher. Like Katsushiro and the farmers, Kikuchiyo learns from Kanbei many important lessons about responsibility, compassion, and camaraderie; at the same time, Kikuchiyo's presence and action also lead to Kanbei's deeper self-understanding concerning his samurai identity and position in history. Thus, through his subtle manipulation of an otherwise conventional shot/reverse-shot scene, Kurosawa successfully establishes Kanbei and Kikuchiyo as two indispensable characters who are mutually attracted to each other yet do not know the exact reason for their attraction at this point in the narrative.

The samurai-farmer alliance is a fragile one. The farmers are understandably afraid of the samurai, and the samurai do not have a good grasp of the psychology of the farmers. To maintain this alliance, a constant readjustment of expectations and a willingness to learn about the other are demanded from both groups. And it is here that Kikuchiyo, who was born into a farmer's family yet joins the samurai as the seventh member, plays a crucial role of mediating between the two groups. For the six other samurai, the process of enlightenment involves their gradual realization that they are not free individuals but a product of history. Despite their selfless determination to protect the farmers against the bandits, the six samurai cannot escape the fact that their class identity puts them in the position of oppressors. To prepare for the bandits' attack, the samurai desperately need more arms for themselves and their farmer foot soldiers. Kikuchiyo, who has intimate knowledge of farmers' life and behavior, discovers many swords, spears, arrows, and armors hidden at Manzo's house, and brings them to the six samurai. Apparently, the villagers have been hunting down and killing injured or exhausted samurai on the run for armor and other valuables. Kanbei and the other samurai are visibly upset when they see a pile of arms stolen from dead samurai. Kyuzo, a stoic master swordsman, even bluntly says that he wants to kill every villager with a sword. Clearly, this is the most critical moment of crisis in the samurai-farmer alliance. Then, suddenly, Kikuchiyo bursts out in anger and accuses the samurai of hypocrisy: "Farmers are miserly, craven . . . , mean, stupid . . . , murderous! . . . You make me laugh so hard I'm crying. . . . But then, who made animals out of them? You! . . . You did—you samurai! All of you damned samurai! . . . And each time you fight you burn villages, you destroy the fields, you take away the food, you rape the women and enslave the men. And you kill them when they resist. . . . You hear me—you damned samurai!" At this point, the six samurai, who had apparently identified themselves with the defeated samurai who were murdered with bamboo spears, realize that they are not simply innocent victims but also victimizers who are not in a position to criticize the villagers as perpetrators of violence. When the village patriarch Gisaku comes to see what is going on, Kanbei tells him nothing happened.

This is a very important scene because it demonstrates that the difference between the samurai and the bandits is not as absolute as it may seem at first. In fact, throughout the film they are presented as a mirror image of each other. As a symbol of unity, Heihachi, who humorously introduces himself as a master of the "wood-cutting school" during the recruitment sequence, makes a banner representing each group in the alliance: the Japanese letter *ta* stands for the farmers, a triangle for Kikuchiyo, and six circles for the six samurai. Interestingly, the bandits are also represented by circles on the strategy map drawn by Kanbei. The similarity between the samurai and the bandits is further emphasized by their parallel actions: the samurai set fire to the bandits' hideout as part of their preemptive attack; in return, the bandits destroy farmhouses by fire. The arrival of the bandits and of the samurai at the village are similarly represented by high-angle shots of the village seen from the top of a mountain. Unlike the bandits, the samurai do not loot the village; nonetheless, they eat rice while the villagers have only foxtail and Japanese millet, which taste so terrible that they are almost inedible.

Needless to say, however, the film does not equate the samurai with the bandits, and keeps reminding the audience of their differences through a series of dichotomies such as the orderliness of the village's fortification versus the unguarded chaos of the bandits' fort. Why, then, does the film underline their similarity through visual and narrative details? The samurai's superiority over the bandits is undeniable in terms of their moral standards and skill in martial arts. Yet the samurai cannot simply dismiss the bandits as the dregs of society—not only because under different circumstances they may have to become brigands for their own survival, but also because even in their current state the samurai are as parasitic as the bandits on the farmers, the producers of rice and other staple foodstuffs. In other words, for the samurai, the bandits are their alter ego, not a simple enemy to be defeated. Diegetically, the samurai's battle against the bandits is presented as a difficult one because of the latter's overwhelming numerical advantage over the former (i.e., forty versus seven) and their possession of guns (four samurai are killed by guns, while three survive). Symbolically, however, the difficulty lies in the fact that in this battle the samurai are forced to ask who they really are and to kill part of themselves in order to defend the village.

Visual Language

The effectiveness of the scene in which Kikuchiyo confronts the six samurai and reveals what lies behind their sentimental view of the farmers' plight partly derives from Kurosawa's strategic displacement of language as a means of communicating important narrative information to the audience. As Joseph L. Anderson argues, from time to time, Kurosawa uses "speech to establish situations and to set up quick characterization but he takes every opportunity to accomplish these tasks through physical action or other visual description" (57). By making use of speech and dialogue selectively, Kurosawa succeeds in creating some of the film's most memorable scenes, in which words express far more than what they literally mean.

A simple discussion of a film's narrative without any reference to its images and sounds often ends up misinterpreting the narrative and missing the richness and complexity of what we actually see and hear. This is especially true in the case of *Seven Samurai* not only because the film problematizes the instrumentalist view of language as a mere communicative tool, but more importantly because it develops its own distinct visual vocabulary and nonverbal codes as more than just stylistic play or formal embellishment.

Visually speaking, perhaps the most important feature of *Seven Samurai* is its treatment of spatial relations as a form of visual language. For instance, the highly self-conscious use of the contrast between the foreground and the background forcefully articulates what is at stake in a given scene. A striking example of the juxtaposition of two planes in screen space appears in the scene in which Kanbei agrees to defend the village against the bandits. Although he sympathizes with the farmers and even is intrigued by tactical aspects of the assignment, Kanbei gives an indirect refusal to the farmers' request, giving several reasons for refusing, including his advancing age and his weariness of war. Especially when no material reward is promised except free meals, risking one's life does not make much sense for Kanbei or, for that matter, for any other unemployed samurai. When he hears Kanbei's answer, unable to control his feeling of utter disappointment, Rikichi starts crying. Watching this, one of the laborers, who has been observing the scene, derides the farmers and their miserable existence by comparing it unfavorably to a dog's life. Katsushiro scolds the laborer for being insensitive, yet quickly learns his own limited power as a merely sympathetic bystander. The laborer challenges Kanbei and Katsushiro by shouting that sympathy without action means nothing to the suffering farmers. He then grabs a bowl of rice from Yohei and, while thrusting it at Kanbei, says that rice may not seem particularly valuable to the samurai, but it means a great deal to the farmers who eat only millet. On hearing the laborer's desperate plea, Kanbei takes the bowl from him and tells the farmers, "I won't waste this bowl of rice." When Kanbei says this, he is actually out of frame. The shot is instead dominated by the bowl of rice in the foreground's center. In the lower left side of the foreground, Kanbei's right arm and hand holding the bowl can be seen. In the background, against the wall, stand from left to right Mosuke, Rikichi, and Manzo. Diegetically speaking, what happens here is simply that Kanbei agrees to help the farmers to defend their village from the bandits' attack. Yet, what is more important is the crystalline shot of the bowl of rice in the foreground and the three farmers in the background: it saves the scene from becoming merely an occasion for expressing sentimental emotion. The indirectness of Kanbei's expression and the conspicuously geometric shot composition together help to make the audience realize that what is at stake is not just one samurai's personal decision but the historical destinies of the three groups—samurai, farmers, and bandits—which are closely tied to the question of who finally gains control of rice, which Kurosawa foregrounds in this shot.

The contrast between the foreground and the background is not always as static as in this scene. By introducing movement into a shot with multiple planes, Kurosawa transforms the flat surface of the screen into a genuinely cinematic space of pure kinetic energy and graphic tension. The beginning of the farmers' unsuccessful recruitment sequence is a particularly good example, showing Kurosawa's remarkably creative use of movement as a dynamic component of cinematic space. Rikichi, Manzo, Mosuke, and Yohei have just arrived in town and are looking for "hungry samurai" as the village patriarch Gisaku has suggested. Yet, the four farmers from a mountainous village seem utterly out of place in an urban space bustling with life, and they have of course no ability to pick out good samurai among so many walking on the street. The bewilderment of the farmers and the hustle and bustle of the town are not indicated by dialogue nor represented by a conventional combination of an (panoramic) establishing shot and closer views of the urban environment. Instead, Kurosawa constructs a complex montage of twelve shots, whose beginning and end are marked by wipes; through the lateral movement of people on multiple planes, tight shot composition, and panning of the camera, Kurosawa effectively articulates the farmers' confusion and the energy of an anonymous crowd. Except for the first shot, the scene consists of a series of shot/reverse-shots, i.e., the alternation of a close-up of the farmers intently watching samurai walking along a street and a medium close-up of the samurai they are watching. Kurosawa maximizes the sense of speed and confusion by using a telephoto lens throughout the scene and by putting moving obstacles in the frame. Because of the telephoto lens, the distance between the foreground and the background is collapsed, and the shots seem extremely cramped and abstract, without clear markers of depth, which can help the audience to situate what they see in a larger diegetic space. The sense of confusion is further accentuated by people constantly walking not only behind but also in front of the farmers laterally in both directions. The use of a long focal-length lens (i.e., a telephoto lens) makes any lateral movement on the screen seem exaggeratedly fast. When a samurai is shown in a reverse shot, the camera pans to follow his movement and keep him at the center of the shot. These following shots make it easy for the audience to see the object of the farmers' looks, the samurai, yet the panning movement of the camera exaggerates the speed of other moving people in the foreground and background, who enter and leave the screen space in a split second. Throughout the scene, there is no dialogue, and the cramped and confusing shots do not reveal any useful information about the town, such as its size and location. Thus, these twelve shots powerfully show the farmers' confusion and ineptitude in a dramatically different environment characterized by an anonymous crowd, speed, and dynamic energy, which are all absent in their native village.

Nation as an Impossible Community

Seven Samurai does not reproduce but only represents the Japanese warring-states period on the screen. No matter how realistic it may appear, Seven Samurai does not show an actual past. This is an obvious fact to those who know Japanese history, yet the distinction between the reproduction and the representation of history is not always respected in critical writings on the film. Whereas in Japan Seven Samurai is often criticized for its alleged historical misrepresentation or inaccuracy, in the United States many critics discuss the film as if it directly dealt with the social reality of sixteenth-century Japan. History exists in Seven Samurai only as a mediated intertext, not as some explicitly represented or self-evident content, as some have seen in the social relationships among and within the three distinct groups of characters—farmers, samurai, and bandits. Stephen Prince writes that "Kambei [sic] tells the [farmers] that everyone must work together as a group and that those who think only of themselves will destroy themselves and all others" because "the material of the past discloses no spaces in which the individual can move, no spaces not already inhabited by groups and their demands" (210). Prince attempts to explain the power of a social group over its members by using the notion of the "interactionist self"; that is, in the social space of sixteenth-century Japan, a self did not exist as an autonomous individual but as an effect of interaction among members of a self-contained group. But there is no need to exoticize Japanese history by emphasizing Japan's alleged collectivism. *Seven Samurai* is after all a war film, and Kanbei simply teaches the farmers how a modern military battle should be fought.

A noted Japanese scholar, Kuwabara Takeo, argues that *Seven Samurai* creates a misleading impression of Japan's warring-states period by depicting farmers as servile and craven. The boundary between samurai and farmers was actually much more fluid, and farmers sometimes fought in battles as common foot soldiers. Nor did masterless samurai see themselves as complete outsiders to farming culture, so that, according to Kuwabara, if *Seven Samurai* were a real story, at the end of the film Kanbei and Katsushiro would probably stay in the village as its new leader and the husband of a village girl, Shino, respectively.

Kuwabara's speculation may be right or wrong, but the important thing is that even for those audiences who are not familiar with the historical reality of the Japanese middle ages, the film's ending seems unsettling or puzzling. *Seven Samurai* concludes with what are arguably the most famous words of Kanbei: "Again we are defeated. The winners are those farmers. Not us." What do these words really mean? How does Kanbei's mysterious remark affect the audience's understanding of the film as a whole? In what sense are the samurai defeated when all of the bandits are killed by the joint forces of the samurai and the farmers? It is obvious that without the samurai's help the farmers would have had to give almost all of their newly harvested barley to the bandits and perhaps even give up a young woman as the bandits' sexual slave to save themselves from starvation. The samurai, together with the farmers, are clearly the winners in the military battles against the bandits. Then, in what other battle do the samurai emerge as the losers?

What initially connects the samurai and the villagers is the bowl of rice Kanbei accepts in the recruitment sequence. A laborer accuses Kanbei of being a sympathetic yet ultimately ignorant bystander who does not understand the significance of a bowl of rice. When he hears this accusation, which is also a desperate plea for help, Kanbei changes his mind and agrees to defend the village; that is, he thinks that he finally understands what the bowl of rice represents. Yet what the last scene of the film reveals is precisely that Kanbei did not quite understand what was at stake in the defense of the village until the end. The villagers were not interested simply in defeating the bandits; that is, their primary goal is not to win the battles but to defend the village, which holds an irreplaceable significance in their daily lives. This is why, for instance, Mosuke and three other families are initially so upset about Kanbei's decision to sacrifice their homes for strategic reasons, and also why, instead of abandoning his own house, Gisaku chooses to stay even if as a result he is killed by the bandits. In other words, what underlies the farmers' decision to hire samurai to defend their village is their attachment to their land and their home. The successful achievement of this ideal is vividly represented in the film's last sequence. Against the backdrop of the peaceful countryside, the villagers collectively plant rice seedlings. They all look cheerful and self-assured; Rikichi sings a festive work song to the accompaniment of a flute and drums, and women rhythmically plant seedlings in sync with the music. The scene shows a happy image of harmony between work and play and the unity of the village whose identity and cohesiveness emerge through the collective act of labor and attachment to the land. Because rice is often regarded as a Japanese national symbol, it is not difficult to see the village in this last scene as an image of the Japanese nation. Of course, such an image of national identity is always an ideological construct, and *Seven Samurai* presents the village-nation as an organic unity by suppressing the principles of realism. In reality, although they would have no need for samurai for the time being, the villagers still would not be living an idyllic life without any worry. Just one victory over a group of bandits would not guarantee the long-term security of the village, which would still remain vulnerable to the threat of other bandits and military campaigns. By concealing the continuing possibility of violence and destruction, *Seven Samurai* shows a romanticized image of the nation as an organic community, which probably exists only as a utopian construct.

The three remaining samurai, Kanbei, Katsushiro, and Shichiroji, watch the scene of the villagers' festive labor from afar. The peace and harmony of the village as a farming community are now restored, and precisely because of the success of the mission, the three samurai, who have neither ties to the land nor the ability to work as farmers, are absolutely excluded from this community. Though defenders of the village (and, by extension, national) ideal at any cost, they have no home to return to and suffer from a permanent state of alienation. They are excluded from the image of the nation as an organic unity. Yet they are not, in the end, alone. The organic community of the farmers is a fragile, temporary one, just as an originating myth of the Japanese nation shown as the unity of land and people has never been a historical reality. If, as Kanbei admits, the samurai are the losers, so are the farmers. *Seven Samurai* presents a powerful allegory of the birth of a nation only to finally dismantle the possibility of a national collective as a harmonious unity.

Conclusion

Seven Samurai breaks many genre conventions of the period film (*jidaigeki*) prevalent until the early 1950s. At the same time, however, it is frequently regarded or criticized as the most representative—that is, the best yet most typical—work of this genre. Many are awed by its dynamic montage and the geometric precision of its composition, while others find the film's plot and structure too mechanical and formalistic. Kanbei's last remark ("Again we are defeated . . .") has also been interpreted in diametrically opposed ways, as an instance of either a sentimental romanticization of the farmers or an elitist condescension toward the farmers. In short, *Seven Samurai* is a profoundly paradoxical film that resists any univocal interpretation or analysis. Yet it is precisely because of its paradoxical features that *Seven Samurai* continues to fascinate viewers. It poses questions not only of what constitutes an epic film, but whether a film can ultimately present a coherent image of a national collective.

Credits

Japan, 1954, Toho

Director: Kurosawa Akira
Producer: Motogi Sojiro
Screenplay: Kurosawa Akira, Hashimoto Shinobu, and Oguni Hideo
Cinematography: Nakai Asakazu
Editing: Iwashita Koichi
Music: Hayasaka Fumio
Sound Recording: Yanoguchi Fumio
Art Direction: Matsuyama Takashi
Sound Effects: Minawa Ichiro

CAST:

Shimada Kanbei	Shimura Takashi
Kikuchiyo	Mifune Toshiro
Gorobei	Inaba Yoshio
Kyuzo	Miyaguchi Seiji
Heihachi	Chiaki Minoru
Shichiroji	Kato Daisuke
Katsushiro	Kimura Isao
Gisaku	Kodo Kokuten
Manzo	Fujiwara Kamatari
Shino	Shino Keiko
Yohei	Hidari Bokuzen
Mosuke	Kosugi Yoshio
Rikichi	Tsuchiya Yoshio
Blind lute player	Kamiyama Sojin

Bibliography

Anderson, Joseph L. "When the Twain Meet: Hollywood's Remake of *The Seven Samurai.*" *Film Quarterly* 15.3 (1962): 55–58.

Bock, Audie. *Japanese Film Directors.* Tokyo: Kodansha International, 1978.

Burch, Noël. "Akira Kurosawa." *Cinema: A Critical Dictionary.* Ed. Richard Roud. Vol. 2. New York: Viking, 1980. 571–82.

———. *To the Distant Observer: Form and Meaning in the Japanese Cinema.* Berkeley: U of California P, 1979.

Cardullo, Bert. "The Circumstance of the East, the Fate of the West: Notes, Mostly on *The Seven Samurai.*" *Literature/Film Quarterly* 13.2 (1985): 112–17.

Chang, Kevin K. W., ed. *Kurosawa: Perceptions on Life, an Anthology of Essays.* Honolulu: Honolulu Academy of Arts, 1991.

Desser, David. *The Samurai Films of Akira Kurosawa.* Ann Arbor: UMI Research, 1983.

Goodwin, James. *Akira Kurosawa and Intertextual Cinema.* Baltimore: Johns Hopkins UP, 1994.

———, ed. *Perspectives on Akira Kurosawa.* New York: G. K. Hall, 1994.

Kaplan, Frederick. "A Second Look: Akira Kurosawa's *Seven Samurai.*" *Cineaste* 10 (1979–80): 42+.

Kida Jun'ichiro. "*Shichinin no samurai*: Tsuso Teion." *Kurosawa Akira shusei.* Vol. 1. Tokyo: Kinema Junpasha, 1989.

Kurosawa Akira. "*Seven Samurai*" and Other Screenplays. London: Faber, 1992.

———. *Something Like an Autobiography.* Trans. Audie E. Bock. New York: Vintage, 1983.

Kuwabara Takeo. "*Shichinin no samurai.*" *Kaizo* June 1954: 132–34.

Nolletti, Arthur, Jr., and David Desser, eds. *Reframing Japanese Cinema: Authorship, Genre, History.* Bloomington: Indiana UP, 1992.

Prince, Stephen. *The Warrior's Camera: The Cinema of Akira Kurosawa.* Princeton: Princeton UP, 1999.

Richie, Donald. *The Films of Akira Kurosawa.* 3rd ed. Berkeley: U of California P, 1998.

Sato Tadao. *Kurosawa Akira no sekai.* Tokyo: Asahi Shinbunsha, 1986.

Tada Michitaro. "The Destiny of Samurai Films." *East-West Film Journal* 1.1 (1986): 48–58.

Tarkovsky, Andrey. *Sculpting in Time: Reflections on the Cinema.* Trans. Kitty Hunter-Blair. New York: Knopf, 1987.

Yoshimoto Mitsuhiro. *Kurosawa: Film Studies and Japanese Cinema.* Durham: Duke UP, 2000.

Pather Panchali (1955)

NEEPA MAJUMDAR

From Neorealism to Melodrama

Context

Satyajit Ray's *Pather Panchali* (*Song of the Road,* 1955) is the first film of the so-called Apu trilogy based on Bibhutibhushan Bandopadhyay's Bengali-language novel of the same title published in India in 1929. It was one of the earliest independent films to be made entirely outside the circuit of commercial film production in India, and the story of its making has become an inextricable part of the film's reception. The financial obstacles encountered by the then amateur Ray, his experience watching Jean Renoir at work filming *The River* (1951) in India, and his eventual international success have lent support to auteurist readings of the Apu trilogy. After a two-year period, Ray eventually completed the film with financial support from the West Bengal state government, which is now the copyright holder of the film. Whether by coincidence or design, West Bengal's Department of Roads became the source of funding for this film titled *Song of the Road.*

    Pather Panchali offers a useful example of cross-cultural reception and the meanings that different audiences invest in films. It was a winner in the category of "Best Human Document" at the Cannes Film Festival in 1956 and was the second Indian film to be recognized at Cannes, the first being *Do bigha zamin* (*Two Acres of Land,* Bimal Roy, 1953) in 1954. Yet it was the first film to put India on the international cinematic map. Until recently, Satyajit Ray and the Apu trilogy were often the only cinematic associations by which India was known in the West, even though India had already become the world's largest producer of films by the 1950s. With an Academy Award for lifetime achievement at the end of his career in 1992 and the Cannes award at the beginning, Satyajit Ray has been defined more by his international reception than by his national significance in India.

The Auteurist Approach

Over the decades since 1956, the approach to *Pather Panchali* in both India and the West has been auteurist, with every study focusing on continuities and changes in Ray's vision and style and remarking on the place of the Apu trilogy in the entire body of his work. It is difficult to see the trilogy in any other way, given the circumstances of its production outside the mainstream, the prolific writings of its director, and the film's reception in Europe at a time when the category of "art cinema" was emerging in connection with the spread of film societies and film festivals worldwide. Ray himself was cofounder of the Calcutta Film Society in 1947, which became a conduit for films outside the mainstream of Hollywood and Indian commercial cinema. Despite significant differences among specific films labeled as "art films," the category of "art cinema" assumes seriousness, personal vision, and an alternative aesthetics, all of which dovetail easily into the auteurist approach that became increasingly commonplace in the 1960s (Nowell-Smith 569). Thus, for example, Satyajit Ray has been placed, alongside directors such as Ingmar Bergman and Kurosawa Akira, in the category of "art cinema," rather than Indian cinema, in a recent film history textbook (Sklar 305–6).

As Ashish Rajadhyaksha points out, it was Ray's early films, including the Apu trilogy, that became the basis in the West "for the notion of a 'Ray movie' that would remain remarkably fixed, whatever the film under discussion" (32). The following *Newsweek* quote might stand in for any Ray film reviewed in the West, while also pointing to the tendency of critics, when confronted with Ray's work, to wax eloquent at the expense of analysis: "Ray's genius is for the lyrical, for the contemplation of life as a blend of material and spiritual beauty" (qtd. in Rajadhyaksha 32). Following an auteurist approach, most readings of Ray and the Apu trilogy emphasize certain recurrent concerns in his work, such as his interest in social transformations from rural to urban and from feudal to modern, often rooted specifically in turn-of-the-century concerns; in shorthand, "Ray's great theme is change" (Nyce 3). The emphasis on lyricism, poetry, and humanism in the "Ray movie" also ends up ignoring the satiric and humorous elements in his films, elements whose flavor comes from a similar sensibility at work in the children's magazine *Sandesh*, started by Ray's grandfather and revived by Ray in the 1960s.

Authenticity and Expectations

Films from unfamiliar cultures often must bear the burden of representing more than just their individual characters, dramatic situations, and locations. In the absence of any other images of a foreign culture, every image and action in a single film might unwittingly come to stand in for the entire culture and are "instantly generalized as typical. . . . Representations thus become allegorical; within hegemonic discourse, every subaltern performer/role is seen as synecdochically summing up a vast but putatively homogenous community. Representations of dominant groups, on the other hand, are seen not as allegorical but as 'naturally' diverse" (Shohat and Stam 182). Furthermore, the reception of non-Western films is frequently marked by the unspoken ethnographic expectation of being afforded a voyeuristic look into "native" cultures as seen through native eyes. For Paolo Chiozzi, for example, "the value [of African cinema] as an ethno-anthropological document is without question" (11). David MacDougall notes that "the 'foreignness' of a film may . . . have a bearing on the ethnographic qualities which we attribute to it. To Western eyes *Pather Panchali* has the force of a cultural document, yet because it was not made by a Westerner, its ethnographic content is implicit" (137). Ironically, Ray himself was fully aware of such appropriations of his work in the West: "There is no reason why we should not cash in on the foreigner's curiosity about the Orient. But this does not mean pandering to their love of the false exotic" (42).

To a certain extent, the allegorical function of unfamiliar locations might enter even the films themselves. In the Apu trilogy, the village of Nishchintipur becomes a representative, rather than unique, place. For example, in the second film of the trilogy, *Aparajito* (*The Unvanquished*, 1957), even though Apu and his mother return to a different village after his father's death, the first glimpse of this new village is greeted with the theme music associated with the village in *Pather Panchali*, functioning for the viewer (and the characters) as a cue to a return to an already known place. Similarly, when Apu pauses at the sound of a train, the *mise-en-scène* reinforces the impression of the sameness of rural Bengal. While Western viewers might be tempted to read any Indian film as representative of all of India, urban Indian viewers (and filmmakers such as Satyajit Ray) might be similarly inclined to view any filmic Indian village as representative of all of rural India.

The issue of the representation of poverty in *Pather Panchali* is at the heart of both Western and Indian responses to the film. Contemporary Western reviews were marked by an aesthetic response to poverty, framed in terms of visual poetics, beauty, and universal humanism, which T. G. Vaidyanathan critiques as the "strained and positively gory aestheticism that results in a complete failure to engage seriously with the moral intentions of the film" (137). In contrast, like Vaidyanathan, Chidananda Dasgupta finds the "poverty in the trilogy, especially *Pather Panchali*, grim, unadorned, real. . . . Yet how different it is from the antheaps of Louis Malle! The poor are no statistic here" (44). Although Dasgupta and other critics regard the film's strength to be precisely its unsentimental look at poverty, the overall Indian response has been more conflicted. Typical of a general reaction in India to Ray's international status is the famous and controversial diatribe against *Pather Panchali* by Nargis, the popular Indian star-turned-politician who attacked Ray's films in the Indian parliament in 1980, charging him with betraying his country by selling images of Indian poverty to the West.

The representation of rural poverty is related to questions of authenticity and the vexed issue of realism in the cinema. Paradoxically, the aesthetic response to *Pather Panchali* combines easily with its opposite, which is the expectation of a documentary representation of India in the film. For Western reviewers such as Lindsay Anderson, the film performs an ethnographic function as a window onto an authentic "Indian," as opposed to a Bengali, village: "To make *Pather Panchali*, Ray must have lived as closely with his characters as Flaherty had to live with his Polynesians, when he made *Moana*." Ironically, Anderson is right insofar as Ray himself admitted to being alienated enough from rural Bengal to feel the need to immerse himself in rural experience before starting to film (Ray 33). For Indian reviewers, questions of authenticity are invariably understood in terms of an implicit difference from mainstream Indian film. Niranjan Majumdar, who reviewed the film when it came out, saw *Pather Panchali* as "the first Indian film which is Indian in every inch," presenting a "truer picture of life in an Indian village than any we have seen" (111), presumably in more conventional Indian films.

Reactions in India
In India, not only has Ray's image changed over time, but he is regarded differently in his native Bengal than in the rest of the country.

While *Pather Panchali* was received in the international context as art cinema, no such separate category existed in India at the time. Rather, as Ashish Rajadhyaksha notes, the early reception of Ray in India placed *Pather Panchali* in the context of postindependence Indian artists such as the members of the Indian Peoples' Theatre Association (IPTA), whose work moved away from a "pre-War emphasis on village-craft indigenism," expressing instead their link to the "industrial programme and to the theme of nation-building" closely aligned with the technological optimism and socialist ideals of independent India's first prime minister, Jawaharlal Nehru (34).[1] Such artists included Khwaja Ahmad Abbas, whose *Dharti ke lal* (*Children of the Earth*, 1946) was, for Satyajit Ray, an example of "rare glimpses of an enlightened approach in a handful of recent [Indian] films" (23).

An aspect of Ray's work that has been central to his reception in Bengal, but is generally overlooked elsewhere, is his popular film and detective series aimed at a juvenile audience.[2] This long-term commitment to children's film and literature (as a writer and illustrator) left its mark on Ray's other films as well. In *Pather Panchali*, for example, the sequence of nature shots heralding the start of the monsoon rains has been typically received as central evidence of Ray's visual poetics, but such a reception has often obscured the characteristically *Sandesh*-style witticism with which this sequence opens as it focuses on the first drop of rain splashing on the unsuspecting bald head of a dozing man. This is one of many instances of the fluid shifting of emotional registers, from children's magazine-style humor to a poetic evocation of the Bengal countryside drawn from the novel. Likewise, visually and in its sound track, the first appearance of the sweet vendor also belongs to the world of *Sandesh*, with the initial framing of the final shot focused on a pair of waddling geese whose steps match the rhythm of the music and lead the procession of the sweet vendor and two children.

By the 1970s, Ray's reputation in India had declined significantly, partly in response to the ongoing international celebration of his work to the exclusion of all other cinematic products from India

---

[1]India won independence from British colonial rule in 1947.

[2]For example, the Goopy and Bagha film series—e.g., *Goopy Gyne Bagha Byne* (*The Adventures of Goopy and Bagha*, 1968)—and the Felu-da mystery series, some of which Ray made into films. Many of these stories originally appeared in the Ray family's children's magazine, *Sandesh*.

(Rajadhyaksha 32). In the early 1970s, "art cinema," or "parallel cinema," became established as a separate category in Indian cinema, with a growing number of alternative filmmakers defining their work in terms of social and political commitment. The critique of Ray at this time centered around the perceived absence of any social analysis of poverty in his work. Subsequently, there was a "demand on Ray to turn more Indian" and "to be more socially relevant" (Nandy 43). The discomfort with Ray among Indian intellectuals also came from the fact that he himself characterized his work in terms of the universal humanism by which he had been received in the West, as when, for example, he stated that he "chose *Pather Panchali* for the qualities that made it a great book: its humanism, its lyricism, and its ring of truth" (33). The social analysis that does in fact occur in the Apu trilogy was thus underplayed equally by those who celebrated the "Ray movie" and by those who critiqued it.

Commercial Indian Cinema/Entertainment

The vast body of Indian commercial cinema is usually associated with the Hindi-language films produced in Bombay, which actually account for only approximately 20 percent of India's total output of films, the rest coming from various regional-language commercial film industries in other parts of the country. But in terms of their formal characteristics, popularity across India, and box-office returns, Bombay films have been the implicit (and usually negatively viewed) norm against which all Indian cinematic practice has been viewed. The 1950s saw the consolidation of the Bombay film "formula," which offers not just a story and stars, but an all-inclusive entertainment that includes something for everyone in the audience: songs, dances, fights, romance, stunts, and comedy packaged in a melodramatic narrative form that privileges moral polarities, coincidence, and multiple subplots. Given the commercial imperative of distributing Hindi films among non-Hindi-speaking viewers across India, Bombay films came to rely on spectacle and often conveyed psychological and narrative information through specifically cinematic means. For example, in the film *Zanjeer* (*The Chain,* Prakash Mehra, 1973), visual techniques convey a climactic moment of recognition when the hero realizes that the man he has associated with is the murderer of his father: point-of-view shots of a talisman around the villain's wrist are combined with emphatic zooms, dramatic music, and rapid shot/reverse shots of the talisman and the hero's eyes as an adult and as a child witnessing the murder and noticing the talisman. The hallmark of Bombay cinema's melodramatic form is the transfer of inner psychological and moral realities onto externalized icons, such as the talisman in this example, whose meaning is immediately legible. Until recently, critics had negatively emphasized the melodramatic aspects of Bombay films, often overlooking their efficient use of the cinematic medium to convey meaning.

Like other intellectuals in India, Ray found few redeeming qualities in the mainstream commercial cinema coming out of Bombay or even the regional commercial cinema in his part of India, Bengal. His critique of Indian cinema in his 1948 essay "What Is Wrong with Indian Films?" points to his own preferences. He opposes commercial cinema's "penchant for the convolutions of plot and counter-plot" with "strong, simple unidirectional narrative" (23). Most of all, Ray complains about the visual dissonance of commercial cinema (22–23) and its propensity toward melodrama, which he sees as resulting from a confusion of movement (which is basic to the cinematic medium) with action and action with melodrama (21). In his writings and cinematic practice, Ray unquestionably defined himself against Bombay film, as evidenced in another essay, "Film Making" (1965), in which he writes that "coexisting with [his] admiration for the best of Hollywood was a growing despair with the uncinematic methods displayed in the home-grown product" (49). However, despite his dislike of Bombay films, Ray did not see himself at the time of making *Pather Panchali* as an "art" filmmaker, but rather as a "serious commercial filmmaker" (39). Such a self-definition also appears in *Pather Panchali,* in the father's ambitions as a playwright of original, rather than formulaic, plays that will gain a popular following.

"Realism" in the cinema and cultural "authenticity" are closely related in that both appear to be universally understood and natural, when in fact they are the product of conventions and specific historical and cultural configurations. "Realism," for instance, is the effect of certain stylistic choices that have come to be associated with the "real." Some of these techniques include location filming, natural lighting, and the use of unknown actors. Ray, like others in postindependence India, faulted Bombay films in terms of both realism and authentic "Indianness." For example, in his view, both realism and cultural authenticity are violated in Bombay cinema's "habit of shooting indoors [i.e., in the studio] in a country which is all landscape [i.e., location filming]" (42). Defining his own work against such practices, Ray says of *Pather Panchali* that its authenticity came from both stylistic choices and subject matter. In narrative form, for example, his film retained the "rambling quality of the novel" because "life in a poor Bengali village does ramble" (33). In terms of subject matter, Ray felt "obliged morally and artistically to make films that have their roots in the soil of our province" (42).

In keeping with Ray's negative views on mainstream Indian cinema, the Apu trilogy prominently features non-cinematic forms of entertainment. *Pather Panchali* invests considerable screen time in showcasing rural attractions ranging from Bengali folk theater, or *jatra*, to the music of the wedding band (playing "It's a Long Way to Tipperary") to traveling vendors with optical devices that function as a vicarious form of tourism. In the second film, *Aparajito*, Apu's alienation from his rural identity is measured in terms of his jaded response to the same village entertainments that had enthralled him earlier in *Pather Panchali*. Although such entertainments may seem to be more "traditional" and authentically Indian than the commercial cinema coming out of Bombay, historically these two kinds of entertainment are closely related. It is widely known, for example, that the prototype for Bombay films were folk theaters such as the Bengali *jatra* or the Marathi *tamasha*, in addition to the urban Parsi theater. It can also be argued that village entertainments are no more culturally "pure" than the Bombay film. Both categories of entertainment are hybrid forms that draw on various Indian, Western, rural, and urban sources. In *Pather Panchali*, examples of hybrid cultural forms are the music played by the rural wedding band and the Western optical technology used to feature places of Indian interest.

Analysis

From Neorealism to Melodrama

In 1953, Cesare Zavattini, screenwriter and theorist of Italian neorealism, wrote, "A blow struck for the cinema in Rome could have repercussions all over the world" (55). *Ladri di biciclette* (*Bicycle Thieves,*

Vittorio De Sica, 1948), which was screened at India's first International Film Festival, in Calcutta in 1951, had an enormous impact on filmmakers in India such as Bimal Roy (e.g., *Do bigha zamin*) and Raj Kapoor (e.g., *Awaara* [*The Vagabond,* 1951]). Ray saw it earlier in London and he "knew immediately that if [he] ever made *Pather Panchali* . . . [he] would make it in the same way, using natural locations and unknown actors" (9). When Indian reviewers invoked Italian neorealism in praising Ray's film, there was a similar emphasis on filmmaking practice as the basis for evaluating the authenticity of location and acting. Yet, *Pather Panchali* arguably also shares other aspects of Italian neorealism, such as the goal of not merely representing poverty but also analyzing it and the equation of the everyday with the dramatic (Zavattini 51–52).

As a corollary to understanding *Pather Panchali* in terms of Italian neorealism, critics have read Ray's work as going against the melodramatic means of representation employed in Bombay films. Suranjan Ganguly, for example, writes, "The Apu trilogy, it could be argued, is the first work of the Indian cinema that shifts the emphasis from exteriority to interiority," by which he means an investment in the inner subjectivity of "psychological realism." For Ganguly and other critics, "Ray tells Apu's story not within a melodramatic framework, but in terms of an evolving male consciousness" (11). While Ray's cinematic style certainly favors understatement as opposed to melodrama, one could equally argue that the Apu trilogy shares with mainstream Indian cinema the avoidance of spoken words in favor of visual images, thereby opening the way for a non-Bengali audience.

For instance, the scene of Durga's death taps into the same repository of associations from which commercial Bombay cinema would also draw. This scene can be read as toying with the Indian viewer's expectations based on conditioned responses in commercial cinema. The melodramatic ingredients are there: night, the storm, lightning flashes, point-of-view shots of meaningful details such as the rattling door bolt and the lamp flame, the camera slowly moving in to the unsteady statue of Ganesh.[3] While the film avoids actually blowing out the flame or toppling the Ganesh shrine, as might be expected in an overtly symbolic representation of death, the emotion of the moment

---

[3]Fittingly, Ganesh is the god who is both the remover and the placer of obstacles.

is nonetheless transferred onto external objects charged with religious and cultural meaning as it draws on the connection between the rain of this scene and the rain of the scene that initiated Durga's death. In this sequence as in others, *Pather Panchali*, like Bombay cinema, transfers emotion and meaning onto certain recurrent external icons. Yet, the film also reigns in the symbolic meaning of such scenes by anchoring them in the materiality of the everyday, as for example when the storm of the night of Durga's death remains a visual presence the following morning in a high-angle pan over the devastated courtyard, with a dead frog prominent in the foreground. Another significant example of *Pather Panchali*'s technique of transferring emotion onto objects is in the scene of Harihar's return home after the death of Durga. His list of presents is sufficient to signify the loss. Even more painful than the wedding sari for Durga is the misplaced joy with which he brings out the framed image of the goddess Lakshmi, who is associated with both wealth and home.

Narrative/Framing/Social Analysis

Despite its literary source, *Pather Panchali*, like much of mainstream Indian cinema, employs predominantly visual, rather than verbal, forms of narration. Its visual strategies are often in tandem with the indirect mode of narration that structures the film from one sequence to the next, from one shot to the next, and sometimes even in the mobile framing of individual shots. This oblique mode of narration works by presenting, in effect, an analysis of the events being represented. In *Pather Panchali*, social analysis is made characteristically at the familial and individual levels. For example, the indirect narration with which the film opens effectively presents the power hierarchies that structure the lives of this impoverished Bengali Brahmin family.

There are two parts to the opening sequence. The first part begins with a low-angle shot of the rich woman whose words frame and introduce both Durga and her mother. But this first section is dominated by shots of Durga stealing guava fruit, privileging the point of view of childhood and the visual over the verbal. Such moments celebrating childhood punctuate the entire film and account for the "lyricism" and humanist optimism in the face of poverty that critics have celebrated in the film. The full narrative meaning of Durga's theft is withheld and becomes apparent only in the second part of the opening sequence, which starts with a medium shot of Durga's mother at the well as she is defined and literally put in her place by the offscreen railing voice of the wealthy relative. Centered around the stolen fruit, the insults with which the film opens are then transferred from mother to daughter, and then to the old aunt (Pishi), ending in the shot of Pishi's bundle being dropped on the kitten, who comes at the end of this chain of transferred insults. This chain of oppression from wealthy landowner to domestic animals establishes the social and domestic networks of power relations in which every character, including animals, is placed, producing, in effect, an analysis of rural exploitation.

A further meaning to Durga's theft is saved for later in the film, when a conversation between her parents reveals to us that the theft was not really a theft after all, since the orchard had originally belonged to Durga's family and was stolen from them. This scenario of impoverishment of the landed gentry in rural India is a familiar one in Indian literature and film, pointing to the migration from village to city with which *Pather Panchali* ends. The film also frames this loss of land in terms of another familiar opposition in Bengali fiction, between aesthetic and commercial worldviews, between the poet-playwright father and his business-minded relatives.

In a narrative that privileges the everyday over the dramatic, such a mode of narration, which initially withholds information, serves to invest the everyday with drama, while providing social and emotional commentary. The framing in individual shots also follows a pattern of indirect narration. When Durga is sick, the shot of her final conversation with Apu cuts to a long shot of the sweet seller in the distance. Following the conversation between Durga and Apu about going to see trains, this shot appears initially to continue in the same emotional register of childhood pleasures. But the actual meaning of its initial framing is withheld until the camera pulls back to reveal the sweet seller framed in a window and then tilts down from the window to rest on a medium shot of Durga lying listless and barely conscious on the bed. Here, the oblique framing works to recontextualize the meaning of the sweet seller and sharpens the emotional resonance of Durga's illness by drawing on the viewer's memory of the previous appearance of this vendor in their village.

Another instance in which the framing withholds meaning, this time to satiric effect, is in the scene with the grocer who doubles as the village schoolteacher. The initial medium shot of the grocer excludes his pupils from the frame so that his words cannot immediately be understood as dictation to his students. This shot then cuts to a boy in the foreground holding his ears, a classic form of punishment in Bengal, which, together with the grocer-schoolteacher, strongly evokes the visual flavor of the stories and drawings in Bengali children's literature. In this long take, the camera leisurely tilts down to show us the other boys goofing around. The sequence ends with the use of offscreen sound to signify the abuse of authority. On-screen, the face of the grocer-schoolteacher is accompanied by the offscreen sounds of his cane hitting the boy, a sound that carries across the cut into the next shot.

The aural equivalent to oblique narrative and framing techniques is the frequent use of offscreen sound. As with the film's first shot of Sarbojaya, *Pather Panchali* consistently uses offscreen sound to signal a controlling voice and to render what we see more vulnerable, such as a shot of Durga tugging on old Pishi's hand to try to stop her from leaving, while Sarbojaya's offscreen voice scolds Durga for doing so. This technique is used to represent benevolent authority as well, as in the shot that shows Pishi begging her other relative, Raju, to take her in temporarily. In this shot, the offscreen voice of Raju, who is never seen in the film, grants her refuge in his house. Such techniques contribute to the impression of the film's understated style; yet they also constitute a mode of indirect social commentary for which Ray has rarely been credited.

A sequence that performs an implicit social analysis begins with three shots unified by the theme of wealth. The first shot shows Pishi in close-up singing a lullaby as she rocks baby Apu. The lyrics of the lullaby signify a fantasy of future wealth for the baby. In the second shot, this fantasy translates into the material wealth of childhood as we see Durga carefully counting her treasures. The third shot shows Sarbojaya cooking, and thus cuts to the heart of the family's actual economic status, which is measured in this film by the availability of food. The offscreen sound of Pishi's lullaby of fantasized wealth accompanies and comments ironically on both shots of Durga and Sarbojaya. In the rest of this sequence, Durga's parents discuss their economic future in deep-focus shots that center Pishi rocking Apu in the extreme background, thus retaining a visual reminder of her lullaby. The sequence ends as it began with a close-up of Pishi and a return to the song that punctuated it.

We see similar social commentary at work as Pishi is thrown out by Sarbojaya, the composition framing her slowly walking out in the background with a dog in the foreground occupying her hut. This shot is placed between two identical shots of Sarbojaya eating and looking offscreen. The layering of visual detail and the editing serve to comment on the hierarchies by which domestic animals, as part of the social structure, have greater value than the old woman.

Mise-en-Scène *and Memory*

Pather Panchali operates at multiple emotional registers, with a narrative pace that refuses to linger over any specific emotional moment. For instance, there is no pause for expressions of grief after Pishi's funeral, which is literally cut off by a direct edit to a shot of a village entertainer. Responding to a seeming absence of overt emotional responses in characters, critics have remarked on Ray's understated style, contrasting it with the excess of emotional expression in Bombay films. In fact, *Pather Panchali* transfers emotion from characters to the *mise-en-scène*. Through strategic repetition, objects and scenarios function as repositories of memory, acting, in effect, as memory-saturated images. The film harnesses and efficiently uses the emotional investment in memory on the part of both characters and viewers.

Along with the humming of the electric pylons, the train sequence occupies a central place in audiences' memories of *Pather Panchali*. For Ray, too, the sequence was memorable, because the first scene to be filmed was the one preceding the arrival of the train, in which Durga and Apu are in the field of *kaash* flowers. In *Our Films Their Films*, Ray describes this first day of filming in meticulous detail. It is thus a central memory both of viewers and of the filmmaker himself. While some critics have read the train sequence and the electric pylons in *Pather Panchali* as an ambivalent reference to postindependence India's vision of industrial progress, they also function in the narrative as a memory image to be drawn on later.

When Durga is sick, she promises Apu another visit to see the trains. The memory of the train sequence weighs on this scene, which in turn functions as a memory of loss in every subsequent use of trains in the Apu trilogy. In the second film, *Aparajito,* for example, when

Apu stops at the sound of a train, his initial delight gives way to a somber expression that is in no need of any explanation because the sound of the train functions as a memory trigger for the scene of his last conversation with Durga. The use of train sounds to signify loss or death continues for Ray well beyond the Apu trilogy. For example, in his 1984 film, *Ghare-Baire* (*The Home and the World*), the husband's realization of his wife's infidelity is signaled by the (nondiegetic) sound of a train over a point-of-view close-up on a spilled jar of vermillion, with its associations of failed marriage.

Not only does Ray draw on the memory of the central train sequence later in the Apu trilogy, but its significance is built up in *Pather Panchali* itself through repeated aural references that invariably connote change and loss. In one night scene, we hear the sound of a train passing as Harihar and Sarbojaya discuss the possibility of moving to the city. Here, the sound track is further layered with the offscreen voice of Pishi singing a folk song, whose lyrics are a prayer to be ferried across the river at the end of life.[4] In this layered sound track, then, the train sound accompanies a song of a death wish as well as a conversation about a major change, both of which assume significance in the narrative of the trilogy as a whole.

Scenes such as the one in which Apu is being prepared by his mother and sister for school may be read in terms of the neorealist insistence on including the nondramatic aspects of everyday life. But in the context of the film as a whole, such a scene is also an investment in memory that will be drawn on later. For example, certain details of this scene are repeated much later in the film, immediately after the death of Durga, making the shots of Apu brushing his teeth and combing his hair become charged with the memory of Durga. In the first scene, it was Durga who combed his hair, and here, as Apu himself does it, he falters and pauses, thereby immediately recalling the memory of the earlier scene. This shot of Apu brushing his teeth cuts to Sarbojaya at the well, which recalls the opening sequence so closely associated with Durga. Other instances of memory-saturated images include the stolen necklace that Apu finds at the end of the film and

---

[4]Although the song can be heard in this scene, subtitles provide a translation of the lyrics only later, in the next sequence.

the mangoes that the wealthy relative offers the family prior to their departure. The mangoes have a double mnemonic association with Durga: not only do they invoke Durga's theft, but they also "fell in the storm" that accompanied her death.

The film also draws on social memory, as for instance in the close-up shot of a stack of empty rice jars that Sarbojaya's neighbor searches through, finding only a few grains in the bottom jar. In 1955, this shot would have resonated with memories of the Bengal famine of 1943:

> In those early years after Independence [in 1947], you couldn't . . . forget what those placid paddy fields and the city of Calcutta had just been through, although few foreign reviewers ever mention it. Independence, as an event, brought to a climax a series of earlier events that had already caused a traumatic shift in the realist model: the 1943 Bengal famine; the 1946–47 Partition [of the country into two separate nations, India and Pakistan]. (Rajadhyaksha 34–35)

Such cultural memories shape more specific local meanings and work against the universalist tendencies of many responses to the film. The use of such memory-saturated images aligns *Pather Panchali* equally with the melodramatic operations that invest meaning in the external, as with the neorealist aesthetics that critics have seen in it.

Conclusion

Unlike the unfulfilled ambitions of Apu's playwright father in *Pather Panchali,* Satyajit Ray's own aspirations as a "serious commercial film-maker" were successful. Since its release in 1955, the responses to *Pather Panchali* have been variously accounted for in terms of visual poetry, ethnographic interest, authentic Indian values, universal humanism, neorealist aesthetics, and anticommercial imperatives, all themselves the effects of specific cinematic strategies in the film. Through the various debates in India around the value of the film and the West's long-standing conflation of Ray with Indian cinema as a whole, *Pather Panchali* demonstrates the shifting meanings of films as they travel across multiple contexts of reception.

Credits

India, 1955, Government of West Bengal

Director: Satyajit Ray
Screenplay: Bibhutibhushan Bandopadhyay (author of the novel) and Satyajit Ray
Cinematography: Subrata Mitra
Music: Ravi Shankar
Art Direction and Production Design: Banshi Chandragupta

CAST:

Apu	Subir Bannerjee
Little Durga	Runki Banerjee
Durga	Uma Dasgupta
Indir Pishi (old aunt)	Chunibala Devi
Harihar (father)	Kanu Bannerjee
Sarbojaya (mother)	Karuna Bannerjee

Bibliography

Anderson, Lindsay. "Panorama at Cannes." *Sight and Sound* 26.1 (1956): 16–21. 1955. Excerpt part. rpt. in Das 112.

Chiozzi, Paolo. "Reflections on Ethnographic Film with a General Bibliography." Trans. Denise Dresner. *Visual Anthropology* 2.1 (1998): 1–84.

Das, Santi, ed. *Satyajit Ray: An Intimate Master.* New Delhi: Allied, 1998.

Dasgupta, Chidananda. *The Cinema of Satyajit Ray.* New Delhi: National Book Trust, 2001.

Ganguly, Suranjan. *Satyajit Ray: In Search of the Modern.* Lanham, MD: Scarecrow, 2000.

Jaffrey, Saeed. "Memories of Ray." *Sight and Sound* 12.4 (1992): 30–31.

MacDougall, David. "Prospects of the Ethnographic Film." *Movies and Methods* Ed. Bill Nichols. Vol. I. Berkeley: U of California P, 1976. 135–50.

Majumdar, Niranjan. Rev. of *Pather Panchali,* dir. Satyajit Ray. *Hindustan Standard* [Calcutta] 2 Sept. 1955. Rpt. in Das 111–12.

Nandy, Ashis. "How 'Indian' is Ray?" *Cinemaya* 20 (1993): 40–45. <http://www.usc.edu/isd/archives/asianfilm/india/index-cin.html>.

Nowell-Smith, Geoffrey. "Art Cinema." *The Oxford History of World Cinema.* Oxford: Oxford UP, 1996. 567–75.

Nyce, Ben. *Satyajit Ray.* New York: Praeger, 1988.

Rajadhyaksha, Ashish. "Beyond Orientalism." *Sight and Sound* 12.4 (1992): 32–35.

Ray, Satyajit. *Our Films Their Films.* Calcutta: Orient Longman, 1976.

Shohat, Ella, and Robert Stam. *Unthinking Eurocentrism: Multiculturalism and the Media.* London: Routledge, 1994.

Sklar, Robert. *Film: An International History of the Medium.* 2nd ed. Englewood Cliffs: Prentice, 2002.

Vaidyanathan, T. G. *Hours in the Dark: Essays on Cinema.* Delhi, India: Oxford UP, 1996.

Zavattini, Cesare. "Some Ideas on the Cinema." *Sight and Sound* 23.2 (1953): 64–69. Rpt. in *Vittorio De Sica: Contemporary Perspectives.* Ed. Howard Curle and Stephen Snyder. Toronto: U of Toronto P, 2000. 50–61.

The Seventh Seal (1956)

MARILYN JOHNS BLACKWELL

Cinematic Form and Cultural Criticism

Context

Ingmar Bergman's virtually inarguable status as a director rests on a corpus within which *The Seventh Seal* (*Det sjunde inseglet*) occupies a privileged position, acknowledged as one of his two or three most central films. Indeed upon its release and afterward it fascinated a generation of American and European filmgoers. The film is certainly "classic" Bergman, typical at least of the first half of his career. Its serious subject matter (his detractors would say "morbid"), the assimilation of the surreal, the narrative emphasis on the psychological states of individuals in crisis, and the striking visual imagery are all hallmarks of his work. Critics argue that "Seldom has film managed to aim so high and so completely realize its ambitions" (Donner 151), and, "Stop it at almost every frame and you will find yourself looking at a striking, distinguished, and often very beautiful composition" (Wood 85). Terms like "visual splendour" (Mosley 65), "technically impeccable" (Taylor 135), and "one of the most beautiful films ever made" (Rohmer 134) drop from their pens. Jean Mambrino even goes so far as to claim that it is "the most bounteous and most unadorned work, the most complex and the most transparent, all illuminated by an exuberance of language and yet suffused with a severe silence" (50). But *The Seventh Seal* was not merely a critical success; it has also become part and parcel of our wider cultural frame of reference: verbal and visual allusions to it still reverberate throughout contemporary films and television.

The question, then, arises as to why this film in particular riveted the attention of an entire generation of filmgoers and continues to engage our cultural imagination, even though it has lost favor among many postmodernist critics who see it—and much of the rest of

Bergman's work—as iconoclastic and preoccupied with irrelevant metaphysical issues. A major impetus behind the international fascination with *The Seventh Seal* lies in the political climate of the mid-1950s. During this period the pervasive sense of despair of the postwar, post-Holocaust West, the impact of existentialist thought, and the threat of a nuclear Armageddon provided fertile ground for a film that questions whether or not there can be a divine structure in a world of death-dealing and madness, and then asks how the individual can impart significance to his or her life and act meaningfully in that world. Almost fifty years later, *The Seventh Seal* continues to exercise a hold on viewers' imaginations, less for its crystallization of metaphysical and existentialist concerns than for its stunning mergence of artistic form and content and for its representation of quite contemporary notions of subjectivity, power, and gender, for, like virtually all of Bergman's films, this one centers on the problem of a culture in extremis. Virtually all Bergman films foreground a search for meaning and for meaningful human connection, but the critical intellectual vocabulary of the last several decades allows us to see the ways in which, for Bergman, this search takes place against the background of a failed patriarchal ideology and culture.

Background

Ingmar Bergman was born into a middle-class family in which the father was a minister in the Lutheran state church who later went on to become chaplain to Sweden's royal family. Because of his father's connection with the powerful political hierarchy of both church and state, his extremely strict nineteenth-century child-rearing practices, and the young man's troubled relationship with him, Bergman has throughout his life questioned all forms of authority, one of his many points of contact with postmodernist sensibilities. Thus the director came early to acknowledge the connection between the familial and the divine father and to reject the patriarchy in all its religious, social, and political manifestations, a position that has also informed much of literary and visual criticism of the late twentieth century. Indeed, Bergman's entire production evinces a cultural criticism of the institutions of power and the ways in which these institutions impact the lives of individual human beings. The patriarchy, as both the social organizational structure and the practice of power that prevails in our culture (thus the film's relevance to contemporary viewers) is a central concern throughout Bergman's films. From the self-deluding and ultimately dethroned Fredrik who is mocked in *Smiles of a Summer Night* (*Sommarnattens leende*, 1955), through the warlike and vacuous power structures of films like *Winter Light* (*Nattvardsgästerna*, 1962) and *The Silence* (*Tystnaden*, 1963) from the early 1960s, to the brutal Bishop Edvard in Bergman's self-avowedly last film *Fanny and Alexander* (1982), his work consistently critiques the role of the patriarchy in Western culture.[1]

But his experiences as a boy growing up in the Sweden of the 1920s and early 1930s also left an indelible mark on his development. Although Sweden is justifiably renowned for its progressive leadership in the areas of political and social change, it is also an extremely conservative country in terms of interpersonal relationships that are often characterized by reserve, formality, and, many would say, coldness. Not surprisingly, then, an emphasis on openness, intimacy, and community in such relationships and a valorization of self-scrutiny and self-awareness also mark Bergman's work.

Equally important to his worldview is the fact that Sweden was industrialized quite late in comparison with other Western nations, as a result of which rural farm life lies only a generation or two in the past for most Swedes. Part and parcel of this small-town/village agrarian past are, on the one hand, cooperation and social community and, on the other, conformity and narrow-mindedness, all of which Bergman's production consistently problematizes. But the proximity of this rural past also manifests itself in Bergman's extraordinarily sensitive and evocative representation of nature, a cherished national value in Sweden.

Another aspect of Swedish culture that marks Bergman's work is the fact that women have historically enjoyed much higher legal and social status in Sweden than in virtually any other country in the world. Bergman acknowledged early in his career the ways in which male culture "others" women and their experience, an acknowledgment that leads to an assertion of the essential value of female experience. Because he sees patriarchal culture as marginalizing artists, women, and all those who threaten its autonomy by noncompliance, he identifies with women, an identification that culminated in the

---

[1]For further study of structures of the patriarchy as developing through Western civilization, see Lerner.

centrality of female alter-ego protagonists in his later films. Women like the sisters in *The Silence,* the two main characters in *Persona* (1966), and Helena in *Fanny and Alexander* are all directorial surrogates who embody the crisis of culture, identity, and gendered subjectivity that is the central concern of his post-1960 films. Thus, Bergman's relatively progressive (if at times problematic) representation of women and female values is rooted both in the culture into which he was born as well as in his understanding of dominant cultural and social institutions.

Artistically, Bergman's legacy can be traced to three major influences—the Expressionistic cinema of the 1920s (and Victor Sjöström's films in particular), the theater, and the works of Swedish playwright August Strindberg, who, along with his fellow Scandinavian Henrik Ibsen, has been dubbed the father of modern drama. The theater is a central concern throughout Bergman's life and works. Already at the age of ten, Bergman traded Christmas presents with his brother Dag in order to obtain a *laterna magica* (magic lantern), with which he played constantly. He also made a toy theater for which he wrote his own plays and also staged a number of Strindberg productions. Strindberg has remained a constant influence throughout his life, as the last lines of *Fanny and Alexander* (surely, given the fact that he considered this his last film, a "marked" positioning if ever there was one) make evident: they consist of a reading from the preface of Strindberg's influential, experimental masterpiece *Ett drömspel* (*A Dreamplay*). For over seventy years, the theater has been central both as a vocation and as a motif for Bergman; thus, from his first film in 1946 to his last in 1982, he has divided his time almost equally between the film studio and the theater. Indeed, in the early 1960s, while he was making such critically acclaimed films as *Winter Light* and *The Silence,* Bergman also worked as director of the Royal Dramatic Theater, the equivalent of Sweden's national stage. Not surprisingly, then, a preoccupation with theater, theatricality, masks, and role-playing surface in virtually all his films, and many of his protagonists are actors and actresses.

But ultimately, Bergman's biography is context, helpful perhaps, but still context. The text of his production lies in a body of work seldom paralleled for its visual sophistication and in which he grapples with many of the most important questions of both the last and the current century.

Analysis

Because of their meticulous craftsmanship, Ingmar Bergman's films almost beg for a "close-reading" approach: for careful scrutiny of the striking compositions that critics have lauded since the film appeared. But *The Seventh Seal* is by no means art for art's sake. In addition to its raising the metaphysical and existential questions that so captivated its first generation of viewers, it also problematizes a number of concerns that figure in contemporary critical and cultural debate; the whole notion of subjectivity, the extent to which it is gendered, and issues of ideology and hierarchies of power are central to twenty-first-century thought. As a result, the film retains its ability to engage viewers.

The first shot is characteristic of Bergman's work in that throughout his production no single shot, no camera angle, no composition, and no editing choice is left to chance. His cinematographer, Gunnar Fischer, and later Fischer's successor, Sven Nykvist, were both extraordinarily sensitive visual artists who partnered very effectively with the compulsively perfectionist Bergman. This opening shot sets the tonality for the entire work, as it reveals an intensively bright light crashing through dark gray clouds, an image that establishes a sharp contrast in tone and lighting that pervades the film. The Dies Irae, a medieval Latin hymn about Judgment Day, explodes on the sound track. A cut reveals a low-angle shot of a sea eagle, motionless against a flat gray sky, an image that, especially within the context of the subsequent narrative, suggests paralysis and stasis. During this shot there is complete silence on the sound track, after which we see an extreme long shot of a rocky cliff that forms a diagonal line down to the sea below. A voice (that of Death, we later learn) reads: "When the lamb had opened the seventh seal, there arose in heaven a silence which lasted about half an hour" (Revelation 8:1).

This silence is, of course, the silence of God that the protagonist, Antonius Block (played by Max von Sydow, who also functions as a directorial surrogate in *The Magician* [*Ansiktet,* 1958] and *Hour of the Wolf* [*Vargtimmen,* 1968]), will, throughout the narrative, try to break through in his attempts to find proof of God's existence, to coerce him into speaking to him. The whole concept of language and its effectiveness and ideological grounding has, of course, been prominent in our thinking about subjectivity and culture for a number of decades.

Language, we know, is ideologically coded, grounded, in Western culture at least, in an equation between God and "the Word": that language which precedes and supersedes all other language. From a post-structuralist perspective, this equation renders language ideologically spurious, compromised, and incapable of fully expressing individual subjectivity. This is certainly the case in feminist thought, which has seen language as unalterably male-gendered and thus inadequate to a communication of female reality, and further argues that silence is a potential strategy of resistance to male discourse. Thus *The Seventh Seal* can be seen as focusing on human connection and communication and the ways in which these are impeded by patriarchal power structures. It treats the destructive impact of the patriarchy, especially but not exclusively the patriarchal Christian church, on the lives of individual human beings. Significantly, Bergman's protagonist, Antonius Block, has, by dedicating himself to the Crusades, attempted to effect the will of God, the ultimate patriarch. From the eleventh to the fourteenth century (*The Seventh Seal* is set in the late 1100s), the church urged the faithful to embark on a series of Crusades, a sort of jihad to convert the "heathen" Muslims, as a result of which untold numbers were slaughtered in the name of the Christian God. Bergman himself holds that "the idea of a Christian God [is] something destructive and fatalistically dangerous, something filled with risk for people and bringing out in them dark destructive forces instead of the opposite" (qtd. in Björkman, Manns, and Sima 164). The only positive force in a reality corrupted by God and his representatives are traditionally female values that lie outside patriarchal structures.

Bergman further associates this God with human devastation by locating his film during the Black Death. During this period, the plague swept through Europe killing fully one-quarter to one-third of the population. Thus Bergman finds this historical moment an appropriate equivalent to the mid-twentieth century, as both eras raise for him certain questions: Can a God exist if he allows such horror? What role do powerful but corrupt social, religious, and political institutions play in this horror? How can individuals forge a meaningful life in a chaotic and apparently senseless world? What does it mean to be human, to possess subjectivity, in an inhuman universe?

The first scene of the narrative shows the Knight in a diagonal composition lying on a rocky beach, his eyes wide open as he is unable to sleep. We note that on his clothing there is a cross that identifies him as a participant in the Crusades. As the viewer later learns, he has become disillusioned with his religious mission of the last ten years, a perspective the viewer is directed to share as the corruption of the church and the patriarchal power structure of which it is a part becomes evident.

When the Knight tries unsuccessfully to pray, the figure of Death appears and announces that he has come to take the Knight, but Block forestalls him by challenging him to a chess match. This scene cinematically as well as narratively characterizes the Knight as a man tormented by his own doubts, at conflict with the natural world, and isolated from his fellow human beings. The natural environment is rigid and harsh, a rocky shoreline with pounding surf and sharp cliff faces. As Birgitta Steene rightly observes, landscape for Bergman is a "reflection of a state of mind, a metaphor for the self" (*Ingmar Bergman* 69). Here it suggests turbulence, disquiet, and discomfort. Because they are neither horizontal (a line that connotes peace and rest) nor vertical (a line of stability and strength), the diagonals of the cliffs surrounding the beach and in the Knight's compositions connote disharmony. The starkly contrastive lighting and coloring is also noteworthy: only dead, flat grays mediate between the bright white of the Knight and his mail, on the one hand, and the total blackness of Death's large cape, on the other. Even the figure of Death himself is visualized in this binary color scheme, his chalk-white face contrasting with his black head wrapping and cape. It is also significant that the Knight is alone; his squire Jöns is on the beach but is sleeping some distance away, and the Knight makes no effort to communicate his torment and anguish to his constant companion of the past ten years. The shock of the Dies Irae juxtaposed with the silence that begins the film, the Knight's vain attempt to pray, the binary coloration, the dominant diagonals, and the compositions showing the Knight in isolation all conjoin.

The binarization of the Knight's reality culminates visually in the last shot of the scene, one that has become an icon for the film and that Robin Wood describes as "a striking quasi-surrealist image, the transitory game of life played out against eternity" (82). The Knight and Death sit opposite each other at a black-and-white chessboard playing with black-and-white pieces against a leaden gray sky and a stormy sea. Chess is, of course, a game designated as "intellectual" and rational, a designation that achieves resonance when Jof and Mia are introduced. For the Knight, as we later learn, has lost contact with an authentic, intuitive reality, largely as a result of his disillusionment with the morally dubious Crusades. It is telling that for him, faith in God is inadequate; he demands *empirical proof* of God's existence.

A short scene follows in which Bergman establishes the fact that the plague is ravaging the countryside. As this scene concludes, the Knight and the Squire ride past a wagon where the camera stops and introduces the second major character constellation: the traveling actor troupe with Jof, Mia, and their child Mikael. Throughout this scene, Bergman draws a sharp distinction, in terms of both narrative and visual presentation, between the Knight and the actor family. One of the clearest differences between the two character groupings centers on isolation versus community. Whereas Block awakened alone on a rocky beach, the actors have been sleeping close together inside their arched wagon; they are protected as Block is not. While Block awakens alone and speaks only with Death, Jof wakes up, speaks with his wife, and then goes outside humming a tune. There he joyfully turns a somersault and greets their horse; his is a communal reality, Block's an isolated one. While the landscape—emblematic of the Knight's state of mind—consists of rocks and barren cliffs, Jof and Mia are surrounded by soft grasses and smoothly undulating trees that allow dappled sunlight to play on the actors' faces; sterility is juxtaposed with fertility. The aural frame of reference allotted to the Knight consists of pounding surf, the ominous Dies Irae, and absolute silence, while the sound track accompanying the family is filled with a horse neighing, the chirping of birds, gentle harp music, a women's choir, and the simple song about heaven's rejoicing in the beauty of nature that Jof sings for his wife. Important, too, is the fact that the use of language in the two scenes is quite different: the Knight uses syntactically complex, stilted rhetoric, whereas the artists express themselves with simple declarative sentences and, in Jof's case, with a song of his own composition. Bergman, who was working at this time as director of the Malmö theater, saw these actors as manifesting "sheer joy, pure vitality. . . . Even today those medieval actors still represent the sort of theatre I love most of all; robust, direct, concrete, substantial, sensual" (qtd. in Björkman, Manns, and Sima 116).

The visions in these scenes underscore this distinction: Block sees Death with his binary coloration against a rocky cliff, while Jof sees, through soft foliage, a vision of the Virgin Mary and the baby Jesus in a brightly lit meadow. The subject matter here is an important marker in characterizing Block and Jof; the Knight sees, of course, the male figure of Death, whereas Jof sees a woman and a baby. Throughout the film, Block is aligned with a harsh and merciless male-centered metaphysics, while Jof, in part through his wife, Mia (they are, as Bergman himself and critics have noted, clearly an iconic figuration of the holy family [Björkman, Manns, and Sima 116; Sarris 83; Steene, *Ingmar Bergman* 64]), is associated with a benevolent and loving female divinity who is visualized caring for her child and who Jof says "smiled" at him. Jof and Mia's religion is nature based, female centered, and intuitive; Block's, abstract, male centered, and grounded in rationalism. The Knight has a vision of Death, Jof of life, fecundity, and futurity. Block sees the death-dealing divine paternal, Jof the life-giving divine maternal. The Knight communicates his vision to no one, tacitly affirming his isolation, whereas Jof shares his vision with Mia, who, to be sure, doesn't believe him, but she nonetheless expresses her love for him and accepts his perception of himself as a visionary, as does the spectator, who sees what he sees.

The distinction between this couple and Block is reinforced by other visuals. The lighting in the Knight's scene is characterized by a contrast between a blistering sun and cold gray skies and sea, while Jof and Mia are photographed in soft, even, light-toned grays. Block's high-contrast lighting expresses the binarism of his reality, the extent to which he has adopted the black/white, good/evil dichotomous thinking characteristic of patriarchal Western culture, while the softer light on Jof and Mia speaks to a more fluid and harmonious worldview. The Knight, too, is shot primarily in close-ups that reveal his anguish or in long shots that emphasize his loneliness and isolation, while Jof and Mia are characterized neither by the anguished self-obsession of the Knight's close-ups nor by the isolation of his long shots. Rather, they are seen mostly in medium shots that reveal a context of nature and community and intimacy with others. For the most part, the Knight is rendered in one-shots of rigid verticals or in diagonals that connote disharmony, while Jof and Mia are repeatedly filmed in two-shots under arches formed by the wagon or tree branches, compositions reminiscent of medieval iconography in which the Virgin Mary is often painted under a vaulting arch that figures divine protection. We note, too, that while death is very real for the Knight, it is nothing more than a player's mask in the Jof and Mia scene; the female-centered (at least in the Western tradition) values of intimacy and family and these characters' close relationship with the natural world dispel, at least for the time being, the threat posed by death.

As the film proceeds, the Knight and Jöns enter a church. The Squire passes the time by talking with a mural painter who tells him about the physical agonies of those dying from the plague and about groups of flagellants who wander the countryside flailing themselves and one another. During the Black Death, such apocalyptic cults roamed the countrysides of Europe and called on the populace to repent. Thus the flagellants foreground the irony of religious belief for Bergman; even while faith aligns itself with life and redemption, it spreads death and destruction. The painter says these images frighten people, and Jöns rejoins, "And then they'll run straight into the arms of the priests."[2] The latter then shares his experiences of the divinely sanctioned Crusades: "For ten years we sat in the Holy Land and let snakes bite us, fleas sting us, wild animals eat us, heathens butcher us, the wine poison us, the women give us lice, the lice devour us, [and] the fevers rot us. . . . And all to the glory of God!"

Both in the vestibule, then, and in the confessional, traditional Christianity is represented as folly, delusion, trickery, and/or evil. The Knight communicates his anguished search for God to a black-robed man behind the iron grid:

> Through my indifference to other people I have isolated myself from the company of other human beings. Now I live in a world of ghosts imprisoned by my dreams and imaginings. . . .
> I want knowledge [of God], not faith, not suppositions, but knowledge. . . . I call out to him in the dark but no one seems to be there. . . . Life is an outrageous horror. No one can live in the face of death, knowing that all is meaningless. . . . In our fear,

---

[2]Throughout this discussion, the translations are my own in those cases when the English screenplay deviates from the meaning of the original Swedish or is, in my view, somewhat dated.

> we make an image, and that image we call God. . . . My life has
> been a futile searching. . . .

It is this speech in particular that prompts many critics to see *The Seventh Seal* as centering on an existential quest for truth and affirmation in a world in which there is no meaning (Steene, *Ingmar Bergman* 66; Steene, *Focus* 4; Donner 137, 145; Sarris 81ff.). Certainly an existentialist reading of the film is a plausible one, especially given Bergman's interest in the French existentialists and the central role that issues of faith and doubt and their impact on the individual's ability to take meaningful action play in his production. Furthermore, the film was made during the Cold War, when fear of a nuclear holocaust was at its most intense. But such a reading alone cannot account for the passionate indictment of the patriarchy so central to the film.

The Knight's quest for God has rendered impossible an authentic life of genuine connection with others. Indeed, during this monologue, the film cuts to an extreme low-angle foreshortened diagonal close-up of the grotesque face of a suffering Christ on the crucifix; the Knight's search for the divine leads only to pain. His existence has become a reflection of God himself—a silence filled only with empty rhetoric. Throughout the film, God is represented as a kind of brutal and destructive "present absence" (Blackwell 71–73) that wreaks devastation in the world. He becomes for Bergman a fictive signifier of patriarchal ideology. During this scene in the church, religion and its organized institutions are represented as terrorism (the painter's statement as to why he was commissioned to do the mural) and trickery (Block is deceived into thinking that he is confessing to a priest, whereas it is Death who uses the Knight's agonized confession to elicit his chess strategy). The Expressionistic low-angle diagonal shots of the agonized and contorted Christ on the crucifix also suggest a God who allows his own son to endure agonies in his name. In this film, God, as the ultimate patriarch, is consistently depicted as indifferent to the sufferings of humankind and represented on earth by the morally bankrupt patriarchy.

Visually, the confessional scene reiterates the notion of the Knight as trapped within and isolated by an abstract, binary view of the world. Especially notable in this scene is the stark contrast between light and shadow: the Knight's face is illuminated in bright white that contrasts with the iron grid on the confessional window, the shadow of which casts a geometric pattern onto his face. These images suggest that the Knight is imprisoned by the male-associated, logically structured intellectual seeking to which he has dedicated his life, to the exclusion of the female-associated values of intimacy, connection, and emotion that Jof and Mia embody. One should note here that even as Bergman's representation of the patriarchy is quite progressive, the film affirms Western culture's very problematic equation between the female and emotion, nature, and family. The high-angle shots that position the spectator literally looking down on the Knight make it clear that, within the context of the film, he is pitiable and his values spurious. Finally, he clenches his fist triumphantly and exclaims, "I, Antonius Block, am playing chess with Death," but his elation is visually undercut by the black-and-white iron grid at the left of the frame and its shadow on the right.

As this segment ends, Block and Jöns exit the church and encounter a young girl (Tyan) who is tied to a stake, moaning and bleeding, as soldiers guard her and a monk reads a religious text over her. Significantly, the Knight approaches Tyan and, without expressing concern for her plight, asks whether or not she has seen the Devil: his humanity has been eroded by his quest for God. It is noteworthy that these soldiers represent civil authority, for religious and civil institutions cohere in the corrupt and destructive patriarchy. The young woman is accused by the church of being a witch and of having had sex with the Devil, and thus of being the cause of the plague, an accusation belied not only by the spectator's (presumed) knowledge that there are no witches but also by her youth, her innocence, and her suffering. Yet the church, God's manifest presence on earth, has not only victimized this innocent, it has also succeeded in making her believe that she is indeed the Devil's handmaiden. The patriarchy, as embodied in God and his representatives—Death, the monk, and the soldiers—is a social, political, and religious authority aligned with brainwashing, victimization, corruption, and death.

A short scene at a farmhouse serves at least two functions: to demonstrate the devastation of the plague and to underline the moral bankruptcy of the church by introducing the ex-priest Raval, who convinced Block to go on the Crusades and is now a robber of the dead and a would-be rapist. This scene also introduces the Silent Woman, who will play a major role at the conclusion of the film. As Raval is about to rape her, he says, "Don't try to scream. There is no one around to hear you, neither God nor people." God is absence, and the only appropriate response to this absence is silence.

The film then proceeds to the village square where Jof, Mia, and their actor companion Skat present several short skits of a rather primitive but nonetheless joyous nature. Their singing is either soft or upbeat, unlike any other music in the film except the harp and women's voices that accompany Jof's vision of the Virgin Mary. But the audience scoffs at their "art," booing and throwing fruit at them. As so often in Bergman, the artist is misunderstood and unappreciated by society, and his or her art is the subject of society's ridicule and scorn.

But as Jof and Mia perform their simple skits and songs, they are interrupted by the entrance of a group of flagellants wailing and moaning, both representatives and victims of the patriarchy. These benighted souls stagger under the weight of immense wooden crosses (Christianity is figured literally as an oppressive burden) and scourge themselves and each other into agonies of self-inflicted torture. Some of them have even donned crowns of thorns. The many monks in this group again suggest the church's complicity in this delusion-filled, self-induced agony. In response, the townspeople cower in fear alongside the Knight, Jöns, the Silent Woman, Jof, and Mia; Bergman here foregrounds the effect of this madness on women and the innocent, religion's "brutalization of a fear-crazed society" (Sarris 85). As the flagellants collapse, a monk rises and harangues the gathered citizenry, threatening them: "Do you know, you insensible fools, that you will die today, tomorrow, or the next day, because all of you have been sentenced? Do you hear what I say? Do you hear the word? You are doomed, doomed, doomed!" Not only is the monk's language brutal (he attacks, among others, a pregnant woman), but Bergman again equates language, "the Word," with the bankrupt religious patriarchy. Finally, an extreme high-angle long shot shows the flagellants trailing off into the distance: a diagonal shot reminiscent of the Knight's "line."

The scene then shifts to the local tavern to demonstrate the effect that God's plague is having on the larger population and thereby to expand the representation of the destructive patriarchy. The horrors of present-day reality lead these people to superstitious and morbid speculation of the worst kind and to complicity, as Raval tortures Jof.

Following a transition scene, the film then shifts to a cliff overlooking the sea where the Knight rises from his chessboard (as a diagonal composition again suggests disharmony) and joins Mia, who is playing with Mikael. After some small talk, she expresses concern for him in an exchange that further demonstrates her empathic connection with people. Cinematic technique reinforces narrative content in this scene as the strong horizontal lines of the landscape and the sea impart a sense of peace that is enhanced by the omnipresent protective arch of the wagon. Long and medium shots that place the characters in a positive relationship with others and with their natural environment dominate and contrast with the isolating long shots of Block in the opening sequence.

Jof returns from the tavern whimpering melodramatically, and Mia comforts him. As in the earlier sequence, he plays with his son, an action that further distinguishes him from the other patriarchal figures in the film. The Knight offers to accompany them through the forest and invites them to stay at his castle until it is safe for them to move on, following which Mia offers a simple meal of milk and wild strawberries.

After Jöns and the Silent Woman join them and are welcomed into Jof and Mia's community, Mia and Block engage in a serious conversation; her pleasant natural manner draws Block out, and, for the first time, he talks about his life. As Mia articulates her worldview of connection to nature and others, she is shot in a diagonal close-up, which lends authority (and potentially spectator identification) to what she is saying and also suggests, because of the diagonals associated with the Knight, that she truly does understand his dilemma. The Knight then shares his personal experiences with her; he speaks fondly of his wife and their life together before the Crusades, concluding, "Faith is a torment . . . like loving someone who is out there in the darkness but never appears, no matter how loudly you call. . . . But all that is unreal when I sit here with you and your husband. How unimportant it all suddenly becomes." We note that it is Mia rather than Jof who is the spokesperson for their spontaneous, intuitive approach to life, a fact that reinforces their alignment with conventionally female rather than male values. As long as the Knight is interacting with Mia, he is seen in medium long shots; Bergman reverts to medium close-ups only when the Knight brings the bowl of milk to his lips and says, "I shall remember this moment with you and your husband. Your faces in the twilight

. . . I'll carry this memory between my hands as carefully as if it were a bowl filled with fresh milk. And it will be a sign to me—it will be a great sufficiency." Block affirms the lesson Mia has just imparted, but his stilted rhetoric indicates that he has not truly integrated the lesson of a simple, intuitive approach to life, of a joyous connection with others and with the natural world. Furthermore, he is filmed in close-up; the two-shot suggestive of connection is replaced by a close-up of isolation. And, indeed, he concludes his speech to return to his chessboard, that visual emblem of his rationality-based quest.

The next scene aligns the "witch" Tyan with Block both visually and verbally, for both embody a delusional belief in God. Then a forest scene brings the Silent Woman into focus (thereby foreshadowing the conclusion of the film, where her point of view is especially privileged), reiterates Jof's visionary abilities, and depicts Block knocking over the chess pieces to distract Death, whereby he performs his one "meaningful deed." After another brief scene in which Jof and Mia flee through the forest amid fierce winds, the film dissolves to the Knight's face and the travelers climbing a steep hill, a shot that foreshadows the visual composition of Jof's vision of the dance of Death. The sky is dark, filled with rain and lightning, and the wind is howling on the sound track. A concluding shot shows lightning superimposed on them: just as previously, nature reflects psychological reality. A static camera shows them winding their way through the Knight's castle, but, importantly, as they file by, the Silent Woman comes nearer to the camera than the others and lingers in a close-up, an indication that she will play a more prominent role in this scene than she has hitherto. The silence that defines her character lends her authority, for silence articulates disillusionment with the patriarchy and insight into the corruption of language inherent in it.

Block is reunited with his wife, Karin, and a close-up of him then dissolves into a close-up of the Silent Woman's face. Karin's voice is heard in the background reading from the section of the Book of Revelation from which the film's title is taken, a technique that establishes an equation between the two women and foreshadows the conclusion of the scene. Another dissolve reveals a long shot of the table where Karin continues reading and the others eat. Virtually the only language left in the narrative is linguistically inauthentic patriarchal Scripture; if God is a pernicious present absence, "the Word" is compromised and ineffective.

Throughout this penultimate scene, women are allotted greater visual prominence than the men. Specifically, the Silent Woman has more visual agency than the other characters: long shots zoom out to include her face in close-up in the foreground, she has a number of point-of-view shots and more close-ups than anyone else, and the camera even adjusts to her movements, moving back as she moves toward it and angling down when she kneels. When Death arrives, she is centered in the shot of four people, while the Knight stands in the background praying one last time for proof of God's existence. While the Silent Woman remains the visual center of the composition, he and Jöns engage in another futile metaphysical debate, until Karin gently hushes them. Philip Mosley's observation that "as so often in Bergman's films, it is the women who cut through the intellectual posturings and dishonesty of the men" is particularly well taken here (65).

The Silent Woman kneels, and the camera zooms in on her face, the left side of which, because of a bright light coming from screen right, is almost completely shadowed. She exclaims ecstatically, "Det är fullbordat," following which she closes her eyes, receiving the same high-contrast lighting and black-and-white coloration as does the Knight. Her statement is the Swedish text of Christ's last words on the cross (John 19:30). But in Swedish (and Bergman is, of course, working with the Swedish Bible), this expression means not merely "It is finished," but also "It is consummated" or "It is accomplished." What is consummated or accomplished here is almost inarguably the will of a merciless and indifferent God, the supreme figure of the patriarchy of which humankind is the victim.

But students and critics alike frequently wonder at the seemingly sudden prominence of the Silent Woman at this climactic moment in the film. Her role might, I think, be read in terms of her association with silence throughout the narrative, for empty rhetoric directed at God has been the hallmark of the Knight's futile and alienating quest. The Silent Woman's words do not derive from her own experience, as "authentic" speech (i.e., speech genuinely expressive of subjectivity) would, but rather are ritual speech, a statement from the Bible, that most male of all Western male texts. She speaks a truth that is specifically gendered as male, as does Karin in her reading from the Book of Revelation. Thus the Silent Woman's last line is fitting. She breaks the silence that is an authentic response to corrupted patriarchal discourse.

The quotation from the Bible is ironically appropriate in asserting that patriarchal Christian ideology is consummated in death—even as the quoted Scripture ostensibly affirms that ideology.

While this statement certainly associates her with Christ and his sufferings, thereby underscoring her victimization by God and the patriarchy, it also points up Bergman's frequently problematic relationship with female experience. Deeply critical of patriarchal ideology, Bergman often aligns himself with and valorizes female experience. But he does not in *The Seventh Seal,* with the exception of Mia (who is defined in terms of her biology as a mother), grant them the agency of authentic speech. Bergman recognizes and is deeply critical of the ways in which women are victimized by the patriarchy, but, at least at this point in his career, women are not granted the authority of visionary image-making, as are both Jof and the Knight, and thus are forever cut off from "true" artistry, which remains for him a male-gendered activity.

The camera dissolves from the Silent Woman's face to Mia's as she awakens to sunshine and birdsong. A zoom-out reveals the whole family, a camera choice that again suggests that it is she who represents this family's values. A long shot shows Jof climbing down with Mikael in his arms and cuts to a harmonious, symmetrical composition of the family with their horse. In a close-up that again privileges spectator identification, Jof recounts his vision: an extreme long shot in stark black-and-white contrast shows the dance of Death, as Death leads the characters struggling up a hillside that lies on a diagonal line within the frame.

After several cuts, Mia affectionately teases Jof: "You and your visions!" and in a long shot they are iconically framed as a family unit with the arch of the wagon top rising protectively above. They circle the wagon in a graceful arc and walk off as the heavenly harps and women's voices from Jof's first vision are heard on the sound track. The dark vision of the dance of Death is countered by the "divine" music that accompanies their departure and the end of the film. But because in film, images tend to have more authority than does sound or language (and this is especially true in Bergman's films), the music cannot completely cancel out the power of Jof's last vision.

The dance-of-Death image entails a significant shift from Jof's previous vision of the Virgin Mary and child, for, in its subject matter, shot length, binary coloration, and diagonal line, it coheres with both the Knight's vision of Death and the camera work that delineates his character. Jof inherits from the Knight the legacy of the patriarchy. While Bergman probably intends Jof's two visions to function as a merging of two opposing modes of human experience that together form a whole and rich understanding of human reality, the final vision serves to recoup Jof for the male forces of the film. It is important here to emphasize that Jof's final vision "is inspired by a creative imagination rather than a Divine Revelation" (Sarris 89); for Bergman, the male artist must acknowledge the power of the patriarchy in order for his art to be fully authentic. At the same time, he reiterates the traditional idealization of a family unit centered on female values.

Conclusion

In *The Seventh Seal*, Bergman creates a film of stunning visual beauty that addresses issues of central concern to our day: patriarchal power structures, genderedness, the ideological grounding of both institutions and language, the constitution of human subjectivity, and the struggle to achieve meaning within a seemingly chaotic and senseless world. While, to be sure, the film's definition of the feminine is still relatively conventional (and it will become markedly more radical after 1960) and the ending of the film reinscribes the notion of art as a male-gendered activity, the film nonetheless is remarkably progressive in its cultural criticism. Like all of us, Bergman can never completely escape the influence of the culture into which he was born. Thus while a confluence of circumstances (his father's profession, his authoritarian upbringing, his innate insight, his personal psychology, and the accident of his birth into a particular country) results in a singular sensitivity to cultural perspectives that would not achieve widespread acceptance until many years later, Bergman also retains some of the thinking of the conservative, patriarchal religious tradition that he, in other respects, rejects. Not surprisingly, then, his work both contests and affirms the ideology of his culture. Nonetheless, the core of this film of extraordinary cinematic depth and richness asserts that God and the patriarchal philosophical, social, and linguistic forces that locate their power in him are potent but empty structures.

Credits

Sweden, 1956, Svensk Filmindustri

Director: Ingmar Bergman
Screenplay: Ingmar Bergman
Cinematography: Gunnar Fischer
Editing: Lennart Wallen
Music: Erik Nordgren
Art Direction: P. A. Lundgren

CAST:

Antonius Block (the Knight)	Max von Sydow
Death	Bengt Ekerot
Jöns (the Squire)	Gunnar Björnstrand
Jof	Nils Poppe
Mia	Bibi Andersson
Skat	Erik Strandmark
Painter	Gunnar Olsson
Tyan	Maud Hansson
Raval	Bertil Anderberg
Plog	Åke Fridell
Lisa	Inga Gill
Mad monk	Anders Ek
Karin	Inga Landgré
Silent Woman	Gunnel Lindblom

Bibliography

Bergman, Ingmar. *Four Screenplays ("Smiles of a Summer Night," "The Seventh Seal," "Wild Strawberries," and "The Magician")*. Trans. Lars Malmström and David Kushner. New York: Simon, 1960.
———. *Images: My Life in Film*. New York: Little, 1994.
———. *The Magic Lantern*. Trans. Joan Tate. New York: Viking, 1988.
Björkman, Stig, Torsten Manns, and Jonas Sima. *Bergman on Bergman*. Trans. Paul Britten-Austin. New York: Simon, 1973.
Blackwell, Marilyn. *Gender and Representation in the Films of Ingmar Bergman*. Columbia: Camden, 1997.
Cowie, Peter. *Ingmar Bergman: A Critical Biography*. New York: Scribner's, 1983.
Donner, Jörn. *The Films of Ingmar Bergman: From "Torment" to "All These Women."* Trans. Holger Lundbergh. New York: Dover, 1972.
Gado, Frank. *The Passion of Ingmar Bergman*. Durham: Duke UP, 1986.
Holland, Norman. "Iconography in *The Seventh Seal*." *Hudson Review* 12.2 (1959): 266–70.
Lerner, Gerda. *The Creation of Patriarchy*. Oxford: Oxford UP, 1986.

Mambrino, Jean. *"The Seventh Seal."* Trans. Marie Georgette Steisel. Steene, *Focus* 50–54.

Mosley, Philip. *Ingmar Bergman: The Cinema as Mistress.* London: Marion Boyars, 1981.

Rohmer, Eric. "With *The Seventh Seal* Ingmar Bergman Offers Us His Faust." Steene, *Focus* 134–35.

Sarris, Andrew. *"The Seventh Seal."* Steene, *Focus* 81–91.

Steene, Birgitta, ed. *Focus on "The Seventh Seal."* Englewood Cliffs: Prentice, 1972.

———. *Ingmar Bergman.* New York: Twayne, 1968.

———. "The Milk and Strawberries Sequence in *The Seventh Seal." Film Heritage* 8.4 (1973): 10–18.

Taylor, John Russel. *"The Seventh Seal."* Steene, *Focus* 135–36.

Wood, Robin. *Ingmar Bergman.* London: Studio Vista, 1969.

The 400 Blows (1959)

ALASTAIR PHILLIPS

Youth and Entrapment in the French New Wave

One never forgets one's first viewing of the ending of François Truffaut's passionate yet melancholy debut feature film *Les quatre cents coups* (*The 400 Blows*). The young teenager Antoine Doinel's determined escape from the reform institution to the sea, choreographed through a combination of extended traveling shots and a yearning musical score, ends as he turns from the waves on the beach to face the gaze of the camera. Unexpectedly, the image freezes, and the camera then tracks in further to register a quizzical uncertainty on the face of the film's young protagonist. Antoine is now captured forever on the cusp of adolescence and adulthood, hesitating somewhere between sea and shore and between the prospect of renewed motion or permanent stillness. *The 400 Blows* is preoccupied with this theme of transition, in terms of both its practice of visual representation and its articulation of the semiautobiographical concerns of its twenty-six-year-old director. It explores the shifting relationship between the formality of the French public education system and the fertility of Antoine's private imagination. It also moves between the affective and spatial restriction of the Doinel family home and the emotional liberation of the Parisian street. It is fascinated, as befitting of the work of a young print journalist just turned filmmaker like Truffaut, with the promising intersection between writing and seeing. Throughout, these ideas are mediated by the idea of youth. Indeed, one can trace the patterns of youth that the film initiates in order to suggest that one of the strongest factors determining the film's longstanding presence in the minds of film audiences may well rest in its prescient conflation of a youthful film culture with a youthful film style. However, this youthfulness is also characterized by an emotional undercurrent of restlessness and a sense of inevitable mortality. For a film held by many as a landmark example of the exuberance and brio of the French New Wave, *The 400 Blows* is also remarkably constrained by a vision of yet one more temporal boundary: that between what has been achieved so far by its director and main character and the issue of what will happen next in an uncertain world marked so clearly by questions of disaffection and transience.

Context

The 400 Blows first needs to be seen in the context of its time and its relationship to developments in France in the years following the end of the Second World War. These developments had a profound impact on how Truffaut's representation of youth intersected with other discourses of innovation and youthfulness taken up more broadly by the French New Wave. As the critic and film journalist Antoine de Baecque has noted, the novelty and the coherence of this seminal moment in French film rested in the very fact that it was "a youth movement"; the French New Wave was "the first cinema movement to have styled itself within the immediacy of its own history, within the world in which its contemporaries lived" (16). It fashioned a new youthful identity for French cinema and deployed ways of capturing the vitality of a broader emergent youth culture on-screen.

An emphasis on transition and change lay at the heart of the new self-identity France was forging in the 1950s, as the nation rapidly modernized from being a predominantly conservative and Catholic rural economy to a more urbanized, consumer culture fascinated by new forms of popular culture and self-expression. The speed of this modernization was matched by a widely perceived sense of restless mobility on the part of young people, who were seen to be forming new patterns of affiliation, appearance, and behavior primarily based around separate tastes in fashion and music. By the mid-1950s, the number of French young people between the ages of fifteen and twenty-nine was at its highest point that century (Baecque 43). This spread of a distinctive youth culture coincided with the dissemination of other new material phenomena, such as the use of artificial fabrics for clothing, the prevalence of color photography in advertising and photojournalism, and the development of the car as the mainstream form of private transportation.

For an older generation who had gone through the economic and political privations of the wartime occupation, there was widespread discussion about the direction society was taking, and this was marked by a sense of a gulf between generations and a break with the certainties of the past. The term "New Wave," later taken to denote the collective sensibility behind the emerging work of such filmmakers as Claude Chabrol, Jean-Luc Godard, Alain Resnais, Agnès Varda, Jacques Rozier, and others, was in fact coined by the journalist Françoise Giroud in an investigative report on the state of the nation's youth in *L'express* in August 1957. Her article was but one of an avalanche of documents, articles, and books whose general tone may be summarized in the form of the titular question posed by the March 1955 special edition of *La nef:* "Youth: Who Are You?" (Baecque 51). This explicit tension between conventionally hierarchical forms of knowledge and behavior and a resistant mentality may well account for so much of the initial acclaim and publicity for *The 400 Blows*. In its suggestive semiautobiographical mode, it clearly seemed to speak to its audience about a broader set of concerns already demonstrably present within contemporary French culture.

Perhaps the most explicit way in which the film embodied an almost manifesto-like commitment to the contemporary rested in its relationship to the fact that Truffaut had been a prolific film critic for papers like *Arts, Radio-Cinéma-Télévision,* and *France-Observateur* before turning filmmaker. Truffaut's good fortune as a young man had been to grow up in the exuberant postwar phase of France's vital film culture, in which there had been a boom in theater construction, film-book publishing, cine-clubs, and, most important, a new raft of influential periodicals including *Cahiers du cinéma* (founded in 1951) and *Positif* (founded in 1952). Here, he had been deeply influenced by the critic André Bazin, who had taken Truffaut under his wing as the secretary of his popular Travail et Culture film club in the late 1940s. As the director was to say later, in *Cahiers du cinéma,* "Bazin helped me make the leap from film buff to critic, to director: he was the Just Man by whom one likes to be judged and, for me, a father whose very reprimands were sweet, like the marks of an affectionate interest I had been deprived of in childhood" ("Il faisait"). Truffaut had subsequently been the author of a tendentious and highly polemical article published by *Cahiers du cinéma* in January 1954 entitled *"Une certaine tendance du cinéma français"* (A Certain Tendency of the French Cinema), which savaged what he saw as the then prevailing trend of the "tradition of quality," a term originally coined in positive terms by the writer Jean-Pierre Barrot in the weekly film magazine *L'ecran français*. Truffaut took exception to the tradition of quality's apparently conventional conception of aesthetic value and respectful projection of "Frenchness," and argued that it tended to favor literary adaptation over original screenwriting and an elaborate and costly artificial *mise-en-scène* at the expense of a more naturalistic screen space. The young film critic thus called for a new form of cinematic engagement that would overturn the ascendancy of the prosaic *metteur en scène* who simply added pictures to a preexisting script. This figure would be replaced with the inventive visual imagination of the *auteur*—the true "man of the cinema." These concerns were elaborated in a second, more widely circulated article, "Le cinéma français crève sous les fausses legends" (The French Cinema Is Crushed by False Legends), which was published in *Arts* in May 1957.

Truffaut believed there were influential and valuable filmmakers at work in France, like the directors Jacques Becker, Robert Bresson, and Jean-Pierre Melville, but their work was at odds with the dominant formality and controlled artifice of figures like Christian-Jaque, director of *Adorables créatures* (*Adorable Creatures*, 1952) and *Nana* (1955), and Jean Aurenche and Pierre Bost, who coscripted film adaptations like *La symphonie pastorale* (Jean Delannoy, 1946) and *Le rouge et le noir* (*The Red and the Black*, Claude Autant-Lara, 1954). Having said this, it is worth pointing out that there were definite hesitations on the part of *Cahiers* editors André Bazin and Jacques Doniol-Valcroze about publishing the rebarbative nature of Truffaut's prose. It is also important to temper Truffaut's remonstrations somewhat, not least for the reason that they clearly took a reductive approach to the complexities of popular French cinema in the 1950s. This is true both in terms of the aesthetics and politics of contemporary genre and stardom and in terms of the creative use of existing and emerging technologies involving cinematography and the magnetic recording of sound.

The 400 Blows can certainly be viewed in relation to this appeal for a new kind of cinema, but its genesis and production history also reveal a more ambivalent and textured story. There are a remarkable series of porous boundaries, for instance, between Truffaut's own family, the story of the Doinel family represented within the narrative, and the familial nature of the organization of the project. If *The 400 Blows* is a film demonstrably about youthful subjectivity, it is also haunted by notions of paternity and belonging that can be said to relate to a longer and richer sense of personal, social, and cinematic history. The film was financed, for example, by Truffaut's father-in-law, Ignace Morgenstern, who had been persuaded of the potential of taking a risk on the would-be feature filmmaker despite aesthetic misgivings about his preceding debut short film, *Les mistons* (*The Mischief Makers,* 1957). In its initial stages, *The 400 Blows* drew quite directly on the young director's reminiscences about family and school life, his friendship with his boyhood friend Robert Lacheney, and his stay in detention at the Villejuif Observation Center in 1948. The film explicitly shows a fictionalized version of the hurt Truffaut himself experienced in not having a real father, especially in the scenes when the stepfather surrenders Antoine to the authorities. The script, as it progressed, was then significantly enhanced by the contribution of another of Truffaut's surrogate father figures when the novelist and screen and television writer Marcel Moussy helped to organize Truffaut's ideas more rigorously. In turn, Truffaut himself adopted a fathering role toward the young man selected to play the lead character of Antoine Doinel, Jean-Pierre Léaud. As close correspondences emerged between Léaud's troubled past and Truffaut's own life—both had been caught for acts of juvenile delinquence—Truffaut became a sort of guardian figure, and the young boy a creative collaborator. All along, however, Truffaut was anxious about the emotional pain that this scenario might cause his parents, and he went to some lengths to fictionalize aspects of his screen father's persona, even replacing his stepfather's enthusiasm for mountaineering with an on-screen passion for car racing.

Perhaps the greatest sense in which the film resisted making a full break with the past was the self-conscious way in which it carefully transcribed existing traditions of French cinema. Truffaut's fondness for the charismatic and subtle work of the 1930s director Jean Vigo, for example, is apparent in many of the early school scenes, which are indebted to Vigo's short film *Zéro de conduite* (*Zero for Conduct,* 1933). Perhaps *The 400 Blows'* greatest influence, though, came through Truffaut's close friend and critical inspiration, André Bazin. As we have seen, Bazin had been the first to publish the director's lambast against the French filmmaking establishment, and he had also served as the director's intellectual mentor. The film is dedicated to Bazin's memory, since he died during the night after *The 400 Blows'* first day of shooting.

Many others within Truffaut's circle were either directly or indirectly included in the process. The name Doinel is an amalgam of part of the family name of *Cahiers du cinéma* editor Jacques Doniol-Valcroze and Ginette Doynel, who had been a close collaborator of one of Truffaut's heroes, Jean Renoir. The film uses various veteran film actors, such as Guy Decomble (the schoolteacher) and Georges Flamant (René's father) in many of its central roles. Also, crucial to the visualization of the words of the script was the work of the cinematographer Henri Decaë, whose sharply contoured and naturalistic cinematography had caught Truffaut's eye in such influential pre–New Wave Parisian films as *Bob le flambeur* (*Bob the Gambler*, Jean-Pierre Melville, 1955). In his analysis of the aesthetic determinants of the New Wave, French film critic Michel Marie specifically argues that Decaë "was willing from the start to adapt to the most precarious and audacious demands of production, and it was he who liberated the camera from its fixed tripod. . . . He made the New Wave possible" (*French New Wave* 89). Decaë's work on Louis Malle's *Ascenseur pour l'échafaud* (*Lift to the Scaffold*, 1958) and his *Les amants* (*The Lovers*, 1958) and Claude Chabrol's *Les cousins* (1959) are other good examples of this atmospheric turn to the street.

If one important generational transition had occurred on the eve of the film's production, another happened at the instance of the film's immediate critical reception at the Cannes Film Festival in May 1958, when the film was rapturously received and awarded the festival prize for Best Direction. Escorted by one more "father" of French cinema, the playwright and director Jean Cocteau, Léaud and Truffaut became the faces of a new generation of French film culture overnight. *The 400 Blows'* intricate conflation of autobiography, fiction, and pressing social issues assured the phenomenal scale of the subsequent press coverage, with the likes of *Elle* magazine declaring, "never has the festival been so youthful, so happy to live for the glory of an art which youth loves. The twelfth film festival has the honour of announcing to you the rebirth of French cinema" (qtd. in Baecque and Toubiana 134). In characteristically epigrammatic fashion, Truffaut's fellow critic and director Jean-Luc Godard declared, "To sum it up, what shall I say? This: *The 400 Blows* will be a film signed Frankness. Rapidity. Art. Novelty. Cinematograph. Originality. Impertinence. Seriousness. Tragedy. Renovation. Ubu-Roi. Fantasy. Ferocity. Affection. Universality. Tenderness."

But it was the French Iranian critic Fereydoun Hoveyda, then also based at *Cahiers du cinéma,* who noted the melancholic reality of the film's observations about the transition between youth and adulthood. He wrote, "*The 400 Blows* is an episode in the difficulty of simply being, the confusion of the individual who has been thrust into the world without asking, and who is denied any means to adapt to it," continuing, "It is the child's responsibility to create an acceptable world with the means at hand. But how can one escape the tragedy of everyday life when he remains torn between his parents, fallen idols, and an indifferent, often hostile, universe?"

Analysis

In many ways, then, *The 400 Blows* is indicative of the French New Wave in the sense that the emphasis placed on transition and change in its critical reception related both to the film's thematic content and to its means of visualization. Truffaut's film concerned a conception of cinema based on youth and movement, in which new ways of seeing were articulated through a sense of constant motion in both camera work and editing. Throughout, albeit in an astutely crafted fashion, it maintained a tone of improvisation, as if to suggest that cinematic language itself was in a state of reinvention. This mobility, however, was not completely matched by the film's treatment of its youthful protagonist's aspirations. One can also glimpse a sense of containment, even in the often relatively critically ignored opening passage of the narrative.

The film begins in motion, as if coming out of the darkness, with a silhouette of the Eiffel Tower rising above the intersection of two lines of apartment buildings. There is a corresponding surge of music, which relays the sense of expectation and potential linked to this classic Parisian icon. Yet as we move closer, it disappears, to be replaced by the more oblique patterns of the city's architecture. Jean Constantin's music likewise shifts register and begins to construct a plaintive, yet also tentative, sense of melancholy and yearning, which is underscored by the grayness and gloom of the late winter afternoon. This pattern is repeated by subsequent extended traveling shots, whose rhythm and duration carefully match the periodization of the orchestral arrangement. Through the imposing central columns of a more contemporary building we see the Eiffel Tower again, and, just briefly, there is a lapse in the melodic sadness on the sound track as if to suggest a feeling of security and respite. This may be no accident, for we are looking at the Palais de Chaillot, home of France's national Cinémathèque, where the young Truffaut had recently watched so many influential films. Shortly afterward, we cut across the river to the foot of the Eiffel Tower. Yet no sooner are we there than the process of continual tracking shots moves into reverse, and with an emphatic slowing down of the musical arrangement, the structure begins to recede from our field of vision. The film's opening thus elliptically suggests a feeling of aspiration and loss that will now be explored more fully through the persona of Antoine. Parallel to this is a sense of the mechanism of cinema, in terms of its being both a significant means of recording and ordering reality and an institutional forum for the dissemination of knowledge and experience about the world. The importance of this heuristic function of film is underlined by the subsequent written dedication to the memory of Truffaut's deceased friend and educator, Bazin. The next shot of the film humorously underpins the idea when it shows a schoolboy diligently writing on a desk, only to open the desk and mischievously replace his text with an image taken from a glamour model calendar.

The transition between authority and youthful spontaneity is repeatedly featured in the film, not least in the ways in which the narrative contrasts the disinterest and constriction of Antoine's family home with the freedom of the city streets that he shares with his friend René. Truffaut delineates Paris with evocative precision in order to explore two key interrelated issues: a sense of playful openness and a new sense of the primacy of the young individual rather than the social group. By choosing, with Henri Decaë's assistance, to shoot much of the film on location—particularly in the nontouristed and thus relatively underexplored urban spaces of the ninth and eighteenth arrondissements—Truffaut was opening the door to the outside world and turning his back on the conventions and artifice of studio-bound filmmaking. As the critic Jean Douchet has written (and Douchet himself is actually in the film briefly as Antoine's mother's secret lover), "The street as seen by the New Wave reflected the aspirations of the young people who made it theirs. . . . Paris was at their feet. It was a place of unlimited possibility" (123). This idea of filming *en plein air* was not new, of course. The tradition of using outdoors urban space can be traced back to the early years of French cinema, which relates to the ways that the paintings of the Impressionists broke with academy-sanctioned studio genre painting earlier on in the nineteenth century. But what was new in *The 400 Blows* was the sense of a definitive rejection of the spatial iconography of French city-based genre cinema. The film features no police detective rooms or chic nightclubs and restaurants, for example. Instead, the emphasis is on the surfaces of the ordinary and inconsequential, which are then transformed through the subjectivity of the protagonist into realms of both imaginative possibility and mournful longing. This is important for a film that became a key instance in the New Wave's more general move away from the narrative and stylistic patterns of popular French cinema. *The 400 Blows,* along with its contemporaneous success at Cannes that year, *Hiroshima, mon amour* (Alain Resnais, 1959), marked the beginnings of a broader trend in France toward the relationship between *auteur* cinema and a middle-class, metropolitan, cinephilic culture.

The streets, cafés, and monuments around Montmartre and the Place de Clichy are shot in available light as if to transmit a sense of authenticity, fluidity, and immediacy, though the quality of these images is certainly not amateurish. Both Decaë and Truffaut had a keen eye for detailed and careful composition, and there is a deliberate rhythm to the way in which individual shots interrelate. In a 1962 pamphlet, *Nouvelle vague,* following on the subsequent success of other important early New Wave films, such as *À bout de souffle* (*Breathless,* Jean-Luc Godard, 1960) and *Paris nous appartient* (*Paris Belongs to Us,* Jacques Rivette, 1960), Raymond Borde specifically argued that the movement's apparent spontaneity was a trained illusion. But there is no denying that the look of *The 400 Blows* was distinctive, with its location cinematography being aided by the implementation of new, portable recording technologies that allowed a more intimate contact with the surface of reality. It used variable focal-length lenses, which had spread earlier on in the decade, to suggest the facilitation of new sensations of movement and distance and proximity; Edgar Morin and Jean Rouch's Parisian street documentary, *Chronique d'un été* (*Chronicle of a Summer,* 1961), shot later in 1959, went on to break further ground by linking these new camera technologies to the use of 35 mm and direct sound.

All of these factors assisted in the promotional links made between the individual figure of the film's director/*auteur* and its protagonist. *The 400 Blows* abounded with a sense of youthful individualism, since Truffaut's filmmaking demonstrably aimed to be a cinema of the first person. Paris was not seen as a space of warm or convivial community—a dominant model of representation in French cinema of the classical period. Instead, it became a somewhat indifferent public environment viewed through the lens of psychological intimacy. The film proliferates with aerial views that isolate a person or a moment. There is a predominance of impressionistic, fleeting gazes at ordinary sites of encounter, movement, and transition. The family, such as it is, is kept for the most part inside the home, with the streets of the capital becoming a place of temporary release and invention.

These ideas are visible in the sequence that follows Antoine's departure from the family apartment after breakfast. Here, Truffaut contrasts the claustrophobic kitchen with the liberty and promise of the surrounding neighborhood streets. The almost imprisoning static final interior shot ends with the boy closing the door behind him so that it nearly fills the frame. There is a dissolve to an angled long shot of Antoine running out of the main building between two parked vehicles. The camera pans to the left, following this line of movement, and in the center of the tiny square outside, Antoine intersects with his friend René. The patterning of the direction of their twin paths is an exact inverse of the spatial geometry of the square as it is viewed in relation to the field of vision temporarily established by the position of the camera. As the two friends walk leftward, there is no cut. Instead, the camera tracks the movement of the boys, maintaining their central position within the frame. For a final moment it pauses, as we watch René about to lead Antoine across the street. The sense of everydayness and the insistence on the use of the gray, milky hues of the available Parisian winter morning light belie the fact that the film's apparently spontaneous capturing of ordinary reality is, in fact, extraordinarily coordinated. There is then a striking, extreme long shot of the boys walking up an anonymous street conversing and laughing. The buoyant and jaunty music underscores a sense of improvised pleasure and creative freedom away from the confines of the classroom. It is important that they are the only two figures walking in this direction, for their dark clothing allows the viewer's eye to pick them out against the pallor of the city around them without the distraction of other figures. Again, the shot is carefully composed so that the image is succinctly cut in half, allowing the camera to discreetly, but also complicitly, track and pan to the left as the boys turn the corner and hide their school belongings behind an anonymous doorway. The next shot is emblematic of the thematic and aesthetic principles being established here. We cut to a view of the painted placard above a cinema advertising a sensational sexual drama, which is at comical odds with both the quotidian surroundings of the street and the scholastic work the schoolboys should be doing. The camera tilts downward, and in extreme long shot we view Antoine and René make off leftward down the street. A rapid zip pan (or swish pan) then tracks the boys as they run across the street, but the image simultaneously dissolves so that by the time the camera actually comes to a halt, the figures have already rematerialized on the sidewalk on the other side. This showmanship is no accident. It reiterates in overtly self-conscious filmic terms the same pleasurable energy and spectacle that the characters themselves are taking in by playing hooky to go to the cinema. The youthfulness of the action within the narrative is being inscribed within a *mise-en-scène* of matching invention and vigor.

We can explore this alignment of ideas around the representation of cinema in *The 400 Blows* by looking briefly at a subsequent sequence within the film that has been widely admired. Antoine and René visit a funfair attraction that consists of a vast cylinder in which people stand against the interior wall as the drum of the machine begins to rotate. The surface of the cylinder consists of a series of metal panels that in themselves resemble a set of frames on a roll of film or the canister-like apparatus of a zoetrope. There are three principal camera positions that articulate the phenomenon of Antoine "riding" the machine. First, we look down into the cylinder from the perspective of the audience above. Second, we look up at the audience from the rim of the cylinder as if to approximate the dislocated sensation of Antoine's point of view. Finally, we examine Antoine more carefully in shots that frame him shifting as he loses the pull of gravity and is able to twist and contort his body, now pinned against the wall of the circulating drum. This attempt to visualize the phenomenon from Antoine's perspective articulates the process and experience of identifying with moving images, and further suggests the many ways in which early cinematic culture intersected with other sensational entertainments and phenomena of industrial modernity.

More specifically, it inscribes in miniature a set of issues pertinent to the film as a whole. Again, the point is that this is a cinema of the first person. The emphasis is on vision, subjectivity, feeling, and action—all the things that Truffaut the film critic valued in his earlier writings on the values of classical Hollywood cinema. Through its detailed investigation of Antoine's face and gestures, the sequence prioritizes intimate dramatic visual experience over crafted verbal interaction. What is interesting, however, is that the experience also points to the limitations of the freedom that the film's protagonist is enjoying. The visceral spatial sensation of the ride is linked to a finite process. Critics such as Anne Gillain have even pointed to the womb-like nature of the ride for Antoine, here suspended in a near fetal position. She argues that "the circular and playful space [of the machine] is also clearly a maternal one where . . . time is suspended" (190). But ironically, we can also see the ride as an emblematic prison that recalls the schoolroom, the family home, the detention cell in the police station, and even the very ending of the film itself, which freezes Antoine, poised within the logic of a permanently static final frame. As elsewhere in *The 400 Blows,* a sense of youthful energy is tempered with a sense of the limits of duration and possibility. Furthermore, even while transfixed by pleasure, Antoine is separated from the world around him. Gillain may well be right to argue that both in the film and in real life, cinema represented for Truffaut "a place of affective compensation for parental neglect" (190). Even in his debut feature, however, the director is also pointing toward the inevitable transience of its miraculous and escapist pleasures.

The 400 Blows abounds with other sensations of displacement and separation. In a telling analysis of the sequence in which the troupe of schoolchildren gradually separate from the gym teacher on the streets of Paris, Gillain further argues that as well as capturing the "boundless energy of childhood [the sequence also becomes] an allegory of its dispersion within the currents of life" (189). There are other more mournful examples, such as when Antoine is punished by the reform institution and is unable to see his friend René. Earlier, Antoine has also suffered seeing his prized private shrine to the writer Balzac go up in flames. Again and again, the film suggests a longing for a durable coherence and stability, but then represents this sentiment in terms of something located beyond the boundary of what's possible. The snatched and furtive scent of Antoine's mother's perfume evokes a lost innocence. The enraptured responses of the children at the Punch-and-Judy show in the park, captured with evocative precision by the discretion and fluency of the editing, also remind us, when we see Antoine and René in the audience, that such endearing childhood innocence is only fleeting. Perhaps the most devastating image of affective displacement in the film occurs when Antoine is taken away from the police station in the van. The camera tracks in on the vehicle as the door is closed, sealing the young boy from the city night outside. It remains in a static position as the van pulls away, emphasizing dislocation in the departure. We then cut to a subjective shot of streets passing by that are no longer within playful reach. In the subsequent extended image, the camera captures the troubled feelings registering on Antoine's face through the cell window. It veers closer, then recedes and eddies closer again in a form of secondary collaboration with the uneven and destabilizing movement of the vehicle. Truffaut subsequently moves inside the van to reveal a broader sense of the boy's field of vision. We hear a reprise of the previously jaunty signature of the score and see Antoine bleakly gazing out at a world now forever beyond his reach.

Conclusion

The moment the reels of *The 400 Blows* were first unwound in public, it entered into a wider discourse of youthfulness and innovation that became central to the way the French New Wave spoke of itself to a public willing to see new screen images of French society and culture. Truffaut's film drew on the privations of his personal life, but in its depiction of the young male protagonist Antoine Doinel it also clearly touched a broader nerve. Part of its success related to its style, which combined an immediacy and apparent spontaneity with a form of representation of adolescence that was both decisive and honest. But was its success also, in part, a result of the film's apparent rejection of any fixed position toward politics? The limited choices the film proposes in its analysis hardly meet the needs of an affirmative call for transformative social action. Its explanation of the plight of Antoine is neither systematic nor conclusive. A debut feature by a young film director on the edge of a brilliant career, the film is nonetheless haunted by feelings of loss and estrangement.

At one stage early in the narrative, the teacher asks sarcastically, "What will France be like in ten years?" On one level, this is the voice of an out-of-touch instructor caught up in an inadequate education system, but in another sense, this is also a question the film asks of itself and its audience. In terms of its appearance near the beginning of a defining moment in the nation's film culture, the film offers an indisputably hopeful response, at least in terms of cinema. However, as a film about that society's own youth, it is bleak indeed. Truffaut did go on to try and answer the question in an indirect fashion, making further films starring Jean-Pierre Léaud as Antoine Doinel, which depicted the adolescent's transition into a young man: the segment "Antoine et Colette" in *L'amour à vingt ans* (*Love at Twenty*, 1962), *Baisers volés* (*Stolen Kisses*, 1968), *Domicile conjugal* (*Bed and Board*, 1970), and *L'amour en fuite* (*Love on the Run*, 1979). In terms of his career, though, he was often primarily remembered for the sad and vibrant images of youth within *The 400 Blows*. Despite numerous successes such as *Jules et Jim* (1961), *La nuit américaine* (*Day for Night*, 1973), and *Le dernier métro* (*The Last Metro*, 1980), and especially after his untimely death at the age of fifty-two from a brain tumor, one could almost say that his persona became as trapped as Antoine's in that final remarkable, but nonetheless inconclusive, still frame on the beach.

Credits

France, 1959, Les Films du Carosse/SEDIF

Director: François Truffaut
Screenplay: François Truffaut and Marcel Moussy
Cinematography: Henri Decaë
Editing: Marie-Josèph Yoyotte
Music: Jean Constantin
Art Department: Raymond Lemoigne
Set Decoration: Bernard Evein

CAST:
Antoine Doinel   Jean-Pierre Léaud
M. Doinel   Albert Rémy
Mme. Doinel   Claire Maurier
René Bigey   Patrick Auffay

M. Bigey   Georges Flamant
Schoolteacher   Guy Decomble

Bibliography

Allen, Don. *Finally Truffaut*. London: Secker, 1985.

Baecque, Antoine de. *La nouvelle vague: Portrait d'une jeunesse*. Paris: Flammarion, 1998.

Baecque, Antoine de, and Serge Toubiana. *Truffaut. A Biography*. Berkeley: U of California P, 2000.

Borde, Raymonde, Freddy Buache, and Jean Curtelin. *Nouvelle vague*. Lyon: Serdoc, 1962.

Crisp, V. G. *François Truffaut*. London: November Books, 1972.

Douchet, Jean. *New Wave*. New York: DAP in association with Editions Hazan/Cinématèque Française, 1999.

Gillain, Anne. "The Script of Delinquency: François Truffaut's *Les 400 coups* (1959)." *French Film: Texts and Contexts*. Ed. Susan Hayward and Ginette Vincendeau. London: Routledge, 1990. 187–99.

Godard, Jean-Luc. "La photo du mois." *Cahiers du cinéma* 92 (1959): 44.

Graham, Peter. *The New Wave*. London: Secker, 1968.

Hillier, Jim, ed. *Cahiers du Cinéma: The 1950s*. London: Routledge in association with the BFI, 1985.

Holmes, Diana, and Robert Ingram. *François Truffaut*. Manchester: Manchester UP, 1998.

Hoveyda, Fereydoun. "La première personne du pluriel." *Cahiers du cinéma* 97 (1959): 53.

Insdorf, Annette. *François Truffaut*. Rev. ed. Cambridge: Cambridge UP, 1994.

Marie, Michel. "Les deambulations Parisiennes de la nouvelle vague." *Paris vu par le cinéma d'avant-garde 1923–1983*. Paris: Editions Experimental, 1985. 51–56.

———. *The French New Wave. An Artistic School*. Oxford: Blackwell, 2003.

Neupert, Richard. *A History of the French New Wave*. Madison: U of Wisconsin P, 2002.

Ross, Kristin. *Fast Cars, Clean Bodies: Decolonisation and the Reordering of French Culture*. Cambridge, MA: MIT Press, 1995.

Truffaut, François. "Il faisait bon vivre." *Cahiers du cinéma* 91 (1959): 25.

———. "Une certaine tendance du cinéma français." *Cahiers du cinéma* 31 (1954): 15–29.

———. "Vous êtes tous témoins dans ce procès. Le cinéma français crève sous les fausses legends." *Arts* 619 (May 1957): 3–4.

Vincendeau, Ginette. *A Companion to French Cinema*. London: Cassell and BFI, 1996.

Breathless (1960)

RICHARD NEUPERT

Godard Jumps Ahead

Context

As Jean-Luc Godard likes to point out, D. W. Griffith used to claim that all you need for a film is a girl and a gun. Godard adds that when he saw Roberto Rossellini's *Voyage to Italy* in 1953, he realized you could also make a movie about two people in a car, just talking (qtd. in Rancière and Tesson 34). A perfect synthesis of these two models is *Breathless* (*À bout de souffle*), which owes a great deal to early film practice and 1950s aesthetic and social forces but still manages to catapult film language in new, unexpected directions. Godard's history as a film critic strongly determined his historical perspective on filmmaking. He began writing film reviews for his friend Eric Rohmer's short-lived *Gazette du cinéma* in 1950 and after 1952 for *Cahiers du cinéma*. His early reviews addressed classical Hollywood films, documentaries, and Soviet films that inspired him to write about political cinema. While many of Godard's reviews have been called "confused and badly organized" (Milne 7), and "quirky and elliptical" (Monaco 107), they were nonetheless marked by a passionate, confident, and even reckless cinephilia.

At a time when the cultural power of the cinema was rising to a near frenzy in France, reviewers like Jean-Luc Godard established their own voice by retelling cinema history from their own perspective. Godard's reviews provide a valuable context for his later film practice, and he often proclaimed that writing criticism was a form of filmmaking and vice versa: "All of us at *Cahiers* thought of ourselves as future directors. Frequenting *ciné-clubs* and the Cinémathèque was already a way of thinking cinema. . . . Writing was already a way of making films" (qtd. in Milne 171; Godard, Interview). Early on, Godard found a distinctive approach to film criticism, an approach that often opposed him to André Bazin's faith in long takes and deep-space filmmaking. For instance, in "Towards a Political Cinema" (September 1950), which addresses Soviet and German films, Godard already refers to images in terms from the field of semiotics, in which all meaning is said to derive from culturally determined signs, which are composed of a concrete signifier and the concept, or signified. As Godard writes in his review, "Here the idea of a shot . . . takes on its real function of sign, indicating something in whose place it appears." Godard even adds a footnote to refer the reader to philosopher Brice Parain's claim that "the sign forces us to see through its significance" (qtd. in Milne 16). His reviews combine the auteurist assumption that the director controls the film's ultimate meaning, a position common to *Cahiers du cinéma,* with an awareness that films are cultural representations built from signs, rather than faithful recordings of reality. For Godard, the film screen was never an objective window onto the world.

Another important aspect of Godard's earliest criticism lies in its "quirky and elliptical" organization. As a reviewer, Godard already leaps from topic to topic, with incredible numbers of references to literature, theater, and painting as well as movies. While able to refer to a vast array of artistic, political, and historical background information, Godard nonetheless jumbles these references together in demanding and highly subjective ways. It is quite fitting, therefore, that Godard's first feature film, *Breathless,* should be as bold as his writing style and include references to Pierre-Auguste Renoir, William Faulkner, Guillaume Apollinaire, as well as a host of other intertextual citations. There is also a brash self-confidence in Godard's film criticism that carries over into his production of *Breathless;* it is no coincidence that his first feature opened with titles composed of white block letters on a black background, similar to *Citizen Kane* (Orson Welles, 1941).

French films like *Breathless* were also shaped by the upheaval and revitalization underway in all aspects of cultural practice in France during the 1950s. In 1957, the magazine *L'express* went so far as to announce that this post–World War II French generation of late teens and twentysomethings comprised a *nouvelle vague,* or "New Wave," population possessing very different perspectives from those of their parents, which was reflected in the arts as well as real-world lifestyle shifts. Thus, the New Wave was initially a journalistic slogan that prompted reporters and the population at large to look for a cinematic manifestation from this young generation. They did not have to wait long. Marks of a *jeune cinéma*, or young French cinema, were identified in sexy new movies such as Roger Vadim's *And God Created Woman* (*Et Dieu créa la femme*, 1956) and Louis Malle's *The Lovers* (*Les amants*, 1958). By 1958 and 1959, when Claude Chabrol's *Le beau serge* and *The Cousins* appeared, followed quickly by François Truffaut's *The 400 Blows* (*Le quatre cents coups*) and Alain Resnais's *Hiroshima, mon amour*, movies by Jean-Luc Godard, Jacques Rivette, and Eric Rohmer, among others, were going into production. This burst of new *jeune cinéma* movies was labeled New Wave cinema. These first features would all be evaluated in the context of one another.

Most of the hundreds of movies that could be called New Wave—typically films by directors who had never directed a feature film before the period of 1958–64—were produced under unusual and often striking conditions. These movies were not merely new in the stories they told, but also in their mode of production and resulting styles. Typically, New Wave films were shot quickly, on location, with recently discovered, often amateurish actors and minimal crews, to reduce costs. These conditions helped determine the trend toward contemporary stories and settings. This less-industrial mode of production was also made possible by a new generation of lighter, cheaper 35 mm cameras and sound-recording equipment. *Breathless* pushed the new shooting style further, using only available light and a film stock not even meant for cinema. The resulting New Wave stories were loosely constructed art-film narratives that followed characters whose desires and goals often remained a bit confused, or at least unfocused. Further, the unpolished, sometimes disjointed film styles fit these rather chaotic, spontaneous tales of youths wandering through contemporary France.

But while the New Wave as a whole looked a bit unprofessional and even careless in contrast to classical Hollywood and mainstream "quality" French films, *Breathless* managed to stand out as one of the more extreme and challenging products of this experimental movement. As Claude-Jean Philippe explains, "It is with [*Breathless*] that the first real blows against syntax, or rather the conventional forms of film language were struck." *Breathless,* with its ellipses and jump cuts, opened up a new world of filmmaking options (qtd. in Douin 37). For such critics, *Breathless* follows in the steps of *The Rules of the Game* (*La règle du jeu*, Renoir, 1939) and *Citizen Kane* as an important marker of a new era in film history. Godard had brought his own personal experiences and aesthetic views from the rich context of 1950s French cinephilia to produce one of the greatest films of all time during a period when many important groundbreaking films were appearing in France. The story and style of *Breathless* set it apart from much of that parallel film practice during the New Wave, and close analysis helps us rediscover some of what has made Godard's first feature so fresh and intriguing for over forty years now.

Analysis

With *Breathless*, Godard managed to synthesize his own critical concerns and revitalize the fiction film while celebrating key elements from cinema history. Part of the dynamism and loose spontaneity of Godard's story springs from its unusual development process, as Godard gradually managed to convince producer Georges de Beauregard to fund his first feature. Godard worked briefly with Beauregard, editing several travelogues and touching up dialogue on a number of scripts, before pitching the idea of a low-budget gangster film. Beauregard became interested, thanks in large part to the recent triumphs of Godard's friends Claude Chabrol and François Truffaut. Godard's story came from a newspaper article that Truffaut had noticed. Godard and Truffaut had discussed it as a possible movie idea, but only had brief notes. At Godard's request, Truffaut wrote up a fifteen-page script outline, which convinced Beauregard. That treatment reveals that while Godard took liberties with character names and some events, the overall plot structure still owes a great deal to Truffaut's summary (Andrew 153–60). Claude Chabrol served as "technical adviser," and Beauregard insisted on Raoul Coutard, a young cinematographer with documentary experience. Jean Douchet notes that Coutard brought "rough and tumble" experimental camera techniques with him (253). Godard's unusual lighting and camera-mobility demands further motivated Coutard to give *Breathless* a radical visual style. Coutard and Godard mixed documentary and fiction film tactics for a new synthesis. The film was shot quickly, August 17 to September 15, 1959, for approximately $85,000, with the largest paycheck going to star Jean Seberg, then under contract to 20th Century–Fox.

Godard's story of Michel Poiccard's three-day pursuit of money and Patricia is deeply indebted to plot devices and icons from a wide range of movies from the past, and thus analyzing it as a dialectical text poised between classical genre filmmaking and art-cinema experimentation proves very useful. As Bordwell and Thompson explain, Godard here does not criticize classical Hollywood so much as update 1940s *film noir* conventions by mixing them with a modern, self-conscious treatment. Gone are the clear plot and character development of classical cinema. Moreover, they point out that the halting plot, with a fair amount of seemingly inconsequential dialogue and action, "make Michel's story quirky, uncertain, deglamorized" (367). Much like Godard's "quirky" critical reviews, his first feature film's story leaps about in loosely connected fits and starts as it delivers bits and pieces of information about Michel, Patricia, and the fictional world they inhabit.

Breathless is a movie that boldly acknowledges its debt to other films, genres, and directors via intertextual references and quotations. Godard even dedicates it to Monogram Pictures, which made many B movies. Monogram was "famous for their ability to turn out tightly paced films on short shooting schedules and poverty-line budgets. This was precisely the ideal of the New Wave" (Cook 444). Dedicating *Breathless* to Monogram was part provocation and part tribute; so when Michel finds a pistol in the American car, Godard further demonstrates his debt to American genre films—Hollywood provides the gun and the girl (Seberg, via 20th Century–Fox). Both Dudley Andrew and Michel Marie (in *The French New Wave*) provide useful lists of genre films referred to in *Breathless,* including many gangster films. For Andrew, *film noir* is the genre that most promotes but also problematizes freedom, proving that Michel, like *Breathless* itself, struggles to escape the limits of genre (12). It is also a genre populated by exploited women and *femmes fatales* trying to survive in a man's world. Moreover, Patricia, standing over the dead Michel, echoes Ida Lupino at the close of *High Sierra* (Raoul Walsh, 1941): both are confused and shocked over the outcome. Romance and happy endings are not part of this generic world. As James Naremore notes, many European *auteurs* have reworked *film noir* self-consciously. In the process they "grounded their work in allusion and hypertextuality rather than a straightforward attempt to keep a formula alive." Godard's version includes reducing the gangster film to comic-book stereotypes (202).

Evidence of a tension between classical genre films and Godard's art-film variation can be seen in just about every scene in *Breathless.*

While the film is dotted with genre references, those scenes which would prove the very stuff of action and characterization in a classical *film noir* seem almost tangential, rarely advancing the key story events. For instance, at one point, Michel is unaware that the police inspectors have been tipped off and are close behind him. He casually exits the metro onto the Champs-Elysées and pauses before a picture of Humphrey Bogart's face, advertising his last film, *The Harder They Fall* (Mark Robson, 1956). A moment of silence follows in tribute to Bogart, who had died of lung cancer, during which a starry-eyed Michel blows smoke and says "Bogey." An iris-out ends the scene, but not before revealing that the police are right behind Michel, though they fail to see him. Thus this plot point is left unresolved; the chase is interrupted by Michel's tribute to his role model, but his idle moment does not help the bumbling police catch him.

Next, there is a fade-in on Patricia asking Michel if he will take her to dinner. But the transition produces a gap between the iris-out and the fade-in, leaving the time and space unclear; no explanation is provided about where the police are now. The pursuit is simply suspended. Michel, broke, heads down to the café restroom, where he knocks out a man to rob him, in a scene that Andrew notes is a citation from Bogart's *The Enforcer* (Bretaigne Windust, 1951) (13). But once he and Patricia are back on the street together, Michel shows no sign of the tough-guy cop killer who just assaulted a man for dinner money. Rather, he recounts the tale he read of a thief who robbed in order to have money to impress a girl, which of course is what Michel just did in the café. Michel finishes the story by explaining that the woman became the man's accomplice until they were both caught. This situation impresses Michel, as if he is providing Patricia with a blueprint for their possible relationship. However, Patricia suddenly remembers a prior engagement, so she will not be joining Michel for dinner after all. Thus, Michel's assault in the café for dinner money becomes pointless and inconsequential, because Patricia dines with another man anyway. Michel's violent act becomes a silly gesture in Godard's comic-book reworking of *film noir*. The generic bits are there, but Michel ends up less a tough thug than a cartoonish criminal crossed with a spurned lover.

This series of events is typical of the plot structure and resulting characterization of *Breathless*. Godard offers up Michel and Patricia as modified art-film characters whose goals drive the large narrative structure but whose individual actions often lead off on tangents or to anecdotal situations. For instance, Patricia goes to meet her editor from the *New York Herald Tribune,* Van Doude, and he gives her a book about a pregnant woman dying from an abortion and says he hopes she avoids the same fate. At this point we are not yet aware Patricia is pregnant, so the story seems pointless, unless her job is to review the book. At the end of the scene, Van Doude says, "You're coming with me, of course," to which Patricia replies three times, in different tones, "Of course." For spectators, it is unclear whether any or all of the conversation is important for theme or character. Patricia's line to Van Doude, "I don't know if I'm unhappy because I'm not free, or if I'm not free because I'm unhappy," explains her deep malaise in an excessively melodramatic manner. But her language seems artificial, as if Godard were suddenly mocking her naive, college-girl attitudes. That she leaves with Van Doude after saying "Of course" further causes the viewer to question her motives and ponder whether her relations with Van Doude also make her "not free." Is she with this man because she wants the writing assignments he can provide or because she actually likes him? And, is she happy to be with him in order to avoid Michel? Answering such questions is difficult, in part, because Patricia, like Michel, displays few strong feelings about what she does (Bordwell and Thompson 369). For instance, it is only when Patricia learns that Michel is a married cop killer that she says she loves him. She seems excited to help steal a car and hide out with him. But in the morning she rather inexplicably decides to call the police to inform on Michel's location. She follows her declaration of love quickly with betrayal. The film's final moments, with Patricia running to Michel shot down on the street, does not fully resolve her situation. She drags her thumb across her lips, mimicking Michel's repeated gesture: Maybe a clue, but of what exactly?

As spectators, we typically construct characters from textual cues, such as gestures, elements of *mise-en-scène,* editing patterns, and character traits, in part so we can better forge hypotheses about where they, and the story, are headed. However, *Breathless* complicates that process of expectation, often forcing us to readjust our hypotheses retrospectively. Michel, even more than Patricia, challenges attempts either to construct a unified character or to anticipate his actions. For instance, he claims his grandfather drove a Rolls-Royce and his father was a clarinet player. But none of this explains how he came to be the thug he is today, and the ashtray of a Rolls-Royce that he shows Patricia as evidence of his love of those cars was stolen from his former girlfriend earlier in the film. He seems to make up his life as he goes. Similarly, he mentions that he is one of the few in his crowd who actually likes cops, so why was he so quick to kill one? Godard's narrator provides fragments of character only. Most puzzling is Michel's behavior at the end. Michel, who has finally arranged to receive his cash and a getaway car for Italy, decides instead to stay with Patricia, who has just betrayed him: "I'm all messed up. Anyway, I feel like going to prison." Moments later, he will be shot dead, but even at the end he makes his funny smirking gestures at Patricia, finishes his cigarette, grumbles, and dies. The story retains many gaps, and reading the events retroactively against the ending fails to fill in basic information. The only thing Michel's death seems to complete is the same ambition as that of the writer Parvalesco—to become immortal (Patricia is probably carrying his child) and then die—rather than encapsulating any trait of his own. Such narrative ambiguity in Godard's characters provides a perfect test case for how we make sense of cinematic characters in the first place and where *Breathless* frustrates easy comprehension of character motivation.

One telling result of such ambivalent characterization is the film's failure to build a consistent "structure of sympathy" that allows the audience to identify fully with Michel and Patricia. Murray Smith argues convincingly from a cognitive theory approach that viewers respond to characters in systematic ways that involve three levels of engagement: recognition, alignment, and, finally, allegiance. Recognition involves our perception of characters as "integral, discrete textual constructs" and allows us to identify characters by their physical and behavioral traits. Alignment is an active process by which "spectators are placed in relation to characters," in part by the narrative's range and depth of information, which includes which events we witness and whether we see and hear from the character's point of view or even share their mental perspective via flashbacks or dreams. Thus, we not only recognize Michel Poiccard as the fellow checking how much money he has in his hand; we then watch as he robs the man in the café. We as viewers begin to see the world through Michel's eyes as we are shown both the problem and Michel's solution. But the final stage of the structure of sympathy—allegiance—requires that spectators take a moral stand based on our understanding of the character's motivation and our decision of whether to empathize with the character's goals and actions (Smith 81–85). Reducing Michel's assault to a cartoonish pastiche derails the process. Godard's excessive style and elliptical plot make it difficult for viewers to "identify" with Michel and Patricia as fully as we might with more generic film characters.

The plot organization of *Breathless* fails to align us consistently and restricts much of the information that could help us further understand Michel and Patricia's experiences. We witness Michel's displeasure at seeing Patricia kiss Van Doude, for instance, and get a great deal of information during the long discussions in her room the next day. However, the plot denies us other information that would help us understand their basic motivations. First of all, we never find out exactly why Michel is owed the money. If it were from some ghastly crime, this fact would certainly affect our opinion of him (and Patricia). Similarly, we never get any view of Patricia and Michel's initial meeting during her vacation. If *Breathless* provided the sort of mental subjective flashback present in *Casablanca* (Michael Curtiz, 1942), when Bogart's Rick recalls the "good times" from the past, we might better understand Michel's obsession with Patricia as well as her reticence to continue the relationship. A final example of denied information is that the plot does not show us any of Patricia's evening with Van Doude beyond what Michel sees. Thus, while she may explain to the jealous Michel in the morning that she did not have sex with Van Doude, we, like the suspicious Michel, have no evidence. Godard's incommunicative narration playfully shifts alignment and short-term allegiance back and forth. In this same scene, Patricia is frustrated that Michel has invaded her room, Michel is frustrated over his money and jealousy, Patricia blurts that she is pregnant, and he scolds her. But the situation is still complicated by the fact that she "thinks" she is pregnant by Michel. Nothing is certain.

Godard offers a fragmented, complex, and incomplete structure of sympathy, especially in contrast to classical *film noir*. By the end, when Patricia tells Inspector Vital where to find Michel, and Michel refuses to leave and is shot in the back, any definite alignment or moral allegiance for either character has been weakened. Both seem to be acting against our expectations. But it is not only the lack of character information that complicates our ability to judge Michel's and Patricia's every action. The narrative discourse and its stylistic devices interfere with any simple structure of sympathy. As Smith explains:

> One of the central actions of the story—Michel's killing of the policeman—is represented in such a discontinuous, elliptical fashion that it is impossible to make a confident moral assessment of the action and therefore, to some degree, of the character. Does Michel simply reach for the gun as the cop approaches him, and casually fill him with lead? Or is the shooting an impulsive act of desperation? . . . Godard's discombobulated montage sequences obscure rather than clarify the moral valence of the action. (215)

The visual style, and the discontinuity of the editing, in particular, disrupts further the spectator's labor of reconstructing a unified story with clear character traits, much less a conclusive sense of allegiance with the protagonists.

If *Breathless* seemed radical, even among the narrative experiments of the French New Wave, this had much to do with its editing and sound mixing. Marie-Claire Ropars-Wuilleumier has famously summed up Godard's contribution:

> It all begins with the disruption of a certain mode of communication. . . . Once Godard removes, in *Breathless*, all the dramatic connections between scenes, but also within a scene and even a shot, he is attacking the logical continuity and thus the completeness of the narrative itself. By cutting out transitions and explanations, he draws the spectator's attention to each image that remains . . . leading to the invention of a new aesthetic. (18–19)

The disruptive editing, and especially the jarring use of jump cuts, has invited detailed attention from critics and historians. As David Bordwell explains in "Jump Cuts and Blind Spots," 1960s *auteur* criticism was particularly interested in distinguishing authorial interventions, so the jump cuts in *Breathless*, in which a temporal ellipsis is created within what could have been a continuous shot, have figured prominently in all accounts of Godard's first feature (8–9). While the jump cuts contributed to some hostile attacks on the supposed unprofessionalism of *Breathless*, for most film historians they are one more way that Godard's film referred to cinema's past—Georges Méliès and Soviet montage directors, in particular—while repackaging it as part of a new film language.

But it is important to remember that the jump cut is one exemplary strategy among many significant stylistic innovations in *Breathless*. Godard as a critic had boldly attacked many mainstream filmmakers for their stories and styles, so he was very conscious of the high stakes in presenting his own feature. He was also aware that he was trailing just behind the first part of the New Wave: "Godard, filming after Chabrol, Truffaut, and Resnais, wanted to make *À bout de souffle* the standard-bearer of a new aesthetics, that of the French New Wave" (Marie, "'It Really Makes You Sick!'" 162). Godard saw his first feature as a chance to build on his own critical and historical perspective: "What I wanted was to take a conventional story and remake, but differently, everything the cinema had done. I also wanted to give the feeling that the techniques of film-making had just been discovered or experienced for the first time" (qtd. in Milne 173). It is worth remembering that only a few months before shooting *Breathless*, Godard had written a review of Chabrol's *The Cousins* that concluded, "When I say that Chabrol gives me the impression of having invented the pan—as Alain Resnais invented the track, Griffith the close-up, and Ophuls reframing—I can speak no greater praise" (qtd. in Milne 129). With *Breathless*, Godard seems to have set out to give the impression of rediscovering editing in particular.

Godard's overall style for *Breathless* involves the exploration of sound-to-image relations and their obvious construction and even disruption of the fictional events. Nearly every scene lays out a complex approach to narrative style. The narrator manipulates information on the micro level of individual jump cuts and musical interventions, as well as in larger scene-to-scene juxtapositions. Godard signals from the beginning that *Breathless* will provide highly overt marks of narration, acknowledging that this is all a fictional construct. For instance, while Michel is driving to Paris, he not only outlines his character's goals, he also hums continuously during jump cuts of the road ahead of him. This micro-level disruption foregrounds diegetic sound that is continuous, but an image that is discontinuous. *Breathless* reminds viewers that sound is recorded and edited separately from the image, and the final print can accommodate what would be impossible in the "real" or profilmic world. This is a movie about cinema that goes far beyond the level of intertextual references to Bogart and *film noir*, referring now to the filmmaking apparatus as well.

As Michel drives, he even addresses the camera/spectator directly. But once he breaks the traffic rules, the disorienting editing and hectic sound track assault the viewer with fast-paced pandemonium. In the eight shots that make up the seventeen-second initial chase, a police whistle sounds as the car crosses the center line; the editing gets more discontinuous, with short, jarring takes; and the music increases in volume and intensity, mixing clumsily with engine noises, a horn, and even squealing tires on the dirt road. During the disorienting montage of the chase, his car changes screen direction repeatedly, traveling right to left, then left to right, and back again. This is all further complicated by rapid pans from inside his car and jump cuts. Once on the dirt road there is a short respite as Michel opens his hood, but then, in a rather conventional point-of-view shot, Michel sees one motorcycle pass, but soon return. Suddenly, the camera work and editing seem to leap into action along with Michel as he ducks into his car. Next we hear the voice of the officer proclaim, "Don't move or I'll shoot," but the accompanying camera shot wanders down Michel's head to his arm. Michel is standing upright now, facing screen right, even though the police officer was last seen to the left. There is no reestablishing shot, and the sound track is silent for a moment, providing no cue as to what happened in that small gap. Next there is a jump cut as the camera follows along Michel's arm to his revolver and cuts in to an even tighter shot of the gun itself, and then, bang, to the falling officer. The series of camera shots overtly resembles a comic strip, with variously posed elements of a conflict. But the final one is of Michel running across a field, with the music again rising loudly before dissolving into the more lyrical theme music as the image fades to black and inexplicably fades up on Michel getting a ride in Paris.

This important sequence reveals the narrator's manipulation of the narration on small and larger levels. During the chase, the disjointed montage provides images that do not easily line up. It is unclear how long this chase took, how Michel got far enough in front of the motorcycles to turn off the highway unseen, where the second police officer ended up, or where exactly the doomed officer was in relation to Michel. The larger leap, of course, is how Michel managed to escape to Paris. It is a disorienting film style that nonetheless preserves its *film noir* milieu while violating classical narrative norms. The editing, camera work, and sound track complicate the narrative events, often denying the viewer access to everything from tiny bits of information (the middle of Michel's arm in a jump cut during a pan) to large portions of the action (the location of the second police officer).

Throughout *Breathless,* Godard's playfully overt manipulation of the viewer's comprehension becomes a consistent strategy. For instance, at the end of the nearly three-minute-long shot sequence of Michel finding Patricia selling papers and chatting with her, he exits after making plans to meet later, when suddenly Patricia runs off-screen in pursuit of him. During the entire sequence, the camera has been in a low position (with cinematographer Raoul Coutard sitting in a mail pushcart), but now loud music blares, diegetic sound is eliminated, and the camera cuts to a high-angle shot looking down on Patricia as she runs in the opposite screen direction. She stops Michel at a newsstand and seems to tell him something, perhaps changing the location of their rendezvous, and he walks off. This transition is a condensed version of the car chase: there are abrupt violations of screen direction, and the sudden music is exactly the same as that in the scene in which Michel runs across the field after shooting the officer. Moreover, after three minutes of hearing spontaneous discussions, the viewer does not hear how the conversation ends. Michel walks off, refuses to buy a *Cahiers du cinéma,* sees a man killed, reads in the newspaper about his murder of the highway patrol officer, and enters the travel agency, where the camera, again in the low cart-level position, tracks around to follow him during his conversation with the travel agent, mirroring the earlier scene's shot sequence.

Godard's narrative style emphasizes the arbitrariness of the story construction, creates permanent ambiguity, and calls the viewer's attention abruptly to the labor of signification. Throughout *Breathless,* whether in the conversations in Patricia's apartment, or when Michel steals a car while Patricia waits, or when Michel and Patricia dodge into a movie theater to hide, every shot and sequence plays with micro- and macro-level disruptions that challenge our expectations as well as the conventions of narrative cinema.

Conclusion

In the end, *Breathless* kills off Michel in a manner fitting the overall *noir* themes as well as the film's ongoing narrative inventiveness. First,

Patricia tries to explain her betrayal to Michel, during which the camera tracks around the room with her, then arcs in the opposite direction as Michel makes a sort of reply, treating them as if they were two satellites in opposed orbits. Next, Michel runs out to the street. Michel's conversation with his friend Berruti is composed from a jumble of editing devices. Further, the police arrive, but there is no establishing shot showing the pursued Michel and the firing police. Godard has assembled the basic pieces of a genre film: Michel is the doomed romantic hero, echoing *film noir* but also Jean Gabin's poetic-realist roles; Patricia is the betraying *femme fatale;* and the malevolent police detectives arrive to gloat. The pieces are there, but it is the craft of the puzzle master that finally impresses the viewer rather than any internal logic of character, theme, or closure.

Breathless lived up to Godard's hopes of becoming the standard-bearer of New Wave aesthetics. Though he never returned to exploring systematically the jump cut, Godard has managed to investigate a multitude of other cinematic techniques and narrative options throughout his amazingly productive career. His cinema revolutionized film language at a time when a few French film critics were just beginning to use new linguistic theories and vocabulary to analyze the cinema. Clearly, Jean-Luc Godard jumped ahead of other filmmakers, but also of most film critics. The legacy of *Breathless* can be seen far beyond the New Wave. It was one of those exemplary films whose imprint can be detected in a host of later films, from a variety of traditions. Films as diverse as *Bonnie and Clyde* (Arthur Penn, 1967), *Pulp Fiction* (Quentin Tarantino, 1994), and *Run Lola Run* (Tom Tykwer, 1998) owe a debt to *Breathless.* Godard's first feature provided film studies with one of its richest texts for the simple reason that *Breathless,* like Godard, springs from cinema history itself.

Credits

France, 1960, Georges de Beauregard

Director: Jean-Luc Godard
Screenplay: Jean-Luc Godard, based on a scenario by François Truffaut
Cinematography: Raoul Coutard
Editing: Cécile Decugis
Music: Martial Solal, Mozart's Clarinet Concerto K. 622

Sound: Jacques Maumont
Technical Director: Claude Chabrol
Camera Operator: Claude Beausoleil

CAST:

Michel Poiccard	Jean-Paul Belmondo
Patricia Franchini	Jean Seberg
Inspector Vital	Daniel Boulanger
Van Doude	Van Doude
Antonio Berruti	Henri-James Huet
Carl Zumbach	Roger Hanin
Parvelesco	Jean-Pierre Melville

Bibliography

Andrew, Dudley, ed. *"Breathless."* New Brunswick: Rutgers UP, 1995.

Bordwell, David. "Jump Cuts and Blind Spots." *Wide Angle* 6 (1984): 4–11.

Bordwell, David, and Kristin Thompson. *Film Art.* New York: McGraw, 2001.

Cook, David A. *A History of Narrative Film.* 4th ed. New York: Norton, 2004.

Douchet, Jean. *Nouvelle Vague [The French New Wave].* Paris: Cinématique Française/Hazan, 1998.

Douin, Jean Luc, ed. *La nouvelle vague 25 ans après.* Paris: Cerf, 1983.

Godard, Jean-Luc. *Histoire(s) du cinéma.* 4 vols. Paris: Gallimard, 1998.

———. Interview. *Cahiers du cinéma* 138 (1962): 21.

Hillier, James. *Cahiers du Cinéma: The 1960s.* Cambridge, MA: Harvard UP, 1986.

Marie, Michel. *"À bout de souffle": Etude critique.* Paris: Nathan, 1999.

———. *The French New Wave: An Artistic School.* Trans. Richard Neupert. Oxford: Blackwell, 2003.

———. "'It Really Makes You Sick!' Jean-Luc Godard's *À bout de souffle* (1959)." *French Film: Texts and Contexts.* Ed. Susan Hayward and Ginette Vincendeau. London: Routledge, 2000. 158–73.

Martin, Marcel. *"À bout de souffle." Cinéma 60* 46 (1960): 117–19.

Milne, Tom. *Godard on Godard.* New York: Viking, 1972.

Monaco, James. *The New Wave: Truffaut, Godard, Chabrol, Rohmer, Rivette.* New York: Oxford UP, 1976.

Moullet, Luc. "Jean-Luc Godard." Hillier 35–48.

Naremore, James. *More Than Night: Film Noir in Its Contexts.* Berkeley: U of California P, 1998.

Neupert, Richard. *A History of the French New Wave.* Madison: U of Wisconsin P, 2003.

Rancière, Jacques, and Charles Tesson. "Jean-Luc Godard: Une longue histoire." *Cahiers du cinéma* 557 (2001): 28–36.

Ropars-Wuilleumier, Marie-Claire. "La forme et le fond ou les avatars du récit." *Etudes Cinématographiques* 57–61 (1967): 17–34.

Smith, Murray. *Engaging Characters: Fiction, Emotion, and the Cinema.* New York: Oxford UP, 1995.

Fellini's 8½ (1963)

KRISS RAVETTO-BIAGIOLI

The Circus of the Self

I am a liar, but an honest one. (Federico Fellini)

Context

Like the protagonist of *8½* (*Otto e mezzo*, 1963)—Guido Anselmi, a famous filmmaker suffering from an artistic block—Federico Fellini later claimed to have lied to his producers about having a completed script for what was to become his most acclaimed film. Guido (played by Marcello Mastroianni) exhibits several other of Fellini's own characteristics: he goes through a midlife crisis, has a reputation for philandering, shares some childhood memories with Fellini, and, like Fellini, goes to a spa to recover from a mental and physical breakdown. But as striking as these biographical analogies between Fellini and Guido may be, they should not be taken at face value. Fellini, in fact, was unapologetic about his tendency to lie about his past: "People reproach me for not always telling the same story in the same way. But this happens because I've invented the whole tale from the start and it seems boring to me and unkind to other people to repeat myself. . . . I have invented myself entirely: a childhood, a personality, longings, dreams, memories, all in order to enable me to tell them" (49–51).

What is clear, however, is that the very film that delineates Guido's failure to make a film has become Fellini's masterwork, cementing the high international visibility he had gained with films like *I vitelloni* (1953), *La strada* (1954), *Le notti di Cabiria* (*Nights of Cabiria*, 1957), and *La dolce vita* (1960). Yet the reception of his early films was not always positive. Italian critics attacked *La strada* for betraying neorealism and its political commitment, indulging instead in sentimentalism, decadence, and solipsism. *La dolce vita* triggered more violent responses: it caused riots, sparked vicious public intellectual debates, and was even the subject of parliamentary hearings.

Unlike Fellini's early films like *La strada* and *Le notti di Cabiria*, which sentimentalize poverty, *La dolce vita, 8½,* and *Giulietta degli spiriti* (*Juliet of the Spirits,* 1965) privilege decadence and personal crises (creative, spiritual, intellectual, and sexual) as their main themes. But they do so from a radically subjective perspective—what Gilles Deleuze calls Fellini's style of "knowing subjectivism" (5–10). That led Italian critics of the film journal *Cinema nuovo* (Guido Aristarco and Luigi Chiarini) and Italian intellectuals (Alberto Moravia and Elio Vittorini) to take issue with what they saw as Fellini's self-indulgent, egoistic promotion of debauchery, and his simultaneous endorsement of Catholicism, mysticism, and bourgeois individualism. It was primarily his "subjective view of reality" and decadent themes that were considered to break with neorealist aesthetic codes, and what critics believed to be its political and moral commitment (Aristarco 20–21). While *La strada* was reproached for submerging the real in spectacle, *La dolce vita* was said to organize the everyday into a traveling spectacle, and *8½* to achieve the deliberate confusion of reality with spectacle. Fellini responded to such accusations by declaring that "realism is a bad word. In a certain sense everything is realistic. I see no dividing line between imagination and reality. . . . A lie is always more interesting than the truth. Lies are the soul of showmanship and I adore shows. Fiction has a greater truth than everyday, obvious reality" (152, 100).

French film critics Georges Sadoul and André Bazin were more sympathetic than their Italian counterparts. They contended that what made postwar neorealist and Italian cinema important was not its sociopolitical content but its formal, aesthetic criteria. Taking his cue from Cesare Zavattini, the neorealist filmmaker and critic who described neorealism as the art of the encounter (fragmentary, ephemeral, elliptical, with deliberately weak connections and floating events), Bazin pointed out that neorealism was less about "real" politics than about the uncertainty of reality. For Bazin, neorealist cinema "rejects implicitly or explicitly the realism it uses" (21). As Deleuze puts it, in neorealism, "the real is no longer represented but aimed at," that is, "rather than representing an already deciphered real, Neorealism aimed at an always ambiguous real" (1). For critics like Bazin and Deleuze, neorealism is not just *in crisis* but is about the crisis of reality—whether political, historical, intellectual, or individual. According to both Bazin and Deleuze, neorealism was radicalized not by Fellini alone, but also by Michelangelo Antonioni, Luchino Visconti, and Pier Paolo Pasolini. All of them went beyond simply capturing the social reality of the street, and exposed the cultural, spiritual, and intellectual emptiness that accompanied Europe's (and particularly Italy's) economic miracle—the overcoming of the devastation and poverty in the aftermath of World War II and the shift toward a consumer-driven economy. These filmmakers saw their role as artists changing from one who speaks in the name of the disempowered poor, who had no social recourse, to one who, as Fellini put forward, "unmasks the lies, identifies the inauthentic, and takes apart the indefinite or false absolutes. This is the only corrective recourse against our bankrupt history" (qtd. in Bondanella 230).

For many filmmakers, the economic boom years of 1958–63 were marked by moral ambiguity and uncertainty. Reflecting the dystopia of Europe's entrance into its "Dolce Vita," Fellini's films *La dolce vita* and *8½*, Visconti's *Rocco e i suoi fratelli* (*Rocco and His Brothers*, 1960), and Antonioni's *L'avventura* (1960) capture the sterility of the bourgeoisie. These films represent the inability of filmmakers, artists, and intellectuals to promote national heroes, solidarity, or any cultural or political account based on "accepted" ideological truths. All of these films bespeak another social crisis—the crisis of representation. While Visconti, Pasolini, and Godard directly confronted the political dimensions of these ideological and social crises, Fellini was reluctant to participate in social politics and was therefore singled out by the press and accused of being a traitor to neorealism—the very movement that put Italy at the forefront of avant-garde filmmaking from the mid-1940s to the early 1950s. Fellini marveled at the wreckage of ideological constructs and social conventions (neorealism included) but preferred not to give any moral conclusion or closure to his films, thus leaving the audience with feelings of uneasiness and anxiety. As he put it, "there is no objective reality in my films, any more than there is in life" (qtd. in Bachmann 85).

While many critics argue that it was *La dolce vita* that marked Fellini's radical break with neorealist aesthetics, *8½* achieved a new aesthetic form in which subjectivity—imagination, dreams, memories, and hallucinations—becomes spectacle. As Deleuze explains, in *8½* "we no longer know what is imaginary or real, physical or mental in the situation, not because we are confused, but because . . . there is no longer even a place from which to ask" (7). The collapse of the real into the spectacle and the open-ended narrative of *8½* make it impossible to establish one conclusive way of reading the film. Instead, *8½* offers multiple, even contradictory ways to read the film: as a self-conscious and self-critical look at the filmmaking process, replete with references to other films (especially Fellini's own); as an experimental treatment of time in terms of what Bergson (in *Matter and Memory*) called *durée*— the rhythms and flows of time as memory, lived experience, history, myth, etc.; and as a psychoanalytic (both Freudian and Jungian) exploration of themes of unconscious sexual guilt (manifested in dreams and fantasies) and imaginary constructions of identity.

Analysis

La Bella Confusione, *or a Squalid Catalog of Mistakes?*

More than a film within a film, or a film about filmmaking, *8½* is a film about the making of *8½* itself. Christian Metz suggests that "it is not only a film about the cinema, it is a film about a film that is presumably itself about the cinema; it is not only a film about a director, but a film about a director who is reflecting himself onto his film" (230). This cinematic rumination on the process of filmmaking constitutes what Metz calls a "mirror construction" (*contruction en abyme*), which confuses as much as it multiplies the levels on which it operates. On one level, we are led to believe this is a film about a director who fails to make a pseudo-science-fiction or pseudo-religious-salvation film in which the pope and his cardinals will lead the exodus of the survivors of a nuclear war into outer space. Yet, even before the episode in which the producer, the production crew, Guido, his wife Luisa, and her friend Rossella visit the film set (the scaffolding of the spaceship's launch pad), it has already become apparent that the actual film Guido is trying to make is not about surviving a nuclear holocaust but about the very film we are watching.

Although we hear frequent remarks about the expense of building the spaceship's launch pad, discussions of nuclear holocaust and intergalactic exodus are nowhere to be found in *8½*. Instead, Daumier— the philosopher/critic who has been brought in to help Guido with the script—often comments on scenes and figures that have just appeared, like the first apparition of Claudia at the spa. In the following sequence, when Guido waits at the train station for his mistress (Carla), he reads Daumier's critical comments, and we hear Daumier's voice: "of all the capricious apparitions, what is the meaning of the girl of the spring? . . . purity? . . . Out of all symbols that abound in the story, this is the worst." Similarly, in the scene following Guido's recollection of La Saraghina (the prostitute he visits with his friends as a young boy), Daumier asks, "what does this mean? This is a character inspired by your childhood memories with no connection to a real critical consciousness. . . . Your tender ignorance has a negative effect. . . . Your little memories bathed in nostalgia . . . intend to denounce [Catholicism] but end up being its accomplice."

Ironically, at the same time that Daumier denounces the incorporation of what appear to be Guido's incoherent personal fantasies (about Claudia) and childhood memories (of La Saraghina) into the text of the film, he reveals some of the film's intended themes and motifs. Daumier explains the connection of Guido's own memories to the themes of Catholic guilt and punishment for illicit sexual desires, confession and concealment, his fantasies of and longings for salvation, purity and fulfillment, and the "stringing together [of] the tatters of his life" to the "vague memories and faces of people that he was never able to love." Daumier excoriates not only Guido's film, for its general mystification and absence of a specific philosophical premise, but also 8½ itself, for its overall incoherence. He functions as the film's autocriticism, which can be seen to predict (and possibly preempt) critiques of Guido (and Fellini) for being self-indulgent, sexist, decadent, and bourgeois.

Yet, Daumier (played by philosopher/critic Jean Rougeul) is not given privileged status, but instead is in turn made fun of by the film. He is a parody of the film critic (particularly film critics of *Cinema nuovo* and possibly Rougeul himself), whom Guido, in a sight gag, fantasizes about executing, but more important, he is ridiculed for advocating the censorship of film itself. Daumier suggests it is better not to produce than to create a work of art that is imperfect. An example of this ironic mirror construction in which the critic is also caught up in and exposed by his own criticism is when Daumier prolongs his monologue by declaring that "We need some hygiene, some cleansing, disinfectant. We are already suffocated by words, sounds and images that have no reason to exist, that come from and are bound for nothingness. . . . If we can't have everything, true perfection is nothingness." What makes this scene funny is that he cannot see that he is suffocating (himself, Guido, and the audience) with words, sounds, and images, and it is his discourse that is bound for nothingness. By the end of the film, Daumier is literally silenced and his image is bleached out.

If Guido were to listen to Daumier's advice, the "real" film would have to end here, with this artistic and intellectual suicide. In this reading of the film's conclusion, Guido abandons the film because it is too incoherent and too close to his own muddled life experiences. The last sequence, in which the important figures in Guido's life are amassed, simply denotes another fantasy, but an imperfect one. Metz offers two other possible ways of reading the denouement of the film. In the second version, Guido does not complete his film but returns to the confusion of his life, asking his wife to accept things as they are, that is, without any "hope of bringing profound meaning" or a "messianic salvation," but celebrating life as it is. In the third version, "the film will be made out of the very confusion of life," but without a "central message" (233). Each possible conclusion radically modifies how we read the film, but unlike the clarity of Daumier's assessment, it is impossible for us to tell which one is the right or definitive version.

Seeing all the characters dressed in white (a motif previously reserved only for Claudia) and the dead appearing next to the living, we are led to believe that the finale is just another one of Guido's fantasies. In this version, the role of the critic is magnified by the press conference, and Guido is silenced not only by his suicide but also by the critics who ridicule him for "having nothing to say." The voice of the critic becomes something of a last judgment, leaving Guido only with images from his life flashing before him. On the other hand, we also know that Guido realizes that he cannot find salvation through his fantasies—neither of Claudia nor of his turning the farm of his childhood into his private harem peopled by all the women of his life. Not only do the real women of his life rebel against their representation in Guido's imaginary, but even his imaginary constructions rebel against his fantasies, undermining his marriage and deriding the inspiration for his film. His interior monologue addressed to Luisa seems to reflect his enlightened consciousness—he expresses his sudden happiness and ability to accept and love himself and others for what they are, to recognize his own confusion, and to overcome the fear of telling the truth about his desires and longings, even his desire to live with her and love others at the same time. But the very conclusion of the film *8½*—a film structured on the flow of Guido's consciousness, however fragmentary, fantastic, and nonlinear it may be—seems to double for the finale (which could also serve as a beginning) of Guido's film. Here, we finally (start to) see Guido play the role of the director, yet by this time we are aware that this is the actor (Mastroianni) playing the role of the director, who is directed to direct.

The uncertainty of roles—even of the role of the film within the film—draws attention to the film's commentary on, and performance of, role playing. Aside from the slippage involved in Mastroianni's acting the part of Guido, who in turn acts as if he were directing a film when he knows that he does not have an idea for a film, there are pervasive confusions between actors, characters, and their roles (both actual and symbolic). The French actress Madeleine LeBeau, who plays the French actress Madeleine, is promised a role in Guido's film, although he does not have a film or a role for her. Yet, we know that she was meant to play a role in the film since we see the costume designer creating her dress when Guido visits his production office. There is also Claudia Cardinale, who plays both the role of Claudia in Guido's own fantasies about the film and his life and the actress Claudia who comes to Guido (much like Madeleine) to find out what role she is to play. With Claudia, however, Guido confesses that there is no role and there is no film. Yet, this admission on the part of Guido comes after his obvious disappointment that Claudia does not live up to his fantasies of her. In opposition to his imaginary construction of Claudia (where she appears in white, drenched in white light), she appears at night, wearing black, and instead of telling him that she has come to "create order and to cleanse" or save Guido (consenting to sacrifice everything for him), she tells him that he looks old and goofy, insisting that he (the character that plays his part) does not know how to love and is therefore very unsympathetic to his predicament. Claudia upsets his internal reality and his attempt to escape this reality (confusion of his own making) through her love (self-sacrifice) (Micciché 267).

The act of role playing is put in crisis by actors playing characters (or caricatures of themselves). These characters often reject their fictional (filmic) incarnation and criticize roles that we have just seen enacted. This makes it hard to discern the various levels of performance—of fictional roles from real, social, or symbolic ones presented in the film. The sequence in which the screen tests are reviewed exemplifies this collapse of reality, fiction, and symbolic meaning. The multiple Olympias (who are doubles of Carla, played by Sandra Milo, who was Fellini's real-life lover), Saraghinas, cardinals, and actors who try out for the part of Guido at eight years old, as well as the actress who tries out for the part of "the wife" make the association of Guido's film to his personal experiences explicit. However, the presence of Luisa in the screening room in the film, and of Giulietta Masina (Fellini's wife) on the set of *8½* that day, reveals multiple tensions between reality and fiction.[1] Luisa must witness not only the tests for the role of "the mistress" (who is clearly a double of Carla) but also that of "the wife" (an obvious likeness to herself), only to have her sister comment that the lines are "straight out of his life." Because the fictionalization of characters does not fool anyone, and the script is read by the audience as a reenactment of an actual scene between Luisa and Guido, Guido's cinematic inventions can substitute for truth. Luisa bemoans his power to project his subjective view of his life through his work. Although she recognizes herself in Guido's film, she reads the role constructed by him both as another lie made to stroke his ego and as his real inability to tell the truth. These representations are at the same time objective lies (they only present Guido's imaginary construction of reality) and subjective truths (they represent Guido's true feelings about Luisa). It is a vicious circle in which reality affects fiction and fiction reality, and where public appearance and private anguish break down into public spectacle and scandal.

While Luisa views her filmic incarnation as the mirror of Guido's reflection on her and takes this representation as cause to end their marriage, Guido—who is unable to tell Luisa he loves her—tells her that she should not be so "melodramatic, it is just a film." But he earlier tells Rossella, "I want to make an honest film, without any lies . . . a film that could help everyone to lay to rest all that is dead that we carry around within. Instead, I cannot lay anything to rest. . . . I find

---

[1]According to Deena Boyer in her diary of the making of *8½*, Giullietta Masina visited the set when Fellini filmed the screen tests, which were later cut into the sequence in which Luisa and her friends join Guido and the production company in the theater to watch the screen tests (18).

myself in a great confusion." Furthermore, he responds to the screen test of the actress playing the role of "the wife" as if it were a manifestation of the real Luisa, by saying, "Luisa, I love you." In a shot/reverse shot, the actress on the screen seems to reply to him, "You lie with every breath." That Guido objectifies his personal life by using it as the material of the film and that he responds emotionally to a fiction of his own making suggest that the film is more than just a fiction. As Deleuze puts it, 8½ "is clearly a subjective recollection or fantasy, but it is not organized into spectacle without becoming objective, without going behind the senses into the reality of the spectacle of those who make it, who live from it, who are absorbed by it" (7). Yet, this also means that Guido "does not act without seeing himself acting, making the viewer complicit in the role he himself is playing . . . and that [he can] love only in dreams or in recollection" (Deleuze 56). Guido can only touch or be touched by reality through the fiction of his own making.

Ruptured Gaze, Rhythm, and Ritornello

8½'s narrative traces Guido's stream of consciousness, mapping out the connections between his dreams and his waking reality, fantasies, and recollections. Guido's subjective point of view is buttressed by Gianni Di Venanzo's camera work: while the narrative follows Guido's thoughts, the camera often seems to replace Guido's eyes. For example, in the opening sequence, when Guido takes flight from the traffic jam and is roped in by Claudia's press agent, we look down at Guido's foot dangling as if it were our own. Similarly, when Guido enters the spa, the camera scans the various characters that directly address the camera as if it were Guido. But as frequently as Venanzo's camera mimics Guido's viewpoint, it also turns its gaze back at him: we watch Guido watching, and being watched by other characters. As John Orr explains, Guido is "caught in the act of preparing his film by all sorts of acolytes and hangers-on. . . . The collective gaze is turned back on him, and he is unable to escape it. [Guido] who aspires to film the world as a carousel which never escapes his panning camera is constantly being watched, hounded, questioned and assailed by those inhabiting the milieu his celebrity embraces" (63).

This symbolic turning of the camera back on the film's creator subverts any one character's claim to control the gaze, yet it also produces a deliberate confusion of spectator and spectacle. The scene in which Guido enters the spa—accompanied by Wagner's "Ride of the Valkyries"—starts as a series of traveling shots that pan the faces of various women who salute the camera (Guido), blowing kisses, waving, and smiling. But each take becomes shorter, less continuous, and more disorienting until the camera pulls back to a long overhead shot—a shot that moves back down into the crowd only to change perspective from Guido to an anonymous point of view, while the music changes from Wagner to Rossini's "The Barber of Seville." While in the initial shots the camera seems to impersonate Guido's vision, it becomes increasingly less clear just who is doing the looking. As the music changes, there is a cut to another traveling shot, but instead of following Guido's line of vision, we surprisingly find him standing in a line for spa water, only to return to his point of view the moment Guido pulls his sunglasses down. At this point the sequence is interrupted by his fantasy of Claudia—this part is marked by the disappearance of diegetic sound and by the overexposure of the image.

Even in the opening scene, which is clearly inscribed as Guido's dream (subjective point of view), there is a rupture between Guido's point of view and that of the camera. When the camera pans over the traffic jam, circling over Guido's car and eventually entering it, it follows his gaze as he scans the passengers in the other cars, but circles back on Guido as he anxiously attempts to escape. The opening sequence is obviously unreal, dreamlike, and subjective: there are only isolated diegetic sounds, Guido's anxious breathing, the rubbing of his hand against the fogged-up window, and then the sound of the wind. There is a complete lack of movement, with the exception of the slow-motion pan over the motionless traffic jam. The combination of subjective point of view and the obsessive framing of Guido from behind produces a curious detachment of Guido from his own dream. Rather than becoming the hero of his own narrative, he anxiously watches himself watching, even in dreams. Guido, as Deleuze writes, finds himself a powerless spectator of his own narrative, "prey to visual and sound sensations which have lost their motor extension" (55).

Fellini defies conventional cinematic constructions of a subjective point of view by exposing the camera's typically anonymous viewpoint, and then by refusing to establish Guido as the one who directs the gaze through the usual series of shot/reverse shots beginning with a close-up. In fact, the first close-up shot of Guido does not come in the opening sequence, but is delayed until the third sequence, and even then it is an indirect one. We do not see Guido himself but his reflection in a mirror. Rather than mimicking a human gaze, the gaze seems to reveal a cinematic (self-)consciousness. Just as Guido is seen looking at himself in the mirror, the set is lit up with an arc light, drawing attention to the image's artificiality. The perception of an independent aesthetic consciousness is not only visualized by the overtly theatrical lighting or the shooting of unfinished parts of the set—the hotel lobby—but also through the use of overt cinematic devices like slow motion (to illustrate Guido's fantasy of Claudia), the suspension of car passengers in a freeze frame (as Guido scans the scene of the traffic jam), and the speeding up of the film (when the young Guido runs on the beach in an attempt to evade capture by the priests from his school). Such cinematic devices reveal just how much Guido's way of seeing is inscribed in cinema: his childhood memories are like slapstick comedies from the age of silent cinema; his romantic fantasies are highlighted by slow-motion photography; and his dreams mimic a photograph's ability to immobilize a moment of time and to capture an image.

But the camera asserts its own point of view, constructing what Pier Paolo Pasolini calls a "free indirect point-of-view-shot" (178–79; my translation). As the camera movement mirrors Guido's subjective gaze, it breaks away from his perspective, constituting a gaze that reflects on his point of view from a metacritical distance. The camera establishes itself not only with Guido as a spectator (director) of the scene, but also as independent from Guido as a spectator on the scene. This splitting of perspective is clear in the opening sequence when the camera takes Guido's perspective as he looks down at the beach below his feet but then shifts to a disembodied bird's-eye view as we watch him falling down into the water.

Constructed as a series of traveling shots, 8½ confuses our sense of spatiality. It offers no geographical markers—establishing shots of exteriors (hotels, the train station, Guido's childhood family home)—and only a few of its scenes are shot on location. With the exception of the piazza in the town of Filacciano, where Claudia drives Guido at the end of the film, all of the other scenes were shot on sets designed by Piero Gherardi. Ironically, Claudia calls the piazza in Filacciano unreal, indicating that the theatrical spaces (stage sets in Cinecittà Studios) are simultaneously more "real" than shooting on location and yet difficult to discern from Guido's imaginary spaces. This uncertainty is only increased by the amount of detail Gherardi put into each set and the fact that most of the film was shot on sets containing an array of eccentric characters that could stand either for real characters or for Guido's fantastic constructs. Similarly, the settings Guido awakes to in the second scene—a pageantry of aging characters at the spa—seems just as surreal as his anxious dreams about death, claustrophobia, and escape. Guido's imaginary world imposes itself even on allegedly "real" spaces. Although the calendar at Guido's hotel reads 1962, the hotel itself, the costumes of the extras, the posters in the train station, the diegetic music, and the props are modeled on 1930s fashion. Even the famous 1930s actress Caterina Boratto—an icon of the movies of Fellini's and Guido's childhood—plays a nameless stranger whom Guido fantasizes about. Her face also appears on the statue of the Madonna at Guido's school.

Because the scenes set in contemporary Italy partially restage Guido's childhood memories, they confirm that we are seeing through his cinematic perspective. But there is in fact a radical disjuncture between the main characters (clearly set in the 1960s) and the background sets and characters (which reflect Guido's memories as a young boy). The nightclub scene that opens with a woman singing Franz Girard's 1922 "Gigolette" demonstrates this dichotomy. As "Gigolette" plays, we see older couples dancing in 1930s attire, but as the music changes to "Cadillac," the older couples leave, and Guido's friend Mezzabotta (whose name literally means "half punch") enters the frame with his new girlfriend, Gloria (one of his daughter's classmates). Mezzabotta looks ridiculous as he attempts to dance with Gloria, but he looks even more foolish as he tells Guido that despite knowing that she only wants his money, he "has never felt closer to anyone in his life." At the same time, Gloria (played by Barbara Steele) appears to be a parody of a young dilettante, who rambles on about the "first cherries of spring" and how "the horrible bees suck the life out of the flowers." Such discrepancies in aesthetics, age, and character are supplemented by the constant interruption of Guido's "reality" through the interjection of his memories, hallucinations, fantasies, and even biting criticisms.

Although 8½ takes place over a five-day period, it displays different and even contradictory time frames. The film incorporates natural types of linear and cyclical time: the chronological progression of days, the pervasive references to aging and the inevitability of death, the chronicling of Guido's sexual development, the alternation of day and night (light to dark and dark to light) and between sleeping and waking states. At the same time, it also depicts what Henri Bergson calls inorganic flows of time: the compulsive reiteration of gestures like Guido's repetition of his mother's wiping or cleaning, Guido's compulsion to touch his nose when he is lying (like Pinocchio), or the repetition of La Saraghina's facial expression by Carla and the American dancer in the harem scene. Such repetitions are often emphasized by an aural refrain: the absence of diegetic sound in the case of Guido's attempt to clean up and be cleansed by others and the use of the rumba as a musical leitmotif for all the female characters associated with La Saraghina. The same sense of repetition applies to spaces (as in the likening of the elevator to the confessional), to figures (the substitution of the mother by Luisa, of La Saraghina by Carla, and of the Madonna's face by that of the actress Caterina Boratto), to the fantasies of salvation and of return to Guido's family farm, to the uncanny reappearance of the dead (such as when Guido visits his father at the cemetery), to the constant interruption of present moments by memories, recollections, and fantasies about the future.

The coexistence of present, past, and possible events demonstrates the film's temporal fluidity. As Deleuze puts it, Guido's "unstable set of floating memories, images of a past . . . move past at dizzying speed, as if time were achieving a profound freedom" (55). Actually, the fluidity of time increases as the film unfolds. The first imaginary sequences are clearly delineated: Guido awakes violently from his first dream, gasping for breath with outstretched hands; at the spa he is woken from his daydream about Claudia by the woman dispensing water; and he is then jarred from his second, more fragmentary daydream about Claudia by the ringing of the phone. As Claudia's role in Guido's film and in his life becomes more untenable, his imaginary construction of her becomes more fragmentary and, ultimately, repetitive. In fact, the more he criticizes his own fantasies about Claudia as "lacking inspiration," the more he likens her to his mother (a distant figure that creates and enforces order). Far from loving, his mother agrees with the church's pronouncements—"shame on you, it is a mortal sin" to have visited La Saraghina—denying the young Guido any consolation, and in the finale she cannot even come to Guido when he calls her; instead, she shrugs and joins Guido's father in the circle dance. Guido even imagines that Claudia, too, has become judgmental, laughing as she reads the part he has for her in the script. This might account for the fact that neither Guido's mother nor Claudia appears in the harem scene.

By the time Guido has his second dream, we see the dream world creep into the "real" world. As Guido sleeps, his mother appears in Carla's hotel room, seemingly wiping the air with her handkerchief (reminiscent of Guido's wiping the window of his car in his first dream). This contemporaneous framing of dreamer and dream slowly dissolves into a double exposure (of the cemetery and the bedroom), and then segues into his dream, which begins with his mother cleaning his father's crypt and ends with his mother attempting to passionately kiss him. But when he pushes her away, he discovers it is Luisa dressed in his mother's clothing, signaling both his conflation of Luisa with his mother and his duplication of his parents' relationship. Guido seems to have adopted his father's evasiveness. Like Guido, his father is first seen attempting to escape the camera, evading Guido and his questions. Both father and son seem more irresponsible than patriarchal, wanting to be babied by their wives (and mistresses) while at the same time treated like real men; but they leave "decorum," order, and responsibility to their wives. Luisa replaces his mother, who like Luisa is presented as both asexual and on the side of moral authority (both criticize Guido for his sexual activities). Luisa is even dressed in white with a high, rounded collar much like a priest. In fact, women play the role of the priests at Guido's school, challenging conventional gender roles without undermining patriarchal and moral orders. When Luisa first appears in the dream, she consoles him ("poor Guido") allegedly for his father's death, but as he pushes her away she responds: "I am Luisa, your wife. Don't you recognize me? What were you thinking about?" He neither recognizes Luisa nor his mother—he has to ask his mother if she indeed is his mother. In the last image of the dream, Guido has disappeared, leaving Luisa standing alone in the cemetery. We are left to wonder just who or what has died. The dream's ending, therefore, questions not only its symbolic meaning, but also the role of dreams as hidden truths.

The next frame after the dream sequence cuts straight to Guido walking down his hotel's hallway humming the "The Barber of Seville." There is no indication of how much time has passed between these two sequences, nor any clues as to how Guido got back to his hotel, and his next visit to Carla sets off a series of sequences that blur the lines between dreams and reality. After Carla develops a fever, Guido finally goes to see her, and she asks him, "Why do you stay with me?" He doesn't answer her but thinks about what he will say to the cardinal when he meets him the next day. In the next cut we see Guido escorted by two of the priests we have already seen accompanying the cardinal in the elevator. Yet, we cannot be sure this is a real encounter or Guido's rehearsal of the encounter that is to take place the next day. Furthermore, as the cardinal digresses into his otherworldly reverie about the birds (making him seem senile), Guido becomes disinterested. As he looks away from the cardinal and his entourage, he spots a woman coming down the hill—a sight that triggers his memory of his encounter with La Saraghina and his subsequent punishment by the priests at his school. This digression does not end by returning Guido to the meeting with the cardinal (in the woods), but shifts to Daumier (in the restaurant), who delivers a scathing criticism of the scene we just watched. The status of this memory, therefore, becomes questionable— is it embedded in a daydream, or is it the visualization of the script?

But, ironically, it is this memory that anchors the preceding scene to the later ones. Daumier's criticism of the scene, in fact, performs a double movement: as it brings the scene into question, it simultaneously establishes a bridge between Guido's memory (of being punished by the church for his sexual desires) and the two scenes in which Guido meets with the cardinal to discuss the position of the church on salvation. His previous encounter with the cardinal triggered his memory of La Saraghina and his punishment at the hands of the church, but in the scene in the restaurant he overhears the cardinal telling a sexual joke about a priest. Rather than provoking a guilty memory, the cardinal's joke triggers Guido's fantasy about meeting the cardinal in what seems to be an adaptation of Dante's *Inferno* (made to look like the spa). In this sequence, the cardinal tells him, "there is no salvation without the church." The juxtaposition of the three scenes—the priest telling the young Guido that La Saraghina is the Devil (in Guido's memory), the cardinal telling a sexual joke (in the restaurant), and the cardinal telling Guido that there is no salvation outside of the church (in Guido's fantasy encounter with the cardinal in the spa)—reveals that the promise of spiritual salvation may be just another lie, one that has been culturally sanctioned by the church.

It is at this point that dissolves and super-impositions arrive with a vengeance. As narrative time becomes harder to follow, these various paradigms of time collide and flow more poetically. Time, Bergson argues, is not experienced chronologically but as a series of flows from the present into the past or (possible) futures (212). Deleuze distinguishes these times as corresponding to two cinematic and musical practices: the "Gallop" (time that gallops toward the infinite possibilities of the future) and the "Ritornello" (literally a "small return," a short musical phrase or song that repeats, in order to preserve the past) (83–97). Although both rhythms of time are present in *8½*, Fellini privileges the ritornello. The ritornello—the modified return of a musical or narrative theme—usually interrupts narrative or musical progression (gallop) with the interjection of a melodic and melancholic reminiscence of what has passed. Yet, as Deleuze explains, "for Fellini, it seems to be the opposite: the gallop accompanies the world which runs to its end . . . but the ritornello immortalizes a beginning of a world and removes it from passing time" (93). Despite its often frenetic pace, *8½*'s sound track functions as a ritornello.

The repetition of Wagner's "Ride of the Valkyries," Rossini's "The Barber of Seville," Nino Rota's theme music, the rumba, and La Saraghina's song (all of which are ritornelli) in the film emphasizes a return to the past, not as a refrain or repetition but as a way of beginning over and over again. For example, the lullaby that accompanies the nannies in Guido's first memory, triggered by the childish cipher "asa nisi masa" (a code word for "anima"),[2] is repeated by La Saraghina when the young Guido goes alone to see her on the beach, and then by Carla in the fantasy in which Luisa introduces herself to Carla just before they dance together at the café. This musical leitmotif marks the connection between the nannies who lovingly nurse and mother the young Guido and the various women who represent his

---

[2]If we take away "sa" and "si" from each word, it leaves "anima." For a further explanation about how "asa nisi masa" becomes "anima," see Albert Benderson's *Critical Approaches to Fellini's "8½."*

sexual objects of desire at different times in his life. The nannies are idealized as women who tend to all of his desires; La Saraghina is his first object of desire as a schoolboy; and Carla is the adult version of these women (she is voluptuous and desires food, sex, and material objects). Even Guido's image of Claudia reflects this return to his infantile fantasies: she is dressed as a nurse who will sacrifice everything to fulfill his needs, and, like La Saraghina, she wears a white veil, suggesting that each woman represents not a new beginning but a ritornello (the starting over of a musical phrase). The film ends with another ritornello, the melodic phrase (which succeeds the opening gallop) of Nino Rota's theme music for *8½*. Rather than providing a conclusion, the music (which returns da capo) suggests that the end is not final but just another possible, modified beginning.

The film presents the past as an idealized space into which all time seems to flow. The present, as illustrated by Guido's relationship to Luisa and the people in the film world, in contrast seems unstable, a time of anxiety, fear, and uncertainty. Guido dreams of escaping this chaotic present by constructing Claudia as his imaginary salvation, yet this gallop toward the future is tempered by his ever-present fear of aging. For instance, the ironic use of Wagnerian music at the spa accompanies his first close-up look at himself in the mirror, the image of a crowd of aging people seeking salvation (the spring of youth), and Guido's search for a woman to nurse him back to youth.

When the music of Wagner recurs, it is in the context of Guido's harem fantasy, in which he replaces the singular figure of deliverance, purity, and devotion (Claudia) with almost all of the women of his past. Instead of representing the various archetypes (Madonna, whore, virgin), these women are transformed into maternal figures that bathe and entertain him, and tend to his various needs. But rather than underlining Guido's mastery over his imaginary harem, Wagner's "Ride of the Valkyries" marks the women's rebellion. Aside from Guido's nannies, Luisa is the only woman of the harem who does not rebel. She is uncharacteristically cast as mother, maid, cook, and nanny to Guido and his women. Although Luisa reminds him that she is his wife, her status as wife has become problematic. As she utters the words "do you remember the day we got married, Guido, do you remember?" she echoes the words of Jacqueline Bonbon ("do you remember when, Guido, I used to dance for you in Bologna, do you remember?"), who has been banished from Guido's presence because she is too old. Like Jacqueline, Luisa is given the spotlight, but instead of dancing for Guido (this time), she dutifully scrubs the floor.

Here, Guido has blended his fantasy world with his childhood memories of the family farm. He transports all of the women of his life (with the exception of Claudia and his mother) back to the farm of his youth, since his fondest memories seem to be those of being there, where he is pampered by his nannies (nurses). Yet, the harem scene does not present a simple desire to become a child or an adolescent again. Rather than galloping to the future (into the arms of Claudia or the church), his fantasy of salvation is replaced by a fantasy about cleansing the past. In the last sequence of the film, everyone from Guido's past reappears. This time, however, they appear in white, as if they (or Guido's memories) have been purified and idealized. By the end of the film, the aging Guido disappears, and we are left with the image of an actor who plays him as a child, dressed in an all-white version of his schoolboy uniform, the one we see him wear both as a boy in his memories and as a man in his dreams. Because there are many possible readings of and returns in the film, Deleuze asks, "on whom will the ritornello place itself, calming the anxiety in *8½*, on Claudia, on [Luisa], or even on [Carla], or only on the white child, the internal or contemporary of all the pasts, who saves everything that can be saved?" (92).

Credits

Italy, 1963, Cineriz

Director: Federico Fellini
Producer: Angelo Rizzoli
Screenplay: Ennio Flaiano, Tullio Pinelli, Federico Fellini, and Brunello Rondi
Story: Federico Fellini and Ennio Flaiano
Cinematography: Gianni Di Venanzo
Editing: Leo Cattozzo
Music: Nino Rota
Art Direction, Costume Design: Piero Gherardi

CAST:
Guido Anselmi	Marcello Mastroianni
Claudia	Claudia Cardinale
Luisa Anselmi	Anouk Aimee
Carla	Sandra Milo

Rossella	Rossella Falk
Gloria Morin	Barbara Steele
French actress (Madeleine)	Madeleine LeBeau
Fashionable woman	Caterina Boratto
La Saraghina	Eddra Gale
Producer	Guido Alberti
Director	Mario Conocchia
Writer (Daumier)	Jean Rougeul
Mezzabotta	Mario Pisu
Jacqueline Bonbon	Yvonne Casadei

Bibliography

Aristarco, Guido. "Guido Aristarco Answers Fellini." *Film Culture* 4.2 (1958): 20–21.

Bachmann, Gideon. "Interview with Federico Fellini." *Cinema 65* 99 (1965): 85–87.

Bazin, André. *What Is Cinema?* Trans. and ed. Hugh Gray. Vol. 2. Berkeley: U of California P, 1972.

Benderson, Albert Edward. *Critical Approaches to Federico Fellini's "8½."* New York: Arno, 1976.

Bergson, Henri. *Matter and Memory.* Trans. Paul and W. S. Palmer. New York: Zone, 1988.

Bondanella, Peter. *Italian Cinema: From Neorealism to the Present.* New York: Continuum, 1991.

Boyer, Deena. *The Two Hundred Days of "8½."* New York: Macmillan, 1964.

Deleuze, Gilles. *Cinema 2: The Time-Image.* Trans. Hugh Tomlinson and Robert Galeta. Minneapolis: U of Minnesota P, 1986.

Fellini, Federico. *Fellini on Fellini.* Trans. Isabel Quigley. New York: Da Capo, 1976.

Metz, Christian. "Mirror Construction in Fellini's 8½." *Film Language: A Semiotics of the Cinema.* Trans. Michael Taylor. Chicago: U of Chicago P, 1974. 228–34.

Micciché, Lino. *Cinema italiano: Gli anni '60 e oltre.* Venice: Marsilio, 2002.

Orr, John. *Cinema and Modernity.* Cambridge: Polity, 1993.

Pasolini, Pier Paolo. *Empirismo Eretico.* Milan: Garzanti, 1972.

2001: A Space Odyssey (1968)

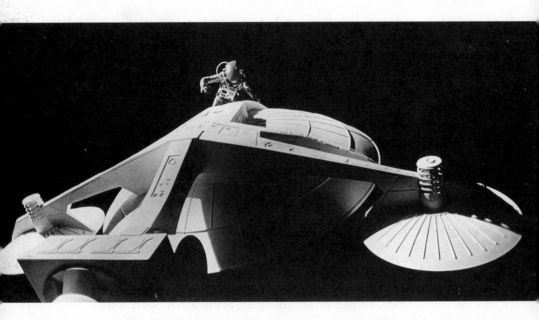

ROBERT KOLKER

— "I'm afraid . . . I can feel it"

Context

From A Trip to the Moon to the Cold War: Sci Fi Origins

Science fiction has been a staple of film since its earliest days. Right after the turn of the twentieth century, the French pioneer of special effects, Georges Méliès, made a fanciful short film called—and about—*A Trip to the Moon*. Scientists enter a projectile that lands them in the eye of the Man in the Moon. They meet strange little creatures. When they return, they wind up under the sea, where they meet more strange creatures. With this film, the movies began looking to the stars or speculating on the look of the future, and using visual spectacle—fantastic images that call attention as much to themselves as to the story they are telling—to make their points.

The science-fiction genre has had its ups and downs in popularity, as all genres do: people's tastes change; the culture changes; and film genres, which are a complex combination of repeated conventions of time, place, character, and narrative, interact with the culture and what the audience agrees to see. When history changes cultural perceptions, a genre can wither and sometimes die. But science fiction has endured, despite small dips in its popularity in the thirties and forties. Fritz Lang's groundbreaking *Metropolis* (released in Germany in 1927, a few years after the Soviet Union produced their science-fiction film *Aelita*) set the mark for the genre, and introduced one of the first great robots, created by what would be a staple of the genre, the mad scientist. The thirties produced a few large studio productions, such as *Just Imagine* (David Butler, 1930), a kind of world's fair exposition of modernity, and there were many serials—short films like the Flash Gordon and Buck Rogers series and *The Phantom Menace*, which ended each week with a cliff-hanger that was resolved in the next week's episode. Most of these serials focused on mad scientists and robots and the heroes that fought them. The thirties culminated in a big-budget film, William Cameron Menzies's *Things to Come,* in 1936, written by H. G. Wells, who also wrote the original novel, *The Shape of Things to Come.* Here, a streamlined modern city—a modern, scientific wonder—arises from war. Progress, in the form of a trip to the stars, is its conclusion. On the opposite side was science fiction about alien invasion. H. G. Wells's *War of the Worlds* (1898) was broadcast in Orson Welles's radio version in 1938, and presented a rather grim view, which was ultimately responsible for the rash of fifties science-fiction films. The United States was in a prewar state of hysteria, and Welles's pseudodocumentary caused wide panic, people believing aliens had landed in New Jersey. Perhaps this is why the forties was mostly a low period for science fiction—World War II kept people's eyes on the ground, or looking for real enemy bombers in the sky. In the fifties, science-fiction films like *The Thing* (Hawks/Nyby) kept imploring us to "watch the skies."

During the thirties and forties, the genre began to mix two narrative elements. The thirties saw the great explosion of monster films: *Frankenstein* and *Dracula* were introduced by Universal Pictures in the early thirties, and their popularity spun off many sequels. The forties saw the birth of the Wolf Man. *Frankenstein* contains aspects of science fiction, including the mad scientist. Horror and science fiction joined inextricably when the genre burst back into extraordinary dominance during the 1950s.[1]

Strange Loves and Strong Fears

The reasons for the genre's reinvigoration are multifold. Much of it had to do with the dropping of atomic bombs on Hiroshima and Nagasaki in 1945. The A-bomb raised people's fears of science run amok and added to peoples' anxiety over the effects of radiation. Hollywood picked up on these fears, as well as the attractions of atomic power, with films that ranged from those about traveling to outer space with atomic fuel to (the more prevalent) ones about monsters being created by atomic radiation. The Godzilla films got started in

---

[1] I wish to thank Jay Telotte for his thoughts on early science-fiction films. His history of the genre is in his book *Science Fiction.* Vivian Sobchack's *Screening Space* is another excellent history of the genre.

Japan in the mid-1950s, coming out of that country's own experience on the receiving end of atomic devastation. In the United States, a few brilliantly conceived films, like Jack Arnold's *The Incredible Shrinking Man* (1957), took on the gruesome or, in this case, cosmic effects of radiation. But something else pushed the genre. The political invention in the United States of a "Communist menace" led not only to a wholesale purging from their jobs of intellectuals, teachers, dentists, screenwriters, and film directors—in fact, anyone with a slightly left-of-center point of view—but also to a growing hysteria throughout the culture that a takeover by an "alien" ideology was as imminent as atomic war.

The science-fiction genre was reborn with a large number of films that were pretty straightforward allegories of alien invasion and infiltration, full of threats that our emotions, our bodies, our very selves were being taken over. Aliens were a substitute for flesh-and-blood (though, of course, barely human) Communists. Don Siegel's 1956 *Invasion of the Body Snatchers* is one of the best examples. "Pods" land on earth and recreate humans as mirror images of themselves, without emotion, without morality—humanoid automatons. These films were obviously extremely conservative in their politics (an exception is Robert Wise's 1951 *The Day the Earth Stood Still,* in which the alien—backed by a threat of extinction from his robot companion—calls for an interstellar political community) and steeped in the milieu of the McCarthy-led anti-Communist witch-hunts of the period. Some, however, worked on the level of spectacle, of eye-popping effects and a sense of the strangeness in the beyond. George Pal's effects for *Destination Moon* (1950) are an example, as is the visual spectacle of Fred M. Wilcox's *Forbidden Planet* (1956). This latter film, made by a major studio, MGM, rather than the small, cheap independents that churned out much fifties science fiction, introduced the best cinematic robot since *Metropolis,* named Robbie. It told its tale of the return of the unconscious in the form of a destructive monster on a foreign planet that is inhabited by an elderly earthling and his daughter (and Robbie)—all by means of a *re*telling of Shakespeare's *The Tempest.* The film is one of the most beautifully designed of fifties science fiction, including its Disney-animated "creatures from the Id."

When the hysteria over homegrown anti-Communism died down by the late fifties, and the Cold War continued to heat up, science fiction went into relative decline. The Cold War lent itself mainly to spy and war films, but a combination of both the war and science-fiction genres reached its climax in Stanley Kubrick's 1964 film *Dr. Strangelove; or, How I Learned to Stop Worrying and Love the Bomb*. After so many films that threatened nuclear or alien Armageddon, Kubrick and screenwriter Terry Southern shrugged their shoulders, laughed, and pointed out that anti-Communism and the Cold War were in fact the idiot machinations of rigid, stupid men who possessed the cunning only to create the means of their own self-destruction . . . and blow up the world. That was that. This film, visually and thematically dark and, simultaneously, hysterically funny, had some small influence in quieting down Cold War rhetoric. After all, after hearing the absurd exaggerations of warmongering in Kubrick's film—"Mr. President, I'm not saying we wouldn't get our hair mussed. But I do say no more than ten to twenty million killed. Tops. Ahh . . . depending on the breaks!"—how could any self-aware person speak such rhetoric seriously? The politics of science fiction were never lost on Kubrick, nor was its inherent spectacle. In fact, he had been thinking about an outer-space science-fiction film (as opposed to a film occupying the kind of inner, political space of *Dr. Strangelove*) since the late fifties (Baxter 199–201). He was aware of the monster–mad scientist mix so important to the horror/science-fiction genre (who appears as the title character in *Strangelove*), and he refined it and then reimagined the whole genre. The film that he created immediately following *Dr. Strangelove* was *2001: A Space Odyssey*, which premiered in 1968, a year of cultural upheaval as well as a high point of cinematic creativity the world over.

Science Fiction and the Art of the Intellect

When I speak of Kubrick "thinking" about a film, I'm not referring to any ordinary filmmaker's process. Kubrick worked mostly alone with a few assistants, researching his projects extensively, organizing and planning down to the minutest detail. *2001* was no exception—quite the contrary: this was to be the science-fiction film that would not merely bring the genre to a climax, but take it to a point of complexity and visual splendor, not to mention mystery, that no other science-fiction film had managed. At the same time, there would be a suggestion of scientific accuracy. Aerospace scientists from NASA were consulted (Bernstein 66). Special effects were painstakingly created and many were invented. *2001* was made long before the revolution in digital composition, now used in all films, that allows any visual effects, or even characters, to be created through computer-based design and animation. Kubrick used models, paintings, carefully synchronized stop-action motion, a few early computer graphics, and some advanced optics to create images that are fantastic and almost tactile at the same time. There is a presence to the images of this film, a sense that they *could* exist, that if you were to flip one of the switches or press one of the buttons that appear in the film, something might actually happen.

He also built large structures, particularly the central interior of the Jupiter spaceship, complete with a revolving centrifuge to allow for some extraordinary tracking shots. All of this was done with a sense of detail never before seen in science fiction. At all times, the screen we look at is filled with images of space and the humans and the tools they use attempting to penetrate it. Interiors are overwhelmed by screens continually presenting graphic, textual, and mathematical data, with buttons waiting to be pushed to create more data, with words that are printed small and large, with brand names and a general minute articulation of things—these are spaceships not with smooth surfaces but covered with conduits and equipment that all look like they could actually be operational. This sense of the presence and immediacy of the environment and instrumentation in *2001* led its co-screenwriter, the science-fiction author Arthur C. Clarke, to say that the next science-fiction film would have to be shot on location!

All this detail and spectacle had a twofold purpose. Keep in mind that Kubrick was an "independent" director. He was unattached to any studio, except, beginning with *A Clockwork Orange* (1971), a long-term, hands-off relationship with Warner Bros.: they would finance and distribute his films but not even have an advanced look at a script, not to mention the film in progress. Kubrick assumed full responsibility for a film from inception through distribution. He worked more like a novelist than a film *auteur,* in complete control of all the massive elements that go into a film as well as the publicity that attends its release. And, as an independent, he knew that each film had to be a commercial success, and therefore had to have spectacular elements, small and large, to attract an audience. The promotional tagline on the posters that accompanied the film's release read, "The Ultimate Trip." In the days of the counterculture and hallucinogenic drugs, Kubrick knew what would attract the audience favored by the film business.

Working alone, though always in consultation with others, and depending on each film for his continued income and productivity made Kubrick aware of the commercial necessities his work had to have, and he failed in this only twice, in the magnificent, ironic, and slow-paced *Barry Lyndon* (1975) and in his problematic last film, also slow paced (something contemporary audiences seem unwilling to put up with), *Eyes Wide Shut* (1999). These are extraordinary films, but they lack some of the spectacle of his other films and instead focus entirely on the intricate and contradictory interactions of characters and their environment that are present in all of Kubrick's work. This was not the case with *2001*, whose spectacle would attract where its complexity might not.

But *2001*, among the most visually spectacular films, is also dense with ideas and speculation. Like all of Kubrick's work, it is full of intricate, interconnected inward- and outward-looking ideas, ideas as complex and minutely defined as the settings and spaces of the visual structure of the film itself—which are themselves, in fact, aspects of the ideas at work in the film. Kubrick was a master of irony, that particular kind of irony that allows for multiple points of view to be held simultaneously—serious and comic, the expected and the unexpected. His films are a mixture of a type of form and content that forces us, as the audience, to think twice, three times, or more to understand what exactly is going on—which forces us to hold multiple ideas in our head at the same time.

Kubrick was also a master of the hidden joke, which is a function of his ironic stance. Each of his films, no matter how serious, has deep within it an often cruel joke played on the main characters, and on the viewers. His characters are never quite aware of the fact that the miseries that befall them are of their own making. These complexities are part of the reality of any Kubrick film: each viewing reveals something missed in the previous one—a gesture, a detail, a repetition of an image, the sudden revelation of another idea that lay dormant—until all the layers of meaning and multiplicity of points of view are either revealed or, as is the case in *2001*, remain hidden.

Analysis

Structure and Composition

2001 poses a multitude of large questions: Is there such a thing as extra-terrestrial life? Does it guide human progress? What happens when humans make computers as smart or smarter than they (this an extension of the old Frankenstein story)? As human emotions become diminished rather than enlarged by what they see, what is the future of human emotions and humans themselves? Can humans be reborn into a greater consciousness? What, ultimately, is the place of human consciousness in the vastness of space? These and other questions are posed through the film's characters and its *mise-en-scène*. *2001* is almost totally, with the exception of a few key sequences, dependent on its visuals, often complex, always extremely articulate. That is, they tell us much more than the characters do about what goes on in the film. The visual spectacle of the film itself engenders its complex ideas.

Let's begin with an image in the penultimate sequence of the film: the "Jupiter Room," that strange place that astronaut David Bowman arrives at after his trip through the infinite tunnel of space, what we might call a black hole (well known since the days of Einstein). The room is simultaneously familiar and unfamiliar. It looks vaguely like something from the seventeenth century, with gray blue walls, French Provincial chairs and tables, statuary, seventeenth-century paintings on the walls, a bed, and, as in almost all of Kubrick's films, a bathroom—this one especially tidy. The floor of this strange place is made up of fluorescent tiles that are arranged in a forced perspective, throwing our perceptions off kilter. We first see the room from astronaut Bowman's point of view, through the port of the space pod in which he traveled across the fields of the infinite. Kubrick cuts to his face, shuddering, in shock. His face reflects the lights of the pod, whose computer screens now read "Non Function." The future has become the past and is now nonfunctional. The past has been cast into the future—or a future that exists inside the astronaut's head.

Kubrick cuts to a shot of the pod standing in the room and then pulls further back for other shots of the utter strangeness of this space, viewed through a distorting wide-angle lens, enforcing a sense of a reality that could not actually exist outside the film. Viewed, but by whom, other than us? Finally, returning to the original point-of-view shot from inside the pod, we now see Bowman himself standing outside the pod in the room. His labored breathing persists on the sound track. In further shots in the sequence, we see Bowman eating a meal and breaking a glass at the table—at which point he looks over his shoulder and sees his ancient dying self in bed!

Is this an astronaut's dream of the perfect hotel room? Or is it the holding cage of extraterrestrial beings? (The music and sounds on the sound track are a mixture of Bowman's breathing, shrieking sounds, and the atonal, anxiety-producing music of the composer György Ligeti, a favorite of Kubrick's.) Whatever or wherever it is, this is the place where Bowman's life will end and, perhaps, begin again. The warped perceptions of this scene are emphasized by the way Kubrick tricks us by playing on the standard cinematic conventions of the shot/reverse shot, in which we see the character and then what the character sees. Instead, in each reverse shot in the room, we see through Bowman's eyes Bowman himself, growing older in each reverse. Bowman looks at Bowman and we at him: at dinner, breaking a glass, alone, and dying, then seemingly reborn, through the monolith, as a fetus circling the Earth.

Fearful Symmetry
What kind of joke is this? For one, it is a joke on the conventions of filmmaking, with this use of the shot/reverse shot to show not the character looking at something or someone else, but the character seeing, instead, only himself. The entire sequence is surreal and apparently inexplicable, and it moves from the sublime to the ridiculous with Bowman's doll-like fetus circling the Earth—if that, indeed, is what's actually happening. But the joke, and the irony, go deeper, and to understand them, we need to probe more deeply into the events that precede this final sequence.

2001, like many of Kubrick's films, is symmetrical, in fact, doubly so. Many of the images of his films are composed symmetrically, providing a bizarre vision of order that not only mocks the disorder of the characters' situation, but confines them within the symmetrical composition itself. 2001's symmetry is subtle and is reflected in the narrative as well as the images. The sequence "The Dawn of Man," which opens the film, is echoed by the sequence "Jupiter and Beyond the Infinite," which ends it. "Man" is "born" at the beginning, dies, and is (apparently) reborn at the end—all of this, it would appear, through the impetus of the monolith. The protoman, in that startling series of shots that begin the film, wordless, speaking only through images of gesture and response, is born into violence. The monolith apparently teaches him how to use tools (there is a flash to the monolith when the ape picks up the bone and figures out what to do with it). Interestingly, maybe even frighteningly, the tools are not used to create but to uncreate, to kill the interlopers from the opposing tribe. "The Dawn of Man" is man's propensity to violence.

At the end, Bowman seems to pass through the monolith to become reborn—but as what? A helpless fetus, passive and entrapped in his cosmic womb? What is he going to do, to become? Kubrick leaves the mystery intact, with only one hint: the look of wide-eyed wonder in the eyes of the encapsulated fetus. Has the monolith and what it stands for undone the damage done at the dawn of man? (It is interesting to note that Kubrick's original notion of the last shot was to have the fetus viewing the Earth as it is covered with atomic-bomb bursts.)

The Perpetuation of Violence through the Art of Editing

The film as a whole suggests intriguing answers, even more enigmas, and spectacular ideas. None is greater than what is contained in the famous cut from the bone that the ape hurls in the air in his euphoria over killing the marauder to a spaceship on its way to a space station near the moon. Actually, the cut is made on a fall: the bone rises and then falls. Cut. The bone-white spaceship falls gracefully in the interstellar ballet that synchronizes its movements with that of the space station. Johann Strauss's waltz "The Blue Danube" plays on the sound track—nineteenth-century music accompanying twenty-first-century space technology. Death (the bone) seems to give way instantly to life—the exciting future of space travel. The edit hides everything, every aeon that intervenes; time itself is swallowed up. Only the ironic presence of an elegant nineteenth-century waltz reminds us of the past.

Editing was one of the most important devices developed in early cinema. In films's very beginnings, one-reelers consisted of one shot, which showed some event: a dancer dancing, two people kissing, a train arriving at a station. As cinematic storytelling developed, the discovery was made that by placing two bits of action that are occurring at the same time but in different places next to each other, or even by dividing a single scene into separate parts—a wide shot that shows the whole scene, a close-up of a face, a hand, a gesture—one could create the architecture of a narrative, its structure, spaces, and meaning. Later, methods other than, or in addition to, cutting were developed. The sequence shot, in which no cutting occurs within a given narrative sequence, allowed movement, positioning, and space alone to describe what the characters were doing.[2] Sergei Eisenstein rethought editing and developed a theory and practice of montage that, in effect, made editing the central purveyor of meaning by using a cut to create a collision of images, to retard or speed up time, or to produce ideas by the juxtaposition of shots, thus eliciting a visceral reaction from the viewer.

It is Eisenstein's influence we see in the bone–spaceship cut in *2001*. With it, Kubrick creates a continuity, but with a discontinuity inside. By leaping through ages of history, he uses the cut literally: he cuts out everything between the bone and the spaceship. At the same time, in Eisensteinian fashion, he creates an association. He cuts on motion (typical of continuity editing), but the motion seems to have no explicit association beyond the visual similarity of floating objects and their color. But what is being implied? The answer is, violence. Even though the sequences that immediately follow the cut show an unusual calm and galactic beauty, the violence that seemed to initiate this calm remains in the back of our minds and moves like a shadow, and then a reality, throughout the film.

Humans as Computers

Actually, it exists more like a negative image than a shadow, the reverse of what we seem to see. One of the enigmas of the film is the contrast between what we, as the audience, see and what the characters in the film see and do. We are, and are meant to be, in awe of the spatial realm Kubrick has created. We know we are looking at models and optical tricks; we feel as if what we are seeing could be a *representation* of the real thing—or at least the real things in Kubrick's imagination,

---

[2]Information on early film practice comes from Gunning, "The Cinema of Attractions."

which he was able to manifest through a variety of optical trickery on the screen. But the characters? They are in awe of nothing. When Heywood Floyd, the emissary of the National Council of Astronautics, arrives at the space station, he phones home. Behind him through a window, a gigantic Earth turns in orbit. Floyd does not once turn around to look, and instead continues a rather bland phone-screen conversation with his daughter (actually Kubrick's daughter; it is also interesting to note that, a few years after the "real" 2001, we now have picture phones much smaller than the ones Kubrick imagined).

Floyd is a blank-faced bureaucrat, evading questions about what's happening on the moon (the discovery of the monolith) and, once he's there, delivering a humdrum speech to a humdrum audience. Some members of this audience accompany him to the monolith site. Do they discuss the enormous possibilities and ramifications of their discovery? No, they make more banal conversation, some of it about the monolith but most of it concentrating on the state of the synthetic food they have for lunch. At the end of the sequence, Kubrick lets us in on the irony of all of this by making a pun. Floyd says, "Well, I must say, you guys have certainly come up with something." One of the men on the shuttle is pouring Floyd a cup of coffee. His words, "Careful, this is hot!" are cut into by the next sequence of the group entering the site, pursued by Kubrick's handheld camera and the wild keening of Ligeti's music. This is hot indeed. But what do they do? They pose for a group photograph, interrupted when the monolith emits an ear-splitting signal, and another time-severing cut takes us to the voyage of the Discovery One to Jupiter and "beyond the infinite." We don't hear again from Floyd for a long time. When we do, the next to the last joke of the film is revealed.

In the mysterious and mysteriously mournful journey of the Jupiter mission—the music on the sound track sounds like a dirge—whose purpose is to find the origins of (presumably) extraterrestrial life, we are presented with two of the most blasé, inexpressive characters in the film, the astronauts David Bowman and Frank Poole, whose behavior is almost robotic. Meanwhile, we, once again, watch the spectacle outside and inside of this extraordinarily imagined ship, which looks like a spermatozoon out to fertilize the universe (an image that is repeated with more emphasis during the passage through the infinite). Kubrick then executes an amazing tracking shot of Poole jogging around the centrifugal hall of the ship, past the rows of instrumentation and the hibernating passengers, soon to be murdered. The sequence is a quiet, elegiac movement that calls attention to itself, to the marvels it shows, and to the utterly ordinary Poole doing another mundane, earth-bound piece of business—jogging, the ordinariness duplicated when Poole lies on a tanning table while viewing the transmitted images of his parents wishing him a happy birthday. He is totally impassive. The extraordinary is forced into the banality of the everyday. *2001* is a film that not only speculates on the possibility of higher intelligence, but directly comments on the diminution of humans and their response. It is about detachment from the wonders of the world and the universe, about the loss of emotional response. The only representative of human (or, in this case, prehuman) life that has exhibited any emotion in *2001* up to this point is the ape who discovers the bone. His joy in violence is a prelude to everything that follows—and everything that follows within the film is entirely without joy or emotion of any kind. The future, in *2001*, is not so different from the present, as Kubrick sees it. Human response has become truncated, men and women are alienated from their own consciousness and from an understanding of the events of the present. All human activity in the film is *run* by something or someone else—perhaps the monolith, but more logically a kind of lethargy born of duty, of carrying out the mission, of plain weariness with wonder. Humans in the film act like automatons.

Computers Smarter Than Humans

And the automaton acts most like a human. The HAL 9000 computer aboard Discovery One is the best in the future world and the end point of scientific research into artificial intelligence. (Don't underestimate the influence of this film: a book on artificial intelligence was published by MIT called *HAL's Legacy* [Stork].) It is a member of a long line of movie robots and computers before and after *2001* that have threatened their masters. There is also a relationship between HAL and that archetype of man-made monsters with consciousness and questions, the monster at the center of Mary Shelley's *Frankenstein*. HAL was built to control and think through everything on the spaceship. He, up to a crucial point, is as calm and emotionless as Poole and Bowman. His red eye stares at their every move (and we, in turn, see them from HAL's point of view). He offers advice, even reads their lips, and begins to take over the ship, killing all but one of its passengers. Does this machine go crazy? Is the film warning us about the dangers of depending too much on technology? After all, Kubrick had already done this in *Dr. Strangelove,* when he indicated that humans can set up destructive machines and then yield so much control to them that their destructive power cannot be stopped. Or, like Frankenstein's monster, has HAL acquired self-consciousness?

Unlike the Doomsday Machine in *Dr. Strangelove,* HAL is not originally set up as a destructive device; it is designed as a controlling companion on a complex space mission. What happens to him? I don't think he goes mad, at least at first. Does he get ahead of his humans and attempt to take over the mission? Yes, but this was, in part, planned for. The information we gather from the film seems to be clear: HAL begins to act up when he claims to detect a fault in an outside antenna. This allows Kubrick to represent the spectacle of a walk in deep space and prepare us for the use of the pod to blast back into Discovery One later in the voyage, as well as to provide HAL an opportunity—while Bowman is trying to rescue Poole, whom HAL has sent flying into the void—to kill all the hibernating astronauts. But besides the visual spectacle of these events—perhaps none more unexpected, imaginative, and hair-raising than the depiction of the murder of the hibernating crewmen through the use of a chart of their diminishing life functions—these are really small plot points.

Plot is never the most important element in Kubrick's development of narrative. There is something else going on, and when we find what it is, we begin to understand that it is something stranger than anything we have seen so far. The revelation begins when Bowman returns from his abortive attempt to save Poole. Locked out of the spaceship by HAL, he explodes his way in and then, with the most determination and emotion we have so far seen from him, enters HAL's "brain" and begins to lobotomize him by ejecting his memory modules. In the process, HAL utters words expressing things that *no one else in the film has expressed:* "I'm *afraid* . . . , I'm *afraid,* Dave. . . . I can *feel* it. . . . I can *feel* it. . . ." The computer, as his mind dies, speaks about the one thing that the humans with presumably whole minds never express: emotion. The machine feels in ways they do not—but that the apes did. They too felt fear. But there is more: we discover that HAL knew more about the mission than Poole and Bowman did.

As the lobotomy is completed, HAL begins singing an inane tune, though one with a telling lyric: "Daisy, Daisy, give me your answer, do/I'm half crazy. . . ." He may be half crazy at this point, but right now, a television monitor goes on in a corner of the chamber. It displays a prerecorded message by Heywood Floyd, with amazing information, which, in typically Kubrick fashion, goes by all but unnoticed. The recording informs Bowman and us that, for security reasons, no one on the mission knew what it was about *except* HAL. In other words, HAL knew about the monolith, knew that the signal it sent was from the moon to Jupiter, and knew that the Discovery's mission was to go to Jupiter and find the source of the monoliths.

Why, then, does HAL go "half crazy" and kill everyone, assuming, as he says while attempting to prevent Poole's reentry into Discovery One, that the mission is too important to allow it to be jeopardized by a suddenly angry human. The answer or, more appropriately, an interpretation of all this is linked directly to the monoliths.

Speculations and Ambiguities:
The Unanswerable Questions of 2001

The monoliths can be understood as images or representations—ideas, actually—given the shape of matte black rectangles, blank, impenetrable, and potent. They have no apparent meaning in themselves, but rather attract meaning to them, or make it. They are defined by the reaction to them by the characters in the film and the viewers of it. Each appearance of a monolith signals a movement of some kind: the ape discovers the bone can be used as a weapon, Floyd and company hear a signal from the monolith and send Bowman and Poole to Jupiter. Once there, before entering the "infinite," we see a kind of ballet of monoliths floating around the universe, an echo, perhaps, of the ballet of the spaceship and space station that opens the second part of the film. At one point, a monolith forms the horizontal section of a cross, with an alignment of astral bodies serving as the vertical. The last time we see a monolith is at the foot of the old Bowman's bed, and the camera, perhaps assuming his point of view, tracks to it until it fills the screen, and we cut to Bowman's fetus circling the Earth.

Are the monoliths messengers sent by extraterrestrials? I don't think so. The monoliths are Kubrick's own speculation on the never-to-be-answered question about whether we are alone in the universe, his intervention into the culture's confused desire/terror of "aliens" coming to change us, probe us, invade our very bodies. We are always afraid of and attracted to the Other, that which is not us. The monoliths are our own Other, the desire of something new. The monoliths indeed seem to cause change. Every time they appear, something happens. But here is where an understanding of a filmmaker's thinking, garnered from the rest of his films, can fruitfully come into play. Kubrick does not, in his films, believe in any power beyond what people, their societies, and their politics create. All of his characters want power, and most develop vast schemes to get it and keep it. They all lose sight of the fact that the systems are of their own making—that they *are* the system. They yield power to the mechanisms they have made, giving up their own responsibility to it. They are destroyed by their surrender. The monoliths can be read as a manifestation of surrender. While they seem to be part of the legend held by some that extraterrestrials are responsible for great human monuments (like the pyramids or Stonehenge—which was, incidentally, built of monolithic stones), the monoliths are passive signs and, of course, not extraterrestrials at all (as I read it) but, if anything, representatives of great change. In other words, they themselves, in their grand impenetrability, are nothing but manifestations of human will, emblems of change.[3]

Again, Kubrick indicates in no other film sympathy with the idea of the existence of any kind of "higher power" or advanced civilization. Quite the contrary. The monoliths are images of human desire and repression. They don't come from a higher power but represent what our very own possibilities and limitations are. This leads to a reinterpretation of the ape and the bone. The appearance of the monolith is a kind of "break" in the impasse of evolution, a visible idea of an imperative to advance. That the advance involves learning how to use tools as weapons is accidental, a product of the apes' intuition. This further illuminates the extraordinary cut from the bone to the spaceship: the latter, an image of beauty and human progress, is tinged by the violence that precedes it— and tinged as well by the passivity of the humans in space in the face of the spectacular unknown and the tools that bring them to it.

---

[3]Leonard Wheat notes that the monoliths may be human attributes (91–93).

The blank face of the monolith is a mirror of the blankness of the characters who inhabit the film, who only react and very occasionally act; they seem not to feel; they respond without response. The only human anger in the film is Bowman's aimed at HAL, and that response is, perhaps, part of his awakening—as is the shuddering trauma throughout his voyage "beyond the infinite." The blankness of the monolith can be read as a representation of the blankness of the mind; it confronts itself and provokes and excites itself, thereby causing change. The monoliths are, like so much in Kubrick films, an idea given form. Not extraterrestrial form, necessarily, but an image of the need for humans to offer a response and to change.

Why is it only HAL who is given knowledge of both the monoliths and the voyage to Jupiter? Perhaps the command of the mission has no faith in the "grunts" who will be actually managing the mission. But the fact is that even the management has put its faith in HAL. Kubrick is very perceptive about the nature of hierarchies, and they are apparent in most of his films: society is divided by class and rank, and those below are always treated badly by those above, and those above are undone by their own actions. Bowman and Poole are tools, and act that way. HAL, however, who should be a tool, is in fact a feeling entity with responsibilities. He acts, has responses, and is violent. He is a murderer with a purpose, like the ape with the bone—in fact, HAL can be thought of as the direct descendent of the ape; he uses his tools to kill in order to advance.

But what if HAL is right that, as he implies, he is the only one who knows enough about the mission and will not jeopardize it in the face of mere humans? Here's something more curious still. If we examine carefully the sequence in which Bowman lobotomizes HAL, we notice that the lucite panels that are extruded every time Bowman turns a key look like miniature, translucent versions of the monoliths. This may be a very fanciful reading, but it's worth considering, because *2001* is so open to multiple interpretations. Imagine that the consciousness of HAL (and there is no doubt that he is a machine with consciousness) envelopes the narrative of *2001*, that somehow the monoliths are harbingers or creations of HAL, or both.

HAL is the beginning and the end, whose creation somehow manages to embrace all of pre-, current, and future history. He reproduces in the form of the monoliths, which coax apes and humans forward to confront finally their own end within the black hole of the universe. This helps explain the utterly enigmatic image that ends the film, the fetus floating in a bubble. What we see is *not* a reborn "star child," but a reborn HAL child, floating endlessly in space, looking—finally— with eyes both amazed and fearful.

Based on this, we could also argue that the apparently perfect linear narrative of the film—from the Dawn to the End of Man—is, in fact, not linear at all, but a kind of ever-repeating cycle, spun by the HAL 9000, contained by him, the clockwork entity that acts when human machinery is breaking down. This would fit with the symmetry, the fearful symmetry, that Kubrick so much loved, from the compositions of individual shots to the shape of the narratives of his films themselves.

Conclusion

The narrative path of *2001* is quite complex, precisely because of its apparent linearity, which implies that Kubrick believes progress is inevitable and goes forward without a hitch. If this *is* what he's saying, then *2001* is the only film of his in which he makes such a statement. But it is simply unlike a filmmaker like Kubrick, all of whose films, as different as their subject matter may be, make a similar statement about the inevitable entrapment of their central character (exactly as the Bowman-fetus is entrapped in a bubble at the end of *2001*). The film ends with this figure circling the Earth, and Kubrick is suggesting that the straight line that the film seems to be following is, in fact, a cycle. *2001* is a kind of envelope of human development (or the lack thereof). Humans seem to move forward but continually get caught in traps. They make incredible machines, which then chew them up. They are, finally—and this is probably not speculation—alone in the universe.

Credits

United States, 1968, MGM

Director and Producer: Stanley Kubrick
Screenplay: Stanley Kubrick and Arthur C. Clarke, based on Clarke's story
    "The Sentinel"

Cinematography (Super Panavision): Geoffrey Unsworth
Additional Photography: John Alcott
Editing: Ray Lovejoy
Music: Richard Strauss, Johann Strauss, Aram Khachaturian, and György Ligeti
Production Design: Tony Masters, Harry Lange, and Ernie Archer
Special Photographic Effects Design and Direction: Stanley Kubrick
Special Photographic Effects Supervision: Wally Veevers, Douglas Trumbull, Con
    Pederson, and Tom Howard
Costume Design: Hardy Amies

CAST:

David Bowman	Keir Dullea
Frank Poole	Gary Lockwood
Dr. Heywood Floyd	William Sylvester
Moonwatcher	Daniel Richter
Voice of HAL 9000	Douglas Rain
Smyslov	Leonard Rossiter
Elena	Margaret Tyzack
Halvorsen	Robert Beatty
Michaels	Sean Sullivan
Mission Control	Frank Miller
Stewardess	Penny Brahms
Poole's father	Alan Gifford
Poole's mother	Ann Gillis

Bibliography

Baxter, John. *Stanley Kubrick, A Biography*. New York: Carroll, 1997.

Bernstein, Jeremy. "Profile: Stanley Kubrick." *The Making of Kubrick's 2001*. Ed. Jerome Agel. New York: Signet, 1970. 58–70.

Ciment, Michel. *Kubrick*. Trans. Gilbert Adair. New York: Holt, 1983.

Coyle, Wallace. *Stanley Kubrick: A Guide to References and Resources*. Boston: G. K. Hall, 1980.

Falsetto, Mario. *Stanley Kubrick: A Narrative and Stylistic Analysis*. Westport: Greenwood, 1994.

Gunning, Tom. "The Cinema of Attractions: Early Film, Its Spectator and the Avant-Garde." *Early Cinema: Space, Frame, Narrative*. Ed. Thomas Elsaesser. London: BFI, 1990. 56–62.

Kagan, Norman. *The Cinema of Stanley Kubrick*. 3rd ed. New York: Continuum, 2000.

Kolker, Robert. *A Cinema of Loneliness: Penn, Stone, Kubrick, Scorsese, Altman*. 3rd ed. New York: Oxford UP, 2000.

Nelson, Thomas Allen. *Kubrick: Inside a Film Artist's Maze*. Bloomington: Indiana UP, 1982.

Phillips, Gene D. *Stanley Kubrick: A Film Odyssey*. New York: Popular Library, 1975.

Sobchack, Vivian. *Screening Space*. New Brunswick: Rutgers UP, 1997.

Stork, David G., ed. *HAL's Legacy: "2001"'s Computer as Dream and Reality.* Cambridge, MA: MIT Press, 1998.

Telotte, J. P. *Science Fiction.* Cambridge: Cambridge UP, 2001.

Walker, Alexander, Sybil Taylor, and Ulrich Ruchti. *Stanley Kubrick, Director: A Visual Analysis.* Rev. and expanded ed. New York: Norton, 1999.

Wheat, Leonard F. *Kubrick's "2001": A Triple Allegory.* Lanham, MD: Scarecrow, 2000.

The Godfather (1972)

JON LEWIS

"Nothing personal, it's only business"

The Godfather is widely acknowledged to be a cinematic masterpiece.[1] But its significance in film history has to do with not only its relative cinematic or artistic quality but its larger role as the first big film in a very new "*auteur* Hollywood," marked by an eight-year run of terrific moviemaking between 1972 and 1979.

The Godfather marked a transition in American filmmaking, which is to say that its style and content proved in various ways ground-breaking. Its success—as a work of art, as a creative "property" exploited by its studio Paramount Pictures, as a model for would-be *auteur* filmmakers awaiting their first big break—changed Hollywood forever. The account of the film that follows looks at the film from a variety of points of intervention; it includes a long look at the movie industry in the early 1970s, a critical and historical discussion of the crime or gangster film genre, some pertinent notes on style and form, and a brief discussion of auteurism. The discussion is necessarily complex given the way the film changed the course of Hollywood history.

Context

Hollywood in 1970

In 1970, Paramount Pictures ranked ninth in the industry, behind the other six majors and two independents, National General and Cinerama.[2] With industry unemployment reaching 42.8 percent, an

---

[1] In a poll of fifteen hundred so-called movie buffs mounted by the American Film Institute (AFI), The Godfather was ranked third in a list of the hundred best films of all time. The British journal Sight and Sound polled film directors in 1992. They ranked The Godfather the sixth all-time best film.

[2] A far longer and more detailed business history is presented in Jon Lewis, "If History Has Taught Us Anything."

all-time high, and short-term interest rates (on loans used to finance motion pictures) soaring up to 20 percent, Gulf and Western, the studio's conglomerate owner, made a bold move to get out of the movie business forever. Gulf and Western entered into a deal with a local real estate developer to unload the legendary Melrose Avenue Paramount production facility, a move nixed at the eleventh hour by a local zoning board that looked unfavorably on the developer's plan to move an adjacent cemetery.

When the real estate deal fell through, Gulf and Western CEO Charles Bluhdorn staked the studio's future on three very different men: Hollywood veteran Stanley Jaffe; sales and advertising expert Frank Yablans; and a former actor and fashion industry executive, Robert Evans. Jaffe bowed out before he had the chance to do much, clearing the way for Yablans, who became the first in what is now a long list of former marketing executives to take over a studio. While a vice president at Paramount, Yablans helped Bluhdorn downsize the studio operation by firing over eleven hundred employees. As president, Yablans promised to cut production costs to an average of $2.5 million a picture—a simply ridiculous figure that was more symbolic than practical. It was out of his gesture of fiscal austerity that *The Godfather* was born.

Evans, unlike Yablans, was a flamboyant character; media interest in his private life rivaled that of the movie stars who appeared in his films. Evans was also an instinctive showman. While in charge of production, he dramatically increased Paramount's worth within the Gulf and Western family of companies, upping the studio's share of the multinational's annual revenues from 5 percent in 1967 to almost 50 percent in 1976. Twice in the first three years of the 1970s, Paramount posted the number one box-office film for the year—*Love Story* (Arthur Hiller, released December 1970) in 1971 and then *The Godfather* the following year. Both projects originated with and were developed by Evans.

To acquire the rights to *Love Story*, Evans advanced $25,000 to publisher Harper and Row to help finance a first printing of twenty-five thousand copies of the novel. Evans's investment dramatically changed the way the publishing house promoted the book. The marketing campaign mounted by Evans made the novel a best seller. Because they owned the rights to the novel so early on, Paramount was able to produce the movie version while the novel was still selling strong.

End of the year figures for 1971 show the movie *Love Story* grossing in excess of $50 million domestically, accounting for roughly a third of Paramount Pictures' gross revenues for the year and earning over three times as much as the year's number two film, Arthur Penn's *Little Big Man* (released December 1970). The dramatic box-office success of *Love Story* sent a clear message to the rest of the industry that one film by itself could save a studio. It also sent a clear message to Yablans that Evans had found a way to use Gulf and Western's publishing empire to develop movies, a formula he then employed to even greater success with *The Godfather.*

Development

As Evans tells the story in his 1994 memoir, *The Kid Stays in the Picture,* in the spring of 1968, novelist Mario Puzo came to him with "fifty or sixty rumpled pages" of a book tentatively titled *Mafia.* At the time, Puzo owed bookies approximately $10,000 he didn't have. Evans advanced Puzo $12,500 and virtually stole the screen rights to one of the biggest novels of the decade (182).

A slightly different version of Evans's colorful story is told by Coppola biographer Peter Cowie. As Cowie tells it, by the time Puzo approached Paramount, he had already received a $5,000 advance to write the novel for G. P. Putnam and Sons. Hoping to presell the movie rights to the book, Puzo showed sixty pages of an early draft to George Wieser, a story editor at Paramount. Wieser liked it because he thought it "read like a Harold Robbins best seller." Wieser then took the manuscript to Evans and his assistant, Peter Bart. At first Evans wasn't interested because the studio had lost money on Martin Ritt's gangster picture, *The Brotherhood* (1969). But Wieser persisted, and eventually Evans agreed to purchase an option for the lowball figure of $12,500 ("Whole Godfather" 90). After purchasing the option, Evans began to develop the project. But he did so cautiously, still unconvinced that there would be an audience for a movie about organized crime.

Evans did not warm to the project until he got nervous that actor Burt Lancaster might take the project away from him. In 1970, Lancaster's production company approached Paramount and offered to help finance the production so long as Lancaster got to star in the film. Evans opposed making a deal with Lancaster for a couple of reasons: he did not think the actor was right for the title role, but, more important, he did not want to diminish studio interest in the project by selling off profit points to Lancaster's company.

When Peter Bart first suggested to Evans that they hire Francis Ford Coppola to direct *The Godfather*, Evans found the idea preposterous. Coppola had at the time directed one B movie (*Dementia 13* [1963]) and three studio films (the comedy *You're a Big Boy Now* [1966]; the musical *Finian's Rainbow* [1968]; and *The Rain People* [1969], a realist road picture), none of which did well at the box office. Moreover, Coppola had a reputation for playing fast and loose with studio money; in 1969 he took $600,000 in development money from Warner Bros. and spent it all on state-of-the-art production equipment. When the studio rejected all of his (and his fledgling company, American Zoetrope's) projects (including *American Graffiti, Apocalypse Now,* and *The Conversation*) and asked for their money back, Coppola had to tell them the money had been spent. In order to pay Warner back, Coppola hired himself out to shoot television commercials and industrial films, but so considerable was his debt to Warner that when rumors circulated that Paramount intended to offer Coppola the chance to direct *The Godfather*, Warner Bros. executives called Evans to tell him that he might as well send the check to them.

Evans offered *The Godfather* to Coppola only after Richard Brooks, Constantin Costa-Gavras, Elia Kazan, Arthur Penn, Franklin Schaffner, Fred Zinnemann, Lewis Gilbert, and Peter Yates turned him down. Though the book was by then a best seller, directors were nervous about the film adaptation because the script and the novel seemed to glorify organized crime. Several directors expressed concern about being associated with a potentially incendiary ethnic picture, which is to say they worried about making what might be taken to be an anti-Italian-American movie.

Bart continued to lobby for Coppola, at one point telling Evans that if he ever wanted to get the film made, he would eventually have to choose between Coppola and Lancaster. In order to maintain studio control over the project, Evans made an offer to Coppola. But to his astonishment, Coppola turned him down, not because of the film's politics but because he had no interest in directing a mainstream genre picture. Legend has it that it was Coppola's friend, George Lucas, who finally convinced him to accept Evans's offer, arguing that if he directed *The Godfather* he would never have to make another commercial film again.

After three days of negotiations with the studio, Coppola took Lucas's advice and provisionally agreed, so long as, in Evans's recounting of Coppola's terms, "it's not a film about organized gangsters, but a family chronicle. A metaphor for capitalism in America" (220). Evans found such a concept for the film ridiculous, even pretentious. But, confident that the studio's final cut left *him* in control of the picture, Evans had a contract drawn up, and Coppola signed for $150,000 plus 7.5 percent of the net to direct the picture.

Evans's notion that he could control Coppola was immediately put to the test when Coppola decided to cast Al Pacino as Michael Corleone. Evans thought Pacino was too short and that all three of his screen tests were awful. Coppola steadfastly held that Pacino was the only actor for the part. After much wrangling, Evans finally made the offer to Pacino, but by then the actor had signed with MGM to appear in *The Gang That Couldn't Shoot Straight* (James Goldstone, 1971).

In 1971, MGM was owned by Las Vegas billionaire Kirk Kerkorian and run by a notorious hard case named James Aubrey. According to Evans, in order to keep Coppola happy, he asked his friend, the reputed Mafia lawyer Sidney Korshak to help him out with Kerkorian and Aubrey. As Evans tells the story, twenty minutes after hanging up with Korshak, Aubrey called Evans: "You no-good motherfucker, cocksucker. I'll get you for this. . . . The midget's [Pacino's] yours." According to Evans, Korshak had called Aubrey's boss, suggesting that he release Pacino from his contract. Evans asked Korshak what he said to convince Kerkorian to cooperate, and Korshak responded, "I asked him if he wanted to finish building his hotel" (223–24). The notion that folks in organized crime quietly made offers one dared not refuse was part of *The Godfather* narrative well before the first foot of film was shot.

Evans also opposed Coppola's plan to cast Marlon Brando in the title role. Coppola finally sold Evans on Brando by shooting a silent screen test in which the actor stuffed his cheeks with cotton to create the image of the older, heavier Don Corleone. It is hard to imagine the film without Brando and Pacino.

Production

Film historians routinely acknowledge that *The Godfather* is an *auteur* film, which is to say that the artistic and financial success of the film has largely been attributed to Coppola, its writer-director. The *auteur* theory dates to the mid-1950s in France when a handful of young film critics for the film magazine *Cahiers du cinéma* developed a historical argument based on the notion that despite the ever-intrusive Hollywood production system, American movies could be seen as the product of a single *auteur,* or author: the director.

The *auteur* theory is central to *The Godfather*'s significance to American studio-film history and to Coppola's role within that history. For many film historians and critics, *The Godfather* marks the beginning of a "golden age," an "*auteur* renaissance." It is hard to dispute such an observation. Consider the following studio titles all in general release in commercial theaters between 1971 and 1974: *A Clockwork Orange* (Stanley Kubrick), *The French Connection* (William Friedkin), *Klute* (Alan Pakula), *Dirty Harry* (Don Siegel), *The Last Picture Show* (Peter Bogdanovich), *Deliverance* (John Boorman), *The Godfather* (Francis Ford Coppola), *Cabaret* (Bob Fosse), *2001: A Space Odyssey* (in reissue; Kubrick), *American Graffiti* (George Lucas), *Mean Streets* (Martin Scorsese), *High Plains Drifter* (Clint Eastwood), *Pat Garrett and Billy the Kid* (Sam Peckinpah), *Badlands* (Terrence Malick), *The Exorcist* (Friedkin), *Serpico* (Sidney Lumet), *Chinatown* (Roman Polanski), *The Conversation* (Coppola), *The Godfather, Part II* (Coppola), and *Blazing Saddles* (Mel Brooks).

Coppola attended film school at UCLA at a time when film studies professors enthusiastically taught the films of the French New Wave and the *auteur* theory promoted by its most famous directors. As a would-be film director, Coppola embraced the *auteur* argument. The *auteur* theory placed importance on a director's personal signature: a recognizable visual style, a repeated interest in certain themes or stories. *Auteurs* could work within the system. Alfred Hitchcock, John Ford, and Howard Hawks did. But in the process of making commercial, genre films, an *auteur* nonetheless made every film recognizably his or her own.

Coppola, the *auteur,* transformed Puzo's tawdry gangster novel into an epic movie chronicle of an Italian-American family. He tempered Puzo's lurid, pulp sensibility and in doing so offered a deft analysis of criminal enterprise as a means of cultural assimilation and social legitimacy. The film's size and scope and even its length became early indications of what would soon become recognizable as Coppola's distinctive, operatic visual style. Like Orson Welles, with whom he shares many qualities, Coppola is a theatrical director. He is fond of set pieces and places an extraordinary emphasis on set design, lighting, and camera work. For example, in a scene about an hour into the film, Tom (Robert Duvall), the family's attorney, is kidnapped by the Don's would-be assassin, the drug lord Sollozzo. Tom is hurried off to Sollozzo's hideout in a Christmas-tree lot. The camera introduces the scene using a long-angle lens inside what looks like a trailer. We can see shadowy figures in the foreground and in the background, but the room itself is almost completely dark. Sollozzo then crosses in front of the camera and is frozen for a moment in grotesque close-up, bathed in monstrous orange light. When we finally see Tom, he is seated, half-lit and half-dark (an apt physical portrait of the man whose ties to the mob are at best semi-legit). The scene opens and closes with the strange establishing shot, an image of the interior of the trailer that tells us absolutely nothing about where we are and everything about how we should feel about the setting and the characters. Coppola is an "academic filmmaker," which is to say that he has taken what he has learned in the classroom (in this case, what he has learned about German Expressionism) and used it to advantage on-screen.

A later scene has Michael (Al Pacino) rehearsing his eventual assassination of Sollozzo and a corrupt New York City cop. As the family henchman Clemenza gives Michael some lessons on how to make a successful "hit," the two men sit below a framed portrait of the pope. The irony, made apparent in the set design, visually portrays the nexus of family business and family life for the Corleones.

The film's climactic scene shows Michael in the warmly lit interior of a church (lit and introduced visually much like the trailer scene) attending the baptism of his nephew and future godson match-cut with shots of the perfect execution of his plan to assassinate all of his criminal rivals and enemies. We see shots inside the darkly lit church alternated with sunlit shots of the various hired guns going about their business. The montage sequence, a set piece par excellence, is so well executed that in the end, when Michael's henchman whispers in his ear that all went well, it is hard not to share a sense of elation at his accomplishment, though what we have seen is little more than the ruthless execution of five or six people.

As with all great *auteurs*, Coppola's visual style is in evidence in all of his work. The operatic scale and scope introduced in *The Godfather* is integral to his Vietnam War film *Apocalypse Now* (1979), the gangster musical *The Cotton Club* (1984), the biopic *Tucker: The Man and His Dream* (1988), and the horror film *Bram Stoker's Dracula* (1992). With the notable exception of *The Conversation* (1974), which seems on reflection a miracle of understatement for Coppola, the common denominator is a penchant for elaboration, a penchant for making films and characters larger than life (the Don, Michael, Kurtz in *Apocalypse Now*, Tucker in *Tucker: The Man and His Dream*).

Montage sequences structured much like the set piece near the end of *The Godfather* render the climax of things in *The Cotton Club*, where a dance number and a series of murders are intercut, and in *The Godfather, Part III* (1990), as a staged opera is intercut with a failed attempt on Michael's life. An emphasis on lighting and set decoration dominate even his lesser-known films: the lavishly produced musical romance *One from the Heart* (1982) features moving stage scrims to highlight the film's theatricality. The eccentric, black-and-white teenpic *Rumble Fish* (1983) is made to look like it was shot in Germany in the 1920s, in what may well have been nothing more or less than a display of Coppola's impatience with formula and genius with film style.

Coppola was by all accounts the godfather of a new American *auteur* cinema. The extent of his success at the box office, with critics (who have routinely acknowledged the genius of the first two *Godfather* films) and with the Motion Picture Academy (*The Godfather* and *The Godfather, Part II* both won Best Picture), made possible, albeit for just a handful of years, commercial opportunities for other young and ambitious directors. After the blockbuster box-office success of *The Godfather*, studio executives came to understand that the surest way to make money was to make really good movies—and, though it pained them to admit it, the only way to make really good movies was to support and trust really good filmmakers.

Coppola versus Evans

Authorship in Hollywood is never clear, never simple. In the years following the release of *The Godfather*, Evans has persistently bristled at the ways in which the film has been routinely acknowledged as a hallmark of a new sort of American *auteur* moviemaking and the ways in which Coppola has been celebrated as the genius who all by himself made *The Godfather*. In a 1984 interview, Evans contended that Coppola's final cut of *The Godfather* "looked like a section out of [the television show] *The*

Untouchables"; it was so bad, Evans further argued, *he* had to recut and "[change] the picture around entirely" (qtd. in Saloman).[3] In his 1994 memoir, Evans recounts an exchange of telegrams between the two men in mid-December 1983. The first, unsigned but supposedly sent by Coppola, read as follows: "Dear Bob Evans, I've been a real gentleman regarding your claims of involvement in *The Godfather*. I've never talked about your throwing out the Nino Rota music, your barring the casting of Pacino and Brando, etc. But continually your stupid babbling about cutting *The Godfather* comes back and angers me for its ridiculous pomposity." The second telegram was sent and signed by Evans the following day: "Thank you for your charming cable. I cannot imagine what prompted this venomous diatribe. I am both annoyed and exasperated by your fallacious accusations. . . . I am affronted by your gall in daring to send this Machiavellian epistle. The content of which is not only ludicrous, but totally misrepresents the truth" (Evans 344).[4]

Evans's challenge to Coppola's authority over *The Godfather* is significant beyond their perhaps petty (but nonetheless fascinating) feud. Though both men remain bitter about, and divided over, who exactly cut the entire movie, Evans and Coppola agree that it is Evans's and not Coppola's ending that audiences saw in 1972. Coppola shot and hoped to use a final scene of Kay (Diane Keaton), Michael's wife, in church lighting a candle for Michael's sins. The released version of the film ends instead as the door slowly closes in Kay's face. Coppola's ending returns us to the film's thematic conflation of family and religion and Michael's necessary betrayal of both in his seizure of power. Evans's ending accounts only for Michael's criminal success and Kay's growing irrelevance in his life.

---

[3]Evans originally developed *The Cotton Club* as a historical picture about the titular legendary Harlem jazz club. His plan was to direct the film himself. He was soon overwhelmed by the dual role as producer-director and turned to Coppola, despite all the animosity, to fix the script and maybe shoot the film. In a matter of months, Coppola took over as writer-director. Evans got a producer's credit, albeit along with seven other players who later entered the scene. That Coppola had stolen his film and then turned it into a strange gangster/musical hybrid rekindled the old feud, ably encouraged by Julie Saloman in her interview/article "Budget Busters: *The Cotton Club*'s Battle of the Bulge."

[4]As with so many Hollywood stories, one has to consider the source. Also in play here is Evans's characteristic hyperbole.

Attribution of authorship is further complicated by the various deals that impacted on the production of the picture. Well before Coppola shot a single foot of film, negotiations were held between *Godfather* producer Al Ruddy and the New York chapter of the Italian American Civil Rights League, after which Ruddy announced that Paramount would eliminate all references to the Mafia and La Cosa Nostra from the *Godfather* screenplay (in exchange for full cooperation of the New York City unions, many of which were, ironically, controlled by Italian American gangsters). It was a comical concession, of course; by 1971, more than seven hundred thousand hardcover editions and three million paperback copies of the novel, which was originally titled *Mafia*, had been sold.

Though it forced the director's hand a bit, Ruddy's deal in the end supported Coppola's take on the novel: that it should be more a family chronicle than a gangster story. In place of "Mafia" and "La Cosa Nostra," Coppola used the term "five families."

Early on in the production of *The Godfather*, Vic Damone, cast as Johnny Fontaine, the singer-actor (many believe based on Frank Sinatra) whose career is rescued by Don Corleone, walked off the set claiming that his part and the film as a whole was demeaning to Italian Americans. Rumor had it that Damone backed out under pressure from Sinatra and/or the mob. True or not, the marketing guys at Paramount allowed the mob backstory to play out in the press because it kept the film, well before its release, in the news. Coppola set about making a complex film about cultural assimilation and capitalist enterprise and their impact on an Italian American family. The studio marketing crew endeavored to keep the public "on point," that *The Godfather* was about scary American gangsters who maybe feared or at least did not look kindly upon the truth the studio planned to put up there on the big screen.

The Release

The Godfather was originally scheduled for a Christmas 1971 release. But the premiere was put off until March 14, 1972, in order to allow Coppola to edit the scenes he shot in Sicily back into the film. Studio executives routinely contract for films to run two hours or less because they are easier for theaters to screen multiple times per night. After seeing Coppola's two-hour rough cut, Evans and the rest of the production team at Paramount were smart enough to see the value in making *The Godfather* an epic.

Evans's gamble paid off. *The Godfather* turned a profit before it played in a single theater.[5] By the time its first run was complete, the film had grossed over $81 million domestically, the most ever to that date, and posted a record twenty-three consecutive weekly grosses in excess of $2 million. It is at least ironic that such a legendary *auteur* picture was also the first big film in a new era of marketing in Hollywood.

It is hard to overestimate the impact of the astonishing box-office success of *The Godfather* on Paramount and on the industry as a whole. Through the first six months of 1972, *The Godfather* grossed in excess of $30 million, roughly twice what Paramount's blockbuster *Love Story* earned in the same time period the year before and four times the revenue earned by the number one film (from January to June) in 1970, *Airport* (George Seaton).

The film's success had an immediate impact on Wall Street as well. Within a month of its premiere, Gulf and Western stock traded at $44.75 per share, an all-time high. By year's end, the Paramount Pictures Leisure Division of Gulf and Western posted record pretax operating profits of $31.2 million, up 55 percent from the previous year.

Analysis

Genre

The opening line of *The Godfather* is delivered in the Don's warmly lit study as a wedding guest, an undertaker seeking a favor (a hit, of course), intones: "I love America." Like *Scarface* (Howard Hawks, 1932), the early sound-era gangster film Coppola perhaps saw in a film history class at UCLA, the gangsters in *The Godfather* turn to crime as a means of social mobility. But success is fleeting, and crime offers a temporary solution at best. After Michael takes over the family business, he and his father, the Don, talk about what might have been. The Don confesses that he never wanted Michael to run the family business, that he wanted his son to be a congressman or senator.

---

[5]In order to secure an exclusive showing of *The Godfather*, exhibitors were asked to advance a fee (as a guarantee against box-office receipts). By March 15, these cash advances had exceeded $15 million. Once the film was in general release, Paramount received a 90/10 split—they received 90 percent of the gate after theater expenses—at all of the 340 venues scheduled to show the film nationwide.

Michael is a modern gangster. He is not like the Italian American and Irish American gangsters in the early sound classics: *Scarface, Little Caesar* (Mervyn LeRoy, 1931), and *The Public Enemy* (William A. Wellman, 1931). Instead, he is by all outward appearances a businessman. That said, Coppola makes clear that a successful business of the magnitude of the Corleone family criminal enterprise, however much it parallels or duplicates more superficially legitimate business enterprises, is incompatible with a happy family life. *The Godfather* ends with Michael arranging a hit on Carlo, his brother-in-law. *The Godfather, Part II* (1974) ends with Michael sitting all alone in the sunroom of his Lake Tahoe compound having just ordered the murder of his brother Fredo. *The Godfather, Part III* ends with the death of Michael's daughter, who is shot in a failed attempt on his life. The business, which was once such a necessity for the family to rise up out of poverty, ends up destroying any chance, even late in life, for Michael to have the sort of happy American life that more ordinary folks routinely enjoy.

The American gangster or crime picture dates to 1903 and *The Great Train Robbery.* Though it is thought of today as a Western, it was produced by Thomas Edison to compete with a series of British-made crime pictures. True crime emerged as a popular genre in 1907 with two films made about the first of several "crimes of the century." *The Unwritten Law* (subtitled *A Thrilling Drama Based on the Thaw-White Tragedy*) and *The Great Thaw Trial* both dramatized Harry Thaw's 1906 murder of Stanford White and the trial that followed. Thaw, a Pittsburgh-born blue blood, shot White, the wealthy architect who designed Madison Square Garden, over a woman: the showgirl-actress Evelyn Nesbit. Thaw was sent to an asylum for the criminally insane (where he remained for eight years), and Nesbit, who was bilked out of a million dollars by Thaw's mother, went on to become a celebrity and sometime actress, starring in, among other pictures, the aptly titled *Redemption* (Joseph A. Golden and Julius Steger, 1917), which costarred her son, Russell Thaw.

Raoul Walsh's 1918 *The Woman and the Law* attended a second crime of the century. It told the story of Bianca De Saulles, a wronged woman who gunned down her husband. What we now call docudramas were common fare in early and silent cinema. D. W. Griffith's 1912 short *The Musketeers of Pig Alley* (shot on location on the notoriously rough East 14th Street in New York City with local "talent," including, legend has it, a fifteen-year-old Charlie "Lucky" Luciano, the future mafioso), Walsh's bowery-gang melodrama *Regeneration* (1915) and his later dockside silent/sound hybrid *Me Gangster* (1928), *The City Gone Wild* (James Cruze, 1927), and Josef von Sternberg's *Underworld* (1927) established the setting and the formula for what became, in the early 1930s, one of the Hollywood studios' most interesting dramatic genres.

Most early gangster films were framed by a reformist message or theme; an opening title card would remind us that crime is bad and that it is up to law-abiding citizens, the police, and the courts to make the lawless city (usually New York or Chicago) safe once again. Within this public-service frame one finds the gangster, at once monstrous and fascinating, free to live his life independent of social norms and moral constraint. The gangster's life on film is a success story of sorts: rags to riches to rags. His path to glory ends at the end of a rope or at the business end of a rain of bullets. He dies because he is bad, of course, and because he has so enjoyed his ill-won success.

During Prohibition, gangsters were all too real; Al Capone, alias Scarface, made the cover of *Time* magazine in 1930, and John Dillinger's thirteen-month crime spree in 1933 and 1934 was front-page news nearly every day for a full year. However frightening Capone and Dillinger might have been in real life, they were nonetheless romanticized in an American popular culture that increasingly celebrated such iconoclastic and dangerous characters. That they found themselves mythologized on the silver screen was at once inevitable and a little disquieting.

At its core, the gangster film is about capitalism: the accumulation of capital, its risks and consequences. In most of the early sound films, the gangster is a recent immigrant—the accent and lifestyle tell us that. The gangster forges ahead on the wrong side of the law because on the right side he has no chance.

Coppola showed an awareness of the genre's inherent social critique. As we discover in *The Godfather, Part II*, the Don first turns to crime to support his family. He becomes violent and ruthless only when a local big shot forces his hand. What the Don wants, and he tells us so in the first film's pivotal scene in the family garden with Michael, is not success, or at least not wealth, but economic security and social justice for his family—the promise of some future in which his sons might have legitimate access to opportunities denied him. "I refused to be a fool dangling on a string," the Don muses to his son; "when it was your time, I hoped it would be you who would hold the strings . . . Senator Corleone . . . Governor Corleone . . . there just wasn't enough time."

By this point in the film (over two hours in), Michael has come to acknowledge that ruthlessness on the political or economic stage is less a matter of moral certainty than a matter of degree. When, after a brief exile in Sicily, Michael sets out to reclaim Kay, his former para-mour, he tells her of his plans to make the family business completely legitimate in five years time. She does not believe him, so he takes a different tack. "My father's not so different from other powerful men," he tells her, "a senator or president." "Don't be naive," she replies quickly, "senators and presidents don't have people killed." In 1972, when *The Godfather* was released, the United States was still very much involved in the war in Vietnam. When Michael counters that she is the one who is naive, the audience was inclined to appreciate his side in the debate.

Reception

Our fascination with gangsters on-screen hinges on a morbid curios-ity. What, after all, attracts us to films about violent characters com-mitting crimes? But it also relates to a sort of jealousy for those who live "better" or "more freely" than we do, and thus there is a need to see such wealth and freedom punished somehow in the end. In the 1930s, the gangster's adventure in a world of plenty was complex and fraught with temptation and punishment. He succeeded because he was willing to act on impulses civilized Americans repressed; he rou-tinely gave in to temptation and in doing so risked or courted punish-ment. The inevitable violent end came about because he was so successful, because like other successful people, he had to play fast and dirty to get where he had gotten. In the movies, at least, there is a cosmic payback for those who dare to enjoy themselves so deeply, so unself-consciously.

This cosmic payback was a matter of some concern to the authors of the 1930 Production Code. Prohibitions against showing instances in which crime, in the end, paid, were strictly enforced from 1934, when the Production Code Administration began enforcing the Code, through 1968, when the Motion Picture Association of America (MPAA) introduced a new film classification system. In 1972, Coppola was able to keep his gangster alive (now through three incarnations, three films) because the 1968 rating system said he could.

One can easily argue that *The Godfather* glorifies the American gangster, or at least the Corleone gangster family. The Don is shown as a mostly warm, moral family man (this despite the murders orchestrated on his behalf, the criminal empire built in his name). Michael poses a more complex heroic figure, albeit one that suggests the modernist notion that heroes exist to be doomed. Michael's first act as the undisputed head of the family and the criminal enterprise formerly run by his father is to arrange for the murder of his brother-in-law (for setting up the assassination of Michael's brother Sonny) and his father's former right-hand man, Tessio, who has betrayed Michael to a rival gangster. What we feel—what we are led to feel—at this moment is (perhaps guilty) elation at the freedom Michael enjoys, the success he has *won*. But as Robert Warshow so cannily argued in 1948, "at bottom, the gangster is doomed because he is under the obligation to succeed, not because the methods he employs are unlawful." Michael's ascension is finally unenviable because it is ruinous, and antisocial. Success, as Warshow reminds us, is "evil and dangerous" (133).

Conclusion

A Parting Glance

Approximately two weeks after the premiere of *The Godfather, Part III*, former Paramount executive Peter Bart introduced a fascinating gangland backstory. In a page-one article titled "How Par[amount] Wised Up to Wiseguys on the Backlot," Bart contended that in 1972, "interests closely linked to the mob had managed to establish a secret beachhead at Paramount," and, moreover, that they did so as the result of a significant investment in the studio made by a notorious Sicilian financier named Michele Sindona (1, 110). According to Bart, in the early 1970s, Sindona entered into a complex deal with then Gulf and Western chairman, Charles Bluhdorn, one that was central to the dramatic turnaround at Paramount at the very moment the studio was developing *The Godfather*. First, Bluhdorn helped Sindona purchase a 20 percent share in a Vatican-held company, the Societa General Immobiliare. Immobiliare, in turn, purchased a significant interest in Paramount, providing the studio with much-needed capital.

Sindona had mob connections; it was alleged that he was one of the Gambino family's financial advisers. Well after the Immobiliare deal went through, Sindona was arrested and convicted of fraud and was subsequently extradited to Italy to stand trial for murder. In 1986, he died in jail under mysterious circumstances. According to Bart, in an effort to convince Coppola to make a third *Godfather* film, Bluhdorn told Coppola what he knew about Sindona, about the deal with the Vatican, and about the mysterious death of the so-called Smiling Pope, John Paul I (1, 110). In *The Godfather, Part III,* Michael Corleone attempts to buy a controlling interest in the shadowy Vatican-based conglomerate Immobiliare and then loses his advantage when a pope is assassinated after little more than a month in office. It is in acknowledgment of his meeting with Bluhdorn and the various connections between the executive's story and the one told in *The Godfather, Part III* that Coppola ultimately decided to dedicate the film to Bluhdorn's memory.

Looking back, it is hard to miss the irony in Bart's story; ultimately, it was a secret investment by a reputed Sicilian gangster that made the production of *The Godfather,* the best gangster film ever made, possible. That the film played such a large part in the industry's turnaround in the early 1970s seems to suggest that Sindona's investment dramatically changed the fortunes of not only the studio but all of Hollywood as well.

Credits

United States, 1972, Paramount Pictures

Director: Francis Ford Coppola
Producer: Albert S. Ruddy
Screenplay: Francis Ford Coppola and Mario Puzo
Cinematography: Gordon Willis
Editing: William Reynolds and Peter Zinner
Music: Nino Rota
Art Direction: Warren Clymer
Set Decoration: Philip Smith
Costume Design: Anna Hill Johnstone

CAST:
Don Vito Corleone   Marlon Brando
Michael Corleone   Al Pacino
Sonny Corleone   James Caan

Peter Clemenza	Richard S. Castellano
Tom Hagen	Robert Duvall
Captain McCluskey	Sterling Hayden
Jack Woltz	John Marley
Barzini	Richard Conte
Sollozzo	Al Lettieri
Kay Adams	Diane Keaton
Sal Tessio	Abe Vigoda
Connie Corleone	Talia Shire
Carlo Rizzi	Gianni Russo
Fredo Corleone	John Cazale
Cuneo	Rudy Bond
Johnny Fontane	Al Martino
Mama	Morgana King
Luca Brasi	Lenny Montana

Bibliography

Arnell, Gene. "Yablans into Paramount Presidency; He and Jaffe on Ideal Budgets." *Variety* 5 May 1971: 3.

Bart, Peter. "How Par Wised Up to Wiseguys on the Backlot." *Variety* 7 Jan. 1991: 1+.

"Brando's Mute Test Copped Role; Godfather Funnier Than Mafia Picnic." *Variety* 8 Mar. 1972: 6.

Cowie, Peter. *Coppola*. New York: Scribner's, 1990.

———. "The Whole Godfather." *Connoisseur* (Dec. 1990): 90.

"Damone Drops Role in 'Godfather' Film." *New York Times* 5 Apr 1971: 31.

Evans, Robert. *The Kid Stays in the Picture*. New York: Hyperion, 1994.

Kaufman, Dave. "Hollywood Unemployment at 42.8%." *Variety* 4 Mar. 1970: 3.

Lewis, Jon. "If History Has Taught Us Anything . . . Francis Coppola, Paramount Studios and *The Godfather, Parts I, II* and *III*." *Francis Ford Coppola's "The Godfather" Trilogy*. Ed. Nick Browne. Cambridge: Cambridge UP, 1999. 25–56.

———. *Whom God Wishes to Destroy . . . Francis Coppola and the New Hollywood*. Durham: Duke UP, 1995.

Lichtenstein, Grace. "'Godfather' Film Won't Mention Mafia." *New York Times* 20 Mar. 1971: 1+.

Murray, William. "Playboy Interview: Francis Ford Coppola." *Playboy* 22 (1975): 53–60.

"Paramount Studio Buy Talks, but No Deal Yet into Focus; Realty Value Runs $29–32 Mil." *Variety* 8 Apr. 1970: 5.

Pryor, Thomas. "Hollywood Future Riding on Box Office." *Variety* 1 July 1970: 1.

Pye, Michael, and Lynda Myles. *The Movie Brats*. New York: Holt, 1975.

Saloman, Julie. "Budget Busters: *The Cotton Club*'s Battle of the Bulge." *Wall Street Journal* 13 Dec. 1984: 22.

Warshow, Robert. "The Gangster as Tragic Hero." 1948. Rpt. in *The Immediate Experience: Movies, Comics, Theatre and Other Aspects of Popular Culture*. New York: Atheneum, 1970. 127–33.

Ali: Fear Eats the Soul (1974)

SHOHINI CHAUDHURI

An Anatomy of Racism

Context

Ali: Fear Eats the Soul (*Angst essen Seele auf*) was made in fifteen days on location in Munich, in September 1973, on a budget of 260,000 DM—which is typical of the breakneck pace at which its director, Rainer Werner Fassbinder, produced his films. He made over forty films from his debut in 1965 to his death from a drug overdose in 1982, at the age of thirty-seven. He was one of the first internationally fêted filmmakers to say unreservedly that he was gay, and he gained notoriety during his lifetime for his unkempt appearance and his controversial lifestyle. He was a leading exponent of the New German Cinema movement, which emerged in the late 1960s and included other well-known directors such as Wim Wenders and Werner Herzog. Launched as a rejection of the attitude and practice of Germany's commercial film industry, the movement virtually came to an end in 1982, leading one obituary commentator to suggest that with Fassbinder's death the "heart" of New German Cinema stopped beating (qtd. in Kaes 75).

    Ali was one of Fassbinder's first popular breakthrough films, along with *The Merchant of Four Seasons* (*Der Händler der vier Jahreszeiten*, 1972) and *Effi Briest* (1974), helping to seal his reputation abroad. *Ali* loosely adapts visual and story elements from a classical Hollywood melodrama, *All That Heaven Allows* (1955), directed by Douglas Sirk. It tells the story of Emmi, a white, widowed cleaning woman around sixty, and her much younger lover Ali, a Moroccan *Gastarbeiter* (immigrant worker), dwelling on the hostile reactions of Emmi's adult children, fellow workers, and other acquaintances to the relationship. Although *Ali* was shot on 35 mm film in color with post-synchronized sound (by no means the norm for low-budget filmmaking), Fassbinder kept costs down with his small cast and crew, drawn from a team of regular collaborators, including his mother and his boyfriend, El Hedi ben Salem, a nonprofessional actor, who plays the Moroccan *Gastarbeiter*. Fassbinder himself appears in the film, as Emmi's thoroughly unpleasant and disapproving son-in-law, Eugen.

In 1967, Fassbinder joined a theater group called the Action-Theater, and shortly thereafter re-created it under the name Anti-Theater, after he failed to get into the German Film and Television Academy. He met most of his regular collaborators there—actors and technicians who worked with him from film to film. This way of working guaranteed the speed, efficiency, and prolific output that were key to Fassbinder's ascendancy within New German Cinema and that propelled him to international stardom as a European art-cinema *auteur*.

The roots of New German Cinema are often traced to the Ober-hausen Manifesto of 1962, signed by a number of young German film-makers demanding the chance to build a noncommercial cinema. In order to renew cinema in Germany, these filmmakers announced that they were "prepared to take economic risks" (Rentschler 2). New German Cinema appeared a few years later, promoting itself as a cinema of *auteurs:* underlying it was the vision of film as the artistic expression of the individual filmmaker. Its films share a common concern with German national identity, focusing on outsiders and social misfits and adopting a critical attitude to Germany's recent history. Domestic audiences generally greeted these films unenthusiastically, but the movement did much to enhance the international profile of postwar German cinema.

A number of historically contingent factors worked in New German Cinema's favor, including the culture of national self-scrutiny promoted by Willy Brandt, who was elected as chancellor of West Germany in 1969. The movement may have worked to the diplomatic advantage of a government keen to make amends for the nation's Nazi past. In such a sociopolitical climate, financial sponsors were more likely to be receptive to the movement's revisionist projects than they would be later, during the government formed under Helmut Kohl's chancellorship in 1982—the year of Fassbinder's death and the "death" of New German Cinema.

Fassbinder is in many ways a symptomatic product of New German Cinema and its most versatile entrepreneur. He greatly admired the work of classical Hollywood directors such as Douglas Sirk, Raoul Walsh, and Alfred Hitchcock. This populist streak distinguished him from most of his New German Cinema contemporaries, but it was nonetheless pivotal to his achievements. He excelled at selling his projects to funding bodies. If would-be sponsors withdrew, he paid for the film himself instead of abandoning it. Fassbinder could take these economic risks because of the cooperation of his collective of family, friends, and team workers (who would often have to wait for the returns before being paid for their work). His rapid turnout of films helped recoup costs, with funded projects subsidizing the self-financed ones.

Fassbinder is the very embodiment of New German Cinema's cult of *auteur* personality, as legends lying in his wake testify. His thematic preoccupations with marginal and oppressed groups, misfits and out-siders are also exemplary. Most of his films deal with urban working-class or lower-middle-class characters in everyday settings—bars, apartment blocks, corner shops, factories, and other places of work. In exterior shots, cities and towns appear deserted, providing minimalis-tic backdrops, while interiors are cluttered with kitsch and tawdry decor, wall posters and paintings, claustrophobic in their box-within-a-box layout, partitioned by mirrors, consecutive door frames, and screens. Fassbinder's work perfectly typifies New German Cinema's excavation of Germany's recent past, foraying even further into the past to discover the roots of National Socialism in the nineteenth cen-tury (such as in *Effi Briest*) or ascertaining its aftereffects in the present.

Ali examines the persistence of neo-Nazi attitudes in contemporary (1970s) society. It draws on postwar West Germany's social and histor-ical particularities to bring these themes to light—namely, the *Gastar-beiter* phenomenon. Starting from ruins after the Second World War, West Germany's economy underwent phenomenal reconstruction and recovery in the "economic miracle" years of the 1950s and 1960s. At this time, workers from less-industrially-advanced southern Euro-pean and North African countries were invited to fill low-paid, menial jobs to compensate for the short native labor supply. During the 1960s and early 1970s, they became crucial to the booming economy. West German society exploited the cheap labor of these immigrant workers, treating them as a different class of citizen, even as subhuman (as an epithet for Italian *Gastarbeiter*, "*Macaronifresser*," indicates—*fressen* is the verb for eating that is applied to animals). By 1973–74, recession struck. Racial tensions rose as people began, unjustifiably, to blame *Gastarbeiter* for the rising unemployment—even though *Gastarbeiter* themselves made up large numbers of the unemployed.

West German capitalist democracy was built on ideals of self-discipline, responsibility, and citizenship. It was believed that these would banish fascist modes of thinking and behavior (Elsaesser, *Fassbinder's Germany* 70). Although West German society overtly condemned the Nazi system and was trying to purge its Nazi elements (in a process of "de-Nazification"), most people, Fassbinder implies in *Ali*, took cover under the work ethic and did not learn from their experiences.

The following analysis looks at the critical perspectives that have governed the film's interpretation to date. In the final section, I move toward a new psychoanalytic reading, developing existing psychoanalytic threads, since in my view, these best befit Fassbinder's exploration of group psychology and unconsciously held beliefs.

Analysis

Brechtian and Sirkian Interpretations

The story kernel of *Ali* appears in an earlier Fassbinder film, *The American Soldier* (1970), in which a chambermaid narrates the love affair between Emmi and Ali. This version ends with Emmi's death and Ali being charged with her murder. In *Ali*, Fassbinder gives the pair a chance to live together. Between 1970 and 1973, the single most important factor in his changed conception of his story was his viewing of melodramas by Douglas Sirk, an émigré Hollywood director of Danish background who had learned his craft in Germany (studying drama and working in the German film industry). Fassbinder first saw Sirk's films in 1971, and claimed that his films were among the most beautiful he had ever seen. He announced that he wanted to make films that were as wonderful and powerful as Hollywood films but that were at the same time critical of the status quo (Jansen and Schütte 93–94).

Fassbinder's reading of Sirkian melodrama shows an ironic and elegiac awareness of the disparity between the way things *are* and how they *appear*, that everyday roles are necessarily a masquerade. He reacts with a campy aestheticism to what he perceives to be a hostile world: "Sirk has said you can't make films about something, you can only make films with something, with people, with light, with flowers, with mirrors, with blood, with all these crazy things that make it worthwhile" (Fassbinder 77). If *Ali* is a "remake" of *All That Heaven Allows,* it is based more on Fassbinder's experience of watching Sirk's film than on the film itself, as is apparent in all-important differences between the two.

In *All That Heaven Allows,* Cary (played by Jane Wyman), a white middle-class woman, falls in love with her white working-class bohemian gardener Ron (Rock Hudson). In *Ali,* Fassbinder increased the age difference between the leads and shifted the emphasis from class differences to racial differences. This stresses the breaking of taboos to a far greater degree, emphasizing more than Sirk's film does that this is a story about—as the gay American independent film director Todd Haynes puts it in his remarks on *Ali*—"forbidden love" (97). Fassbinder's casting of his boyfriend, El Hedi ben Salem, was a nod to Rock Hudson (whose gay sexuality was a secret when *All That Heaven Allows* was made). One of Emmi's children, Bruno, responds to her relationship with sudden but ineffectual violence by kicking in her TV set—a direct reference to the earlier film, where Cary's children give her a TV for Christmas after she has split up with Ron for her children's sake. In Sirk's film, TV is "the last refuge for a lonely woman" (we see the despondent Cary reflected in the TV frame, left in the knowledge that her sacrifice was all for nothing, as both children are about to flee the nest), but in *Ali,* Emmi has already fended off loneliness. Her children can do nothing.

A key scene in *All That Heaven Allows* shows Cary and Ron at a party facing the gossips' vicious delight and the faint alarm of the snobbish. The film portrays the hypocrisy of its characters' age and class prejudices and their readiness to reduce Cary's love for Ron to brute physical attraction—they marvel at his tan and his good set of muscles ("from working outdoors"). Sirk undermines their petty-minded and money-oriented concerns by emphasizing Ron's virtue and honesty and idealizing his bohemian lifestyle—semi-self-sufficient, sensibly opting out of the capitalist rat race. His melodramas gave Fassbinder a model for making films that could perform "a moral critique of an immoral society" within the framework of what was still a commercial system—even for Fassbinder, an independent director working in Germany, free from Hollywood restrictions (Kellner 32). Still, in many respects, Fassbinder's critique is more challenging than Sirk's could ever be.

Both films end with images of compromised happiness: although the couples are reunited, Ron is injured by a fall, and Ali collapses from a burst stomach ulcer. In each case, the woman is left looking after the damaged man. But in *All That Heaven Allows,* Cary and Ron's reunion has significations auguring well for their future together: a wild deer (earlier associated with Ron, Cary's "nature boy") appears in the idyllic snowy landscape outside the window. The outlook in *Ali,* by contrast, is unremittingly grim. A hospital doctor tells Emmi that Ali's ailment is common among immigrant workers, who endure particular stresses. They are not entitled to the rest cures they really need, only operations; in all likelihood, illness will simply recur. At Ali's bedside, Emmi turns, weeping, to the window, which reveals only a flat grayness. A faint melody is heard—one of three instances of nondiegetic music in the film, an ironic gesture to melodrama's use of music as an emotional cue. While Sirk only indirectly relates Ron's injury to society (through Cary's hesitation to return to him, an internalization of outward pressures to conform), Fassbinder traces Ali's collapse and illness to the heart of an immoral capitalist system, which mistreats its workers even as it thrives at their expense. Ali's psychosomatic illness reveals that it is the body, rather than "the soul" of the film's title, that is literally being eaten away, a target for capitalist power relations.

Fassbinder himself read Sirk's ending as being ambivalent, the couple's happy reunion at odds with a story that, *he* thought, demonstrated the incompatibility of Cary's and Ron's respective worlds (Fassbinder 81). He defended his own unhappy endings, refusing to limit happiness, utopia, and revolution to the fantasies of the screen. He designed his films' closures to create another "ending" in the audience's head—to make it obvious to them that they must change their lives, even if society restricts their choices.

Sirkian influences also inspire *Ali's mise-en-scène:* pools of saturated color in the Asphalt Pub scenes; the use of mirrors, doorways, partitions, and grilles to internally frame characters within the cinematic frame. Crucially, though, *Ali* lacks the glamorous surfaces of the Hollywood film, and some are put off by its harsher appearance. Hollywood seduces us with ideals with which we narcissistically identify.

Ali, on the other hand, makes visible the gap between ourselves and the ideals to which we aspire (for example, in the tawdry glamour of the bar girls). Sirk cast stars who personify ideals such as virtue, honesty, and beauty, while Fassbinder used relatively unknown actors and tried to get his audience to empathize with characters' situations rather than with such narcissistically gratifying traits.

Just as Fassbinder was discovering Sirk, Laura Mulvey and other feminist critics were reevaluating Hollywood melodrama, and Sirk figured highly in their adjudication of its critical potential. Formerly dismissed as simply affirming dominant middle-class American ideologies (such as the security of the family and the all-conquering power of romantic love), the genre began to be seen in a new light. Since melodrama focuses on women's desires and experiences of dissatisfaction with the existing order, Mulvey and others believed it thereby exposed the flaws in oppressive ideological structures. Mulvey herself offered one of the first critical discussions of *Ali,* setting a precedent for the interpretive models that were to dominate in readings of the film in particular and Fassbinder's cinema more generally: that is, Sirkian and Brechtian models.

The German playwright Bertolt Brecht advocated a kind of theater that would neither produce an illusion of reality nor make spectators identify emotionally with the characters. He instructed actors to keep a distance from their roles. The audience would always be reminded that this is not reality but a representation, enabling them to think and act rather than becoming involved in the play. This has become known as "the alienation effect" (*Verfremdungseffekt*). Mulvey underlines the relevance of this approach to both Fassbinder and Sirk: "Both come from the theatre, both brought to cinema a sense of theatrical distanciation . . . that works against the tendency of film to absorb the spectator into itself" (46).

Ali contains many Brechtian devices. Some of the acting is typically stylized, giving characters' actions and looks a "ritualistic" or nonnaturalistic quality (Mayne 62). The film's long shots constrain emotional identification by placing a concrete distance between the audience and the characters, while its long takes temporarily arrest the action and amplify a given shot's meaning. Emmi and Ali have their honeymoon dinner in a restaurant where, Emmi affirms, Hitler used to eat. A long shot traps them in the tight internal frame of a doorway, as they sit in front of a painting, looking incongruous in this plush upper-class set-ting, alone but for the hostile stare of the waiter (whom we see in a re-verse shot). The shot is perfectly symmetrical in composition, containing a potentially infinite regress of frames-within-its-frame. It puts the characters "onstage," self-reflexively pointing up its status as a cinematic representation. This is a metacinematic procedure—going beyond cinematic conventions to reflect on, or call attention to, cin-ema's processes of enunciation (that is, how cinema functions, how it structures what we see).

In the next sections we will see how *Ali*'s emphasis on vision *ex-ceeds* the Brechtian paradigm, which Fassbinder himself rejected: "With Brecht you see the emotions and you reflect upon them as you witness them but you never feel them. . . . I think I go farther than he did in that I let the audience *feel and think*" (qtd. in Sparrow 20). This tactic gathers momentum at the film's turning point, in an outdoor café, just before Emmi and Ali decide to take a vacation. The camera cuts away to reveal a static, nonnaturalistic tableau of gaping by-standers, at whom Emmi shouts, "Stare, bloody swine! This is my hus-band! My husband!" The loneliness and despair of the couple's situation is palpable, as Emmi begins to cry and Ali comforts her, their social exclusion being the only thing that holds them together. Fass-binder allows us to have "Hollywood emotions" and reflect on them at the same time.

Exhibitionism and the Gaze
A fair amount of film criticism has focused on the way hostility to-ward Emmi and Ali is conveyed through the look. These readings are informed by the psychoanalytic theory of Jacques Lacan, as well as by Mulvey's essay on "the male gaze," which argues that narrative film is structured by a controlling, objectifying male gaze that reduces the fe-male body to a spectacle. *Ali* problematizes this notion of the gaze, not least because one body of spectacle here is male. As Judith Mayne notes, from the outset, "our attention is drawn, as spectators, to the act of looking, relentlessly portrayed here as the interplay of objectifying gazes" (62). As soon as Emmi enters the Asphalt Pub, she is trapped by aggressive stares, marking her as an outsider in this milieu. The camera objectifies the characters in a similar fashion, through long shots and long takes—blurring the differences between our "stares" as

spectators and the smirks of people in the film and making us unwillingly complicit in Emmi and Ali's oppression (Mayne 62).

Mayne and other commentators have discussed these scenes in terms of their deployment of the shot/reverse-shot structure that continually defines the viewer's place in the film narrative. Through such a structure, viewers are able to oscillate from one character's look to another, while forgetting or repressing the presence of the camera, the Other that ultimately structures what they see. However, what Mayne does not emphasize enough is that in *Ali* the shot/reverse-shot structure does not give the reassurances that it does in conventional narrative film. Oppressive looks dominate in the film, nearly depriving us of a place in the narrative that would allow us to transcend the racism and ageism of the Germany of the film's day. At the very least, the film does not offer us a politically correct position from which to view either Emmi or Ali (as, for example, Todd Haynes does with his characters in *Far From Heaven*, a 2002 remake of *All That Heaven Allows* that also turns the cross-class relationship into an interracial one). Emmi always appears too old for those who look at her, and Ali too "black." Because of Fassbinder's camera technique and his casting choices, we as viewers are disquietingly forced to share these attitudes for the duration of the film.

Conventional narrative film represses the look of the camera by identifying it with an optical or narrational point of view. It makes spectators feel "on top" of the action—giving access to the fictional world while also providing an illusion of mastery over the field of vision. In *Ali*, the look of the camera is not repressed. Our illusion of mastery is punctured, particularly in the scene in which Emmi and Ali part in the morning. The camera starts filming at street level: we see the couple emerge from the apartment block, shake hands, walk their separate ways, turn around, wave farewell, and then exit the screen space. Suddenly, the camera tilts up to reveal Emmi's neighbor Frau Kargus leaning out of the window, her gaze following the parting lovers. This shot does not merely inform us that, unbeknownst to them, Emmi and Ali are in danger from gossipy neighbors. The look of the neighbor reminds us that *we are not in control of what we see,* nor do we have a privileged access to Ali and Emmi's intimacy. As Thomas Elsaesser puts it, it pulls the rug out from under our feet (*Fassbinder's Germany* 61). Far from giving us a vantage "on top" of the characters, the scene gestures to another dynamic in the film: the couple deliberately puts themselves in front of the other characters' disapproving looks. This exhibitionism is the medium through which the couple's defiance of society's conventions takes shape, for the relationship prospers only insofar as it is bound together by these disapproving looks from the outside. When this hostility subsides, problems *within* the relationship surface: the lovers' mutual gaze is not enough.

Exhibitionism blurs binary distinctions between the subject and the object of the look; we are neither subjects nor objects but both at the same time. Both observer and observed are "locked into the spectacle relationship as a form of power" (Mayne 74). For Elsaesser, the exhibitionism in Fassbinder's films is a subversive parody of the German fascist subject's "pleasure of being seen," displaying his/her conformism and good behavior "in view of the all-seeing eye of the state" ("Primary Identification" 544–55). Whether or not they directly refer to specific events in Germany (Elsaesser refers to West Germany's postwar bureaucratic crackdown on terrorism as well as to Nazism), Fassbinder's films represent the social in its entirety *as* a machinery of surveillance. This is why *Ali*'s emphasis on vision goes beyond the Brechtian paradigm discussed above. Neither simply reflecting the conditions of cinematic representation nor reflecting those of visual objectification per se, Fassbinder's films reveal "spectacle as a social form . . . *through* the basic elements of cinema" (Mayne 74).

Kaja Silverman reads this in Lacanian terms. Following Lacan, she distinguishes between the gaze and the look. In Lacan, the gaze arises from all sides, not from one person or group. The gaze "confirms and sustains" identity, controlling and oppressing us, although it doesn't account for the *form* that identity assumes (72). The look, on the other hand, emanates from a subject or subjects. In Lacanian psychoanalysis, the subject is always split, self-divided and alienated from its desire, that is, "castrated." Lacan reads castration metaphorically, so for him the look (as well as language), rather than the anatomical body, is the site of castration. The look conveys the looker's desire and *lack*, as Emmi acknowledges her own lack of sexual appeal when she sees Ali showering ("You're very handsome, Ali"). The looks of the bar girls fuming with sexual jealousy over Ali consorting with Emmi would be another example, as jealousy signifies privation, frustration, lack.

However, people can also project their own insufficiency/lack/desire onto another, "through a sadistic identification with the gaze"

(Silverman 71). In *Ali*, all the oppressive looks operate in this way, as characters collude with the gaze that controls and confirms identity—including the patronizing looks of Emmi's fellow workers when they feel up Ali's muscles after they have reconciled their differences with Emmi. As Silverman says, "they exchange him amongst themselves," treating him like a commodity while denying their own desire (69).

Certain scenes that make Ali into an erotic spectacle escape the oppressive look. When Ali, now alienated from Emmi, seeks solace in the home of the bar owner Barbara, we see him in long shot through the doorway, and Barbara, peeling off his shirt, lovingly clasps his torso from behind. Another scene turns from a shot of Barbara in the bathroom mirror to a long shot through the doorway, showing Ali undressing in the darkened bedroom, ending with the lovers falling on the bed lit by an irislike effect at the center of the frame. To us, these scenes might seem to reflect a "female gaze"—albeit one constructed by a gay male director—with the male body as the object of desire. Silverman's reading contests such assumptions. For, in mainstream narrative film, it is not that men desire women that is the problem, she argues, but that they identify with a controlling gaze that enables them to displace their own insufficiencies onto women (who become the figure of castration). It is no use switching the gender of "the gaze," for the gaze itself is oppressive.

In the aforementioned scenes, the gaze is "redefined through its alignment with Barbara's desiring and accepting look" (Silverman 71). Even though Ali goes to Barbara out of desperation and as someone who knows the price of his flesh (when Barbara tells Emmi that she is the bar owner, she is also hinting that Ali is her possession), what has happened here is that even we the viewers see Ali in a different way, through a different "filter" or "screen." In Lacanian terminology, the "screen" is the image, or set of images, that determine how we view any subject of representation (Lacan, *Four Fundamental Concepts* 107). Silverman suggests that we see the screen as a culturally variable repertoire of images (75–76). For example, when most characters look at Ali, what they see is "the very 'picture' of social and sexual marginality," for that is the identity conferred on him by the dominant cultural screen of race in 1970s Germany (72). Thus, "the cultural representations through which we see and are seen" should be the focus of our political struggle, not the gaze (78).

A Psychoanalytic Critique of Racism and Everyday Fascism

> This supposed *jouissance* is one of the key components of racism: the Other (Jew, Arab, Negro) is always presumed to have access to some specific enjoyment, and that is what really bothers us. (Žižek 187)

In its portrait of racism, *Ali* manages to be both socially and historically specific and more universal. As I stated earlier, it doesn't let even contemporary audiences off the hook regarding their own susceptibility to these attitudes. This is perhaps the film's most obvious feature but also the one that is the least (psycho)analyzed.

Fassbinder refused to represent oppressed groups positively just for the sake of it, and this has exposed him at various times to attacks of anti-Semitism, homophobia, and misogyny from activist groups. He shows that his oppressed groups have failings like anyone else but does not exculpate himself from perpetuating certain cultural stereotypes in his characterizations. Ali, for example, speaks ungrammatically and occasionally shows a childlike lack of understanding, a typical representational strategy used by white authors to denote the supposed inadequacy and inarticulacy of characters from other cultures. Yet the film undercuts this when a Bavarian-accented racist shopkeeper refuses to serve Ali because, he says, Ali cannot speak German properly. The shopkeeper pretends to misunderstand Ali when he asks for Libella, a type of margarine, offering him lemonade instead. "He can speak better German than you can!" Emmi cries in exasperation, in Ali's defense. Furthermore, the film gives a privileged place to Ali's brand of German in its title. *Angst essen Seele auf* ("Fear eats the soul") is Ali's phrase; as Emmi points out, it is ungrammatical (the verb should be *isst*, not *essen*), yet she expresses her preference for Ali's variant, pidgin German over the standard German.

Ali is not poised to turn the tables on his oppressors. He, just like the white characters, is alienated from his desire, as illustrated when he, by now utterly ruining his relationship with Emmi and gambling away all his money, slaps himself in front of a mirror. This is one of Fassbinder's numerous reconstructions of Lacan's "mirror stage," a stage in a child's development when it identifies with its image in the mirror. The mirror image forms the basis of the child's self-knowledge, but at the same time creates the conditions of self-alienation, due to the disparity between the image offered by the mirror and how the child feels itself, in its lived reality, to be. The child becomes captured by its image, split and alienated from itself—a dress rehearsal for its alienation from others, for others, too, only have "an exterior image" of us, "analogous to the one seen in the mirror," and "inevitably there is conflict between the *me* as I feel myself and the *me* as . . . others see me" (Merleau-Ponty 136–37).

Fassbinder was familiar with psychoanalytic theory. He once said that Freud was more important than Marx (Elsaesser, *Fassbinder's Germany* 54). He lacked Marx's faith in the ability of the working classes to transcend their oppression and thereby end all social conflict. Like Freud, he did not believe that society would inevitably become more tolerant toward oppressed groups.

Freud sees our antipathy toward strangers as a deflection of hatred and aggression *within* the in-group. Any group or intimate relationship "contains a sediment of feelings of aversion and hostility, which only escapes perception as a result of repression." "No one," says Freud, "can tolerate a too intimate approach to his neighbor" (130). Yet, as one of Emmi's fellow workers warns her in the film, no one can live without others (or neighbors), either. Hatred against outsiders unifies the group and controls ambivalences simmering within. We see this clearly in the married couple Krista (Emmi's daughter) and Eugen: as soon as Emmi announces her love for a Moroccan *Gastarbeiter*, their hostile bickering with each other gives way to bemused disbelief; their relationship coheres again having identified an outsider. When Emmi introduces Ali to her children, the camera pans from one stony face to the next in a continuous pass, showing the children's solidarity in their hostility to the newlyweds. "Come on, Eugen," Krista says after Bruno has kicked in the TV, "we will not stay in this pigsty."

In Nazi Germany, *race* became "the pseudo-natural criterion" by which people were either rejected or chosen to be in the group (Adorno 129). *Ali* analyzes how such fascist tendencies continue in the present, with some startling results. We have already discussed how exclusionist tactics are conveyed visually—the way groups stare in a unified way at an outsider, the long shots and framings that emphasize a given character's exclusion and isolation. The look that fixes you is a key element in racial subjugation, as Frantz Fanon has pointed out, remembering how children stared at him, crying, "Look, a Negro!" (109). It is a look that confiscates your subjectivity. The fantasies and cultural representations of others immediately overdetermine you from the outside, harking back to your "original" self-alienation at the mirror stage. In *Ali,* Emmi's neighbors let their imaginations loose when they see her take Ali upstairs: "Frau Kurowski has a foreigner with her, a black one," Frau Kargus announces. "Really, a Negro?" the other neighbor gasps.

Emmi's neighbors seethe with disapproval about Emmi and Ali's relationship, while their landlord's son coolly takes it in stride. "There *is* such a thing as decency," insists Frau Münchmeyer (played by Fassbinder's mother), yet he, for one, "can't see anything indecent about it." Likewise, when the neighbors call the police, they find the latter unbothered by the fact that Emmi has four Arabs partying in her flat, even though Arabs are "dangerous, with bombs and that." Not all Arabs are terrorists, the police assure them, presenting the paradox that the police and the state have become "liberal"—an ostensible change in public attitudes—while a residual fascism remains in ordinary people.

Fassbinder shows how the dichotomy between insider and outsider groups is so ingrained that it affects those whose social position, beliefs, and conduct would seem to exclude such attitudes. Even Ali just stares in silence along with his ageist coworkers when Emmi comes to his workplace to plead with him to return to her. "Who is she, Ali? Your grandmother from Morocco?" they ask, laughing, as Emmi hurries out.

Emmi is culpable, too, nostalgically reminiscing about Hitler and being in the in-group: she herself was a Nazi Party member, "like most people." However, for her neighbors she doesn't belong to the in-group; when she brings Ali home they remind themselves that she was never really a "true" German: "Frau Kurowski, what sort of name is that?" Emmi's former husband, Franciszek, was a Polish immigrant, who came to Germany during the war as a forced laborer. At that time, Emmi tells Ali, immigrant workers were known as *Fremdarbeiter* (literally, "strange workers" or "alien workers") rather than *Gastarbeiter* ("guest workers"). As the film shows, the euphemistic transition from *Fremdarbeiter* to *Gastarbeiter* conceals the unfair and persisting social exclusion of these workers who keep the country's economy going.

Emmi's latent prejudices resurface when she refuses to let Ali eat couscous, saying, "In Germany people don't eat couscous." In order to solidify her regained ties with her fellow workers, she readily excludes another outsider, her new Yugoslavian coworker, Yolanda. The film depicts Emmi's complicity with the strategies that oppress Yolanda by repeating an early shot in which Emmi was framed behind the prisonlike bars of the stairway banisters eating her lunch alone because her fellow workers had moved away; Yolanda literally occupies the position Emmi has vacated.

When Emmi and Ali return from their vacation to find people strangely accepting of them, crude economic motives quickly become apparent. Emmi's neighbor requests extra storage space in the cellar. Bruno, who broke the TV, comes along with a conciliatory check—he wants a babysitter while his wife takes a part-time job to keep up with rising living costs. The shopkeeper, facing competition from the supermarket, needs Emmi's business. The external demands of a capitalist society confirm what Emmi recognizes as the psychological basis of the enmity against her: envy. "They're just envious [*neidisch*], that's all," she explains to Ali. The English-subtitled Connoisseur Video release of *Ali* translates *neidisch* as "jealous," perhaps not unintentionally, for both envy and jealousy are riveted by a "seen spectacle" (Merleau-Ponty 145). Envy usually revolves around possessions, a vision of the Other possessing and enjoying it all. Jealousy is its sexualized counterpart, a sexualization of that enjoyment. In both instances, the self feels invaded by another's success.

Emmi's neighbors are understandably perplexed at her explanation. This is because this kind of envy is barely acceptable to the conscious mind, although according to Freud it is everywhere apparent in civilized societies "in the shape of *Gemeinschaft, esprit de corps*, 'group spirit,'" which, he writes, originate in envy (*Neid*), expressing as they do the sentiment that "no one must want to put himself forward, everyone must be the same and have the same" (152). According to Theodor Adorno, the same grudging spirit manifests under fascism as an "undercurrent of malicious egalitarianism": no one must be better off; no one should "indulge in individual pleasures" (131). The jealousy and envy that have been stifled in the group is projected onto outsiders. This clearly has a counterpart in contemporary racist discourse, where the Other is assumed to be enjoying more than its "fair share" (of jobs, benefits, and state welfare, for example). Indeed, in *Ali,* it is the Other's apparent enjoyment that becomes a source of resentment. Emmi's fellow workers assume that Arabs are after sex only; the German women they fraternize with, too, think about nothing but sex. The Arabs' "strange music" (the film's main use of diegetic music) wafts out of the Asphalt Pub's jukebox and, later, out of the stereo in Emmi's flat and down the stairs, to her neighbors' opprobrium—another marker of the Arabs' "obscene" and "excessive" enjoyment. By situating this racist anxiety within the complexities of group dynamics and exclusionary tactics, *Ali* makes its critique of racism all the more pertinent and penetrating.

Conclusion

As well as pinpointing the socioeconomic conditions that generate racism in *Ali,* Fassbinder adds vital psychoanalytic dimensions—the hostile look that colludes with the dominant cultural "screens" or representations of race (or age) of the day and the unconscious ambivalence in every emotional tie that makes us disburden repressed envy and hatred onto strangers and outsiders. Emmi and Ali pursue their intimacy at the risk of censure and ostracism. Whether or not we interpret their public contravention of social norms as a subversive form of self-display, as Elsaesser suggests ("Primary Identification" 545), or as a "poignant" and "personal" fable of gay love (Haynes 97), *Ali* offers us a searing analysis of relations between oppressors and the oppressed, insiders and outsiders, in ways that reach well beyond Fassbinder's Germany. These two aspects, the critique of racism and the story of forbidden love, converge in the figure of Ali, played by Fassbinder's own lover. Like other New German Cinema productions, Fassbinder's films indict authoritarianism and fascism, yet actors, friends, and lovers have alleged that he behaved in an authoritarian way toward them, both on and off the set. His films consciously display this streak in himself; being aware of it, they address and reflect on it, forcing audiences, too, to face their complicity with what he depicts.

Credits

West Germany, 1974, Tango-Film (Rainer Werner Fassbinder and Michael Fengler)

Director: Rainer Werner Fassbinder
Screenplay: Rainer Werner Fassbinder
Cinematography: Jürgen Jürges
Editing: Thea Eymèsz
Sound: Fritz Müller-Hertz
Lighting: Ekkehard Heinrich
Art Direction: Rainer Werner Fassbinder

CAST:

Emmi	Brigitte Mira
Ali	El Hedi ben Salem
Barbara	Barbara Valentin
Krista	Irm Hermann
Eugen	Rainer Werner Fassbinder
Albert	Karl Scheydt
Bruno	Peter Gavhe
Frau Kargus	Elma Karlowe
Frau Ellis	Anita Bucher
Frau Münchmeyer	Liselotte Eder, aka Lilo Pempeit
Paula	Gusti Kreissl
Hedwig	Margit Symo
Frieda	Elisabeth Bertram
Bar girl	Katharina Herberg
Landlord's son	Marquard Böhm
Waiter	Hannes Gromball
Doctor	Hark Bohm
Shopkeeper	Walter Sedlmayr
Yolanda	Helga Ballhaus

Bibiliography

Adorno, Theodor W. "Freudian Theory and the Pattern of Fascist Propaganda." *The Essential Frankfurt School Reader.* Ed. Andrew Arato and Eike Gebhardt. New York: Continuum, 2000. 118–37.

Babuscio, Jack. "Camp and the Gay Sensibility." *Gays and Film.* Ed. Richard Dyer. London: BFI, 1980. 40–57.

Elsaesser, Thomas. *Fassbinder's Germany: History, Identity, Subject.* Amsterdam: Amsterdam UP, 1996.

————. "Primary Identification and the Historical Subject: Fassbinder and Germany." *Narrative, Apparatus, Ideology: A Film Theory Reader.* Ed. Philip Rosen. New York: Columbia UP, 1986. 535–549.

Fanon, Frantz. *Black Skin, White Masks.* Trans. Charles Lam Markmann. New York: Grove, 1967.

Fassbinder, Rainer Werner. *The Anarchy of the Imagination: Interviews, Essays, Notes.* Ed. Michael Töteberg and Leo A. Lensing. Trans. Krishna Winston. Baltimore: Johns Hopkins UP, 1992.

Franklin, James C. "Method and Message: Forms of Communication in Fassbinder's *Angst Essen Seele Auf.*" *Literature/Film Quarterly* 7.3 (1979): 182–200.

Freud, Sigmund. "Group Psychology and the Analysis of the Ego." *Penguin Freud Library Volume 12: Civilization, Society and Religion.* Trans. James Strachey. London: Penguin, 1991. 91–178. Rpt. of *Massenpsychologie und Ich-Analyse.* Vienna: International Psychoanalytic, 1921.

Hartsough, Denise. "Cine-Feminism Renegotiated: Fassbinder's *Ali* as Interventionist Cinema." *Wide Angle* 12.1 (1990): 18–29.

Haynes, Todd. "Personal Pick: *Ali: Fear Eats the Soul.*" *Premiere* 5.11 (1992): 97.

Iden, Peter, et al. *Fassbinder.* Trans. Ruth McCormick. New York: Tanam, 1981.

Jansen, Peter W., and Wolfram Schütte. *Rainer Werner Fassbinder.* Frankfurt am Main: Fischer, 1992.

Johnston, Sheila. "A Star Is Born: Fassbinder and the New German Cinema." *New German Critique* 24–25 (1981–82): 57–72.

Kaes, Anton. *From Hitler to Heimat: The Return of History as Film.* Cambridge, MA: Harvard UP, 1992.

Kardish, Laurence. *Rainer Werner Fassbinder.* New York: Museum of Modern Art, 1997.

Katz, Robert. *Love Is Colder Than Death: The Life and Times of Rainer Werner Fassbinder.* London: Jonathan Cape, 1987.

Kellner, Douglas. "Fassbinder, Women, and Melodrama: Critical Interrogations." *Triangulated Visions: Women in Recent German Cinema.* Ed. Ingerborg Majer O'Sickey and Ingeborg Von Zadow. Albany: State U of New York P, 1998. 29–41.

Lacan, Jacques. *Écrits.* Trans. Alan Sheridan. London: Routledge, 1993.

————. *The Four Fundamental Concepts of Psychoanalysis.* Trans. Alan Sheridan. London: Penguin, 1994.

Mayne, Judith. "Fassbinder and Spectatorship." *New German Critique* 12 (1977): 61–74.

Merleau-Ponty, Maurice. "The Child's Relations with Others." Trans. William Cobb. *The Primacy of Perception.* Evanston, IL: Northwestern UP, 1964. 96–155.

Mulvey, Laura. *Visual and Other Pleasures.* Basingstoke: Macmillan, 1989.

Paterson, Susanne F. "Fassbinder's *Ali: Fear Eats the Soul* and the Expropriation of a National *Heim.*" *Postscript* 18.3 (1999): 46–57.

Rayns, Tony, ed. *Fassbinder.* London: BFI, 1976.

Reimer, Robert C. "A Comparison of Douglas Sirk's *All That Heaven Allows* and R. W. Fassbinder's *Ali: Fear Eats the Soul;* or, How Hollywood's New England Dropouts Became Germany's Marginalized Other." *Literature/Film Quarterly* 24.3 (1996): 281–87.

Rentschler, Eric, ed. *West German Filmmakers on Film: Visions and Voices.* New York: Holmes, 1988.

Shuttac, Jane. *Television, Tabloids, and Tears: Fassbinder and Popular Cinema.* Minneapolis: U of Minnesota P, 1995.

Silverman, Kaja. "Fassbinder and Lacan: A Reconsideration of Gaze, Look and Image." *Camera Obscura* 19 (1989): 54–85.

Sparrow, Norbert. "'I Let the Audience Feel and Think': An Interview with Rainer Werner Fassbinder." *Cineaste* 8.2 (1977): 20–21.

Watson, Wallace Steadman. *Understanding Rainer Werner Fassbinder: Film as Private and Public Art.* Columbia: U of South Carolina P, 1996.

Žižek, Slavoj. *The Sublime Object of Ideology.* London: Verso, 1997.

Chinatown (1974)

STEVE NEALE

Early 1970s Hollywood Cinema

Context

"Forget it, Jake. It's Chinatown." *Chinatown*'s last line was first heard by the public on its initial release in the United States by Paramount Pictures in June 1974. Since then, *Chinatown* has been hailed as a film that addresses historical, political, and philosophical issues in a serious and radical manner; as a film that both deploys and undermines the conventions of the Hollywood detective film; and as an unusually complex and intricate film with a nevertheless typical narrative structure. For some or all of these reasons, it has also been said to typify what Hollywood's historians have referred to sometimes as "the New Hollywood" and sometimes as "the Hollywood Renaissance" of the late 1960s and early 1970s.

This discussion will begin by looking at notions of the New Hollywood and the Hollywood Renaissance, and at factors inside and outside the American film industry at the time that helped account for *Chinatown*'s production. These include changes in management, ownership, personnel, and policy at Paramount and other major studios. They also include widespread disillusion with America's political regime, its actions and policies at home and abroad, and the values perceived to underpin them. I then go on to look at *Chinatown*'s generic and structural features: in particular, the extent to which they undercut generic conventions while at the same time adhering to many of the structural norms of "classical" Hollywood cinema. Finally, attention will turn to *Chinatown*'s stylistic features, to its biblical, optical, and aquatic motifs, and to the unusually dense, allusive, and enigmatic texture they each help to generate.

Hollywood and America in the Late 1960s and Early 1970s

As Peter Krämer suggests, "Hollywood Renaissance" and "New Hollywood" are terms that have both been used to label changes in the structure, practice, personnel, and output in Hollywood in the late 1960s and early 1970s. As he also explains, "New Hollywood" now tends to refer to the era of the contemporary blockbuster inaugurated by *Jaws* (Steven Spielberg) in 1975, while "Hollywood Renaissance" tends to stress aesthetic rather than industrial factors and issues. Whatever term is used, it is clear that the period between 1966 and 1975 witnessed significant changes at a number of levels in Hollywood, and that *Chinatown* was a product of this period of change.

During the so-called golden age of Hollywood studios, a company like Paramount not only produced films; it also owned theater chains and could "block book" the films it distributed. A landmark ruling against Paramount by the Supreme Court in 1948 declared the studios guilty of violating antitrust laws, initiating a disintegration of the studio system. Studios were deprived of guaranteed outlets for films, but also were divested of the potential financial liability of owning theaters during a period of rapid decline in cinema attendance. Paramount, like other major companies, increasingly opted to produce smaller numbers of bigger-budget films in-house and to distribute and cofinance films made by independent production companies. It increasingly opted, too, to make money by selling or renting packages of its older films to television. However, during the late 1950s and early 1960s, most of the big-budget films it produced or financed, films like *The Buccaneer* (Anthony Quinn, 1958), *Circus World* (Henry Hathaway, 1964), and *The Fall of the Roman Empire* (Anthony Mann, 1964), failed at the box office. With the possible exception of its Elvis Presley films, it also seemed unable to make films that appealed to the youth market, the only sector of the population in the United States still regularly going to the cinema.

One reason for this was that Paramount, like a number of other companies, was run by executives whose careers were forged in an earlier era. Yet if Paramount lacked effective leadership, it did not lack assets. It possessed real estate, a music publishing company and a back catalog of films worth millions of dollars in television revenue. This was the era that saw the Hollywood studio rapidly undergoing transformation and absorption into corporate conglomerates. In 1966, Paramount was acquired by Gulf and Western Industries, while the following year United Artists was acquired by Transamerica. Two years later, Warner Bros. was acquired by Kinney National Services and MGM by Kirk Kerkorian. Management changes ensued, brought on by retirements, by the shifting priorities of the new conglomerate owners, and by a recession brought about by overspending and over-production in the American film industry as a whole.[1]

At Paramount, a team of producers and executives that included Robert Evans, Peter Bart, Stanley Jaffe—all of them under forty—was installed by Gulf and Western. Evans was to play a key role in the making of *Chinatown*. Having turned Paramount's fortunes around with such hits as *Love Story* (Arthur Hiller, 1970) and *The Godfather* (Francis Ford Coppola, 1972), he was permitted to produce a film of his own each year for a five year period. *Chinatown* was the first. In the meantime, however, the recession crystallized a number of problems and paved the way for changes in policy and product as well as in per-sonnel. The increasing failure of big-budget films aimed at older audi-ences (coupled with the increasing success of overseas productions with artistic credentials and of domestic productions with obvious youth appeal) coincided with research indicating that young people with a college education went to the cinema more often than any other group. It also coincided with changes in censorship practices. With in-dependent exhibition and production now the norm, the Motion Pic-ture Association of America found itself no longer able to enforce a Production Code that was initially drawn up in the late 1920s and that many now considered to be out of date. The rating system, introduced in 1968, differentiated audiences by age and relaxed restrictions on films aimed at those over sixteen. It thus paved the way for "adult" films that would appeal to college-educated audiences in their twen-ties and early thirties.[2] With incest and corruption at the heart of its narrative, *Chinatown* was clearly one such film.

By the time *Chinatown* was made, nearly all Hollywood studios were run by younger executives who employed younger writers and directors, and nearly all were making a number of films with appeal to

---

[1]For details on Paramount and the film industry in America in the 1950s and 1960s, see Dick 37–108 and Balio 401–73.

[2]For an account of Hollywood, audiences, censorship, and the introduction of the rating system, see Lewis.

college-educated audiences. This was the period in which young, college-educated "movie brats" like Francis Ford Coppola, Martin Scorsese, and Brian De Palma joined an earlier influx of directors like Robert Altman, Sam Peckinpah, and Arthur Penn and made their first films.[3] This was also when European directors such as Michelangelo Antonioni and Roman Polanski were making films for Hollywood. Given their currency among film company executives, it seemed to some as though Hollywood might come to resemble a "European style auteur cinema" (Cook xvii).

Such hopes were clearly exaggerated. Hollywood continued to produce a range of films, by no means all of which were films of the more sophisticated type made by these directors. Among the biggest box-office hits in 1974 and 1975 were *Herbie Rides Again* (Robert Stevenson), *Earthquake* (Mark Robson), *Benji* (Joe Camp), *Murder on the Orient Express* (Sidney Lumet), and *Funny Lady* (Herbert Ross). It is true, however, that the range of styles and genres was broader at this time than it had been for a number of years. It is also true that many of these directors, often influenced by trends overseas, made films that broke stylistically, generically, or thematically with Hollywood's past. Prompted by the Vietnam War, the struggles of ethnic minorities, the assassinations of Martin Luther King Jr. and Robert Kennedy, and the Watergate break-in and subsequent impeachment of Richard Nixon, they tended, too, to share the anti-establishment, countercultural views of their target audience. The same is true of younger actors and writers. It is no accident that Faye Dunaway and Jack Nicholson, *Chinatown*'s stars, had made their names in countercultural classics like *Bonnie and Clyde* (Arthur Penn, 1967) and *Easy Rider* (Dennis Hopper, 1969), respectively, or that *Chinatown*'s screenwriter, Robert Towne, had worked in an uncredited capacity on the script of *Bonnie and Clyde*.

Released two months prior to Nixon's resignation, *Chinatown*'s story of power and corruption in Los Angeles clearly struck a contemporary chord. It was followed by a number of other "conspiracy thrillers" (or "paranoid" conspiracy films), such as *The Conversation* (Francis Ford Coppola, 1974), *The Parallax View* (Alan J. Pakula, 1974), *Three Days of the Condor* (Sydney Pollack, 1975), and *All the President's*

---

[3]The classic account of this can be found in Pye and Myles.

Men (Pakula, 1976), all of which have been related to the Watergate scandal by writers like Paul Cobley (5–14), David A. Cook (198–205), and Martin Rubin (146–50). But noting that their origins as projects lay for the most part in the late 1960s and early 1970s, Geoff King has cautioned against seeing them in terms of Watergate alone (22–23). I believe that King is right. According to Robert Towne's account on the *Chinatown* DVD, the first version of the script was written in 1971 and prompted by an interest in the history of Los Angeles. But Watergate clearly had a major impact on the reception of these films. It is thus all the more ironic that it was the Nixon government that legislated for tax shelter syndicates of the kind that, according to *Variety*'s review, provided 25 percent of *Chinatown*'s $3.2 million budget (Rev. of *Chinatown*).

Analysis

Genre and Narrative Structure

If *Chinatown* can be seen as a 1970s conspiracy thriller, it can also be seen as a 1970s detective film, and as one among a number of films in the late 1960s and early 1970s that revived, transformed, or revised long-established genre conventions.[4] Detective films of all kinds had been a staple in Hollywood in the 1930s, 1940s, and early 1950s. Sherlock Holmes and Charlie Chan films were made in series, taking their place alongside Nancy Drew mysteries, adaptations of the novels of S. S. Van Dine, and adaptations of the "hard-boiled" novels of Raymond Chandler, Dashiell Hammett, and Mickey Spillane. The hard-boiled tradition and the private-eye heroes of Hammett and Chandler were highly influential. When the detective film was revived in the 1960s and early 1970s, films such as *Marlowe* (Paul Bogart, 1969), *The Long Goodbye* (Robert Altman, 1973), and *Farewell, My Lovely* (Dick Richards, 1975), all of them adaptations of Chandler novels, took their place alongside *Tony Rome* (Gordon Douglas, 1967), *The Detective* (Douglas, 1968), *Lady in Cement* (Douglas, 1968), *Chandler* (Paul Magwood, 1971), *The Mackintosh Man* (John Huston, 1973), *Night Moves* (Arthur Penn, 1975), and other extensions and reincarnations of the hard-boiled tradition.

---

[4]For a detailed overview, see Cook 159–257.

However, there were differences among these films in their attitude to the detective or private eye and in the way they treated the basic conventions of the detective film itself. In nearly all of the detective films prior to the 1970s, detectives solved crimes and brought their perpetrators to justice. The heroic status of the detective as a successful investigative agent and as a successful fighter of crime was therefore affirmed. Since most of these detectives were men, masculine prowess was often affirmed as well. This was particularly true in hard-boiled films, where action as well as deduction was central to the narrative, and where the hero's moral, intellectual, and physical superiority was often marked by his independent status. Also, he usually had either to resist the seductions and machinations of villainous female characters or to investigate female characters whose allegiances were unclear.

While some or all of these elements were reinforced in films like *Tony Rome* and *Farewell, My Lovely,* they were qualified or undermined in films like *The Long Goodbye, Night Moves,* and *Chinatown.* In *Night Moves,* the private eye is ultimately unable to fathom the mysteries with which he is confronted. In *The Long Goodbye,* his morally superior stance and carefree manner are revealed as ineffectually naive. And in *Chinatown,* as John G. Cawelti points out, "Instead of bringing justice to a corrupt society, the detective's actions leave the basic source of corruption untouched. Instead of protecting the innocent, his investigation leads to the death of one victim and the deeper moral destruction of another. Instead of surmounting the web of conspiracy with honor and integrity intact, the detective is overwhelmed by what has happened to him" (186–87). Although he remains a well-meaning and likable character with whom the audience is aligned throughout, Gittes's involvement in divorce work, and even his name, contravene the heroic conventions of the hard-boiled detective film. In the meantime, while Evelyn Mulwray is an evasive and indeed at times duplicitous female character, she is clearly not a *femme fatale.* Her evasiveness and duplicity stem from a wish to protect her daughter. Her feelings for Gittes are genuine. Along with her husband, she alone understands her father's true nature. Gittes himself grasps all of these things too late. In these and in other ways, too (the telling of a sexual joke while Evelyn is standing behind him, the slitting of his nose, the beating he takes from the farmers in Orange County), Gittes's male prowess is undermined. The patriarchal power of Noah Cross, on the other hand, is revealed for the monstrous thing it is.

Polanski himself has written that he wanted *Chinatown* to be evocative of the world and period of Dashiell Hammett and Raymond Chandler (305). Casting John Huston, writer and director of the 1941 adaptation of Hammett's *The Maltese Falcon,* was one way of doing so. In setting his story in the 1930s rather than in the pre–World War I period in which most of the historical events that form its backdrop took place,[5] Robert Towne evoked the era of "classical Hollywood" as well. These evocations find their echo in the retro styling of the film's credits and costume design. To that extent, *Chinatown* might seem to be an example of "nostalgic reincarnation": one of four modes of "generic transformation" identified by Cawelti as marking Hollywood's output at this time. Polanski claims, however, that he saw *Chinatown* "not as a 'retro' piece or conscious imitation of classic movies shot in black and white, but as a film about the thirties seen through the camera eye of the seventies" (303), a point we shall return to below. And Cawelti himself sees *Chinatown* as an instance not of nostalgia but of "demythologization," as a film that undermines the generic traditions and myths it evokes: because *Chinatown* "places the hard-boiled detective story within a view of the world that is deeper and more catastrophic, more enigmatic in its evil, more sudden and inexplicable in its outbreaks of violent chance" than is normally the case, "the image of heroic, moral action embedded in the traditional private-eye myth turns out to be totally inadequate to overcome the destructive realities revealed during the course of the story" (189).

This aspect of *Chinatown* can be ascribed to Polanski, who altered its initial script in a number ways. According to Syd Field, there were three drafts of the script overall. In the first, written by Towne, Jake Gittes opens and closes the story with a voice-over narration, just as Raymond Chandler did in most of his stories (63). Evelyn kills Cross, Gittes rescues her daughter, and Cross's land scheme results in a profit. There is clearly an irony in this last point. According to Field, "Towne's point of view in *Chinatown* is that those who commit certain types of

---

[5]A detailed account of these events can be found in Field 90–92. A group of businessmen acquired the rights to the Owens River and to worthless land in the San Fernando Valley. They planned to build an aquaduct, then sell off the land for a fortune. A drought in 1906 gave them their chance. They were aided by William Mulholland at the Department of Water and Power, who at the height of the drought arranged for thousands of gallons of water to be dumped into the ocean.

crimes, like murder, robbery, rape or arson, are punished by being sent to prison, but those who commit crimes against an entire community are often rewarded by having streets named after them or plaques dedicated to them at City Hall" (64). However, this point of view is fully consonant with hard-boiled mythology: the flip side of hard-boiled individualism is very often a cynical attitude toward public institutions, officials, and power. In all other respects, the "resolution of this first draft is that justice and order prevail" (63). The hiring of Polanski resulted in a second draft with no voice-over and a very different ending, in which Evelyn is killed and Cross survives: "The last scene shows Noah Cross weeping over Evelyn's body while a stunned Gittes tells Escobar that Cross is the man 'responsible' for everything." In the third draft, the ending is even more downbeat: "Horrified by Evelyn's death, Cross puts his arm protectively around his daughter/granddaughter and forcefully whisks her away into the darkness. Noah Cross gets away with it all: murder, the water scandal, the girl" (65).

The pessimism evident in this ending can be found in Polanski's earlier films as well. In *Repulsion* (1965), the virginal central character is driven to suicide. In *The Fearless Vampire Killers* (1967), vampirism wins out. In *Rosemary's Baby* (1968), the devil's child is adopted rather than rejected by Rosemary. And *Macbeth* (1971) ends not just with the downfall of Macbeth, but with the cycle of corrupt power and ambition renewed. In all of these films, as in *Chinatown,* innocence of any kind is always ineffectual. Polanski's biographers attribute this outlook to a childhood spent in the Cracow ghetto and his exposure to the horrors of the Nazi regime. Whatever the reasons, it is his innocence, rather than his worldly-wise ways, that leads Gittes to mistake the nature of Evelyn's relationship with Katherine and that thus helps Cross to triumph. Knowledge is a crucial issue in all detective films. In *Chinatown,* its dimensions are biblical. The ultimate transition from ignorance to knowledge in *Chinatown* occurs in the scene in which Evelyn Mulwray is beaten into confessing that Katherine is her daughter *and* her sister, that Evelyn's father is also Katherine's father, and that Evelyn herself was a willing participant in sex with him. This scene conjoins the film's romance plot with its political and criminal plots while centering them all on a character called Noah.

The interweaving of these plots is one of the hallmarks of *Chinatown*'s widely admired screenplay. So, too, are numerous references to knowledge and innocence (Evelyn tells Gittes that "Hollis seems to think you're an innocent man"; Cross says to Gittes, "You may think you know what you're dealing with, but believe me you don't"). Arguably, there are one or two minor flaws. As Robert McKee points out, Ida Sessions would not have known enough about the water conspiracy to tip Gittes off in a phone call (371), while Gittes's motivation for meeting with Cross near the end remains unclear. (This is clearly a version of the scene in the first draft in which Evelyn meets with Cross in order to kill him. While it serves as another example of Gittes's innocence and of his naively self-confident belief that he can assert control over villainy and the subsequent course of events, it seems more likely at this stage of events that he would try to avoid Cross rather than meet with him.) For the most part, however, McKee, Field and other writers of screenplay manuals agree that *Chinatown*'s script is exemplary.

For Field, especially, all successful screenplays possess a three-act structure comprising a setup, a confrontation, and a resolution. These acts are linked by "plot points." Field uses *Chinatown*'s script as a model, with its setup introducing Jake Gittes, his associates, and the character who turns out to be Ida Sessions. Posing as Mrs. Mulwray, Sessions tells Gittes that her husband is having an affair. She hires him to find out whom it is with. Gittes follows and photographs Hollis Mulwray and a younger woman. A newspaper story claims that Hollis has been caught in a "love nest." At this point, Evelyn Mulwray and her lawyer appear in Jake's office and threaten to sue. This for Fields is the plot point that leads to act two, comprising Jake's attempts to discover who set him up, the murder of Hollis Mulwray, the development of Jake's relationship with Evelyn, the discovery of a plot to run off water and acquire land cheaply in the midst of a drought, Jake's first meeting with Cross, and Cross's attempt to discover the whereabouts of the younger woman. The discovery of a pair of glasses in Mulwray's pool is the plot point that leads to act three. The glasses belong either to Mulwray or to Mulwray's killer. Jake confronts Evelyn with the evidence and his suspicion that she is holding Katherine, the younger woman, against her will. Evelyn reveals that Katherine is her daughter and that Cross is Katherine's father. She also reveals that the glasses did not belong to Hollis. Realizing that they belonged to Noah Cross, and that Cross killed Hollis, set him up, and is the man behind the conspiracy to run off water and buy up cheap land, Gittes arranges to confront him. Cross, however, forces Gittes to reveal the whereabouts of Evelyn and Katherine, and the final denouement in Chinatown ensues.

One of the features of Field's three-act model is the length of its second act. Kristin Thompson points out that the second act is nearly always twice as long as the first and the third, and proposes an alternative, four-part model comprising a "setup," a "complicating action," a "development," and a "climax." Each is linked by "turning points," and each is of roughly equal length, with "a crucial turning point more or less at dead center" (28). If analyzed in these terms, *Chinatown* exemplifies Thompson's four-part model as well. Here, the turning point between the setup and the complicating action occurs just after Mulwray's death, when Evelyn tells Jake she has hired him. Thirty-one minutes into the film, this opens the way for a relationship between Jake and Evelyn and changes the focus of Jake's investigations. The turning point between the complicating action and the development occurs in the first scene between Gittes and Cross. Cross hires Jake to find Mulwray's "girlfriend," turning Jake's attention to her whereabouts. This scene ends precisely halfway through the film. Finally, the turning point leading to the climax occurs just over an hour and half into the film. Having received an unsatisfactory explanation as to Katherine's identity, Jake has abandoned Evelyn. Lying alone in bed, he receives a phone call from Escobar. Ida Sessions wants to see him. He puts down the phone, and it rings again. Escobar insists and gives Jake her address.

The models proposed by Field and Thompson raise a number of interesting issues, not the least of which is the nature and definition of turning points and acts.[6] The point to make here, though, is that neither Thompson nor Field see her or his models as historically specific. Field refers to *Casablanca* (Michael Curtiz, 1942) as well as to *Chinatown*. Thompson argues specifically that 1970s, 1980s, and 1990s Hollywood films are as "classical" in their narrative structures as films of the 1930s, 1940s, and 1950s. The implication is that the historical hallmarks of a 1970s film like *Chinatown* lie beyond its script and its narrowly

---

[6] For further discussion of *Chinatown* and its narrative structure from a screenwriter's point of view, see Eaton.

defined 1970s context. If so, as we have seen, they certainly lie in its treatment of genre. Perhaps they also lie in what Polanski, as noted earlier, called "the camera eye of the seventies," or aspects of the film's style.

Style, Motifs, and Tone

In amplifying his comment about style, Polanski specifically cites Panavision and color as significant developments (306). Color had been the norm for Hollywood films of all kinds since the mid-1960s. Making a 1970s film with retro ingredients in black and white, as Peter Bogdanovich had done in *The Last Picture Show* (1971), would in *Chinatown*'s case have produced an aura of nostalgia inappropriate in a film with revisionist aims. Panavision is an anamorphic widescreen process with an aspect ratio (the ratio of width to height) of 2:35 to 1. By the early 1960s, it had supplanted CinemaScope as the process used most often to make anamorphic widescreen films. CinemaScope had itself in the 1950s helped supplant the Academy ratio of 1.33 to 1, the ratio used in most 1930s and 1940s Hollywood films. Panavision and color thus both help to mark a difference between *Chinatown* and films of the past. This is augmented by the use made in *Chinatown* of Panavision's new handheld Panaflex camera. The Panaflex was used instead of dollies, cranes, and other traditional devices to produce most of the film's mobile shots, though *Chinatown* is not simply marked by a rejection of past techniques, as the use of a crane in its last shot and the original choice of veteran Stanley Cortez as cinematographer indicate. Cortez was replaced by John Alonzo soon after filming began, but Alonzo's account of his work on the film is as full of references to classical, even old-fashioned, techniques as it is to new ones. While noting that "shooting Faye Dunaway without diffusion . . . would never have been done in the 'classic' period," he also notes that Polanski "wanted a bit of the classic depth of field that Gregg Toland used to achieve" (565). Recalling that Panavision's faster lenses "gave us a little edge over our predecessors," he also notes that he "resurrected an old-fashioned type of light . . . called a 'chicken coop'" (586). And although he used a zoom lens, he notes that he never used it "strictly as a move," that is as a substitute for moving the camera (572).

Alonzo's account indicates that *Chinatown*'s visual style is equally as marked by its avoidance of a number of contemporary trends as it is by its use of new technology. This is evident in its use of long takes and its average shot length (ASL). Barry Salt further points out that the trend toward faster cutting in the 1960s "reached a peak" in the 1970s, "with by far the most common ASL being about 6 seconds. ASLs of 4 seconds or less were now fairly common, and hardly any ordinary commercial American films had ASLs longer than 13 seconds. . . . Long ASLs were now almost exclusively associated with high artistic ambition" (283). Consonant with this last point, perhaps, *Chinatown* has an ASL of 15 seconds. As in all films, the cutting rate varies from sequence to sequence. One of the longest shots in the film occurs toward the end, when Jake confronts Cross with the glasses retrieved from the pond. This is a single-take conversation scene. But even in an action scene like the one in which Jake gets beaten up in the orange grove, Polanski and Alonzo tend to use a handheld moving camera and continuous choreography rather than rapid cuts to articulate the action. This is in keeping with the tendency to show characters moving into and out of locations and spaces, whether in cars or on foot, and with a general tendency to preserve the spatial and temporal integrity of movements and actions.

Despite its widescreen format, *Chinatown* tends to use long takes and a mobile camera rather than lateral framings and stagings as means of preserving this integrity. This is a sign of the changing status and use of widescreen formats in the 1970s. Widescreen formats like CinemaScope were introduced in the 1950s as a means of distinguishing films from television. However, the screening of films on television became an increasingly important source of revenue for the film industry in the 1960s. Because of the differences in shape, films shot in widescreen formats caused problems when shown on television:

> If the full height of a widescreen frame filled the TV screen, then only a portion of the width could be seen. . . . When transmitted on a 4:3 TV screen attempts were made to "pan" the image to keep significant action within the transmission frame. The "pan and scan" conversion of widescreen to 4:3 aspect ratio often introduced unmotivated pans following dialogue from one side of the widescreen to the other. . . . Pan and scan either took a portion of the frame that was considered the most important (usually dialogue led) or panned from subject to subject to follow dialogue or cut from one portion of the screen

to another portion of the screen (again following dialogue) introducing a cutting rate that never occurred when the film was originally produced. (Ward 108–9)

From the early 1960s on, directors and cinematographers were increasingly urged to bear the dimensions of the television screen in mind when composing their shots.

One tendency was to group narratively central actions and characters in a sector of the frame whose dimensions were compatible with those of the television image. Examples in *Chinatown* can be found in the conversation scene between Evelyn and Jake in the restaurant, in the earlier conversation scene between Evelyn and Jake on Evelyn's patio, and in the second scene involving Jake and the secretary in the Department of Water and Power. During the restaurant scene, a number of alternating two-shots frame Evelyn and Jake together at center left and center right of the image. During the scene on the patio, Evelyn and Jake are framed in two-shot center left then center right. During the scene with the secretary, Jake sits down to light a cigarette, and he is framed foreground right with the secretary seated behind the desk midground center. In each of these shots, only a portion of the frame— a portion compatible with the aspect ratio of the television image—is occupied by the principal characters. This does not mean, though, that the remainder of the widescreen frame is empty. Diners can be seen at the edges of the frame in the restaurant scene; hot water and tea are poured by Evelyn's servant, first on the right-hand edge of the frame and then on the left; flowers in a vase of water are visible on the secretary's desk on the left-hand side of the frame. These elements tend to be cropped when *Chinatown* is panned and scanned for 4:3 television (and video) formats. In widescreen, however, they serve not only to help fill the frame; in the last two instances, they help articulate one of the film's central motifs—the motif of water—as well.

If water is central to *Chinatown*'s plot, it is also central to the interwoven patterns of imagery that pervade *Chinatown*'s image track and sound track alike. Aside from the sequences set near the ocean and the reservoir, and aside from tea and vases of flowers, water is audibly or visibly alluded to: in the dispenser on the left-hand side of frame in the joke-telling sequence, in the steam emitted from the car in the street behind Jake in the barber shop, in the newspaper headline

"Seabiscuit Idol of Race Fans," in the pool in Mulwray's garden, in all the images of fish in the film, in lines such as "Echo Park. Water again," in the squeaking sound of the car being washed when Jake first visits Mulwray's house, in the sound of the dripping tap in Ida Sessions's apartment, in the "dripping" sounds evident in the opening in bars of the "Love Theme from *Chinatown*," and in the piano figure marking the "J. J. Gittes" segment of Jerry Goldsmith's score.

A link between these aquatic motifs and motifs from the Bible, meanwhile, is implied not just in the association between a patriarch called Noah and a flood, but in the image of the fish that adorns the flag of Albacore, Noah Cross's yacht club; in the fish that Cross and Gittes eat for lunch; and in Cross's reference to Mulwray's fascination with tide pools: "That's where life begins." Herbert Eagle suggests, therefore, that the images of fish may recall early Christian symbolism (151). Whatever the case may be, the discovery of Cross's glasses in the pool in Mulwray's garden provides not just another link between *Chinatown*'s aquatic and biblical motifs, but a link between its aquatic, biblical, and optical motifs as well.

The optical motifs in *Chinatown* center on the capacities and limitations of human vision, of visual representation, of the human eye, and of the means and devices used to extend its capacities, counteract its flaws, and fix the appearances with which it is confronted. They thus include the photographs that open the film, the photographs that Gittes takes of Mulwray and Katherine, and the photographs—still dripping water—that Duffy takes of Mulwray and Cross. As well as Cross's glasses, Mulwray's glasses, and the "flaw" in Evelyn's eye, they also include the rearview mirror in Jake's car, Jake's binoculars, the lens in Jake's camera, and the window through which he first sees Evelyn and Katherine together. This last example highlights the extent to which vision and visual appearances in *Chinatown* are marked as inadequate: on the basis of what he sees, Jake thinks that Mulwray is having an affair with a younger woman and that Evelyn is holding Katherine against her will. He is wrong in both cases.

These motifs, like all motifs, are governed by a logic of repetition. They are also governed by the logic of puns. Here optical motifs pun on the figure of the private eye, and the first line of the film puns on "blinds," while the film as a whole could be said to be organized around puns on "Water and Power." These forms of logic intertwine with one another and with the logic of investigative fiction—a logic that depends on mystery, suspense, and the generation of clues and red herrings. The result, as Garrett Stewart shows, is that "ordinary narrative suspense, the train of multiplying clues and partial discoveries, is to a large extent replaced by a sense of foreboding divorced from plot, and more importantly by a suspension in symbolic details themselves, a consistently withheld relevance that defines the true plotline of the film" (28).

Conclusion

Stewart continues: "What does it mean that Noah Cross eats whole fish? Or that he is named Noah for that matter? That Mrs. Mulwray has a black flaw in her left green eye?" (28). These questions might be multiplied. Why is this the eye shot out by Loach at the end of the film? Why is this image prefigured by the taillights, one normally lit, one dark and deliberately damaged by Jake, on Mrs. Mulwray's car? Why is it also prefigured by the image of two circular stopwatches, one functioning normally, one smashed by Mulwray's car early on in the film? Why is it prefigured, too, by the missing lens in Jake's sunglasses following his fight with the farmers in the orange grove, and by Curly's wife's black eye? Why is "albacore" mistaken for "apple core" and "grass" mispronounced as "glass"? Why is the insistence on repetition so great that Jake is doomed, to adopt Hollis Mulwray's words, "to make the same mistake twice"? There is in the end simply no answer to all of these questions, for it is one of the hallmarks of *Chinatown*, as Stewart goes on to point out, that it presents itself as an allegory without a key, a riddle to which there is no single or final solution. That, perhaps, however dependent it may be on the stereotype of "Oriental inscrutability," is the significance of "Chinatown" itself, not as a location, but as a sign in the minds of its principal characters.

Credits

United States, 1974, Long Road Productions, Paramount-Penthouse

Director: Roman Polanski
Producer: Robert Evans
Screenplay: Robert Towne
Cinematography: John A. Alonzo
Editing: Sam O'Steen
Music: Jerry Goldsmith
Art Direction: W. Stewart Campbell
Costume Design: Anthea Sylbert

CAST:

J. J. Gittes	Jack Nicholson
Evelyn Mulwray	Faye Dunaway
Noah Cross	John Huston
Escobar	Perry Lopez
Hollis Mulwray	Darrell Zwerling
Ida Sessions	Diane Ladd
Detective Loach	Richard Bakalyan

Bibiliography

Alonzo, John. "Behind the Scenes of *Chinatown.*" *American Cinematographer* 56.5 (1975): 526–91.

Balio, Tino, ed. *The American Film Industry.* Madison: Wisconsin UP, 1985.

Cawelti, John G. "*Chinatown* and Generic Transformation in Recent American Films." *Film Genre Reader.* Ed. Barry Keith Grant. Austin: U of Texas P, 1986. 181–201.

Chinatown. Dir. Roman Polanski. 1974. DVD. Paramount, 2000.

Cobley, Paul. *The American Thriller: Generic Innovation and Social Change in the 1970s.* Houndmills: Palgrave, 2000.

Cook, David A. *Lost Illusions: American Cinema in the Shadow of Watergate and Vietnam.* New York: Scribner's, 2000.

Dick, Bernard F. *Engulfed: The Death of Paramount Pictures and the Birth of Corporate Hollywood.* Lexington: UP of Kentucky, 2001.

Eagle, Herbert. "Polanski." *Five Filmmakers: Tarkovsky, Forman, Polanski, Szabo, Makaveyev.* Ed. Daniel J. Goulding. Bloomington: Indiana UP, 1974.

Eaton, Michael. "*Chinatown.*" London: BFI, 1997.

Field, Syd. *Screenplay: The Foundations of Screenwriting.* New York: Dell, 1994.

King, Geoff. *New Hollywood Cinema.* London: Tauris, 2002.

Krämer, Peter. "Post-Classical Hollywood." *The Oxford Guide to Film Studies.* Ed.

John Hill and Pamela Church Gibson. Oxford: Oxford UP, 1998. 289–309.

Lewis, Jon. *Hollywood v. Hard Core: How the Struggle over Censorship Saved the Modern Film Industry.* New York: New York UP, 2000.

McKee, Robert. *Story: Substance, Structure, Style, and the Principles of Screenwriting.* New York: Methuen, 1997.

Polanski, Roman. *Roman.* London: Heinemann, 1984.

Pye, Michael, and Linda Myles. *The Movie Brats: How the Film Generation Took Over Hollywood.* London: Faber, 1979.

Rev. of *Chinatown,* dir. Roman Polanski. *Variety* 9 June 1974: 16.

Rubin, Martin. *Thrillers.* Cambridge: Cambridge UP, 1999.

Salt, Barry. *Film Style and Technology: History and Analysis.* London: Starword, 1992.

Stewart, Garrett. "'The Long Goodbye' to 'Chinatown.'" *Film Quarterly* 28.2 (1974–75): 25–32.

Thompson, Kristin. *Storytelling in the New Hollywood: Understanding Classical Narrative Technique.* Cambridge, MA: Harvard UP, 1999.

Ward, Peter. *Picture Composition for Film and Television.* Oxford: Focal, 2003.

The Last Supper (1976)

GILBERTO M. BLASINI

Cinema, History, and Decolonization

Context

In his essay "The Viewer's Dialectic," Tomás Gutiérrez Alea (1928–1996) states that "Film not only entertains and informs, it also shapes taste, intellectual judgment and states of consciousness. If filmmakers fully assume their own social and historical responsibilities, they will come face to face with the inevitable need to promote the theoretical development of their artistic practice" (110). These words clearly exemplify the creative vision and political accountability that mark the films of Gutiérrez Alea, the most prolific and renowned film director of postrevolutionary Cuba. His body of work, both documentaries and fiction films, serves as an example of a responsible filmmaking practice that looks to promote social change while experimenting with the aesthetic and narrative possibilities proffered by cinema. His films question governmental inefficiency and incompetence (*The Death of a Bureaucrat* [*La muerte de un burócrata*, 1966]), intellectual responsibility in the light of radical social changes (*Memories of Underdevelopment* [*Memorias del subdesarrollo*, 1968]), sexism and its connections to class issues (*Up to a Certain Point* [*Hasta cierto punto*, 1983]), homophobia (*Strawberry and Chocolate* [*Fresa y chocolate*, 1993]), and political corruption (*Guantanamera*, 1995), among many other social problems extant in Cuba. A complex exploration of the harmful and pervasive ramifications of racism and colonialism is best represented in *The Last Supper* (*La última cena*, 1976).

However, in contrast to Gutiérrez Alea's other films, whose stories are all set in the twentieth century, *The Last Supper* takes place in the eighteenth century. By locating the film's story in the past, Gutiérrez Alea presents a critical rewriting of Cuban history. The film allows, in particular, for a reassessment of the island's colonial legacy and the specific hierarchies of power that were established principally through the plantation system and its dependence on slavery. At the core of this rewriting is the drive to engage audiences in decolonizing processes that seek to recuperate and include those marginalized voices that have been disregarded or silenced by the official version of history. Hence, the film serves as an act of resistance against what had been society's dominant groups not only by presenting alternative versions of particular events, but also by establishing and validating a historical ground for the construction of unique cultural identities. *The Last Supper* is a critical revision that also resuscitates and makes palpable the importance of African cultures in the constitution of the country's idiosyncratic and hybrid nationality. Outside of the Cuban national context, Gutiérrez Alea's revisionist approach to history aligns with cinematic movements such as the New Latin American Cinema as well as with other cultural expressions in the Caribbean. This approach also makes *The Last Supper* part of a larger group of films that, according to Teshome H. Gabriel, exemplify how cinema can be the guardian of popular memory. In his words, these films "delve into the past, not only to reconstruct, but also to redefine and to redeem what the official versions of history have overlooked" (57).

Background

To understand the driving impetus behind *The Last Supper*, it is necessary to place Gutiérrez Alea's work in the context of the cultural agenda of postrevolutionary Cuba. After seizing power on January 1, 1959, and declaring Cuba an independent republic, the new government under Fidel Castro's leadership attempted to create a new society, one that sought to eliminate the decadence, corruption, and social disparity that dictator Fulgencio Batista had left behind. Batista's legacy of social and political deterioration was in large part due to the U.S. presence on the island (which had become official after the end of the Spanish-American War in 1898), and its political ends—to maintain very profitable economic holdings (advantageous trade relations, particularly of sugar) and military properties (which gave the United States a strategic geographical location in relation to the rest of the Caribbean and Latin America). As a corrective counteraction, the Cuban government (which officially became socialist in 1961) initiated agrarian reforms that divided up large landholdings in rural areas, lowered rents paid in the cities, and promoted literacy (by 1988, 98 percent of the population was able to read and write). Within the newly constituted republic, cinema became a high priority. Just three months after independence, the government approved Law 169, which created the Instituto Cubano del Arte e Industria Cinematográficos (ICAIC). As Gutiérrez Alea puts it, "Cuban cinema emerged as one more facet of reality within the Revolution" ("Viewer's Dialectic" 108).

In general terms, cinema had two main purposes in the post-1959 political context: to help educate people and to promote revolutionary ideals that would allow citizens to become active participants in the social changes taking place in their country. In order to pursue cinema's potential as a tool for social and political awareness, people needed to be taught how to become more critical readers of films. For that purpose, the ICAIC eventually created a cinematheque, a film magazine, a television show, and mobile cinema units, among other things, that would help in the diffusion of films and in the literacy campaign (as it relates both to reading and writing Spanish and to understanding cinema and its artifices) throughout the island. Although strongly influenced by the ideals of the revolution, the filmic work of Gutiérrez Alea—and, for that matter, that of many other film directors who have been part of the ICAIC—should not be understood as propaganda. In fact, even though Gutiérrez Alea always showed support for the revolution, his films openly reflect on the problems and contradictions that emerged throughout this social process (e.g., *Memories of Underdevelopment, Strawberry and Chocolate,* and *Guantanamera*).

The abrupt changes taking place in Cuba during the first decade of the revolution led filmmakers such as Gutiérrez Alea to focus initially on documentaries. This trend is important because even though these filmmakers moved on to fiction films, they continued infusing their work with a keen historical observation of their island's social realities. In Gutiérrez Alea's case, this observation was also heightened by two distinct experiences. First, his academic training as a filmmaker took place at the Centro Sperimentale di Cinematografia in Rome, from 1951 to 1953. The Centro was closely linked with Italian neorealism, which sought to reveal the social struggles of the poor and working classes in Italy. Second, Gutiérrez Alea was affected by the particular political situation in Cuba not only after his return from Italy, but also during the first decade of the

Cuban Revolution. As a result, Gutiérrez Alea's filmmaking became one where

> art's function is to contribute to the best enjoyment of life, at the aesthetic level, and it does this not by offering a ludicrous parenthesis in the middle of everyday reality but by enriching that very reality. At a cognitive level, it contributes to a more profound comprehension of the world. This helps viewers develop criteria consistent with the path traced by society. On the ideological level, finally, art also contributes to reaffirming the new society's values and, consequently, to fighting for its preservation and development. ("Viewer's Dialectic" 116)

Although these ideas directly apply to the particular national project shaping Cuba, Gutiérrez Alea's work also dialogued with the New Latin American Cinema, a pan-national film movement that officially started in 1967, in Viña del Mar, Chile. At the core of this movement was an attempt to use cinema as a cultural weapon against the ubiquity of imperialism and neocolonialism still rampant in Latin American countries during the latter part of the twentieth century. For that purpose, the New Latin American Cinema had as its primary project "producing a distinctive cinema that would directly address and promote the social, cultural and political transformations and empowerment of its audience" (Blasini 194). To be able to effect major changes that would potentially produce political agency in audiences, one of the principal strategies employed by Latin American filmmakers was to use cinema as a medium to revisit and rewrite the history of the Americas. This strategy would allow them to challenge what Frantz Fanon has called the perverted logic of colonialism that "turns to the past of the oppressed people, and distorts, disfigures, and destroys it" (210).

In many instances, this revisionist approach sought to unearth the role that African cultures have played in the transformation of the Americas. For example, in 1969, Caliban, the character from William Shakespeare's play *The Tempest* (1611), was reclaimed in three different languages by three Caribbean artists. In Martinique, Aimé Césaire wrote *Une tempête: d'après "La tempête" de Shakespeare* in an adaptation for a "black theater" ("un théâtre nègre"). Barbadian Edward Brathwaite wrote a long poem titled "Caliban" as part of his book of poetry

Islands. Finally, Cuban Roberto Fernández Retamar wrote the essay "Cuba hasta Fidel," in which he compared Cubans to the figure of Caliban. These three texts passionately reclaim the figure of Caliban as a symbol of resistance, and as a denouncement against the oppressions suffered by Caribbean countries and their inhabitants—particularly due to issues of race and class—at the hands of European colonizers. As Michael Chanan informs, "aspects of the Caliban theme found expression in Cuban cinema during the course of the '70s in which the image of the slave is powerfully deconstructed" (270). These films include *The Other Francisco* (*El otro Francisco,* 1974), *Rancheador* (1975), and *Maluala* (1979), a trilogy by filmmaker Sergio Giral, as well as a series of documentaries. Gutiérrez Alea himself had written a screen adaptation of *The Tempest* in collaboration with Michael Chanan.[1] Even though Gutiérrez Alea was never able to turn his script into a film, he explored issues related to slavery, religion, and colonialism in *The Last Supper.*

Analysis

Narrative Structure
As a starting point for unmasking the oppressive imperialist enterprises of colonialism and its use of slavery for economic profit, Gutiérrez Alea based his film on an anecdote found in a historical study of the Cuban sugar industry entitled *El ingenio* (1964), by Manuel Moreno Fraginals.[2] Briefly, both the anecdote and the film revolve around a Count who, in a moment of religious hubris, decides to restage Jesus Christ's Last Supper but with twelve of his slaves in the roles of Christ's disciples. Due to cultural misunderstandings and abuses of power, this supper has very unsettling effects on all of its participants. It leads to a slave revolt that is quickly suppressed through the execution of the slaves who attended the Count's banquet. Importantly, contrary to the historical document, the film allows for one slave, Sebastián, to escape from the massacre. This change has meaningful ideological ramifications because it creates Sebastián as a revolutionary subject who does not allow the world of the Count (which stands as a symbol of capitalism) to annihilate him.

---

[1]Gutiérrez Alea describes part of this screenplay in an essay entitled "El verdadero rostro de Calibán" which appeared in *Cine Cubano.*
[2]The anecdote can be found in Spanish in Fornet 146–47.

Blasini

On the surface, the film follows a linear temporal progression during Holy Week: from Good Wednesday, when the Count arrives at the sugar mill, to Easter Sunday, when the Count declares his intention to build a church where the sugar mill once stood while Sebastián freely roams through the mountains. This particular structure is important because it provides the film with a chronology that invokes the conventional notion of history as an ordering of facts that supposedly lead to an understanding of events and, consequently, the world. However, this exterior structure is purposefully used to call attention to the constructedness of history. On the one hand, the fact that the action takes place during Holy Week ironically exposes not only the Count's hypocritical use of Catholicism, but also how the slaves' lives were severely regulated through contradictory messages about their duties to work and to religion. On the other hand, the twelve chosen slaves challenge in various degrees the dominant order of things—spatial as well as historical—through the oral stories, the songs, and the myths that they interject throughout the film. These political interventions become particularly evident during their "Last Supper" with the Count on Holy Thursday. The sequence, which lasts more than half of the film's running time, uncovers the contradictory discourses employed by the different branches of Eurocentric thought—religion, science, and economics—to justify slavery and the oppression of African cultures. Key to the film's deployment of this uncovering process is the fact that the slaves find ways of questioning and even contesting these discourses without the Count's ever noticing it.

African Cultures and Subversive Anticolonial Acts

At different points in the film, Gutiérrez Alea calls attention to the particular survival tactics that slaves had to develop in order to preserve their cultures and contest the authority of Eurocentric discourses. Congo, the storyteller, exemplifies these tactics. During the "Last Supper," Congo tells the Count, "Master, black people carry God's curse. Blacks were born to suffer. You don't realize it when you see them singing and dancing. When you hear them singing, ask yourself, 'who's crying?'" Immediately after this statement, Congo tells a story about how Africans found themselves implicated in the inhumanity of the slave trade in order to meet their basic needs, such as having food to eat. In the story, an African man tries to sell his own son to slave

684

traders, but when the son realizes this, he sells his father instead. After returning with food to his family, the son is punished for his deed, and he is also sold to slave traders. The story ends when Congo says, "With the money obtained from the son's sale, the family ate twice that week." After hearing this conclusion, all the other slaves laugh—a reaction that the Count reads as a natural response to the entertaining show put together by Congo. The Count's misunderstanding of what the story and the performance were all about is evidenced by the fact that he decides to provide some entertainment of his own (he stands and starts singing a Spanish song).

Along with providing an alternative version of history, this scene emphasizes performance and oral storytelling in at least two ways. First, it establishes a connection with African oral traditions and its main figure, the *griot*. In African cultures, the *griot* is a storyteller who keeps communal history alive by continuously enacting tales, anecdotes, and myths, using song, dance, narration, declamations, and, most important, direct interaction with the audience.[3] Thus, the inclusion of Congo as a storyteller functions to highlight the existence of alternative histories that privilege an understanding of the world based on collectivity and not individualism. Second, it reveals the subversive qualities of Afro-diasporic cultures. In order to survive and subvert power, African groups were forced to invent codes that would be unintelligible to their oppressors. *The Last Supper*'s visual style during the banquet sequence further reinforces the element of subversion. The sequence takes place in a claustrophobic environment that is further limited by the use of static cameras, which pan from side to side and zoom in and out of characters, but never quite move. Characters, especially slaves, are rendered captives in a *mise-en-scène* that constrains their movement. The visual constraint works as a visual metaphor for slaves' living conditions under colonial regimes. As a counterpoint, when the story takes place outdoors, particularly when the slaves revolt and try to escape, the action is depicted through handheld cameras. Although this stylistic choice helps to infuse these

---

[3]An important difference between the conventional African *griot* and its cinematic counterpart is the fact that the former's stories advocate a return to a conservative, traditional order, while the latter attempts to create a new social order. For more details, see Diawara.

scenes with a sense of anxiety and immediacy related to the tension and discontent between oppressors and oppressed, it also works to represent an alternative spatial possibility for the latter, particularly since Sebastián flees to the mountains where runaway slaves have established free settlements (called *palenques*).

The construction of Cuba as well as the entire Caribbean as a singularized slave society based on plantation systems involved what Gordon K. Lewis calls "a virulent negrophobia," which promoted the idea that African slaves were inferior to their European masters (5–9). This "negrophobia" led to oppressive practices by the hegemonic European-identified groups. Official government documents, historical chronicles, and literary texts created stereotypes by representing slaves as savages who were lazy and irresponsible and who had an inferior mentality as well as an aggressive sexuality (Lewis 7). Indeed, Shakespeare's *The Tempest* falls into this category of stigmatizing texts. According to Gutiérrez Alea, the play represents the enslaved world as one that is "corrupt, savage, irrational, violent, cruel, impotent, and incapable of doing anything else but serve as the slave of that other world that builds itself as legitimate, clean, wise, just, as the chosen one—surely by God—to rule the universe's destiny" ("El verdadero" 15). This antislave/"negrophobic" mentality was also reflected in the strivings to control and even eliminate any religious practice from Africa in the colonies. Yet, these suppressive attempts only worked to nurture the desire among slaves to perform their social and religious traditions, both as acts of preservation and celebration of diasporic African cultures and as acts of subversion and resistance against the dominant groups.

In the film, Sebastián uses African culture, in his case Yoruba beliefs, to challenge the Eurocentric colonial order imposed and sustained in Cuba by people like the Count. His retelling of Olofi's creation of the world—including the concepts of and relationship between Truth and Lie—provides a framework for understanding how colonizers manipulated ideologies into a "common sense" that justified and perpetuated the subjugation of people of African ancestry.[4] The fact that this retelling happens while the Count has passed out from drinking too much wine represents how slaves needed to become resourceful to subvert the hierarchies of inequality in colonial

---

[4]A version of Olofi's story can be found in Downing.

societies in the Americas. However, Sebastián does not limit his transgressive behavior to moments when he is unobserved. At one point during the banquet, the Count sits Sebastián next to him and asks him, "Who am I?" After waiting for more than a minute, Sebastián responds by spitting in the Count's face. This moment is crucial since Sebastián refuses to acknowledge the Count both as a subject and as "his master." As Stuart Hall states, "identities actually come from the outside, they are the way in which we are recognized and then come to step into the place of that recognition which others give us. Without the others there is no self, there is no self-recognition" (8). Consequently, Sebastián's gesture becomes radically political since his denial of recognition implies a lack of acquiescence to the power of the Count, even if the larger historical circumstances place him in a disadvantageous position, socially and materially speaking, as a slave.

The role of the slave, nevertheless, holds a privileged position in Marxist philosophical discourse (based on G. W. F. Hegel's concept of the master-slave dialectic in *The Phenomenology of the Spirit*). Indeed, it is the slave—as well as its other iterations, such as the working classes—who moves history forward by continuously rebelling against the oppressive powers of capitalism. As a result, the film redefines power through Sebastián's agency to contest and, in the long run, to prevail over the Count. This redefinition of power functions less as a rewriting of history and more as an ideological construct that asks Cuban audiences to show strength and tenacity in the face of powerful enemies and adverse times. In many ways, Cuba was still trying to break "the vicious circle of underdevelopment" by attempting "to diversify production and lessen the country's dependence on sugar" as well as by combating the U.S. embargo (Chanan 256).[5] During the 1970s, "the economy remained plagued by major problems. Low productivity, mismanage-

---

[5]Two points need to be made here for clarity's sake. The first one relates to Cuba's dependence on sugar. Like other Latin American countries that underwent European colonization, Cuba's economy had developed through monoculture (i.e., the cultivation or exploitation of a single crop) in order to create a cycle of colonial dependence. This cycle was still in place during the 1960s and 1970s. The second one relates to the U.S. embargo. In 1960, after an unsuccessful attempt to invade Cuba (the Bay of Pigs fiasco), the United States looked for other ways to weaken Castro's government economically. One of the solutions was to cease having any kind of commerce with the island. This is what is known as the U.S. embargo on Cuba.

ment, inefficiency, underemployment, and overly ambitious goals were the more persistent ones" (Suchlicki 182). As a result, "on the ideological front, greater emphasis was placed on the need for sacrifice" (Suchlicki 181). Given this historical context, the film's final scene, showing Sebastián running up a mountain, provided audiences with a model of perseverance through the film's main character. At the same time, the scene links Sebastián with a history of revolutionary groups who used the mountains as their safe haven. On the one hand, the mountains reference the *palenques,* which, much like the *quilombos* in Brazil, stand for a sense of freedom and rebellion, since they were communities founded by slaves who ran away from oppressive living conditions in the plantations. On the other hand, they also allude to the July 26 Movement, which, under the leadership of Fidel Castro, was able to make Cuba an independent country. During critical moments before seizing the island, members of the July 26 Movement—along with the many peasants who joined them in what became known as the Rebel Army—took refuge in the Sierra Maestra, a mountain chain that proved to be an ideal place to hide from Batista's armed forces.

Race and the Hierarchy of Power

In terms of its revisionist approach to Cuban history, one of *The Last Supper*'s most outstanding achievements is how it makes a point of addressing the multiplicity of positions held by the sugar mill's slaves. Historically, even though social and cultural diversity existed among the different African groups that were brought to the Americas, they were all homogenized under rubrics such as "blacks" and "Africans." In the film, audiences learn that one of the slaves is Carabalí (a group that presumably practiced cannibalism) and another is Lucumí. This last slave, whose name is Bangoché, narrates how he was a king in Africa before being sold as a slave in Guinea. His sale becomes ironic given that Bangoché himself was implicated in the slave trade during his kingship. Gutiérrez Alea includes these details as a way of suggesting both the existence of social hierarchies in Africa as well as the complicity of some Africans in the capitalistic enterprise of selling people as slaves.[6]

---

[6]Works like Peter Gerhard's "A Black Conquistador in Mexico" offer evidence of the presence of Africans in the colonizing of the Americas before the slave trade had officially started.

Along with the differences that Africans brought with them to the Americas, *The Last Supper* also shows how the colonial system placed slaves and their descendants in separate hierarchies of valuation and importance according to factors such as place of work and skin color. These structures of power put into place through the plantation system promoted division as well as animosity among the slaves. For example, both Edmundo, the Count's personal slave, and Antonio, a house slave from another of the Count's residences, consider themselves not only different from but also better than the slaves who cut cane and live in barracks. Both of these characters use phrases such as "dirty blacks" and "stupid blacks" when referring to the other slaves. Antonio even displays appropriate table manners during the Last Supper reenactment; he knows how to use a fork and a knife and how to wipe his face with a napkin.

Don Manuel, the overseer, constitutes yet another strata in the plantation system: the mulatto. As a half-breed with Spanish blood in him (made visible through his lighter skin), Don Manuel is able to enjoy privileges—such as freedom—denied to the slaves. At the same time, he is considered less than those who are pure Spaniards, e.g., white people like the Count. Given his in-between racial status (i.e., not totally white but not totally black either), Don Manuel is subjected to manipulation by the Count. At the beginning, Don Manuel is the middleman who does all the dirty work that keeps the sugar mill economically productive, particularly ordering and disciplining the slaves into arduous work. By the end, after being vengefully slain at the hands of Sebastián, Don Manuel conveniently becomes an "innocent victim" of the slaves' "savagery" in the Count's perverted version of the facts. In fact, the Count goes so far as to compare Don Manuel with Jesus Christ and decides to construct a church in his name. This last example is one of the numerous critiques that the film presents of Catholicism. Throughout the film, Gutiérrez Alea portrays the way in which the Catholic Church became complacent in regard to the inhumanities committed through the colonization of the Americas.

Before looking at *The Last Supper*'s critique of Catholicism, another character needs to be examined in relation to the film's articulation of racial hierarchies. Don Gaspar, the French engineer in charge of the sugar mill's technology (or, as he is diegetically called, the sugar maestro), stands out as an example of a white character who shows sympathy toward the slaves—even though he never directly intervenes on their behalf to stop the abuses committed against them. The existence of a white dissident voice in regard to the treatment of slaves is crucial since it allows for a less Manichaean construction of race relations. As a character, Don Gaspar signifies the ideas of the Enlightenment. For him, science and technology are major instruments for progress, and freedom and equality should be extended to everyone in a society. However, like Sergio, the bourgeois intellectual who remains in Cuba after the revolution in Gutiérrez Alea's *Memories of Underdevelopment*, Don Gaspar never acts on his thoughts; he might recognize the brutality used against the slaves, but he does not intercede to change the situation. In other words, he is all thought and no action.

Catholicism: Salvation or Domination?

Catholicism's centrality to the text is evident in the film's title. However, what the narrative reveals, particularly during the Count's reenactment of the Last Supper, is Gutiérrez Alea's ironic stance toward Christianity and its ambivalent and sometimes ambiguous role in the colonization of Cuba. The priest clearly illustrates both the religious institution's ambivalence and its ambiguity. Right after the Count arrives at the sugar mill, the priest tells him how difficult it is to teach the Catholic precepts to "these stupid blacks." Given that this kind of prejudicial language and biased attitude frames the introduction of the priest as a character, it becomes difficult to read any of his actions without being suspicious of his motivations. In fact, his interactions with the slaves are always imprinted with tones of paternalism and condescension (e.g., when he accompanies them while they bathe in the river). In addition, his interventions on behalf of the slaves after Don Manuel has forced them to work during Good Friday are remarkably ineffectual. The priest fails not only to persuade the Count that the slaves should not be forced to work on a religious holiday, but also to oppose the Count's vengeful rampage that leads to the murder and public display of the heads of eleven slaves. As the film evidences, the Catholic Church often remained silent concerning the brutality and injustices committed against colonized peoples. This silence led to further complicity, especially when it came to finding financial support for the church, exemplified in the film by the new chapel that the Count promises to build where the sugar mill once stood.

Catholicism also finds expression through the Count and his supposedly humble yet terribly arrogant behavior. In a purging gesture during Holy Week, the Count decides to emulate Jesus Christ, particularly the actions that took place during the Last Supper he had with his disciples. As the film progresses and the Count becomes more drunk, his real feelings and ideological stands come to the surface. The slaves as well as the audience get to see how the Count tries to justify the existence of slavery using religious ideas. Through the story of Saint Francis and Fray León, the Count tries to make the slaves believe that "real happiness does not consist in being free. Instead, perfect happiness resides in suffering silently, if that's what God wants. If cruelty is endured patiently, with joy, that's what perfect happiness is all about; to tolerate sadness, ill-treatment and opprobrium for the love of Christ. Pain is the one thing that we can truly claim to belong to us in life." These words function as a way of explaining why Pascual, the very old slave to whom the Count had granted freedom, would never experience true happiness. What really comes to the fore during Pascual's scene is the lack of a social and economic structure that would help ex-slaves (i.e., those slaves who were able to buy their freedom) to find a way of life outside of the plantation system.

Through the rest of the banquet, the Count continues to use religion to vindicate the oppression of black people through slavery. He even states that God gave black people the disposition to cut cane and work hard, something that white people have not been created to do. It is at the height of this presumptuous speech that he places Sebastián in the role of Judas. Yet, given how the whole film operates as a rewriting of Eurocentric stories and histories, it is not surprising that the film affirms Sebastián's Judas figure rather than the Count's colonialist identification with Christ—who is also linked, as previously noted, to the overseer Don Manuel. If, from the Count's colonialist perspective, Sebastián (or any rebellious slave) represents a betrayal of the "natural order" established by God, the film suggests that this notion of religion is not natural at all, but complicit in colonial domination. Indeed, the film's portrayal of Sebastián after his escape links him explicitly to nature. Sebastián's visual insertion in a sequence that includes a wild river, a falcon flying, falling rocks, and horses galloping suggests that freedom is possible because he has "betrayed" the seduction of the Eurocentric (which in this case also equates to an anthropocentric) understanding of life whereby hierarchies exist not only among people, but also between people and their surroundings. It is precisely these hierarchies that sustain "unnatural" and untenable institutions such as slavery. Rather than a romanticizing gesture that suggests returning to a pristine, precolonized era, the film's last sequence argues that a new (Cuban) society could only come to be through a holistic understanding of the world: one in which each component is believed to be as equal and vital as the other.

Conclusion

The Last Supper represents a cinematic attempt to rewrite the history of colonization that marked not only Cuba but also the rest of the Americas starting in 1492 (and that arguably continues in different forms up to the present day). In his denunciation of the power structures put into place by the plantation system, particularly through the inhumanities committed against Africans and their descendents via slavery, Gutiérrez Alea provides an incisive criticism of capitalism and other institutions, such as the Catholic Church, that participated (either directly or indirectly) in the exploitation of African cultures and in the sociopolitical transformation of the Americas. By moving African slaves to the center of the story as principal characters, the film not only incorporates a multiplicity of voices generally silenced by colonial history, but also gives visibility to the survival tactics that slaves had to employ to maintain themselves and their culture, keeping them alive and vital. The tales and myths narrated and performed by slaves like Congo and Sebastián function to emphasize the crucial role that African cultures have played in the formation of what can be understood not only as a Cuban identity, but also as a Caribbean identity. Indeed, the legacies of the African diaspora link *The Last Supper* with other films such as *The Harder They Come* (Perry Henzell, Jamaica, 1973), *Sugar Cane Alley* (*Rue cases nègres*, Euzhan Palcy, Martinique, 1983), *Quilombo* (Carlos Diegues, Brazil, 1984), *Almacita, Soul of Desolato* (*Almacita di desolato*, Felix de Rooy, Curaçao, 1986), *Daughters of the Dust* (Julie Dash, United States, 1991), and *Brincando el charco: Portrait of a Puerto Rican* (Frances Negrón-Muntaner, Puerto Rico, 1994). All these texts attempt to show how beliefs aligned with African cultures helped marginalized people to resist giving in to colonial knowledges.

In these films, diasporic African cultures become a symbolic space where social, cultural, and political elements converge and transform into a discourse that can be called "Caribbean *créolité.*" This discourse provides an opportunity to rescue those stories, subjectivities, and cultural manifestations that have been suppressed, erased, or forgotten by Eurocentric versions of the area's history, as well as by mainstream cinema, such as Hollywood. According to the latter, the Caribbean continues to be a "foreign" and "exotic" region that needs to be continuously discovered and conquered—materially as well as symbolically—by "privileged" outsiders (particularly from the United States and Europe) who come to the area to bring "civilization" and "progress," and to indulge in its many available pleasures. Gutiérrez Alea set out to combat these troublesome and detrimental colonialist renditions of the Caribbean through his films and theoretical writings, which can be read as cultural manifestos urging people to decolonize their minds—particularly, but not exclusively, as film spectators—in order to promote the construction of new social realities based on respect, equality, and freedom.

Credits

Cuba, 1976, Instituto Cubano del Arte e Industria Cinematográficos (ICAIC)

Director: Tomás Gutiérrez Alea
Screenplay: Tomás González and Tomás Gutiérrez Alea with the collaboration of María Eugenia Haya and Constante Diego
Cinematography: Mario García Joya
Editing: Nelson Rodríguez
Music: Leo Brouwer
Art Direction: Carlos Ardití

CAST:
Sebastián   Silvano Rey
Conde/Count   Nelson Villagra
Don Manuel   Luis Alberto García

Bibliography

Blasini, Gilberto M. "The World According to *Plaff*: Reassessing Cuban Cinema in the 1980s." *Visible Nations: Latin American Cinema and Video.* Ed. Chon Noriega. Minneapolis: U of Minnesota P, 2000. 193–216.

Chanan, Michael. *The Cuban Image: Cinema and Cultural Politics in Cuba.* London: BFI, 1985.

Diawara, Manthia. "Oral Literature and African Film: Narratology in *Wend Kuuni.*" *Questions of Third Cinema.* Ed. Jim Pines and Paul Willemen. London: BFI, 1989. 199–211.

Downing, John. "Four Films of Tomás Gutiérrez Alea." *Film and Politics in the Third World.* Ed. John D. H. Downing. Brooklyn: Automedia, 1987. 292–93.

Fanon, Frantz. *The Wretched of the Earth.* Trans. Constance Farrington. New York: Grove, 1963.

Fernández Retamar, Roberto. *Calibán: Apuntes sobre la cultura en nuestra América.* Mexico City: Editorial Diógenes, 1972.

Fornet, Ambrosio, ed. *Alea: Una retrospectiva crítica.* La Habana: Editorial Letras Cubanas, 1987.

Gabriel, Teshome H. "Third Cinema as Guardian of Popular Memory: Towards a Third Aesthetics." *Questions of Third Cinema.* Ed. Jim Pines and Paul Willemen. London: BFI, 1989. 53–64.

Gerhard, Peter. "A Black Conquistador in Mexico." *Slavery and Beyond: The African Impact on Latin America and the Caribbean.* Ed. Darién Davis. Wilmington: Scholarly Resources, 1995. 1–9.

Gutiérrez Alea, Tomás. "El verdadero rostro de Calibán." *Cine Cubano* 126 (1989): 12–22.

———. "The Viewer's Dialectic." *New Latin American Cinema: Theory, Practices and Transcontinental Articulations.* Ed. Michael T. Martin. Detroit: Wayne State UP, 1997. 108–31.

Hall, Stuart. "Negotiating Caribbean Identities." *New Left Review* 209 (1995): 3–12.

Lewis, Gordon K. *Main Currents in Caribbean Thought: The Historical Evolution of Caribbean Society in Its Ideological Aspects, 1492–1900.* Baltimore: Johns Hopkins UP, 1983.

Suchlicki, Jaime. *Cuba: From Columbus to Castro and Beyond.* 4th ed. Washington, DC: Brassey's, 1997.

Taxi Driver (1976)

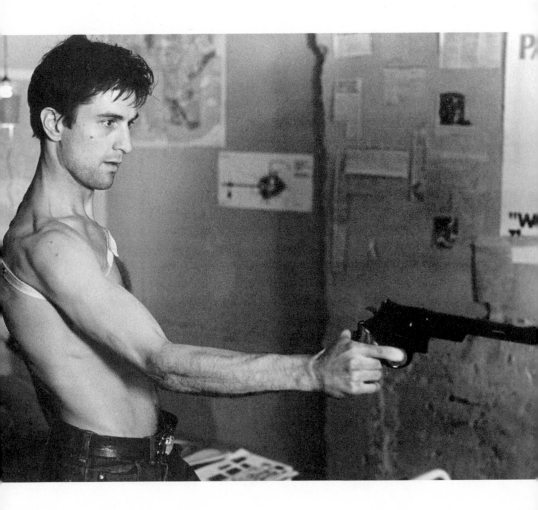

CYNTHIA FUCHS

"I got some bad ideas in my head"

There is much to like in *Taxi Driver* if one doesn't mind the
disorder in the narrative. (Andrew Sarris)

Context

Travis Bickle's cab first appears in *Taxi Driver* under the opening credits,
rolling as if through hell. Emerging from steam and darkness, the vehicle floats across the screen, slowly. The image seems propelled by
Bernard Herrmann's ominous saxophone-heavy score and punctuated
by neon flares and stoplights reflected in the rain-slicked windshield.
As the film cuts to shots of Travis's eyes in red-lit, anxious close-up, it
becomes clear that the hellishness exists simultaneously within and
without. The cab becomes a character unto itself, cruising the streets, repeatedly caught in close-ups or from a distance, whether in motion or
paused, as a fare enters or exits. But for Travis (Robert De Niro), the taxi
driver, there is no exit.

As the film goes on to reveal, this sense of restriction is largely a
function of Travis's own perception, his increasing failure to see beyond himself. Written by Paul Schrader, directed by Martin Scorsese,
and shot by Michael Chapman, *Taxi Driver* has achieved a kind of
mythic status, and not only because John Hinckley cited it as the inspiration for his attempted assassination of Ronald Reagan. (Ironically,
Schrader claims he was inspired to critique the perverse machinations
of "celebrity" by Lynette "Squeaky" Frome, whose attack on President
Ford landed her on the cover of *Time* magazine.) The product of an
apparently remarkable conversion of talents and historical circumstances, *Taxi Driver* is frequently cited as a sort of apotheosis of
groundbreaking 1970s cinema. The movie combines fragments of rage
and intelligence, violence and vulnerability, filtered through the debil-
itated, difficult psyche of Travis Bickle.

Briefly, the film tracks Travis's descent: a New York City cab driver and Vietnam War veteran, he meets Betsy (Cybill Shepherd), a campaign worker for presidential candidate Charles Palantine (Leonard Harris); when she rejects him after a miserable "date," Travis's frustration turns violent. Thwarted in his attempt to assassinate Palantine, Travis shoots a pimp, "Sport" (Harvey Keitel), whom he has met briefly through his burgeoning friendship with a twelve-year-old prostitute, Iris (Jodie Foster). This violent act—Travis shoots the pimp, a john, and a couple of associates—is particularly gruesome, rendered for maximum horror. At the film's end, newspapers hail Travis as a "hero," but viewers are left to wrestle with the fact that his targeting of criminals was quite accidental. Here and elsewhere, *Taxi Driver* reveals clear debts to pornography's clinical observation, situational awkwardness, and visual excess, as well as to horror film techniques: all are framed by Travis's peculiar constellation of obsessions and compulsions, his inability to distance himself from the urban environment that so appalls him.

Reading Disorder

Though *Taxi Driver* has surely garnered much praise and respect over the years, on its release in 1976, reviewers were polarized over its darkness and excess. Some complaints focused on its seeming narrative "disorder," bluntly described by Andrew Sarris in the *Village Voice*: "*Taxi Driver* made very little sense to me" (146). Others disparaged its (literal and metaphoric) overkill. According to *New York* magazine's John Simon, "This imagery of the *ville tentaculaire* is overdone and hammily shot by Chapman" (68). *Time*'s Richard Schickel criticized what he called a "shocked innocence about the tawdry quality of city life that is gratingly naïve," adding, "Unfortunately, social comment does not come easily to [Scorsese], and the strain shows. It is a conflict he can resolve only in a violence that seems forced and—coming after so much dreariness—ridiculously pyrotechnical" (62, 63). Lenny Rubenstein worried that Schrader and Scorsese were "themselves entranced by his kind of psychosis," and so, "their film is unable to break out of its madman's straitjacket, even at the finish, when the audience has to tell itself that Travis couldn't possibly end up a hero" (35). Later writers, such as Robin Wood, have likewise called out the film's ethical "incoherence." Wood contends this is produced by "a relatively clear-cut conflict of auteurs," that is, "the Scorsese/Schrader collision" (50).

Still, the film has not been without its champions, even back in 1976. *Newsweek*'s Jack Kroll proclaimed, "The real poetry of the film is in its rich texture. Scorsese and cinematographer Michael Chapman create a funky, overripe New York that's like a nightmare" (83). More effusively, the *New Yorker*'s Pauline Kael (not incidentally, former film critic Schrader's mentor and tireless defender of pioneering filmmakers such as Robert Altman and Francis Ford Coppola) lauded almost exactly what her fellow reviewers disliked, celebrating the film's daring refusal to judge its frightening protagonist's actions or motives. She also saw something in it that other writers tended to ignore, its intricate political sensibility, having to do not only with violence and tabloid media, whores and presidential campaigns, but also with consumption, that is, the process of making sense of art, pornography, horror movies, or any experience on the street. She writes:

> There is practically no sex in it. But no sex can be as disturbing as sex. And that's what it's about: the absence of sex—bottled up, impacted energy and emotion, with a blood-spattering release. The fact that we experience Travis's need for an explosion viscerally, and that the explosion itself has the quality of consummation, makes *Taxi Driver* one of the truly modern horror films. (85–86)

What makes the film horrific, according to Kael, is its understanding and representation of spectatorship. Here, that spectatorship is layered—as Travis views his world and himself, you view him; at the same time, you also view others viewing him, and him viewing them, too. Here, as well, spectatorship is a process of identification, leading to emotional and sensate "release" delivered by the "explosive" conflation of sex and violence on-screen. What Kael's observation leaves out, however, is Iris, cowering in the hotel room as Travis rampages, shooting the men around her, splattering brains and skull on the wall when she begs, "Don't shoot him!" The awful thrill of the shoot-out assumes your connection with Travis and ignores the denouement that follows, when Travis appears healed from his wounds and a hero in the newspaper clippings taped to his dingy walls. Given *Taxi Driver*'s deliberate evocation and subversion of such "need for an explosion viscerally," easy identification with the violence and its intention is impossible.

What makes the film most *truly* horrific, then, is the violent consummation evoked in its audience, its pornographic linking of pain with pleasure. Much as any horror film reflects its cultural moment, *Taxi Driver* reflects its own—the end of the Vietnam War, a swelling distrust of the U.S. government, the still-unresolved fears as well as hopes raised by the civil rights, women's lib, and other identity-based protest movements. The film, within and without all these contexts, speaks directly to a combined sense of dread and desire. It articulates a need for collective as well as individual "release," while also recontaining such need by making it into art, a consumable object.

For all this controversy (and, likely, because of it), the film retains an undeniable appeal, for this very disjointedness, as well as for its structural and thematic complexity. *Taxi Driver* has proved a useful text for a range of readers—auteurists and cultural-studies theorists, formalists and feminists—precisely because it seems at once so confusing and so profound, so inadvertent and so precise, so relevant to its moment and its makers and yet so timeless. Approaches to the film are as varied as those who take it on: it reads as an example of Scorsese's struggles with Catholicism or Schrader's with Calvinism (see Michael Bliss's *The Word Made Flesh: Catholicism and Conflict in the Films of Martin Scorsese*); Schrader's interest in a sort of metaphysical cinema (see his own *Transcendental Style in Film: Ozu, Bresson, Dreyer*); or even an earnest social critique, with targets ranging from capitalism to racism to systemic political corruption.

At the same time, and along the same thematic lines, *Taxi Driver* examines the strained relation between "realism" (as a set of cinematic conventions that change over time) and "reality" (as a cultural concept, constructed by consensus as much as experience). Frequent internal frames indicate the subjective nature of Travis's, or any, view—cab and apartment windows, doorways, television and movie screens all underline your alignment with Travis as an observer and interpreter of what's visible, since such frames mark surfaces rather than indicating psyches or motives. When, in one sequence of shots, Travis plops a couple of Alka-Seltzer tablets into a glass of water and watches the fizz, the camera zooms in slowly on him (from the glass's point of view), then cuts to his overhead view of the fizz: roiling and strangely sinister.

Rather than distancing you from Travis's perspective, such images lock you into his gloomy disaffection. Whether Travis describes the outside world using sexualized rebukes ("You fuckers, you screwheads") or racist epithets ("Some won't even take spooks, but it don't make no difference to me"), he judges his fares, by behavior and appearance. In his world, language doesn't signify, except as a means to dissemble. In this violent, pornographic world, the fluidity of meaning becomes more threatening and vile. Travis doesn't trust his fares, himself, or his friends. When, desperate for comfort, he asks Wizard (Peter Boyle) for advice, the ostensibly wiser, more weathered cabbie suggests he "get laid," because "You got no choice anyway, because we're all fucked, more or less," at which point Travis exhibits his one moment of good judgment in the film, responding, "That's just about the dumbest thing I've ever heard."

Throughout *Taxi Driver*, audience identification with Travis is made uncomfortable to the point where its final distance from him, during the shoot-out, offers only scant "pleasure," more a kind of shell-shocked reprieve from the terror in which you've been implicated. His disorientation mirrors a world where language is elusive and imagery is imprecise, where internal states can only be approximately conveyed.

Analysis

God's Lonely Man

As a psychological excavation of Travis Bickle, the film is at once earnest, ironic, and chilling. Schrader calls him "a particular kind of breed of white boy," a desperate, lonely, and specifically urban individual, who takes out his rage on the nearest available targets. That is, he's more typical than he is deviant, and this is what makes him so utterly disturbing. Not only do many viewers sympathize with his distress; they also understand (even appreciate) his drive to target. Roger Ebert notes that his "utter aloneness is at the center of *Taxi Driver*, one of the best and most powerful of all films, and perhaps it is why so many people connect with it even though Travis Bickle would seem to be the most alienating of movie heroes" (1). This potential identification with a character who appears, on his surface, so shocking was a more alarming idea pre–Freddy Krueger, who was born into the *Nightmare on Elm Street* series in 1984; now, Travis looks self-possessed, even introspective, compared to Freddy or *Halloween*'s Michael Myers (John Carpenter, 1978), or even *Seven*'s John Doe (David Fincher, 1995). In part, this effect is achieved through the use of Travis's voice-over diary, ostensibly revealing his thinking as he becomes increasingly despondent and focused on his new regimen, designed to refit him for a mission: "Too much sitting has ruined my body," he says, as a montage shows him going through rigorous exercise and weapons training. As social and political commentary, *Taxi Driver* offers Travis up as an extreme version of the damaged Vietnam veteran, honorably discharged in May 1973, before the fall of Saigon but well after the war had turned sour for the troops, the U.S. administration, and the U.S. public alike.

At the same time, *Taxi Driver* challenges assumptions about film as art and commercial product. As it breaks down and reassembles multiple film genres, it challenges viewer expectations. The film borrows from and rethinks horror movies, social-problem films (through its representation of racism, prostitution, and political campaigning), romances, hyperviolent psycho-killer flicks, character studies (evoking, as Schrader claims, Robert Bresson's *Diary of a Country Priest* [*Journal d'un curé de campagne*, 1951]), vigilante pictures, and revisionist Westerns (more than one observer, including its creators, have noted its resemblances, in plot and metaphor, to John Ford's *The Searchers* [1956]). With so many themes and references in play, *Taxi Driver* makes all these groupings seem inadequate.

That there is little consensus regarding *Taxi Driver*—its possible meaning, cultural significance, or aesthetic value—is, of course, one reason it is popular among acting students, film instructors, and filmmakers (Travis's "Are you talkin' to me?" monologue remains a staple for auditions). This seeming instability makes the film all the more provocative. It also makes *Taxi Driver* an especially productive case for investigation of the many ways that meaning might be made of a film. Jonathan Rosenbaum, for instance, points to the contradictions inherent in the film: "Perhaps the most formally ravishing—as well as the most morally and ideologically problematic—film ever directed by Martin Scorsese, the 1976 *Taxi Driver* remains a disturbing landmark for the kind of voluptuous doublethink it helped ratify and extend in

American movies." Rosenbaum's concern over the film's "moral-ity"—as it is collapsed onto that of the protagonist—is typical. As Patricia Patterson and Manny Farber write in *Film Comment*, "The intense De Niro is sold as a misfit psychotic and, at the same time, a charismatic star who centers every single shot and is given a prismatic detailing by a director who moves like crazy multiplying the effects of mythic glamour and down-to-earth feistiness in his star" (28). Other theorists see in this same imagery a kind of exactness and insight into the culture that produces him; for example, Robert Kolker argues, "*Taxi Driver* rigorously structures a path that is separate from community, separate from the exigencies of any 'normal' life, separate from any rational comprehension and need. "What's left," he writes, is "only the explosion of an individual attempting to escape from his self-made prison, an individual who, in his madness, attempts to act out the role of movie hero" (182). In this estimation, Travis's trajectory is darkly ironic—his violent surfeit at the film's end is no path to hero-ism or health, much less community or friendship. He's left, at last, alone, still roiling, still wretched.

Morbid Self-Attention

As the film opens, the twenty-six-year-old Travis is caught between as-pirations, to find intimacy or to remain safely alone; repeatedly, the film makes visible his frustration and immobility, his restlessness and fear. The first scene has the camera track behind Travis as he enters a cab company's personnel office. The camera on him from the personnel officer's low-angled point of view, Travis fidgets and looks away, telling the officer that he's unable to sleep: "I ride around nights mostly. Subways, buses. Figured, you know, I might as well get paid for it." Though Travis has trouble expressing himself, here speaking as if his own intention eludes him, when he mentions his combat experi-ence, the officer, also a marine, warms up. At the same time, the camera position shifts, moving up along the line of Travis's arm to show the patch on his sleeve, "King Kong Company." Even as this reframing briefly insinuates the two men's shared bond, especially the officer's sympathy for Travis's insomnia, the scene soon reverts to its previous tension, when the officer asks whether he is "moonlighting." Again, Travis falters, unsure what the word means but absolutely certain he wants to work "long hours" and, especially, "anywhere, any time."

His new job grants Travis a spectacular and disheartening perspective of the city that so enthralls and repulses him. Driving to Harlem, the Bronx, and Brooklyn, he sees all the city has to offer: "All the animals come out at night," he says in voice-over while the camera frames glimpses of nighttime activities. "Whores, skunk pussies, buggers, queens, fairies, dopers, junkies, sick, venal. Someday a real rain will come and wash all this scum off the streets." In effect, his word choice creates the scene before you; his list of debauchery refers to no one in particular, yet to everyone you see. New York, here, is specific and generic, an emblem of the sort of corruption and selfishness that he observes around him, and also as generic as the taxi driver himself.

From Travis's point of view, which becomes increasingly disturbed and constricted, anyone who looks "different" makes him uneasy. He is shown consistently framed—through the side window or the windshield or from the back of the cab as if the viewer were riding as a fare. Looking outside, emulating his gaze, the camera shows wet pavement and splashy puddles, pimps in platform shoes and prostitutes in hot pants, street vendors and cheap hotels. Still unable to sleep, Travis goes to 42nd Street porn theaters, and worries, even as he sees women on-screen reduced to objects of near-clinical inspection. These movies serve as both his panacea and his provocation, signaling his paradoxical alienation from and immersion in the noirish nightscape he so urgently reviles. The porn films link his interest in violence (which he sees outside, as he drives) with images of female aggression (whores who come on to him, porn performers who make noise on-screen) and with sexual dissipation (his fares' backseat activities). As Travis's psychic descent parallels the film's structural breakdown, its seeming "incoherence," images of his safe spectatorship in the theater or in his cab (indeed, any perspective resembling Laura Mulvey's notoriously self-sustaining "male gaze") become the film's primary spectacle.

The very narrowness of his vision leads to repeated textual ruptures, of cause and effect, or linear time; the film is laced through with jump cuts, time-lapse images, and eerie dissolves. This subjective chaos invites you to see inside Travis, to comprehend his nonsense, while implicating your vision in his. Even as Travis is fixed by the camera—as object or subject—his voice-over suggests that he's self-conscious, at least enough to see his isolation and fret over his preoccupations: "I don't believe that one should devote his life to morbid self-attention," he says, his language self-distancing. The camera hovers over him lying atop his bed, fully clothed and jaw clenched. "I believe that someone should become a person like other people." That he has no idea who this "person" would be, or even what "other people" are like seriously retards his personal-development program. Still, he presses on. "All my life needed," he says, "was a sense of direction, a sense of someplace to go."

Like an Angel

And then, he sees her. He first spots Betsy from a distance, and instantly (in the film's compacting of time) deems her his ideal. "She appeared like an angel," he asserts in voice-over, while Betsy strides in slow motion, her blond hair flipping gently, her white dress bright against the crowd's colorful clothing. "Out of this filthy mass. She is alone. They. Cannot. Touch. Her." The halting rhythm of his speech indicates that Travis is struck by his vision, shaped by his need. She is alone, she is like him. She closes the glass door of the storefront office where she works, as the shot dissolves to Travis's diary: he is writing his vision into existence, with Doritos and Coke on his table—consuming junk food, he consumes himself as well, exacerbating his agitation. That he knows nothing about Betsy is precisely why he worships and desires her. In separating her from "them," he imagines himself as not "them," and therefore able to "touch her." He parks outside her office, the presidential campaign headquarters for Senator Charles Palantine, sucking on a soda straw as if he were in a porn theater. When he is spotted, he scoots off in a hurry, afraid to be looked at while looking.

When he approaches her inside the office, the camera emulates his point of view as he walks across the floor toward her, cutting to show people's responses to him; dressed up in his red velvet jacket and freshly washed shirt, he is both polite and persistent. The camera takes an overhead view of Betsy's desk as his hand passes over it: "You're a lonely person. And all this means nothing." Reading her cluttered workstation as "nothing," Travis imbues it with his own meaning. But if his flawed, irrational, and self-serving vision makes him pathological, your own ostensibly rational reading of him draws you into the construction of that same pathology. The camera's positioning of your look with his at once secures and complicates your identification with him.

Betsy's view of Travis is even more slippery than his of her. During their conversation, the film cuts, in more or less standard shot/reverse-shot pattern, between Travis's view of Betsy and hers of him. She looks tentative (leaning back from him, twirling her pencil), and her protective coworker Tom (Albert Brooks) comically positions himself in the background and pokes his head around corners, monitoring their progress. Tom's thick glasses, pink shirt, and powder blue vest make him look pleasant and pathetic, like the office worker he is. As Betsy fiddles with her pencil, glancing from Travis to Tom, the former looks relatively "masculine," perversely intriguing in his awkwardness and intensity. Her perspective is emphasized during their first "coffee and pie" date (Betsy orders fruit salad, but, as he says in voice-over, "She could have had anything she wanted"). As traffic and pedestrians pass by the diner window behind them, Betsy's look is fixed on Travis, who, in turn, tries to hold her gaze, but fumbles, as with the personnel officer, unable to declare his desire for her (instead disparaging his perceived rival, Tom, as in, "His energy seems to go in the wrong places") and unable to understand her jokes or rhythms. For now, Betsy appears drawn to his very strangeness: "I don't believe I've ever met anyone quite like you." And with that, she calls on a song lyric by Kris Kristofferson to articulate what she sees in Travis, that is, "a walking contradiction."

Even in Betsy's gaze, then, Travis eludes definition. At the same time, his self-identity depends increasingly on his ability to define the world around him, including Betsy. Tellingly, *Taxi Driver* signifies his mounting interest in her in scenes where she's safely nowhere in sight, when he seeks out and purchases the Kristofferson record she mentioned or when he picks up Palantine in his cab. The camera cuts between fixed shots of the senator and his aides in the backseat and of Travis in the front, profiles and front views, medium shots and close-ups framed by the rearview mirror. All this visual activity suggests a rising tension in the cab, despite the fact that Palantine does his best to contain the conversation, to turn it into another version of his basic stump speech ("I have learned more about America from riding in cabs than in all the limos in the country"). However, Travis hijacks the conversation when the senator asks him what "bugs him the most," launching into a tirade about the city, which is like "an open sewer, full of filth and scum, and sometimes I can hardly take it. . . The president should just clean up this whole mess here, he should just flush it right down the fucking toilet." Suddenly, the senator looks quite alone, even flanked by his aides: "Well, um," he fumbles, much like Travis has before in the film, "I think I know what you mean, Travis." But of course he doesn't. And when the politicians emerge from the cab—where they supposedly "learned . . . about America"—they shake their heads in disbelief as well as in an effort to underline their distance from this alarming display of outrage, the America that Palantine can never know.

While this scene clearly sets Travis apart from the "official" or mainstream white guys' experience, it also underlines his alienation from Betsy, despite his best efforts to imagine their similarity. Just so, their one and only evening "date" is a disaster: he takes her to a dirty movie, *Sometime Sweet Susan*, a voyeuristic activity, premised on watching from a distance, not interacting. Betsy stomps off in a rage, the camera tracking Travis as he follows her up the theater aisle to the street, pausing with him as he watches her hail a cab, and waiting with him as he stands, forlorn and angry, unable to think what to do, before a hardly interested audience of the sort that hangs around outside porn theaters. When, at last, he puts his hand up, pathetically seeking escape from his embarrassment, Travis stops himself. "But I got a taxi," he whimpers, furious and, again, alone. That taxi is becoming as much a trap as a means of escape from his sleeplessness and fear.

Though Travis endeavors to contact her again, Betsy staunchly refuses to see him. If she can understand a distinction between surface and substance (she sees working for Palantine as "selling toothpaste"), Travis only sees the packaging. Everything is too "real" for him; his life is a pornographic movie, authentic as advertised. His devastation at his loss of control over his "reality" (as if he ever had control) is exemplified in a justly famous shot in which he calls her from a pay phone in an otherwise empty hallway. As you hear his half of the conversation ("We could, uh . . . Oh, okay, okay . . . Yeah, well, okay"), the camera pans right, leaving Travis at the phone, to look down the hallway at a glass door in the distance. People walk by, horns honk, and Travis finally walks into frame and away from the stationary camera; his voice-over relates what follows, accompanied by the sad saxophone theme that marks Travis's alienation throughout the film: "After the first call she wouldn't come to the phone any longer. I also sent flowers but with no luck." The camera cuts to a slow pan of Travis's apartment, filled with hundreds of flowers. "The smell of the flowers only made me sicker. The headaches got worse. I think I got stomach cancer." At this point, Travis has turned wholly inside, his point of view—and yours—slowed and warped by his torment.

Like a Union

Travis is moved to step outside his wallowing worldview by his "realization" that Betsy has betrayed him, that the problem is not him, but, as he's told Senator Palantine, the filthy city. The film illustrates this realization, at first, as Travis's increased mobility. Just as he closes his self-pitying journal entry—"I shouldn't complain, though. You're . . . only . . . as . . . healthy . . . as . . . you . . . feel"—the shot cuts abruptly to the next scene. He barges through the campaign headquarters' door, striding toward the camera and Betsy (Tom, plaid-jacketed, feebly intercedes: "Let's not have any trouble"). She rejects him outright, and Tom steps in to defend her. At last Travis relents, allowing Tom to lead him to the door, where he stops briefly to face his enemy again: "I wanna tell you, you're in a hell and you're gonna die in a hell like the rest of them!" This takes place as he stands by the door, surrounded by Palantine poster imagery, with Betsy in the foreground, her back to the camera and her blond hair perfectly set, like a helmet. Once outside, Travis walks to and past—through—the frame, left to right, and as he exits your view, his voice-over asserts his new perspective: "I realize now how much she's just like all the others. Cold and distant, and many people are like that. Women for sure. It's like a union."

The only character who appears to counter Travis's dire sensibility is Iris, whom he meets one dark night when she enters his cab, his sanctuary, in an effort to escape her pimp, Matthew, or "Sport." The scene is one of several that lay out Travis's sense of mobile isolation and self-enclosure in the taxi. The first shot, from outside the cab, shows them both, with Iris in the backseat ("Come on, man. Just get me outta here, all right?"), the light that notes his availability bright above both their heads, and with Travis in deep shadow, to the right. The shot cuts to her approximate view, as he turns to look at her, the traffic sounds seeming like a dull roar, strangely following his slow movement. Cut back to her, more urgent now, the shot closer on her heavily made-up face and white-brimmed hat, as the door opens and a shadow falls across her face: Sport's torso appears, and he grabs at her while she and the camera scoot across the backseat, holding on Travis as he blocks your view of Iris. A cut to the rearview mirror indicates that he's watching the backseat action, from his safe distance; a "One Way" road sign pointed directly at the mirror is visible, as if suggesting that Iris will be his "way."

Indeed, Sport emphasizes the moment's significance: "Come on. Don't make no scene," he instructs, but to no avail. This scene is primal for Travis, the inspiration for his ensuing mission, to "clean up" the streets. The camera shows his eyes in murky close-up, reflected in his mirror, then shows Iris exiting the cab, making one last effort to break from Sport's grasp, only their torsos visible in the backseat side window. The camera pans as Sport moves into Travis's front-seat view, his big-ringed hand in focus while Travis's profile is blurred. Sport throws a crumpled $20 bill on the seat beside Travis, whose look down at the payment for his awful inaction is revealed by what might be termed a "money's-eye view," just as Sport again directs his property to behave: "Be cool, bitch!" The saxophonic theme music comes up, and the scene closes on Travis's profile, again from the backseat, but now without Iris as the embodiment of the camera's gaze.

As this scene suggests, the distinction that Travis sees between himself and the "cesspool" he sees outside is penetrable. This vulnerability is frighteningly represented in the scene that directly follows Travis's break with Betsy, featuring Scorsese as a fare who has Travis park outside an apartment building. The scene is the longest devoted to any one fare, and is the film's turning point, illustrating the intersection of gender and race that will focus Travis's forthcoming frenzy, as the female body and blackness are collapsed into a single emblem of hateful "difference." From here, Travis descends beyond mournful agitation, into violence.

From the dark backseat, the fare describes a particular "light," on the second floor, "closest to the edge of the building," while the camera approximates Travis's obliging look, slowly—very slowly—moving up and over, to rest on the designated window. There stands the silhouette of a woman, smoking a cigarette, partitioned by the windowpanes and remote as if on a movie screen. "See the woman in the window?" asks the fare, just as she moves out of sight. Travis answers at last, "Yeah," his profile now the same as the one observed by Iris earlier. Now, however, the fare specifically directs his gaze outward. "You know who lives there, huh?" he grimaces. "A nigger lives there. How do you like that?" The fare goes on to describe the violence he plans to wreak on his wife. "I'm gonna kill her," he smiles, "with a .44 magnum pistol." And, after asking Travis to imagine what this weapon would do to a "woman's face" ("It'd blow it right apart"), he further makes his point by giggling about what it might do to a "woman's pussy." "Now *that* you should see," he says, then suddenly self-conscious: "You must think I'm pretty sick." In fact, the film suggests that this sentiment, however extreme-seeming in this fare, coincides with Travis's increasing agitation.

The racism explicitly voiced in this scene echoes not only Travis's own casual use of the term "spooks," but also the attitude expressed repeatedly by his fellow cabbies, including Wizard, who calls Harlem "fuckin' Mau-Mau Land." Several scenes show the cabbies hunkered over their coffees at the Belmore Cafeteria, talking trash about their fares, from rhinestone T-shirted "fags" to prostitutes. During one conversation, as Doughboy (Harry Northup) observes that Travis "runs all over town," the camera passes over a couple of black pimps, in big hats and sunglasses, leaning back into their chairs, looking stereotypically menacing from Travis's perspective, indicated by the cut back to him looking over his shoulder at the pimps, the camera moving in the same sort of lazy sweep that introduced the pimps—the resentment here is mutual, at least in Travis's mind.

Harder and Harder

The connections between seeing and sexuality, violence and difference, come to a crescendo in the scene in which Travis buys an arsenal of firearms from Doughboy's associate, Fast Andy (Steven Prince). The camera caresses the weapons in a way that suggests its previous negotiations of Betsy's slow-motion form, Iris on the street, or even the "pretty sick" fare's wife: the gleaming guns are equally objectified and sexualized forms. Travis practices by pointing a .38 out the hotel window ("It's got a really nice action to it," narrates Andy, "and a heck of a wallop"), the camera panning from traffic to a couple of people with umbrellas, a point-of-view shot that keeps Travis's arm and the gun barrel in frame, again aligning you with his paradoxically dissociated and yet self-enclosing vision.

This vision is focused again and again on images that underline his isolation, and they are repeatedly framed by a gun, material or metaphoric. He practices cocking, releasing, and aiming his weapons before the mirror, fashioning an intricate apparatus on which one gun might slide down his arm, hidden under the sleeve of his military jacket. The "You talkin' to me?" scene makes this fiercely damaged vision explicit: he speaks to and aims at himself in the mirror, in an arrangement of shots that also draw you, the spectator, into his line of fire, simultaneously directed at himself and the other. Time out from this regimen takes him back to the porn theater; as the film builds to one of its climaxes (a woman on-screen says, "It's getting harder and harder, it's throbbing now"), you see Travis in the dark theater, pointing at the screen as if his finger were a gun. Lest this allusion be missed, his narration overlaps with her voice: "The idea had been growing in my brain for some time." The film cuts from this shot of his careful aim at the movie to a shot of his gun pointed at a Palantine poster in his apartment.

The recurrent symptom of Travis's deviance—but also his conformity—is his compulsive spectatorship, his efforts to control the world outside his windshield, in a window frame, or on a movie screen. This desire for control inspires Travis to take out his vengeance on Betsy through Palantine, her representative and arguably her pimp (or maybe just the "people's" pimp; on this same point, note also Tom's comedic phone conversation with a campaign-button manufacturer about the difference in meanings between "We *Are* the People" and "*We* Are the People," a scene Brooks and Scorsese added to Schrader's script). Within this logic, the foiled assassination of Palantine leads directly to his attack on Sport and his associates. Also within this logic, Travis's shooting of a black convenience-store robber serves as visual foreplay for the film's climax, using similar framings (handheld and low-angle shots) and camera movements (swift pans, slow cruises from overhead), but fewer in number and less elaborate. Here the storeowner both reinforces Travis's judgment ("Maricon!" he calls the body bleeding all over the floor, "Mau-mau!") and makes Travis look relatively sane, by beating the robber with a baseball bat after he instructs Travis (whose gun is, of course, illegal) to get out. "That's the fifth motherfucker this year," the owner exclaims as he goes after him with a calculated fury.

The final shoot-out with Sport and company is the seemingly inevitable result of Travis's self-immersion, his inability to see himself. When he does attempt, following Iris's advice, to "Look at [his] own eyeballs in the mirror," the only reflection he sees is the enemy's. This lack of perspective is represented in the audaciously Mohawk-sporting "disguise" he adopts for the mission (reflecting Sport's own "Indian" pretense and evoking, again, *The Searchers*, only in some perverse inversion). Shooting Sport or Palantine has the same ostensible effect, to exorcise Travis's amorphous "bad ideas." This exorcism takes the form of a terrible, hyperstylized, excessive pornography: many weapons and penetrations, objectification and dismemberment, and money shots (spurting blood). Iris is the traumatized viewer now, and the film includes her in the last shots—in which Travis shoots the john's brains against the wall, then tries to shoot out his own—which emphasize the horrific effect of Travis's actions. Seeking vengeance but disallowed the catharsis of a Dirty Harry, a John McClane, or a Blade, Travis is plainly a monster in the eyes of the most significant viewer in the scene. Suddenly, you can see him from another perspective.

Conclusion

Taxi Driver's ironic coda reinforces this different perspective. The camera pans the walls of his apartment, papered with headlines and clippings heralding him as a "hero" who has returned Iris to her parents. Now the voice-over belongs not to Travis (silenced following his self-release?), but to Iris's father, reading a letter he has written to thank Travis. Still, the film can't leave well enough alone, following Travis to one last fare, Betsy again, an angel in a white pantsuit intrigued by the sensational reports of his exploits. Desexualized and disembodied, her face floats in his rearview mirror, another point-of-view shot that suggests Travis has hardly shifted his position or his thinking. "I read about you in the papers," she says, riding in the back of his cab, like the "sick" fare, like the pimps and johns and politicians, like Iris. When he drops her off, she recedes from view as he drives away, hanging in the darkness like the dream she has always been.

Cut to Travis's eyes in his mirror once again: he is still riding in his taxi, still seeing risk at every turn. Upping the Expressionist ante of traditional *noir* stylistics, Travis's internal disease denotes an irreversible loss of subjective balance. With his cab a rolling metaphor for his hostility and loneliness, he can indeed go "anywhere," still feeling and, importantly, still seeing, the same way he always has, at once limited and inventive, subjective and reflective.

Credits

United States, 1976, Columbia Pictures

Director: Martin Scorsese
Producers: Michael Phillips and Julia Phillips
Screenplay: Paul Schrader
Cinematography: Michael Chapman
Editing: Tom Rolf and Melvin Shapiro
Music: Bernard Herrmann
Art Direction: Charles Rosen

CAST:

Travis Bickle	Robert De Niro
Betsy	Cybill Shepherd
Wizard	Peter Boyle
Iris Steensma	Jodie Foster
Matthew ("Sport")	Harvey Keitel
Senator Charles Palantine	Leonard Harris
Tom	Albert Brooks
Doughboy	Harry Northup
Fast Andy	Steven Prince

Bibliography

Bliss, Michael. *The Word Made Flesh: Catholicism and Conflict in the Films of Martin Scorsese.* Lanham, MD: Scarecrow, 1995.

Brunette, Peter, ed. *Martin Scorsese: Interviews.* U of Mississippi P, 1999.

Canby, Vincent. "Scorsese's Disturbing *Taxi Driver." New York Times* 15 Feb. 1976, sec. 2:1+.

Ebert, Roger. "Review: *Taxi Driver:* 20th Anniversary Edition." *Chicago Sun-Times.* 1 Mar. 1996. <http://www.suntimes.com/ebert/ebert_reviews/1996/03/1023026.html>.

Friedman, Lawrence S. *The Cinema of Martin Scorsese.* New York: Continuum, 1997.

Fuchs, Cynthia J. "'All the Animals Come Out at Night': Vietnam Meets *Noir* in *Taxi Driver." Inventing Vietnam: The War in Film and Television.* Ed. Michael Anderegg. Philadelphia: Temple UP, 1991.

Kael, Pauline. "Underground Man: A Review of *Taxi Driver." New Yorker* 9 Feb. 1976.

Kolker, Robert. *A Cinema of Loneliness.* 2nd ed. New York: Oxford UP, 1988.

Kroll, Jack. "Hackie in Hell." *Newsweek* 1 Mar. 1976: 82–83.

Mulvey, Laura. "Visual Pleasure and Narrative Cinema." *Screen* 16.3 (1975): 6–18.

Patterson, Patricia, and Manny Farber. "The Power and the Gory." *Film Comment* 12.3 (1976): 27–30.

Ray, Robert B. *A Certain Tendency of the Hollywood Cinema, 1930–1980.* Princeton: Princeton UP, 1985.

Rosenbaum, Jonathan. "Hell on Wheels." *Chicago Reader* 1 Mar. 1996. <http://www.chireader.com/movies/archives/0496/04016.html>.

Rubenstein, Lenny. Rev. of *Taxi Driver. Cineaste* 7.3 (1976): 34–35.

Sarris, Andrew. "Confessions of a Wishy Washy Critic." *Village Voice* 16 Feb. 1976: 145–46.

Schickel, Richard. "Potholes." *Time* 16 Feb. 1976: 62–63.

Schrader, Paul. *Taxi Driver.* New York: Faber, 1990.

———. *Transcendental Style in Film: Ozu, Bresson, Dreyer.* Berkeley: U of California P, 1972.

Scorsese, Martin. *Scorsese on Scorsese.* New York: Faber, 1996.

Simon, John. "Hack Work." *New York Magazine* 23 Feb. 1976: 68+.

Stern, Lesley. *The Scorsese Connection.* Bloomington: Indiana UP; London: BFI, 1995.

Taubin, Amy. *"Taxi Driver."* London: BFI, 2000.

Wood, Robin. *Hollywood from Vietnam to Reagan.* New York: Columbia UP, 1986.

Ceddo (1977)

PHILIP ROSEN

Discursive Space and Historical Time

Context

Ousmane Sembene, African Postcoloniality, and Film

Ceddo was written and directed by the most storied filmmaker from sub-Saharan Africa, Ousmane Sembene. Sembene was already an important Francophone novelist when he made his first, short film in 1963, not long after his native Senegal achieved independence as part of the great wave of African decolonization in the late 1950s and early 1960s. He is now generally regarded as a pathbreaker for postcolonial sub-Saharan cinema. His 1966 film *La noire de . . .* (*Black Girl*) is usually described as the first feature-length fiction film from sub-Saharan Africa, and his next film, *Mandabi* (*The Money Order,* 1968) is regarded as the first feature in an African language. At the time of this writing, he has released nine features and is generally regarded as the most influential of the first generation of sub-Saharan filmmakers. Many believe he virtually defined the major stylistic and ideological tendencies for that generation. His fifth feature film, *Ceddo,* came at the end of his most productive period (he was not able to make another film for thirteen years).

Nine feature films is a significant body of work, but it may not seem a large output for forty years of filmmaking, especially when compared to similarly towering figures in Western cinemas, such as Jean-Luc Godard or Steven Spielberg. Sembene is also a productive writer, but this quantitative point still suggests the difficulties of sub-Saharan filmmaking. The history of cinema in this region is inseparable from the history of colonialism and its aftermath. In the late nineteenth century, a handful of European powers climaxed a long period of incursions and occupations by dividing much of the huge continent among themselves. After World War II and in the geopolitical

717

context of the Cold War, European empires collapsed, and leaders of resistance movements often became the founders of new African nation-states. In the sub-Saharan region, decolonization started in 1957 with Ghana, and in 1960 alone fourteen new African states were admitted to the United Nations—including Sembene's Senegal. Despite the early euphoria of national liberation, most new African nation-states remained economically and technologically reliant on the old colonial powers. Terms such as "dependency" and "neocolonialism" were commonly invoked to describe the situation.

The concept of neocolonialism seemed to fit the context of postindependence sub-Saharan filmmaking all too well. For more than half of film history, the African continent had been administered and exploited by Western European nation-states, predominantly England and France. The colonizing powers included some of the dominant national film cultures of Europe. The colonizers discouraged the growth of any African industries that might compete with their own, as well as indigenous cultural innovation in their colonies. Colonialist ideologies, which helped to justify and naturalize exploitative economic policies, included explicit and/or implicit racism. They often conceived African culture as falling under the anthropological category of the "primitive" and rationalized the exclusion of Africans from leading positions in machine-based or technologically intensive practices. All these factors prevented the participation of Africans in film and mass media.

After independence, filmmaking in sub-Saharan Africa was in a classic neocolonial situation. Not only did distribution remain dominated by non-African firms and films, but resources necessary for film production were too often available only from the former colonizers. Efforts to establish nationally supported film industries or regional production cooperatives were heroic but achieved only occasional and temporary realization. To this day, there is no broad feature-film industry identified with sub-Saharan Africa, but there are a number of important filmmakers who manage to find financial support and generally achieve limited distribution, in the manner of independent and art cinema in the West (although recently a new model has emerged in the Nigerian video film; see Haynes).

At the same time, the history of anticolonial struggles, the emergence of new nation-states, and neocolonialism often provided the first generation of African filmmakers with subject matter as well as a driving motivation to make new kinds of films for Africa. This certainly seems to have been the case with Sembene. Sembene and other African filmmakers in the 1960s and early 1970s wished to make films that would speak of, to, and for Africans in ways that films never had. The anticolonial struggles seemed to show that political independence was inseparable from cultural independence. African film culture was therefore political from the start. Making this cultural politics more complex was the fact that many filmmakers saw the neocolonial situation as corrupting their own national leaders. Thus, their promotion of African independence involved not only narrativizing anticolonial struggles and life in postcolonial Africa, but also criticizing structures of leadership and class hierarchy in the new African states. Sembene was one of the most daring in this regard.

In the broadest possible terms, we can say that there were three streams of ideas shaping the original ambitions of postcolonial African cinema. The first was national liberation. As in many other regions, African anticolonialist intellectuals and statesmen conceived of themselves as acting for the common interests of "the people," described this unified "people" as a nation, and articulated the political interests and rights of these citizen-masses as national interests and rights. This meant promoting—or interrogating—internal unity across social and cultural divisions in the struggle against foreign economic exploitation and political oppression. It therefore called not only for a realization of the best of African values but also for a modernizing revision of seemingly traditional internal hierarchies such as caste, gender, and age (Cabral 46–48, 54–55).

Second, there was the international idea of third world cinema, or third cinema. As proposed by Latin American filmmakers in the 1960s and 1970s, third cinema sought to make films that would not accede to the norms of Hollywood cinema but would also not be like Western avant-garde or art cinema, whose oppositional strategies chiefly concerned the most educated cultural strata. Third cinema would support and articulate the struggle of the masses for liberation from exploitation and colonialism. It would make new kinds of films by adapting itself to local political ideas and struggles, cultural practices, and technical resources. The result would be new modes of filmic representation and new functions for cinema, devised in anticolonial or neocolonial contexts (Solanas and Getino).

The third stream shaping African cinema was the value of specifically African cultural practices set against the colonialist devaluation of African culture. But defining an African cultural commonality was difficult, given the myriad differences in African languages, histories, cultures, and ethnicities. Some proposed an enduring pan-African cultural core that could now be fully realized under conditions of independence. Others argued that African cultural processes and values had developed historically, were therefore flexible, and had always been practiced in interaction with non-African forces and ideas (Fanon). Indeed, both the nation-state and cinema might be seen as "importations" to be refashioned in novel ways appropriate to African history.

For filmmakers, this often led to the question of whether there would be a uniquely African mode of filmic representation, an African "film language." The idea was not only to film previously unfilmed aspects of Africa, but to devise specifically African modes of *cinematic* representation (see Ukadike). One of the most widely invoked influences in this regard was the African oral tradition. The oral tradition provided a reservoir of narrative resources—story formats, character types, and so forth. Even more fundamentally, it seemed to provide a distinctive attitude toward representation—the way stories are told, the way audiences are addressed. Unlike print, the oral tradition assumes the possibility of verbal interplay between speaker and audience. It assumes that the making and receiving of a text are social, collective processes. Some saw this oral tradition as closely related to an idea of community and argued that African culture emphasizes community and collectivity over individuality. This emphasis on popular collectivity linked African culture to both national liberation theory and the objectives of third cinema (Gabriel, "Third Cinema"; "Towards a Critical Theory").

Analysis

History in Ceddo

By 1976, when he made *Ceddo*, Sembene was recognized as a leading figure in an emergent African cinema. In this film one can detect the impact of all three streams of ideas that shaped the first generation of African cinema. It deals with difficulties of national unification and resistance to foreign incursions, it utilizes local resources in order to tell its story from the perspective of popular masses, and, as we will see, it is concerned with specifically African modes of representation.

Yet *Ceddo* seems unique, even within Sembene's body of work. All his other films deal with resistance to European colonialism during the twentieth century or the difficulties of life after decolonization. Some critics therefore identify Sembene with a straightforward, didactic social realism, although this hardly captures what makes his films so interesting and influential. But *Ceddo* depicts some of the pageantry and glory of African culture and history before European colonialization. Its richly proclamatory and figurative speech, its costumes, its violence, its representation of older customs, its unusual musical score—these and other elements seemed to make it a stylized, spectacular project. Nevertheless, there are fundamental ways in which it is connected to his other films, for it critically analyzes not only foreign exploiters of Africa, but also African political and cultural structures. *Ceddo* is not simply a tribute to the glory of a previously suppressed history. It reveals a web of tensions and conflicts that structured modern African society in general and Senegalese society in particular. It puts him squarely on the side of those who see distinctively African cultural practices as engaging with history and change.

Sub-Saharan African cinema is rooted in both the present and the past, for the problems of the postcolonial present mandate rethinking the history and culture of Africans in opposition to the official versions promoted by the colonizers. *Ceddo* restores previously repressed aspects of the African past, but, as we will see, it does not deal only in the past. Partly because of this, it is an unusual historical film. For example, unlike most historical films, the exact place and time of *Ceddo* are never precisely specified. Story events occur in an unidentified Wolof-speaking kingdom, which means it is in the West African region that now includes Senegal, where the film was shot. The time appears to be during the late eighteenth or early nineteenth century. This historical imprecision suggests the story is not about a particular event. Rather, it is about something more general and abstract. It gives us a microcosm of a historical *process,* when an old order is ending and a new order is emerging. The transformation represented in *Ceddo* was fundamental in defining modern Africa.

Other aspects of *Ceddo* also suggest it should not be taken as a literal depiction of historical events. In particular, the basic story structure seems more like a folk tale than a historical account. The film begins with the disruption of a preexisiting state of affairs: a beautiful princess has been kidnapped. As a result, handsome prince-heroes are sent by the father-king to rescue her, and the chain of events can only end when she has been returned home as the betrothed of a rescuer. However, this tale-like structure takes unexpected turns. The kidnapping and rescue of the princess turns out to be a matter of power and politics rather than villainy, sexual desire, or romance. Indeed, in the end the princess transfers allegiances, in effect rescuing herself from her rescuers. Furthermore, the story does not simply follow the actions of kidnapper and rescuers. Instead, it includes a great number of scenes in which other characters act out and discuss their situations, and these situations are always defined in terms of the politics of social and political groups.

This way of structuring the story is related to the film's conception of history. In *Ceddo,* the beginning of modern Africa is a result not of conflicts among individual desires, but of conflicts of interest among groups or collectivities. Individual characters do freely verbalize motivations, but motivations stem from political and social positions. Most of the key conflicts and issues at stake in this historical microcosm are openly debated and analyzed by characters, and the various positions interact in complex ways. Four of the most important conflicts are the following: First, there is the conflict between foreign influence and indigenous, Black African power. The European slave trader, the European Catholic priest, and the Arab imam contend for influence over the king and his aristocracy, and through that for political control of the nation. The common people resist these imported influences in a time-honored way, kidnapping Princess Dior as a hostage in order to demand that the king restore their traditional rights (Pfaff, "Entretien" 56). The imam and his disciples must thus overcome the common people when the imam violently usurps the kingship and assumes authority over the nation. From a postcolonial perspective, the opposition of indigenous and foreign might seem to allegorize European colonialism, represented by the slave trader and the priest. However, things are more complicated. This is demonstrated by a second major conflict, which seems to dominate the opposition between foreign and indigenous: religious conflict.

Given the overwhelming prevelance of Islam in present-day Senegal, a remarkable aspect of the film is Sembene's representation of Islam as a historically foreign, invasive force. He portrays the imam as a short, lighter-skinned Arab, clearly an outsider single-mindedly working toward his goal of a universal Islamic society. Sembene is not necessarily anti-Islamic; one of his late films with a contemporary setting, *Guelwaar* (1992), depicts a humane, sympathetic imam. But in *Ceddo* the figure of the imam defamiliarizes institutions that many contemporary West Africans embrace. It also implies that relations between indigenous and foreign have long defined African history and culture.

But furthermore, religious division exists *within* the foreign and *within* the indigenous. Not only Arab Islam, but European Christianity is vying for converts from the traditional fetish religion. At the beginning of the film, the king, his family, and most aristocrats have already accepted Islam. Thus, the Catholic priest and his tiny group of followers are silent and weak. But the bulk of the population is "ceddo" and holds to the traditional fetish religion. The word *ceddo* appears in several Senegalese languages. In the precolonial period, it designated a special caste of slaves to the crown who had certain rights and could have a voice in decision making, partly because their political and military power supported the power of the king (Colvin; Diop 46–47). Since then, the term has acquired other meanings. Sembene once said that it signifies those who cling to the old ways and resist the onslaught of the foreign. In the film, the ceddo resist changes imposed on them, including the increasingly powerful Muslim influence.

A third structuring conflict is thus political and social division within the Wolof. The ceddo are the common people as opposed to the aristocrats, so the religious division within the Wolof is partly one between the official rulers and the ruled. The ceddo, having lost many of their old rights and under pressure to convert, formally announce their opposition and the reasons for the hostage taking according to traditional practices when they plant the ritualistic challenge stick (the *samp*) in the ground. But scheming and competition appear within the aristocracy itself, and, later, treasonous nobles betray the king. On the other side, the anti-Islamic forces are divided by caste distinctions and rivalries: the warrior Saxewar holds to his fetishes, but he despises the lower-caste ceddo, and is killed by the ceddo hostage taker; Prince Madior recants Islam in order to maintain his claim to inherit the throne, but as a rival of Saxewar for Dior and separated from the ceddo by caste, he becomes an outsider. In this social and political context, no national unity is possible to oppose the new and the foreign. Ironically, then, when the ceddo lose, so does the aristocracy that subordinates them.

At this level, the film raises the problem of overcoming social and ethnic divisions, central to both national liberation theory and contemporary African political culture. These internal conflicts also demonstrate that cultural and religious structures are systematically linked to power structures. The weakening of traditional religion undermines the institutional continuity of African political institutions. The final example of this rupture is the shift from settling disputes by ritualistically circumscribed individual combat to the pragmatic, anything-goes tactics ordered by the imam.

The connection of power and culture is also demonstrated by a fourth opposition, one that seems more specific and yet crystallizes all these divisions: the opposition between matrilateral succession and patrilineal succession. Matrilateral succession, in which a nephew inherits from the maternal uncle, is associated with traditional political and religious practices. Patrilineal succession, in which a son inherits from the father, is foreign, imported through Islam. As others explain to the king at one point, when he accepts Islam, he unwittingly undermines the basis of his authority, for he himself inherited it matrilaterally from his mother's brother.

Matrilateral succession implies that institutions of legitimate authority must acknowledge the presence of women. By excluding women from legitimate lines of inheritance, patrilineal succession strengthens authoritarianism, patriarchy, and the social, political, and cultural subordination of women. In fact, the conflict between these two modes of succession is part of a network of narrative elements having to do with women, ranging from the carved female figure at the tip of the *samp* to the fact that Princess Dior is the only female character with a speaking role and, most startlingly, to the fact that the story climaxes when Princess Dior shoots the imam in the genitals. Sembene once suggested that the only reason the film was banned in Senegal for a number of years was the symbolic significance of the princess (qtd. in Pfaff, *Cinema* 174).

Space, Discourse, and Models of Address

Every one of these four conflicts—the relation of foreign to indigenous practices and identities, religious and ethnic differences, internal social divisions, and the cultural and political status of women and femininity—resonates with issues in postcolonial Africa. But part of postcoloniality is also the possibility and complexity of making an African film about the African past. This means we may ask how African history is represented in this unusual, postcolonial film. And this, in turn, requires close attention to the way film space and time are organized in images and sounds.

Careful study of *Ceddo* will demonstrate that it is a different sort of historical film, but this does not mean it is visually "difficult." The camera work and editing provide the spectator with clear access to the most pertinent narrative events and discussions of them. This is not all they do; for example, pans and horizontal movements of characters within the frame subtly emphasize the flatness of the terrain, giving a sense of an elemental rural environment within which the story occurs. But if we are looking for a specifically African mode of representation, it may at first seem that the editing is not the place to look.

Some critics argue that first-generation African cinema, with Sembene as a leading figure, had an affinity for long takes and minimal editing. These techniques are said to correspond to African practices of oral storytelling because they emphasize the time of the telling rather than the suspenseful chain of events of the tale itself or, for some, because they construct a unity of time and space that corresponds with rural African experience. This is sometimes connected to the observation that first-generation African films are "slower" than Western films (Diawara, "Popular Culture"; Gabriel, "Third Cinema"). However, there is more stylistic variety in *Ceddo* than such generalizations allow. Even in significant conversational scenes, such as the first one between Princess Dior and her captor, or the grand meeting of the Wolof nation that follows, the film is edited to *analyze* the scene for the spectator, emphasizing one aspect or another in order to direct the spectator through the conversations.

These scenes provide grounds for comparing the mode of representation in *Ceddo* to mainstream Western filmmaking, for analytic editing is fundamental to mainstream cinema. In mainstream films, scenic space is broken down into shots that are ordered to (a) provide the spectator with a coherent and "readable" fictional time and space and (b) to allow the filmmakers to emphasize particular components of the scene at specific points. In Hollywood and much other first world cinema, cutting between medium shots and close-ups is standard practice.

A special and revealing case is the importance of facial close-ups in Hollywood cinema. Facial close-ups signify access to the emotions, psychology, and moral interiority of *individual* characters, and mainstream cinema gravitates toward stories centered on individuals and their desires. There are certainly other ways to use analytic editing, for example, as in Eisenstein's films about revolutionary masses. But the conventional stylistic systems of mainstream narrative film have always been broadly associated with ideologies of individualism. One of the most typical conventions of mainstream analytic editing is the presentation of dialogue in shot/reverse shot. In its textbook form, a scene is presented from two roughly symmetrical camera positions showing a speaker and an interlocutor, with the resulting shots edited to alternate between the two perspectives as the conversation progresses. This alternation constructs a strongly dualized space. On the other hand, all camera positions are on one side of the action (establishing an axis of action or so-called 180-degree line) in order to maintain continuity of screen direction from shot to shot. A sense of spatial unity from shot to shot is promoted by the flow of conversation on the sound track and the directionally opposed eyelines, which make it appear that the two characters are facing one another. Shot/reverse-shot editing does not have to be used for conversations or individualized character interaction; however, it is probably fair to say it is the most common way of filming conversations in mainstream cinema.

Now compare the first dialogue scene in *Ceddo*, in which Princess Dior confronts her ceddo kidnapper. It looks like a standard shot/reverse-shot construction. (It even exploits subtleties possible within a mainstream system: the priority of Dior is implied because her head remains in frame even in shots of the kidnapper.) However, there is a peculiarity. The scene is not really a dialogue in the sense of a conversation between two people, for there is a third person named Fara present. Instead of directly addressing each other, the princess and her kidnapper address each other through him, saying things like "Fara, tell her that . . . " This is clearly a ceremonial procedure, described by the Wolof communicative concept of *jottali*, or the formal relaying of an utterance (Cham 35ff.). It is one example of how *Ceddo* refers to traditional social and cultural practices from the Senegambian region. But there are two things of special interest here. First, this first dialogue of the film provides a model of indirect address, for speech is mediated by a third party. Second, while the dual space of the shot/ reverse shot is maintained, there is an odd contradiction precisely because speech must flow through a third. This "third" continually complicates the duality, intimacy, and implied emotional and psychological interiority common in dialogues and facial close-ups in Western filmmaking.

Both this model of addressing someone and the presence of the third are taken to a more elaborate level in the next scene, the meeting of the entire nation called by the king to investigate the kidnapping and decide on a response. It is composed of a succession of verbal confrontations that reveals the interests of all parties. Most of these verbal confrontations are between pairs of individuals: the ceddo elder Diogomay versus the king, Prince Biram versus Diogomay, Diogomay versus the imam, Saxewar versus Prince Madior, Madior versus Biram, and so forth. These dualized debates seem perfectly suited to the dualization of space in conventional shot/reverse-shot editing, except that once again speech must flow through a third, whose presence is now emphasized. Like Fara in the earlier scene, Jaraaf in this scene performs the function of formally passing on an utterance. However, his style is different. He introduces speakers and comments on their words with rhetorical flourish, even taking sides in the debate.

The succession of debates between pairs of participants takes place in a kind of giant circle defined by the positions of the various factions around a large open area. This circle constitutes a national arena of debate and decision making. Jaraaf stands inside it, and debaters enter it to speak. But what is the nature of address here? To whom do the debaters speak? There are at least five answers. As in the previous scene, they address one another (1), but only do so through a third (2). Simultaneously, however, they are also addressing the king (3), who initiates the debates and will make any final decisions (though the king also must be addessed through Jaraaf). In addition, the formality of the whole system of debate, along with the verbal virtuosity of the participants, identifies what we see as *public* performance; that is, there is a more diffuse addressee: the nation as a whole (4), whose fate is in the balance. But once we allow for the diegetic publicness of the performance, we must acknowledge that there is another public that is not in the film at all, namely the film audience (5). The whole network of debate and multiple-spoken address, which depicts the disputes and power relations of a past society, is addressed to *us* now. The space and time of the film must address a film spectator in the present.

Because of this multiplicity of addressees, the spatial construction is more complex than in the dialogue between Dior and the kidnapper. The shots alternate not between two debaters in the center of the enclosure, but between shots of the center and cutaways to those on its rim, with the king—the decision maker—occupying the most powerful "reverse field." That is, any sense of dual spatial alternation is between the inside and the border of the enclosure.

Within the enclosure, where the paired debaters are positioned, the editing avoids the dual spatial alternation so common in Western cinema. For example, during the interchange between Madior and Saxewar, the camera is placed in the reverse field of the court, and the debaters occasionally play directly and frontally to the camera, something rare in mainstream film. In the next debate, which explicates the connections among religion, political power, and matrilateral succession, Madior, Biram, and Jaraaf are in a triangular configuration within the circle, and the camera cuts to all sides of the triangle, frontally centering whichever one is speaking. It is possible to say much more about this rich scene and its editing, but this is enough for now to make the point.

Both of these early scenes utilize analytic editing and evince knowledge of mainstream conventions, and yet seem subtly or systematically different from dominant Western constructions. Given the context of Sembene's career, the next logical question is whether this difference in spatial constructions and complexities of address can be connected tö the promotion of African cultural autonomy and a distinctive African "film language." In fact, the film itself points in this direction, with its references to the African oral tradition. The flamboyance of Jaraaf's costume and verbal imagery as well as the fact that Fara has a musical instrument makes it clear that there is a cultural reference for the "third" troubling the space of dialogue scenes: the much-noted West African figure of the *griot*. *Griots* are a caste of specialists in the spoken word. A *griot* may be a poet, a public storyteller, a communal historian, a hired praise singer, and more. For many West Africans, the *griot* is a symbol of the oral tradition, and in *Ceddo*, the *griots'* link to the oral tradition is emphasized.

Spectacle seems central to *Ceddo,* with its pageantry, violence, and dramatic confrontations, as well as its detailed vision of particular aspects of precolonial life, such as dress. Yet, much of the film is also intensely verbal, filled with talk. In fact, there are many additional references to the African oral tradition. Throughout the film, language is generally declamatory, acting and gesture are expressively stylized, and conversations are consistently punctuated by the skillful use of proverbs and figures of speech. In this fictional world, verbal display and performance are part of everyday life. Even some objects incorporated into actions are overtly symbolic, which emphasizes the expectation that acts, like words, are *performed* as signs—"spoken," as it were, in a social, public setting.

Foreigners provide a contrasting model of discourse and language, especially the imam, who always cites an authoritative book—the Koran. In comparison with speech, a book is hierarchical. It cannot itself engage in question and reply, as can a speaker, for a book is a fixed (printed) discourse that addresses all readers in the same way, no matter what the situation. Of course, verbal interchange can also be shot through with structures of power (as *Ceddo* shows), but this is not inherent in its "technology"; quite the contrary. Thus, the imam does not permit conversation or debate; rather, he bases the authority of his own voice on the book, and renames each ceddo after persons in the Koran (Daney 52).

But *Ceddo* is actually engaged not so much in a glorification of the African oral tradition as in an interrogation of it. Note the contrast between the impoverished and minimalist rhetorical style of Fara and the spectacular, grandiose style of Jaraaf. One *griot* is identified with the common people and the transmission of truth, and the other uses the cultural force of speech in pursuit of power and riches. This may actually relate to a West African view of language, which conceives of speech as necessary in order to seek and convey truth, but sees it simultaneously as flawed, for it also makes trickery and lying possible (Miller; Cham). Thus, silence can actually be the repository of truth—and yet at the same time the repository of powerlessness. From this perspective, *Ceddo* may be seen as investigating the relations between speech and power, on the one hand, and truth and silence, on the other. Think of the silent ceddo masses in the great meeting scene, who are repositories of an ancient virtue; however, their silence must be compared to that of the Christian missionary, in whom it signifies powerlessness, and the European trader, in whom it implies insidious power.

Most generally, there is something emblematic in the fact that it is the *griot* that serves as the "third," complicating the standard shot/reverse-shot spatial division. For this makes the third a cultural code, the embodiment of a sociocultural function. This "third" therefore connotes that an utterance is never just addressed to an individual but is also a public act; hence the performative, theatrical, proclamatory nature of speaking in *Ceddo*. Even in the most restricted conversational scene, the individual is positioned in relation to the collective public, an audience beyond the immediate speech situation. Diegetically, that audience is the Wolof nation, which defines itself and its internal and external struggles through speech. But there is also the filmgoing public, which, if African, parallels that collective, Wolof public in the film.

The very space of the film is thus connected to a narrative and historical logic. Characters act as agents of social and historical groups and speak for and about collectives. The ritualization or theatricalization of speech and narrative invokes African cultural concerns in relation to specifically African political questions. This moves the film toward a politicized rather than psychologized representation of history.

From Discursive Space to Historical Time

We have seen that *Ceddo* does not just depict the oral tradition, but both interrogates it and deploys it to inflect the way the film addresses an audience. How does this affect the film's presentation of African history? There are two collective publics ultimately addressed by the speakers in *Ceddo*: the Wolof nation in the past and the film audience in the present. How does *Ceddo* relate an African past to spectators in the present?

We can start answering this question by looking at the scene in which the European priest sees Prince Madior observing his church. The priest approaches Madior and looks up, apparently to the heavens. The image dissolves to a low-angle shot looking straight up at the interior of a cathedral dome painted with Christian iconography of Black figures, accompanied by an African choral mass. This introduces the extended sequence that follows: an outdoor, twentieth-century African Christian Communion service, filmed in documentary, *cinéma vérité* style. All the major characters of the film are present—Muslims and traditionalists—with Madior presiding as a bishop and the priest appearing as an honored corpse. We then return to the historical past and the shot of the priest that opened the sequence. Such a dissolve from a facial close-up to distant events conventionally signifies the beginning of a dream, a memory, or the thoughts of the individual, something reinforced by the apparent point-of-view editing of the transition. Furthermore, the content of the sequence—in which the actors playing both ceddo and Muslims are shown as twentieth-century Christians—evidently displays the priest's goal, a Christianized Africa of the future.

Yet, this impression of interiority is countered by other elements of the sequence. First, the twentieth-century detail—the clothing, the music—is too correct; if this is the priest's dream, how could the priest know how people would actually dress and sing in the twentieth century? Second, there is something startling about this sequence; this surprise is partly formal, because there is no preparation for such a break in the film's straightforward chain of "objective" story events, but the surprise is also *historical*: contemporary Senegal is overwhelmingly Muslim, but here we see a modern Senegal in which Christianity is triumphant. Thus, the sequence presents a counterfactual outcome of the precolonial struggles in the Wolof nation. It gives us a kind of flash-forward from the precolonial struggles that seem central to the story. But it is a historically shocking flash-forward, insofar as the spectator recognizes the inaccuracy of what she or he is seeing.

Again, a mainstream cinematic code is invoked, only to be twisted away from its usual functions. In this case, this transformation involves an unusual conflation of the subjectivity of the image (as the priest's dream) and the objectivity of the image (the correctness about present-day dress codes). At this moment, *Ceddo* becomes a very different kind of historical film indeed—for it unsettles the status of the film image itself.

Conventional historical films present the spectator with a restoration of what objects and people are supposed to have looked like in the past. In them, the image serves as a reliable conveyance for what the film takes as historical truth. Any departures from this convention are presented as the delusions or imaginings of an individual character. This scene from *Ceddo* gestures toward that practice, by seeming to signify a character's dream, but then goes beyond it and broaches another possibility for historical cinema: the image can give us a variation on African history that did not happen, a historical option lost.

There are other examples in the film of historical options lost. One occurs when the ceddo kidnapper is killed. Again the film dissolves from a close-up of Princess Dior's reaction to the killing to shots of her offering water to the kidnapper, not in submission but in a traditional regional gesture of respect (Pfaff, *Cinema* 176). According to conventional filmic coding, this should be the interior, subjective vision of an individual character (Dior's gesture certainly represents her changed attitude toward the ceddo), for such mutual respect between Wolof social strata divided by caste is another historical eventuality that did not occur. Had it occurred, it might well have been the basis for staving off Islam as well as Christianity in the name of indigenous tradition.

But the film's most remarkable example of the historical counterfactual is its ending. The princess, as Wolof nobility and the bearer of matrilateral succession, kills the imam while the ceddo protect her by placing their bodies in front of Muslim rifles. Narratively, this resolves the original story problem—her kidnapping—but only with complicated reversals: Dior is finally rescued from the kidnapper, but then she rescues herself from her putative rescuer, the imam, and in alliance with those who planned her original kidnapping. This climax enacts an historical possibility never realized in Senegalese history, a unification of the old nobility and the ceddo against foreign incursions. But crucially, unlike the earlier counterfactual scenes, this resolution is *not* cinematically coded as subjective, but presented as an "objective" story event. Thus, the camera work and editing convey an action as narratively truthful that a contemporary audience knows was historically unrealized.

This ending unsettles the film image by splitting it into a double function. It remains a trustworthy vehicle for narrative information (the story is indeed ended by the princess's action), yet it is not the final arbiter of historical truth. In turn, this makes history itself subject to a double vision, a possibility introduced by the shock of the priest's "dream." On the one hand, like almost any historical film, *Ceddo* gives us images of the past, inviting spectators to take pleasure in its reconstruction of details of precolonial society, its careful dramatization of the logic of power at that time, and the dynamics and spectacle of its story. On the other hand, it challenges the spectators to think through contradictions between the image and historical truth, from a position in the present.

This historical double vision pervades the film, even beyond story events and the image. One of the most praised examples is the film's music. Title and background music are made up of African-oriented modern jazz by Manu Dibango. But according to Sembene, it is based on "authentic music created by a griot more than a hundred years ago" (qtd. in Pfaff, "Entretien"). (The film seems to pay homage to this source at an early point, when the nondiegetic music takes up a theme being played by the *griot* Fara.) This mixture of contemporary musical styles and period music is another element in the film's historical double vision. While the music draws on historical sources, its jazz style acknowledges a late-twentieth-century performance. This musical double vision is also apparent in the film's inclusion of the African American gospel song "I'll Make It Home Someday" during sequences showing the suffering slaves bought by the White slave trader. The gospel song was a mode developed by descendents of such slaves in the New World, who also invented jazz. Within music history, then, this gospel song is a historical middle term between indigenous African music and Dibango's jazz stylings. But within the film's narration of African history, it points to a disastrous historical outcome of some of the actions in the narrative: the African diaspora and the economy of Western chattel slavery. The gospel song is from a future that—unlike the priest's dream—did indeed occur.

History for the Present

Although slavery is never explicitly discussed in *Ceddo*, it pervades the social world of the film. The White trader promotes a European exchange economy, whose medium of exchange is suffering black bodies, something emphasized by the branding scenes. Yet, the film implies that something in indigenous African culture makes it vulnerable to these methods of exchange. Indeed, slavery is shown to be completely naturalized within Wolof society. The best of traditionalist aristocrats, Madior and Saxewar, show only contempt for slaves, and even the rebellious ceddo can only imagine obtaining guns by reluctantly trading their own children to the White slave trader.

While interrogating oral cultural traditions, *Ceddo* has its narrative agents speak of many of the problems and options confronting them, often with eloquence and always with clarity and logic. Yet, Black-over-Black caste slavery and the trading of Black slaves to the Whites in a foreign exchange system remain unquestioned by any character. This silence, this repression, is a condemnation of traditional Africa's failure to take care of its own. Here is a historical aspect of tradition that *needed* change.

In this perspective, the film's ending can be better understood. Dior's final act of killing the imam is possible only after she acquires new respect for crown slaves and thus overcomes the caste division that separates her from them. And for the spectator in the present who knows of the historical persistence of caste and the existence of New World slavery, this ending will appear not only as counterfactual, but as critical and utopian at the same time. It is no accident that the agent of this critical, utopian ending is the only female character with a speaking part. It is through Dior, in fact, that social transformation becomes conceivable. Note that this resolution makes Dior the leader of the traditionalist forces, which is itself a contradiction. For according to tradition, the maternal nephew should inherit the throne, and the idea that Dior should govern is alien to all factions.

Thus, African resistance and identity must consider what modifications are necessary in the very tradition being defended. This issue is familiar in debates over national liberation and postcoloniality. After all, what was national liberation if not an experience of radical historical change? For national liberation theory and third cinema, the question was how culture and film might be modified to support liberation. The problem has sometimes too quickly been summarized as the interplay of indigenous and foreign or tradition and modernity, as if the indigenous and the traditional were not themselves components of modern experience (see Mudimbe).

This is not just a question for the past, but one addressed to the spectator in the postcolonial/neocolonial present, which takes us back to how the film organizes historical representation. The film ultimately understands history as a set of options that may lead to differing futures—including the present in which we live as one possibility. For *Ceddo*, then, historical comprehension does not occur when we understand the beginning, middle, and inevitable end of a true story, but rather when we consider futures that did not occur in comparison with those that did.

This promotes awareness of the strategies leading collective forces to make certain choices and not others, and it requires revising both African history and conventional Western cinematic devices—engaging with "film language" in new ways. Thus, clearly well aware of international mainstream cinematic conventions, Sembene plays off of them, inviting the spectator to engage in critical questioning. Part of the originality of *Ceddo* is that it invents a kind of historical cinema that depends on a complex temporal awareness: the interaction of the past and the present (where the spectator lives) in the construction of history. And this in turn depends on confronting the spectator with the possibility of different histories.

This is figured in the film's final shot, an uneasy freeze-frame that pictures Dior isolated from her new ceddo allies, surrounded by Muslims, as she stares directly at the camera. If the story's climax is counterfactual, even utopian, it also leaves much unsettled. First, even within the story world, the Muslim faction remains strong, so that the coexistence among religions demanded by the ceddo is by no means secure; and within the world of the spectator, Senegal in fact became predominantly Muslim. Second, the prerogatives of the White slave trader have never been questioned, and they are associated with the unseen, actual horrors of New World slavery. Third, with both the king and the imam dead, the political problem has not been solved. Or rather, the solution poses its own questions, because it involves the breakthrough of female agency into the world of politics and power.

Conclusion

The project of the film is to confront the spectator with current problems and difficulties, rather than certainties and solutions, even certainties about the inevitability of what happened in the past. *Ceddo* anchors consideration of the past in the present. The elementary problem of historical knowledge is the fact that any representation of the reality of the past can only occur in the present. Historical knowledge is therefore always divided between truth claims about the past and the fact that it is written in the present according to the needs of the present. Much historical representation suppresses this problem and the suspicions of unreliability it engenders. But in *Ceddo*, this division between past and present becomes part and parcel of the representation of history, and of the film image itself. For by the end of the film, the image cannot be read only as depicting the past. It addresses the present, for purposes of the present. This aesthetics of history is a challenge to the viewer, encouraging an active consideration of the historical possibilities not only of "then" but of "now." This makes the splittings of historical knowledge that affect understandings of the image into a politics of representation. The desire for such spectator activity may partly reflect the heritage of the African oral tradition, which the film examines; it was also a goal of third cinema theory, but politically it is closely tied to the context of postcolonial Africa. The cinematic and historiographical innovations of *Ceddo* are of wide-reaching importance, yet remain rooted in the fact that it situates itself as an African film dealing with African histories and African issues.

Credits

Senegal, 1977, Films Domireew

Director: Ousmane Sembene
Screenplay: Ousmane Sembene
Cinematography: Georges Caristan
Editing: Florence Eymon
Music: Manu Dibango

CAST:

Princess Dior	Tabata Ndiaye
Madior	Moustapha Yade
The kidnapper	Ismaila Diagne
The king	Matoura Dia
Jaraaf	Oumar Gueye
Prince Biram	Mamadou Dioumé
Saxewar	Nar Modou
Diogomay	Ousmane Camara
A ceddo renamed Ibrahima	Ousmane Sembene

Bibliography

Cabral, Amilcar. "National Liberation and Culture." *Return to the Source: Selected Speeches of Amilcar Cabral.* Ed. Africa Information Service. New York: Monthly Review, 1973. 39–56.

Cham, Mbye Baboucar. "Ousmane Sembene and the Aesthetics of African Oral Traditions." *Africana Journal* 13.1–4 (1982): 24–40.

Colvin, Lucie Gallistel. *Historical Dictionary of Senegal.* Metuchen, NJ: Scarecrow, 1981.

Daney, Serge. "*Ceddo.*" *Cahiers du cinéma* 304 (1979): 51–53

Diawara, Manthia. "Oral Literature and African Film: Narratology in *Wend Kuuni.*" Pines and Willemen 199–211.

———. "Popular Culture and Oral Traditions in African Film." *Film Quarterly* 41.3 (1988): 6–14.

Diop, Cheikh Anta. *Precolonial Black Africa.* Trenton: Africa World, 1987.

Fanon, Frantz. "On National Culture." *The Wretched of the Earth.* Trans. Constance Farrington. New York: Grove, 1981. 206–49.

Gabriel, Teshome H. "Third Cinema as a Guardian of Popular Memory: Towards a Third Aesthetics." Pines and Willemen 53–64.

———. "Towards a Critical Theory of Third World Films." Pines and Willemen 30–52.

Haynes, Jonathan, ed. *Nigerian Video Films.* Rev. ed. Athens: Ohio UP, 2000.

Miller, Christopher. *Theories of Africans: Francophone Literature and Anthropology in Africa.* Chicago: U of Chicago P, 1990.

Mudimbe, V. Y. *The Invention of Africa: Gnosis, Philosophy and the Order of Knowledge.* Bloomington: Indiana UP, 1988.

Pfaff, Françoise. *The Cinema of Ousmane Sembene, a Pioneer of African Film.* Westport: Greenwood, 1984.

———. "Entretien avec Ousmane Sembène," *Positif* 235 (1980): 56.

Pines, Jim, and Paul Willemen, eds. *Questions of Third Cinema.* Bloomington: Indiana UP, 1989.

Solanas, Fernando, and Octavio Getino. "Toward a Third Cinema." *Reviewing Histories: Selections from New Latin American Cinema.* Ed. Coco Fusco. Buffalo, NY: Hallwall's, 1987. 56–81.

Ukadike, Nwachukwu Frank. *Black African Cinema.* Berkeley: U of California P, 1994.

Peking Opera Blues (1986)

JENNY KWOK WAH LAU

Imploding Genre, Gender, and History

Context

It is almost a cliché by now to say that Hong Kong cinema has produced one of the world's most influential cinemas, especially when it comes to the action genre. A recent and well-known name that comes to mind is John Woo, whose film *A Better Tomorrow* (1986) took U.S. audiences by surprise. He is now regarded as the most representative director from that area of the globe. However, in Hong Kong, most people realize that it is Tsui Hark, the *producer* of *A Better Tomorrow,* who almost single-handedly revised and modernized the action genre and thus directly or indirectly launched the Hollywood careers of John Woo and superstars Chow Yun-Fat (through the same film) and Jet Li (through *Once Upon a Time in China* [1991], which Tsui directed). The combined work of these talents has forever changed the cinemascape of Hollywood. Within the Asian market Tsui is considered the Steven Spielberg of Hong Kong.

Tsui is a rare *auteur* in a cinema where a cutthroat commercial system reigns so tightly that it is hard to imagine the possibility of idiosyncrasy, let alone authorship. Throughout the last twenty years, Tsui has directed or produced some sixty films. This is an unusually high output, especially considering the fact that his films were not made with the support of a big studio system with standing sets, production crews, casts, and distribution networks. (The Shaw Brothers studio is an example of the latter, whose established factory production-line style rendered possible a prolonged high production rate.) After the success of *Zu: Warriors of the Magic Mountain* (1983), Tsui finally established his own production company, Film Workshop, in 1984. But this was not a large studio-style company. Furthermore, Tsui's achievements are not only quantitative but also qualitative, some in the artistic sense, others in terms of mass appeal. Tsui directed or produced three of the top

739

box-office hits of the eighties: *Aces Go Places III* (1984), *Zu: Warriors of the Magic Mountain,* and *A Better Tomorrow.* The latter two won a number of prizes at the Hong Kong Film Awards, an equivalent to the Oscars.

Tsui is a director who does not confine his work to a single genre. Although his most well-known films, such as *Zu,* the *Once Upon a Time in China* series (1991–97), and his two U.S. productions, *The Blade* (1995) and *Time and Tide* (2000), all belong to the martial-arts genre, and *A Better Tomorrow, A Chinese Ghost Story* (1987, producer), and *The Killer* (1989, producer) are action thrillers, he has also made sentimental comic melodramas, such as *Shanghai Blues* (1984), *Peking Opera Blues* (1986), and *I Love Maria* (1988, producer). Earlier in his career, during the 1980s, he was also one of the major producers/directors of Cinema City (then a new production company), whose *Aces Go Places* comedy series toppled the box-office records of Michael Hui, the Hong Kong comedy king of the time.

Tsui's greatest contribution lies in how he renewed and redefined Hong Kong cinema, contributing significantly to what became known as the Hong Kong New Wave. The New Wave began in 1979 when a number of young media makers, mostly television serial-drama directors, were given a chance to make films with a level of creative freedom unprecedented in the history of Hong Kong media. This happened as a result of the failure of traditional cinema, which, throughout the 1970s, suffered a precipitous loss of audience due to the popularization of television. Instead of investing in established directors who were used to following the traditional formats and could not recoup their losses, investors took advantage of the crisis and tried their luck with a new group of young filmmakers. Within one year (1979–80), thirty to forty directors were able to make their debuts. Tsui Hark's *The Butterfly Murders* (1979) and Ann Hui's *The Secret* (1979) were among the most impressive films to appear. During the subsequent two years, the movement came into full bloom. Allen Fong's *Father and Son* (1981) won the first prize at the Edinburgh Film Festival, the first Hong Kong film to gain an international "Best Film" award. *Dangerous Encounter—First Kind* (1980) and *Zu* by Tsui; *Man on the Brink* (1981) by Alex Cheung Kwok Ming; *The Story of Woo Viet* (1981) and *Boat People* (1982) by Ann Hui; *The Sword* (1980), *Love Massacre* (1981), and *Nomad* (1982) by Patrick Tam; *Last Affair* (1983) by Tony Au; and *Homecoming* (1984) by Yim Ho are all classics of the period.

The difference between the New Wave and the previous cinema can be summarized by looking at three major areas: visual expression, themes or subject matter, and self-reflexivity in its interpretation of Hong Kong cinema and society. Although social realism has been a noted characteristic of the New Wave, this description is only partially true; a number of the New Wave films, such as *Last Affair* and *Nomad*, are highly stylized or "unreal." This kind of stylization is particularly evident in the martial-arts genre, where the New Wave classic *Zu* is a good example. In this film, Tsui uses unusual camera angles and *mise-en-scène*, rapid editing techniques, and what was considered the first extensive use of high-tech special effects in Hong Kong, thus revolutionizing the very cinematic language of the genre. It is also a film whose unusual level of self-reflexivity deconstructs the action genre itself while at the same time celebrating its tropes. This practice created a new Hong Kong interpretation of the tradition of martial arts (and to a certain extent a new interpretation of China).[1] Almost all of Tsui's subsequent productions included these elements, which became his most recognizable trademarks.

The three films that eventually secured Tsui's name as a director and producer, both within and outside of Hong Kong, are *Zu, Peking Opera Blues*, and *A Better Tomorrow*. These films were all wildly popular with audiences in Hong Kong, Japan, Taiwan, Korea, and with fans in the West. Interestingly, while *Zu* belongs to the martial-arts genre and *A Better Tomorrow* is a modernized gunplay, *Peking Opera Blues* is a combination of the two. Furthermore, while the first two films are male dominated, *Peking Opera Blues* can be considered one of the best female action films. Perhaps because of its very successful comic characters (it was among the top ten box-office hits of the year), *Opera Blues* is sometimes undervalued as a film of exuberance, cartoon kung fu violence, and slapstick. But to view *Opera Blues* as simple mass entertainment is to miss its complexity. This oversight in the interpretation and understanding of Hong Kong films, whose exciting action and high entertainment value may deceive the critical mind, is found in many writings about the cinema.[2] Careful reading will show that

---

[1] For a discussion of Tsui's nationalism see Stephen Teo's *Hong Kong Cinema*.

[2] Examples can be found at Chris Dashiell's 2002 website: <www.rottentomatoes.com/click/movie1032460/reviews.php?critic=all&sortby=deault&page=1&rid=287408> and in David Bordwell's *Planet Hong Kong*.

the film exemplifies the best of the Hong Kong New Wave in its visual expression and in its self-reflexive interpretation of old themes.

Analysis

First, clarification of the title of the film is needed since it is commonly misunderstood by Western audiences. The literal translation of the Chinese title of the film is "Knife Horse Opera Actress(es)," which is a term for male actors impersonating women warriors, archetypal characters in the tradition of Peking opera. Some Western reviewers, however, have mistranslated the title as "Knife, Horse, Dawn." This perhaps is because the Chinese character for "dawn" and that for "opera actress" is the same. But the meaning of the word is determined by the context, which in this case does not allow for the translation as "dawn." Obviously, Peking opera itself is a major motif in the film. The three female characters in the film are presented in a double reversal of gender roles, playing the role of men, who play the role of the women warriors, or the "knife horse opera actresses," both onstage and offstage.[3]

The story of *Peking Opera Blues* takes place in 1913 China, when republican revolutionary fighters were struggling to overthrow imperial China. Three women, Tsao Wan (played by Brigitte Lin), an intellectual revolutionary; Sheung Hung (played by Cherie Chung), a greedy musician; and Pat Neil (played by Sally Yeh), the daughter of a local opera theater owner, meet each other by accident. While each of them has a different personal goal, they manage to help each other and the revolutionary project. After accomplishing the political goal, half by luck and half by willing sacrifice, they part from each other, hoping for the best for the country.

As a colorful, visually dynamic film, *Opera Blues* exhibits Tsui's cinematic style and innovations in the best possible way. In the following analysis, one can see how the film adopts a strategy of mixing genres (action and comedy), gender, and narratives (drama and commentary) in order to create a new story that provides different voices and perspectives, which undermine or even subvert traditions in all three areas.

---

[3]There is no intention to endorse an essentialist view of gender here. This essay uses a "traditional" conception of male and female, which is in line with the spirit of the film.

Narrative Structure

The structure of the film's story is complicated but clever. First, it borrows the traditional revolutionary narrative of an enlightened scholar (coming back from the West, represented by Tsao Wan) ready to sacrifice him or herself for the cause. But while this is a familiar narrative from Chinese and Hong Kong cinema of the past, Tsui adds another two characters, each of whom has her own story line—Sheung Hung and Pat Neil. Under normal circumstances, the lives of these three women would barely intersect. But they are linked in the film by the overwhelming situation of the civil war. Tsao embodies the rhetoric of a traditional revolutionary, who "betrays" her father (General Tsao), a corrupt general, in order to save the country. Her task is to steal a document from her father that is needed by the president, who is in fact planning to crown himself monarch. General Tsao, not knowing that his daughter is fighting for the other side, confides to her where the document is hidden and hands her a gun (a forbidden weapon) for self-protection. The standard narrative of a conflict between loyalty to one's parent and loyalty to one's country plays out in ways familiar to the Hong Kong audience. But instead of reproducing a clichéd story, the film uses the two characters Sheung Hung and Pat Neil, with their separate and vastly different lifestyles, to produce a different narrative space, in which complex plot, silly farce, and serious social commentary coincide.

Sheung Hung first appears in a musical performance held in a private home for a Stalin-like general (Tun), who despite a riot taking place outside is frantically scheming to make Sheung his twenty-ninth wife. But Sheung's sole interest is in gold. She outmaneuvers the general and evades the riot while pursuing a box of jewelry, which has slipped out of the hand of its owner in the midst of the chaos. Yet her luck fails her, as the box gets accidentally transported to a theater troupe. However, she will not give up because of this mishap. She pursues the jewelry throughout most of the film, thus setting up her chance meeting with Pat Neil later in the story. This simple scene, set in the beginning of the film, succinctly reveals Sheung's flirtatious, materialistic nature; her shrewdness in tricking and cheating; her strong survival instinct; and her complete lack of concern for politics. Yet, these characteristics will be put to use (or, better said, forced into use) for a noble revolutionary goal.

Pat Neil is the last character to be introduced. She is seen trying to sneak onto the stage with the other opera actors in violation of the rule that only males are allowed to perform. Her father catches on to her and throws her out. Her attraction to drama and her agony about being a female are immediately obvious. Ironically, it is her love for acting that ends up saving the revolution at the end of the film.

While Tsao's endeavor in the revolution drives the main narrative, subsidiary narrative strands are created by the accidental entanglement of the lives of Sheung and Pat, which in many instances creates comic relief. Tsao first meets Sheung briefly on the street, where she rescues her from harassment by soldiers. Later, Sheung accidentally gets into Tsao's home and is again rescued by Tsao from lascivious soldiers. Thus, a narrative connection is made in which Sheung is indebted to Tsao. Pat Neil first meets Tsao and Sheung when during one dramatic night the latter rush into her theater with a wounded revolutionary fighter. Sympathetic to their situation, Pat is caught between helping the strangers and her fierce father, who is not on the revolutionary side. Pat reluctantly helps Tsao behind her father's back and consequently becomes sensitized to the revolutionary underground.

Up to this point, the three women are still living separate lives, Sheung in pursuit of jewelry, Tsao committed to the revolution, and Pat taking care of the theater and helping the lead actor escape from Tun's persecution. Soon the three strands of story line merge in an unexpected way. Sheung, in chasing after the jewelry box, dresses as the female lead character of an opera that is being performed onstage. Pat, in order to hide the absence of the male actor who used to play that role but has run away, is substituting for him. But the big surprise comes when Sheung, out of ignorance, steps on a fake door backstage and falls onto the front stage. Suddenly there are two versions of the same character dressed in identical fashion onstage with one not knowing what to do. Hilarious as it may sound, they are able to maintain this deception until a fight backstage interrupts the performance. Soon General Tsao, who is among the audience, becomes interested in Pat and Sheung. Seeing this, Tsao takes advantage of her father's promiscuous nature and recruits Sheung and Pat for her cause.

The plot is, no doubt, complex. But more interesting is the way narrative agency and voice oscillate among Tsao, Sheung, and Pat in a seamless fashion. Although each of the three women has her own unique goal, as the narrative progresses they learn to help one another. As already noted, the main narrative dealing with Tsao's revolutionary goal is a rather traditional trope in Chinese cinema. In contrast, the two lines of events generated by Sheung and Pat are significant in the ways they add voices and perspectives previously not represented concerning the (historical) revolution.[4] Sheung's attitude is almost irreverent. History, meaning, and even political injustices are, at best, irrelevant to her. Pat is the opposite. Although she is not a revolutionary fighter and does not really understand much about Tsao's task, she is willing to help on the basis that "it is the right thing to do." The two voices create a new narrative that demystifies both the heroism and the old revolutionary story of political transformation accomplished by a small group of dedicated fighters. Sheung and Pat represent very ordinary people who are, either intentionally or unintentionally, nevertheless involved. Their motives, as with Sheung's, may be self-invested. Their actions might even be accidental. Yet again and again they save the situation. Thus, the line that traditionally separates the hero (Tsao) from the nonhero (Sheung) is never clear.

One final point worth noting about the film's narrative structure is that both before the story begins and after the last subtitle, there is a scene of a laughing "painted face." The painted face, also called *jing,* is another (male) archetypal character in Peking opera, usually a powerful general. His face is traditionally painted according to one or another particular style and color, which signifies his role. A black painted face, which is the one used in this film, represents an honest and uncompromising hero. This laughing face is obviously a nondiegetic character, one that is outside of the story world of *Opera Blues.* His laugh adds another voice to the story itself: the characters' efforts in fighting and killing all end up in vain. As the ending subtitle says, "Tsao's documents proved to be unnecessary as the President crowned himself monarch anyway. But then he died two years later and the country was in chaos. Thus the revolution had to start all over again." Here, history seems to have a mind of its own and is presented as cyclical in nature.

---

[4]Note that the film uses the actual name of the historical president Yuan Sai Hoi (Yuen Shi-kai), who did indeed return to the monarchy in 1915 and died in 1916. In this way, although the story is imaginary, there is a measure of commentary expressed about the historical revolution.

The planned task of destroying General Tsao's documents turns out to be futile. Sheung and Pat, who never planned to help the revolution, end up playing major roles. Thus, human affairs are shown to be unpredictable and uncontrollable. In the end, all actions become laughable. The mocking gesture of the painted face signifies a somewhat Taoist notion of the irrelevance of human action within the grand plan of the universe. By framing the story within this laugh, the film presents a level of self-reflexivity, undermining an old nationalistic myth.

Female Bonding

Opera Blues explores an intriguing notion of "gender mixing"; female characters cross-dress as males to then play females onstage. Through this foregrounding of gender issues, the film expresses an interesting view on femininity and female relationships. While John Woo's films portray male bonding, a common theme in the action genre, Tsui stands out in his exploration of female bonding. Ever since his first film, *The Butterfly Murders,* the portrayal of feminine power has been part of his films. His other films, such as *Shanghai Blues, Green Snake* (1993), and *Tristar* (1996), all include strong female friendships. Although it is true that strong female warriors are a part of the tradition of Chinese martial-arts films, *Opera Blues* is not just about strong females. It explores the intricacies and the many dimensions of female relationships. Its investigation of trust, mutual dependence, admiration, and support among the three women serves as a counterpart to the male relationships in, for example, *A Better Tomorrow.*

It is interesting to note that the three women bond exactly at the moment when they leave "home." Two of them are literally kicked out by men. Pat is thrown out of the theater by her father, and Sheung by the opera troupe. After Tsao says good-bye to her father, the three accidentally meet on the street where Sheung and Pat are shivering in the cold. Tsao offers her handsome overcoat to share. In the midst of the falling snow, they decide to "go out and have a little wine" to celebrate their newfound friendship. The next scene is of a candlelit interior in Tsao's Western-style mansion. The three get drunk in Tsao's house. This experience creates a strong sense of solidarity from then on.

While the use of strong women is not totally absent in U.S. cinema—for example, *Thelma and Louise* (Ridley Scott, 1991)—there is a difference here. In Tsui's films, women are strong not because they have taken on masculine traits, but exactly because they make full use of their femininity (not just sexuality). For instance, the three women, being physically weaker than the men, do not engage in any of the major combats. Instead, every time a fight or a chase breaks out, they try to run away. However, it is their wit, their acrobatic skill, their attention to detail, their capacity to console and take care of others, as well as their use of sexuality, that ends up supporting the revolutionary goal. Thus, Tsui portrays a kind of femininity quite different from what one sees in Hollywood films.

Tsao's cross-dressing helps her move through a male-dominated society. But her strength and later success comes only after she bonds with the other two women. Pat Neil is a strong woman who would not give up her dream to perform despite her father's objections. Although she wants to play the woman warrior onstage, in life she is full of "feminine" softness. Again and again she is engaged in helping and enabling others. When Tsao's group escapes into her theater, she is about to kick them out. But seeing a wounded fighter, she softens and helps, even though she is putting herself at risk. A few scenes later, Pat helps the male opera actor escape the ticket officer's pursuit. A moving scene reveals a feminine (or motherly) concern for details when she hands him costumes and jewelry and says, "take this . . . just in case you need it (on your way south)." In another scene, when the three women finally get hold of the documents, they are again chased by a large group of soldiers. But this time Tsao chooses to return home to save her father, leaving Pat and Sheung to escape on their own. The two women, who have no experience in any warfare, are terrified. But Pat is the stronger one, and she continues to protect and calm Sheung down. In one shot, the two women embrace each other for mutual consolation and encouragement. In the rest of the film, Pat continues to use her protective instinct to help complete the plan.

Among the three women in *Opera Blues*, Sheung could be considered the most traditionally "feminine," as represented by her profession (as a singsong girl), her dress code (mostly attractive dresses), and her ability to use her sexuality and sensuality to seduce men. Because of this quality, she can rescue Pat from General Tsao when their attempt to steal the key fails. She is also the one who, while pretending to engage in sex with Tun, kills him and retrieves the document needed by Tsao. But, of course, Sheung would not have done any of this if not for the bonding and trust that has developed among Pat, Tsao, and herself. The comic drama runs like this: Sheung accidentally shoots dead Tun in his office. The sound of the gunshot causes the guards to rush into the room. But Sheung takes advantage of the few minutes that she has to rescue Tsao before the guards can break open the door. When the guards come in, Sheung and Tsao are able to set up a charade with Tsao hiding behind and holding up the torso of Tun, while Sheung pretends to be engaged in sex play with him. Embarrassed by the scene, the guards immediately retreat.

The different characters of the three women, and especially the variation of their Cantonese dialects, can be taken as representing the different groups of Chinese. Tsao is a Western-educated intellectual. From the Cantonese dialect that she speaks, it is also clear that she is from southern China (including Hong Kong), where the republicans historically succeeded in leading the revolution in the early 1900s.[5] Her enlightened status is most noticeable in the scene in which the three women drink together in her house. A global map raises the curiosity of the other two women, and Tsao takes the opportunity to educate them about the world.

Sheung's connection to the grass roots is strong, through both her profession and her provincial language. Her interest in wealth and lack of interest in politics is part of her survival mentality. She is pretty, attractive, and full of wit. Whether it is true or not, these characteristics are usually seen as a reflection of Hong Kong. But most of all, her Cantonese is specifically Hong Kong in style. In one scene, she cannot understand Tsao's more formal language. When Tsao interrogates her "motive" for coming to her house, Sheung's reply is, "what does the word 'motive' mean?" Tsao has to rephrase her question in a more colloquial form: "Why do you come here?"

Pat's accent makes it clear that she is not a native Cantonese speaker. This implies that she is not from southern China or Hong Kong. Since her family is engaged in the trade of Peking opera, she is

---

[5]The republicans believed that China should become a democratic republic. They fought a prolonged revolutionary war that from 1911 on gradually succeeded in ending the three thousand years of dynastic rule of emperors. Their leader, Dr. Sun Yat Sen was a southerner, based in Canton and Hong Kong. Later, in 1949, after four years of a fierce civil war, the Communists overthrew the republican government and converted China into a socialist state.

probably from the North, the center of Communist China. Thus, the three women, to a certain extent, also represent the three different parts or epochs or even ideologies of three diverse Chinas, which at times were at odds with each other.[6] But now, as their life paths cross, a certain kind of mixing has enabled them to come to a state of cooperation and reconnection.

Comedy Action Thriller

Opera Blues is a comedy and an action thriller. It is interesting to see how fight and chaotic scenes are well orchestrated as visual fantasy and integrated into the story line. At the same time, verbal or physical humor is thrown in even in the most emotional or tension-filled moments. This kind of shift in tone persists throughout the entire film and at times creates a roller-coaster-ride form of excitement and confusion.

Among the three women, Sheung is the most comic character. In the beginning of the film, when a riot occurs, a jewelry box falls down the stairway, and a soldier catches it. He cannot believe his "good luck" and murmurs to himself, "I must be dreaming." But Sheung will not allow such good luck to fall to someone else. She knocks the soldier out with her *pipa* (a Chinese musical instrument similar to a guitar). When she is finished putting everything back in the box, she hits the soldier with the instrument again, murmuring to him, "now you can continue to dream (sleep)." A few scenes later, a frightened Sheung is surrounded by hostile soldiers. Again the moment is filled with tension. But Tsao sympathizes with Sheung's (female) reluctance to be frisked by a group of male soldiers. She breaks in and takes over frisking Sheung. To the viewer's surprise, the latter is ticklish and starts giggling. This not only strikes a comic tone but also serves to illustrate Sheung's alignment with Tsao.

Pat Neil's comic role derives from her overseriousness. When she is given a password to guard against intruders into the theater's backstage area, the idea is to keep the pursuing soldiers out. But she takes

---

[6]The term "three Chinas," the Republican China, the Communist China, and the Hong Kong China, should be taken only metaphorically. There is no political intention in the use of the term, which is strongly opposed by the mainland Chinese government.

her job so literally that she even asks her father for the password—"Peking Duck" (a northern Chinese dish). The latter is angered and yells back "Guo Bao Chicken" (another non-Cantonese dish). Pat does not know what to do with this unexpected response, semi-right and semi-wrong. In frustration, her father simply breaks open the door.

Another comic moment occurs after Pat and her newfound friends decide to spend the night in a room in the theater's backstage space rather than staying out in the cold snowy night. When morning comes, her father receives an order from General Tsao to have Pat perform in the opera that evening. The perturbed old man, who is against females performing, darts into Pat's room with the news. But there are actually four more people in the room, and they have to hide in any way they can—huddling under a blanket, scuttling around the father's back, or even climbing up to the roof. The movements of these characters and the camera are so well choreographed that one is reminded of the physical humor of Buster Keaton, except that this scene is even more complicated.

One of the most hilarious scenes comes from Fa, the opera's "female" lead. He has the misfortune of attracting the attention of the ticket agent, Mr. Liu, who is so taken with him/her that he makes a sexual proposal. When Fa rejects Liu, the latter tortures him/her with a finger-crushing device. The scene is excruciating to watch. But surprisingly, a comic effect is produced by Fa's exaggerated response. First Fa falls off the stairway on hearing the lewd proposal. Then, when he recovers, he cries like a baby. This excess in Fa's behavior creates a sense of self-awareness about the generic narrative of the old Cantonese opera, in which a rich man forces a poor opera actor to provide sexual favors. Thus, Tsui's comic moments are meant for both laughing and crying, providing extreme emotional and tone shifts. Another example would be the scene in which Tsao is tortured. The moment may seem gruesome, but it is soon followed by the above-mentioned comic scene of Sheung seducing Tun. Tsui, by exaggerating old generic narratives and by juxtaposing such moments with either humor or self-reflexivity, both celebrates and deconstructs aspects of the old cinema.

Action Scenes
Action and suspense are designed in *Opera Blues* so that they are integrated into the narrative, moving it forward rather than stopping it for

the sake of performance.[7] A number of chase scenes between the soldiers and the revolutionary fighters end with well-choreographed large-scale action. For instance, one pursuit at the beginning of the film turns into a gunfight, followed by a fistfight, and ends only when the two male revolutionary fighters escape in Tsao's luxurious automobile. Thus, the narrative space is transported to the street, which becomes the stage for the next episode. Similar chase-fight-escape sequences can be found elsewhere in the film, which move the setting and the story forward.

Several attempts to steal the documents fail. The fighters then try to dupe General Tsao by putting a drug into his food while he is watching an opera performance. Here, intercutting between two major actions, onstage and backstage, creates two scenes that mirror each other. Onstage, as discussed earlier, there are two females playing the same warrior character. This happens because after the male actor runs away, Pat gets her chance to perform. But while she is onstage, Sheung, who masquerades as one of the actresses so that she can ransack the backstage to find her jewelry box, accidentally falls on the backstage trapdoor and gets thrown onto the front stage. The theater audience does not realize what is happening and thinks that it is part of the performance, which means that Sheung has to immediately pick up the same role as Pat, since she is dressed in the same costume. Tension is built as Pat has to twist the plot and "teach" Sheung about her lines and the acrobatic skill as the play goes on. This onstage performance is intercut with images of General Tsao's lack of interest in his food while his gluttonous girlfriend swallows his share and thus the drug. The girl visits the restroom and runs into revolutionary fighters there. In the dimly lit environment, a skirmish takes place during which the revolutionaries mistakenly assume that she is the general. Soon the real identity of the fighters backstage and the real identity of the woman warriors onstage are revealed. The whole theater, both front stage and backstage, turns into a battleground. Again, a chase-and-fight scene takes place, this time intermingled with the opera

---

[7]Tom Gunning's idea of the "cinema of attractions" has been used by various scholars in the study of musicals. The musical piece within the film functions like the "cinema of attractions," where the narrative stops for the sake of the performance. This idea can also be seen in many action films where the story pauses for the sake of presenting the fighting.

actors and actresses, who just a moment before were acting out a fight scene. Thus, there is a complete intermingling of "real life" and fictional drama within the film, highlighting its own fictional status.

While Ching Siu-Tung choreographed the movements in the film,[8] it is Tsui who expressed them in dynamic cinematic form. The operatic costumes create a dazzling, colorful visual, while movements are accentuated by creative camera angles and editing. In the above-mentioned scene, the fighters escape by sliding across the curtain and the fabric hanging from the roof of the theater. This also foreshadows the last climactic moment of the film, when the three women and all the fighters masquerade as actors/actresses in the onstage drama of *Eight Fairies Cross the Sea*. The plan is to escape through the rooftop of the theater. This last scene of the film provides a grand finale of motion and color. The fighters, who are completely surrounded by the soldiers, come up with the idea of doing a drama to escape. *Eight Fairies Cross the Sea* is a clever choice of plays, since there are a number of fighters in it who need to run, and the drama involves a large number of "lead actors." In addition, "crossing the sea" has a double meaning of both a journey (in the story, these fairies are taking a journey to a birthday party) and, in Cantonese, "running away and leaving things (a mess) behind," as the fighters are planning to do. Again, not only a sense of humor, but a sense of the interconnectedness of life and drama is displayed.

The opera *Eight Fairies* is shot using a number of bird's-eye-view shots intercut with close-ups and side shots. There are only a few wide-angle shots, which do not really serve as establishing or master shots. This approach demonstrates the overall visual style of the film, in which different camera angles construct a space that is not completely defined but remains fluid enough for the expansion of action. Cuts are made among contrasting movements, colors, tones, and even styles. In the end, the fighters' ploy is revealed to the soldiers. The fighters actually try to use the dramatic plot element of "crossing the sea" to create a route to get out of the theater even as it is surrounded by soldiers. As a prop for the drama, long blue fabric is thrown out across the roof so

---

[8]Ching is among a group of major action choreographers in Hong Kong, including such outstanding talents as Yuen Woo-Ping. The latter choreographed the action scenes of *The Matrix* (1999) and *Crouching Tiger, Hidden Dragon* (2000).

that the actors can "slide" across the "sea." But the soldiers have already realized the scheme, and shooting begins. The "journey" turns into a gunfight chase across the roof. Acrobatic movements shown in slow motion intensify the action and create strong visual tension. Close-up shots of the blood-drenched hands of the women grasping each other create sensational evocations of camaraderie in ways that prefigure the male camaraderie of John Woo's *A Better Tomorrow*. When the bloodbath ends, the audience is left uncertain, not knowing exactly which characters are dead and which are alive.

The last scene begins with an empty shot of a semicloudy sky. The three women and two male revolutionary fighters are seen each riding a horse. They form a circle and bid each other farewell. Now that the mission of getting the documents is accomplished, each one of them plans to go back to her or his old trade, hoping that they may run into one another again in the future. The same operatic music is played as that at the beginning of the film, and the subtitles tell us that everything comes full circle again. A loud laugh from the painted face is heard, which seems to serve as a comment on the futility of human action.

Conclusion

While Tsui is not shy about being commercial, *Peking Opera Blues* is definitely not an escapist film. It is true that sentimentalism and emotionalism are employed in the film, but they are not without the tension of double meanings. This reflexive doubling of meaning is successfully achieved by creating new narratives that incorporate different voices, by mixing the action genre with comedy, by reversing gender, and by mixing reality with drama. Some popular critics may find the slapstick humor silly or naive, but the jokes can also serve as parody, a way of talking back to the past. Thus, one of the secrets of *Opera Blues* is that one can enjoy it on several different levels. *Opera Blues'* rich costumes, extravagant visual settings, and well-choreographed actions (which mix martial arts with modernized weapons) also contribute to its attractiveness. But most of all, it is the implosion of forms, articulated through the dynamic interactions among the three "transgendered" women, that creates an unorthodox interpretation of history and leaves the most lasting impression on its audience.

Kwok Wah Lau

Credits

Hong Kong, 1986, Cinema City Film Productions

Director and Producer: Tsui Hark
Action Director: Ching Siu-Tung
Screenplay: Raymod To Kwok-Wai
Cinematography: Poon Hang-Seng
Editing: David Wu Dai-Wai
Original Music: James Wong and David Wu Dai-Wai
Art Direction: Ho Kim-Sing, Leung Chi-Hing, and Vincent Wai Kai-San
Costume Design: Ng Po-Ling

CAST:

Tsao Wan	Brigitte Lin Ching-Hsia
Sheung Hung	Cherie Chung Cho-Hung
Pat Neil	Sally Yeh
General Tsao	Kenneth Tsang Kong
General Tun	Cheung Kwok-Keung
Pat's father	Wu Ma

Bibliography

Bordwell, David. *Planet Hong Kong: Popular Cinema and the Art of Entertainment.* Cambridge, MA: Harvard UP, 2000.

Fu, Poshek, and David Desser. *The Cinema of Hong Kong: History, Arts, Identity.* Cambridge: Cambridge UP, 2000.

Gunning, Tom. "The Cinema of Attractions: Early Film, Its Spectator and the Avant-Garde." *Early Cinema: Space, Frame, Narrative.* Ed. Thomas Elsaesser and Adam Barker. London: BFI, 1990. 56–62.

Teo, Stephen. *Hong Kong Cinema: The Extra Dimension.* London: BFI, 1997.

Yau, Esther C. M., ed. *At Full Speed: Hong Kong Cinema in a Borderless World.* Minneapolis: U of Minnesota P, 2001.

Yeelen (1987)

N. FRANK UKADIKE

Dialectical and Experiential Interplay between Art and Culture

From the mid-1980s to the present, scholars and critics have observed fundamental shifts in the subject, theme, voice, and tone of many recent African films. While the pioneering African filmmakers often made didactic films that treated important issues concerning African people and dialectical ones blending new and traditional ways of living, a new breed of African filmmakers has challenged the dominant paradigms of African and other cinematic traditions.

The proliferation of experimental trends in recent African cinema—that is, films that serve to heighten political consciousness and thematically audacious and innovative films that openly exhibit affinities with culture and history—demonstrates a characteristic emphasis on film as cultural practice. Souleymane Cissé's work exemplifies this shift and these changes; while his work can be regarded as a bridge between the old and the new, his radical approach to narrative construction is best understood from the perspective of the ideological underpinnings of the pioneering years.

Context

The earliest films made during the pioneering years of African cinema, from the late 1960s to the 1970s, were inundated with politics and were often deliberately didactic. The primary goal was to use the medium to inform and educate people and to project authentic visions of Africa and its peoples. The medium also helped reverse the demeaning stereotypical images of Africa found in dominant representations of the continent. Considering that this cinema was born out of oppression and resistance, coming only after the independence of the producing countries, the prevailing mood of nationalism propelled filmmakers to link cinema with national development. Simply put, the pioneers developed a cinema grounded in the belief that the film medium could speak for the people while also being an impetus for social change. Some of the films that addressed the challenges and contradictions of (post)colonial Africa include *La noire de . . .* (*Black Girl*) and *Xala*, both Ousmane Sembene, Senegal, 1966 and 1974, respectively), *Cabascabo* (Oumarou Ganda, Niger, 1969), *Soleil O* (Med Hondo, Mauritania, 1969), *Harvest 3,000 Years* (*Mirt sost shi amit*, Haile Gerima, Ethiopia, 1976), and *Sambizanga* (Sarah Maldoror, Angola, 1972).

Also from this early beginning, the films initiated polemical discussions about film aesthetics, leading critics to question whether there can be an African language of the cinema. This concern arose when it became obvious that even when images are situated and read within the "universalist" notion of cinema, the means of signification are specific to the traditions and cultures of the producing nations. In effect, the construction of African narratives was imbued with cultural sensibilities and political specificities. It is in this context, for example, that the ideology of the man widely considered to be the "father" of African cinema, Ousmane Sembene of Senegal, can be seen in the narrative style employed in his film *Borom Sarret* (1963). This twenty-minute short, many will argue, initiated a model for African film, in which the synthesis of fiction, documentary, meticulous attention to detail, and oral narrative technique all coalesce to produce an indigenous aesthetic.

Sembene's approach to narrative construction suggests new ways of seeing and interpreting African history through cinematic images. It brought attention to the dichotomy between African cinema and Euro-American cinema—in this case, a dichotomy between a social cinema geared toward education and enlightenment (or, more important, toward liberation) and a commercial cinema oriented toward profit.

Sembene's influence on other African filmmakers, including Souleymane Cissé, has been enormous and continues to this day, even having an impact on the radical younger filmmakers whose notion of aesthetics is markedly different from the more linear and lugubrious structure of the pioneering films. As can be seen from the films of the 1960s and 1970s, African narrative styles are not at all monolithic, as Sembene's narrative style is neither prescriptive nor binding on other pioneer filmmakers such as Med Hondo, Haile Gerima, Safi Faye, Sarah Maldoror, and Souleymane Cissé. Yet, while it is true that differences abound in narrative style and orientation, ideologically, these pioneers unanimously display their contempt for the dominant notion of commercial cinema.

From this perspective, my discussion of Cissé's *Yeelen* (*Brightness*) will emphasize the use of indigenous aesthetics to foster innovation and imaginative narrative patterns. Cissé, like most of his counterparts, aspires to this goal through the appropriation and subversion of dominant aesthetic formulas which, blended with one's own cultural codes (oral narrative art), create an invigorating aesthetic.

The overarching drive behind African moviemaking in its early days was to intervene in the sociopolitical sphere in an effort to reassess history. Now, what was once strictly documentation on educational and political levels has become a more diversified art form that is not only constantly changing but also confronting dissension within its own domain. This dissension revolves around how to negotiate the relationship between individual and collective prerogatives, and emphasizes the value of juxtaposing innovative methods of filmmaking with traditional paradigms to enable imaginative invention—thus keeping the art forms forever changing along with the constantly evolving African world and aesthetic sphere. While the pioneering films tell important stories, it is their point of view and originality in general that make them uniquely African. This point of view, fully embraced by innovative directors such as Cissé, breaks the mold of traditional paradigms and allows new "revolutionary" forms of expression and interrogative models of narrative patterns and aesthetics to proliferate, thus challenging entrenched notions of cinematic orthodoxy.[1] For example, when *Yeelen* was released in 1987, it was hailed as the cinema of the fantastic; it was respected and glorified, though not in all circles.[2]

Indeed, the 1980s was the decade par excellence for African cinema, the golden age of unprecedented creativity that saw the realization of great films. These films, which include *Yaaba* (1989) and *Tilaï* (*The Law*, 1990), both by Idrissa Ouedraogo; *Bal poussière* (*Dancing in the Dust*, 1988) by Henri Duparc; *Zan Boko* (*Homeland/The Placenta*, 1988) and

---

[1]Some observations in this segment came out of the conversations I had with twenty African filmmakers. For more details, see the introduction to my book *Questioning African Cinema: Conversations with African Filmmakers*. Some portions of my analysis of *Yeelen* are taken from my book *Black African Cinema* (1994) and modified for this project. Thanks to the University of California Press for letting me use my work.

[2]Even among African audiences, there are some who believe that *Yeelen*'s structure is too complicated and confusing and wonder if the desired effects have really been achieved.

Wend Kuuni (*God's Gift,* 1982), both by Gaston Kaboré; *Sarraounia* (1986) by Med Hondo; *La vie est belle* (*Life Is Rosy,* 1987) by Ngangura Mweze and Benoît Lamy; *Heritage Africa* (1989) by Kwaw Ansah; and *Camp de Thiaroye* (*The Camp at Thiaroye,* 1987) by Ousmane Sembene and Thierno Faty Sow, solidified the respect accorded to the continent's cinematic endeavor.

If the 1960s and 1970s were the decades of experimentation and soul searching for African cinema, the African cinematic practice of the 1980s, if nothing else, has done an enormous job of restating and refocusing its original goals: the drive for more autonomy, the elimination of aesthetic constraints, and the liberation of the artist's mind. With the success of *Yeelen* and other African films, one can conveniently declare that the popularity of these films enhanced the position of this cinema within the stylistic repertoire of world cinema. With the protean notion of Africa as a "cinematographic desert" now rendered obsolete, the question of whether or not quality films can emerge out of Africa no longer exists. The unprecedented success of *Yeelen* and some other African films of this period, in terms of critical acclaim as well as box-office receipts (in Africa, Europe, and the United States), has prompted speculation regarding the emerging trend of new African cinema. Even though they are encircled by the constraints of production, exhibition, and distribution (Cissé once stated, for example, that "one must be crazy to think about making films in Africa" [qtd. in Ukadike, *Questioning* 20]), African filmmakers have been able to assert distinctive indigenous voices in the reproduction of African experiences on film by upholding a critical cultural agenda. This essay assesses Cissé's contribution to those voices. His cinema reflects the cultural dynamics of Africa as well as his quest for cinematic autonomy, which, I argue, is demonstrated in *Yeelen*'s compelling and imaginative experimentation. African film practice has stressed indigenous characteristics, particularly the relationship between the environment and the characters. Part of what is in question here is whether these characteristics constitute what might be considered the quintessential elements of Cissé's cinematographic art and, by extension, African film style. The dynamics of culture and image will be examined within the overall method by which *Yeelen* conveys meaning. Also examined will be how, as a cultural product, the film's message can be scrutinized and synthesized as part of a larger African cultural discourse.

Milieu

Born in Bamako, the capital city of Mali, Souleymane Cissé, a pioneer in the development of Malian cinema, is one of Africa's most acclaimed filmmakers. In the 1960s, Cissé joined the ranks of other Africans who were offered a full scholarship to study in the Soviet Union. From 1963 to 1969 he studied filmmaking at the VGIK, the State Institute of Cinema in Moscow. There, he had the opportunity to be taught by the Soviet Union's eminent filmmaker Mark Donskoi, whose former African film students included Ousmane Sembene and Sarah Maldoror. In 1969, Cissé returned to Mali to work as film director at the Service Cinématographique du Ministère de l'Information du Mali (SCINFOMA); there he produced more than thirty newsreels and several documentary films dealing with Malian issues. It was not until 1972 that the young director shot his first independently produced fiction film, *Cinq jours d'une vie* (*Five Days in a Life*, 1972), which, in terms of creativity and ideology, was full of promise and excitement.

"The films of Souleymane Cissé," notes Clyde Taylor, "have found a form that lies somewhere between the extended parables of Sembene and the disrupting strategies of Med Hondo and Haile Gerima" (55). Roy Armes also observes that Sembene's work is matched for critical rigor and creative excitement by Cissé in three masterly features of increasing stylistic complexity: *Den Muso* (*The Young Girl*, 1974), *Baara* (*Work*, 1978), and *Finye* (*The Wind*, 1982) (*Third World Film Making* 223)—to which one should now add *Yeelen*.

In the first years of his career, coinciding with the period when the pioneers of African cinema were advocating a cinema of awareness for the African people, Cissé's films, as social commentaries, could not have avoided being political and didactic. For him, film must "address issues of the utmost concern and implication to his [the filmmaker's] society, with the hope of positive change" (qtd. in Ukadike, *Black African Cinema* 188). In fact, the first fiction film he made after his Moscow education, *Cinq jours d'une vie*, criticized the poor practical education offered by Africa's Koranic schools. In *Den Muso*, Cissé denounced parental attitudes toward daughters who are ostracized for going against tradition. *Baara* introduced a critical view of trade unionism never before explored in African cinema, in the same way that *Finye* offered insight into Africa's military regimes (188).

Cissé's political views have put him at odds with his country's ruling oligarchs. However, he has managed to adapt to the repressive political establishment when, on occasion, genuine criticism of the system has been prohibited. According to Cissé:

> There are certain changes or transformations during a lifetime that force one to rethink his ways of doing things. . . . If *Yeelen* is different from *Finye* and *Baara*, it may be because of . . . certain impulses driving each creation. The change of style may also be deliberate. After I made *Finye* and *Baara*, I was labeled a political filmmaker; some said my films are too didactic. But an artist should have the freedom to experiment with theme, content and narrative strategy. As my own experiences have shown, what you narrate may also put you into trouble. Sometimes, in order to survive a hostile environment one is forced, not necessarily to disarm, but to construct a narrative that is not too political nor devoid of pungent criticism of the system. (Qtd. in Ukadike, *Questioning* 21)

Cissé's fiction films have captivated audiences all over the world. *Baara* enjoyed immense popular success in Africa and Europe, becoming in 1982 the first African film shown on a prime-time French television station (FR3). *Finye* captured the 1983 FESPACO grand prize, the Étalon de Yennega. This film, which has earned audience acclaim worldwide, was also one of the first African films to be released on video and DVD. If these features were imbued with creative excitement and stylistic virtuosity, *Yeelen* confirmed Cissé's mastery of cinematic conventions. A talented artist, Cissé claims he is still searching for an original form or style of expression—an acceptable film language. His most ambitious film, *Yeelen,* described by critic Jonathan Rosenbaum as "the greatest African film ever made," seems to have satisfied this quest. It won the Jury's Prize at the 1987 Cannes Film Festival.

Analysis

Dynamics of Culture and Image

Yeelen epitomizes the daring stance shared by African cinema pioneers. In every respect, the filmmaker's quest for an indigenous film structure parallels the film's exploratory tactics and is realized in a complex cinematic style. The film narrates an initiation journey that puts father (Soma Diarra) and son (Nianankoro) on a collision course as they struggle for supremacy in the possession of a special knowledge that is exclusive to the Bambara people of Mali—the secrets of nature. The father, seeking to prevent his son from acquiring this special knowledge, plans to kill him. But Nianankoro's mother intervenes by sending her son away (on an initiation journey that introduces him to the oral cultures and traditions common to the Sahel region). This pilgrimage takes him across the semiarid regions spanning the Bambara to Dogon and Fulani lands, enabling him to acquire the ultimate knowledge that lets him establish his own supernatural powers.

At the Fulani kingdom of Boulla, for example, Nianankoro is captured because he is thought to be a cattle thief. Once in front of the king and his paramount chiefs and subjects, he brags about his power; then, on being attacked, he displays this power by making a guard stiffen and by putting a sword in flames. This display of prowess, reminiscent of the great warriors of Mali who sustained the Malian empire in the thirteenth century as one of the greatest in world history, amazes the king. He enlists Nianankoro to help repel a strong group of invading enemy forces. The enemy is defeated, and Nianankoro's success ultimately earns him respect and special treatment like that accorded a king's son; the king even admits him to live beside him in his palace as one of the admired members of the kingdom. However, as enticing as this offer may be, Nianankoro cannot accept it, as he must continue with his journey if he is to escape the wrath of his father. Meanwhile, Soma, his father, is conducting his own magical rites for help in discovering Nianankoro's escape route. He is aided by two male followers, presumably low-ranking neophytes of the Komo society, who carry the magic post that guides them through the desert as he commands the gods to dry up the lakes and level the mountains so that Nianankoro can be tracked down and destroyed.

The stories and images associated with *Yeelen* are never disconnected from the villages or the Sahel region in which they are set; they thereby act as concrete examples of the linkage between narration and the presentation of culture. During the father's search for his son, Cissé offers a vignette of rural life as a backdrop for the eventual encounter between them, showcasing activities such as cultivating crops, cattle rearing, and blacksmithing. When Soma comes into one town, the scene highlighting the profession of blacksmithing is quite pronounced. This is an important scene because the Komo cult has a respected blacksmithing origin, and its people are proud of it. This journey also calls attention to the behavior and mannerisms maintained throughout by the protagonists in the film: Soma is showy, loud, forward, talkative, and arrogant; Nianankoro is reticent, respectful, calm, and calculated, and has a resolute expression and gait like his mother, who is extremely taciturn and displays the angelic mannerisms of Sana, the old woman in Idrissa Ouedraogo's *Yaaba*. As one admirer of *Yeelen* observed, "it is through the crypto-Oedipal setting that supernatural and spiritual things come forth clearly in the filming of the diegesis."[3] Through this setting, symbols are invoked to buttress the social and personal issues connecting the father, mother, and son.

When History and Myth are invoked at the beginning and throughout, it is because Cissé wants us to be aware that in this tapestry of history and culture lies the omnipotent spiritual power of the *nyama,* the intrinsic spiritual force responsible for giving life and for the maintenance of all living things. Consider, for instance, the beginning of the film, when a squawking fowl that has been set on a magic post (*Kolonkalanni*) is set aflame by the invocations of Soma to Mari, a Bamana god. This is followed by Soma setting off brush fires with his magic and displaying an unrelenting determination to kill his own son by pleading with the gods "to scour the earth and dry the seas" to find Nianankoro. Consider also the scene in which Nianankoro is sitting with his aging mother and, looking into a bowl of water, sees an image of his uncle, Baafing Diarra, who is also on the move (armed with another *Kolonkalanni*) to capture his nephew. All of this invokes terror. The audience, bombarded with these powerful images and symbols, cannot avoid recognizing that the Bamana universe is at a turning point; generational transition is at the heart of this impending disaster. The film is replete with powerful images such as these, that the filmmaker uses to create suspense.

Cissé belongs to the class of African filmmakers who strongly believe that a powerful film medium should and can be harnessed to fit the agenda of those seeking to probe African issues (precolonial,

---

[3]From discussing *Yeelen* with students and audiences.

colonial, and neocolonial) to illuminate "the system." The dilemma, though, has always been that, as in most areas of civil society, the means of production and dissemination of cinema, the arts, culture, and science are controlled by "the enemy." For this reason, the objective of the proponents of a distinctly African cinema has been to "decolonize culture," to put it rightfully in the hands of the people, and use it to indict the oppressors and stimulate radical discourse for genuine change. This ideology has translated into a very powerful film style, as evidenced by *Yeelen*. At its most basic level, the director rejects the traditional Hollywood narrative structure and production method. There is an avoidance of the use of professional actors, a rejection of continuity editing, and an elimination of the traditional linear-progressive story line associated with Western cinema in favor of a more episodic and cyclical rendering. This might well be called the style for indigenizing filmmaking. However, the ideology of indigenous cinema has an even deeper resonance and implication for Cissé's method of Africanizing cinema. For him, it is better to "approach issues differently in order to arrive at, if not a new meaning, a new synthesis." On the criteria for reaching this level, the filmmaker explains:

> *Yeelen* is embedded in deep cultural codes. Filming *Yeelen* was an extraordinary lesson for me. It was a discovery of a new thing, . . . one aspect of Malian culture—and there are many cultures in Mali—just as there are numerous aspects of other cultures in Africa. . . . Certain elements and codes resonating from a particular culture may influence film form and film style. [It means] looking intensely to be able to interpret what was going on . . . with the creative device I felt was appropriate. It is this discovery which compelled me to reveal, and in this revelation the content dictated the form and the strategy with which to shape the film style. (Qtd. in Ukadike, *Questioning* 22)

Sheila Petty sees many sub-Saharan African cinematic texts making progress toward a "reorganization of knowledge [by which] the filmmakers demonstrate the impossibility of retrieving an 'original' moment" (11). While this may not be feasible in a real sense, and while the films may no longer explicitly aspire to repossess African space or decolonize minds, the manner in which they have investigated the complexities and complications illuminating the African subject builds cultural awareness for the protagonists and for the audience. In other words, they avoid the ambiguities and dichotomies that support Eurocentric, colonial patrimony. Cissé's concern for form and content clearly has resonance in his exploration of camera pyrotechnics, special effects, and the social aspects of narratological patterns that reinforce cinematic codes and cultural conventions.

Cissé documents that this film was accomplished through mutual understanding and respect, by placing the significations of form and content within social, cultural, and historical contexts and in a transgressive mode of address far removed from dogmatic codes and conventions. For example, *Yeelen* could either be seen as promulgating a strict reflectionist or deterministic notion of cultural and social connotations or, more daringly, as an antitraditionalist allegory that presents "parallels" and "opposites" as dichotomous canons for the critique of tradition and change.[4] Admitting that the images may not be accessible to everyone, "not even to Malians not initiated into the Komo cult," what matters most for Cissé is that the film interprets the rituals honestly by carefully depicting the "rich imagery and symbolisms . . . to achieve a specific goal and significance." This goal, according to Cissé, is attained only if the film is able to "invite the spectator to seek for the deeper meaning which transcends the literary meaning of what the entire film signifies. [Thus] *Yeelen* compels spectators to ask questions about the secrets of the Komo; makes you an active observer, and provokes discussion and participation" (Ukadike, *Questioning* 22). Without this sense of active investigation, the very depiction of the "Komo" secret society, in which the camera lens witnesses the actual initiation, rituals, and ceremonies, would have been regarded as sacrilegious and intrusive.

In fact, traditional Malians have long been suspicious of what they term "diabolic images" of the magic machine of the devil's creation named *tiyatra* (Malian dialect designating "cinema") (Hampaté Bâ 67). Simply put, the people of Mali make no secret of their disdain for the superficial images projected by the colonial propaganda machine. But

---

[4]For example, *Yeelen* can be read as a critique of traditionalist culture (the Komo cult), since Mali is 90 percent Islamic, and Cissé, the filmmaker, is Muslim. However, skilled as Cissé is in obfuscation, the film evades this primary source of influence.

Cissé holds the middle ground between the Western ethnographic conception of the moving image, which seeks out the misery of the third world, and the falsehood of repressing it on the grounds of cultural intrusion. Therefore, *Yeelen* is important for a number of reasons: the film creates a dialectic of old and new, between the disgruntled younger generation and those who maintain the status quo (a topic I shall return to later); as a critique of culture, the film displays new ideas, and as a critique of convention, the filmic strategy suggests a resolute trend in creativity, fresh and focused on African film language. Out of this practice, however, emerge certain questions of Cissé's perspicacity and of possible ideological contradictions. I attempt to discuss these questions by examining Cissé's concern for authenticity and for the respectful treatment of the subject, and by considering related cinematic strategies for representing fact and fiction.

Articulating the Codes

Yeelen displays Cissé's powers of directorial invention in its combination of forms. As a poetic celebration of Malian culture, it is dynamic. In the sense of its authenticity and cultural iconography, and as an indigenous African art form, it is a classic in the Bambara epic tradition, similar to the Sanjata legend, weaving aspects of repressed cultural motifs—rituals, folklore, and symbols—into a historical tapestry of ritual values. As a cinematic summa encompassing the indigenous and the mainstream, it specifically alludes to styles ranging from Sembene's candid didacticism to Hondo's eruptive style. In it we find the fusion of fiction, ethnographic and documentary modes like cinéma vérité, and oral literature.

Structured around mythological patterns, *Yeelen*'s narrative allows one to critically explore the articulation of the precolonial and the traditional. The film's binary structure emphasizes the distinctive dynamic of traditional culture, revealing contradictions indicative of what Kwame Anthony Appiah, in another context, terms the "exclusivity of insight" (346). By drawing attention to the dynamics of opposition and rejection inherent in traditional systems, Cissé's projection of their inevitability thus centers around apostasy, or the challenge to traditional pinciples. This works as a revisionist code that, though not on a par with traditional systems, enables him to construct a narrative driven by a cultural and moral dialectic. Because of Soma's refusal to transfer generations of secrets to his son, the viewer is forced to sympathize with Nianankoro when he attempts to obtain this knowledge by force. In this respect, the father's action nullifies one of Africa's most cherished traditions—the quest for knowledge—while the son's rebellion appears to be just another case of the nonchalant negation of the tradition of respect and loyalty to elders. The film does not show us, however, that Soma is obligated not to reveal such secrets to his son because he is too young to be entrusted with the secrets of the Komo, which only members who have attained the rank of "Kore" can possess.

In describing the Komo society, Rachel Hoffman states that "as a policy agency, Komo manages anti-social behavior; as a spiritual assembly, it cultivates and protects a community's mythology; as a professional organization, its members possess that awesome ability to create material objects through which the spiritual world becomes incarnate" (100). Yet this knowledge does not come easily. Kate Ezra notes that it takes a neophyte "seven-year cycles through six grades of progressively more arcane knowledge" to reach, at old age, the Kore stage (qtd. in Hoffman 100). From this perspective, one can see why Soma would see it as imperative to invoke the powers at his disposal for his advantage and for the advantage of the Komo cult, whose members do not question his motive for taking such draconian action. Ratifying the need to implement the will of, if not to pacify, the gods and spirits, the Grand Master of the Komo gladly tells Soma to "cry like the sacred goat, like the divine hyena that banned slavery on both shores when mothers deserted their babies to save their lives! Sacred ram, cry so I can hear you, cry like the Komo Nango Djago! Sacred beast of Bala, cry so all can hear you!" The Grand Master's invocation makes a powerful statement that has both continental significance and historical implications for the African diaspora. This scene displays a deep commitment that renders the *mise-en-scène* authentic; we hardly question whether the ritual is real or whether the characters, as arbiters of tradition, are serious in their endeavor to reach the "divine justice" being sought. They speak in tongues, adding to the impression of authenticity, and their dress helps convince even the skeptics that these are members of an influential organization whose rules they want to protect at all cost.

There are other seeming contradictions in the film's structure. For example, Soma's stated reason for wanting to kill his son is that he stole the Komo secret. Yet at the beginning of the film, the audience is told during a conversation between mother and son that Soma had wanted to kill Nianankoro from birth, possibly because he sees his son as a potential challenge to his spiritual and sociopolitical authority. This revelation is, in a sense, a coded way of illuminating the discourses of power and potential transformation that have marked the African precolonial, colonial, and postcolonial worlds. Recall those two servants who carried Soma's pestle of destruction, servants depicted as impotents incapable of doing anything except carrying out orders without question. This passivity is indeed disturbing, considering that the young men are of the same age as Nianankoro, at the prime of their youth, and they are expected to join the progressive forces of change that Nianankoro represents. Will they be transformed and continue from where Nianankoro left off since they are witnesses to the struggle? Or are they simply a new breed of henchmen destined to further entrench the philosophies of the Komo cult?

Because the Komo society is highly restrictive, and because the powers woven by the members are all-encompassing, as in other secret societies all over the world, it is prone to criticism and rejection. But considering that Cissé's background is in the Soninke, a clan of early Islamized marabouts (Hoffman 100), is it possible that the director is speaking on behalf of his own clan, which may be deprived of admission into this impregnable Bambara knowledge? Indeed, the nation of Mali is ninety percent Islamic, but Cissé's work, while focusing mainly on contemporary Muslim urban and rural societies, does not necessarily indicate that traditional systems should be discounted. While reflecting on what has plagued African sensibility for many years—namely endemic corruption and paralyzing underdevelopment—he also ponders the potentials of traditional culture. For example, he considers the practice of witchcraft, and of all the supernatural powers and scientific inquisitions it evokes, showing its inability to promote social advancement. Put another way, this implies that Cissé is advocating a new way of thinking beyond witchcraft's present scope, a refinement in which such powers are no longer misused but are transformed from destruction to invention, placed in parallel to the inspirations that have shaped Western scientific and technological prowess.

In terms of form, *Yeelen* is not exactly a film that fits well into the tradition of social realism, yet it reflects a synthesis of ideology and aesthetics that is reminiscent of early Soviet filmmaking. For instance, Dziga

Vertov's radical documentary practice was distinguished by artistic and innovative editing and camerawork. Similarly, *Yeelen* fuses formal innovations with the cultural conventions of African oral traditions to produce a distinctive narrative structure and rhythmic pattern. It is here that Cissé succeeds where many have failed. However, our concern is not to appraise the film as the "most beautiful film ever to have emerged out of Africa" (Adair 284), because it would be naïve to subscribe to that view, but rather to see it as a dynamic construction whose beautiful photography also demystifies conventional notions of beauty.

Yeelen's inventiveness is also notable in its subversion of a linear narrative structure, which had hitherto plagued numerous African films. For example, its favoring of short vignettes over lengthy narrative development, it could be argued, is instrumental to the film's coherence in spite of its complex structure. This structure emanates from the diverse mixture of cultures presented in each episode, which forces the viewer to acknowledge the complex relationship of precolonial structures to the present. For instance, the film's flashbacks draw attention to the interplay between past and present history and myth, and since the film is replete with so many allusions, it also illuminates the interrelationship between fact and fantasy. The film therefore bridges the distinction between the traditional African mode of address (precolonial past) and a technologically inspired mode of representation like cinema (neocolonial present). This dialectical connection between traditional and present-day art forms enables an affirmation of cultural continuity and change, of cultural existence and identity.

Though the majority of African films employ natural settings, in Cissé's *Yeelen*, nature becomes a focal point of the film. Most of the events take place in the bush, such as the initiations, or on the parched grounds of the Sahel; but they are neither romanticized nor reduced to exotic decor in the Hollywood fashion that denies Africans their culture. In *Yeelen*, nature's gifts are accorded universal significance; for example, ancestral soil, water, and trees are assigned symbolic values. In the scene in which Nianankoro and Attou are seen bathing, water symbolizes purity and fecundity, and the respect attached to the shooting of this sequence clearly indicates the African notion of the human body as a sacred entity. The scene's nudity is presented in a wholesome, nonsensational way. Colors are also significant, as in the black pigmentation of Attou, Nianankoro, and the close-up shot of Nianankoro's mother as her fingers mix the water in the bowl before she uses it to purify her son. Consider also the shot of the stream of water and blue sky, together with the shadows cast by the sunlight; these are captured in their purest naturalism. This attention to visual simplicity and the profundity of nature is also apparent in the close-up shots of the cliff leading to the stream as Cissé's camera pans slowly, highlighting its natural beauty.

Cissés interest in the natural world extends to the significance of the cosmological origins presented in the film. During the 1980s, it could be argued that African films no longer had to repossess African space nor to decolonize minds; more important was the urge to investigate the complexities of illuminating—both in form and content, directly or indirectly—African affairs. The film begins with narration and accompanying cosmograms for the elements: "Heat makes fire and the two worlds (earth and sky) exist through light." In Bamana dialect, *yeelen* means "brightness," and cinematographically, the style of presentation compels the viewer to reflect on this cosmological and mythological point of the narration, to uncover the meaning of "light," which has several connotations in the film.

The characters in the film relate to the word "light" in various ways: brightness/light can suggest enlightenment, creation, wisdom, and knowledge, but also destruction, purity, and regeneration. For Djigui Diarra, Soma's twin brother, exposure to "brightness" from trying to acquire Komo power too fast made him lose his sight. Brightness for Soma may be seen in the magic he wields throughout and in the rays that emanate from his magic post, which obliterate the very landscape when he encounters his son. For Nianankoro, brightness comes from his youthful exuberance, as pointed out by the hybrid simian albino creature in the trees, who tells him between laughs: "Your life will be radiant . . . your death will be luminous." This prophecy not only foreshadows the mystical encounter in which both father and son are armed with magical tools of annihilating brightness; it also defines Nianankoro's life and his death in terms of light. Light is not contrasted to darkness here, as it is in the Western tradition, but becomes an overarching symbol of power and knowledge, through which the dualities of the film are resolved: tradition and youth, the natural and the mystical, earth and sky, even life and death.

Thus, in *Yeelen*, the characters must go through a series of encounters as part of an initiation process that will enable them to acquire light—

power and knowledge. In the end, both father and son perish. For Nianankoro to attain the level of maturity necessary to confront his father's prowess means an acquisition of occult powers. He must recover a scepter—the wing of the Kore, a long piece of carved wood shaped like a wing that symbolizes knowledge and power—the only thing capable of destroying the Komo. He has already been given parts of the missing wing from his mother, and she reveals to him that the remaining part of the Kore is in the possession of his father's identical twin brother, Djigui, who fled the Bambara land. As already noted, Djigui himself lost his sight trying to acquire the Komo secrets. Through this series of encounters, the whole process of acquiring mystical knowledge is presented as double-edged: the getting of wisdom is linked to destruction. Meanwhile, on the other side of the conflict, members of the Komo cult meet secretly and decide what kind of punishment to inflict on Nianankoro. He must be stopped before he acquires the power to destroy them. It is not surprising then that his father, armed with the pestle of the Komo, embarks on the dreadful journey of tracking him down. When they finally meet, Cissé unleashes one of cinema's most dramatic moments. Nianankoro, armed with the wing of the Kore, and his father, with the pestle of Komo, stand gazing at each other. To highlight this confrontation Cissé employs a powerful and unpretentious visual composition; the extreme close-ups of both men's faces compel us to engage with a wide range of moving emotions. Few words are exchanged. We see both men perspiring feverishly, and when the tears in Nianankoro's eyes begin to trickle down, both the wing and the pestle emit magical rays. The screen turns translucent, an indication that the competition is over. Both men are destroyed, and the earth is scorched.

In staging the battle of father versus son, *Yeelen* positions viewers in sympathy with Nianankoro against the tyrannical power of his father and the Komo cult. In doing so, it also presents a political critique of the concentration of power in the hands of a small, tradition-bound, patriarchal group. Yet, the film does not dismiss the cultural significance of the Komo, nor of traditional cultural knowledge more generally. Indeed, the film pays respect to the knowledge and power of the Komo, in much the same way that Nianankoro gives respect to his father, even as he stands against him. Essentially, then, film does not criticize the power of traditional culture and cultural knowledge, only the restriction of that power and knowledge, and its hardening into an inflexible, inaccessible system. In a sense, "brightness" is a metaphor for Cissé's attempt to open the door on the secrecy associated with traditional cultural knowledge, to bring it to light.

Along these lines, the film's use of myth and tradition also suggests the importance of allowing culture and cultural identity to take shape freely, to keep evolving, or, in Stuart Hall's words, to remain a process of "becoming" as well as "being" (225). Here, Amie Williams's observation that *Yeelen* and other African films "dip into the ancient past not to escape the present or lapse into nostalgia but to extract knowledge and history relevant to the present condition of its viewers as dispersed postcolonial subjects" (93) echoes Cissé's desire to transform spectator intractability (African or Western) into openness, a transformation involving active processes of looking, interpreting, and discovering.

This transformation is also associated with the ability of light to bring openness and regeneration, as suggested in the last shots of the film. In the last scene, Nianankoro's son is seen walking over the open terrain of a large sand dune in a beautifully lit desert. He uncovers two egglike orbs, gives one to his mother, Attou, who, in turn, gives him Nianankoro's *grand boubou* (robe), symbolizing the passing down of Nianankoro's cultural heritage. The position of Nianankoro's son not only exemplifies hope for Africa, but also ratifies, once again, what many Africans have wished for in the postcolonial era: the eradication of all forms of dictatorship and the sweeping away of all tyrants and corruption, thus making way for a new generation to emerge. This dramatic ending—reminiscent of many African films, à la Sembene—leaves the future open and shining brightly, even as it retains its connection to the past.

Conclusion

Cissé tells his legendary tale without resorting to reductionist conventions. His well-known attention to detail is not simply exploitive, illustrative, or didactic. Cissé is meticulous in, for example, his use of *mise-en-scène,* relying on carefully chosen locations that represent the natural and cultural landscape that the film traverses, but never indulging in the exotic or oversimplified stereotypes that dominate depictions of Africa in Western-style films. Cissé has argued that his work is based on a philosophy in which the "mastery of content" forces one "to select forms that are appropriate" (Cissé). In keeping with this philosophy, he makes extensive use of composition in depth, camera movement, and sound to portray the characters and narrative action of *Yeelen* as taking place within appropriate cultural and natural surroundings. Although Western observers sometimes tend to see African films as straightforward or simple in both content and style, *Yeelen* is a richly complex film at both levels.

Cissé has argued that "knowledge is built and consolidated by one generation [precolonial], it is destroyed by another [colonialism], and recreated by a new generation [indigenous practices]" (Cissé). If *Yeelen's* narrative serves to exemplify this kind cultural transformation, it can also be said that Cissé performs a similar transformation in his filmmaking practice. Drawing on traditional, indigenous materials, cultural conventions, and codes, he attempts to integrate past and present, mythic and natural, content and style. Writing in light, Cissé transforms these supposedly entrenched oppositions into a dynamic new cultural perspective, an open space for the future.

Credits

Mali, 1987, Les Films Cissé

Director, Producer, and Screenplay: Souleymane Cissé
Cinematography: Jean-Noël Ferragut and Jean-Michel Humeau
Editing: André Davanture
Music: Salif Keita and Michel Portal
Art Direction and Costume Design: Kossa Mody Keita
Special Effects: Frederic Duru

CAST:

Nianankoro	Issiaka Kane
Attou	Aoua Sangare
Soma Diarra and Djigui Diarra	Niamanto Sanogo
Rouma Boll, king of the Fulani/Peul	Balla Moussa Keita
Mah, the mother	Soumba Traore
Uncle Bofing	Ismaila Sarr

Bibliography

Adair, Gilbert. "The Artificial Eye (*Yeelen*)." *Sight and Sound* 57.4 (1988): 284–85.
Appiah, Kwame Anthony. "Is the Post- in Postmodernism the Post- in Postcolo-

nial?" *Critical Inquiry* 17.2 (1991): 336–57.

Armes, Roy. "Black African Cinema in the Eighties." *Screen* 26.3–4 (1985): 60–73.

———. *Third World Film Making and the West.* Berkeley: U of California P, 1987.

Bakari, Imruh, and Mbye B. Cham, eds. *African Experiences of Cinema.* London: BFI, 1996.

Cissé, Souleymane. "Souleymane Cissé's *Light on Africa.*" Interview. *Black Film Review* 4.4 (1988): 12.

Diawara, Manthia. *African Cinema, Politics and Culture.* Bloomington: Indiana UP, 1992.

Gabriel, Teshome H. *Third Cinema in the Third World: The Aesthetics of Liberation.* Ann Arbor: UMI Research, 1982.

Goldfarb, Brian. "A Pedagogical Cinema: Development Theory, Colonialism and Post-Liberation African Film." Ukadike, *New Discourses* 7–24.

Hall, Stuart. "Cultural Identity and Diaspora." *Identity: Community, Culture, Performance.* Ed. J. Rutherford. London: Lawrence and Wishart, 1990. 225.

Hampaté Bâ, Amadou. "Le dit du cinéma Africain." *Films ethnographiques sur l'Afrique noire.* Paris: UNESCO, 1967.

Hoffman, Rachel. "*Yeelen.*" *African Arts* 22.2 (1989): 100–101.

Martin, Michael T., ed. *Cinemas of the Black Diaspora.* Detroit: Wayne State UP, 1995.

Mazrui, Ali A. *The Africans: A Triple Heritage.* Toronto: Little, 1986.

Mbiti, John. *African Religions and Philosophy.* New York: Doubleday, 1970.

Mudimbe, V. Y. *The Invention of Africa: Gnosis, Philosophy, and the Order of Knowledge.* Bloomington: Indiana UP, 1988.

Ngugi wa Thiong'o. *Decolonising the Mind: The Politics of Language in African Literature.* London: James Currey/Heinemann, 1986.

Pfaff, Françoise. *Twenty-five Black African Filmmakers: A Critical Study of Filmography and Bio-bibliography.* New York: Greenwood, 1986.

Petty, Sheila. "Cities, Subjects, Sites: Sub-Saharan Cinema and the Reorganization of Knowledge." *Afterimage* Summer 1991: 10+.

Said, Edward W. *Culture and Imperialism.* New York: Vintage, 1993.

Stam, Robert, and Ella Shohat. *Unthinking Eurocentrism: Multiculturalism and the Media.* New York: Routledge, 1994.

Taylor, Clyde. "Africa, the Last Cinema." *Journey across Three Continents.* Ed. Renee Tajima. New York: Third World Newsreel, 1985. 50–58.

Tomaselli, Keyan. *The Cinema of Apartheid.* Chicago: Smyrna, 1988.

Ukadike, N. Frank. *Black African Cinema.* Berkeley: U of California P, 1994.

———, ed. *New Discourses of African Cinema.* Special issue of *Iris: A Journal of Theory on Image and Sound* 18 (1995).

———. *Questioning African Cinema: Conversations with Filmmakers.* Minneapolis: U of Minnesota P, 2002.

Willemen, Paul. *Looks and Frictions: Essays in Cultural Studies and Film Theory.* London: BFI, 1994.

Williams, Amie. Rev. of *Zan Boko* by Gaston Kabore. *African Arts* 23.2 (1990): 91–93.

Do the Right Thing (1989)

SHARON WILLIS

A Theater of Interruptions

Context

Authenticity and Audience

Upon its release in 1989, *Do the Right Thing* provoked intense debate among mainstream popular reviewers. In this popular context, the film's "message" became a site of struggle as numerous magazines set up the debate in terms like those of *U.S. News and World Report*: "Doing the Controversial Thing: A Provocative Discussion of Race Relations in the 1980s or a Racist Incitement to Riot?" (Sanoff 38). Sensationalizing the subject of race, this either/or structure also implicitly characterized African American resistance as itself racist in origin. This symmetrical structure also conflated violence against persons and violence against property, on one level, and conflated the cinematic staging of fantasy and the advocacy of violence in daily life, on another.

Those critiques that insistently focused on the burning of Sal's pizzeria also consistently related representation—which in this case these critics figured as targeting an African American audience—to reality by imagining that stable identifications shape spectator responses to both images and fantasy. To imagine that spectator identification originates in recognizable resemblances and slides into imitation, as these critics might argue, requires an impoverished theory of fantasy's relationship to agency in the world. This version of fantasy's function disallows the ways in which our access to the fantasies cinema stages is multiple, mobile, and intermittent. It ignores the ways that we invest our fantasmatic identifications in spaces, in scenes, in gestures and movements, and in the technical apparatus of cinema itself—as well as in characters and stories.

In exemplary fashion, *Newsweek* staged the *Do the Right Thing* debate under this heading "'How Hot Is Too Hot?': Spike Lee has always provoked discord—but not like this. Is his new movie irresponsible or

777

vitally important? *Newsweek*'s critics disagree" (Kroll). Representing the negative position, Jack Kroll asserted: "People are going to argue about this film for a long time. That's fine, as long as things stay on the arguing level. But this movie is dynamite under every seat. Sadly, the fuse has been lit by a filmmaker tripped up by muddled motives." Kroll locates the source of this muddle in an ambivalence that leads Lee "to substitute pizza politics for the hard realities of urban racial conflict," in an "evasion of the issues." And Kroll finds that ambivalence further reflected in the famous juxtaposed quotations about violence—one from Malcolm X and one from Martin Luther King—that conclude the film. Paradoxically enough, he has to advance his own position in a framework that is itself ambivalent, as his article faces off with a positive assessment of the film.

As in Kroll's account, *Do the Right Thing* often appeared as an organic extension of the director's person, in the language of much popular critique. Richard Corliss, for instance, offers this bizarre comment: "He holds the film like a can of beer in a paper bag—the cool sip of salvation on a blistering day—until it is revealed as a Molotov cocktail." Interweaving an anxiety about the film's effects in the real with a fantasy about Lee himself, this quote reminds us that one of the stunning aspects of the "Spike Lee phenomenon" in dominant popular discourse is its compulsive focus on the director as a public figure, and its utter neglect of his screen persona.

If mainstream popular culture sought to acclaim or reject *Do the Right Thing* in terms of the correctness of its "argument," the roots of this impulse lay in a more widespread collapsing of cinematic "real effects" with social reality, and in the corollary impulse of constructing Lee as its privileged interlocutor, speaking for a whole African American population. But in this question of the "real effect," popular journalism begins, surprisingly enough, at times to agree with African American critical reception. Wahneema Lubiano describes a pressure within African American reception that at times constructs a "realist" film as continuous with referential reality and, concomitantly, constructs its producer as a delegate for a community (176). This is the "burden of representation" that Kobena Mercer describes as the "predicament" whereby "the artistic discourse of hitherto marginalized subjects is circumscribed by the assumption that such artists speak as 'representatives' of the communities from which they come" (214).

Under this burden of representation, the black cultural producer becomes something like an anthropological native informant, charged with providing an enthographic, documentary account of his community.

Realism, Lubiano writes, "suggests disclosure of the truth (and then closure of the representation)" (182). These lines suggest the very paradigms of reception, she goes on to argue, that operate within the dominant representational regime to confine African American film production to an arena of competing claims for realist authority, which is construed as access to sociological "truth." Such paradigms of course foreclose consideration of reality as constructed through representations that are produced within a historical context constituted by competing political interests. But they also shape the concerns of debates that are organized around "positive" and "negative" images, taken as appropriate or inappropriate models for an audience imagined to consume through imitation.

"The question of representation and what anyone should say about his/her community," Lubiano writes, "is a constant pressure under which African American cultural workers produce." "But it is a question," she further contends, "that constantly disenfranchises even as it reinforces the notion of absolutes." That is, for those critics and commentators who evaluate representations through a strict opposition of good and bad, "then 'good' or 'real' cultural production is impervious to reader or audience misbehavior (misreading)," while "'bad' or 'nonrepresentative' or 'unrealistic' cultural production" reinforces racism or "misleads African-Americans" (185).

In various contemporary debates, the failure to see cinematic realist effects as, precisely, representational strategies, elides the tensions within "black representation." Flattening this tension by conflating realism with "reality," or truth, forecloses the complexities of audience response: the critical and analytical side of people's responses to everyday entertainment. As Sasha Torres puts it in her persuasive critique of arguments that base their authority on an identification of stereotypes, such readings leave little room for the complex and "unpredictable effects" of "complex, and often resistant, spectatorship," just as they tend to "flatten textual objects" and to overlook specific *textual* detail (2). Failure to acknowledge these tensions reduces the cinematic text to an argument that does not allow us room to think through any relationship to fantasy structures, or to acknowledge the ways that hegemonic representation may be challenged at the level of other cinematic strategies, such as antirealism.

Analysis

Antirealism

Like a number of "classic" directors, from Alfred Hitchcock to Jean-Luc Godard to Roman Polanski, Spike Lee frequently casts himself in his films as an ambivalent or treacherous character. Think of Lee's characters in the films whose production bookends that of *Do the Right Thing*. Half-Pint, the socially desperate misfit in *School Daze* (1988) resides at the center of the debates the film wishes to showcase: he waffles between adherence to the "jigaboo" and "wannabe" factions of fraternity culture, while conducting ongoing debates with more politically conscious classmates. Lee also plays Giant, the manipulative manager of Bleek Gilliam in *Mo' Better Blues* (1990), who maintains a gambling addiction that leads him to deceive his friend, eventually drawing him into a physical conflict, the aftereffects of which end his career as a trumpeter. Finally, in *Jungle Fever* (1991), Lee's character, Cyrus, betrays his best friend's affair to his wife. In each case, Lee portrays a shady character toward whom the film is implicitly critical. But equally important, the presence of the "real" director operates as an extradiegetic interruption within the narrative texture.

As a textual figure, Lee circulates his own image through his films as he does the images of many of his regular actors, whose roles from film to film vary dramatically. Such an effect interrupts any easy correlation between on-screen and offscreen realities. *Do the Right Thing* is replete with such extradiegetic effects, borne in and around the faces and bodies of its actors. The film maps and anchors its restricted arena of action, the single block of brownstones and stores in Bedford Stuyvesant, through two iconic figures: Mother Sister (Ruby Dee) and Da Mayor (Ossie Davis). Marked off from the rest of the characters by a generational difference as maternal and paternal poles, they also figure the opposition between mobility and stasis that structures the film, since Da Mayor restlessly roams up and down the street, while Mother Sister, by her own account, "always watches" from a perch in her open window or on her stoop. Significantly, these distinguished actors of both stage and screen call up a whole history of African

American characters and productions. At the same time, their long-term marriage immediately lends an ironic cast to their antagonism within the diegesis.

Likewise, by casting his real sister (Joie Lee) as his fictional one, Lee ruptures the fictional space from the beginning, setting it in dialogue with an outside space, a world beyond the screen. On another level, the four-minute opening credit sequence introduces Rosie Perez in an extradiegetic role. Organized much like a music video, this sequence features Perez's "flygirl" dance moves, and her boxing poses, over the sound track of Public Enemy's "Fight the Power." Established here as the film's "theme song," "Fight the Power" will recur as localized diegetic sound that blares obtrusively into the scene, and fades again, following the movements of Radio Raheem (Bill Nunn) and his boom box.

Meanwhile, like the song, Perez is imported into the narrative place. As the mother of Mookie's child, Hector, however, she is haunted by her initial construction as a maternal figure. She relentlessly scolds (hectors?) Mookie in stunning verbal performances of curse and insult that exceed and suspend dramatic action. Her discourse thus links her through association to the hysterical racist diatribes by men that emerge autonomously from the narrative in a later montage sequence of pure performativity. Troubling the stable and seamless fictional frame that realism requires, Lee's film consistently resists the demand to provide a documentary "window" onto African American culture.

Fundamental to *Do the Right Thing*'s antirealist project is its plainly "classical" structure, based on the prescribed rules of classical Greek drama. It adheres strictly to the unities of time and place: set in a single-block location and transpiring within a twenty-four-hour period, the film circles thematically back to the image that introduces Mookie, counting his money on awakening. We can surely see the "Corner Men," Coconut Sid (Frankie Faison), ML (Paul Benjamin), and Sweet Dick Willy (Robin Harris) as an ironic gesture toward the chorus of classical Greek tragedy, as their running patter comments on unfolding events, while they remain strictly apart from the action until the climactic riot scene. Some of the film's funniest riffs come from the Corner Men, theatrically displayed against a solid wall of bright red and framed under umbrellas. Situated outside the zone of the film's action, the stationary Corner Men regularly interrupt the plot with verbal performance. (Not insignificantly, in this regard, Robin Harris was primarily known as a stand-up comic.)

This film could not be more self-conscious about the ways it sets performance against narrative. In an early incident, the band of four friends who move about *en bloc* stop to berate Da Mayor for his drunkenness. When he responds by giving them a speech about his failed paternity and their disrespect, Ahmad (Steve White) responds with a direct theatrical reference, "I hope you've finished your little soliloquy," thus commenting on the film's proliferation of soliloquies that interrupt dramatic action and verbal exchange. Punctuating the action, the Corner Men call attention to the film's violation of conventional Hollywood plotting. Instead of building action and suspense, this film offers vignettes, a series of mostly verbal confrontations of seemingly equal weight, always unresolved, trailing off as the characters wander away, apparently losing interest or becoming distracted. We will see later in the essay how the camera frequently mimics their behavior, picking up and dropping characters with a kind of free-floating distracted attentiveness, like Da Mayor's and Mother Sister's.

Throughout the film, we find moments of distraction, where layers of message collide or interfere. To take just one example, when Mookie has dragged Jade out of Sal's pizzeria because he interprets Sal's attentions to her as overtly sexual, we see the siblings against a bright red wall under the painted message: "Tawana Told the Truth." This reference to what were then recent news events (the disputed and subsequently retracted charges by African American teenager Tawana Brawley that she had been raped by a group of white police officers) suggests a resistance to the generally accepted facts of the case, and disrupts the scene thoroughly to the extent that we simply don't know how to *read* this message. Is the film endorsing this position? Does it mean to suggest a connection between the Brawley case and Sal's attraction to Jade? Its ornery resistance to clear interpretation both interrupts our absorption in the sibling dispute and calls attention to the interpretive effort this film foregrounds for both the spectator and the characters, who themselves are trying to work through some of these questions. Significantly, the substance of the dispute itself takes a detour: as Mookie insists that Jade stop coming to the pizzeria because of Sal's intentions, she retaliates: "Stop trying to play big brother. I'm a grown woman. You gotta lotta nerve. Mookie, you can hardly pay your rent and you're gonna tell me what to do. Come off it." Though Mookie insists, "One has nuthin' to do with the other," the discussion turns definitively to his meager earning history.

This veering off is completely coherent within the film's overarching cinematic strategies: the camera consistently picks up characters and incidents, leaving them in the middle of things to investigate another conversation or event, which it will drop in order to return to a previous one. The event that serves as a catalyst for Jade and Mookie's argument begins just after the film's temporal midpoint, with Sal's flirtatious conversation with Jade in the pizzeria. As Sal (Danny Aiello) speaks, the camera migrates to examine Mookie's and Pino's (John Turturro) reactions, captured in medium close-up as it slowly pans back and forth between their hostile looks at Sal and Jade. But before developing Mookie's reaction, the film leaves the pizzeria to pick up Radio Raheem, just as his music begins to distort and fade. We follow him to the Fruit-N-Veg Delight, the Korean-owned grocery store, where he rudely enters into a transaction for twenty "D" Energizer batteries. As he argues with the store's owners (Steve Park and Ginny Yang), insulting their English, we see him from their point of view. Through the distorting effects of a fish-eye lens in medium close-up, the film suggests the couple's subjective view of Raheem as menacing. Significantly, this scene recalls the film's one other use of the fish-eye effect: in Sal's first confrontation with Raheem about his music.

As in most of its scenes of dispute and hostility, beginning with Da Mayor and Mother Sister's first encounter, the film structures this sequence through canted frames, in which the characters emerge on opposing diagonals: Raheem's frame is canted to the right, the couple's to the left. Thus the film seems intent on visually inscribing hostility or opposition, but it also suggests in the same gesture that verbal violence incites a distorting subjectification of view. Like so many of the film's confrontations, this one ends with Raheem relenting, for no particular reason, after the store owner reciprocates with the insult "Motherfucker you!" Raheem concludes: "Motherfucker you. You're alright."

As Raheem exits the store, the film picks up Da Mayor arriving to purchase flowers. We see his arrival from a point of view inside the pizzeria, one that captures Sal's silhouette as it looks through the window. After following Da Mayor to Mother Sister's stoop, where he presents the flowers, the film detours away to pick up Radio Raheem again and follow him to the Corner Men, who register their annoyance and launch into another exchange of playful insults, beginning with ML remarking, "At least my moms didn't name me Sweet Dick Willie." Sweet Dick Willie picks up on the mother reference and purports to take this as an insult to his mother. The exchange culminates in ML's pronouncing, "Negroes kill me, always holdin' onto, talkin' about their dicks." This remark leads to a back-and-forth discussion about having sex in the heat. The whole scene recalls Richard Pryor's famous comedy routines from the 1970s and 1980s, which frequently deployed racist stereotypes about black sexuality.

An ice cart moving into frame introduces the next sequence. This cart draws the little boy, Eddie (Richard Habersham), into traffic, and forces Da Mayor to knock him to safety at the curb. This, in turn, prompts Eddie's mother to launch into a scathing reprimand, first of Da Mayor and, subsequently, of her injured son. Erupting in a performance of harsh maternal disciplinarity, consonant with the feminine role in this film of judging and managing men, this mother provides a thematic match with Mookie's failed attempt to manage Jade's sexuality, to which the film returns now after some seven minutes of wandering through various vignettes.

This exemplary series of intercut episodes produces a variety of encounters among the neighborhood "types." These are hardly characters, but rather figures, who mark out areas of friction and tension in the public spaces: gender dynamics, struggles around property rights and consumerism, and competing masculine postures. Here, as throughout the film, all the women seem to speak with one voice, and to function primarily as spectators watching the diverse male figures. While mobility is reserved for men, women are confined in place. Though Tina has a job, we never see her leave her apartment. Prior to the riot scene, we see Jade emerging from her apartment only in Mookie's company. Mother Sister remains perched at home, surveying those who pass by, and consistently berating and excoriating Da Mayor.

Likewise, Tina and Jade continually criticize Mookie. Jade consistently pressures him about his earning power and responsibilities, while Tina berates him with the coarsest possible attacks on his masculinity. *Do the Right Thing* charges its women—figured as mothers and sisters—with judging and disciplining masculinity. They are seen mostly castigating—and occasionally rewarding—men for conduct that lives up to the proper masculine role: as wage earners and fathers.

In their judgmental function, the women are aligned in this one respect with the police and the Corner Men; while in their mobile patrol of the borders of the community, the police serve not only as law enforcers, but as judges. In a striking scene built of sustained shot/reverse shots, the film tracks a prolonged and mutually suspicious exchange of looks between the police and the Corner Men. As Officer Ponte (Miguel Sandoval) comments, "What a waste!" one of the Corner Men reads his lips. (We might note that Lee repeats this moment, with the same actors playing the police, in *Jungle Fever*, when the officers make this comment in regard to the interracial couple.) In a strange ricochet effect, the Corner Men turn their attention from the police to the steady business at the Korean grocery store. Coconut Sid begins, "As I was saying before we were so rudely interrupted by the finest . . . ," while ML blurts out, "It's a fucking shame." We see that he means to direct their attention to the store. Though the remark might be directed toward the role and conduct of the interrupting police, it also functions to cast the Corner Men as hostile judges of the Korean entrepreneurs, and it leads to a brutal self-critique about the failure of black enterprise.

Interruption and Alienation

Lee's antirealist project in *Do the Right Thing* brings it closely in line with the theatrical practices of Bertolt Brecht. Walter Benjamin describes Brecht's "epic theater" as a theater that relies centrally on "alienation" effects, eschewing "empathy" in favor of "astonishment" and focusing on situation rather than plot. The two procedures are interdependent. "Instead of identifying with the characters," Benjamin writes, "the audience should be educated to be astonished at the circumstances under which they function" ("What Is Epic Theater?" 150). Epic theater "obtains such conditions . . . by interrupting the plot" (*Reflections* 234). Appropriately enough to the context of film, the "principle of interruption" that Benjamin sees as epic theater's organizing function finds its analogue in montage, where "the superimposed element disrupts the context in which it is inserted" (*Reflections* 234). Taken in the broadest sense, montage refers not only to editing, but to the complex articulations of shots and sequences spliced together. In its assertive preference for interruption and vignette, parallel plotting and editing, Lee's montage is aggressive. But the film is similarly obtrusive in its camera work and framing, as these help to concatenate scenes that attract and *dis*tract our interpretive gaze. Committed to studying social boundaries and their policing as manifestations of institutionalized racism's mark on public space, this film inscribes these concerns within its visual texture: in the cinematic articulation of space, in its cuttings and framings.

While its technical means intervene to interrupt and mediate any direct identification with the characters, *Do the Right Thing*'s camera nonetheless resembles some of its characters—it behaves like them. It is highly mobile, and given to assertive advancing and retreating. The film's opening sequence introduces its principals through an equalizing montage in which the camera obtrudes into private spaces—zooming in and zooming out. As the establishing shot pans across the city block, after a cut, the camera zeroes in on the body behind the voice of the DJ Mister Señor Love Daddy (Samuel L. Jackson), hovering in extreme close-up on his mouth. Only as it pulls back to reveal his whole face does the camera pick up the glint of light reflecting on the glass of his broadcasting booth, the screen that partitions him off from the world of the street that he surveys, as he offers the first of his many "public service" announcements: "Jheri Curl alert." When it comes to Smiley (Roger Guenver Smith), apparently the film's most unbalanced character, the camera captures him in a striking low-angle shot. In its frequent advance and retreat, the camera appears to be sneaking into apartments whose inhabitants are just arising. In Mookie's apartment, we note, the use of the handheld camera suggests amplified and invasive intimacy, as the slight movement that troubles the image signals an invisible body entering the character's space.

In this opening sequence, *Do the Right Thing* establishes the zooming-in and zooming-out structure that marks a strikingly stylized performance sequence that emerges about one-third of the way into the film. Mookie has indirectly entered the debate about Sal's "Wall of Fame," which seems to exclude African Americans from representation as it remains entirely dedicated to Italian American celebrities and sports figures. He questions Pino about his favorite athlete, actor, and rock star: Magic Johnson, Eddie Murphy, and Prince. Against the background of a cheesy wall mural figuring a Roman ruin, Mookie points to the apparent contradiction between Pino's racist pronouncements and the blackness of his favorite performers. Pino contends, "It's different. Magic, Eddie, and Prince are not niggers, I mean are not black. I mean they're black, but not really black. They're more than black." Mookie suggests that Pino's racism is related to a kind of "color envy": "Deep down inside, I think you wish you were black. . . . Your hair is kinkier than mine." Pino erupts in an aggressive rant that mocks African American public figures like Al Sharpton ("Mr. Doo, Sharp Tone"), Jesse Jackson ("Keep hope alive"), and Louis Farrakhan ("Farraman?"). The dispute ends with a ridiculous reciprocity, as Mookie responds, "Fuck you, and fuck Frank Sinatra." To which Pino replies, "Fuck Michael Jackson."

This exchange gives way to a cut that opens a sequence marked by the actors' stationary postures, as in stand-up routines, while the camera zooms in and out dramatically to begin and end each speech. Presenting five performances composed entirely of epithets and stereotypes, the sequence shows Mookie slurring Italians, Pino attacking blacks, Latino Stevie (Luis Ramos) slandering Koreans, Officer Long (Rick Aiello) insulting Latinos, and the Korean grocery owner slurring Jews. As the camera zooms in and out on each, to dizzying effect, it also suggests a kind of equivalency and a random circulation of epithets—as if these insults were free-floating slogans to be taken up by anyone toward anyone in a moment of aggression. Significantly, this sequence is *interrupted*—"Time out!"—by the voice of Mister Señor Love Daddy, whose name sounds like a pileup of honorifics, or positive epithets. When Love Daddy comes into view, he is propelled toward the camera on a rolling chair, which produces the effect of a reverse zoom, as the character rushes in on the camera. This sequence of stand-up performances that do not communicate with each other clearly anticipates the incommunicative language that marks the confrontation between Radio Raheem and Sal, which begins in an explosion of racist epithets. That later moment imports the nonnarrative, racist performance directly into the plot, and may remind us of the strategies epic theater employs to enforce the spectator's critical distance from the staged events.

Icons, Slogans, Static

This centrally pivotal sequence abruptly gives way, through a cut, to a reestablished order in the pizzeria. We hear Mookie trying to coerce Sal into paying him before closing time. Money seems to be Mookie's mantra. He talks about getting paid all the time; in our final image of him, he is collecting crumpled hundred dollar bills from the debris-strewn sidewalk. As Mookie sets out on a delivery, we see a little girl and her cheerful sidewalk chalk drawing from directly above, and then we rejoin him as Radio Raheem comes into view. This key scene is shot with a handheld camera, coding it for intimacy by suggesting the felt presence of the body behind the camera, a body that brings us into close proximity with the menacing Radio Raheem. It opens with Mookie noticing Raheem's brass knuckles, shaped (in another inter-textual reference, here to Robert Mitchum's menacing preacher in *The Night of the Hunter* [Charles Laughton, 1955]) to spell out "LOVE" on one hand, and "HATE" on the other. As Mookie disappears out of the lower right corner of the frame, Raheem begins to tell "the story of love and hate," boxing in front of the camera, his fists thrusting to-ward it and withdrawing. In this image, it is as if Raheem were giving with one hand and taking away with the other. Raheem's performance may remind us of Pino's ambivalent love-hate relationship to blacks. "The story of life is this . . . ," he asserts, "Static! One hand is always fighting the other." But he ends enigmatically, "Brother Mookie, if I love you, I love you, but if I hate you . . ." In this unfinished and in-conclusive utterance, failing to generate any clear or stable meaning, we hear an echo of the film's own conclusion, seeming to weigh the words of Martin Luther King Jr. against those of Malcolm X but with-out ever deciding between them.

Do the Right Thing's characters regularly move forward and back, toward and away from the camera, as with an adversary. But the film complements these movements with the restless lateral mobility it grants most of its male characters, whose comings and goings map the public space. Primary among these is, of course, Mookie, whose pur-poseful progress on his deliveries the camera tracks, and whose con-tinual interruption by bystanders brings other characters into view and allows them to barrage him with free-floating slogans: "Stay black," for instance, or "Always do the right thing." Buggin' Out (Gi-ancarlo Esposito) is, like Mookie, driven by purposeful mobility as he campaigns to mount a boycott of Sal's because the "Wall of Fame" fails to represent blacks.

In a key scene, a white man interrupts Buggin' Out's progress by carelessly stepping on his brand-new—white—Jordans. Buggin' Out pursues Clifton (John Savage), who sports a green Boston Celtics T-shirt bearing Larry Bird's name and number. As the two argue about rights and privilege in public space, Clifton recurs to property rights. "I own this brownstone," he argues, while Buggin' Out contends that he does not belong in the neighborhood. When Clifton refers to his "freedom" to live where he wants, in a stunningly ironic reminder of both the contemporary gentrification and the historic segregation and redlining of neighborhoods—Buggin' Out reads off his shirt and tells him to go back to Massachusetts. As irony proliferates here, a serious conflict involving public space and private property is reduced to a war of slogans: Michael Jordan or Larry Bird, fetishized shoes as opposed to a brownstone. Here Buggin' Out looks as superficial and misguided as Clifton. *Do the Right Thing*'s shifting and multiple critical angles leave no one standing; no one is above reproach.

Clifton's shirt, like Buggin' Out's shoes, fits seamlessly into the film's continual circulation of icons relating to sports, celebrity, and commodity—brand names. Our characters inhabit a world awash in slogans whose messages are uncertain, names and images whose meaning is unstable, and recorded sound that functions as an anthem or trademark. Think of the brilliantly staged standoff between Stevie, with his stationary boom box blasting Latin music, and Radio Raheem, who interrupts Stevie by invading this space with his blaring anthem, "Fight the Power." Here the comparative electronic volume capacity seems to stand in for masculine force, and thus the scene mocks male posturing. Music constitutes a bid for dominance, an invasion, a form of violent interruption, as the film's tragic climax will bear out. But it also highlights the discursive, as well as the social and economic, impotence of the characters.

In this proliferation of icons we find another reiteration of the film's opposition between movement and stasis, perhaps this time best understood as inscribed in real property versus identity. To Sal's "Wall of Fame" the film juxtaposes Smiley's nomadic advertising of his postcard image of Malcolm X and Martin Luther King Jr. as a commodity for sale. Everywhere presenting this image, Smiley interrupts as often as he is interrupted. He blocks Mookie's progress several times, and he interrupts Sal and Pino's intimate conversation about the pizzeria and the family, about their competing loyalties.

Smiley's postcard image is thickly iconic. First of all, this well-known and widely reproduced photo represents the only meeting of these two leaders (Torres 127). It memorializes an encounter as a relationship, and thus it represents fantasy as much as, if not more than, reality. Since Smiley inscribes the image with his own abstract symbols—a crown for King and an X for Malcolm X—he overlays it with icons in the strictest meaning of the term. Finally, this image circulates throughout the film, ending up as the single picture on the burned and "blackened" "Wall of Fame," and it returns to close the film, following on the citations from the two leaders that Lee juxtaposes there without comment. If we consider the film's conclusion as Brechtian in its inconclusiveness, we must nonetheless also understand that, in its frozen stillness, and depicting an amity that never existed between the two men and the positions they represented, the image functions as a fetish, freezing history and presenting a forced symmetry.

Like slogans, of course, racial and ethnic epithets ricochet throughout the film, and at times they seem only tenuously anchored in conscious agency. The ready availability of epithets and people's susceptibility to resort to them in moments of violence are centrally thematized in the film's climactic sequence in Sal's. By resorting to violence and smashing Raheem's boom box, Sal precipitates Raheem's murder at the hands of the police, an act that in turn sparks a riot. This sequence presents violence as escalating organically from Sal's entirely uncharacteristic recourse to a racial slur. To judge by the shooting script, this scene was clearly improvised. And, for Lee, this improvisational scene seems to be a moment of authenticity.

In an interview with Barbara Grizzutti Harrison, Lee gave this account of shooting the film's final showdown: "We wanted Danny [Aiello] to say the word 'nigger' and he would not say it, and we all knew he had said the word many times. What finally got him to say it was when [the character named] Buggin' Out called him a fat guinea bastard." "And something snapped in Danny," Lee continued, "and he just vomited all this 'black cocksucker nigger motherfucker.' He didn't want to be perceived as being racist or prejudiced, and that's why he had trouble saying the word." To conclude, Lee asserted, "We all knew he had said those words many times. Once he was hit with 'fat guinea bastard,' the floodgates started opening. You have all said the word many times" (135).

When Lee credits this sequence with exposing a special psychic "truth," he seems to share a common conviction that no matter how we may repress them, all of us find racial and ethnic stereotypes readily available in the form of epithets that erupt in moments of extreme stress. This is another way of saying that we all maintain an arsenal of hate speech in the reservoir of the unconscious, which functions like a psychic septic tank. But to treat such discourse as somehow truest and most essential because it is most buried is to ignore the interaction of our psychic lives with the external social world, to ignore our tendencies to project the psychic onto the social, and to leave out of the account the truths that conscious discourse produces when it confronts unconscious effects.

As events unfold amid the assembled crowd, which has faced off across the street from Sal's, Mookie appears to be physically aligned with the three white men. Deliberately and dispassionately, Mookie breaks rank, crosses the street, and returns to hurl a trash can through the pizzeria's window, igniting the riot that culminates in the crowd's vandalizing and torching the restaurant. At this point, and even at the film's inconclusive conclusion, Mookie remains silent about this gesture. And, like him, the film leaves it inarticulate and unexplained. Significantly, while the crowd produces a cacophony in fragments of angry speech, the voice we hear most clearly in the riot is Mother Sister's, first ordering "Burn it down!" and later reduced to ragged cries. Contained within the female space of commentary and critique, she is ultimately reduced to the inarticulateness of a hysterical scream.

Conclusion

Concluding indecisively, the film circles back to where it began, as Mookie awakens to thoughts of money. Meeting Sal at the ruins of the pizzeria, he demands his weekly pay: $250. Sal crumples five one-hundred-dollar bills and bounces them one by one off Mookie's chest, so that they land in the debris below. Mookie stoops to collect them, throws back two of the bills, insisting that Sal keep the extra money, but leaving him short $50. As the balled up bills volley back and forth, so the conversation volleys: Mookie's main concern is his pay, while Sal's is for his "place," in the sense both of his life's work and of his belonging to the neighborhood. As the exchange meanders inarticulately, like so much static, the men end up on common ground: discussing the weather. If they appear to part amicably, Mookie waffles once again, stooping to snatch the remaining bills from the debris. Thus, the film freezes Mookie in the debased posture of self-interest, leaving the higher ground to Sal. What are we to make of this?

Out of the static and interference that has marked all verbal exchange in this film emerge first the written text citing King and Malcolm X and then the image that Smiley has circulated obsessively. No analysis mediates the juxtaposed citations about violence or their relation to the image. The film leaves us with competing and fragmentary "messages." Since it is organized by collisions among competing discourses, *Do the Right Thing* presents contradictions that are highly resistant to resolution as a clear assertion or statement—precisely the inadequate form required by a dominant discourse that seeks to restrict the film to an "argument" that fits within the binary framework mainstream culture provides for its ongoing story of contemporary race relations.

Credits

United States, 1989, 40 Acres and a Mule Filmworks

Director, Producer, and Screenplay: Spike Lee
Coproducer: Monty Ross
Cinematography: Ernest Dickerson
First Assistant Director: Randy Fletcher
Editing: Barry Alexander Brown
Music: Bill Lee
Sound: Skip Livesay
Costume Design: Ruthe Carter
Production Supervisor: Preston Holmes

CAST:

Sal	Danny Aiello
Da Mayor	Ossie Davis
Mother Sister	Ruby Dee
Vito	Richard Edson
Buggin' Out	Giancarlo Esposito
Mookie	Spike Lee
Radio Raheem	Bill Nunn
Pino	John Turturro
ML	Paul Benjamin
Coconut Sid	Frankie Faison
Sweet Dick Willie	Robin Harris
Jade	Joie Lee
Officer Ponte	Miguel Sandoval
Officer Long	Rick Aiello
Clifton	John Savage
Mister Señor Love Daddy	Samuel L. Jackson
Tina	Rosie Perez
Smiley	Roger Guenver Smith
Ahmad	Steve White
Cee	Martin Lawrence

Bibiliography

Benjamin, Walter. *Reflections: Essays, Aphorisms, Autobiographical Writings.* Ed. Peter Demetz. Trans. Harry Zohn. New York: Harcourt, 1978.

———. "What Is Epic Theater?" *Illuminations: Essays and Reflections.* Ed. Hannah Arendt. Trans. Harry Zohn. New York: Schocken, 1969. 147–54.

Corliss, Richard. "Hot Time in Bed-Stuy Tonight." *Time* 3 July 1989: 62.

Harrison, Barbara Grizzutti. "Spike Lee Hates Your Cracker Ass." Interview with Spike Lee. *Esquire* Oct. 1992: 132–39.

Kroll, Jack. "How Hot Is Too Hot?" *Newsweek* 3 July 1989: 64.

Lubiano, Wahneema. "But Compared to What? Reading Realism, Representation, and Essentialism in *School Daze, Do the Right Thing* and the Spike Lee Discourse." *Representing Black Men.* Ed. Marcellus Blount and George P. Cunningham. New York: Routledge, 1996. 173–204.

Mercer, Kobena. *Welcome to the Jungle: New Positions in Black Cultural Studies.* New York: Routledge, 1994.

Sanoff, Alvin. "Doing the Controversial Thing." *U.S. News and World Report* 10 July 1989: 38–39.

Torres, Sasha. *Black, White, and in Color: Television and Black Civil Rights.* Princeton: Princeton UP, 2003.

Close-up (1989)

HAMID NAFICY

Questioning Reality, Realism, and Neorealism

Context

Biographical Sketch and Stylistic Features

No Iranian filmmaker has received more critical and popular acclaim in the West than Abbas Kiarostami, whose picture appeared on the cover of the July–August 1995 issue of *Cahiers du cinéma* above a caption that simply declared, "Kiarostami le magnifique." Inside, nearly fifty pages were devoted to discussing his work. Kurosawa Akira said this about him: "The films of Abbas Kiarostami are extraordinary. Words cannot describe my feelings about them and I simply advise you to see his films. . . . When Satyajit Ray passed on, I was very depressed. But after seeing Kiarostami's films, I thanked God for giving us just the right person to take his place" (*Cinématheque Ontario* 23). The winner of many international awards, Kiarostami was born in 1940 in Tehran, where he received his BA in painting from the Fine Arts College of the University of Tehran in 1973. It took him thirteen years to complete this degree because he had to support himself by working in jobs that seem in retrospect to have had a decisive impact on his cinematic career and on his distinctive film style. Upon his admittance to college, he was employed by Tehran's Office of Highway Patrol and Traffic, where he supervised road repairs and construction at night while attending classes during the day. His concern with the road and with traveling as a cinematic trope and a philosophical topic, which mark many of his later films, dubbed by critics as "road movies," may have its origins in this early experience.[1]

---

[1]His "road movies" include *And Life Goes On* (*Zendegi va digar hich*, 1991), *Taste of Cherry* (Ta'm-e gilas, 1997), *The Wind Will Carry Us* (*Bad ma ra khahad bord*, 1999), and *Ten* (*Dah*, 2002).

In 1961, Kiarostami began working in advertising agencies, for which he designed book covers, book posters, film posters, and advertising films, including a stint at Tabli Film, an ad agency headed by Bijan Jazani, an anti-Shah Marxist who in the years to come would become the leader of the urban guerrilla movement Fadaiyan-e Khalq, for which he would be executed. Kiarostami's first fifty advertising films featured no women, a fact that surprised him when it was pointed out to him. Despite this realization, however, lack of female representation continued in all his subsequent short and feature films, until *Ten* (*Dah,* 2002), which features a female taxi driver in the lead. Overall, he made a total of 150 advertising films. Working in the format of brief, one-minute ads impacted his later film style. As he noted, in these films "you had to tell the introduction, the body, the message, and the theme and convince the viewers quickly, immediately, and concisely" (qtd. in Baharlu 17). From them he learned to appreciate temporal precision and economy of cinematic expression, which became hallmarks of his style.

The institutional conditions under which he made most of his films also had a profound impact on his career and cinema. Unlike most Iranian art-cinema directors, Kiarostami has made a majority of his films under the sponsorship of commercial advertising agencies and government organizations. In the late 1960s, he was hired to head the filmmaking division of the Center for the Intellectual Development of Children and Young Adults, a dynamic government-supported national cultural arts organization, under whose auspices he made the center's and his own first film, *Bread and Alley* (*Nan va Kucheh,* 1970), and all his subsequent short-subject and feature films until 1994. In line with the center's charter, a majority of his films there involved children as primary diegetic subjects, but they were not necessarily aimed at children.

For over two decades, both during the Shah's period, which ended with the 1978–79 revolution, and during the subsequent Islamic period, while employed by the center, Kiarostami was in essence a civil-servant filmmaker on the government's payroll, an arrangement that most New Wave filmmakers (before the revolution) and art-cinema directors (after the revolution) shunned for fear of being coopted and censored more heavily. In fact, because of his work at the center, some critics dubbed his films—which did not claim to be "politically committed," as was expected of intellectuals—"official" films and called his cinema a "commissioned" cinema. However, this was an unfair characterization, for on further scrutiny, it becomes clear that his films offer often incisive explications, analyses, and even critiques of Iranian culture and society, not in a politically overt, or politically correct, manner, but in an ironic and sly fashion.

Throughout his career, Kiarostami has thrived by going against the grain and by deliberately working within limitations of various sorts. These include limitations of film form and technique, sponsorship, and government censorship, against all of which he has tested his creativity, discovered his individual voice, and honed his authorial style. Some of these limitations, such as the choice of film form and technique, were internal, self-imposed by the director, and some, such as financing and censorship, were external, driven by commercial and governmental exigencies. As a result of these experiences, unlike most art-cinema directors and critics who have complained of the deleterious effects both of rapacious commercial film financiers and of draconian state funding bodies and censors, Kiarostami has often pointed to the unexpected positive outcomes of limits, even censorship, for they force filmmakers to be more creative and to think through their films more thoroughly (qtd. in Rosen 39–40).

Kiarostami's cinema is a situated cinema, in that his films generally emanate from the specific social worlds around him or from his own encounters. However, at the same time that they treat these social worlds and encounters with the ethos and aesthetics of realism and neorealism, his films embody certain deconstructive practices that counter or problematize realism and neorealism, resulting in formally rigorous works that are quietly operatic in their humanism and in their celebration of life's small victories. These practices, which include self-referentiality, self-inscription, self-reflexivity, and other forms of "distantiation," are discussed throughout this essay.

Analysis

Close-up: *A Close Reading of the Story*

The film *Close-up* (*Nema-ye nazdik,* 1989), produced under the aegis of the Center for the Intellectual Development of Children and Young Adults, is about an ordinary man, a print-shop worker named Hossain Sabzian who is an extraordinary fan of the renowned film director

797

Mohsen Makhmalbaf and his film *The Cyclist* (*Bicycleran,* 1987). His identification with the director is both total and expedient, as he deftly impersonates Makhmalbaf for the entertainment of his friends and to impress strangers, among them Mrs. Ahankhah, whom he meets on a city bus. During this bus encounter, he successfully passes as Makhmalbaf by endorsing for her a copy of the director's published screenplay of *The Cyclist* as though it were penned by him, thereby gaining access to the Ahankhah family heart and hearth. He visits their middle-class home, pretending to be the director reconnoitering it as a possible location for an upcoming movie. The family members, who have never seen the famous director but have heard of him, at first believe his story, welcome him, and agree to act in his film. However, because of certain discrepancies in his story, they begin to suspect that he is an imposter and perhaps a member of a gang of thieves casing their home for robbery. And when days pass without the arrival of any film crew and equipment, a suspicious family member finally reports Sabzian to the authorities and sues him both for operating under false pretenses and for borrowing money without the intention to repay. At this point, a journalist named Hasan Farazmand gets wind of the story and publishes an account of it in the weekly journal *Sorush,* which reaches Kiarostami.

In this apparently simple story of the power of cinematic identification and fandom, culled from his own social milieu, Kiarostami finds larger social and philosophical meanings, turning it into a humanist and sly tale of a man's desperate search for identity and dignity.

Close-up begins with Farazmand the journalist accompanied by two policemen in a taxicab on their way to the Ahankhah home to arrest the imposter Sabzian. After much questioning of passersby about directions, the taxi finally arrives at the house.[2] Farazmand and the policemen enter it, but the camera remains outside for quite some time with the waiting taxi driver, who wanders about, picks up a few flowers from a pile of cuttings, and inadvertently kicks a metal spray can down the steep alley. In what has become a hallmark of Kiarostami's film style, in essence a visual pun or aside, the camera fixates for some time on this seemingly spontaneous and mundane event, as the can rolls noisily down the alley until it comes to a stop by a curb. After a

---

[2]This car ride may have been the seed for other car rides, which became a dominant trope and narrative agent of Kiarostami's subsequent "road movies."

while, the policemen and Sabzian emerge from the Ahankhah house and speed away in the taxi to the Ozgol police station, while the journalist, in another narrative aside, scours the neighborhood in search of a tape recorder.

There is an air of make-do and improvisation in the film's narrative that adds to Kiarostami's visual asides and to what appears to be his unscripted and spontaneous filming style. However, his style is highly planned and calculated at the same time that it is open to chance and discovery. The accumulation of these whimsical asides and seemingly improvised moments of discovery help to constitute not only the philosophical core of the film, but also its critique of Iranian society. For example, the can rolling down the hill can be read philosophically, as a symbol of Sabzian's lowly life at the mercy of fate. The fact that the policemen do not have a patrol car and are forced to visit the crime scene in a taxi and that a professional journalist owns neither sufficient funds to pay for the taxi he has hired nor a tape recorder for his interviews may be read as a critique of poverty in Iran and of the lack of professionalism of the police and journalists. However, Farazmand improvises by borrowing money from Mr. Ahankhah to pay for the taxi, and someone in the neighborhood finally lends him a tape recorder. The same scenes, therefore, can be read as demonstrating the resourcefulness of both the policemen and the journalist in the face of limited or unreliable resources, symbolizing the manner in which art-cinema directors must turn limitations and contingencies to advantages.

Kiarostami appears as himself in the film, although not so much visually (only glimpses of him are shown from the back), but as the voice of the investigative filmmaker just outside the frame who is researching the magazine story on the incident, visiting locations, interviewing players, and re-creating and directing scenes. This investigative structure inscribes Kiarostami as both author and actor, who simultaneously records the film and invents it as he goes along, mixing documentary footage with fictional accounts. He interviews in their home the Ahankhah family members, who attempt to save face by pretending not to have been fooled by Sabzian's impersonation. In Qasr prison, he interviews Sabzian, who confesses to having impersonated Makhmalbaf, an act that, he admits, appears to have been fraudulent but deep down was very sincere, since it was motivated by his love for cinema and by his respect and admiration for the director.

When Kiarostami asks Sabzian's permission to film him, the savvy printer immediately and remarkably responds, "Yes, I give you permission because you are my subject, my audience." Kiarostami also interviews the judge in his chamber to obtain permission to film Sabzian's trial, whose crime the judge regards as not worth filming. In addition, he re-creates many scenes, including Sabzian's bus encounter with Mrs. Ahankhah and the scene of his arrest. The latter is reenacted twice, once from outside the Ahankhah home and a second time from the inside, playing into the Iranian dichotomous orientation involving inside and outside (discussed further below).

Kiarostami provokes, distorts, and directs the profilmic reality throughout, but he does so most remarkably in the court trial, where, alluding to his earlier jailhouse interview in which Sabzian had made a distinction between manifest reality and latent meaning, he explains to Sabzian that there are two cameras in the court. The one that is filming in long shots, he tells Sabzian, "belongs to the court," that is, it is for outsiders, designed to film external reality. On the other hand, he tells Sabzian, the camera that films in close-up "is for us and not for the court," that is, it is for the insiders, intended to record the internal reality—the truth. This point is further driven home when Kiarostami tells him, "if any time during the trial you need to explain something in particular, something that seems unbelievable or unacceptable to the court, then tell it to this close-up camera." Much has been written about the centrality of the concept of sincerity or inner purity (*safa-ye baten*) among Iranians as a core value (Beeman; Bateson, Clinton, Kassarjian, Safavi, and Soraya; Bateson). Inner purity is achieved when there is a balance between exterior behavior and interior feelings, and many films, including Dariush Mehrjui's clever *The School We Went To* (*Madreseh'i keh miraftim,* 1980–89), have dealt with it. In linking this psychological orientation, which distrusts manifest reality but highly values inner reality, to shot size and shot composition, Kiarostami deftly visualizes that psychology.

It is in this context that Sabzian's courtroom elaboration and defense of his behavior must be viewed. According to him, his impersonation was not based on fraud, but was driven by his sincere love for Makhmalbaf's films, which powerfully depict the terrible social conditions of downtrodden Iranians, including himself. As a result, he elaborates: "I loved Makhmalbaf and wanted to be in his place. . . .

Playing him gave me self-confidence and earned me respect." As a poor, lowly printer, no one had taken him seriously, while as a film director, people recognized him, respected him, and followed what he asked of them (apparently, the Ahankhahs were willing to cut down a large tree in their garden to make a better shot possible). By confessing to his fraud and by justifying it in such deeply personal terms, he makes himself vulnerable, displaying intimacy and sincerity instead of calculation and cleverness. However, as Kiarostami astutely observes "his lies reflect his inner reality better than the superficial truth" that the other characters mouth (qtd. in Lopate 359).

Finally, by setting up the close-up shot as belonging to "us," Kiarostami conflates the position of the film's subject with those of the director and the spectators, creating a powerful suturing mechanism that makes the audience complicit in both Sabzian's fraud and Kiarostami's sly film.

Cinéma Vérité

By stating his two-camera filming instructions to Sabzian in the presence of the judge, the plaintiffs, and the spectators, Kiarostami provokes a new filmic reality that is different from the courtroom reality without an activist camera, thereby transforming his film *Close-up*, as Roland Barthes might have described it, from a univocal direct cinema "work" to a multivocal *cinéma vérité* "text" (156–57). In the process, the spectator is also potentially transformed, from a passive consumer of the film to the producer of its meaning. The distinction between direct cinema and *cinéma vérité* has largely been lost in film criticism. If direct cinema, as practiced by pioneers such as Albert Maysles, Richard Leacock, and Frederick Wiseman, is devoted to recording the profilmic reality in an unvarnished and unmediated manner, *cinéma vérité*, particularly as practiced by trailblazers such as Jean Rouch, Errol Morris, and Jean-Luc Godard, intends to investigate and question reality by intervening in it or provoking it. *Close-up* is not a straight documentary, nor is it entirely fictional; rather, it is a hybridized film partaking of both forms, made in the *cinéma vérité* style. It is no surprise, therefore, that the judge asks Kiarostami, "Are you ready?" before beginning his court session. In a *cinéma vérité* film, the real court proceedings cannot begin without filming, whereas in a direct cinema film, the camera is meant to have no bearing on the profilmic world.

Once begun, Kiarostami continues to provoke and interact with Sabzian, the judge, and the plaintiffs, as well as directing and retaking actual court scenes. As a result, the one-hour, scheduled court session was extended into a ten-hour *vérité* filming, which Kiarostami then condensed into a long sequence.

The distinction that the diegetic Kiarostami makes between the long-shot camera and the close-up camera and between external reality and internal meaning is the Iranian figuration of the distinction between direct cinema and *cinéma vérité*. And it is this distinction, this tension between manifest and latent meanings, that informs and propels the drama not only of this film, but also of Kiarostami's filmic style in general, turning his films into subtle and sly treatises on reality, realism, and the human condition.

Another example of Kiarostami's provoking reality to get at deeper meanings is the powerful sequence that brings the film to a close, during which Kiarostami arranges a surprise meeting between Sabzian and his idol. As Sabzian is exiting the court and entering a noisy, traffic-laden street, Makhmalbaf suddenly appears before him and introduces himself. Taken aback, the lowly fan bends down to kiss his hand in the traditional gesture of humility and great respect. However, Makhmalbaf, in the equally traditional gesture of magnanimity, prevents him from doing so and, instead, embraces him, whereupon Sabzian breaks into what appears to be heartfelt tears. These expressions of humility and emotion demonstrate Sabzian's sincerity.

Significantly, instead of filming this touching scene in a direct cinema style, which would have emphasized Sabzian's sincerity, Kiarostami manipulates the sound track to create intermittent interruptions, thus undermining both Sabzian's sincerity and the documentary veracity of his own film. Like most of his interventions, this one, too, is made to appear spontaneous, for he and his crew seem surprised by the faulty connection in Makhmalbaf's microphone. Apparently unaware of the problem, Makhmalbaf and Sabzian proceed to purchase a bouquet of red flowers to take to the Ahankhah family as a gesture of reconciliation, now that Sabzian has been acquitted thanks to his confession and apology. The ensuing scene that shows Makhmalbaf driving his motorcycle with Sabzian seated behind him with the flowers, while holding onto his idol, is reminiscent of stereotypical love scenes in which lost lovers are reunited. They engage in conversation, but the bad connection makes it difficult to understand what they are saying. It is important to point out that the bad connection is in fact only a ruse, deliberately manufactured in postproduction. In doing this, Kiarostami has acted like Sabzian: by engaging in a game of pretense. Unlike Sabzian, however, he does not confess on film to his fraud. Perhaps with this ruse he is telling us that the content of their conversation is not important; what is important is that the lover and the beloved, the fan and the star, the disciple and the master are united—a classic trope in Persian mystic poetry and philosophy. As a result of these deliberate interjections, this most intimate moment of unrehearsed reality is turned into a highly mediated scene about cinema and filmmaking, which critiques both film realism and the Iranian valorization of sincerity. Because of these interjections, the spectators, too, are placed in an ambivalent or split position. On the one hand, they sympathize with Sabzian and with his cathartic union with his object of desire. On the other hand, the audacious use of various alienation strategies distances them, forcing them to question the expediency of sincerity and the sincerity both of realist cinema and of Kiarostami.

Director as Star

Sabzian's justification of his fraud points to the power both of cinema and of film directors as stars among Iranians. He did not impersonate a soccer star, a religious figure, or a war veteran—the only officially sanctioned heroic models of emulation then available in Iran. Instead, he chose a film director who, although widely known, did not at the time have wide picture recognition. In the United States, the names most prominently displayed on theater marquees are generally those not of directors but of movie stars. In prerevolutionary Iran, too, mainstream films were often keyed to the drawing power of the stars. However, after the revolution, the star system was dismantled due to its association with corruption, idolatry, and the degradation and commodification of women (Naficy 164). As a result, the Iranian stars whose names dominate the theater marquees today are primarily the directors, particularly art-cinema directors—although in recent years, actors as stars have been on the rise again. What is even more remarkable is that these star directors are both popular as entertainers and respected as intellectuals, who with each film offer a new treatise on

Iranian history, identity, and society or on some universal philosophical, existential, moral, or authorial dilemma. Filmmakers seem to have replaced, at least for the nonce, writers and poets as public intellectuals of great import.

The concept of director as author, star, and public intellectual is undergirded by the self-inscriptional, self-referential, and self-reflexive strategies in which art-cinema directors, in particular Kiarostami, engage—strategies that give Kiarostami's films both their authorial regularities and their authorial innovations.

Authorial "Camera Pen"

Kiarostami has served multiple functions in most of his films, including as director, screenplay writer, editor, and actor, as is the case in *Close-up*. Such multifunctionality has ensured his authority and authorship and has given his films a remarkable continuity of content and form and what Godfrey Cheshire calls "interrelatedness" (9). With few exceptions (Dariush Mehrjui and Bahram Beizai, for example), no other Iranian director has maintained his style while evolving with it so organically. Another factor contributing to his style is the manner in which he discovers his film ideas, actors, and locations often in his own biography, in his immediate social milieu, in ordinary events, or in his previous films. His Koker trilogy, consisting of *Where Is the Friend's Home? (Khaneh-ye doust kojast?*, 1987), *And Life Goes On (Zendehgi va digar hich*, 1991), and *Under the Olive Trees (Zir-e darakhtan-e Zaitun*, 1994), provides examples of how one film begets another and how one film refers to, and instigates, another. *Close-up*, on the other hand, demonstrates the manner in which Kiarostami finds his film ideas, actors, and locations in ordinary events and in his immediate surroundings. But how does he weave these ordinary events into a philosophical treatise of extraordinary complexity? To answer this question I invoke what the French critic Alexandre Astruc presciently prophesied in 1948 as a new age of cinema, the age of the camera pen (*caméra-stylo*). By this he meant a cinema that "would gradually break free from the tyranny of what is visual, from the image for its own sake, from the immediate and concrete demands of the narrative, to become a means of writing just as flexible and subtle as written language." He went so far as to suggest that only cinema could do justice to the contemporary ideas and philosophies of life. According to

Astruc, if the philosopher Descartes lived today, he would be making films (17–18). In that case, Descartes' famous dictum would have to be reformulated to read, "I make films, therefore I am."

This is just as true for Kiarostami because his films are so intricately and intimately tied to his own existence and subjectivity that it is difficult to conceive of his life without his films or of his films without him.[3] That is why many of those who imitate his style fail to produce his effect, for his style without him is nothing; or rather, it is something else! This is also true of Kiarostami's photography and poetry, both of which are driven by the same intimate connection between author, autobiography, and the work.[4]

Kiarostami is doing precisely what Astruc had demanded over half a century ago; he *writes* with his camera pen, and he *thinks* with his films, concretely, philosophically, and poetically, all at the same time. He expresses his private obsessions and desires, his hopeful and humanistic philosophy of life, and his sly social criticism with film, the way great writers express themselves with a pen (or with the keyboard). His films are like essays, short stories, or poems, which offer a slice of life or a personal rumination on existence, on what it means to be human, and on what constitutes reality or the cinema. And like great writers, he accomplishes his cine writing with such seeming effortlessness, clarity, and precision, with minimum use of the usual rhetorical devices of art-cinema films or the special effects of mainstream cinema that it is refreshing and awe inspiring. However, as noted, his films in general, and *Close-up* in particular, are imbued with authorial artifices of one sort or another. I discuss two more such artifices in the remainder of the essay.

Neorealism

Much has been made of Kiarostami's debt to Italian neorealism, to which he readily admits (qtd. in Lopate 352–53); however, his relationship to it is quite complex. The spirit and style of neorealism is

[3]In this intimate coincidence of authorship and autobiography, Kiarostami is like another great *auteur* filmmaker, Chris Marker, who in his seminal film *Sunless* (*Sans soleil*, 1983) used the revised Descartean dictum of "I film, therefore I am."
[4]For his book of poetry, see Kiarostami, *Walking with the Wind*; for his book of photographs, see Kiarostami, *Abbas Kiarostami*.

strongly present particularly in his early films, in which his actors were ordinary people untrained in the art of acting. They were often male children on a dogged quest or journey to get something, to redress a wrong, or to prove something. In these, he showed himself to be an artist of the everyday, but not of everydayness, for he did not seek the tediousness, repetitiveness, and degradation of the everyday but instead searched and discovered the moments of rupture, tension, and glory hidden in the quotidian. Inspired by the neorealist style and ethos, almost all of his films are shot on location—not in the studio— and in available light, using a small crew and simple equipment. The apparent casualness and improvisation of his visual style consolidates his connection both to Italian neorealism and to the French New Wave. However, these are manufactured impressions of casualness and realism that Kiarostami has striven hard to produce, not innocent recordings of unfolding reality, as many believe. They conceal his considerable planning and tinkering with locations, prop arrangements, acting and dialogue, and filming.

Many of his films, particularly his later films, use shot/reverse shots sparingly, relying on long shots and long takes. Considered the engine of the continuity filmmaking of the classical realist style, shot/reverse-shot filming and editing creates audience identification with characters by suturing them into the diegesis. As such, the classical realist style is highly psychological and fictional, while Kiarostami's sparing use of these strategies renders his films more social and realistic, even didactic. The understated characters in many of his films do not actually seem to discover much in their quests, and, if they do, they seem unaware of it. They are determined but often not transformed by their own discoveries, as the characters in modernist novels and films are. We get this impression because they rarely have subjectivity, which is usually signaled by point-of-view filming and by shot/reverse-shot editing.[5] Instead, Kiarostami's filming style, involving long shots and long takes, tells us more about his own subjectivity than about the characters' point of view. However, thanks to his films' didactic structure it is the audience that discovers something universal, by which it

---

[5]*Close-up* is an exception, for Sabzian has subjectivity and undergoes change when he admits to his fraud, confesses to his love for Makhmalbaf's movies, and meets up with his idol.

is potentially transformed. Because Kiarostami breaks the fourth wall and inserts the process of filmmaking into his stories, the focus of inquiry is turned from the characters to the camera, the cinema, the director, and, ultimately, the spectators, who become aware of their own act of film watching. His latest films, therefore, constitute a *trompe l'oeil* cinema (Mulvey 26), for they mix illusion and reality and create an uncertainty about which is which—a far cry from the classical neorealist concerns and style.

Self-Reflexivity

In its broadest definition, self-reflexivity in Iranian cinema, and in Kiarostami's films in particular, takes several forms. Two of these have already been noted as they play out in *Close-up*: the dynamic relationship between interiority and exteriority, which is driven by mistrusting appearances and prizing hidden meanings; and self-referentiality, which results from films referring to, or quoting, one another, creating an intertextual nexus within a director's oeuvre. Another form, prominent in Kiarostami's films, is self-inscription, by which the filmmaker inserts himself into his films diegetically, sometimes as himself and sometimes by proxy. As in many of his films, Kiarostami is a diegetic agent in *Close-up*, appearing as himself, investigating Sabzian's story, instigating certain scenes, and in general directing the film. This self-inscription, however, is not so much in the interest of heightened filmic realism as it is in the interest of undermining it in order to investigate the truth both of reality and of cinema.

Such self-inscription is part and parcel of the self-reflexive structure of his films. Such a structure is usually considered to be a modernist device and a Western trope of avant-garde artists. However, in Kiarostami's case it emanates not only from his contact with the West but also from what he has absorbed from traditional Iranian theatrical performances, among them the Shi'i religious passion plays called *taziyeh*. Performed annually during the holy month of Moharram, they commemorate the martyrdom in the planes of Karbala (today's Iraq) of Imam Hossein, the grandson of the prophet Muhammad, at the hands of the Umayyad caliphate. This event, which in its regular recreation across the country has become an archetype of unjust usurpation of power in Shi'i cosmology, has been called the "Karbala paradigm" (Fischer 21). Its impact on Iranian psychology and aesthetics has been significant. This is because this paradigm provides a framework for thinking about how to live; it channels grief and rage caused by loss and by injustice into stoicism and quiet determination; it embodies a tragic vision of the world and of grief, guilt, repentance, and anger in religiously motivated emotions; and it creates total identification with the martyrs. The invocation of this paradigm has allowed Iranians to continue to express grief and to channel outrage at an unjust world, even up to contemporary times, in a socially sanctioned and personally meaningful and redemptive fashion. The 1978–79 revolution, which toppled Shah Mohammad Reza Pahlavi and ushered in the Islamic Republic, was but one recent example of the "work" of this paradigm (among other factors).

Kiarostami does not so much mobilize the tragic, grief-ridden, or justice-seeking contents of the Karbala paradigm as he does its self-reflexive "distantiation" structure, as exemplified in the passion plays. In these performances, the apparatus of the stage is made visible, as no curtain separates the circular stage from the audience that surrounds it. In addition, men and boys play the parts of women, and they read their parts from scripts that they hold in their hands. In this way, "the script serves as a barrier to any suggestion that the actor actually becomes the person he portrays" (Chelkowski 5). Moreover, the actors speak in a declamatory fashion not only to each other but also to the audience. In these direct addresses, they sometimes narrate the story, sometimes verbalize the characters' feelings, and sometimes tell of their own feelings of shame and humiliation as actors who must play the parts of evil people and the killers of the Imam. They apologize to the audience and tearfully confess to their own personal devotion to the Imam, emphasizing that they are only acting as the bad guys and are not themselves bad or evil. The *taziyeh* audience, in turn, responds by emitting appropriate cries of commiseration, weeping, and slapping their faces, foreheads, and thighs. The hard differentiation between being an empirical person and an actor onstage, which is so crucial to Western performing arts is a fragile and a negotiated one in Iran, for under certain circumstances, being (*budan*) and acting or representing (*nemudan*) are conflated, with disastrous consequences for the players. Sometimes the *taziyeh* actors who play evil roles are socially shunned or physically harmed because of this conflation of the part with the person playing the part.[6] This same principle was at work immediately after the revolution, when actors and stars who had played bad guys or immoral women in prerevolution films were forbidden from the screens completely, as though they had been bad or immoral in their own offscreen lives. Many lives and careers were thus ruined.

Kiarostami's answer to a question about whether he used Brechtian "distantiation" in his films underscores his debts not only to Western modernism but also to indigenous Iranian and Muslim performance practices. It is worth quoting at length:

> Yes, but I haven't taken it from the theory of Brecht only. I came to that through experience. We are never able to construct truth as it is in the reality of our daily lives, and we are always witnessing things from far away while we are trying to depict them as close as we can to reality. So if we distance the audience from the film and even [the] film from itself, it helps to understand the subject matter better. I found distantiation in Taazieh [*taziyeh*].
>
> Many of the audiences believe my films are documentaries, as if it just *happened* that there was a camera there to record them. I think if the audience knows they are watching a performance, something which has been constructed, they will understand it more than they would in a documentary film. . . . This year I went to a village near Teheran to watch a Taazieh. In the scene of the Yazid's and Imam Hossein's battle, Imam Hossein's sword suddenly became bent because it was made of very cheap, soft metal. Yazid went to him and took his sword and put it on a big stone and straightened it with another stone and gave it back to him and then they continued fighting.

---

[6]Jean Baronnet's fascinating 1970s documentary about a *taziyeh* performance in the city of Natanz, *Le Lion de Dieu: Theatre Ta'Ziyeh à Natanza,* contains interviews with players who were subjected to such treatment.

This is exactly the opposite to what at the moment Hollywood is doing, which is brainwashing the audience to such an extent that it strips them of any imagination, decision-making or intellectual capacity, in order to captivate them for two whole hours. In my films, there are always some breaks—such as when a prop assistant brings a bowl of water, and hands it to an actor in the film. This gives the audience time to breathe a little and stops them from becoming emotionally involved and reminds them that, "Yes, I'm watching a film." In *Under the Olive Trees* I always keep this distance between the reality of the scene and the reality of the subject matter. (Qtd. in Hamid 24)

Similar to a *taziyeh* performance, in *Close-up* the impostor Sabzian, the Ahankhah family members, the judge, the journalist, and the film directors Makhmalbaf and Kiarostami are all both themselves and actors self-consciously playing their own parts. They re-create certain scenes (Sabzian impersonating Makhmalbaf in the Ahankhah home or on the bus), act in new scenes (Sabzian and Makhmalbaf meeting for the first time), and sometimes directly address the camera either in interview situations (Sabzian, the judge, and Ahankhah family members) or in what amounts to an internal monologue (Sabzian speaking to the close-up camera). In the process, the real, the re-created, and the fictional are juxtaposed so seamlessly in a *trompe l'oeil* fashion that they are impossible to tell apart. The status of the film itself, too, is equally complicated and thrown into doubt, for it is neither a direct cinema documentary faithfully reproducing a pro-filmic reality nor a fiction film producing a new fictive reality. In Kiarostami's own words, it represents an attempt to "reach fiction through the documentary" (qtd. in Doraiswamy 20), with the result that it promotes both "distantiation" and identification—both cognition and emotion, belief and disbelief. The production of doubt and ambiguity at so many different levels is deeply counterhegemonic. It is counterhegemonic both vis-à-vis the dominant classical realist cinema—exemplified by Hollywood films—which is driven by the invisibility of its style, and vis-à-vis the dominant Islamist political regime in Iran, which is given to the production of visible certainties. Significantly, however, Kiarostami's criticism against these two hegemons is offered, astutely, primarily at the level of filmic style, not content.

Conclusion

Overall, Kiarostami's films are films of indirection, implication, and restraint—a kind of tantric cinema. Iranians appear to draw particular pleasure from and seem to have perfected the tantric arts. Some would call this evasiveness, but I would prefer to characterize it in Homi Bhabha's words as "sly civility" (93–101), for in the works of the best poets and filmmakers, such as Kiarostami, indirection, implication, restraint, and limitation become strategies of creative agency, involving resistance, criticism, and authorship of various sorts, which open up the hermeneutically rich texts to audience input and to multiple interpretations.

Credits

Iran, 1989, Center for the Intellectual Development of Children and Young Adults

Director, Screenplay, and Editing: Abbas Kiarostami
Producer: Alireza Zarrin
Cinematography: Alireza Zarrindast
Assistant Directors: Jahangir Azad and Aliasghar Mirzai
Sound: Mohammad Haqiqi, Ahmad Asgari, Jahangir Mirshekari, Hasan Zahedi, and Changiz Sayyad
Makeup: Fariba Zandpur
Production Manager: Hasan Aqakarimi

CAST (all playing themselves):
Hossain Sabzian
Hasan Farazmand
Abbas Kiarostami
Mohsen Makhmalbaf
Hushang Samai
Abolfazl Ahankhah
Mehrdad Ahankhah
Mahrokh Ahankhah
Manuchehr Ahankhah
Nayer Mohseni Zonnuzi
Ahmadreza Moayyed Mohseni
Davud Gudarzi
Mohammadali Barati
Moslem Oshreh
Hasan Komeili
Alireza Ahmadi
Davud Hemmat

Bibiliography

Astruc, Alexandre. "The Birth of a New Avant-Garde: *La Caméra Stylo.*" *The New Wave: Critical Landmarks.* Ed. Peter Graham. New York: Doubleday, 1968. 17–23.

Baharlu, Abbas. *Abbas Kiarostami.* Tehran: Noruz-e Honar, 2000.

Barthes, Roland. *Image, Music, Text.* Trans. Stephen Heath. New York: Hill and Wang, 1977.

Bateson, Catherine. "'This Figure of Tinsel': A Study of Themes of Hypocrisy and Pessimism in Iranian Culture." *Daedalus* (Summer 1979): 125–34.

Bateson, Catherine, J. W. Clinton, J. B. M. Kassarjian, H. Safavi, and M. Soraya. "Safay-i Batin: A Study of the Interrelations of a Set of Iranian Ideal Character Types." *Psychological Dimensions of Near Eastern Studies.* Ed. L. C. Brown and N. Itzkowitz. Princeton: Darwin, 1977. 257–74.

Beeman, William. *Language, Status, and Power in Iran.* Bloomington: Indiana UP, 1986.

Bhabha, Homi K. *The Location of Culture.* London: Routledge, 1994.

Chelkowski, Peter J. "Ta'ziyeh: Indigenous Avant-Garde Theatre of Iran." *Ta'ziyeh: Ritual and Drama in Iran.* Ed. Peter Chelkowski. New York: New York UP; Tehran: Soroush, 1979. 1–11.

Cheshire, Godfrey. "How to Read Kiarostami." *Cineaste* 25.4 (2000): 8–15.

Cinématheque Ontario Film Programme Guide, Winter 1995.

Doraiswamy, Rashmi. "Abbas Kiarostami: Life and Much More." *Cinemaya* 16 (1992): 18–20.

Fischer, Michael. *Iran: From Religious Dispute to Revolution.* Cambridge, MA: Harvard UP, 1980.

Hamid, Nassia. "Near and Far." *Sight and Sound* (Feb. 1997): 22–24.

Kiarostami, Abbas. *Abbas Kiarostami: Photo Collection.* Tehran: Nashr-e Honar, 2000.

———. *Walking with the Wind/Hamrah ba Bad.* Trans. Ahmad Karimi-Hakkak and Michael Beard. Cambridge, MA: Harvard Film Archive/Harvard UP, 2001.

Lopate, Philip. Interview with Abbas Kiarostami. *Totally, Tenderly, Tragically: Essays and Criticism from a Lifelong Love Affair with the Movies.* New York: Anchor, 1998. 352–67.

Mulvey, Laura. "Kiarostami's Uncertainty Principle," *Sight and Sound* (June 1998): 24–27.

Naficy, Hamid. "Iranian Cinema." *Companion Encyclopedia of Middle Eastern and North African Film.* Ed. Oliver Leaman. London: Routledge, 2001. 130–222.

Qukasian, Zaven. *Majmueh Maqalat dar Naqd va Moareffi-ye Asar-e Abbas Kiarostami.* Tehran: Didar, 1996.

Rosen, Miriam. "The Camera of Art: An Interview with Abbas Kiarostami." *Cineaste* 19.2–3 (1992): 38–40.

Shabani Pirposhteh, Mohammad. *Tarhi az Doust: Negahi beh Zendigi va Asar-e Filmasz-e Andishmand Abbas Kiarostami.* Tehran: Entesharat-e Rowzaneh, 1997.

To Sleep with Anger (1990)

VALERIE SMITH

Migration and Masculinity

Context

At a key moment in Charles Burnett's *To Sleep with Anger* (1990), Gideon, the patriarch of the family on which the film focuses, lies semi-conscious in bed, recovering from a stroke. His pastor and members of his church choir surround him and prepare to pray for his recovery. As the pastor places his hand near the bottom of the bed, he feels something, pulls the cover back, and sees scattered dried palma christi leaves that Suzie, Gideon's wife, has placed there. In an ever-so-admonitory tone of voice, he asks her what other remedies she has given Gideon. Somewhat chagrined, she admits that she has "crossed his chest with cold oil and given him some cow tea." The pastor gently chastises her for relying on these folkways instead of turning to prayer. (Interestingly, he does not suggest that she trust conventional medicine.) At this moment, we see enacted the clash of cultures at the heart of one of the central dilemmas with which the film is concerned—the complex position that African American migrants from the South occupy, long after their geographical journey is complete. Gideon and Suzie may have left the South thirty years before the moment at which the film is set, but the old ways are still with them, in the form of the oral tradition, music, food, values, remedies, friendships, and memories.

Born in 1944 in Vicksburg, Mississippi, Charles Burnett is the son of a career military man and a nurse's aide who moved to the Watts section of Los Angeles when he was three years old. He and his brother were raised by their grandmother in a neighborhood populated primarily by other black migrants from the South. Burnett was educated at Los Angeles Community College and UCLA, from which he received a BA and an MFA degree in film. During this time, he became part of a group of young African American filmmakers known as the

Los Angeles School, which included such figures as Ben Caldwell, Larry Clark, Julie Dash, Haile Gerima, Billy Woodberry, and others. And he received the Louis B. Mayer Award, which financed his master's thesis and first film, *Killer of Sheep* (1977). An eighty-seven-minute black-and-white movie that features amateur actors, for the most part, and was made for less than ten thousand dollars, *Killer of Sheep* focuses on the lives of black migrants to Los Angeles. In its subject matter, subtle use of imagery, and sensitivity to the nuances of domestic relations, it anticipates the content and techniques evident in two of Burnett's most important subsequent films: *My Brother's Wedding* (1983), and *To Sleep with Anger* (1990). *Killer of Sheep* won the Critics' Prize at the 1981 Berlin Film Festival, and in 1990 it was designated one of twenty-five culturally and artistically significant motion pictures included in the National Film Registry of the Library of Congress.

We should not be surprised by the fact that the experience of black migrants in Los Angeles is central to much of Burnett's work when we consider that the mass movement of black people from the South to the urban West, Midwest, and Northeast was one of the most transformative and significant processes in African American history and culture. Burnett's family was part of a wave of African Americans that went to Los Angeles in search of the financial prosperity, social mobility, and freedom from segregation that the booming wartime economy seemed to promise. New industries, the manufacturing and shipping of materials and supplies that supported the war effort, the Japanese internment, and the growth of the U.S. economy due to expanding Latin American markets and initiatives to rebuild post-World War II Europe all contributed to the formation of an expanded black working and middle class on the West Coast. Before 1940, the vast majority of African Americans lived in the South, almost half of them in the rural South. From 1910 to 1970, six and a half million blacks moved from the rural South to the urban West, Midwest, North, and Northeast: five million of these moved after 1940. By 1970, black America was one-half southern and less than one-quarter rural. "Urban" had thus come to be synonymous with "black" in the American imagination.[1]

---

[1]Although an extensive body of sources exists on the subject of African American migration, one might productively begin an exploration of this topic with Malaika Adero, *Up South*; Farah Jasmine Griffin, *"Who Set You Flowin'?"*; Alferdteen Harrison, ed., *Black Exodus*; and Nicholas Lemann, *The Promised Land*.

Analysis

In *To Sleep with Anger,* as in *Killer of Sheep* and *My Brother's Wedding,* Burnett meditates on the impact of the process of migration on individuals (principally men), on family relations, and within African American communities. In different ways, the characters in *To Sleep with Anger* are pulled between West and South, urban and rural, the promise of the future and memories of the past, material gain and spiritual meaning. Each generation bequeaths some version of this tension to the next; the migrant experience thus emerges as a place of fertile but potentially destructive contradictions. The film is replete with allusions and techniques that emphasize the inextricable connections between apparent oppositions in the characters' lives. The music, verbal and visual references to folklore, and the strategic use of crosscutting all underscore this rich ambivalence.

To Sleep with Anger focuses on a multigenerational African American family in Los Angeles during the post–civil rights era. Theirs is not the Los Angeles of "new jack pictures" such as *Boyz N the Hood* (John Singleton, 1991), *South Central* (Steve Anderson, 1992), or *Menace II Society* (Allen Hughes and Albert Hughes, 1993), riddled with graffiti, gang culture, and drive-by shootings. Nor is the sound track of their lives the hard-driving bass of hip-hop music. Rather, Gideon (Paul Butler) and Suzie (Mary Alice) are part of the wave of black migrants who left Alabama, Mississippi, Arkansas, and Louisiana for the West Coast during the postwar boom. Thirty years later, Gideon, retired on a comfortable pension, and Suzie, a midwife, live in a Craftsman bungalow in a middle-class African American neighborhood, not far from their two sons and their families. The sense of proportion in their comfortable home, with its elaborate woodwork, wide doorways, built-in cupboards, and '50s kitchen, underscores their substantial reliability and sense of security. The landscape they inhabit evokes the southernness of Los Angeles—a mild climate that makes gardening and backyard chicken coops possible. The sound track to their lives is traditional gospel and the blues from the Mississippi delta.

The "good son," Junior (Carl Lumbly), who is the elder son, and his wife, Pat (Vonetta McGee), live in a home architecturally reminiscent of their parents' and adhere to the values Gideon and Suzie embody. Devoted to family, they are attentive to their daughter, Rhonda (Reina

King), as well as to their parents, and eagerly anticipate the birth of their second child. Pat plans to have her baby at home, with her mother-in-law's assistance. They volunteer at a food pantry, work hard, and attend church. But if Junior represents the continuation of Gideon and Suzie's values, Babe Brother (Richard Brooks), the rebellious younger son, struggles to define himself against them. He and his wife, Linda (Sheryl Lee Ralph), are successful professionals, more concerned with making money than they are with religion or family. Sunny (DeVaughn Nixon), their son, and his grandparents spend more time together than Babe Brother and Linda spend with either. While Junior is quick to help his parents with their home repairs and gardening chores, and is shown working on his own home, Babe Brother considers manual labor demeaning and will usually find some excuse to avoid it. Repelled by the notion that Pat kept her first child's afterbirth in the refrigerator, Linda is proud of the fact that she had Sunny at Cedars-Sinai (or "Cedar and Sinai, and that ain't no county hospital," as she says playfully).[2] In contrast to the homes his brother and parents inhabit, Babe Brother's is more contemporary in style and more lavishly furnished.

To Sleep with Anger can be read as a struggle for the soul of Babe Brother within the context of a narrative of black migration. Babe Brother is forced to decide what kind of man he will be when his path crosses that of Harry Mention (Danny Glover), a friend of Gideon and Suzie's from back home who stops by for an unexpected, extended visit. Harry becomes a mentor of sorts, an alternative father to Babe Brother. As Linda puts it during a pivotal scene in the film, "You're not like the rest of Gideon's friends. Most of them believe if you're not hard at work, then you're hard at sin." To which Harry replies, as he cleans his nails with his switchblade knife, "I'm more modern in my ways, I don't believe in sin, though there is good and evil and evil is something that you work at."

Linda wants to believe that Harry is less "country," more worldly than her in-laws and their friends. But she soon discovers that in

---

[2]Presumably, Pat keeps the placenta until the family can dispose of it according to a black southern ritual, perhaps by burying it. As is the case with other folkloric allusions, the film does not explain this practice.

profound ways he embodies the worst of the old. Harry has been implicated in the violence from which so many migrants fled: from the stories he and others tell, he may have been responsible for at least two murders, one of which was made to look like a lynching and almost caused a race riot back home. He holds to outmoded, misogynist ideas about sexual and family relations. As if to undermine her marriage, he reintroduces Suzie to her old flame Okra Tate. He advises Babe Brother that real men are not monogamous. His own sons are dead. In short, he reveals himself to be a contaminating, parasitic presence in the community that welcomes him. During his visit, tensions in the family come to a head: Gideon suffers a stroke after an argument with Babe Brother, Linda and Babe Brother separate, and Suzie is injured as she tries to stop Babe Brother and Junior from killing each other. Only after Harry is expelled from the household—Suzie tells him he must leave, and the next day he drops dead on the kitchen floor—is order restored and Gideon healed.

Although the film presents the engrossing, linear narrative of a crisis in the lives of one family, its textured allusiveness encourages a vertical reading. The opening dream sequence, as well as recurring scenes of two neighbor boys, one who learns to play the trumpet and the other who trains homing pigeons (both figures associated with Babe Brother's quest for identity and self-knowledge), might seem initially to be distracting, if not irrelevant. However, moments such as these, as well as explicit or implied references to folkloric figures such as John Henry or the trickster, the recurrence of proverbial speech, and passing allusions to superstitions, expand the meaning of the film beyond the lives of the characters who are its ostensible focus. These references and motifs mark the film as a folkloric document in and of itself, an artifact of precisely the sort of cultural syncretism that shapes the lives of southern migrants.[3]

---

[3]For a compelling discussion of the use of folklore in the film, see Karen Chandler. In an intriguing interview with Burnett ("Talking with Charles Burnett"), Sojin Kim and R. Mark Livengood analyze Burnett's own observations about the function of folklore in the film.

Close Readings

The film opens with a shot of a man who turns out to be Gideon decked out in a gray, three-piece suit, wearing a matching fedora, shoes, and socks, and seated in a wooden dining room side chair as he stares off into space. To his left is a dining room table covered with a lace tablecloth. On the table sits a bowl of fruit and beside it, a slice of an apple. Above the bowl of fruit is a large, framed photograph of a well-dressed black woman, probably taken during the 1930s, who may well be Gideon's mother. (We see this same photograph on the wall of the bedroom in which Sunny sleeps at his grandparents' house.) Sister Rosetta Tharpe's classic, twangy, deliberate, blues-inflected recording of Thomas A. Dorsey's "Precious Memories," in which her guitar responds to the call sounded by the vocal, plays on the sound track:

> *Precious Memories,*
> *How they linger,*
> *How they ever flood my soul.*
> *In the stillness,*
> *Of the midnight,*
> *Precious, sacred scenes unfold.*

As the camera moves from an abrupt close-up of Gideon's face, it pans upward to the picture, and then downward to the bowl of fruit. Flames spontaneously burst from the fruit, and then the camera moves to Gideon, as if seeking a reaction shot, but he remains oblivious. The camera then moves back to the burning fruit, to the table leg, which has also burst into flame, and then back to Gideon, who not only fails to respond, but has begun to twiddle his thumbs idly. Then Gideon's feet catch fire; as the flames move up his body so that they are almost at the level of his chin, he appears to nod off to sleep. Just as Tharpe begins to repeat the lyric, a shot of Gideon's flaming feet fades into his bare feet, and we see him in what turns out to be the narrative present, wearing jeans and a khaki work shirt and sitting on a bench near his backyard chicken coop, holding his Bible and sleeping. He jerks himself awake, and we realize that what we have just seen was a dream.

In retrospect, we recognize that the opening sequence introduces both the issues central to and the style of the film. The sequence suggests the resonant, inescapable links between urban and rural,

West and South that shape the migrant experience.[4] Gideon's formal attire in the first shot positions him in the urban context, but the lyrics that accompany the image underscore the enduring memories that connect him to people and places from his rural past. Likewise, his backyard in Los Angeles, as well as the work clothes he wears there, are more evocative of "down South" than "up North." Moreover, the flames that threaten to consume the fruit, the table, and Gideon himself anticipate Harry's arrival and the threat he poses to Gideon's family, indeed to Gideon's life itself.

It is not insignificant that this warning is conveyed through Gideon's dream. The use of a dream here both establishes the vocabulary and strategies of address through which meaning is conveyed in the film and pays homage to folklore as a discursive mode. Gideon is sufficiently disturbed by the premonition his dream contains that he complains to Suzie that he still can't find his toby, the charm his grandmother gave him that he believes protects him from evil.

But beyond that, this opening, disorienting as it is, prepares viewers for the position we must occupy in relation to the film. As is often the case when we are confronted with a dream, we don't know where we are, who the players are, and how we are meant to understand it. If the scene is meant to refer to something, what is its referent? Are there multiple referents? Even retrospectively, our interpretation of this scene, like our understanding of a dream, is only partial. Is the photograph Gideon's mother, Big Mama, or is it someone else? Why do the flames fail to consume Gideon, the fruit, and the table? Is the sliced apple meant to signify temptation? The world of *To Sleep with Anger* is a community constituted by its own vernacular, rituals, foodways, and superstitions. Burnett does not spoon-feed explanations to us. As outsiders, we are required to work to make connections and to accept only partial explanations. According to the logic of this world, as in

---

[4]In her brilliant forthcoming essay on Sister Rosetta Tharpe, Gayle Wald makes a compelling case for Tharpe's central role in debates over the distinction between sacred and secular music as well as larger controversies concerning African American cultural identity at the middle of the twentieth century. By this light, the selection of one of Tharpe's recordings as the backdrop for this opening scene is especially significant.

dreams, knowledge is organized and conveyed in a variety of ways and according to multivalent processes and practices.

Harry's arrival likewise evokes the continuities associated with the migrant experience. The fact that Harry appears at a time when Gideon expects something to go very wrong is one sign that he is not the friend they believe him to be. A series of omens warn the viewer that Harry is not to be trusted, although the family members (like Gideon in the dream sequence) take longer to recognize this. An egg and a teapot both break the morning he arrives, and the fetus Pat is carrying kicks her each time she tries to shake Harry's hand.

Shortly after Harry appears unannounced and Suzie and Gideon invite him to stay as long as he likes, Sunny touches Harry's foot with a broom, which alarms all three.[5] Gideon makes Sunny apologize; Harry quickly grabs the broom and spits on it; and without missing a beat, Suzie brings out a saucer of salt from which Harry takes a couple of pinches to toss over his shoulders. They may not have seen each other for thirty years, but these superstitions are still fresh in their minds. Involuntarily and nonverbally, these ritual practices connect the migrants to their past history and bind them together in a community with friends and relatives from whom they have become separated.

In an interview with Sojin Kim and R. Mark Livengood, Burnett said that he based the character of Harry on a folk character called the Hairy Man. Part trickster, a figure derived from West African antecedents, Harry appears when the family in general (and Babe Brother in particular) is at a crossroads and thus especially vulnerable. He disturbs the status quo and "creates the possibility for renewal and forgiveness by provoking suffering and rage"(70). Part badman (a classic figure from African American folklore), Harry is associated with a type of outlaw figure who refuses to be constrained by societal norms, whether imposed by African American or white cultural practices.

To his friends, in contrast, Gideon is associated with the folk figure of John Henry. The focus of a famous African American blues ballad, John Henry is legendary because of his capacity for hard work. According to the song, John Henry challenges a steam drill to a race to

---

[5]In *Shuckin' and Jivin'*, Daryl Cumber Dance includes the superstition that "If you touch somebody with a broom, they going to jail. But if he spits on the broom, that cures it" (308).

speed the construction of a railway tunnel. In a show of superhuman strength, John Henry wins the race, but in the process he works himself to death. The character can thus be read as a figure either of black hypermasculinity or of self-destructiveness. In Babe Brother's mind, his father's commitment to hard work has rendered him little more than a "farm animal." It is thus hardly surprising that he is intrigued by the alternative that Harry presents with his slick, peripatetic ways.

We are invited to contrast Harry's power and values with Gideon's in a variety of ways. Among the most striking is the repetition of Tharpe's cover of "Precious Memories" in the sequence in which Harry is left alone while Gideon and Suzie have gone to church. The use of this distinctive music here speaks back to its use at the beginning of the film. In the dream sequence, the first time we hear the song, the lyrics suggest something of the inescapable presence of Gideon's southern past in his northern life. When it reappears, it provides a background for shots of Harry examining and touching Gideon and Suzie's family photographs, a predator prying through their drawers and curios, groping for private information he can use against them in the future.

Later that same Sunday morning, while everyone else is at church, Babe Brother and Harry play cards at Gideon and Suzie's kitchen table while Linda and Sunny look on. The use of crosscutting here alternates the kitchen scene with the Scripture reading and a baptismal service at church, underscoring the fact that Babe Brother is at a crossroads, traditionally the place over which the trickster figure presides. As Harry reels in Babe Brother, Linda, and Sunny with stories of his younger days in Memphis, in the church scenes the pastor reads from Matthew 10:34–35, in which Christ declares his mission on earth in terms that invoke Harry's trickster function: "Think not that I am come to send peace on earth: I came not to send peace, but a sword. For I am come to set a man at variance against his father, and the daughter against her mother, and the daughter-in-law against her mother-in-law." And as the young worshipper is baptized (while the choir sings "Take Me to the Water" in the background), Babe Brother is gradually drawn in by the spell Harry casts. This technique thus also highlights the contradictory and yet inextricable pulls of sacred and secular experience so central to the migrant experience: crosscutting conveys not only chronological simultaneity but cultural syncretism as well.

In its own way, the scene in the kitchen, like the baptism, is an initiation rite of sorts; Babe Brother is won over by Harry's tales of knife fights, fast women, and hard-drinking men. At first Linda also appears to be taken in by Harry, but she quickly senses that he may pose a serious danger. She seems concerned about the impact Harry's stories will have on Sunny. Harry's overfamiliarity with her (at one point he puts his arm around her and caresses her shoulder) makes her uncomfortable. And she mistrusts Harry's impact on Babe Brother. For Harry is clearly more interested in Babe Brother than he is in her; as the conversation progresses, she becomes more a spectator and less an interlocutor. Indeed, Harry's story speaks so powerfully to Babe Brother that it seems to transform him subtly but profoundly. In the course of the telling, he aligns himself with Harry, to the point that he speaks harshly to Linda when she picks up one of Harry's cards out of curiosity, saying, "Don't touch the cards, you're not in the game!" Indeed, in Babe Brother's struggle to define his masculinity, she is not "in the game."[6]

At Harry's suggestion, Gideon and Suzie host an old-fashioned fish fry to which they invite many of their old friends from back home. A marvelous set piece, this scene features compelling blues and gospel performances by their old friends Percy (Jimmy Witherspoon performing "See, See Rider") and Hattie (Ethel Ayler performing "Stand By Me"). The use of music here further emphasizes the proximity of sacred and secular experience in African American communities and history and highlights the concealed tensions in the party and the family. In the public space of the living room, the guests are clearly enjoying themselves. But the memory and the threat of violence are just below the surface, as evidenced in the confrontation between Marsh (Sy Richardson) and Harry in the kitchen and Gideon and Babe Brother's conversation in front of the house.

Early in the scene, Witherspoon, the legendary jazz, blues, and R & B artist, sings the classic lyrics of love gone bad, violence, and men who escape, a tale all too familiar to Harry:

> See, see Rider
> See what you have done
> Lord, see, see Rider

---

[6] See Karen Chandler's extensive and thoughtful reading of this scene.

See what you have done
Stole my girl
Now that man's done gone.

Gonna buy me a pistol
Just as long as I am tall
Gonna buy me a pistol
Just as long as I am tall
Shoot that girl
Catch that Cannonball.

Shortly thereafter, when the men gather in the kitchen to drink corn liquor, Marsh confronts Harry about his role in the death of his cousin Emory and his old friend from home Harker, and blames Harry for almost causing a race riot. Almost as a gloss on his own function in Gideon and Suzie's household, Harry brushes off the accusation, saying, "Strange as it may seem, it might have cleared the water. Sometimes the right action comes from the wrong reason."

The use of crosscutting later in the scene underscores and then defuses the heightened atmosphere of conflict. Near the end of Marsh's conversation with Harry, Gideon and Babe Brother begin to argue outside about Babe Brother and Linda's priorities, and Hattie, accompanied by a guitarist, starts to sing "Stand by Me" in the living room:

In the midst of tribulation,
Stand by me.
In the midst of tribulation,
Stand by me.
When my life becomes a burden,
And I'm crossing chilly Jordan,
Thou who never lost a battle,
Stand by me.

Marsh leaves Harry in the kitchen as other men come in to get a drink. The tension between these two seems almost to migrate to the front steps, for the confrontation situated there escalates as the other dissipates; Babe Brother explodes when Gideon, like clockwork, compares his behavior to Junior's. As if to foreshadow subsequent developments in the film, Suzie warns that arguing with Babe Brother will cause Gideon to have a stroke. She insists that the two men shake hands before they separate, perhaps fearing what will happen if they go to sleep angry. Despite the tension of this scene, the visual juxtaposition of Hattie's wistful performance of the song, as well as its persistence as a background vocal, bestows on it the power of a prayer, an act of faith that order will be restored within the family.

The pressure of the confrontation between Gideon and Babe Brother has already taken its toll, however. The next time we see Gideon, he is unwell, walking with Harry in the heat of the day along a railroad track, an obvious allusion both to Gideon as a John Henry figure and to the migrants who relied on this mode of transportation to take them from the South to the North. Gideon is on the verge of collapse, and yet Harry keeps him moving. When they finally stop for a rest, in the distance, sepia-toned, spectral images of black men hammering railroad ties dissolve into each other, the sound of the hammers echoing in the distance. As Harry reflects, "So many memories, stretched along tracks like these." Given Gideon's disorientation, Harry's words, and the techniques with which the image of the men are produced, viewers might well ask if the men we see working on the tracks are Gideon's hallucinations, images of their shared recollections, or a digression meant to represent these evocative, pivotal figures from African American cultural history.

By the next day, Gideon is unable to get out of bed and soon suffers a stroke. As Gideon's health deteriorates, Babe Brother loses his mooring. Wandering around as if in a stupor, he becomes more deeply connected to Harry, despite the toll Gideon's decline and this association take on his family. On the evening of a dinner party he and Linda host for Harry and his friends, for example, Babe Brother takes her to task for failing to see to it that Sunny's shoes are on the right feet. When she asks him to leave the pots alone so she can finish cooking, he slaps her and she threatens to stab him with a serving fork. During the party she cries and refuses to engage with him. Because he will not stop seeing Harry, she takes Sunny and moves in with Junior and Pat.

Freed of responsibility, Babe Brother plans to leave his marriage and ailing father behind and go on the road with Harry. But in the most dramatic scene of the film, Babe Brother and Junior fight in their parents' kitchen. Babe Brother pulls the knife that Harry has given him, Junior wrestles it away from him, and fueled by his rage, disappointment, and perhaps envy of his brother, Junior seems ready to kill him. But Suzie, Pat, and Linda are able to keep the two men apart, and Suzie places her hand around the knife to prevent the stabbing. Her sacrifice brings the family together as her sons reunite in order to care for her. Reconstituted on firmer ground, the family no longer needs Harry to play his symbolic role. Prodded by Hattie, Suzie tells Harry to leave, but before he can collect his belongings, he drops dead on the kitchen floor. As the film ends, Gideon has recovered sufficiently to be able to come downstairs, and their neighbors join forces to help the family deal with the dead body in their midst.

Conclusion

Although this film raises subtle questions about the impact of migration on the men in the film, it relegates women to the conventional roles of maintaining culture and tradition. Suzie, the midwife and gardener, epitomizes the good wife and mother. Hattie, Harry's old girlfriend, has left her wild ways behind and "is in church now." Pat possesses many of the qualities we associate with Suzie. And even Linda, who is edgy and driven when we first meet her and has little time for her son, falls into step as an attentive wife, daughter-in-law, and mother when Babe Brother begins to lose his way. Notwithstanding the subtleties of (especially) Sheryl Lee Ralph's and Mary Alice's performances, the film might have taken us even more deeply into the experience of black middle-class women migrants and their "daughters."

To Sleep with Anger has a quiet, meditative, contemplative tone and focuses on a community of attractive, but largely unexceptional, characters. Since the time of its release, it has enjoyed critical acclaim, having won the Special Jury Prize at the Sundance Film Festival in 1990 and been selected for inclusion in the same year at both the Cannes and the Toronto Film Festivals. But perhaps because it demands that viewers accustom themselves to a world that is for many unfamiliar and not fully comprehensible, it has yet to find a wide audience. The issues with which it grapples are central to what it means to live in communities in the postmodern age, however. Its modest focus casts into relief complex questions about the ways in which socioeconomic status, labor markets, mobility, and history interact with constructions of race and gender to shape how we live our lives from one generation to the next.

Credits

United States, 1990, SVS Films

Director: Charles Burnett
Producers: Thomas S. Byrnes, Caldecot Chubb, and David Scott
Screenplay: Charles Burnett
Cinematography: Walt Lloyd
Editing: Nancy Richardson
Art Director: Troy Myers
Production Design: Penny Barrett
Costume Design: Gaye Shannon-Burnett

CAST:
Gideon	Paul Butler
Sunny	DeVaughn Nixon
Suzie	Mary Alice
Rhonda	Reina King
Skip	Cory Curtis
Babe Brother	Richard Brooks
Linda	Sheryl Lee Ralph
Junior	Carl Lumbly
Pat	Vonetta McGee
Harry Mention	Danny Glover
Percy	Jimmy Witherspoon
Hattie	Ethel Ayler
Marsh	Sy Richardson

Bibiliography

Adero, Malaika. *Up South: Stories, Studies and Letters of This Century's Black Migrations.* New York: New P, 1993.

Chandler, Karen. "Folk Culture and Masculine Identity in Charles Burnett's *To Sleep With Anger.*" *African American Review* 33 (1999): 299–311.

Dance, Daryl Cumber. *From My People: 400 Years of African American Folklore.* New York: Norton, 2002.

———. *Shuckin' and Jivin': Folklore from Contemporary African Americans.* Bloomington: Indiana UP, 1978.

Goodwin, E. Marvin. *Black Migration in America from 1915 to 1960.* Lewiston, NY: Edwin Mellen, 1990.

Griffin, Farah Jasmine. *"Who Set You Flowin'?" The African American Migration Narrative.* New York: Oxford UP, 1995.

Guerrero, Ed. *Framing Blackness: The African American Image in Film.* Philadelphia: Temple UP, 1993.

Harrison, Alferdteen, ed. *Black Exodus: The Great Migration from the American South.* Jackson: UP of Mississippi, 1991.

Jones, Jacquie. "The Black South in Contemporary Film." *African American Review* 27 (1993): 19–24.

Kim, Sojin, and R. Mark Livengood. "Talking with Charles Burnett." *Journal of American Folklore III* (1998): 69–73.

Lemann, Nicholas. *The Promised Land: The Great Migration and How It Changed America.* New York: Vintage, 1991.

Roberts, John. *From Trickster to Badman: The Black Folk Hero in Slavery and Freedom.* Philadelphia: U of Pennsylvania P, 1989.

Wald, Gayle. "From Spirituals to Swing: Sister Rosetta Tharpe and Gospel Crossover." *American Quarterly*, forthcoming.

White, Armond. *The Resistance: Ten Years of Pop Culture That Shook the World.* Woodstock, NY: Overlook, 1995.

Raise the Red Lantern (1991)

SHUQIN CUI

The Cinematic Orient and Female Conflict

Context

In the 1980s, the emergence of the Fifth Generation of Chinese film directors and their New Wave films began to draw international attention.[1] China became a visual icon to a worldwide audience. In the process of screening China, filmmakers treated historical memories and national trauma as major themes. In their revision of Chinese history, filmmakers questioned the ideological orthodoxy of official discourses and uncovered personal or familial experiences formerly repressed. Three films, Chen Kaige's *Farewell My Concubine* (1993), Tian Zhuangzhuang's *The Blue Kite* (1993), and Zhang Yimou's *To Live* (1994), for instance, collectively unveil China's social and political history, but they do so from different angles. *Farewell My Concubine* places the personal drama of two opera singers within the framework of fifty years of Chinese history. Chen uses the form of an opera-within-the-film and the saga of a biological male becoming a cultural female to question whether one can remain true to anything or anyone in the face of extraordinary historical circumstances. *The Blue Kite,* seen from a child's point of view and with his voice-over narration, presents the death of three fathers. Each father's death punctuates a specific political moment. Together the deaths signify the political confrontation between the individual fathers of the child and the collective father symbol of the state apparatus. The child, as witness to and narrator of his fathers' stories, reinforces memory as well as revises history. *To Live* similarly focuses on a family melodrama during China's decades of sociopolitical upheaval. Presenting children as the victims of various

---

[1]The Fifth Generation of film directors refers chronologically and aesthetically to the 1982 graduates of the Beijing Film Academy.

"progressive" campaigns (the son dies in the Great Leap Forward, the daughter during the Cultural Revolution), the film shows ordinary people struggling to survive amid the brutal effects of waves of political change.

In their thematic pursuit of history and tradition, New Wave films demonstrate a radical departure from films in the theatrical-melodramatic tradition as well as from models of socialist production. New Wave experiments in visual articulation, cinematography, and *mise-en-scène* brought Chinese cinema—heretofore politically manipulated and aesthetically ignored—into the international arena. Significantly, the visual images are culturally specific and ethnographically appealing. For instance, Chen Kaige's unusual framing in *Yellow Earth* (1984)—heaven above, earth below, and humans between—visually illustrates the philosophical interdependence between human beings and nature. By inserting a Communist figure into the frame and the discourse, however, the director invites the audience to witness an allegorical confrontation between ancient conceptions and Communist ideology. Tian Zhuangzhuang's stunning cinematography in *Horse Thief* (1986) reveals a marginal culture exotic to the eyes of Han Chinese as well as to international audiences. The embodiment of religious discourse within the cinematic form appears allegorical: a horse thief is shunned by the very god he venerates. Huang Jianxin's urban setting and Expressionist *mise-en-scène* in *Dislocation* (1986) create a modernist art that satirizes the absurdity of socialist bureaucracy. In having a robot replace the protagonist to attend endless meetings, the film describes a futuristic condition where human and machine answer to the concepts of control and obedience.

Beyond the thematic and semiotic aspects of the discursive and visual representation of China, the concept of gender is centrally important. In fact, gendering the nation and sexualizing representation become linked strategies for constructing national images and for attracting international spectatorship. The sign of woman carries dual implications: as repressed Other, she defines sociocultural oppression, and as an erotic icon, she offers a seductive display. The appeal of Zhang Yimou's films lies precisely in his visual articulation of female images, signifying many faces of social repression as well as of visual attraction.

The Director and His Films

As the leading figure of the Fifth Generation of filmmakers, Zhang Yimou has inscribed his name into Chinese film history and has achieved international recognition. His film career began as a cinematographer for *One and Eight* (1983), *Yellow Earth* (1984), and *The Big Parade* (1985). His early films as a director, *Red Sorghum* (1987), *Ju Dou* (1990), and *Raise the Red Lantern* (1991), established Zhang's reputation not only as a master of visual art—*mise-en-scène,* color tone, and cinematography—but also as a female-image maker. In particular, the star image of Gong Li became an international icon identified with Zhang's work. While known for his highly stylized visuals and drama, Zhang has often surprised the audience with unusual experiments. *The Story of Qiu Ju* (1992) and *Not One Less* (1999), for instance, return to the essence of realism. The use of nonprofessional actors, location shooting, and minimal camera work foregrounds ordinary people as central characters and crafts their experiences into a narrative. However, Zhang refuses to be identified as a single kind of director. His *Keep Cool* (1997) turns the camera lens to Beijing for a black comedy about the urban milieu of contemporary China. A more recent big-budget martial arts epic, *Hero* (2002), demonstrates Zhang's persistence in the provocative use of visual form and his desire for commercial success.

A standout in his prolific career, Zhang Yimou's *Raise the Red Lantern* presents us with a stunning example of how gendered construction and visual signs can constitute a national allegory and attract international spectators. In *Raise the Red Lantern,* Zhang's critique of patriarchal discourse—its family structure, concubine system, gender relations—is an essential part of the process of visualization. The "iron-house" *mise-en-scène,* for example, suggests how national traditions may confine and repress the desires of individuals. The red lanterns and foot massages offer a spectacle of ethnographic detail, while conflicts among the women lend drama to the narrative, drawing in the international viewer. The critical reception of *Raise the Red Lantern,* international and domestic, has varied widely, however. The film received a Silver Lion at the Venice International Film Festival in 1991 and an Academy Award nomination for Best Foreign Language Film in 1992. Meanwhile, the film was banned at home. Critics generally see Zhang as the director who introduced Chinese films to international screens. Some viewers, however, have accused him of staging ethnographic scenes to please foreign audiences. Taking Zhang's *Raise the Red Lantern* as an example, this essay examines how the director uses a visual language system and gender relations to construct national allegories. And more broadly, we will see how a "cooperative orientalism" emerges as national production and international perception meet.

Analysis

Iron-House Mise-en-Scène *and National Allegories*

The "iron-house" *mise-en-scène* is a trademark of Zhang Yimou's films, as illustrated by the dye mill in *Ju Dou* and the courtyard house in *Raise the Red Lantern*. The iron house, a literary metaphor drawn from Lu Xun's fiction in the early twentieth century,[2] signifies the nation as a sealed space in which citizens languish lethargically and nearly suffocate. Through this metaphor, Lu Xun called for national salvation, hoping that the voice of enlightenment might destroy the iron house and awaken the sleeping citizens by overturning the oppressive nature of Chinese tradition.

Zhang transforms the literary version of the iron house into a visual closed form. In depicting the iron house, *Raise the Red Lantern* intends not to destroy it but to use it as the ideal setting in which to explore the oppressive nature of tradition. Zhang describes his intentions clearly in his interview with Mayfair Yang: "I was so excited when I discovered the walled gentry mansion, which is hundreds of years old, in Shanxi Province. Its high walls formed a rigid square grid pattern that perfectly expresses the age-old obsession with strict order. The Chinese people have for a long time confined themselves within a restricted walled space. . . . We have a historical legacy of extinguishing human desire" (301–2). The ancient mansion provided Zhang with a space where he could exercise his directorial authority and critique national tradition. In its closed form, the set manipulates the narrative and confines the characters to a single locale. In fact, it dominates the field of viewing.

---

[2]Lu Xun (1881–1936), best known for his short stories and critical essays, is considered the father of modern Chinese literature.

The master's mansion, for instance, displays a confined space on the arrival of the fourth wife. In a telephoto shot, Songlian is positioned against an overwhelming stone tablet and under an arched entrance. The entrance leads the female protagonist into a patriarchal household, symbolically echoed in the surrounding architectural forms. The high, massive walls divide the wives and concubines according to their status yet combine them under the same roof of patriarchal authority. The successions of doors prevent any possible transgressions. The narrative is restricted entirely to the framed courtyard house. Often, the camera anticipates the action, and the setting elaborates its implications. Placed in such a setting and facing the weight of tradition, the characters have little freedom.

Inside the sealed house, the drama unfolds as the four wives and concubines compete for the master's favor.[3] The daily rituals begin when each appears in her doorway to await the master's nightly selection. After the lantern is placed in front of the chosen one, the drama of female competition takes center stage inside the walls and between the chambers. A woman cannot simply express her desire by walking beyond the walls; this would violate the patriarchal restrictions and earn punishment. The rooftop presents the only available space extending beyond the walls. Here Songlian is able to engage in a brief communication with the master's son. Also attached to the mansion is a "death house," where women in previous generations were executed for their failure to obey traditional rules. The third mistress is hanged here when her affair with the family doctor becomes known.

While it visually defines the repression of women, the iron-house *mise-en-scène* can also be understood as a comment on the state of China. With the narrative confined to the master's mansion and detached from historical context, the audience, especially international viewers, may readily read this *mise-en-scène* as a national allegory: China is an iron house that denies any possible freedom to its people. Indeed, the visual attractiveness of the film in the absence of historical

---

[3]*Wives and Concubines* is the original title of Su Tong's novella, from which the film *Raise the Red Lantern* is adapted. In terms of the narrative, the title indicates the four female characters: Master Chen's first, second, third, and fourth wives or concubines. From a sociolinguistic perspective, the term "wives and concubines" (*qiqie*) reflects a patriarchal tradition that allowed a man to obtain multiple wives and concubines to serve his various needs and interests.

context may encourage such an interpretation. This notion of national allegory originates from Fredric Jameson's reading of third world literary texts, especially Lu Xun's short stories. Jameson's thesis states that all third world texts present national allegories, as the private individual stories often imply the embattled situation of the public third world culture and society; yet he argues that the interplay between political and personal makes such texts alien and resistant to conventional Western habits of reading (69). For Jameson, the task of reading third world texts is to look behind personal experience for the inevitable political implications responsible for the text's meaning. This reading is fraught with difficulties, however, because Western readers may not recognize the allegorical subtext. Not surprisingly, Jameson's belief that "all third-world texts" are to be read from a political perspective as national allegories has provoked constant debate and criticism (69). Opposing arguments, posed by Aijaz Ahmad, for instance, challenge the exclusiveness of third world literature, the tendency of division between self and Other, and the narrowness of taking national oppression as the only source of representation (3–25).

Raise the Red Lantern, however, does invite the viewer to see the film as a visual allegory of China. Moreover, by visualizing the nation in a way aimed at engaging with international audiences, the film alters the division between self and Other, or between third world texts and first world readings. Whereas Lu Xun called for tearing down the iron house, Zhang Yimou invites viewers to gaze into the iron-house space. Moreover, the global geopolitical shifts since Lu Xun's era have reordered the world. Under present conditions of international commerce, we need to ask what happens when national cultural productions do not resist but correspond to transnational perception. For instance, in taking the iron-house metaphor from written to visual form, the director transfers China's oppressive tradition onto the screen. The new representation, however, emphasizes visual construction rather than discursive exploration. In addition, the visual form suggests a subjective directorship that is more concerned with form than content. As Zhang explained in his interview with Mayfair Yang, the film attempts "to give a concrete form to the oppression. When tragedy is made aesthetic, then it is all the more overpowering" (305). The audience of the closed form is lured or willingly drawn into a realm of imprisonment, where the world beyond the boundaries of the screen disappears.

The Red Lanterns, the Foot Massage, and the Cinematic Orient

In addition to the iron-house form, the film's visual power and ethnographic allure can be credited to visual and sound motifs that include the deployment of the red lanterns and the hammering sounds of foot massage. A ritual sequence of lighting, extinguishing, and covering the lanterns indicates the privilege of the one concubine chosen to spend the night with the master at the expense of the rest. The lantern is lit as the master arrives for the night, extinguished as he leaves, and permanently veiled should a wife violate the master's rules. As a visual and patriarchal symbol, the lantern indicates male possession of the female body, and suggests the controlling forces behind both the narrative and spectatorship. For instance, the lighting of lanterns along the courtyard and inside the chamber announces the coming of the fourth wife, Songlian. The red lanterns, in symmetrical composition, create an empowering aura as the newlywed is prepared for the master. The color red, of course, suggests sexual engagement. When Songlian realizes that to keep the master she must possess the lanterns, she fakes a pregnancy. When her ruse becomes apparent, the lanterns are veiled. Thus the lanterns signify the rise and fall of the woman in the sexual economy of the household.

The sealed mansion embellished with lanterns stages a female drama and establishes the realm of spectatorship. As a concubine is selected for the night and the lit lantern goes up, the film acknowledges the right of the master to possess the female body and invites the audience to share his vision. Thus, the spectator enjoys the voyeuristic pleasure of gazing into a private space and sharing the concubine's body. It is from this perspective that the audience views the catfight among the women. The third wife charms the master with her opera singing and challenges the "sisters" with her competitive force. The second wife, who possesses neither youth nor skill but "a Buddha's face and a scorpion's heart," stirs up conflict among the wives by setting one party against another. The cinematic tactic of raising the red lantern dramatizes not only the conflict among the wives but also the act of spectatorship.

Along with the red-lantern imagery, the film reinforces the idea of female sexuality and cinematic ethnography through sound effects. For example, the audience receives the image and sound of foot massage as the second wife has the treatment in her chamber. The sound changes to offscreen as Songlian and her maid, Yan'er, separately yet simultaneously indulge themselves in an imagined foot massage and sexual fantasy. The transition of sound from on-screen to offscreen space creates an aural and visual atmosphere of sexual desire that encompasses the three women. The pervasive sounds of foot massage signify the force that regulates each woman and organizes the wives into a network of power struggles. As Suzie Young-Sau Fong suggests, the foot massage is a kind of "mechanical foreplay to prepare the vagina as a receptacle for the penis, in his own words, to help her better serve him. Like the lighting of the red lanterns, it is a treatment rather than a treat" (16). When maid and mistress engage in the pleasure (or illusion) of the foot massage, the sounds transgress not only spatial divisions but also class differences. However, the foot massage announces the privilege accorded to one wife while denied to the others. As a consequence, Songlian orders Yan'er to manually massage her feet, and Yan'er reluctantly obeys. From the concubine's perspective, the sound of the foot massage indicates a female sexual desire under the control of the master.

The images of red lanterns and the sounds of foot massage present the audience with an imaginative ethnography and an exoticized Orient. Such inventions have drawn varied reactions. Dai Qing, a Chinese critic, responds to the film with "a pair of raised eyebrows" as she discovers historical inaccuracies regarding the ethnographic rituals and the characters (333–37). It is appropriate for Dai Qing to clarify the impossibility of using red lanterns to flaunt the details of a master's sexual life and of massaging a woman's feet to induce sexual arousal. Nonetheless, she fails to realize that *Raise the Red Lantern* is not a film *as* ethnography but rather ethnography in imaginative fashion. Zha Jianying, a Chinese writer living in the United States, observes that her Chinese friends in America dislike the film because of its "tendency of catering to the Westerners with oriental exoticism" (331). Her Western friends, however, are fascinated by the film. The following commentary from Roger Ebert is typical of the praise lavished on the abundant visual pleasure offered in the film: "*Raise the Red Lantern* exists solely for the eyes. Entirely apart from the plot, there is the sensuous pleasure of the architecture, the fabrics, the color contrasts, the faces of the actresses."

The different perceptions of the film raise the issue of cooperative orientalism: the production side "orientalizes" to satisfy the international gaze, while the reception side embraces such self-exhibition with fascination. Rey Chow has termed this tendency toward self-exhibition the "oriental's orientalism." In her view, Zhang's films exhibit a self-representation that places the voyeurism of orientalism on display (171). Arif Dirlik further explains the history behind self-representation or self-orientalization. From the beginning, he argues, Asians participated in constructing the constellation of ideas and images known as the Orient. Orientalism was a product of *interactions* between Euro-American and Asian intellectuals that tended to blur the lines between self and Other and between subject and object (95). The issue calls for further explanation: When the Orient has for so long been articulated as the Eastern "Other," what does it mean for Asian filmmakers to engage in self-exhibition and self-orientalization?

In contemporary filmmaking, when national productions try to accommodate international perceptions and consumption, the national marker starts to lose its legitimacy. Intent on introducing Chinese cinema to the world, Zhang Yimou and other directors seriously consider what kind of film will signify Chinese ethnicity while appealing to a world audience. Ethnographic elements help fulfill that need. The ethnographic details in Chinese films often make for compelling spectacles: wedding processions and folk music of *xintian you* in *Yellow Earth,* the Tibetan's one hundred thousand prostrations to Buddha in *Horse Thief,* the dye mill in *Ju Dou,* wine making in *Red Sorghum,* and red lanterns and foot massage in *Raise the Red Lantern.* Films with such images are by no means ethnographic in the sense of scientific studies and documentaries produced by academic anthropologists and professional filmmakers. Yet although films inscribed with ethnographic coding do not necessarily pursue cultural authenticity, they may share the primary task of representation or self-representation of one culture to another. Moreover, the mission of screening China to the world inverts the customary order of ethnographic production: rather than studying an Other, a self presents its own image. Mary Louise Pratt expounds on this auto-ethnographic representation or self-orientalization:

> If ethnographic texts are a means by which Europeans represent to themselves their (usually subjugated) others, auto-ethnographic texts are those the others construct in response to

> or in dialogue with those metropolitan representations. . . .
> Auto-ethnographic texts are not, then, what are usually
> thought of as "authentic" or autochthonous forms of represen-
> tation. . . . Rather auto-ethnography involves partial collabora-
> tion with and appropriation of the idioms of the conqueror. (7)

To consider Chinese film productions in terms of either auto-
ethnography or cooperative orientalism is problematic. Yet, the concept of collaboration sheds light on our exploration of how the
screened China relates to its viewers.

For instance, Chinese film directors have often portrayed a repressive
cultural tradition through visual and ethnographic images. Such representations, drawn from an indefinite past and often placed in primitive
settings, meet the expectations of the spectators' *imagined* China: oppressive yet visually stunning. The discourse of China in the Western imagination is encouraged and reinforced by this visual ethnography.
Depictions of the unknown past suggest historical authenticity, while the
primitive settings imply social reality. It is precisely this indefinite time
and space that ensure the notion of an *imagined* China. For instance,
Zhang Yimou's *Red Sorghum* begins with a voice-over in which the narrator traces the legends of his grandparents. Against the setting of a
sorghum field, the tales of the grandmother's arranged marriage, sexual
encounter with a bandit, and brutalization at the hands of Japanese soldiers turn into screen images. The legend and the homeland evoke a past
and a place that witness the stifling burden of tradition while celebrating
the passion of human desire. Zhang's *Ju Dou* ties its female protagonist
to a socially abusive patriarch and to "incest" with her "nephew." The
mise-en-scène of a preindustrial dye mill and its colorful products indicate
the weight of gender oppressions as well as the vitality of sexual desire.
Here again, time and space belong to a tradition more imagined than authentic. For its part *Raise the Red Lantern* stages the drama of one master
with his four concubines. The ancient, stone-walled mansion and the
narrative transition through the seasons turn the past into an ethnographic museum available for visual representation. Thus, when self-
exhibition meets the cinematic gaze and corresponds to the discourse of
an international spectatorship, we have a cooperative orientalism.

As auto-ethnographic exhibitions travel across national borders,
they ultimately become cultural commodities in the global market and

require transnational capital. In this sense, a further explanation for the phenomenon of cooperative orientalism lies in the engagement between cultural artifact and the market system. Film culture and production in China share certain similarities with German cinema, and, as Thomas Elsaesser observes, German cinema was "created around the very contradictions of culture and commodity, or (self)-expression value and self-exhibition value, in a modern capitalist economy that depends on export to sustain internal growth" (302). In this era of accelerating globalization, the filmmaker must secure a public screening space and cross-national capital. For the Chinese filmmaker, however, access to public space depends on the dictates of governmental censorship and ideological correctness. If willing to reproduce the official discourse, one is assured of financing for production and for distribution on release. To counter the official discourse, however, film directors must manage to find a way of their own, usually by attracting foreign capital and winning international recognition. Caught between political pressures at home and the global marketing system, directors find themselves in an awkward position. International viewers acknowledge them as image makers bringing the icon of China to the world screen. Chinese viewers, by contrast, may see a national betrayal in disclosing domestic dirty laundry to foreigners. In this context, an important question must be considered: Who or what is exoticized and exhibited and to whom? To put the question in the more specific terms of this essay, what is the role of the female image in self-orientalization?

Female Conflict

Raise the Red Lantern stages a theater of female competition and social punishment. Louise Bernikow describes conflict between women in literature as a "carnival," and notes that "masculine writers love to describe these scenes and set them in stories where women are passive in relation to men but hostile to each other" (207). In line with Bernikow's position, I argue that the female drama in *Raise the Red Lantern* suggests a gendered relationship between women as the represented and men as directors and spectators. Displayed at center stage, the female body is a contested site, as the editors of *Writing on the Body* declare, "a battleground for competing ideologies" (Conboy, Medina, and Stanbury 7). The concubine in *Raise the Red Lantern* is confined inside the master's patriarchal house. Her image is captured by the camera and framed or imprisoned on-screen. In this central position, therefore, woman becomes the primary source for the construction of the film's narrative and visual articulation, and international spectatorship. Furthermore, a close analysis of female conflicts in *Raise the Red Lantern* shows that women compete against each other through the destruction of their own bodies, or via feminine conditions such as menstruation, miscarriage, and pregnancy, or through death. A question arises: Does this central position at all enable woman's identity, voice, and perspective to emerge, or is the female image shaped for other purposes?

Consider the contest between Songlian and the third wife, Meishan. The wedding night marks the moment when the female body submits to the master's sexual possession and the female image becomes the central object of the viewer's attention. The voice-over of the third wife's maid asks the master to return, as the third wife is "terribly sick." Two concubines who have never met are thus engaged in a contest between the body of sexuality and the body of sickness. As the new bride, Songlian has traditional legitimacy and can claim visual dominance. The third wife resorts to sickness to call for the master's attention and resorts to a voice-over for cinematic recognition. She must challenge Songlian however she can. The master does abandon the bride to return to the "sick" wife, yet in actual fact neither concubine holds the power to decide the course of events. The master, or, ultimately, the law of the father, decides which woman is chosen or neglected.

The drama of female rivalry darkens to violent hostility when pregnancy and miscarriage are used as competing tactics. Meishan tells the story of how she and the second wife became pregnant at about the same time. The second wife then poisoned Meishan with a drug designed to cause a miscarriage. The second wife wanted to assume motherhood of the master's heir, but her plan failed when she gave birth to a girl, while Meishan gave birth to a boy. The second wife is represented as no better than an attempted murderer. By presenting the women at each other's throats, the film's narrative leads audience attention toward a female catfight. The critique of gender oppression is subsumed to spectacle as we realize that the rivals are reduced to desperately competing to give birth to a male heir. The second wife,

Zhuoyun, never relinquishes her thoughts of exacting revenge against the third wife. Finally, she makes public Meishan's sexual affair with the family doctor, and thus compels the master to hang Meishan in the death house. Meishan's pursuit of a sexual affair is a transgression of the iron house; it expresses her desire to seek love on her own terms. For Zhuoyun, the third wife's sexual affair hands her the ideal weapon with which to vanquish her foe. The root cause of Meishan's death, however, is not female jealousy at all, but the Confucian ideal of female chastity.

Realizing the importance of gaining the master's favor, Songlian decides to feign a pregnancy. She understands that bearing the master a male heir will secure her a permanent privilege. Unfortunately for Songlian, the maid Yan'er notices Songlian's menstrual blood and reports this to the second wife. The master responds by having Songlian's lanterns covered, never to be lit again. This conflict between mistress and maid is also a matter of class difference. Yan'er, of low social status, nevertheless has strong sexual desires and fantasies of herself as a wife. In fact, she keeps lanterns concealed in her room. When Songlian discovers the lanterns, she punishes Yan'er by forcing her to kneel in the courtyard in the winter cold. Songlian's authority stems from her position as a mouthpiece of patriarchal discourse. "According to the family rules," she declares, "the maid who conceals the lanterns should be punished accordingly." Yan'er silently dies of humiliation and illness caused by her mistreatment.

The answer to the question of what a woman wants is narrowed to the singular desire of winning over the master: spend the night with him, bear him a male child, be fondled by him, serve at his side. In return, the chosen wife receives signs of her status: the privilege of ordering favorite foods from the menu, having the lanterns lit in her chamber, and having her feet massaged. The film shows that a woman's desire to meet the master's demands requires the sacrifice of the female body. The destructive consequences of the female body—sickness, pregnancy, menstruation, sexual affairs—are turned into elements of competition between the women themselves, ensuring that patriarchal ideology controls the discourse and dominates visual representation. Thus, the theater of female conflict and social punishment shifts the focus of gender relations from the social dynamics between men and women to those between women themselves. Women take the positions of both oppressor and oppressed. This allows men to retreat from the scene and deflect accusations of patriarchal oppression. While women are staged for the spectacle, patriarchal discourse, or the male figure, manipulates the show from the background. Perhaps suggesting this absent yet controlling force, the figure of the master appears infrequently, often only partially, in *Raise the Red Lantern*.

The presence of women at center stage while the master is absent also calls attention to the issue of international spectatorship. An attentive audience will recognize that the master takes a marginal position in the frame as a screen character, but as a patriarchal symbol he represents the dominant force. His absence as a figure does not negate the ever-present authority of patriarchal rules. The invisibility of the male figure leaves a space that invites international spectatorship to project its gaze directly and exclusively on the female image. Thus, Western perception meets an already orientalized exhibition organized around a sense of female captivity. Moreover, the absence of the male figure ensures that the spectators will assume the position of the authoritative viewing subject.

This subject position enables the viewer to enter an exotic visual world where ethnographic displays and female images are presented as pleasurable. To this end, the master is not so much absent as replaced by international spectators. When both Chinese patriarchy and international spectators participate in the construction and perception of an oriental display, little room is left for a local or female spectatorship. Thus, it is not surprising that the female Chinese scholar Dai Qing criticizes the film's *imagined* ethnography and false ritual practices. She correctly observes that the red lanterns, foot massage, and competition to spend the night with the master present the Orient, especially oriental women, as a metaphor for sexuality. Indeed, cooperative orientalism can be seen as a business transaction between the oriental exhibitionist and the international viewing public. The ethnographic attraction and the female images are commodities displayed and consumed in a system of exchange. The star image of Gong Li, for instance, personifies how woman is socially repressed yet sexually seductive. From Zhang's first film, *Red Sorghum*, to his last one with Gong Li as his lead, *Shanghai Triad* (1995), no one can deny the evocative power of Gong Li's face.

That face, in close-up or in fragments, invites and returns a gaze filled with all possible desires. When applied to the Chinese New Wave, this concept of the gaze implies not only sexual pleasure in looking, but also a transnational engagement in perception. For international audiences, the female image, focused in close-up and framed in detail, comes to signify either oriental myth or cultural ritual.

First, as an ethnographic emblem and social sign, the image presents to the international gaze the woman's socially violated body or culturally ascribed identity. Thematic issues such as the arranged marriage, the concubine system, and sexual abuse might lead the audience's imagination toward an unknown and oppressive non-Western culture. In this manner, the engagement in looking is complicit with colonialism. "The spectator," as Ella Shohat explains, "is subliminally invited on an ethnographic tour of a celluloid preserved culture" (32). Second, as a visual icon of stunning beauty and sexual appeal, the female image directs the gaze to voyeuristic pleasure. The female body typically stars in a spectacle of difference: jolted in the wedding sedan in the sorghum field, lighting the red lantern to select the concubine, having her naked feet pounded to prepare her to serve the man in bed. These self-exhibitions of oriental women as ethnographic and sexual images encourage viewing as a mode of fantasy and possession. As self-representation and international perception cooperatively constitute and consume visual images of oriental women, one occasionally does hear a woman's voice—in the form of madness.

The Female Voice of Madness and Silence

A force occasionally able to transgress the sealed walls and thereby resist patriarchal authority in *Raise the Red Lantern* is the female voice, associated first with music, then with madness. The role of music, as embodied in a female singing voice, provides a temporary means for women to assert their desires and frustrations. For instance, the third wife, Meishan, expresses her longings through opera singing. In early morning, the sound of opera singing awakens the master and Songlian. Following Songlian, and from her point of view, we see the third wife in theatrical dress as she practices her opera performance on the rooftop of the compound. Meishan's emotions and frustrations transcend the confinement of the patriarchal household as her voice penetrates the cells of the compound, disrupting or displeasing those who are asleep. Two women, one in white, one in black, face each other with intense suspicion. The third wife warns Songlian that in this household, it is better to be awake than asleep.

The music links Meishan, the singer, to Songlian, the listener, in a transgression of culturally prescribed gender roles. In a different sequence, the master selects Zhuoyun for the night and ignores the third and fourth wives. In the courtyard of her chamber, Meishan tries to release her frustration by singing. Songlian, on top of the house, observes her. As the two join for a conversation, Songlian declares that the residents of the household are like dogs, cats, rats, and mice, not human beings. Meishan announces that she will meet her lover immediately and see what the authority dares to do to her. Enhanced by the two-shot of the characters on the upper level of the house and the choir singing in the background, the scene is one of female subversion.

Music also points to the invisible and the unspeakable. Meishan, Songlian, and two male friends engage in a game of mah-jongg. Meishan's lover, the family doctor, turns on the phonograph to play Meishan's early recorded opera aria. The music and the voice indicate Meishan's identity as a former opera star as well as her intimate relation with the doctor. As she bends to pick up a mah-jongg tile from under the table, Songlian discovers that Meishan is rubbing the doctor's leg with her foot. Songlian hears the music and witnesses the affair, while the decorous setting invites a voyeuristic gaze into female space. Unfortunately, the female voice as a gesture of resistance brings down the wrath of authority. Ultimately, the voice is silenced, the body extinguished.

Near the end of the film, we see the transformation of the female voice from song to madness. The figure of the madwoman and the voices of madness are the consequences of female resistance against patriarchal authority. From Songlian's point of view, the audience watches, via a handheld camera, as a group of male servants carry Meishan, bound and gagged, to the death house. Songlian screams wildly as Meishan is hanged, and so the death of one woman's body leads to another woman's mad voice. Again, the response to the disobedient woman is to silence her voice, as is evident in a confrontation between the master and Songlian:

THE MASTER: What did you see?
SONGLIAN: Meishan is dead. You murdered her.
THE MASTER: Nonsense! You saw nothing. You are mad!

The master condemns Songlian as a madwoman. However, the "madwoman" refuses to be silenced and uses her madness to bring back the murdered woman's voice. First, Songlian lights the lanterns in Meishan's chamber and lets her singing voice come to life through the gramophone; it pierces the silence and returns a voice not just to Meishan, but to the dead women of past generations. Opera music, from solo to choir, plays, and opera masks fill the frame, giving voice to female desires. The connection of music to madness underscores the suffocating world in which the women live and die. The "madwoman" goes on to light the lanterns in her own room, which the master had permanently covered. The gramophone and the madwoman seize the sound track and the image, for a moment asserting a female force. The image reinforces the voice, and the voice sustains the image.

Conclusion

In *Raise the Red Lantern,* however, madness as resistance is only a temporary emancipation. The mad voice fades as the wheels of tradition grind on. By the following summer, the master's mansion prepares for the coming of the fifth concubine with the usual rituals. Images of lanterns and sounds of foot massage suggest her potential ascendancy in this patriarchal household. "Who is that woman?" the new bride asks. "The former fourth mistress, who has gone mad," the maid replies. From the fifth mistress's point of view, we see the madwoman, Songlian, in her student dress, pacing within the walled compound. Her ceaseless motion, in a succession of dissolves and superimpositions, suggests agitation: "she is a wound that will not heal; her feminine madness is the disease invading the masculine body of tradition" (Fong 19). Such a metaphor of disturbance remains merely a visual gesture, however. Silenced by the patriarchal discourse and trapped within the visual *mise-en-scène*—door frames, walls, and roof lines—Songlian stays quarantined, lost in her feverish madness.

Credits

China, 1991, China Film Coproduction

Director: Zhang Yimou
Producer: Chiu Fu-Sheng and Hou Hsiao-hsien
Screenplay: Ni Zhen
Cinematography: Zhao Fei
Editing: Du Yuan
Music: Naoki Tachikawa and Zhao Jipeng
Art Direction: Caio Jiuping

CAST:

Songlian, the fourth wife	Gong Li
Meishan, the third wife	He Saifei
Zhuoyun, the second wife	Cao Cuifeng
The master	Ma Jingwu
Yan'er	Kong Lin

Bibiliography

Ahmad, Aijaz. "Jameson's Rhetoric of Otherness and the National Allegory." *Social Text* 17 (1987): 3–25.

Bernikow, Louise. *Among Women.* New York: Harper Colophon, 1981.

Chow, Rey. *Primitive Passions: Visuality, Sexuality, Ethnography, and Contemporary Chinese Cinema.* New York: Columbia UP, 1995.

Conboy, Katie, Nadia Medina, and Sarah Stanbury, eds. *Writing on the Body: Female Embodiment and Feminist Theory.* New York: Columbia UP, 1997.

Cui, Shuqin. *Women through the Lens: Gender and Nation in a Century of Chinese Cinema.* Honolulu: U of Hawai'i P, 2003.

Dai Qing, "Raised Eyebrows for *Raise the Red Lantern.*" *Public Culture* 10 (1993): 333–37.

Dirlik, Arif. "Chinese History and the Question of Orientalism." *History and Theory* 35 (1996): 95–117.

Ebert, Roger. *"Raise the Red Lantern." Chicago Sun-Times* 27 Mar. 1992. <www.suntimes.com/ebert/ebert_reviews/1992/03/748213.html>.

Elsaesser, Thomas. *New German Cinema: A History.* New Brunswick: Rutgers UP, 1989.

Fong, Suzie Young-Sau. "The Voice of Feminine Madness in Zhang Yimou's *Raise the Red Lantern.*" *Asian Cinema* 7.1 (1995): 12–23.

Jameson, Fredric. "Third-World Literature in the Era of Multinational Capitalism." *Social Text* 15 (1986): 65–88.

Pratt, Mary Louise. *Imperial Eyes: Travel Writing and Transculturation.* London: Routledge, 1992.

Shohat, Ella. "Gender and Culture of Empire: Toward a Feminist Ethnography of the Cinema." *Visions of the East: Orientalism in Film.* Ed. Matthew Bernstein and Gaylyn Studlar. New Brunswick: Rutgers UP, 1997. 19–66.

Yang, Mayfair. "Of Gender, State Censorship, and Overseas Capital: An Interview with Director Zhang Yimou." *Public Culture: Society for Transnational Cultural Studies* 10 (1993): 297–316.

Zha, Jianying. "Excerpts from 'Lore Segal, Red Lantern, and Exoticism.'" *Public Culture* 10 (1993): 329–32.

Daughters of the Dust (1991)

ANNA EVERETT

Toward a Womanist/Diasporic Film Aesthetic

Context

When Julie Dash defied the odds by getting *Daughters of the Dust* funded, produced, distributed, and finally exhibited in mainstream film theaters and later on television, the achievement signaled in a powerful way that "independent Black cinema had come of age" (Bambara xiv). Not surprisingly, Dash was immediately compared to that mercurial independent filmmaker par excellence, Spike Lee. For here was an audacious, uncompromising, and determined young black woman filmmaker who refused to be deterred by the fact that every major Hollywood studio rejected the film on the grounds that it was not commercial enough to support financially and not familiar enough for audiences to embrace emotionally.

Like Lee, Dash was trained at one of the nation's premiere film schools—UCLA, in her case—and she also trained for a time at the American Film Institute (AFI). Like Lee, Dash was able to realize her dream of creating a highly "personal film" (as she put it) that ultimately garnered both commercial and critical success. And like Lee's early films, Dash's *Daughters* owes much of its visual power to the virtuosity of its director of cinematography, Arthur Jafa (A.J.) (Bambara xv). Similarly, both Lee's and Dash's first films are marked by highly stylized and experimental formal structures—an avant-garde sensibility.

The similitude ends there. Although both Lee's and Dash's first feature-length films are tales centered around the black woman, Dash's film, unlike Lee's *She's Gotta Have It* (1986), is narrativized and focalized from a black woman's perspective. Questions involving the politics of representation and gender differences were also in play more broadly with the release of Dash's film, as *Daughters* became a standout amid the new cycle of black films during the 1990s in light of the dominance of black male directors and masculinist discourses at the heart of this trend. Male-directed films such as *Boyz N the Hood* (John Singleton, 1991), *A Rage in Harlem* (Bill Duke, 1991), *Straight out of Brooklyn* (Matty Rich, 1991), *New Jack City* (Mario Van Peebles, 1991), *Deep Cover* (Duke, 1992), and *Juice* (Ernest R. Dickerson, 1992), among others, exemplify this masculine-focused, post-blaxploitation cycle of popular urban black films easily embraced by Hollywood.

Ed Guerrero has described these films of urban decay and blight in terms of an ethos that he's dubbed "ghettocentricity" (186). Whereas these "ghettocentric" masculinist films are primarily pessimistic depictions of black communities devastated by "the pressures of ghetto life" (178), Dash's film proffers a more cautiously optimistic portrayal of black feminist survival. As Guerrero puts it, "*Daughters of the Dust* pointedly sets out to reconstruct, to recover a sense of black women's history, and to affirm their cultural and political space in the expanding arena of black cinema production" (175).

Production Background

> I never planned a career as a filmmaker. . . . None of the images I saw of African American people, especially the women, suggested that we could actually make movies. We were rarely even in them. (Dash, "*Daughters*" 1)

There is perhaps one more similarity between Spike Lee and Julie Dash. Replicating Lee's successful tie-in strategy with his book *The Making of "Do the Right Thing"* (1989), Dash's *"Daughters of the Dust": The Making of an African American Woman's Film* (1992) similarly functions as a sort of user's guide for her film. The book's useful behind-the-scenes details do not merely document the ten-year ordeal she endured to get the cinematic idea and ideal from her imagination onto the screen. They also provide pertinent information that aids spectators in deciphering many of the film's highly symbolic and "culturally specific" codifications. To better understand the breakthrough significance of *Daughters of the Dust*, it is important to consider key aspects of this film's production history and background that Dash divulges in her book and in personal interviews.

In her instructive and well-informed preface to Dash's book, Toni Cade Bambara notes that shortly after its release, *Daughters* enjoyed a cult status. Bambara adds, "It is not unreasonable to predict that it will shortly achieve the status it deserves—classic. . . . Perhaps, finally with the breakthrough of *Daughters* into the theatrical circuit, new audiences are developing for the culturally-specific works of filmmakers, producers, directors, and videographers within community media, public television, the independent sector, and the commercial industry" (Bambara xvi). Indeed, *Daughters* eventually achieved unanticipated success, beyond what I call the "prestige ghettos" of film festivals, art-house film circuits, museum venues, and elite university audiences. Moreover, Dash achieved this on her own terms, with both integrity and tenacity. As a result, *Daughters* received tremendous responses at film-festivals across the globe in 1991, culminating in Sundance's Best Cinematography award for Arthur Jafa (Brouwer 13). Irrespective of these accolades, *Daughters* languished for a year without a distribution deal (Guerrero 177). It is telling that Dash was unable to parlay her successes on the prestige film-festival circuit into a lucrative film distribution deal with the big studios. By contrast, that same year, novice filmmaker Matty Rich won a Special Jury Prize at Sundance for his film *Straight out of Brooklyn*, which *was* snapped up for distribution by Samuel Goldwyn (178).

Perhaps the difference in the reception of these two films by Hollywood's patriarchal establishment can be attributed to gender politics. Dash has asserted, "most white men don't want to be a black woman for two hours" (qtd. in Guerrero 177). However, it is equally important to bear in mind Guerrero's observation that the popular black film audience is largely a youth market, habituated to violent, formulaic action-adventure films. Expectedly then, *Daughters'* ability to appeal to this demographic would be limited. Notwithstanding such a formidable limitation, *Daughters'* surprising resilience and profitability hinged on its unmitigated success with a sizable middle-class black female demographic, which constituted the film's primary audience (Brouwer 13). Jacqueline Bobo reminds us that *Daughters* was "not simply a tale of black women reclaiming their past. As a work deliberately conceived as a film about black women, with black women intended as its primary audience, it intervenes strongly in a tradition of derogatory portrayals of black women in dominant cinema" (165). It is true that *Daughters* challenges and reimages portrayals of black women, but Dash's film also intervenes in historic portrayals of black life in general in terms of how both genders would have experienced the horrific system of slavery. I am arguing that *Daughters'* critical response to the racial oppression of both black women and black men and to black men's phallocentric constructions of black women positions it as a prototypical "womanist" film text. *Daughters* can be considered a womanist text because it not only denounces white racism and patriarchy; it also "assumes that it can talk effectively and productively about men" (Williams 70).

According to Sherley Anne Williams, productive talk about black men that encompasses a trenchant critique of their negative, stereotypical, and "'phallocentric' constructions of the black female image" is a key feature of womanist critiques. At the same time, womanist criticism takes in its purview black men's constructions of themselves (70). Viewed as a counternarrative to the popular films compromised by sexist constructions of black women, *Daughters* functions as a womanist film text that complements the highly regarded literary output of such womanist authors as Lorraine Hansberry, Alice Walker, and Toni Morrison. Like these black women writers, Dash understands too well how the "corruption wrought by slavery" continues to undermine gender relations within the black community (71). *Daughters*, then, is a powerful cinematic treatise on the persistence of African cultural traditions, rituals, and values in the black community that includes a restoration of loving and compassionate gender relations between black men and women in the aftermath of slavery's destructions.

Dash also understood too well the difficulties of attracting large audiences to yet another painful story about slavery's degradations. Her aim was to defamiliarize the story of slavery to such an extent that audiences would have to engage with it differently, to see it with fresh eyes. Drawing on specific memories and stories from her family history that were grounded in the history of slavery, Dash became interested in telling her family's origins from within the Sea Islands culture off the coast of South Carolina. Though family stories inspired the film, she reveals in her book her surprise at her family members' newfound reluctance to discuss their histories in South Carolina or their migration to New York. Perhaps the idea of painful family stories writ large on celluloid sparked the reticence; still, Dash was compelled to tell the story and create images that would "touch an audience the way it touched my family" (5).

In her effort to tell a novel story about slavery, and simultaneously get the story right by imbuing it with historically authentic details, Dash embarked on a daunting research agenda that included hours of research at the nation's premiere archives of black history. Among the numerous archival institutions that she culled for factual data were New York's Shomburg Center for Research in Black Culture, in Harlem, and the National Archives and the Library of Congress, both in Washington, D.C. (Dash, *"Daughters"* 5). Dash elaborated further on the significance of her research findings in a videotaped interview at the University of Colorado at Boulder in 1995. Dash explained her passion for the subject matter of *Daughters* and her decision to use the South Carolina Gullah dialect in this way:

> My family comes from the Sea Islands area, and they spoke like that. I started doing research on that whole region when I was at UCLA. The Sea Islands represents Ellis Island for us; that is where the slave ships came in. That is *our* Ellis Island. It is sacred ground for us. Why was this particular microcosm of the African American slavery culture different from slavery in Mississippi or Alabama? It is because they were so isolated. Why on these islands [where] there was so much yellow fever?
> . . . The sickle cell trait helped the West Africans survive malaria [although they were] killed in the end. It is a heavy site of African resistance. There was much to mine there.

Mining this particular aspect of African resistance to slavery, Dash found "the existence of over sixty thousand West African words or phrases in use in the English language" that were "a direct result of the slave trade" (*"Daughters"* 5). Her discovery and incorporation of such words are among the many examples of "authentic" historical facts that aided in the preparation of *Daughters of the Dust*'s compelling narrative. This wealth of information convinced Dash that only a feature-length film could do the subject matter the justice it commanded. In 1985, she realized that "a short film would not be large enough for the story. I knew I would have to make a feature. There was too much information, and it had to be shared" (6).

Sharing her newfound vision proved more frustrating than she imagined given the new trend in Hollywood to capitalize on what Dash has termed "urban testosterone films" (Interview). Armed with her script, revised numerous times to present what she thought was a novel take on the slavery episode, Dash sought financing for her film. After pitching her concept to numerous unreceptive production companies, Dash realized the need to "shoot an example of the film" because it was an "'untraditional' black movie" (*"Daughters"* 6–7). It was untraditional for studio executives in Hollywood because it did not feature characters living in urban ghettos, "killing each other and burning things down," and it was devoid of "explicit sex scenes" (8). Dash found little difference in the reception from potential European film backers who either did not understand the film, thought it too typically American, or thought it too radical for their audiences to grasp.

Ultimately, major financial backing for the film came from the Public Broadcasting System's American Playhouse, the Rockefeller Foundation, the National Black Programming Consortium, and smaller investors. In addition to scraping together a budget of approximately $800,000, Dash succeeded in securing the independent New York distributor Kino International. Dash credits Kino's wisdom to hire an African American publicity firm, KJM3 Entertainment Group, for the film's impressive publicity campaign when it finally opened to sold-out crowds at the Film Forum in New York on January 15, 1992 (*"Daughters"* 25–26). *Daughters* replicated this feat of unexpected box-office success at most theaters where it screened in spite of its limited release "on a staggered schedule throughout 1992." In fact, *Daughters'* success is all the more remarkable because a staggered schedule during an initial release is understood widely as the kiss of death for mainstream and independent films alike, as they often are "pulled before the audience has a chance to find them" (26). Still, *Daughters'* striking box-office draw was buoyed by word-of-mouth advertising, which sustained it beyond the crucial make-or-break opening-weekend standard (Bobo 168). Despite its relegation to only one or two screens per market, *Daughters* consistently sold out, even requiring extra screenings. Jacqueline Bobo points out that at one point *"Daughters of the Dust* had the highest per-screen average for the week, beating such films as *The Hand that Rocks The Cradle, Fried Green Tomatoes, Father of the Bride* and *Grand Canyon* (168). Clearly confounding expectations, *Daughters* had become *the little film that could.*

Analysis

Daughters of the Dust was not universally embraced, however. Interestingly, criticisms that the film encountered on its release were contradictory. On the one hand, there were charges claiming that the film essentially played "like a two-hour Laura Ashley commercial" (Guerrero 177). On the other hand, *Daughters* was deemed too demanding and idiosyncratic for audiences to grasp. Worse still, the film was dismissed in Hollywood because such a film had never been done before (Brouwer 12–13). The fact that Dash had intentionally broken with mainstream filmmaking approaches that too often reduce the complexities of black life to homogenized, ready-made film commodities apparently was lost on most critics who reviewed the film for the popular press. In the years since the film's initial release, many academic critics have drawn on published interviews with Dash as a means of demystifying many of *Daughters'* seemingly arcane symbolisms and its culturally specific and visually complex representations.

In the 1995 interview cited earlier, Dash confronted several misconceptions about the demanding nature of *Daughters.* First, regarding the film's putative lack of structure, she emphasized several points: (1) *Daughters* pays homage to another film, *Ganja and Hess* (1973), by black filmmaker Bill Gunn. (2) The film has a firm structure, with a definite beginning, middle, and end. (3) Her goal was "to tell the story as an African *griot* would, with an unfolding, like women's weaving." (4) The film employs a flash-forward structural approach that best suited her vision of the film. (5) "*Daughters* is not plot driven," Dash stresses. "I was heavily influenced by foreign films. . . . There are passages from the film that stay with you forever. Since [*Daughters*] is a film about family, I wanted to do a film that was like an heirloom itself. I wanted to create these tableaux images like frescos in your mind. . . . I was going for the visual impact. . . . most of the shots are tableaux." (6) Jafa experimented with *Daughters'* film speed. He used a computer capable of manipulating the film speed from between 24, 40, and 60 frames per second. (7) Ultimately, *Daughters* is a work of "speculative fiction, it's a science fiction story—a what-if story." As Dash puts it, "I wanted to do a voudoun [erroneously termed "voodoo"] film without zombies, and I did." This last remark leads us to *Daughters'* more accurate representations of African disaporic cultural traditions.

Second, Dash explained the film's many allusions and references to African disaporic cultural traditions and symbols: (1) The Gullah dialect of the film's characters reflects the dislocated Africans' retention of remnants or "scraps" of their Gambian and Senegambian language heritage. Dash tells the audience, "I wanted it to be in the Gullah dialect. English words are spoken with an African syntax and cadence. You hear English, but the grammatical placement is more African than English. So you really have to listen" to appreciate the "Senegambian and Gambian" influences, for example. (2) African American jazz and blues tonalities were strong influences on *Daughters'* visual aesthetic. Dash elaborates on the musical influences:

> We wanted the music to transcend the visuals in some way. We wanted it to reflect the New World realities that these people were experiencing during the Middle Passage. . . . What music would they have heard? A Santeria priest sang and played percussion for the film and women sang songs that were never heard on film before. It was emotional music.

(3) America's "miscegenation taboo" and its concomitant "color-struck" problematic in *Daughters* are signified by Yellow Mary's name, Trula's very fair complexion, and Eula's rape by a white plantation overseer.[1] For Dash, Yellow Mary's name and Trula's "yellow" skin color are significant indeed. Although Yellow Mary's skin tone is fairer than that of her Peazant family relatives, her lover Trula's is fairer still. This conscious choice in casting the "yellow" characters was important for Dash to foreground the "the relativity of the term," which is used to designate black people's fair skin tones while calling attention

---

[1]The hypocrisy of laws that prohibited interracial unions is often revealed by the so-called color-struck phenomenon, wherein fair-skinned blacks (the product of race mixing between white slave masters and their black women chattel) are considered simultaneously desirable and repulsive by both blacks and whites.

to the white-skin privilege that accrues to it. (4) W. E. B. DuBois's potent concept of "double-consciousness" is another important African American theme in *Daughters*. Of all the characters in the film, Yellow Mary, who is in voluntary exile from the mainland, embodies this concept most. Dash comments, "As African Americans, we've learned to constantly translate. We speak one way in public. We speak another way at home. We are constantly translating emotions, dialects, all of that. But everyone else has not been forced to do that." The fact that black people's everyday survival depends on their successful negotiation of black and white cultural norms is at the heart of DuBois's double-consciousness concept, and it contributes to Yellow Mary's alienation from the racist demands of the mainland.

A third issue of importance in *Daughters* deals with the film's focus on black women. Clearly, the film's title alone announces its womanist orientation: The film's title is a rewriting of a biblical passage that Dash changed from "sons of the dust," to "daughters of the dust." This is not Dash's only rewriting. *Daughters'* counterhegemonic discourse was motivated by Dash's desire to rewrite cinematic images of black women and break completely with traditional film stereotypes. In her book, Dash confesses that both she and Jafa were "on a mission to redefine how black women look on the screen and what they're doing" (52). Judging from criticisms of the film's supposed "Laura Ashley" commercial look, they apparently succeeded. *Daughters* refocuses traditional cinema's distorted gaze by crafting some of the most beautifully compelling images of black women of all skin tones and hues (Bambara xiv). Most important, however, the film disrupts and rewrites popular cinematic portrayals of black female victimization with a counterhegemonic narrative focus on black women's power and agency. Despite its strong womanist treatment, "This film is not so much matriarchal as it reflects my decision to position the film from the point of view of the women" (Dash, Interview). Bambara sums up Dash's project as a fitting and long overdue answer to singer Abby Lincoln's question, "Who will revere the black woman?" Bambara writes, "Dash composes a woman validation ceremony within a film that has already assured the black woman spectator that we are not, as usual, going to be mugged in the dark" (xv).

Issues four and five center on spectatorial positioning in *Daughters* and certain audience responses to the film as Dash described them in her 1995 interview. It is difficult to improve on Dash's own commentary as she contextualizes matters of spectatorship and the reception of her film. First, she discusses the centrality of the character Trula, Yellow Mary's implied lover, who is silent throughout the film. Trula's silence serves a pivotal function. Dash explains: "Trula was the vehicle used to represent the audience. This is why she does not speak. She is like the audience—she does not understand the dialect [nor] the religion. Trula witnesses Nana Peazant making a talisman. She runs away, signifying the West's tendency of fearing and refusing to know something that is not familiar." Dash also talks of how differently European and American audiences received *Daughters*. Dash begins by situating the film's positive reception in Europe following a wave of popularity for African American films (Hollywood and independent ones) in Europe from 1979 to 1986. Dash refuses to speak for European audiences, but her successes there had a profound impact:

> I can't speak for them. I can't say how they saw me or us [other black filmmakers]. In Europe, there are so many different countries, with people who speak many different languages and cultures. They find the work more accessible because they are not put off by a Geechee [or Gullah] dialect. They are not put off by an African American tradition that they've never seen before on television. They just ask you about it. They watch it and study it, whereas in the States, people tend to resent information that they didn't know beforehand but should have. It's like, "Wait a minute. What is this? I have not seen it on *60 Minutes*; it doesn't exist." We need to start learning about other cultures.

Dash is getting at the need for American audiences especially to cultivate an understanding and appreciation of other cultures despite the interpretive work and effort this might entail. She makes the point by describing her own experience grappling with one such unfamiliar film text that nonetheless gives her great spectatorial pleasure:

> In this country, we tend to operate from the position of privilege in the sense of knowing it all . . . and not being tolerant of other tongues and dialects as much as other people who come

in contact with different dialects and tongues. For example, as an African American growing up in New York City, I had to come to understand the Irish American, Chinese American, Scottish American, and Italian American, all of that. To this day, *Miller's Crossing* [1990] is one of my favorite films. But when I watch the tape, I have to rewind back because they are speaking in the slang from the period as well as this Irish accent that I do not understand. They can go through an entire passage and I don't know a word that is said.

This personal anecdote is revealing of Dash's penchant for indulging cinematic complexity as both a spectator and filmmaker. As some critics have pointed out, *Daughters* "is a 'demanding' film" for spectators, which opens up narratively to a varying range of interpretations (Brouwer 12), but this passage makes it clear that she only demands from an audience what she herself is willing give.

Myth versus Fiction

By now it should be clear that *Daughters of the Dust* does not reside easily in filmdom's traditional generic categories or accepted subgenre hybrids, because its African diasporic cultural specificities and aesthetic sensibilities require different evaluative criteria. Perhaps bell hooks's comparison of *Daughters* to a "mythopoetic" aesthetic shared by such postcolonial writers as Michael Ondaatje and Theresa Hak Kyung Cha comes closest to an acceptable positioning of the film. According to hooks, this aesthetic means "bringing certain factual information into a kind of mythopoetic context" (qtd. in Dash, *"Daughters"* 29). Dash accepts this mythopoetic rubric because it accommodates her film's speculative fiction or "what if" scenario, as she calls it. Dash reminds hooks that, "Myth, of course, plays a very important part in all our lives, in everyone's culture. Without myth and tradition," she asks, "what is there?" (29).

It is to Dash's effective and seamless incorporation of African Americans' historically factual experiences of slavery into a compelling fictional film narrative that we now turn. In fact, Dash has remarked on the discomfiting realization that many people base their historical knowledge on cinematic depictions. For such people, Dash observed, "History is on the screen. History is not from the textbook."

Dash, however, distinguishes her project by affirming the fact that *Daughters'* historical base does not depend "on the whim of the production designer" (Interview). Instead, she based her creative treatment of specific historical facts about slavery on her own painstaking historical research. In this way, *Daughters* might be said to possess a documentary effect, as its docudrama-style mythopoetics are consistent with John Grierson's documentary tradition, which celebrates the creative treatment of actuality.

For Dash, it was important to tell a different story of slavery, one that considers the facts and fictions of slavery but from a heroic survivalist perspective rich in symbolic significance. Among slavery's facts and fictions that *Daughters* engages are slave revolts, African religions, indigo plantations, and de facto black slavery beyond America's southern states. True to her intent to tell a different story of slavery, *Daughters* represents these slavery atrocities through myth, black oral histories, and symbolic indirection. For example, Dash symbolizes the fact of African revolts against slavery by suicidal drownings through the image of a carved wooden African statute floating in a river off the inlet Ibo Landing. The myth of the Ibo Landing scene in *Daughters* is based on historical records from the logs of slave ships (Dash, Interview). Eula Peazant, a central character and one of the film's two narrators, recites such instances of slave revolt from black oral history versions popularized by Paule Marshall's book *Praise Song for the Widow* (1983). As Dash tells it:

> There are two myths and one reality. . . . Ibo captives, African captives of the Ibo tribe, when they were brought to the New World, they refused to live in slavery. There are accounts of them having walked into the water, and then on top of the water all the way back to Africa, you know, rather than live in slavery in chains. There are also myths of them having flown from the water, flown all the way back to Africa. And then there is the story—the truth or the myth—of them walking into the water and drowning themselves in front of the captors. ("*Daughters*" 29–30)

Dash uncovered research that claimed that sailors and crew members on slave ships had nervous breakdowns watching "Ibo men, women and children in shackles, walking into the water and holding themselves under the water until they in fact drowned" (30).

The character of Bilal Muhammed preserves the historical record of African religious traditions that existed alongside Christianity among enslaved African Americans. Dash's research turned up the fact that a Sudanese man named Bilal Muhammed, a Muslim with five daughters, actually lived during the slavery era. His diaries and papers, on permanent display at the Smithsonian Institution, tell of his family's efforts to practice their "tradition of Islam" even in captivity (Dash, *"Daughters"* 36). Dash saw Muhammed's Islamic tradition as an important narrative counterpoint to Viola's uncritical acceptance of Christianity despite its complicity in slavery and other forms of colonialist oppression (37). In *Daughters,* Viola returns from the mainland as a missionary who reflects the Western view that unfamiliar religions are dealing with the Devil. She embodies the view of some black people that anything Western bests anything African and thus will uplift them. Apparently, as part of an educated and enlightened black elite coming back to Ibo Landing to film the primitives, Viola also represents flawed tendencies in the DuBoisian notion of "the talented tenth," the idea that the "best" of the black community need to focus on achieving higher education in order to develop a leadership capacity (Dash, Interview).

Dash addresses traditional history's diminution of black people's de facto slave status in the North and in other locales through the overdetermined lead character of Yellow Mary. Yellow Mary, a prostitute, is not only a narrative counterpoint to Viola's womanly Christian virtue, Dash also positions Yellow Mary as a survivor of the mainland's racist oppression. Whereas Viola brings religion to Ibo Landing, Yellow Mary brings her girlfriend (Dash, Interview). Although Yellow Mary returns as a woman of means, signified by her fancy clothes and expensive trinkets (the memory box, for example), she recounts her painful bondage experiences as a wet nurse for rich women in Cuba. Her plight of providing mother's milk for suckling white babies from her breast was a common one for slave women. Yellow Mary's account of refusing this abject slave condition and her ultimate decision to return to Ibo Landing permanently is meant to be a caution for those members of the Peazant family planning their northern migration to the mythological promised land. As symbols of the mainland, it is ironic that Yellow Mary and Trula run away from the very oppressive conditions that the Peazants are running toward (Dash, Interview). Yellow Mary understands what the Peazants cannot know, which is the impossibility of sustaining the family's basic needs in the North in any way commensurate with the natural and free agricultural bounty of Ibo Landing. This is one symbolic reference and significance of the Peazant family's gumbo feast, its allegorical Last Supper.

Close Reading

What makes *Daughters of the Dust* an important film within the context of womanist diasporic cultural production is its ability to adroitly engage issues of postslavery migration, historical memory, feminine identity, and cultural dislocation through character development. *Daughters* is a formally experimental avant-garde treatise on the psychosocial location of African Americans astride two distinct cultures, that of the Ibo of West Nigeria and that of American slavery in Confederate Georgia, and a treatise that is abundantly rife with narrative conflict and potential. The future, pregnant with possibilities, is expressed metaphorically in the members of the Peazant family who plan to migrate north from Ibo Landing. Conflict, although situated in a not-too-distant past, is represented in such a manner that its relevance to contemporary issues is inescapable. It is the film's emphasis on conflict, then, that marks its seditious potential. Dash acknowledges that she privileges female characters in her films. Because of the mythic role played by women in traditional African societies, it is not surprising that Dash would imbue her female characters with traits such as strength, wisdom, tenacity, and adaptability, all of which have sustained Africans throughout the diaspora. Lest it be mistakenly thought to contain only mythical characters that are paragons of virtue, *Daughters* does present complex characters in support of the script's more realist impulses. Nana, Yellow Mary, and Haagar are the characters, in my view, charged with carrying out the film's ideological imperative and who contextualize and historicize the Africanness of African American cultural and traditional practices.

In the elderly family matriarch Nana, we are presented with a historical link to the African past of African Americans. To the extent that she fiercely clings to memories of a time "before freedom come," as well as preserves many of the ancient customs and ways, Nana functions as the repository of a certain history that can serve as support for an uncertain future. It has often been stated that history is less concerned with an accurate accounting of past events than it is with providing a framework from which to apprehend the future. It is in upholding this concept of historical utility that the following exchange between Nana Peazant and her grandson Eli Peazant becomes especially meaningful. Nana insists that Eli keep in touch with the lessons to be learned through valuing and remembering his African ancestors:

> I'm trying to give ya something to take Nort with ya along with all you great, big dreams. Rely upon those old Africans, Eli. . . . Let them feed your head with wisdom that is from this day in time. 'Cause when ya leave this island, Eli Peazant, you ain't going to no land of milk and honey. Eli, I'm putting my trust in you to keep the family togedder up Nort. That's the challenge facing all you Negro people what free. Celebrate our ways.

Clearly, the historical economy in Nana's remarks is directed to African American spectators who, for any number of reasons, know too little about their histories prior to the slavery episode. Nana's invocation that "it's up to the living to keep in touch with the dead" is simply an allusion to the responsibility of blacks to educate themselves about their histories, which are intentionally elided and distorted in official Western interpretations of black history. In reminding Eli that the African ancestors did not "forget everything they once knew," and that he should "celebrate our way," Nana's message is clear: African Americans need to recoup and revere their cultural traditions, and to respect the fact that blacks survived slavery, a four-hundred-year holocaust, and have gained some important and useful survival techniques that must be tapped in amassing the courage and strength necessary to face future obstacles.

To situate the character of Yellow Mary Peazant requires at once the establishment of her centrality in the articulation of a diasporic genre of cinematic expression and the recognition of her interrogative function vis-à-vis the changing status of women throughout the African diaspora—her womanist function. With respect to Yellow Mary as a signifier of principles that typify womanist diasporic cinema, I think a few quotes from the film can prove illustrative. At one point during the film's progression, several adolescent girls voice their curiosity about Yellow Mary, who has just arrived on the island. The dialogue proceeds thus:

FIRST GIRL: What kind of 'oman she is?
SECOND GIRL: Yellow Mary ain't no family 'oman.
THIRD GIRL: She a scary 'oman.
FOURTH GIRL: She a new kind of 'oman!

We have already noted that the language itself is a diasporic marker, a reflection of the Gullah dialects that Dash researched extensively. Here, however, Yellow Mary's dual function is suggested. First of all, as a new woman, Yellow Mary is considered scary because she breaks with established notions of female identity and agency. Second, the allusion to family here, as in she "ain't no family 'oman," suggests her rejection of an essentialist notion of what it means to be a woman in a traditional extended black family as represented by the Peazants of Ibo Landing. Yellow Mary has reconciled the binarism of the African American diaspora. She can love her African past, as represented by Nana, and she can enjoy her present and future, as demonstrated by her delight at being different from the women who have yet to see the mainland. Yellow Mary signifies the integrated African American who is confident in her dual cultural identity and national heritages. Yellow Mary is comfortable with her Gullah identity, astride her black and white cultures, and does not accord one primacy over the other. Her own comments flag at least one key diasporic iconography:

I got ta keep movin, people settin' still don't get it with me ya know. . . . Eula, you a real backwater, Geechee girl. Wish I could find me a good man, Eula, somebody I could depend on. Not that I want to depend on him, just to know that I could if I had to. You know, I sure hope they fixin' some gumbo. It's been a long time since I had some *good* gumbo. I had some in Savannah you know, but they didn't put everyting in it. I haven't had some good food in a long time.

Referring to the traditional women who cook, Yellow Mary's desire for gumbo should be recognized instantly for its Creole symbolism.

The term "gumbo," naming a Creole dish, is deployed here deliberately to overdetermine both diasporic consciousness and cinema. Kobena Mercer regards the Creolizing tendency as a "dynamic which critically appropriates elements from the master-codes of the dominant culture . . . disarticulating given signs and rearticulating their symbolic meaning otherwise" (57). Yellow Mary yearns for a "good man," but her insistence on self-reliance signals an important component of feminine space within the African diaspora. The implications for women filmmakers hold here as well. Yellow Mary's strength and resolve are central to the ideological discourse in *Daughters* because they suggest black women's myriad coping mechanisms to confront their triple oppression: sexism, racism, and classism (hooks 14).

For Yellow Mary, her identity is firmly rooted in a past that she can touch, Nana Peazant and Ibo Landing, and a future and present that will be determined based on her choice to remain behind or depart with the others. As it gets closer to the time for the family to load up the boat and head for the mainland, Yellow Mary realizes that she may not see Nana again, as Nana is getting on in age. After a hostile exchange with Haagar, a Peazant through marriage, Yellow Mary confesses to Nana, "I've been on my own since I was a lil girl. . . . I know I'm not like the other 'omen here. But I need to know that I can come and hold on to what I come from, I need to know that the people who know my name, Yellow Mary Peazant, and know I'm a proud 'oman. I want for stay with you here."

Where Yellow Mary represents the ability to fuse her "third world" and "first world" cultural heritages with equanimity, Haagar Peazant seeks to fully embrace one at the expense of the other. Haagar's character could be said to reflect the total assimilationist impulse exhibited by one faction of the African diaspora. Her myopic assessment that the Gullah traditions of the past and the modern ways of the present are completely incompatible proves to be a painful miscalculation as the story progresses. In voicing her opposition to the rest of the family's attempts to convince Nana to migrate north with them, Haagar emphatically lets her feelings be known: "I'm a educated person, and I'm tired of those old stories, watching her make those root potions. Who do she be talking to, washing up in the river with her clothes on like those saltwater folks used to do? My children ain't going to be like those old Africans, fresh off the boat. My god, I still remember." Dash is perhaps sounding a cautionary note on the dangers of being brainwashed by an educational system that overemphasizes Western history and that deemphasizes the role of Africa and its peoples in world civilization and American history. For Haagar, the past is meant to be forgotten so that she and her children can finally inhabit that dreamed of future in an imagined land of milk and honey. Haagar is not without some redeeming qualities, however. That she possesses a dogged determination and force of will speaks to the filmmaker's grasp of the ambiguities and complexities of effective character development. By fleshing out characters such as Haagar, who hates Yellow Mary, resents Nana, and dominates the lives of her daughters, Dash almost proffers this character to spectators as one who will likely survive the harsh realities of life on the mainland. Consider this statement by Haggar: "I might not've been born into this family, but I'm here now. And I say let Nana Peazant stay behind, that's what she wants. We're moving into a new day. She's too much a part of the past." And in response to possible male resistance to her stance, she replies, "I'm a fully grown 'oman, and I don't have to mind what I say. I done born five children into the world, and put two in the ground alongside their daddy. I worked all my life, and ain't got nothing to show for it, and if I can't say what's on my mind, then damn everybody to hell."

The stark contrast between Nana, who knows nothing of the world outside Ibo Landing and who lives her life at first glance as a fossil of that which she guards so vigilantly, and the rigid and pragmatic Haagar, whose forward-looking posture blinds her to the concept of compromise, appears almost so calculated that one character could be in danger of canceling out the other. But the strong mitigating influences exerted by the other characters act to temper Nana's extreme valorization of past customs. Likewise, the gentleness of spirit and family loyalty ascribed to Viola, Eula, Eli, and other characters softens the impact of Haagar's domineering persona. Dash's characters are so diverse that they effectively counter attempts to perpetuate an essentialist perspective of black cultural, social, political, and sexual identity. Indeed, *Daughters* celebrates the diversity of "the black experience" with a critical consciousness that interpolates the official histories that are too widely circulated and, at the same time, exposes unofficial histories to a wider audience.

By deliberately pointing up, in a graphic albeit creative way, the horrors of slavery's abuses, *Daughters* counters the popular recollection of slavery as recast and sanitized by such specious representations as *Roots*. Produced for network television in the 1970s, *Roots* was at the time the most popular miniseries in broadcasting history. As the episodes of *Roots* progressed through the generations, the specifics of African experiences in America were increasingly accommodated to America's mythology of immigration. *Daughters* represents an act of contestation by a black woman filmmaker that is in keeping with the scholarly interventionist mode of postmodern struggle to disrupt the master narrative of postcoloniality and its xenophobic construction of the African diasporic Other. Metaphorically speaking, then, just as the Peazant family in *Daughters of the Dust* signifies a modern crossing over to the mainland from the South Carolina Sea Islands, so Dash's film's success signifies a significant crossing over to the male-dominated mainstream of theatrical film production for black women filmmakers.

Conclusion

Finally, there are a few remaining points about *Daughters of the Dust* that bear mentioning. Several concern further elements of the film's symbolism. Eula's pregnancy and her ethereal "unborn child" represents the promise and future of postemancipation African peoples in America despite a horrific engendering or birth under amoral conditions. For example, Eula's rape brings forth a beautiful young daughter, which appears analogous to the rape of Africa's bringing forth the rebirth of Africans as African Americans and their contributions to American culture—in spite of slavery's degradations. The Native American character Julian Last Child represents Dash's desire to rewrite the history of the Cherokee nation's forced relocation from the South and the Sea Islands to Oklahoma. Dash wanted Julian Last Child to represent the idea that at least one of the indigenous peoples remained behind and enjoyed a life of freedom and autonomy. The names of Haagar Peazant's daughters, Iona and Myown, are significant in their reference to one of slavery's most abhorrent practices: selling black women and their children separately. Through these names, Dash evokes the inhumane practice without stating it, as such.

Everett

The marriage of Julian Last Child and Iona is also meant to illustrate the long history of intermarriage between African Americans and Native Americans. The glass-bottle tree gains its significance when Eli breaks many of the bottles. Eli's breaking of the bottles represents an act of cultural sacrilege, in that it is equivalent to "taking a hatchet to the Bible" (Dash, Interview). When Mr. Snead, the photographer, unnecessarily uses the flash on his camera in the daytime, it is not a sign of his incompetence. Rather, it is meant to provide an insight into his character. He is a show-off who makes a spectacle of himself because he is full of himself (Dash, Interview). Finally, *Daughters* took Dash twenty-three days to shoot. When asked in 1995 if she was 100 percent happy with the film, Dash indicated that she was 90 percent happy with it because, as she stated, "it is difficult to realize a film in actuality as faithfully as it appears in your imagination" (Dash, Interview).

Credits

United States, 1991, American Playhouse, Geechee Girls

Director, Producer, and Screenplay: Julie Dash
Cinematography: Arthur Jafa
Editing: Joseph Burton and Amy Carey
Music: John Barnes
Art Direction: Michael Kelly Williams
Costume Design: Arline Burks

CAST:

Nana Peazant	Cora Lee Day
Eula Peazant	Alva Rogers
Yellow Mary	Barbara O. Jones
Trula	Trula Hoosier
Bilal Muhammed	Umar Abdurrahamn
Eli Peazant	Adisa Anderson
Haagar Peazant	Kaycee Moore
Iona Peazant	Bahni Turpin
Viola Peazant	Cheryl Lynn Bruce
Mr. Snead	Tommy Redmond Hicks
St. Julien Lastchild	M. Cochise Anderson
Unborn child	Kai-Lynn Warren

Bibliography

Bambara, Toni Cade. Preface. Dash, *Daughters* xi–xvi.

Bobo, Jacqueline. *Black Women as Cultural Readers.* New York: Columbia UP, 1995.

Brouwer, Joel R. "Repositioning: Center and Margin in Julie Dash's *Daughters of the Dust." African American Review* 29.1 (1995): 5–17.

Dash, Julie. *"Daughters of the Dust": The Making of an African American Woman's Film.* New York: New P, 1992.

———. Interview with faculty and students of University of Colorado, Boulder. Unreleased video. 25–27 Sept. 1995.

Guerrero, Ed. *Framing Blackness: The African American Image in Film.* Philadephia: Temple UP, 1993.

Hall, Stuart. "New Ethnicities." *ICA Documents.* Ed. Kobena Mercer. London: Inst. Contemporary Arts, 1988. 2–31.

hooks, bell. *Feminist Theory: From Margin to Center.* Boston: South End, 1984.

Lee, Spike, and Lisa Jones. *"Do the Right Thing": A Companion Volume to the Universal Pictures Film.* New York: Fireside, 1989.

Mercer, Kobena. "Diaspora Culture and the Dialogic Imagination: The Aesthetics of Black Independent Film in Britain." *Black Frames.* Ed. Mbye B. Cham and Claire Andrade-Watkins. Cambridge, MA: MIT P, 1988. 50–61.

Williams, Sherley Anne. "Some Implications of Womanist Theory." *Reading Black, Reading Feminist: A Critical Anthology.* Ed. Henry Louis Gates, Jr. New York: Meridian, 1990. 68–75.

All About My Mother (1999)

PAUL JULIAN SMITH

Narrative, Themes, and Technique

Context

Pedro Almodóvar's *All About My Mother* (*Todo sobre mi madre*) premiered in Spain on April 8, 1999, and has rapidly come to be seen as a
classic. The recipient of a large number of awards around the world,
most importantly the Cannes prize for Best Director and the Oscar for
Best Foreign Language Film, it was also a resounding commercial success, attracting more than two million spectators in both Spain and
France and grossing $8 million in the United States, a more than re-
spectable figure for a European movie. But in many ways its success is
anomalous. *All About My Mother* came from a nation whose film industry has been in near-perpetual crisis since it came into being. Its
narrative is complex and irreducible to Hollywood formulas. Its
themes are apparently of minority interest. As some disgruntled critics
noted, its unusually large cast lacks a single sympathetic heterosexual
male. Finally, its technique is arty, boasting a stylized look and shooting style likely to alienate a general audience. Almodóvar had come to
fame with stylish farces such as *Women on the Verge of a Nervous Breakdown* (*Mujeres al borde de un ataque de nervios*, 1988). Why is it that the
superficially unattractive *All About My Mother,* an uncompromising
study of a mother's grief after the death of her teenage son, became
such an unqualified success?

   It might help briefly to place the film within the commercial context
of production, distribution, and exhibition. After the difficult days of
the early 1990s, Spanish cinema was enjoying "the good years" of the
second half of the decade (Heredero and Santamarina 107). Feature
production boomed to a high of eigthy-two films in 1999, and, greatly
helped by Almodóvar himself, Spanish cinema's share of its own market rose to a respectable 13.8 percent (*Focus 2000* 30). *All About My*

Mother was the eighth of Almodóvar's features to be made by his own company, El Deseo, helmed by his brother Agustín. El Deseo coproduced *All About My Mother* with the French company Renn Productions, the production arm of Pathé, which claims to be the biggest independent filmmaker in Europe. Further funding came from the French and Spanish TV sectors, including Canal+, at that time a powerful player in the film industries of both countries. Given this strong backing and Almodóvar's track record (no feature he has made has failed to turn a profit), Almodóvar enjoyed enviable artistic freedom as a screenwriter and director.

In the film's distribution around the world, the primacy of the Almodóvar signature was reconfirmed in the promotion of the film. The same one-sheet poster was used in all territories: a stylized image of a young woman, arms crossed and lips pursed, drawn in thick black outline and shaded in primary colors: blue, red, and yellow. The single credit read: "A film by Almodóvar." This distinctive image positioned the film as a "quality" choice for an educated audience: the promotional material stood out from among the more familiar posters of commercial movies, which are usually based on photographic rather than hand-drawn material. (Only the U.S. video release showed a more conventional design: a main photograph of principal Cecilia Roth, with smaller shots of her fellow female costars below.) Trailers for the film reveal how distributors tailored it for different national audiences. The French trailer employs Ismaël Lô's romantic song (played in the film over the sequence in which Manuela arrives in Barcelona) and a great deal of dubbed dialogue. The U.S. version features frantic bongo music (taken from Almodóvar's *Kika* [1993]) over images of the characters laughing and joking. The British trailer covers both bases, beginning with Lô and Alberto Iglesias's poignant original score, before switching to bongos. While all the trailers stress the overwhelming presence of women in the film (as does the poster), the different versions clearly reveal the volatility of the film's genre: Is it a comedy (as fans of Almodóvar's earlier work might tend to suppose), or rather a serious story of female friendship? As we shall see, it is precisely the strength of Almodóvar's filmmaking that it plays to a wide range of audiences by blurring the boundaries between genres.

While the film was a huge popular success in Spain and France, *All About My Mother*'s distribution in English-speaking territories where few foreign films are seen was more problematic. The American and British trailers feature no dialogue whatsoever, hoping not to frighten conservative audiences. Rather, they both stress the film's universality by using the same sequence of English intertitles: "Part of every woman is a mother"; "Part of every woman is an actress"; "Part of every woman is a saint"; "Part of every woman is a sinner"; and, finally (humorously), "Part of every man is a woman." But the method of exhibition was vital, too. Foreign-language movies are generally seen in dedicated art houses in the United Kingdom and the United States. At best, distributors seek to "go wide" only after successfully opening on a few screens. Sony Classics followed this strategy in the United States, where the film debuted on just two screens in New York and Los Angeles on November 21, 1999, hoping to generate "want to see" through word of mouth. This strategy clearly worked, as the film peaked at 145 screens on April 2, 2000. More confident of a wider initial market for Almodóvar in London, Pathé opened the film on August 29, 1999, on twenty-two screens, including a number of multiplexes where foreign-language films rarely play. It seems likely, then, that *All About My Mother* served, almost uniquely, as a "crossover" movie between the art-house ghetto and more commercial fare. Indeed, this was precisely the term used by the positive *New York Times* review (Maslin).

Spain itself had also experienced changes in exhibition methods, which tended to support Almodóvar's move upmarket from the kitsch comedies of the 1980s. Exhibitors had upgraded theaters and increased ticket prices. Average Spanish film viewers, especially those that preferred domestic films, were now wealthier, more educated, and more urban than ever before (SGAE 78). If it was a critical commonplace that with *All About My Mother* Almodóvar was now "more mature" (and this was a backhanded compliment), his films had grown with their large target audience. The newly expert screenplay and technique, not to mention the more somber themes, were pluses rather than minuses when it came to attracting a local public to a local film.

Analysis

Narrative

The Internet Movie Database (IMDb) gives the following plot synopsis of *All About My Mother:*

> A single mother in Madrid sees her only son die on his 17th birthday as he runs to seek an actress's autograph. She goes to Barcelona to find the lad's father, a transvestite named Lola who does not know he has a child. First she finds her friend, Agrado, also a transvestite; through him she meets Rosa, a young nun bound for El Salvador, and by happenstance, becomes the personal assistant of Huma Rojo, the actress her son admired. She helps Huma manage Nina, the costar and Huma's lover, and she becomes Rosa's caretaker during a dicey pregnancy. With echoes of Lorca, "All About Eve," and "Streetcar Named Desire," the mothers (and fathers and actors) live out grief, love, and friendship.

It is interesting to contrast this with the first paragraph of Almodóvar's own short synopsis, as given in the press book:

> A Greek saying states that only women who have washed their eyes with tears can see clearly. The saying does not hold true for Manuela. The night a car ran over her son Esteban, Manuela cried until she was completely dry. And far from seeing clearly, the present and the future become mixed up in the same darkness. (El Deseo 5)

Almodóvar's synopsis breaks off only twenty minutes into the film's running time ("Manuela goes to Barcelona in search of Lola, her son's father"). But it is clear that, unlike the IMDb version, what concerns him is not the surface or objective action of the plot (Manuela's encounters with a transvestite, a nun, and an actress), but rather the deeper or subjective reality. He leads us here, as in the film itself, to identify with the mourning mother's point of view: with her grief, her confusion, and her disorientation.

Yet if we examine the plot more closely, we see that it is highly self-conscious and artistically crafted. There are frequent parallels and repetitions that suggest that, unlike a Hollywood plot, which tends to proceed in a linear fashion, Almodóvar's narrative is circular. For example, there are three characters called Esteban: the son who is run over toward the start of the film, the father reencountered toward the end (now in the guise of the HIV-positive transvestite Lola), and the baby fathered by Lola with the nun Sister Rosa. Echoes are often ironic or tragic. Manuela returns to see Huma onstage in *A Streetcar Named Desire*. But where first she was accompanied by her son, now there is an empty seat beside her. She will even take the place of Huma's girlfriend Nina onstage one night, weeping bitter tears as a fictional mother, tears that cannot but remind us of those she shed for her real son. The teenage Esteban never sees a photo of his father, but the latter is shown, too late, a photo of his son, whom he has never seen before. In daringly brief train sequences, Manuela makes a circular journey from Madrid to Barcelona, Barcelona to Madrid, and then back once more. On the last journey, she brings with her the child Esteban, the last character by that name, who has neutralized the virus bequeathed to him by his father.

As we watch the film, however, we are unaware of these complex patterns and symmetries. Indeed, as Mark Allinson, author of the most recent of several English-language books on Almodóvar, notes:

> The story unfolds using simple linear time (one event after the other in chronological order). . . . There are only two flashbacks, justified diegetically: Manuela, on returning to the performance of Tennessee William's *A Streetcar Named Desire* . . . , has a visual memory of him as he was waiting for her on the night of the play; and when she tells actress Huma about her son, Huma also recalls the night, and remembers seeing the boy's face through the taxi window asking her for an autograph. (140)

The circularity of the plot, potentially disturbing, even monotonous, is thus combined in more traditional style with a linear dynamic that moves, like the train, swiftly toward its final destination.

Allinson's discussion of the narrative is in the context of his discussion of *All About My Mother*'s genre, which he identifies as melodrama. The appeal to coincidence (Manuela encounters each of her new friends by accident) and the use of *mise-en-scène* as a form of "expressive power" also reconfirm this genre identification (140). It is worth noting, however, that the film's genre is, like its plot, contested. The IMDb, once more, defines *All About My Mother* as a "comedy/drama." Almodóvar himself calls it, ironically perhaps, a "screwball drama" (that is, a serious film that relies nonetheless on the wit and elegance of classical Hollywood "screwball" comedy). The section titles of the press book, composed as always by Almodóvar himself, attempt to anticipate and direct reviews by highlighting certain aspects of the narrative: "Faking It" suggests that women are born actors, calling attention to Manuela's initial simulation of a "wounded maternity" she will later come to experience for real (Manuela works as a nurse simulating organ-donation scenarios) (El Deseo 15). The next sections, "Actresses" and "Actresses and Women," further this equation, tracing it back to cinematic and personal precedents: Bette Davis in *All About Eve* (1950; the acknowledged source of *All About My Mother*) and the child Pedro's memory of a patio where village women gathered ("three or four women talking represent for me the origin of life . . . of fiction, and of narration") (El Deseo 16). But Almodóvar also draws attention to a scene we will examine in more detail later: "La Agrado's Monologue." Since this transvestite character is the only broadly comic character of the film (and even she is shown with some dignity), Almodóvar hints that humor is by no means incompatible with this newly serious and "mature" style.

Themes

If its narrative is problematic, at once complex and simple, intricate and transparent, then the themes of *All About My Mother* are equally debatable. In the only book devoted entirely to the film (a critical guide intended for students), Silvia Colmenero Salgado offers the following themes: the body in chains, in the heart of time, a return journey, wounded maternity, the impossible encounter with the father, the wheel of destiny, the face of death, the lying game, the monologue in the film or the film in a monologue, the persecuted look, a dialogue between texts, and giving birth (11). While some of these themes are more readily identifiable than others ("the face of death" is that of the dying father; "the persecuted look" that of the woman, especially the woman who loves another woman), it is clear from the vocabulary used in Colmenero Salgado's list that these are highly abstract categories. After all, no theme could be more universal than that of destiny. The chapter headings on the French DVD are equally abstract: "death . . . and after," "once upon a time," "life goes on."

Almodóvar's cinematic world is indeed stylized, irreducible to everyday life. But *All About My Mother* does treat broad themes that have social implications in Spain and go perhaps unrecognized in other places. As I have suggested elsewhere (*Desire Unlimited* 2), the main themes of the film are gender, nationality, and homosexuality. Almodóvar is universally known as a "woman's director," an impression reinforced by publicity material in all countries and (like his supposedly newfound "maturity") a backhanded compliment. In fact, *All About My Mother* followed *Live Flesh* (1997), a crime melodrama that boasted at least three strong and complex male characters. In pigeonholing Almodóvar as a director of films about and for women, therefore, critics are actively constructing an image that does not correspond to the totality of his work. It remains the case, however, that the male characters in *All About My Mother* either disappear after the opening sequences (Esteban), appear only in the closing sequences (Esteban-Lola), or are marginalized in the middle (Mario is a crudely insensitive actor as unsympathetic as the Stanley character he plays onstage in *Streetcar*). It is no accident that this last role is played by Carlos Lozano, an actor familiar to Spanish TV audiences as the host of tacky game and reality shows.

All About My Mother does, then, focus almost exclusively on women, a welcome and still rare emphasis in feature-film production. But its representation of women is controversial. While the main character, Manuela, is independent and, initially at least, self-assured (she is a single working mother who has escaped an abusive relationship to bring up her child alone), she is also defined primarily by her motherhood. In the opening sequences that establish her character, we see her easy familiarity with her teenage son: they sit together on the sofa watching *All About Eve* on television. As in maternal melodrama of the 1940s, it seems motherhood is irreconcilable with sexual expression. Even by the end of the film, Manuela (now recovered from her loss and the happy surrogate parent of the new Esteban) is not shown to have a lover. Exploiting the deep resonances of Catholicism that persist in a largely secular Spain, Almodóvar suggests that Manuela is a new Mary (a new mourning, virgin mother), even having her drive past the Sagrada Familia, the celebrated church named for the Holy Family, as soon as she reaches Barcelona.

Manuela may be active and enterprising in searching for her former lover. But her role is the altruistic and nurturing one that is traditional for women: she cares not only for the two Estebans but for Agrado, who has been beaten up by a trick, and for Sister Rosa, the nun whom she discovers is dying of AIDS. What is significant, however, is that Rosa has been rejected by her own unsympathetic biological mother. The "natural" family is thus shown to be unnatural in its affections. And while the film may be suggesting that women are particularly qualified as caretakers, it also proposes, more subtly, that traditional family structures are no longer valid and that the improvised arrangements we make with our friends may be more solid and valuable. In this it coincides with social changes in Spain, where the collapse of the birthrate to the lowest in the world has thrown traditional family values into crisis. If this new world is one of "the strangeness of kinship" (Maslin), it is also one in which the notion of family has been generously extended to embrace the kindness of strangers.

Another area in which Spain has experienced fundamental change is nationality. In *Spanish National Cinema*, Núria Triana-Toribio has recently revealed the shifting and contradictory ways in which the national has been represented and conceived in relation to film. She argues that in the 1990s Spanishness was conceived under the useful "generic umbrella" of a "discourse on diversity" (146). This ideology has been used to co-opt different generations of directors, different autonomous areas within the Spanish state, and different genders and sexualities (the boom in both women directors and gay themes). While Almodóvar's profile might seem to correspond quite closely to this capacious model, Triana-Toribio also notes the unease with which Spain's best-known director is at the same time viewed by his fellow filmmakers: "Widely seen as the main representative of Spanish cinema outside Spain, and the recipient of numerous international accolades . . . Almodóvar is still the source of some embarrassment in his own country." Indeed, it was only when *All About My Mother* won the

Goya (Spanish Oscar equivalent) for best director that Almodóvar "received major recognition within Spain" (158).

One clear way in which Almodóvar has been out of step with democratic Spain has been his stubborn identification with Madrid, the old centralist capital. Perhaps the most important structural change in the post-Franco period was the establishment of a new state of self-governing areas in which Basques, Catalans, and Galicians achieved a high degree of autonomy. While the idea of Almodóvar making a film in Barcelona seemed as unlikely as Woody Allen or Spike Lee working in LA, the very fact that most of *All About My Mother* was shot on location in Barcelona was taken as a long delayed gesture toward this reality of devolution. Almodóvar, diplomatic as ever, was extravagant in his praise for the Catalan capital, a favor that was generally returned by the local press (Smith, *Contemporary Spanish Culture* 164). Just as, however, there are contradictions in *All About My Mother*'s representation of women, so there are problems in Almodóvar's newly diverse vision of Spain. Although in reality the Catalan language has been "normalized" even in the capital, the film shows barely a trace of Barcelona's bilingualism. While there are postcard shots of Barcelona's distinctive architectural style known as *modernisme* (equivalent to art nouveau), the Catalan city serves merely as a backdrop to the Spanish-speaking characters. Although the varieties of Spanish spoken are themselves diverse (Manuela has a soft Argentine accent, Agrado a marked Andalusian pronunciation), well-known Catalan actors such as Rosa María Sardà as Rosa's unsympathetic mother speak not one word of their native tongue. Similarly, the role of foreign immigration to Barcelona is reduced to background: as Rosa is taken ill in the street, multiracial children play behind her, mere extras in a drama whose focus is on other themes.

But Almodóvar was not making a documentary. And it would be unfair to require his films to restrict themselves to national issues that are themselves difficult to delimit. And just as apparently traditional gender roles hide new forms of family structure, so *All About My Mother*'s apparent neglect of changes in the character of the Spanish state can be reread in a positive light. The nomadic Manuela, commuting between Madrid and Barcelona, suggests that the two cities are dependent on one another. The newly flexible caretaking she embodies cannot be identified with only one geographic location.

A similar fluidity applies to my final theme: sexuality. Outside Spain, Almodóvar is often said to be an "openly gay director." Indeed, in the United States, the Catholic League attacked him as a "devout homosexual" in its angry denunciation of *All About My Mother*. It is important to note, however, that Almodóvar has never presented himself in such terms and is rarely asked about the topic by the discreet Spanish press. While the 1990s were a decade of increased visibility in Spain for gay men, that visibility does not register in Almodóvar's filmmaking. His first and last feature to center on male homosexuality was *Law of Desire* (*La ley del deseo*), in 1987. *All About My Mother* does focus, however, on a stormy lesbian affair between the diva Huma and her junkie lover Nina. This is the only sexual relationship shown in the film, and one that, as always in Almodóvar, is doomed by the impossibility of the couple. While it would be possible to read this relationship as repeating negative stereotypes of lesbians (the notorious *The Killing of Sister George* [Robert Aldrich, 1968] also focuses on a destructive affair between an older and a younger woman), what is vital here is that their love is taken for granted. No one who encounters the couple expresses the slightest surprise at their affair, and Huma, a grande dame of the theater, is (like Almodóvar) clearly unconcerned by the effect such a revelation might have on her adoring audience. As he has done since at least *Dark Habits (Entre tinieblas,* 1983), which focused on an unlikely love between a Mother Superior and a nightclub singer, Almodóvar depicts a utopian Spain in which homosexuality is indifferent and poses no particular problems for its practitioners.

When Huma first meets Manuela and solicits her help in searching for Nina, she echoes *Streetcar*'s most famous line: "I have always depended on the kindness of strangers." While foreign viewers might take Huma's references to Tennessee Williams and Bette Davis (she has modeled her smoking on Davis) as pointing to a "gay sensibility" in the film, it is important to stress once more that Almodóvar himself has consistently denied the existence of such a concept and that his mass audience in Spain would most likely be mystified by this suggestion. While homosexuality has been vital to the promotion of Almodóvar to niche audiences abroad, in Spain itself it remains (like gender or nationality) forbidden territory, often the cause of embarrassment and denial. It is not the least of the contradictions that coalesce around *All About My Mother* that a film that so thoroughly marginalizes heterosexual men and boasts one of the most sympathetic transvestites in cinematic history should have crossed over so successfully to a mainstream audience around the world. As José Arroyo puts it in his review in *Sight and Sound*, "That a paean to motherhood should be so queer might be a commonplace. That such a queer film dramatises a general condition with formal elegance, nuanced observations and emotional resonance is rare indeed."

Technique

The formal elegance of Almodóvar itself has emotional resonance. Or to put it another way, his technique is not merely technical. An acknowledged master of film form, Almodóvar exploits *mise-en-scène*, cinematography, and editing to unexpected effect. Technique can be used to work against the narrative and themes we have previously examined, rather than to reinforce them. Indeed, this is precisely the way it functions in the classical melodrama of directors such as Douglas Sirk, an acknowledged influence on Almodóvar.

Before *All About My Mother*, Almodóvar had sometimes been criticized for an obsession with visual pleasure, which is viewed as feminine or effeminate. One critic accused *High Heels* (*Tacones lejanos*, 1991) of being made by an "interior decorator" (Thompson 62). The art design of *All About My Mother* is typically meticulous but less ostentatious than in his earlier films. The color coding is based initially on the primary colors displayed in the poster for the film. These colors are used to differentiate clearly between spaces. For example, the stage backdrop to the *Streetcar* production is an intense saturated blue, which appears nowhere else in the film. Elsewhere, primary colors recur in complex patterns. Manuela's umbrella, unfurled on the rainy night when her son is killed, is red, blue, and yellow. But her red raincoat matches her son's red-and-white-striped top. It also rhymes with the walls and ashtray of the bar in which he sits waiting for Manuela and with the huge red lips of the poster of Huma in front of which Manuela herself waits. Colors thus serve to bring together diverse elements in a single sequence.

But that precise tone of red recurs unpredictably throughout the film, suggesting identifications between characters that the viewer may not consciously register. When Rosa takes Manuela to her mother's house, her coat is red, and when Manuela meets Huma in her dressing room, the latter's tight tailored jacket is the same color.

Almodóvar thus suggests similarities between these superficially different women: the loving mother, the sacrificial nun, and the self-obsessed diva. While each has, in her different way, been disappointed in love, soon they will be sharing a sofa together, the best of friends. Clothes are not simply used implicitly to bring together diverse characters and plot strands, however. They are also explicitly thematized and play a role in the narrative. Manuela herself remarks on the slutty outfit Agrado has given her on the day she will visit Rosa's priggish mother; Agrado cheers herself up on that same day with a knockoff of a ladylike Chanel suit (in *High Heels*, Victoria Abril got to wear the genuine article). Clothing is an index to class and character as well as a source of aesthetic pleasure.

This primary palette is contrasted with secondary colors. Manuela's new apartment in Barcelona is decorated in 1970s style: muddy brown, sage green, and sickly orange (in a typically careful detail, the same fashionably retro design is printed on the face of the CD of the sound track). Often costume and background compete with clashing colors and designs. The actors seem positively overwhelmed by the intricate modernist decor in Rosa's mother's flat. Art design here works against psychology to suggest that people cannot be separated from their environment, that citizens are at one with their city. Indeed, this distinctive decoration is typical of a few moneyed blocks of Barcelona's Eixample, a celebrated example of nineteenth-century town planning. Details of the *mise-en-scène* also raise unsettling questions. When Esteban waits for his mother in the café, prisonlike bars can be seen on the windows behind, breaking up the poster of Huma that looms out of focus in the background. Is it he who is threatened (by impending death), or she (held captive by tragic love and celebrity)? Or again, the first appearance of the primary palette is ominous indeed: in the opening credits, the camera pans slowly over medical equipment, whose knobs and charts are accented in red, blue, and yellow. Is the gravity of the hospital setting, which will also recur throughout the film, undercut or reinforced by this aestheticization, this universal color coding?

Almodóvar's camera is mobile, snaking along corridors, tracking along city streets, and even (as we will see) taking off in a helicopter. But sometimes it simply comes to rest on the characters, paying its respects to an everyday life that will be shattered by mourning and melancholia. Thus, when Manuela and Esteban watch TV, they share the frame just as they share the family flat in a domestic life that will end all too soon. The most mobile scenes, the train journeys, are shot most simply and economically: the shattered Manuela caught in close-up in her seat; the gaping mouth of a tunnel; and (later) a train speeding in and out of the shot, caught momentarily by a camera that holds still once more. Almodóvar, who showed the characters of *Kika* arriving at the glamorous new Atocha station in Madrid, does not bother here with such frippery.

If the *mise-en-scène* remains relatively lush, the editing, like much of the cinematography, is severely economical. *All About My Mother* appeals to laconic intertitles to signal gaps in time ("Two weeks later," "Two years later"), and grueling scenes of emotional distress are not held too long. When Manuela tells Rosa's mother of her dead son, Almodóvar shows Manuela closing the door and holds the shot from behind just for a second. We hear her renewed sobs but do not see her face. But just as the *mise-en-scène* raises curious questions that go beyond the plot (Esteban's prison bars, the gaily colored medical paraphernalia), so the editing establishes connections that remain ambiguous. Snaking down the theater corridor, the camera disappears into the mouth of a rubbish bin only to reemerge once more in the black hole of the railway tunnel, a strange and disturbing graphic match. Throughout, the cutting is deliberate. The grid of Esteban's notebook, in which he sought Huma's autograph, slowly dissolves into the pattern of flashing lights on the facade of the theater: the life of a budding writer is linked to the unwitting cause of his death. In such moments, narrative and technique fuse in a form of imagistic storytelling that is both eloquent and elegant.

Close Reading

Let us look, finally, at three scenes that reveal the diversity of Almodóvar's technique. The death of Esteban occurs eleven minutes into the film. As mother and son discuss Esteban's missing father, they are shown characteristically in a tight two-shot. The camera holds still during this long unbroken take. Sheltering beneath the rainbow-hued umbrella, they are shadowed by the prison bars of the café behind them. When Huma and Nina emerge from the theater on the other side of the street, they are shown from Manuela and Esteban's point of view and from further away, in medium shot. Alberto Iglesias's main theme, a probing piano phrase, starts up. As the two actresses leave, we see first Esteban, indistinct and imploring outside the taxi window, and then Huma, looking back at Esteban as the taxi recedes into the distance. Iglesias adds urgent string motifs on the sound track. Suddenly, the camera tracks away, leaving Manuela alone in the distance. A very brief shot follows from inside an unidentified car: a suddenly shattered windshield signals the accident we do not see. The score ceases abruptly, and Almodóvar cuts to an equally enigmatic shot: a slow blurry pan of the street at night, upside down. As the camera comes to rest in an unusual canted position (i.e., at an angle to the horizontal), Manuela comes into the shot, her hair drenched by the rain, screaming "Hijo mío!" ("My son!"). We realize this is the dying Esteban's perspective. Not only is the picture blurred and distorted, the sound is no longer synchronized with the image. As Esteban sinks quickly into unconsciousness (the shot fades to black), he is as shocked and disorientated as the audience. It is perhaps this single scene that justifies the first person of the title. If the whole film is called *All About* My *Mother*, it is because here at the turning point Manuela is shown from her dying son's point of view. If Esteban is identified as the "author" of the film (he makes notes for a project that bears the same name as the film we are watching), his early exclusion from the narrative is troubling, denying the audience an authoritative commentary on the action we will see.

The simplicity of this pivotal sequence contrasts with the treatment of another vital plot point, Manuela's arrival in Barcelona. To the sound of Ismaël Lô's lyrical "Tajabone" (whose lyrics are in an African language few of the film's audience are likely to understand), Almodóvar offers a gorgeous aerial shot of the city at night. The camera flies over a hill and hovers, as if mesmerized by the spectacle laid out before it. Almodóvar cuts to a traveling shot of Manuela in a taxi. The glamorous facade of the Sagrada Familia, Barcelona's most emblematic monument, gleams gold in a special lighting design. It then dissolves, reflected in the taxi window. We then cut to more traveling shots from Manuela's point of view of the Nou Camp, a peripheral area of the city and a site of transvestite prostitution. The girls and their clients gleam in the flickering light of bonfires and headlights. One high-angle shot echoes the aerial shot of the city: the cars circle around the field as if in some strange mechanical choreography. What is striking about this sequence is the use of sound to unify very diverse images. The same song (gentle, enigmatic, unsettling) plays throughout. The mobile camera here mimics the mobile Manuela, trekking from place to place in her search for closure. But soon it will come to rest on Agrado: Manuela reencounters her old friend, begins to piece together a new life by confronting the old.

Both of these sequences are purely cinematic: we cannot imagine them taking place onstage. The third and final scene I have chosen is overtly theatrical: Agrado's monologue. The sequence begins with a characteristic camera tracking shot along the red curtain in front of the stage. It then advances down the aisle to where Agrado addresses the audience in a pink sweater and black PVC pants. As the monologue continues, the camera cuts ever closer but remains in frontal position throughout. Occasional cutaways to the audience cue our own reaction: delighted humor at Agrado's confessions of plastic surgery, climaxing in her declaration that a woman is only authentic in so far as she resembles her dream of herself. Eschewing virtuoso camera movement, editing, or music, Almodóvar relies here on the performance skills of Antonia San Juan, an artist known for her cabaret work but previously unskilled in cinema. In spite of his mastery of film technique, then, Almodóvar is equally at home in the discovery and direction of actresses. The wide range of performance styles in *All About My Mother* testifies both to his ability to mix genres (comedy and tragedy) and to his subtle orchestration of varied registers of narrative and technique.

Conclusion

The self-invented transvestite Agrado, who calls ironic attention to her own artificiality, appears to reconfirm one stereotype about Almodóvar: that his cinema is "postmodern." Critics generally use this term not in its philosophical sense, but as a loose synonym for "superficial," "campy," or "kitschy." We have seen, however, that this side of the film is fused with a more characteristic tendency toward an emotion that is frankly expressed, however well dressed and expertly shot it may be. Perhaps this explains the enigma with which I began: how an apparently marginal film in milieu and origin could have had such a broad-based success. The formal perfection and queer references of *All About My Mother* will attract a select audience. The universal themes of motherhood and bereavement will ring true for many more. Expertly pitched between niche and mainstream, *All About My Mother* shows that European cinema can cross over to a wide audience without abandoning its artistic vision.

Credits

Spain, 1999, El Deseo S. A. and Renn Productions, with Canal+

Director and Screenplay: Pedro Almodóvar
Cinematography: Affonso Beato
Editing: José Salcedo
Music: Alberto Iglesias
Art Design: Antxón Gómez
Costume Design: José María De Cossío and Sabine Daigeler

CAST:

Manuela	Cecilia Roth
Huma	Marisa Paredes
Nina	Candela Peña
Agrado	Antonia San Juan
Sister Rosa	Penélope Cruz
Rosa's mother	Rosa María Sardà
Esteban	Eloy Azorín
Mario	Carlos Lozano
Lola	Toni Cantó

Bibliography

Allinson, Mark. *A Spanish Labyrinth: The Films of Pedro Almodóvar.* London: Tauris, 2001.

Arroyo, José. Rev. of *All About My Mother* (*Todo sobre mi madre*), dir. Pedro Almodóvar. *Sight and Sound* Sept. 1999. 22 Mar. 2003 <http://www.bfi.org.uk/sightandsound/reviews/details.php?id=185>.

Catholic League. "*All About My Mother* Rips Nuns." Press release 12 Nov. 1999. 22 Mar. 2003 <http://www.catholicleague.org/99press_releases/pr0499.htm#ANOTHER%20CATHOLIC-BASHING%20MOVIE?>.

Colmenero Salgado, Silvia. *Pedro Almodóvar: Todo sobre mi madre.* Barcelona: Paidós, 2001.

El Deseo S. A. "*Todo sobre mi madre*": Un film de Almodóvar. Press book. Madrid: El Deseo, 1999.

Focus 2000. Cannes: European Audiovisual Observatory, 2000.

Heredero, Carlos F., and Antonio Santamarina. *Semillas del futuro: Cine español 1990–2001*. Madrid: Nuevo Ministerio, 2002.

Maslin, Janet. Rev. of *All About My Mother*, dir. Pedro Almodóvar. *New York Times* 24 Sept. 1999. 22 Mar. 2003 <http://www.nytimes.com/library/film/092499ny-mother-film-review.html>.

Internet Movie Database (IMDb). "Plot Summary for *Todo sobre mi madre* (1999)." 22 Mar. 2003 <http://www.imdb.com/title/tt0185125/plotsummary>.

Smith, Paul Julian. *Contemporary Spanish Culture: TV, Fashion, Art, and Film*. Oxford: Polity, 2003.

———. *Desire Unlimited: The Cinema of Pedro Almodóvar*. London: Verso, 2000.

Sociedad General de Autores y Editores (SGAE). *Hábitos de consumo cultural*. Madrid: SGAE, 2000.

Thompson, David. Rev. of *High Heels* (*Tacones lejanos*), dir. Pedro Almodóvar. *Sight and Sound* (Apr. 1992): 61–62.

Triana-Toribio, Núria. *Spanish National Cinema*. London: Routledge, 2003.

Glossary of Critical Terms

Academy ratio: The **frame** size established by the Academy of Motion Picture Arts and Sciences to standardize the sound film in 1932. It indicated an **aspect ratio** of 4:3, or 1.33:1. The ratio was 1.37:1 before the sound track was incorporated into the film. Non-widescreen televisions still use this ratio. See also **Panavision; widescreen.**

action match: See **match-on-action cut.**

aerial shot: A **shot** from above, usually made from a plane, helicopter, or crane. See also **crane shot.**

aerial view: Also known as *bird's-eye view;* an **omniscient-point-of-view shot** that is taken from an aircraft or extremely high crane and implies an omniscient perspective.

alienation effect: Also known as distancing effect or **distantiation;** in theater, an effect that strives to draw attention to the play's own artifice (via, among other possible devices, highly artificial acting styles, props, sets, and so on) creating a psychological distance between the audience and the action on the stage. As advocated by German playwright Bertolt Brecht, this effect limits the audience's emotional identification with the characters and events depicted while encouraging an intellectual response.

ambient sound: Sound that emanates from the ambience (or background) of the setting or environment being filmed, either recorded during **production** or added during **postproduction.**

analog format: One of the two ways of storing recorded sound, either monaurally or stereophonically (the other is the digital format). This format involves an analogous (or 1:1) relationship between the sound wave and its storage; in other words, the recorded sound wave is a copy of the original wave.

anamorphic lens: A **lens** that squeezes a wide image to fit the dimensions of a standard 35 mm film **frame.** In projection, an anamorphic lens on the projector reverses the process and redistributes the wide image onto the screen. See also **widescreen.**

animation: All techniques that make inanimate objects move on the screen, such as drawing directly on the film, individually photographing animation **cels,** and photographing the objects one **frame** at a time while adjusting their position between frames. See also **pixillation; stop-motion photography.**

answer print: The first combined print, incorporating the picture, the sound, and the special effects, from which the **editor** determines whether further changes are needed before creating the **final print.**

antagonist: The major character whose values or behavior are in conflict with those of the **protagonist.**

antirealism: A treatment that goes against the dominant tendencies of **realism.** However, realism and antirealism (like realism and fantasy) are not strictly opposed polarities.

aperture: The camera opening that defines the exposure of each **frame** of film.

arc light: The source of high-energy illumination on the movie **set** and in the projector; the principle source of film lighting during the 1920s and for three-strip Technicolor. It is produced by an electric current that arcs across the gap between two pieces of carbon (the direct-current carbon arc) or, more recently, by a mercury arc between tungsten electrodes sealed in a glass bulb.

Arriflex: A light, portable camera first used in the late 1950s; it was essential to the mobile, handheld photography of the **New Wave** and to most contemporary **cinematography. Mitchell cameras,** however, are the industry standard.

art director: The person responsible for **set** design and graphics.

art houses: Small theaters that sprang up in the major cities of the United States during the 1950s to show "art films" as opposed to "commercial films"—a distinction that can no longer be so clearly made, due to international funding mechanisms and studio acquisitions of independent distribution companies.

aspect ratio: The relationship between the **frame**'s two dimensions: the width of the image to its height. See, for example, **Academy ratio.**

assembly edit: A preliminary edited version of a movie, in which selected **sequences** and **shots** are arranged in approximate relationship without further regard to rhythm, continuity, or other conventions of editing.

associative editing: The cutting together of **shots** to establish their metaphoric or symbolic—as opposed to their **narrative**—relationship. The prehistoric bone that becomes a futuristic space station in Kubrick's *2001* (1968) is a prime example. See also **match cut.**

asynchronous sound: Sound that is not precisely matched temporally with the actions occurring in it (as opposed to **synchronous sound**).

auteur: A director or other creative intelligence with a recognizable and distinctive style who is considered the prime "author" of a film. See also *politique des auteurs.*

automatic dialogue replacement (ADR): Rerecording done via computer, a faster, less expensive, and more technically sophisticated process than via live actors.

average shot length (ASL): Roughly how long each **shot** in a given film lasts; the ASL is important for determining the overall pace of the film.

backlight: Lighting, usually positioned behind and in line with the subject and the camera, generally used to create highlights on the subject as a means of separating it from the background and increasing its appearance of three-dimensionality, but which can also produce silhouettes.

back lots: Large tracts of open land owned by the studios and used to simulate various locations.

best boy: First assistant electrician to the **gaffer** on a movie **production set.**

B films: Also called B features, B pictures, B movies; films made cheaply and quickly, often reusing sets and costumes of more expensive productions. They were used to fill the bottom half of a double bill when double features were standard.

bit players: Actors who hold small speaking parts.

Black Maria: The first movie studio—a crude, hot, cramped shack in New Jersey where Thomas A. Edison and his staff began making movies.

blimp: An awkward soundproofing cover for the camera first used in the early years of sound. Most cameras today are constructed with their own internal soundproofing.

block booking: The practice whereby distributors forced exhibitors to rent a **production** company's films in large groups, or "blocks," tied to several desirable titles in advance of production. Initiated by Adolph Zukor in 1916, block booking became fundamental to the studio-system monopoly and was ruled illegal by the U.S. Supreme Court in 1948 as part of the "Paramount decrees." Elements of block booking persist in the practice of blind bidding for films in the **preproduction** stage, a source of constant complaint among contemporary exhibitors.

blockbuster: A film that is enormously popular or one that was so costly to make that it must be highly successful to make a profit. The first blockbusters were probably Italian superspectacles like *Cabiria* (Giovanni Pastrone, 1914), followed by the D. W. Griffith epics *The Birth of a Nation* (1915) and *Intolerance* (1916). During the 1920s, films like *The Thief of Bagdad* (Raoul Walsh, 1924) and *Ben-Hur* (Fred Niblo, 1925) were conceived and marketed as blockbusters, as was the producer David O. Selznick's *Gone with the Wind* (Victor Fleming, 1939) in the sound era. In the 1950s and 1960s, the epic-scale **widescreen** blockbuster (e.g., Cecil B. DeMille's *The Ten Commandments* [1956]) became a veritable genre.

blocking: Actual physical and spatial relationships among figures and settings on the stage or in the **frame.**

bluescreen photography: A **special-effects** process that involves shooting live action, models, or miniatures in front of a bright blue screen, leaving the background of the **shot** unexposed. This produces footage that can later be composited with other elements such as traveling mattes into the primary film. See **matte shot.** Now often supplanted by **greenscreen photography** used in **CGI.**

boom: A mechanical device for holding the microphone in the air, out of camera range, and movable in almost any direction.

Cahiers du cinéma: Paris-based film journal founded by André Bazin, Jacques Doniol-Valcroze, and Lo Duca in 1951 that featured important articles by future directors of the French **New Wave.**

cameos: Small but significant roles often taken by famous actors.

camera angle: The perspective that the camera takes on the subject being shot. Low angle, high angle, or tilt angle are the three most common.

camera obscura: Literally, "dark chamber"; a box (or a room in which a viewer stands); light entering through a tiny hole (later a **lens**) on one side of the box (or room) projects an image from the outside onto the opposite side or wall.

caméra-stylo: Literally, "camera pen"; phrase first used by Alexandre Astruc in 1948 to suggest that cinema could be as multidimensional and personal as the older literary arts.

canted framing: See **Dutch angle.**

cel: A transparent sheet of celluloid or similar plastic on which drawings or lettering may be made for use in **animation** or **intertitles.**

celluloid roll film: Also known as *motion-picture film,* **film stock,** or **raw film stock;** consists of long strips of perforated cellulose acetate on which a rapid succession of still photographs known as **frames** can be recorded. One side of the strip is layered with an emulsion consisting of light-sensitive crystals and dyes; the other side is covered with a backing that reduces reflections. Each strip is perforated with **sprocket** holes that facilitate the movement of the **stock** through the sprocket wheels of the camera, the processor, and the projector. Manufactured in several standard **formats.**

CGI: Standard abbreviation for "computer-generated imagery." See **computer-generated effects** and **digital effects.**

chanbara: A Japanese sword-fight film.

character roles: Actors' parts that represent distinctive character types (sometimes stereotypes): society leaders, judges, doctors, diplomats, and so on.

chiaroscuro: The use of deep gradations and subtle variations of lights and darks within an image.

cinéaste: An artistically committed filmmaker.

Cinecittà: The largest Italian studio complex; it is located in Rome.

cinema novo: Literally, "new cinema"; politically committed Brazilian cinema of the 1960s.

CinemaScope: The trade name used by 20th Century–Fox for its anamorphic **widescreen** process. The word is frequently used today to refer to all anamorphic processes.

cinematic time: The imaginary time in which a movie's images appear or its **narrative** occurs; time that has been manipulated through editing. As a result, a five-minute film **sequence** might cover, say, two years, or two seconds. See also **real time.**

Cinématographe: A compact, portable, hand-cranked machine invented by Auguste and Louis Lumière and first exhibited in 1895 in Paris. It was a camera, processing device, and projector all in one.

cinematographer: The **director of photography (DP),** who is responsible for the camera technique and the lighting of a film in **production.**

cinematography: Motion-picture photography.

cinéma vérité: Literally, "cinema truth," the French translation of Dziga Vertov's *Kino-pravda;* as originally used in 1950s France by filmmaker Jean Rouch, the term described a kind of nonfiction cinema that utilized lightweight camera and sound equipment, small crews, and direct (and often confrontational) interviews. The term now often refers to a visual style characterized by handheld camera work and **direct sound.**

Cinerama: A **widescreen** process invented by Fred Waller that requires three electronically synchronized cameras; it was first used in the 1952 film *This Is Cinerama* and was abandoned in 1962 in favor of an anamorphic process marketed under the same name.

clapperboard: Sometimes called *clapboard;* it consists of two short wooden boards, hinged together, on which essential identifying information—some of which changes with each take—is written in chalk. The person handling the device claps the boards together in front of the camera and says the number of the take. The resulting reference marks, on both the photographic film and the sound-recording tape, facilitate the rematching of sounds and images during editing. The "clap" has been widely replaced by electronic syncing devices.

close-up: Sometimes designated CU; a **shot** that often shows a part of the body filling the **frame**—traditionally a face. More generally, any close shot.

coherence: Logical or aesthetic consistency within a movie; the organization of all the basic elements of cinematic form into a harmonious or credible whole.

colorization: The use of digital technology, in a process much like hand-tinting, to "paint" colors on movies meant to be seen in black and white.

color timing: The color balance of an image or **scene,** or any process used to color-correct or balance an image or scene, so that color continuity is maintained throughout the film.

composition: The process of visualizing and putting visualization plans into practice; more precisely, the organization, distribution, balance, and general relationship of stationary objects and figures, as well as of light, shade, line, and color within the **frame.**

compressing: Also known as *companding;* the process of combining **sound tracks** that preserves signals but reduces or eliminates noise ("hissing") on the tape.

computer-generated effects: One category of **special effects** (the others are **in-camera effects** and **laboratory effects**). This kind is created by digital technology and transferred to film.

computer graphics: Electronically generated **animation,** used since the late 1970s to provide credit **sequences** (*Superman,* [1978]) and **special effects** (*Star Wars,* [1977]) for theatrical films.

conforming: See **negative cut.**

Constructivism: A movement in the arts during the 1920s, closely related to Russian **Futurism.** It advocated the use of modern architectural and/or mechanical designs and emphasized the constructed nature of all representations.

content curve: In terms of cinematic duration, an arc that measures information in a **shot;** at the curve's peak, the viewer has absorbed the information from a shot and is ready to move on to the next **composition.**

continuity editing: Sometimes called *classical Hollywood style* and now the dominant style of editing (the other style is **discontinuity editing**). It seeks to achieve logic, smoothness, sequentiality, and the temporal and spatial orientation of viewers to what they see on the screen; ensures the flow from **shot** to shot; creates a rhythm based on the relationship between cinematic space and **cinematic time;** creates filmic unity (beginning, middle, and end); establishes and resolves problems. In short, it delivers a story as clearly and coherently as possible, absorbing the viewer into the film's **narrative.** Sometimes called *invisible cutting.*

contract director: A director who works on projects from contract to contract rather than on an annual salary, as was common under the studio system. A *contract player* was an actor in the same system.

contrapuntal sound: Sound used in counterpoint, or contrast, to the image.

costumes: The clothing worn by an actor in a movie (sometimes called *wardrobe,* a term that also designates the department in a studio in which clothing is made and stored).

Glossary of Critical Terms

crane shot: Movement of a camera mounted on an elevating arm that, in turn, is mounted on a vehicle capable of moving on its own power. A crane may also be mounted on a vehicle that can be pushed along tracks.

crosscutting: Juxtaposing **shots** from two or more **sequences,** actions, or stories to suggest parallel action, as in D. W. Griffith's *Intolerance* (1916).

cut: A direct change from one **shot** to another, i.e., the precise point at which shot A ends and shot B begins; one result of **cutting.**

cutting: Also known as **splicing;** the actual joining together of two **shots.** The **editor** must first **cut** (or splice) each shot from its respective roll of film before gluing or taping all the shots together.

cutting continuity script: A specialized document that not only reflects the changes made between the **shooting script** and the actual shooting but also includes the number, kind, and duration of **shots,** the kind of transitions, the exact dialogue, and the musical and **sound effects.**

dailies: Also known as **rushes;** usually synchronized picture/sound **workprints** of a day's shooting that can be studied by the director, **editor,** and other crew members before the next day's shooting begins.

day for night: The technique used to shoot night **scenes** during the day. The effect is created by stopping down the **lens** aperture or by using special lens filters. **Night-for-night** shooting characterized the harsher **realism** of film styles such as *film noir.*

deep-focus cinematography: Using the **short-focal-length lens,** this technique captures **deep-space composition** and its illusion of depth.

deep-space composition: A visual composition that occupies all three **planes** of the **frame,** thus creating an illusion of depth, and usually shot with **deep-focus cinematography.**

definition: A term used to describe the facility of **film stock** to articulate the separate elements of an image. See also **resolution.**

depth of field: The distance in front of a camera and its **lens** in which objects are in apparent sharp focus.

dialectical montage: Also known as *intellectual montage;* a form of **discontinuity editing** pioneered by Soviet film theorist and filmmaker Sergei Eisenstein, in which **shots** "collide" or noticeably conflict with one another. It is based on the Marxist concept of dialectical materialism, which posits the history of human society as the history of the struggle between the classes.

dialogue: The lip-synchronous speech of characters who are either visible on-screen or speaking offscreen, say from another part of the room that is not visible or from an adjacent space.

diaphragm: Also called *iris diaphragm;* a louvered disk, located midway between the front and rear elements of a **lens,** with an opening (the **aperture**) that can be made smaller or larger to regulate the amount of light that passes through the lens. See also *f*-**stop.**

diegesis: The total world of the film's **story.** The diegesis includes events and actions that are not shown on-screen but that nonetheless pertain to the story.

diegetic elements: The elements—events, characters, objects, settings, sounds—that form the world in which the film's **story** occurs; see also **diegesis** and **nondiegetic elements.**

diegetic sound: Sound that originates from a source within the world created by the film, such as on-screen and offscreen sounds heard by characters (as opposed to **nondiegetic sound**).

digital effects: Effects created directly by the use of computer imaging, so that the actual image is generated and/or manipulated by computer software. Also known as **CGI** (computer-generated imagery).

digital intermediate process: The process by which a film **negative** is converted into digital files in order to undergo digital manipulation (such as **color timing** or the addition of **computer-generated effects**) before being converted back into film.

director of photography (DP): See **cinematographer.**

direct point of view: One of two main categories of **subjective point of view** (the other is **indirect point of view**). It occurs when a character is in the **frame** and we see directly what he or she sees; this preserves time and space and creates a greater sense of **verisimilitude.**

direct sound: Sometimes called *real sound;* sound that is recorded "live," simultaneously with the image. With modern developments such as portable tape recorders and soundproofed cameras, direct sound has become common.

discontinuity editing: Also known as *constructive* or *nonlinear editing;* less widely used than **continuity editing;** often but not exclusively used in **experimental films.** This style joins **shot** A and shot B to produce an effect or meaning beyond that conveyed by either shot alone.

dissolve: Also known as an *overlap dissolve,* or simply **lap dissolve;** a transitional device in which **shot** B, superimposed, gradually appears over shot A and begins to replace it at midpoint in the transitional process. It usually indicates the passing of time.

distance: In short, the amount of space between the viewer and the characters on the screen, which varies with varying **shot** lengths. Identification with characters depends on manipulating this virtual distance to suppress recognition of the "dead space" between the audience and the screen.

distancing effect: See **alienation effect.**

documentary: A term widely attributed to John Grierson and his review of Robert Flaherty's *Moana* in 1926, though probably in use earlier; it now generally describes most kinds of films, beginning with those made with the Lumières' *Cinématographe,* that present themselves as nonfictional and are collectively regarded as truthful or authentic representations of reality. See also **mock documentary.**

Dolby: A system (named for its inventor, Ray Dolby) for audio recording and playback that reduces background noise and improves frequency response.

dolly: A moveable platform for carrying lights, cameras, and other kinds of filming equipment. A *dolly shot* is a moving camera **shot** filmed from a dolly (often mounted on wheels or on a flatbed truck). *Dolly in* and *dolly out* are dolly shots that respectively move toward or away from the subject being filmed.

double exposure: A **special effect** in which one **shot** is superimposed over another; may be expanded to a **multiple-exposure.**

double-system recording: The standard technique of recording film sound on a medium separate from the picture; it allows both for maximum quality control of the medium and for the many aspects of manipulating sound during **post-production** editing, mixing, and synchronization.

DP: Standard abbreviation for **director of photography.**

dramatic irony: An effect felt when the audience learns something before the characters on the screen do.

dubbing: The recording and **postsynchronization** of a **dialogue** or **sound-effects** track—for example, foreign-language dubbing.

Dutch angle: Also known as *Dutch tilt* or *oblique angle* or **canted framing.** In a Dutch-angle **shot,** the camera is tilted from its normal horizontal position so that it is no longer straight, giving the viewer the impression that the world in the **frame** is out of balance.

editor: The person who supervises the **splicing** or **cutting** together of the **shots** of a film into their final structure.

ellipsis: In filmmaking, generally an omission of time—the time that separates one **shot** from another—to create dramatic or comedic impact.

emulsion: A thin, light-sensitive coating of chemicals covering the base of the **film stock.**

emulsion speed: A measure of a **film stock**'s sensitivity to light. According to a scale established by the American Standards Association (ASA), the faster emulsion speeds are more sensitive to light and have a higher ASA number.

establishing shot: A **shot** that ordinarily begins a **sequence** of shots by showing the location of the ensuing action. While usually a **long shot,** it may also be a **medium shot** or a **close-up** that includes some sign or other cue to identify the location. It is also called a **master shot** or *cover shot* because the **editor** can repeat it later in the film to remind the audience of the location, thus "covering" the director by avoiding the need to **reshoot.**

experimental films: Also known as *avant-garde films,* a term implying that they are in the vanguard, out in front of traditional films. Such films are usually about unfamiliar, unorthodox, or obscure subject matter and are ordinarily made by independent (even underground) filmmakers, not studios, often with innovative techniques that call attention to, question, and even challenge their own artifice.

exposition: The images, action, and **dialogue** necessary to give the audience the background of the characters and the nature of the situation they are in, laying the foundation for the storytelling.

exposure: The amount of light allowed to strike the surface of the film. Film can be underexposed to create dark, murky images or overexposed to create lighter ones.

Expressionism: An artistic (including cinematic) style originating in Germany in the early twentieth century that sought to express an emotional state or subjective responses to objective and social reality. Expressionist films were usually characterized by an **antirealist** or explicitly psychological *mise-en-scène* and hard, **chiaroscuro** lighting.

external sound: A form of **diegetic sound** that comes from a place within the world of the **story,** which both we and the characters in the scene hear but do not see the source of.

extras: Actors who, usually, appear in nonspeaking or crowd roles and receive no screen credit.

extreme close-up: Sometimes designated ECU; a very close **shot** of some detail, such as a person's eye, a ring on a finger, or a watch face.

extreme long shot: Sometimes designated ELS; a **shot** that places the human figure far away from the camera, thus revealing much of the landscape.

eye level: An eye-level **shot** is made from the observer's eye level and usually implies neutrality with respect to the camera's attitude toward the subject being photographed.

eyeline match cut: This type of **match cut** joins **shot** A, a **point-of-view** shot of a person looking offscreen in one direction, and shot B, the person or object at which he or she is looking.

fade-in and fade-out: Transitional devices in which a **shot** made on black-and-white film fades in from a black field (on color film, from a color field) or fades out to a black field (or to a color field). A fade should not be confused with a **dissolve.**

fast motion: Photography that accelerates action by photographing it at a filming rate less than the normal 24 fps and then projecting it at normal speed, so that it takes place cinematically at a more rapid rate.

feature: The main film in a program of several films, or any film over four reels (approximately 45 minutes) in length. Standard theatrical feature length is 90 to 120 minutes.

fill light: Lighting, positioned at the opposite side of the camera from the **key light,** that can fill in the shadows created by the brighter key light. Fill light may also come from a **reflector board.**

film d'art: A movement in French cinema, beginning around 1908, that attempted to produce cinematic records of stage **productions;** it featured renowned dramatic personalities such as Sarah Bernhardt.

film noir: Literally, "black film"; a French term for films, beginning in the 1940s, that share certain "dark" characteristics, such as sordid urban atmospheres, **low-key lighting, night-for-night** shooting, shady characters, and **plots** dealing with illicit passions and violent crimes.

filmography: A listing of films, their directors, and their dates; similar to a bibliography.

film plane: The front surface of the film as it lies in the camera or projector gate (i.e., the film **aperture**).

film stock: See **celluloid roll film.**

filters: Pieces of plastic or glass placed in front of a **lens** to manipulate the quality of light—the tone or intensity of its illumination.

final cut: The final edited version of the film, created by mixing the **sound tracks,** inserting the desired optical or **special effects,** fine-tuning the rhythm of the film, balancing details and the bigger picture, bringing out subtleties and masking flaws, and approving the fidelity and acoustic quality of the mixed sound; not to be confused with **final print** or **fine cut.**

final print: An edited version of the film that contains everything that is to appear in the **release print;** do not confuse with **final cut** or **fine cut.**

fine cut: The result of the **editor**'s fine-tuning the **rough cut** (through as many versions as necessary), in consultation with the director and the producer.

first run: The distribution of a new film to showcase theaters. On its second run, the film is usually distributed to theaters in less-exclusive locations.

fish-eye lens: A radically distorting **wide-angle lens** with an angle of view that approaches 180 degrees.

flashback: A device for presenting or reawakening the memory of the camera, a character, the audience, or all three; a **cut** from the **narrative** present to a past event, which may or may not have already appeared in the movie either directly or through inference.

flash-forward: A device for presenting the anticipation of the camera, a character, the audience, or all three; a **cut** from the **narrative** present to a future time, one in which, for example, the omniscient camera reveals directly or a character imagines, from his or her **point of view,** what is going to happen.

flatbed: One type of predigital editing machine; a table on which the footage on the reels is pulled horizontally from left to right.

focal length: The distance from the optical center of a **lens** to the focal point (the film plane) when the lens is focused at infinity.

focus plane: The plane at which the **lens** forms a clear image when focused on a given **scene,** measured as the distance from the **film plane.** See also **depth of field.**

focus puller: An assistant camera operator responsible for following and maintaining the focus during **shots.**

Foley sounds: A special category of **sound effects,** invented in the 1930s by Jack Foley, a sound technician at Universal Studios. Technicians known as Foley artists, or footsteps artists, create these sounds in specially equipped studios, where they use a variety of props and other equipment to simulate sounds such as footsteps, doors opening, jingling car keys, cutlery hitting a plate, punching or kicking people or objects, and so on.

Formalism: An artistic style that focuses on form rather than content. The philosophy of Formalism posits that meaning is a function of the formal features of a discourse and deemphasizes the content or the referent of the content.

format: The dimensions of a **film stock** and its perforations, and the size and shape of the image **frame** as seen on the screen. The format extends from Super 8 mm through 70 mm (and beyond, into such specialized formats as IMAX) but is generally limited to three standard gauges: Super 8 mm, 16 mm, and 35 mm.

frame: The smallest compositional unit of film structure, the frame is the individual photographic image both in projection and on the film strip. The term also designates the boundaries of the image as an anchor for the **composition.**

frames per second (fps): The number of still images that pass through the camera or projector per second. Sound film usually runs at 24 fps, video at 25 fps.

freeze-frame: Also known as *stop frame* and *hold frame*; a **still** image within a movie, created by repetitive printing in the laboratory of the same **frame** so that it can be seen without movement for whatever length of time the filmmaker desires.

front projection: A process in which **stills** or footage are projected from the same direction as the camera onto the process screen; used in **process shots.**

***f*-stop:** The setting on a **lens** that indicates the diameter of the **aperture** (e.g., *f*-1, *f*-1.4, *f*-2, *f*-2.8, *f*-4, *f*-5.6, *f*-8, *f*-11, *f*-16, *f*-22, *f*-32, *f*-45, *f*-64). The size of the aperture determines how much light the lens will transmit to the **emulsion** surface of the film and therefore determines the visual quality of the image imprinted on the **negative stock.** The larger the *f*-number, the smaller the aperture and the greater the **depth of field.** See also **diaphragm.**

full shot: A **shot** that includes the subject's entire body and often a three-fourths view of the **set.**

Futurism: (1) Italian Futurism was an artistic movement that glorified power, speed, technology, and even war, and has sometimes been linked to the rise of Fascism in Italy. (2) Russian Futurism, which was closely allied to Russian Formalism and to Constructivism in the 1920s, emphasized the similarities between artistic forms and modern technology.

gaffer: The chief electrician on a movie **production set.**

gauge: Also known as **format;** the width of the **film stock** and its perforations, measured in millimeters, extending typically from Super 8 mm through 70 mm.

gel: A sheet of colored filter material placed in front of lighting instruments on a movie **production set** to alter the tone, color, or quality of their illumination. Not to be confused with a **cel.**

gendai-geki: One of two major Japanese film genres, the *gendai-geki* deals with stories of contemporary life. A popular subtype is the *shomin-geki,* or story of middle-class and lower-middle-class family life. See also *jidai-geki.*

greenscreen photography: Photography in which live action is filmed in front of a green screen, which will allow **CGI** to be added to the filmed action.

grip: All-around handyperson on a movie **production set,** most often working with the camera crews and electrical crews on lights and props.

handheld shot: A type of **shot** made possible by portable, single-operator cameras. See also **Arriflex.**

high angle: A high-angle **shot** (or *downward-angle shot*) that is made with the camera above the action.

high-key lighting: Lighting **setup** in which there is a high ratio of **fill light** to **key light,** producing a relatively shadow-free, even-toned image with very little contrast between the darks and the lights. Its opposite is **low-key lighting.**

improvisation: (1) Actors' extemporization—that is, delivering lines based only loosely on the written script or without the preparation that comes with studying a script before rehearsing it; (2) "playing through" a moment, making up lines to keep **scenes** going when actors forget their written lines, stumble on lines, or have some other mishap.

in-camera effects: One category of **special effects** (the others are **laboratory effects** and **computer-generated effects**). This kind is created in the **production** camera (the regular camera used for shooting the rest of the film) on the original **negative** and includes such effects as **montage** and **split-screen.**

indirect point of view: One of two main categories of **subjective point of view** (the other is **direct point of view**). It affords us the opportunity to see and hear what a character does, but as the result of at least two consecutive **shots.**

intercutting: See **crosscutting.**

interior monologue: One variation on the mental, **subjective point of view** of an individual character (see **point of view**), which allows us to see a character and hear that character's thoughts (in his or her own voice, even though the character's lips don't move).

901

Glossary of Critical Terms

internal sound: A form of **diegetic sound** that occurs whenever we hear the thoughts of a character we see on-screen and assume that other characters cannot hear them.

intertitles: Printed titles that appear within the main body of a film to convey **dialogue** and other **narrative** information. Intertitles are common in (but not essential to) the silent cinema. Sometimes referred to as *title cards.*

iris-in and iris-out: Optical **wipe** effects in which the wipe line is a circle; named after the *iris diaphragm,* which controls the amount of light passing through a camera **lens.** The iris-in begins with a small circle, which expands to a partial or full image; the iris-out is the reverse.

iris shot: A **shot** in which a circular, **lens**-masking device contracts or expands to isolate or reveal an area of the **frame** for symbolic or **narrative** visual effect.

jidai-geki: One of two major Japanese film genres, the *jidai-geki* is a period film set before the Meiji Restoration of 1868. All samurai films are *jidai-geki.* See also ***gendai-geki.***

jump cut: A **cut** that is made in the midst of a continuous **shot,** or a mismatched cut between shots (the opposite of a **match cut**'s apparent seamlessness). Jump cuts create discontinuity in filmic time and space and draw attention to the medium itself, as opposed to its content. Some critics define jump cuts as cuts that defy the **30-degree rule** and the **180-degree system.**

key light: The main light on a **set,** normally placed at a 45-degree angle to the camera-subject axis, mixed in a contrast ratio with **fill light,** depending on the desired effect.

Kinetograph: The first viable motion-picture camera, invented in 1889 by W. K. L. Dickson for the Thomas Edison Laboratories. See also ***Cinématographe;*** **Kinetoscope.**

Kinetoscope: Invented before the projector, this was the Thomas Edison Company's peep-show device in which short, very basic moving pictures could be seen.

laboratory effects: One category of **special effects** (the others are **in-camera effects** and **computer-generated effects**). This kind, created on a fresh piece of **film stock,** includes a wide range of procedures, from **dissolves** to complex **multiple-exposure** techniques.

lap dissolve: See **dissolve.**

latent images: The invisible images that are created when light hits the **emulsion** on photographic film or paper. The latent images become visible during the developing process.

Latham loop: In early projection systems, a set of **sprockets** that looped the film to keep it from breaking as a result of its own inertia.

lens: The optical device used in cameras and projectors to focus light rays by refraction.

letterboxing: The process of blacking out the top and bottom of a television's **Academy ratio frame** to reproduce a **widescreen** image.

linkage: Soviet filmmaker V. I. Pudovkin's description of **montage,** a concept to which Sergei Eisenstein took exception.

location shooting: Any shooting not done inside a studio or on the studio's **back lots.**

locked print: The crucial stage in editing after which no further changes are made; the **editor** cuts the original **negative** to conform to this print.

long-focal-length lens: Also known as the **telephoto lens,** and one of the four major types of lenses (the others are the **short-focal-length lens,** the **middle-focal-length lens,** and the **zoom lens**). It flattens the space and depth of the image and thus distorts perspective relations.

long shot: Sometimes designated LS; a **shot** that shows the full human body, usually filling the **frame,** and some of its surroundings.

long take: A single unbroken **shot,** moving or stationary, that describes a complex action that might otherwise be represented through **montage.** It is essential to *mise-en-scène* aesthetics. See also **sequence.**

low angle: Also known as *upward angle.* A low-angle **shot** is made with the camera below the action.

low-grain: Describes **film stock** that exhibits very little film grain (the silver-halide crystals that capture the image when exposed to light) when projected. Low-grain stock aids in producing crisp, clear images.

low-key lighting: Lighting that creates strong contrasts; sharp, dark shadows; and an overall gloomy atmosphere. Its contrasts between light and dark often imply ethical judgments. Its opposite is **high-key lighting.**

magic lantern: A device for projecting images onto a wall or screen, consisting of a powerful light source, transparent slide, and magnifying lens. First described by Giovanni de Fontana in the fifteenth century, it was later integrated into elaborate theatrical shows featuring fantastic images and **special effects.** A *stereopticon* combines two or three magic lanterns to focus several images in one area, allowing for combinations of images or **dissolves** between them.

magnetic recording: One of two ways of recording and storing sound in the **analog format** (the other is **optical recording**), and for years the most popular medium and the one most commonly found in professional **production;** in this method, signals are stored on magnetic recording tape of various sizes and formats (open reels, cassettes, etc.).

mask: A covering of some type placed before the camera **lens** to block off part of the photographed image. A mask can also refer to an **aperture** plate inserted behind a projector lens in order to obtain a desired **aspect ratio.** See also **matte shot.**

master shot: A **shot,** usually a **long** or **full** one, that establishes the spatial relationships among characters and objects within a dramatic **scene** before it is broken up into closer, more discrete shots through editing. See also **establishing shot.**

match cut: A **cut** in which two different **shots** are linked together by visual and/or aural continuity.

match-on-action cut: A **match cut** at the moment of a specific action (such as the opening of a door) in a **shot** that is closely paralleled or continued in the shot that immediately follows, giving the illusion of a fluid or seamless motion.

matte shot: A **shot** that is partially opaque in the **frame** area so that it can be printed together with another frame, masking unwanted content and allowing for the addition of another **scene** on a reverse matte. In a *traveling matte shot* the contours of the opaque areas can be varied from **frame** to frame.

matting: The process of blocking or masking the top and bottom of standard **Academy ratio** 35 mm **frame** for the purpose of producing a **widescreen** effect. An *open matte* can be removed for television broadcast and video release. Not to be confused with **letterboxing.**

medium close-up: A **shot** distanced midway between a **close-up** and a **medium shot;** e.g., a human subject's face and torso from the chest up.

medium long shot: Sometimes designated MLS; also known as the *American shot* and the *plan américain;* a **shot** that is taken from the knees up and includes most of a person's body.

medium shot: Often designated MS; a **shot** showing the human body, usually from the waist up.

Method acting: Also known as *the Method;* a naturalistic acting style, loosely adapted from the ideas of Russian director Konstantin Stanislavsky by American directors Elia Kazan and Lee Strasberg, that encourages actors to speak, move, and gesture not in a traditional stage manner but in the same way they would in their own lives.

metteur en scène: Term used in *auteur* theory to describe a director who is technically competent but whose work does not possess the broader thematic, aesthetic, and psychological dimensions of the *auteur.*

middle-focal-length lens: Also called the *normal lens,* and one of the four major types of lenses (the others are the **short-focal-length lens,** the **long-focal-length lens,** and the **zoom lens**). It does not distort perspectival relations.

mise-en-scène: Literally, "putting in the scene"; a term that describes the action, lighting, decor, and other elements within the **shot** itself, as opposed to the effects created by **cutting.** Purveyors of **realism** generally prefer the process of *mise-en-scène* to the more manipulative techniques of **montage.**

Mitchell camera: The standard Hollywood studio camera of the 1930s, 1940s, and 1950s, introduced in 1921 to compete with the Bell & Howell 2709 (the industry standard from about 1920 until the introduction of sound) and still heavily used.

mix: Optically, a **dissolve.** Aurally, the combination of several different **sound tracks,** such as dialogue and music.

mixing: The work of the general sound **editor,** who refines, balances, and combines different **sound tracks.**

mock documentary: Also known as *mockumentary;* this type of film tends to combine stylistic elements identified with the **documentary** form while delivering a fictional or largely fictional story. Audiences can sometimes be "tricked" into believing in the film's authenticity, or the effect can be used to heighten the film's **verisimilitude.**

modeling: In **computer graphics,** the process of digitally creating three-dimensional objects, environments, and **scenes.**

model shot: A **shot** that uses miniatures instead of real locations, especially useful in disaster or science-fiction films.

montage: (1) In France, the word for editing, from the verb *monter,* "to assemble or put together"; (2) in the former Soviet Union in the 1920s, the various forms of editing that expressed ideas developed by theorists and filmmakers such as Sergei Eisenstein, who argued that contiguous **shots** relate to each other in a way that generates concepts not materially present in the content of the individual shots themselves; (3) in Hollywood, beginning in the 1930s, a **sequence** of shots, often with superimpositions and **optical effects,** showing a condensed series of events.

morphing: The **digital effects** process whereby one image is gradually transformed into another.

motion blur: The blurred visual effect that occurs when the object being recorded is moving faster than the **shutter** speed of the camera. A characteristic of **swish pans.**

Moviola: For years the most familiar and popular upright editing machine; a portable device, operated by foot pedals and leaving the **editor**'s hands free, it is based on the same technical principle as the movie projector and contains a built-in viewing screen.

multiple exposure: See **double exposure.**

narration: (1) The commentary spoken by either offscreen or on-screen voices, frequently used in **narrative films,** where it may emanate from an omniscient voice (and thus not one of the characters) or from a character in the movie. (2) The process through which the **plot** reveals or withholds information pertaining to the **story.** Narration can be *restricted* or *partially restricted* to the knowledge of a character or characters; it can also be *omniscient.* In film, omniscient narration tends to be dominant, though **point of view** can shift from character to character.

narrative: The overall connection of events within the world of a movie; see also **plot; story.**

narrative films: A general term for movies that tell **stories**—with characters, places, and events—conceived in the minds of the films' creators. These stories may be wholly imaginary or based on true occurrences, realistic or unrealistic or both.

negative: A photographic image on transparent material in which light and dark shades are inverted; makes possible the reproduction of the image.

negative cost: The cost of producing a film, exclusive of advertising, studio overhead, and distribution prints.

negative cut: The penultimate stage of editing, in which a specialist **editor,** often called the *negative cutter,* or *neg-cutter,* cuts the original **negative** to conform to the **locked print,** resulting in the **final print.**

neorealism: A post–World War II movement in filmmaking associated primarily with the films of Roberto Rossellini, Luchino Visconti, and Vittorio De Sica in Italy. It was characterized by leftist political sympathies, **location shooting,** and the use of nonprofessional actors.

neue Kino, das: Literally, "the new cinema," referring to the cinema of West Germany in the late 1960s and 1970s.

newsreels: Filmed news reports shown along with the main feature in American theaters in the 1930s, 1940s, and 1950s; eclipsed by television news.

New Wave (*nouvelle vague*): Originally a school of French filmmakers who, in the 1950s, started their careers as critics for *Cahiers du cinéma.* The year 1959 can be said to mark the beginning of this movement since it was the release date of François Truffaut's *Les quatre cents coups* (*The 400 Blows*) and Alain Resnais' *Hiroshima, mon amour.* The phrase is often used to describe any new group of directors in any country whose approach to filmmaking is radically different from that of the established tradition, as in the Taiwanese or Iranian New Wave.

nickelodeon: The first permanent movie theaters, converted from storefronts. From *nickel* (the price of admission) plus *odeon* (Greek for "theater").

night for night: See **day for night.**

nondiegetic elements: The things we see and hear on the screen that come from outside the world of the **story** (including background music, titles and credits, or voice-over comment from an omniscient narrator). See **diegesis.**

nondiegetic sound: Sound that originates from a source outside a film's world and thus not heard by the characters, such as musical scores and voice-overs (as opposed to **diegetic sound**).

offscreen sound: A form of sound, either **diegetic** or **nondiegetic,** that derives from a source we do not see. When diegetic, it consists of **sound effects,** music, or vocals that emanate from the world of the **story.** When nondiegetic, it takes the form of a musical score or **narration** by someone who is not a character in the story.

offscreen space: Space outside the **frame;** one of two kinds of cinematic space (the other is **on-screen space**).

omnidirectional microphones: Sound-recording equipment that responds to sound coming from all directions.

omniscient point of view: The most basic and most common **point of view.** "Omniscient" means "all-knowing"; in film, the camera has complete or unlimited perception of events. The camera maintains the status of an all-knowing observer that presents various restricted perspectives as the **story** evolves.

180-degree system: Also known as the *180-degree rule,* the *axis of action,* and the *center line;* the fundamental means by which filmmakers maintain consistent screen direction, orienting the viewer and ensuring a sense of the cinematic space in which the action occurs. The system assumes three things: the action within a **scene** will always advance along a straight line, either from left to right or from right to left of the **frame;** the camera will remain consistently on one side of that action; and everyone on the **production set** will understand and adhere to this system.

on-screen sound: A form of **diegetic sound** that emanates from a source we see. It may be **internal** or **external sound.**

on-screen space: Space inside the **frame;** one of two kinds of cinematic space (the other is **offscreen space**).

optical effects: Effects created using special cameras, **optical printers, animation,** rotoscoping, or motion-control devices that cannot be done in front of the camera. Unlike **digital effects,** all of them involve some manipulation of the photographic process itself.

optical printer: The machine that performs many **postproduction** optical processes such as **dissolves,** color balancing, and some **special effects.** Film prints are duplicated in a contact printer.

optical recording: One of two ways of recording and storing sound in the **analog format** (the other is **magnetic recording**) and until the 1950s the standard method; the conversion of sound waves into light, which is recorded photographically onto 16 mm or 35 mm **film stock.**

orthochromatic stock: A kind of black-and-white **film stock** that reacts particularly to the blue and green areas of the color spectrum rather than the red; widely replaced by **panchromatic stock** in the 1920s but still used for special applications.

outtakes: Material not used in either the **rough cut** or the **final cut,** cataloged and saved.

pan: Any pivotal movement of the camera around an imaginary vertical axis running through it. The camera is usually mounted on the gyroscopic head of a stationary tripod; from "panorama."

Panavision: The anamorphic process that is most commonly used today, with a standard aspect ratio of 1.85:1 (though the "true" **widescreen** ratio remains 2.40:1); it replaced **CinemaScope** in the early 1960s. Super Panavision (originally called Panavision 70) uses 70 mm **film stock** to produce a 65 mm **negative** without squeezing the image. Ultra Panavision produces a 65 mm negative anamorphically compressed in filming by a ratio of 1.25:1. The process now referred to as Panavision 70 is an optical printing method that allows 70 mm **release prints** to be blown up from 35 mm negatives, either anamorphic or spherical. Panavision is also the trade name of a widely used camera based on the design of the **Mitchell camera.**

panchromatic stock: Black-and-white **film stock** that is sensitive to all the colors of the spectrum, from red to blue. It became the film stock of choice during the late 1920s in Hollywood. The introduction of **widescreen** processes in the 1950s greatly enhanced panchromatic **depth of field.**

parallel editing: Also called **crosscutting;** the **intercutting** of two or more lines of action that occur simultaneously and usually lead to a common end; a very familiar convention for producing tension in chase or rescue **sequences.**

persistence of vision: Often called the physiological foundation of the cinema: an image remains on the retina of the eye for a short period of time after it disappears from the actual field of vision; when a successive image replaces it immediately, as on a moving strip of film, the illusion of continuous motion is produced.

pitch: The level of a sound, defined by its frequency.

pixillation: A technique used for animating models by photographing them one **frame** at a time (as in *King Kong* [1933]). The technique can also be applied to the opposite effect, so that the illusion of continuous motion is disrupted. This effect is achieved either by **stop-motion photography** or by culling out particular frames from the **negative** of the **film stock.**

planes: The theoretical regions or areas that mark distance from the camera—foreground, middle ground, and background—or areas within the **frame.** See also **rule of thirds.**

plot: A structure for presenting everything we see and hear in a film, with an emphasis on causality, consisting of two factors: (1) the arrangement of the diegetic events in a certain order or structure and (2) added nondiegetic material. See also **diegetic** and **nondiegetic elements.**

plot duration: The elapsed time of those events within a **story** that a film chooses to tell.

point of view: Abbreviated as POV; the position from which a film presents the actions of the **story;** not only the relation of the narrator(s) to the story but also the camera's act of seeing and hearing. The two fundamental types of cinematic point of view are **omniscient** and **subjective** (or **restricted**), which can be either **direct** or **indirect points of view.**

point-of-view editing: The joining together of a **point-of-view shot** with a **match cut** to show, in the first shot, a character looking and, in the second, what he or she is looking at.

politique des auteurs: First postulated by the film critics of the *Cahiers du cinéma.* The "policy of authors" argues that film directors can be considered *auteurs* if they are able to impose a specifically cinematic vision on the form of their films. Although the *politique des auteurs* was not really a theory but a polemic, it has led to the elaboration of numerous versions of "*auteur* theory" (as Andrew Sarris called his revision of these ideas).

postproduction: The third stage of the **production** process, consisting of editing, preparing the **final print,** and bringing the film to the public (marketing and distribution).

postsynchronization: Synchronization of sound and image after the film has been shot—an important step forward in the liberation of the early sound-film camera from its glass-paneled booth. Also called **dubbing.**

preproduction: The initial, planning-and-preparation stage of the **production** process.

process shot: Live shooting against a background that is **front-** or **rear-projected** on a translucent screen.

production: The second stage of the production process, the actual shooting.

production sounds: Those **synchronous sounds** recorded during **production** (most of which, including **dialogue,** are changed, cleaned up, or rerecorded during **postproduction**).

production values: The amount of human and physical resources devoted to the image, including the style of its lighting. High production values are often associated with slick, expensive films; low production values with **B films** or independents.

protagonist: The major character who serves as the "hero," or who is singled out as the primary figure for positive viewer identification.

pull-down claw: Within the movie camera, the mechanism that controls the intermittent cycle of shooting individual **frames** and advances the film frame by frame.

rack focus: A **shallow-focus** technique that forcibly directs the vision of the spectator from one subject to another. The focus is pulled or changed to shift the **focus plane.**

raw film stock: See **celluloid roll film.**

reaction shot: A **shot** that cuts away from the central action to show a character's reaction to it.

realism: In cinema, this term often describes a type of filmmaking in which the purveyors attempt to be faithful to the nature of the subject itself and avoid obvious creative manipulation of the subject matter. It concerns itself with reproducing a sense of the actual or real and tends to privilege **long takes, location shooting,** and naturalistic acting styles over more artificial studio effects in an effort to produce the impression of unmediated authenticity. As familiarity with "non-Western" cinemas and cultures has increased over the years, the opposition of realist and antirealist cinematic representations has increasingly come to be questioned as a specifically Western concern.

real time: Time that is chronological and continuous, as usually experienced in everyday life. It is one possible aspect of a film's duration (the other is **cinematic time**). Directors can use real time within films to create periods of uninterrupted "reality" on the screen; in other cases, a whole film might be produced in real time.

rear projection: A technique in which a **scene** is projected onto a translucent screen located behind the actors so that it appears as if they are in a specific location.

reel: The casing and holder for the film or tape. The feed reel supplies the film, and the take-up reel rewinds it. A 35 mm reel holds up to 1,000 feet; a 16 mm reel, 400 feet. At sound speed (24 **fps**), a full 35 mm reel runs about 10 minutes; at silent speed (approximately 16 fps), between 14 and 16 minutes.

reflector board: A piece of lighting equipment, but not really a lighting instrument, because it does not rely on bulbs to produce illumination. Essentially, it is a double-sided board that pivots in a U-shaped holder. One side is a hard, smooth surface that reflects hard light; the other is a soft, textured surface that provides softer **fill light.**

release print: The version of the **final print** used by the filmmakers to create prints for distribution.

rerecording: Sometimes called *looping* or dubbing; the replacing of **dialogue**, which can be done manually (i.e., with the actors watching the footage, synchronizing their lips with it, and rereading the lines) or, more likely today, through **automatic dialogue replacement (ADR).** (Dubbing also refers to the process of replacing dialogue in a foreign language with English, or the reverse, throughout a film.)

resolution: The capability of a camera **lens** to define images in sharp detail.

restricted point of view: See **subjective point of view.**

reverse-angle shot: A **shot** taken at a 180-degree angle from the preceding shot—in practice rarely used. Instead, filmmakers have adopted **shot/reverse-shot** editing, in which the angle separating the two perspectives is usually between 120 degrees and 160 degrees.

reverse field shot: See **reverse shot**.

reverse motion: Shooting a subject so that the action runs backward—achieved either by turning the camera upside down (so long as the film is double-sprocketed) and then turning the processed film end over end or by running the film backward through an **optical printer.**

rough cut: A further refinement of the **assembly edit**—close enough to the **final cut** to begin to give a sense of the finished movie.

rule of thirds: A compositional principle that enables filmmakers to maximize the potential of the image, put its elements into balance, and create the illusion of depth. A grid pattern, when superimposed on the image, divides it into horizontal thirds representing the foreground, middle-ground, and background **planes** and vertical thirds that break up those planes into further elements. Generally, objects of interest are placed where the horizontal and vertical lines of the grid intersect.

rushes: See **dailies.**

scale: The size and placement of a particular object or a part of a **scene** in relation to the rest, a relationship determined by the type of **shot** used and the placement of the camera.

scene: A complete unit of **plot** action incorporating one or more **shots;** the setting of that action.

Schüfftan process: A process-photography technique that combines mirror **shots** and **model shots** to create a composite image. It was invented by the German **cinematographer** Eugen Schüfftan (later Eugene Schuftan) and was first used on a large scale by Fritz Lang to create the futuristic vistas of *Metropolis* (1926).

score: The musical **sound track** for a film; also used as a verb.

screenplay: The script of a film. It may be no more than a rough outline that the director fills in, or it may be detailed, complete with **dialogue,** continuity, and camera movements, as were most Hollywood studio scripts of the 1930s and 1940s.

screen test: A filming undertaken by an actor to try out for a particular role.

screwball comedy: A type of comedy popular in American films of the 1930s; characterized by frantic action and a great deal of verbal wit. The focal point of the **plot** is usually a couple in a bizarre predicament, as in Frank Capra's *It Happened One Night* (1934) and Howard Hawks's *Bringing Up Baby* (1938).

second unit: In an elaborate **production,** a supplementary film crew that photographs routine **scenes** not shot by the first unit. Background and **establishing shots,** for instance, are usually shot by the second unit.

self-reflexivity: In film, the quality of a film's formal elements that reflects, mirrors, and even critiques the film's own content; more generally, any means by which a film makes reference to its constructedness, artifice, or its status as a film.

sequence: A series of edited **shots** characterized by an inherent unity of theme and purpose.

series photography: The use of a series of still photographs to record the phases of an action.

set: The location where a **scene** is shot, often, but not exclusively, constructed on a **soundstage.**

setting: The time and space in which a **story** takes place.

setup: One camera position and everything associated with it. While the **shot** is the basic building block of the film, the setup is the basic component of the film's **production.**

shallow focus: A technique that deliberately uses a shallow **depth of field** in order to direct the viewer's perception along a shallow, or limited, **focus plane.** See also **deep-focus cinematography; rack focus.**

shooting angle: The level and height of the camera in relation to the subject being photographed.

shooting script: A guide and reference point for all members of the **production** unit, in which the details of each **shot** are listed and can thus be followed during filming.

short-focal-length lens: Also known as the *short-focus* or **wide-angle lens,** and one of the four major types of lenses (the others are the **middle-focal-length lens,** the **long-focal-length lens,** and the **zoom lens**). It creates the illusion of depth within the **frame,** albeit with some distortion at the edges of the frame.

shot: A continuously exposed, unedited piece of film of any length: the basic signifying unit of film structure.

shot/reverse shot: One of the most prevalent and familiar of all editing patterns, which cuts between **shots** of different characters, usually in a conversation or confrontation, following the 180 degree rule. When used in **continuity editing,** the shots are typically framed over each character's shoulder to preserve the screen direction.

shutter: A device that shields the film from light at the **aperture** while the film moves from one **frame** to another.

slapstick: A type of comedy that relies on acrobatic physical gags and exaggerated pantomine rather than on verbal humor.

slow motion: Photography that decelerates action by photographing it at a rate greater than the normal 24 fps, so that it takes place in **cinematic time** at a rate that is less rapid than the rate of real action that took place before the camera.

soft focus: A dreamy or romantic effect (often making an actor or actress appear younger) produced by means of **lens** filters, special lenses, or even petroleum jelly smeared directly on a normal lens such that the **definition** of a subject is blurred or softened.

sound bridge: Also known as a *sound transition;* sound carried from a first **shot** over to the next before the sound of that second shot begins, or vice versa.

sound design: A concept given its name by film editor Walter Murch, combining the crafts of editing and mixing and, like them, involving both theoretical and practical issues. In essence, it represents advocacy for movie sound (to counter some people's tendency to favor the movie image).

sound effects: All sounds artificially created for the **sound track** that have a definite function in telling the **story.**

soundstage: A windowless, soundproofed, professional shooting environment, which is usually several stories high and can cover an acre or more of floor space.

sound track: A separate recording tape, occupied by each type of sound recorded for a movie (one track for vocals, one for **sound effects,** one for music, etc.).

special effects: A term used to describe a range of synthetic processes used to enhance or manipulate the filmic image. They include **optical effects,** such as **front projection, model shots,** and **rear projection;** mechanical or physical effects, such as explosions, fires, fog, flying and falling objects or people, and so on; makeup effects, such as animatronics, the use of blood bags and prosthetics, and so on; and **digital effects.**

splicer: An editing device with an edge for **cutting** film evenly on a **frame** line and a bed on which to align and tape together **cuts** that will be invisible to the audience.

splicing: See **cutting.**

split screen: A method of splitting the **frame** into parts, which may be created in the camera or during the editing process. Unlike **parallel editing,** which cuts back and forth between **shots** for contrast, the split screen can tell multiple stories within the same **frame.**

sprockets: The evenly spaced holes on the edge of the film strip that allow it to be moved forward mechanically; also, the wheeled gears that engage these holes in the camera and projector.

Glossary of Critical Terms

stand-ins: Actors who look reasonably like movie stars (or at least like the actors playing the major roles) in height, weight, coloring, and so on, and who substitute for them during the tedious process of preparing **setups** or taking light readings.

Stanislavsky system: A system of acting developed by Russian theater director Konstantin Stanislavsky in the late nineteenth century that encourages students to strive for **realism,** both social and psychological, and to bring their past experiences and emotions to their roles. It influenced the development of **Method acting** in the United States.

steadicam: A camera actually worn by the cameraman, so it is not "handheld"; it removes jumpiness, and it is now much used for smooth, fast, and intimate camera movement.

stereophonic sound: The use of two or more high-fidelity speakers and **sound tracks** to approximate the actual dimensionality of hearing with two ears.

still: A photograph that re-creates a **scene** from a film for publicity purposes, or a single-**frame** enlargement from a film that looks like a photograph.

stock: See **film stock.**

stock footage: Film borrowed from a collection or library that consists of standard, often-used **shots** such as of World War II combat or street crowds in New York City.

stop-motion photography: A technique used for trick photography and **special effects** in which one **frame** is exposed at a time so that the subject can be adjusted between frames; reputedly discovered by Georges Méliès. See also **pixillation.**

story: In a movie: (1) all the events we see or hear on the screen and (2) all the events that are implicit or that we infer to have happened but that are not explicitly presented. See also **diegesis.**

storyboard: A **scene**-by-scene (sometimes a **shot**-by-shot) breakdown that combines sketches or photographs of how each shot is to look along with written descriptions of the other elements that are to go with each shot, including **dialogue,** sound, and music.

story conferences: Sessions during which the **treatment** is discussed, developed, and transformed from an outline into what is known as a *rough-draft screenplay* or *scenario.*

stunt persons: Performers who double for other actors in **scenes** requiring special skills or involving hazardous actions, such as crashing cars, jumping from high places, swimming, and riding (or falling off) horses.

subjective point of view: Also known as **restricted point of view, point of view** that shows a **shot** or **scene** as viewed by a character.

surrealism: A movement in painting, film, and literature, originating in Paris in the 1920s, that aimed to depict the workings of the subconscious by combining incongruous imagery or presenting a situation in dreamlike, irrational terms; more generally, surrealism may suggest a fantastic style of representation.

swish pan: Also called *zip pan;* a horizontal camera movement so fast that it blurs the photographic image. Often used in films of the French **New Wave.**

synchronous sound: The type of film sound we are most familiar with, which comes from and matches a source apparent in the image, as when **dialogue** matches characters' lip movements (as opposed to **asynchronous sound**).

synopsis: See **treatment.**

take: A director shoots one or more versions of each **shot** in a given **setup,** only one of which appears in the final version of the film; each of these versions is a take.

take-up spool: A device that winds the film inside the movie camera after it has been exposed.

telephoto lens: A **lens** with a long **focal length** that functions like a telescope to magnify distant objects. Because its angle of view is very narrow, it flattens the depth perspective.

30-degree rule: A rule governing camera **setup** and shooting that requires an angle of not less than 30 degrees between successive **shots** (to avoid the appearance of repeating shots or jump cuts).

tilt shot: The vertical movement of a camera mounted on the gyroscopic head of a stationary tripod. Like the pan **shot,** it is a simple movement with dynamic possibilities for creating meaning.

Todd-AO: A widescreen process very popular in the 1950s and 1960s that used a 65 mm negative printed onto 70 mm film, with a high-quality, six-track **sound track.** The final projected print had a 2.35:1 **aspect ratio.**

track: A single recording channel on a **sound track** that can be **mixed** with others and modified to create a variety of effects.

tracking shot: A **shot** produced with a smooth camera movement that moves with the action (alongside, above, beneath, behind, or ahead of it); an effect made possible by mounting the camera on a set of tracks, a **dolly,** a crane, or an aerial device, such as an airplane, helicopter, or balloon.

treatment: Also known as a **synopsis;** an outline of the action that briefly describes the essential ideas and structure for a film.

two-reeler: A film running about 30 minutes, the standard length of early silent comedies.

two-shot: A standard Hollywood **shot** in which two characters appear; ordinarily a **medium shot** or a **medium long shot.**

typecasting: The casting of actors because of their looks or "type" rather than for their acting talent or experience.

undercrank: To run a camera at a speed of less than 24 **fps.** When the film is projected at normal speed, the subject appears in **fast motion.** See also **slow motion.**

unidirectional microphones: Sound-recording equipment that responds, and has great sensitivity, to sound coming from one direction.

verisimilitude: A convincing appearance of truth; films produce verisimilitude when they convince the viewer that the things they see on the screen—people, places, events, no matter how fantastic—are "really there."

viewfinder: On a camera, the small window one looks through when taking a picture; its **frame** indicates the boundaries of the camera's **point of view.**

VistaVision: A nonanamorphic **widescreen** process developed by Paramount to compete with Fox's **CinemaScope** in 1954. It ran 35 mm **film stock** through the camera horizontally rather than vertically to produce a double-**frame** image twice as wide as the conventional 35 mm frame. The positive print could be projected horizontally with special equipment to cast a huge image on the screen, or it could be reduced anamorphically for standard vertical 35 mm projection. Because the process is very expensive, VistaVision since 1961 has been used only for **special effects.**

Glossary of Critical Terms

visual-effects (VFX) supervisor: The person in charge of the technical and creative aspects of **special-effects production,** including computer-generated imaging, **bluescreen** and **greenscreen photography,** and the use of miniatures.

voice-over: A voice track laid over the other **tracks** in a film's sound **mix** to comment on or narrate the action on-screen.

walk-ons: Roles even smaller than **cameos,** reserved for highly recognizable actors or personalities.

wide-angle lens: A lens whose broad angle of view increases the illusion of depth but distorts the linear dimensions of the image. See also **fish-eye lens; telephoto lens.**

widescreen: Sometimes reserved to describe any flat (i.e., nonprocessed) film format with an **aspect ratio** of 1.66:1 (European standard) or 1.85:1 (American standard), the term "widescreen" may also refer broadly to any format that produces a screen image wider than the **Academy ratio** of 1.33:1, whether processed or not. Most widescreen processes use **anamorphic lenses,** but some employ wide-gauge film (**Panavision** 70, **Todd-AO**) or multiple-camera processes (**Cinerama**).

wild recording: Recording sound (usually to be used later as **sound effects**) independently of the visuals. Also known as *wild sound.*

wild shooting: Shooting a film without simultaneously recording the **sound track.**

wipe: A transitional device in which **shot** B wipes across shot A, either vertically or horizontally, to replace it. Although (or because) the device reminds us of early eras in filmmaking, directors continue to use it, especially in video effects.

work print: Any positive print (either print or sound or both, but not yet timed or color-corrected) intended for use in the initial trial **cuttings** of the editing process.

zoom lens: One of the four major types of **lenses** (the others are the **short-focal-length lens,** the **middle-focal-length lens,** and the **long-focal-length lens**). It allows for continuous motion toward and away from the subject being photographed; it has a continuously variable **focal length.**

Contributors

Daniel Bernardi is an associate professor in the Hispanic Research Center at Arizona State University. He is the author of *Star Trek and History: Racing Toward a White Future* (1998), and the editor of *The Birth of Whiteness: Race and the Emergence of U.S. Cinema* (1996) and *Classic Hollywood/Classic Whiteness* (2001).

Joanne Bernardi is an associate professor of Japanese at the University of Rochester. She is the author of, among other works, *Writing in Light: The Silent Scenario and the Japanese Pure Film Movement* (2001).

Matthew Bernstein teaches film studies at Emory University. He is the author of *Walter Wanger, Hollywood Independent* (1994), editor of *Controlling Hollywood: Censorship and Regulation in the Studio Era* (2000), and coeditor of *John Ford Made Westerns: Filming the Legend in the Sound Era* (2001).

Marilyn Johns Blackwell is the Vorman-Anderson Professor of Scandinavian Studies at Ohio State University. In addition to numerous articles on film, drama, and the novel in Sweden, Denmark, and Norway, as well as books on C. J. L. Almqvist and August Strindberg, she has also written *Persona: The Transcendent Image* (1986) and *Gender and Representation in the Films of Ingmar Bergman* (1997).

Gilberto M. Blasini is an assistant professor of film and television studies in the English Department at the University of Wisconsin, Milwaukee. His research, teaching, and publications focus on Caribbean and Latin American cinemas and cultures, post-1967 U.S. cinema (with special emphasis on the road movie genre), and television theory and criticism.

Shohini Chaudhuri is a lecturer in the Department of Literature, Film, and Theatre Studies at the University of Essex. Her articles have appeared in *Camera Obscura; Strategies: Journal of Theory, Culture and Politics;* and *Screen*. She has just published *Contemporary World Cinema: Europe, the Middle-East, East-Asia and the Indian Sub-continent* (2005).

Paul Coates is a professor of film studies in the Department of English and Film Studies at the University of Aberdeen, Scotland. His publications include *The Story of the Lost Reflection* (1985); *The Gorgon's Gaze: German Cinema, Expressionism, and the Image of Horror* (1991); *Cinema, Religion and the Romantic Legacy* (2003); and *The Red and the White: Exploring the Cinema of People's Poland* (forthcoming).

Contributors

Tom Conley, professor of romance languages and visual/environmental studies at Harvard University, has authored *Film Hieroglyphs: Ruptures in Classical Cinema* (1991), *The Self-Made Map: Cartographic Writing in Early Modern France* (1996), and *L'inconscient graphique* (2000).

Elizabeth Cowie teaches film studies at the University of Kent, England. She was a cofounder and editor of the feminist journal *m/f* and edited *The Woman in Question* with Parveen Adams. She published *Representing the Woman: Cinema and Psychoanalysis* in 1997 and has written more recently on the horror in the Georges Franju film *Eyes Without a Face*, on the cinematic dream work in Ingmar Bergman's *Wild Strawberries*, and on memory and trauma in Alain Resnais' documentary film *Hiroshima, mon amour*. She is currently completing a book on documentary film, television, and video art.

Shuqin Cui is an associate professor of Asian studies at Bowdoin College. Her teaching and research interests include cinema studies, women's writing, and cultural history. She is the author of *Women Through the Lens: Gender and Nation in a Century of Chinese Cinema* (2003).

David Desser is a professor of cinema studies at the University of Illinois, where he teaches courses on Japanese, Chinese, Korean, and Hollywood cinema. He has authored or edited numerous books, including *Ozu's "Tokyo Story"* (1997); *The Cinema of Hong Kong: History, Arts, Identity* (2002); and *American Jewish Filmmakers* (2003). He provided the commentary for the Criterion DVD release of *Tokyo Story* (2003).

Anna Everett is an associate professor of film and TV history and theory and of new media studies and the director of the Center for Black Studies at the University of California at Santa Barbara. She has published numerous books and articles, including *Returning the Gaze: A Genealogy of Black Film Criticism, 1909–1949* (2001); *New Media: Theories and Practices of Digitextuality* (coedited with John Caldwell) (2003); and the forthcoming *Digital Diaspora: A Race for Cyberspace.*

Christopher Faulkner is a professor of film studies and director of the PhD program in cultural mediations at Carleton University, Ottawa, Canada. He has written widely on French cinema and is the author of *The Social Cinema of Jean Renoir* (1986) and, with Olivier Curchod, of *"La règle du jeu": scénario original de Jean Renoir* (1999). He also provided the commentary for the Criterion DVD release of *The Rules of the Game* (2004).

Jane Feuer is a professor of English at the University of Pittsburgh. She is the author of *The Hollywood Musical* (1982) and *Seeing through the Eighties: Television and Reaganism* (1995).

Cynthia Fuchs teaches at George Mason University and is film editor for PopMatters.com. She has also published numerous articles on popular film, music, and culture. She edited *Spike Lee: Interviews* (2002) and coedited *Between the Sheets, In the Streets: Queer, Lesbian, and Gay Documentary* (1997).

916

Jeffrey Geiger teaches at the University of Essex, where he was founding director of the Centre for Film Studies. His work on documentary film and American studies has appeared in a number of books and journals, such as *Third Text, Cinema Journal,* and *PMLA*. He is currently completing a study of representations of the South Pacific.

Hal Gladfelder is an associate professor of English at the University of Rochester, specializing in the eighteenth-century novel, narrative theory, and British cinema; his most recent book is *Criminality and Narrative in Eighteenth-Century England: Beyond the Law* (2001).

Tom Gunning teaches film studies at the University of Chicago, where he is Edwin A. and Betty L. Bergman Distinguished Service Professor in the Department of Art History and the Committee on Cinema and Media. He is the author of *D. W. Griffith and the Origins of American Cinema* (1994) and *The Films of Fritz Lang: Allegories of Vision and Modernity* (2000).

Robert Kolker is professor emeritus of English at the University of Maryland and visiting professor of media studies at the University of Virginia. His publications include *A Cinema of Loneliness: Penn, Stone, Kubrick, Scorsese, Spielberg, and Altman* (1980); *The Altering Eye: Contemporary International Cinema* (1983); *Film, Form, and Culture* (textbook and CD-ROM, 2001); and *Alfred Hitchcock's "Psycho": A Casebook* (2004).

Marcia Landy is Distinguished Service Professor of English and Film Studies at the University of Pittsburgh, with a secondary appointment in the Department of French and Italian. In addition to numerous essays in journals and anthologies, her publications include *Fascism in Film: The Italian Commercial Cinema, 1930–1943* (1986); *Film, Politics, and Gramsci* (1994); *Italian Film* (2000); *The Historical Film: History and Memory in Media* (2000); and *Stars: A Reader,* with Lucy Fischer (2004).

Jenny Kwok Wah Lau is an assistant professor in the Cinema Department at San Francisco State University. She has published works on film and culture in U.S. and international journals and recently edited the book *Multiple Modernities: Cinemas and Popular Media in Transcultural East Asia* (2003).

Jon Lewis is a professor in the English Department at Oregon State University and the editor of *Cinema Journal*. His publications include *Whom God Wishes to Destroy . . . Francis Coppola and the New Hollywood* (1995), *Hollywood v. Hard Core: How the Struggle over Censorship Saved the Modern Film Industry* (2000), and *The End of Cinema as We Know It: American Film in the Nineties* (2002).

Karin Littau is currently the director of the Centre for Film Studies at the University of Essex. Her publications include an article on early cinema for a collection called *Crash Cultures,* an article on G. W. Pabst's film adaptation of *Pandora's Box* in *MLN,* and an essay on David Cronenberg's *The Fly* for *Alien Identities: Exploring Differences in Film and Fiction*. She is the author of the forthcoming *Theories of Reading*.

917

Contributors

Neepa Majumdar is an assistant professor of English and film studies at the University of Pittsburgh. She has published essays on film music and stardom in Indian cinema and is currently preparing a manuscript titled *Wanted Cultured Ladies Only! Female Stardom and Cinema in India, 1930s to 1950s.*

Charles J. Maland teaches cinema studies and American studies in the English Department of the University of Tennessee. He is the author of, among other works, *Chaplin and American Culture* (1989), which won the Theater Library Association Award for best book in the area of recorded performance (radio, TV, or film) in 1990.

Richard Maltby is a professor of screen studies and head of the School of Humanities at Flinders University, South Australia. His publications include *Dreams for Sale: Popular Culture in the Twentieth Century* (1989); *Hollywood Cinema*, 2nd ed. (2003); as well as numerous articles and essays. With Ruth Vasey, he is currently writing *Reforming the Movies: Politics, Censorship and the Institutions of the American Cinema, 1908–1939.*

Hamid Naficy is Nina J. Cullinan Professor of Art and Art History/Film and Media Studies and chair of the Department of Art History at Rice University. He has published extensively about theories of exile and displacement; exilic and diasporic cultures, films, and media; and Iranian, Middle Eastern, and Third World cinemas. His latest English-language books are *The Making of Exile Cultures: Iranian Television in Los Angeles* (1993); *Home, Exile, Homeland: Film, Media, and the Politics of Place* (1999); and *An Accented Cinema: Exilic and Diasporic Filmmaking* (2001). His forthcoming book is *Cinema and National Identity: A Social History of Iranian Cinema.*

James Naremore is Chancellors' Professor of Communication and Culture at Indiana University. His publications include *The Magic World of Orson Welles* (1978; rev. ed., 1989), *Acting in the Cinema* (1989), *The Films of Vincente Minnelli* (1993), and *More Than Night: Film Noir in Its Contexts* (1998).

Steve Neale is chair of film studies in the School of English at Exeter University. He is the author of *Genre and Hollywood* (2000), editor of *Genre and Contemporary Hollywood* (2002), and coeditor of *Contemporary Hollywood Cinema* (1998).

Richard Neupert teaches film studies at the University of Georgia. His books include *The End* (1995) and *A History of the French New Wave Cinema* (2002).

Bill Nichols is director of the Graduate Program in Cinema Studies at San Francisco State University. His publications include *Movies and Methods*, vols. 1 and 2; (1976, 1985); *Blurred Boundaries: Questions of Meaning in Contemporary Culture* (1994); *Introduction to Documentary* (2001); and *Maya Deren and the American Avant-Garde* (2001).

Geoffrey Nowell-Smith was until recently a professor of cinema cultures at the University of Luton, England, and is now a senior research fellow in the

Department of History at Queen Mary, University of London. He is the editor of *The Oxford History of World Cinema* (1996) and the author of various works on European cinema, most recently *Visconti* (2003).

Alastair Phillips is a lecturer in film studies in the Department of Film, Theatre and Television at the University of Reading, England. He is the author of *City of Darkness, City of Light: Emigré Filmmakers in Paris 1929–1939* (2004) and coeditor (with Ginette Vincendeau) of *Journeys of Desire: European Actors in Hollywood* (forthcoming). He is currently writing a book titled *Du Rififi chez les hommes.*

Dana Polan is a professor of critical studies in the University of Southern California's School of Cinema-TV. He is the author of, among other works, *In a Lonely Place* (1993), *Pulp Fiction* (2000), and the forthcoming *Beginnings of the American Study of Film.*

Kriss Ravetto-Biagioli teaches at Emerson College. She is the author of *The Unmaking of Fascist Aesthetics* (2001) and is currently working on a book on mythopoetic cinema entitled *Killing Gravity.*

Philip Rosen is a professor of modern culture and media and of English at Brown University, and is the director of graduate studies in modern culture and media. He has published widely in film theory and history, including articles on Ousmane Sembene. His books include *Narrative, Apparatus, Ideology: A Film Theory Reader* (1986) and *Change Mummified: Cinema, Historicity, Theory* (2001).

R. L. Rutsky teaches in the Cinema Department at San Francisco State University and is the author of *High Technè: Art and Technology from the Machine Aesthetic to the Posthuman* (1999) and coeditor of *Strategies for Theory: From Marx to Madonna* (2003). His forthcoming work includes the edited volume *Consumption in an Age of Information* and *Surfing Cultures.*

S. I. Salamensky has taught at Harvard University and Williams College and is currently an assistant professor of theater at the University of California, Los Angeles. She is the editor of the volume *Talk Talk Talk: The Cultural Life of Everyday Conversation* (2001) and is completing a book on anxieties over language and performance from the fin de siècle to the Nazi period.

Paul Julian Smith is a professor of Spanish at the University of Cambridge. His books include *Desire Unlimited: The Cinema of Pedro Almodóvar* (2000); *The Moderns: Time, Space, and Subjectivity in Contemporary Spanish Culture* (2001); *Contemporary Spanish Culture: TV, Fashion, Art and Film* (2003); and *"Amores Perros": Modern Classic* (2003). He is a regular contributor to *Sight and Sound.*

Valerie Smith is director of the Program in African American Studies and Woodrow Wilson Professor of Literature in the Department of English at Princeton University. The author of *Self-Discovery and Authority in Afro-American Narrative* (1987) and *Not Just Race, Not Just Gender: Black Feminist Readings* (1998), and

Contributors

the editor of *Representing Blackness: Issues in Film and Video* (1997), she is currently writing a book on memory and the U.S. civil rights movement.

Gaylyn Studlar is Rudolf Arnheim Collegiate Professor of Film Studies and director of the Program in Film and Video Studies at the University of Michigan. Her publications include *In the Realm of Pleasure: Von Sternberg, Dietrich, and the Masochistic Aesthetic* (1988); *Reflections in a Male Eye: John Huston and the American Experience* (1993); *This Mad Masquerade: Stardom and Masculinity in the Jazz Age* (1996); and *Visions of the East: Orientalism in Film* (1997).

N. Frank Ukadike is an associate professor of film and of African and African Diaspora studies at Tulane University. He is the author of, among other works, *Black African Cinema* (1994) and *Questioning African Cinema: Conversations with Filmmakers* (2002).

Sharon Willis is a professor of French and of visual and cultural studies at the University of Rochester. A coeditor of *Camera Obscura,* she is the author of *Marguerite Duras: Writing on the Body* (1987) and *High Contrast: Race and Gender in Contemporary Hollywood Film* (1997). She is currently completing a book on cinema and the civil rights movement.

Mitsuhiro Yoshimoto is an associate professor of East Asian studies at New York University. He is the author of *Kurosawa: Film Studies and Japanese Cinema* (2000) and of numerous articles on film, media, and theory in both English and Japanese.

Photo Credits

p. 20, Photo of tree, Courtesy of J. D. Cady; p. 42, *Arrival of a Train at La Ciotat*, Courtesy of the Kobal Collection/Lumière; p. 64, *A Trip to the Moon (Le voyage dans la lune)*, Courtesy of the Kobal Collection/Méliès; p. 82, *The Birth of a Nation*, Courtesy of the Kobal Collection/EPIC; p. 98, *The Cabinet of Dr. Caligari*, Courtesy of the Kobal Collection/ Decla-Bioscop; p. 118, *Nanook of the North*, Courtesy of the Kobal Collection/Flaherty; p. 138, *Sherlock Jr.*, Courtesy of the Kobal Collection/Metro; p. 158; *Battleship Potemkin*, Courtesy of the Kobal Collection/Goskino; p. 178, *Metropolis* Courtesy of the Kobal Collection/UFA; p. 196, *Un chien andalou*, Courtesy of the Kobal Collection/Buñuel–Dalí; p. 216, *It Happened One Night*, Courtesy of the Kobal Collection/Columbia; p. 238, *Modern Times*, Courtesy of the Kobal Collection/Chaplin/United Artists; p. 260, *Osaka Elegy*, Courtesy of the British Film Institute; p. 282, *Bringing Up Baby*, Courtesy of the Kobal Collection/RKO; p. 300, *The Rules of the Game (La Règle de jeu)*, Courtesy of the Kobal Collection/Nouvelle Edition Francaise; p. 318, *Stagecoach*, Courtesy of the Kobal Collection/United Artists; p. 340, *Citizen Kane*, Courtesy of the Kobal Collection/RKO; p. 362, *Casablanca*, Courtesy of the Kobal Collection/Warner Bros.; p. 380, *Double Indemnity*, Courtesy of the Kobal Collection/Paramount; p. 400, *Roma città aperta (Rome Open City)*, Courtesy of the Museum of Modern Art/Film Stills Archive, New York; p. 422, *Bicycle Thieves*, Courtesy of the Museum of Modern Art/Film Stills Archive, New York; p. 440, *Singin' in the Rain*, Courtesy of the Kobal Collection/MGM; p. 456, *Tokyo Story*, Courtesy of the Museum of Modern Art Film Stills Archive, New York; p. 474, *Rear Window*, Courtesy of the Kobal Collection/Paramount; p. 494, *Seven Samurai (Shichinin no samurai)*, Courtesy of the Kobal Collection/TOHO; p. 510, *Pather Panchali (Song of the Road)*, Courtesy of the Kobal

Photo Credits

Collection/Government. of West Bengal; p.528, *The Seventh Seal*, Courtesy of the Kobal Collection/Svensk Filmindustri; p. 550, *The 400 Blows*, Courtesy of the Museum of Modern Art/Film Stills Archive, New York; p. 566, *Breathless*, Courtesy of the Museum of Modern Art/Film Stills Archive, New York; p. 582, *8½ (Otto e mezzo)*, Courtesy of the Kobal Collection/Cineriz; p. 602, *2001: A Space Odyssey*, Courtesy of the Kobal Collection/MGM; p. 622, *The Godfather*, Courtesy of the Kobal Collection/Paramount; p. 640, *Ali: Fear Eats the Soul (Angst essen Seele auf)*, Courtesy of the Kobal Collection/Tango Film; p. 660, *Chinatown*, Courtesy of the Kobal Collection/Paramount; p. 678, *The Last Supper*, Courtesy of Unifilm; p. 696, *Taxi Driver*, Courtesy of the Kobal Collection/Columbia; p. 716, *Ceddo*, Courtesy of the Kobal Collection/Films Domireew/Sembene; p. 738, *Peking Opera Blues*, Courtesy of the Kobal Collection/Cinema City; p. 756, *Yeelen (Brightness)*, Courtesy of the Kobal Collection/Films Cisse/Government of Mali; p. 776, *Do the Right Thing*, Courtesy of the Kobal Collection/Universal; p. 794, *Close-up*, Courtesy of the Kobal Collection/Institute of Intellectual Development; p. 814, *To Sleep with Anger*, Courtesy of the Kobal Collection/SVS Films; p. 830, *Raise the Red Lantern*, Courtesy of the Kobal Collection/ERA International; p. 850, *Daughters of the Dust*, Courtesy of the Kobal Collection/American Playhouse/WMG/Geechee; p. 872, *All About My Mother*, Courtesy of the Kobal Collection/El Deseo/Renn/France 2.

Index

Index

Index

Index

Index

Index

Index

Index

Index

Nixon, Richard, 356
Ni Zhen, 847
Noda Kogo 471
noir, see film noir
Noire de . . . Le, (Black Girl), 717, 758
Nolletti, Arthur, Jr., 457
Nomad, 740
Nordgren, Erik, 547
North by Northwest, 490n
Northup, Harry, 710, 713
Not One Less, 833
Notorious, 478
Notti di Cabiria, Le (Nights of Cabiria), 583, 584
Nouvelle Edition Française, La 316
Nouvelle vague, 559
Nowell-Smith, Geoffrey, 423–37
Nuit américaine, La (Day for Night), 564
Nunn, Bill, 781, 793
"Nuremberg" light, 347
Nykvist, Sven, 533

Oberhausen Manifesto, 642
O'Connell, Arthur, 359
O'Connor, Donald, 442, 449, 452, 454
Odets, Clifford, 244
"Oedipal revolt," 105–9, 113
Oedipus Rex (Sophocles), 186
Offenbach, Jacques, 70, 71, 73
Office of War Information (OWI), 381–82
Oguni Hideo, 507
Okada Saburo, 265, 267–68, 279
    konto coined by, 268n
Oklahoma!, 444
Okura Chiyoko, 280
Old Comedy, vs. New Comedy, 291
Old Wives for New, 225
Olsson, Gunnar, 547
Once Upon a Time in China, 739, 740
Ondaatje, Michael, 861
One and Eight, 833
One from the Heart, 630
One Hour With You, 225
180–degree rule, 276, 333–34, 466, 726
one scene-one cut, 275–76
Only Angels Have Wings, 286
On the Town, 442
optical printing, 355
orientalism, 838–41

Orr, John, 591–92
Orry-Kelly, 377
orthochromatic film stock, 130
Osaka, 269–71, 278
Osaka Elegy, 260–81
    Ayako as center of, 277–78; casting of, 275; choice of location for, 269–71; class focus of, 274; critical response to, 265–66; dialogue of, 273; director deviations from screenplay in, 277, 278; editing style in, 263, 276; patriarchy condemned in, 266; portrayal of women in, 263–64, 267, 268–69; production of, 265–66; screenplay of, 273, 277, 278; shooting schedule of, 275; social realism of, 265, 274; sources for, 267–68, 276
Oshreh, Moslem, 811
Ossessione, 411
O'Steen, Sam, 676
Other Francisco, The (El otro Francisco), 683
Ouedraogo, Idrissa, 760
Our Films Their Films, 523
Our Hospitality, 143
Owen, Wilfred, 105
Ozu Yasujiro, 37, 261, 457, 471
    background of, 458–59; cinematic hallmarks of, 458, 459–62, 466; creative freedom of, 459; critical assessments of work by, 459–60; favored camera position of, 459, 461; as most Japanese of Japan's directors, 458, 459–60; penchant for dedramatization of, 460, 463; reputation of, 458–59

Pacino, Al, 627, 629, 631, 638
Pagliero, Marcello, 406, 420
Paisà, 402
Pakula, Alan J., 628, 664, 665
Pal, George, 605
Palcy, Euzhan, 692
Panaflex cameras, 671
Pan-American Exposition of 1901, 73–74
Panavision, 671
pantomime, 69, 70, 240, 248, 252
Paper Doll's Whisper of Spring, A (Kami ningyo haru no sasayaki), 275
Parain, Brice, 568
Parallax View, The, 664

948

Index

Index

Index

Index